Criminal Law Today

D0166097

Criminal Law Today

FIFTH EDITION

FRANK SCHMALLEGER, PH.D.

Distinguished Professor Emeritus,
The University of North Carolina at Pembroke

DANIEL E. HALL, J.D., ED.D.

Professor and Director of Criminal Justice, Professor of Political Science,
and Affiliate Professor of Black World Studies, Miami University,
and Visiting Professor of Law, Sun Yat-sen University, Guangzhou, China

PEARSON

Boston   Columbus   Indianapolis   New York   San Francisco   Upper Saddle River
Amsterdam   Cape Town   Dubai   London   Madrid   Milan   Munich   Paris   Montréal   Toronto
Delhi   Mexico City   São Paulo   Sydney   Hong Kong   Seoul   Singapore   Taipei   Tokyo

Editorial Director: Vernon R. Anthony
Editor, Digital Projects: Nichole Caldwell
Senior Acquisitions Editor: Gary Bauer
Development Editor: Elisa Rogers, 4development
Editorial Assistant: Lynda Cramer
Director of Marketing: David Gesell
Marketing Manager: Mary Salzman
Senior Marketing Coordinator: Alicia Wozniak
Marketing Assistant: Les Roberts
Senior Managing Editor: Joellen Gohr
Senior Project Manager: Steve Robb
Senior Operations Supervisor: Pat Tonneman

Creative Director: Andrea Nix
Art Director: Diane Y. Ernsberger
Cover Designer: CFISHDESIGN, Candace Rowley
Cover Image: © ER 09/Shutterstock
Media Project Manager: Karen Bretz
Full-Service Project Management: Linda Zuk, WordCraft LLC
Composition: S4Carlisle Publishing Services
Printer/Binder: Courier/Kendallville
Cover Printer: Lehigh/Phoenix Color Hagerstown
Text Font: Goudy Oldstyle Std 10.5/13.5

Credits and acknowledgments borrowed from other sources and reproduced, with permission, in this textbook appear on the appropriate page within the text.

Copyright © 2014, 2010, 2006 by Pearson Education, Inc. All rights reserved. Manufactured in the United States of America. This publication is protected by Copyright, and permission should be obtained from the publisher prior to any prohibited reproduction, storage in a retrieval system, or transmission in any form or by any means, electronic, mechanical, photocopying, recording, or likewise. To obtain permission(s) to use material from this work, please submit a written request to Pearson Education, Inc., Permissions Department, One Lake Street, Upper Saddle River, New Jersey 07458, or you may fax your request to 201-236-3290.

Many of the designations by manufacturers and sellers to distinguish their products are claimed as trademarks. Where those designations appear in this book, and the publisher was aware of a trademark claim, the designations have been printed in initial caps or all caps.

Library of Congress Cataloging-in-Publication Data
Schmalleger, Frank.
    Criminal law today / Frank Schmalleger, Daniel E. Hall. -- 5th ed.
      p. cm.
    ISBN 0-13-300858-4 (978-0-13-300858-6)
    1. Criminal law--United States. I. Hall, Daniel (Daniel E.) II. Title.

KF9219.S36 2014
345.73--dc23   2012041212

10 9 8 7 6 5 4 3 2 1

PEARSON

ISBN 10:   0-13-300858-4
ISBN 13: 978-0-13-300858-6

For Michelle Lallos, who could have
written this book, and Eva Joan Hall,
the smallest Hall of all.

ADVISORY PANEL FOR CRIMINAL LAW TODAY

K. Lee Derr, J.D., *The Senate of Pennsylvania*

Thayne D. Gray, J.D., *Assistant Prosecuting Attorney, Clinton County, Ohio*

Gerald W. Hildebrand, *Austin Community College*

Morris Jenkins, Ph.D., *University of Toledo*

Thomas Lateano, J.D., *Kean University*

Daria La Torre, J.D., *Alvernia College*

Dennis Murphy, J.D., Ph.D., *Armstrong Atlantic State University*

Charles B. Noel, *Community College of Allegheny County*

Cliff Roberson, J.D., L.L.M., Ph.D., *Kaplan University*

Michael A. Sullivan, J.D., *Assistant County Prosecutor, Cuyahoga County, Ohio*

Reece Trimmer, J.D., *The North Carolina Justice Academy*

David J. W. Vanderhoof, L.L.M., *Criminal Justice Studies, University of North Carolina at Pembroke*

Gregory Warchol, Ph.D., *Northern Michigan University*

Beth Warriner, *Naugatuck Valley Community College*

Brief Contents

Contents

CHAPTER 3

Expanding the Concept of Crime 65

CHAPTER 7

Legal and Social Dimensions of Personal Crime: Homicide 209

CHAPTER 8

Legal and Social Dimensions of Personal Crime: Assault, Battery, and Other Personal Crimes 239

CHAPTER 9

Legal and Social Dimensions of Property and Computer Crimes 268

CHAPTER 10

Offenses against Public Order and the Administration of Justice   323

CHAPTER 13   Victims and the Law   423

CHAPTER 14   Punishment and Sentencing   457

Preface

Our purpose in writing this textbook has been to provide students with an appreciation for the fundamental nature of law, an overview of general legal principles, and a special understanding of the historical development of criminal law and its contemporary form and function in American society today. Stories from real life, engaging graphics, up-to-date examples and issues, and interactive media bring the law to life in this comprehensive, timely, and user-friendly introduction to criminal law. Key features include the following.

Capstone Cases in each chapter provide excerpts from actual court opinions illustrating important themes in the law. The cases offer significant insights into the everyday workings of American jurisprudence and demonstrate the logic behind appellate decisions. Court opinions, statutes, and other quoted materials have occasionally been redacted and edited slightly for clarity. Many case citations and references have been removed without the use of ellipses or other omission signifiers in order to keep the flow of reading uninterrupted.

Graphics such as full-color diagrams, illustrations, and other figures throughout the text reinforce key points and illustrate important, complex, and challenging concepts for easier understanding.

Criminal Law in the News boxes in each chapter highlight recent news stories/issues that illustrate the variety of legal perspectives found at federal, state, and local levels and make students aware of jurisdictional differences in the law.

Our approach has been strongly influenced by our belief that the law has always been, and remains, a vital policymaking tool. As a topic for study and discussion, the nature and life of the law is more important today than ever before. The law faces challenges as it continues to adapt to the needs of a complex and rapidly changing society. These challenges are highlighted in this text and serve to emphasize for readers the contemporary relevance of our ever-evolving American criminal law.

Frank Schmalleger
Distinguished Professor Emeritus, University of North Carolina at Pembroke

Daniel E. Hall
Professor and Director of Criminal Justice, Professor of Political Science,
and Affiliate Professor of Black World Studies, Miami University
and Visiting Professor of Law, Sun Yat-sen University, China

New to the Fifth Edition

Chapter-Specific Changes

- In Chapter 1, updated information has been provided on cases involving O. J. Simpson and Jack Kevorkian. Added are a new figure depicting the structure of the U.S. federal courts; a brief discussion of the ancient legal Code of Ur-Nammu from Mesopotamia; and the concepts of selective incorporation, damages, and punitive damages. Also, the chapter now distinguishes the three forms of tort, and the discussion of the rule of law has been expanded to include mention of the World Justice Project.

- In Chapter 2, the discussion of involuntary acts has been clarified, as have the discussions of possession and constructive possession, criminal negligence, and free speech. The discussion of strict liability and *mens rea* has been elevated in importance and highlighted. The requirement that some states have for reporting a crime of which one has knowledge is discussed in the context of the child sexual abuse scandal that enveloped Pennsylvania State University in 2011. In the wake of the Treyvon Martin shooting, a new key term, *deadly weapon doctrine*, has been added.

- In Chapter 3, the discussion of the *sine qua non*, or "but for," test has been enhanced and the concept of bill of attainder has been clarified.

- In Chapter 4, explanation of the co-conspirator hearsay rule has been added, and additional information is provided about acts in furtherance of a conspiracy, including the Pinkerton Rule. A discussion has been added about punishing those who can be held vicariously liable for an offense. Changes have been made to the attempt, corporate liability, and conspiracy discussions, including incorporating a new framework for understanding corporate liability.

- In Chapter 5, a new chapter-opening story about the shooting of Treyvon Martin and a new discussion of stand-your-ground laws have been added.

- In Chapter 6, a section has been added on civil commitment, including confining individuals who are mentally ill or a danger to themselves.

- In Chapter 7, the discussion of the "year-and-a-day rule" has been enhanced, and the case of *Kennedy* v. *Louisiana* is now discussed.

- In Chapter 8, the discussion of assault and of aggravated assault has been improved, and the concept of terroristic threat is introduced. The concept of spousal rape has been clarified, the status of the offense under state laws has been updated, and the discussion of kidnapping has been expanded.

- In Chapter 9, the property crime statistics and the discussion of computer crimes have been updated. A new section on the grading of theft crimes has been added.

- In Chapter 10, a new section on weapons crimes has been added to include discussion of the 2010 U.S. Supreme Court case of *McDonald* v. *Chicago*. The discussion of First Amendment free speech protections has been expanded to include consideration of the case of Westboro Baptist Church of Topeka, Kansas, whose members protested at the funerals of fallen U.S. soldiers, believing that God hates the United States because of its acceptance of homosexuality. The discussion of immigration crimes has been expanded to include the question of how much authority states have over immigration, and the discussion of environmental crimes has been expanded to include the 2011 Gulf oil spill.

- In Chapter 11, Nevada prostitution laws have been clarified, the examination of pornography has been expanded, and the discussion of laws regulating child pornography has been enhanced.

- In Chapter 12, the chapter-opening story relating to terrorism has been updated and expanded. The free speech terrorism-related case of *Holder* v. *Humanitarian Law Project* is now discussed.

- In Chapter 13, statistics on violent victimization have been updated and a discussion has been added concerning due-process limits to the admission of victim impact evidence.

- In Chapter 14, a new section has been added on constitutuonal limitations on criminal punishments, including the excessive fines clause of the Eighth Amendment, and the discussion of sentencing enhancements has been expanded. The discussions of lethal injections in capital cases and the use of DNA testing to identify wrongful convictions have been expanded.

General Changes

NEW! Additional Case Applications

Sixty Additional Application features now follow many of the Capstone Cases throughout the text. Provided by Dr. John Forren of Miami University in Hamilton, Ohio, each Additional Application consists of a brief summary and holding of a case that relates to—and builds on—the issues addressed in the Capstone Case. Additional Applications appear where an important distinction in the application of the law will enhance students' understanding of the concept. The Additional Applications (1) delve deeply into the subject matter represented by Capstone Case opinions through the use of lower court cases and (2) attempt to grapple with issues and questions left unanswered by previous court decisions.

Additional Applications

What is a "substantial step"? Why require it?

United States v. Gladish, 536 F.3d 646 (7th Cir. 2008)

The Case: The defendant, a 35-year-old man from southern Indiana, visited an Internet chat room called "Indiana regional romance" and solicited "Abagail"—a purported 14-year-old Indiana girl who, in reality, was an undercover (adult female) federal law enforcement agent—to have sex with him. In their online chats, "Abagail" agreed to a sexual encounter with the defendant and, in one conversation, he raised the possibility of her traveling from her purported home in northern Indiana to meet him "in a couple of weeks." No specific travel or meeting arrangements were made, however. The defendant was arrested and charged by federal prosecutors of attempting to "persuade, induce, entice, or coerce a person under 18" to engage in criminal sexual activity. On appeal, the defendant claimed that he had not taken a "substantial step" toward the completion of the specified crime; thus, the criminal charges were invalid.

The Finding: A three-judge panel of the U.S. Court of Appeals for the Seventh Circuit ruled that the defendant, in these circumstances, could not be found guilty of criminal attempt. Writing for the panel, Judge Richard A. Posner focused largely on the purposes underlying the law of criminal attempts and the rationale of its "substantial

meet his purported victim in person. All of the defendant's actions, Posner concluded, were "consistent with his having intended to obtain sexual satisfaction vicariously." Indeed, he added, "since [the agent] furnished no proof of her age, he could not have been sure and may indeed have doubted that she was a girl, or even a woman. He may have thought (this is common in Internet relationships) that they were both enacting a fantasy."

Is the gathering of some—but not all—necessary drug lab components a "substantial step"?

United States v. Spencer, 439 F.3d 905 (8th Cir. 2006)

The Case: Following a tip provided by a delivery truck driver, state law enforcement officers in June 2000 searched the Monona County, Iowa, residence of Joseph Spencer and found over 2,000 marijuana plants along with significant quantities of red phosphorus, an iodine container, a cache of pseudoephedrine, various flasks and tubes, acid, striker tabs, and coffee filters—the latter items, a state expert later testified at trial, are all associated with the operation of an illegal methamphetamine lab. After a nine-day trial, a federal district court jury found the defendant guilty on several gun possession and drug trafficking charges, including violation of 21 U.S.C. Sec. 846, which prohibits an "attempt to manufacture five grams or more" of actual (pure) methamphetamine. On appeal, Spencer challenged his conviction on criminal attempt charges on the grounds that the government had failed to prove that he had taken a "substantial step" toward

---

NEW! Critical Thinking and Application Problems

At the end of each chapter, these problems based on real-life scenarios challenge students to think critically and apply their knowledge of the chapter material to real-life, contemporary legal problems.

CRITICAL THINKING AND APPLICATION PROBLEMS

Use the following facts to answer problems 1 and 2:

Timothy V. Oyer, a 42-year-old male, decided to jog in a municipal park near his home on a beautiful June day. After jogging three miles, he slowed to a walk to cool down. During his walk he noticed a woman sitting under a tree not far from the sidewalk he was on. As he moved closer to her he was surprised to discover that she was not wearing any clothes above the waist. She appeared to be in her mid-20s and he found her attractive. As he neared her, she smiled at him and greeted him with a "hello." Then the following discussion occurred:

Timothy: It is a beautiful day.

Woman: Yes it is. You out running?

Timothy: Yes, not as far as I wanted. I am not in the shape I used to be.

Woman: Nonsense, you look great. I am the one that is out of shape.

Timothy: Are you kidding, you are beautiful with a body to match.

Woman: Sit down here. Take a break.

Timothy accepted the invitation to sit with her and they talked for 15 minutes. They discussed physical fitness and the weather, she laughed at his jokes, and she told him that he was a handsome man. At one point, she placed one of her legs on his shoulder in a demonstration of her flexibility. After 15 minutes of conversation and flirting, she asked to see his

APPLYING THE CONCEPT

CAPSTONE CASE

How Shall a Court Interpret a Criminal Statute That Is Silent on *Mens Rea*?

People v. Jensen,
Mich. App. 439 (1998)

THE CASE Following a jury trial, defendant was convicted of three counts of knowing that she was HIV positive and engaging in sexual penetration without informing her partner of her HIV status, MCL 333.5210; MSA 14.15(5210). Thereafter, the trial court sentenced defendant to concurrent terms of two years and eight months to four years' imprisonment on each of the three counts. . . . [The case made its way to the Michigan Supreme Court, which remanded to the Michigan Court of Appeals to review constitutional claims.]

THE FINDING On remand, we find that the HIV notice statute is neither unconstitutionally overbroad nor violative of defendant's rights to privacy or against compelled speech. . . .

First, defendant asserts that MCL 333.5210; MSA 14.15(5210), which makes it a crime to fail to inform a person's body or of any object into the genital or anal openings of another person's body, but emission of semen is not required. . . .

Defendant . . . argues that the statute is unconstitutional because it does not contain an intent, or *mens rea*, requirement. More specifically, defendant asserts that because the statute does not require a specific intent to harm, one who does not understand or appreciate the consequences of his or her acts can be found criminally responsible. We disagree.

In light of defendant's repeated argument that mentally deficient individuals will be prosecuted under this statute, we reiterate and remind defendant that, even though the evidence in the instant case does not support this factual scenario, if a "person lacks substantial capacity either to appreciate the wrongfulness of his conduct or to conform his conduct to the requirements of the law," he or she will be found lacking in criminal responsibility under the legal insanity defense statute.

Capstone Cases

The cases throughout the chapters have been updated and shortened. New cases include *Illinois v. Lara* and *Smith v. Doe* in Chapter 3, *Kansas v. Hendricks* in Chapter 6, *McDonald v. Chicago* in Chapter 10, and *Maples v. Thomas* and *Miller v. Alabama* in Chapter 14. Complete versions of the Capstone Cases, links to Web Extras and Legal Resources, a Guide to Reading Legal Citations, and topical learning modules can be accessed by going to **www.pearsonhighered.com/careers.**

Learning Objectives

The Learning Objectives at the beginning of each chapter have been shortened and rewritten in plain language to provide readers with a concise overview of what they can expect to learn from each chapter.

OBJECTIVES

After reading this chapter, you should be able to

- Describe the legal essence of criminal conduct.
- Explain *actus reus* and what constitutes a criminal act.
- Explain *mens rea* and the different types of intent.
- Describe strict liability offenses, and explain why some crimes are punished solely on the basis of strict liability.
- Summarize concurrence, and describe how concurrence relates to *mens rea* and *actus reus*.

Criminal Law in the News

All Criminal Law in the News boxes have been replaced with entirely new stories drawn from today's media. New story topics:

- The possible corporate criminal liability of British Petroleum for the 2010 Gulf oil spill
- The activities of Westboro Baptist Church members who protest at military funerals
- A honeymooner who may have been tried twice for the death of his new wife
- Gun rights in the wake of infamous mass shootings
- The possible use of the defense of addiction in cases of shoplifting
- Abortion doctors who were charged with murder under Maryland law
- Faith-healing parents who were convicted in the death of their son after refusing medical treatment
- Online piracy charges against New Zealand multimillionaire Kim Dotcom (a.k.a Megaupload)
- A federal appellate court's action in overturning California's Proposition 8, which banned same-sex marriages
- The story of Colleen LaRose ("Jihad Jane")
- The role of DNA testing in identifying wrongful convictions
- The political scandal involving former Illinois Democratic Governor Rod Blagojevich

CRIMINAL LAW IN THE NEWS

Faith-Healing Parents Convicted in Son's Death

As members of a small Oregon sect, the Followers of Christ, Jeff and Marci Beagley ruled out traditional medical care in favor of faith healing. When their 16-year-old son Neil died in June 2008 without receiving medical attention, they were convicted of criminally negligent homicide and sent to prison.

The cause of Neil Beagley's death was kidney failure due to a congenital condition in his urinary tract, which could have been treated by inserting a catheter to remove a blockage, but he never saw a physician. When the teenager suddenly became very ill, at least 60 members of the faith gathered around him, anointed his body with oil, and used "laying on of hands" while praying for him. No one ever called for medical help.

Neil Beagley's death was the second case tried under a 1999 Oregon law specifically passed to stop an alarmingly high mortality rate due to untreated illnesses among children in the Followers of Christ. An Oregon medical examiner found that children in this 1,000-member sect had a death rate 26 times higher than children in the general population. The new law excludes faith healing as a defense

Jeff Beagley leaving the courthouse. What led to his conviction of criminally negligent homicide? *Newscom*

pushed for a stiff sentence to deter future deaths of children in the sect. "The court has the opportunity to deliver a clear

Instructor Supplements

The following supplementary materials are available to support instructors' use of the main text:

- *eBooks*. *Criminal Law Today* is available in two eBook formats, CourseSmart and Adobe Reader. CourseSmart is an exciting new choice for students looking to save money. As an alternative to purchasing the printed textbook, students can purchase an electronic version of the same content. With a CourseSmart eTextbook, students can search the text, make notes online, print out reading assignments that incorporate lecture notes, and bookmark important passages for later review. For more information, or to purchase access to the CourseSmart eTextbook, visit **www.coursesmart.com**.

- **MyBank** and **MyTest**. Whether you use the basic **TestBank** or generate questions electronically through **MyTest**, every question is linked to the text's learning objective and page number and to level of difficulty. This allows for quick reference in the text and an easy way to check the difficulty level and variety of your questions. **MyTest** can be accessed at **www.PearsonMyTest.com**.

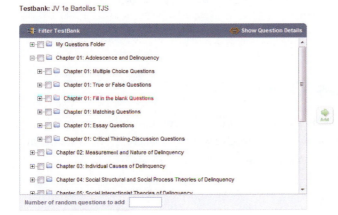

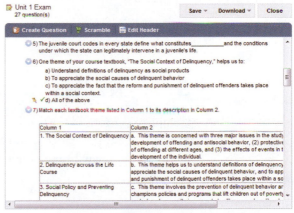

- *Interactive Lecture PowerPoint® Presentations*. This supplement will enhance lectures like never before. Award-winning presentation designers worked with our authors to develop PowerPoint presentations that truly engage the student. Much like the text, the PowerPoint illustrations are full of instructionally sound graphics, tables, charts, and photos that do what presentation software was meant to do: support and enhance your lecture. Data and difficult concepts are presented in a truly interactive way, helping students connect the dots and stay focused on the lecture. The Interactive Lecture PowerPoint Presentations also include in-depth lecture notes and teaching tips so you have all your lecture material in one place.

> To access these supplementary materials online, instructors need to request an instructor access code at **www.pearsonhighered.com/irc**. Within 48 hours after registering, you will receive a confirmation e-mail that includes an instructor access code. When you receive your code, go to the site and log on for full instructions on downloading materials you wish to use.

- *The Pearson Criminal Justice Online Community*. Available at www.mycriminaljusticecommunity.com, this site is a place for educators to connect and exchange ideas and advice on courses, content, CJ Interactive, and so much more.

STUDENT RESOURCES ONLINE

Complete versions of the Capstone Cases, links to WebExtras and Legal Resources, a Guide to Reading Legal Citations, and topical learning modules may be accessed by students and instructors at **www.pearsonhighered.com/careers.**

Acknowledgments

Criminal Law Today owes much to the efforts of many people. Members of the Advisory Panel, who reviewed drafts of this text as it developed and showered us with comments and suggestions, deserve special thanks. Advisory Panel members are listed on page vi.

Others who have contributed to this text and to whom we are very grateful are Keiser University's John J. Dolotowski, Miami University's John Forren for providing the Additional Applications features, Lance Parr of California's Grossmont College, and Mike Gray at Maryland's Eastern Shore Criminal Justice Academy. Thanks also to Morgan Peterson at California's Palomar College for assistance in tracking down thorny permissions issues. David Graff at Kent State University did an excellent job of Web content development, and we are in his debt.

This edition has benefited substantially from the suggestions and ideas provided by these reviewers: Beth Bjerregaard, University of North Carolina, Charlotte; Ellen Eason-Montgomery, Harold Washington College; Barry Langford, Columbia College; Thomas Lateano, Kean University; Larry Lewis, Davenport University, Grand Rapids; Marshall Lloyd, San Antonio College; Daniel Maxwell, University of New Haven; John Milliken, Trine University; Kerry Muehlenbeck, Mesa Community College; Greg Plumb, Park University; Scott Teague, Forsyth Technical Community College; and Patricia Wagner, Youngstown State University.

Thanks also to Nina Amster at the American Law Institute for help in working through the process necessary to obtain permission to reprint selected portions of the Model Penal Code.

We are especially indebted to the fine folks at the Legal Information Institute at Cornell Law School (including codirectors Thomas R. Bruce and Peter W. Martin), which offers U.S. Supreme Court opinions under the auspices of the Court's electronic-dissemination Project Hermes.

Special thanks go to Elisa Rogers at 4development for immense help in creation of the manuscript and to Linda Zuk at WordCraft LLC for guiding this project from manuscript to book. Last but not least, we wish to thank the staff at Pearson Prentice Hall who have made this book the quality product that it is. Many thanks to Vern Anthony, Gary Bauer, Tanika Henderson, JoEllen Gohr, Steve Robb, Pat Tonneman, Diane Ernsberger, David Gesell, and many other staffers (some of whom remain anonymous) who have brought this book to fruition. Thank you, each and every one!

About the Authors

Frank Schmalleger, Ph.D., is Distinguished Professor Emeritus at the University of North Carolina at Pembroke. Dr. Schmalleger holds degrees from the University of Notre Dame and Ohio State University, having earned both a master's (1970) and doctorate (1974) from Ohio State University, with a special emphasis in criminology. From 1976 to 1994, he taught criminal justice courses at the University of North Carolina at Pembroke. For the last 16 of those years, he chaired the university's Department of Sociology, Social Work, and Criminal Justice. He was named Professor Emeritus in 2001. As an adjunct professor with Webster University in St. Louis, Missouri, Schmalleger helped develop the university's graduate program in security administration and loss prevention. He taught courses in that curriculum for more than a decade. Schmalleger has also taught in the New School for Social Research's online graduate program, helping to build the world's first electronic classrooms in support of distance learning through computer telecommunications. An avid Internet user, Schmalleger is also the creator of a number of award-winning websites, including one that supports this textbook.

Frank Schmalleger is the author of numerous articles and many books, including the widely used *Criminal Justice Today* (Pearson, 2013), *Criminology Today* (Pearson, 2012), and *Criminal Justice: A Brief Introduction* (Pearson, 2014). See his website at www.schmalleger .com.

Daniel E. Hall, J.D., Ed.D., a native of Indiana, earned his bachelor's degree at Indiana University, his Juris Doctor at Washburn University, and his Doctor of Education at the University of Central Florida. He practiced law in both the United States and the Federated States of Micronesia. He has been on the faculties of the Department of Criminal Justice and Legal Studies at the University of Central Florida and the Department of Criminal Justice at the University of Toledo, where he was chair and associate professor. He is currently professor and director of criminal justice, with a joint appointment in political science and affiliate status in Black World Studies, at Miami University Hamilton. He is also visiting professor of law at Sun Yat-sen University in Guangzhou, China. Dr. Hall is the author or coauthor of 20 textbooks and many journal articles on public law subjects. Daniel lives in Ohio with his two daughters, Eva and Grace. You can learn more about Daniel at www.danielhall.org and he may be reached at hallslaw@yahoo.com.

Let reverence for the laws,

be breathed by every American mother,

to the lisping babe, that prattles on her lap;

let it be taught in schools, in seminaries, and in colleges;

let it be written in Primers, spelling books, and in Almanacs;

let it be preached from the pulpit, proclaimed in legislative halls,

and enforced in courts of justice.

And, in short, let it become the political religion of the nation;

and let the old and the young, the rich and the poor, the grave and the gay,

of all sexes and tongues, and colors and conditions,

sacrifice unceasingly upon its altars.

—ABRAHAM LINCOLN (1838)

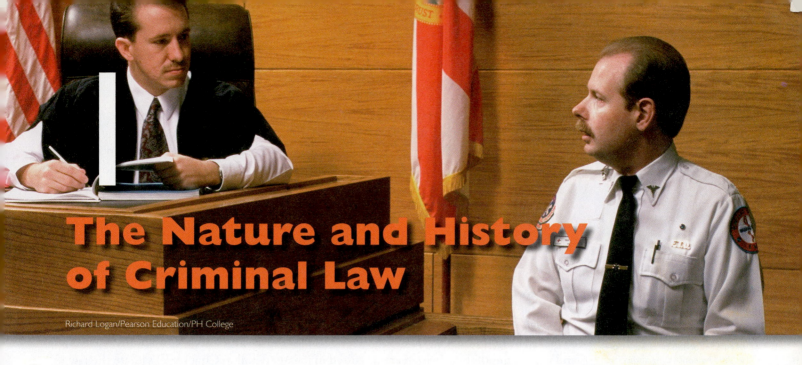

The Nature and History of Criminal Law

Richard Logan/Pearson Education/PH College

CHAPTER OUTLINE

Introduction

What Is Criminal Law?

Historical and Philosophical Perspectives

Common Law

Types of Crimes

The Purpose of Criminal Law

Sources of Criminal Law

The Modern U.S. Legal System

An Adversarial, Accusatorial Due-Process System

The Rule of Law

OBJECTIVES

After reading this chapter, you should be able to

- Define crime and criminal law.
- Summarize the origins and development of criminal law.
- Describe the role of common law in modern criminal law, and explain the differences between procedural and substantive criminal law.
- Describe the various ways in which crimes can be classified, and list the four traditional types of crimes.
- Identify the purposes served by criminal law.
- Identify the various sources of criminal law, including the principle of *stare decisis*.
- Describe the structure of the U.S. legal system, including jurisdiction.
- Describe the adversarial and accusatorial qualities of the U.S. system of criminal justice.
- Expound upon the "rule of law" and explain why due process is an integral part of the rule of law.

Law is the art of the good and the fair.
— Ulpian, Roman judge (circa AD 200)

[D]ue process . . . embodies a system of rights based on moral principles so deeply embedded in the traditions and feelings of our people as to be deemed fundamental to a civilized society as conceived by our whole history. Due process is that which comports with the deepest notions of what is fair and right and just.
— Justice Hugo Black (1886–1971)[1]

The law is that which protects everybody who can afford a good lawyer.
— Anonymous

1

INTRODUCTION

In June 2000, Larico Garrett, 22, of Manchester, Connecticut, was arrested for car theft after he pulled the stolen vehicle he was driving into a convenience store parking lot to ask a police officer for directions to a nearby street.[2] Although he answered the man's questions, Officer Robert Johnson found the 2 a.m. encounter suspicious and ran a radio check of the license plate on the Cadillac that Garrett was driving. When dispatchers reported the vehicle stolen, Johnson summoned help and drove to the street where Garrett was headed. Garrett was arrested and charged under Connecticut law with taking a vehicle without the owner's permission, a misdemeanor punishable by less than a year in jail.

WHAT IS CRIMINAL LAW?

Although most people would agree that it is not very smart for a car thief to ask directions from a police officer, it is not a crime to be stupid. Car theft, of course, is another matter, and most forms of theft (which are discussed in greater detail in Chapter 9) violate the law. *Black's Law Dictionary*, an authoritative source on legal terminology, defines the word **law** as follows: "that which is laid down, ordained, or established . . . a body of rules of action or conduct prescribed by controlling authority, and having binding *legal* force."[3]

However, not all rules are laws, fewer still are criminal laws, and not all have "binding legal force." Sociologists, for example, distinguish between **norms** and **mores**, while philosophers and ethicists talk of **morals** and morality. Morals are ethical principles, and moral behavior is behavior that conforms to some ethical principle or moral code. Norms are rules that underlie and are inherent in the fabric of society. For example, it is regarded as inappropriate to belch in public. Anyone who intentionally violates a social norm may be seen as inadequately socialized (others might say "uncivilized"), offensive, and even dangerous (if the violation is a serious one) to an accepted way of life. When social norms are *unintentionally* violated (as may be the case with a belch at the dinner table), a mere request to be excused generally allows social interaction to proceed with little or no interruption. Mores, on the other hand, are rules that govern serious violations of the social code, including what social scientists call "taboos." Violations of both mores and norms are forms of deviance and can properly be called "deviant behavior." Even so, few violations of social norms are illegal, and fewer still are **crimes** (Figure 1–1). Because

law
"That which is laid down, ordained, or established . . . a body of rules of action or conduct prescribed by controlling authority, and having binding *legal* force."

norms
Unwritten rules that underlie and are inherent in the fabric of society.

mores
Unwritten, but generally known, rules that govern serious violations of the social code.

morals
Ethical principles, or principles meant to guide human conduct and behavior; principles or standards of right and wrong.

crime
Any act or omission in violation of penal law, committed without defense or justification, and made punishable by the state in a judicial proceeding.

FIGURE 1–1

Crime, Deviance, and Norm Violation.

Note: Although there are many ways rules can be violated, only a select few offenses are actually "criminal" acts.

TYPES OF OFFENSES

Criminal Acts

Taboo Acts
"Defiant" Behavior
Violation of Mores

Violation of Norms
"Uncivilized" Behavior
Immoral Behavior

laws have not been enacted against quite a large number of generally recognized taboos, it is possible for behavior to be contrary to accepted principles of social interaction and perhaps even immoral—but still legal. As you read through this book, it is important to remember that only human conduct that violates the criminal law can properly be called "criminal." Although other forms of nonconformist behavior may be undesirable or even reprehensible, they are not crimes.[4] Accordingly, the distinguishing characteristic between a crime and other deviance is the presence of a public prohibition and the authority of the government to enforce the prohibition.

Criminal law can be understood, then, as the body of rules and regulations that defines and specifies punishments for offenses of a public nature or for wrongs committed against the state or society. Criminal law is also called *penal law* and is usually embodied in the penal codes of various jurisdictions. In short, criminal law defines what conduct is criminal, and violations of the criminal law are referred to as *crimes*.

> *"Law" is a solemn expression of the will of the supreme power of the state.*
>
> —*Montana Code Annotated, Section 1–1–101*

criminal law
The body of rules and regulations that defines and specifies punishments for offenses of a public nature or for wrongs committed against the state or society. Also called *penal law.*

HISTORICAL AND PHILOSOPHICAL PERSPECTIVES

Laws in the United States have been shaped by a number of historical developments and philosophical perspectives. Criminal law, in particular, has been greatly influenced by natural law theories.

Natural and Positive Law

Natural law dates back to the Greek philosopher Aristotle. Adherents believe that some laws are fundamental to human nature and discoverable by human reason, intuition, or inspiration, without the need to refer to man-made laws. Such people believe that an intuitive and rational basis for many of our criminal laws can be found in immutable moral principles or some identifiable aspects of the natural order.

One authoritative source has this to say about natural law:

> This expression, "natural law," or *jus naturale*, was largely used in the philosophical speculations of the Roman jurists of the Antonine age, and was intended to denote a system of rules and principles for the guidance of human conduct which, independently of enacted law or the systems peculiar to any one people, might be discovered by the rational intelligence of man, and would be found to grow out of and conform to his *nature*, meaning by that word his whole mental, moral, and physical constitution.[5]

Ideally, say natural law advocates, man-made laws should conform to principles inherent in natural law. The great theologian Thomas Aquinas (1225–1274), for example, wrote in his *Summa Theologica* that any man-made law that contradicts natural law is corrupt in the eyes of God.[6] A philosophical outgrowth of natural law is natural rights theory. This theory holds that individuals naturally possess certain freedoms that may not be encroached upon by other individuals or governments.

A contrasting construct is **positive law**, which is simply the law that is enforced by the government. Natural law and natural rights philosophers don't deny the authority of governments to establish positive law, but instead they believe such authority is bounded by the natural rights of individuals. Some positivists also contend that for law to be legitimate, it must be created and implemented in ways that are acceptable to most people (democratic or contractualist positivism).

Natural law principles continue to be influential in many spheres. The modern debate over abortion, for example, relies on the use of natural law

natural law
The rules of conduct inherent in human nature and in the natural order, which are thought to be knowable through intuition, inspiration, and the exercise of reason without the need to refer to man-made laws.

positive law
Law that is legitimately created and enforced by governments.

> *Law is born from despair of human nature.*
>
> —*José Ortega y Gasset, Spanish philosopher (1883–1955)*

CRIMINAL LAW IN THE NEWS

Politicians Who Violate the "Rule of Law" Get Tough Prison Sentences

The United States has always embraced the principle that no one, not even a powerful politician, can violate the law. George Washington, speaking about political power, advised, "never for a moment should it be left to irresponsible action." President Theodore Roosevelt added, "No man is above the law and no man is below it."

Today, enforcement of the "rule of law" appears to be stricter than ever, producing some eye-popping prison terms for convicted politicians. Former Illinois Democratic Gov. Rod Blagojevich was sentenced to 14 years in prison in 2011, more than twice the 6½-year term given to his predecessor, former Republican Gov. George Ryan, who was convicted on federal fraud and racketeering charges in 2006.

Blagojevich was all over the news for his most notable crime, trying to sell President Obama's former Senate seat, and he was unrepentant until almost the end. But was he twice as guilty as Ryan, whose administration quashed a probe into bribes paid to state officials for issuing illegal truck drivers' licenses that led to highway deaths? And was Ryan twice as guilty as former Democratic Gov. Otto Kerner of Illinois, who got three years in prison in 1973 for accepting bribes from a racetrack owner?

Sentencing is a matter for individual judges to decide, but the overall trend for convicted politicians is upward. In 2009, former Rep. William J. Jefferson (D-La.), who famously stored bribe money in his freezer, was given 13 years in prison. It was the longest sentence ever given to a former congressman, easily topping the eight years and four months in prison given in 2006 to former Rep. Randy Cunningham (R-Calif.), who accepted bribes for tens of millions of dollars in defense contracts.

Pleas for mercy now seem to fall on deaf ears. In the 1970s, Kerner was released early due to terminal cancer, but in 2011 a judge refused former Governor Ryan's request for a leave to visit his wife who was dying of cancer. The only way Ryan got to see her at all was through the mercy of his prison warden.

Some judges compare the destruction of citizens' trust in the political system to violent crimes. According to former U.S. Attorney Patrick Collins, who prosecuted Ryan, "judges are now looking at these corruption cases like guns and drug cases." As U.S. District Judge James Zagel put it in sentencing Blagojevich: "When it is the

Former Illinois Democratic Gov. Rod Blagojevich, who was sentenced to 14 years in prison in 2011, for trying to sell President Obama's former Senate seat. What is the rule of law, and why is it important?

Tannen Maury/EPA/Newscom

governor who goes bad, the fabric of Illinois is torn and disfigured and not easily or quickly repaired."

Some errant politicians still get relatively short sentences but are hammered if convicted again. In 2008, former Democratic Mayor Kwame Kilpatrick of Detroit was sentenced to four months in prison for covering up an affair with his chief of staff and assaulting a police officer. But when he violated parole, the judge lambasted him for his "lack of contriteness and lack of humility," and he received 18 months to 5 years in prison in 2010.

Politicians embrace high standards for their enemies, but not so much for themselves. When President Bill Clinton was impeached in 1998, Rep. Tom Delay (D-Texas), the House majority whip at the time, advocated "the higher road of the rule of law." He continued: "Sometimes hard, sometimes unpleasant, this path relies on truth, justice and the rigorous application of the principle that no man is above the law."

Then in 2011, Delay was convicted for money laundering and sentenced to three years in prison. He has never accepted blame for what he did, arguing that he was the victim of his own political enemies in Texas.

"The criminalization of politics undermines our very system and I'm very disappointed in the outcome," he said.

Resources

"'Sorry' Blagojevich Gets 14-Year Prison Sentence," *Chicago Sun-Times*, December 7, 2011, http://www.suntimes.com/news/metro/blagojevich/9300810-452/sorry-blagojevich-gets-14-year-prison-sentence.html.

"Tom DeLay Gets 3 Years in Prison for Money Laundering," Fox News, January 10, 2011, http://www.foxnews.com/politics/2011/01/10/tom-delay-gets-years-prison-money-laundering. "Former Rep. William Jefferson sentenced to 13 years in prison," *Christian Science Monitor*, November 13, 2009, http://www.csmonitor.com/USA/Politics/2009/1113/former-rep-william-jefferson-sentenced-to-13-years-in-prison.

---

arguments to support both sides in the dispute. Before the 1973 U.S. Supreme Court decision of *Roe* v. *Wade*,[7] abortion was a crime in most states (although abortions were sometimes permitted in cases of rape or incest or when the mother's life was in danger). In *Roe*, the justices held, "State criminal abortion laws . . . that except from criminality only a life-saving procedure on the mother's behalf without regard to the stage of her pregnancy and other interests involved violate the due process clause of the Fourteenth Amendment, which protects against state action the right to privacy, including a woman's qualified right to terminate her pregnancy." The Court set limits on the availability of abortion, however, when it said that, although "the State cannot override that right, it has legitimate interests in protecting both the pregnant woman's health and the potentiality of human life, each of which interests grows and reaches a 'compelling' point at various stages of the woman's approach to term." Natural law supporters of the *Roe* standard argue that abortion must remain a "right" of any woman because she is naturally entitled to be in control of her own body. They claim that the legal system must continue to protect this "natural right" of women.

In contrast, antiabortion forces—sometimes called "pro-lifers"—claim that the unborn fetus is a person and that he or she is entitled to all the protections that can reasonably and ethically be given to any living human being. Such protection, they suggest, is basic and humane and lies in the natural relationship of one human being to another. If antiabortion forces have their way, abortion will one day again be outlawed.

Natural law became an issue in confirmation hearings conducted for U.S. Supreme Court justice nominee Clarence Thomas in 1991. Because Thomas had mentioned natural law and natural rights in speeches given before his nomination to the Court, Senate Judiciary Committee Chairman Joseph Biden (and others) grilled him about the concept. Biden suggested that natural law was a defunct philosophical perspective, no longer worthy of serious consideration, and that the duty of a U.S. Supreme Court justice was to follow the Constitution. Thomas responded by pointing out that natural law concepts contributed greatly to the principles underlying the Constitution. It was the natural law writing of John Locke, Thomas suggested, that inspired the Framers to declare: "All men are created equal."

> *This law of nature, being . . . dictated by God himself, is of course superior in obligation to any other. It is binding over all the globe, and all countries, and at all times; no human laws are of any validity if contrary to this; and such of them as are valid derive all their force, and all their authority immediately, or immediately from this original.*
>
> —Sir William Blackstone, 1 Cooley's Blackstone 41

> *Natural law provides a basis in human dignity by which we can judge whether human beings are just or unjust, noble or ignoble.*
>
> —Justice Clarence Thomas (1987)

History of Western Law

Just as philosophical perspectives have contributed to the modern legal system in the United States, so have many ancient forms of law. Consequently, our laws today reflect many of the principles developed by legal thinkers throughout history.

> *Law is whatever is boldly asserted and plausibly maintained.*
>
> —Aaron Burr, former vice president of the United States (1756–1836)

Ancient Laws   The development of criminal codes can be traced back several thousand years. Although references to older codes of law have been discovered, the oldest written law that has been found, although only in part, is the Code of Ur-Nammu from Mesopotamia. It is dated to approximately 2100 BC. Similar to contemporary U.S. law, it distinguished between compensation and punishment—or in contemporary terms, civil law and criminal law. For example, the code provided monetary compensation for personal injuries and punishment (death) for murder, rape, and other "crimes."

Another ancient law that was found in more complete condition is the Code of Hammurabi. This code was inscribed on a stone pillar near the ancient city of Susa around the year 1750 BC. The Hammurabi Code, named after the Babylonian king Hammurabi (1792–1750 BC), specified a number of property rights, crimes, and associated punishments. Hammurabi's laws spoke to issues of ownership, theft, sexual relationships, and interpersonal violence. Although the Hammurabi Code specified a variety of corporal punishments, and even death, for named offenses, its major contribution was that it routinized the practice of justice in Babylonian society by lending predictability to punishments. Before the code, captured offenders often faced the most barbarous and capricious of punishments, frequently at the hands of revenge-seeking victims, no matter how minor their offenses had been. As Marvin Wolfgang has observed, "In its day, . . . the Hammurabi Code, with its emphasis on retribution, amounted to a brilliant advance in penal philosophy mainly because it represented an attempt to keep cruelty within bounds."[8] Although it is of considerable archeological importance, the Code of Hammurabi probably had little impact on the development of Western legal traditions. Even though they had little direct impact on the development of Western law, we learn from these ancient codes that some legal principles (e.g., distinguishing compensation from punishment, and the idea of proportionality of punishment) are innate, meaning that they have held significance for people for a long time.

The first requirement of a sound body of law is that it should correspond with the actual feelings and demands of the community, whether right or wrong.

—Justice Oliver Wendell Holmes, Jr.
(The Common Law, 1881)

Civil and Common Law Traditions   In contrast to the Hammurabi Code, Roman law influenced our own legal tradition in many ways. Roman law derived from the Twelve Tables, which were written about 450 BC. The Tables, a collection of basic rules related to family, religious, and economic life, appear to have been based on common and fair practices generally accepted among early tribes that existed before the establishment of the Roman republic. Roman law was codified by order of Emperor Justinian I, who ruled the Byzantine Empire between AD 527 and 565. In its complete form, the Justinian Code, or *Corpus Juris Civilis* (CJC), consisted of three lengthy legal documents: (1) the Institutes, (2) the Digest, and (3) the Code itself. Justinian's code distinguished between two major legal categories: public laws and private laws. Public laws dealt with the organization of the Roman state, its senate, and governmental offices. Private law concerned itself with contracts, personal possessions, the legal status of various types of persons (citizens, free persons, slaves, freedmen, guardians, husbands and wives, and so on), and injuries to citizens. Emperor Claudius conquered England in the middle of the first century, and Roman authority over "Britannia" was consolidated by later rulers who built walls and fortifications to keep out the still-hostile Scots. Roman customs, law, and language were forced on the English population during the succeeding three centuries under the *Pax Romana*—a peace imposed by the military might of Rome.[9] The CJC was abandoned and lost for several centuries. But it was rediscovered in the eleventh century and thereafter influenced the development of civil codes throughout Europe, including the Napoleonic and German codes. Indeed, Napoleon transplanted his code throughout the territories he conquered. Today, many nations fall into the civil law tradition, including France, Italy, Spain, Germany,

French Africa, French South America, and French Central America. The law of the Catholic Church, canon law, was influential in the development of the civil law tradition. Although the civil law tradition spread throughout continental Europe and much of the rest of the world, it was not transplanted to England, where a separate legal tradition developed.

The criminal law . . . is an expression of the moral sense of the community.

—United States v. Freeman, 357 F.2d 606 (2d Cir. 1966)

COMMON LAW

Before the Norman conquest of 1066, most law in England was local. It was created by lords and applied within their realms. Accordingly, law was decentralized and varying. When William the Conqueror invaded England in 1066, he declared Saxon law absolute and announced that he was "the guardian of the laws of Edward," his English predecessor. William, however, in seeking to add uniformity to the law, planted legal seeds that would grow and eventually merge into one **common law**. He established courts that would be hierarchical and have national jurisdiction. The decisions of the highest court, Kings Court, were binding all across England. Over time, these courts developed their own processes and rules. One such development was the doctrine of *stare decisis*.

common law
Law originating from use and custom rather than from written statutes. The term refers to non-statutory customs, traditions, and precedents that help guide judicial decision making.

Stare decisis, which means "let the decision stand," embodies the idea that cases with like facts should have the same law applied. The earlier case is commonly known as *precedent*. The final element in the equation is the absence of a legislature. Unlike the civil law tradition, which is legislative in nature, courts developed common law, case by case. In most cases, courts looked to local custom and practice to make the law. However, the diversity of the law that characterized the feudal era was reduced by having a hierarchical system of courts, with higher court decisions binding lower courts.

The common law of England is not to be taken in all respects to be that of America. Our ancestors brought with them its general principles, and claimed it as their birthright; but they brought with them and adopted only that portion which was applicable to their situation.

—Van Ness v. Pacard, 27 U.S. (2 Pet.) 137, 144 (1829)

The fusion of these developments effectively resulted in the creation of new laws, through courts, that applied throughout England. For the first time, England had a unified set of laws that were common to all the English; hence this legal tradition is known as the *common law tradition*. As Clarence Ray Jeffery, a sociologist of law, observes, "It was during the reign of Henry II (1154–1189) that the old tribal-feudal system of law disappeared and a new system of common law emerged in England."[10] By the year 1200, common law was firmly entrenched in England. Because it depended so heavily on judicial interpretation, common law has often been referred to as *judge-made law*. As noted author Howard Abadinsky observes, "Common law involved the transformation of community rules into a national legal system. The controlling element [was] precedent."[11] The common law tradition is evolutionary in nature. Its change came incrementally, as courts adapted the law to different facts or societal changes. The civil law tradition, on the other hand, is planned and statutory. Civil law is conceived of by some authority, is established, and then changes abruptly when the legislative authority revises the code.

The common law tradition was carried to the United States by the early English immigrants, and today it forms the basis of much statutory and case law in this country. The influence of common law on contemporary criminal law is so great that it is often regarded as *the* major source of modern criminal law. The American frontier provided an especially fertile ground for the acceptance of common law principles. The scarcity of churches and infrequent visits by traveling ministers prompted many territories to recognize common law marriages. Similarly, the lack of formal legal agencies led to informal recognition that a meeting of minds (and a person's "word") constituted a valid contract in most areas of human endeavor.

The strength of the common law tradition in early America was highlighted in 1811, when the famous English prison reformer and jurist Jeremy Bentham wrote to President

James Madison offering to codify the law of the United States in its entirety. Bentham told Madison that the case-by-case approach of the common law, based solely on precedent, was too "fragmented, flexible, and uncertain" to support the continued economic and social development of the country. Madison, however, rejected the offer and directed John Quincy Adams to reply to Bentham, telling him "[either] I greatly overrate or [Bentham] greatly underrates the task . . . not only of digesting our Statutes into a concise and clear system, but [of reducing] our unwritten to a text law." A short time later, Madison also rejected federal use of the written legal code developed by Edward Livingston, an American follower of Bentham.[12]

By the late 1800s, however, common law principles were giving way across America to written civil and penal codes. The Married Women's Property Act of 1875, for example, which provided a model for state legislatures of the period, gave married women control over wages earned independently of their husbands. The act effectively dissolved the older common law doctrine of unity of husband and wife, a principle that had given husbands control over their wives' wages and property. About the same time, the nineteenth-century jurist David Dudley Field drafted what came to be known as the Field Code—a set of proposed standardized criminal and civil procedures and uniform criminal statutes that were adopted by the state of New York and served as a model for other states that sought to codify their laws.

Although modern American substantive and procedural criminal law is largely codified, some states still explicitly acknowledge the common law roots of contemporary penal legislation. For example, the Florida Criminal Code states, "The common law of England in relation to crimes, except so far as the same relates to the modes and degrees of punishment, shall be of full force in this state where there is no existing provision by statute on the subject."[13] With regard to "punishment of common law offenses," the Florida Code says, "When there exists no such provision by statute, the court shall proceed to punish such offense by fine or imprisonment, but the fine shall not exceed $500, nor the imprisonment 12 months."[14] Arizona Revised Statutes contain a similar provision, which reads, "The common law only so far as it is consistent with and adapted to the natural and physical conditions of this state and the necessities of the people thereof, and not repugnant to or inconsistent with the Constitution of the United States or the constitution or laws of this state, or established customs of the people of this state, is adopted and shall be the rule of decision in all courts of this state."[15]

Occasionally individuals are arrested and tried under common law when appropriate statutory provisions are not in place. In 1996, for example, euthanasia advocate Dr. Jack Kevorkian was arrested and tried in Michigan on charges of violating the state's common law against suicide. After Kevorkian was acquitted, jury foreman Dean Gauthier told reporters, "We felt there was a lack of evidence regarding the interpretation of the common law."[16] In 1999, however, after Michigan enacted statutory legislation outlawing physician-assisted suicide, Kevorkian was convicted of a number of crimes and sentenced to 10 to 25 years in prison. Evidence against Kevorkian came largely from a videotape aired on CBS's *60 Minutes*, showing the doctor giving a lethal injection to 52-year-old Thomas Youk, who suffered from amyotrophic lateral sclerosis, also known as ALS, or Lou Gehrig's disease. After spending more than eight years in prison Kevorkian was paroled for good behavior in 2007. He died in 2011 from pneumonia at the age of 83.[17]

No one, sir, is above the law. No one.

—Judge Jessica Cooper, ruling in the trial of Jack Kevorkian

Although Florida and a few other states have passed legislation officially institutionalizing common law principles, all states today, with the exception of Louisiana, which employs a modified civil law system because it was once a territory of France, remain **common law states**. Even though today's primary lawmakers are legislatures, both the common law and judges continue to play a significant role in the development of the law. Statutes are often broadly drafted, and interpretation and "gap filling" are necessary. The responsibility

common law state
A jurisdiction in which the principles and precedents of common law continue to hold sway.

of interpreting and applying the law belongs to judges, who, through their interpretation of both statutes and precedent, continue to develop the existing body of common law. The common law continues to be significant in this way and others. Often, statutes are simply codifications of the common law. For example, to understand what a legislature meant when it referred to "malice aforethought," a judge would have to determine if the body simply codified the common law principle. If so, then the judge would turn to common law decisions to understand the meaning of the term. It is important to realize, however, that the common law, except interpretations of state and federal constitutions, is a lower form of law than statutes. As such, statutes prevail when in conflict with the common law.

Regardless of whether a state more closely affiliates with a common law or civil law tradition, there is considerable uniformity of law, particularly criminal law. There are several causes of the similarities. First, the U.S. Constitution applies equally and identically to all states. For reasons you will learn later, the Constitution has had considerable impact on both substantive and procedural criminal law in recent decades.

Second, there has been a convergence of all legal traditions, not just within the United States, but around the world (Figure 1–2). As people from different legal traditions interact, through war, conquest, business transactions, and travel, legal convergence occurs. Today, all common law nations have legislative bodies that are the primary lawmakers. England has its Parliament, the United States has its Congress, and the states have their state legislatures. Conversely, judges play a larger role in interpreting the law in civil law nations than in the past. The emergence of legislative authority is a significant change to the common law tradition. Its impact has been significant in criminal law, where the doctrine of *nullum crimen sine lege*, also known as the *principle of legality*, has taken hold. The Latin phrase translates to "there is no crime if there is no statute." Today, the idea that crimes must be declared by statute in advance of the criminal act is embodied in the due-process clauses of

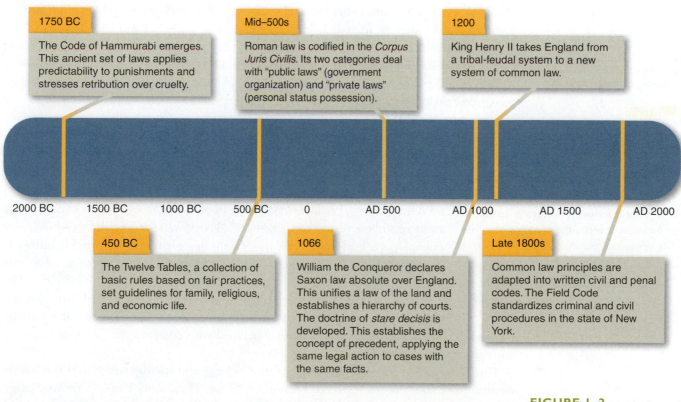

1750 BC
The Code of Hammurabi emerges. This ancient set of laws applies predictability to punishments and stresses retribution over cruelty.

Mid–500s
Roman law is codified in the *Corpus Juris Civilis*. Its two categories deal with "public laws" (government organization) and "private laws" (personal status possession).

1200
King Henry II takes England from a tribal-feudal system to a new system of common law.

450 BC
The Twelve Tables, a collection of basic rules based on fair practices, set guidelines for family, religious, and economic life.

1066
William the Conqueror declares Saxon law absolute over England. This unifies a law of the land and establishes a hierarchy of courts. The doctrine of *stare decisis* is developed. This establishes the concept of precedent, applying the same legal action to cases with the same facts.

Late 1800s
Common law principles are adapted into written civil and penal codes. The Field Code standardizes criminal and civil procedures in the state of New York.

2000 BC   1500 BC   1000 BC   500 BC   0   AD 500   AD 1000   AD 1500   AD 2000

FIGURE 1–2

A Timeline of Developments in the Law.

TABLE 1–1 Civil and Common Law Legal Traditions Compared

The Civil Law Legal Tradition	The Common Law Legal Tradition
Where: France, Italy, Portugal, Spain, Franco-Africa, Latin America, Louisiana (limited)	Where: England, United States, Australia, New Zealand, Belize, Canada, Anglo-Africa
Judges play minimal role in development of law	Judges play major role in development of law
Periodic, sometimes abrupt, legislative change	More evolutionary change through judicial decisions with occasional legislative change
Rational and forward thinking	More likely to change in response to current conditions

the Constitution. Indeed, although exceptions can be found, in both legislation and judicial decisions, for very well-defined and recognized common law crimes, the rule is widely adhered to today.

Additionally, civil law nations are increasingly adopting accusatorial processes, which were founded in common law systems, and common law nations are adopting a few inquisitorial practices, which have their origin in civil law nations. Finally, other factors influencing the uniformity of law are the similarity of values among all citizens and the national and international nature of business and social life. Table 1–1 compares and summarizes the two legal traditions.

Civil Law Distinguished

civil law
The form of the law that governs relationships between parties.

At this point, criminal law should be distinguished from civil law. Whereas criminal law concerns the government's decision to prohibit and punish conduct, **civil law** (not to be confused with the civil law legal tradition) governs relationships between private parties. Civil codes regulate private relationships of all sorts, including marriages, divorces, inheritance, adoption, and many other forms of personal and business relationships. Civil actions come in many varieties, including breach of contract, domestic, and tort. A **tort** is "the unlawful violation of a private legal right other than a mere breach of contract, express or implied. A tort may also be the violation of a public duty if, as a result of the violation, some special damage accrues to the individual."[18] An individual, business, or other legally recognized entity that commits a tort is called a **tortfeasor**.

tort
A private or civil wrong or injury; "the unlawful violation of a private legal right other than a mere breach of contract, express or implied."[ii]

tortfeasor
An individual, business, or other legally recognized entity that commits a tort.

There are three forms of tort. The first, negligence, occurs when a tortfeasor injures another through unintentional but careless behavior. Car accidents and slips and falls are examples. Intentional behavior that harms another is the second form of tort. Many crimes are also intentional torts. The third form of tort is strict liability. In these cases, which are rare, defendants are liable if they are the cause of harm, even if they are not negligent, because they engage in ultrahazardous activities and liability exists regardless of the care exercised. The storage and use of explosives, for example, may lead to strict liability claims in some instances. Strict liability encourages potential defendants to take every possible precaution to guard against harm to others.

Stare decisis *is ordinarily a wise rule of action. But it is not a universal, inexorable command. The instances in which the court has disregarded its admonition are many.*

—Justice Louis D. Brandeis, dissenting in
Washington v. W.C. Dawson & Co.,
264 U.S. 219, 238 (1924)

A tort may give rise to civil liability, under which the injured party may sue the person or entity that caused the injury and ask that the offending party be ordered to pay damages. Civil law is more concerned with compensating injuries than it is with punishment.

Parties to a civil suit are referred to as the *plaintiff* and the *defendant*, and the names of civil suits take the form *Named Plaintiff* v. *Named Defendant*. Unlike criminal cases, in which the state prosecutes wrongdoers, most civil suits are brought by individuals. On occasion, however, the plaintiff in a civil suit may be the state or a government office or agency. For example, the state may bring a suit to protect the public welfare, such as to condemn a dangerous building, to stop the sale of a dangerous product, or to revoke an attorney's right to practice law or a doctor's right to practice medicine. A government may also sue in the same manner and for the same reasons as private individuals, such as when someone breaches a contract with the government or harms the government through negligence.

The primary intention of civil actions is to provide compensation for losses, known as **damages**. In some cases, declaratory and injunctive relief may be sought. That is, the plaintiff may want the court to make a declaration of law (e.g., the statute is unconstitutional) or may want the court to order someone to do something or not to do something (e.g., remove a fence that crossed onto the plaintiff's property). A second financial remedy represents an area of overlap with criminal law. In instances of extremely negligent or intentional behavior, civil suit plaintiffs may be awarded **punitive damages**. Punitive damages are monies beyond compensation; they are intended to punish or to deter, two objectives of criminal law. Punitive damages have been challenged as unconstitutional because defendants in civil actions are not protected by all the rights of criminal defendants. The Supreme Court has upheld the constitutionality of civil punitive damages with limitations as to amount and how they are calculated.[19]

damages (actual)
A financial award in a civil suit intended to compensate for injuries to person or property.

punitive damages
A financial award in a civil suit that is intended to punish the defendant and/or to deter similar future misconduct. Punitive damages are monies beyond the actual damages suffered by the plaintiff.

For example, in 1989 the *Exxon Valdez*, an oil tanker, struck ground in Alaskan waters. The injury to the ship resulted in hundreds of thousands of barrels of oil spilling into the ocean, the largest spill by a tanker in U.S. history and the second largest spill of any kind next to the Deepwater Horizon spill of 2010. Subsequently a jury awarded plaintiffs $5 billion in punitive damages. That award was reduced on a couple of occasions by appellate courts, and the Supreme Court later reduced the amount equal to the actual damages awarded by the jury (approximately $500 million), because the spill was caused by negligence. Punitive damages may exceed the 1:1 ratio in cases of intentional torts.[20]

While Justice Cardozo pointed out with great accuracy that the power of the precedent is only "the power of the beaten track"; still the mere fact that a path is a beaten one is a persuasive reason for following it.

—Justice Robert H. Jackson (1945)

Of course, violations of the criminal law can also lead to civil actions—even though the defendant may not be convicted of the criminal charges. In 1996, for example, Bernhard Goetz, also known as the "subway vigilante," was ordered to pay $43 million in damages to Darrell Cabey, one of four young black men he shot on a New York City subway train in 1984. Goetz did not deny that he shot the men but claimed that they were trying to rob him. After the shooting, Goetz was acquitted of attempted murder and assault charges at a criminal trial but served eight months in prison on weapons charges. Immediately after the civil award, Goetz filed for bankruptcy, listing $17,000 in assets and $60 million in liabilities.

Perhaps the most famous example of such an instance, however, was the 1995 wrongful death suit filed against O. J. Simpson by the family of murder victim Ronald Goldman. The suit demanded monetary damages for what the plaintiffs claimed was Simpson's role in the wrongful death of Ronald Goldman, and it alleged that Simpson (and possibly other unknown defendants) caused Goldman's death. In 1997, Simpson was ordered to pay $33.5 million to the family of Ron Goldman and to Nicole Simpson's estate, after a California civil jury found that he was responsible for their deaths.[21] California Superior Court Judge Hiroshi Fujisaki, who had also presided over the trial, denied Simpson's request for a new trial.[22] In 2008, Simpson was convicted by a Las Vegas jury on 12 felony counts stemming from a confrontation in a hotel room in 2007. The convictions came 13 years to the day after his 1995 acquittal.[23] As of this writing, the 64-year-old Simpson is serving his sentence of up to 33 years in prison at the Lovelock Correctional Center in Lovelock, Nevada.[24]

Because criminal law and civil law are conceptually distinct, both in function and in process, a person can be held accountable under both types of law for the same instance of misbehavior without violating constitutional prohibitions against double jeopardy.

Criminal Procedure Distinguished

substantive criminal law
The part of the law that defines crimes and specifies punishments.

Whereas **substantive criminal law** defines what conduct is criminal, criminal procedure defines the processes that may be used by law enforcement, prosecutors, victims, and courts to investigate and adjudicate criminal cases. As an academic field, criminal procedure also includes the study of the Constitution's role in the process. For example, the Fourth Amendment's privilege against unreasonable searches and seizures, the Fifth Amendment's privilege against self-incrimination, and the Sixth Amendment's right to counsel, to a speedy and public trial, and to confront one's accusers are all criminal procedure topics. This text does not explore criminal procedure. Instead, it provides a comprehensive survey of criminal law.

TYPES OF CRIMES

felony
A serious crime, generally one punishable by death or by incarceration in a state or federal prison facility as opposed to a jail.

misdemeanor
A minor crime; an offense punishable by incarceration, usually in a local confinement facility, for a period of which the upper limit is prescribed by statute in a given jurisdiction, typically one year or less.

There are many different ways to classify crimes. One way is to distinguish crimes by their seriousness. It is common, for example, to distinguish among felonies, misdemeanors, and infractions.[25] A crucial feature that distinguishes one type of crime from another is the degree of punishment. Hence **felonies** are thought of as serious crimes that are punishable by at least a year in prison. To the founders of the United States, the highest crime an individual could commit, and the only crime mentioned in the Constitution, is treason (which is defined and discussed in more detail in Chapter 11). **Misdemeanors** are less serious offenses, generally thought of as punishable by less than a year's incarceration (Figure 1–3). The Texas Penal Code, for example, defines a felony as "an offense so designated by law or punishable by death or confinement in a penitentiary." A misdemeanor, according to the Texas Code, "means an offense so designated by law or punishable by fine, by confinement in jail, or by both fine and confinement in jail."

Other states use similar definitions. The California Penal Code describes a felony as "a crime which is punishable with death or by imprisonment in the state prison." The code

FIGURE 1–3

Common Punishments for Criminal Acts.

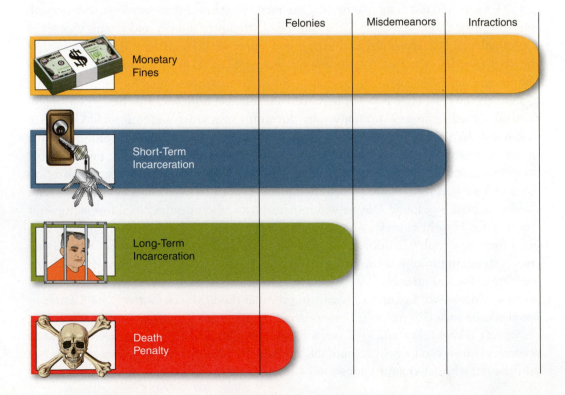

continues, "Every other crime or public offense is a misdemeanor except those offenses that are classified as infractions." Consistent with its emphasis on degree of punishment as a distinguishing feature between felonies and misdemeanors, California law states, "Except in cases where a different punishment is prescribed by any law of this state, every offense declared to be a misdemeanor is punishable by imprisonment in the county jail not exceeding six months, or by fine not exceeding one thousand dollars ($1,000), or by both." In California, "[a]n infraction is not punishable by imprisonment." Some jurisdictions refer to **infractions** as *ticketable offenses*, to indicate that such minor crimes usually result in the issuance of citations, which can often be paid through the mail.

Another important distinction can be drawn between crimes that are completed and those that are attempted or are still in the planning stage. The term *inchoate*, which means "partial" or "unfinished," is applied to crimes such as conspiracy to commit a criminal act, solicitation of others to engage in criminal acts, and attempts to commit crimes. Inchoate crimes are discussed in greater detail later in this book.

Crimes can also be classified as either **mala in se** or **mala prohibita**. *Mala in se* crimes are those that are regarded, by tradition and convention, as wrong in themselves. Such acts are said to be inherently evil and immoral and are sometimes called *acts against conscience*. *Mala in se* crimes, such as murder, rape, and other serious offenses, are almost universally condemned and probably would be so even if strictures against such behaviors were not specified in the criminal law.[26] Jeffery says that just as there is a natural law, there are also "natural crimes." "The notion of natural crime," he says, as "a crime against a law of nature rather than against a legal law, was present in the criminal law at its inception. This led to the definition of crimes as *mala in se*, acts bad in themselves, and *mala prohibita*, acts which are crimes mainly because they are prohibited by positive law."[27]

As Jeffery observed, *mala prohibita* crimes (*malum prohibitum* is the singular term that refers to one such crime) are considered "wrongs" only because there is a law against them. Without a statute specifically proscribing them, *mala prohibita* offenses might *not* be regarded as "wrong" by a large number of people. *Mala prohibita* offenses often include the category of "victimless crimes," such as prostitution, drug use, and gambling, in which a clear-cut victim is difficult to identify and whose commission rarely leads to complaints from the parties directly involved in the offense.

Many other distinctions can be drawn between types of crimes, but space does not permit discussion of them all. One final division should be mentioned, however—the traditional classification of offenses into four types: (1) **property crimes**, (2) **personal crimes**, (3) **public-order offenses**, and (4) **morals offenses**. The distinction between property and personal crimes is of special importance in most state penal codes. Official reports on the incidence of crime, such as the FBI's Uniform Crime Reports (UCR), are structured along such a division. Crimes against property include burglary, larceny, arson, criminal mischief (vandalism), property damage, motor vehicle theft, passing bad checks, commission of fraud or forgery, and so on (see Chapter 9). Personal crimes, or offenses against persons, include criminal homicide, kidnapping and false imprisonment, various forms of assault, and rape (see Chapters 7 and 8). Personal crimes are also called *violent crimes*. Public-order offenses, or crimes against the public order, include offenses such as fighting, breach of peace, disorderly conduct, vagrancy, loitering, unlawful assembly, public intoxication, obstructing public passage, and (illegally) carrying weapons (see Chapter 10). Finally, morals offenses denote a category of unlawful conduct that was criminalized originally to protect the family and related social institutions (see Chapter 12). This category includes lewdness, indecency, sodomy, and other sex-related offenses, such as seduction, fornication, adultery, bigamy, pornography, obscenity, cohabitation, and prostitution.

---

infraction
A violation of a state statute or local ordinance punishable by a fine or other penalty, but not by incarceration. Also called *summary offense*.

mala in se
Acts that are regarded, by tradition and convention, as wrong in themselves.

mala prohibita
Acts that are considered "wrongs" only because there is a law against them.

The purpose of all law, and the criminal law in particular, is to conform conduct to the norms expressed in that law.

—United States v. Granada, 565 F.2d 922, 926 (5th Cir. 1978)

 Know 3 for each one

property crime
A crime committed against property, including (according to the FBI's UCR Program) burglary, larceny, motor vehicle theft, and arson.

personal crime
A crime committed against a person, including (according to the FBI's UCR Program) murder, rape, aggravated assault, and robbery. Also called *violent crime*.

public-order offense
An act that is willfully committed and that disturbs public peace or tranquility. Included are offenses such as fighting, breach of peace, disorderly conduct, vagrancy, loitering, unlawful assembly, public intoxication, obstructing public passage, and (illegally) carrying weapons.

morals offense
An offense that was originally defined to protect the family and related social institutions. Included in this category are crimes such as lewdness, indecency, sodomy, and other sex-related offenses, including seduction, fornication, adultery, bigamy, pornography, obscenity, cohabitation, and prostitution.

THE PURPOSES OF CRIMINAL LAW

Max Weber (1864–1920), an eminent sociologist of the early twentieth century, said that the primary purpose of law is to regulate the flow of human interaction.[28] Without laws of some sort, modern society probably could not exist, and social organization would be unable to rise above the level found in primitive societies, where mores and norms were the primary regulatory forces. Laws make for predictability in human events by using the authority of government to ensure that socially agreed-on standards of behavior will be followed and enforced. They allow people to plan their lives by guaranteeing a relative degree of safety to well-intentioned individuals, while constraining the behavior of those who would unfairly victimize others. Laws provide a stable foundation for individuals wishing to join together in a legitimate undertaking by enforcing rights over the control and ownership of property. They also provide for individual freedoms and personal safety by sanctioning the conduct of anyone who violates the legitimate expectations of others. Hence the first and most significant purpose of the law can be simply stated: Laws support social order.

To many people, a society without laws is unthinkable. Were such a society to exist, however, it would doubtless be ruled by individuals and groups powerful enough to usurp control over others. The personal whims of the powerful would rule, and the less powerful would live in constant fear of attack. The closest we have come in modern times to lawlessness can be seen in war-torn regions of the world. The genocidal activities of warring parties in Bosnia and Herzegovina, Croatia, and Rwanda and the wholesale looting and the frequent sexual attacks on Kuwaiti women by Iraqi troops during the Gulf War provide a glimpse of what can happen when the rule of law breaks down.

Crime is a technical word. It is the law's name for certain acts which it is pleased to define and punish with a penalty.

— Saturday Evening Post writer Melville D. Post (1897)

Like laws in general, the criminal law has a variety of purposes. Some say that the primary purpose of the criminal law is to "make society safe for its members, and to punish and rehabilitate those who commit offenses."[29] Others contend that the basic purpose of the criminal law is "to declare public disapproval of an offender's conduct by means of public trial and conviction and to punish the offender by imposing a penal sanction."[30]

The criminal law also serves to restrain those whom society considers dangerous, often through imprisonment, home confinement, or other means. It deters potential offenders through examples of punishments applied to those found guilty of crimes, and it protects honest and innocent citizens by removing society's most threatening members. In short, criminal law protects law-abiding individuals while maintaining social order through the conviction and sentencing of criminals. A more complete list shows that criminal law functions to

- Protect members of the public from harm
- Preserve and maintain social order
- Support fundamental social values
- Distinguish criminal wrongs from civil wrongs[31]
- Express communal condemnation of criminal behavior
- Deter people from criminal activity
- Stipulate the degree of seriousness of criminal conduct
- Establish criteria for the clear determination of guilt or innocence at trial
- Punish those who commit crimes
- Rehabilitate offenders
- Assuage victims of crime

SOURCES OF CRIMINAL LAW

Today's laws can be found in a number of sources, each of which is briefly discussed in the pages that follow. These "living" sources of the law can be distinguished from historical underpinnings of the law, such as ancient codes.

Constitutions

The highest form of law in the United States is the Constitution of the United States. The Constitution, however, is not a source of specific laws or criminal prohibitions (although it does define treason as a crime). Instead it serves as a constraint on the **police power** of the government. The Constitution sets limits on the nature and extent of criminal law that the government can enact. It guards personal liberties by restricting undue government interference in the lives of individuals and by *implicitly* ensuring personal privacy. The **Bill of Rights** contains most of the Constitution's limits on the authority of the government to regulate people.

The Constitution can be seen as the sole piece of legislation by which all other laws and legislation are judged acceptable or unacceptable. For example, the Constitution enshrines the notion that people should only be held accountable for that which they do (actions) or do not do (omissions), rather than for what they think or believe. Hence if a state legislature were to enact a law prohibiting thoughts of a seditious or carnal nature, the law would likely be overturned if it ever came before the U.S. Supreme Court, which serves as our nation's constitutional interpreter.

Constitutional provisions determine the nature of criminal law by setting limits on just what can be **criminalized**, or made illegal. Generally speaking, constitutional requirements hold that criminal laws can only be enacted where there is a compelling public need to regulate conduct. The U.S. Supreme Court has held that "to justify the exercise of police power the public interest must require the interference, and the measures adopted must be reasonably necessary for the accomplishment of the purpose."[32]

As mentioned earlier in this chapter, the Constitution also demands that anyone accused of criminal activity be accorded due process. Similarly, the Constitution helps ensure that the accused are provided with the opportunity to offer a well-crafted defense.

The Constitution imposes a number of specific requirements and restrictions on both the state and federal governments, and it protects individual rights in the area of criminal law. Most of the restrictions, requirements, protections, and rights inherent in the Constitution, as they relate to criminal law, are discussed elsewhere in this textbook. For now, we should recognize that they include

- Limits on the government's police power
- Limits on strict liability crimes
- Protection against *ex post facto* laws
- Protection against laws that are vague and unclear
- Protection of free thought and free speech
- Protection of the right to keep and bear arms
- Freedom of religion
- Freedom of the press
- Freedom to assemble peaceably
- Freedom from unfair deprivation of life, liberty, and property
- Prohibitions against unreasonable searches and seizures
- Protection against warrants issued without probable cause
- Protection against double jeopardy in criminal proceedings

police power
The authority of a state to enact and enforce a criminal statute.[iii]

Bill of Rights
The first ten amendments to the U.S. Constitution, which were made part of the Constitution in 1791.

criminalize
To make criminal; to declare an act or omission to be criminal or in violation of a law making it so.

- Protection against self-incrimination
- Right to a speedy and public trial before an impartial jury
- Right to be informed of the nature of the charges
- Right to confront witnesses
- Right to the assistance of defense counsel
- Prohibition against excessive bail
- Prohibition against excessive fines
- Prohibition against cruel and unusual punishments
- Guarantees of equal protection of the laws

Even though the rights found in the Constitution were originally intended to limit only the federal government, the U.S. Supreme Court has determined that the addition of the Fourteenth Amendment's due-process and equal protection clauses immediately following the Civil War were intended to extend (incorporate) most of the rights found in the Constitution to the states. As such, most of the rights just listed apply to state law enforcement officers and in state courts.

In addition to the federal Constitution, each state has its own constitution. Although states may not reduce the rights found in the U.S. Constitution, some expand on them, either through their state constitutions or by statute. Here are a few examples of state constitutional provisions that go beyond the U.S. Constitution in the protection of individual liberties:

- Many states—including Alaska, Arizona, California, Florida, Hawaii, Illinois, Louisiana, Montana, South Carolina, and Washington—expressly protect privacy, whereas the federal constitution does so implicitly. A federal right to privacy was only recently declared by the Supreme Court (as a *penumbra*, or implied protection), and it is controversial because of the absence of express language in the Constitution establishing the right.

- Many states provide for education through their constitutions, although the federal Constitution does not contain a right to education.

- In addition to protecting freedom of religion, as the First Amendment of the federal Constitution does, Georgia's constitution protects freedom of "conscience."

Statutes, Ordinances, and Regulations

Courts of law follow precedent, on the general theory that experience is more than just individual decision. Precedent, however, tends to carry forward the ignorance and injustice of the past. Mankind is constantly learning, getting new views of truth, seeing new values in social justice. Precedent clogs this advance.

—Frank Crane, noted author (1919)

As you have already learned, the source of most criminal statutes, as well as most criminal procedure today, is the legislature. In addition to the Congress of the United States, the legislature of each state has the authority to define crimes. The laws of a legislature are known as *public laws* or *statutes*. Statutes are commonly organized by topic, such as the Code of Criminal Laws. The vast majority of crimes are defined by state legislatures, most investigations by law enforcement are for state crimes, and more than 90 percent of felonies and serious misdemeanors are prosecuted in state courts.

In addition to state and federal crimes, municipalities are often empowered by state law to define and punish crimes, usually misdemeanors and infractions. Local laws are commonly known as *ordinances*. Another source of law is administrative regulations. Legitimately promulgated regulations have the full authority of legislation. Administrative regulations can be penal and can result in incarceration, fines, and other punishments.[33]

Common Law

For reasons discussed earlier, the common law, both historical and newly developed, continues to be important. Specifically, courts mold the law and contribute to the uniformity and predictability of the law through interpretation. As you read earlier, the doctrine of *stare decisis* has played a major role. The extent to which a court should follow precedent is a perennial question. Should a lower court follow a higher court's decision if it is over 100 years old and was premised on social or economic circumstances that have changed? Should the Supreme Court be bound by its own precedent if the composition of the Court has changed significantly?

The U.S. Supreme Court has ruled, "*Stare decisis* is of fundamental importance to the rule of law."[34] **Case law** and **statutory law** make for predictability in the law. Criminal defendants and their attorneys entering a modern courtroom can generally gauge with a fair degree of accuracy what the law will expect of them. In the words of the Court: "[A]cknowledgments of precedent serve the principal purposes of *stare decisis*, which are to protect reliance interests and to foster stability in the law."[35] In a strongly worded acknowledgment of the importance of *stare decisis*, the majority opinion of the U.S. Supreme Court in the 1986 case of *Vasquez* v. *Hillary* says that *stare decisis* "permits society to presume that bedrock principles are founded in the law rather than in the proclivities of individuals, and thereby contributes to the integrity of our constitutional system of government, both in appearance and in fact."[36] Even so, a number of justices have, in various cases, recognized that *stare decisis* "is not an imprisonment of reason."[37] In other words, although *stare decisis* is a central guiding principle in Western law, it does not dictate blind obedience to precedent.

Although lower courts are bound by the decisions of higher courts, any court is free to set aside its own previous decisions, assuming that a higher court has not ruled on the subject. Although the rationale undergirding the doctrine of *stare decisis* applies to courts when reviewing their own decisions, the willingness of the highest court of any jurisdiction to set aside its own decisions is more important than for other courts because there is no higher court to correct errors. Indeed, Justice Robert Jackson said it best in *Brown* v. *Allen*, "We are not right because we are infallible, but we are infallible only because we are final."[38] In *Payne* v. *Tennessee*,[39] the Supreme Court discussed the doctrine of *stare decisis* in the context of deciding to reverse itself for the second time on the same issue.

Many cases, of course, are not subject to *stare decisis* because they are unlike previous cases. They may deal with new subject matter or novel situations, raise unusual legal questions, or fall outside the principles established by earlier decisions. A case is precedential only if the facts are similar to those of the case that is being heard. If it is possible to **distinguish** the facts of a new case from the facts of earlier ones, then the law of the precedential case will not be applied, or only applied in part, to the case under review.

There is a hierarchy in American law that should not be forgotten. The Constitution of the United States is the highest form of law. All other law, including state constitutions, must be consistent with it. After the U.S. Constitution, the U.S. Code is the highest form of federal law, with administrative regulations following. At the state level, state constitutions fall below the federal constitution, with state codes and then administrative regulations following, in that order. The common law, except interpretations of state and federal constitutions, is a lower form of law than statutes. As such, statutes prevail when in conflict with the common law.

The Model Penal Code

The **Model Penal Code (MPC)** deserves special mention. The MPC is not law but a proposed model, which states can use in developing or revising their statutory codes. The MPC was published as a "Proposed Official Draft" by the American Law Institute (ALI) in 1962. It had undergone 13 previous revisions and represented the culmination of efforts that had been ongoing since the ALI's inception.

case law
The body of previous decisions, or precedents, that has accumulated over time and to which attorneys refer when arguing cases and that judges use in deciding the merits of new cases.

statutory law
Law in the form of statutes or formal written codes made by a legislature or governing body with the power to make law.

stare decisis
The legal principle that requires that courts be bound by their own earlier decisions and by those of higher courts having jurisdiction over them regarding subsequent cases on similar issues of law and fact. The term literally means "standing by decided matters."

distinguish
To argue or to find that a rule established by an earlier appellate court decision does not apply to a case currently under consideration even though an apparent similarity exists between the cases.

Model Penal Code (MPC)
A model code of criminal laws intended to standardize general provisions of criminal liability, sentencing, defenses, and the definitions of specific crimes between and among the states. The Model Penal Code was developed by the American Law Institute.

APPLYING THE CONCEPT

CAPSTONE CASE

Does the Eighth Amendment Bar the Admission of Victim Impact Evidence During the Penalty Phase of a Capital Trial?

Payne v. *Tennessee,*
501 U.S. 808 (1991)

CHIEF JUSTICE REHNQUIST delivered the opinion of the court.

In this case we reconsider our holdings in *Booth* v. *Maryland,* 482 U.S. 496 (1987), and *South Carolina* v. *Gathers,* 490 U.S. 805 (1989), that the Eighth Amendment bars the admission of victim impact evidence during the penalty phase of a capital trial.

THE CASE   The petitioner, Pervis Tyrone Payne, was convicted by a jury on two counts of first-degree murder and one count of assault with intent to commit murder in the first degree. He was sentenced to death for each of the murders, and to 30 years in prison for the assault.

The victims of Payne's offenses were 28-year-old Charisse Christopher, her 2-year-old daughter Lacie, and her 3-year-old son Nicholas. The three lived together in an apartment in Millington, Tennessee, across the hall from Payne's girlfriend, Bobbie Thomas. On Saturday, June 27, 1987, Payne visited Thomas' apartment several times in expectation of her return from her mother's house in Arkansas, but found no one at home. On one visit, he left his overnight bag, containing clothes and other items for his weekend stay, in the hallway outside Thomas' apartment. With the bag were three cans of malt liquor.

Payne passed the morning and early afternoon injecting cocaine and drinking beer. Later, he drove around the town with a friend in the friend's car, each of them taking turns reading a pornographic magazine. Sometime around 3 p.m., Payne returned to the apartment complex, entered the Christophers' apartment, and began making sexual advances towards Charisse. Charisse resisted and Payne became violent. A neighbor who resided in the apartment directly beneath the Christophers heard Charisse screaming, "'Get out, get out,' as if she were telling the children to leave." The noise briefly subsided and then began, "horribly loud." The neighbor called the police after she heard a "blood-curdling scream" from the Christophers' apartment.

When the first police officer arrived at the scene, he immediately encountered Payne, who was leaving the apartment building, so covered with blood that he appeared to be "sweating blood." The officer confronted Payne, who responded, "I'm the complainant." When the officer asked, "What's going on up there?" Payne struck the officer with the overnight bag, dropped his tennis shoes, and fled.

Inside the apartment, the police encountered a horrifying scene. Blood covered the walls and floor throughout the unit. Charisse and her children were lying on the floor in the kitchen. Nicholas, despite several wounds inflicted by a butcher knife that completely penetrated through his body from front to back, was still breathing. Miraculously, he survived, but not until after undergoing seven hours of surgery and a transfusion of 1,700 cc's of blood—400 to 500 cc's more than his estimated normal blood volume. Charisse and Lacie were dead.

Charisse's body was found on the kitchen floor on her back, her legs fully extended. She had sustained 42 direct knife wounds and 42 defensive wounds on her arms and hands. The wounds were caused by 41 separate thrusts of a butcher knife. None of the 84 wounds inflicted by Payne were individually fatal; rather, the cause of death was most likely bleeding from all of the wounds.

Lacie's body was on the kitchen floor near her mother. She had suffered stab wounds to the chest, abdomen, back, and head. The murder weapon, a butcher knife, was found at her feet. Payne's baseball cap was snapped on her arm near her elbow. Three cans of malt liquor bearing Payne's fingerprints were found on a table near her body, and a fourth empty one was on the landing outside the apartment door.

Payne was apprehended later that day hiding in the attic of the home of a former girlfriend. As he descended the stairs of the attic, he stated to the arresting officers, "Man, I ain't killed no woman." According to one of the officers, Payne had "a wild look about him. His pupils were contracted. He was foaming at the mouth, saliva.

He appeared to be very nervous. He was breathing real rapid." He had blood on his body and clothes and several scratches across his chest. It was later determined that the blood stains matched the victims' blood types. A search of his pockets revealed a packet containing cocaine residue, a hypodermic syringe wrapper, and a cap from a hypodermic syringe. His overnight bag, containing a bloody white shirt, was found in a nearby dumpster.

At trial, Payne took the stand and, despite the overwhelming and relatively uncontroverted evidence against him, testified that he had not harmed any of the Christophers. Rather, he asserted that another man had raced by him as he was walking up the stairs to the floor where the Christophers lived. He stated that he had gotten blood on himself when, after hearing moans from the Christophers' apartment, he had tried to help the victims. According to his testimony, he panicked and fled when he heard police sirens and noticed the blood on his clothes. The jury returned guilty verdicts against Payne on all counts.

THE FINDING During the sentencing phase of the trial, Payne presented the testimony of four witnesses: his mother and father, Bobbie Thomas, and Dr. John T. Huston, a clinical psychologist specializing in criminal court evaluation work. Bobbie Thomas testified that she met Payne at church, during a time when she was being abused by her husband. She stated that Payne was a very caring person, and that he devoted much time and attention to her three children, who were being affected by her marital difficulties. She said that the children had come to love him very much and would miss him, and that he "behaved just like a father that loved his kids." She asserted that he did not drink, nor did he use drugs, and that it was generally inconsistent with Payne's character to have committed these crimes.

Dr. Huston testified that based on Payne's low score on an IQ test, Payne was "mentally handicapped." Huston also said that Payne was neither psychotic nor schizophrenic, and that Payne was the most polite prisoner he had ever met. Payne's parents testified that their son had no prior criminal record and had never been arrested. They also stated that Payne had no history of alcohol or drug abuse, he worked with his father as a painter, he was good with children, and he was a good son.

The State presented the testimony of Charisse's mother, Mary Zvolanek. When asked how Nicholas had been affected by the murders of his mother and sister, she responded:

> He cries for his mom. He doesn't seem to understand why she doesn't come home. And he cries for his sister,

Lacie. He comes to me many times during the week and asks me, "Grandmama, do you miss my Lacie?" And I tell him yes. He says, "I'm worried about my Lacie."

In arguing for the death penalty during closing argument, the prosecutor commented on the continuing effects of Nicholas's experience, stating:

> But we do know that Nicholas was alive. And Nicholas was in the same room. Nicholas was still conscious. His eyes were open. He responded to the paramedics. He was able to follow their directions. He was able to hold his intestines in as he was carried to the ambulance. So he knew what happened to his mother and baby sister.
>
> There is nothing you can do to ease the pain of any of the families involved in this case. There is nothing you can do to ease the pain of Bernice or Carl Payne, and that's a tragedy. There is nothing you can do basically to ease the pain of Mr. and Mrs. Zvolanek, and that's a tragedy. They will have to live with it the rest of their lives. There is obviously nothing you can do for Charisse and Lacie Jo. But there is something that you can do for Nicholas.
>
> Somewhere down the road Nicholas is going to grow up, hopefully. He's going to want to know what happened. And he is going to know what happened to his baby sister and his mother. He is going to want to know what type of justice was done. He is going to want to know what happened. With your verdict, you will provide the answer. . . .

The jury sentenced Payne to death on each of the murder counts.

The Supreme Court of Tennessee affirmed the conviction and sentence. The court rejected Payne's contention that the admission of the grandmother's testimony and the State's closing argument constituted prejudicial violations of his rights under the Eighth Amendment as applied in *Booth* v. *Maryland*, 482 U.S. 496 (1987), and *South Carolina* v. *Gathers*, 490 U.S. 805 (1989). The court characterized the grandmother's testimony as "technically irrelevant," but concluded that it "did not create a constitutionally unacceptable risk of an arbitrary imposition of the death penalty and was harmless beyond a reasonable doubt." The court determined that the prosecutor's comments during closing argument were "relevant to [Payne's] personal responsibility and moral guilt."

> . . . We granted certiorari, 498 U.S. (1991), to reconsider our holdings in *Booth* and *Gathers* that the Eighth Amendment prohibits a capital sentencing jury from considering "victim impact" evidence relating to the personal characteristics of the victim and the emotional impact of the crimes on the victim's family.

(continued)

This Court held by a 5-to-4 vote [in *Booth*] that the Eighth Amendment prohibits a jury from considering a victim impact statement at the sentencing phase of a capital trial.

The Court made clear that the admissibility of victim impact evidence was not to be determined on a case-by-case basis, but that such evidence was per se inadmissible in the sentencing phase of a capital case except to the extent that it "related directly to the circumstances of the crime." In *Gathers*, decided two years later, the Court extended the rule announced in *Booth* to statements made by a prosecutor to the sentencing jury regarding the personal qualities of the victim.

The *Booth* Court began its analysis with the observation that the capital defendant must be treated as a "uniquely individual human being, and therefore the Constitution requires the jury to make an individualized determination as to whether the defendant should be executed based on the 'character of the individual and the circumstances of the crime.'" The Court concluded that while no prior decision of this Court had mandated that only the defendant's character and immediate characteristics of the crime may constitutionally be considered, other factors are irrelevant to the capital sentencing decision unless they have "some bearing on the defendant's 'personal responsibility and moral guilt.'" To the extent that victim impact evidence presents "factors about which the defendant was unaware, and that were irrelevant to the decision to kill," the Court concluded, it has nothing to do with the "blameworthiness of a particular defendant." Evidence of the victim's character, the Court observed, "could well distract the sentencing jury from its constitutionally required task [of] determining whether the death penalty is appropriate in light of the background and record of the accused and the particular circumstances of the crime."

... *Booth* and *Gathers* were based on two premises: that evidence relating to a particular victim or to the harm that a capital defendant causes a victim's family do[es] not in general reflect on the defendant's "blameworthiness," and that only evidence relating to "blameworthiness" is relevant to the capital sentencing decision. However, the assessment of harm caused by the defendant as a result of the crime charged has understandably been an important concern of the criminal law, both in determining the elements of the offense and in determining the appropriate punishment. Thus, two equally blameworthy criminal defendants may be guilty of different offenses solely because their acts cause differing amounts of harm. "If a bank robber aims his gun at a guard, pulls the trigger, and kills his target, he may be put to death. If the gun unexpectedly misfires, he may not. His moral guilt in both cases is identical, but his responsibility in the former is greater." ...

Wherever judges in recent years have had discretion to impose sentence, the consideration of the harm caused by the crime has been an important factor in the exercise of that discretion. . . .

Whatever the prevailing sentencing philosophy, the sentencing authority has always been free to consider a wide range of relevant material. . . .

The Maryland statute involved in *Booth* required that the presentence report in all felony cases include a "victim impact statement" which would describe the effect of the crime on the victim and his family. Congress and most of the States have, in recent years, enacted similar legislation to enable the sentencing authority to consider information about the harm caused by the crime committed by the defendant. The evidence involved in the present case was not admitted pursuant to any such enactment, but its purpose and effect was much the same as if it had been. While the admission of this particular kind of evidence—designed to portray for the sentencing authority the actual harm caused by a particular crime—is of recent origin, this fact hardly renders it unconstitutional. . . .

"We have held that a State cannot preclude the sentencer from considering 'any relevant mitigating evidence' that the defendant proffers in support of a sentence less than death." . . . . But it was never held or even suggested in any of our cases preceding *Booth* that the defendant, entitled as he was to individualized consideration, was to receive that consideration wholly apart from the crime which he had committed. . . . *Booth* reasoned that victim impact evidence must be excluded because it would be difficult, if not impossible, for the defendant to rebut such evidence without shifting the focus of the sentencing hearing away from the defendant, thus creating a "'mini-trial' on the victim's character."

Payne echoes the concern voiced in Booth's case that the admission of victim impact evidence permits a jury to find that defendants whose victims were assets to their community are more deserving of punishment than those whose victims are perceived to be less worthy. As a general matter, however, victim impact evidence is not offered to encourage comparative judgments of this kind—for instance, that the killer of a hardworking, devoted parent deserves the death penalty, but that the murderer of a reprobate does not. It is designed to show instead each victim's "uniqueness as an individual human being," whatever the jury might think the loss to the community resulting from his death might be.

Under our constitutional system, the primary responsibility for defining crimes against state law, fixing punishments for the commission of these crimes, and establishing procedures for criminal trials rests with the States. The state laws respecting crimes, punishments, and criminal procedure are of course subject to the overriding provisions of the United States Constitution. Where the State imposes the death penalty for a particular crime, we have held that the Eighth Amendment imposes special limitations upon that process.

"First, there is a required threshold below which the death penalty cannot be imposed. In this context, the State must establish rational criteria that narrow the decisionmaker's judgment as to whether the circumstances of a particular defendant's case meet the threshold. Moreover, a societal consensus that the death penalty is disproportionate to a particular offense prevents a State from imposing the death penalty for that offense. Second, States cannot limit the sentencer's consideration of any relevant circumstance that could cause it to decline to impose the penalty. In this respect, the State cannot challenge the sentencer's discretion, but must allow it to consider any relevant information offered by the defendant." But, as we noted in *California* v. *Ramos*, 463 U.S. 992, 1001 (1983), "beyond these limitations . . . the Court has deferred to the State's choice of substantive factors relevant to the penalty determination."

"Within the constitutional limitations defined by our cases, the States enjoy their traditional latitude to prescribe the method by which those who commit murder should be punished." *Blystone* v. *Pennsylvania*, 494 U.S. 299, 309 (1990). The States remain free, in capital cases, as well as others, to devise new procedures and new remedies to meet felt needs. Victim impact evidence is simply another form or method of informing the sentencing authority about the specific harm caused by the crime in question, evidence of a general type long considered by sentencing authorities. We think the *Booth* Court was wrong in stating that this kind of evidence leads to the arbitrary imposition of the death penalty. In the majority of cases, and in this case, victim impact evidence serves entirely legitimate purposes. In the event that evidence is introduced that is so unduly prejudicial that it renders the trial fundamentally unfair, the Due Process Clause of the Fourteenth Amendment provides a mechanism for relief. We are now of the view that a State may properly conclude that for the jury to assess meaningfully the defendant's moral culpability and blameworthiness, it should have before it at the sentencing phase evidence of the specific harm caused by the defendant. "The State has a legitimate interest in countering the mitigating evidence which the defendant is entitled to put in, by reminding the sentencer that just as the murderer should be considered as an individual, so too the victim is an individual whose death represents a unique loss to society and in particular to his family." By turning the victim into a "faceless stranger at the penalty phase of a capital trial," *Booth* deprives the State of the full moral force of its evidence and may prevent the jury from having before it all the information necessary to determine the proper punishment for a first-degree murder.

The present case is an example of the potential for such unfairness. The capital sentencing jury heard testimony from Payne's girlfriend that they met at church; that he was affectionate, caring, kind to her children; that he was not an abuser of drugs or alcohol; and that it was inconsistent with his character to have committed the murders. Payne's parents testified that he was a good son, and a clinical psychologist testified that Payne was an extremely polite prisoner and suffered from a low IQ. None of this testimony was related to the circumstances of Payne's brutal crimes. In contrast, the only evidence of the impact of Payne's offenses during the sentencing phase was Nicholas's grandmother's description—in response to a single question—that the child misses his mother and baby sister. Payne argues that the Eighth Amendment commands that the jury's death sentence must be set aside because the jury heard this testimony. But the testimony illustrated quite poignantly some of the harm that Payne's killing had caused; there is nothing unfair about allowing the jury to bear in mind that harm at the same time as it considers the mitigating evidence introduced by the defendant. The Supreme Court of Tennessee in this case obviously felt the unfairness of the rule pronounced by *Booth* when it said, "It is an affront to the civilized members of the human race to say that at sentencing in a capital case, a parade of witnesses may praise the background, character and good deeds of Defendant (as was done in this case), without limitation as to relevancy, but nothing may be said that bears upon the character of, or the harm imposed, upon the victims." . . . .

We thus hold that if the State chooses to permit the admission of victim impact evidence and prosecutorial argument on that subject, the Eighth Amendment erects no per se bar.

Payne and his amicus argue that despite these numerous infirmities in the rule created by *Booth* and *Gathers*, we should adhere to the doctrine of *stare decisis* and stop short of overruling those cases. *Stare decisis* is the preferred course because it promotes the evenhanded, predictable, and consistent development of legal principles, fosters reliance on judicial decisions, and contributes to the actual and perceived integrity of the judicial process. Adhering to precedent "is usually the wise policy, because in most matters it is more important that the applicable rule of law be settled than it be settled right." Nevertheless, when governing decisions are unworkable or are badly reasoned, "this Court has

(continued)

never felt constrained to follow precedent." . . . . This is particularly true in constitutional cases, because in such cases "correction through legislative action is practically impossible." Considerations in favor of *stare decisis* are at their acme in cases involving property and contract rights, where reliance interests are involved. . . .

[T]he opposite is true in cases such as the present one involving procedural and evidentiary rules.

Applying these general principles, the Court has during the past 20 Terms overruled in whole or in part 33 of its previous constitutional decisions. *Booth* and *Gathers* were decided by the narrowest of margins, over spirited dissents challenging the basic underpinnings of those decisions. . . .

Reconsidering these decisions now, we conclude for the reasons heretofore stated, that they were wrongly decided and should be, and now are, overruled. We accordingly affirm the judgment of the Supreme Court of Tennessee.

What Do *You* Think?

1. What does the Court mean when it says, "*Stare decisis* is not an inexorable command; rather, it 'is a principle of policy and not a mechanical formula of adherence to the latest decision'"?

2. What would it mean for the American system of criminal justice if *stare decisis* actually were an "inexorable command" or "a mechanical formula of adherence to the latest decision"?

3. Should the doctrine of *stare decisis* apply differently in the highest court of a jurisdiction than in its lower courts?

4. What principles should guide the U.S. Supreme Court in deciding whether to adhere to one of its precedents?

Additional Applications

Who counts as a "victim"?

United States v. *Whitten et al.*, 610 F.3d 168 (2nd Cir. 2010)

The Case: In December 2006, a federal court in New York convicted a Staten Island gang member on five capital counts in connection with the robbery and shooting deaths of two undercover police detectives who had been investigating illegal gun trafficking. At the penalty phase of the trial, federal prosecutors rested their argument for the death penalty in part on evidence of the defendant's future dangerousness. They also relied on courtroom testimony about victim impact from ten people—including

three police officers who recounted to the jury how the murders had caused them great personal anguish and had also profoundly affected others who had worked alongside the slain detectives. The jury sentenced the defendant to death on all five capital counts. On appeal, the defendant argued, among other things, that *Payne* v. *Tennessee* permitted only family members to testify at trial about the impact of a violent crime.

The Finding: In a unanimous ruling, a three-judge panel of the U.S. Court of Appeals for the Second Circuit rejected the defendant's narrow "family-only" interpretation of *Payne*. The 1991 *Payne* ruling itself, the appeals court conceded, had indeed focused specifically on victim impact testimony given by a family member. Yet since *Payne*, at least three other federal appeals courts have interpreted the Supreme Court's ruling to allow evidence from non-relatives "about their own grief and about the loss felt by other non-family members." What's more, the appeals panel noted, "nothing in the Court's reasoning" suggests that the ruling was intended to have a narrow application. To the contrary, *Payne* suggests, "a fact-finder should be allowed to measure the 'specific harm' the defendant caused by committing the murder, a phrase broad enough to embrace the loss felt by friends or co-workers who were close to the victim. The opinion refers repeatedly to the specific harm caused as encompassing loss felt by 'community' or 'society.'" Consequently, the Second Circuit concluded, the trial court in New York did not commit error when admitting evidence that the detectives' shootings had adversely affected the victims' former police department colleagues.

How much victim impact testimony is allowed in the sentencing phase?

United States v. *McVeigh*, 153 F. 3d 1166 (3rd Cir. 1998)

The Case: On the morning of April 19, 1995, a bomb destroyed the Alfred P. Murrah Federal Building in Oklahoma City, killing 168 people. Two years later, Timothy J. McVeigh was convicted on 11 criminal counts and sentenced to death for his part in the bombing. During the penalty phase of his trial, federal prosecutors presented victim impact testimony from 38 witnesses, including 26 relatives of deceased victims, 3 injured survivors, 1 employee of the Murrah Building day-care center, and 8 rescue and medical workers. McVeigh challenged the use of victim impact testimony in his sentencing, arguing, among other things, that the cumulative effect of this testimony from 38 separate witnesses unfairly influenced the jury's deliberations by inviting jurors to use emotion rather than reason as required in *Payne v. Tennessee*.

The Finding: In upholding the death penalty, the Third Circuit held that *Payne* provides no bright-line rule for determining how much victim impact testimony is permissible in sentencing. Instead, trial courts may allow even a "substantial amount" of "poignant and emotional" impact testimony whenever that testimony aids the jury in making a "reasoned moral response" to a capital defendant's crime. In this case, the appeals court noted, the "sheer number of actual victims and the horrific things done to them" necessarily allowed for a broader showing of harm during sentencing so that jurors could fully understand the consequences of the crime. At the same time, the trial judge and federal prosecutors carefully limited the scope of impact testimony presented to the jury, "saying nothing about the vast majority of the 168 people who died in the blast." Viewed in its entirety, the appeals court held, the victim impact testimony at trial—although unusual in terms of numbers of witnesses—did not move the jury to impose a sentence based on passion and thus preserved fundamental fairness as required by the U.S. Constitution.

Doubts about *Payne* in the lower courts?

Humphries v. Ozmint, 397 F.3d 206 (3rd Cir. 2005)

The Case: In August 2004, a Greenville County, South Carolina, court sentenced a local man to death after finding that he had murdered a convenience store operator during a botched New Year's Day robbery attempt. During the sentencing phase of the trial, the state prosecutor spoke to the jury at length about the victim's childhood, his family—including his newly orphaned six-year-old daughter—and his various contributions to the local community. The prosecutor then urged the jury to "look at the character" of the defendant in light of his victim's exemplary life and then determine whether it would be "profane to give this man a gift of life under these circumstances." In petitioning for federal review, the defendant argued that the prosecutor had violated the strictures of *Payne v. Tennessee* by effectively inviting the jury to compare his relative worth as an individual to that of his victim.

The Finding: In affirming the state court judgment, a Fourth Circuit panel found *Payne v. Tennessee* to be directly controlling. *Payne*, the panel noted, prohibited comparisons between the victim and other members of the

community generally—but it did not specifically prohibit implicit victim-to-defendant comparisons during closing arguments. Indeed, *Payne* "[u]nquestionably" permitted the prosecutor to argue both that the victim was "unique" as an individual and that the jury at sentencing should consider the consequences of his death. As such, the defendant's sentencing proceedings met the fundamental fairness requirements articulated by the Supreme Court in *Payne*.

Even while adhering to *Payne*, though, the appellate panel questioned the fairness of the Supreme Court's victim impact approach:

> We note that a consequence of *Payne* is that a defendant can be put to death for the murder of a person more "unique" than another, even though the defendant is, in fact, unaware of the victim's uniqueness. This does give us some pause for concern, as does the notion that, under *Payne*, a sentence of death can turn on the severity of the harm caused to the victim's family and society, even though the defendant did not know the victim or the victim's family.

Nonetheless, the panel concluded, "these are the inevitable consequences of *Payne*'s comparative framework; a framework that we, as judges of an inferior court, are without liberty to change."

Is *stare decisis* stronger with older precedents?

Lawrence v. Texas, 539 U.S. 558 (2003)

The Case: In *Bowers v. Hardwick*, 478 U.S. 186 (1986), a closely divided U.S. Supreme Court upheld a Georgia criminal law that declared the act of sodomy—even when engaged in by consenting adults in the privacy of their own homes—a felony offense punishable by up to 20 years in state prison. Distinguishing its own earlier rulings that had limited state authority over contraception and abortion, the *Bowers* Court held that state criminal prohibitions on homosexual sodomy were unrelated to "family, marriage or procreation"—values that, according to *Bowers*, had animated the Court's earlier development of a limited constitutional right to privacy. State criminal sodomy laws, the *Bowers* court concluded, have "ancient roots" and fall clearly with the state's traditional police powers.

Twelve years after *Bowers* was decided, police in Houston, Texas, charged two adult men with violating Texas Penal Code Ann. Sec. 21.06(a), which made it a crime to engage in "deviate sexual intercourse with another individual of the same sex." Police officers had witnessed the intimate acts in question while responding to reports

(*continued*)

that an armed man was "going crazy" in Lawrence's private residence. After being held in custody overnight, the two men were convicted before a justice of the peace and fined $200 each. On appeal, both men challenged the validity of the state's criminal statute under the federal and Texas constitutions. State courts, following *Bowers*, rejected the men's federal constitutional claims.

The Finding: In a 6–3 ruling, the U.S. Supreme Court reversed the convictions and explicitly overruled the 17-year-old precedent in *Bowers*. Texas state courts, the *Lawrence* majority ruled, had acted appropriately in following *Bowers* because the "facts in *Bowers* had some similarities to the instant case" and *Bowers* was an "authoritative" federal precedent at the time of their decisions. Nonetheless, Justice Anthony Kennedy wrote in *Lawrence*, "the [doctrinal] foundations of *Bowers*" had sustained "serious erosion" in recent years due to the Supreme Court's rulings in other areas such as abortion rights and state civil rights laws. Meanwhile, criticism of

Bowers within the legal community had been "substantial and continuing" and "disapproving of its reasoning in all respects." What's more, the historical analysis at the heart of *Bowers*—suggesting that criminal prohibitions against sodomy had existed for centuries—had been overstated "at the very least." At the same time, Kennedy noted, the *Bowers* Court's narrow conception of the rights of consenting homosexual adults stood sharply at odds with broader declaration of rights on the same basic questions by the European Court of Human Rights.

The doctrine of *stare decisis*, the *Lawrence* Court concluded, "is essential to the respect accorded to the judgments of the Court and to the stability of the law." Yet in this case, there had been "no individual or societal reliance on *Bowers* of the sort that could counsel against overturning its holding once there are compelling reasons to do so. *Bowers* itself causes uncertainty, for the precedents before and after its issuance contradict its central holding. The rationale of *Bowers* does not withstand careful analysis. . . . *Bowers* was not correct when it was decided, and it is not correct today." ■

The American Law Institute was organized in 1923, after a study was conducted by a group of prominent American judges, lawyers, and teachers who formed the Committee on the Establishment of a Permanent Organization for the Improvement of the Law.[40] A report of the committee highlighted two chief defects in American law—uncertainty and complexity—that had combined to produce a "general dissatisfaction with the administration of justice" throughout the country.

The committee recommended that a lawyers' organization be formed to improve the law and its administration. That recommendation led to the creation of the ALI. The institute's charter declared its purpose to be "to promote the clarification and simplification of the law and its better adaptation to social needs, to secure the better administration of justice, and to encourage and carry on scholarly and scientific legal work."

The MPC serves today as a suggested model for the creation and revision of state criminal laws. It is divided into four parts: general provisions, definitions of specific crimes, treatment and correction, and the organization of correction. A fundamental standard underlying the MPC is "the principle that the sole purpose of the criminal law [is] the control of harmful conduct" instead of punishment, as many had previously believed. Because the code's authors believed that "faultless conduct should be shielded from punishment,"[41] the MPC limited criminal liability for a number of law violators, especially those who served merely as accomplices or who acted without an accompanying culpable mental state.

Although no state has adopted the MPC in its entirety, aspects of the MPC have been incorporated into the penal codes of nearly all the states. Moreover, in 1966, the U.S. Congress established the National Commission on Reform of Federal Criminal Laws. The commission eventually produced a recommended revision of Title 18 of the U.S. Code (which contains the bulk of federal criminal laws), in part based on MPC provisions. Some of the recommended revisions have since been enacted into law. As the great legal scholar Sanford Kadish once said, the MPC has "permeated and transformed" the body of American criminal law.[42]

The Model Penal Code is the most influential work in American substantive criminal law.

—James B. Jacobs, the Warren E. Burger Professor of Law at New York University

The MPC is an important document, not only because it attempts to achieve standardization in American criminal law and has served as a model for many state criminal statutes, but also because it contains legal formulations created by some of the most cogent thinkers in American jurisprudence. As a consequence, we frequently contrast MPC provisions with existing state statutes throughout this book. One area in which such a contrast is not possible, however, is the area of high-technology and computer crimes. The MPC, originally drafted more than 45 years ago, makes no specific mention of crimes committed with the use of computers and other crimes involving advanced technology. For your reference, the MPC is excerpted in Appendix C.

THE MODERN U.S. LEGAL SYSTEM

The U.S. Constitution establishes the basic architecture of American government. To avoid the centralization of power, the Framers designed a federal system of government. Unfortunately, however, when federalism is discussed, confusion frequently arises over use of the term *federal government*.

Federalism

Federalism refers to a system of government that has both local and national elements. This is contrasted with unitary systems, which have only one national or centralized government, although regional or local subunits may exist.

"A federal system of government is one in which two governments have jurisdiction over the inhabitants."[43] Under federalism, a central government coexists with various state and local governments. Each governing body has control over activities that occur within its legal sphere of influence. The Constitution gives our national government jurisdiction over activities such as interstate and international commerce, foreign relations, warfare, immigration, bankruptcy, civil rights, and certain crimes committed on the high seas and against the "law of nations" (international law). Individual states are prohibited from entering into treaties with foreign governments, from printing their own money, from granting titles of nobility (as is the national government), and various other things.

States retain the power, however, to make laws regulating or criminalizing activity within their boundaries. The general authority of the states to regulate for the health, safety, and welfare of their citizens is the police power. There are policy areas and individuals over which both the federal government and one or more states may have concurrent jurisdiction. For example, it is a violation of both federal and state law to assassinate a federal official, to rob a federally insured bank, or to commit acts of terrorism. In such cases, individuals may be prosecuted and punished by multiple jurisdictions. In cases where concurrent jurisdiction exists and there is a conflict between federal and state laws, federal law prevails under the supremacy clause of Article VI of the U.S. Constitution.

However, the supremacy clause does not authorize the federal government to regulate in areas that belong to the states. The sovereignty of the states is preserved in the Tenth Amendment, which reads, "The powers not delegated to the United States by the Constitution, nor prohibited by it to the States, are reserved to the States respectively, or to the people." Accordingly, the federal government may not assume general police powers and begin to punish thieves, robbers, rapists, and murderers whose crimes have no connection to the federal government. Furthermore, the Constitution protects several individual rights, with narrow exceptions, from government intrusion.

In recent decades, the expansion of federal jurisdiction has been facilitated by several constitutional provisions, including the Bill of Rights, the commerce clause, the Fourteenth and Fifteenth Amendments, and the necessary and proper clause. The commerce clause in particular was used by Congress for many decades to expand federal authority. The Supreme Court has stemmed this growth in recent years. The 1995 case *U.S.* v. *Lopez* provides an example of the Court's limiting federal authority under the commerce clause.[44] In *Lopez*, the Court held that Congress had overstepped its authority to regulate interstate commerce in passing the 1990 Gun-Free School Zones Act. The legislation made it a crime to possess a firearm in a school zone. Attorneys for the government defended the act, arguing that, among other things, guns in schools have a negative impact on education, which in turn has an adverse effect on citizens' productivity. Hence, they claimed, interstate commerce would be negatively affected by allowing guns to be carried in school zones. The Supreme Court disagreed and invalidated the law, finding that the legislation exceeded Congress's authority to regulate commerce among the states.

Similarly, in 2000, the U.S. Supreme Court overturned the federal arson conviction of a man who had firebombed his cousin's home.[45] The defendant had been arrested and prosecuted under Section 844 of Title 18 of the U.S. Code, which makes it a federal crime to maliciously damage or destroy, by means of fire or an explosive, any building used in interstate or foreign commerce or in any activity affecting interstate or foreign commerce. The Court found that this particular instance of arson could not be prosecuted under the law because the residence was *not* used in interstate or foreign commerce. In its ruling, the Court rejected the government's argument that the Indiana residence involved in this case was constantly used in at least three activities affecting commerce: (1) it was "used" as collateral to obtain and secure a mortgage from an Oklahoma lender, who, in turn, "used" it as security for the loan; (2) it was "used" to obtain from a Wisconsin insurer a casualty insurance policy, which safeguarded the interests of the homeowner and the mortgagee; and (3) it was "used" to receive natural gas from sources outside Indiana.

Then, again in 2000, the Supreme Court invalidated the federal Violence against Women Act of 1994, which provided a civil cause of action for victims of gender crimes. The plaintiff was a woman who alleged that the defendants raped her. Because rape is "not, in any sense of the phrase, economic activity," the Court found that Congress lacked authority to regulate it under the commerce clause. Further, the Court returned to basic federalism principles when it stated that the "Constitution requires a distinction between what is truly national and what is truly local. . . . The regulation and punishment of intrastate violence that is not directed at instrumentalities, channels, or goods involved in interstate commerce [have] always been the province of the states."[46]

Even though these decisions have established a limit, federal authority is still substantial. For example, in the 2005 case *Gonzales* v. *Raich*,[47] a federal statute that criminalized the cultivation of marijuana was upheld against a state law that specifically legitimized the use of marijuana for medical purposes. The Court wrote, "Given the enforcement difficulties that attend distinguishing between marijuana cultivated locally and marijuana grown elsewhere, and concerns about diversion into illicit channels, we have no difficulty concluding that Congress had a rational basis for believing that failure to regulate the intrastate manufacture and possession of marijuana would leave a gaping hole in the [federal government's law]."

Practically speaking, American federalism has resulted in the creation of 50 state criminal codes, the creation of a separate U.S. criminal code, and numerous city and local ordinances detailing many types of violations. As a consequence, crimes can have different descriptions and associated penalties depending on the **jurisdiction** involved. Still, considerable commonality exists in practice because all state codes criminalize serious misconduct such as murder, rape, robbery, assault and battery, burglary, and theft. Although statutory terminology may differ from state to state, and although particular crimes themselves may

jurisdiction
(1) The geographic district or subject matter over which the authority of a government body, especially a court, extends. (2) The authority of a court to hear and decide an action or lawsuit.

even be given different names, commonalities can be found among almost all of the states in terms of the types of behaviors they define as criminal. The Model Penal Code, discussed earlier in this chapter, represents one attempt to standardize American criminal law among jurisdictions.

Separation of Powers

Just as federalism's horizontal division of authority prevents the centralization of power, so does the vertical separation of powers between the branches of government. The U.S. government and the governments of all the states are divided into three branches: legislative, executive, and judicial.

Legislative   Article I of the Constitution established a bicameral (two-chambered) Congress. The two houses of Congress, the House of Representatives and the Senate, are the primary federal lawmaking body. Accordingly, Congress declares what acts are criminal, defines the criminal process and the respective authorities of the government players (police, judges, corrections), and establishes the punishments for each crime.

Congress may delegate the authority to make laws to federal administrative agencies. However, each delegation must be accompanied with guidance, or in legal terms, an intelligible principle, that steers the agency in the correct policy direction or otherwise limits its discretion. In addition to delegating noncriminal regulatory and service rule-making authority, Congress occasionally delegates criminal rule-making authority to agencies.[48]

Each state has its own legislature, of various names, that makes its own set of criminal laws. Most municipalities are empowered under state law with limited penal rule-making authority as well.

Executive   The role of the president is established in Article II of the Constitution. All executive authority is vested in the president and any lower offices that are created. The president is the chief law enforcement officer of the United States. Under the president's authority are a host of federal law enforcement agencies, including the Department of Justice, the Federal Bureau of Investigation, the Drug Enforcement Administration, the Secret Service, the Department of Homeland Security, Immigration and Customs Enforcement, and the Transportation Security Administration. It is the responsibility of executive officials to investigate, prevent, and prosecute crime.

There are more than 20,000 law enforcement agencies in state and local government, and they are responsible for the investigation and prosecution of more than 90 percent of all crime in the United States. At the federal level, prosecutions occur primarily through the many offices of the U.S. attorneys. The attorney general's office also handles some prosecutions. At the state level, prosecutors are known by many titles, including state's attorney and prosecutor.

Judicial   Article III established the Supreme Court and such inferior courts that Congress chooses to create. In 2012 the federal judiciary included one Supreme Court, 13 appellate courts, and 94 district courts. In addition, several specialty federal courts, such as bankruptcy and the Court of Claims, were part of the system (see Figure 1–4).

Each state has its own court system, each varying in its architecture. Most states have two or more trial courts, one appellate court or a system of appellate courts that hear cases by geographic district or subject matter (e.g., Texas Court of Criminal Appeals), and one high court. Court titles vary. The high court in most states is known as the supreme court, but New York's highest court is the court of appeals and its supreme courts are trial courts. A few states, such as West Virginia and Delaware, have only one level of appeal. The Framers

FIGURE 1–4

The Structure of the
Federal Courts.

Schmalleger, Frank J., *Criminal Justice
Today: An Introduction Text for the
21st Century*, 12th Ed., © 2013.
Reprinted and electronically reproduced
by permission of Pearson Education, Inc.,
Upper Saddle River, New Jersey.

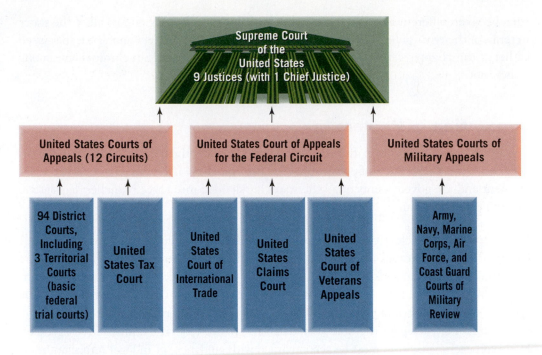

of the Constitution structured their new government with the intention that state courts would hear most state and federal cases, and as a consequence of the federal architecture they created, most crimes fall within the jurisdiction of the states. Although federal jurisdiction has grown since the Constitution was ratified, state courts continue to hear more than 90 percent of all criminal cases. In 2008, for example, 106 million cases were heard in state courts—58 million traffic, 21 million criminal, 19 million civil, 6 million domestic, and 2 million juvenile. In contrast, 56,000 cases were filed in federal appellate courts, 374,000 cases (104,000 were criminal) were filed in district courts, and 1.6 million cases were filed in bankruptcy courts in statistical year 2011. In recent years the Supreme Court of the United States has typically seen about 10,000 appeals, from which it hears and decides 80 to 90 cases.[49]

It is the responsibility of courts to administer justice, both civil and criminal. Courts hear and resolve legal disputes, oversee specific dimensions of the criminal investigatory process, oversee the prosecution of cases once charges are filed (and occasionally before they are filed), and act as guardians of governmental architecture and civil liberties. Courts necessarily interpret statutes, regulations, and judicial precedent. An awesome authority that courts possess is **judicial review**. Although the authority is not explicit in the Constitution, the Supreme Court has asserted this authority ever since Chief Justice John Marshall penned the following in the famous case *Marbury* v. *Madison* in 1803: "It is emphatically the province and duty of the judicial department to say what the law is. Those who apply the rule to particular cases, must of necessity expound and interpret that rule. If two laws conflict with each other, the courts must decide on the operation of each."[50] Judicial review has played a significant role in criminal law. Through it, the Supreme Court and lower courts have invalidated many state and federal criminal laws and procedures.[51]

Although judicial systems vary in structure, common elements can be identified in the context of criminal cases. First, all systems have trial courts where criminal cases are filed, warrants are issued, juries are found, witnesses and evidence are received, verdicts are rendered, and sentences are passed. In the federal system, there are 94 trial courts, known as *U.S. district courts*. There is at least one district court in each state.

All systems also have at least one appellate court. These courts do not impanel juries or hear evidence. Instead, they review the decisions of trial judges for legal error. They do this

judicial review
The authority of a court to review the actions of the executive and legislative branches and to declare as void those not consonant with the Constitution.

through written and sometimes oral arguments. In the federal system, the 11 U.S. courts of appeals are the first, and often last, rung of appeal. They are often final because not all cases continue to the highest level of appeal, the U.S. Supreme Court. The Supreme Court has discretionary jurisdiction over nearly all cases that are appealed to it; the Court typically hears about 3 percent of those cases.

AN ADVERSARIAL, ACCUSATORIAL DUE-PROCESS SYSTEM

Like other common law nations, the United States employs an adversarial and accusatorial system. An adversarial, accusatorial system is like a contest in which the prosecution is pitted against the defense, in contrast to an inquisitorial system, which is more like an ongoing inquiry with both the prosecution and the defense seeking the truth (Table 1–2). In many inquisitorial systems, a magistrate leads the investigation, and the transition from investigation to trial is seamless. Accusatorial systems are punctuated by processes. Police in the United States conduct their investigations with little judicial oversight, except when they seek warrants and in a few other situations. The situation changes when the date of arrest occurs. A new player, the public prosecutor, enters the contest. In most cases, the defense counsel does too.

From this point forward, the defense and the prosecution are adversaries. The accusatorial process assumes that truth is best found by having competing forces searching, analyzing, and ultimately presenting their facts and theories. The judge plays a more passive role in the **adversarial system** than in the inquisitorial system, largely acting as umpire between the parties and generally overseeing the process. The accusatorial nature of the U.S. system refers to the balance that is struck between the defendant and the government. The entire process is designed to protect the accused. The ultimate goal is to protect the civil liberties of all by protecting the rights of the one individual accused of the crime.

There are several basic tenets of this system. First, the government bears the burden of proof. It files the action, and it has the responsibility of proving guilt. The defense, on the other hand, has no obligation to prove innocence. In fact, defendants do not have to present any case whatsoever at trial. They may sit silent, call no witnesses, and present no facts. Nonetheless, defendants often choose to present a defense, such as an alibi or an alternative theory of who committed the crime.

In any case, the **burden of proof** requirement mandates that prosecutors must prove guilt beyond a **reasonable doubt**. Although the **reasonable doubt standard** is intertwined with the burden of proof requirement, the difference between the two is important (Table 1–3). One is an *obligation* imposed on the prosecution; the other is a *criterion* that must be met if a conviction is to be obtained.

adversarial system
The court system that pits the prosecution against the defense in the belief that truth can best be realized through effective debate over the merits of the opposing sides.

burden of proof
The mandate, operative in American criminal courts, that an accused person is presumed innocent until proven guilty and that the prosecution must prove the defendant's guilt beyond a reasonable doubt.

reasonable doubt
In legal proceedings, an actual and substantial doubt arising from the evidence, from the facts or circumstances shown by the evidence, or from the lack of evidence.[iv] Also, that state of the case, which after the entire comparison and consideration of all the evidence, leaves the minds of the jurors in such a condition that they cannot say they feel an abiding conviction of the truth of the charge.[v]

reasonable doubt standard
The standard of proof necessary for conviction in criminal trials.

TABLE 1–2   The Inquisitorial System versus the Adversarial System

Inquisitorial System	Adversarial System
One continuous investigation/trial overseen by judge	Investigation overseen by police and separate judicial phase initiated by prosecutor with minimal judicial involvement in early stages
Judges play active role throughout process	Judges are more passive, and attorneys play more active role
Truth is sought through investigation	Truth is sought through competition between prosecution and defense
Process is less formal than in an adversarial system	Process is highly formal and technical, especially once charges are filed

TABLE 1–3 Standards of Proof Compared

Standard	Definition	Use
Beyond a reasonable doubt	High or moral certainty, but not 100% confidence	For convictions in criminal cases
Clear and convincing evidence	Greater than preponderance of evidence but less than beyond a reasonable doubt	To decide specific issues in criminal and quasi-criminal cases
Preponderance of evidence	Greater than 50% probability	For verdicts in civil cases
Probable cause	Reasonable grounds to make or believe an accusation	Default standard for warrants and arrests
Reasonable suspicion	A general and reasonable belief that a crime has occurred	Needed for police stops & frisks and other special situations

In 1970, the majority opinion of the U.S. Supreme Court in the case of *In re Winship* held that "the reasonable-doubt standard plays a vital role in the American scheme of criminal procedure. . . . The standard provides concrete substance for the presumption of innocence—that bedrock 'axiomatic and elementary' principle whose 'enforcement lies at the foundation of the administration of our criminal law.'"[52] The Court went on to say, "It is critical that the moral force of the criminal law not be diluted by a standard of proof that leaves people in doubt [about] whether innocent men are being condemned."[53]

The Court, however, has not precisely defined "reasonable doubt"—leaving it to the states to communicate the essence of the concept to juries. During his charge to the jury in the O. J. Simpson murder trial, for example, Judge Lance Ito, following standard California jury instructions, defined "reasonable doubt" as follows: "It is not a mere possible doubt, because everything relating to human affairs is open to some possible or imaginary doubt. It is that state of the case which, after the entire comparison and consideration of all the evidence, leaves the minds of the jurors in that condition that they cannot say they feel an abiding conviction of the truth of the charge."[54]

Other states define the concept differently. A Nebraska jury instruction, for example, that was held to be constitutional by the U.S. Supreme Court in 1994 explains reasonable doubt this way: "A reasonable doubt is an actual and substantial doubt arising from the evidence, from the facts or circumstances shown by the evidence, or from the lack of evidence."[55]

In contrast to criminal cases, where the reasonable doubt standard prevails, a lesser standard of proof is needed in civil cases. A finding for the plaintiff in a civil case requires only the determination that a **preponderance of the evidence** shows that the defendant should be held accountable. A preponderance of the evidence can mean a probability of just over 50 percent that the defendant did what is claimed. Following the criterion of the preponderance of the evidence, a judge or jury can find for the plaintiff if they conclude that it is more likely than not that the allegation against the defendant is true.

A third standard of proof, which requires **clear and convincing evidence**, falls somewhere between the standards of proof beyond a reasonable doubt and a preponderance of the evidence. Clear and convincing evidence establishes the reasonable certainty of a claim. The clear and convincing evidence standard requires less than proof beyond a reasonable doubt but more than a preponderance of the evidence. Oklahoma jury instructions on clear and convincing evidence, for example, read as follows: "By requiring proof by clear and convincing evidence, I mean that you must be persuaded, considering all the evidence in the case, that each of these elements is highly probable and free from serious doubt."[56] Clear and convincing evidence is applied to specific issues in criminal cases. For example, some jurisdictions require defendants to prove insanity by clear and convincing evidence.

Bluster, sputter, question, cavil; but be sure your argument is intricate enough to confound the court.

—William Wycherley, English dramatist (1640–1716)

preponderance of the evidence
A standard for determining legal liability, which requires a probability of just over 50 percent that the defendant did what is claimed.

clear and convincing evidence
The level of factual proof used in civil cases involving issues of personal liberty. The standard requires greater certainty than "more probable than not" but is not as demanding as "no reasonable doubt."

In criminal trials, the government is the accuser and shoulders a high burden of proof (beyond a reasonable doubt). The accused enjoys a presumption of innocence, freedom from self-incrimination, the right to a jury trial in most cases, the right to counsel (including free counsel, if the defendant is indigent), the right to be free from unreasonable searches and seizures, and a host of other protections. The breach of some of these rights by the government can lead to dismissal of charges or to lesser remedies.

It is common to characterize criminal justice systems by where they fall on the crime-control and due-process models continuum. The crime-control pole of the continuum is characterized by its emphasis on preventing, detecting, and prosecuting criminals. Efficiency is a value of the system. The due-process pole emphasizes the preservation of individual liberties over the rights of the community to be free of crime or to have an efficient system. The crime-control model is satisfied when crimes are prevented or a crime is detected and the factual guilt of an offender is found in an efficient manner. The due-process model, on the other hand, emphasizes legal guilt. Legal guilt incorporates factual guilt, but it also includes a fair process. A defendant is legally guilty only if he or she is factually guilty and the government respected the defendant's rights while investigating and prosecuting the case. Advocates of the due-process model prefer to risk freeing a few guilty people than to have a system that doesn't discourage governmental abuses. These are only models, and no system can be defined as purely one or the other. The United States, though, with its abundant constitutional and statutory protections, clearly falls on the due-process end of the continuum.[57]

> *All sides in a trial want to hide at least some of the truth.*
>
> —Alan M. Dershowitz, the Felix Frankfurter
> Professor of Law at Harvard Law School

THE RULE OF LAW

In 1739, David Hume asked the following question:

> Here are two persons who dispute for an estate; of whom one is rich, a fool, and a bachelor; the other poor, a man of sense, and has a numerous family. The first is my enemy; the second my friend. To whom should the estate be awarded?[58]

To Hume, the morally correct decision would have been to award the estate based on principles of law without regard to personal passions, individual motives, or the economic power or social position of those involved. By following this course of action, Hume said, we are adhering to the "rule of law," not the "rule of man."

The **rule of law**, sometimes also referred to as the *supremacy of law*, involves the belief that an orderly society must be governed by established principles and known codes that are applied uniformly and fairly to all of its members. Under the rule of law, no one is above the law, and those who enforce the law must abide by it.

The rule of law has been called "the greatest political achievement of our culture,"[59] for without it few other human achievements—especially those that require the efforts of a large number of people working together—would be possible. The American Bar Association (ABA) defines the rule of law to include the following:[60]

rule of law
The maxim that an orderly society must be governed by established principles and known codes that are applied uniformly and fairly to all of its members. Also called *supremacy of law*.

- Freedom from private lawlessness provided by the legal system of a politically organized society
- A relatively high degree of objectivity in the formulation of legal norms and a like degree of evenhandedness in their application
- Legal ideas and juristic devices for the attainment of individual and group objectives within the bounds of ordered liberty
- Substantive and procedural limitations on governmental power in the interest of the individual for the enforcement of which there are appropriate legal institutions and machinery

due process of law
The procedures that effectively guarantee individual rights in the face of criminal prosecution; the due course of legal proceedings according to the rules and forms that have been established for the protection of private rights; formal adherence to fundamental rules for fair and orderly legal proceedings. Due process of law is a constitutional guarantee.

As the ABA definition indicates, the rule of law also includes the notion that **due process of law**, or those procedures that effectively guarantee individual rights in the face of criminal prosecution, is necessary before the imposition of any punishments on lawbreakers. Due process of law can be defined as "the due course of legal proceedings according to the rules and forms which have been established for the protection of private rights,"[61] or as formal adherence to fundamental rules for fair and orderly legal proceedings. Due process means that laws may not be created or enforced in arbitrary or unreasonable fashion. In this context, rule of law acts to restrain government. The World Justice Project identified the following elements as essential to rule of law: the accountability of government officials; whether laws are enacted and implemented in a fair and efficient manner; the degree of clarity of laws; the degree to which laws protect fundamental rights; and whether access to justice is administered by fair and independent judicial officers. The World Justice Project issued its first report on rule around the world in 2010.[62] In the United States, many elements of rule of law—including governmental accountability, the preservation of fundamental rights, and an independent judiciary—are protected by the separation of powers architecture and through judicial review.

Due process is protected by the Fifth and Fourteenth Amendments. The Fifth Amendment reads: "No person shall be held to answer for a capital, or otherwise infamous crime . . .; nor shall any person be subject for the same offence to be twice put in jeopardy of life or limb; nor shall be compelled in any criminal case to be a witness against himself, nor be deprived of life, liberty, or property, without due process of law." The Framers of the Constitution intended for all the amendments, including the Fifth, to restrict the power of the federal government, but not the states. They trusted state governments to protect civil rights more than the federal government. This changed as a consequence of the Fourteenth Amendment, which was one of three post–Civil War amendments. The Thirteenth Amendment, adopted in 1865, prohibits slavery and involuntary servitude, except as punishment for crimes. The Fifteenth Amendment, adopted in 1870, extends the vote to all, regardless of race.

The Fourteenth Amendment states the due-process requirement of the rule of law rather succinctly in these words: "No State shall make or enforce any law which shall abridge the privileges or immunities of citizens of the United States; nor shall any State deprive any person of life, liberty, or property, without due process of law; nor deny to any person within its jurisdiction the equal protection of the laws." Although that amendment applies primarily to state governments, the Fifth Amendment imposes due-process requirements upon the federal government as well.

selective incorporation (aka incorporation)
A constitutional doctrine that holds that rights found in the Bill of Rights, which were originally intended to only restrict the federal government, apply to the states through the Fourteenth Amendment's due-process clause. Only rights found by the Supreme Court to be fundamental and necessary to an ordered liberty are incorporated.

The Fourteenth Amendment doesn't define due process. Through a process known as **selective incorporation**, the Supreme Court has applied the rights found elsewhere in the Bill of Rights to the states, through the Fourteenth Amendment's due-process clause. They are not applied directly. Instead they are applied only when the Court finds them necessary to fairness. Today, defendants in state criminal proceedings are protected by nearly all the rights found in the Bill of Rights, including *inter alia* the Fourth Amendment's protection against unreasonable searches and seizures, as well as probable cause and warrant requirements; the Fifth Amendment's privilege against self-incrimination; the Sixth Amendment's rights to counsel, to confront one's accusers, and to a speedy public trial; and the Eighth Amendment's prohibition of cruel and unusual punishments.

The words, "due process of law," were undoubtedly intended to convey the same meaning as the words, "by the law of the land."

Murray's Lessee v. Hoboken Land and Improvement Co., 59 U.S. (18 How.) 272, 276 (1856)

SUMMARY

- Criminal law refers to the body of rules and regulations that define and specify punishments for offenses of a public nature, or for wrongs committed against the state or society. A crime is any act or omission in violation of penal law, committed without defense or justification, and made punishable by the state in a judicial proceeding.

- Laws derive from many different sources. The development of criminal law in the United States was strongly influenced by English common law. Common law derived from generally accepted use and custom, rather than from written guidelines or statutes. Two important forms of the criminal law are substantive and procedural. Substantive criminal law defines crimes and specifies punishments for violations of the law. Procedural criminal law specifies the methods to be used in enforcing substantive law.

- Crimes can be classified in various ways. One is by their degree of seriousness, resulting in categories such as felonies, misdemeanors, and infractions. Crimes can also be classified according to whether they have been completed or are still being planned. Another way of classifying crimes is according to whether they are thought to be wrong in themselves, or wrong simply because there is a law against them. Finally, the four traditional types of crimes provide another typology: (1) property crimes, (2) personal crimes, (3) public-order offenses, and (4) morals offenses.

- All laws, including criminal and civil law, facilitate predictable social interaction and guarantee a relative degree of safety to society's members. Laws exist to provide predictability in human events and to provide a stable foundation for human interaction. Criminal law, in particular, is intended to make life safe for members of society, to restrain dangerous behavior, and to punish those who commit crimes.

- Criminal law devolves from a number of sources, some of which are historical and others of which can be regarded as "living." Historical sources include ancient codes, religious principles, commonly accepted practices (from which the common law derives), and the U.S. Constitution. Living sources include statutes, ordinances, regulations, and the common law principle of *stare decisis*—which generally holds that a court should follow precedent in rendering its decisions.

- The American legal system is a form of federalism, in which two governments—the governments of the states and the federal government—have jurisdiction over inhabitants. States retain the power to make laws regulating or criminalizing activity within their boundaries, and there are policy areas and individuals over which both the federal government and one or more states may have concurrent jurisdiction.

- The United States employs an adversarial, accusatorial system, which is like a contest in which the prosecution is pitted against the defense. The adversarial system can be contrasted with an inquisitorial system, which is more like an ongoing inquiry, with both the prosecution and the defense seeking the truth.

- The rule of law, sometimes also referred to as the *supremacy of law*, involves the belief that an orderly society must be governed by established principles and known codes that are applied uniformly and fairly to all of its members. Under the rule of law, no one is above the law, and those who enforce the law must abide by it. The rule of law also includes the notion that due process of law, or those procedures that effectively guarantee individual rights in the face of criminal prosecution, is necessary before the imposition of any punishments on lawbreakers.

KEY TERMS

adversarial system, 29

Bill of Rights, 15

burden of proof, 29

case law, 17

civil law, 10

clear and convincing
   evidence, 30

common law, 7

common law state, 8

crime, 2

criminal law, 3

criminalize, 15

damages, 11

distinguish, 17

due process of law, 32

felony, 12

infraction, 13

judicial review, 28

jurisdiction, 26

law, 2

mala in se, 13

mala prohibita, 13

misdemeanor, 12

Model Penal Code
   (MPC), 17

morals, 2

morals offense, 13

more, 2

natural law, 3

norm, 2

personal crime, 13

police power, 15

positive law, 3

preponderance of the
   evidence, 30

property crime, 13

public-order offense, 13

punitive damages, 11

reasonable doubt, 31

reasonable doubt
   standard, 29

rule of law, 31

selective incorporation, 32

stare decisis, 17

statutory law, 17

substantive criminal law, 12

tort, 10

tortfeasor, 10

QUESTIONS FOR DISCUSSION

1. How does this textbook define criminal law? What is the significance of each of the definition's components?

2. Explain the history of law in Western society and of criminal law in particular.

3. What is the role of common law in modern criminal law?

4. How do laws of criminal procedure differ from substantive criminal laws?

5. What purposes are served by the criminal law today? Why are those purposes significant for society and social order?

6. What are the various sources of criminal law?

7. Describe the U.S. legal system, including jurisdictions.

8. What are the differences between the adversarial and inquisitorial systems of prosecution?

9. What is the rule of law? Why is due process an integral part of the rule of law?

CRITICAL THINKING AND APPLICATION PROBLEMS

1. Draft two statutes, one defining a *mala prohibitum crime* and the other a *mala in se crime*. Both statutes must regulate the ownership, care, control, or use of animals in some manner. Explain why each statute represents the type of crime (*mala in se* or *mala prohibitum*) you have defined.

2. Identify a feature of the current American legal system that appears to be more of the civil law tradition than the common law tradition. Fully explain why the feature relates more to the civil law tradition than to the common law tradition.

LEGAL RESOURCES ON THE WEB

Legal research involves the ability to fully and authoritatively explore all aspects of a question of law. It includes ascertaining the current status of relevant law in the proper jurisdiction, finding all cross-references and parallel case citations needed to properly analyze a question as well as the arguments of the opposing side, finding relevant law in the proper format and context (including annotations and history), and verifying that the law the researcher has uncovered is still valid and has not been replaced or overruled. Proprietary electronic databases, which are available either online or as stand-alone software tools, offer complete resources for legal research. Primary among such databases are LexisNexis® and Westlaw®, both of which are available for a fee. For anyone undertaking serious legal research, a subscription to one or both of those services (or others like them) is probably mandatory.

The Web offers a limited ability to perform some aspects of legal research—although the quality and availability of free materials on the Web may never be a replacement for proprietary legal databases. This is so because most free Web-based materials are not subject to peer review and may contain gaps and delays in the availability of crucial subject matter. Similarly, few free materials allow for easy cross-referencing and comprehensive analysis.

Nonetheless, a number of readily available Web-based resources in the legal area can give students of the law a sense of the issues involved in legal research, and they permit anyone with the requisite computer equipment and necessary skills to access a wealth of potentially useful information. To build on those resources, each chapter in this book contains a section like this one titled "Legal Resources on the Web." A variety of Web-based legal resources and law-related services are highlighted in the chapters that follow, and issues pertaining to Web-based legal resources are discussed. Listed below are a number of legal research links that you may find useful as starting points in any research effort:

Cornell University's Legal Information Institute
http://www.law.cornell.edu.

An excellent starting point for online legal research.

FindLaw®
http://www.findlaw.com.

An extensive collection of legal information, ranging from links to state and federal court cases and statutes to an analysis of the U.S. Constitution and Bill of Rights with case law annotations.

Georgetown Law Library
http://www.ll.georgetown.edu/guides/history_crime_punish.cfm.

The Georgetown Law Library's History of Crime and Punishment Research Guide.

International Rule of Law Resource Center
http://www.lexisnexis.com/community/international-foreignlaw/landing/international-rule-of-law.aspx.

Provides international advocates engaged in the rule of law access to critical information, such as applicable law, news, and expert analysis.

Legal Research Using the Internet
http://www2.lib.uchicago.edu/~llou/mpoctalk.html.

An overview of Internet legal research with links to useful sites.

LexisOne Community
http://law.lexisnexis.com/webcenters/lexisone

A free resource from LexisNexis. LexisOne provides free case law research, free legal forms, the Legal Internet Guide, and more.

United Nations Rule of Law
http://www.unrol.org.

Provides information on the work of the United Nations to promote rule of law.

USAID Democracy and Governance
http://www.usaid.gov/our_work/democracy_and_governance/technical_areas/rule_of_law.

Emphasis is on strengthening the rule of law and on respect for human rights.

U.S. Institute of Peace's Rule of Law Center of Innovation
http://www.usip.org/ruleoflaw/index.html.

The U.S. Institute of Peace conducts research, identifies best practices, and develops new tools for policymakers and practitioners working to promote the rule of law.

World Justice Project Rule of Law Index
http://worldjusticeproject.org/about.

Identifies the elements of rule of law and measures it around the world.

SUGGESTED READINGS AND CLASSIC WORKS

Atiyah, P. S., and R. S. Summers. *Form and Substance in Anglo-American Law: A Comparative Study in Legal Reasoning, Legal Theory, and Legal Institutions.* Oxford: Oxford University Press, 1987.

Becker, Howard S. *Outsiders: Studies in the Sociology of Deviance.* New York: Free Press, 1963.

Eldefonso, Edward, and Alan R. Coffey. *Criminal Law: History, Philosophy, Enforcement.* New York: Harper and Row, 1981.

Finnis, John. "Natural Law: The Classical Theory." In *The Oxford Handbook of Jurisprudence and Philosophy of Law*, edited by Jules Coleman and Scott Shapiro. Oxford: Oxford University Press, 2002.

Fletcher, George P. *Basic Concepts of Criminal Law.* New York: Oxford University Press, 1998.

———. *Basic Concepts of Legal Thought.* New York: Oxford University Press, 1996.

Friedman, Lawrence M. *A History of American Law.* New York: Simon and Schuster, 1973.

Hall, Kermit L. *Crime and Criminal Law: Major Historical Interpretations.* New York: Garland, 1987.

Hart, Herbert Lionel Adolphus. *The Concept of Law.* New York: Oxford University Press, 1961.

Holmes, Oliver Wendell. *The Common Law.* Boston: Little, Brown, 1881.

Maine, Henry Sumner. *Ancient Law: Its Connection with the Early History of Society and Its Relation to Modern Ideas.* New York: Dorset, 1986.

Nelson, William E. *Americanization of the Common Law: The Impact of Legal Change on Massachusetts Society, 1760–1830.* Cambridge, MA: Harvard University Press, 1975.

Pound, Roscoe. *The Spirit of the Common Law.* Norwood, MA: Plimpton Press, 1921.

Seagle, William. *The Quest for Law.* New York: Alfred A. Knopf, 1941.

Stephen, Sir James Fitzjames. *A History of the Criminal Law of England.* New York: Macmillan, 1883.

Sumner, William Graham. *Folkways.* New York: Dover, 1906.

Wilson, James Q. *The Moral Sense.* New York: Free Press, 1993.

NOTES

1. *Solesbree* v. *Balkcom*, 339 U.S. 9 (1950).

2. Richard Zitrin, "Man in Stolen Car Asks Cop for Directions," APBnews, June 22, 2000, http://www.apbnews.com/newscenter/breakingnews/2000/06/22/driver0622_01.html (accessed July 2, 2001).

3. Henry Campbell Black, Joseph R. Nolan, and Jacqueline M. Nolan-Haley, *Black's Law Dictionary*, 6th ed. (St. Paul: West, 1990), 1026. Italics added.

4. However, they may be subject to civil, administrative, or other sanctions.

5. See Henry Sumner Maine, *Ancient Law: Its Connection with the Early History of Society and Its Relation to Modern Ideas* (New York: Dorset, 1986), 50.

6. Thomas Aquinas, *Summa Theologica* (Notre Dame, IN: University of Notre Dame Press, 1983).

7. See *Roe* v. *Wade*, 410 U.S. 113 (1973).

8. Marvin Wolfgang, "The Key Reporter," *Phi Beta Kappa* 52.

9. Roman influence in England had ended by AD 442, according to Crane Brinton, John B. Christopher, and Robert L. Wolff, *A History of Civilization*, 3rd ed. (Englewood Cliffs, NJ: Prentice Hall, 1967), 1:180.

10. Clarence Ray Jeffery, "The Development of Crime in Early English Society," *Journal of Criminal Law, Criminology, and Police Science* 47 (1957): 647–666.

11. Howard Abadinsky, *Law and Justice* (Chicago: Nelson-Hall, 1988), 6.

12. See William D. Bader, "Some Thoughts on Blackstone, Precedent, and Originalism," *Vermont Law Review* 5 (1994): 9–11.

13. Florida Criminal Code, Chapter 775, Section 1.

14. Ibid, Section 2.

15. Arizona Revised Statutes, Title 1, Section 201.

16. Todd Nissen, "Suicide Advocate Kevorkian Acquitted for Third Time," Reuters.com, May 14, 1996 (accessed July 5, 1996).

17. Keith Schneider, "Dr. Jack Kevorkian Dies at 83; A Doctor Who Helped End Lives," *The New York Times*, June 3, 2011, www.nytimes.com/2011/06/04/us/04kevorkian.html (accessed March 7, 2012).

18. General Statutes of Georgia, 51–1–1.

19. See *Exxon Shipping* v. *Baker*, 554 U.S. 471 (2008); *Phillip Morris USA* v. *Williams*, 549 U.S. 346 (2007); and *State Farm Mutual Automobile Insurance Co.* v. *Campbell*, 538 U.S. 408 (2003).

20. "U.S. Justices Cut Punitive Damages in Exxon Valdez Disaster Case," *New York Times*, June 25, 2008, http://www.nytimes.com/2008/06/25/world/americas/25iht-25scotusexxon.13993179.html.

21. B. Drummond Ayres, "Jury Decides Simpson Must Pay $25 Million in Punitive Award," *The New York Times*, February 11, 1997.

22. Jane E. Allen, "Simpson Appeal Rejected," *USA Today*, April 29, 1997.

23. Steve Friess, "O. J. Simpson Found Guilty in Robbery Trial," *New York Times*, October 4, 2008, http://www.nytimes.com/2008/10/04/us/04simpson.html (accessed November 3, 2008).

24. Pipe, "O.J. Simpson Leads Lovelock Inmates to Dramatic Win against the Guards," *The Sparky Times*, July 11, 2011, http://www.sparkytimes.com/archives/426/oj-simpson-leads-the-lovelock-inmates-to-dramatic-win-against-the-guard (accessed March 7, 2012).

25. "Infractions" are not considered crimes under the Model Penal Code.

26. See, for example, James Q. Wilson, *The Moral Sense* (New York: Free Press, 1993).

27. Jeffery, "The Development of Crime."

28. Max Rheinstein, ed., *Max Weber on Law in Economy and Society* (Cambridge, MA: Harvard University Press, 1954).

29. British Columbia Superior Courts website, http://www.courts.gov.bc.ca/LegalCompendium/Chapter9.htm.

30. A. Ashworth, "Punishment and Compensation: Victims and the State," *Oxford Journal of Legal Studies* 6 (1986): 89.

31. See M. Findlay, S. Odgers, and S. Yeo, *Australian Criminal Justice*, 2nd ed. (Oxford: Oxford University Press, 1999).

32. *California Reduction Company* v. *Sanitary Reduction Works*, 199 U.S. 306 (1905), citing *Lawton* v. *Steele*, 152 U.S. 133 (1894).

33. For more on this subject, see Daniel E. Hall, *Administrative Law: Bureaucracy in a Democracy*, 4th ed. (Upper Saddle River: Prentice Hall, 2009).

34. *Welch* v. *Texas Highways and Public Transp. Dept.*, 483 U.S. 468, 494 (1987).

35. *Itel Containers International Corp.* v. *Huddleston*, 507 U.S. 60 (1993).

36. *Vasquez* v. *Hillary*, 474 U.S. 254, 265–266 (1986).

37. *Guardians Assn.* v. *Civil Service Comm'n of New York City*, 463 U.S. 582, 618 (1983); *United States* v. *International Boxing Club of New York, Inc.*, 348 U.S. 236, 249 (1955); and *Payne* v. *Tennessee*, 501 U.S. 808 (1991).

38. *Brown* v. *Allen*, 344 U.S. 433 (1953).

39. *Payne* v. *Tennessee*, 501 U.S. 808 (1991).

40. Some of the material in this section, as well as wording, is taken from "About the American Law Institute," at the American Law Institute's website, http://www.ali.org.

41. Stephen A. Saltzburg and others, *Criminal Law: Cases and Materials* (Charlottesville, VA: Michie, 1994), 53.

42. Quoted in Saltzburg and others, *Criminal Law*.

43. Clarence B. Carson, "The Meaning of Federalism," September 20, 2000, http://www.libertyhaven.com/politicsandcurrentevents/governmentreformitsrealrole/federalism.html (accessed January 4, 2002).

44. *United States* v. *Lopez*, 514 U.S. 549 (1995).

45. *Jones* v. *United States*, 529 U.S. 848 (2000).

46. *United States* v. *Morrison*, 529 U.S. 598 (2000).

47. *Gonzales* v. *Raich*, 545 U.S. 1 (2005).

48. Daniel E. Hall, *Administrative Law: Bureaucracy in a Democracy*, 4th ed. (Upper Saddle River, NJ: Prentice Hall, 2009).

49. National Center for State Courts, Court Statistics Project, http://www.courtstatistics.org (accessed May 22, 2012); federal data from http://www.uscourts.gov/statistics (accessed May 22, 2012).

50. *Marbury* v. *Madison*, 5 U.S. 137 (1803).

51. For a more thorough discussion of judicial review, see Daniel E. Hall and John P. Feldmeier, chap. 1 in *Constitutional Values: Governmental Powers and Individual Freedoms*, 2nd ed. (Upper Saddle River, NJ: Prentice Hall, 2013).

52. *In re Winship*, 397 U.S. 358 (1970).

53. Although the main thrust of *Winship* was in the area of the rights of juveniles facing adjudication by the juvenile court, the case has been held applicable to adult defendants facing criminal prosecution as well. See, for example, *Victor* v. *Nebraska*, 511 U.S. 1 (1994).

54. The Lectric Law Library, "Judge Ito's 9/95 Jury Instructions in O.J.'s Criminal Case," http://www.lectlaw.com/files/cas62.htm (accessed July 2, 2009).

55. *Victor* v. *Nebraska*, 511 U.S. 1 (1994).

56. Oklahoma Uniform Jury Instructions—Civil, 2nd ed., no. 3.2 (1993).

57. For more on the crime-control and due-process models, see N. Gary Holten and Lawson Lamar, chap. 1 in *The Criminal Courts* (New York: McGraw-Hill, 1991).

58. The question has been edited to make it easier to read. Taken from David Hume, *A Treatise of Human Nature*, vol. II, book III, "Of Morals," sec. VI, "Some Further Reflections Concerning Justice and Injustice," as found in Clarence Morris, ed., *The Great Legal Philosophers: Selected Readings in Jurisprudence* (Philadelphia: University of Pennsylvania Press, 1959).

59. John S. Baker, Jr., and others, *Hall's Criminal Law: Cases and Materials*, 5th ed. (Charlottesville, VA: Michie, 1993), 3.

60. American Bar Association Section of International and Comparative Law, *The Rule of Law in the United States* (Chicago: American Bar Association, 1958).

61. Bureau of Justice Statistics, *Dictionary of Criminal Justice Data Terminology*, 2nd ed. (Washington, DC: U.S. Government Printing Office, 1982).

62. The World Justice Project, Rule of Law Index, http://worldjusticeproject.org/about.

© Michael Matthews – Police Images/Alamy

2
Criminal Liability and the Essence of Crime

CHAPTER OUTLINE

Introduction

The Legal Essence of Criminal Conduct

The Criminal Act

State of Mind

Strict Liability and *Mens Rea*

Concurrence

OBJECTIVES

After reading this chapter, you should be able to

- Describe the legal essence of criminal conduct.
- Explain *actus reus* and what constitutes a criminal act.
- Explain *mens rea* and the different types of intent.
- Describe strict liability offenses, and explain why some crimes are punished solely on the basis of strict liability.
- Summarize concurrence, and describe how concurrence relates to *mens rea* and *actus reus*.

> *The love of justice is, in most men, nothing more than the fear of suffering injustice.*
>
> —François, duc de La Rochefoucauld (1613–1680)
>
> *Who thinks the Law has anything to do with Justice? It's what we have because we can't have Justice.*
>
> —William McIlvanney (b. 1936)

INTRODUCTION

Near the close of the 1995 California double-murder trial of O. J. Simpson, Judge Lance Ito began his final **jury instructions** with these words: "All right, ladies and gentlemen of the jury, you have heard all the evidence, and it is now my duty to instruct you on the law that applies to this case. . . . The law requires that I read these instructions to you here in open court. Please listen carefully." Judge Ito's instructions to the jury that day included the following:

> No person may be convicted of a criminal offense unless there is some proof of each element of the crime independent of any admission made by him outside of this trial. . . .

> A defendant in a criminal action is presumed to be innocent until the contrary is proved, and in case of a reasonable doubt whether his guilt is satisfactorily shown, he is entitled to a verdict of not guilty. This presumption places upon the prosecution the burden of proving him guilty beyond a reasonable doubt. . . .

> The prosecution has the burden of proving beyond a reasonable doubt each element of the crimes charged in the information and that the defendant was the perpetrator of any such charged crimes. The defendant is not required to prove himself innocent or to prove that any other person committed the crimes charged. . . .

> The defendant is accused in counts one and two of having committed the crime of murder, a violation of Penal Code, Section 187. Every person who unlawfully kills a human being with malice aforethought is guilty of the crime of murder, in violation of Section 187 of the California Penal Code. In order to prove such crime, each of the following elements must be proved: one, a human being was killed; two, the killing was unlawful; and, three, the killing was done with malice aforethought. . . .

> All killing that is perpetrated by any kind of willful, deliberate and premeditated killing, with express malice aforethought, is murder of the first degree. . . . Murder of the second degree is the unlawful killing of a human being with malice aforethought, where there is manifested an intention unlawfully to kill a human being, but the evidence is insufficient to establish deliberation and premeditation. Murder is classified into two degrees and if you should find the defendant guilty of murder, you must determine and state in your verdict, whether you find the murder to be of the first or second degree. . . .

> The purpose of the court's instructions is to provide you with the applicable law so that you may arrive at a just and lawful verdict. . . .[1]

THE LEGAL ESSENCE OF CRIMINAL CONDUCT

From the perspective of Western jurisprudence, all crimes can be said to share certain features, or elements, and the notion of crime itself can be said to rest on such general principles. Taken together, these features compose the legal essence of the concept of crime. They are referred to in legal parlance as the **elements of crime** and describe the most essential aspects of criminal conduct. All crimes can be said to have these general elements in one form or another. Because each state has the authority to define crimes as it wants, the same crime may have different elements between states.

Don't confuse these general, conceptual elements with the specific, statutory elements of crimes. To convict a defendant of a particular crime, prosecutors must prove to a judge or jury that all the statutory elements are present.[2] If even one element of an offense cannot be established beyond a reasonable doubt, criminal liability has not been demonstrated, and the defendant will be found not guilty. Later chapters examine the elements of *specific* crimes as well as defenses to charges of **criminal liability**. For now, we will turn our

---

jury instructions
Directions given by a judge to a jury concerning the law of the case.

A reasonable doubt is nothing more than a doubt for which reasons can be given. The fact that one or two men out of twelve differ from the others does not establish that their doubts are reasonable.

—*Quintin Hogg, nineteenth-century British statesman*

elements of crime
(1) The basic components of crime. (2) In a specific crime, the essential features of that crime, as specified by law or statute.

criminal liability
The degree of blameworthiness assigned to a defendant by a criminal court and the concomitant extent to which the defendant is subject to penalties prescribed by the criminal law.

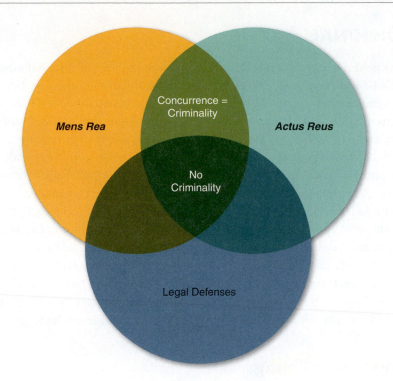

FIGURE 2–1

The Essence of Criminal Conduct.

attention to the most fundamental features of crimes in general. These essential concepts were developed under common law and continue today.

There are three essential aspects of all crimes: (1) the criminal act (which, in legal parlance, is termed the *actus reus*), (2) a culpable mental state (*mens rea*), and (3) a concurrence of the two. Figure 2–1 illustrates the relationship between *mens rea* and *actus reus*. Criminality exists when the two concur and where no defense, as characterized in the figure, exists. Defenses in this figure refer to the zone of individual liberties over which governments have no authority to regulate and to those instances where other factual or legal defenses free an individual from criminal responsibility. Hence, as discussed in this chapter, the essence of criminal conduct consists of a concurrence of a criminal act with a culpable mental state. The critical issue of concurrence is what distinguishes murder from homicide committed in self-defense, for example, or rape from consensual sex.

Some legal scholars add the concept of harm, or a harmful result, to the list of elements that conceptually constitute the essence of crime. We do not do so here, however, because—as we shall later see—some crimes do not involve a clear-cut harm, whereas others can be effectively committed before actual harm occurs.

Commonly we say a judgment falls upon a man for something in him we cannot abide.

—John Selden, English jurist (1584–1654)

Through years of effort, legal scholars have refined considerably each of the elements that comprise the conceptual essence of criminality. Some suggest that additional elements are inherent in the concept. These additional elements are (1) causation, (2) a resulting harm (as previously mentioned), (3) the principle of legality, and (4) necessary attendant circumstances. In the remainder of this chapter, we discuss the three essential aspects of crime. In Chapter 3, we describe the remaining four elements as they relate to contemporary understandings of criminality.

Before beginning our discussion of the essential elements of crime, however, it is necessary to point out that when attorneys speak of "conduct," they routinely mean more than mere behavior or action. The term **conduct**, as it is used in the discussion that follows, encompasses both the behavior and the mental state that were present at the time of the behavior.

conduct
In the criminal law, behavior and its accompanying mental state.

THE CRIMINAL ACT

Generally, a person must commit some act before being subject to criminal sanctions, and a necessary first feature of most crimes is some act in violation of the law. Such an act is termed the **actus reus** of a crime. The term (which, like much other legal terminology, is Latin) means a "guilty act." For purposes of the criminal law, the word *act* is often said to mean a performance, a deed, or a movement, as distinguished from remaining at rest. In keeping with common law tradition, Arizona law, for example, couches the idea of an act squarely in terms of physical conduct. The "definitions" section of the Arizona Revised Statutes says, quite simply, "'Act' means a bodily movement."[3] The same words are found in Part I, Article 1, Section 1.13(2) of the Model Penal Code (MPC) (see Appendix C).

Some bodily movements may appear relatively minor, even though they result in considerable criminal liability. An individual who hires someone to kill another person, for example, may move only the tongue, but he or she is still liable to a criminal charge. Hence words are "acts" in the sense that the term is used by the criminal law. In this same regard, given technology, it takes little bodily movement to actually kill someone—merely the pull of a finger on the trigger of a gun.

actus reus
An act in violation of the law; a guilty act.

If there were no bad people there would be no good lawyers.

—Charles Dickens, English novelist (1812–1870)

Thinking Is Not Doing

Some religious traditions hold that evil or bad thoughts are sins. But thoughts are not actions in the sense of an *actus reus*. Hence, although people might feel guilty about their own thoughts, even to the point of considerable mental anguish, one cannot be arrested merely for thinking something. The philosophical basis of this principle may lie in the belief that "thoughts are not susceptible of proof except when demonstrated by outward action."[4] Moreover, there are people who think all kinds of things but never act on their thoughts. People may more easily control their actions than their thoughts, and it is, after all, their actions that cause harm to others.[5]

Being Is Not Doing

To *be* something is not a crime, but to *do* something may be. A person who admits (perhaps on a TV talk show) to being a drug user, for example, cannot be arrested on that basis. However, a police detective who hears the admission might begin gathering evidence to prove some specific law violation in that person's past, or perhaps the detective might watch that individual for future conduct in violation of the law. An arrest might then occur. If it does, it will be based on a specific action in violation of the law pertaining to controlled substances.

Voluntary Acts

Some forms of human action are inherently noncriminal. The laws of most jurisdictions specify that a person's actions must be voluntary for them to carry criminal liability. The Indiana Code, for example, reads: "A person commits an offense only if he voluntarily engages in conduct in violation of the statute defining the offense. However, a person who omits to perform an act commits an offense only if he has a statutory, common law, or contractual duty to perform the act."[6] Many states, such as Texas,[7] have followed the lead of the Model Penal Code, which requires that all acts be voluntary and specifically lists the following to be involuntary:

1. Reflexes and convulsions;
2. Bodily movements during unconsciousness or sleep;

3. Conduct during hypnosis or resulting from hypnotic suggestion; and

4. Movements caused by another person.[8]

Because the laws of most jurisdictions, like those of Texas, require action to be voluntarily undertaken before criminal liability can accrue, a person who kills another during a "bad dream" or while sleepwalking may not be criminally liable for his or her actions. In 1988, in just such a case, 24-year-old Kenneth Parks was acquitted by a Canadian jury of second-degree murder charges after he admittedly drove 14 miles to his mother-in-law's home and beat her to death with a tire iron.[9] Parks claimed he was sleepwalking during the killing. During the trial, friends of Parks said he had a history of sleepwalking, and doctors testified that medical literature describes about 30 cases of murder committed by sleepwalkers.[10]

In 1999, however, Scott Falater, 43, of Phoenix, Arizona, was convicted in Maricopa County Superior Court of first-degree murder after a jury refused to believe his claim that he stabbed his wife 44 times, dragged her to a backyard swimming pool, and held her head under water until she died—all while he was sleepwalking.[11]

Falater admitted that he must have killed his wife of 20 years and later removed his blood-stained clothes and hid them in his Volvo with the knife used in the slaying. But, he said, he was asleep at the time of the 1997 killing and had no memory of his actions. Although two sleep experts cited a family history of sleepwalking, job stress, and lack of recent sleep as explanations for Falater's supposedly violent sleepwalking episode, jurors sided with prosecutors who said that Falater's actions were too deliberate to constitute sleepwalking.

Possession

Possession is generally considered to be another form of action. Possession, like any other act, may not always be voluntary. The Model Penal Code declares possession to be an act if the item was knowingly received or was within the control of the individual for a period long enough to terminate possession. Texas[12] and Arizona[13] are examples of states that have adopted the Model Penal Code's approach of distinguishing **knowing possession** and **mere possession**. A person who knowingly possesses something is well aware of what he or she has and has probably taken steps to obtain it. Someone who merely transports something for another, on the other hand, may be unaware of what he or she possesses. Similarly, a person on whom drugs are "planted," and who remains unaware of their presence, cannot be found guilty of drug possession. Nonetheless, both knowing possession and mere possession constitute **actual possession**, meaning that the person is actually in direct physical control of the object in question.

An individual may also exercise **constructive possession** over property and objects. Constructive possession means that, at a given time, a person may not have actual physical custody of the material in question, but he or she is still able to control or influence it. Issues of constructive possession commonly arise in automobiles where the driver and other occupants of an automobile know that one occupant is in possession of narcotics, an open alcohol container, or some other contraband. To be in constructive possession, actual knowledge of the item is required, as is the ability to exercise dominion and control over the contraband. Jurisdictions vary considerably in the application of constructive possession but a few general principles apply widely. Although being in close proximity to the contraband is insufficient to establish constructive possession, "ownership" is not required. If the driver is the owner of the automobile, dominion and control over the contraband is likely to be found. Control may be proven for other occupants as well, although it will be more difficult. Any factor that bears on control will be considered in making the constructive possession finding. Constructive possession issues are not limited to automobiles. Similar questions arise in multi-occupant homes and businesses as well. Under the Model Penal

knowing possession
Possession with awareness of what one possesses.

mere possession
Possession in which one may or may not be aware of what he or she possesses.

actual possession
Possession in which one has direct physical control over the object or objects in question.

constructive possession
The ability to exercise control over property or objects, even though they are not in one's physical custody.

Code, a defendant must be in possession, actual or constructive, for a period long enough to terminate possession in order to be criminally liable for possession.

In most circumstances, seconds is long enough to establish possession. But it could be longer. For example, Simon and Linda share a safety deposit box in a bank. Simon calls Linda Saturday at 6 p.m. to tell her that he has placed illegal drugs in the box. She objected and immediately drove to the bank to remove the drugs from the box but the bank was closed and wasn't scheduled to reopen until Monday morning. Linda sent the bank manager an email message requesting access to the box as soon as possible. The message wasn't read until Monday morning. The police, who had Simon under surveillance, obtained a warrant for the box and made arrangements with the bank's management to open the box on Sunday. In this case, although Linda may be guilty of another crime, such as failure to report a felony, she is not guilty of drug possession. Although she had knowledge of the drugs in her safety deposit box, she didn't have adequate time to divest herself of their possession.

Failure to Act

In times past, people could be routinely arrested for doing nothing at all. Vagrancy laws, for example, were popular in the early part of the twentieth century, but they have generally been invalidated by the courts because they did not specify what act violated the law. In fact, the *less* a person did, the more vagrant he or she was.

An **omission to act**, or a failure to act, however, may be criminal when the person in question is required by law to do something, that is, when the law specifies a duty to act. Classic federal examples of such offenses include the failure to file a tax return or to register for the military draft. As a consequence of the accounting firm crimes of the early 2000s, the federal government now requires securities attorneys to report securities crimes to their supervisors.[14]

An example of a state-imposed duty to act is child-neglect laws, which focus on parents and child guardians who do not live up to their responsibility to care for their children, and have recently received considerable attention, as discussed shortly. Similarly, intentionally withholding needed medication from a critically ill individual might constitute the basis for a charge of homicide.

In a real-life example, Ginger and David Twitchell were convicted in 1990 of involuntary manslaughter after their two-year-old son, Robyn, died of a bowel obstruction that could easily have been treated surgically.[15] The Twitchells, members of the Christian Science Church,[16] believed in the efficacy of "scientific prayer" as the sole way to treat illness and refused medical treatment for their son. Their conviction was overturned in 1993, however, when the Massachusetts Supreme Court ruled that the Twitchells should have been allowed to argue at trial that they believed they were within their parental rights to choose spiritual treatment.

Statutes requiring the reporting of crimes are also common. Ohio, for example, requires that all felonies be reported. Like other states, Ohio also requires the reporting of deaths and life-threatening injuries.[17] Most states require child neglect and child abuse to be reported as well. Statutes vary in what must be reported, who must report, and to whom the reports must be made. In some states, all individuals who suspect child abuse or neglect must report. In others, only individuals who have a special relationship with the child, such as a guardian, teacher, or health-care employee, must report. Some states require all reports of abuse and neglect be made to law enforcement or child protective agency authorities, whereas others mandate reporting to a supervisor, who is then required to report to authorities.

These questions received national attention in the Penn State University child-abuse scandal that began in 2011 when young male victims alleged that 68-year-old Jerry Sandusky, former Penn State football defense coordinator, sexually abused them. Sandusky,

omission to act
An intentional or unintentional failure to act, which may impose criminal liability if a duty to act under the circumstances is specified by law.

who continued to use Penn State facilities after his retirement from the university in order to help troubled youths, was alleged to have committed the offenses for many years, dating back to his employment with Penn State. Following a grand jury investigation, Sandusky was charged with 52 counts of abusive conduct with children ages 10 to 15.[18] Failing to act became an issue in this case because at least one report of the abuse was made by a university employee who alleged that he witnessed Sandusky sexually assaulting a youth in Penn State's athletic showers. He reported the incident to the late Joe Paterno, then Penn State football coach, who subsequently reported the incident to his bosses, Tim Curley and Gary Schultz, at Penn State. Pennsylvania law requires employees of public or private institutions to report suspected child abuse to the "person in charge." That individual then has the responsibility to report the suspected abuse to the authorities.[19] Questions have been raised about Paterno's reporting. It has been alleged that he "watered down" the report he had received, and some question whether he was the "person in charge" and therefore should have reported the incident to the authorities, not his supervisor.[20] There is also a question whether Paterno's bosses reported the incident to authorities. At the time of this writing, Sandusky, Curley, and Schultz have been charged with a variety of crimes. The president of Penn State at the time of the incidents, Graham Spanier, has also been charged with several felonies and misdemeanors, including perjury, child endangerment, and failing to report suspect child abuse. Joe Paterno died shortly after the scandal broke, but civil suits against his estate, as well as against Penn State and other employees, by the victims remain a possibility.

Finally, we should note that *reasonable* failures to act may be noncriminal, even when serious harm results. Hence the captain of a passenger airplane may decide to avoid an emergency landing that would save the life of a heart attack victim if such a landing might endanger the other passengers.

Speech as an Act

Unlike a thought, speech and nonverbal expressions are physical acts. But the First Amendment to the U.S. Constitution provides that "Congress shall make no law . . . abridging the freedom of speech." Although the Framers used the term *speech*, the Supreme Court has found that they intended to protect all forms of expression, verbal and otherwise. Also, as you learned in the last chapter, the First Amendment applies to the states today through the process of incorporation. Even though the First Amendment's protection of expression is strong, there are limits. Expression that creates a clear and present danger to others, that is likely to incite another person to immediate violence (fighting words), that presents a threat of bodily harm to another, that is libelous, or that is obscene may be regulated. Telling someone "I'm going to kill you" might result in an arrest for the offense of "communicating threats." Similarly, threatening the president of the United States may be a crime under federal law and is taken seriously by the Secret Service, which regularly arrests individuals for boasting about planned violence directed at the president.[21]

A high standard of protection of speech has been established, and consequently many unpopular forms of expression have been protected. The protests of the Westboro Baptist Church are an example. The church's congregation, led by its Pastor Fred Phelps, believes that the United States is evil, and its members espouse hatred of many groups, including homosexuals, Jews, Catholics, and many others. To advance their message, members began protesting at the funerals of American military personnel who had been killed in combat. In 2006, church members protested at the funeral of a marine who died in Iraq. They carried signs that read "America is doomed," "Thank God for Dead Soldiers," "God Hates You," "Fag Troops," as well as many others. The father of the fallen marine sued the Westboro Baptist Church, Fred Phelps, and other members of the Phelps family for the intentional infliction of emotional distress. The father won at the trial level; lost in the appellate court;

and, in an 8–1 2011 decision, the Supreme Court decided that the church's expression was protected by the First Amendment. Chief Justice Roberts wrote:

> Westboro believes that America is morally flawed; many Americans might feel the same about Westboro. Westboro's funeral picketing is certainly hurtful and its contribution to public discourse may be negligible. But Westboro addressed matters of public import on public property, in a peaceful manner, in full compliance with the guidance of local officials. The speech was indeed planned to coincide with Matthew Snyder's funeral, but did not itself disrupt that funeral, and Westboro's choice to conduct its picketing at that time and place did not alter the nature of its speech.
>
> Speech is powerful. It can stir people to action, move them to tears of both joy and sorrow, and—as it did here—inflict great pain. On the facts before us, we cannot react to that pain by punishing the speaker. As a Nation we have chosen a different course—to protect even hurtful speech on public issues to ensure that we do not stifle public debate. That choice requires that we shield Westboro from tort liability for its picketing in this case.

Justice Alito, the one dissenting justice, commented that "to have a society in which public issues can be openly and vigorously debated, it is not necessary to allow the brutalization of innocent victims like petitioner."[22]

Part II, Article 2, Section 211.3, of the Model Penal Code provides for the offense of "terroristic threat" and says: "A person is guilty of a felony of the third degree if he threatens to commit any crime of violence with purpose to terrorize another or to cause evacuation of a building, place of assembly, or facility of public transportation, or otherwise to cause serious public inconvenience, or in reckless disregard of the risk of causing such terror or inconvenience." Threats made for the purpose of illegally acquiring money or other things of value are described separately in most state penal codes as extortion and blackmail.

STATE OF MIND

mens rea
The specific mental state of the defendant at the time of the crime; a guilty mind.

Mens rea is the second general element of crime. The term, which literally means "guilty mind," refers to the specific mental state of the defendant at the time of the crime. The importance of *mens rea* as a component of crime cannot be overemphasized, which can be seen in the fact that some courts have held that "[a]ll crime exists primarily in the mind."[23]

Specific, General, and Transferred Intent

general intent
The form of intent that can be assumed from the defendant's behavior. General intent refers to an actor's physical conduct.

specific intent
A thoughtful, conscious intention to perform a specific act in order to achieve a particular result.

At the common law, two forms of *mens rea* were recognized: **general intent** and **specific intent**. The distinction between the two was very important. In the early years, specific intent distinguished a felony, which was punished with death, from a misdemeanor, which was punished in other ways.

If the defendant intended to cause the outcome of the act, then specific intent exists. If the defendant intended to act but did not intend the consequence, then general intent is present. For example, suppose a defendant struck a victim in the leg with an axe. The defendant intended to frighten the victim into complying with his request to not trespass on his property. Later, the victim died from a resulting infection. At common law, the defendant committed a general-intent crime. The outcome would have been different if the defendant had hit the victim with the axe with the specific intent of causing her death. If such were the case, then the defendant would be responsible for the specific-intent crime of murder.

scienter
Knowledge; guilty knowledge.

A specific form of *mens rea* is known as **scienter**. Although sometimes used interchangeably with *mens rea* or the common law specific intent, it is different. Scienter refers to a defendant's "guilty knowledge," whereas *mens rea* refers to a defendant's "guilty intent." To prove scienter, the prosecution must establish that a defendant knew a particular fact when

CRIMINAL LAW IN THE NEWS

Supreme Court Rules in Favor of Church Picketers at Marine's Funeral

Citing free speech rights in the Constitution, the Supreme Court upheld the right of a church group to display controversial and demeaning signs when picketing at the funeral of a U.S. Marine who was killed in Iraq.

Six members of the Westboro Baptist Church, who oppose gays serving in the military, held signs that read, for example: "Thank God for Dead Soldiers," "You're Going to Hell," and "God Hates the USA/Thank God for 9/11."

Albert Snyder, the father of the dead soldier, sued the church group for intentional infliction of emotional distress. He said the Westboro pickets, led by the Rev. Fred Phelps, robbed him of the "last moment" he had with his son, Lance Cpl. Matthew A. Snyder. The father said he often became tearful, angry and physically ill when he remembered the protest, which took place in Westminster, Maryland, in March 2006.

The Westboro Baptist Church group, based in Topeka, Kansas, has picketed almost 600 funerals around the country in the past 20 years. Even though members carried signs like "God Hates Fags" at the Maryland funeral, they said they did not believe the younger Snyder was gay, but were protesting military policy.

Snyder initially won a $5 million verdict against Westboro in federal court, but the decision was overturned on appeal and then the Supreme Court decided to take up the case. In preparation, attorneys general from 49 states filed friend-of-the-court briefs in support of the grieving father and called the Rev. Phelps's tactics "psychological terrorism."

But in an 8–1 decision in March 2011, the justices ruled that the church group's free speech rights trumped the father's emotional distress. Chief Justice John Roberts, writing for the majority, said the father might have had a case if the Westboro group had been protesting a purely private matter, but they were protesting policies of the U.S. military.

The jury in the original trial found that the Westboro picketing did not deserve free speech protections because it was "outrageous." But the chief justice wrote that outrageousness "is a highly malleable standard."

Citing a 1988 Supreme Court decision, Roberts wrote that a parody of the Rev. Jerry Falwell in *Hustler* magazine might be seen as outrageous, but the Court still accorded the porn publication free speech protections. Like the soldier's father, Falwell claimed intentional infliction of emotional distress. The parody suggested he had lost his virginity to his mother in an outhouse. But Roberts, citing the *Hustler* decision, said liability could

Westboro Baptist Church members picketing at a funeral for a fallen soldier in Dallas, Texas. Picketers claim that America is evil, and that God will punish the country. One of their sayings is "Thank God for dead (American) soldiers." Is speech like this protected by the Constitution?
Reuters/Tim Sharp

(continued)

not be imposed on "the basis of jurors' tastes or views, or perhaps on the basis of their dislike of a particular expression."

"Speech is powerful," Roberts concluded. "It can stir people to action, move them to tears of both joy and sorrow, and—as it did here—inflict great pain. On the facts before us, we cannot react to that pain by punishing the speaker. As a nation we have chosen a different course—to protect even hurtful speech on public issues to ensure that we do not stifle public debate."

In a lone dissent, Justice Samuel Alito insisted the soldier's funeral was a private matter that did not allow the protesters free speech protections. "In order to have a society in which public issues can be openly and vigorously debated, it is not necessary to allow the brutalization of innocent victims," he wrote.

Roberts did, however, endorse a buffer zone for such protests and cited past decisions. In a case involving an abortion clinic, for example, the court allowed a buffer

zone between protesters and the clinic entrance. He said the Westboro picketers were 1,000 feet from the funeral and "the protest was not unruly; there was no shouting, profanity, or violence."

Resources

Snyder v. *Phelps et al.*, U.S. Supreme Court opinion, March 2, 2011, **http://www.supremecourt.gov/opinions/10pdf/ 09-751.pdf.**
"Westboro Free-Speech Ruling Has Its Limits," *USA Today*, March 3, 2011, **http://www.usatoday.com/news/washington/ judicial/2011-03-03-courtinside03_ST_N.htm.**
"High Court Rules for Anti-Gay Protesters at Funerals," National Public Radio (NPR), March 2, 2011, **http://www.npr.org/2011/03/02/134194491/ high-court-rules-for-military-funeral-protesters.**

the act occurred. In 1994, for example, the Illinois Supreme Court validated a state law making it a felony to knowingly expose uninformed others to HIV through sexual contact.[24] Under the law, people who are aware that they are infected with HIV must avoid sexual contact with those who are unaware of their condition, or they risk felony prosecution. The court held that the law had been properly applied in two cases: that of a woman who knew she was infected with HIV when she had sex with a man without telling him, and a case involving a man with HIV infection who was charged with raping a woman. In neither case was the purpose of sexual intercourse to intentionally transmit the disease-causing agent.

Scienter is also required in the crime of receiving stolen property. If the receiving party doesn't know the property's stolen character, the crime has not been committed. In some cases actual knowledge is not required to prove scienter. Instead the prosecution has proved its case if it can demonstrate that the defendant should have known the fact that is the subject of the scienter requirement. Statutes that contain a scienter element usually also have a *mens rea* requirement. In the case of stolen property, actual knowledge of the stolen character is required, as is the intention to both receive and deprive its owner of the property.

Additional doctrines elaborating general and specific intent were developed in early common law. For example, through the doctrine of **transferred intent**, a defendant's specific intent to cause harm to one person is transferred to the victim on whom the harm actually falls. To apply, the harm that befalls the unintended victim must be similar to the intended harm, and the transference cannot increase the defendant's criminal liability. If a defendant acts in self-defense but inadvertently harms a third party, the defendant's self-defense applies against the third party, even though that individual posed no threat to the defendant.

transferred intent
A legal construction by which an unintended act that results from intentional action undertaken in the commission of a crime may also be illegal.

The Model Penal Code's *Mens Rea* Scheme

Over time, the distinction between general and specific intent proved to be too unsophisticated to address the variety of different cases and states of mind that can occur, and courts and legislatures began to develop many terms to describe *mens rea*. In time, hundreds of terms could be found in state codes, the federal code, and judicial decisions that described *mens rea*. Of course, hundreds of different states of mind were not described; instead, many referred to the same state of mind.

FIGURE 2–2

Types of *Mens Rea*.

To bring some clarity to the situation, the Model Penal Code (MPC) established a general scheme that outlines four states of mind: purposeful, knowing, reckless, and negligent (Figure 2–2). *Mens rea* is most clearly present when a person acts purposefully and knowingly, but *mens rea* sufficient for criminal prosecution may also result from reckless or negligent behavior.

Purposeful is the MPC equivalent of specific intent at the common law; hence it refers to a desire to cause the outcome that resulted. **Knowing behavior** is action undertaken with awareness that the outcome is practically certain. This is different than purposeful behavior, which requires more than an awareness that the result is likely; it requires the actor to want it to happen.

The third state of mind under the Model Penal Code is recklessness, or **reckless behavior,** which is defined as behavior that consciously disregards a substantial and unjustifiable risk that the result will occur. The risk must be of such nature and degree that disregard of such risk constitutes a gross deviation from the standard of conduct that a law-abiding person would observe. The difference between knowing and reckless behavior is the degree of risk that is taken. A person acts knowingly if the outcome is nearly certain, whereas the lesser conscious disregard of a substantial and unjustifiable risk satisfies the reckless standard. For example, Elton John's song about Princess Diana (originally written for Marilyn Monroe) says, "You lived your life like a candle in the wind." The wind is, of course, a risky place to keep a lighted candle—and doing so increases the likelihood that its flame will be

The trial court is the most important agency of the judicial branch of the government precisely because on it rests the responsibility of ascertaining the facts.

—Jerome N. Frank, United States v. Forness, 125 F.2d 928, 942-43 (2d Cir. 1942)

knowing behavior
Action undertaken with awareness.

reckless behavior (also recklessness)
An activity that increases the risk of harm.

CRIMINAL LAW IN THE NEWS

Man Shooting Gun into Air Accidently Kills Girl

Ohio authorities report that an Amish girl was accidently killed by a man who discharged his muzzle-loaded rifle into the air to clean it, hitting her from 1.5 miles away.

Rachel M. Yoder was returning home alone from a Christmas party in 2011, driving a horse-drawn buggy on a dark rural road. The bullet struck the 15-year-old girl in the head, and the horse took the unguided buggy back home—leaving behind a trail of blood from the point where she was shot. The girl's father came out and found her lying in a pool of blood. The bullet was not discovered until she went to the hospital, where she was taken off life support and died.

News of the shooting sent shock waves through the Amish community. Within days, a man who lived nearby told police he had fired his gun into the air around the time the girl was shot, and neighbors confirmed they heard a shot at that time. The bullet found in the girl's head matched the man's unusual muzzle-loaded bullets.

The man said that after hunting deer, he fired his gun into the air in order to clean it. Authorities did not identify him, but one news report assumed he was Amish. The accident occurred in Amish country and he was using an old-style weapon identified with the religious group. Muzzle-loaded rifles, used through the Civil War, require pushing gunpowder and the bullet down the barrel with a ramrod. Some sport-hunters, however, still use this dated technology.

Authorities in Holmes County, Ohio, accepted the man's story and deemed the killing an accident, but because firing weapons into the air is not safe, they forwarded the case to the county prosecutor to consider criminal charges. "Any time you shoot, normal practice is to shoot into a bank or a backstop," said County Sheriff Timothy Zimmerly. "You should never shoot up into the air."

Can someone be killed this way?

This freak accident was greeted with disbelief on Internet chat sites for gun owners, but subsequent discussions brought supporting evidence to light. The debates focused on two aspects of the case.

First, can a bullet from a muzzle-loaded gun travel that far? Such weapons aren't as powerful as modern breach-loading rifles, but a Civil War officer was reportedly killed by a bullet shot more than a mile away. And in a 2007 study for U.S. Army Armament Research the Mountaintop Technologies research firm, a bullet fired from a muzzle-loaded rifle at a 35-degree angle traveled 9,197 feet, a little more than 1.5 miles.

Second, can a bullet shot into the air actually kill someone as it comes down? A bullet falling through the air never reaches the force it originally had coming out of the gun. A 1962 study by Major General Julian S. Hatcher, a U.S. Army ordnance expert, determined that a bullet weighing 0.021 pounds shot straight up would hit

An Amish buggy, like the one 15-year-old Rachel M. Yoder was driving when she was struck and killed by a bullet fired by a man who discharged his rifle into the air. Was such action reckless behavior?

Shutterstock

ground at a force of 30 foot-pounds, about half of what it takes to create a disabling wound.

However, a December 1994 study in the *Journal of Trauma* suggested that bullets shot into the air can occasionally be deadly. From 1985–1992, King/Drew Medical Center in Los Angeles treated 118 people for what appeared to be injuries from such bullets, and 38 of them died.

Resources
"Sheriff: Ohio Man Cleaning Gun Killed Amish Girl," CBS News, December 20, 2011,

http://www.cbsnews.com/8301-201_162-57345561/ sheriff-ohio-man-cleaning-gun-killed-amish-girl/.

"Round from Mile-Plus away Killed Girl: Man Cleaning Muzzleloader Fires Shot That Accidentally Hits Rachel Yoder," Daily Record, December 21, 2011,

http://www.the-daily-record.com/news/ article/5138144.

"'It Was a Freak Accident': Amish Girl, 15, Was Shot in Head by Rogue Bullet from Hunting Gun a MILE Away," Daily Mail, December 21, 2011,

http://www.dailymail.co.uk/news/article-2076431/ Rachel-Yoder-shot-gun-1-5-miles-away-Amish-girl-15- killed-freak-accident.html.

extinguished. But there is no certainty that the flame will be blown out or, if so, when it might happen. As a practical example, reckless driving is a common charge in many jurisdictions; it is generally brought when a driver engages in risky activity that endangers others. A person who creates such a risk but is unaware of such risk solely by reason of voluntary intoxication also acts recklessly with respect to such risk. Hence, in most other jurisdictions, intoxication is no bar to prosecution of reckless behavior undertaken while intoxicated.

The fourth state of mind under the Model Penal Code is negligence. Arizona has incorporated the MPC standard for **criminal negligence** in its statutes, as follows:[25] "'Criminal negligence' means, with respect to a result or to a circumstance described by a statute defining an offense, that a person fails to perceive a *substantial and unjustifiable risk* that the result will occur or that the circumstance exists. The risk must be of such nature and degree that the failure to perceive it constitutes a *gross* deviation from the standard of care that a reasonable person would observe in the situation."[26] The difference between recklessness and negligence is that a defendant must be aware that a substantial and justifiable risk was taken to be reckless. No awareness is required to be negligent. In the case of negligent behavior, the law is imposing a "you should have known better" standard. A person who acts negligently, and thereby endangers others, may be found guilty of a crime when harm occurs, even though no negative consequences were intended and when the risk was not foreseen. For example, a mother who leaves her 12-month-old child alone in the bathtub can later be prosecuted for negligent homicide if the child drowns.[27]

Statutes that impose criminal liability for negligent behavior have survived constitutional scrutiny. This was the issue in the *Hanousek* case, discussed in the Capstone Case box.

Even though negligence may be criminalized, it is generally not punished as severely as purposeful, knowing, or reckless behavior. As Supreme Court Justice Oliver Wendell Holmes once remarked, "Even a dog distinguishes between being stumbled over and being kicked."[28]

A person's state of mind during the commission of an offense can rarely be known directly, unless the person confesses. Hence juries often construct *mens rea* from **inferences** they draw from a person's actions and from all the circumstances surrounding those actions. For example, assume that a corporation's accountant transferred corporate funds to an account opened by the accountant in a false name in a bank in the Caribbean islands. Assuming he has not confessed to embezzlement, a jury has the authority to infer from his actions that he intended to take and keep the money for herself. Similarly, the **deadly weapon doctrine** used in murder cases is an example of an inference. The Model Penal Code defines a deadly weapon as "any firearm, or other weapon, device, instrument, material, or

criminal negligence
(1) Behavior in which a person fails to reasonably perceive substantial and unjustifiable risks of dangerous consequences. (2) Negligence of such a nature and to such a degree that it is punishable as a crime. (3) Flagrant and reckless disregard for the safety of others, or willful indifference to the safety and welfare of others.

inference
A conclusion drawn from other facts. Juries often infer intent from a defendant's behavior.

deadly weapon doctrine
A rule that empowers a jury to infer a defendant's specific intent to take the life of the victim when the defendant used an item in such a manner that it is known to be capable of causing death or serious bodily injury.

APPLYING THE CONCEPT

CAPSTONE CASE

Can a Person Be Criminally Punished for Ordinary Negligence?

United States v. Hanousek, 176 F.3d 1116 (9th Cir. 1999)
THOMPSON, Circuit Judge.

Edward Hanousek, Jr., appeals his conviction and sentence for negligently discharging a harmful quantity of oil into a navigable water of the United States, in violation of the Clean Water Act, 33 U.S.C. §§ 1319(c)(1)(A) & 1321(b) 3). Hanousek . . . argues that section 1319(c)(1)(A) violates due process if it permits a criminal conviction for ordinary negligence. We affirm.

THE CASE   Hanousek was employed by the Pacific & Arctic Railway and Navigation Company . . . As roadmaster, Hanousek was responsible under his contract "for every detail of the safe and efficient maintenance and construction of track, structures and marine facilities of the entire railroad . . . and [was to] assume similar duties with special projects."

One of the special projects under Hanousek's supervision was a rock-quarrying project at a site alongside the railroad referred to as "6-mile," located on an embankment 200 feet above the Skagway River. The project was designed to realign a sharp curve in the railroad and to obtain armor rock for a ship dock in Skagway. The project involved blasting rock outcroppings alongside the railroad, working the fractured rock toward railroad cars, and loading the rock onto railroad cars with a backhoe. . . . At 6-mile, a high-pressure petroleum products pipeline owned by Pacific & Arctic's sister company, Pacific & Arctic Pipeline, Inc., runs parallel to the railroad at or above ground level, within a few feet of the tracks. To protect the pipeline during the project, a work platform of sand and gravel was constructed on which the backhoe operated to load rocks over the pipeline and into railroad cars. The location of the work platform changed as the location of the work progressed along the railroad tracks. In addition, when work initially began, Hunz & Hunz covered an approximately 300-foot section of the pipeline with railroad ties, sand, and ballast material to protect the pipeline, as was customary. After Hanousek took over responsibility for the project, no further sections of the pipeline along the 1,000-foot work site were protected, with the exception of the movable backhoe work platform. [See Figure 2–3.]

On the evening of October 1, 1994, Shane Thoe, a Hunz & Hunz backhoe operator, used the backhoe on the work platform to load a train with rocks. . . . While using the backhoe bucket to sweep the rocks from the tracks, Thoe struck the pipeline, causing a rupture. The pipeline was carrying heating oil, and an estimated 1,000 to 5,000 gallons of oil were discharged over the course of many days into the adjacent Skagway River, a navigable water of the United States.

Following an investigation, Hanousek was charged with one count of negligently discharging a harmful quantity of oil into a navigable water of the United States, in violation of the Clean Water Act. . . .

After a twenty-day trial, the jury convicted Hanousek of negligently discharging a harmful quantity of oil into a navigable water of the United States. . . . The district court imposed a sentence of six months of imprisonment, six months in a halfway house and six months of supervised release, as well as a fine of $5,000. This appeal followed.

THE FINDING

A. Jury Instructions   Hanousek contends the district court erred by failing to instruct the jury that . . ., the government had to prove that Hanousek acted with criminal negligence, as opposed to ordinary negligence, in discharging a harmful quantity of oil into the Skagway River. In his proposed jury instruction, Hanousek defined criminal negligence as "a gross deviation from the standard of care that a reasonable person would observe in the situation." Over Hanousek's objection, the district court instructed the jury that the government was required to prove only that Hanousek acted negligently, which the district court defined as "the failure to use reasonable care." . . .

Statutory interpretation begins with the plain language of the statute. . . . If the language of the statute is clear, we need look no further than that language in determining

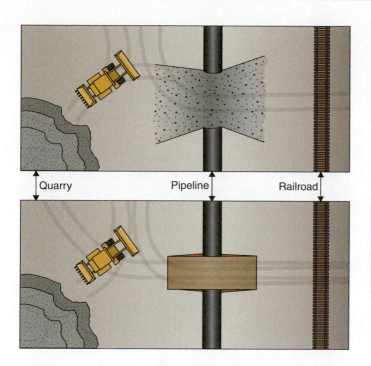

STANDARD PRACTICE

A sturdy platform made of sand, gravel, and railroad ties protects the Pacific & Arctic Pipeline.

Quarry   Pipeline   Railroad

NEGLIGENT PRACTICE

Under Hanousek's authority, the Pacific & Arctic Pipeline is protected only by a movable platform.

FIGURE 2–3

Criminal Negligence in *United States* v. *Hanousek* (1999).

the statute's meaning. Particular phrases must be construed in light of the overall purpose and structure of the whole statutory scheme. When we look to the plain language of a statute in order to interpret its meaning, we do more than view words or subsections in isolation. We derive meaning from context, and this requires reading the relevant statutory provisions as a whole.

Sections 1319(c)(1)(A) & 1321(b)(3) of the Clean Water Act work in tandem to criminalize the conduct of which Hanousek was convicted. . . . . Neither section defines the term "negligently," nor is that term defined elsewhere in the CWA. In this circumstance, we start with the assumption that the legislative purpose is expressed by the ordinary meaning of the words used. The ordinary meaning of "negligently" is a failure to use such care as a reasonably prudent and careful person would use under similar circumstances. If Congress intended to prescribe a heightened negligence standard, it could have done so explicitly, as it did in 33 U.S.C. § 1321(b)(7)(D). This section of the CWA provides for increased civil penalties "in any case in which a violation of [33 U.S.C. § 1321(b)(3)] was the result of gross negligence or willful misconduct." 33 U.S.C. § 1321(b)(7)(D). This is significant. Where Congress includes particular language in one section of a statute but omits it in another section of the same Act, it is generally presumed that Congress acts intentionally and purposely in the disparate inclusion or exclusion.

We conclude from the plain language of 33 U.S.C. § 1319(c)(1)(A) that Congress intended that a person who acts with ordinary negligence in violating 33 U.S.C.

§ 1321(b)(3) may be subject to criminal penalties. We next consider Hanousek's argument that, by imposing an ordinary negligence standard for a criminal violation, section 1319(c)(1)(A) violates the due process clause of the Constitution.

B. Due Process   The criminal provisions of the CWA constitute public welfare legislation. The criminal provisions of the CWA are clearly designed to protect the public at large from the potentially dire consequences of water pollution, and as such fall within the category of public welfare legislation. . . .

It is well established that a public welfare statute may subject a person to criminal liability for his or her ordinary negligence without violating due process. Where one deals with others and his mere negligence may be dangerous to them, as in selling diseased food or poison, the policy of the law may, in order to stimulate proper care, require the punishment of the negligent person though he be ignorant of the noxious character of what he sells. . . .

Hanousek argues that . . . he was simply the roadmaster of the White Pass & Yukon railroad charged with overseeing a rock-quarrying project and was not in a position to know what the law required under the CWA. This is a distinction without a difference. In the context of a public welfare statute, as long as a defendant knows he is dealing with a dangerous device of a character that places him in responsible relation to a public danger, he should be alerted to the probability of strict regulation. . . .

The totality of this evidence is sufficient to support Hanousek's conviction for negligently discharging a harmful

(continued)

quantity of oil into a navigable water of the United States, in violation of 33 U.S.C. §§ 1319(c)(1)(A) & 1321(b)(3).

In light of the plain language of 33 U.S.C. § 1319(c)(1)(A), we conclude Congress intended that a person who acts with ordinary negligence in violating 33 U.S.C. § 1321(b)(3) may be subjected to criminal penalties. These sections, as so construed, do not violate due process. . . . AFFIRMED

What Do *You* Think?

1. Do the dangers of pollution require the approach taken by Congress in the statute involved in this case?

2. Should simple negligence be a basis for criminal liability?

Additional Applications

Are all violations of the Clean Water Act public welfare offenses?

United States v. *Ahmad*, 101 F.3d 386 (5th Cir. 1996)

The Case: After discovering that water had leaked into a large gasoline storage tank at his Conroe, Texas, gas station, the station owner used a rented hand-held pump to discharge 5,220 gallons of liquid—including approximately 4,700 gallons of gasoline—directly into the city sewer system and a local creek. The owner alleged that he thought that he was pumping only water and thus lacked the requisite *mens rea* to violate the law. Nonetheless, federal prosecutors charged him with violating the Clean Water Act's felony provisions by "knowingly discharging a pollutant . . . into a navigable water of the United States without a permit" and by "knowingly operating a source in violation of a pretreatment standard." In countering defense challenges to the trial judge's jury instructions, government lawyers relied in significant part on the argument that violations of the Clean Water Act are "public welfare offenses."

The Finding: In finding reversible error in the jury instructions, the Fifth Circuit panel rejected the government's argument that the Clean Water Act was a public welfare statute. "On its face," the panel conceded, "the CWA certainly does appear to implicate public welfare." Yet public welfare offenses "have virtually always been crimes punishable by relatively light penalties such as fines or short jail sentences." Serious felonies, by contrast, "should not fall within the exception 'absent a clear statement from Congress.'" ■

---

substance, whether animate or inanimate, which in the manner it is used or is intended to be used is known to be capable of producing death or serious bodily injury."[29] Under this definition, almost anything can be a deadly weapon, and more traditional weapons are not deadly if not used in a manner designed to cause death. For example, a dog that is trained to bring a person down and then tear open the jugular vein is a deadly weapon and a handgun is not, if the gun is thrown at a person in anger, even if it accidentally discharges and kills the victim.

It is important to note that *mens rea*, even in the sense of intent, is not the same thing as **motive**. A motive refers to a person's reason for committing a crime. To prove murder at the common law, a defendant's specific intent (or "purpose" under the MPC) to cause the victim's death is required. The defendant's motive (for example, to silence the victim or to steal the victim's money) does not have to be proved as a matter of law. Prosecutors, however, often find it strategically necessary to prove motive in order to convince juries of guilt beyond a reasonable doubt. Although motive is not legally required to prove guilt, it may be a factor in sentencing.

motive
A person's reason for committing a crime.

STRICT LIABILITY AND *MENS REA*

strict liability crime
A violation of law for which one may incur criminal liability without fault or intention. Strict liability offenses do not require *mens rea*.

strict liability
Liability without fault or intention.

A special category of crimes, called **strict liability crimes**, requires no culpable mental state and presents a significant exception to the principle that all crimes require a conjunction of action and *mens rea*. Strict liability offenses (also called *absolute liability offenses*) make it a crime simply to *do* something, even if the offender has no intention of violating the law or causing the resulting harm. **Strict liability** is based philosophically on the presumption that causing harm is in itself blameworthy, regardless of the actor's intent.

Routine traffic offenses are generally considered strict liability offenses that do not require intent and may even be committed by drivers who are not consciously aware of what they are doing. A driver commits minor violations of his or her state motor vehicle code simply by doing that which is forbidden. Hence driving 65 mph in a 55-mph zone is a violation of the law, even though the driver may be listening to music, thinking, or simply going with the flow of traffic, entirely unaware that his or her vehicle is exceeding the posted speed limit.

Statutory rape provides another example of the concept of strict liability.[30] Unlike rape statutes, which require the use of force or coercion of the victim, statutory rape occurs between two consenting individuals and requires only that the offender have sexual intercourse with a person under the age of legal consent. Statutes describing the crime routinely avoid any mention of a culpable mental state. California law, for example, prohibits the crime of "unlawful sexual intercourse," which it describes as "an act of sexual intercourse accomplished with a person who is not the spouse of the perpetrator, if the person is a minor. For the purposes of this section, a 'minor' is a person under the age of 18 years."[31] The law goes on to say, "Any person who engages in an act of unlawful sexual intercourse with a minor who is not more than three years older or three years younger than the perpetrator is guilty of a misdemeanor," and "[a]ny person who engages in an act of unlawful sexual intercourse with a minor who is more than three years younger than the perpetrator is guilty of either a misdemeanor or a felony, and shall be punished by imprisonment in a county jail not exceeding one year, or by imprisonment in the state prison."

In many jurisdictions, it matters little in the crime of statutory rape whether the "perpetrator" knew the exact age of the "victim," or whether the "victim" lied about his or her age or gave consent, because such laws are "an attempt to prevent the sexual exploitation of persons deemed legally incapable of giving consent."[32] They assume that such individuals are "too innocent and naïve to understand the implications and nature of [the sexual] act."[33]

> It is better that ten guilty persons escape than one innocent suffer.
>
> —Sir William Blackstone,
> English jurist (1723–1780)

Some legal experts maintain that strict liability offenses can never be "true crimes" because they require no mental element. In fact, most strict liability offenses are violations of regulatory statutes, such as those that declare it a violation to sell misbranded items, possess a motor vehicle with an altered serial number, or operate a car with a burned-out taillight. Because violations of health regulations can cause considerable harm to a large number of people, even though the violator neither intends harm nor knowingly violates the law, courts may assess liability according to a principle articulated in 1943 by the U.S. Court of Appeals for the Third Circuit, which held: "Where the offenses prohibited and made punishable are capable of inflicting widespread injury, and where the requirement of proof of the offender's guilty knowledge and wrongful intent would render enforcement of the prohibition difficult if not impossible . . . the legislative intent to dispense with *mens rea* as an element of the offense has justifiable basis."[34] Under the Model Penal Code and some state codes, strict liability offenses are termed "violations" rather than crimes and are punishable only by fines or forfeiture.

Some laws require a culpable mental state *and* contain strict liability provisions that may increase criminal liability when other elements can be demonstrated. In an interesting 1996 Missouri Supreme Court case,[35] for example, the drug-dealing convictions of two men were upheld, although the men claimed that the state statute under which they were convicted was a strict liability statute. The statute in question read: "A person commits the offense of distribution of a controlled substance near public housing or other governmental assisted housing if he . . . unlawfully distribute[s] or deliver[s] any controlled substance to a person in or on, or within one thousand feet of the real property comprising public housing or other governmental assisted housing." The appellants admitted that they had sold drugs but contended that they were unaware of the fact that they were close to a public housing project. Their attorney claimed that "because the language of [the statute] contains no *mens rea* or knowledge requirement (i.e., it is a 'strict liability' statute according to appellants), . . . a conviction is easier to obtain, and a criminal defendant left more vulnerable than he would be otherwise, when the prosecution is relieved of a major obstacle—the burden of proving defendant's bad intent."

In finding against the men, the Missouri court held that the state law under which they were convicted "is not a strict liability statute." The words "within 1,000 feet . . . of public housing" are merely a punishment-enhancement provision and do not create a separate crime, said the court. "Appellants' real complaint," said the court,

> is that they did not know they were within one thousand feet of public housing when they carried out their plan to sell crack cocaine. This ignorance is not a product of appellants' inability to understand the statute. It is the result of their failure to determine the existence of and their distance from public housing. The burden of ascertaining those facts lies with appellants under the statute. The due process clause simply does not require that the state prove appellant's knowledge of his proximity to public housing, nor does it require the state prove appellant's knowledge that the property is classified as public housing, before it will allow the state to enhance the punishment for a crime appellant intentionally committed.

Strict liability statutes have been challenged as violating the U.S. Constitution on many occasions. The challenges commonly assert a due-process violation. With few exceptions, strict criminal liability statutes have been upheld. In *Lambert* v. *California*, 355 U.S. 225 (1957), for example, the U.S. Supreme Court stated that it does not agree with "Blackstone in saying that 'a vicious will' is necessary to constitute a crime, for conduct alone, without regard to the intent of the doer, is often sufficient." Yet in the same case, the Court invalidated a statute that punished a convict's failure to register because of its lack of *mens rea* requirement. The Court's rationale for distinguishing the registration law from other legitimate strict liability crimes was the passive nature of the act. The law made it a crime not to register, even if there was no knowledge of the requirement. This decision, of course, defies the basic principle that mistake of law is no defense. This rule is examined later in this book.

When Statutes Are Silent on *Mens Rea*

Some statutes are altogether silent on *mens rea*. Because strict liability crimes are not favored by some legal scholars, courts will usually make an effort to determine if a *mens rea* requirement is imbedded in the statute. To accomplish this, courts have to interpret the statute. There are many interpretation rules, or **canons of construction**, that are used to guide courts in criminal cases. For example, the *canon of presumptive constitutionality* holds that if two interpretations of a statute are possible, one constitutional and another not, the statute is to be interpreted as constitutional. Another canon requires that criminal statutes are to be interpreted narrowly and, if possible, in a defendant's favor. Yet another requires the plain meaning of laws to be enforced without further interpretation unless a plain-meaning understanding is absurd.

But if a statute's meaning is not plain, then a court must dig further. A court can attempt to deduce its meaning by looking at the common law, if it influenced the statute, by examining relevant case law, by looking at similar statutes, by looking to the law of other jurisdictions, and by checking the **legislative history** of the statute. The legislative history is the record of debates, committee reports and meetings, legislators' statements, and other evidence of what the legislature intended when it enacted the law. In *People* v. *Jensen*, highlighted in a Capstone Case in this chapter, the Michigan Court of Appeals had to go beyond the text of the statute to determine whether a *mens rea* requirement was intended for the crime of having sex with someone without notifying him or her of HIV infection. As the case illustrates, there is a strong preference for requiring some form of intent for serious crimes, even when a legislature doesn't explicitly include a *mens rea* element in the law.

canon of construction
A rule that guides courts in interpreting constitutions, statutes, and other law.

legislative history
The record of debates, committee reports and meetings, legislators' statements, and other evidence of what the legislature intended when it enacted a particular statute.

APPLYING THE CONCEPT

CAPSTONE CASE

How Shall a Court Interpret a Criminal Statute That Is Silent on *Mens Rea?*

People v. *Jensen,*
Mich. App. 439 (1998)

THE CASE Following a jury trial, defendant was convicted of three counts of knowing that she was HIV positive and engaging in sexual penetration without informing her partner of her HIV status, MCL 333.5210; MSA 14.15(5210). Thereafter, the trial court sentenced defendant to concurrent terms of two years and eight months to four years' imprisonment on each of the three counts. . . . [The case made its way to the Michigan Supreme Court, which remanded to the Michigan Court of Appeals to review constitutional claims.]

THE FINDING On remand, we find that the HIV notice statute is neither unconstitutionally overbroad nor violative of defendant's rights to privacy or against compelled speech. . . .

First, defendant asserts that MCL 333.5210; MSA 14.15(5210), which makes it a crime to fail to inform a sexual partner that one has AIDS or is HIV positive, is unconstitutionally overbroad because it (1) includes both consensual and nonconsensual sexual acts and (2) fails to require an intent to cause harm. We believe that defendant's constitutional challenges on these grounds fail.

MCL 333.5210; MSA 14.15(5210) states as follows:

> A person who knows that he or she has or has been diagnosed as having acquired immunodeficiency syndrome or acquired immunodeficiency syndrome related complex, or who knows that he or she is HIV infected, and who engages in sexual penetration with another person without having first informed the other person that he or she has acquired immunodeficiency syndrome or acquired immunodeficiency syndrome related complex or is HIV infected, is guilty of a felony.

As used in this section, "sexual penetration" means sexual intercourse, cunnilingus, fellatio, anal intercourse, or any other intrusion, however slight, of any part of a person's body or of any object into the genital or anal openings of another person's body, but emission of semen is not required. . . .

Defendant . . . argues that the statute is unconstitutional because it does not contain an intent, or *mens rea*, requirement. More specifically, defendant asserts that because the statute does not require a specific intent to harm, one who does not understand or appreciate the consequences of his or her acts can be found criminally responsible. We disagree.

In light of defendant's repeated argument that mentally deficient individuals will be prosecuted under this statute, we reiterate and remind defendant that, even though the evidence in the instant case does not support this factual scenario, if a "person lacks substantial capacity either to appreciate the wrongfulness of his conduct or to conform his conduct to the requirements of the law," he or she will be found lacking in criminal responsibility under the legal insanity defense statute.

With respect to defendant's *mens rea* argument, we note that fewer than half the states have criminal statutes penalizing the exposure of others to the HIV virus, and only a few of those contain an explicit *mens rea* requirement. . . . The others, including Michigan's statute, are silent on this topic except to require that the defendant know of his or her HIV or AIDS infection and fail to reveal it before donating blood, engaging in sexual penetration, or engaging a prostitute. . . . Notably, however, in *People* v. *Lardie*, 452 Mich 231, 256; 551 NW2d 656 (1996), our Supreme Court recently upheld the constitutionality of the statute that criminalizes causing death by operating a vehicle while intoxicated. The statute was challenged after the trial court held that it unconstitutionally precluded the jury from determining the defendant's mental state or intent, but this Court upheld the statute as creating a "strict liability, public welfare offense" without requiring the prosecutor to prove *mens rea*. In upholding the constitutionality

(continued)

of this statute, our Supreme Court made the following observations:

> In order to determine whether a statute imposes strict liability or requires proof of a mens rea, that is, guilty mind, this Court first examines the statute itself and seeks to determine the Legislature's intent. *People* v. *Quinn*, 440 Mich 178, 185; 487 NW2d 194 (1992). In interpreting a statute in which the Legislature has not expressly included language indicating that fault is a necessary element of a crime, this Court must focus on whether the Legislature nevertheless intended to require some fault as a predicate to finding guilt. In this statute, the Legislature did not expressly state that a defendant must have a criminal intent to commit this crime.
>
> Criminal intent is ordinarily an element of a crime even where the crime is created by statute. Statutes that create strict liability for all of their elements are not favored. Nevertheless, a state may decide under its police power that certain acts or omissions are to be punished irrespective of the actor's intent. Many of the crimes that impose strict liability have been termed "public welfare regulation." . . .
>
> See *Quinn*, supra at 185–186.

Where the offense in question does not codify the common law and omits reference to the element of intent, this Court will examine the Legislature's intent in enacting the legislation to determine whether there is a *mens rea* requirement.

Our Supreme Court in *Lardie* concluded that the Legislature intended to eliminate the gross negligence requirement that attended common-law involuntary manslaughter, the crime with which intoxicated drivers who killed were charged before the statute was enacted. Rather, the Legislature essentially presumed that voluntarily driving while one knows he or she could be intoxicated is gross negligence as a matter of law. Nevertheless, the Court believed that the Legislature presumably intended to require proof of a criminal intent for the criminal act of intoxicated driving. "[W]e conclude that the statute requires the people to prove that a defendant, who kills someone by driving while intoxicated, acted knowingly in consuming an intoxicating liquor or a controlled substance and acted voluntarily in deciding to drive after such consumption."

Applying the rationale of *Lardie* to the case at bar, we believe it likely that the Legislature intended to require some type of intent as a predicate to finding guilt under MCL 333.5210; MSA 14.15(5210), but that here the requisite intent is inherent in the HIV-infected person's socially and morally irresponsible actions. Moreover, the Legislature

could reasonably have presumed that it is grossly negligent for an HIV-infected person to engage in *any* sexual penetration with another person without full disclosure of his or her HIV infection. What does nondisclosure achieve? Only further dissemination of a lethal, incurable disease in order to gratify the sexual or other physical pleasures of the already infected individual. Disclosure would permit the other person to either refuse sexual contact or consent with knowledge of the risks he or she is taking. We also believe that the Legislature's primary concern is stemming the spread of HIV and AIDS throughout the population (similar to curtailing people from voluntarily driving while under the influence, as in *Lardie, supra*). Failure to disclose not only places the unwitting participant but also that participant's other sexual partners at serious risk of premature death. Indeed, the probable results accompanying nondisclosure are fairly predictable: death to innocent third parties.

Moreover, in *Lardie*, our Supreme Court also found that the death caused by intoxicated driving statute required a "causal relationship" between the defendant's culpable state of mind, i.e., intentionally driving while intoxicated, and the other person's resulting death. Here, the same causal connection exists despite the variety of methods by which one may contract AIDS or HIV or a myriad of other diseases that could end one's life. Knowingly engaging in sexual conduct capable of transmitting the AIDS virus or HIV without telling a partner about one's HIV-positive status is the culpable state of mind that can cause the partner's resulting infection and eventual death. Accordingly, although the MCL 333.5210; MSA 14.15(5210) contains no express *mens rea* requirement, we presume that the Legislature intended to require that the prosecution prove that the defendant had a general intent to commit the wrongful act, i.e., to engage in sexual penetration with another person while withholding the defendant's positive AIDS or HIV status.

Thus, the statute does not require strict liability because, if the defendant explains his or her HIV status and the other person consents to the physical contact despite the risks associated with such contact, there is no criminal liability. Finally, the statute requires that the culpable mental state have a causal relationship to the harm that the statute seeks to prevent, *id.*, i.e., requiring disclosure of one's HIV status will reduce the unwitting spread of AIDS and HIV-related diseases. We therefore find that MCL 333.5210; MSA 14.15(5210) is not unconstitutionally infirm on the basis that it lacks an explicit *mens rea* requirement. . . .

We therefore affirm the constitutionality of MCL 333.5210; MSA 14.15(5210) and defendant's convictions pursuant to the statute.

What Do *You* Think?

1. What kinds of crimes require intent? Which do not?

2. What is the difference between specific intent and general intent? Is either concept relevant in this case? Why?

3. Why does the court find that the statute on which this case is based "does not require strict liability"?

4. Some people argue that the kind of law discussed in this case turns a personal status (being infected with the AIDS virus) into a crime. Do you agree or disagree? Why?

5. Do you agree with the court's ruling in this case? Why or why not?

Additional Applications

What kinds of federal crimes require intent?

Morissette v. United States, 342 U.S. 246 (1952)

The Case: While hunting for deer in a remote area, a part-time scrap metal collector entered a U.S. Air Force bombing range in Michigan and gathered roughly three tons of rusting bomb casings from piles scattered on the ground. After selling the casings at a local junk market—for a total profit of $84—the collector was charged with violating 18 U.S.C. 641 by "knowingly steal[ing] and convert[ing]" government property for personal use. At trial, the sole question for decision was whether Congress, in failing to address *mens rea* explicitly in the statute, had intended to impose liability regardless of criminal intent. (The defendant had freely admitted gathering the casings; he claimed, however, that he had reasonably thought them to be abandoned property.) The trial judge ruled that Congress had indeed imposed strict liability in the statute; consequently, Morissette was not permitted to argue to the jury that he had acted with innocent intention.

The Finding: In a unanimous ruling, the U.S. Supreme Court reversed Morissette's conviction. Writing for the Court, Justice Robert H. Jackson noted that, although there is no "precise line or . . . comprehensive criteria for distinguishing between crimes that require a mental element and those that do not," American courts have long recognized that "crime, as a compound concept, generally constituted only from concurrence of an evil-meaning mind with an evil-doing hand." Thus, federal statutes that codify common law crimes such as murder, assault, conspiracy—and as here, theft and conversion of property—are generally understood to include a *mens rea*

requirement absent "any affirmative instruction from Congress to eliminate" it.

Nonetheless, Jackson noted, the general presumption against strict criminal liability is significantly weaker in statutes that define public welfare offenses such as violations of food safety standards, drug purity laws, labor/workplace rules, and regulations of tenement housing. Unlike crimes at common law, Jackson noted, violations of essentially regulatory laws typically "result in no direct or immediate injury to person or property." Likewise, criminal convictions for public welfare offenses generally do "no grave damage to an offender's reputation." Consequently, courts in the latter context may exercise greater latitude when inferring from statutory silence that Congress intended to omit the traditional *mens rea* requirement.

When can state courts infer a *mens rea* requirement?

People v. Troiano, 552 N.Y.S.2d 541 (1990)

The Case: On May 1, 1987, Alicia Troiano was involved in a two-car accident in Oceanside, New York, that resulted in the other driver's death. Troiano was not charged with fault for the accident itself or the resulting fatality—an investigation revealed that the decedent had been driving while intoxicated and had failed to yield at a stop sign—but a post-accident inspection of Troiano's car (a 1972 Oldsmobile station wagon) showed that the brakes on the right rear wheel did not meet state minimum safety standards. Troiano claimed no knowledge of the brake defect—the car's brake system had been operating normally and had been inspected only a few months before—but state officials nonetheless charged her with a misdemeanor violation of the state's Vehicle and Traffic Law requirement that "[e]very motor vehicle, operated or driven upon the highways of the state, shall be provided with adequate brakes." At trial, Troiano moved for dismissal on the grounds that the statute in question—which was completely silent on the issue of *mens rea*—did not create a strict liability crime.

The Finding: The New York court granted Troiano's motion to dismiss, finding that a *mens rea* requirement must be presumed to be present in the state's motor vehicle regulations. "It is a well-known principle of statutory construction," the court noted, "that absent the Legislature's clear indication of an intent to impose strict liability, a statute should be construed to require a *mens rea*." Accordingly, the mere existence of a mechanical defect alone was insufficient to establish that a crime had been committed. Proof beyond a reasonable doubt of the existence of a "culpable mental state" was required as well.

Lest there remain any doubt about the constitutional stature of the reasonable-doubt standard, we explicitly hold that the Due Process Clause protects the accused against conviction except upon proof beyond a reasonable doubt of every fact necessary to constitute the crime with which he is charged.

—Justice William J. Brennan, Jr., In re Winship,
397 U.S. 358, 364 (1970)

Insanity and *Mens Rea*

The ability to form a statute's requisite *mens rea* can be prevented or hindered by mental illness. Indeed, the insanity defense is a *mens rea* defense. As a defense, insanity has many forms, and special rules regulate its use. These will be discussed in Chapter 6. For the moment, be aware that insanity as a *mens rea* defense refers to the defendant's state of mind at the time the act occurred. Insanity at the time of trial is a different matter. It is also covered in Chapter 6.

CONCURRENCE

concurrence
The simultaneous coexistence of (1) an act in violation of the law and (2) a culpable mental state.

The concurrence of an unlawful act and a culpable mental state provides the third fundamental aspect of crime, for those crimes that require *mens rea*. **Concurrence** requires that the act and the mental state occur together in order for a crime to take place. Even more, the two must be connected and they must occur in the proper sequence, *mens rea* followed by the act. Indeed, it is the *mens rea* that sets the act into motion. A defendant must form the intention to kill, even if it is only a second, before taking the act that resulted in the death of another person for there to be purposeful or intentional murder. However, it is not enough that the *mens rea* was formed before the act. There must also be a causal relationship between the two. The act must be the product of the mental state of the actor. For example, a person may intend to kill a rival. As she drives carefully to the intended victim's house, gun beside her, fantasizing about how she will commit the murder, the intended victim is crossing the street on the way home from grocery shopping. If the two accidentally collide and the intended victim dies, there has been no concurrence of act and intent—even though the driver may later rejoice in her "good fortune" at having killed her enemy without incurring criminal liability.

Some jurisdictions make the need for concurrence a clear part of their legal codes. The California Penal Code, for example, requires that "[i]n every crime or public offense there must exist a union, or joint operation of act and intent, or criminal negligence."[36] The absence of concurrence is not a common defense in American criminal law.

SUMMARY

- The legal essence of criminal conduct consists of three essential elements: *actus reus* (an act in violation of the law), *mens rea* (a guilty mind), and the concurrence of the two. Some scholars suggest that another four elements are also inherent in the concept of crime: causation, a resulting harm, the principle of legality, and necessary attendant circumstances. In contrast to the elements common to all crimes, particular offenses are statutorily defined in terms of specific statutory elements. To convict a defendant of a given crime, prosecutors must prove to a judge or jury that all of the statutory elements of a crime are present. If even one statutory element of an offense cannot be established beyond a reasonable doubt, criminal liability will not have been demonstrated, and the defendant will be found not guilty.

- To *be* something is not a crime, but to *do* something may be. Following tradition, the criminal act is referred to as the *actus reus* of an offense. For purposes of the criminal law, the word *act* means a performance, a deed, or a movement, as distinguished from remaining at rest.

- The term *mens rea* literally means "a guilty mind." Various degrees of culpability, or types of *mens rea*, can be distinguished. At the common law, the distinction between specific and general intent was important. Today, the four most commonly specified levels of culpability are purposeful, knowing, reckless, and negligent. It is important to note that *mens rea* is not the same thing as motive. A motive refers to a person's reason for committing a crime. *Mens rea* refers to the offender's mental state at the time the crime was committed. Strict liability offenses, which are based on the presumption that causing harm is in itself blameworthy, represent an exception to general understandings of the nature of crime because they require no accompanying culpable mental state.

- Strict liability offenses, a special category of crimes, require no culpable mental state, and present a significant exception to the principle that all crimes require a conjunction of action and *mens rea*. Strict liability is based on the presumption that causing harm is in itself blameworthy, regardless of the actor's intent.

- The concurrence of an unlawful act and a culpable mental state provides the third fundamental aspect of crime. Concurrence requires that the act and the mental state occur together in order for a crime to take place.

KEY TERMS

actual possession, 43	elements of crime, 40	motive, 54
actus reus, 42	general intent, 46	omission to act, 44
canon of construction, 56	inference, 51	reckless behavior, 49
concurrence, 60	jury instructions, 40	scienter, 46
conduct, 41	knowing behavior, 49	specific intent, 46
constructive possession, 43	knowing possession, 43	strict liability, 54
criminal liability, 40	legislative history, 56	strict liability crime, 54
criminal negligence, 51	*mens rea*, 46	transferred intent, 42
deadly weapon doctrine, 51	mere possession, 43	

QUESTIONS FOR DISCUSSION

1. What are the three fundamental aspects of crime? How is each central to the concept of crime?

2. What is meant by the term *actus reus*? What are the basic elements of *actus reus*?

3. What is *mens rea*? What were the two forms of *mens rea* recognized by the common law?

4. What are the various states of mind outlined by the Model Penal Code?

5. What is strict liability? Why are some crimes punished solely on the basis of strict liability?

6. Are strict liability offenses as worthy of "blame" as other offenses that require *mens rea*? Why or why not?

7. How does the concept of concurrence relate to *mens rea* and *actus reus*?

CRITICAL THINKING AND APPLICATION PROBLEMS

1. You work for a state legislator. She is very concerned about the state's environment, particularly the introduction of nonnative, invasive species of plants. She asks you to draft a bill that makes it a crime to introduce such plants into the state's environment. Assume you have a definition of a nonnative, invasive species. Draft a bill for her that applies the Model Penal Code's four states of mind to different offenses. Grade the offenses from the highest to the lowest. Explain how each offense is different and why you graded the offenses as you did.

2. As you learned, statutory rape is a strict liability crime in many jurisdictions. A defendant doesn't have to intend to have sex with a minor to commit the crime. Even more, evidence that the victim appeared to be an adult or that the defendant was misled by the victim about his or her age are not defenses to the crime. Divide into teams of four, two defending the crime as strict liability and two opposing it. Take 20 minutes to construct your best arguments and debate the question of whether fairness (due process) or some other constitutional provision is violated by a strict liability statutory rape statute.

3. The following was enacted by the Congress of the United States:

   Breach of Loyalty: Any citizen of the United States who believes that the government of the United States shall be overthrown or abolished through force and rebellion shall be guilty of breach of loyalty and punished with life imprisonment.

   I. B. Extreme, a 55-year-old male who lives in Florida, was in a bar playing poker with five individuals whom he had met for the first time earlier in the evening. The discussion during the game turned to politics and Extreme commented, "I believe the government is all corrupt. Jefferson said a rebellion now and then is a good thing. Americans should load their guns and teach Washington a lesson." His statements were reported to the Federal Bureau of Investigation by one of his poker friends who turned out to be a local police officer. Extreme has been charged with violating the Breach of Loyalty statute. Discuss his best defense, as you learned in this chapter.

LEGAL RESOURCES ON THE WEB

Law dictionaries can be especially useful to students using this textbook and to anyone beginning the study of law. Quite a few law dictionaries are available on the Web, including the following:

Court TV Glossary of Legal Terms

http://www.courttv.com/legalterms/glossary.html
A comprehensive glossary of legal terms.

Nolo's Free Dictionary of Law Terms and Legal Definitions

http://www.nolo.com/lawcenter/dictionary/wordindex.cfm
Plain-English definitions of hundreds of legal terms from Nolo Press.

Jurist's Basic U.S. Legal Terminology

http://jurist.law.pitt.edu/dictionary.htm
A dictionary of basic terminology with a focus on legal procedure. Includes hyperlinks to relevant websites.

Law.com Dictionary

http://dictionary.law.com
A real-life dictionary of the law.

Merriam-Webster's Dictionary of the Law

http://dictionary.reference.com/legal

A searchable legal dictionary from a definitive source.

The FindLaw Dictionary

http://dictionary.lp.findlaw.com

A service of FindLaw.com.

SUGGESTED READINGS AND CLASSIC WORKS

American Law Institute. *Model Penal Code and Commentaries*. Philadelphia: American Law Institute, 1985.

Fletcher, George P. *Rethinking Criminal Law*. New York: Oxford University Press, 2000.

Friedman, Lawrence M. *American Law*. New York: Norton, 1984.

———. *A History of American Law*. New York: Simon and Schuster, 1973.

Hall, Jerome. *General Principles of Criminal Law*, 2nd ed. Indianapolis: Bobbs-Merrill, 1960.

Katz, Leo. *Bad Acts and Guilty Minds: Conundrums of the Criminal Law*. Chicago: University of Chicago Press, 1987.

Murray, Peter. *Basic Trial Advocacy*. Boston: Little, Brown, 1995.

Packer, Herbert L. *The Limits of the Criminal Sanction*. Palo Alto, CA: Stanford University Press, 1968.

Patterson, Dennis. *Law and Truth*. New York: Oxford University Press, 1996.

Perkins, Rollin M., and Ronald N. Boyce. *Criminal Law*, 3rd ed. Mineola, NY: Foundation Press, 1982.

Shute, Stephen, and A. P. Simester. *Criminal Law Theory: Doctrines of the General Part*. Oxford: Oxford University Press, 2002.

Turow, Scott. *Presumed Innocent* [novel]. New York: Farrar Straus Giroux, 1987.

Williams, Gianville L. *Criminal Law: The General Part*. London: Stephens and Sons, 1953.

NOTES

1. You can read Judge Ito's full instructions at The 'Lectric Law Library, http://www.lectlaw.com/files/cas62.htm.

2. Common law crimes, of course, are not based on statutory elements.

3. Arizona Revised Statutes, Title 13, Section 105.

4. Wayne R. LaFave and Austin W. Scott, Jr., *Criminal Law* (St. Paul: West, 1986).

5. Recent studies that appear to demonstrate the efficacy of prayer, as well as certain New Age and Eastern beliefs in "thought manifestation," are not subsumed under this principle.

6. Indiana Code, Title 35, Article 41, Chapter 2, Section 1.

7. Texas Penal Code, Title 2, Section 6.01.

8. Model Penal Code §2.01.

9. The woman, Barbara Woods, was also stabbed.

10. "Sleepwalker Acquitted in Mother-in-Law Slaying," *San Francisco Examiner*, May 28, 1988.

11. Matt Kelley, "Jury Convicts Husband in Sleepwalking Murder Trial," Associated Press, June 27, 1999, http://www.trib.com/HOMENEWS/WASH/SleepwalkTrial.html (accessed July 8, 2009).

12. Texas Penal Code, Title 2, Section 6.01.

13. Arizona Revised Statutes, Title 13, Section 105, paragraphs 30 and 31.

14. 17 C.F.R.§205.

15. Fred Bayles, "Spiritual Healing," Associated Press, November 27, 1993.

16. The Boston-based church is officially known as the First Church of Christ, Scientist.

17. O.R.C. §2921.22.

18. Kevin Johnson, "Sandusky Child Sex-abuse Case Lacks Key Details," *USA Today*, March 4, 2012, http://www.usatoday.com/news/nation/story/2012-03-04/sandusky-penn-state-abuse-case/53358684/1 (accessed March 10, 2012).

19. 23 Pa. Const. Stat. §6311, et seq. and 55 P.S. §3490 et seq.

20. See "United States: Child Reporting Laws—Penn State Scandal," Mondaq, http://www.mondaq.com/unitedstates/x/153566/Commercial/Child+Abuse+Reporting+Laws+Penn+State+Scandal.

21. The free speech clause of the First Amendment may allow one to say that the president deserves to die, but to actually threaten the president is an offense under Title 18, Chapter 41, Section 871, of the federal criminal code.

22. *Snyder* v. *Phelps*, 131 S.Ct. 1207 (2011).

23. *Gordon* v. *State*, 52 Ala. 3008, 23 Am. Rep. 575 (1875).

24. Gregory Tejeda, "Supreme Court Backs State Law Making Knowing HIV Transmission a Crime," United Press, January 20, 1994.

25. All Arizona definitions in this section are taken from Arizona Revised Statutes, Title 13, Section 105.

26. Italics added.

27. But she cannot be prosecuted for more serious degrees of homicide because leaving a young child alone in a tub of water, even if intentional, does not necessarily mean that the person who does so intends the child to drown.

28. Oliver Wendell Holmes, *The Common Law* (Boston: Little, Brown & Co., 1881), 3.

29. Model Penal Code §210.0(4).

30. There is disagreement, however, among jurists as to whether or not the crime of statutory rape is a strict liability offense. Some jurisdictions treat it as such and will not accept a reasonable mistake about the victim's age. Others, however, do accept such a mistake as a defense.

31. California Penal Code, Part I, Title 9, Chapter 1, Section 261.5.

32. *State* v. *Stiffler*, 763 P.2d 308 (Idaho App. 1988).

33. *People* v. *Hernandez*, 393 P.2d 673 (Cal. 1964).

34. *U.S.* v. *Greenbaum*, 138 F.2d 437 (3d Cir. 1943).

35. *Missouri* v. *Hatton*, No. 78277 (consolidated with) *Missouri* v. *Richard Troy, Jr.*, No. 78278 (Missouri Supreme Court cases).

36. California Penal Code, Preliminary Provisions, Section 20.

Shutterstock

3

Expanding the Concept of Crime

CHAPTER OUTLINE

Introduction

Corpus Delicti

Additional Principles of Criminality

OBJECTIVES

After reading this chapter, you should be able to

- Explain the concept of *corpus delicti*.
- Explain the concepts of causation and proximate cause.
- Distinguish between causation in fact and proximate cause.
- Explain the concept of felony murder, and describe how it differs from other forms of murder.
- Illustrate the nature of an *ex post facto* law, and explain why our legal system does not permit the creation of *ex post facto* criminal laws.

> *Law should be like death, which spares no one.*
>
> —Montesquieu (1689–1755)
>
> *Justice is a machine that, when someone has once given it the starting push, rolls on of itself.*
>
> —John Galsworthy (1867–1933)

INTRODUCTION

On March 30, 1992, David Smith's double-wide mobile home in Orangeburg County, South Carolina, suffered damage from a fire. Investigators determined that the fire had started in the kitchen and was the result of cooking oil igniting after being heated in a deep-fat fryer for at least an hour. Although no accelerant was discovered, investigators found evidence that the house had been "sterilized" prior to the fire. Outside the trailer, a trash can filled with children's toys was found. In a pump house adjacent to the trailer, personal items were discovered in two suitcases, one bearing an identification tag with David Smith's name on it. The items included photo albums, love notes, costume jewelry, and "sex toys." Moreover, the back door—a sliding glass door—was open three inches. One investigator suggested that the door had been left open to provide an oxygen supply to facilitate the burning of the fire.

Smith and two associates were arrested and charged with arson. Before trial, however, defense counsel moved that the trial court conduct an evidentiary hearing out of the presence of the jury for the purpose of determining whether sufficient evidence of the **corpus delicti** existed to proceed to trial. Counsel argued that "the government must establish the incendiary nature of the fire before it can get into the issue of statements or admissions." The trial court agreed and conducted a hearing at which two arson investigators testified. At the conclusion of the hearing, the trial court held: "In order for the State to establish *corpus delicti* in this case, it must provide evidence that the burning was by a willful act and not a result of natural or accidental causes. There has been no testimony whatsoever to suggest that this fire was the result of a willful act; that any criminal agency was involved whatsoever; that these defendants had any connection whatsoever with the fire that resulted. . . . There was no testimony that would even support the theory of circumstantial evidence, wherein if employed it would have to exclude every other reasonable hypothesis, except point toward the guilt of these defendants."

The trial court then dismissed the arson charges against all three defendants.

corpus delicti
The facts that show that a crime has occurred. Literally, the "body of crime."

CORPUS DELICTI

A trial is still an ordeal by battle. For the broadsword there is the weight of evidence; for the battle-ax, the force of logic; for the sharp spear, the blazing gleam of truth; for the rapier, the quick and flashing knife of wit.

—Lloyd Paul Stryker, criminal attorney

These chapter-opening paragraphs were taken from the 1996 South Carolina appellate case of *State* v. *Williams*.[1] They highlight the importance of *corpus delicti* in the judicial process and give some insight into the nature of the concept itself.

The term *corpus delicti* literally means "body of crime." The term is often confused with the statutory elements of a crime (which will be discussed in future chapters) or taken literally to mean the body of a murder victim or some other physical results of criminal activity. The concept actually means something quite different. One way to understand the concept of *corpus delicti* is to realize that a person cannot be tried for a crime unless it can first be shown that the offense has occurred. In other words, to establish the *corpus delicti* of a crime, the state has to demonstrate that a criminal law has been violated and that someone violated it. Hence there are only two components of the *corpus delicti* of a crime: (1) that a certain result has been produced, and (2) that a person is criminally responsible for it (Figure 3–1). As one court said, "*Corpus delicti* consists of a showing of: (1) the occurrence of the specific kind of injury and (2) someone's criminal act as the cause of the injury."[2] So, for example, the crime of larceny requires proof that the property of another has been stolen—that is, taken unlawfully with the intent to permanently deprive the owner of its possession.[3] Hence evidence offered to prove the *corpus delicti* in a trial for larceny is insufficient when the evidence fails to prove that property has been stolen from another or when property found in the accused's possession cannot be identified as having been stolen. Similarly, "[i]n an arson

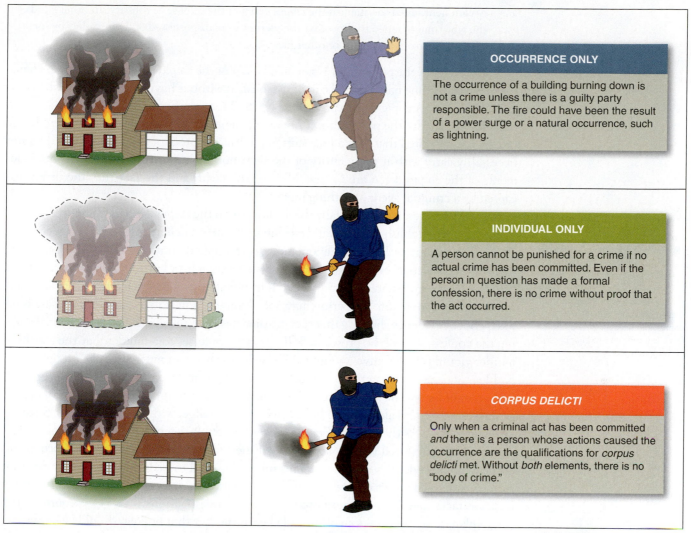

OCCURRENCE ONLY

The occurrence of a building burning down is not a crime unless there is a guilty party responsible. The fire could have been the result of a power surge or a natural occurrence, such as lightning.

INDIVIDUAL ONLY

A person cannot be punished for a crime if no actual crime has been committed. Even if the person in question has made a formal confession, there is no crime without proof that the act occurred.

CORPUS DELICTI

Only when a criminal act has been committed *and* there is a person whose actions caused the occurrence are the qualifications for *corpus delicti* met. Without *both* elements, there is no "body of crime."

FIGURE 3–1

The *Corpus Delicti* of Crime.

case, the *corpus delicti* consists of (1) a burned building or other property, and (2) some criminal agency which caused the burning. . . . In other words, the *corpus delicti* includes not only the fact of burning, but it must also appear that the burning was by the willful act of some person, and not as a result of a natural or accidental cause."[4]

Another court described the concept this way: "The rule in criminal cases is that the coincidence of circumstances tending to indicate guilt, however strong and numerous they may be, avails nothing unless the *corpus delicti*, the fact that the crime has been actually perpetrated, be first established. So long as the least doubt exists as to the act there can be no certainty as to the criminal agent."[5] As a general rule, *corpus delicti* must be established beyond a reasonable doubt.

Here's how one court, in a pocket-picking case, explained the central role played by *corpus delicti*:

> We conclude that the government failed to prove beyond a reasonable doubt that Zanders and Harris took the wallets from the immediate actual possession of Dr. Sokolov and Mr. Routson, or from their persons, or that a pick-pocketing even took place. There was no direct evidence that Zanders and Harris took the wallets, and no expert testimony as to the methods used by pickpockets to remove wallets from the clothing of individuals, or the amount of force necessary to pick a pocket. Hence, there was neither direct nor indirect evidence of a taking of property from Dr. Sokolov or Mr. Routson by anyone, much less by Zanders or Harris. . . . The evidence presented is just as consistent, at least on a reasonable doubt standard, with both victims having lost their wallets and the defendants having found them and having used the credit cards without authority. In short, the

government failed to establish the *corpus delicti* of the offense of robbery. In other words, the government failed to show that the victims were dispossessed of their wallets by some person or persons by stealth or other means.[6]

The identity of the perpetrator is not an element of the *corpus delicti* of an offense. Hence the fact that a crime has occurred can be established without having any sense of who committed it. This principle was clearly stated by the Montana Supreme Court when it noted that "the identity of the perpetrator is not an element of the *corpus delicti*. In *State* v. *Kindle* (1924) . . . we stated that '[i]n a prosecution for murder, proof of the *corpus delicti* does not necessarily carry with it the identity of the slain nor of the slayer.' . . . The essential elements of the *corpus delicti* are . . . establishing the death and the fact that the death was caused by a criminal agency, nothing more."[7]

Confessions present an especially thorny area when the *corpus delicti* of a crime cannot be independently established. Generally speaking, the **corpus delicti rule** holds that a criminal conviction cannot be based solely on the uncorroborated confession or admission of the accused. As one court explained it, "It is a settled principle of law that a mere extrajudicial confession, uncorroborated by other facts, is insufficient to show the *corpus delicti* and cannot support a conviction." A person may, for example, confess to a crime, but if there is no independent evidence showing that such a crime has even taken place, the individual making the confession can't be prosecuted. If a person confesses to a murder, but the supposed murder victim is found alive and in good health, no charge of murder can be brought. The problem of demonstrating the *corpus delicti* of a crime is more difficult when a person confesses to murder but the murder victim's remains cannot be found. Most states do not permit a confession to stand alone as the basis of a criminal charge, without independent corroborating evidence. As the Indiana Supreme Court held: "A defendant's extrajudicial confession may be introduced into evidence only if the State establishes the *corpus delicti* of the crime by independent evidence. . . . This rule is designed to 'reduce the risk of convicting a defendant based on his confession for a crime that did not occur,' prevent coercive interrogation tactics, and encourage thorough criminal investigations."[8] A Texas court offered this explanation: "The wisdom of this rule lies in the fact that no man should be convicted of a crime, the commission of which he confesses, unless the state shows, by testimony other than the accused's confession, that the confessed crime was in fact committed."[9]

In the case of *Illinois* v. *Lara*,[10] from the Court of Appeals of Texas, a confession to sexual assault was found inadequate to establish *corpus delicti* because there was no corroborating evidence.

A determination of the *corpus delicti* of a crime is important for another reason: A crime will generally be prosecuted in the location where it was committed—that is, where the *corpus delicti* of the crime exists. Following this principle, the Wyoming Constitution, for example, provides in part: "When the location of the offense cannot be established with certainty, venue may be placed in the county or district where the *corpus delicti* is found."[11]

Finally, federal courts and a few state courts have abandoned the requirement of establishing the *corpus delicti* of a crime because doing so is not always possible. Attempted crimes, some high-technology crimes, conspiracies, and crimes such as income tax evasion make the *corpus delicti* requirement difficult, if not impossible, to meet.

corpus delicti rule
(1) The body or essence of a criminal offense that proves that the alleged crime has been committed, but not who committed the crime. (2) In practice, a principle of law that says that an out-of-court confession, unsupported by other facts, is insufficient to support a criminal conviction.

Life and liberty can be as much endangered from illegal methods used to convict those thought to be criminals as from the actual criminals themselves.

—Chief Justice Earl Warren, writing for the majority in Spano v. New York, 360 U.S. 315 (1959)

ADDITIONAL PRINCIPLES OF CRIMINALITY

Many scholars contend that the three features of crime (which we outlined in the last chapter)—*actus reus*, *mens rea*, and concurrence—are sufficient to describe the essence of the legal concept of crime. Other scholars, however, see modern Western law as more complex. They argue that four additional principles are necessary to fully appreciate contemporary understandings of crime: (1) causation, (2) a resulting harm, (3) the principle of legality, and (4) necessary attendant circumstances. Each of these is discussed in the pages that follow. Although these are not legal elements that prosecutors must prove, they act as limitations on the authority of government to prosecute. This distinction will become clearer as you read further.

Causation

Causation refers to the fact that the concurrence of a guilty mind and a criminal act must produce or *cause* harm. Whereas some statutes criminalize only conduct, others subsume the notion of concurrence under causation and specify that a causal relationship is a necessary element of a given crime. They require that the offender *cause* a particular result before criminal liability can be incurred. In wording reflective of the Model Penal Code, for example, the Texas Penal Code defines *homicide* in this way: "A person commits criminal homicide if he intentionally, knowingly, recklessly, or with criminal negligence causes the death of an individual."[12] If there is no death of a human being *caused* by another person, the statute does not apply.

Although the Texas statute seems clear enough, the word *causes* may be open to a number of interpretations. Does a person cause the death of another if he or she fires a weapon at someone, intending to kill the person, and misses, but the target drops dead from fright? Does a person cause the death of another if he or she shoots the person, who dies six months later in the hospital from pneumonia—never having fully recovered from the gunshot wound? Does a person cause the death of another if he or she contracts with a witch doctor to curse that individual, and the person soon dies in an accident or from disease?

When discussing a specific ultimate harm, such as death, which is referred to in homicide statutes, it is necessary to recognize the difference between **causation in fact** and **proximate cause**. If there is an actual link between the actor's conduct and the resulting harm, causation in fact exists. Even so, a cause in fact cannot be said to be the sole cause, or even the primary cause, of a particular event. If a person fires a gun, for example, and the bullet strikes a building, causing it to ricochet and hit a person standing next to the shooter, it can be said that the person who fired the weapon shot the bystander or, at the very least, *caused* him to be shot. In this case, other causes clearly contributed to the event, including the presence and movements of the bystander who was struck (Figure 3–2). Each

causation in fact
An actual link between an actor's conduct and a result.

proximate cause
The primary or moving cause that plays a substantial part in bringing about injury or damage. It may be a first cause that sets in motion a string of events whose ultimate outcome is reasonably foreseeable.

FIGURE 3–2

Cause in Fact.

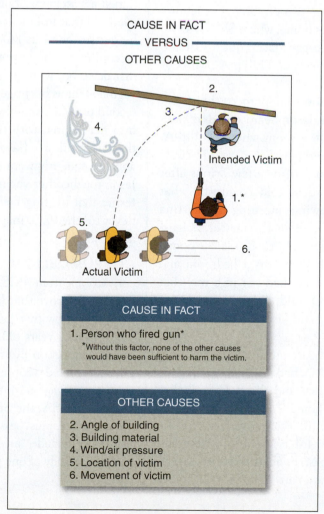

CAUSE IN FACT
VERSUS
OTHER CAUSES

2.
3.
4.
Intended Victim
1.*
5.
6.
Actual Victim

CAUSE IN FACT

1. Person who fired gun*
   *Without this factor, none of the other causes would have been sufficient to harm the victim.

OTHER CAUSES

2. Angle of building
3. Building material
4. Wind/air pressure
5. Location of victim
6. Movement of victim

APPLYING THE CONCEPT

CAPSTONE CASE

Does a Defendant's Confession of a Sex Crime Have to Be Supported by Other Evidence for Conviction?

Illinois v. Lara (Ill. App. 1st Dist. 2011)

THE CASE A jury found the defendant, Jason Lara, guilty of two counts of predatory criminal sexual assault (PCSA) for inserting his finger into the vagina of an eight-year-old girl, J.O. On appeal, Jason argues that the State failed to prove the *corpus delicti* of the offense, because the State failed to present any evidence corroborating Jason's confession that he put his finger inside J.O. We agree. . . .

Augustina P. had two children, J.O. and C.A. Augustina, who worked many evenings, often asked her friend, Shelley Lara, to look after her two children. Sometimes J.O. and C.A. slept at Shelley's home, where Shelley's son, Jason, also slept. Augustina began dating John Cordero after she separated from her husband, Phillip A., who was C.A.'s father.

On February 11, 2005, Jason told Cordero that once, when Phillip A. came to visit, Jason heard sounds of licking and sucking coming from a room where Phillip A. and J.O. were alone together. On February 17, 2005, Cordero and Augustina went out for a few drinks after Augustina got off work. Cordero told Augustina what Jason had said. The following morning, Augustina asked Cordero to talk to J.O. about the matter. Augustina's sister brought J.O. and C.A. to Cordero's home, before school. Cordero took J.O. into a bedroom and asked her if Phillip had ever touched her in a way that made her uncomfortable. J.O. said, "Yes, he has but it wasn't Phillip." Instead, J.O. said Jason had touched her inappropriately.

Augustina came into the bedroom to talk to J.O., and again J.O. said Jason, not Phillip, had touched her "private part." Augustina called Shelley and the police. Shelley and Jason came to Cordero's home. Police officers arrested Jason. Carey Kato, a forensic interviewer working for the Children's Advocacy Center, interviewed J.O. later that day. J.O. said that on two occasions about a month earlier, Jason had touched her "private part." She pointed to her vagina. J.O. explained that when she and her sister slept at Shelley's home, they would sleep on the floor next to the bed in the living room where Jason slept. One night she woke up to find her pants and underpants pulled down to her knees, and Jason's hand resting on her "private part." A few days later, when she came back to lie on the floor after going to the bathroom late at night, Jason put his hand inside her panties and on her vagina. Kato specifically asked whether Jason put his hand inside her, and J.O. said it was outside her vagina on both occasions. Jason signed a statement about the incident later that day. He admitted that in January 2005, on two separate occasions, he put his hand in J.O.'s pants and touched her vagina. According to the written statement, he said that on the first occasion, while J.O. slept, he put his finger into her vagina as far as his fingernail, and then J.O. woke up. The second time J.O. was already awake when he put his finger into her vagina, with the finger again entering as far as the fingernail. . . . [Jason was indicted on several charges and subsequently went to trial. J.O. testified at trial that Jason touched her vagina on two occasions but she didn't testify that his finger entered her. Jason testified that he never touched J.O. inappropriately, contrary to his earlier admission.]

CORPUS DELICTI Next, Jason asks us to reduce his convictions from PCSA to [aggravated sexual assault] ACSA. To prove that Jason committed ACSA, the State needed to show that Jason was over 17 years old and J.O. was under 13 years old when Jason committed an act of sexual conduct on J.O. The statutory definition of "sexual conduct" includes contact between a defendant's finger and the victim's vagina for the purpose of sexual gratification. To prove PCSA, the State needed to prove the facts that prove ACSA, plus "sexual penetration," which the statute defines to include "any intrusion, however slight, of any part of the body of one person *into the sex organ* of another person" . . . .

Illinois has long followed the rule that "proof of the *corpus delicti* may not rest exclusively on a defendant's extrajudicial confession, admission, or other statement." . . .

The corroboration rule has changed very little since our supreme court applied it in [1856]. . . .

[In 1982 our *Supreme Court*] explained:

> The corroboration rule requires that the *corpus delicti* be proved by some evidence *aliunde* admission of a defendant. *** The corroboration rule was the result of an historical mistrust of extrajudicial confessions. Two reasons for this mistrust have commonly been cited: confessions are unreliable if coerced; and, for various psychological reasons persons 'confess' to crimes that either have never occurred or for which they are not legally responsible.

. . . we find sufficient corroboration for Jason's confession that he committed ACSA when he touched J.O.'s vagina, but we find no corroboration for the single element, sexual penetration, that distinguishes ACSA from PCSA. . . .

Augustina, Cordero and J.O. presented no evidence that any part of Jason's body intruded into J.O.'s vagina. Paraday [a police detective who investigated the case] admitted that in the forensic interview, in response to a direct question about the extent of the contact, J.O. said that Jason's hand stayed outside her vagina in both incidents. The only evidence of penetration came from the written statement Jason signed. . . .

Accordingly, we reverse both convictions for PCSA and vacate Jason's sentences on those charges. [Jason's convictions on the (ASCA) charges that did not require penetration were upheld and the case was remanded for sentencing.]

What Do *You* Think?

1. Change the facts of the case. Create two factual examples of how *corpus delicti* could be proven for the more serious PCSA crime at issue in the case.

2. Do you believe that *corpus delicti* serves an important purpose, or should confessions be allowed to stand alone as evidence to support convictions?

Additional Applications

Is circumstantial evidence enough to establish the *corpus delicti*?

South Dakota v. Bates, 71 N.W.2d 641 (S.D. 1955)

The Case: After a brief jury trial in a South Dakota municipal court, H. O. Bates, a licensed big game hunter, was convicted and fined $100 for illegally hunting an elk

out of season. On appeal, Bates conceded that he had killed an elk on the day in question and that that action *would* have been a crime if it had actually occurred at the location of his arrest—a remote canyon in Lawrence County where state game wardens had discovered the freshly dressed carcass. Bates insisted, however, that he had actually shot the elk several miles away, in neighboring Pennington County—where elk hunting was allowed under a special state regulation. At trial, state game officials produced no physical or eyewitness evidence to indicate where Bates had actually shot the elk. To establish the *corpus delicti*, state officials relied on the circumstances of Bates's arrest as well as extrajudicial statements allegedly made at the scene that suggested his initial lack of familiarity with the area and with the state's elk hunting rules.

The Finding: The Supreme Court of South Dakota affirmed the conviction. In this case, the court noted, a showing that the elk had been killed in Lawrence County was an essential element of the *corpus delicti*—which the state bore the burden of establishing beyond a reasonable doubt. Yet although a *corpus delicti* "cannot be presumed" on the basis of a defendant's admissions standing alone, state officials here presented such statements alongside corroborating circumstantial evidence to the jury, which carried the primary duty of determining whether the reasonable doubt standard had been met. When establishing that a crime has, in fact, been committed, the court stressed, the available corroborating evidence standing alone "need not be conclusive in character." To the contrary, such evidence is sufficient "even though it is wholly circumstantial and furnishes only slight corroboration" if, taken with the defendant's statements, it "convince[s] the jury that the crime charged is real and not imaginary."

Can evidence of a defendant's motive, intent, and opportunity contribute to proof that a "murder" has occurred?

California v. Towler, 641 P.2d 1253 (Cal. 1982)

The Case: Following a bench trial, Christopher Towler was convicted of second-degree murder in the death of Ron Stone, who, as a drug informant, had earlier set up Towler in a drug sting that had resulted in Towler's felony drug conviction. Both before his trial and while awaiting sentencing, Towler told several people that he hated "snitches" and thought they should be killed. Further, he stated that there was a "plan" to "get" Stone before his sentencing—and that when Stone's body was found, it

(continued)

would "be like an accident . . . there would be no evidence . . . or it would be so gone . . . that nobody would know how it was done." Shortly before Towler's sentencing hearing, then—while Towler was out on bail—Stone disappeared without notice. His body was found about two months later on a remote riverbank several miles away; because of decomposition, medical examiners could not establish the cause or time of death—although they noted that Stone probably had not been shot, stabbed, strangled, or beaten. At trial, Towler's lawyers contested the existence of *corpus delicti* by introducing evidence suggesting that Stone could have drowned, overdosed on drugs, or committed suicide.

The Finding: The Supreme Court of California affirmed the conviction, holding that the existing evidence, exclusive of any statements made by the defendant, was sufficient to support a finding that a crime had in fact occurred. A prosecutor, the court noted, is "not required to establish the *corpus delicti* by proof as clear and convincing as is necessary to establish the fact of guilt; rather, slight or *prima facie* proof is sufficient for such purpose." More specifically, the court, citing one of its own earlier rulings on the issue, held that "the prosecution need not eliminate all inferences tending to show a noncriminal cause of death." Rather, it is sufficient to produce information "which creates a reasonable inference that the death could have been caused by a criminal agency even in the presence of an equally plausible noncriminal explanation of the event." Here, the court found, the available evidence "did not rule out the possibility that Stone had died from noncriminal causes." Yet the countervailing evidence of the defendant's motive, intent, and opportunity, alongside the particular circumstances in which Stone's body was discovered, was sufficient to support the trial court's finding that a felony murder had indeed taken place. ∎

of the features of the event may be said to be causes in fact, for without each being present, the harm in question would not have occurred.

Factual causality can be determined through the *sine qua non* test, which holds, in effect, that "without this, that would not be." The *sine qua non* test is also referred to as the "had not" test and as the **"but for" rule** because it means that some injury would not have happened *but for* the conduct of the accused. In our earlier example, the bystander would not have been shot but for the actions of the shooter. Similarly, he would not have been shot but for the fact that someone had chosen to build a wall out of, say, steel-reinforced concrete, which caused the bullet fired by the shooter to ricochet. Even when factual cause can be demonstrated, however, it might not provide the basis for a criminal prosecution because the government must then prove that it is also a legally recognized cause. Proof of factual cause may be *necessary* for a conviction, but it alone is not *sufficient* for a conviction to result.

"but for" rule
A method for determining causality that holds that "without this, that would not be," or "*but for* the conduct of the accused, the harm in question would not have occurred."

The idea of proximate cause is a more useful legal concept than factual cause. Proximate cause holds individuals criminally liable for causing harm when it can logically be shown that the harm caused was reasonably foreseeable from their conduct. Proximate cause can also be thought of as the first cause in a string of events that ultimately produced the harm in question. If, for example, a woman poisons her husband's dinner, intending to kill him, but he stays late at the office and she puts the meal in the refrigerator, she may still be held liable for the crime of homicide if a boarder staying in the house gets up in the middle of the night, eats the meal, and dies (Figure 3–3). In this case, the actions of the woman who intended to cause the death of her husband become the proximate cause of the death of the boarder. Proximate cause exists in this example for two reasons: First, the woman set in motion a chain of events with potentially deadly consequences; and second, the boarder's consumption of food in the refrigerator was a reasonably foreseeable event, and his death was therefore a foreseeable consequence of the woman's actions. Hence, even though the wrong person died, the death should have been reasonably foreseeable from the defendant's actions. As a result, legal liability exists.

A proximate cause is also a primary cause. The U.S. Supreme Court observed that "'proximate cause' requires some direct relation between the injury asserted and the injurious

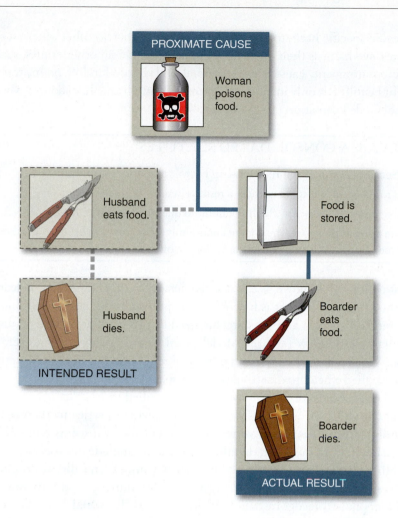

FIGURE 3–3

Proximate Cause.

Although the death of the boarder was not the woman's intended result, there is a clear chain of events leading directly to that outcome.

conduct alleged."[13] If, for example, one person assaults another and chases him out of a building and through a driving rainstorm, the assault cannot be said to be the proximate cause of the victim's death if he is struck by lightning (the primary cause of the death) and killed during the pursuit, even though one might argue that but for the initial assault, he would not have been exposed to the elements and would therefore have lived. This is so because the lightning strike was not related to the assault; that is, it was not brought on by it in the same sense that an infection might be produced by a gunshot wound. The bolt of lightning, in this instance, was independent of any harm caused by the assailant and could not have been reasonably foreseen.

To clarify the issue of causation, the American Law Institute suggests the use of the term **legal cause** rather than *proximate cause* in order to emphasize the notion of a legally recognizable cause and to preclude any assumption that such a cause must be close in time and space to the result it produces. Legal causes can be distinguished from those causes that may have produced the result in question but that may not provide the basis for a criminal prosecution because they are too complex, too indistinguishable from other causes, not knowable, or not provable in a court of law.

Resulting Harm

The need for some identifiable **harm** as an actual or potential consequence of culpable activity is often cited as a general feature of crime. If an action held no potential to cause harm, it would make little sense to pass a law prohibiting it. Personal crimes, such as murder

legal cause
A legally recognizable cause; the type of cause that is required to be demonstrated in court in order to hold an individual criminally liable for causing harm.

harm
Loss, disadvantage, injury, or anything so regarded by the person affected, including loss, disadvantage, or injury to any other person in whose welfare he or she is interested. Also called *resulting harm*.

and rape, cause specific harm to nameable individuals, whereas other offenses, such as attempts, may have harm as their goal but fail to achieve it. Still other crimes, such as those against the environment, cause a more general and diffuse kind of harm, the impact of which might be fully felt only in later generations. Pennsylvania has adopted, verbatim, the Model Penal Code's causation provision, as follows:[14]

PENNSYLVANIA CONSOLIDATED STATUTES

Title 18, Section 303. Causal relationship between conduct and result.

(a) General rule.—Conduct is the cause of a result when:

(1) it is an antecedent but for which the result in question would not have occurred; and

(2) the relationship between the conduct and result satisfies any additional causal requirements imposed by this title or by the law defining the offense. . . .

The first definition is known as the *sine qua non* or "but for" test that you learned about earlier in this chapter. This test is favored by the prosecutor because little connection between a defendant's action and the outcome need be proved. The second provision in the Pennsylvania causation law (and the Model Penal Code's) requires a stronger, proximate connection. This applies when statutes otherwise require it. So, the but for test is the default that is applied when proximate cause is not specifically required.

A special offense category, however, sometimes called *social-order offenses* or *victimless crimes*, denotes a type of criminal law violation in which parties to the crime willfully (even joyfully) participate and in which the element of harm seems remote. Victimless crimes, which will be discussed in detail in Chapter 12, include offenses such as prostitution, gambling, "crimes against nature" (sexual deviance), and illegal drug use. People involved in such crimes argue that, if anyone is being hurt, it is only themselves. What these offenders fail to recognize, say legal theorists, is the social harm caused by their conduct. Areas afflicted with chronic prostitution, drug use, sexual deviance, and illegal gambling usually also experience property values falling, family life disintegrating, and other, more traditional crimes increasing as money is sought to support the "victimless" activities. As a result, law-abiding citizens flee the area. As Joel Feinberg, a well-known contemporary analyst of the law, says, "It is legitimate for the state to prohibit conduct that causes . . . harm to important public institutions and practices."[15] Feinberg's dictum agrees with our conclusion, reached in Chapter 1, that crimes can be distinguished from other law violations by the fact that they are essentially offenses against the community or the public.

All laws are an attempt to domesticate the natural ferocity of the species. . . . We can't stop a banker from stealing a widow's money, but we can make it harder for him to steal.

—*John W. Gardner, American writer and former U.S. Secretary of Health, Education, and Welfare*

An important point to remember, however, is that, from a legal perspective, "the question is not whether in some sense, ethical or sociological, the defendant has committed a harm. Rather, the question is whether the defendant's conduct has caused the harm, which the law in question sought to prevent."[16] In a criminal prosecution, it is rarely necessary to prove harm as a separate element of a crime because it is subsumed under the notion of a guilty act. In the crime of murder, for example, the "killing of a human being" brings about a harm but is, properly speaking, an act that, when done with the requisite *mens rea*, becomes a crime. A similar type of reasoning applies to the criminalization of attempts. Some writers have used the example of throwing rocks at blind people to illustrate that behavior need not actually produce harm for it to be criminal. One could imagine a scenario in which vandals decide to throw rocks at visually impaired individuals, but because of bad aim, the rocks never hit anyone and the intended targets remain blissfully unaware that anyone is trying to harm them. In such a case, shouldn't throwing rocks provide a basis for criminal liability? As one authority on the subject observes, "Criticism of the principle of harm has . . . been based on the view that the harm actually caused may be a matter of sheer accident and that the rational thing to do is to base the punishment on the *mens rea*, and the action, disregarding any actual harm or lack of harm or its degree."[17] Similarly, the prominent contemporary legal scholar George P. Fletcher says, "The emphasis on intention as the core of crime [highlights] the offender's attitude as the essence of criminality."[18] This is why we have said that the essence of criminality consists only of three things: (1) an *actus reus*, (2) a *mens rea*, and (3) the concurrence of an illegal act and a culpable mental state.

Although the need for an identifiable harm is sometimes specified by law as an element of an offense, at other times the degree of harm increases the seriousness of an offense. Indiana law, for example, allows greater punishment for the crime of product tampering when harm results. The law reads: "A person who: (1) recklessly, knowingly, or intentionally introduces a poison, a harmful substance, or a harmful foreign object into a consumer product; or (2) with intent to mislead a consumer of a consumer product, tampers with the labeling of a consumer product that has been introduced into commerce, commits consumer product tampering, a class D felony. However, the offense is a class C felony if it results in harm to a person, and it is a class B felony if it results in serious bodily injury to another person."[19] North Dakota defines *harm* to mean loss, disadvantage, or injury to the person affected and includes loss, disadvantage, or injury to any other person in whose welfare he or she is interested.[20]

Where a particular result *is* specified by law as a necessary element of a given crime, however, a successful prosecution requires both a concurrence of *mens rea* and the act, as well as a concurrence of *mens rea* and the resulting harm. When the harm that results from criminal activity is different in *degree* from the intended harm, the concurrence requirement is still met. Hence if I shoot someone, intending only to wound the individual, but the person dies, I may still be liable for homicide. If, on the other hand, the resulting harm is of a different *kind* than that intended, the needed concurrence may be lacking. If I leave a getaway car whose engine is running parked in the garage under an apartment in the middle of the night while I break into a nearby bank, and the person sleeping in the apartment above the car dies from carbon monoxide poisoning, I would not be guilty of homicide, even though my actions may have caused the person's death.

The felony murder rule, however, is an exception to the general notion that criminal liability does not accrue when the harm that results is different in kind from the harm intended. Felony murder statutes hold a person involved in the commission of a felony responsible for homicide if another person dies during the offense, even though the death may have been unintentional. For example, if two armed robbers enter a bank and one is shot by security guards, the surviving robber may be guilty of homicide even though he never fired his weapon or pointed it at anyone. Some jurisdictions have even prosecuted surviving drug users under felony murder statutes when a friend's death resulted from an overdose brought on by the sharing of drugs. The felony murder rule is discussed more thoroughly in Chapter 8.

The Principle of Legality

The **principle of legality** reflects the fact that behavior cannot be criminal if no law exists that both defines it as illegal and prescribes a punishment for it. The principle of legality is ancient, having developed at the common law. It is all right to drink beer in most places today, if you are of "drinking age," because there is no statute on the books prohibiting it.[21] During Prohibition, of course, the situation was quite different.

principle of legality
An axiom that holds that behavior cannot be criminal if no law exists that defines it as such. Today, the principle of legality is commonly analyzed as a due-process principle.

The need for a specified punishment is also part of the principle of legality. Larceny, for example, would not be a crime if the law simply said, "It is illegal to steal." Punishment must be specified by law so that if a person is found guilty of violating the law, sanctions can be lawfully imposed. Two legal dicta capture the role of state-sanctioned punishment in the principle of legality. The first is *nullen crimen, nulla poena, sine lege*, which means "there is no crime, there is no punishment, without law." The second is *nullum crimen sine poena*, which means "no crime without punishment."

As you will see, the principle of legality has been subsumed into the general protections provided by the due-process clauses of the Fifth and Fourteenth Amendments, which require a fair process (and "substance," or outcome) before a government may take life, liberty, or property from a person. Today, the limitations on government authority that were imposed by the principle of legality represent only a portion of the rights protected by the due-process clauses. There are other constitutional provisions, such as the prohibition against *ex post facto* laws and bills of attainder, that are specific due-process mandates (Table 3–1).

ex post facto
Formulated, enacted, or operating retrospectively. Literally, "after the fact." As prohibited by the Constitution, no punitive law may be applied to acts committed before the law was enacted and effective.

Game is game, and he who finds may kill. That has been the law in these mountains for forty years, to my certain knowledge; and I think one old law is worth two new ones.

—*James Fenimore Cooper, The Pioneers (1823)*

Ex Post Facto Laws   The ancient principle of legality included the notion that a law cannot be created tomorrow that will hold a person legally responsible for something that he or she does today. These are called **ex post facto** laws. *Ex post facto* is a Latin term that means "after the deed." An *ex post facto* law is one that (1) makes an action done before the passing of the law (and that was legal when done) criminal and punishes such action; (2) aggravates a crime, or makes it more serious than it was when committed; (3) inflicts a greater punishment than existent law did at the time the crime was committed; or (4) alters the legal rules of evidence and requires less, or different, testimony than the law required at the time of the offense in order to convict the offender.[22] The Framers incorporated the prohibition of *ex post facto* laws in the U.S. Constitution,[23] which says that laws are binding only from the date of their creation or from some future date at which they are specified as taking effect.[24]

The constitutional provision against *ex post facto* laws applies only to criminal or penal statutes,[25] although both criminal and civil penalties may be regarded as punitive, depending largely on the intent of the legislative body that created them. In 2003, for example, in the case of *Smith* v. *Doe*,[26] which appears in this chapter as a Capstone Case, the U.S. Supreme Court was asked to consider the legality of the retroactive nature of the Alaska Sex Offender Registration Act.[27]

Similarly, in 2008, a federal appellate court held that Congress's decision to add a crime to a list of deportable offenses could be used to deport an alien, even though he committed the offense before Congress added the crime to the list.[28] In 2007, the decision to revoke

The principle of legality holds that behavior cannot be criminal if no law exists that both defines it as illegal and prescribes a punishment for it. What about common law offenses that have not been codified into written statutes? Are they still punishable as crimes?

Shutterstock

TABLE 3–1   Chapter 3 Overview

Before an Act Is Criminal	The Act	After the Act: Conviction	After the Act: Punishment
Principle of legality (due process): Government must clearly define the act as criminal and set forth its punishment.	Government may not coerce or excessively encourage the act (entrapment).	Burden: Government must prove every element beyond a reasonable doubt.	*Ex post facto*: No law may increase criminal liability of punishment after the act.
Constitutional limitations: Some actions/inactions may not be criminalized.	Government's ability to prevent and monitor conduct is limited by the Constitution and by statutes.	*Corpus delicti* must be proven.	Double jeopardy: Individuals may not be tried twice or have punishment increased after first adjudication.
		Guilt must be determined by courts. Bills of attainder by legislatures are prohibited.	Other constitutional limitations exist, such as the Eighth Amendment's prohibition of cruel and unusual punishments.

the probation of a federal convictee for refusing to submit to DNA collection was upheld, even though the law requiring him to submit a DNA sample was enacted after his conviction. Again, the appellate court found the DNA collection scheme to be nonpunitive in nature.[29] The nonpunitive analysis was also used in the Supreme Court's 1997 decision in *Kansas* v. *Hendricks*,[30] wherein the Court held that a law that permitted the *civil* commitment of those who had committed or had been charged with a sexually violent offense before enactment of the law was not an *ex post facto* law.

Finally, in 2003, the U.S. Supreme Court held that a law enacted after expiration of a previously applicable limitations period violates the *ex post facto* clause when it is applied to revive a previously time-barred prosecution. The case, *Stogner* v. *California*,[31] concerned a state law intended to enact a new criminal statute of limitations permitting prosecution for sex-related child abuse where the prior limitations period had expired if prosecution began within one year of the victim's report to the police.

Of course, a jurisdiction can change its laws in such a way as to reduce the criminality of specified conduct. Doing so would not be a violation of the legality principle. Finally, we should note that the constitutional provision that no state shall pass an *ex post facto* law refers to a legislative enactment and not to a judicial decision.[32] The New Hampshire Supreme Court case of *State* v. *Reynolds*[33] provides an example of a punitive *ex post facto* law.

Bills of Attainder   The Constitution also prohibits bills of attainder.[34] A **bill of attainder** is a legislative act punishing a person or a select group of people without the benefit of judicial trial. The Framers were wary of bills of attainder because of their use by the British monarchy to silence dissent. In cases of Parliament's conviction, offenders were put to death and their families lived with corruption of blood (loss of rights of inheritance and to hold hereditary titles). The bill of attainder clause is a specific application of the separation of powers, which reserves the authority to try cases and to proclaim punishments to the judiciary. The clause also serves to protect due process. Although infrequent, the Supreme Court has invalidated several laws as bills of attainder. The 1946 case *United States* v. *Lovett*[35] provides an example of a noncriminal bill of attainder. In *Lovett* Congress enacted legislation specifically declaring three individuals as subversive and prohibiting their employment by the federal government. The Court found Congress's act to be a bill of attainder because it targeted specific individuals and punished them without judicial trial. Today, and possibly in 1946, the law would likely also be invalidated on First Amendment

bill of attainder
A legislative pronouncement that an individual is guilty of a crime. Bills of attainder are prohibited to the federal and state governments by the U.S. Constitution.

APPLYING THE CONCEPT

CAPSTONE CASE

Does a Retroactive Sex Offender Registration Law Violate the Prohibition of *Ex Post Facto* Laws?

Smith v. *Doe*, 538 U.S. 84 (2003)

The Alaska Sex Offender Registration Act requires convicted sex offenders to register with law enforcement authorities, and much of the information is made public. We must decide whether the registration requirement is a retroactive punishment prohibited by the *Ex Post Facto* Clause.

The State of Alaska enacted the Alaska Sex Offender Registration Act (Act) on May 12, 1994. . . . Like its counterparts in other States, the Act is termed a "Megan's Law." Megan Kanka was a 7-year-old New Jersey girl who was sexually assaulted and murdered in 1994 by a neighbor who, unknown to the victim's family, had prior convictions for sex offenses against children. The crime gave impetus to laws for mandatory registration of sex offenders and corresponding community notification. In 1994, Congress passed the Jacob Wetterling Crimes Against Children and Sexually Violent Offender Registration Act . . . which conditions certain federal law enforcement funding on the States' adoption of sex offender registration laws and sets minimum standards for state programs. By 1996, every State, the District of Columbia, and the Federal Government had enacted some variation of Megan's Law.

The Alaska law, which is our concern in this case, contains two components: a registration requirement and a notification system. Both are retroactive. . . . The Act requires any "sex offender or child kidnapper who is physically present in the state" to register, either with the Department of Corrections (if the individual is incarcerated) or with the local law enforcement authorities (if the individual is at liberty). . . . Prompt registration is mandated. If still in prison, a covered sex offender must register within 30 days before release; otherwise he must do so within a working day of his conviction or of entering the State. . . . The sex offender must provide his name, aliases, identifying features, address, place of employment, date of birth, conviction information, driver's license number, information about vehicles to which he has access, and postconviction treatment history. . . . He must permit the authorities to photograph and fingerprint him. . . .

If the offender was convicted of a single, nonaggravated sex crime, he must provide annual verification of the submitted information for 15 years. . . . If he was convicted of an aggravated sex offense or of two or more sex offenses, he must register for life and verify the information quarterly. . . . The offender must notify his local police department if he moves. . . . A sex offender who knowingly fails to comply with the Act is subject to criminal prosecution. . . .

THE CASE Respondents John Doe I and John Doe II were convicted of sexual abuse of a minor, an aggravated sex offense. John Doe I pleaded *nolo contendere* after a court determination that he had sexually abused his daughter for two years, when she was between the ages of 9 and 11; John Doe II entered a *nolo contendere* plea to sexual abuse of a 14-year-old child. Both were released from prison in 1990 and completed rehabilitative programs for sex offenders. Although convicted before the passage of the Act, respondents are covered by it. After the initial registration, they are required to submit quarterly verifications and notify the authorities of any changes. Both respondents, along with respondent Jane Doe, wife of John Doe I, brought an action under Rev. Stat. §1979, 42 U.S.C. § 1983 seeking to declare the Act void as to them under the *Ex Post Facto* Clause of Article I, §10, cl. 1, of the Constitution and the Due Process Clause of §1 of the Fourteenth Amendment. . . .

The framework for our inquiry, however, is well established. We must "ascertain whether the legislature meant the statute to establish 'civil' proceedings." *Kansas* v. *Hendricks*, 521 U.S. 346, 361 (1997). If the intention of the legislature was to impose punishment, that ends the inquiry. If, however, the intention was to enact a regulatory scheme that is civil and nonpunitive, we must further examine whether the statutory scheme is " 'so punitive either in purpose or effect as to negate [the State's] intention' to deem it 'civil.' " . . .

Whether a statutory scheme is civil or criminal "is first of all a question of statutory construction." *Hendricks* . . . .

The courts "must first ask whether the legislature, in establishing the penalizing mechanism, indicated either expressly or impliedly a preference for one label or the other." . . . Here, the Alaska Legislature expressed the objective of the law in the statutory text itself. The legislature found that "sex offenders pose a high risk of reoffending," and identified "protecting the public from sex offenders" as the "primary governmental interest" of the law. . . .

As we observed in *Hendricks*, where we examined an *ex post facto* challenge to a post-incarceration confinement of sex offenders, an imposition of restrictive measures on sex offenders adjudged to be dangerous is "a legitimate nonpunitive governmental objective and has been historically so regarded." In this case, as in *Hendricks*, "[n]othing on the face of the statute suggests that the legislature sought to create anything other than a civil . . . scheme designed to protect the public from harm." . . .

Other formal attributes of a legislative enactment, such as the manner of its codification or the enforcement procedures it establishes, are probative of the legislature's intent. In this case these factors are open to debate. The notification provisions of the Act are codified in the State's "Health, Safety, and Housing Code," confirming our conclusion that the statute was intended as a nonpunitive regulatory measure. The Act's registration provisions, however, are codified in the State's criminal procedure code, and so might seem to point in the opposite direction. These factors, though, are not dispositive. The location and labels of a statutory provision do not by themselves transform a civil remedy into a criminal one. . . .

Title 12 of Alaska's Code of Criminal Procedure (where the Act's registration provisions are located) contains many provisions that do not involve criminal punishment, such as civil procedures for disposing of recovered and seized property, laws protecting the confidentiality of victims and witnesses, laws governing the security and accuracy of criminal justice information, laws governing civil postconviction actions, and laws governing actions for writs of habeas corpus, which under Alaska law are "independent civil proceeding[s]," . . . Although some of these provisions relate to criminal administration, they are not in themselves punitive.

Our conclusion is strengthened by the fact that, aside from the duty to register, the statute itself mandates no procedures. . . . The Act itself does not require the procedures adopted to contain any safeguards associated with the criminal process. That leads us to infer that the legislature envisioned the Act's implementation to be civil and administrative.

[The Court continued its analysis by examining whether the law had the effect, even if not intended, of punishing sex offenders.]

Although the public availability of the information may have a lasting and painful impact on the convicted sex offender, these consequences flow not from the Act's registration and dissemination provisions, but from the fact of conviction, already a matter of public record. The State makes the facts underlying the offenses and the resulting convictions accessible so members of the public can take the precautions they deem necessary before dealing with the registrant. . . .

The State concedes that the statute might deter future crimes. Respondents seize on this proposition to argue that the law is punitive, because deterrence is one purpose of punishment. This proves too much. Any number of governmental programs might deter crime without imposing punishment. . . .

The Act is nonpunitive, and its retroactive application does not violate the *Ex Post Facto* Clause.

What Do *You* Think?

1. Do you agree with the court—that is, do you think the law in question is not punitive and therefore not an *ex post facto* law? Why or why not?

2. Should restrictions on *ex post facto* laws apply to administrative procedures, such as parole hearings, or should they only apply to laws that define crimes themselves? Why?

Additional Applications

Can courts retroactively apply a common law rule that defines a crime?

Rogers v. Tennessee, 532 U.S. 451 (2001)

The Case: During an altercation on May 6, 1994, Wilbert K. Rogers stabbed James Bowdery in the chest with a butcher knife, necessitating an emergency surgical procedure to repair Bowdery's heart. The stabbing victim survived the heart surgery; as a direct result of these events, though, Bowdery developed a condition known as cerebral hypoxia—which results from a loss of oxygen to the brain—and fell into a coma where he remained until his death 15 months later from a related kidney infection. Following Bowdery's death, Rogers was convicted by a Shelby County, Tennessee, trial court on second-degree murder charges. Rogers contested the charges on appeal, arguing that Tennessee's courts had long recognized a

(continued)

judicially created common law "year-and-a-day rule," which provided that no defendant could be convicted of murder unless the victim had died by the defendant's act within 366 days of that act. On appeal, the Supreme Court of Tennessee agreed that the claimed common law rule had been in place at the time of the defendant's trial. After reviewing the justifications for the common law rule, however, the state supreme court determined that the original reasons for judicial recognition of the rule no longer existed. Accordingly, the state court abolished the common law rule and held that Rogers had been validly convicted of Bowdery's death. Requesting U.S. Supreme Court review, Rogers's lawyers argued that the state supreme court's retroactive application of a new common law rule violated the U.S. Constitution's *ex post facto* and due-process clauses.

The Finding: In a closely divided ruling, the U.S. Supreme Court affirmed the state supreme court's change in common law rules. Noting that "limitations on *ex post facto* judicial decisionmaking are inherent in the notion of due process," Justice Sandra Day O'Connor nonetheless observed that "important institutional and contextual differences" exist between criminal laws passed by legislatures and common law rules developed by courts. The common law, O'Connor stressed, "presupposes a measure of evolution that is incompatible with stringent application of *ex post facto* principles." Consequently, a judicially crafted change in a common law doctrine of criminal law is consistent with due process—even as applied in the same case in which the change is announced—unless it is "unexpected and indefensible by reference to the law which had been expressed prior to the conduct at issue." In this context, O'Connor reasoned, Rogers should have reasonably anticipated that the courts would rule Tennessee's one-year-and-a-day rule to be "an outdated relic" inappropriate for adherence in modern times.

In a spirited dissent, Justice Antonin Scalia (joined by three other members of the Court) voiced strong disagreement with the majority's conclusion that Rogers had "fair warning" that the common law rule in Tennessee was subject to retroactive rescission in his case. More fundamentally, Scalia attacked O'Connor's weighing of the relative fairness concerns in drawing a basic distinction between legislative and judicial changes in applicable criminal law principles. "Today's opinion," Scalia wrote, "produces . . . a curious constitution that only a judge could love. One in which [by virtue of the *ex post facto clause*] the elected representatives of all the people cannot retroactively make murder what was not murder when the act was committed; but in which unelected judges can do precisely that. One in which the predictability of parliamentary lawmaking cannot validate the retroactive creation of crimes, but the predictability of judicial lawmaking can do so."

Can a state retroactively change a law rewarding existing prisoners for good behavior?

Weaver v. *Graham*, 450 U.S. 24 (1981)

The Case: In 1976, a Florida man was convicted in state court of second-degree murder and sentenced to 15 years in prison. At the time, Florida law—like similar laws in many other states—provided an administrative mechanism and mathematical formula by which prisoners could earn specified "gain-time" credits for good behavior; in light of that statutory formula, the incarcerated petitioner began to accumulate credits toward a reduced overall sentence. Two years into his prison term, however, Florida's legislature then repealed its earlier "gain-time" framework and replaced it with a more restrictive formula that, as applied to the petitioner, effectively extended his prison sentence by over two years. On review, the Supreme Court of Florida upheld the application of the new rules to the prisoner on the ground that gain-time crediting was an act of legislative grace rather than a vested right; accordingly, the state could withdraw or modify such credits even retroactively without violating the prisoner's constitutional rights. The petitioner then sought review by the U.S. Supreme Court on the ground that the state's revision of his terms of incarceration had violated the U.S. Constitution's *ex post facto* clause.

The Finding: Writing for the Court, Justice Thurgood Marshall reversed the state court's ruling and held that Florida's new statutory crediting system violated the *ex post facto* clause as applied to inmates already sentenced under the state's previous legislative formula. The *ex post facto clause*, Marshall wrote, precludes a state from imposing a punishment more severe than that assigned by law when the criminal offense occurred—regardless of whether a "vested right" has been impaired by the state's statutory change. Thus, "even if a statute merely alters penal provisions accorded by the grace of the legislature, it violates the Clause if it is both retrospective and more onerous than the law in effect on the date of the offense." The critical question, the Court held, is "whether the law changes the legal consequences of acts completed before its effective date."

free speech and association and Fifth Amendment due-process grounds. The last occasion where the Court voided a law because it was a considered a bill of attainder was in 1965.[36] This case represents the principle that a legislative enactment can be aimed at an entire group and still be a bill of attainder. This case involved a bill that prohibited members of the Communist Party from serving on a labor union's executive board. Congress feared that members of the Communist Party would promote violence or political strikes. The Court found that Congress may prohibit labor leadership from committing certain acts but that such laws had to apply to all persons generally. The law under review targeted specific individuals (communists) and punished them by prohibiting them from holding leadership positions. Similar to the law in *Lovett*, such a law would also be found to violate free speech, free association, *ex post facto*, and due-process protections if heard today.

Double Jeopardy

Similar to the *ex post facto* principle, the Fifth Amendment to the U.S. Constitution states that "no . . . person be subject for the same offense to be twice put in jeopardy of life or limb." Through this **double jeopardy** provision, individuals may not (1) be tried a second time for the same offense or (2) be punished a second time for the same offense. Generally, jeopardy attaches when the first witness is sworn in during jury trials, a guilty plea has been accepted by the trial court, or the first witness is sworn in during bench trials (without a jury). If jeopardy has not attached, then a defendant may be tried. For example, if a judge dismisses a charge early in a case before trial has been scheduled, the defendant may be charged again. There are also a few exceptions to the prohibition of retrying an accused individual after jeopardy has attached, such as when a properly declared mistrial has occurred. Sentences may also be corrected on appeal, even if they increase the sentence. However, a legislative decision to increase the punishment of a crime after it has been committed cannot be applied retroactively. To do so would violate the double jeopardy, *ex post facto*, and due-process clauses.

double jeopardy
A second prosecution or a second punishment for the same offense. Double jeopardy is prohibited by the Fifth Amendment to the U.S. Constitution.

Void-for-Vagueness Principle

Another aspect of due process is the constitutional void-for-vagueness principle. The U.S. Supreme Court gave voice to the **void-for-vagueness principle** in an early ruling in which it held that "a statute which either forbids or requires the doing of an act in terms so vague that men of common intelligence must necessarily guess at its meaning and differ as to its application, violates the first essential of due process of law." Statutes are void when vague because their enforcement would require after-the-fact judicial interpretations of what the law means—an activity akin to *ex post facto* rule creation.

void-for-vagueness principle
A constitutional principle that refers to a statute defining a crime that is so unclear that a reasonable person of at least average intelligence could not determine what the law purports to command or prohibit.

In 1999, in *Chicago* v. *Morales*,[37] for example, the U.S. Supreme Court held that a city ordinance that prohibited criminal street gang members from loitering in public places was unconstitutionally vague and an arbitrary restriction on personal liberties. The Court found that "because the ordinance fails to give the ordinary citizen adequate notice of what is forbidden and what is permitted, it is impermissibly vague."[38] The term *loiter*, said the Court, "may have a common and accepted meaning, but the ordinance's definition of that term— 'to remain in any one place with no apparent purpose'—does not." The Court reasoned that "[i]t is difficult to imagine how any Chicagoan standing in a public place with a group of people would know if he or she had an 'apparent purpose.'" The ordinance, under which 42,000 people had been arrested,[39] was also found to lack sufficient minimal standards to guide law enforcement officers because it failed to provide any gauge by which police officers could judge whether an individual "has an 'apparent purpose.'" The Court concluded that "this vagueness about what loitering is covered and what is not, dooms the ordinance."

Shortly after the *Morales* decision, the Chicago City Council passed an antigang ordinance intended to meet Supreme Court objections.[40] The city's new ordinance permits police officers to arrest suspected gang members or drug dealers if they disregard an order to leave a corner or block that the police have identified as a gang "hot spot." The ordinance

CRIMINAL LAW IN THE NEWS

Was Honeymooner Tried Twice for the Death of His Wife?

American Gabe Watson was convicted in Australia of manslaughter for the death of his new wife, while scuba diving there. Then, due to suspicions he had actually murdered her, Watson was tried again for the same offense in his home state of Alabama. U.S. courts usually prohibit trying someone over again, as noted in the discussion of double jeopardy. But, as this case proves, there are exceptions.

On their honeymoon in 2003, Alabamans Gabe and Tina Watson went scuba diving on the Great Barrier Reef in Australia, and Tina drowned. Her death was initially thought to be of natural causes, but her parents suspected Watson murdered her, and for the next four years they pushed for an investigation.

Finally in 2008, an Australian coroner held an inquest and determined murder may have occurred, based partly on Tina's father's testimony that Watson wanted to cash in on Tina's life insurance policy. Watson's lawyers, however, stated the policy would have paid less than $35,000—hardly a motive for murder—and Tina's father was still listed as the beneficiary.

Australian prosecutors decided not to charge Watson with murder. But noting his failure to rescue Tina, they did charge him with manslaughter. He pleaded guilty and was given 12 months in prison. When prosecutors pushed for a longer sentence, an Australian appeals panel upped it to 18 months. But Tina's parents were unhappy with the light verdict and helped convince prosecutors in Alabama to seek murder charges against Watson.

To answer concerns about double jeopardy, Alabama Attorney General Troy King identified a U.S. Supreme Court decision, *United States* v. *Lanza*, that allowed courts in different U.S. states to try a person for the same crime. This was reportedly done in the case of Timothy McVeigh, the Oklahoma City bomber, who was found guilty and executed in 2001.

To justify a trial in Alabama for a murder in Australia, the indictment alleged Watson had planned his crime before the couple left for their honeymoon. Prosecutors cited testimony from Tina's father that Watson had asked about her life insurance policy. They also alleged that by planning their honeymoon trip to Australia, Watson had plotted to kidnap Tina.

The Australian coroner agreed to share evidence with Alabama authorities, but Australian authorities still hesitated about turning over Watson himself. Australia had signed an international pact never to allow executions, and Alabama endorses capital punishment. King pledged

Gabe Watson (left), tried and convicted in Australia for the death of his wife while the couple was on their honeymoon, talks to his attorney. Watson was deported to Alabama following his Australian conviction, where prosecutors sought to try him on murder charges. How would the concept of double jeopardy apply to his case?

Reuters/Marvin Gentry

Watson would not be executed in Alabama, but Cameron Dick, his Australian counterpart, still hesitated, according to a memo obtained by *The Australian*. "It appears that no matter how Alabama works to comply with your requests, you continue to find new demands," King wrote to Dick.

Even when Watson had completed his Australian prison term and was about to be deported to Alabama in November 2010, Australian authorities were still struggling to comply with international law. *The Australian* reported that Watson had to sign a statement saying, "I am aware that these charges may result in my execution if I am convicted."

Watson was eventually deported, but his Alabama trial in February 2012 quickly fell apart. Prosecutors dropped the kidnapping charge and removed the Australian coroner's testimony, deeming it hearsay. Circuit Judge Tommy Nail allowed for to trial to proceed even in the face of double jeopardy claims, but then released Watson due to lack of evidence. "The only way to convict him of intentional murder is to speculate," Nail said. "Nobody knows exactly what happened in the water. I'm sure we'll never know."

Resources

Eric Velasco, "Gabe Watson's Prosecution in Wife's Australian Honeymoon Death Ends with Judge's Dismissal," *Birmingham (Ala.) News*, February 23, 2012, **http://blog.al.com/spotnews/2012/02/birmingham_judge_finds_gabe_wa.html**.

Hedley Thomas, "Gabe Watson Told: Sign 'Death Warrant'," *The Australian*, November 11, 2010, **http://www.theaustralian.com.au/national-affairs/exclusive-watson-told-sign-death-warrant/story-fn59niix-1225951440987**.

Brad Norington, "Double Jeopardy Argument Dismissed by Court as Gabe Watson Faces Court in Alabama over Wife's Scuba Death," *The Australian*, April 29, 2011, **http://www.theaustralian.com.au/news/double-jeopardy-argument-dismissed-by-court-as-gabe-watson-faces-court-in-alabama-over-wifes-scuba-death/story-e6frg6n6-1226046664168**.

also requires police officers to have a "reasonable belief that gang or drug activity is taking place." The law only permits the jailing of suspects until they can be fingerprinted, and it does not allow them to be held longer unless they are found to be in possession of guns or drugs.

Necessary Attendant Circumstances

Finally, statutes defining crimes may specify that additional elements, called **attendant circumstances**, be present for a conviction to be obtained. Attendant circumstances refer to the "facts surrounding an event"[41] and include such things as time and place (Figure 3–4). Attendant circumstances specified by law as necessary elements of an offense are sometimes referred to as *necessary attendant circumstances* to indicate the fact that the existence of such circumstances is required in order for all of the elements of the crime to be met.

attendant circumstances
The facts surrounding an event.

Florida law, for example, makes it a crime to "[k]nowingly commit any lewd or lascivious act in the presence of any child under the age of sixteen years."[42] In this case, the behavior in question might not be a crime if committed in the presence of someone older than 16. Also, curfew violations are being increasingly criminalized by states, shifting liability for a minor's behavior to his or her parents. To violate a curfew, it is necessary that a juvenile be in a public place between specified times (such as 11 p.m. or midnight and 5 or 6 a.m.). In those states that hold parents liable for the behavior of their children, parents can be jailed or fined if such violations occur.

Sometimes attendant circumstances increase the **degree**, or level of seriousness, of an offense. Under Texas law, for example, the crime of burglary has two degrees, defined by state law as follows: Burglary is a "(1) state jail felony if committed in a building other than a habitation; or (2) felony of the second degree if committed in a habitation." In other words, the degree of the offense of burglary changes depending on the nature of the place burglarized.

degree
The level of seriousness of an offense.

Similarly, Florida law specifies a number of degrees of "sexual battery," depending on the amount of force used to commit the crime, the age of the victim, and whether more

FIGURE 3–4

Attendant Circumstances.

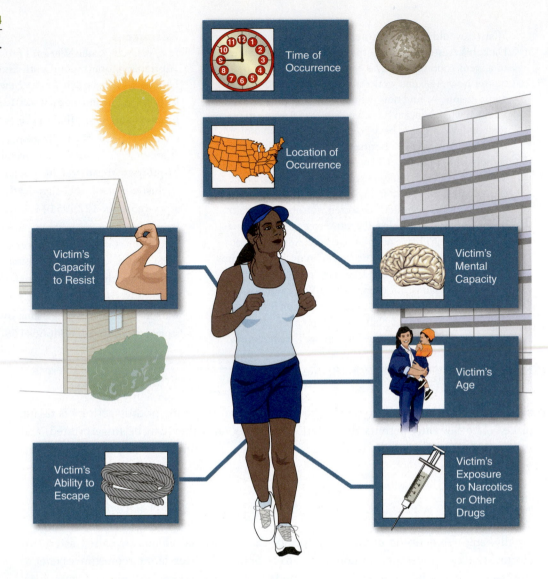

than one perpetrator was involved in the commission of the offense.[43] The relevant statute reads: "The penalty . . . shall be increased as provided in this subsection if it is charged and proven by the prosecution that, during the same criminal transaction or episode, more than one person committed an act of sexual battery on the same victim." Florida law also increases the degree of sexual battery (and associated penalties) "[w]hen the victim is physically helpless to resist . . .; [w]hen the offender, without the prior knowledge or consent of the victim, administers or has knowledge of someone else administering to the victim any narcotic, anesthetic, or other intoxicating substance, which mentally or physically incapacitates the victim . . .; [w]hen the victim is mentally defective and the offender has reason to believe this or has actual knowledge of this fact . . .; [w]hen the victim is physically incapacitated . . .; when the offender is a law enforcement officer, correctional officer, or correctional probation officer"; and under other circumstances.

Circumstances surrounding a crime can also be classified as aggravating or mitigating and may, by law, be used to lessen or increase the penalty that can be imposed on a convicted offender. Aggravating and mitigating circumstances are not elements of an offense, though, because they are primarily relevant at the sentencing stage of a criminal prosecution. They are therefore discussed in Chapter 14.

SUMMARY

- The term *corpus delicti* literally means "body of crime." To prove the *corpus delicti* of a crime is to show that a crime has in fact occurred. Doing so requires the state to demonstrate that a criminal law has been violated and that someone violated it. The *corpus delicti* rule holds that a criminal conviction cannot be based solely on the uncorroborated confession or admission of an accused—that is, a confession, uncorroborated by other facts, is insufficient to show the *corpus delicti* of a crime and cannot support a conviction.

- In addition to the three fundamental elements of crime (*actus reus*, *mens rea*, and concurrence) discussed in the last chapter, four additional principles are necessary to fully appreciate contemporary understandings of crime: (1) causation, (2) a resulting harm, (3) the principle of legality, and (4) necessary attendant circumstances.

- Causation refers to the fact that the concurrence of a guilty mind and a criminal act may produce, or *cause*, harm. Whereas some statutes criminalize only conduct, others subsume the notion of concurrence under causation and specify that a causal relationship is a necessary element of a given crime.

- If there is an actual link between the actor's conduct and the resulting harm, causation in fact is said to exist. The "but for" rule is another way of determining causation. It looks to see whether some injury would not have happened *but for* the conduct of the accused.

- A *proximate cause* is a primary or moving cause that plays a substantial part in bringing about injury or damage. It may be a first cause that sets in motion a string of events whose ultimate outcome is reasonably foreseeable. A *legal cause*, on the other hand, is simply one that is legally significant.

- The principle of legality mirrors the fact that behavior cannot be criminal if no law exists that both defines it as such and prescribes punishment for it.

- The principle of legality also includes the notion that a law cannot be created tomorrow that will hold a person legally responsible for something he or she does today. Such laws are called *ex post facto* laws, their primary feature being that they are retroactive. *Ex post facto* laws are illegal under the U.S. Constitution.

- Statutes defining some crimes specify that additional elements, called *attendant circumstances*, must be present for a conviction to be obtained. Attendant circumstances refer to the "facts surrounding an event" and include such things as time and place. Sometimes attendant circumstances increase the degree, or level of seriousness, of an offense.

KEY TERMS

attendant circumstances, 83
bill of attainder, 77
"but for" rule, 72
causation in fact, 69
corpus delicti, 66

corpus delicti rule, 66
degree, 83
double jeopardy, 81
ex post facto, 76
harm, 73

legal cause, 73
principle of legality, 75
proximate cause, 69
void-for-vagueness
  principle, 75

QUESTIONS FOR DISCUSSION

1. Explain the concept of *corpus delicti*. How does the *corpus delicti* of a crime differ from the elements of a crime?

2. Sometimes people mistakenly say that the body of a murder victim provides the *corpus delicti* of the crime of murder. What actually constitutes the *corpus delicti* of murder?

3. What is the difference between causation in fact and proximate cause?

4. What is meant by *"but for"* causation? What does *legal cause* mean? Give an example of each.

5. What is felony murder? How does it differ from other forms of murder?

6. What is an *ex post facto* law? Why is the creation of *ex post facto* laws regarded as impermissible in our legal system?

7. What are necessary attendant circumstances? How might they play a role in a criminal conviction?

CRITICAL THINKING AND APPLICATION PROBLEMS

The value of metals has been on the rise. Consequently, theft of metals, particularly copper and brass, has increased significantly. Thieves, who steal metals from homes, businesses, and automobiles, commonly sell their contraband to scrap metal dealers. Concerned about the growing metal theft business, the state legislature, with the governor's endorsement, enacts the following:

Section 1: Receiving Stolen Metals: Any person (or persons) who owns, operates, or is employed by a metal recycling business shall (1) make an inquiry into the source of all metals received, (2) photograph prospective sellers and the metals they offer for sale, (3) demand a copy of a photograph identification from the prospective seller, and (4) check the state stolen metals report to determine if the specific metals sold are registered as stolen and to determine if the prospective seller is a registered metals thief. If the metals appear on the report or the seller appears as a registered metals thief, the owner, operator, or employee shall not purchase the metals and shall report the offer of sale, and provide the photographs and other information collected under this section, to the appropriate local law enforcement agency within one hour. Violation of this section is a misdemeanor of the first degree. This section shall apply retroactively, to one year prior to its enactment.

Section 2: Registration as Metal Thief: To reduce theft and to prevent the sale of stolen metals, a state registry of metal thieves and stolen metals shall be established. Any person who is convicted in the State of stealing or receiving stolen metals or who is convicted of violating the Receiving Stolen Metals section above shall register with the Secretary of State. The Secretary of State shall establish and maintain a report of metal thieves, as well as a report of missing metals, which shall be made available to the public generally. A registered metal thief shall remain listed on the report for ten years following conviction.

1. What is the *corpus delicti* of section 1, Receiving Stolen Metals?

2. Is section 1 *ex post facto*? Explain your answer.

3. Is section 2 *ex post facto*? Explain your answer.

LEGAL RESOURCES ON THE WEB

A number of criminal law–related blogs are accessible through the Internet. The following are among the best:

Connecticut Law Blog
http://aconnecticutlawblog.com

A very comprehensive legal news site that covers criminal law, sentencing law, civil law news, and court decisions.

Cornell University Law School's Legal Information Institute Blog
http://blog.law.cornell.edu

An announcements blog that follows events at the U.S. Supreme Court.

Crime and Federalism Blog
http://federalism.typepad.com

A recent law school graduate and an experienced criminal defense and civil rights lawyer discuss recent news and court opinions, emphasizing federal crimes, federalism, and Section 1983 actions.

CrimLaw Blog
http://crimlaw.blogspot.com

A blog devoted to criminal law issues from a Virginia attorney.

Electronic Discovery and Evidence Blog
http://arkfeld.blogs.com

A blog that covers cases and other issues relating to electronic discovery and electronic evidence.

Fourth Amendment Blog
http://www.fourthamendment.com/blog

A daily summary of search-and-seizure cases and news.

Innocence Blog
http://innocenceinstitute.blogspot.com

A blog maintained by the Innocence Institute of Point Park University. The Innocence Institute says that it "investigates claims of wrongful convictions, raises awareness of the frailties associated with the criminal justice system, acts as a resource to those working to reverse injustice, and provides educational training in investigative reporting to college students and professionals."

Public Defender Blog
http://apublicdefender.com

A blog maintained by a Connecticut public defender, with comments on the latest in forensics and investigation technology.

Second Circuit Court Blog
http://circuit2.blogspot.com

Case summaries and commentary provided by attorneys from the Federal Defenders Office in New York City.

Supreme Court of the United States (SCOTUS) Blog
http://www.scotusblog.com/movabletype

A blog that covers all aspects of the Supreme Court beat, including legal decisions and other Court-related news.

Tillers on Evidence and Inference
http://tillerstillers.blogspot.com

A law blog devoted to evidence, emphasizing probability theory and theories of evidence, inference, induction, and proof.

SUGGESTED READINGS AND CLASSIC WORKS

Abadinsky, Howard. *Law and Justice*. Chicago: Nelson-Hall, 1988.

Bazelon, David L. *Questioning Authority: Justice and Criminal Law*. New York: Knopf, 1989.

Duff, Anthony. *Philosophy and the Criminal Law: Principle and Critique*. Cambridge: Cambridge University Press, 1998.

Fletcher, George P. *Rethinking Criminal Law*. Boston: Little, Brown, 1978.

Frank, Jerome. *Law and the Modern Mind*. 1930. Reprint, Garden City, NY: Anchor, 1970.

Friedman, Lawrence M. *Crime and Punishment in American History*. New York: Basic Books, 1993.

Hall, Jerome. *General Principles of Criminal Law*, 2nd ed. Indianapolis: Bobbs-Merrill, 1960.

Hart, H. L. A., and John Gardner. *Punishment and Responsibility: Essays in the Philosophy of Law*, 2nd ed. New York: Oxford University Press USA, 2008.

Thomas, Charles W., and Donna M. Bishop. *Criminal Law: Understanding Basic Principles*. Newbury Park, CA: Sage, 1987.

NOTES

1. *State v. Williams*, South Carolina Supreme Court, Opinion No. 24403. Filed March 25, 1996. LLR 1996.SC.17.

2. *Willoughby v. State*, 552 N.E.2d 462, 466 (1990).

3. See *Maughs v. Commonwealth*, 181 Va. 117, 120, 23 S.E.2d 784, 786 (1943).

4. *State v. Williams*, South Carolina Supreme Court, Opinion No. 24403. Filed March 25, 1996. LLR 1996.SC.17; and *State v. Blocker*, 205 S.C. 303, 31 S.E.2d 908 (1944).

5. *Poulos v. Commonwealth*, 174 Va. 495, 500, 6 S.E.2d 666, 667 (1940).

6. *Zanders v. United States*, No. 91-CF-1394 & Nos. 91-CF-1465 & 94-CO-1558, District of Columbia Court of Appeals.

7. *State v. Arrington* (Mont. 1993), 1993.MT.7, posted at http://www.versuslaw.com.

8. *Willoughby v. State*, 555 N.E.2d at 466 (1990).

9. *East v. State*, 146 Tex. Crim. 396, 175 S.W.2d 603 (1942).

10. *Illinois v. Lara*, WL 2460263 (Ct. App. Texas 2007).

11. Wyoming Constitution, Article 1, Section 10.

12. Texas Penal Code, Title 5, Chapter 19, Section 1.

13. *Holmes v. Securities Investor Protection Corporation*, 503 U.S. 258 (1992).

14. Model Penal Code §2.03.

15. Joel Feinberg, *Harm to Others* (Oxford: Oxford University Press, 1984).

16. John S. Baker, Jr., and others, *Hall's Criminal Law: Cases and Materials*, 5th ed. (Charlottesville, VA: Michie, 1993), 135.

17. Ibid., 138.

18. George P. Fletcher, *Basic Concepts of Criminal Law* (New York: Oxford University Press, 1998), 178.

19. Indiana Code, Article 45, Chapter 8, Section 3.

20. North Dakota Criminal Code, Section 12.1-01-04.

21. In fact, some parts of the United States are still "dry," and the sale, purchase, or public consumption of alcohol can be a violation regardless of age.

22. *Calder v. Bull*, 3 Dall. 386 (1798); and *Mallet v. North Carolina*, 181 U.S. 590 (1901).

23. U.S. Constitution, Article I, Section 10, clause 1.

24. The same is not true for *procedures* within the criminal justice system, which can be modified even after a person has been sentenced and hence become retroactive. See, for example, the U.S. Supreme Court case of *California Department of Corrections v. Morales*, 514 U.S. 499 (1995), which approved of changes in the length of time between parole hearings, even though those changes applied to offenders already sentenced.

25. *Ogden v. Sanders*, 12 Wheat. 213 (1827); *League v. Texas*, 184 U.S. 156 (1902); *Calder v. Bull*, 3 Dall. 386 (1798); and *Locke v. New Orleans*, 4 Wall. 172 (1866).

26. *Smith v. Doe*, 583 U.S. 84 (2003).

27. Alaska Statutes, Section 12.63.100(6)(C)(i) (Michie 2002).

28. *Rodriguez* v. *Carbone*, WL 695377 (2d Cir. 2008).

29. *United States* v. *Reynard*, 473 F.3d 1008 (9th Cir. 2007).

30. *Kansas* v. *Hendricks*, 521 U.S. 346 (1997).

31. *Stogner* v. *California*, 539 U.S. 607 (2003).

32. *Ross* v. *Oregon*, 227 U.S. 150 (1913).

33. *State* v. *Reynolds*, 642 A.2d 1368 (N.H. 1993).

34. U.S. Constitution, Article I, Sections 9, 10.

35. 328 U.S. 303 (1946).

36. 381 U.S. 437 (1965).

37. *Chicago* v. *Morales*, 527 U.S. 41, 56–57 (1999).

38. See, for example, *Coates* v. *Cincinnati*, 402 U.S. 611, 614 (1971).

39. Pam Belluck, "Chicago Anti-Loitering Law Aims to Disrupt Gangs," *New York Times*, August 31, 2000, http://www.nytimes.com/library/national/083100gangs-law.html (accessed July 1, 2005).

40. Ibid.

41. Joseph R. Nolan and Jacqueline M. Nolan-Haley, *Black's Law Dictionary: Definitions of the Terms and Phrases of American and English Jurisprudence, Ancient and Modern*, 6th ed. (St. Paul: West, 1990), 127.

42. The statute also says, "A mother's breastfeeding of her baby does not under any circumstance violate this section."

43. Florida Statutes, Section 794.011.

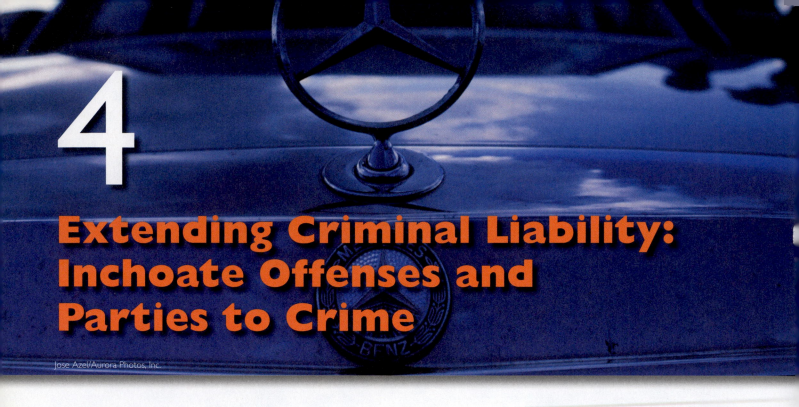

4

Extending Criminal Liability: Inchoate Offenses and Parties to Crime

Jose Azel/Aurora Photos, Inc.

CHAPTER OUTLINE

Introduction

Criminal Attempt

Criminal Conspiracy

Criminal Solicitation

Parties to Crime

OBJECTIVES

After reading this chapter, you should be able to

- Identify the elements of attempt, conspiracy, and solicitation.
- Identify and distinguish among the various tests used to determine if there has been adequate action to establish the crimes of attempt and conspiracy.
- Explain why courts won't punish a person for "evil thoughts" alone.
- Distinguish between a conspiracy and a criminal solicitation.
- Distinguish among a principal in the first degree, a principal in the second degree, and an accomplice.
- Describe the history and contemporary law of corporate criminal liability, including the punishments that are imposed on corporations.
- Describe the conditions under which a corporation may be held liable for the acts of its officers or its employees.

> *Intent to commit a crime is not itself criminal. There is no law against a man's intending to commit a murder the day after tomorrow. The law only deals with conduct.*
>
> —*Oliver Wendell Holmes*
> (The Common Law, 1881)

> *If there are still any citizens interested in protecting human liberty, let them study the conspiracy laws of the United States.*
>
> —*Clarence Darrow*
> (The Story of My Life, 1932)

90

INTRODUCTION

Melvin Lee Davis was convicted in federal court in 1982 and was sentenced to prison. A release date was set for October 2011. In late 1990, while incarcerated at the Federal Correctional Institute in Summers, Connecticut (FCIS), Melvin was an inmate trustee and worked as a law library clerk. On October 18 of that year, the warden's office at FCIS received, through interoffice mail, two official-looking documents describing changes in Davis's case. The first, a letter written on stationery from the "U.S. Department of Justice, Federal Bureau of Prisons, Community Programs Office, Boston, Massachusetts," said that Virginia Department of Corrections officials had dropped an administrative hold on Davis and indicated that Davis's release date had been changed to January 8, 1991. The second document appeared to be an official U.S. government memorandum instructing prison officials to release Davis on January 8, 1991. Authorities at FCIS became suspicious and called the offices from which the letters appeared to originate. They learned that both letters were fraudulent, and further investigation revealed Davis's fingerprints on both documents. Davis was charged with attempted escape from a federal institution, and the U.S. District Court for the District of Connecticut held that his making and passing of two false documents in an attempt to move his release date up by 20 years constituted the offense of attempted escape. The court's decision was upheld by the U.S. Court of Appeals for the Second Circuit.[1]

Inchoate crimes are incipient crimes "which generally lead to other crimes."[2] *Inchoate* means imperfect, partial, or unfinished. They are also referred to as *anticipatory offenses*. Inchoate crimes traditionally include (1) attempts, (2) solicitation, and (3) conspiracies. While language favoring punishment of inchoate misconduct can be found in fourteenth-century judicial opinions, most inchoate crimes were not recognized until the late eighteenth century. Until then, prevailing legal wisdom often held that "a miss is as good as a mile."[3]

A conceptual difficulty with inchoate crimes is that the earlier the police intervene to arrest someone for a crime, the greater the possibility that the person will be arrested for conduct that may appear suspicious but that is actually innocent. On the other hand, the longer the police abstain from intervening in what may be a planned crime, the greater the likelihood that the crime will be successfully completed and that victims will be harmed. Further, if uncompleted crimes could not be punished, police would have no incentive to stop acts of violence and other crimes before they are committed.

There are some crimes that are often thought of as complete crimes but are actually inchoate crimes in disguise.[4] Most of these crimes are discussed in other chapters. Burglary, which is discussed in Chapter 9, is one such offense. In most jurisdictions, the crime of burglary is defined as the entering of a building with the intent to commit a theft or a felony. Technically speaking, the crime of burglary is completed with an illegal entry of a building, although the crime for which the entry was made may never be completed. Other offenses that fall into this nebulous category include possession of burglary tools and stalking.

inchoate crime
An unfinished crime that generally leads to another crime. Also, a crime that consists of actions that are steps toward another offense. Also called *anticipatory offense*.

CRIMINAL ATTEMPT

Joshua Dressler, one of the country's most respected authorities on criminal law and criminal procedure, suggests that it takes six steps for a person to intentionally commit a crime.[5] First, according to Dressler, the individual conceives the idea of the crime. Second, he or she then evaluates the idea. Third, the person forms the intention to go forward. Fourth, he or she prepares to commit the crime. Fifth, the individual commences the acts necessary to complete the crime and, sixth, finishes the actions defined by law as necessary to complete the crime. Dressler notes that a person is not punished during the first three stages of the process. In the first two stages, the individual lacks a *mens rea* (intent). In addition, because people are not punished for thoughts alone, there is no crime until there is an *actus reus*. According to Dressler, it is the activity in the middle range (the fourth and fifth stages), which comes after the formation of the *mens rea* but before the attainment of the criminal goal, that is legally considered inchoate, or incomplete, conduct.[6]

Statutory definitions of the crime of attempt are generally brief and often fail to provide a complete understanding as to what constitutes an attempt.[7] New York, for example, describes the crime of attempt as follows: "A person is guilty of an attempt to commit a crime when, with the intent to commit a crime, he engages in conduct which tends to effect the commission of such crime."[8] In California, the statute on criminal attempts provides: "A person commits an attempt when, with the intent to commit a specific offense, he does any act which constitutes a substantial step toward the commission of that offense."[9] Illinois takes an approach similar to California's. According to the Illinois statute on attempts, a criminal attempt occurs when a person, with the intent to commit an offense, performs any act that constitutes a **substantial step** toward the commission of that offense.[10] Federal courts[11] and the Model Penal Code (MPC)[12] also acknowledge the substantial-step principle.

As these definitions note, attempt is a specific-intent crime. For an individual to commit the crime of attempted murder (criminal homicide), for example, the individual must specifically intend to commit murder. On the other hand, an individual may commit murder without necessarily intending to do so, as in the case of felony murder (discussed in Chapter 7). Hence in some cases there is a substantial difference in the *mens rea* required for the completed crime and the attempt. Speaking generally, then, the crime of attempt can be said to have two elements:

- Specific intent to commit a criminal offense
- A substantial step undertaken toward the commission of the intended offense

The Act Requirement

Attempted criminal activity encompasses a broad area. Almost any crime that can be envisioned can be attempted, and under the penal codes of most states, any crime defined by statute has as its adjunct an attempt to commit that crime. Florida law, for example, says that "a person who attempts to commit an offense prohibited by law and in such attempt does any act toward the commission of such offense, but fails in the perpetration or is intercepted or prevented in the execution thereof, commits the offense of criminal attempt."[13] The Model Penal Code, sounding much like the examples from California and Illinois cited earlier, requires a substantial step to corroborate intent.[14] Its suggested wording is also reflected in Alaska law, which reads: "A person is guilty of an attempt to commit a crime if, with intent to commit a crime, the person engages in conduct which constitutes a substantial step toward the commission of that crime."[15] Hence, under the laws of most states, for the crime of homicide there is the corresponding crime of attempted homicide, for the crime of rape there is the corresponding crime of attempted rape, and so on.

For an attempt to be charged, an act of some sort is necessary. But what kinds of acts are sufficient to constitute attempts? Generally speaking, courts have held that **mere preparation** to commit an offense is not sufficient to support a charge of attempted criminal activity and that some specific action must be taken toward the actual completion of the intended offense. Consider, for example, the Texas Penal Code, which describes the crime of "aiding suicide" with these words: "A person commits an offense if, with intent to promote or assist the commission of suicide by another, he aids or attempts to aid the other to commit or attempt to commit suicide."[16]

substantial step
(1) Significant activity undertaken in furtherance of some goal. (2) An act or omission that is a significant part of a series of acts or omissions, constituting a course of conduct planned to culminate in the commission of a crime. (3) An important or essential step toward the commission of a crime that is considered sufficient to constitute the crime of criminal attempt. A substantial step is conduct that is strongly corroborative of the actor's criminal purpose. According to one court, a substantial step is "behavior of such a nature that a reasonable observer, viewing it in context, could conclude beyond a reasonable doubt that it was undertaken in accordance with a design to violate the statute."[i]

mere preparation
An act or omission that may be part of a series of acts or omissions constituting a course of conduct planned to culminate in the commission of a crime but that fails to meet the requirements for a substantial step. Also, preparatory actions or steps taken toward the completion of a crime that are remote from the actual commission of the crime.

Just what constitutes "an attempt to aid"? On that issue, the Texas statute is silent. Texas law, however, says that a person is generally guilty of attempted criminal activity if "he does an act amounting to more than mere preparation that tends but fails to effect the commission of the offense intended." Under Texas law, then, would a person be guilty of attempting to aid another to commit suicide if he or she purchased a copy of the book *Final Exit*,[17] which describes various methods of suicide and tells readers how to enact them, and gave the book to a person contemplating suicide? Would the person have gone beyond "mere preparation" in the provision of aid? Similarly, if someone requested literature from the Hemlock Society, an association of suicide rights activists, would that be an act beyond mere preparation? If a person feigned symptoms to a physician in order to obtain tranquilizers that could be used in a suicide, would that be more than mere preparation? What if that person provided such pills to someone seeking to die? What constitutes a substantial step is discussed in this chapter's Capstone Case, *Tennessee* v. *Reeves*.

> *Your verdict will be "Guilty" or "Not Guilty." Your job is not to find innocence.*
>
> —Judge Russell R. Leggett,
> Westchester County Court, New York

Preparation

Mere preparation to commit a crime is generally insufficient to constitute the crime of criminal attempt. As mentioned, the Model Penal Code provides that conduct is not an attempt unless it involves a substantial step toward the commission of the offense and is strongly corroborative of the actor's criminal purpose.[18] A central issue becomes one of deciding when the conduct in question is no longer considered to be "mere preparation" and becomes an attempt within the meaning of an applicable statute. The U.S. Court of Appeals for the Fifth Circuit, in *Mims* v. *United States*,[19] recognized the difficulty involved in resolving the issue and observed that "[m]uch ink has been spilt in an attempt to arrive at a satisfactory standard for telling where preparation ends and attempt begins" (Figure 4–1).

In the oft-cited case of *People* v. *Rizzo*,[20] four defendants were cruising the streets of New York searching for a victim they knew as Charles Rao. Rao was a payroll clerk, and the defendants felt certain that he would be walking from a bank carrying a deposit bag, which they thought would be full of money to meet an upcoming payroll at the company where Rao worked. One of the defendants, Charles Rizzo, told the others that he would be able to identify Rao and would point him out to them before the robbery. Although the defendants never found Rao, their suspicious activity attracted the attention of police. They were arrested and charged with attempted robbery. At trial, all four defendants were convicted of attempted first-degree robbery and sentenced to prison. Rizzo appealed his conviction, arguing that he had not legally attempted the crime of robbery because he never came close to carrying out the offense. The New York Court of Appeals agreed and reversed Rizzo's conviction. The appellate court based its decision, in large part, on an earlier court's finding that "acts constituting an attempt" are those that come "very near to the accomplishment of the crime."[21] Holding that the actions of the defendants constituted "mere preparation," the appeals court asked:

> Did the acts . . . come dangerously near to the taking of Rao's property? Did the acts come so near to the commission of robbery that there was reasonable likelihood of its accomplishment but for the interference [of the police]? Rao was not found; the defendants were still looking for him; no attempt to rob him could be made, at least until he came in sight. . . . There was no man there with the payroll for the United Lathing Company whom these defendants could rob. Apparently no money had been drawn from the bank for the payroll by anybody at the time of the arrest. In a word, these defendants had planned to break into a building and were arrested while they were hunting about the streets for the building, not knowing where it was. Neither would a man be guilty of an attempt to commit murder if he armed himself and started out to find the person whom he had planned to kill but could not find him. So here these defendants were not guilty of an attempt to commit robbery in the first degree when they had not found or reached the presence of the person they intended to rob.

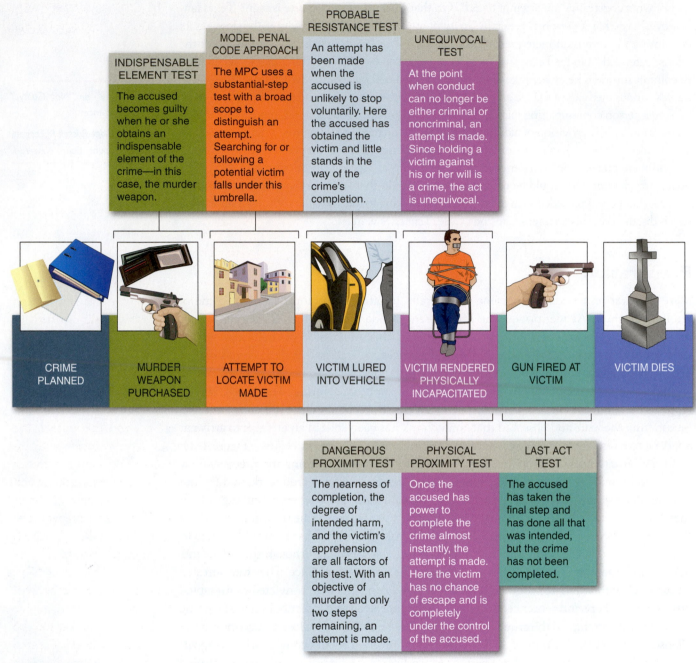

FIGURE 4–1

Criminal Preparation, Criminal Attempt, and Crime Commission.

"For these reasons," concluded the court, "the judgment of conviction of this defendant appellant must be reversed."[22]

Courts have used various formulations to distinguish between preparation and a substantial step:

- The last-act test, which asks whether the conduct completed is dangerously close to completing the crime itself

- The notion that the more serious the threatened harm, the more justified the court would be in examining acts further back in the series of acts that would lead to crime completion

- The idea that the clearer the intent to commit the offense is, the less proximate the acts need to be to the completion of the crime to constitute the crime of attempt

APPLYING THE CONCEPT

CAPSTONE CASE

If Students Plan to Kill a Teacher by Poisoning, Is It Attempted Murder for the Students to Bring the Poison to School, or Must They Actually Put the Poison in a Place Where the Teacher Might Consume It?

Tennessee v. Reeves, 917 S.W.2d 825 (Tenn. 1996)

THE CASE On the evening of January 5, 1993, Tracie Reeves and Molly Coffman, both twelve years of age and students at West Carroll Middle School, spoke on the telephone and decided to kill their homeroom teacher, Janice Geiger. The girls agreed that Coffman would bring rat poison to school the following day so that it could be placed in Geiger's drink. The girls also agreed that they would thereafter steal Geiger's car and drive to the Smoky Mountains. Reeves then contacted Dean Foutch, a local high school student, informed him of the plan, and asked him to drive Geiger's car. Foutch refused this request.

On the morning of January 6, Coffman placed a packet of rat poison in her purse and boarded the school bus. During the bus ride Coffman told another student, Christy Hernandez, of the plan; Coffman also showed Hernandez the packet of rat poison. Upon their arrival at school, Hernandez informed her homeroom teacher, Sherry Cockrill, of the plan. Cockrill then relayed this information to the principal of the school, Claudia Argo.

When Geiger entered her classroom that morning she observed Reeves and Coffman leaning over her desk; when the girls noticed her, they giggled and ran back to their seats. At that time Geiger saw a purse lying next to her coffee cup on top of the desk. Shortly thereafter Argo called Coffman to the principal's office. Rat poison was found in Coffman's purse, and it was turned over to a Sheriff's Department investigator. Both Reeves and Coffman gave written statements to the investigator concerning their plan to poison Geiger and steal her car.

Reeves and Coffman were found to be delinquent by the Carroll County Juvenile Court [and a jury convicted them of attempt to commit second-degree murder] and both appealed from that ruling. . . . Because we have not addressed the law of criminal attempt since the comprehensive reform of our criminal law undertaken by the legislature in 1989, we granted that application.

THE FINDING Before the passage of the reform legislation in 1989, the law of criminal attempt, though sanctioned by various statutes, was judicially defined. In order to submit an issue of criminal attempt to the jury, the State was required to present legally sufficient evidence of: (1) an intent to commit a specific crime; (2) an overt act toward the commission of that crime; and (3) a failure to consummate the crime.

Of the elements of criminal attempt, the second, the "overt-act" requirement, was by far the most problematic. By attempting to draw a sharp distinction between "mere preparation" to commit a criminal act, which did not constitute the required overt act, and a "direct movement toward the commission after the preparations had been made," *Dupuy*, 325 S.W.2d at 239, 240, which did, Tennessee courts construed the term "overt act" very narrowly. . . .

In 1989, however, the legislature enacted a general criminal attempt statute, as part of its comprehensive overhaul of Tennessee's criminal law. In that statute, the legislature did not simply codify the judicially created elements of the crime, but utilized language that had up to then been entirely foreign to Tennessee attempt law. Section 39-12-101 provides, in pertinent part, as follows:

a. A person commits criminal attempt who, acting with the kind of culpability otherwise required for the offense:
   1. Intentionally engages in action or causes a result that would constitute an offense if the circumstances surrounding the conduct were as the person believes them to be;
   2. Acts with intent to cause a result that is an element of the offense, and believes the conduct will cause the result without further conduct on the person's part; or

(continued)

3. Acts with intent to complete a course of action or cause a result that would constitute the offense, under the circumstances surrounding the conduct as the person believes them to be, and the conduct constitutes a substantial step toward the commission of the offense.

b. Conduct does not constitute a substantial step under subdivision (a)(3) unless the person's entire course of action is corroborative of the intent to commit the offense. . . .

As stated above, our task is to determine whether the defendant's actions in this case constitute a "substantial step" toward the commission of second-degree murder under the new statute. . . .

In addressing this issue, we first note that the legislature, in enacting Section(s) 39-12-101, clearly looked to the criminal attempt section set forth in the Model Penal Code. . . .

The State argues that the striking similarity of Tenn. Code Ann. 39-12-101 and the Model Penal Code evidences the legislature's intention to abandon the old law of criminal attempt and instead adopt the Model Penal Code approach. The State then avers that the model code contains examples of conduct which, if proven, would entitle, but not require, the jury to find that the defendant had taken a "substantial step" and that two of these examples are applicable to this case. The section of the model code relied upon by the State, Section(s) 5.01(2), provides, in pertinent part, as follows:

1. Conduct which may be held substantial step under paragraph (1)(c). Conduct shall not be held to constitute a substantial step under paragraph (1)(c) of this Section unless it is strongly corroborative of the actor's criminal purpose. Without negating the sufficiency of other conduct, the following, if strongly corroborative of the actor's criminal purpose, shall not be held insufficient as a matter of law. . . .
   e. possession of materials to be employed in the commission of the crime, which are specially designed for such unlawful use or which can serve no lawful purpose of the actor under the circumstances;
   f. possession, collection, or fabrication of materials to be employed in the commission of the crime, at or near the place contemplated for its commission, where such possession, collection, or fabrication serves no lawful purpose of the actor under the circumstances. . . .

The State concludes that because the issue of whether the defendant's conduct constitutes a substantial step may be a jury question under the model code, the jury was justified in finding her guilty of attempting to commit second-degree murder. . . .

Initially, we cannot accept the argument that the legislature intended to explicitly adopt the Model Penal Code approach, including the examples set forth in Section(s) 5.01(2). Although Section(s) 39-12-101 is obviously based on the model code, we agree with the defendant that the legislature could have, if it had so desired, simply included the specific examples in the Tennessee statute. That it did not do so prohibits us from concluding that the legislature explicitly intended to adopt the model code approach in all its particulars.

This conclusion does not mean, however, that the legislature intended to retain the distinction between "mere preparation" and the "act itself." Moreover, while we concede that a strong argument can be made that the conviction conflicts with *Dupuy* because the defendant did not place the poison in the cup, but simply brought it to the crime scene, we also are well aware that the *Dupuy* approach to attempt law has been consistently and effectively criticized. . . . The other principal ground of criticism of the *Dupuy* approach bears directly on the primary objective of the law—that of preventing inchoate crimes from becoming full-blown ones. Many courts and commentators have argued that failing to attach criminal responsibility to the actor—and therefore prohibiting law enforcement officers from taking action—until the actor is on the brink of consummating the crime endangers the public and undermines the preventative goal of attempt law.

The shortcomings of the *Dupuy* rule with respect to the goal of prevention are particularly evident in this case. As stated above, it is likely that under *Dupuy* no criminal responsibility would have attached unless the poison had actually been placed in the teacher's cup. This rigid requirement, however, severely undercuts the objective of prevention because of the surreptitious nature of the act of poisoning. Once a person secretly places a toxic substance into a container from which another person is likely to eat or drink, the damage is done. Here, if it had not been for the intervention of the teacher, she could have been rendered powerless to protect herself from harm.

After carefully weighing considerations of *stare decisis* against the persuasive criticisms of the *Dupuy* rule, we conclude that this artificial and potentially harmful rule must be abandoned. We hold that when an actor possesses materials to be used in the commission of a crime, at or near the scene of the crime, and where the possession of those materials can serve no lawful purpose of the actor under the circumstances, the jury is entitled, but not required, to find that the actor has taken a "substantial step" toward the commission of the crime if such action is strongly corroborative of the actor's overall criminal purpose. For the foregoing reasons, the judgment of the Court of Appeals is affirmed. . . .

What Do You Think?

1. Do you agree that the girls had taken a substantial step toward the commission of a targeted offense?

What test does the court establish for Tennessee to determine if a substantial step has been taken?

2. Would your answer be different if Tennessee used the last-step test or the physical proximity test? If so, how?

3. Do you think that the court, in using common law rules of construction, modifies the legislative enactment? Is the court using its judgment to replace that of the drafters of the statute?

Additional Applications

What is a "substantial step"? Why require it?

United States v. *Gladish*, 536 F.3d 646 (7th Cir. 2008)

The Case: The defendant, a 35-year-old man from southern Indiana, visited an Internet chat room called "Indiana regional romance" and solicited "Abagail"—a purported 14-year-old Indiana girl who, in reality, was an undercover (adult female) federal law enforcement agent—to have sex with him. In their online chats, "Abagail" agreed to a sexual encounter with the defendant and, in one conversation, he raised the possibility of her traveling from her purported home in northern Indiana to meet him "in a couple of weeks." No specific travel or meeting arrangements were made, however. The defendant was arrested and charged by federal prosecutors of attempting to "persuade, induce, entice, or coerce a person under 18" to engage in criminal sexual activity. On appeal, the defendant claimed that he had not taken a "substantial step" toward the completion of the specified crime; thus, the criminal charges were invalid.

The Finding: A three-judge panel of the U.S. Court of Appeals for the Seventh Circuit ruled that the defendant, in these circumstances, could not be found guilty of criminal attempt. Writing for the panel, Judge Richard A. Posner focused largely on the purposes underlying the law of criminal attempts and the rationale of its "substantial step" requirement. Unlike in tort law, Posner argued, a criminal attempt is punishable even in the absence of completion of the intended crime because "the criminal law . . . aims at taking dangerous people out of circulation before they do harm." Yet even so, Posner continued, citing attempted murder as an example, "[y]ou are not punished just for saying that you want or even intend to kill someone, because most talk doesn't lead to action. You have to do something that makes it reasonably clear that had you not been interrupted or made a mistake—for example, the person you thought you were shooting was actually a clothier's manikin (*sic*)—you would have

completed the crime." That "something," Posner wrote, "marks you as genuinely dangerous—a doer . . . ."

In this particular case, the appeals panel found, the defendant had engaged in "explicit sex talk" with the purported underage girl, but he never took the legally required "significant step" toward completing the crime of engaging in illegal sex with a minor. The defendant never indicated that he would actually travel to northern Indiana; more generally, he apparently never made any concrete plans to meet his purported victim in person. All of the defendant's actions, Posner concluded, were "consistent with his having intended to obtain sexual satisfaction vicariously." Indeed, he added, "since [the agent] furnished no proof of her age, he could not have been sure and may indeed have doubted that she was a girl, or even a woman. He may have thought (this is common in Internet relationships) that they were both enacting a fantasy."

Is the gathering of some—but not all—necessary drug lab components a "substantial step"?

United States v. *Spencer*, 439 F.3d 905 (8th Cir. 2006)

The Case: Following a tip provided by a delivery truck driver, state law enforcement officers in June 2000 searched the Monona County, Iowa, residence of Joseph Spencer and found over 2,000 marijuana plants along with significant quantities of red phosphorus, an iodine container, a cache of pseudoephedrine, various flasks and tubes, acid, striker tabs, and coffee filters—the latter items, a state expert later testified at trial, are all associated with the operation of an illegal methamphetamine lab. After a nine-day trial, a federal district court jury found the defendant guilty on several gun possession and drug trafficking charges, including violation of 21 U.S.C. Sec. 846, which prohibits an "attempt to manufacture five grams or more" of actual (pure) methamphetamine. On appeal, Spencer challenged his conviction on criminal attempt charges on the grounds that the government had failed to prove that he had taken a "substantial step" toward the actual production of methamphetamine.

The Finding: A unanimous panel of the Eighth Circuit rejected Spencer's claim. Whether a defendant's conduct constitutes a "substantial step," the panel noted, necessarily "depends on the particular factual circumstances." And in this case, the defendant had not yet assembled all of the necessary components of a fully functioning drug lab on his property. Further, agents had not found any actual methamphetamine at the residence. Nonetheless, the court held, "there was a combination of items" at the scene that an expert witness had associated at trial with a

(*continued*)

commonly used method of methamphetamine production. What's more, a delivery driver had testified at trial that he had delivered methanol—"a hazardous material used as a solvent" in illegal drug labs—to the residence. Given all the facts at hand, the panel concluded, "the evidence was sufficient for the jury to find [that] Spencer attempted to manufacture methamphetamine." Quoting from a 2001 ruling from the Tenth Circuit, the panel added: the defendant "need not possess a full 'working lab' to be convicted" of attempting to manufacture illicit drugs. ∎

The Proximity Approach

The proximity approach was the traditional test used at common law.[23] Under this approach, acts remotely leading toward the commission of the offense are not considered as attempts to commit the crime, but acts immediately connected with it are. The proximity test was based on the **last-act test**.

last-act test
In the crime of attempt, a test that asks whether the accused had taken the last step or act toward commission of the offense, had performed all that he or she intended and was able to do in an attempt to commit the crime, but for some reason did not complete the crime.

The last-act test originated from the frequently cited English case of *Regina* v. *Eagleton*.[24] The defendant in *Eagleton* was a baker who was hired by the welfare office to provide bread for the poor. He was to receive credit vouchers from the poor for each loaf of bread that he provided them and was then to take the vouchers to the welfare office, which would then credit him for his efforts. He was to be paid later, based on the number of vouchers submitted. Soon, however, the baker was charged with attempting to obtain money by false pretenses for having delivered underweight loaves and for turning in the credit vouchers he had received for them.

Eagleton defended himself on the grounds that turning the tickets in to the welfare office earned him credit, not money. In effect, he argued that his activity did not amount to an attempt to obtain money, only credits. He was, nonetheless, convicted based on the fact that after he turned in the vouchers to the welfare office, he was not required to perform any other act in order to be paid. Hence, the court reasoned, he had completed the last act necessary for payment.

The last-act test required that the accused has taken the last step or act, has performed all that he or she intended and was able to do in an attempt to commit the crime, but for some reason did not complete the crime. Using this test in a murder by shooting, for example, an attempt would not be completed until the accused fired the weapon. The last-act test was popular in England during the latter part of the nineteenth century,[25] but it was eventually abandoned amidst charges that the test made it virtually impossible for law enforcement personnel to prevent the commission of a substantive crime.

physical proximity test
A test traditionally used under common law to determine whether a person was guilty of attempted criminal activity. The physical proximity test requires that the accused has it within his or her power to complete the crime almost immediately.

In an effort to reduce the strict provisions of the last-act test, the **physical proximity test** was developed. Under the physical proximity test, the substantial step need not be the last act, but it must approach sufficiently near to it in order to stand as a substantial step in the direct movement toward commission of the intended crime.[26] Under the physical proximity test, which was well articulated in the 1948 Pennsylvania case of *Commonwealth* v. *Kelly*,[27] the required substantial step is not held to have been completed until the accused has it within his or her power to enact the crime almost immediately. Under this test, for example, in order to be found guilty of attempted rape, the accused would need to have the victim under his control and have started taking the necessary steps to force the victim to have sexual relations with him. In the *Kelly* case, two men intending to trick a victim out of his money convinced him to go to the bank to withdraw funds. The men were arrested at the bank before the potential victim withdrew the funds. The court held that their conduct did not amount to criminal attempt because the money had not actually been removed from the intended victim's account.

dangerous proximity test
A test for assessing attempts, under which a person is guilty of an attempt when his or her conduct comes dangerously close to success.

Justice Oliver Wendell Holmes developed the **dangerous proximity test**. This test incorporates the physical proximity standard but is more flexible. According to the dangerous proximity test, a person is guilty of an attempt when his or her conduct is in "dangerous proximity" to success. According to Holmes, courts should consider three factors: the nearness of completion, the degree of intended harm, and the degree of apprehension felt by the intended victim.[28] For example, a drug-dealing defendant intending to buy a large quantity of cocaine in an illegal transaction from a wholesaler may meet with the higher-level dealer, examine the goods, and then reject the drugs for quality reasons. Under the dangerous proximity test, however, the defendant could still be found guilty of attempted possession of a controlled substance with intent to sell because the acts that were undertaken were dangerously close to completing the targeted offense.

Alternatives to the Proximity Approach   Alternatives to the proximity approach include the indispensable element test, the unequivocal test, and the probable desistance test (Table 4–1). Under the indispensable element test, the accused is not guilty of an attempt if he or she has yet to obtain control of an indispensable feature of the crime. For example, an accused who intends to commit armed robbery is not guilty of an attempted armed robbery before obtaining a weapon because that is an indispensable element of armed robbery. Critics of the indispensable element test say that it does little to consider an actor's actual degree of culpability.

Under the unequivocal test, an act does not become an attempt until it ceases to be equivocal.[29] This test requires that an act or acts committed by the defendant must unequivocally manifest his or her criminal intent in order to constitute an attempt. Conduct that may indicate *either* noncriminal *or* criminal intent is not sufficient to demonstrate attempt. This test has been criticized on the grounds that there is no act that is completely unequivocal, as all human behavior is open to interpretation.

A third alternative is the probable desistance approach. Under this approach, the defendant's conduct constitutes an attempt if it has gone beyond the point where the defendant is likely to *voluntarily* stop short of completing the offense. This test has been criticized on the grounds that it is difficult to determine whether a defendant is likely to stop a course of action.

> We hold that the reckless disregard for human life implied in knowingly engaging in criminal activity known to carry a grave risk of death represents a highly culpable mental state.
>
> —Justice Sandra Day O'Connor, writing on accomplice liability in Tison v. Arizona, 481 U.S. 137 (1987)

The Model Penal Code Approach   As noted earlier, the Model Penal Code (MPC) makes use of the substantial-step test. The MPC approach, which is used in most states and in the federal courts, incorporates aspects of both the proximity test and the unequivocal test. Any conduct that meets any of the variations of either test is sufficient to constitute an attempt, as it constitutes a substantial step toward crime completion. Under this approach, an attempt will be found to have occurred in many cases where the defendant does not move very far along the path toward consummation of the intended offense.

TABLE 4–1   Attempt: Summary of Tests

Proximity Test	Definition
Dangerous proximity	Defendant must act in dangerous proximity to the crime to be culpable. Acts remotely connected to the crime are not adequate.
Physical proximity	Defendant is culpable if completion of the crime is within grasp, although the defendant's act need not be the penultimate act.
Indispensable element	Defendant is culpable once he or she has committed an indispensable act.
Unequivocal	Defendant is culpable if he or she has unequivocally manifested an intent to commit the crime.
Probable desistance	Defendant is culpable if it is likely that he or she would have followed through with the crime.
Substantial step	Defendant is culpable if he or she took substantial steps toward the commission of the crime.

The MPC approach reflects a continuing trend during the past 30 years toward a broadening of attempt liability. The code lists the following examples of activity that might meet the substantial-step criterion, providing that the behavior in question is thought to corroborate the defendant's criminal purpose:[30]

- Lying in wait or searching for or following the contemplated victim[31]
- Enticing or seeking to entice the contemplated victim of the crime to go to the place contemplated for the commission of the crime
- Reconnoitering the place contemplated for the commission of the crime
- Unlawful entry of a structure, vehicle, or enclosure in which it is contemplated that the crime will be committed
- Possession of materials to be employed in the commission of the crime, which are specially designed for such unlawful use or that can serve no lawful purpose of the actor under the circumstances
- Possession, collection, or fabrication of material to be employed in the commission of the crime, at or near the place contemplated for its commission, where such possession, collection, or fabrication serves no lawful useful purpose of the actor under the circumstances
- Soliciting an innocent agent to engage in conduct constituting an element of the crime

Defenses to Charges of Criminal Attempts

During the Vietnam conflict, Father Phillip Berrigan and another prisoner in a federal correctional institution were charged with attempting to violate a federal statute prohibiting the sending of letters into and out of a federal institution without the warden's consent. Both were apprehended as they attempted to mail the letters. In presenting evidence in the case, an assistant U.S. attorney established that, unknown to the defendants, the warden had been aware that the letters were being prepared and were about to be sent. Apparently, the warden let the conduct leading up to the actual mailing of the letters occur in order to help the government build a case against the defendants.[32] In this situation, Father Berrigan clearly did all that he intended to do in order to commit the targeted crime.

Berrigan was convicted by a trial court of an attempted violation, but his conviction was overturned by a federal appellate court, which ruled that, although the priest's conduct amounted to more than mere preparation, it was legally impossible for him to commit the crime because the warden had, in effect, consented to the conduct when he did not interfere with it. Although Berrigan's case may have been unusual, anyone charged with an attempt may generally raise two defenses: abandonment and impossibility (Figure 4–2).

abandonment
The voluntary and complete abandonment of the intent and purpose to commit a criminal offense. Abandonment is a defense to a charge of attempted criminal activity. Also called *renunciation*.

Abandonment
The defense of **abandonment** claims that the defendant voluntarily decided to renounce continued attempts to commit the crime. Indiana law reads: "[I]t is a defense that the person who engaged in the prohibited conduct voluntarily abandoned his effort to commit the underlying crime and voluntarily prevented its commission."[33] In some jurisdictions, the term *renunciation* is used instead of abandonment. Texas law, for example, states: "It is an affirmative defense to prosecution . . . that under circumstances manifesting a voluntary and complete renunciation of his criminal objective the actor avoided commission of the offense attempted by abandoning his criminal conduct."

Similarly, Florida law reads: "It is a defense to a charge of criminal attempt, criminal solicitation, or criminal conspiracy that, under circumstances manifesting a complete and voluntary renunciation of his criminal purpose, the defendant: (a) abandoned his attempt to commit the offense or otherwise prevented its commission; (b) after soliciting another person to commit an offense, persuaded such other person not to do so or otherwise prevented commission of the offense; or (c) after conspiring with one or more persons to

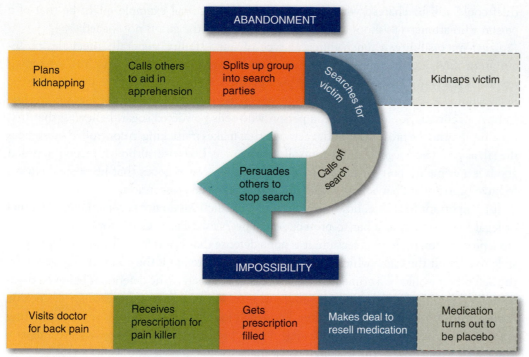

FIGURE 4–2

The Defenses of Abandonment and Impossibility.

commit an offense, persuaded such persons not to do so or otherwise prevented commission of the offense."[34]

There are a number of arguments in favor of allowing abandonment or renunciation as a defense: (1) It encourages desistance, (2) it indicates a lack of dangerousness on the part of the offender, and (3) it shows a lack of intent on the part of the defendant to carry the crime to completion. On the other hand, critics argue that (1) it has little deterrent effect, (2) it fails to show whether the defendant will prove dangerous in the future, and (3) the accused has already completed the crime of attempt. Even so, courts in most American jurisdictions today recognize the abandonment defense.

The Model Penal Code also allows for the defense of abandonment. The code states that "it is an affirmative defense that the defendant has abandoned his effort to commit the crime or otherwise prevented its commission."[35] Virtually all jurisdictions require that abandonment be voluntary. Postponement of the crime in anticipation of a better time for its commission, the defendant's decision to find a different victim, or disappointment in the anticipated fruits of the crime are not considered to constitute voluntary abandonment. Involuntary abandonment is not a bar to prosecution because a defendant may be forced to abandon attempts to commit a crime because of police intervention, inclement weather, a debilitating accident, or some other inability to continue. Even when the defense is successful, it does not affect the criminal liability of an accomplice who does not join in such abandonment or renunciation.

Impossibility Impossibility, the second defense to a charge of attempted criminal activity, may be of either the factual or legal variety. Factual impossibility, which is rarely successful as a defense, claims that the defendant could not have committed the envisioned offense even if he or she had been able to carry through the attempt to do so. It is factually impossible, for example, to rob a person who has no possessions, even though a robbery might be attempted; it is similarly impossible to kill someone who is already dead (although an attempt might be made by someone who lacks knowledge of the person's death[36]). Another example of factual impossibility is that of a pickpocket who tries to pick an empty pocket. Even though the intended victim had nothing in his or her pockets, the would-be

impossibility
A defense to a charge of attempted criminal activity that claims the defendant could not have factually or legally committed the envisioned offense even if he or she had been able to carry through the attempt to do so. It is, for example, factually impossible to kill someone who is already dead.

thief could still be charged with an attempt to steal. A final example might be that of a person who attempts to shoot another, only to find that the gun is not loaded.

Legal impossibility, a much different type of impossibility, generally precludes prosecution in most jurisdictions. The defense of legal impossibility claims that the attempted offense is really no offense at all, either because there is no law against the imagined crime or because the actions in question do not meet the requirements of the law for a crime to have occurred. So, for example, a person who sells powdered sugar, believing that it is cocaine, may not be prosecuted under a statute that makes trafficking in controlled substances illegal, as powdered sugar is not a controlled substance. Likewise, although receiving stolen goods is a crime in most jurisdictions, someone who receives goods that he or she believes to have been stolen, but actually were not, will rarely face prosecution.

It is important to realize, however, that some jurisdictions do not accept claims of factual or legal impossibility as a bar to prosecution. The Alaska Penal Code, for example, reads: "In a prosecution under this section, it is not a defense that it was factually or legally impossible to commit the crime which was the object of the attempt if the conduct engaged in by the defendant would be a crime had the circumstances been as the defendant believed them to be." Although the intent of the provision is no doubt to allow prosecution of cocaine dealers who sell powdered sugar (often knowingly) and the like, it raises some interesting possibilities under which one could imagine the prosecution of a person who attempts a crime that exists only in the imagination of the actor.

Completed Offense

In most jurisdictions, if a defendant is charged with a substantive crime but evidence indicates that the defendant only completed an attempt, he or she may be found guilty only of the *lesser included offense* of an attempt. If the crime is completed, however, then the attempt is usually considered to have merged into the completed offense, and the defendant would be guilty only of the substantive offense and not of both the substantive offense *and* an attempt to complete that offense.

Suppose, however, that the defendant is charged *only* with an attempt but evidence establishes that he or she actually completed the offense. May the defendant then be found guilty of the substantive crime? The answer is no, as virtually all jurisdictions hold that a defendant may not be found guilty of a greater offense than the one with which he or she is charged. On the other hand, the fact that the substantive crime was actually committed cannot be used as a defense to a charge of attempt to commit that crime.

Punishment for Criminal Attempts

At common law, all attempts were punishable as misdemeanors. Accordingly, offenders convicted of attempt were punished less severely than they would have been had the contemplated crime been completed. Over the years, legislatures in this country have struggled to establish appropriate punishments for criminal attempts.

Noted jurist H. L. A. Hart reasoned that attempts should be punished because "there must be many who are not completely confident that they will succeed in their criminal objective, but will be prepared to run the risk of punishment if they can be assured that they have to pay nothing for attempts which fail; whereas if unsuccessful attempts were also punished, the price might appear to them to be too high. Again, there must be many cases where men might with good or bad reason believe that if they succeed in committing some crime they will escape, but if they fail they may be caught."[37]

Today, punishment schemes relating to offenses are usually closely related to the grading system established for the intended offense, and in many states the punishment for an attempt is one classification below that for the intended offense itself. The Model Penal Code, on the other hand, provides the same punishment for attempts that it does for completed crimes (except in cases of crimes punishable by life imprisonment or death). Supporters of the MPC approach argue that the same *mens rea* exists in an offender's mind when a crime is attempted as when it is completed—and that, consequently, the same punishment is justified. For purposes of punishment, they say, it matters little whether the attempted crime actually occurred or failed for some reason to be completed. According to commentaries on the Model Penal Code, an appropriate sentence can best be determined by the antisocial disposition of the offender and by the demonstrated need for a corrective sanction. Therefore, in most instances, it makes little difference when applying sanctions whether the offender was able to consummate the attempted criminal activity or not.[38]

CRIMINAL CONSPIRACY

A **criminal conspiracy** is an agreement between two or more people to commit or to effect the commission of an unlawful act or to use unlawful means to accomplish an act that is not unlawful. The notion of conspiracy was first formulated by the English Star Chamber in 1611. Under English common law, the term had much the same meaning as it does today. However, while conspiracy was generally considered to be a misdemeanor under common law, most states and the federal government today classify it as a felony. The U.S. Supreme Court has said that "the agreement to commit an unlawful act is a distinct evil, which may exist and be punished whether or not the substantive crime ensues."[39]

The Commentaries on the Model Penal Code state, "Conspiracy as an offense has two different aspects, reflecting the different functions it serves in the legal system. In the first place, conspiracy is an inchoate crime, complementing the provisions dealing with attempt and solicitation in reaching preparatory conduct before it has matured into commission of a substantive offense. Second, it is a means of striking against the special danger incident to group activity, facilitating prosecution of the group, and yielding a basis for imposing added penalties when combination is involved."

According to legal commentator Paul Marcus, striking changes in criminal conspiracy prosecutions during the past two decades include an enormous growth in the number of cases involving many defendants, an increase in the prevalence of complex evidentiary issues, and increasingly complicated charges brought against defendants in conspiracy cases.[40] Cases he cites as examples include (1) *United States* v. *Casamento* (1989),[41] involving 21 defendants, 275 witnesses, and 40,000 pages of transcripts; (2) *United States* v. *Ianniello* (1989),[42] a 13-month trial with 11 defendants; (3) *United States* v. *Kopituk* (1982),[43] a case that had 12 defendants and 130 witnesses; and (4) *United States* v. *Martino* (1981),[44] with 20 defendants and more than 200 witnesses. Many of today's conspiracy cases involve drug trafficking, in which several people agree to work in concert to manufacture, transport, and distribute controlled substances.

Doctrine of Complicity

Conspiracy is a complex and controversial crime. Some judges and legal scholars have advocated its reform or abolition.[45] Criticisms of the crime of conspiracy include charges that it provides the state with a potent, and possibly unfair, weapon because it gives prosecutors extraordinary latitude in prosecuting behavior that would not otherwise be criminal. Similarly, prosecutors pursuing conspiracy cases have available to them a number of procedural advantages that are not available in other cases. Procedural advantages favoring the prosecution include the use of joint trials, the admission of **hearsay** evidence, and the fact

criminal conspiracy
An agreement between two or more people to commit or to effect the commission of an unlawful act or to use unlawful means to accomplish an act that is not unlawful.

hearsay
Something that is not based on the personal knowledge of a witness. Witnesses who testify about something they have heard, for example, are offering hearsay by repeating information about a matter of which they have no direct knowledge.

CRIMINAL LAW IN THE NEWS

Can Hearsay Be the Primary Evidence in a Murder Case?

In September 2012, Drew Peterson, a retired police officer, was convicted of murdering Kathleen Savio, his third wife. They were divorced at the time of the murder. In what was initially believed to be an accidental death, Peterson was charged with Savio's murder after his fourth wife, Stacy Peterson, disappeared. After the disappearance Savio's body was exhumed and re-examined. Described as cocky and brash, Peterson taunted authorities on national television shows, drawing national attention to the case. Prosecutors had little physical evidence to prove Peterson a murderer. Instead they relied on the hearsay of Peterson's fourth wife, Stacy, whom authorities believe Peterson killed to keep her from testifying. People close to Stacy testified that she told them that Peterson told her he could kill her and make it look like an accident, that she kept a knife under her bed to protect herself from him, and that Peterson left the house at the time of the murder. The evidence, which would have been inadmissible previously, was admissible at Peterson's trial because the Illinois legislature changed evidence law specifically to make prosecution of Peterson with the hearsay possible. For that reason the law is commonly known as Drew's Law. Peterson's challenges to the admissibility of the evidence failed at the trial level, he was convicted, and he appealed. The Supreme Court of the United States has issued several decisions that have reinforced the importance of the Sixth Amendment's Confrontation Clause. In the 2004 case *Crawford* v. *Washington*, the Court held that testimonial evidence, or evidence that tends to prove a fact, should be subject to cross-examination. Previously the test for confrontation was focused on the reliability of the evidence. In its decision the Court remarked that dispensing with confrontation because evidence is reliable is the same as dispensing with trial because a defendant is obviously guilty. The Court said in *Crawford* that statements made in response to ongoing emergencies are not testimonial. Applying this principle, the Court found a dying man's statement identifying his assailant to police admissible at trial because the statement was made shortly after the shooting and while the shooter was still at large in the 2010 case *Michigan* v. *Bryant*. The hearsay used to convict Peterson doesn't appear to satisfy the Court's ongoing emergency test and, as such, his conviction may be reversed on appeal.

SOURCES: Michael Tarm, Jury convicts Peterson of killing 3rd wife, September 6, 2012. USA Today. http://usatoday30.usatoday.com/news/nation/story/2012-09-06/drew-peterson-verdict/57643462/1

Drew Peterson, Wikipedia, October 1, 2012. http://en.wikipedia.org/wiki/Stacy_Peterson#Stacy_Peterson

---

that the case may be tried in any jurisdiction in which any element of the offense occurred. Other criticisms include the charge that the crime of conspiracy is so vague that it defies definition and the claim that conspiracy is predominantly mental in composition, resulting in prosecutions based more on thought than on activity.

Because conspiracy statutes give prosecutors a broad authority to charge individuals for what often appear to be rather nebulous offenses, Justice Learned Hand once described the crime of conspiracy as "the darling of the modern prosecutor's nursery."[46] Justice Hand noted that the crime of conspiracy is fundamentally "formless" and therefore serves as a powerful tool of prosecutors. Many contend that because of conspiracy's emphasis on *mens rea* and its corresponding de-emphasis on conduct, there is a greater risk that people will be punished for what they say or think rather than for what they do. In a famous English case, for example, the House of Lords upheld a conviction for "conspiracy to corrupt public morals."[47] The defendants were convicted based on an agreement made between them to publish a directory listing prostitutes and their services (the agreement was regarded as illegal because it had the intention of promoting immoral acts). The publishing of the directory never occurred. If it had, however, it would not in itself have been a crime.

Elements of the Crime

The crime of conspiracy has four elements:

- An agreement between two or more people
- The intention to carry out an act that is unlawful or one that is lawful but is to be accomplished by unlawful means
- A culpable intent on the part of the defendants
- Depending on the jurisdiction, preparation, an overt act, or a substantial step in furtherance of the conspiracy

When a conspiracy unfolds, the ultimate act that it aims to bring about does not have to occur for the parties to the conspiracy to be arrested. When people plan to bomb a public building, for example, they can be legally stopped before the bombing. As soon as they take steps to further their plan, they have met the requirement for an act. Buying explosives, telephoning one another, and drawing plans of the building may all be actions "in furtherance of the conspiracy."

Plurality Requirement

The essence of the crime of conspiracy is an *agreement* for the joint purpose of unlawful ends. Because conspiracy is defined in terms of an agreement, it necessarily involves two or more people. This aspect of the offense is called the **plurality requirement**. This requirement has both *mens rea* and *actus reus* elements. The *mens rea* is the conspirators' mutual intention of committing the underlying offense. The process of coming to agreement is part of the crime's *actus reus*. However, agreement between two individuals on a desired outcome without a plan to achieve the outcome is not a conspiracy. This issue came into sharp focus in the federal prosecutions of members of a Christian militia group, known as Hutaree, between 2010 and 2012. The United States alleged that members of the Hutaree conspired to overthrow the government of the United States, constituting the crime of sedition. In furtherance of their seditious intentions, the defendants had a vague plan that involved murdering a local law enforcement officer or a family member of such a person and subsequently attacking the fallen officer's funeral procession with weapons of mass destruction. Without detailing how it would occur, the members believed that these events would lead to a general uprising against the United States.

The federal trial judge who presided at trial found an absence of agreement, no "unity of purpose," between the conspirators on each element of the plan because the evidence at trial demonstrated different plans by the conspirators. There was evidence about the antigovernment beliefs of the group and about the desires of the defendants to kill police officers and to overthrow the government, but there was no evidence that every conspirator possessed the intention to commit all of these acts. Similarly, there was no evidence of an agreement between the conspirators to commit all of these acts. Also fatal to the prosecution, the trial judge found no connection between the murder of a local law enforcement officer, an assault on police who attended the funeral, and the overthrow of the U.S. government. The First Amendment's protection of free speech also played a role in the decision. Although hateful and vile, the defendants' statements were opinions protected by the First Amendment, not concrete plans to overthrow the government. After two years of pretrial detention and six weeks of trial, the trial judge granted the defendants' motions for acquittal on the seditious conspiracy charges in 2012.[48]

Any implied agreement is sufficient for prosecution under most conspiracy statutes. One party may, for example, by his or her actions indicate to another party that he or she will pursue a joint venture. Courts are generally very liberal as to the types of proof that may be used

plurality requirement
The logical and legal requirement that a conspiracy must involve two or more parties.

to prove an agreement. In *Williams* v. *United States*, the government was allowed to prove an agreement by circumstantial evidence that strongly suggested that there must have been a common plan. In *United States* v. *James*, defendants were convicted of a conspiracy to assault a federal officer based on the fact that they attended drills designed to train for an anticipated attack by law enforcement personnel. Defendants who were present for some of the drills, but were not present at the shoot-out, were found guilty of conspiracy because attendance at the drills established that they must have been part of the agreement to attack the officer.[49]

Wharton's Rule   Some crimes, by their very nature, require two or more criminal participants for their commission. Adultery, for example, requires at least two people (generally a man and a woman, one of whom must be married to someone else). Other crimes may be committed by solitary offenders but sometimes involve more than one criminal participant. Murder, for example, requires only one person—the murderer—for its commission. The crime of conspiracy to commit murder, however, involves at least two people.

Wharton's rule

A rule applicable to conspiracy cases holding that an agreement by two persons to commit a particular crime cannot be prosecuted as a conspiracy when the crime is of such a nature as to necessarily require the participation of two persons.

Wharton's rule provides that where the targeted crime by its very nature takes more than one person to commit, then there can be no conspiracy when no more than the number of people required to commit the offense participate in it. In the crime of adultery, for example, there can be no conspiracy to commit adultery unless more than two people are involved in the offense (as when a married couple conspires to lure others into adulterous relationships).[50] Wharton's rule was named after Francis Wharton, the criminal law author who first articulated it. The rationale behind the rule is that where the crime requires more than one person to commit it, the legislature presumably factored into the prescribed punishment for the offense the dangers stemming from group criminality.

Wharton's rule does not apply to those situations in which the crime is defined so as to require two or more people to commit but only where one of the offenders is punishable under the targeted crime statute. The rule is irrelevant, for example, in the case of a statute that punishes the selling of liquor during certain hours of the day but that prescribes a punishment only for the seller. In some jurisdictions and under federal law, Wharton's rule is only a presumption that does not apply if it is clear that the legislature did not intend to bar convictions for conspiracy.[51]

Similarly, Wharton's rule has not been incorporated into the Model Penal Code. According to code commentaries, the fact that an offense inevitably requires concert is no reason to immunize criminal preparation to commit it. The code does indicate that in those situations in which the minimum number of participants required to commit the crime are involved, those offenders may not be convicted of both the substantive crime and the conspiracy to commit it.[52]

Required Intent

As noted earlier, the essence of the crime of conspiracy is an agreement to commit an illegal activity or to commit some legal activity via illegal means. Accordingly, conspiracy is a specific-intent crime, and someone who appears to conspire to commit a crime may not be guilty of conspiracy if intent to commit the crime is lacking.[53] As noted in Chapter 2, specific intent requires a thoughtful, conscious intention to perform a specific act in order to achieve a particular result. Hence, to prove the crime of conspiracy, the government is required to prove that the defendant specifically intended to effect the commission of an unlawful act. Courts have held that knowledge of a conspiracy's objective is necessary to show requisite criminal intent.[54] At a minimum, it must be shown that a defendant has knowledge of the conspiracy's illegal purpose when he or she performs acts that further that illicit purpose.[55] Moreover, a defendant's knowledge of the purpose of the criminal conspiracy must be shown by "clear, unequivocal evidence."[56] Similarly, an apparent co-conspirator does not need to have any criminal intent for the other party in a conspiracy to be convicted of the offense of conspiracy. In the case of an undercover police officer, for example, the officer may appear to be involved with others in a criminal conspiracy while lacking the actual intent to commit the crime envisioned.

Some states require a "corrupt motive" to establish conspiracy. In the well-known case of *People* v. *Powell*,[57] for example, the defendants were charged with conspiracy to violate a statute requiring municipal officials to advertise for bids before buying supplies for the city. The defendants had offered a substantial discount to the city, if the city would forgo the bidding process. The defendants were successful in arguing that they could not be convicted of a conspiracy because they acted in good-faith ignorance of the bidding requirement. The court held that they could not be convicted unless there was proof that the defendants acted with "an evil purpose." Most states and the Model Penal Code, however, emphasize the responsibility of potential conspirators to know the law relevant to their actions and do not require a "corrupt motive" for proof of conspiracy.

> *If a man intentionally adopts certain conduct in certain circumstances known to him, and that conduct is forbidden by the law under those circumstances, he intentionally breaks the law in the only sense in which the law ever considers intent.*
>
> —Justice Oliver Wendell Holmes, Jr., Ellis v. United States, 206 U.S. 246, 257 (1907)

Parties to a Conspiracy

When people participate in a conspiracy, the law does not require that each party form an agreement with all of the other parties involved. In complex conspiracies, for example, the parties may not all know one another and may not even be aware of the involvement of all of the other parties. This is particularly true in cases involving organized crime, drug dealing and distribution, illicit gambling, and organized prostitution.

Elaborate conspiracies, in which the parties to the conspiracy may not all be aware of one another's identity or even involvement, are sometimes described as *wheel* or *chain conspiracies* (Figure 4–3). In wheel conspiracies, the conspirators deal only with a ringleader and not with one another. The leader of the conspiracy can be thought of as a hub around which each of the others—like spokes on a wheel—revolves. To establish whether a wheel conspiracy is a single conspiracy or a series of conspiracies for purposes of the law, courts have developed a community-of-interests test. A single conspiracy exists if (1) each "spoke" knows that other "spokes" exist, although they need not know their precise identity, and (2) the various "spokes" have a community of shared interests. In one early case in which this test was applied, a woman was convicted of conspiracy to perform illegal abortions as part of a wheel conspiracy. The convicted woman had referred pregnant women to a doctor (who was also a defendant) in violation of the law. In declaring that a wheel-type conspiracy existed, the trial court held that the defendant had been aware that others were also referring pregnant women to the same doctor for illegal abortions.[58]

The second type of conspiracy, the chain conspiracy, involves a sequence of individuals. Conspiracies of this type are often found in illegal drug distribution schemes (in which controlled substances move sequentially from importer to wholesaler to retailer and, ultimately, to the consumer) and in other activities associated with racketeering. The community-of-interests test may also be used to determine whether a chain-type conspiracy consists of a single conspiracy or a group of conspiracies. Under both wheel and chain conspiracies, the precise identity of the other conspirators is not important, as long as it can be demonstrated that charged conspirators had knowledge of the fact that others were involved in the scheme and that they acted in terms of a shared interest.

Because two or more individuals are required to establish a conspiracy, at least two individuals must be convicted of the crime. It is illogical for one of two conspirators to be acquitted and the second convicted. If this happens, both defendants must be acquitted by the court. If there are multiple defendants, only two must be convicted in order for the verdicts to be legitimate.

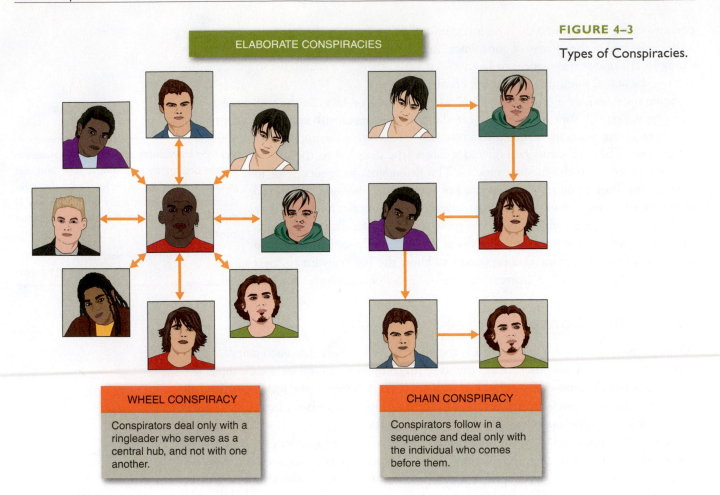

FIGURE 4–3

Types of Conspiracies.

ELABORATE CONSPIRACIES

WHEEL CONSPIRACY

Conspirators deal only with a ringleader who serves as a central hub, and not with one another.

CHAIN CONSPIRACY

Conspirators follow in a sequence and deal only with the individual who comes before them.

A couple of special evidentiary rules exist in conspiracy cases that concern the plural nature of the crime. First, there must be at least genuine conspirators. If an undercover police officer is one of two conspirators, the crime has not been committed.

The **co-conspirator hearsay rule** is another unique feature of conspiracy trials. Hearsay, or statements made out of court, is generally inadmissible at trial. But in conspiracy cases, the statements of conspirators made during planning in furtherance of the crime are admissible, even if the co-conspirator is not available to testify.

co-conspirator hearsay rule
This rule is an exception to the general rule that hearsay, or statements made out of court by a person who is not in court to testify, is inadmissible. In conspiracy trials, statements made by conspirators out of court and who are not available to testify are admissible.

Acts in Furtherance of the Conspiracy

All jurisdictions require that some act in furtherance of the conspiracy occur to satisfy the *actus reus* requirement. In some jurisdictions, merely planning the crime satisfies this requirement. In others, the defendants must commit an overt act. Any act, beyond preparation, in furtherance of the commission of the crime satisfies this requirement. In a minority of states, the standard is higher than proof of an overt act; it must be shown that the defendants took a substantial step toward completion of the crime. The Model Penal Code requires proof of an overt act for misdemeanors and the lowest felonies but not for higher felonies.[59]

Pinkerton's Rule
A doctrine holding that all conspirators are liable for the acts of co-conspirators that are taken in furtherance of the conspiracy.

In the federal system and many states, the so-called **Pinkerton's Rule** applies in conspiracy cases. Deriving its name from a Supreme Court case,[60] the rule provides that conspirators are responsible for the acts of their co-conspirators that are taken in furtherance of the conspiracy. This liability rests with all co-conspirators even if they individually didn't authorize, or were unaware of, the act. The Pinkerton Rule applies to overt acts. So if a jurisdiction requires an overt act, only one conspirator has to commit the act for it to apply to all the conspirators. The rule also encompasses crimes that underpin the conspiracy. So if one conspirator commits a crime in furtherance of the larger conspiracy, all the conspirators are criminally liable for the lesser crime.

Generally speaking, a conspiracy can be said to continue until the crime it anticipates is either completed or is abandoned by all of the parties involved. If a crime involves multiple conspirators and a single conspirator withdraws, the conspiracy continues for purposes of the law as long as two or more parties continue to be involved in it. It is often important to establish when an individual conspirator withdrew for a variety of purposes, including (1) prosecution under a statute of limitations, (2) defense challenges to declarations made by other conspirators after withdrawal, and (3) defense claims of nonliability for crimes committed by others after the date of a defendant's withdrawal. To effectively constitute withdrawal, however, the individual withdrawing generally must give notice of having withdrawn to other conspirators or to law enforcement officials. Intent to withdraw is not the same as withdrawal. For a defense based on withdrawal to be successful under Model Penal Code guidelines, the defendant must show that withdrawal was voluntary and that the "success of the conspiracy" was "thwarted."[61] A withdrawal motivated by fear of immediate detection is not considered voluntary.

In 2003, in the case of *United States* v. *Recio*,[62] the U.S. Supreme Court ruled that "a conspiracy does not automatically terminate simply because the government has defeated its object." In *Recio*, police officers stopped a truck carrying illegal drugs and seized the drugs. With the help of the truck's driver, they arranged a sting. The driver paged a contact who called two men who came to meet him and pick up the truck. The men were arrested and were convicted of conspiring to possess and distribute unlawful drugs, but they won an appeal in which they claimed that any conspiracy that might have existed effectively ended once the truck and its contents were in police custody, as it would no longer have been possible to achieve the object of the conspiracy. The Supreme Court disagreed, however, and reinstated the men's convictions, holding that "where police have frustrated a conspiracy's specific objective but conspirators (unaware of that fact) have neither abandoned the conspiracy nor withdrawn," the essence of the conspiracy (the agreement to commit the crime) remains.

CRIMINAL SOLICITATION

Under common law, **criminal solicitation** occurs when one person requests or encourages another to perform a criminal act. Consider the following scenario: Jerry Jones's daughter has been dating Tim Collins, but Jones does not like Collins. Soon Jones learns that his neighbor, William White, is an important organized crime figure. Jones conceals this knowledge from White. He also knows that Collins is one of White's employees and is apparently involved in illegal activity. During a casual conversation with his neighbor, Jones tells White that Collins is a police informant. Could Jones be charged with solicitation to commit murder?[63] Although this is a question with no clear answer, if a jury were to find that Jones's purpose in disclosing that information was to encourage White to commit a crime, then the crime of criminal solicitation has been committed.

All states have codified the crime of criminal solicitation. Florida law, for example, reads: "A person who solicits another to commit an offense prohibited by law and in the course of such solicitation commands, encourages, hires, or requests another person to engage in specific conduct which would constitute such offense or an attempt to commit such offense commits the offense of criminal solicitation. . . ."[64] Most states consider it immaterial whether the solicitee agrees to perform the act solicited.

Consider a second scenario in which Joe asks Jim to kill his wife, Joyce. Because criminal solicitation consists of the requesting or encouraging of another to commit a crime, Joe's

criminal solicitation
The encouraging, requesting, or commanding of another person to commit a crime.

request clearly constitutes the crime of solicitation. The crime is completed upon the transmission of the request or the encouragement. If Jim agrees to the request, generally both parties will be guilty of conspiracy when an overt act is taken in furtherance of the conspiracy (such as Jim's buying a gun to be used to kill Joe's wife). If Jim does in fact kill Joyce, then both Joe and Jim would be guilty of murder. Criminal solicitation, unlike conspiracy, requires no overt act. It does, however, require a mental state such that the defendant must have intended to induce the other person to perform the crime, and a successful prosecution must establish that the defendant had the mental state required for the completed crime. Hence, in the example just described, Joe must have intended to induce Jim to kill Joyce and must in fact have intended that Joyce be murdered.

It is not necessary that the solicitor intend that the person he or she solicits commit the crime. It would, for example, also be criminal solicitation for Joe to ask Jim to find someone else to kill Joyce. Similarly, solicitation does not need to be addressed to one person and may also be addressed to members of a group. A communication to a large and undefined group will not normally, however, be considered a solicitation.[65]

Consider another possible scenario: Joe calls Jim's home, but Jim is not at home, so Joe leaves a message on his answering machine asking for help in killing his wife. Before Jim receives the message, Jim's wife turns it over to the police. Has Joe committed the crime of criminal solicitation? In some states, the answer would be no because these jurisdictions require that the solicitation be communicated before the crime can be considered to have been completed. Other states, however, and the Model Penal Code declare it irrelevant that the defendant failed to communicate with the person who was the object of the solicitation as long as the defendant's conduct was designed to produce such a communication.[66] In this scenario, leaving the message on the answering machine was evidence of conduct designed to produce communication. Hence, under the Model Penal Code, Joe would be guilty of criminal solicitation.

Finally, no jurisdiction in the United States defines the use of an innocent person in the commission of an offense as criminal solicitation. If, for example, Joe asks Bill to bring him his briefcase, which is lying on the table in the hotel lounge, but unbeknownst to Bill, the briefcase does not in fact belong to Joe, then no criminal solicitation (for the crime of theft) occurs. Joe may, however, be guilty of an attempted larceny by trying to commit the offense with the use of an innocent instrumentality.

In an unusual case, Donald Winniewicz, 36, of Houston, Pennsylvania, was arrested in 2004 and charged with criminal solicitation to commit homicide after he confessed to playing an audiotape to his sleeping ten-year-old stepson.[67] The audiotape, made by Winniewicz, was an apparent attempt to plant suggestions in the sleeping boy's mind that he should smother his four-year-old sibling with a pillow. Those who listened to the tape reported that they heard Winniewicz saying things like, "Why haven't you done this yet? If you love Grandma, you will do this."[68] The tape, which was discovered by Winniewicz's wife in a drawer in the family's Pittsburgh home, was confiscated by police.

PARTIES TO CRIME

Common law developed a fairly complex scheme of labeling those involved in a crime, known as the **parties to crime**, according to their relationship to the criminal act. It distinguished between those who actually committed the crime and others who assisted the perpetrator either before, during, or after the crime had been committed. Common law categories included (1) **principal in the first degree**—the individual who actually committed the crime; (2) **principal in the second degree**—anyone who was present at the crime scene and who aided, abetted, counseled, or encouraged the principal in the

parties to crime
All those who take part in the commission of a crime, including those who aid and abet and are therefore criminally liable for the offense.

principal in the first degree
A person whose acts directly resulted in the criminal misconduct in question.

principal in the second degree
A person who was present at the crime scene and who aided, abetted, counseled, or encouraged the principal.

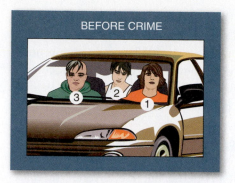

BEFORE CRIME

CRIMINAL 1

ACCESSORY BEFORE THE FACT

Aids in the preparation for a crime. Here Criminal 1 transports other offenders to the scene of the crime.

DURING CRIME

CRIMINAL 2

PRINCIPAL IN THE SECOND DEGREE

Is present at the scene of the crime and aids in the crime itself. Criminal 2 has restrained the victim by binding and gagging.

CRIMINAL 3

PRINCIPAL IN THE FIRST DEGREE

Actually commits the crime itself. Criminal 3 is the participant who performs the act of murder.

AFTER CRIME

CRIMINAL 4

ACCESSORY AFTER THE FACT

Furnishes postcrime assistance. In this case, Criminal 4 provides a hiding place for the offenders and also cleans the murder weapon to prevent detection.

FIGURE 4–4

Parties to Crime Under Common Law.

commission of the crime; (3) **accessory before the fact**—anyone who aided and abetted in the preparation for the crime but was not present at the crime scene; and (4) **accessory after the fact**—anyone who did not participate in the crime but knew that the crime had been committed and furnished postcrime assistance to keep the criminal from being detected or from being arrested (Figure 4–4).

Common law also took note of whether a principal in the second degree assumed a "constructive presence," as in the case of a lookout who stayed outside the building in which a crime was being committed, or an "actual presence," as in the case of a person who more directly assisted in the actual commission of the offense.

Under common law, such distinctions were quite important because an indictment charging a defendant as an accessory would not allow his or her conviction as a principal, and vice versa. Additionally, an accessory could not be tried until the principal was first convicted. Such rules no longer exist in the United States today, and any participant in a crime may be tried and convicted even if the individual who actually committed the crime has not yet been apprehended.

Relationship of Complicity

A trend in modern American law has been to eliminate distinctions between principals and accessories before the fact. Most jurisdictions within the United States, along with the Model Penal Code, no longer distinguish between the principal in the first or second degree or an accessory before the fact. The degree of a person's criminal liability today is rarely dependent on his or her presence or absence at the crime scene, and most jurisdictions draw distinctions only between principals and accessories. They recognize an **accessory** only as one who assists the felon after the crime has been committed.

accessory before the fact
A person who aids and abets in preparation for crime commission, but who was not present at the crime scene.

accessory after the fact
A person who did not participate in a crime but who furnished postcrime assistance to keep the offender from being detected or from being arrested.

accessory
One who knowingly gives assistance to a person who has committed a felony for the purpose of helping that individual avoid apprehension or detection. An accessory is liable for separate, lesser offenses following a crime.

The old common law categories of principal in the first degree, principal in the second degree, and accessory before the fact are now often legislatively combined into our modern understanding of "principal." Federal law, for example, says: "(a) Whoever commits an offense against the United States or aids, abets, counsels, commands, induces or procures its commission, is punishable as a principal. (b) Whoever willfully causes an act to be done which, if directly performed by him or another would be an offense against the United States, is punishable as a principal."[69]

This section of the U.S. Code makes clear the legislative intent to punish as a principal not only one who directly commits an offense, as well as one who "aids, abets, counsels, commands, induces or procures" another to commit an offense, but also anyone who *causes* the doing of an act that, if done by him or her directly, would render that person guilty of an offense against the United States. It removes all doubt that one who puts in motion or assists in the illegal enterprise, and thus causes the commission of an indispensable element of the offense by another agent or instrumentality, is guilty as a principal even though he or she intentionally refrained from the direct act that constituted the completed offense.

Accomplice Liability

accomplice
A person who, with intent to promote or facilitate the commission of a crime, gives assistance or encouragement to the principal. An accomplice is liable as a principal before and during a crime.

complicity
Involvement in crime either as a principal or as an accomplice. The term also refers to the activities of conspirators and may therefore be taken to mean conduct that is intended to encourage or aid another person to commit a crime, to escape, or to avoid prosecution.

accomplice liability
The degree of criminal blameworthiness of one who aids, abets, encourages, or assists another person in the commission of a crime.

Generally, one who assists in the commission of a crime but does not commit the *actus reus* is called an **accomplice**. Unlike a mere accessory, an accomplice is often present or directly aids in the commission of the crime. The relationship between the person who commits the crime and his or her accomplice is one of **complicity**. The principle of **accomplice liability** is based on the notion that any individual who aids, abets, encourages, or assists another person to commit a crime should share in the criminal liability that accrues under law.

Although we often think of an accomplice as playing a central role in the commission of a crime, words alone may be sufficient to establish accomplice liability if the words constitute approval or encouragement and thus further the actions that constitute the offense. Generally, however, mere presence at the scene of the crime is not, by itself, sufficient to render one an accomplice because it would not make sense to charge mere bystanders with a crime. Likewise, one who is present at the scene when a crime is committed and who then flees from the scene cannot, on that basis alone, be charged with an offense. Only if an individual is present at the crime scene for the purpose of approving, encouraging, or assisting in the commission of the crime may the person be charged under the principle of accomplice liability. Furthermore, to be liable as an accomplice, a defendant must (1) know what the criminal is trying to do, (2) intentionally aid or encourage another person to commit a crime, and (3) believe that the aid or encouragement would make the criminal's success likely.[70] For his or her actions to be considered intentional, the defendant must have intended to (1) commit the acts that in fact gave aid or encouragement and (2) bring about the other party's commission of the offense by committing those acts.

As noted in the preceding section, under the law of most jurisdictions today, an accomplice may share in the same charge and punishment as the principal criminal.

Accessory

As previously mentioned, the emphasis in substantive and procedural laws in most American jurisdictions today is to distinguish between those who are involved in crime as principals and those who are involved as accessories. The contemporary concept of a person as an accessory to criminal activity evolved from the common law idea of an accessory after the fact. Hence the crime of being an accessory after the fact remains on the books in most states. Under the laws of most jurisdictions today, one who knowingly gives assistance to a person who has committed a felony for the purpose of helping that individual avoid apprehension or detection is guilty as an accessory. For example, the U.S. Code says: "Whoever, knowing that an offense against the United States has been committed, receives, relieves, comforts or assists the offender in order to hinder or prevent his apprehension, trial or punishment, is an accessory after the fact."[71]

Proving an accessory's guilt requires a showing that (1) a crime has been completed, (2) the defendant knew that the crime had been committed, (3) the defendant knew that the crime was committed by the individual who was being assisted, and (4) the assistance was personally given by the defendant to the individual who committed the crime. A person who is coerced or forced into giving assistance to a criminal offender, however, will not generally be charged as an accessory after the fact because the assistance was given unwillingly. Such would be the case where an innocent bystander is forced to drive a getaway car at gunpoint and is later released.

It is not necessary that an accessory be aware of the precise details of the crime in order to be charged. In one example, a defendant was found guilty as an accessory after the fact in an aggravated assault case for providing assistance to an individual who had attacked a prison guard. Although the accessory knew that an assault had occurred, he did not know that the person who had been assaulted was a prison guard (which, under state law, raised the level of seriousness of the offense and resulted in the accessory receiving a higher sentence). His conviction and sentence were later upheld by an appellate court.[72]

Some states no longer charge people with the offense of accessory after the fact. They have instead codified new crimes of aiding and abetting, aiding a felon, aiding an escape, interference with a police officer, and so on.

Under common law, the failure to report a known crime was considered a **misprision of felony** and was chargeable as such. In most jurisdictions today, however, no such crime exists. To be charged as an accessory after the fact, a defendant must have taken affirmative acts to hinder the felon's arrest or detection. Mere failure to inform authorities of an offender's presence or failure to come forward and provide authorities with suspicions about a person's guilt is not sufficient unless there is a legal duty to inform (as is the case in many jurisdictions with child-protection personnel, physicians, nurses, and other medical personnel who suspect cases of child abuse). A few states, however, have created the statutory crime of compounding a felony. This offense is basically an agreement not to prosecute or inform on one who has committed a crime in return for money or some benefit from the criminal.

misprision of felony
The failure to report a known crime; the concealment of a crime.

The Criminal Liability of Corporations

Can a corporation be a party to a crime? At the early common law the answer was no. In the late 1700s the famous jurist Sir William Blackstone wrote in his *Commentaries* that "a corporation cannot commit treason or felony or other crimes in its corporate capacity, though its members may in their distinct individual capacities."[73] Blackstone reasoned that a corporation could not commit a criminal act: It has no physical body and because it cannot form the necessary *mens rea* required for many serious crimes because it is literally a mindless organization.

The law began changing in the nineteenth century when courts began to recognize corporations as individuals could commit crimes. Legal scholar Jeffrey P. Grogin identified three theories of, or approaches to, corporate criminal liability that have developed in the subsequent years. The first holds corporations liable for the acts of their agents under traditional principal–agent theory that was developed at the common law for contracts and other civil law actions. The second theory holds that corporations should be liable for their policymakers but not liable for the actions of employees generally. The third theory posits that corporations are liable for their agents and employees only when the corporation's policies and practices fail to prevent the commission of a crime.[74]

CRIMINAL LAW IN THE NEWS

Can Corporations Be Convicted of Crimes?

In 2012, the U.S. Department of Justice filed criminal charges against British Petroleum (BP) for the 2010 oil spill in the Gulf of Mexico. To some people, the charges seemed strange. People commit crimes—and serve prison time for them—but can a company? Wouldn't it make more sense to file a civil lawsuit, which would force companies to pay large fines and change harmful policies?

Actually, state and federal governments file criminal charges against corporations all the time, because it has several key advantages, legal experts say. The first advantage comes during evidence gathering. In a civil lawsuit, prosecutors have to contend with the company's right to have an attorney present and make sure the evidence is closely related to the charge. But in a criminal investigation, prosecutors can force employees to testify without a company lawyer and the criminal grand jury has virtually no limits on what it investigates.

The biggest advantage for prosecutors, however, is how the mere threat of a criminal conviction motivates a company to cooperate. A court can't send a convicted company to prison, but it can place it under a judge's supervision for many years, which CEOs would find intolerable. Moreover, a criminal conviction could remove the company from basic activities such as participating in government contracts or holding certain licenses—quickly bringing it to extinction.

Consider the 2002 criminal conviction of Arthur Andersen, the once-prestigious accounting firm. As the certified public accountant (CPA) for the energy company Enron, Arthur Andersen was found guilty of helping destroy documents essential to the government's investigation of Enron. When it was convicted, Arthur Andersen had to surrender its CPA licenses, cutting off its main source of income. Two years later, the Supreme Court overturned the conviction on a technicality, but Arthur Andersen was already out of business.

In most cases, however, prosecutors would rather work with live companies rather than destroy them. In November, 2012, BP agreed to plead guilty to 14 criminal counts, including manslaughter, and accepted a criminal fine of $4 billion, payable over five years--the largest criminal fine in U.S. history.

Murder and Manslaughter

Corporations can even be charged with murder and manslaughter for the deaths of people victimized by company actions. Using murder and manslaughter charges, several state attorneys general have gone after corporations in high-profile cases that captured public outrage.

Oil spill workers collect tainted debris and dark patches of oil along the beach on June 10, 2010, at Perdido Pass, Alabama, following the blowout of a well owned by British Petroleum in the Gulf of Mexico. Under what legal theory can a corporation be held criminally responsible?

AP Photo/Sun Herald, Drew Tarter

In 2006, a woman driving through a traffic tunnel in Boston was killed when 26 tons of concrete panels fell on her car. It turned out that the panels had been glued to the tunnel ceiling with the wrong type of epoxy as part of the city's Big Dig project. New York–based Powers Fasteners, which provided the glue, was charged with manslaughter. The company agreed to pay $16 million in exchange for dropping the criminal charge. In comparison, the criminal charge would have yielded a $1,000 maximum fine, but the stigma would have harmed the company's ability to do business.

If company policies led to a person's death, company officials can be found guilty of murder even when they did not personally kill anyone. In 1983, an employee of Film Recovery Systems died from cyanide poisoning at the company's silver reclamation plant in Elk Grove Village, Illinois. The company's employees, mostly immigrants who did not understand warnings stated in English, had no idea of the deadly conditions. Three top corporate officers were convicted of second-degree murder and sentenced to 25 years each in prison. The company went bankrupt.

Resources

"Criminal Charges Are Prepared in BP Spill," *Wall Street Journal*, December 29, 2011,
http://online.wsj.com/article/SB1000142405297020389950457712687159162457 2.html.

"Can a Company Be Charged with a Crime?" *Slate*, August 12, 2002,
http://www.slate.com/articles/news_and_politics/explainer/2002/04/can_a_company_be_charged_with_a_crime.html.

"Corporations Can Kill Too: After Film Recovery, Are Individuals Accountable for Corporate Crimes?" *Digital Commons—Loyola of Los Angeles Law Review*, June 1, 1986 (pdf),
http://tinyurl.com/7ngoxxm.

Corporate criminal liability has evolved to include all types of offenses, including traditional crimes against the person such as battery and murder. In a landmark Illinois case in the early 1980s, three corporations and five corporate officers were convicted of murdering an employee who died as a result of unsafe working conditions.[75] In 1981, New York courts held that corporations can be held criminally liable for manslaughter, although in the specific case before the courts no liability was found.[76] In a 2007 case, Massachusetts prosecutors charged Powers Fasteners, a Brewster, New York–based company, with manslaughter in the collapse of concrete ceiling panels in Boston's Big Dig tunnel construction project after one of the panels fell on a car, crushing it and killing a passenger in the vehicle.[77] The company, said prosecutors, was criminally negligent in the tunnel collapse. In 2008, however, prosecutors dropped criminal charges against the company after it agreed to pay $16 million to settle a civil suit stemming from the incident.[78] Powers Fasteners also agreed to take steps to prevent future use of the wrong type of epoxy by its customers.

Although the principle that a company can be prosecuted for a criminal offense is generally well accepted, the question of whether a particular statute imposes such liability is rarely, if ever, spelled out. Although some criminal statutes explicitly state that corporations can be treated, for purposes of the law, as people, others are less clear. Hence, in this still-emerging area of the criminal law, it is often up to the courts to decide whether a company can be held criminally liable for violation of a particular statute.[79]

The Model Penal Code provides that a corporation may be held criminally liable if any of the following conditions are met:[80]

1. The offense is a minor offense, and the conduct was performed by an agent acting on the corporation's behalf within the scope of the agent's employment.

2. The offense is defined by another statute and is made applicable to corporations.

3. The offense consists of a failure to perform a specific duty imposed on the corporation by law, such as failing to file a tax return.

4. The criminal acts were approved, authorized, permitted, or recklessly tolerated by the board of directors or a high management official acting on behalf of the corporation and within the scope of his or her employment.

Some U.S. jurisdictions take the approach that a corporation may be held criminally liable for crimes committed by any employee who has been given the power and duty, or responsibility and authority, to act on behalf of the corporation. This approach is based on the belief that it should be incumbent on boards of directors and high management officials to be sufficiently informed so as not to condone criminal misconduct on behalf of the corporation.

Courts have adopted a number of doctrines that enlarge the scope of corporate liability for employee misconduct. One of the most significant, the collective knowledge doctrine, imputes to a corporation the knowledge of all employees, thereby imposing liability on companies even when no single employee has sufficient knowledge to be liable.[81] As some authors have observed,[82] the court in the prosecution of Arthur Andersen seemed to go even one step further, creating a kind of collective corporate liability by instructing the jury that it could convict Andersen without agreeing on which employee committed the crime. Another doctrine adopted by the courts is the *willful blindness doctrine*, under which criminal liability can accrue where a corporation deliberately disregards criminal misconduct.[83]

Enactment of the federal Sarbanes-Oxley Act in 2002 (officially known as the Public Company Accounting Reform and Investor Protection Act)[84] created the potential for high fines and other criminal sanctions. Corporations can also be placed on probation, resulting in close government scrutiny of their activities during the probationary period.

In the not-too-distant past, corporate officers and business managers had only limited legal ability to effectively protect their companies. Until recently, federal law made no provision for leniency in cases in which corporations reported wrongdoing by their employees, and managers could not effectively reduce corporate liability either by attempting to prevent crime or by reporting it to the government once it had been detected within the company. Today, however, official U.S. Department of Justice policy encourages federal prosecutors not to indict a corporation for employee wrongdoing if the corporation had in place an effective program to deter wrongdoing at the time the crimes were committed or if it reported detected wrongdoing to the government and cooperated fully in further investigations.[85] Moreover, new federal sentencing guidelines, enacted in 2003, protect businesses that have established effective compliance and ethics programs for their employees.[86]

Some of the better-known recent cases in which corporations have been held criminally liable include the 2002 federal conviction of accounting firm Arthur Andersen on obstruction-of-justice charges after its employees shredded documents related to the bankruptcy of Enron Corporation; Ford Motor Corporation's conviction in 1978 on three counts of reckless homicide in the deaths of three teenage girls in a Ford Pinto whose gas tank exploded in a crash; Exxon Corporation's agreement to pay $100 million in criminal fines (and more than $1 billion in civil damages) in charges stemming from the 1989 *Exxon Valdez* oil spill in Alaska; General Electric Corporation's 1990 conviction on charges of defrauding the U.S. Army;[87] and a $20,000 fine paid by a Wisconsin corporation after it was found guilty of two counts of reckless homicide in the misreading of Pap smears that led to the deaths of two women in 1996.[88]

Vicarious Liability

vicarious liability
The criminal liability of one party for the criminal acts of another party.

Vicarious liability imposes criminal liability on one party for the criminal acts of another party. Corporate liability, which you just learned about, is a form of vicarious liability because through the doctrine, a corporation or its officers may be criminally liable for the conduct of its employees. Vicarious liability is not limited to corporate settings. An automobile owner may be criminally liable for the acts of an individual to whom she lends her automobile, and parents are sometimes liable for the actions of their children. So, for example, a person who loans a vehicle to an individual who parks it in a fire zone may be responsible for paying the fine associated with the illegal parking.

Those who advocate holding offenders responsible under the concept of vicarious liability argue that doing so is necessary for the effective enforcement of important regulatory schemes, such as pure food and drug regulations, child labor laws, alcoholic beverage control laws, and so on. Those who oppose the concept of vicarious liability argue that it is inconsistent with the basic principles of criminal law and that individuals should only be held accountable when they are clearly and morally blameworthy.

It is, however, important to distinguish between accomplice liability and vicarious liability. Accomplice liability is based on affirmative participation in a crime, whereas vicarious liability is based solely on a recognizable relationship between the defendant and the perpetrator. Hence, as in the previous example, vicarious liability may be imposed when the defendant is made legally accountable by statute for the crimes committed by others, even though he or she lacked any knowledge of the crime's commission.[89]

Most states require that before vicarious liability may be imposed on an individual, the individual must have control over the perpetrator. In those states, accordingly, vicarious liability is limited to employer–employee relationships and similar situations.[90] Precedent appears to limit vicarious liability to situations in which the potential for punishment is not extreme. This "punishment limitation" is based on the fact that, although there are social interests in imposing some degree of vicarious liability, anyone who lacks knowledge of an offense should not be too severely punished because of it, even when technically liable for its prevention.[91]

Although strict liability and vicarious liability are both forms of liability without fault, they dispense with the fault requirement in entirely different ways. Strict liability is imposed in situations in which the *mens rea* requirement has been eliminated. Vicarious liability, on the other hand, may be imposed in situations in which the act requirement has been eliminated.

Punishing the Vicariously Liable   Persons who are vicariously liable may be punished in the same manner and to the same extent as the individual who committed the act leading to liability. As you learned in this chapter, this can include, although rare, prison sentences for murder and manslaughter. Corporations are different. Although a corporation can be convicted of committing virtually any crime, it cannot be imprisoned. But a corporation can be fined, ordered to pay restitution, and ordered to do or not do something (e.g., return stocks or securities to defrauded customers), and its officers can be dismissed and its license to operate can be disciplined. Although it is common for there to be a public outcry for harsh punishments of corporations, it must be remembered that corporations are more than abstract, faceless entities. They employ and serve people, often innocent of the crimes that corporations have committed, and often provide needed services. Revoking a license to operate or fines so large as to cause a business to fail can result in a serious loss of jobs and the loss of a needed service in the community.

SUMMARY

- Inchoate offenses are incipient crimes that generally lead to other crimes. *Inchoate* means imperfect, partial, or unfinished. Inchoate crimes include (1) attempts, (2) conspiracies, and (3) solicitation.

- Almost any crime that can be envisioned can be attempted, and under the penal codes of most states, any crime defined by statute has as its adjunct an attempt to commit that crime.

- To constitute an attempt, an act of some sort is necessary. Mere preparation to commit an offense is not sufficient to support a charge of attempted criminal activity.

- The crime of attempt is a specific-intent crime. It has two elements: (1) the specific intent to commit a criminal offense and (2) a substantial step toward the commission of the intended offense.

- In most jurisdictions, anyone charged with an attempt may raise the defenses of abandonment and impossibility. Virtually all jurisdictions require that the abandonment be voluntary. The defense does not affect the criminal liability of an accomplice who does not join in the abandonment.

- Impossibility may be of either the factual or legal variety. Factual impossibility, which is rarely useful as a defense, means that a person could not commit the envisioned offense even if he or she were successful in the attempt. Legal impossibility means that the attempted offense is really no offense at all, perhaps because there is no law against the imagined crime, or because the actions in question do not meet the requirements of the law for a crime to have occurred. Legal impossibility generally precludes prosecution in most jurisdictions.

- Under common law, all attempts were punishable as misdemeanors. Today, punishments for attempts are usually based on the punishments specified for the intended offense. Many state statutes assign a lesser degree of punishment for attempts than for the intended crime. Except for crimes punishable by life imprisonment or death, the Model Penal Code provides the same punishment for attempts as for the crimes attempted.

- The common law crime of conspiracy is an agreement between two or more people to commit an unlawful act or a lawful act by unlawful means. Under common law, conspiracy was a misdemeanor. However, in most states today, and under federal jurisdiction, conspiracy is classified as a felony.

- The elements of the crime of conspiracy are (1) an agreement between two or more people; (2) the intention to carry out an act that is unlawful, or a lawful act that is to be accomplished by unlawful means; and (3) a culpable intent on the part of the defendants.

- For people to be charged with a conspiracy, it is not necessary that each party form an agreement with all other parties involved in the conspiracy. In complex conspiracies, the parties may not know one another and may not even be aware of what other parties are involved. This is particularly true in cases involving organized crime.

- Under common law, criminal solicitation occurs when one asks or encourages another to perform a criminal act. Criminal solicitation, unlike conspiracy, requires no overt act. The required mental state is one in which the defendant must have intended to induce the other person to perform the crime. In addition, a successful prosecution must establish that the defendant possessed the mental state required for the completed crime.

- Under common law, a fairly complex scheme was developed for labeling those involved in a felony according to their relationship to the criminal act. Offenders could be classified as (1) a principal in the first degree, (2) a principal in the second degree, (3) an accessory before the fact, or (4) an accessory after the fact.

- States have abolished the distinction between a principal in the second degree and an accessory before the fact. The degree of an offender's criminal liability is today assessed independently of the individual's presence or absence at the crime scene. Generally, one who assists in the commission of a crime but does not commit the *actus reus* is considered to be an accomplice. The individual who commits the actual crime is considered to be the principal.

- To be held guilty as an accomplice, a defendant must have intentionally aided or encouraged another person to commit a crime. "Intentionally," in this instance, means that (1) the defendant must have intended to commit the acts that in fact gave aid or encouragement; and (2) by committing those acts, the defendant must have intended to bring about the other party's commission of the offense.

- Someone who knowingly gives assistance to a person who has committed a felony for the purposes of helping that individual avoid apprehension or detection is guilty as an accessory after the fact.

KEY TERMS

abandonment, 100

accessory, 111

accessory after the
    fact, 111

accessory before the
    fact, 111

accomplice, 112

accomplice liability, 112

co-conspirator hearsay
    rule, 108

complicity, 112

criminal conspiracy, 103

criminal solicitation, 109

dangerous proximity
    test, 98

hearsay, 103

impossibility, 101

inchoate crime, 91

last-act test, 98

mere preparation, 92

misprision of felony, 113

parties to crime, 110

physical proximity test, 98

Pinkerton's rule, 108

plurality
    requirement, 105

principal in the first
    degree, 110

principal in the
    second degree, 110

substantial step, 92

vicarious liability, 116

Wharton's rule, 106

QUESTIONS FOR DISCUSSION

1. Why is it necessary to require a "substantial step" before mere plans become a criminal attempt?

2. Why are courts hesitant to punish a person for "evil thoughts" alone?

3. What is the difference between conspiracy and criminal solicitation?

4. Why is it easier for prosecutors to build a case when they are not required to establish whether the defendant is a principal in the first degree, a principal in the second degree, or an accomplice?

5. When is a corporation liable for the acts of its officers?

6. Under the statutes of many states, a bar owner is criminally liable when an employee-bartender sells liquor to juveniles. What if the bar owner instructs the bartender not to sell liquor to juveniles, but the bartender disregards those instructions and sells to juveniles anyway? Should the owner then be held criminally liable? Why or why not?

7. Should vicarious criminal liability exist? What are the implications of holding a corporation liable for the actions of its employees? What about holding parents responsible for the actions of their children? Who benefits from such liability, and who can be harmed by it?

CRITICAL THINKING AND APPLICATIONS PROBLEMS

Narcissa, Carolyn, and Henry are drinking in a bar. All three were laid off from their jobs as bank tellers at 4EverSafe Bank three months earlier. They remain unemployed in spite of serious efforts by all three to find employment. Unhappy, broke, and drunk, the discussion turns to quick ways to make money. Narcissa comments, "We should rob 4EverSafe. We know how to do it." Carolyn responds, "Really. 4 o'clock is the right time, right before the money is moved into the vault and the guards are transitioning." Henry nods and says, "That is the right time," and waves to the server to bring him another beer. The conversation about this subject continued for 15 minutes. During that time, they discussed the timing, point of entry, how they would disguise themselves, and where they would hide the stolen money. An hour later they all went their separate ways. The next day Narcissa called Carolyn and asked her to go with her to the store to purchase the disguises they had discussed in the bar, which they did.

While at the store, they decided that they would also need weapons for the robbery, so they each applied for a handgun license. They picked up the handguns together two days later after the background checks were completed. That evening, they met at Narcissa's home to further discuss the plans and texted the following message to Henry from Carolyn's phone: 2moro is the day in re money plan. B @ location at 3:50. Nrssa & Crlyn. On her way home after leaving Narcissa's, Carolyn was stopped by a police officer for speeding. He observed the mask, the new handgun, and a bag in the back seat of her car. He arrested her for the traffic violation and obtained a search warrant to seize the items in the back seat and to search through her phone. After reading the text sent to Henry, the officer concluded that she was a member of a conspiracy to commit a robbery. After consulting with an attorney, Carolyn agreed to confess in exchange for a reduced charge. The next day, Narcissa arrived at the bank at the appointed time. Undeterred by the absence of Henry and Carolyn, she donned her mask, put the gun in her purse, and entered the bank, only to be surprised by the police. She was arrested, and all three—Narcissa, Carolyn, and Henry—were charged with attempted bank robbery and conspiracy to commit a robbery.

1. Applying the mere-preparation test for attempt, has Narcissa committed attempted robbery/conspiracy to rob? Has Carolyn? Has Henry?

2. Applying the overt-act test for attempt, has Narcissa committed attempted robbery/conspiracy to rob? Has Carolyn? Has Henry?

3. Applying the substantial test for attempt, has Narcissa committed attempted robbery/conspiracy to rob? Has Carolyn? Has Henry?

LEGAL RESOURCES ON THE WEB

A variety of law-related associations, such as the American Bar Association and the National Lawyers Association, can be reached via the World Wide Web. Following are some associations of interest to students of criminal law:

American Association for Justice
http://www.justice.org

The largest national association of attorneys involved in criminal defense and personal injury litigation.

American Bar Association (ABA)
http://www.abanet.org

The largest and most influential national association of attorneys. Information about the positions taken by the association and model rules of ethics are available at this site.

American Bar Association's Criminal Justice Section
http://www.abanet.org/crimjust/home.html

The mission of the ABA's Criminal Justice Section is to improve the criminal justice system. The site offers publications and press releases.

National Association of Criminal Defense Lawyers (NACDL)
http://www.criminaljustice.org

NACDL promotes the mission of the nation's criminal defense lawyers in an effort to ensure justice and due process for persons accused of crimes or other misconduct.

National District Attorneys Association (NDAA)
http://www.ndaa.org

A national organization of local prosecutors that offers members the opportunity to network with fellow prosecutors throughout the nation to enhance their knowledge and skills.

National Lawyers Association (NLA)
http://www.nla.org

A national bar association organized to improve the image of the legal profession, to advance legal institutions and respect for the law, and to educate the public on such matters.

National Legal Aid and Defender Association (NLADA)
http://www.nlada.org

A professional membership organization of sentencing advocates and defense-based mitigation specialists.

SUGGESTED READINGS AND CLASSIC WORKS

Arnold, Thurmon. "Criminal Attempts: The Rise and Fall of an Abstraction." *Yale Law Journal* 90 (1930): 53.

Ashworth, Andrew. "Criminal Attempts and the Role of Resulting Harm under the Code and the Common Law." *Rutgers Law Journal* 19 (1988): 725.

Curran, John W. "Solicitation: A Substantive Crime." *Minnesota Law Review* 17 (1933): 499.

Duff, Robert A. "The Circumstances of an Attempt." *Cambridge Law Journal* 50 (1991): 100.

Johnson, Phillip E. "The Unnecessary Crime of Conspiracy." *California Law Review* 61 (1973): 1137.

Kadish, Sanford H. "Complicity, Cause and Blame." *California Law Review* 73 (1985): 323.

Moriarty, David. "Extending the Defense of Renunciation." *Temple Law Review* 62 (1989): 1.

Syre, Francis B. "Criminal Conspiracy." *Harvard Law Review* 35 (1922): 393.

NOTES

1. *United States* v. *Davis*, 8 F.3d 923 (2d Cir. 1993).
2. Joseph R. Nolan and Jacqueline M. Nolan-Haley, *Black's Law Dictionary: Definitions of the Terms and Phrases of American and English Jurisprudence, Ancient and Modern*, 6th ed. (St. Paul: West, 1990), 761.
3. Jerome Hall, *General Principles of Criminal Law*, 2nd ed. (Charlottesville, VA: Michie, 1960).
4. Joshua Dressler, *Understanding Criminal Law*, 2nd Ed. (Boston: Matthew Bender, 1995), 351.
5. Ibid.
6. Ibid., p. 347.
7. Stanford H. Kadish and Stephen J. Schulhofer, *Criminal Law and Its Processes*, 6th ed. (Boston: Little, Brown, 1995), 581.
8. New York Penal Law, Section 110.0.
9. California Penal Code, Section 664.
10. Illinois Annotated Statutes, Chapter 38, Section 8–4.
11. See *United States* v. *Mandujano*, 499 F.2d 370, 376 (5th Cir. 1974), cert. denied, 419 U.S. 1114, 95 S. Ct. 792, 42 L. Ed. 2d 812 (1975).
12. Model Penal Code, Section 5.01(2).
13. Florida Penal Code, Chapter 777, Section 4, paragraph 1.
14. Model Penal Code, Section 5.01(2).
15. Alaska Statutes, Section 11.31.100.
16. Texas Penal Code, Title 5, Chapter 22, Section 8.
17. Derek Humphry, *Final Exit* (New York: Dell, 1992).
18. Model Penal Code, Section 5.01(2).
19. *Mims* v. *United States*, 373 F.2d 135, 148 (5th Cir. 1967).
20. *People* v. *Rizzo*, 246 N.Y. 334, 158 N.E. 888 (1927).
21. *Commonwealth* v. *Peaslee*, 177 Mass. 267, 59 N.E. 55 (Sup. Judicial Ct. of Mass. 1901).
22. *People* v. *Rizzo*, 246 N.Y. 334, 158 N.E. 888 (1927).
23. *Commonwealth* v. *Peaslee*, 177 Mass. 267, 59 N.E. 55 (Sup. Judicial Ct. of Mass. 1901).
24. *Regina* v. *Eagleton*, 6 Cox Criminal Cases 559 (Eng. 1855).
25. Ibid.
26. *Commonwealth* v. *Kelly*, 58 A.2d 375 (Pa. Super. Ct. 1948).
27. Ibid., 377.

28. *People* v. *Rizzo*, 246 N.Y. 334, 158 N.E. 888 (1927).

29. *King* v. *Barker*, 1924 N.Z.L.R. 865 (N.Z. 1924).

30. Model Penal Code, Sections 5.01(2)(a) through (g).

31. Note that this example would overrule the case of *People v. Rizzo* discussed earlier.

32. *United States* v. *Berrigan*, 482 F.2d 171 (3d Cir. 1973).

33. Indiana Code, Title 35, Article 41, Chapter 3, Section 10.

34. Florida Penal Code, Chapter 777, Section 4, paragraph 5.

35. Model Penal Code, Section 5.01(4).

36. See, for example, *People v. Dlugash*, 363 N.E.2d 1155 (N.Y. 1977).

37. H. L. A. Hart, *Punishment and Responsibility* (London: Oxford University Press, 1968), 130.

38. Model Penal Code and Commentaries, Comment to Section 5.05 at 490 (1985).

39. *United States* v. *Recio*, 537 U.S. 270 (2003); and *Salings* v. *United States*, 522 U.S. 52, 65 (1997).

40. Paul Marcus, "Criminal Conspiracy Law: Time to Turn Back from an Ever Expanding, Ever More Troubling Area," *Bill of Rights Journal* 1 (1992): 8–11.

41. *United States* v. *Casamento*, 887 F.2d 1141 (2d Cir. 1989).

42. *United States* v. *Ianniello*, 866 F.2d 540 (2d Cir. 1989).

43. *United States* v. *Kopituk*, 690 F.2d 1289 (11th Cir. 1982).

44. *United States* v. *Martino*, 648 F.2d 367 (5th Cir. 1981).

45. Dressler, *Understanding Criminal Law*, 393.

46. *Harrison* v. *United States*, 7 F.259 (2d Cir. 1925).

47. *Shaw* v. *Director of Public Prosecutions*, A.C. 220 at p. 294 (1962).

48. *United States* v. *Stone, et al.*, Order Granting Defendants' Motions for Judgment of Acquittal on Counts 1–7, U.S. Dist. E.D. Mich., Case No. 10–20123, March 27, 2012. See also Robert Snell and Christine Ferretti, "7 Hutaree Acquitted of Most Serious Charges," *The Detroit News*, March 27, 2012, http://detroitnews.com/article/20120327/METRO/203270433/.../7-Hutaree-acquitted-most-serious-charges.

49. *United States* v. *James*, 528 F.2d 999 (5th Cir. 1976).

50. *Gebardi* v. *United States*, 287 U.S. 112 (1932).

51. *Iannelli* v. *United States*, 420 U.S. 770 (1975).

52. Model Penal Code, Section 1.07(1)(b).

53. See *United States* v. *Boyd*, 149 F.3d 1062, 1067 (10th Cir. 1998); and *U.S.* v. *Rahseparian*, 231 F.3d 1257 (10th Cir. 2000).

54. *United States* v. *Klein*, 515 F.2d 751, 753 (3d Cir. 1975).

55. See, e.g., *United States* v. *Austin*, 786 F.2d 986, 988 (10th Cir. 1986).

56. See ibid., at 988.

57. *People* v. *Powell*, 63 N.Y. 88 (1875).

58. *Anderson* v. *Superior Court*, 177 P.2d 315 (Cal. Super. Ct. 1947).

59. Model Penal Code, §5.03(5)

60. *United States* v. *Pinkerton*, 328 U.S. 640 (1946).

61. Model Penal Code, Section 5.03(6).

62. *United States* v. *Recio*, 537 U.S. 270 (2003).

63. This problem is an adaptation of a hypothetical point made by Kent Greenawalt in "Speech and Crime," *American Bar Foundation Research Journal* (1980): 662.

64. Florida Penal Code, Chapter 777, Section 4, paragraph 2.

65. *People* v. *Quentin*, 296 N.Y.S.2d 443 (Sup. Ct. 1968).

66. Model Penal Code, Section 5.02(2).

67. "Stepfather Accused of Fratricide Plot," *USA Today*, January 23, 2004.

68. Stu Brown, "Winniewicz Ordered to Stand Trial," WPXI.com, January 28, 2004, http://v.i.v.free.fr/image/nv-subliminal-28–01–2004.html (accessed November 2, 2004).

69. U.S. Code, Title 18, Section 2.

70. *United States* v. *Ortega*, 44 F.3d 505 (7th Cir. 1995).

71. U.S. Code, Title 18, Section 3.

72. *United States* v. *Hobson*, 519 F.2d 765 (9th Cir. 1975).

73. Sir William Blackstone, *Commentaries on the Law of England* (Oxford, England: Clarendon Press, 1765–69), chap. 18, sec. 12.

74. Jefrey P. Grogin, "Corporations Can Kill Too: After Film Recovery, Are Individuals Accountable for Corporate Crimes," *Loyola of Los Angeles Law Review* 19 (1986): 1411, 1413–1414, http://digitalcommons.lmu.edu/llr/vol19/iss4/12.

75. Id, discussing *People* v. *Film Recovery Systems*.

76. *People* v. *Warner-Lambert Co.*, 51 N.Y.2d 295, 414 N.E.2d 660 (1980), cert. den., 450 U.S. 1031(1981). The absence of a foreseeability of the accident that resulted in the employee's death was the reason no liability was found.

77. Elizabeth M. Taurasi, "Big Dig Epoxy Provider Pleads Not Guilty to Involuntary Manslaughter," *Design News*, September 5, 2007, http://www.designnews.com/article/1304-Big_Dig_Epoxy_Provider_Pleads_ Not_Guilty_to_Involuntary_Manslaughter.php (accessed December 3, 2008).

78. "Company Pays Millions in Big Dig Settlement," *Palm Beach Post*, December 18, 2008.

79. Ibid.

80. Model Penal Code, Section 2.07.

81. See *United States* v. *Bank of New England, N.A.*, 821 F.2d 844, 856 (1st Cir. 1987).

82. Taylor and Coie, "Shelter from the Storm," citing Seth C. Farber and Melanie R. Moss, "Cooperating with the Government in Corporate Criminal Investigations: Has Andersen Changed the Landscape?" *Criminal Litigation Newsletter* (winter 2002–2003): 3–10.

83. See *United States* v. *Bank of New England, N.A.*, 821 F.2d 844, 856 (1st Cir. 1987).

84. Pub. L. 107–204, 116 Stat. 745 (July 30, 2002).

85. Jennifer Arlen and Reinier Kraakman, "Controlling Corporate Misconduct: An Analysis of Corporate Liability Regimes," *New York University Law Review* 72 (1997): 687, 702.

86. Federal guidelines for the sentencing of organizations and businesses are set out in the *U.S. Sentencing Guidelines Manual*, §§ 8A 1.1–8E1.3. The guidelines are used by federal judges to determine appropriate sentences for businesses and other organizations that have been convicted of crimes.

87. Project on Government Oversight, *Defense and Health Care Industries: Rather Than Clean Up Their Act, They Attack the Act* (Washington, DC: Author, February 1997).

88. See James A. Filkins, "With No Evil Intent: The Criminal Prosecution of Physicians for Medical Negligence," *Journal of Legal Medicine* 22, no. 4 (October 2001): 467–99.

89. *United States* v. *Dotterweich*, 320 U.S. 277 (1943).

90. *People* v. *Forbath*, 5 Cal. App. 2d 767 (1935).

91. *Commonwealth* v. *Koczwara*, 155 A.2d 825 (Pa. 1959).

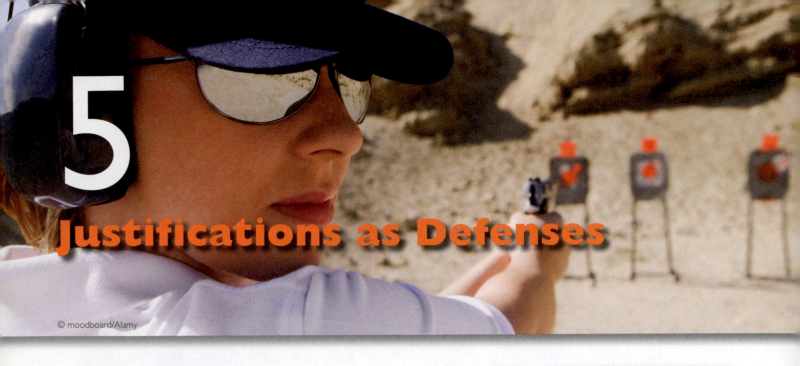

© moodboard/Alamy

5
Justifications as Defenses

CHAPTER OUTLINE

Introduction

Types of Defenses

The Nature of Defenses

Justification as a Defense

OBJECTIVES

After reading this chapter, you should be able to

- Explain the purpose of a defense to a criminal charge, and distinguish between factual and legal defenses.
- Explain the nature of affirmative defenses.
- Distinguish between justifications and excuses.
- Describe the necessity defense.
- Summarize the use of force and deadly force in self-defense.
- Explain the execution-of-public-duty defense, and describe when and by whom it might be used.

> If someone comes to kill you, rise up and kill him first.
>
> —The Talmud, Sanhedrin 72a
>
> The end must justify the means.
>
> —Matthew Prior (1664–1721)
>
> Men use thought only to justify their wrongdoings.
>
> —Voltaire (1694–1778)

INTRODUCTION

On February 26, 2012, in Sanford, Florida, 17-year-old Treyvon Martin was shot and killed by George Zimmerman, a 28-year-old community watch coordinator, during what appears to have been a struggle between the two men. Zimmerman told police that he shot Martin in self-defense. Initially, the prosecutor who reviewed the case decided that the shooting was justified, but Zimmerman was later arrested amidst public outcry and charged with second-degree murder by a special prosecutor appointed by Florida's governor.[1]

The night of the shooting, Martin was visiting with his father and his father's fiancée at her home. They had been watching a sporting event on TV, and Martin left the home to walk to a convenience store. Zimmerman saw Martin walking through his neighborhood during the young man's return from the store, thought him suspicious, followed him, called the police, apparently ignored a suggestion to discontinue the pursuit by the police dispatcher, and ultimately confronted and fatally shot Martin. What happened at the time of the confrontation has yet to be determined as this book goes to press. Some news accounts reported that Zimmerman claimed Martin had knocked him down and banged his head against the ground. Photos taken immediately after the incident appear to show a bleeding wound on Zimmerman's head, and a battered nose.

Claims that Zimmerman, who is Hispanic, was motivated to follow Martin because he was African American contributed to making the incident a national cause célèbre. The media frenzy and rush to judgment was fast and furious. Protests calling for Zimmerman's arrest, and in some instances immediate punishment, sprang up around the nation in the weeks following the shooting.

At the time of this writing, Zimmerman has not been tried. He is expected to assert self-defense, a defense that has a stronger foundation in law in Florida than in some states because Florida employs what has become popularly known as a "stand-your-ground" law. Stand-your-ground laws empower individuals to use deadly force to resist life-threatening or limb-threatening attacks without having to first retreat. Central to Zimmerman's defense will be the injuries he allegedly received from Martin. The cause of his suspicion and his apparent decision to ignore the suggestion of the dispatcher not to pursue Martin will also be important. To fully explain his decisions on that evening, Zimmerman's attorney will likely paint a picture of the history of the neighborhood for the jury. Hard hit by the economic recession, property values had declined considerably and there had been a rash of burglaries, break-ins, and other problems. The residents of the community came to rely on Zimmerman

George Zimmerman, the Florida neighborhood watch volunteer who killed Treyvon Martin in 2012. Although he was not arrested immediately following the shooting, he was later charged with second-degree murder amidst an organized outpouring of social protest. What kind of defense might Zimmerman use?

EPA/Gary W. Green/POOL/Newscom

for security and support. Local police recommended the creation of a neighborhood watch, and in response to a problem with a vicious dog, authorities recommended that Zimmerman buy a gun. Zimmerman bought his gun, the community created a neighborhood watch, and Zimmerman was asked to be the watch coordinator. Acting in this role, Zimmerman had called the police on many occasions before the night of the shooting. One source credits him with catching at least one thief who was ultimately arrested by police. Whether race was a factor in Zimmerman's decision to follow and confront Martin will likely be an issue at trial. An investigation of Zimmerman's life by Reuters News revealed a complex man who was reared in a multi-ethnic household, who respected the boundaries between police and citizens during his time as watch coordinator, but who was frustrated by the lack of success the authorities had in addressing the growing crime problem in his neighborhood.[2]

TYPES OF DEFENSES

defense
Evidence and arguments offered by a defendant and his or her attorney(s) to show why that person should not be held liable for a criminal charge.

A **defense** consists of evidence and arguments offered by a defendant and his or her attorney(s) to show why that person should not be held liable for a criminal charge. Generally, there are two types of defenses, *factual* and *legal* (Figure 5–1). A factual defense is one in which the defendant simply asserts that he or she didn't do it. Alibi (when a defendant claims not to have been present at the location of the crime) is an example of a factual defense. In some cases, even when a defendant *has* committed the illegal act in question, legal defenses available through the court can have a significant effect on disposition of the case (that is, they can be *dispositive*). It is therefore possible for a defendant to have committed the crime but face no legal liability.

justification
A type of legal defense in which the defendant admits to committing the act in question but claims it was necessary in order to avoid some greater evil.

Two forms of legal defense are **justifications**, in which the defendant admits to committing the act in question but claims it was necessary in order to avoid some greater evil, and **excuses**, in which the defendant claims that some personal condition or circumstance at the time of the act was such that he or she should not be held accountable under the criminal law. This chapter concerns itself with justifications; the chapter that follows examines excuses.

excuse
A type of legal defense in which the defendant claims that some personal condition or circumstance at the time of the act was such that he or she should not be held accountable under the criminal law.

As the well-known jurist Jerome Hall says, "'Justification' and 'excuse' are very old concepts. Indeed these words have long been parts of everyday speech; Anglo-American law has used them for centuries. . . . What is common to both concepts is that an injury or damage has been caused by a human being. The difference is that in the former, the actor did the right thing in the circumstances, e.g., he defended himself against an assailant or destroyed property to save life; while in 'excuse' the rectitude of the actor or his action is

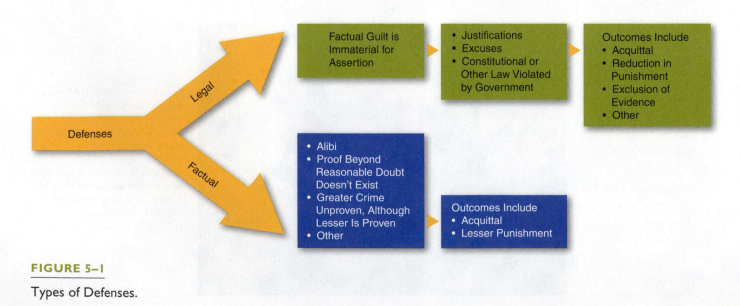

FIGURE 5–1

Types of Defenses.

simply irrelevant. What is relevant in excuse, i.e., relevant to penal law, is that for reasons either of incapacity or of extreme pressure, such as the threat of immediate death, the actor should not be held criminally liable; instead he is excused."[3]

Another author explains the difference between justification and excuse this way: "A justified actor engages in conduct that is not culpable because its benefits outweigh the harm or evil of the offense; an excused actor admits the harm or evil but nonetheless claims an absence of personal culpability."[4]

Generally speaking, conduct that a person believes is necessary to avoid a harm or evil to himself or herself, or to avoid harm to another, is justifiable if the harm or evil to be avoided is greater than that which the law defining the offense seeks to avoid. Hence justifications may apply when people find themselves facing a choice between a "lesser of two evils." The correct choice will, of course, be the morally correct one. The "right choice" may then reduce or eliminate criminal liability for the act in question. A frequently used example is that of firefighters who set a controlled fire in order to create a firebreak to head off a conflagration threatening a community. Whereas intentionally setting a fire may constitute arson, doing so to save a town may be justifiable behavior in the eyes of the community *and* in the eyes of the law.

An excuse, in contrast, does not claim that the conduct in question was justified but that the actor who engaged in it was, at the time, not legally responsible for his or her actions. So, for example, a person who assaults a police officer thinking that the officer is really a disguised "space alien" who has come to abduct him may be found not guilty of the charge of assault by reason of insanity.

As we begin our discussion of justifications and excuses, it is important to realize that not all states have codified defenses, and those that have them do not necessarily address all of the defenses that are discussed here. As the Model Penal Code (MPC) explains, "The main aim of a criminal code is to differentiate conduct that warrants criminal sanctions from conduct that does not. If it is clear that conduct will not be subject to criminal sanctions, the effort to establish precisely in each case whether that conduct is actually justified or only excused does not seem worthwhile."[5]

> *He who excuses himself accuses himself.*
>
> —*William Shakespeare,* King John

THE NATURE OF DEFENSES

Justifications and excuses are **affirmative defenses**; that is, they must be raised or asserted by the defendant independently of any claims made by the prosecutor. This is a variance from the general rule that places the burden of production and persuasion on the government. For affirmative defenses, defendants bear the burden of production; that is, they must assert the defense at the time required by law. Failure to raise an affirmative defense in a timely manner acts as a waiver of the defense. States vary concerning the burden of persuasion placed on the defendant. Some require the defendant to prove the defense; others shift the burden to the prosecution to disprove the defense.

A successfully raised defense may have the effect of completely exonerating the defendant of any criminal liability. At times, however, the defense raised is less than perfect—that is, the defendant is unable to meet all of the requirements necessary to demonstrate that a particular justification or excuse should be entirely accepted in his or her case. When claims offered by the defendant are not sufficient for a verdict of not guilty, they may still mitigate the defendant's liability and result in a lesser punishment.

Because most criminal cases are complex, it is difficult to be certain whether a specific defense will be accepted by a judge or jury in a given instance. Moreover, those charged with crimes may be particularly inventive in their efforts to "bend" traditional defenses in order to apply them to their cases. Other defendants may offer creative excuses that have not previously been heard in American courts. Still others may attempt to apply traditionally

affirmative defense
An answer to a criminal charge in which a defendant takes the offensive and responds to the allegations with his or her own assertions based on legal principles. Affirmative defenses must be raised and supported by the defendant independently of any claims made by the prosecutor. Affirmative defenses include justifications and excuses.

accepted defenses under novel circumstances. All this makes it difficult to generalize about the applicability of any particular defense to a given set of circumstances.

JUSTIFICATION AS A DEFENSE

Conduct that violates the law may be justifiable. A person who kills another in self-defense, for example, may be completely innocent of criminal homicide. Justifications include (1) necessity, (2) self-defense, (3) defense of others, (4) defense of home and property, (5) resisting unlawful arrest, and (6) consent. We will discuss each of these defenses in the pages that follow. Keep in mind that the applicability of any particular defense may vary between jurisdictions. Some jurisdictions have codified a wide number of defenses, whereas others continue to follow common law tradition in the acceptability of some defenses.

necessity

A defense to a criminal charge that claims that it was necessary to commit some unlawful act in order to prevent or avoid a greater harm.

Necessity

Strictly speaking, the concept of **necessity** forms the basis of all justifications (Figure 5–2). A defendant offering the defense of necessity makes the claim that it was necessary to commit some unlawful act in order to prevent or avoid a greater harm.

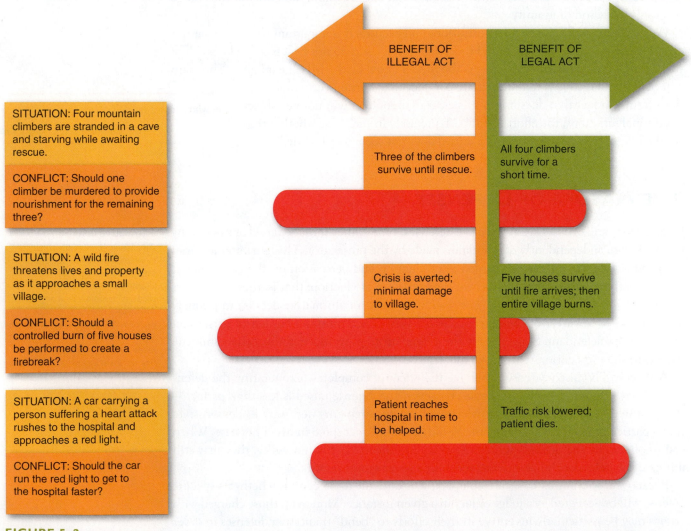

FIGURE 5–2

The Defense of Necessity.

Sometimes the harm avoided is one that otherwise would have affected the defendant; sometimes it is a harm that would have affected others. In a third type of situation, both the person taking the necessary action and others whom he or she was acting to protect might have been harmed.

The Model Penal Code (MPC) says that the principle of necessity "is essential to the rationality and justice of the criminal law," and official commentaries on the code recognize specific instances in which necessity may provide an effective defense to a criminal charge, including the running of a red light by an emergency vehicle, the jettisoning of cargo to save a sinking ship, the breaking and entering of someone seeking shelter in a blizzard, and the emergency dispensing of medication by a pharmacist without a prescription.

A number of state laws refer specifically to the defense of necessity, whereas the Model Penal Code contains a "choice-of-evils" provision under which necessity is subsumed.[6] MPC Section 3.02, which is titled "Justifications Generally: Choice of Evils," reads:

> "Conduct that the actor believes to be necessary to avoid a harm or evil to himself or to another is justifiable, provided that: (a) the harm or evil sought to be avoided by such conduct is greater than that sought to be prevented by the law defining the offense charged," and the actor was not negligent or reckless "in bringing about the situation requiring a choice of harms or evils in appraising the necessity for his conduct."[7]

As the Model Penal Code points out, necessity can only be claimed where the "evil" to be avoided is less than the harm caused. A person who throws luggage out of a falling aircraft to save the aircraft and its passengers will be far more justified in his actions in the eyes of the law than, for example, a person who kills another to avoid a financial loss. Texas law includes this concept, as shown in the following excerpt.

TEXAS PENAL CODE § 9.22

Conduct is justified if:

1. the actor reasonably believes the conduct is immediately necessary to avoid imminent harm;
2. the desirability and urgency of avoiding the harm clearly outweigh, according to ordinary standards of reasonableness, the harm sought to be prevented by the law proscribing the conduct; and
3. a legislative purpose to exclude the justification claimed for the conduct does not otherwise plainly appear.

One of the earliest and best-known cases involving a necessity defense is that of *Regina* v. *Dudley and Stephens*.[8] The case began in 1884 when an English ship sank in a squall about 1,600 miles off the Cape of Good Hope. Three seamen, Thomas Dudley, Edward Stephens, and a man named Brooks, found themselves in a lifeboat with a 17-year-old cabin boy named Richard Parker. Although none of the four had sustained serious injuries in the sinking of their vessel, little food had been stowed away on the lifeboat. After 12 days adrift the men ran out of food, and eight days later Dudley and Stephens decided to kill and eat the cabin boy, which they did. The men ate the boy's flesh and drank his blood. Brooks did not participate in the killing, and four days later, the three surviving seamen were rescued by a passing ship. Dudley and Stephens were arrested and charged with murder. At trial, they offered the defense of necessity, saying that it had been necessary to kill the cabin boy so that at least some of those on the lifeboat might survive.

The court found that "the prisoners were subject to terrible temptation, to sufferings which might break down the bodily power of the strongest man, and try the conscience of the best." Moreover, the court continued, "[I]f the men had not fed upon the body of the

Every jurisdiction recognizes that special circumstances can justify conduct that otherwise would be an offense.

—Paul H. Robinson, Northwestern University Law School

boy they would probably not have survived," and "the boy being in a much weaker condition was likely to have died before them." Nonetheless, the court ruled that "the deliberate killing of this unoffending and unresisting boy was clearly murder, unless the killing can be justified by some well-recognized excuse admitted by law. . . . [I]n this case there was no such excuse, unless the killing was justified by what has been called 'necessity.'" The court continued:

> Though law and morality are not the same, and many things may be immoral which are not necessarily illegal, yet the absolute divorce of law from morality would be of fatal consequence; and such divorce would follow if the temptation to murder in this case were to be held by law an absolute defense of it. It is not so. To preserve one's life is generally speaking a duty, but it may be the plainest and the highest duty to sacrifice it. War is full of instances in which it is a man's duty not to live but to die. The duty, in case of shipwreck, of a captain to his crew, of the crew to the passengers, of soldiers to women and children; these duties impose on men the moral necessity, not of the preservation, but of the sacrifice of their lives for others. . . . It is not correct, therefore, to say that there is any absolute or unqualified necessity to preserve one's life.

Found guilty of murder, Dudley and Stephens were sentenced to die—a sentence that was later commuted by the queen to six months' imprisonment.

As a defense against criminal liability, necessity has generally been far more effective in protecting defendants facing grave physical threats that are immediately present than it has been in protecting defendants who are facing economic or psychological challenges. For example, a person who destroys a house to stop a fire advancing on a town is far less likely to incur criminal liability than one who steals because of hunger or another who breaks into a pharmacy to acquire the drugs needed to feed a powerful addiction.

Self-Defense

self-defense
A defense to a criminal charge that is based on the recognition that a person has an inherent right to self-protection and that to reasonably defend oneself from unlawful attack is a natural response to threatening situations.

Defense of self has long been accepted as justification for activities that might otherwise confer criminal liability. **Self-defense** is based on the recognition that individuals have an inherent right to protect themselves and that to reasonably defend oneself from unlawful attack is a natural response to threatening situations. Similarly, it can be argued that a person who acts in self-defense lacks the requisite *mens rea* for the commission of a crime—that is, a person who kills an attacker does not have as his or her primary purpose the taking of another's life, but rather the preservation of his or her own.

Texas law reads: "A person is justified in using force against another when and to the degree he reasonably believes the force is immediately necessary to protect himself against the other's use or attempted use of unlawful force."[9] The wording of the Model Penal Code is similar. It reads: "The use of force upon or toward another person is justifiable when the actor believes that such force is immediately necessary for the purpose of protecting himself against the use of unlawful force by such other persons on the present occasion."[10] A significant difference between the two, however, is the *reasonableness requirement* of the Texas law—a requirement also found in the laws of many other states. In judging the validity of a claim of self-defense, the Model Penal Code asks us to decide whether the defendant *subjectively* believed that the use of force was necessary; Texas law judges the actor's decision *objectively*—that is, from the point of view of a reasonable person. The difference can be a crucial one.

reasonable person
A person who acts with common sense and who has the mental capacity of an average, normal, sensible human being. The reasonable person criterion requires that the assumptions and ideas on which a defendant acted must have been reasonable in that the circumstances as they appeared to the defendant would have created the same beliefs in the mind of an ordinary person.

As we will see in Chapter 6, the requirement that the use of force in self-defense be reasonable mandates that the accused behave as a reasonable person would under the same circumstances. The concept of a **reasonable person** envisions a person who acts with common sense and who has the mental capacity of an average, normal, sensible human being. In judging any activity, the reasonable person criterion requires that the assumptions and ideas on which the defendant acted must have been objectively reasonable, in that the circumstances as they appeared to the defendant would have created the same beliefs in the mind of an ordinary person. Hence anyone motivated by special needs or driven by psychological forces not routinely present in the average person may find that the claim of self-defense is not available to them in jurisdictions that impose the reasonableness requirement.

Apparent danger is another concept associated with self-defense (Figure 5–3). Apparent danger exists when the conduct or activity of an attacker makes the threat of danger obvious. Danger, for example, becomes apparent when a threatening individual draws a gun or a knife and approaches another person in a menacing fashion. The emphasis on "immediacy" and "present occasion" found in many state codes classifies forceful activities undertaken in self-defense as justifiable only when they occur within the context of a face-to-face encounter. Hence, whereas a person who uses force to fight off an unlawful attack is justified in doing so, someone who stalks and kills a potential attacker in a preemptive strike would be hard-pressed to claim self-defense. Likewise, a person who "takes the law into her own hands" and exacts vengeance on a person who has previously victimized her cannot be said to be acting in self-defense. In short, "the victim had it coming" is not a valid self-defense justification.

Force, as the term is used within the context of self-defense, means physical force; it does not extend to emotional, psychological, economic, psychic, or other forms of coercion. A person who turns the tables on a robber and assaults him during the robbery attempt, for example, may be able to claim self-defense, but a businessperson who assaults a financial rival to prevent a hostile takeover of her company will have no such recourse.

Individuals may also protect themselves in the face of threats when the threat implies that danger is present in a given situation even though the precise nature of that danger may not be immediately apparent. Situations involving present danger include circumstances in

apparent danger
A form of imminent danger that is said to exist when the conduct or activity of an attacker makes the threat of danger obvious.

Once someone uses the term "reasonable person," it's awfully hard to define it.

—*Richard J. Bartlett, former Dean, Albany Law School, Union University*

FIGURE 5–3

Apparent Danger.

which the threatened individual can anticipate the danger that he or she is about to face. For example, if a threatening individual says, "I'm going to kill you!" and advances on another while reaching into his pocket, the threatened individual can reasonably assume that the attacker is reaching for a weapon and can act on that basis. Difficulties may arise, however, when defensive force is used on an attacker who may be incapable of carrying out the threat. Someone who says "I'm going to kill you," for example, while searching for the key to a locked gun cabinet would appear to represent a less immediate danger than one who has the key in hand. Most jurisdictions recognize, however, that a reasonable amount of force can be used to protect oneself in the face of threats that seem to clearly imply that the use of unlawful force is imminent.

The amount of force used by those who seek to defend themselves from unlawful attack must be proportionate to the amount of force or the perceived degree of threat that they are seeking to defend themselves against. Hence, **reasonable force** is the degree of force that is appropriate and not excessive in a given situation. Reasonable force can also be thought of as the minimum degree of force necessary to protect oneself, one's property, a third party, or the property of another in the face of a substantial threat.

Deadly force, the highest degree of force, is considered reasonable only when used to counter an immediate threat of death or great bodily harm (as may be the case in situations involving attempted murder, rape, kidnapping, and attempted assault). Deadly force cannot be used against nondeadly force. If a lesser degree of injury can be anticipated or if a lesser degree of force affords an effective defense, it must be used. Similarly, once danger has been averted, the use of force must cease. A person who overcomes an attacker, for example, leaving him incapable of further attack, is unjustified in then taking the attacker's life. Once a threat has been deterred, it is improper for a person who has successfully defended him- or herself to continue using force. Doing so effectively reverses the role of attacker and victim. For example, a person walking home alone at night might be accosted by a robber who beats him. If the would-be victim turns the tables on the robber by using a can of pepper spray, disabling and temporarily blinding the robber, he would be unjustified if he then picked up a rock and smashed the skull of the incapacitated robber.

In 1997, a Bluffton, South Carolina, woman was arrested after trying to run over a man who allegedly raped her repeatedly just minutes before. The woman told police that the suspect, 24-year-old Charles Edward Hayward, broke into her house at night while she was alone and sleeping. Hayward apparently forced his way into the woman's bedroom, beat her severely, took what money she had in the home, and raped her twice. He then forced her out of the home and into her car, ordering her to drive him out of the area. The woman, however, jumped quickly into the car and locked the doors before the suspect could enter. As a detective put it the following morning: "She was fortunate enough to jump in the car and lock the doors. She started the vehicle up and tried her damnedest to run over him. In doing so, she ended up stuck in the ditch by a neighbor's house."[11] The woman blew the car horn, waking neighbors who called 911. She was taken to a local hospital where she was arrested on charges of assault with a deadly weapon.

Similarly, a person who is facing assault cannot exceed the bounds of necessary force in repelling the attack. If a large and robust person is struck by an unarmed, small and weak—but angry—individual, for example, it would be unreasonable for the much stronger person to break the smaller person's neck if instead he could merely restrain the attacker.

The claim of self-defense is usually unavailable to those who precipitate or incite an attack on themselves. In other words, one who initiates a confrontation cannot later be reasonably afforded the protection of a self-defense claim. A verbally and physically abusive person, for example, cannot claim self-defense if the person being abused responds with

---

reasonable force
A degree of force that is appropriate in a given situation and is not excessive; the minimum degree of force necessary to protect oneself, one's property, a third party, or the property of another in the face of a substantial threat.

deadly force
A force likely to cause death or great bodily harm.

When you are surrounded by four people, one of them smiling, taunting, demanding, terrorizing, you don't have a complete grasp or perfect vision.

—Bernhard Goetz (March 1985)

APPLYING THE CONCEPTS

CAPSTONE CASE

May an Aggressor Assert Self-Defense?

United States v. *Thomas*, 34 F.3d 44 (2nd Cir. 1994)

THE CASE On October 30th, 1990, Wallie Howard, a Syracuse police officer working undercover for the Federal Drug Enforcement Administration (DEA), was shot and killed during a cocaine "buy-bust" taking place in the parking lot of "Mario's Big M Market" in Syracuse.

According to the testimony adduced at trial, Davidson was the head and supplier of a cocaine conspiracy that had begun in Syracuse in or around 1988. The conspiracy allegedly sold between ten thousand and fifty thousand dollars of cocaine weekly, with Davidson supplying the cocaine and receiving the bulk of the proceeds. The testimony indicated that Parke was a chief lieutenant of Davidson's and that Parke and Morales frequently delivered cocaine to customers who had called them on their beepers to place orders. Lawrence was a seller at one of the conspiracy's drug apartments; he also functioned as "muscle" for the conspiracy. Stewart had dealt cocaine for the conspiracy in the past, and he owed the group a debt for cocaine he had purchased three weeks earlier, which turned out to be "bad." He was invited to participate in the events of the thirtieth as a means of paying off the debt he owed to the conspiracy for this cocaine.

On October 18, 1990, Agent Howard and confidential informant Luther Gregory purchased three ounces of cocaine from Morales for $2,700. While the deal took place in Gregory's apartment, Parke walked around the apartment house, apparently conducting countersurveillance. On October 22, Howard and Gregory purchased another four ounces of cocaine from Morales. Parke waited in the car outside while Morales delivered the cocaine and collected the money. At that purchase, Howard and Gregory inquired about the possibility of buying an additional one and one-half kilograms of cocaine. Morales indicated that he would be able to supply that amount. . . . On the morning of October 30, the DEA drug task force met to schedule the buy-bust. Because more than $40,000 in cash was to change hands, the agents were concerned about the possibility of a robbery and attempted to arrange the purchase in a public location. Their fears were well-founded; Davidson had made plans to rob Gregory, because he felt Gregory had robbed him in the past.

The defendants also met the morning of the 30th, and Davidson laid out his plan to rob Gregory of the money. Parke supplied Lawrence with a .357-caliber revolver, and Stewart was armed with a .22-caliber handgun. Morales was to negotiate the deal and act as the driver, and Lawrence and Stewart were to conduct the actual robbery. Davidson and Parke remained behind as the others left to meet Gregory.

Morales met with Agent Howard and Gregory at Gregory's apartment, and they agreed to do the deal in the parking lot of Mario's Big M. When the buyers arrived at the parking lot, Morales told Gregory to come with him to Morales' apartment to check the quality of the cocaine. When they arrived at Morales' apartment, Lawrence and Stewart emerged with guns drawn. They bound and gagged Gregory, breaking his wrist in the process. Morales, Lawrence, and Stewart then returned to Mario's Big M. While Morales waited in his car, Lawrence and Stewart, both armed, approached Gregory's vehicle, where Agent Howard was seated in the passenger seat. Stewart proceeded to the driver's side and got in the driver's seat, while Lawrence went around the back of the vehicle to the passenger side. The following conversation was recorded on the agent's equipment:

STEWART: What the f_____'s up?
HOWARD: Huh?
LAWRENCE: Open up the door.
STEWART: Tell me where the money is.
HOWARD: What money?
LAWRENCE: Hey, hey, hey . . .
STEWART: Hey, don't shut . . .
LAWRENCE: Open the door, man.

At that point, conversation ceased and background noises are heard on the recording. According to trial testimony, Stewart had the loaded .22 in his hand and tried to shoot but was unsuccessful because no round had been placed in the chamber. Agent Howard got three shots off, one of which struck Stewart in the shoulder. From behind Howard, Lawrence, who was standing at the rear passenger side of the vehicle, fired the .357 at Agent Howard, striking him in the rear of the head and killing him. Stewart

(continued)

was arrested seconds later, slumped against a wall with the .22 nearby. Morales and Lawrence attempted to flee but were both apprehended within moments; the murder weapon was recovered from the floor of Morales' vehicle. Both Morales and Stewart waived their *Miranda* rights, made admissions, and signed confessional affidavits. . . .

In his confession, Morales recounted the events of the day largely as outlined above. He stated that seated in his car in the parking lot, he saw Stewart draw a gun and get shot by Howard. He further testified that Lawrence then shot Howard in the head, threw his gun into Morales' car, and started to run. . . .

At trial, the defendants-appellants were found guilty as charged. All of the defendants were sentenced to life. . . .

Self-Defense: The defendants contend that the district court erred in not specifically charging the jury that it was the government's obligation to prove the absence of self-defense beyond a reasonable doubt. The government generally has the burden of disproving self-defense beyond a reasonable doubt once it is raised by a defendant. For reasons not clear, Judge McCurn agreed to give only a portion of the requested self-defense charge (which was taken virtually verbatim from Leonard B. Sand et al., *Modern Federal Jury Instructions*, 1993). He declined to give the last two paragraphs of the requested charge, which expressly placed the burden on the government to prove beyond a reasonable doubt that the defendants did not act in self-defense. The defendants claim that this omission was in error. . . .

THE FINDING   The defense of self-defense is not available to one who acts as the aggressor, and commits his aggression threatening deadly force, even though the intended victim responds with deadly force so that the original aggressor will be killed if he does not first kill.

It has long been accepted that one cannot support a claim of self-defense by a self-generated necessity to kill. The right of homicidal self-defense is granted only to those free from fault in the difficulty; it is denied to slayers who incite the fatal attack, encourage the fatal quarrel or otherwise promote the necessitous occasion for taking life. . . . In sum, one who is the aggressor in a conflict culminating in death cannot invoke the necessities of self-preservation. Under this principle, the defendants had no entitlement to any self-defense charge. The unrebutted evidence showed that with guns drawn, Lawrence, Stewart, and Morales bound and gagged Gregory, breaking his wrist in the process; they then returned to the parking lot where Stewart and Lawrence, armed with a .22 and a .357, respectively, approached Howard's car from two opposite sides; Lawrence banged on the window, and they demanded the money Howard was carrying. At least Lawrence, and possibly both Lawrence

and Stewart, had their guns drawn as they confronted Howard and demanded the $40,000. Moreover, in finding the defendants guilty of felony murder under Count VI, the jury necessarily found that the killing was done in the attempted perpetration of a robbery. Upon this evidence, it is clear that Lawrence and Stewart were the aggressors, and that their felonious aggression was accompanied at the outset by the threat of deadly force. There was no evidence to the effect that Howard menaced Stewart and Lawrence prior to their assault on him. Even if one believes Stewart's contention that he did not draw his gun until Howard drew on him, that claim would not alter the uncontested evidence that Lawrence menaced Howard with his gun while Lawrence and Stewart approached him. Thus, even on Stewart's asserted facts, the defendants were the first to threaten deadly force. They therefore did not raise an issue of fact calling for an instruction on self-defense.

The charge was therefore unnecessarily favorable to the defendants in that it offered the jury the option to acquit by reason of self-defense. The judge's failure to make clear that the burden on the issue of self-defense rests on the government cannot have prejudiced the defendants when they had no right to have the jury consider the issue at all.

The judgments of conviction are affirmed.

What Do *You* Think?

1. Lawrence fired at Agent Howard and killed him after Howard had already drawn his weapon and fired. Why was Lawrence unable to claim self-defense in the shooting? Do you think he should have been allowed to raise this claim? Why or why not?

2. In this case, the U.S. Court of Appeals for the Second Circuit said: "It has long been accepted that one cannot support a claim of self-defense by a self-generated necessity to kill." What is the logic behind this principle? Do you agree with it? Explain.

3. Under what circumstances, if any, might the defendants have been justified in using force against Agent Howard? Under what circumstances might they have been justified in using deadly force?

Additional Applications

Can state law require the *defendant* to prove self-defense?

Martin v. Ohio, 480 U.S. 228 (1987)

The Case: During a violent argument over grocery money in 1983, Earline Martin shot and killed her husband in the couple's Ohio home. At her subsequent trial—on state aggravated murder charges—the defendant claimed self-defense; specifically, she testified that she had retrieved the gun from an upstairs room only after her husband had already struck her and only with the intent of disposing of it. Yet when she appeared downstairs with the weapon in hand, she claimed, her husband moved to attack her again. She then "lost her head" and fired the weapon several times.

In the jury's instructions, the trial judge noted that state prosecutors carried the burden of proving all of the statutory elements of aggravated murder beyond a reasonable doubt. Yet consistent with Ohio law, the judge distinguished the defendant's self-defense claim and instructed the jury that it was the *defendant* who carried the burden of proof on that point, by a preponderance of the evidence. The jury convicted the defendant of aggravated murder, and on appeal, she claimed that Ohio's statutory burden of proof for self-defense violates the Fourteenth Amendment's requirement of due process of law.

The Finding: In a closely divided ruling, the U.S. Supreme Court upheld the conviction and the state's rule requiring the defendant to prove self-defense by preponderance-of-the-evidence. Writing for the majority, Justice Byron White emphasized the "preeminent role of the States" in defining crimes and allocating the burden of persuasion in criminal cases. States, the Court held, may choose if they wish to differentiate in their own laws between the elements of a crime—which, under the due-process clause, must be proven "beyond a reasonable doubt"—and any affirmative defenses that may be raised. Indeed, White observed, the common law rule had been for centuries that "affirmative defenses, including self-defense, were matters for the defense to prove." And although most states—"for whatever reasons"—had long ago abandoned that common law rule in their own statutes, Ohio bore no constitutional obligation to follow their lead. As White concluded: "We are no more convinced that the Ohio practice of requiring self-defense to be proved by the defendant is unconstitutional than we are that the Constitution requires the prosecution to prove the sanity of a defendant who pleads not guilty by reason of insanity."

When does a failure to retreat negate a self-defense claim?

Brown v. United States, 256 U.S. 335 (1921)

The Case: While working at a post office construction site in Texas, defendant Brown shot a co-worker (Hermes) four times—including once when Hermes was already incapacitated and lying on the ground. According to testimony presented at trial, the two men had had a troubled relationship prior to the shooting; indeed, on two occasions, Hermes had attacked Brown with a knife and had threatened that "the next time, one of them would go off in a black box." Shortly thereafter, Hermes again approached Brown with a knife, and Brown—by now carrying a gun in his coat—ran to get the coat, lying about 25 feet away. Hermes pursued him, and as Hermes approached, Brown fired four times, killing his pursuer. At trial, Brown claimed self-defense; yet in his jury instructions, the judge undercut that defense by emphasizing that "the party assaulted is always under the obligation to retreat, so long as retreat is open to him, provided he can do so without subjecting himself to the danger of death or serious bodily harm." The jury rejected Brown's self-defense argument and convicted him of second-degree murder.

The Finding: The U.S. Supreme Court, in a 7–2 ruling, reversed the conviction on the grounds that the judge's jury instructions had been erroneous. Affirmative claims of self-defense, Justice Oliver Wendell Holmes wrote, had long been limited in English and early American common law. Yet "[t]he law has grown . . . in the direction of rules consistent with human nature," he observed, and a person's failure to retreat in itself is no longer "a categorical proof of guilt" but rather only "a circumstance to be considered with all the others in order to determine whether the defendant went farther than he was justified in doing." And when making that case-by-case factual judgment, Holmes added, a jury should consider that "[d]etached reflection cannot be demanded in the presence of an uplifted knife." Consequently, "if a man reasonably believes that he is in immediate danger of death or grievous bodily harm from his assailant he may stand his ground and . . . if he kills him he has not exceeded the bounds of lawful self-defense." ■

---

force and the situation escalates into a brawl or leads to a homicide. Under such circumstances, the law recognizes the inherent validity of the claim often heard from children: "He started it!" This principle is embodied in the Model Penal Code, which specifically states that the use of deadly force to repel force is not justified if the attack has been provoked.[12] *United States* v. *Thomas*[13] illustrates this point.

retreat rule
A rule in many jurisdictions that requires that a person being attacked retreat in order to avoid the necessity of using force against the attacker if retreat can be accomplished with "complete safety."

A minority of jurisdictions will impose a **retreat rule** upon those who would claim self-defense. Those jurisdictions require that the person being attacked retreat to avoid the necessity of using force if retreat can be accomplished with "complete safety." Jurisdictions that follow a retreat rule, however, often specify that an actor is not obliged to retreat from specific locations, such as his or her home or place of work, before responding forcefully when threatened or assailed. Actors who do not retreat may be judged according to other criteria, such as whether the amount of force with which they responded was reasonable and proportionate to the threat at hand. Some jurists argue that a person who is under attack should have no obligation to retreat, as he or she has a natural right to resist an unprovoked attack under any circumstances.

stand your ground
A statute that permits the use of deadly force to repel life- or limb-threatening force in public spaces with no duty to retreat.

At the other extreme is a minority of states enacting the so-called **stand-your-ground** laws (Figure 5–4) mentioned earlier. Although many states permit the use of deadly force in special venues, such as a person's home, states with stand-your-ground laws permit the use of deadly force, and accordingly there is no duty to retreat, in public spaces. To justify use of deadly force, stand-your-ground laws typically require a reasonable belief that the use of force is needed to repel a threat to life or limb. George Zimmerman, who was featured in the story that opens this chapter, will likely rely on Florida's stand-your-ground law in his defense of the second-degree murder charge that was filed against him for the fatal shooting of Treyvon Martin. Florida's stand-your-ground statute reads, in part:

> A person is justified in using force, except deadly force, against another when and to the extent that the person reasonably believes that such conduct is necessary to defend himself or herself or another against the other's imminent use of unlawful force. However, a person is justified in the use of deadly force and does not have a duty to retreat if:
> 1. He or she reasonably believes that such force is necessary to prevent imminent death or great bodily harm to himself or herself or another or to prevent the imminent commission of a forcible felony; or
> 2. Under those circumstances permitted pursuant to s. 776.013 [Florida's Castle Doctrine, which you will read about later in this chapter][14]

perfect self-defense
A claim of self-defense that meets all of the generally accepted legal conditions for such a claim to be valid. Where deadly force is used, perfect self-defense requires that, in light of the circumstances, the defendant reasonably believed it to be necessary to kill the decedent to avert imminent death or great bodily harm and that the defendant was neither the initial aggressor nor responsible for provoking the fatal confrontation.

Some jurisdictions, such as North Carolina, have developed the notion of **perfect self-defense**. When deadly force is used, perfect self-defense is established "when the evidence, viewed in the light most favorable to the defendant, tends to show that at the time of the killing it appeared to the defendant and she believed it to be necessary to kill the decedent

FIGURE 5–4

States with Stand-Your-Ground Laws.

Brady Campaign to Prevent Gun Violence.

At least 21 states (shown in green) have laws allowing citizens to use deadly force without attempting to retreat when threatened outside the home.

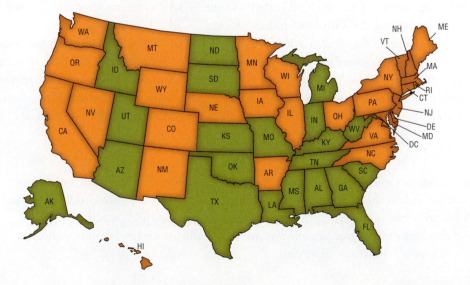

CRIMINAL LAW IN THE NEWS

Some States and Courts Strengthen Gun Rights

When two men broke into her trailer home, an 18-year-old Oklahoma mother called 911 and asked what she could do to defend her baby and not get charged with a crime.

One of the men had a knife. "Do what you have to do to protect your baby," the operator advised in the January 2012 call. The woman then took out a 12-guage shotgun and killed one of the men. Authorities did not prosecute her, citing a new state law allowing homeowners to use guns for protection.

In the past few years, state legislatures and federal courts have substantially strengthened Americans' ability to use firearms to defend their homes. States have passed a bevy of new laws to protect armed homeowners, and the Supreme Court has guaranteed basic gun rights.

However, like the mother who called 911 for legal advice, the courts and law enforcement officials are still sorting out what all these changes mean.

Landmark Supreme Court Decision

For the first time, in 2008 the Supreme Court recognized a constitutional right for private citizens to bear arms. The decision, *District of Columbia* v. *Heller*, was limited to federally administered areas, but in *McDonald* v. *Chicago*, two years later, the High Court extended the right to state and local governments.

Before these landmark decisions, courts applied a limited interpretation to the somewhat ambiguous Second Amendment: "A well regulated Militia, being necessary to the security of a free State, the right of the people to keep and bear Arms, shall not be infringed." Tying gun rights to service in militias, pre-*Heller* courts upheld bans on personal possession of firearms.

The Supreme Court changed all that and guaranteed a right to bear arms, but with some provisos. It specifically excluded felons and the mentally ill and venues such as schools and government buildings.

Subsequent court actions suggest more limitations. In November 2011, the Supreme Court refused to hear *Masciandaro* v. *United States*, involving the right to bear arms in national parks. And in February 2012, a federal judge upheld an Illinois ban on carrying concealed guns, the only statewide ban left. The judge observed that the Supreme Court "has not recognized a right to bear firearms outside the home."

New State Laws to Protect the Home

As the courts wrestle with the Second Amendment, at least 31 states have passed "castle-doctrine" laws since 2005.

Although gun owners already had a right to defend themselves against home invasion, the new laws typically allow the use of firearms without first having to retreat. And although the castle doctrine in many states is limited to the home, it can apply to porches, rental properties, and even cars in some states.

Handgun ammunition overlays a copy of the U.S. Constitution. What important recent U.S. Supreme Court cases speak to the issue of gun control?

Fotolia

In Pennsylvania, a man killed his wife's drunken boyfriend with a bow and arrow when the man came onto his porch, and he was not prosecuted because the state's law covers porches. In South Carolina, a woman visiting one of her rental properties shot a homeless man when he refused to stop approaching her. Police declined to file charges against her.

In Ohio, a suspected drug dealer attempted to use the state's castle doctrine to protect himself against a murder charge. When a rival rammed his car and smashed his car window, the man shot and killed the rival. Although the Ohio castle law extends to cars, the man was still convicted of murder.

Resources

Adam Liptak, "Justices Extend Firearm Rights in 5-to-4 Ruling," *New York Times*, June 28, 2010, **http://www.nytimes.com/2010/06/29/us/29scotus.html.**
Patrik Jonsson, "Oklahoma Mom Kills Home Invader: Why the Law Was on Her Side," *Christian Science Monitor*, January 5, 2012, **http://www.csmonitor.com/USA/Justice/2012/0105/ Oklahoma-mom-kills-home-invader-Why-the-law-was-on-her-side.**
Jim Phillips, "Homicide Verdict Will Be Appealed on 'Castle' Issue," *The Athens News*, November 4, 2010, **http://www.athensnews.com/ohio/article-32527-homicide-verdict-will-be-appealed-on-lscastlers-issue.html**

to save herself from imminent death or great bodily harm. That belief must be reasonable, however, in that the circumstances as they appeared to the defendant would create such a belief in the mind of a person of ordinary firmness. Further, the defendant must not have been the initial aggressor provoking the fatal confrontation. A killing in the proper exercise of the right of perfect self-defense is always completely justified in law and constitutes no legal wrong."[15] Imperfect self-defense may exist when any of the conditions required for perfect self-defense is lacking. In jurisdictions where the concepts of perfect and imperfect self-defense are employed, imperfect self-defense may lower criminal liability but not eliminate it.

> *We cannot lightly . . . allow the perpetrator of a serious crime to go free simply because that person believed his actions were reasonable and necessary to prevent some perceived harm.*
>
> —Judge Sol Wachtler, New York State Court of Appeals, ruling in the case of Bernhard Goetz (1986)

The law of self-defense generally provides that a person is justified in acting to defend him- or herself under circumstances in which a reasonable person would believe him- or herself to be in danger. In the Zimmerman case, discussed at the opening of this chapter, it remains to be seen whether Zimmerman can establish that he had a reasonable belief that Treyvon Martin threatened him with loss of life or great bodily harm.

Defense of Others

The use of force to defend oneself has generally been extended to permit the use of reasonable force to defend others who are, or who appear to be, in imminent danger. Simply put, when another person is being victimized, you can stand in the shoes of the victim and can use whatever force the victim could use in that person's defense.

alter ego rule
A rule of law that, in some jurisdictions, holds that a person can only defend a third party under circumstances and only to the degree that the third party could act on his or her own behalf.

However, the defense of others, sometimes called *defense of a third person*, is circumscribed in some jurisdictions by the **alter ego rule** (Figure 5–5). The alter ego rule holds that a person can only defend a third party under circumstances and only to the degree that the third party could act. Hence, a person who aids a third party whom he sees being accosted may be criminally liable if the third party initiated the attack or if the assault on the third party is a lawful one—that is, being made by a law enforcement officer conducting a lawful arrest of a person who is resisting.

Jurisdictions, such as Texas, that follow Model Penal Code conventions do not recognize the alter ego rule; they allow a person to act in defense of another if "the actor reasonably believes that his intervention is immediately necessary to protect the third person." Even though a person may misperceive a situation, if he or she acts in defense of a third party, thinking that party is in immediate danger, the requisite *mens rea* that might otherwise make the action a crime is lacking.

FIGURE 5–5

The Alter Ego Rule.

Defense of others cannot be claimed by an individual who joins an illegal fight merely to assist a friend or family member. Likewise, one who intentionally aids an offender in an assault, even though the tables have turned and the offender is losing the battle, cannot claim defense of others. In other words, defense of others always requires that the defender be free from fault and that he or she must act to aid an innocent person who is in the process of being victimized. The restrictions that apply to self-defense also apply to defense of a third party. A defender must only act in the face of an immediate threat to another person, cannot use deadly force against less-than-deadly force, and must act only to the extent and use only the degree of force needed to repel the attack.

Finally, force may be used against others to prevent them from hurting themselves. As the following Texas law illustrates, "protection of life or health" may sometimes require that people be forced to do something they do not want to do. A mother searching for her children may be forcefully removed from a burning building that is about to collapse. A weapon may be wrested from the hand of a suicidal person, and someone who is about to jump from a high building may be tackled and saved from death.

TEXAS PENAL CODE § 9.33

A person is justified in using force or deadly force against another to protect a third person if:

1. Under the circumstances as the actor reasonably believes them to be, the actor would be justified under Section 9.31 or 9.32 in using force or deadly force to protect himself against the unlawful force or unlawful deadly force he reasonably believes to be threatening the third person he seeks to protect; and

2. The actor reasonably believes that his intervention is immediately necessary to protect the third person.

Section 9-34. Protection of Life or Health.

    a. A person is justified in using force, but not deadly force, against another when and to the degree he reasonably believes the force is immediately necessary to prevent the other from committing suicide or inflicting serious bodily injury to himself.

    b. A person is justified in using both force and deadly force against another when and to the degree he reasonably believes the force or deadly force is immediately necessary to preserve the other's life in an emergency.

Defense of Home and Property

Defense of property, also called *protection of property*, can apply in the following situations: (1) protection of personal property, (2) defense of home or habitation, (3) defense of another's property, and (4) use of a mechanical device to protect property.

In most jurisdictions, the owner of property can justifiably use reasonable *nondeadly* force to prevent others from unlawfully taking or damaging that property. As a general rule, however, the preservation of human life outweighs protection of property, and the use of deadly force to protect property is not justified unless the perpetrator of the illegal act may intend to commit, or is in the act of committing, a violent act against another human being. A person who shoots a trespasser, for example, cannot use the defense of property to avoid criminal liability, but one who shoots and kills an armed robber while being robbed can. The difference is that a person facing an armed robber has a right to protect his or her property but is also in danger of death or serious bodily harm. An unarmed trespasser represents no such serious threat.[16]

In 1999, for example, businessman Richard H. Mathis, 34, of North Augusta, Georgia, was arrested and charged with assault and battery with intent to kill after he opened fire on two burglars at his mobile home dealership.[17] After the dealership had been repeatedly burglarized, Mathis decided to spend the night at the business protecting his property. On hearing a break-in, Mathis surprised two alleged burglars and fired shots in their direction with a semiautomatic assault rifle. One burglar, 27-year-old Douglas M. West, was slightly wounded on the face and neck by flying shrapnel.

The use of mechanical devices to protect property is a special area of law. Because, generally speaking, deadly force is not permitted in defense of property, the setting of booby traps—such as spring-loaded shotguns, electrified grates, explosive devices, and the like—is generally not permitted to protect property that is unattended and unoccupied. Of course, another problem may arise in the use of such devices: the death or injury of an innocent person. Booby-trapped property may be entered by children trying to recover a baseball, by firemen called to extinguish a fire, or by law enforcement officers with a lawful search warrant. If an individual is injured as a result of a mechanical device intended to cause death or injury in the protection of property, criminal charges may be brought against the person who set the device. These principles were well summarized by the Supreme Court of California in the case of *People* v. *Ceballos* (1974),[18] when it observed: "In the United States, courts have concluded that a person may be held criminally liable under statutes proscribing homicides and shooting with intent to injure, or civilly liable, if he sets upon his premises a deadly mechanical device and that device kills or injures another. . . . However, an exception to the rule that there may be criminal and civil liability for death or injuries caused by such a device has been recognized where the intrusion is, in fact, such that the person, were he present, would be justified in taking the life or inflicting the bodily harm with his own hands."[19]

On the other hand, acts that would otherwise be criminal may carry no criminal liability if undertaken to protect one's home. For purposes of the law, one's "home" is one's dwelling, whether owned, rented, or merely "borrowed." Hotel rooms, rooms onboard vessels, and rented rooms in houses belonging to others are all considered, for purposes of the law, one's "dwelling." The retreat rule, referred to earlier, which requires a person under attack to retreat when possible before resorting to deadly force, is subject to what some call the *castle exception*. The **castle exception** can be traced to the writings of the sixteenth-century English jurist Sir Edward Coke, who said, "A man's house is his castle—for where shall a man be safe if it be not in his house?"[20] The castle exception generally recognizes that a person has a fundamental right to be in his or her home and also recognizes the home as a final and inviolable place of retreat (that is, the home offers a place of retreat from which a person can be expected to retreat no farther). Hence it is not necessary for one to retreat from one's home in the face of an immediate threat, even where such retreat is possible, before resorting to deadly force in protection of the home. Some court decisions have extended the castle exception to include one's place of business, such as a store or office.

The law describing defense of home is far from clear, however. Part of the problem comes from the fact that people defending their homes against intrusion are often acting out of self-defense or defense of family. Another problem arises from the fact that not all states have codified the conditions under which the use of force in defense of the home is justifiable. Some states follow the old common law rule that permits the use of deadly force to prevent an unlawful entry of any kind into the home. Other states, however, especially those that have enacted statutes designed to give the weight of legal authority to defense of one's home, qualify the use of deadly force by authorizing it only for purposes of preventing a felony. Under such statutes, a person would be authorized in using force against a burglar who has illegally entered his or her home with the intent to steal, but the person would not be authorized in using force against someone who mistakenly or lawfully enters the residence.

A few states have extended the castle rule to automobiles but not to public places generally, locating these states between retreat states and stand-your-ground states in terms of self-defense justifications. The Ohio self-defense statute, for example, provides that "an occupant of that person's vehicle or who lawfully is an occupant in a vehicle owned by an immediate family member of the person has no duty to retreat before using force in self-defense or defense of another."[21]

Finally, property in the possession of a third person, or the home of a third person, may be protected by one who assists that person to the same degree and in the same manner that the owner of the property or the home would have been privileged to act. Tennessee's protection-of-property law is similar to MPC Section 3.06 and many other state laws.

castle exception
An exception to the retreat rule that recognizes a person's fundamental right to be in his or her home and also recognizes the home as a final and inviolable place of retreat. Under the castle exception to the retreat rule, it is not necessary to retreat from one's home in the face of an immediate threat, even where retreat is possible, before resorting to deadly force in protection of the home.

TENNESSEE CRIMINAL CODE

Title 39, Section 11-614. Protection of property.

(a) A person in lawful possession of real or personal property is justified in threatening or using force against another when and to the degree it is reasonably believed the force is immediately necessary to prevent or terminate the other's trespass on the land or unlawful interference with the property.

(b) A person who has been unlawfully dispossessed of real or personal property is justified in threatening or using force against the other when and to the degree it is reasonably believed the force is immediately necessary to reenter the land or recover the property if the person threatens or uses the force immediately or in fresh pursuit after the dispossession; and:

   (1) The person reasonably believes the other had no claim of right when the other dispossessed the person; and

   (2) The other accomplished the dispossession by threatening or using force against the person.

(c) A person is not justified in using deadly force to prevent or terminate the other's trespass on real estate or unlawful interference with personal property.

Title 39, Section 11-615. Protection of third person's property.

A person is justified in threatening or using force against another to protect real or personal property of a third person if, under the circumstances as the person reasonably believes them to be, the person would be justified under 39-11-614 in threatening or using force to protect the person's own real or personal property.

Title 39, Section 11-616. Use of device to protect property.

(a) The justification afforded by §§ 39-11-614 and 39-11-615 extends to the use of a device for the purpose of protecting property only if:

   (1) The device is not designed to cause or known to create a substantial risk of causing death or serious bodily harm;

   (2) The use of the particular device to protect the property from entry or trespass is reasonable under the circumstances as the person believes them to be; and

   (3) The device is one customarily used for such a purpose or reasonable care is taken to make known to probable intruders the fact that it is used.

(b) Nothing in this section shall affect the law regarding the use of animals to protect property or persons.

Resisting Unlawful Arrest

All jurisdictions today have laws making it illegal for a person to resist a lawful arrest. Under common law, however, it was lawful to use force to resist an *unlawful* arrest. Following common law tradition, some jurisdictions today continue to consider resistance in the face of an unlawful arrest justifiable, and many have codified statutory provisions detailing the limits imposed on such resistance and the conditions under which it may be used. The Texas statute cited in the preceding section, for example, makes it clear that a person may use a reasonable amount of force, other than deadly force, to resist an unlawful arrest or an unlawful search by a law enforcement officer if the officer "uses or attempts to use greater force than necessary to make the arrest or search" and "when and to the degree the actor reasonably believes the force is immediately necessary to protect himself against the peace officer's use or attempted use of greater force than necessary." A provision of the law makes it inapplicable to cases in which the defendant is the first to resort to force, and deadly force to resist arrest is not justified unless the law enforcement officer resorts to deadly force when it is not called for.

> *When the suspect poses no immediate threat to the officer and no threat to others, the harm resulting from the failure to apprehend him does not justify the use of deadly force to do so.*
>
> —Justice Bryan R. White, writing for the majority in Tennessee v. Garner, 471 U.S. 1, 11 (1985)

On the other hand, some states require a person to submit to any arrest by an authorized law enforcement officer acting on official business. That's because resisting arrest can be a dangerous undertaking for all the parties involved and because the complexities of today's law may make it difficult for those on the scene to decide at the moment of arrest whether an arrest is lawful or not. Moreover, in contrast with common law days, the ready availability of defense counsel makes it unlikely that anyone unlawfully arrested will spend much time in jail. In some jurisdictions, it is an affirmative defense to prosecution if the peace officer involved was out of uniform and did not identify himself or herself as a peace officer by showing his or her credentials to the person whose arrest was attempted. The offense of resisting arrest is discussed in more detail in Chapter 10.

Most jurisdictions provide statutory protections to law enforcement officers who find it necessary to use force to effect an arrest or to prevent individuals in their custody from escaping. Such statutes provide an **execution-of-public-duty defense** and preclude the possibility of arresting officers being prosecuted on charges of assault or battery (if force is needed to effect the arrest or to maintain custody) as long as the officers acted in a lawful manner. Requirements of a lawful arrest typically include (1) making the purpose of the arrest known to the person arrested and (2) using a valid arrest warrant (if the arrest is to be made on the authority of a warrant—something that is not necessary if the crime was committed in the officer's presence). Execution-of-public-duty statutes also protect anyone carrying out the order of a lawful court or tribunal, anyone performing the duties or functions of a public officer, and anyone lawfully involved in the execution of legal processes defined by law. Blanket statutes of this sort legitimize the lawful behavior of public servants, government employees, and elected officials.

The use of deadly force by law enforcement officers is of special concern. If a police officer attempting to make a lawful arrest meets resistance, he or she may use reasonable force to effect the arrest and to protect himself or herself. General rules of self-defense apply in such situations. However, even in those states requiring citizens to retreat before using deadly force, an officer is not required to retreat rather than make an arrest.

Before the U.S. Supreme Court case of *Tennessee v. Garner* (1985),[22] which specified the conditions under which deadly force could be used in the apprehension of suspected felons, most law enforcement departments throughout the United States operated under the **fleeing felon rule**. The fleeing felon rule permitted officers to shoot a suspected felon who attempted to flee from a lawful arrest. In *Garner*, however, the Court ruled that "the use of deadly force to prevent the escape of all felony suspects, whatever the circumstances, is constitutionally unreasonable."[23] According to *Garner*, deadly force may be applied only to prevent death or the threat of serious injury to the public or to protect the law enforcement officer from a defendant who resorts to the use of deadly force. Because *Garner* was a civil case, however, the actions of police officers, although they might violate criteria established by *Garner*, may still not be criminal.

Consent

Consent is the final justification discussed in this chapter. The defense of **consent** makes the claim that the person suffering an injury either (1) agreed to sustain the injury or (2) accepted the possibility of injury before the activity was undertaken. In either case, consent must be voluntarily and legally given if the defense is to be useful. It is also important to note that consent is only available as a defense if lack of consent is an element of the crime (as it is, for example, in the crime of rape).

Consent is inherent in some situations. As one author says, "The act of one who grabs another by the ankles and causes him to fall violently to the ground may result in a substantial jail sentence under some circumstances, but receive thunderous applause if it stops a ball carrier on the gridiron."[24] A person injured in an athletic contest cannot, under most circumstances, bring a charge of battery against another player, as both consented to participate in the game. Of course, some sporting events are much more likely to produce injuries than others, and some involve far more personal contact than others. Football players,

---

execution-of-public-duty defense
A defense to a criminal charge, such as assault, that is often codified and that precludes the possibility of police officers and other public employees from being prosecuted when lawfully exercising their authority.

fleeing felon rule
A now-defunct law enforcement practice that permitted officers to shoot a suspected felon who attempted to flee from a lawful arrest.

consent
A justification, offered as a defense to a criminal charge, claiming that the person suffering an injury either agreed to sustain the injury or accepted the possibility of injury before the activity was undertaken.

for example, are routinely expected to tackle one another, whereas tennis players are not. If an assault continues beyond the point permitted by the rules of the sport, it may become illegal. Fistfights between basketball players, even though they occur on court, provide an example of such illegal activity. In 2004, for example, five Indiana Pacers players and five Detroit Pistons fans were charged with assault and battery in connection with one of the worst brawls in American sports history. The fight broke out near the end of a game in Pontiac, Michigan, after an on-court dispute over a foul. Similarly, violent sports that are not recognized as legitimate by government authorities may leave the participants liable to a criminal charge. Contestants in bare-knuckle or street fighting, for example, can be charged with assault, even though the "contest" may have been informally arranged by the "local community" and sanctioned by numerous observers.

Sexual activity is another area in which the defense of consent is frequently employed. A man might claim in defense to a charge of rape, for example, that a woman consented to his sexual advances and therefore agreed to sexual intercourse. Consent to one thing (sexual advances), however, does not constitute consent to another (sexual intercourse). Problems may arise when one of the parties to a sexual act wrongly believes that the other has consented and proceeds to engage in sexual activity on the basis of that belief. In 1988, for example, 21-year-old Robert Chambers pleaded guilty to a charge of first-degree manslaughter after 18-year-old Jennifer Levin died during what Chambers called consensual "rough sex." Levin, said Chambers, had injured his testicles, causing him to strike out at her in pain, resulting in her death.[25] More recently, in 1993, the "condom rapist" Joel Valdez was found guilty of rape after a jury in Austin, Texas, rejected his claim that the act became consensual once he complied with his victim's request to use a condom. Valdez, who was drunk and armed with a knife at the time of the attack, claimed that his victim's request to use a condom amounted to consent. The woman pledged not to resist, and in fact did not resist, in exchange for his agreeing to use a condom. From that point forward, claimed Valdez, "we were making love."[26]

Although cases like those of the "condom rapist" may be easy to decide, clear consent in cases involving sexual activity may be difficult to establish. The reason is that much sexual activity proceeds on the basis of nonverbal cues, which require a fair degree of subjective interpretation, and both the cues and the manner of their interpretation are the products of strong cultural influences. Members of certain subcultures, for example, believe that a woman is required to offer at least a modicum of resistance to a man's sexual advances even though she may intend to engage in sexual intercourse with him. Men in such subcultures may inaccurately gauge the degree of persistence required to overcome a woman's "resistance," or they may force an encounter by misinterpreting a woman's intentions. Some of the same difficulties may be involved in judging the willingness of homosexual partners or in assessing a man's degree of consent to sexual intercourse when a woman is the aggressor.

express consent
A verbally expressed willingness to engage in a specified activity.

To address these issues, some individuals and institutions have advocated requiring **express consent**. Express consent is a verbally expressed willingness to engage in a specified activity, and in the heterosexual arena it generally places the burden of ensuring that consent has been obtained on the man. In 1990, for example, Antioch College instituted a requirement of "willing and verbal consent for each individual sexual act." The Antioch policy requires express consent from both partners at each stage as the level of sexual activity increases. Although the college's statute does not carry the force of law, it is indicative of the complexities involved in determining consent.

Because the public has an interest in the protection of citizens, consent is generally not available as a defense in cases of homicide or where the injury inflicted causes serious bodily harm. Reflecting such concerns, consent, or lack thereof, is not an element specified by laws contravening homicide and many other crimes. A killer who shoots another person, for example, after being told "There's the gun. Go ahead and shoot me!" cannot effectively offer a consent defense, even though the victim's comments may be substantiated by witnesses.[27] Likewise, a person who complies with the request of a panhandler and cuts off the beggar's hand in order to make him appear more needy can still be prosecuted for battery. Similarly, most jurisdictions do not permit one to consent to one's own death, and consent is not a valid defense in cases of euthanasia, especially where the defendant played an *active* role in the decedent's death or directly caused the death.

Consent cannot be claimed in cases of intimidation or fraud. A person cannot, for example, be forced to give consent. Intimidation or the threatened use of force to obtain consent invalidates the consent given and may result in charges of extortion or blackmail against the threat maker. Similarly, a person tricked into giving consent may later bring charges of fraud against the trickster. Likewise, one who is mentally incompetent, unconscious, or otherwise incapable of giving consent is protected by the law in most matters.

SUMMARY

- A defense consists of evidence and arguments offered by a defendant and his or her attorney(s) to show why that person should not be held liable for a criminal charge. A successful defense may have the effect of completely exonerating the defendant of any criminal liability.

- Defenses may be built upon these bases: (1) alibi, (2) justifications, and (3) excuses.

- Justifications and excuses are affirmative defenses. They must be raised or asserted by the defendant independently of any claims made by the prosecutor.

- An excuse does not claim that the conduct in question is justified; it suggests instead that the actor who engaged in it was, at the time, suffering under some defect of personality or circumstance so as to not be legally responsible for his or her actions.

- Justifications include: (1) necessity, (2) self-defense, (3) defense of others, (4) defense of home and property, (5) resisting unlawful arrest, and (6) consent.

- The defense of necessity claims that it was necessary to commit some unlawful act in order to prevent or to avoid a greater harm. The defense of necessity has generally been far more effective in the face of grave physical threats that are immediately present than it has been in protecting defendants facing economic or psychological hardship.

- Self-defense is based on the recognition that individuals have an inherent right to protect themselves and that to defend oneself from unlawful attack is a natural response to threatening situations. The law of self-defense generally holds that the use of force upon or toward another person is justifiable when the actor believes that such force is immediately necessary for the purpose of protecting him- or herself against the unlawful use of force by the other person. Deadly force, the highest degree of force, can only be used to counter an immediate threat of death or great bodily harm.

- The use of force to defend oneself has generally been extended to permit the use of reasonable force to defend others who are, or who appear to be, in imminent danger. Property in the possession of a third person, or the home of a third person, may be protected by one who assists that person to the same degree and in the same manner that the owner of the property or the home would have been privileged to act.

- In most jurisdictions, the owner of property can justifiably use reasonable *nondeadly* force to prevent others from unlawfully taking or damaging that property. As a general rule, however, the preservation of human life outweighs protection of property, and the use of deadly force to protect property is not justified unless the perpetrator of the illegal act may intend to commit, or is in the act of committing, a violent act against another human being.

- Resistance in the face of an unlawful arrest is considered justifiable in almost all jurisdictions. Many states have codified statutory provisions detailing the limits imposed on such resistance and the conditions under which it can be used.

- Most states also provide statutory protections to law enforcement officers who find it necessary to use force to effect an arrest or to prevent individuals in their custody from escaping. Such statutes provide an execution-of-public-duty defense, which precludes the possibility of arresting officers being prosecuted on charges of assault or battery (if force is needed to effect the arrest or to maintain custody), as long as the officers act in a lawful manner.

- The defense of consent claims that the person suffering an injury either agreed beforehand to sustain the injury or accepted the possibility of injury before the activity was undertaken. Sexual activity is an area in which the defense of consent is frequently employed, as lack of consent is an element of many sex crimes. Consent, however, is generally not available as a defense where the victim's lack of consent is not a statutory element of the offense.

KEY TERMS

affirmative defense, 127

alter ego rule, 138

apparent danger, 131

castle exception, 141

consent, 143

deadly force, 132

defense, 126

excuse, 126

execution-of-public-duty
    defense, 143

express consent, 144

fleeing felon rule, 143

justification, 126

necessity, 128

perfect self-defense, 136

reasonable force, 132

reasonable person, 132

retreat rule, 136

self-defense, 130

stand your ground, 136

QUESTIONS FOR DISCUSSION

1. What is the purpose of a defense to a criminal charge?

2. What is an affirmative defense?

3. What is the difference between justifications and excuses? Give examples of justifications that might serve as defenses.

4. What fundamental claim is raised by the defense of necessity? When are claims of necessity most successful?

5. When may force be used in self-defense? When may deadly force be used?

6. Explain the execution-of-public-duty defense. When and by whom might such a defense be used?

CRITICAL THINKING AND APPLICATION PROBLEMS

Applying Florida's stand-your-ground law (discussed earlier in this chapter), would the defendants in each of the following cases be criminally liable for murder?

1. D. Edley, a healthy forty-year-old man, shot and killed, with a handgun that he lawfully possessed, a seventy-year-old woman, Ida Hungry, who was pushing a shopping cart full of empty bottles and cans on a public street. Weathered by years of homelessness, Hungry was frail and gaunt. She approached Edley on a crowded street, both hands on

the cart, pushed him with the cart against a building, and said to him, "Kiss me or I will kill you." Edley shook his head no and Hungry responded by growling and pushing the cart harder against his body. Edley shot and killed her.

2. D. Edley, a healthy forty-year-old man, shot and killed, with a handgun that he lawfully possessed, a thirty-year-old man, Vic Tim, who was pushing a shopping cart full of empty bottles and cans on a public street. Bulked up after years of weight training while in prison, Vic was muscular and imposing. He approached Edley on a crowded street, both hands on the cart, pushed Edley with the cart against a building, and said to him, "Kiss me or I will kill you." Edley shook his head no and Tim responded by growling and pushing the cart harder against his body. Edley shot and killed him.

3. D. Edley, a healthy forty-year-old man, shot and killed, with a handgun that he lawfully possessed, a thirty-year-old man, Vic Tim, who was pushing a shopping cart full of empty bottles and cans on a public street. Bulked up after years of weight training while in prison, Tim was muscular and imposing. He approached Edley on a crowded street, both hands on the cart, pushed Edley with the cart against a building, and said to him, "Kiss me or I will kill you." Edley shook his head no and Tim responded by growling and pushing the cart harder against his body. Edley took his handgun from holster, exhibited it, and said "Let me go or I'll shoot you. Don't make me do it!" Tim pushed the cart harder and Edley shot and killed him.

LEGAL RESOURCES ON THE WEB

Some websites are virtual law libraries and provide a wealth of links to statutes, important documents, and court opinions. This section lists some of the best such sites:

FindLaw
http://www.findlaw.com
Includes laws, cases, and codes; legal practice materials; legal news; dictionaries; and more.

Law Guru
http://www.lawguru.com/lawlinks/Virtual_Law_Library
Includes links to a number of informative sources relative to American law.

Legal Information Institute
http://www.law.cornell.edu
An excellent collection of legal materials and resources from Cornell University Law School.

University of Southern California Gould School of Law Virtual Library
http://lawweb.usc.edu/library/resources.cfm
A great site with lots of links, including links to international criminal tribunals. Click on "Free Legal Web Resources" for many links to U.S. criminal law sites.

SUGGESTED READINGS AND CLASSIC WORKS

Corrado, Michael Louis. *Justification and Excuse in the Criminal Law: A Collection of Essays.* New York: Garland, 1994.

Dershowitz, Alan M. *The Best Defense.* New York: Random House, 1983.

Fletcher, George. "Justification." In *Encyclopedia of Crime and Justice,* edited by Sanford H. Kadish, 3:941–946. New York: Free Press, 1983.

Katz, Leo. *Bad Acts and Guilty Minds: Conundrums of the Criminal Law*. Chicago: University of Chicago Press, 1987.

Robinson, Paul H. *Criminal Law Defenses*, 2 vols. St. Paul: West, 1984.

NOTES

1. "The Shooting of Treyvon Martin," Wikipedia, http://en.wikipedia.org/wiki/Shooting_of_Trayvon_Martin.

2. "George Zimmerman: Prelude to a Shooting," Reuters News, available at http://www.reuters.com/article/2012/04/25/us-usa-florida-shooting-zimmerman-idusbre83o18h20120425.

3. Jerome Hall, "Comments on Justification and Excuse," *American Journal of Comparative Law* 24 (1976): 638–640.

4. Paul H. Robinson, "Criminal Law Defenses: A Systematic Analysis," *Columbia Law Review* 82 (1982): 190, 203–204.

5. Model Penal Code, Article 3, Commentary.

6. The "Codification of a Principle of Necessity" is discussed in Part I of the code's commentaries.

7. Model Penal Code, Section 3.02.

8. *Regina* v. *Dudley and Stephens*, 14 Q.B.D. 273 (1884).

9. Texas Penal Code, Section 9.31.

10. Model Penal Code, Section 3.04 (1).

11. Carolyn Grant, "Police: Victim Aimed Car at Attacker," *Island Packet*, January 23, 1997.

12. Model Penal Code, Section 3.04(2)(b)(i).

13. *United States* v. *Thomas*, 34 F.3d 44 (2nd Cir. 1994).

14. F.S.A. §776.

15. *State* v. *Norman*, 324 N.C. 253, 378 S.E.2d 8 (1989).

16. The exception, of course, is that of a trespasser who trespasses in order to commit a more serious crime.

17. "Man Charged in Shooting of Burglars," *Island Packet*, February 7, 1999.

18. *People* v. *Ceballos*, 12 Cal. 3d 470, 526 P.2d 241 (1974).

19. Under common law, exceptions were made in instances of attempted arson and attempted burglary of a dwelling house.

20. Sir Edward Coke, *Third Institute*, 162.

21. O.R.C. §2901.09.

22. *Tennessee* v. *Garner*, 471 U.S. 1, 9–10 (1985).

23. Ibid.

24. Rollin M. Perkins and Ronald N. Boyce, *Criminal Law*, 3rd ed. (Mineola, NY: Foundation Press, 1982), 1075.

25. Kirk Johnson, Chambers, "With Jury at Impasse, Admits 1st-Degree Manslaughter," *New York Times*, March 28, 1988, http://query.nytimes.com/gst/fullpage.html?res=940DE2DE143EF935A15750C0A96E948260&sec=&spon=&pagewanted=all(accessed March 15, 2009).

26. "Rapist Who Agreed to Use Condom Gets 40 Years," *New York Times*, May 15, 1993, http://query.nytimes.com/gst/fullpage.html?sec=health&res=9F0CE2DF173FF936A25756C0A965958260 (accessed March 15, 2009).

27. See, for example, *State* v. *Fransua*, 85 N.M. 173, 510 P.2d 106, 58 A.L.R. 3d 656 (Ct. App. 1973).

6

Defenses: Excuses and Insanity

Newscom

CHAPTER OUTLINE

OBJECTIVES

After reading this chapter, you should be able to

- List the main distinguishing features of an excuse.
- Summarize the conditions of the defense of duress.
- Describe the intoxication defense, and explain why voluntary intoxication is usually not accepted as a defense to a criminal charge.
- Explain the defense of mistake, and tell when it is most useful.
- Summarize defenses based on age/immaturity.
- Summarize what constitutes entrapment, and elaborate upon the difference between the subjective and objective approaches to assessing entrapment.
- Summarize various syndrome-based defenses, and provide some examples of this type of defense.
- Distinguish incompetency to stand trial from insanity at the time a crime is committed.
- Explain diminished capacity and diminished responsibility.
- Explain the difference between a finding of NGRI and one of GBMI.
- Describe the insanity defense and the controversy surrounding it.

> *If weakness may excuse, what murderer, what traitor, parricide, incestuous, sacrilegious, but may plead it?*
> —John Milton (1608–1674)

> *Ignorance of the law excuses no man; not that all men know the law, but because 'tis an excuse every man will plead, and no man can tell how to refute him.*
> —John Selden (1584–1654)

> *Two wrongs don't make a right, but they make a good excuse.*
> —Thomas Szasz (b. 1920)

INTRODUCTION

After midnight on February 17, 1992, Alice Mahaffey told police officer Ronald Wright, paramedic Venetia Giger, and neighbor William Tice that Horace Pope had beaten her, stabbed her, and kicked her in the head repeatedly with his cowboy boots. He took her car keys, left her for dead, and drove away in her car with his 18-year-old niece, Marsha Pope, she said. After Pope and Marsha left, Mahaffey managed to drag herself across the street to Tice's residence, where she lay slumped on his sofa, covered in blood, until the police and paramedics arrived. She died in the hospital eight days after surgery from wounds received and from an ensuing infection.

Marsha was an eyewitness to the attack by Pope. She was alone in her parents' home on February 16, 1992, she said, when Pope and Mahaffey, both alcoholics, arrived in Mahaffey's car. Both had been drinking, and while Mahaffey was placing beer in the kitchen, Pope and Marsha were left alone in the living room. Pope told Marsha that he was going to kill Mahaffey and take her car and money. Believing that he was drunk and not to be taken seriously, Marsha retired to her bedroom, leaving Pope and Mahaffey in her parents' bedroom. Later, Pope summoned Marsha to the bathroom and forced her to watch him beat, kick, and stab Mahaffey. Marsha witnessed him beat Mahaffey's head against the sink and wall while she was sitting on the toilet, after which he pushed her off the toilet and stomped on her head and back with his boots. While she was lying facedown on the floor, Pope straddled and stabbed her. When Marsha tried to escape, he threatened to kill her if she attempted to leave.

He then left Mahaffey lying on the bathroom floor and went to the kitchen to wash his hands, after telling Marsha to see if she was dead. To prevent him from inflicting further violence, Marsha confirmed that Mahaffey was dead. Marsha then left with Pope in Mahaffey's car. After being threatened again with death, Marsha persuaded Pope to drop her off at a friend's house, at which time she immediately called 911. After dropping Marsha off, Pope drove to the trailer where his brother's family was staying and attempted to borrow money. Upon being refused, he made the following statement: "Well, I've killed a woman in your house and your bathroom's in a mess." He then drove away in Mahaffey's car and was apprehended by the police, at which time he made two spontaneous statements. He said calmly, "I hope I killed the bitch," and as the officers were discussing Mahaffey's condition, he said loudly, "I hope I didn't go through all that for nothing. I hope she's dead as a doornail."

The trial court found that at the time he attacked Mahaffey, Pope was so intoxicated that his capacity to appreciate the criminality of his conduct or to conform his conduct to the requirements of the law was substantially impaired and that he was suffering from extreme mental or emotional disturbance. In making these findings, the court considered the fact that Pope was an alcoholic who generally consumed between two six-packs and a case of beer per day and who had consumed at least a half case of beer before attacking Mahaffey. The court also considered Pope's family history of mental illness and extreme alcoholism as well as expert opinion that was based in part on that history.

Although Pope refused to be evaluated by the defense's mental health expert, the expert interviewed members of his family and reviewed the facts of the murder. According to the mental health expert, given his history of chronic alcohol abuse and the amount of alcohol he had consumed on the night of the murder, Pope's behavior was impaired such that his impulse control was decreased, his aggression was increased, and his ability to appreciate the criminality of his conduct or to conform his conduct to the law was impaired.[1]

This is a true story, and the wording in these opening paragraphs is adapted from an opinion by the Florida Supreme Court.[2] You might ask yourself the following questions: (1) Should the fact that the defendant was drunk at the time he committed the crimes excuse him of responsibility for his actions or reduce his degree of criminal liability? (2) Should the fact that Alice Mahaffey did not die until eight days until after she was attacked, and that she succumbed to infection while in the hospital, reduce the defendant's degree of criminal liability?

Pope was found guilty of first-degree murder and robbery and was acquitted of kidnapping. He was sentenced to death for the homicide and to a consecutive life term for robbery with a deadly weapon. The Florida Supreme Court upheld his convictions. As you read through this chapter, you will learn about the nature of excuses, and you will see why voluntary intoxication is rarely a successful defense to a criminal charge.

THE NATURE OF EXCUSES

As discussed in Chapter 5, "justification declares the allegedly criminal act legal; excuse admits the act's criminality, but declares the allegedly criminal actor not to be worthy of blame."[3] An excuse admits that the action committed by the defendant was wrong and that it violated the criminal law but claims that the defendant should be excused from criminal liability by virtue of special conditions or circumstances that suggest that the defendant was not responsible for his or her deeds. The majority of excuses are personal in nature; that is, they claim that the defendant acted on the basis of some disability or some abnormal condition, such as intoxication, insanity, or immaturity. Even when a defendant suffers from a disability, however, that disability alone is not sufficient to excuse him or her of criminal responsibility. Only when the disability has the effect of in some way contributing to the criminal activity in question will the actor be excused. Like justifications, excuses are affirmative defenses and must be raised by the defendant.

> *Often times excusing of a fault doth make the fault the worse by the excuse.*
>
> —William Shakespeare, King John

FORMS OF EXCUSES

Several excuses are recognized at law, including (1) duress, (2) involuntary intoxication, (3) mistake, (4) age, (5) entrapment, (6) insanity, and (7) diminished responsibility. All of these excuses are discussed in this chapter. Also discussed here is the special area of syndrome-based defenses, a form of excuse that has recently entered the legal limelight.

Duress

The Model Penal Code (MPC) says: "It is an affirmative defense that the actor engaged in the conduct charged to constitute an offense because he was coerced to do so by the use of, or a threat to use, unlawful force against his person or the person of another, which a person of reasonable firmness in his situation would have been unable to resist."[4]

The defense of **duress**, sometimes also called *compulsion*, is based on the belief that people do not willfully engage in acts they are compelled or coerced to perform. Hence the mother forced to rob a bank by someone holding her children hostage, the captured military officer compelled to provide secrets to an enemy under threat of torture, and the pilot of an airplane who flies off course after her plane has been commandeered by terrorists are all forced to commit acts they would not otherwise perform.

In an interesting 1997 case, 53-year-old Jose Fernandez Pupo, a 30-year veteran of Cuba's military intelligence and police services, was acquitted by a federal jury in Tampa, Florida, on charges stemming from the hijacking of a small Cuban plane flown to U.S.-controlled

> *Things in law tend to be black and white. But we all know that some people are a little bit guilty, while other people are guilty as hell.*
>
> —Donald Cressey, University of California, Santa Barbara

duress
A condition under which one is forced to act against one's will. Also called *compulsion*.

territory.[5] He admitted that he commandeered a Cuba Aero Taxi flight over the eastern part of Cuba on July 7, 1996, and forced it to divert to the U.S. Naval Base at Guantanamo Bay. He also admitted having been armed with two firearms at the time of the hijacking and did not contest allegations that he fired one of the weapons out of an open cockpit window to show that he "meant business." Arrested on federal charges of air piracy, Fernandez Pupo offered a duress defense, saying that he had no alternative to breaking the law because Cuban authorities, aware that he headed an underground anti-Castro movement, were about to arrest him. A colleague, he said, had told him that a warrant had been issued for his arrest. Torture and death, he claimed, would likely follow. At the trial, U.S. District Judge Joyce Hens Green informed the jury that Fernandez Pupo could not be held criminally responsible for his act if jury members agreed that it was carried out "under duress." She said the hijacking could be excused if the defense could prove that Fernandez Pupo acted on the "reasonable belief" that he "would suffer immediate injury or death if he did not commit the crime." The jury concluded that the defense met that standard.

Some legal scholars say that duress may qualify as either a justification or an excuse. The main difference, they point out, is that necessity (which, as a justification for unlawful behavior, was discussed in Chapter 5) is brought about by acts of nature or natural events, whereas duress is imposed by one human being on another. Whenever a person is forced to act in violation of the law, whether by reason of human or natural "pressure," he or she is probably convinced that such action is necessary.

In most jurisdictions, effective use of the duress defense must be based on a showing that the defendant feared for his or her life or was in danger of great bodily harm—or that the defendant was acting to prevent the death or bodily harm of another.[6] Likewise, the threat under which the defendant acted must have been immediate, clear, and inescapable and must not have arisen from some illegal or immoral activity of the defendant. The MPC states that the defense of duress is "unavailable if the actor recklessly placed himself in a situation in which it was probable that he would be subjected to duress." Such a clause, found in many state statutes that codify the defense of duress, is called the *at-fault exception*. For example, one who joins a street gang cannot later claim that the gang "forced" him to engage in illegal acts against his will. Similarly, a prostitute ordered to shoplift by her "pimp" under the threat of being denied drugs to support her habit would be hard-pressed to claim duress as a defense to a larceny charge.

Generally speaking, duress is a defense only when the crime committed is less serious than the harm avoided. Some jurisdictions limit the applicability of the duress defense to less serious crimes; others state that it cannot be used as a defense to a charge of homicide; and still others broaden the ban to all crimes of personal violence. The California Penal Code limits the applicability of duress defenses to noncapital crimes in which the actor's life was threatened. It reads: "All persons are capable of committing crimes except . . . [p]ersons (unless the crime be punishable with death) who committed the act or made the omission charged under threats or menaces sufficient to show that they had reasonable cause to and did believe their lives would be endangered if they refused." During the Vietnam War, several U.S. servicemen were charged with murdering Vietnamese citizens in what became known as the My Lai incident. Lieutenant Calley defended himself by claiming that he was obeying orders.

States that have not codified the defense of duress generally adhere to common law requirements that the alleged coercion involve "a use or threat of harm which is present, imminent, and pending, and of such a nature as to induce a well grounded apprehension of death or serious bodily harm if the act is not done."[7]

Although duress is widely recognized today as a useful defense to a criminal charge, the well-known nineteenth-century English jurist James Stephen suggested that duress should be an ameliorating factor when punishment is considered but that it should not eliminate criminal liability. Stephen wrote, "It is, of course, a misfortune for a man that he should be placed between two fires, but it would be a much greater misfortune for society at large if criminals could confer impunity upon their agents by threatening them with death or violence if they refused to execute their commands." As an example, Stephen says, "The law says to a man intending to commit murder, if you do it I will hang you. Is the law to withdraw its threat if someone else says, if you do not do it I will shoot you?"[8]

Compare the Texas law on duress with Model Penal Code Section 2.09.

TEXAS PENAL CODE

Section 8-05. Duress.

(a) It is an affirmative defense to prosecution that the actor engaged in the proscribed conduct because he was compelled to do so by threat of imminent death or serious bodily injury to himself or another.

(b) In a prosecution for an offense that does not constitute a felony, it is an affirmative defense to prosecution that the actor engaged in the proscribed conduct because he was compelled to do so by force or threat of force.

(c) Compulsion within the meaning of this section exists only if the force or threat of force would render a person of reasonable firmness incapable of resisting the pressure.

(d) The defense provided by this section is unavailable if the actor intentionally, knowingly, or recklessly placed himself in a situation in which it was probable that he would be subjected to compulsion.

(e) It is no defense that a person acted at the command or persuasion of his spouse, unless he acted under compulsion that would establish a defense under this section.

Intoxication

The story that opened this chapter described how an alcoholic, Horace Pope, severely beat and then stabbed a woman named Alice Mahaffey, who later died. Although mental health experts testified at trial that Pope had a history of chronic alcohol abuse and that his ability to control his behavior on the night of the assault had been severely impaired by the large amount of alcohol he had consumed, he was nonetheless convicted of murder and sentenced to die.

> There is never a deed so foul that something couldn't be said for the guy; that's why there are lawyers.
>
> —Melvin Belli, American lawyer (1907–1996)

The verdict in the *Pope* case is consistent with the application of the intoxication defense in most jurisdictions. A claim of intoxication is generally not regarded as an effective defense even when the intoxication results from alcoholism, and laws that codify the defense usually set strict limits on the use of the intoxication defense. Intoxication is not a useful defense because most intoxicated individuals are responsible for their impaired state, and the law generally holds that those who voluntarily put themselves in a condition in which they have little or no control over their actions must be held to have intended whatever consequences ensue. In some jurisdictions and for certain crimes, however, voluntary intoxication may lessen criminal liability. Such is the case where a high level of intoxication makes it impossible for a person to form the *mens rea* necessary for a given offense. For example, because first-degree murder requires premeditation, a defense showing that a defendant was highly intoxicated while committing homicide—and therefore unable to think clearly—may result in a second-degree murder or manslaughter conviction.

In *People* v. *Walker*,[9] for example, California Jury Instruction Number 4.21 was read to the jury:

> In the crime of attempted murder of which the defendant is accused in count 1 of the information, a necessary element is the existence in the mind of the defendant of the

APPLYING THE CONCEPT

CAPSTONE CASE

Is a Soldier's Murder of Civilians Justified Because He Was Ordered to Do It?

United States v.
Calley, 46 C.M.R. 1131 (1975)

THE CASE During midmorning on 16 March 1968 a large number of unresisting Vietnamese were placed in a ditch on the eastern side of My Lai and summarily executed by American soldiers.

[PFC] Meadlo gave the most graphic and damning evidence. He had wandered back into the village alone after the trial incident. Eventually, he met his fire team leader, Specialist Four Grzesik. They took seven or eight Vietnamese to what he labeled a "ravine," where Lieutenants Calley, Sledge, and Dursi and a few other Americans were located with what he estimated as seventy-five to a hundred Vietnamese. Meadlo remembered also that Lieutenant Calley told him, "We got another job to do, Meadlo," and that appellant started shoving people into the ravine and shooting them. Meadlo, in contrast to Dursi . . . fired into the people at the bottom of the "ravine." . . .

Specialist Four Grzesik found PFC Meadlo crying and distraught, sitting on a small dike on the eastern edge of the village. He and Meadlo moved through the village, and came to the ditch, in which Grzesik thought were thirty-five dead bodies. Lieutenant Calley walked past and ordered Grzesik to take his fire team back into the village and help the following platoon in their search. He also remembered that Calley asked him to "finish them off," but he refused. . . .

He saw Lieutenant Calley and Meadlo firing from a distance of five feet into another group of people who were kneeling and squatting in the ditch. . . .

Of the several bases for his argument that he committed no murder at My Lai because he was void of *mens rea*, appellant emphasized most of all that he acted in obedience to orders. . . .

THE FINDING An order of the type appellant says he received is illegal. Its illegality is apparent upon even cursory evaluation by a man of ordinary sense and understanding. . . .

We find no impediment to the findings that appellant acted with murderous *mens rea*, including premeditation.

What Do You Think?

1. Should murder ever be excused because of duress? Can you create a set of facts under which you believe murder should be excused because of duress?

2. Should the rule concerning duress and following orders be different for soldiers in combat?

Additional Applications

Who bears the burden of proving duress (or the lack thereof)?

Dixon v. *United States*, 548 U.S. 1 (2006)

The Case: Defendant Keshia Davis, while purchasing firearms at two Texas gun shows in January 2003, unlawfully provided an incorrect address and falsely stated that she was not under any criminal indictment at the time. At her trial on multiple felony counts, she admitted the factual basis of the charges. She argued, however, that she had not formed the necessary *mens rea* for these crimes because her boyfriend had threatened to kill her or hurt her daughters if she did not buy the guns for him. In instructing the jury on this claim, the trial judge stated that, under federal law, the defendant had to prove duress by a preponderance of the evidence—a burden that the jury concluded had not been met. On appeal, Davis argued that both the Fifth Amendment's due-process clause and modern common law required that the government prove the absence of duress beyond a reasonable doubt.

The Finding: By a 7–2 vote, the U.S. Supreme Court affirmed the trial judge's instructions. Writing for the majority, Justice John Paul Stevens affirmed that the due-process clause required prosecutors to prove all of the elements of the charged crimes—including that the defendant had "knowingly" and "willfully" acted in violation of the law—beyond a reasonable doubt. Yet the existence of duress, Stevens reasoned, was a separate matter to be determined by the jury—and for such excuses, the common law has long assigned the burden of proof to the accused. Without question, Stevens noted, Congress *could* have mandated—as the Model Penal Code suggests for states—that the burden of proof be reallocated to the prosecution. Yet it has not clearly done so in the statutes in question, and in the absence of such a clear congressional intent, the common law approach to duress necessarily prevails.

How imminent must the harm be?

State v. Toscano, 378 A.2d 755 (N.J. 1977)

The Case: Defendant Joseph Toscano, a New Jersey chiropractor, was convicted by state court for his role in a wide-ranging criminal conspiracy to stage "accidents" in public places and then fraudulently collect settlement payouts from insurers. Dr. Toscano—who became involved in the scheme only after another doctor's paperwork mistakes had threatened to expose it—admitted at trial that he had aided in the fraud by completing a false medical report. At trial, however, he sought a jury instruction on duress, claiming that he participated only after repeated threats from a co-conspirator—whom he knew had gang affiliations and a criminal past—that he and his wife would be otherwise harmed. The police, Toscano asserted, would not have been able to offer protection if he had refused to comply.

In refusing the duress instruction, the trial judge followed the state common law standard that the defendant must make a threshold showing to the judge of a "present, imminent and impending" threat of harm; in this case, the judge concluded, Toscano's subjective fears of future harm, even if accepted as real, were negated by his failure to notify police of the scheme for an extended period of time. Thus under specific instructions *not* to consider duress, the jury convicted Toscano of conspiracy as charged.

The Finding: In a landmark ruling on state law, the Supreme Court of New Jersey reversed Toscano's conviction and ordered a new trial. Finding that New Jersey—like most other states—had no applicable statute defining the defense of duress, the court opted to "revise the common law" in the state by eliminating the defendant's preliminary need to show the threat of "present, imminent and impending" harm. Henceforth in New Jersey, the court declared, duress may be established—regardless of immediacy of threat—"if the defendant engaged in conduct because he was coerced to do so by the use of, or threat to use, unlawful force against his person or the person of another, which a person of reasonable firmness in his situation would have been unable to resist." And in asserting this excuse, the state high court stressed, the defendant need initially only convince the trial judge that "the fact of duress is in issue." Once that threshold showing has been made, the judge should then instruct the jury to consider all relevant factors—including "immediacy [of harm] . . . the gravity of harm threatened, the seriousness of the crime committed, the identity of the person endangered, the possibilities for escape or resistance and the opportunities for seeking official assistance"—so as to determine how a person "of reasonable firmness" would respond. Given this "admittedly open-ended" inquiry, the court added, it is "appropriate as a matter of public policy . . . to require the defendant to prove the existence of duress by a preponderance of the evidence."

---

specific intent to kill. If the evidence shows that the defendant was intoxicated at the time of the alleged crime, you should consider that fact in determining whether defendant had such specific intent. If from all the evidence you have reasonable doubt whether the defendant formed such specific intent, you must find that he did not have such specific intent.

The essence of any defense based on intoxication can be found in the effect that an intoxicating substance has on the mental state of the defendant. Of course, intoxication may make it impossible to commit a crime. A man charged with rape, for example, could conceivably use expert testimony to support his contention that it was impossible for him to achieve an erection because of his highly intoxicated condition at the time of the alleged offense. Such a claim, however, does not reference the mental state of the defendant but relies instead on the assertion that the crime in question did not actually occur because the defendant was too intoxicated to commit it. This kind of a defense is far different from the claim that the requisite mental state needed to commit an offense was lacking.

The 1996 case of *Montana* v. *Egelhoff* provides an interesting perspective on *mens rea* and voluntary intoxication. Like the law in many states, Montana law does not permit voluntary intoxication to be used as a defense in criminal proceedings. That restriction was challenged, however, in an appeal that reached the U.S. Supreme Court on the basis that a defendant might be so intoxicated as to be unable to form the *mens rea* needed for a specific crime. Attorneys for the defendant argued that the right of due process requires that defendants be given the opportunity to present "all relevant evidence to rebut the State's evidence on all elements of the offense charged."

There is a critical difference between voluntary and involuntary intoxication. The California Penal Code says that "**voluntary intoxication** includes the voluntary ingestion, injection, or taking by any other means of any intoxicating liquor, drug, or other substance."[10] **Involuntary intoxication**, in contrast, generally results from the unknowing ingestion of an intoxicating substance.

Involuntary intoxication may result from secretly "spiked" punch or LSD-laced desserts, from following medical advice, and from situations in which an individual is tricked or forced into consuming an intoxicating substance. A few years ago, for example, the Drug Enforcement Administration reported on the growing use of the drug Rohypnol (flunitrazepam) by young men who secretly put the substance into women's drinks in order to lower the women's inhibitions. Rohypnol is a powerful sedative, the side effects of which are not entirely known.

Involuntary intoxication is difficult to demonstrate in the case of alcohol because the taste and effects of alcohol are both widely known in our culture, and it can be assumed that most people who consume the substance are aware of its effects. Involuntary intoxication, however, may also result from the use of prescription or over-the-counter drugs containing substances with which the user is unfamiliar. One case,[11] for example, involved a hunter who assaulted other members of his hunting party. Expert witnesses testified that, at the time of the assaults, the man was suffering from toxic psychosis brought on by the excessive use of cough drops containing the chemical dextromethorphan hydrobromide (he had consumed 12 boxes of the cough drops in the 24 hours preceding the attacks), and the defendant was acquitted by a trial court.

Finally, involuntary intoxication can also result from a rare biological condition under which a person's body ferments food. The internal fermentation process, which takes place in the intestines, is caused by the yeast *Candida albicans* and can result in drunkenness, even though the afflicted individual has not consumed alcohol.

Involuntary intoxication may serve as a defense if it either creates in the defendant an incapacity to appreciate the criminality of his or her conduct or creates an incapacity to conform his or her behavior to the requirements of the law.

Mistake

In 1992, 16-year-old Japanese exchange student Yoshihiro Hattori was shot to death in Baton Rouge, Louisiana, by homeowner Rodney Peairs when he went to the wrong house looking for a Halloween party. Hattori, whose command of the English language was very poor, continued to approach Peairs's home when ordered to stop by the armed homeowner. Peairs was acquitted of manslaughter charges after claiming that he mistakenly thought the student was an intruder.

An honest **mistake of fact** will generally preclude criminal liability in instances in which the actions undertaken would have been lawful had the situation been as the person acting reasonably believed them to be. An *honest mistake* is one that is genuine and sincere and not a pretext offered merely to hide criminal intent. A decade ago, for example, many questions were raised when fashion model Jerry Hall was arrested after she picked up a

voluntary intoxication
Willful intoxication; intoxication that is the result of personal choice. Voluntary intoxication includes the voluntary ingestion, injection, or taking by any other means of any intoxicating liquor, drug, or other substance.

involuntary intoxication
Intoxication that is not willful.

mistake of fact
Misinterpretation, misunderstanding, or forgetfulness of a fact relating to the situation at hand; belief in the existence of a thing or condition that does not exist.

APPLYING THE CONCEPT

CAPSTONE CASE

Does a Defendant Have a Constitutional Right to Defend Against a Murder Charge by Claiming Intoxication?

Montana v. Egelhoff,
116 S. Ct. 2013 (1996)

Justice Scalia delivered the opinion of the Court.

THE CASE In July 1992, while camping out in the Yaak region of northwestern Montana to pick mushrooms, respondent made friends with Roberta Pavola and John Christenson, who were doing the same. On Sunday, July 12, the three sold the mushrooms they had collected and spent the rest of the day and evening drinking, in bars and at a private party in Troy, Montana. Some time after 9 *p.m.*, they left the party in Christenson's 1974 Ford Galaxy station wagon. The drinking binge apparently continued, as respondent was seen buying beer at 9:20 *p.m.* and recalled "sitting on a hill or a bank, passing a bottle of Black Velvet back and forth" with Christenson.

At about midnight that night, officers of the Lincoln County, Montana, sheriff's department, responding to reports of a possible drunk driver, discovered Christenson's station wagon stuck in a ditch along U.S. Highway 2. In the front seat were Pavola and Christenson, each dead from a single gunshot to the head. In the rear of the car lay respondent, alive and yelling obscenities. His blood-alcohol content measured .36 percent over one hour later. On the floor of the car, near the brake pedal, lay respondent's .38-caliber handgun, with four loaded rounds and two empty casings; respondent had gunshot residue on his hands.

Respondent was charged with two counts of deliberate homicide, a crime defined by Montana law as "purposely" or "knowingly" causing the death of another human being. Mont. Code Ann. Section(s) 45-5-102 (1995). . . . Respondent's defense at trial was that an unidentified fourth person must have committed the murders; his own extreme intoxication, he claimed, had rendered him physically incapable of committing the murders, and accounted for his inability to recall the events of the night of July 12. Although respondent was allowed to make this use of the evidence that he was intoxicated, the jury was instructed, pursuant to Mont. Code Ann. Section(s) 45-2-203 (1995),

that it could not consider respondent's "intoxicated condition . . . in determining the existence of a mental state which is an element of the offense." The jury found respondent guilty on both counts, and the court sentenced him to eighty-four years' imprisonment.

The Supreme Court of Montana reversed. It reasoned: (1) that respondent "had a due process right to present and have considered by the jury all relevant evidence to rebut the State's evidence on all elements of the offense charged . . . ," and (2) that evidence of respondent's voluntary intoxication was "clear[ly] . . . relevant to the issue of whether [respondent] acted knowingly and purposely. . . ." Because Section(s) 45-2-203 prevented the jury from considering that evidence with regard to that issue, the court concluded that the State had been "relieved of part of its burden to prove beyond a reasonable doubt every fact necessary to constitute the crime charged . . . ," and that respondent had therefore been denied due process. We granted certiorari. . . .

THE FINDING The cornerstone of the Montana Supreme Court's judgment was the proposition that the due process clause guarantees a defendant the right to present and have considered by the jury "*all relevant evidence* to rebut the State's evidence on *all elements* of the offense charged."

The State Supreme Court's proposition that the due process clause guarantees the right to introduce all relevant evidence is indefensible. The clause does place limits upon restriction of the right to introduce evidence, but only where the restriction "offends some principle of justice so rooted in the traditions and conscience of our people as to be ranked as fundamental." Respondent has failed to meet the heavy burden of establishing that a defendant's right to have a jury consider voluntary intoxication evidence in determining whether he possesses the requisite mental state is a "fundamental principle of justice." The primary guide in making such a determination, historical practice, gives respondent little support. It was firmly established at common law that a defendant's voluntary intoxication provided neither an

(continued)

"excuse" nor a "justification" for his crimes; the common law's stern rejection of inebriation as a defense must be understood as also precluding a defendant from arguing that, because of his intoxication, he could not have possessed the *mens rea* necessary to commit the crime. The justifications for this common-law rule persist to this day and have only been strengthened by modern research. Although a rule allowing a jury to consider evidence of a defendant's voluntary intoxication where relevant to *mens rea* has gained considerable acceptance since the nineteenth century, it is of too recent vintage and has not received sufficiently uniform and permanent allegiance to qualify as fundamental, especially since it displaces a lengthy common-law tradition which remains supported by valid justifications. . . .

None of this Court's cases on which the Supreme Court of Montana's conclusion purportedly rested undermines the principle that a state can limit the introduction of relevant evidence for a "valid" reason, as Montana has. The due process clause does not bar states from making changes in their criminal law that have the effect of making it easier for the prosecution to obtain convictions. The judgment is reversed.

What Do You Think?

1. How does a claim that (a) an intoxicated defendant should not be held responsible for his or her criminal activity because of the inability to form the requisite *mens rea* for a specific crime differ from the claim that (b) an intoxicated defendant should be excused because he or she had lowered inhibitions and impaired judgment as a consequence of ingesting alcohol? Do both claims carry the same *moral* weight? Explain.

2. Do you believe that, as a matter of fundamental due-process rights, a defendant should be given the opportunity to present "*all relevant evidence* to rebut the State's evidence on *all elements* of the offense charged"? Why or why not?

3. Do you think that, in circumstances like those described in this box, voluntary intoxication should completely exonerate a defendant of criminal liability because of its impact on the defendant's mental state? Explain.

Additional Applications

When can a defendant claim involuntary intoxication in a DUI case?

Carter v. State, 710 So.2d 110 (Fla. App. 1998)

The Case: Late in the evening, defendant David Carter was arrested by a Broward County, Florida, deputy sheriff

for driving under the influence (DUI). At the scene, Carter refused to take a breath alcohol test; he also failed three road sobriety tests and, on video, admitted that he had consumed three drinks and had smoked cannabis. He was charged with violating Sections 316.193(1) and (2)(b) of Florida's criminal laws by driving under the influence; at trial, he was convicted on those charges and sentenced to 17 months in prison.

At his trial, Carter testified that he had actually consumed only one beer—but on the same night, he had also been at the house of a friend who had given him what she told him were four ibuprofen tablets. That friend, in turn, testified that (1) she had been prescribed amitriptyline (an antidepressant); (2) she kept that medication in a container alongside ibuprofen tablets; and (3) she realized the next day that she had given the defendant a high dose of the antidepressant medication by accident. The director of the University of Miami's DUI lab also testified that Carter's behavior was consistent with intoxication due to the antidepressant—although it was also consistent with excessive alcohol and cannabis ingestion. Carter requested a jury instruction on involuntary intoxication; however, the trial judge refused on the ground that the state's DUI statute imposed strict liability and thus involuntary intoxication was not a valid defense.

The Finding: A Florida appeals court reversed the convictions and remanded the case for a new trial. The state's DUI laws, the court held, indeed required a showing of knowledge and intent—because strict liability "is constitutionally limited to minor infractions such as parking violations or other regulatory offenses." And in this particular case, the defendant had produced evidence both that he had unknowingly ingested a substance that could impair him and that he then drove without knowledge of the possible impairment. Given these circumstances, the due-process protections in federal and state law entitled the defendant to a jury instruction that involuntary intoxication was a possible excuse for his actions.

Is intoxication of a chronic alcoholic truly "voluntary"?

New York v. Tocco, 525 N.Y.S.2d 137 (N.Y.Sup.Ct. 1988)

The Case: On April 24, 1986, Salvatore Tocco—described by the trial court as "an alcoholic of classic dimension, caught in a vortex of a severe drinking problem . . . for upwards of 15 years"—set fire while intoxicated to an apartment in which he resided with his ex-wife and children. Tried without a jury on charges of second-degree arson (defined as "intentionally [damaging] a building . . . by starting a fire") and reckless endangerment, Tocco admitted setting the fire (although he could not recall his arrest); nonetheless, his attorney argued that Tocco had been incapable of formulating the specific intent necessary for second-degree arson. Prosecutors, without conceding the point, urged the court to consider the lesser included offense of reckless (fourth-degree) arson, which requires a lower culpable mental state.

The Finding: Admittedly "seek[ing] some limiting principle whereby application of the cruel and unusual punishment prohibition does not result in exoneration of the chronic alcoholic for criminal conduct," the trial judge ultimately found the defendant not guilty of arson in the second degree but guilty of reckless arson and reckless endangerment. Under prevailing law, the judge explained, a state of intoxication itself is not a defense to a criminal charge; still, in this case, the defendant's state of severe inebriation negated the *mens rea* necessary to prove guilt on charges of "intentionally" damaging a building by fire. At the same time, the judge continued, Tocco's intoxication did *not* negate a finding of recklessness, a lower culpable state of mind—precisely because "[i]f an alcoholic knows that he is prone to commit criminal acts while drunk and that the consumption of even one drink will destroy his ability to resist further drinking. . .

it must follow that his voluntary imbibing of the first drink is the very initiation of a reckless act." For a chronic alcoholic like Tocco, the judge concluded, the very act of taking a first drink was a "voluntary exercise of his will" that commenced a reckless course of action, the natural consequences of which were thus intended.

While so ruling on the basis of current law, the trial judge also speculated more broadly: "Can . . . an alcoholic's inebriated state(s) ever be considered truly voluntary?" After all, the judge noted, "there is a recognition among physicians that alcoholism is a disease characterized by loss of control" over consumption; indeed, the judge continued, "some (though probably not all) alcoholics lack the ability to control the taking of even the first drink." What's more, "if alcoholism is a disease . . . then the imposition of criminal liability for acts performed while drunk would at first blush defy logic." In light of all this, the trial judge concluded, "the law may evolve as new medical research on the nature of alcoholism becomes available." Still, at least at this point, "alcoholism is not, according to the prevailing view, accepted as a defense to any crime." ■

---

marijuana-filled suitcase in a public baggage claim area at an airport in Barbados. Hall, girlfriend of the rock musician Mick Jagger, claimed that she mistakenly grabbed the bag because it looked just like one she owned. She was released after convincing authorities that the mistake was genuine and after spending a night in jail.

A *reasonable mistake* is one that might be made by a typically competent person acting under the same set of circumstances. A man who forces a woman whom he does not know to accompany him on a journey she does not want to take may, for example, be guilty of kidnapping even though he believed she acquiesced to his requests to accompany him. In just such a case, the Indiana Supreme Court found a defendant guilty of kidnapping a woman who offered no physical resistance out of fear of the defendant—although she expressed verbal reservations. Any reasonable man, under the same circumstances, said the court, would have realized that she did not want to go with him. In the words of the court:

> Appellant's assertion that he did not "force" the victim out of the laundromat provides some evidence that he honestly so believed. It is, however, no evidence of the reasonableness of that belief. . . . Apart from this statement, we find nothing in the record to suggest that a reasonable man in appellant's position would have interpreted the victim's actions as indicative of her free consent to accompany appellant. By appellant's own version of the encounter the facts are such that no reasonable person could have believed as appellant alleges he did.[12]

Mistake as to fact should be distinguished from **ignorance of fact**. Ignorance of fact refers to a lack of knowledge of some fact relating to the matter at hand, whereas mistake of fact refers to a misinterpretation or misunderstanding of the facts at hand. Both can be defenses to a criminal charge. As a defense, both ignorance of fact and mistake of fact may negate the *mens rea* required for a specific offense. As one court said, "The criminal intention being of the essence of crime, if the intent is dependent on a knowledge of particular facts, a want of such knowledge, not the result of carelessness or negligence, relieves the act of criminality."[13]

Some mistakes do not relieve a defendant of criminal liability. A drug dealer who mistakenly purchases heroin, thinking it is cocaine, will still be found guilty of trafficking in a

ignorance of fact
Lack of knowledge of some fact relating to the situation at hand.

controlled substance.[14] Likewise, when a person intends to commit one crime but actually commits another, his or her mistake will be no defense. For example, a burglar who breaks into the wrong house seeking money he has heard is hidden under a mattress will still be guilty of the crime of burglary even though he is unable to locate the cash.

mistake of law
A misunderstanding or misinterpretation of the law relevant to the situation at hand.

Another form of mistake is **mistake of law**. Generally speaking, however, courts have held that neither **ignorance of the law** (where one does not know a law exists) nor a misunderstanding of the law provides for an acceptable defense, and criminal proceedings assume that "everyone capable of acting for himself knows the law."[15] This assumption does not mean, of course, that everyone is actually familiar with each and every law, but it effectively compels people to learn the standards set by the law in their sphere of activity. In effect, ignorance of the law is a kind of **culpable ignorance** in which an individual's failure to exercise ordinary care to acquire knowledge of the law may result in criminal liability.

ignorance of the law
A lack of knowledge of the law or of the existence of a law relevant to the situation at hand.

culpable ignorance
The failure to exercise ordinary care to acquire knowledge of the law or of facts that may result in criminal liability.

Although quite rare in practice, ignorance or mistake of law may be a defense in cases in which a given offense requires specific intent or in which mistake of law negates the *mens rea* required by a statute. For example, in the case of *Ratzlaf* v. *United States* (1994),[16] the U.S. Supreme Court ruled that no one can be convicted of trying to evade specific federal bank-reporting requirements that mandate "willfullness" unless it can be shown that they knew they were violating the law. Federal law requires a domestic bank involved in a cash transaction exceeding $10,000 to file a report with the Secretary of the Treasury; makes it illegal to "structure" a transaction—that is, to break up a single transaction above the reporting threshold into two or more separate transactions "for the purpose of evading the reporting requiremen[t]"; and sets out criminal penalties for "[a] person *willfully* violating" the antistructuring provision.

> *Ignorance of the law is no excuse in any country. If it were, the laws would lose their effect, because it can always be pretended.*
>
> —President Thomas Jefferson (1787)

Waldemar Ratzlaf was found guilty of violating the antistructuring provision of the law after he made a number of cash withdrawals just below the $10,000 threshold in order to pay off gambling obligations. He appealed his conviction, claiming that the "willfulness" requirement of the law made it necessary for the government to prove that he acted with knowledge that his structuring activities were illegal. The U.S. Supreme Court agreed, ruling that "[t]o give effect to [the statute's] 'willfulness' requirement, the Government must prove that the defendant acted with knowledge that the structuring he or she undertook was unlawful, not simply that the defendant's purpose was to circumvent a bank's reporting obligation." The Court ruled that "the lower courts erred in treating the 'willfulness' requirement essentially as words of no consequence." The fact that currency structuring is not necessarily an inherently immoral activity bolstered Ratzlaf's contention that the government had to prove his "willfulness" in violating the law. In the words of the Court:

> "Because currency structuring is not inevitably nefarious, this Court is unpersuaded by the United States' argument that structuring is so obviously 'evil' or inherently 'bad' that the 'willfulness' requirement is satisfied irrespective of the defendant's knowledge of the illegality of structuring,"[17] as it might be, for example, in cases of rape or murder.

The Court continued:

> The interpretation adopted in this case does not dishonor the venerable principle that ignorance of the law generally is no defense to a criminal charge, for Congress may decree otherwise in particular contexts, and has done so in the present instance.[18]

Ignorance of the law may also be an excuse where the law is not adequately published or is incapable of being known. An individual who violates a federal law against "knowingly making false statements" by placing his or her signature on a complicated government form may, for example, raise just such a defense. In one such case, a defendant signed a federal form required to obtain a firearm, but the form contained references to federal statutes by numbered sections and subsections, without explaining the content or purpose of the law it cited.

Although the defendant was technically in violation of the law (he was a convicted felon, and the laws referred to on the form prohibited a convicted felon from purchasing a gun), he claimed that he did not knowingly make a false statement because he was ignorant of what the legal nomenclature on the form meant. Although he was convicted, a federal appeals court reversed his conviction, saying that "many lawyers would not have understood" the language of the form and that it was therefore unreasonable to expect a layperson to understand it.[19]

> The man who has maimed, let him be maimed.
> The man who has killed, let him be killed.
>
> —Anonymous

Finally, mistake of law may be a valid defense to a criminal charge if made in good faith under circumstances involving a bona fide attempt to ascertain the meaning of the law through reliance on a public official who is in a position to interpret the statute or through the use of appropriate legal counsel. In some jurisdictions, a defendant may effectively raise such a defense where "before engaging in the conduct, the defendant made a bona fide, diligent effort, adopting a course and resorting to sources and means at least as appropriate as any afforded under our legal system, to ascertain and abide by the law, and where he acted in good faith reliance upon the results of such effort."[20]

Mistake of fact can be asserted by a defendant to show that, based on the defendant's belief at the time of the illegal activity, no crime occurred because the requisite *mens rea* was lacking. In *People* v. *Tolbert* (1996),[21] for example, a California appellate court held that a reasonable but mistaken belief in a victim's death prior to movement of that person by the defendant precludes conviction for kidnapping. In *Tolbert*, the defendant shot the victim (Killingbeck) in the right eye with a shotgun at close range, but the victim didn't die. Because the defendant, thinking the victim was dead, then transported the still-living body of his victim, he was charged with kidnapping. At trial, Tolbert was found guilty and sentenced on three counts. On count 4 (felon in possession of a firearm), the trial court sentenced him to two years in prison; on count 1 (second-degree murder), the trial court imposed an indeterminate term of 24 years to life, to be served consecutively; on count 3, kidnapping for robbery, it imposed an additional life term, plus four years on a personal firearm use enhancement, also to be served consecutively. Tolbert appealed the kidnapping conviction and sentence, claiming that the fact that he believed the victim was dead at the time he transported the body meant he lacked the *mens rea* needed for the crime of kidnapping.

Age

Defenses based on age, also called **infancy defenses** or *immaturity defenses*, make the claim that certain individuals should not be held criminally responsible for their activities by virtue of their youth. The defense of infancy has its origin in early Christian teachings, which held that children under the age of seven were incapable of rational thought and planned action. Under common law, children below the age of seven were presumed to be without criminal capacity—that is, to be incapable of forming the *mens rea* needed for criminal activity. Today that rule still holds, and in most states children below the age of seven cannot be charged even with juvenile offenses, no matter how serious their actions. However, in a startling 1994 case, prosecutors in Cincinnati, Ohio, charged a 12-year-old girl with murder after she confessed to drowning her toddler cousin ten years earlier—when the girl was only two years old! The cousin, 13-month-old Lamar Howell, drowned in 1984 in a bucket of bleach mixed with water. Howell's drowning had been ruled an accidental death until his cousin confessed. In discussing the charges with the media, Hamilton County prosecutor Joe Deters admitted that the girl could not be successfully prosecuted. "Frankly," he said, "anything under seven cannot be an age where you form criminal intent."[22] The prosecution's goal, claimed one of Deters's associates, was simply to "make sure she gets the counseling she needs."

Another rationale for the defense of infancy questions the assertion that children are too young to form the *mens rea* required for a criminal act. It is based instead on the belief that

infancy defense
A defense that claims that certain individuals should not be held criminally responsible for their activities by virtue of their youth. Also called *immaturity defense*.

APPLYING THE CONCEPT

CAPSTONE CASE

Is It Kidnapping to Move a Person Who Is Mistakenly Believed to Be Dead?

People v. Tolbert,
56 Cal. Rptr. 2d 604 (Cal. Ct. App. 1996)

THE CASE   [California] Penal Code, Section 26, recites, generally, that one is incapable of committing a crime who commits an act under a mistake of fact disproving any criminal intent. Penal Code Section 20 provides, "In every crime . . . there must exist a union, or joint operation of act and intent, or criminal negligence." The word "intent" in Section 20 means "wrongful intent." "So basic is this requirement [of a union of act and wrongful intent] that it is an invariable element of every crime unless excluded expressly or by necessary implication."

The kidnapping statute "neither expressly nor by necessary implication negate[s] the continuing requirement that there be a union of act and wrongful intent. The severe penalties imposed for th[is] offense . . . and the serious loss of reputation following conviction make it extremely unlikely that the Legislature intended to exclude as to th[is] offense the element of wrongful intent."

Mistake of fact is an affirmative defense. The defendant therefore has the burden of producing evidence that "he had a *bona fide* and reasonable belief that the [victim] consented to the movement. . . ." The Supreme Court has since held that this burden may be met with evidence supplied by the prosecution. However, because wrongful intent is an element of the crime, the ultimate burden of persuasion is on the people; the defendant is "only required to raise a reasonable doubt as to whether he had such a belief." We find ourselves unable to distinguish a mistake of fact about whether the kidnapping victim consents from a mistake of fact about whether the kidnapping victim is alive. If the victim is dead, he or she is no longer a "person" who can be kidnapped, precisely because he or she can no longer give or withhold consent to the asportation. (Cf. *People v. Kelly* (1992) 1 Cal. 4th 495, 524 [it is legally impossible to rape a dead body because "[a] dead body cannot consent to or protest a rape . . ."]; *People v. Thompson* (1993)

12 Cal. App. 4th 195, 201 ["the crime of rape requires a live victim, because it requires nonconsensual sexual intercourse. . . .) It does appear that under *Mayberry,* knowledge that the victim was alive is not an element of the crime of kidnapping, which the prosecution must prove in all cases; but if there is any evidence that the defendant honestly and reasonably believed the victim was dead, the people must prove beyond a reasonable doubt that the defendant lacked such a belief. . . .

THE FINDING   Here, there was ample evidence that defendant reasonably believed Killingbeck was dead before the asportation began. Indeed, it seems amazing that Killingbeck stayed alive for any time at all. He had been shot in the right eye by a shotgun held six to twelve inches away; there was an exit wound behind his right ear. Some of the pellets left through the exit wound, but "lots of them" remained inside. The force was sufficient to leave his head "slightly deformed." He was rendered unconscious instantly; the wound was inevitably fatal. The pathologist testified that Killingbeck was able to live for a little while because the left side of his brain was uninjured, but this would hardly have been obvious to a layman. The fact that defendant believed Killingbeck was dead is further evidenced by his comment to Tim that there was "a dead body" in the car, even though Killingbeck actually was still alive at the time.

Thus, it is inferable that defendant reasonably believed Killingbeck died immediately after he was shot. On the other hand, there is no evidence that defendant did not reasonably believe Killingbeck died immediately. Certainly one could imagine all sorts of scenarios in which defendant could have realized Killingbeck was still alive; he might have noticed that Killingbeck was still breathing before he closed the trunk; or he might have stopped the car at some point and opened the trunk to check on Killingbeck. "But speculation is not evidence, less still substantial evidence." The only sufficient asportation here consisted of the movement of the car around Rubidoux with Killingbeck in the trunk. There was substantial evidence that at this point defendant honestly and reasonably believed Killingbeck was dead; there was no substantial evidence to the contrary. Accordingly, the kidnapping for robbery conviction must be reversed. Retrial is barred by double jeopardy. . . .

The kidnapping for robbery conviction is reversed, and the case is remanded for resentencing. In all other respects, the judgment is affirmed.

What Do You Think?

1. Should mistake of fact exonerate a defendant who, through criminal activity, brings about a situation (as in this case) that causes him or her to mistake the facts?

2. How does the court's reasoning that a dead body cannot be raped support its position in this case? Do you agree with this reasoning? Why or why not?

Additional Applications

Is it breaking and entering to mistakenly enter a neighbor's house at dark?

State v. Lamson, 330 S.E.2d 68 (N.C.App. 1985)

The Case: On the evening of April 7, 1984, a deputy sheriff responded to a reported burglary attempt at the Concord, North Carolina, home of Joanne Christie. Upon arriving at the scene, he found the defendant David Lamson standing on Christie's back porch; earlier, Christie reported, Lamson had tried to enter the home through an open window on the front porch and had also shaken the back door knob loudly. Lamson—who had been drinking but was not drunk—was found to be carrying a suitcase; no burglary tools, however, were found in his possession.

At trial on aggravated burglary charges, Lamson's defense rested on an asserted mistake of fact. Christie's next-door neighbor testified that a friend of the defendant was staying at his house, and Lamson had visited his friend there on several previous occasions. What's more, Lamson produced photographs showing that the two adjacent houses were very similar in color, design, and appearance. At his sentencing hearing, he adamantly denied any intent to break into Christie's home. Rather, he claimed, he had simply mistaken the house for the neighbor's in the dark, and he had been making noise intentionally at the door and window in order to wake somebody up "to see when

[his friend] would be back to give him a ride to Charlotte." The trial court, after refusing to give a jury instruction on mistake of fact, found Lamson guilty of aggravated burglary and sentenced him to 18 years in prison.

The Finding: On appeal, the Court of Appeals of North Carolina dismissed the aggravated burglary charge and ordered that Lamson be retried on the lesser charge of misdemeanor breaking or entering. The "obvious objective" of the defense, the court held, was to show a mistake of fact—and the jury should have been instructed about the availability of that defense at trial. "A crime is not committed," the court continued, "if the mind of the person doing the act is innocent." Yet there is "nothing in the evidence" in this case "which supports a finding that [Lamson] entered Christie's house with intent to commit larceny."

Is it bigamy to unknowingly marry a second time?

People v. Vogel, 299 P.2d 850(Cal. 1956)

The Case: In September 1950, six years after marrying Peggy Lambert in a New Orleans civil ceremony, defendant Robert Vogel was called to active military duty in the Korean War. Upon his return to the United States in November 1951, he did not return to live with his wife and children, and the following month, Peggy and the children moved out of state. No formal divorce was ever granted. In March 1953, Vogel then married Stelma Roberts in San Diego County, California. Consequently, Vogel was convicted by a jury of committing bigamy in violation of Section 281 of California's Penal Code.

At trial, Vogel conceded that he had not obtained a divorce from Peggy, but argued that he had acted under a good-faith (albeit erroneous) belief that Peggy had divorced him by 1952. On that point, Vogel contended that shortly before his call-up to active Korean War duty, Peggy had told him that she was going to divorce him "in a jurisdiction unknown to him so that he could not contest the custody of their children." What's more, he produced evidence that Peggy had obtained a driver's license in her maiden name in 1951 and had then lived in St. Louis for several months in 1952 as "Mrs. Earl Heck." The trial court, however, rejected Vogel's good-faith belief as immaterial; consequently, the bulk of evidence pertaining to Vogel's claimed mistake of fact was excluded from the jury's consideration.

The Finding: On appeal, the Supreme Court of California reversed Vogel's conviction. Noting that the state's

(continued)

bigamy prohibition was silent on the question of wrongful intent, the Court nonetheless held that "good sense and justice" required that the jury be allowed to consider the defendant's honest-belief defense. As the court explained: "The severe penalty imposed for bigamy, the serious loss of reputation conviction entails, the infrequency of the offense, and the fact that it has been regarded for centuries as a crime involving moral turpitude, make it extremely unlikely that the Legislature meant to include the morally innocent to make sure the guilty did not escape." ■

children—although they may act willfully—are "too young to know any better." As one writer says, "The reason society holds minors free from criminal liability is not because they are too young to form a criminal intent, but because they are presumed to be too young to make a conscious, moral choice between doing good and doing evil."[23]

Most jurisdictions today do not impose full criminal culpability on children under the age of 18, but a number of states set the age of responsibility at 16 and some at 17. Children who violate the criminal law are officially referred to as **juvenile offenders** rather than as "criminals" to avoid the sort of stigmatization that might follow them throughout their lives. Juvenile offenders may be adjudicated "delinquent," but they are not "found guilty" (Figure 6–1).

Children under the age of criminal responsibility are subject to juvenile court jurisdiction, rather than to the jurisdiction of adult criminal courts, although almost all states allow older children to be transferred to criminal court jurisdiction if the crimes they are charged with are especially serious or if the children are habitually in trouble with the law. Transfer to adult court requires a showing by the prosecution that the child was able to "appreciate the wrongfulness of [his or her] conduct," that the child had "a guilty knowledge of wrongdoing," or that the child was "competent to know the nature and consequences of his [or her] conduct and to know that it was wrong." Some states specify that juvenile courts have no jurisdiction over certain excluded offenses. Delaware, Louisiana, and Nevada, for example, do not allow juvenile court jurisdiction over children charged with first-degree murder.

juvenile offender
A child who violates the criminal law or who commits a status offense. Also, a person subject to juvenile court proceedings because a statutorily defined event caused by the person was alleged to have occurred while the person was below the statutorily specified age limit of original jurisdiction of a juvenile court.

FIGURE 6–1

Age as a Defense.

Age	INFANCY TO SEVEN YEARS OLD	SEVEN YEARS OLD TO AGE OF RESPONSIBILITY (VARIES BY STATE)	AGE OF RESPONSIBILITY
If Charged...	Usually *cannot* be charged, even as a minor	Charged as minor unless... SERIOUS OFFENSE → HABITUAL OFFENSE →	Charged as adult
Violators Referred to as...	N/A	Juvenile offenders	Criminals
If Convicted...	N/A	Adjudicated delinquent	Found guilty
Possible Defense of Infancy?	Yes (Automatic)	Yes	No (Regardless of mentality)

In a hearing that made headlines some years ago, Cameron Kocher, a ten-year-old Pennsylvania youngster, was arraigned as an adult for the murder of his seven-year-old neighbor Jessica Carr.[24] Cameron, who was only nine years old at the time of the crime, was alleged to have used his father's scope-sighted hunting rifle to shoot the girl from a bedroom window while she was riding on a snowmobile in a neighbor's yard. The two had argued earlier over who would get to ride on the vehicle. The case was resolved in 1992, when the Pennsylvania Supreme Court overturned Cameron's arraignment as an adult, and the boy was placed on juvenile probation.

The defense of infancy is based on the chronological age of the defendant. It has not been successful when based on claims of *mental* immaturity. Courts have held that those who have passed the chronological age necessary for criminal responsibility cannot raise the defense of infancy based on psychological determinations of mental immaturity because "if by reason of mental disease or defect a particular individual has not acquired [the ability to observe legal requirements] his remedy is a defense based on idiocy or insanity."[25] The following Texas statute defines the relationship between age and criminal responsibility in that state.

TEXAS PENAL CODE 8.07

a. A person may not be prosecuted for or convicted of any offense that he committed when younger than fifteen years of age except:

   (1) perjury and aggravated perjury when it appears by proof that he had sufficient discretion to understand the nature and obligation of an oath;

   (2) a violation of a penal statute cognizable under Chapter 302, Acts of the 55th Legislature, Regular Session, 1957 (Article 67011–4, *Vernon's Texas Civil Statutes*);

   (3) a violation of a motor vehicle traffic ordinance of an incorporated city or town in this state;

   (4) a misdemeanor punishable by fine only, other than public intoxication;

   (5) a violation of a penal ordinance of a political subdivision; OR

   (6) a violation of a penal statute that is, or is a lesser included offense of, a capital felony, an aggravated controlled substance felony, or a felony of the first degree for which the person is transferred to the court under Section 54.02, Family Code, for prosecution if the person committed the offense when fourteen years of age or older.

b. Unless the juvenile court waives jurisdiction under Section 54.02, Family Code, and certifies the individual for criminal prosecution or the juvenile court has previously waived jurisdiction under that section and certified the individual for criminal prosecution, a person may not be prosecuted for or convicted of any offense committed before reaching seventeen years of age except an offense described by subsections (a)(1)-(5). No person may, in any case, be punished by death for an offense committed while he was younger than seventeen years.

Entrapment

On August 23, 2004, federal magistrate David Homer blasted the government's case against 34-year-old Yassin Aref and 49-year-old Mohammed Hossain—two New York Muslim men alleged to have terrorist links.[26] Homer ordered Aref, leader of an Albany mosque, and Hossain, owner of a pizzeria, released from jail, saying that there was no evidence that they were involved in any terrorist activities. The men had been arrested by the Federal Bureau of Investigation (FBI) weeks earlier during an early morning raid on Aref's mosque. The arrest came after an FBI sting operation in which agents used an informant to try to entice the two men to engage in a money-laundering scheme. The informant, who had been convicted of a felony for selling false driver's licenses, reportedly told the men that the money was to be used to purchase a shoulder-fired missile to assassinate a Pakistani diplomat.

Aref and Hossain had apparently been targeted by the sting operation after Aref's name was found in a notebook recovered by the U.S. military at what was described as a "terrorist training camp" in Iraq. The FBI said that Aref's name, written in Kurdish, was associated with the title "kak," which they interpreted to mean "commander."[27]

Aref and Hossain were released following review of the notebook by other FBI translators, who interpreted the entry to mean "brother" or "Mr.," and not "commander"—an error that was explained in a letter that the FBI sent to Judge Homer a few days before he released the two men.

Defense attorney Terence Kindlon said the government had not merely been overzealous but had originally presented false information to the court. Kindlon made it clear that if the government decided to proceed against his clients, he would raise an entrapment defense because the money-laundering idea had originated with the FBI. His clients, who may have thought they were making a loan to the informant, were not otherwise predisposed to engage in illegal activity, Kindlon said.

The defense of **entrapment** is built on the assertion that had it not been for government instigation, no crime would have occurred. Entrapment defenses may be raised where public law enforcement officials or people acting on their behalf induce or encourage an otherwise law-abiding person to engage in illegal activity. In effect, the defense of entrapment claims that law enforcement officers are guilty of manufacturing a crime where none would otherwise exist.

Entrapment activities may include a number of inducements to crime, but the two most common are (1) false representation by enforcement agents that are calculated to induce the belief that the illegal behavior is not prohibited and (2) the use of inducements to crime that are so strong that a person of average will and good intent could not resist (Figure 6–2).

Entrapment cannot be effectively raised as a defense, however, where government employees "merely afford opportunities or facilities for the commission of the offense" or where

entrapment
An improper or illegal inducement to crime by enforcement agents. Also, a defense that may be raised when such inducements occur.

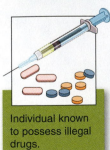 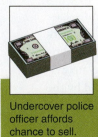  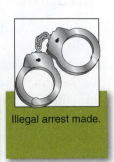

Individual known to possess illegal drugs. | Undercover police officer affords chance to sell. | Individual consents to sale. | Legal arrest made.

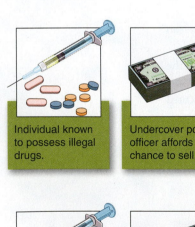 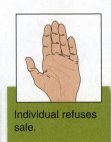   

Individual known to possess illegal drugs. | Undercover police officer affords chance to sell. | Individual refuses sale. | **ENTRAPMENT** Officer offers ten times his original price. | Individual consents to sale. | Illegal arrest made.

FIGURE 6–2

Entrapment.

law enforcement officers or their representatives engage in the "mere fact of deceit."[28] In other words, an undercover "sting" operation set up by the government to lure burglars and thieves who want to sell stolen goods would be legal, whereas government enticements to steal might not be.

U.S. Supreme Court cases have differentiated between a subjective approach to gauging entrapment and an objective approach, which developed later (Table 6–1). The *subjective test* excludes from criminal liability people who are "otherwise innocent, who have been lured to the commission of the prohibited act through the Government's instigation."[29] The subjective test attempts to distinguish between those who are blameworthy and those who are not, by asking whether a person "caught" by the government was predisposed to commit the crime in question. In doing so, it distinguishes "unwary criminals," who are ready and willing to commit the offense when presented with a favorable opportunity, from those who are not. Some courts have held that predisposition can be established by demonstrating a defendant's (1) prior convictions for similar crimes, (2) reputation for committing similar crimes, or (3) readiness to engage in a crime suggested by the police.[30] The subjective test for entrapment uses the criterion of "origin of intent." It asks, "Did the criminal intent start in the mind of the officers, or was the defendant 'predisposed' to commit the offense when the officer first appeared on the scene?"[31] Hence, following the subjective approach, traps may be legitimately laid by the government only for those who are already bent on crime.

The *objective test* to assessing entrapment is based on "the belief that the methods employed on behalf of the Government to bring about conviction cannot be countenanced."[32] If government agents have acted in a way that is likely to instigate or create a criminal offense, regardless of the defendant's predisposition to crime, then—according to the objective approach—the defendant can successfully raise the defense of entrapment. The objective approach to assessing entrapment is sometimes referred to as the defense of **outrageous government conduct**.

Definitive federal cases in the area of the entrapment defense include *Sorrells v. United States* (1932),[33] *Sherman v. United States* (1958),[34] and *Jacobson v. United States* (1992).[35] In *Jacobson*, the U.S. Supreme Court ruled, "In their zeal to enforce the law . . . government agents may not originate a criminal design, implant in an innocent person's mind the disposition to commit a criminal act, and then induce commission of the crime so that the government may prosecute."[36] However, because the decisions by the U.S. Supreme Court in the area of entrapment defense are not based on constitutional principles, they are not binding on the states. Nonetheless, all states recognize the defense of entrapment, and some have codified it. Most states follow a subjective approach in assessing claims of entrapment raised by a defendant. A dozen states, on the other hand, follow an objective approach. No jurisdiction permits the excuse of entrapment to serve as a defense to serious crimes,

outrageous government conduct
A kind of entrapment defense based on an objective criterion involving "the belief that the methods employed on behalf of the Government to bring about conviction cannot be countenanced."[i]

TABLE 6–1 Entrapment: Summary of Tests

Entrapment Test	Standard	Evidence	Effect	Where Used
Subjective test	Is defendant predisposed to commit the crime?	Defendant's record, statements, etc.	If defendant is predisposed, then he or she will be convicted, regardless of government conduct	Federal government and majority of states
Objective test	Does government behavior create substantial risk that someone not predisposed will commit the offense?	Government's conduct	If government's conduct is excessive, then defendant will be acquitted, regardless of predisposition	MPC and minority of states

such as murder and rape, however. Entrapment was found in the Florida case presented in the Capstone Case feature.

Syndrome-Based Defenses

In 1997, 16-year-old Jarred Viktor of Escondido, California, was arrested and charged with the brutal murder of his step-grandmother, 53-year-old Elizabeth Carroll. Carroll, who was killed in the hallway of her home, was slashed and stabbed 61 times in a vicious killing that sent shock waves through the local community. At the time of the murder, Viktor, a troubled teen, had been studying at home after being kicked out of high school. He was arrested hours after the killing, along with his girlfriend, when he crashed his grandmother's stolen Mustang in which the two had been riding. Following the crash, Viktor confessed to the murder. In an interesting twist, however, defense attorney Jeff Martin tried to show jurors that Viktor—because of his use of a powerful antidepressant called Paxil and his intense involvement in a popular Nintendo game called "The Legend of Zelda: A Link to the Past"—was unable to form the intent required for a murder conviction. In Zelda, players arm themselves with a "master sword" and then repeatedly stab at obstacles blocking their progress to higher levels. According to attorney Martin, "He played, excessively, these role-playing video games, for hours at a time. And it's my understanding that Zelda is a game in which you progress through it by stabbing, and being rewarded for that." Martin's gambit was unsuccessful, and Viktor—convicted of first-degree murder—was sentenced to life in prison without the possibility of parole.

The *Viktor* case is characteristic of new and innovative defense strategies that make use of enhancements to traditional defenses—with varying degrees of success. Primary among such strategies has been the use of claimed "syndromes" to broaden the scope of existing defenses. Some defense attorneys, for example, have attempted to employ battered woman's syndrome (BWS) in an effort to show how battered wives who kill their abusive husbands were really acting in self-defense. Others have used syndrome-based defenses to lessen the degree of an offender's criminal liability, where some accountability remains.

Other claimed "syndromes" used for such purposes include battered child's syndrome, rape trauma syndrome, sexual abuse syndrome, urban survival syndrome, and black rage syndrome. Syndromes, because they refer to personal abnormalities, generally supplement defenses based on excuses rather than those claiming justifications. According to mental health law expert Stephen Morse, "[A]bnormalities are usually excusing conditions that bear on the accused's responsibility, rather than objectively justifying conditions that make otherwise wrongful conduct right under the circumstances."[37]

A battered woman. Is the battered woman syndrome defense an excuse or a justification? © *Christelle Vaillant/Alamy*

APPLYING THE CONCEPT

CAPSTONE CASE

Is It Entrapment for a Female Agent of the Police to Offer Romance and Sex to Entice a Man with No Criminal History into Drug Dealing?

Madera v. State,
943 So.2d 960 (Fla. App. 4th Dist. 2006)

THE CASE   The appellant pled no contest to charges of trafficking in MDMA [a controlled substance with the street name Ecstasy], conspiracy to traffic in MDMA, and delivery of MDMA, reserving his right to appeal the trial court's denial of his motion to dismiss. The motion asserted that, on the undisputed facts, he was entrapped as a matter of law. We agree and reverse. . . .

The State argues that because it denied that the defendant lacked a predisposition to commit the crime, a material issue of fact was in dispute, and thus the motion was properly denied. This argument, however ignores the distinction between a subjective and objective theory of entrapment. In the former, a predisposition to commit the crime will defeat the affirmative defense of entrapment. In the latter, predisposition is not an issue. Rather, the question is whether the conduct of law enforcement was so egregious as to violate the due process rights of the defendant.

The facts alleged in the motion that were not specifically denied by the state include the following: The defendant was 37 years old with absolutely no criminal history, unknown to law enforcement officers, and gainfully employed in lawful activity at the time the confidential informant first approached him. The defendant became romantically interested in the CI and she led him to believe that she was similarly interested in him. She first brought up the topic of illegal drug use and continually asked the defendant if he knew where to buy drugs or if he could obtain drugs for her. The defendant repeatedly told her that he did not use or sell illegal drugs, and that, being new to the area, he did not know anyone who used or sold drugs.

The CI made promises of an intimate relationship, to include sexual relations, if the defendant would assist her in obtaining drugs. She discussed her personal medical problems with the defendant and played on his sympathy,

indicating that she needed the drugs to cope with the pain and the stress of cancer. The CI was herself a convicted drug trafficker who had recently received a below guidelines suspended sentence and probation. Unbeknownst to the defendant at the time, the CI was involved in similar transactions with several other individuals, whom she also pretended to befriend.

The facts in this case are remarkably similar to those in [a prior case] in which we found the conduct of law enforcement so egregious as to constitute a violation of due process and, thus, objective entrapment. The conduct in that case was described as follows:

> The record demonstrates that the CI approached Curry sometime before the detective was involved with any investigation. The CI encouraged a romantic relationship with Curry involving sexual activity. The CI also gave Curry money to help pay her mortgage. When the CI asked her to help him sell cocaine, she said no. It was only after an abundance of phone calls from the CI, and later the detective, that she acquiesced. The CI provided the cocaine and repeatedly met with Curry at her place of employment. In sum, there was no crime without the CI's prodding and improper conduct, which rose to the level of egregious. For this reason, Curry's due process rights were violated. The trial court should have found entrapment as a matter of law and granted the motion to dismiss.

Similarly, in this case, there would have been no crime without the CI's prodding and improper conduct. At the time, the defendant was gainfully employed at a lawful occupation, had no prior criminal history, and was not even suspected of criminal activity.

THE FINDING   The CI was used here, not to detect crime, but to manufacture it. Thus, as in *Curry*, we find that the defendant's due process rights were violated by this egregious conduct and that he was objectively entrapped as a matter of law.

(continued)

Accordingly, the judgment and sentence are hereby reversed with directions to set them aside and grant the motion to dismiss.

What Do You Think?

1. Was the conduct of law enforcement in this case so egregious that it was entrapment under both the objective and subjective tests?

2. Is the promise of a romantic relationship, including sex, so alluring or immoral that it is always wrong for the government to use this approach?

3. Would the outcome of this case have been different if the offer had been made by a male confidential informant to a female target?

Additional Applications

Should federal courts use a subjective or objective test of entrapment?

Hampton v. United States, 425 U.S. 484 (1976)

The Case: In late February 1974, the defendant Hampton was playing pool with an undercover DEA agent (Hutton) at a St. Louis bar when Hampton noticed needle marks on Hutton's arms. According to Hutton, Hampton then told the agent that he needed money and could obtain heroin to sell; Hutton responded by setting up two transactions at which Hampton sold small packets of heroin to government agents. Contesting this version of events, Hampton insisted that it had actually been Hutton who initially proposed the illegal drug sales; what's more, Hampton claimed, the undercover DEA agent had engaged in outrageous conduct by actually supplying the drugs that Hampton later sold. Thus at trial, Hutton unsuccessfully requested a jury instruction that embodied his version of the facts and directed the jury to acquit on entrapment grounds if it was found that Hutton had indeed been the heroin supplier. Further, Hampton's requested instruction would have directed the jury not to consider Hampton's predisposition to commit the offense in light of the government's conduct in the case.

The Finding: In a divided 5–3 ruling featuring no majority opinion, the U.S. Supreme Court upheld the conviction and rejected Hampton's entrapment defense. Writing for a three-justice plurality, Justice William Rehnquist adopted a subjective approach to entrapment in emphasizing the "intent or predisposition of the defendant" rather than the conduct of government agents. Previous Supreme Court rulings, Rehnquist argued, had categorically "ruled out the possibility that the defense of entrapment could ever be based upon governmental misconduct in a case . . . where the predisposition of the defendant to commit the crime was established." Two other justices—Lewis Powell and Harry Blackmun—likewise rejected Hampton's entrapment defense while explicitly objecting to Rehnquist's "absolute rule" that "no matter what the circumstances, neither due process principles nor our supervisory power could support a bar to conviction in any case where the Government is able to prove predisposition."

In a dissent joined by two others, Justice William Brennan argued instead for adoption of an objective standard for entrapment that placed primary emphasis on the government's conduct. Brennan wrote: "Where the Government's agent deliberately sets up the accused by supplying him with contraband and then bringing him to another agent as a potential purchaser, the Government's role has passed the point of toleration. The Government is doing nothing less than buying contraband from itself through an intermediary and jailing the intermediary. . . . [S]uch conduct deliberately entices an individual to commit a crime."

Can a federal drug defendant claim "sentencing entrapment"?

United States v. Nanez and Neal, 2006 U.S. App. LEXIS 4258 (6th Cir. 2006) (unpublished decision)

The Case: In January 2002, defendant Kevin Neal was recruited as a driver for an interstate drug-selling operation. During a series of negotiations with undercover agents posing as drug buyers, Neal and a co-defendant discussed details of drug delivery and discussed future cocaine sales, and evidence introduced at trial indicated that the undercover agents had coordinated actively with a federal prosecutor during the operation to ensure that the ensuing transactions included at least five kilograms of cocaine. Upon his arrest, Neal was charged with (among other things) conspiracy to distribute five or more kilograms of cocaine—a crime that, under federal law, carried increased penalties as compared to illicit dealing in smaller amounts. On appeal, Neal argued that he had been predisposed to deal only in small quantities of drugs; the government, however, had induced him to deal in larger quantities so as to increase his ultimate sentence.

The Finding: In upholding Neal's conviction, a three-judge panel of the U.S. Court of Appeals for the Sixth Circuit rejected the defendant's "sentencing entrapment" argument out of hand. "Sentencing entrapment," the panel noted, "is a legal theory that has been recognized by neither this court nor the United States Supreme Court." What's more, the Supreme Court has only outlined two theories of entrapment, objective and subjective—"neither of which applies to sentencing." The record of the case, moreover, "does not indicate that Neal's will was overcome or that he was included only to deal in small quantities." Thus, in this case, the panel concluded, "there is no occasion for us to consider adopting a doctrine of sentencing entrapment."

In the medical literature, a **syndrome** is defined as "a complex of signs and symptoms presenting a clinical picture of a disease or disorder."[38] If it can be demonstrated that a person charged with a crime was "suffering" from a known syndrome at the time that the crime was committed, such a showing may lower or eliminate criminal liability in at least three ways: (1) It may help support the applicability of a traditional defense (including a justification); (2) it may expand the applicability of traditional defenses (including justifications) to novel or unusual situations or to situations in which such defenses might not otherwise apply; or (3) it may negate the *mens rea* needed to prove the offense, leading the jury or trial judge to conclude that a crucial element necessary to prove the crime is missing. Some suggest a fourth possibility, however, and that is "the creation of new affirmative defenses,"[39] in which novel and unique defenses, beyond those now recognized by law, would take their place alongside other, more traditional defenses, such as duress, mistake, and self-defense. Defenses predicated on, or substantially enhanced by, the acceptability of syndrome-related claims are termed **syndrome-based defenses** (Figure 6–3).

As a matter of constitutional law, a defendant is entitled to introduce evidence that might disprove any element of the charged crime. Consequently, many defendants have attempted to use syndromes as proof that they lacked the *mens rea* required for conviction. *Convincing* arguments of this sort, however, have been difficult to make because few syndromes are medically well documented, and fewer still have found an established place within American legal tradition.

Although courts have been reluctant to recognize the claim that syndromes negate *mens rea*, the use of syndromes in expanding the applicability of traditional defenses has met with greater success. In such a role, syndromes—in and of themselves—provide neither a justification nor an excuse for otherwise criminal behavior. Syndromes may be called on, however, to explain why a given individual in a particular situation should be held to a different set of standards than those to which a typical "reasonable person" is held. Should the actions of a battered woman, for example, be judged according to the criterion of a "reasonable battered woman" rather than that of a "reasonable (nonbattered) person"? If so, the fact that a woman suffering from a history of spousal abuse chose to kill her husband might be defensible under the doctrine of self-defense, even though an otherwise "reasonable" person (with no history of spousal abuse) might have been expected to leave the marital relationship rather than kill the batterer. Defenses that might be "expanded" by syndromes include self-defense and diminished responsibility (discussed later in this chapter).

Finally, some suggest that syndrome-based defenses should be recognized as new affirmative defenses and that their legitimacy should be predicated on the widely accepted legal principle that only those who are morally responsible should be punished for their acts. Western jurisprudence has generally held that where moral responsibility does not exist, for whatever reason, it is unjust to punish someone who violates the criminal law. Advocates of such wholesale adoption of syndrome-based defenses suggest a totality-of-circumstances approach that would allow a defendant to present any evidence that may have some bearing on his or her motivation. Under this approach, juries would be faced with deciding the

syndrome
A complex of signs and symptoms presenting a clinical picture of a disease or disorder.[ii]

syndrome-based defense
A defense predicated on, or substantially enhanced by, the acceptability of syndrome-related claims.

FIGURE 6–3

The Structure of a
Syndrome-Based Defense.

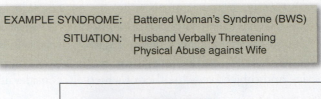

EXAMPLE SYNDROME: Battered Woman's Syndrome (BWS)
SITUATION: Husband Verbally Threatening
Physical Abuse against Wife

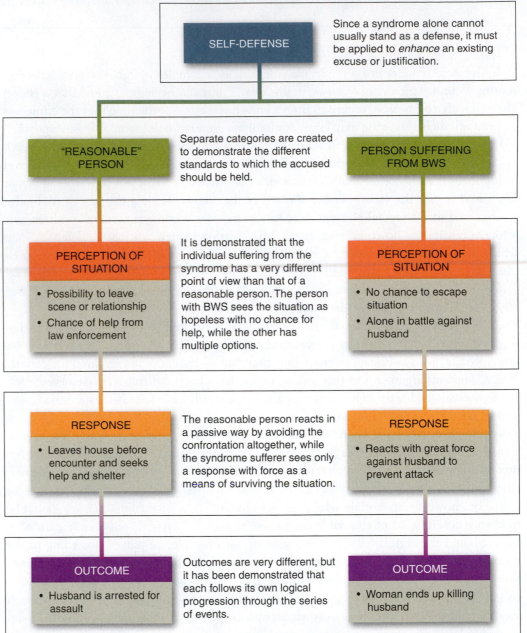

SELF-DEFENSE

Since a syndrome alone cannot usually stand as a defense, it must be applied to *enhance* an existing excuse or justification.

"REASONABLE" PERSON

Separate categories are created to demonstrate the different standards to which the accused should be held.

PERSON SUFFERING FROM BWS

PERCEPTION OF SITUATION
- Possibility to leave scene or relationship
- Chance of help from law enforcement

It is demonstrated that the individual suffering from the syndrome has a very different point of view than that of a reasonable person. The person with BWS sees the situation as hopeless with no chance for help, while the other has multiple options.

PERCEPTION OF SITUATION
- No chance to escape situation
- Alone in battle against husband

RESPONSE
- Leaves house before encounter and seeks help and shelter

The reasonable person reacts in a passive way by avoiding the confrontation altogether, while the syndrome sufferer sees only a response with force as a means of surviving the situation.

RESPONSE
- Reacts with great force against husband to prevent attack

OUTCOME
- Husband is arrested for assault

Outcomes are very different, but it has been demonstrated that each follows its own logical progression through the series of events.

OUTCOME
- Woman ends up killing husband

battered woman's syndrome (BWS)

A condition characterized by a history of repetitive spousal abuse and "learned helplessness" (the subjective inability to leave an abusive situation). Also, "a series of common characteristics that appear in women who are abused physically and psychologically over an extended period of time by the dominant male figure in their lives; a pattern of psychological symptoms that develop after somebody has lived in a battering relationship; or a pattern of responses and perceptions presumed to be characteristic of women who have been subjected to continuous physical abuse by their mate[s]."[iii] Also called *battered person's syndrome.*

question of whether the individual acted "voluntarily" or whether, instead, the individual's behavior was a quasi-automatic product of forces beyond his or her control.

Battered Woman's Syndrome   Battered woman's syndrome (BWS) is the best known of the syndromes on which today's innovative defenses are based. BWS, sometimes also referred to as *battered spouse syndrome* or *battered person's syndrome*, entered contemporary awareness with the 1979 publication of Lenore Walker's book *The Battered Woman.* Defense attorneys were quick to use Walker's idea of "learned helplessness" to explain why battered women were unable to leave abusive situations and why they sometimes found it necessary to resort to violence to free themselves. Walker helped popularize the syndrome in legal circles by testifying at a number of trials as an expert witness. Battered woman's syndrome has been defined by the New Jersey Supreme Court as "a series of common characteristics that appear in women who are abused physically and psychologically over an extended period of time by the dominant male figure in their lives; a pattern of psychological symptoms that develop after somebody has lived in a battering relationship; or a pattern of responses and perceptions presumed to be characteristic of women who have been subjected to continuous physical abuse by their mate[s]."[40]

As is the case with syndromes generally, BWS is not in itself a defense. It is a *condition* said to characterize women who live in abusive relationships. BWS may, however, provide additional justification for a woman who kills a battering spouse during an episode of battering—when the threat of serious bodily harm or death is imminent. As an excuse for killings that do not occur within the context of an immediate threat, however, BWS has proven less effective in eliminating criminal liability, although it may lessen it, as provocation generally does (resulting, for example, in a manslaughter conviction rather than a conviction for first-degree or second-degree murder).

An oft-cited example of BWS is the 1989 North Carolina case of *State* v. *Norman*.[41] The case illustrates some of the difficult issues involved in any defense invoking a BWS claim. In 1987, the defendant, Judy Norman, was arrested and tried for the first-degree murder of her husband, J. T. Norman, whom she shot three times in the back of the head as he slept. The couple's 25 years of marriage had been stormy and fraught with violence. As the state's supreme court later observed:

> The defendant presented evidence tending to show a long history of physical and mental abuse by her husband due to his alcoholism. . . . The defendant testified that her husband had started drinking and abusing her about five years after they were married. His physical abuse of her consisted of frequent assaults that included slapping, punching and kicking her, striking her with various objects, and throwing glasses, beer bottles and other objects at her. The defendant described other specific incidents of abuse, such as her husband putting her cigarettes out on her, throwing hot coffee on her, breaking glass against her face, and crushing food on her face. . . . The defendant's evidence also tended to show other indignities inflicted upon her by her husband. Her evidence tended to show that her husband did not work and forced her to make money by prostitution, and that he made humor of the fact to family and friends. He would beat her if she resisted going out to prostitute herself or if he was unsatisfied with the amounts of money she made. He routinely called the defendant "dog," "bitch" and "whore," and on a few occasions made her eat pet food out of the pet's bowls and bark like a dog. He often made her sleep on the floor. At times, he deprived her of food and refused to let her get food for the family. During those years of abuse, the defendant's husband threatened numerous times to kill her and to maim her in various ways.[42]

> The common characteristics of a battered wife [include] her inability to leave despite . . . constant beatings; her "learned helplessness," her lack of anywhere to go; her feelings that if she tried to leave, she would be subjected to even more merciless treatment; her belief in the omnipotence of her battering husband; and sometimes her hope that her husband will change his ways.
>
> —Chief Justice Robert N. Wilentz, New Jersey Supreme Court, in State v. Kelly, 478 A.2d 364 (1984)

On the day of the killing, J. T. Norman had again beaten his wife, and when nighttime came he ordered her to sleep on the bedroom floor, telling her "that's where dogs sleep." Judy Norman found that she couldn't sleep, walked to a neighbor's house to find pain pills, but discovered a pistol instead. She took the weapon back to her home and shot her husband in the back of the head as he slept. After the first shot had been fired, she felt her husband's chest and, after determining that he was still breathing, shot him twice more in the head.

Two expert witnesses in forensic psychiatry examined Judy Norman after the shooting and testified at trial that the defendant fit the profile of a battered woman. The condition, they testified, "is characterized by such abuse and degradation that the battered wife comes to believe she is unable to help herself and cannot expect help from anyone else." A psychologist testified that Judy Norman believed it was reasonably necessary for her to shoot her husband because she thought herself doomed to "a life of the worst kind of torture and abuse . . . [and] that it would only get worse, and that death was inevitable."

At the close of the trial, Judy Norman's attorneys asked the jury to acquit her of all charges because, they claimed, given her circumstances, the killing of her husband had been an act of reasonable self-defense. The jury, however, returned a verdict of "guilty" on one charge of voluntary manslaughter, and Judy Norman was sentenced to six years' imprisonment. She appealed, saying that the trial court should have more fully considered her claim of self-defense based on BWS. The North Carolina Court of Appeals granted a new trial, ruling that the trial court should have instructed the jury of the possibility of returning a not-guilty verdict based on the claim of self-defense. The court of appeals reasoned that "when there is evidence of battered wife syndrome, neither an actual attack nor threat of attack by the husband at the moment the wife uses deadly force is required to justify the wife's killing of him in . . . self-defense." The appellate court concluded that "to impose such requirements would ignore the 'learned helplessness,' meekness, and other realities of battered wife syndrome and would effectively preclude such women from exercising their right of self-defense." In the words of the court: "A jury, in our view, could find that decedent's sleep was but a momentary hiatus in a continuous reign of terror by the decedent, that defendant merely took advantage of her first opportunity to protect herself, and that defendant's act was not without the provocation required for perfect self-defense."

Eventually the *Norman* case reached the North Carolina Supreme Court. That court overruled the appellate court's decision, finding that an immediate threat to the defendant was lacking because of the nonconfrontational circumstances surrounding the killing. A valid claim of self-defense, the supreme court ruled, can only be based on evidence "tending to show that, at the time of the killing, the defendant reasonably believed herself to be confronted by circumstances which necessitated her killing her husband to save herself from imminent death or great bodily harm." The term *imminent*, said the court, can be defined as "immediate danger, such as must be instantly met, such as cannot be guarded against by calling for the assistance of others or the protection of the law." Because no imminent harm was about to befall the defendant at the time she shot her husband, the court reasoned, the claim of self-defense was not justified.

In this case, the North Carolina Supreme Court judged the actions of Judy Norman according to traditionally accepted standards of self-defense. As mentioned in Chapter 5, such standards rely on the *objective* criterion of what a "reasonable person" would do under the same circumstances. Although the appellate court was willing to modify the standards for a claim of self-defense by allowing a *subjective* evaluation of reasonableness—that is, that a habitually battered woman might reason differently than would an average, normal, and sensible human being—the state's supreme court was not.

BWS is an area of the law that is still in flux. Some states, such as California, specifically permit expert testimony regarding BWS concerning "the physical, emotional, or mental effects upon the beliefs, perceptions, or behavior of victims of domestic violence,"[43] whereas others make no specific provision for the admissibility of BWS testimony. Such testimony, however, when it is available, may help juries better understand claims of self-defense made by battered women. As one Kansas court explained: "Expert testimony on the battered woman syndrome would help dispel the ordinary lay person's perception that a woman in a battering relationship is free to leave at any time. The expert evidence would counter any 'common sense' conclusions by the jury that if the beatings were really that bad the woman would have left her husband much earlier. Popular misconceptions about battered women would be put to rest, including the beliefs the women are masochistic and enjoy the beatings and that they intentionally provoke their husbands into fits of rage."[44] At the same time, defense initiatives based on a view of BWS *as a syndrome* may one day effectively extend the role of BWS beyond that of merely expanding self-defense claims and into the role of an excuse, such as duress or diminished capacity.

Efforts at clarification continue. Section 40507 of the Violent Crime Control and Law Enforcement Act of 1994 requires the U.S. attorney general and the secretary of health and human services to undertake a study of battered woman's syndrome and to "transmit to the House Committee on Energy and Commerce, the Senate Committee on Labor and Human Resources, and the Committees on the Judiciary of the Senate and the House of Representatives a report on the medical and psychological basis of" the syndrome "and on the extent to which evidence of the syndrome has been considered in criminal trials." The report is to include "(1) medical and psychological testimony on the validity of battered women's syndrome as a psychological condition; (2) a compilation of State, tribal, and Federal court cases in which evidence of battered women's syndrome was offered in criminal trials; and (3) an assessment by State, tribal, and Federal judges, prosecutors, and defense attorneys of the effects that evidence of battered women's syndrome may have in criminal trials."

Other Syndromes   BWS was one of the first syndromes to be raised as a defense enhancement in American courtrooms. Many others have since followed. Among them are these:[45] adopted child syndrome, false memory syndrome, premenstrual syndrome (PMS), holocaust survival syndrome (see, for example, *Werner v. State*[46]), attention deficit disorder (raised in defense of Michael Fay, the teenager "caned" in Singapore in 1994), black rage defense (created by William Kunstler and offered in defense of Colin Ferguson, the Long Island Rail Road shooter), elder abuse syndrome, fetal alcohol syndrome (a variation of which was used in defense of Eric Smith, the 14-year-old who sodomized and killed a four-year-old neighborhood boy), Gulf War syndrome, Munchausen by proxy syndrome (wherein a caregiver injures his or her children to gain attention), nicotine withdrawal syndrome, repressed memory syndrome (used by California prosecutors to convict George Franklin, Sr., of the rape and murder of his eight-year-old daughter's friend 20 years after the killing), rotten social background syndrome, parental abuse syndrome (employed by Erik and Lyle Menendez), post-traumatic stress disorder, rape trauma syndrome (see, for example, *State v. Marks*[47]), ritual abuse syndrome (abuse at the hands of Satanic and other cults), UFO survivor syndrome, urban survival syndrome (used to defend Texas killer Daimian Osby), and Vietnam syndrome (see, for example, *State v. Kenneth J. Sharp, Jr.*[48]). One especially recent syndrome to be discussed in the medical literature is Internet addiction disorder (IAD). Specialists studying this disorder say that IAD is as real as alcoholism. People with IAD tend to lose control over their daily activities and crave the use of the Internet. They even have withdrawal symptoms when forced to forgo access to the Internet for an extended period of time.

Because syndromes are clinically viewed as diseases or disorders, we might anticipate the development of defenses based on other disorders, including hypoglycemia, senility, Alzheimer's disease, sleep disorders, postpartum disorders, preexisting genetic conditions, alcoholism, and drug addiction. Proponents of defenses based on chronic alcoholism, for example, suggest that the overpowering nature of addiction is such that alcoholics are unable to control their drinking and that any criminal behavior that follows from a lessening of personal control induced by the consumption of alcohol should be excused because it is the result of disease rather than willful choice. Others make the same argument for those addicted to drugs. Remember that there are two major elements of all crimes: *mens rea* and *actus reus*. If an involuntary physical condition causes one to commit a crime (for example, an epileptic batters someone during a seizure), then there is no *mens rea*, as required to commit a crime.

> We've been abused! The citizens have been abused by abusive excuses! We've been abused by the "dumb excuse syndrome," and because of that we're not responsible . . . as a society.
>
> —Gregory Koukl, Stand to Reason
> radio commentary

Independent of such arguments, defenses based on syndromes, diseases, and disorders (other than "insanity") have yet to meet with widespread success. Even so, the use of syndrome-type defenses is increasing. In 1991, for example, a Fairfax, Virginia, judge dismissed drunk-driving charges against Dr. Geraldine Richter, an orthopedic surgeon, who cited the role PMS played in her behavior.[49] Dr. Richter admitted to drinking four glasses of wine before allegedly kicking and cursing a state trooper who stopped her car because it was weaving down the road. A Breathalyzer test showed a blood-alcohol level of 0.13 percent—higher than the 0.10 percent needed to meet the requirement for drunk driving under Virginia law. A gynecologist who testified as an expert witness on Dr. Richter's behalf, however, said that the behavior she exhibited is characteristically caused by PMS and asserted that PMS "explained away" what would otherwise have been unacceptable behavior on the part of the surgeon.

> If they [the accused] didn't have a moral obligation to do right because of their bad circumstances, why do we have a moral obligation to understand their bad circumstances and exercise leniency?
>
> —Gregory Kould, Stand to Reason radio commentary

The defense of PMS has met with success in England, as well, where a 1980 case resulted in a verdict of not guilty against Christine English, who had killed her live-in lover when he threatened to leave her. An expert witness at the trial, Dr. Katharina Dalton, testified that English had been the victim of PMS for more than a decade. According to Dr. Dalton, PMS had left Ms. English "irritable, aggressive, . . . and confused, with loss of self-control."[50]

Problems with Syndrome-Based Defenses

One of the central problems with all defenses based on syndromes is that there is no syndrome that includes homicide, or any other law-breaking behavior, as a symptom of or as an *inevitable result* of the syndrome. In other words, according to most specialists, most people suffering from syndromes are as capable of controlling their behavior as anyone else.[51] In fact, most do. Speaking loosely, for every 100 people afflicted with some "syndrome," 99 do not violate the criminal law, and far fewer kill.[52] Most women suffering from PMS, for example, are unlikely to attack a highway patrol officer. At the same time, almost everyone has something in his or her background that could be pointed to in an effort to mitigate responsibility for any particular act. That is to say, at one time or another, we have probably all suffered "negative" experiences that could serve as excuses for otherwise irresponsible behavior.

psycholegal error
The mistaken belief that if we identify a cause for conduct, including mental or physical disorders, then the conduct is necessarily excused.[iv]

To conclude that the mere existence of a syndrome supports a legal excuse, claims Stephen J. Morse, is "fundamental psycholegal error."[53] **Psycholegal error**, says Morse, refers to "the mistaken belief that if we identify a cause for conduct, including mental or physical disorders, then the conduct is necessarily excused." He continues, "Causation is not an excuse, nor is a cause identical to compulsion, which may be an excuse." It is not enough, says Morse, that a syndrome be identified as part of the causal chain that led to the commission of a crime; rather the syndrome needs to produce some excusing condition before the defendant can be lawfully excused. "[S]hould the use of syndromes to excuse be expressed doctrinally by the creation of new, discrete excuses for each new syndrome, or by the use of new syndrome evidence simply to support existing excuses?" Morse says, "I strongly favor the latter approach because the former—the creation of a new excuse based on the syndrome—suggests confusingly that it is simply the presence of the syndrome in the causal chain that somehow itself excuses."[54]

Another problem with syndrome-like excuses is that, in a fundamental sense, they seem to rely on a tactic of *blame shifting*, in which the victim of crime is made to seem less like a victim and more like a criminal in hopes that a jury will side with the defendant. Blame shifting attempts to convince the jury that the victim "had it coming" and builds on such notions as a history of abuse that can actually justify homicide. In *The Abuse Excuse*, famed trial lawyer Alan M. Dershowitz says, "At bottom, the subtle message of these abuse-excuse defenses is that the *real* criminal is the dead victim and the defendant performed a public good by dispatching him. Thus, the abuse excuse places the *victim* of the killing or maiming on trial—generally in absentia—and if the defense lawyer can persuade the jury that he or she 'had it coming,' there is a chance that the jury will disregard the established rules of self-defense and take the law into its own hands by acquitting the defendant or reducing the charges."[55]

This kind of thinking quickly became clear in arguments raised by defense attorneys on behalf of Erik and Lyle Menendez, the California brothers who were convicted of murdering their parents. "Good parents do not get shotgunned by their kids. Period," said defense attorney Leslie Abramson.[56] Taken to this extreme, cautions Dershowitz, abuse excuses are "lawless invitation[s] to vigilantism, both on the part of abuse victims and on the part of jurors who sympathize more with them than with those whom they have killed or maimed."[57]

The Future of Syndrome-Based Defenses   The growing tendency among courts in recent years to accept an expansion of criminal defenses based on syndromes reflects an increased willingness by other social institutions to accept sophisticated excuses (especially "scientifically" supported ones) for wrongdoing of all kinds. As a direct result of this society-wide intellectual revolution, says U.S. Supreme Court Justice Clarence Thomas,

> [m]any began questioning whether the poor and minorities could be blamed for the crimes they committed. Our legal institutions and popular culture began identifying those accused of wrongdoing as victims of upbringing and circumstances. The point was made that human actions and choices, like events in the natural world, are often caused by factors outside of one's control. No longer was an individual identified as the cause of a harmful act. Rather, societal conditions or the actions of institutions and others in society became the responsible causes of harm. The external causes might be poverty, poor education, a faltering family structure, systemic racism or some other forms of bigotry, and spousal or child abuse, just to name a few. The consequence of this new way of thinking about accountability and responsibility—or lack thereof—was that a large part of our society could escape being held accountable for the consequences of harmful conduct. The law punishes only those who are responsible for their actions; and in a world of countless uncontrollable causes of aggression or lawlessness, few will have to account for their behavior.[58]

Thomas concludes: "An effective criminal justice system—one that holds people accountable for harmful conduct—simply cannot be sustained under conditions where there are boundless excuses for violent behavior and no moral authority for the state to punish. . . . How can we teach future generations right from wrong if the idea of criminal responsibility is riddled with exceptions . . . ?"[59]

Alan Dershowitz phrases the same sentiments succinctly. He says, "The most profound danger posed by the proliferation of abuse and other excuses is that it may be a symptom of a national abdication of personal responsibility."[60]

Others, however, feel that it is time for syndrome-based excuses to be accorded legitimacy. As one author puts it: "Once it is recognized that excuses are based on notions of justice, and show the law's consideration for the defendant's predicament in particular circumstances, it becomes obvious that the list of excuses need not be regarded as closed. Our judges are so costive in their attitude to defenses that there is perhaps no immediate hope of a change of attitude on their part; but if the call for new defenses is made insistently enough it may be heeded eventually."[61]

MENTAL INCOMPETENCY

Mental competency is an important concept in the law, particularly criminal law. A defendant's mental state is assessed using different legal tests at various points in the criminal justice process (Figure 6–4). The two most significant points are at trial and at the time of the commission of the crime. This discussion begins with the former.

CRIMINAL LAW IN THE NEWS

Is Some Shoplifting an Addiction?

Should shoplifting be added to our long list of addictions? An estimated 1 in 11 Americans steals merchandise from stores—often when they don't even need to, according to the National Association for Shoplifting Prevention.

Whereas conventional wisdom holds that most shoplifters are troubled teenagers or the poor, the association reports that three-quarters are adults, and most of them hold down jobs.

Even in this economic downturn, shoplifters generally aren't taking necessities. "People aren't stealing to feed their families," said Joe LaRocca, senior asset protection advisor of the National Retail Federation. "They're stealing iPods, handbags, and other discretionary items." Retailers also report heavy stealing of expensive cuts of meat, expensive liquor, and electric toothbrushes and tools.

Terry Shulman, founder of Cleptomaniacs and Shoplifters Anonymous, sees similarities between shoplifting and a drug addiction. "An addiction is something a person has difficulty stopping on his or her own, one where there's an escalation of the out-of-control behavior and where there are feelings of withdrawal or preoccupation when not engaging in it," he said. "That fits drug addicts, and it fits thousands of shoplifting addicts I've talked to."

The National Association for Shoplifting Prevention says about one-third of shoplifters have depression. Shulman says they often say something was taken from them and, therefore, "I'm entitled to something extra for my suffering."

Shoplifters can be brazen. In a support group, a petite woman recalled rolling a large executive office chair with a built-in massager out the front door of a store. A man in the group said he stole a 400-pound air compressor and shoved it into his car trunk. "It's an adrenalin rush," he said.

"The excitement they experience from shoplifting entices them back," the National Association of Shoplifting Addiction reports. "The excitement of 'getting away with it' produces a chemical reaction which is described as an incredible 'rush.'"

A woman in the act of shoplifting. Is shoplifting an addiction for some people?
Fotolia

Being Discovered and Recovering

Getting caught quickly ends the rush. Paula Paine, a wealthy Houston socialite addicted to shoplifting, was out jogging one day when she came upon a new house with unpacked furniture inside. She came back in her car, loaded up the furniture and brought it to her own home.

But when Paine's house went up for sale and she held an open house, the neighbor recognized the purloined furniture. Paine was mortified but later realized it was the best thing that could have happened to her because she had to ask for help.

Enrolling in a 12-step program, Paine took responsibility for her addiction and returned all she had stolen. The National Association of Shoplifting Addiction says when shoplifters confront their problem and explore the causes, chances of repeating the offense typically drop from 25% to 2%.

Although stores often drop charges against shoplifters, Shulman favors prosecuting them. He says this forces them to confront their addiction and share their obsession with others in a support group. "It's the secrets that keep us sick," he says. Shoplifters "have nowhere to tell their secret because of the fear and shame."

Like other addictions, the urge to shoplift may never go away. A former shoplifter says she no longer carries a big handbag because "that for me was my major instrument to conceal the items. Now when I go to the store, my bag will hold no more than my cell phone and my wallet."

Resources

"The Last word: Addicted to Shoplifting," *The Week*, February 5, 2009, **http://theweek.com/article/index/92984/ the-last-word-addicted-to-shoplifting.** "Addicted to Stealing: Inside a Shoplifter's Mind," ABC Primetime, July 10, 2007,

http://abcnews.go.com/Primetime/ story?id=1190720&page=1#.T07WExxC8rh. National Association of Shoplifting Prevention, "Psychological Studies on Shoplifting and Kleptomania," **http://www.shopliftingprevention.org/ WhatNASPOffers/NRC/PsychologicalStudies.htm**

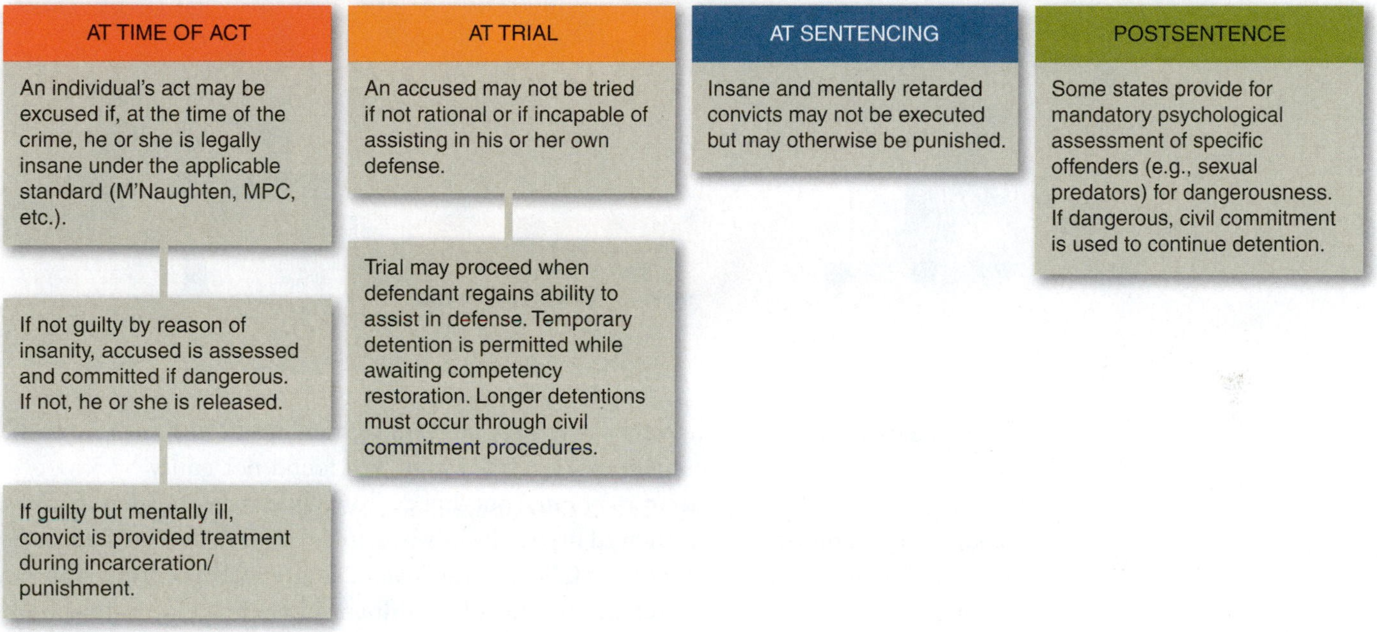

AT TIME OF ACT	AT TRIAL	AT SENTENCING	POSTSENTENCE
An individual's act may be excused if, at the time of the crime, he or she is legally insane under the applicable standard (M'Naughten, MPC, etc.).	An accused may not be tried if not rational or if incapable of assisting in his or her own defense.	Insane and mentally retarded convicts may not be executed but may otherwise be punished.	Some states provide for mandatory psychological assessment of specific offenders (e.g., sexual predators) for dangerousness. If dangerous, civil commitment is used to continue detention.
If not guilty by reason of insanity, accused is assessed and committed if dangerous. If not, he or she is released.	Trial may proceed when defendant regains ability to assist in defense. Temporary detention is permitted while awaiting competency restoration. Longer detentions must occur through civil commitment procedures.		
If guilty but mentally ill, convict is provided treatment during incarceration/ punishment.			

FIGURE 6–4

Insanity and Competency.

Competency to Stand Trial

Due-process requirements prohibit the government from prosecuting a defendant who is legally incompetent to stand trial. Competency to stand trial may become an issue when a defendant appears to be incapable of understanding the proceedings against him or her or is unable to assist in his or her own defense due to mental disease or defect. Conversely, a person is **competent to stand trial** if he or she, at the time of trial, has sufficient present ability to consult with his or her lawyer with a reasonable degree of understanding and a rational as well as factual understanding of the proceedings (Figure 6–5).[62]

In 1996, for example, lawyers for multimillionaire chemical heir John E. du Pont successfully argued at a pretrial hearing that their client was psychotic and, as a consequence, was unable to work effectively with his lawyers in preparing a defense to the charge against him. Du Pont was accused of shooting and killing David Schultz, an Olympic wrestler and 1984 gold medalist who had trained on du Pont's estate near Philadelphia. After the shooting, du Pont was declared schizophrenic by news commentators, pop psychologists, and his own attorneys. His delusions of being the Dalai Lama, Jesus, and "heir to the Third Reich" were all publicized in the national media. "He's not faking it. It's real. He's psychotic," Dr. Robert Sadoff, an expert witness hired by the defense, testified at the pretrial hearing.[63]

competent to stand trial
A finding by a court that the defendant has sufficient present ability to consult with his lawyer with a reasonable degree of rational understanding and that the defendant has a rational as well as factual understanding of the proceeding against him or her.

FIGURE 6–5

Competency to
Stand Trial.

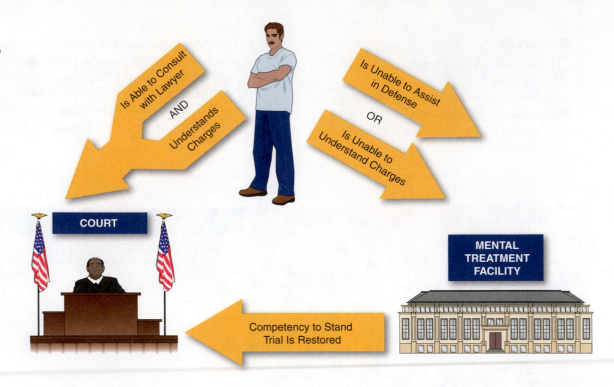

FIGURE 6–5

Competency to
Stand Trial.

Even a psychotic person, however, may be competent to stand trial—although he or she may later be relieved of criminal responsibility if tried and found not guilty by reason of insanity. Before the trial, prosecutors pointed out that du Pont appeared competent because he answered to his own name, showed no psychosis while in jail, and signed his own name on court documents—not that of Jesus Christ or the Dalai Lama. He also continued to run his huge estate, dubbed "Foxcatcher," and handle his financial affairs through telephone calls to his staff from jail. "The defendant is able to conduct his affairs, both financial and legal," Assistant District Attorney Joseph McGettigan told the court.[64] Delaware County Common Pleas Judge Patricia Jenkins sided with du Pont's attorneys, however, declaring that du Pont "is actually psychotic," and ordered him held in a mental hospital for treatment until doctors could decide that he would be able to assist his lawyers in preparing his defense. In 1997, after half a year of treatment with antipsychotic drugs, a judge ruled that du Pont's competency had been restored. He was then tried and found guilty of third-degree murder in the killing of Schultz. He was sentenced to 13 to 30 years in prison or a mental hospital (the place of detention to be decided by Pennsylvania correctional authorities).

Competency to stand trial focuses on the defendant's condition at the time of trial, rather than at the time of the crime. The U.S. Supreme Court has held: "Fundamental principles of due process require that a criminal defendant who is legally incompetent shall not be subjected to trial."[65] In *Pate* v. *Robinson* (1966), the Court held that a failure to observe procedures adequate to protect a defendant's right not to be tried or convicted while incompetent to stand trial deprives the defendant of the right to a fair trial.[66] The federal test to determine whether a defendant is competent to stand trial was set forth in *Dusky* v. *United States* (1960), in which the Supreme Court held that the "test must be whether he has sufficient present ability to consult with his lawyer with a reasonable degree of rational understanding—and whether he has a rational as well as factual understanding of the proceedings against him."[67]

Section 4241 of Title 18 of the U.S. Code, "Determination of Mental Competency to Stand Trial," reads:

If . . . the court finds by a preponderance of the evidence that the defendant is presently suffering from a mental disease or defect rendering him mentally incompetent to the extent that he is unable to understand the nature and consequences of the proceedings against him or to assist properly in his defense, the court shall commit the defendant to the custody of the Attorney General. The Attorney General shall hospitalize the defendant for treatment in a suitable facility.[68]

Once sanity has been recovered, the defendant may be brought to trial.

In *Cooper* v. *Oklahoma* (1996), the U.S. Supreme Court ruled that states must let criminal defendants avoid trials if it's more likely than not that they are incompetent.[69] Until *Cooper*, Oklahoma defendants (and defendants in Pennsylvania, Connecticut, and Rhode Island) were required to provide clear and convincing evidence that they were mentally incompetent and therefore unable to participate in their own trials in a meaningful way. As discussed in Chapter 1, clear and convincing evidence is that which establishes the reasonable certainty of a claim, although the standard requires less than proof beyond a reasonable doubt. In *Cooper*, the Court held that the clear-and-convincing-evidence standard was too strict and ruled that criminal defendants must be allowed to avoid trials if they show by a preponderance of the evidence that they are mentally unfit. Proof by a preponderance of the evidence means that the defendant must only convince the court that it is more likely than not that he or she is mentally incompetent and unable to participate in the trial. At the time of the *Cooper* ruling, most states and all federal courts[70] were already using the preponderance-of-the-evidence standard to determine competency to stand trial.

Once the issue of incompetency is raised, some states and the federal government require the defendant to prove lack of competency in order to avoid trial, whereas other states require that the prosecution prove the defendant competent before trial can proceed. Arizona is typical of the way many states handle competency hearings. Following guidelines set down in *Dusky*, Arizona law says that the term **incompetent to stand trial** means that, "as a result of a mental illness, defect, or disability, a defendant is unable to understand the nature and object of the proceeding or to assist in the defendant's defense." The Arizona law continues: "The presence of a mental illness, defect, or disability alone is not grounds for finding a defendant incompetent to stand trial." In the state of Arizona, at "any time after the prosecutor charges a criminal offense by complaint, information, or indictment, any party or the court on its own motion may request in writing that the defendant be examined to determine the defendant's competency to stand trial, to enter a plea, or to assist the defendant's attorney. . . . Within three working days after a motion is filed . . . the parties shall provide all available medical and criminal history records to the court," and the "court may request that a mental health expert assist the court in determining if reasonable grounds exist for examining a defendant."

Arizona law also says that "[w]ithin thirty days after the report is filed, the court shall hold a hearing to determine a defendant's competency to stand trial. The parties involved may introduce other evidence regarding the defendant's mental condition or may submit the matter by written stipulation on the expert's report. . . . If the court finds that the defendant is competent to stand trial, the proceedings . . . continue without delay." Arizona law specifies that "[i]f the court initially finds that the defendant is incompetent to stand trial, the court shall order treatment for the restoration of competency unless there is clear and convincing evidence that the defendant will not be restored to competency within fifteen months. The court may extend the restoration treatment by six months if the court determines that the defendant is making progress toward the goal of restoration."

When competency cannot be restored, Arizona law stipulates: "If the court finds that a defendant is incompetent to stand trial and that there is no substantial probability that the defendant will regain competency within twenty-one months after the date of the original finding of incompetency, any party may request that the court: (1) Remand the defendant to the custody of the department of health services for the institution of civil commitment

incompetent to stand trial A finding by a court that—as a result of a mental illness, defect, or disability—a defendant is unable to understand the nature and object of the proceeding against him or her or is unable to assist in the preparation of his or her own defense.

proceedings. . . . (2) Appoint a guardian. . . . (3) Release the defendant from custody and dismiss the charges against the defendant."[71]

In like manner, all capital punishment jurisdictions require that a person about to be executed understand the situation he or she faces before execution can occur. Continuing with Arizona law, for example, we find that it provides that "[p]risoners who are sentenced to death are presumed competent to be executed. A prisoner may be found incompetent to be executed only on clear and convincing evidence of incompetency." If a condemned prisoner is found to be incompetent, he or she must be sent to a state hospital and "shall remain confined at the state hospital until the prisoner becomes competent to be executed."[72] The Eighth and Fourteenth Amendments to the U.S. Constitution also prohibit the execution of a convictee who is legally insane.

Insanity at the Time of the Crime

Although the question of competency to stand trial may be vitally important to defendants who claim insanity at the time of trial, another important issue revolves around the need to determine whether a criminal defendant was insane at the time the crime was committed. It is that question with which we will be concerned throughout the remainder of this chapter.

The insanity defense, like other defenses that have found a place in our legal system, exists because, as the famed jurist David Bazelon once observed, "the criminal law [is] an embodiment of society's moral vision." Therefore, says Bazelon, "[f]inding a defendant guilty is not only a factual judgment; it also constitutes a moral condemnation of the person. In our tradition, moral blame cannot attach where an act was not the result of a free choice. The verdict of not guilty by reason of insanity is nothing more than an expression of that moral intuition."[73] Furthermore, other punishment objectives are not satisfied when the offender is insane. For example, specific deterrence may be impossible.

Insanity can influence criminal liability in two ways: (1) It may result in a finding that the *mens rea* required for a specific crime was lacking, leading the court to conclude that no crime occurred, or (2) it may lead to a showing that, although the requisite *mens rea* was present at the time of the crime, the defendant should be excused from legal responsibility because of mental disease or defect. The first perspective allows that a given mental condition may negate an element of an offense, whereas the latter recognizes that a crime took place but excuses the perpetrator due to a lack of moral blameworthiness. If *mens rea* cannot be proven by the prosecution, a finding of not guilty should result. If the defendant possessed the necessary *mens rea* but is able to successfully raise the defense of insanity, a **not guilty by reason of insanity (NGRI)** verdict should be returned. In short, *as a defense*, insanity recognizes that some people, by virtue of mental disease or mental defect, cannot morally and justly be held accountable for their actions.

not guilty by reason of insanity (NGRI)
The plea of a defendant, or the verdict of a jury or judge in a criminal proceeding, that the defendant is not guilty of the offense charged because at the time the crime was committed, the defendant did not have the mental capacity to be held criminally responsible for his or her actions.

THE INSANITY DEFENSE: A COMMON MISUNDERSTANDING

A prevalent misconception in the criminal law, even among some attorneys, is the belief that *mens rea* is *automatically* lacking in an insane defendant and that the purpose of the insanity defense is to advance such a claim. The famed jurist Jerome Hall, for example, once wrote, "If the defendant was insane at the time of the conduct in issue, the requisite *mens rea* was lacking and no crime was committed."[74] Hall believed that a culpable mental state could not be shown to exist in an insane defendant. Similarly, the Court TV website tells visitors: "In the eyes of the law, a defendant is legally insane if he or she is unable, because of a mental problem, to form a *mens rea*, a Latin term meaning a guilty mind. Because the law only punishes people who are mentally responsible for their actions, most states allow juries to find a defendant not guilty if he or she was insane at the time a crime was committed. At the heart of an insanity defense is the notion that, because of mental illness, either the defendant could not understand the difference between right and wrong or could not keep from doing the wrong act."[75]

The ability to distinguish between moral good and evil is, however, quite a different issue than that of demonstrating a culpable *mens rea*, when *mens rea* is understood as purposeful or intentional behavior. Those who are suffering from mental illness may still act purposefully, even though they may not, due to mental disease, be able to fully appreciate the moral implications of their behavior. The difference between intent or purpose and lack of moral sense can be seen in some of the actions of children. Children often act purposefully and intentionally, and they may also act selfishly. A child whose behavior harms another may have intended the behavior, and may even have intended harm, but may not—by virtue of immaturity—have been able to fully realize the moral implications (that is, the "wrongfulness") of his or her actions.[76]

If children can act purposefully but are unable to fully appreciate the consequences of their actions, a similar claim can be made for those who are insane at the time they commit a crime. As one court held: "Even the most psychiatrically ill have the capacity to form intentions, and the existence of intent usually satisfies any *mens rea* requirement."[77] Whether we speak of children or the insane, it would be unjust for society to punish those who lack the capacity to understand the moral consequences of their behavior, however intentional it may have been. Children and the insane are not responsible for their behavior not because they don't intend it, but because to hold them responsible given their lack of moral appreciation is fundamentally unfair. In the one case, that of children, the law distinguishes the immature person from the bad one; in the other case, that of the mentally ill, the law distinguishes the sick from the bad.

WHAT IS INSANITY?

Just what constitutes insanity? The authoritative *Black's Law Dictionary* warns that the term **insanity** is "a social and legal term rather than a medical one." It goes on to define the concept as "a condition which renders the affected person unfit to enjoy liberty of action because of the unreliability of his behavior with concomitant danger to himself and others."[78] *Black's* continues, saying that the term "is used to denote that degree of mental illness which negates the individual's legal responsibility or capacity." In other words, the law has its own definition of insanity, which is sometimes at odds with the psychiatric definition of mental illness. A person may be mentally ill or mentally abnormal and yet be legally sane, and vice versa.

As *Black's* observes, the term *insanity* has no place in the medical literature—which speaks instead of *mental disorders*—a term also used in some statutes. The definitive work on mental disorders is the *Diagnostic and Statistical Manual of Mental Disorders*, published by the American Psychiatric Association.[79] The *Manual*, now in its fourth edition, is referred to as **DSM-IV** and was last revised in 1994 (a new edition is expected to be released at about the time that this book goes to press). It lists 12 major categories of mental disorders, which are presented in Table 6–2. As the table shows, researchers have identified many different mental illnesses of varying severities and complexities. From a psychiatric perspective, it is far too simplistic to describe a severely mentally ill person merely as "insane." In fact, the vast majority of people with a mental illness would be judged "sane" if current legal tests for insanity were applied to them.[80] Hence, although mental illness may explain a person's behavior, it seldom excuses it.

insanity
An affirmative defense to a criminal charge; a social and legal term (rather than a medical one) that refers to "a condition which renders the affected person unfit to enjoy liberty of action because of the unreliability of his behavior with concomitant danger to himself and others."[v] Also, a finding by a court of law.

DSM-IV
The fourth edition of the *Diagnostic and Statistical Manual of Mental Disorders*, published by the American Psychiatric Association.[vi] The DSM-IV lists 12 major categories of mental disorders.

The insane, like young infants, lack one of the essential attributes of personhood—rationality.

—M. Moore, California Law Review (1985)

TABLE 6–2   Classification of Mental Disorders in Medicine

Adjustment Disorders

Anxiety Disorders

Delirium, Dementia, and Amnestic and Other Cognitive Disorders

Disorders Usually First Diagnosed in Infancy, Childhood, or Adolescence

Dissociative Disorders

Easting Disorders

Factitious Disorders

Impulse-Control Disorders Not Elsewhere Classified

Mental Disorders Due to a General Medical Condition Not Elsewhere Classified

Mood Disorders

Personality Disorders

Schizophrenia and Other Psychotic Disorders

Sexual and Gender Identity Disorders

Sleep Disorders

Somatoform Disorders

Substance-Related Disorders

Source: Based on data from American Psychiatric Association, *Diagnostic and Statistical Manual of Mental Disorders,* Fourth Edition, Text Revision (Washington, DC: APA, 2000).

Note: Disorders are listed in alphabetical order; the order of listing is not meant to imply any other significance.

Psychiatric understandings of mental disorder focus on conditions that produce problems in living and are built on therapeutic models. Such understandings are clearly amenable to societal pressures and influences. For example, although the American Psychiatric Association had at one time classified homosexuality as a disorder, a powerful gay rights movement during the 1980s led to the exclusion of sexual preferences from the current list of medically recognized mental disorders.

Even though the term *insanity* is a legal term and not a psychiatric one, legal insanity, as a concept, is still predicated on a disease or disability of the mind. As one judge observed, "It is not enough, to relieve from criminal liability, that the prisoner is morally depraved. It is not enough that he has views of right and wrong at variance with those that find expression in the law. The variance must have its origin in some disease of the mind."[81]

HISTORY OF THE INSANITY DEFENSE

The insanity defense has its modern roots in the 1843 case of Daniel M'Naughten, a woodcutter from Glasgow, Scotland. M'Naughten appears to have suffered from what today might be called paranoia or delusions of persecution. He believed that he was in some way being persecuted by Robert Peel, who was then prime minister of England. M'Naughten traveled to London with the intention of assassinating Peel and would have succeeded but for the fact that Peel chose to ride in the carriage of Queen Victoria (who did not take part in the event) rather than in his own. Peel's carriage was occupied by Edward Drummond, Peel's secretary, and it was Drummond whom M'Naughten killed—believing him to be Peel. Upon his arrest, M'Naughten told police that he had come to London to kill the prime minister because "[t]he Tories in my city follow and persecute me wherever I go, and have entirely destroyed my peace of mind. [T]hey do everything in their power to harass and persecute me; in fact they wish to murder me."

Early English common law tests for determining sanity stressed the defendant's ability "to discern the difference between moral good and evil"[82] and the defendant's knowledge of the nature of the act.[83] The M'Naughten case formalized both tests and brought them together, although it almost led in an entirely new direction. In the course of a lengthy trial, M'Naughten's defense counsel claimed that their client was insane, relying in large part on a new and innovative work by Dr. Isaac Ray, entitled the *Medical Jurisprudence of Insanity*. Dr. Ray's text foreshadowed much of what we know today as modern psychiatry. Jurors in the *M'Naughten* trial, for example, were told that "the human mind is not compartmentalized and . . . a defect in one aspect of the personality could spill over and affect other areas."[84] Seen this way, Ray's thinking represented an enlightened movement away from then-prevalent conceptions, such as phrenology and monomania,[85] which saw the personality as a compartmentalized structure whose various characteristics were in large part determined by the shape of the skull and physical features of the brain. Lord Chief Justice Tindal, obviously impressed with the new perspective on insanity, undertook a clear movement away from established tradition when he charged the *M'Naughten* jury with these words: "The question to be determined is whether at the time the act in question was committed, the prisoner had or had not the use of his understanding, so as to know that he was doing a wrong or wicked act. If the jurors should be of opinion that the prisoner was not sensible, at the time he committed it, that he was violating the laws both of God and man, then he would be entitled to a verdict in his favour; but if, on the contrary, they were of the opinion that when he committed the act he was in a sound state of mind, then their verdict must be against him." M'Naughten, found to be insane, was acquitted.

The M'Naughten Rule: Knowing Right from Wrong

As one judge observed, "M'Naughten's case could have been the turning point for a new approach to more modern methods of determining criminal responsibility."[86] The *M'Naughten* verdict, however, caused much public outcry and angered Queen Victoria, who herself had been the recent target of an assassination attempt. In an effort to bolster traditional common law interpretations of insanity, the leadership of the House of Lords called judges from across the country to a special session. Under strong political pressure, the assembled judges were led to reaffirm the old right–wrong test and to reject emerging medical understandings of insanity. Lord Chief Justice Tindal responded to questions by members of the House of Lords on behalf of the gathered judges. He said, in part,

> Your Lordships are pleased to inquire of us . . . "What are the proper questions to be submitted to the jury, where a person alleged to be afflicted with insane delusions respecting one or more particular subjects or persons, is charged with the commission of a crime (murder, for example), and insanity is set up as a defence?"
>
> . . . We have to submit our opinion to be, that the jurors ought to be told in all cases that every man is to be presumed to be sane, and to possess a sufficient degree of reason to be responsible for his crimes, until the contrary be proved to their satisfaction; and that to establish a defence on the ground of insanity, it must be clearly proved that, at the time of the committing of the act, the party accused was labouring under such a defect of reason, from disease of the mind, as not to know the nature and quality of the act he was doing; or, if he did know it, that he did not know he was doing what was wrong.[87]

As one author observed, "By an accident of history, the rule of M'Naughten's case froze [those primitive] concepts [of phrenology and monomania] into the common law just at a time when they were becoming obsolete"[88] in the medical community. "In this manner," one court wrote, "Dr. Ray's insights were to be lost to the common law for over one hundred years except in the small state of New Hampshire."[89]

Problems with M'Naughten   The **M'Naughten rule** includes two possibilities: (1) a lack of *mens rea* (the person didn't know what he or she was doing) and (2) an acceptable legal excuse (the person didn't know that it was wrong). *Either* alternative provides an acceptable defense under *M'Naughten*.

> *M'Naughten and its antecedents can, in many respects, be seen as examples of the law's conscientious efforts to place in a separate category, people who cannot be justly held "responsible" for their acts.*
>
> —*United States v. Freeman, 357 F.2d 606 (2d Cir. 1966)*

M'Naughten rule
A rule for determining insanity that asks whether the defendant knew what he or she was doing or whether the defendant knew that what he or she was doing was wrong.

Insanity Defense Reform Act (IDRA)
A part of the 1984 Crime Control and Prevention Act that mandated a comprehensive overhaul of the insanity defense as it operated in the federal courts. The IDRA made insanity an affirmative defense to be proved by the defendant by clear and convincing evidence and created a special verdict of not guilty by reason of insanity.

Central to the second alternative provided by the M'Naughten rule is the possibility that defendants may be able to demonstrate insanity by showing that, while they knew what they were doing, they did not know that their behavior was "wrong." The wrongfulness test has been at the center of controversy since its inception. The **Insanity Defense Reform Act (IDRA)** of 1984, the Model Penal Code, the American Psychiatric Association's model standard on legal insanity, and most state penal codes all contain some form of the wrongfulness test, and all make use of the word *wrong* or *wrongfulness* in attempting to assess a defendant's mental condition at the time of the crime.

Considerable disagreement exists, however, over whether the word *wrong* refers to the defendant's ability to appreciate the *legal* or the *moral* wrongfulness of his or her act. For a defendant to know that an act was legally wrong, all that is required is that the defendant be aware of the fact that the act in question is against the law. Defendants who, by reason of mental disease or defect (Alzheimer's disease, for example), are not so aware would be insane from a legal point of view. On the other hand, according to the second school of thought, if a defendant knows that his or her activity is illegal but believes that it is morally acceptable or even righteous, then he or she might be legally insane.

In addition to legal and moral perspectives, the ability to *appreciate* or to *know* the wrongfulness of conduct can be interpreted from a psychiatric point of view. Psychiatrically speaking, the ability to appreciate wrongfulness can involve much more than either a legal or a moral sense. A deeper appreciation of the wrongfulness of one's actions can be had when a well-integrated personality experiences both emotional as well as cognitive and intellectual awareness that give rise to a sense of right and wrong.

Given the complexities of the issues involved, some jurisdictions attempt to solve the question of whether a defendant *knew* his or her action was *wrong* by instructing juries that a defendant must have the capacity to understand the nature of the act. Other jurisdictions leave it up to the jury's common sense to decide what such terms mean.

By the early 1900s, it was generally accepted that strict application of the M'Naughten rule deprives the trier of fact of many of the insights yielded by modern psychiatry. As a result, other proposals for assessing legal insanity were made—primary among them the irresistible impulse test, the Durham rule, and the American Law Institute test. Each will be discussed in the pages that follow.

Insanity became an issue in the 2002 trial of Andrea Yates, the Texas mother who was accused of drowning her five young children in a bathtub. Prosecutors chose to try her on capital murder charges, and her attorneys offered an insanity defense.

The state of Texas employs a modified version of the M'Naughten rule that requires defendants who claim insanity to prove that they did not know that the unlawful act they committed was wrong. Texas law reads, "It is an affirmative defense to prosecution that, at the time of the conduct charged, the actor, as a result of severe mental disease or defect, did not know that his conduct was wrong."[90]

At trial, Yates's attorneys offered evidence intended to show that Yates, who was strongly influenced by religious fundamentalism, believed she was saving her children from eternal damnation by killing them.[91] Testimony from various defense experts purported to show that this distorted belief was the product of delusions and hallucinations from which Yates suffered and that were made worse by postpartum depression following the birth of her last child. From her deranged perspective, the experts suggested, she believed that she was doing right and not wrong.[92] Defense attorneys also pointed to Yates's long history of psychological problems, including confinement in mental institutions, suicide attempts, and a history of prescribed antidepressive drug treatments. Prosecutors countered by pointing to the fact that Yates had rationally and calmly phoned 911 almost immediately after the killings to inform police of what she had done—evidence, they said, that she understood that the killings were criminal.

Following a mere three and a half hours of deliberation, a jury of eight women and four men found Yates guilty of murder. Although she was sentenced to life in prison, her conviction was overturned by a three-judge panel of the First Texas Court of Appeals in 2005. The appellate court found that false testimony by a California psychiatrist had been instrumental in persuading the jury to reject Yates's insanity defense. The testimony, offered by the prosecution's sole mental health expert, Park Dietz, included an inaccurate claim that he had been consulted by the producers of the TV show *Law and Order* about an episode involving a woman who drowned her children. The panel ordered a new trial, and on July 26, 2006, following three days of jury deliberations, Yates was found not guilty by reason of insanity—and committed to the North Texas State Hospital.

The Irresistible Impulse Test: Control Rules

The wrongfulness component of the M'Naughten rule has been criticized because it focuses only on the cognitive component of the personality. In other words, to *know* that one's actions are wrong requires the ability to think and to judge. Moreover, the M'Naughten rule does not allow for degrees of insanity. Under the rule, either a person knows what he or she is doing, and knows that it is wrong, or he or she does not. There is no middle ground. Recognizing this, some authors have said, "The essence of *M'Naughten* is that for mental disease or defect to incapacitate, it must be of such a degree as to leave the person irrational—that is, no rational person lacks criminal capacity by reason of insanity."[93] It is possible to imagine a situation, however, in which a person knows what he or she is doing, knows that it is wrong, and is still unable to stop doing it. A famous potato chip commercial of a few years ago, for example, challenged viewers with the phrase, "You can't eat just one!" The advertisement claimed that once a person tasted one of the chips, he or she would be unable to resist having more.

Although there is nothing legally or morally "wrong" with eating potato chips, it may be that some people find it equally impossible to control other forms of behavior that are against the law. During the 1920s, in the belief that some forms of behavior could not be controlled, many states modified the M'Naughten rule to permit "irresistible impulse" defenses. Defenses based on the **irresistible impulse test** claim that at the time the crime was committed, a mental disease or disorder prevented the defendant from controlling his or her behavior (see Figure 6–6). Some jurisdictions that use the irresistible impulse provision employ a "policeman at the elbow" jury instruction. Jurors are told that "if the accused would not have committed that act had there been a policeman present, he cannot be said to have acted under irresistible impulse."

Critiques of the irresistible impulse defense point out that it may be impossible to really know who can and who cannot control their behavior in specific situations and that such an excuse might apply to all who commit crimes. In the case of the second claim, the inability to control one's impulses might be a general characteristic of criminal personalities, making it possible to argue that all criminal offenders engage in illegal behavior because of lessened behavioral controls. Were it not for such a lack of control, some people suggest, criminals would be law-abiding citizens.

The Durham Rule: Crime as a Product of Mental Disease

In 1954, in the case of *Durham* v. *United States*,[94] the U.S. Court of Appeals for the District of Columbia concluded that all existing tests to determine legal sanity were flawed. The court then went on to develop its own standard, stating that the rule "is simply that an accused is not criminally responsible if his unlawful act was the *product* of mental disease or mental defect." The **Durham rule**, also known as the *product rule*, built on the court's belief

> [The insanity defense] invokes the deepest questions about our society's willingness to pay the price of our moral principles.
>
> —Judge David Bazelon, U.S. Court of Appeals for the District of Columbia Circuit

irresistible impulse test
A test for insanity that evaluates defense claims that at the time the crime was committed, a mental disease or disorder prevented the defendant from controlling his or her behavior in keeping with the requirements of the law.

Durham rule
A rule for determining insanity that holds that an accused is not criminally responsible if his or her unlawful act was the product of mental disease or mental defect. Also called *product rule*.

FIGURE 6–6

Insanity Tests: Expanding
Concepts.

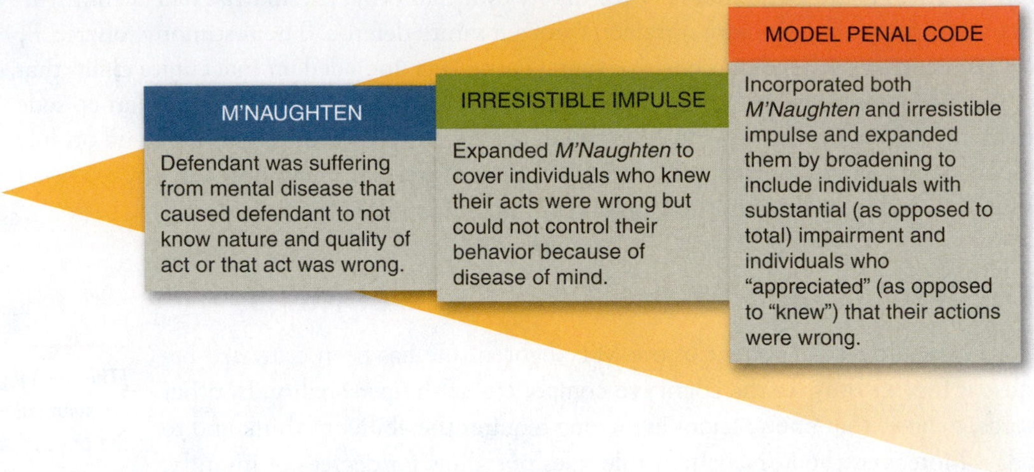

M'NAUGHTEN	IRRESISTIBLE IMPULSE	MODEL PENAL CODE
Defendant was suffering from mental disease that caused defendant to not know nature and quality of act or that act was wrong.	Expanded *M'Naughten* to cover individuals who knew their acts were wrong but could not control their behavior because of disease of mind.	Incorporated both *M'Naughten* and irresistible impulse and expanded them by broadening to include individuals with substantial (as opposed to total) impairment and individuals who "appreciated" (as opposed to "knew") that their actions were wrong.

that an inability to distinguish right from wrong is merely a symptom of mental disease and that behavior resulting from the disease is a more apt determinant of legal insanity.

Unfortunately, however, few mental health professionals could be found who expressed the relationship between mental illness and behavior as the court did. As a result, the Durham rule was quickly criticized by those who said that it was out of touch with medical reality. Others claimed that it was far too vague and provided little guidance to the jury, potentially resulting in far too many acquittals. As one federal appellate court held: "The most significant criticism of *Durham* . . . is that it fails to give the factfinder any standard by which to measure the competency of the accused."[95]

In 1972, the District of Columbia court that had offered the Durham rule 18 years earlier finally rejected it in favor of a "prevailing community standards" approach to assessing criminal liability.[96] In *United States* v. *Brawner*, the court held that "a defendant is not responsible if at the time of his unlawful conduct his mental or emotional processes or behavior controls were impaired to such an extent that he cannot *justly* be held responsible for his act."[97] The *Brawner* ruling effectively defined insanity in terms of social justice rather than in terms of established legal or psychiatric notions.

The American Law Institute Test: Substantial Capacity

substantial capacity test
A test developed by the American Law Institute and embodied in the Model Penal Code that holds that "a person is not responsible for criminal conduct if at the time of such conduct as a result of mental disease or defect he lacks substantial capacity either to appreciate the criminality [wrongfulness] of his conduct or to conform his conduct to the requirements of the law."[vii]

In an effort to clarify standards for assessing legal insanity, the American Law Institute (ALI) incorporated a **substantial capacity test** into the Model Penal Code. In doing so, the ALI noted, "No problem in the drafting of a penal code presents larger intrinsic difficulty than that of determining when individuals whose conduct would otherwise be criminal ought to be exculpated on the ground that they were suffering from mental disease or defect when they acted."[98]

The ALI substantial capacity test is a modernized version of the M'Naughten rule, blended with control rules. It reads: "A person is not responsible for criminal conduct if at the time of such conduct, as a result of mental disease or defect, he lacks substantial capacity either to appreciate the criminality [wrongfulness] of his conduct or to conform his conduct to the requirements of the law."[99]

It is not because their mental disease causes the insane to commit crimes that we excuse them, no more than it is because an infant's lack of rationality causes him to do bad that we excuse him. Rather, in both cases, we excuse because the actors lack the status of moral agents.

—M. Moore, California Law Review (1985)

The ALI test substitutes the word *appreciate* for *know* in the original *M'Naughten* formulation and recognizes the role of impulse through use of the phrase "conform his conduct to the requirements of the law." The test is also written so as to better recognize modern psychiatric knowledge through use of the word *substantial*, which acknowledges that, although portions of a defendant's personality might be affected by mental disease in such a way as to render him or her legally insane, some mental capacity might still remain.

In the mass media, references to defendants who claim temporary insanity are common. *Temporary insanity* is not a legal term. Temporary or lifelong, the applicable jurisdiction's legal standard (for example, M'Naughten) must be proven, as demonstrated in *Miller* v. *State* (1996).

Guilty but Mentally Ill

A definitive moment in the history of the insanity defense in this country came in 1982 with an NGRI verdict in the trial of John Hinckley, who admitted to trying to assassinate President Ronald Reagan for the delusional purpose of proving his love for actress Jodie Foster. After weeks of conflicting testimony by a parade of expert witnesses for both the defense and the prosecution, the judge in the Hinckley trial instructed jurors to weigh the issue of insanity in terms of the Model Penal Code approach and to return a verdict of "not guilty" unless they could agree "beyond a reasonable doubt" that Hinckley was sane. Because the expert witnesses the jury heard from could not agree among themselves as to Hinckley's sanity, the jury instruction virtually ensured the NGRI verdict—and one was promptly returned.

> At bottom, the determination whether a man is or is not held responsible for his conduct is not a medical but a legal, social, or moral judgment.
>
> —*United States v. Freeman, 357 F.2d 606 (2d Cir. 1966)*

Public outcry at the *Hinckley* verdict led about half of the states to rewrite their insanity statutes, with many returning to M'Naughten-like standards. Before *Hinckley*, the Model Penal Code definition of insanity had been adopted by 10 of the 11 federal courts of appeals and by more than half of the states. After *Hinckley*, a few states (Idaho, Montana, and Utah among them) abolished the insanity defense except insofar as insanity could be shown to affect the specific *mens rea* required by statute for a particular crime. Also in response, the U.S. Congress passed the 1984 Crime Control and Prevention Act, which included the Insanity Defense Reform Act (IDRA) of 1984,[100] mentioned briefly earlier in this chapter. With the IDRA, Congress mandated a comprehensive overhaul of the insanity defense as it operated in the federal courts. The act made insanity an affirmative defense to be proven by the defendant by clear and convincing evidence and created a special verdict of not guilty by reason of insanity.[101] Through the IDRA, Congress intended to prohibit the presentation of evidence of mental disease or defect, short of insanity, to excuse conduct.[102]

The IDRA does not, however, prohibit psychiatric evidence that may be relevant to proving whether a crime occurred. If a subjective state of mind is an element of a crime, for example, evidence regarding the existence or absence of that state of mind is relevant to whether a crime was in fact committed. As federal courts have ruled: "Psychiatric evidence which negates *mens rea* . . . negates an element of the offense rather than constituting a justification or excuse"[103] and may be admitted at trial for that purpose. As in federal courts, the use of psychiatric evidence is admissible in all state jurisdictions today to negate *mens rea* where the evidence presented focuses on the defendant's specific state of mind at the time the offense was committed.

The IDRA also created a comprehensive civil commitment procedure under which a defendant found NGRI is held in custody pending a court hearing. The hearing must occur within 40 days of the verdict. At the conclusion of the hearing, the court determines whether the defendant should be hospitalized or released.

In a second type of response to the *Hinckley* verdict, ten states adopted statutes that permitted findings of **guilty but mentally ill (GBMI)**. The states patterned their laws after a 1975 Michigan statute that created the possibility of GBMI verdicts in Michigan criminal trials. GBMI statutes require that when the insanity defense is raised at trial, judges must instruct juries that four verdicts are possible: (1) guilty, (2) not guilty, (3) not guilty by reason of insanity, and (4) guilty but mentally ill. A jury must return a finding of guilty but mentally

guilty but mentally ill (GBMI)
A verdict, equivalent to a finding of guilty, that establishes that "the defendant, although mentally ill, was sufficiently in possession of his faculties to be morally blameworthy for his acts."[viii]

APPLYING THE CONCEPT

CAPSTONE CASE

How Long Does a Person Have to Be Insane to Qualify for the Defense of Insanity?

Miller v. State,
991 P.2d 1183 (Nevada 1996)

THE CASE   On May 8, 1993, Robyn Goring (Goring) was stabbed to death in the apartment she shared with appellant John Kilioi Miller (Miller) and their two children. Maria Jordan (Jordan), an officer on the Las Vegas police force, lived in the apartment directly below Goring and Miller's apartment. Jordan heard loud noises in the apartment above her on May 8, 1993. When Jordan went to the upstairs apartment, Miller opened the door and stated something to the effect that "I blew it" or "I lost it." Jordan noticed blood on Miller's clothes, two children in the apartment's living room, and the body of a young woman on the kitchen floor.

Officers responded to a 911 call by Jordan and observed Goring's body on the kitchen floor with a knife protruding from her torso. While being transported to the police station, Miller stated that he did not deserve to be treated nicely. Before and after Miller was informed of his *Miranda* rights, he volunteered incriminating statements. Miller stated, "I lost control and I just picked her up," and "I'm sorry. I don't want to live anymore. Shoot me." Also, Miller's shirt and the bottom of his pants appeared to be bloodstained.

The medical examiner's office found a total of forty-two stab wounds, many superficial, inflicted upon Goring's body. On June 10, 1993, Miller was charged with first-degree murder with the use of a deadly weapon. At trial, Goring's mother and sister testified that Goring lived with Miller for twelve years but was planning to leave Miller because he oppressively controlled Goring's life and was physically violent toward her. . . .

[Several psychiatrists testified, with differing opinions, about Miller's mental condition.]

At the close of the guilt phase of the trial, the jury found Miller guilty of first-degree murder with the use of a deadly weapon. At the penalty hearing, Miller was sentenced to life in prison without the possibility of parole. . . .

THE FINDING   The *M'Naughten* test for insanity has been applied in Nevada since 1889. To prove a defendant is insane under the *M'Naughten* test, the defense must show that the defendant labors under such a mental defect that the defendant cannot understand the nature of his or her actions, or cannot tell the difference between right and wrong. Because a finding of criminal liability requires a conclusion that a defendant's culpable mental state existed contemporaneously with a culpable act, a successful insanity defense must show the elements of *M'Naughten* existed at the time of the act.

In the trial described here, Miller's defense theory was that he was sane before and after killing Goring, but was insane during the actual killing. Three medical experts testified that his mental condition made him prone to fall into violent seizures while completely sane. Further testimony showed that Miller could then act extremely violent with no ability to appreciate the nature of his actions but would come out of the seizure acting deeply remorseful upon realizing the nature of his conduct. Miller presented evidence that on May 8, 1993, he fell into a violent seizure, stabbed Goring forty-two times, and then came out of the seizure consumed with remorse. Three medical experts concluded that Miller satisfied the *M'Naughten* insanity test during the period in which he stabbed Goring.

At the close of evidence in the trial, the district court instructed the jury to determine whether Miller was legally insane when he killed Goring. The district court also instructed the jury that a finding of insanity required proof that at the time Miller killed Goring, he was laboring under a defect of the mind that caused him not to understand the nature or quality of his actions or that what he was doing was wrong. Finally, the district court instructed the jury to consider Miller's mental condition before and after the killing to throw light on what Miller's mental condition was at the time of the killing.

Concerned that the jury was confused about the time duration component of the insanity defense, Miller proffered two jury instructions. The first proffered instruction was entitled "temporary insanity" and stated that "[r]egardless of its duration, legal insanity which existed at the time of the commission of the crime is a defense to the crime." The second proffered instruction stated that when evidence shows that at times the defendant was legally insane and at other times he was legally sane, he has the burden of proving by a preponderance of the evidence that he was legally insane at the time of the commission of the act. The district court denied Miller's proffered instructions, ruling that the instructions described temporary insanity and that temporary insanity is not a defense in Nevada.

On two occasions during closing arguments in the guilt phase of Miller's trial, the prosecutor told the jury that temporary insanity is not a recognized defense in Nevada. . . .The district court endorsed the prosecutor's statements by overruling Miller's objections to the statements and proclaiming, "He [the prosecutor] can argue that it's not a defense under the law." . . .

Clearly, a person can benefit from the M'Naughten insanity defense if he shows he was insane during the temporal period that coincides with the time of the crime. Technically and semantically, such a finding is temporary insanity. Therefore, if a defendant presents evidence of insanity during the interval that coincides with the commission of the crime charged, that defendant is entitled to a correct and complete instruction that insanity on a temporary basis can be a defense to the crime.

We conclude that the district court properly denied Miller's instructions when they were offered. . . . However, after the instructions were given, the district court and the prosecutor told the jury that "temporary insanity" is not a defense. Even though the jury instructions stated that insanity must be present at the time of the commission of the offense, the jury was not told that the duration of the insanity does not matter. The jury was not told that the insanity defense applied even if the evidence showed Miller to be legally insane at some time and yet legally sane at others.

We conclude that allowing the prosecutor to comment that "temporary insanity is not a defense" materially confused the jury. The jury was then faced with the dilemma of distinguishing between whether insanity existed "for the time interval" that coincides with the time of the criminal act or for a "temporary" time. . . .

In this case, Miller presented competent evidence that he was insane when he killed Goring but was sane before and after the killing. Accordingly, Miller was entitled to a correct and complete instruction that excusable insanity, even for a short period, could be a defense to the crime. Moreover, comments of the prosecutor and the district

court regarding the unavailability of temporary insanity as a defense in Nevada hopelessly confused the jury.

Accordingly, Miller's judgment of conviction is reversed and this matter is remanded for a new trial.

What Do You Think?

1. According to Dr. Norton Roitman, a psychiatrist, when Miller killed Goring, he "could not appreciate the nature of his acts and could not recognize the difference between right and wrong." If Roitman was correct, what legal test for insanity would Miller have met?

2. Dr. Jack Jurasky, a psychiatrist who testified for the prosecution, concluded that Miller's outburst was of such a violent nature that he could not have appreciated the nature of his actions when he stabbed Goring. If Jurasky was correct, what legal test for insanity would Miller have met?

3. Miller claimed to be sane before and after the killing but insane during the time the crime was committed. His attorneys asked that, at the close of trial, the jury be instructed on the issue of temporary insanity and that they be told that "regardless of its duration, legal insanity that existed at the time of the commission of the crime is a defense to the crime." Why do you think that the trial court refused to give to the jury the instructions regarding the insanity defense suggested by the defendant?

4. In this case, the appellate court reversed the defendant's conviction and remanded the case for a new trial. On what basis was that decision reached? Do you agree with the decision? Why or why not?

5. What does this case have to tell us about the difference between insanity and temporary insanity? Are differences between the two terms significant in cases like this one? Explain.

Additional Applications

Can a judge impose an insanity defense over the objections of a competent defendant?

Frendak v. United States, 408 A.2d 364 (D.C. App. 1979)

The Case: After a series of psychiatric examinations over several months, a trial court found Paula Frendak competent to stand trial in Washington, D.C., on first-degree murder charges arising out of the shooting death of a co-worker. Although evidence of Frendak's insanity had been introduced in her competency proceedings, she refused to claim an insanity defense at trial; the jury consequently found her guilty of first-degree murder. Still concerned

(continued)

by the evidence of insanity introduced earlier, however, the judge then opted—over Frendak's objections—to interpose an insanity defense and hold a second "insanity phase" of the trial before the same jury. (In the District of Columbia, such a bifurcated proceeding may be conducted when an insanity defense is to be presented.) After hearing expert testimony that Frendak suffered from "a major psychotic illness" and "reduced behavioral control," the jury ultimately found the defendant not guilty by reason of insanity. On appeal, Frendak challenged the trial judge's decision to raise an insanity defense over her objections.

The Finding: The District of Columbia Court of Appeals reversed the trial judge's decision to impose an insanity defense in the case. A competent defendant, the appeals court found, may reasonably opt to forego an insanity defense for any of several reasons, including "fear that an insanity acquittal will result in the institution of commitment proceedings," objections to the "quality of treatment or the type of confinement" found in an institution for the mentally ill, desire to "avoid the stigma of insanity," or desire to preserve a crime's symbolic value as "a political or religious protest." And in some instances, the appeals court found, such specific considerations may "substantially outweigh" the general goal of "ensur[ing] that some abstract concept of justice is satisfied by protecting one who may be morally blameless from a conviction and punishment which he or she might choose to accept." Consequently, the panel concluded, a trial judge may *not* force an insanity defense on a defendant found competent to stand trial if the individual "intelligently and voluntarily" decides to forego that defense.

How far can a state go in limiting an insanity defense?

Clark v. Arizona, 548 U.S. 735 (2006)

The Case: Early in the morning of June 21, 2000, defendant Eric Clark, a truck driver, shot and killed a police officer during a routine traffic stop in Flagstaff, Arizona. Consequently, Clark was charged with first-degree murder for intentionally or knowingly killing a law enforcement officer in the line of duty. At his bench trial, Clark conceded his role in the crime; his defense, however, introduced evidence that he suffered from paranoid schizophrenia for two reasons: first, to raise an affirmative defense of insanity; and second, to prove a lack of the *mens rea* required under Arizona's first-degree murder law. The trial court ruled that Clark could not rely on evidence bearing on insanity to show a lack of specific intent. As for insanity, the court applied a statutory test adopted by Arizona in 1993—which narrowed the state's insanity defense by abandoning the cognitive incapacity part of the M'Naghten test—and held that Clark could establish insanity only by showing an incapacity to understand that his actions were wrong. On Supreme Court review, Clark challenged the constitutionality of Arizona's 1993 departure from the traditional two-part M'Naghten test.

The Finding: Writing for the Court, Justice David Souter upheld Arizona's legislative decision to modify its insanity test. Although the "landmark" M'Naghten rule has been quite influential, Souter argued, "[h]istory shows no deference to M'*Naghten* that could elevate its formula to the level of fundamental principle, so as to limit the traditional recognition of a State's capacity to define crimes and defenses." Indeed, Souter observed, "[e]ven a cursory examination" of state and federal approaches to insanity reveals "significant differences" among jurisdictions as to how—or whether—the defense is defined. "With this varied background," the Court concluded, "it is clear that . . . the insanity rule, like the conceptualization of criminal offenses, is substantially open to state choice." The Due Process Clause "imposes no single canonical formulation of legal insanity." ■

---

ill if (1) every element necessary for a conviction has been proven beyond a reasonable doubt, (2) the defendant is found to have been *mentally ill* at the time the crime was committed, and (3) the defendant was *not* found to have been *legally insane* at the time the crime was committed. The difference between mental illness and legal insanity is a crucial one.

A finding of GBMI is equivalent to a finding of guilty, and the court will sentence the defendant just as a person found guilty of the crime in question would be sentenced. A GBMI verdict establishes that "the defendant, although mentally ill, was sufficiently in possession of his faculties to be morally blameworthy for his acts."[104] As one author says, "The most obvious and important function of the GBMI verdict is to permit juries to make an unambiguous statement about the factual guilt, mental condition, and moral responsibility of a defendant."[105]

Once sentenced, GBMI offenders are evaluated to determine whether hospitalization or psychiatric treatment is needed. If the offender is hospitalized, he or she will join the "regular" prison population on release from the treatment facility. Time spent in the hospital and in prison both count toward sentence completion, and the offender will be released from custody after the sentence has been served, even if he or she still suffers from mental disease.

The Doctrine of Settled Insanity

For legal purposes, insanity is insanity regardless of its underlying cause. Hence "insanity at the time of an alleged criminal act generally constitutes a defense, regardless of how the condition may have come about."[106] Consequently, insanity may be a useful defense even if it is brought on by the defendant's own actions.

As pointed out earlier, intoxication is generally not regarded as a defense to a criminal charge because it is a condition brought about by the actions of the intoxicated person through the willful consumption of alcohol or other intoxicants. Under the doctrine of settled insanity, however, the habitual and long-term use of intoxicants or other drugs that results in permanent mental disorders "that are symptomatically and organically similar to mental disorders caused by brain disease"[107] can create the basis for a claim of insanity provided that the defendant can meet the required definition of insanity in the relevant jurisdiction. According to some authors, "[T]he nearly unanimous rule is that a mental or brain disease or defect caused by the long-term effects of intoxicants constitutes a mental state that warrants an insanity defense."[108] The same is not true, however, of "mere addiction" to narcotics or the compulsion to abuse alcohol or other consciousness-altering substances. Courts in 29 states and the District of Columbia have recognized the defense of settled insanity, whereas only one state has rejected it.[109] Twenty states have yet to consider the issue.

DIMINISHED CAPACITY

The defense of **diminished capacity**, also called *diminished responsibility*, is available in some jurisdictions. However, "the terms 'diminished responsibility' and 'diminished capacity' do not have a clearly accepted meaning in the courts."[110] Some defendants who offer diminished-capacity defenses do so in recognition of the fact that such claims may be based on a mental condition that would not qualify as mental disease or mental defect, nor would it be sufficient to support the affirmative defense of insanity—but it might still lower criminal culpability. According to UCLA law professor Peter Arenella, "The defense [of diminished capacity] was first recognized by Scottish common law courts to reduce the punishment of the 'partially insane' from murder to culpable homicide, a non-capital offense."[111]

The diminished-capacity defense is similar to the defense of insanity in that it depends on showing that the defendant's mental state was impaired at the time of the crime. As a defense, diminished capacity is most useful when it can be shown that, because of some defect of reason or mental shortcoming, the defendant's capacity to form the *mens rea* required by a specific crime was impaired. Unlike an insanity defense, however, which can result in a finding of not guilty, a diminished capacity defense is built on the recognition that "[m]ental condition, though insufficient to exonerate, may be relevant to specific mental elements of certain crimes or degrees of crime."[112] For example, defendants might present evidence of mental abnormality in an effort to reduce first-degree murder to second-degree murder, or second-degree murder to manslaughter, when a killing occurs under extreme emotional disturbance. Similarly, in some jurisdictions very low intelligence will, if proved, serve to reduce first-degree murder to manslaughter.[113]

The Model Penal Code limits applicability of diminished capacity to cases in which capital punishment might be imposed: "Whenever the jury or the Court is authorized to determine or to recommend whether or not the defendant shall be sentenced to death or imprisonment upon conviction, evidence that the capacity of the defendant to appreciate the criminality

diminished capacity
A defense based on claims of a mental condition that may be insufficient to exonerate a defendant of guilt but that may be relevant to specific mental elements of certain crimes or degrees of crime. Also called *diminished responsibility*.

[wrongfulness] of his conduct or to conform his conduct to the requirements of law was impaired as a result of mental disease or defect is admissible in favor of sentence of imprisonment."[114]

One of the most famous cases of diminished capacity was its successful use in the murder trials of San Francisco's Mayor George Moscone and Harvey Milk, a member of the San Francisco Board of Supervisors (the city's governing body) in 1979. Dan White, a former supervisor and otherwise productive member of the community murdered his former colleagues in front of witnesses, in their offices. In what appeared to be an obvious case of murder for political motives, the jury found White possessed diminished capacity and was only guilty of manslaughter. White presented evidence of depression to support his claim of diminished capacity. One of the experts who testified mentioned that White had substantially changed his diet from healthy to one full of Twinkies and Coke. The expert testified that this change was evidence of depression and that it exacerbated his depressive state. The press locked onto this testimony, the label "Twinkie Defense" was popularized, and White's reduction in culpability became generally, although wrongly, believed to be the consequence of his consumption of Twinkies.[115]

> We have an insanity plea that would have saved Cain.
>
> —Mark Twain, author (1872)

Outraged at the outcome, the California state legislature eliminated the diminished-capacity defense. The California Penal Code today reads: "The defense of diminished capacity is hereby abolished."[116] The code adds that "[a]s a matter of public policy there shall be no defense of diminished capacity, diminished responsibility, or irresistible impulse in a criminal action or juvenile adjudication hearing."[117] Although California law limits the use of certain excuses that might be raised to negate *mens rea*, a showing that the required *mens rea* was in fact lacking can still lead to acquittal. However "evidence of diminished capacity or of a mental disorder may be considered by the court at the time of sentencing or other disposition or commitment."[118]

HOW WIDELY USED IS THE INSANITY DEFENSE?

The insanity defense is not widely used. According to an eight-state study published in 1991, which was funded by the National Institute of Mental Health and reported in the *Bulletin of the American Academy of Psychiatry and the Law*,[119] the insanity defense was used in less than 1% of the cases that came before county-level courts. The study showed that only 26% of all insanity pleas were argued successfully, and further found that 90% of those who employed the defense had been previously diagnosed with a mental illness. As the American Bar Association says, "The best evidence suggests that the mental nonresponsibility defense is raised in less than 1 percent of all felony cases in the United States and is successful in about a fourth of these."[120] In most cases in which a defendant is acquitted on an NGRI finding, it is because the prosecution and the defense have agreed on the appropriateness of the plea before trial. The implication, according to the American Psychiatric Association, is that the insanity defense is rarely used by "fakers."[121]

Other studies show similar results. *Myths and Realities: A Report of the National Commission on the Insanity Defense*, for example, found that in 1982 only 52 of 32,000 adult defendants represented by the public defender's office in New Jersey—less than 0.2%—entered an insanity plea. Of those, only 15 were successful.[122] Similar studies of New York City courts reveal that an insanity plea is entered, on average, in only 1 in 600 or 700 criminal cases.[123] A 1998 report by Hawaii's Legislative Reference Bureau, which reviewed practices throughout the country, found that the insanity defense was raised in fewer than 2% of all cases that go to trial and that it was successful in less than 10% of the cases in which it was raised.[124]

When entered, however, insanity pleas may be used in a wide variety of cases. The eight-state study found that approximately half of those pleading insanity had been indicted for violent crimes, although less than 15% had been charged with murder. The other 50% of insanity pleas were entered in robbery, property damage, and minor felony cases.

CONSEQUENCES OF AN INSANITY FINDING

Few defendants found not guilty by reason of insanity or guilty but mentally ill are immediately released, as would be a person who is acquitted of a crime, although nondangerous defendants may not by law be kept longer than necessary to assess their condition. Generally, those found not guilty by reason of insanity or guilty but mentally ill are subject to a hearing to determine whether they are still mentally ill and dangerous to themselves or others and whether confinement in a treatment facility is justified.[125] Most are so confined, and studies show that people found NGRI are, on average, held at least as long as people found guilty and sent to prison.[126] After a period of time, a person so confined may request a hearing to determine whether he or she is still a danger to self or others or is eligible to be released. At such a hearing, in order for confinement to continue, the state must demonstrate by clear and convincing evidence that the person poses a danger to self or others and requires continued confinement. Such proceedings are civil, not criminal. Accordingly, the constitutional protections afforded criminal defendants do not automatically extend to the subjects of civil commitment proceedings. Of course, however, basic notions of due process apply, and because individuals determined to be dangerous will experience a significant loss of liberty, something more than typical civil law constitutional protections exists. Even more, many legislatures have provided by statute for protections similar to those available in criminal proceedings, including the right to have a high standard of proof, such as beyond a reasonable doubt, for the dangerousness finding; the right to confront and cross-examine witnesses; and the right to compel witnesses.[127]

In *Foucha v. Louisiana* (1992), the U.S. Supreme Court held that it is unconstitutional to put the burden of proving that confinement is no longer justified on the defendant.[128] In *Foucha*, the Court overturned Louisiana's blanket procedure of incarcerating in mental facilities those acquitted of crimes by reason of insanity. The state's scheme, which resulted in the detention of acquitted defendants who were no longer insane, required detainees to prove that they were not dangerous before they could be released. In contrast, the Court concluded that acquitted defendants no longer suffering from mental disease should be released, and held that an assessment of dangerousness that is not based on a clear showing of mental illness does not provide a legal justification for detention. In the words of the Court:

> [T]he State asserts that, because Foucha once committed a criminal act and now has an antisocial personality that sometimes leads to aggressive conduct, a disorder for which there is no effective treatment, he may be held indefinitely. This rationale would permit the State to hold indefinitely any other insanity acquittee not mentally ill who could be shown to have a personality disorder that may lead to criminal conduct. The same would be true of any convicted criminal, even though he has completed his prison term. It would also be only a step away from substituting confinements for dangerousness for our present system which, with only narrow exceptions and aside from permissible confinements for mental illness, incarcerates only those who are proved beyond a reasonable doubt to have violated a criminal law.[129]

After *Foucha*, other courts found it acceptable for states to require offenders found NGRI, and who are no longer deemed mentally ill at the conclusion of trial, to participate in outpatient treatment programs through which they can be monitored.[130]

Today, most persons found NGRI are confined after trial because they continue to be mentally ill. As a result, defense attorneys generally request that juries be informed of the likely consequences of an NGRI verdict. Attorneys want to ensure that the jury doesn't assume that a potentially dangerous or unstable defendant will be immediately released back into the community if an NGRI verdict is returned. In *Shannon v. United States* (1994), however, the U.S. Supreme Court held that federal courts are not required to instruct a jury regarding the potential consequences to the defendant of a verdict of NGRI.[131] Most state courts have not yet ruled on the issue.

ABOLISHING THE INSANITY DEFENSE

Because of the difficulties associated with assessing insanity from a legal perspective, some scholars advocate a strict *mens rea* approach to insanity. That approach would amount to a wholesale elimination of the insanity defense and its replacement with a test to assess the presence or absence of a culpable mental state in a defendant who is thought to be suffering from mental disease or defect.

As mentioned earlier, three states—Montana, Utah, and Idaho—have already moved in just such a direction. Frustration over the inability of medical and legal professionals to agree on the nature of exculpatory insanity, plus the difficulties that attend the application of legal tests for insanity, led to the abolishment of the insanity defense *as an excuse* in those jurisdictions. The Idaho criminal code, for example, succinctly states: "Mental condition shall not be a defense to any charge of criminal conduct."[132] Although states such as Iowa no longer allow defendants to raise the insanity defense as an excuse to a criminal charge, defendants in all jurisdictions may still claim that the presence of mental disease at the time of the crime left them unable to form the *mens rea* needed for criminal activity. In Iowa (and elsewhere), a successful showing that a culpable mental state was lacking would lead a judge or jury to conclude that no crime had occurred.

Rather than focusing on the elements necessary for crime, other authorities suggest that claims of insanity should only be considered at the sentencing phase of a criminal proceeding—once guilt has already been established. Some states do just that and use bifurcated trials, involving two stages. In the first stage, the state attempts to prove the defendant's guilt without considering claims of insanity. If the trier of fact determines that the defendant committed the offense in violation of the law, a second stage then follows in which attention turns to psychiatric testimony and the offender's claim that he or she should be sentenced differently, due to mental problems, than others found guilty of the same offense.

CIVIL COMMITMENT

The states and federal government are increasingly turning to civil law to supplement criminal law to protect the public from dangerously mental ill offenders.

There is a long history of states, under their *parens patriae*, or protective, role, confining individuals who were (1) mentally ill and (2) a danger to themselves or others. The purpose of such confinement is not deterrence or retribution. It is a civil process that may be initiated regardless of whether a crime has been committed or prosecuted.

In most criminal cases a defendant's mental state is raised at trial either through a *mens rea* or insanity defense. Historically it was rare for criminal cases to evolve into civil confinement cases. Today many states, and the federal government, have directly connected criminal cases and civil confinement, particularly for sex predators. These laws are the consequence of the lack of success in treatment of and the high rate of recidivism by sexual predators. These laws typically provide for the civil commitment of dangerous offenders, with periodic reviews for dangerousness and mental illness, following their prison sentences. For such confinement to occur, a separate civil commitment process must be filed by the government near the end of the offender's prison sentence. The connection between civil commitment and criminal cases raises due-process and other constitutional questions. The Supreme Court answered some of these questions in the 1997 case of *Kansas* v. *Hendricks*, which is featured as a Capstone Case in this chapter.

APPLYING THE CONCEPT

CAPSTONE CASE

May a State Confine Someone Because He or She Is Likely to Harm Someone Else in the Future?

Kansas v. Hendricks, 521 U.S. 346 (1997)

THE CASE In 1994, Kansas enacted the Sexually Violent Predator Act, which establishes procedures for the civil commitment of persons who, due to a "mental abnormality" or a "personality disorder," are likely to engage in "predatory acts of sexual violence." The State invoked the Act for the first time to commit Leroy Hendricks, an inmate who had a long history of sexually molesting children, and who was scheduled for release from prison shortly after the Act became law. Hendricks challenged his commitment on, *inter alia*, "substantive" due process . . . grounds. . . . The Kansas Supreme Court invalidated the Act, holding that its pre-commitment condition of a "mental abnormality" did not satisfy what the court perceived to be the "substantive" due process requirement that involuntary civil commitment must be predicated on a finding of "mental illness."

The initial version of the Act, as applied to a currently confined person such as Hendricks, was designed to initiate a specific series of procedures. The custodial agency was required to notify the local prosecutor 60 days before the anticipated release of a person who might have met the Act's criteria. The prosecutor was then obligated, within 45 days, to decide whether to file a petition in state court seeking the person's involuntary commitment. If such a petition were filed, the court was to determine whether "probable cause" existed to support a finding that the person was a "sexually violent predator" and thus eligible for civil commitment. Upon such a determination, transfer of the individual to a secure facility for professional evaluation would occur. After that evaluation, a trial would be held to determine beyond a reasonable doubt whether the individual was a sexually violent predator. If that determination were made, the person would then be transferred to the custody of the Secretary of Social and Rehabilitation Services (Secretary) for "control, care and treatment until such time as the person's mental abnormality or personality disorder has so changed that the person is safe to be at large."

In addition to placing the burden of proof upon the State, the Act afforded the individual a number of other procedural safeguards. In the case of an indigent person, the State was required to provide, at public expense, the assistance of counsel and an examination by mental health care professionals. The individual also received the right to present and cross-examine witnesses, and the opportunity to review documentary evidence presented by the State.

Once an individual was confined, the Act required that "[t]he involuntary detention or commitment . . . shall conform to constitutional requirements for care and treatment." Confined persons were afforded three different avenues of review: First, the committing court was obligated to conduct an annual review to determine whether continued detention was warranted. Second, the Secretary was permitted, at any time, to decide that the confined individual's condition had so changed that release was appropriate, and could then authorize the person to petition for release. Finally, even without the Secretary's permission, the confined person could at any time file a release petition. If the court found that the State could no longer satisfy its burden under the initial commitment standard, the individual would be freed from confinement.

In 1984, Hendricks was convicted of taking "indecent liberties" with two 13-year-old boys. After serving nearly 10 years of his sentence, he was slated for release to a halfway house. Shortly before his scheduled release, however, the State filed a petition in state court seeking Hendricks' civil confinement as a sexually violent predator. . . .

Hendricks subsequently requested a jury trial to determine whether he qualified as a sexually violent predator. During that trial, Hendricks' own testimony revealed a chilling history of repeated child sexual molestation and abuse, beginning in 1955 when he exposed his genitals to two young girls. At that time, he pleaded guilty to indecent exposure. Then, in 1957, he was convicted of lewdness involving a young girl and received a brief jail sentence. In 1960, he molested two young boys while he worked for a

(continued)

carnival. After serving two years in prison for that offense, he was paroled, only to be rearrested for molesting a 7-year-old girl. Attempts were made to treat him for his sexual deviance, and in 1965 he was considered "safe to be at large," and was discharged from a state psychiatric hospital.

Shortly thereafter, however, Hendricks sexually assaulted another young boy and girl—he performed oral sex on the 8-year-old girl and fondled the 11-year-old boy. He was again imprisoned in 1967, but refused to participate in a sex offender treatment program, and thus remained incarcerated until his parole in 1972. Diagnosed as a pedophile, Hendricks entered into, but then abandoned, a treatment program. He testified that despite having received professional help for his pedophilia, he continued to harbor sexual desires for children. Indeed, soon after his 1972 parole, Hendricks began to abuse his own stepdaughter and stepson. He forced the children to engage in sexual activity with him over a period of approximately four years. Then, as noted above, Hendricks was convicted of "taking indecent liberties" with two adolescent boys after he attempted to fondle them. As a result of that conviction, he was once again imprisoned, and was serving that sentence when he reached his conditional release date in September 1994.

Hendricks admitted that he had repeatedly abused children whenever he was not confined. He explained that when he "get[s] stressed out," he "can't control the urge" to molest children. Although Hendricks recognized that his behavior harms children, and he hoped he would not sexually molest children again, he stated that the only sure way he could keep from sexually abusing children in the future was "to die." Hendricks readily agreed with the state physician's diagnosis that he suffers from pedophilia and that he is not cured of the condition; indeed, he told the physician that "treatment is bull" . . . .

THE FINDING   Kansas argues that the Act's definition of "mental abnormality" satisfies "substantive" due process requirements. We agree. Although freedom from physical restraint "has always been at the core of the liberty protected by the Due Process Clause from arbitrary governmental action," *Foucha* v. *Louisiana*, 504 U.S. 71, 80 (1992), that liberty interest is not absolute. The Court has recognized that an individual's constitutionally protected interest in avoiding physical restraint may be overridden even in the civil context:

"[T]he liberty secured by the Constitution of the United States to every person within its jurisdiction does not import an absolute right in each person to be, at all times and in all circumstances, wholly free from restraint. There are manifold restraints to which every person is necessarily subject for the common good. On any other basis organized society could not exist with safety to its members."

Accordingly, States have in certain narrow circumstances provided for the forcible civil detainment of people who are unable to control their behavior and who thereby pose a danger to the public health and safety. . . .

The statute thus requires proof of more than a mere predisposition to violence; rather, it requires evidence of past sexually violent behavior and a present mental condition that creates a likelihood of such conduct in the future if the person is not incapacitated. As we have recognized, "[p]revious instances of violent behavior are an important indicator of future violent tendencies." A finding of dangerousness, standing alone, is ordinarily not a sufficient ground upon which to justify indefinite involuntary commitment. We have sustained civil commitment statutes when they have coupled proof of dangerousness with the proof of some additional factor, such as a "mental illness" or "mental abnormality. . . ."

Hendricks nonetheless argues that our earlier cases dictate a finding of "mental illness" as a prerequisite for civil commitment, citing *Foucha*, and *Addington*. He then asserts that a "mental abnormality" is *not* equivalent to a "mental illness" because it is a term coined by the Kansas Legislature, rather than by the psychiatric community. Contrary to Hendricks' assertion, the term "mental illness" is devoid of any talismanic significance.

Indeed, we have never required State legislatures to adopt any particular nomenclature in drafting civil commitment statutes. Rather, we have traditionally left to legislators the task of defining terms of a medical nature that have legal significance. As a consequence, the States have, over the years, developed numerous specialized terms to define mental health concepts. Often, those definitions do not fit precisely with the definitions employed by the medical community. The legal definitions of "insanity" and "competency," for example, vary substantially from their psychiatric counterparts. . . .

[Accordingly the Court found that the law didn't violate due process. It also rejected Hendrick's double jeopardy and *ex post facto* claims because the Court found the law to be civil, and *ex post facto* and double jeopardy apply only to criminal laws and punishment. That the law does not punish past behavior, protects the public from a future behavior, isn't designed to satisfy retributive or deterrence objectives, is premised on mental illness not criminal behavior, and requires treatment of individuals confined, and annual examination and release of individuals who are found to no longer be dangerous are the reasons the Court found the laws to be civil, not criminal.]

What Do You Think?

1. Should a person be confined for something that *may* happen?

2. Do you accept the distinction between civil commitment and punishing crimes that underpins this decision?

3. How dangerous must an offender be to justify confinement? Is the science of recidivism sufficiently developed to make this prediction?

The Supreme Court's decision in *Hendricks* was focused on substantive due process. That is, it held that it is "fair" for the government to commit a person if two elements are satisfied: a finding of dangerousness and a finding of mental illness. Of course, there are procedural due-process requirements as well. The law in question in *Hendricks* satisfies procedural due process because it established a number of procedural rights, including a trial on the dangerousness and mental illness questions, the rights to appointed counsel and to compulsory process, and to proof beyond a reasonable doubt.

Additional Applications

Must a state demonstrate a complete lack of self-control in civil commitment proceedings?

Kansas v. *Crane*, 534 U.S. 407 (2002)

The Case: After the U.S. Supreme Court's 1997 affirmation of the state's Sexually Violent Predator Act in *Hendricks*, Kansas officials instituted civil confinement proceedings against Michael Crane, a previously convicted sex offender who suffered from both exhibitionism and antisocial personality disorder. After a jury trial, a Kansas district court ordered Crane's civil commitment; the Kansas Supreme Court reversed, however, holding that under *Hendricks*, the due-process clause requires a specific finding in a civil confinement proceeding that the defendant "cannot control his dangerous behavior"—even if problems of "emotional capacity" and not "volitional capacity" provide the "source of bad behavior" that justifies commitment. Seeking U.S. Supreme Court review, Kansas officials argued that the state supreme court wrongly interpreted *Hendricks* as mandating that the state must *always* prove that a dangerous individual is "completely unable" to control his behavior.

The Finding: In a 7–2 ruling, the U.S. Supreme Court vacated the Kansas Supreme Court's judgment and remanded the case for further proceedings. The Fourteenth Amendment's due-process clause, Justice Stephen Breyer wrote for the majority, does not require the state to demonstrate a defendant's "*total* or *complete* lack of control" in a civil commitment proceeding. After all, Breyer noted, "most severely ill people—even those commonly termed 'psychopaths'—retain some ability to control their behavior." At the same time, the Constitution does not permit commitment of a dangerous sex offender "without *any* lack-of-control determination" at all. The *Hendricks* ruling, Breyer wrote, underscored the "constitutional importance of distinguishing a dangerous sexual offender from other dangerous persons who are perhaps more properly dealt with exclusively through criminal proceedings"—a necessary distinction, he continued, "lest 'civil commitment' become a 'mechanism for retribution or general deterrence'. . . ." Consequently, the due-process clause requires the state in each case to produce "proof of serious difficulty in controlling behavior"—a rule that, Breyer admitted, necessarily lacks "mathematical precision."

Does the federal government have the constitutional authority to confine sexual predators through civil commitment?

United States v. *Comstock*, 560 U.S. ___ (2010)

The Case: In late 2006, six days before Graydon Comstock was to have finished a 37-month federal prison sentence for receiving child pornography, the U.S. Department of Justice instituted civil commitment proceedings against him under the Adam Walsh Child Protection and Safety Act. Under that act, a federal district court may order the indefinite civil commitment of an individual currently in federal custody who (1) has previously "engaged or attempted to engage in sexually violent conduct or child molestation"; (2) currently suffers from a serious mental illness, abnormality, or disorder; and (3) as a result of that mental illness, abnormality, or disorder is "sexually dangerous to others" in that "he would have serious difficulty in refraining from sexually violent conduct or child molestation if released." In the lower courts, Comstock (and several others) asserted that the federal government's civil confinement process violated several constitutional provisions, including the *ex post facto* clause, the double jeopardy clause, the due-process and equal protection clauses, and the Sixth and Eighth Amendments. In agreeing to hear Comstock's

(continued)

case, however, the U.S. Supreme Court limited its review only to a question of federal legislative power under the Constitution: did the necessary and proper clause of Article I, Section 8 of the Constitution grant to Congress the authority to enact a comprehensive federal civil commitment program?

The Finding: In a 7–2 ruling, the Court affirmed Congress' power to mandate continued civil confinement of dangerous sex offenders already in federal custody. Justice Breyer, writing for the majority, pointed to "five considerations" that "taken together" provide Congress with ample authority to enact the law: (1) the "Necessary and Proper Clause grants Congress broad authority to enact federal legislation;" (2) the act's civil commitment provision "constitutes a modest addition to a set of federal prison–related mental-health statutes that have existed for many decades;" (3) "Congress reasonably extended its longstanding civil-commitment system to cover mentally ill and sexually dangerous persons who are already in federal custody;" (4) "the statute properly accounts for state interests" in protecting state sovereignty and independence; and (5) the statute is "narrowly tailored" to pursue the federal government's "legitimate interest as a federal custodian in the responsible administration of its prison system." ■

SUMMARY

- This chapter discusses excuses, the second major category of defenses. The other major category, justifications, was discussed in Chapter 5 . Excuses admit that the law-breaking actions committed by a defendant were wrong and that they violated the criminal law, but that the defendant should nonetheless be excused from criminal liability because of special circumstances.

- The majority of excuses are personal in nature. They claim that the defendant acted on the basis of some disability or some abnormal condition—such as intoxication, insanity, or immaturity—and that the defendant should not be held responsible for his or her actions.

- Where a defendant suffers from a known disability, that disability alone is not sufficient to excuse him or her of criminal responsibility. Only when the disability has the effect of in some way producing or contributing to the criminal activity in question will the actor be excused.

- Excuses recognized by law include (1) duress; (2) intoxication; (3) mistake; (4) age; (5) entrapment; (6) insanity; (7) diminished capacity; and, to a limited degree, (8) various "syndromes."

- The defense of duress, sometimes also called *compulsion*, is based on the notion that people do not willfully engage in acts that they are compelled or coerced to perform. In most jurisdictions, effective use of the duress defense must be based on a showing that the defendant feared for his or her life, was in danger of great bodily harm, or was acting so as to prevent the death or bodily harm of another. Likewise, for the duress defense to be effective, the threat under which the defendant acted must have been immediate, clear, and inescapable and must not have arisen from some illegal or immoral activity of the defendant.

- Voluntary intoxication is generally not a defense because individuals are responsible for their impaired state, and the law generally holds that those who voluntarily put themselves in a condition so as to have little or no control over their actions must be held to have intended whatever consequences ensue.

- Involuntary intoxication may serve as a defense if it creates in the defendant either an incapacity to appreciate the criminality of his or her conduct or an incapacity to conform his or her behavior to the requirements of the law.

- Mistake of fact will preclude criminal liability in instances in which the actions undertaken would have been lawful had the situation been as the acting person reasonably believed them to be. However, mistake of law, or ignorance of the law, rarely provides an effective defense.

- Infancy, or immaturity, defenses claim that certain individuals should not be held criminally responsible for their activities by virtue of their youth. Most jurisdictions do not impose full criminal culpability on children under the chronological age of 18, whereas a number of states set the age of responsibility at 16, and some at 17.

- The entrapment defense is built on the assertion that, had it not been for government instigation, no crime would have occurred. Two approaches to assessing entrapment can be found in the law: the subjective and the objective. The subjective approach excludes from criminal liability otherwise innocent individuals who were lured into the commission of the crime through the government's instigation. The objective approach to entrapment, also referred to as the *outrageous government conduct defense*, is based on the claim that methods employed by the government to bring about a conviction in the case are offensive to moral sensibilities.

- In recent years, numerous new and innovative defense strategies based on the use of "syndromes" have been proposed—with varying degrees of success. Among the syndromes through which claims for the expansion of traditional defenses have been made are battered woman's syndrome, premenstrual syndrome, sexual abuse syndrome, urban survival syndrome, and black rage syndrome.

- Although courts have been reluctant to recognize the claim that syndromes negate *mens rea*, the use of syndromes in expanding the applicability of traditional defenses has met with greater success. Nonetheless, the future of syndrome-based defenses remains very much in doubt.

- *Insanity* is a social and legal term rather than a medical one. Psychiatrists speak instead of *mental disorders* and do not use the term *insanity*, making it difficult to fit expert psychiatric testimony into legal categories. Nonetheless, the legal concept of insanity still has its basis in some disease of the mind.

- Competency to stand trial focuses on the defendant's condition at the time of trial rather than at the time of the crime. Competency to stand trial exists when a defendant has sufficient present ability to consult with his or her lawyer with a reasonable degree of rational understanding and has a rational as well as factual understanding of the proceedings against him or her.

- The insanity defense recognizes that some people, by virtue of mental disease or mental defect, cannot morally and justly be held accountable for their actions. Insanity can affect criminal liability in two ways: (1) It may result in a finding that the *mens rea* required for a specific crime was lacking at the time the crime was committed or (2) it may lead to a showing that, although the requisite *mens rea* was present at the time of the crime, the defendant should be excused from legal responsibility because of mental disease or defect.

- The defense of insanity is an affirmative defense and must be raised by the defendant. If successful, an insanity defense results in a verdict of not guilty by reason of insanity (NGRI).

- The M'Naughten rule, an early test, held that a person was insane if he or she "was laboring under such a defect of reason, from disease of mind, as not to know the nature and quality of the act he was doing; or if he did know it, that he did not know he was doing what was wrong."

- The claim of irresistible impulse is a defense in some jurisdictions. The irresistible impulse test asks whether, at the time the crime was committed, a mental disease or disorder prevented the defendant from controlling his or her behavior.

- The Durham rule, also known as the *product rule*, holds that an accused is not criminally responsible if his or her unlawful act was the *product* of mental disease or mental defect.

- The American Law Institute's substantial capacity test, which is incorporated into the Model Penal Code, says that a person is not responsible for criminal conduct if at the time of such conduct, and as a result of mental disease or defect, he or she lacked substantial capacity either to appreciate the criminality of the conduct or to conform the conduct to the requirements of the law.

- A guilty but mentally ill (GBMI) verdict establishes that a defendant, although mentally ill, was sufficiently in possession of his or her faculties to be morally blameworthy for the criminal act.

- The defense of diminished capacity, also called *diminished responsibility*, is available in some jurisdictions. It is based on claims that a defendant's mental condition at the time of the crime, although not sufficient to support the affirmative defense of insanity, might still lower criminal culpability. A finding of diminished capacity may result in a verdict of guilty to lesser charges.

- The insanity defense is not widely used and is raised in only about 1% of all criminal cases. Defendants found "not guilty by reason of insanity" are rarely set free but are instead committed to a mental hospital until confinement is no longer deemed necessary.

- Because of the difficulties associated with assessing insanity from a legal perspective, a number of jurisdictions have eliminated the insanity defense. Although some states no longer allow defendants to raise the insanity defense *as an excuse* to a criminal charge, defendants in all jurisdictions may still claim that the presence of mental disease at the time of the crime left them unable to form the *mens rea* needed for criminal activity.

KEY TERMS

battered woman's syndrome (BWS), 172

competent to stand trial, 179

culpable ignorance, 160

diminished capacity, 193

DSM-IV, 183

duress, 151

Durham rule, 187

entrapment, 166

guilty but mentally ill (GBMI), 189

ignorance of fact, 159

ignorance of the law, 160

incompetent to stand trial, 181

infancy defense, 161

insanity, 183

Insanity Defense Reform Act (IDRA), 186

involuntary intoxication, 156

irresistible impulse test, 187

juvenile offender, 164

mistake of fact, 156

mistake of law, 160

M'Naughten rule, 185

not guilty by reason of insanity (NGRI), 182

outrageous government conduct, 167

psycholegal error, 176

substantial capacity test, 188

syndrome, 171

syndrome-based defense, 171

voluntary intoxication, 156

QUESTIONS FOR DISCUSSION

1. What are the main distinguishing features of an excuse?

2. What are the conditions needed for the successful use of the defense of duress? Why is the defense inapplicable in cases of serious law violations such as murder and rape?

3. Why is voluntary intoxication usually not accepted as a defense to a criminal charge? Should it be? Why or why not?

4. What is the nature of a mistake that is acceptable as a defense to a criminal charge? What kinds of mistakes are not likely to reduce criminal liability?

5. At what age do you think people should be held criminally liable for their actions? Should there be a minimum age and a maximum age for determining culpability?

6. What is the difference between the subjective and the objective approaches to assessing entrapment? Which do you think is most useful? Why?

7. Is a syndrome an excuse, a justification, or an explanation? Are syndromes best viewed as potentially negating *mens rea*, as widening traditional defenses, or as justifying behavior for a particular class of people? Why?

8. How does the legal notion of insanity differ from psychiatric conceptions of mental disorders? What is the significance of such differences from a legal perspective?

9. How is competency to stand trial assessed? How might defendants who are truly incompetent best be distinguished from those who are "faking it"?

10. What is the difference between a finding that, as a result of mental disease or defect, the defendant lacks the specific *mens rea* required for a given crime and a finding that the defendant is insane?

11. What is the difference between a finding of NGRI and one of GBMI?

12. Compare and contrast the various legal "tests" for assessing insanity that are discussed in this chapter. Which do you think is the more useful? Why?

13. Some jurisdictions have eliminated the insanity defense. Why do you think they did so? Do you agree with such reasoning? Explain.

CRITICAL THINKING AND APPLICATION PROBLEMS

Use the following facts to answer problems 1 and 2:

Timothy V. Oyer, a 42-year-old male, decided to jog in a municipal park near his home on a beautiful June day. After jogging three miles, he slowed to a walk to cool down. During his walk he noticed a woman sitting under a tree not far from the sidewalk he was on. As he moved closer to her he was surprised to discover that she was not wearing any clothes above the waist. She appeared to be in her mid-20s and he found her attractive. As he neared her, she smiled at him and greeted him with a "hello." Then the following discussion occurred:

Timothy: It is a beautiful day.

Woman: Yes it is. You out running?

Timothy: Yes, not as far as I wanted. I am not in the shape I used to be.

Woman: Nonsense, you look great. I am the one that is out of shape.

Timothy: Are you kidding, you are beautiful with a body to match.

Woman: Sit down here. Take a break.

Timothy accepted the invitation to sit with her and they talked for 15 minutes. They discussed physical fitness and the weather, she laughed at his jokes, and she told him that he was a handsome man. At one point, she placed one of her legs on his shoulder in a demonstration of her flexibility. After 15 minutes of conversation and flirting, she asked to see his penis. Stunned, Timothy responded, "Really?" She nodded and smiled. Timothy unzipped his pants and displayed his penis. At that moment police officers pulled up in a van, jumped out, and arrested Timothy for indecent exposure. He would later learn that the woman was paid to be part of a sting operation to catch sexual offenders.

Timothy has two criminal convictions in his record. While in college, at the age of 19, he was convicted of public indecency, fined $100, and sentenced to ten days in jail. The jail time was suspended to probation. In this incident he was one of seven fraternity pledges who were caught by campus police running naked outside a sorority. At the age of 31 he was convicted of public indecency for masturbating in the restroom of an adult bookstore. He was fined $500 and sentenced to ten days in jail, which he served. He has been married to his wife for 18 years and he has worked as a data analyst for the same company for 13 years.

1. Applying the subjective test of entrapment to these facts, determine whether Timothy was entrapped. Fully explain your analysis and defend your conclusion.

2. Applying the objective test of entrapment to these facts, determine whether Timothy was entrapped. Fully explain your analysis and defend your conclusion.

LEGAL RESOURCES ON THE WEB

Many law schools maintain websites. Law school sites serve a variety of purposes. They provide admissions information to prospective students, list the credentials of law school faculty, and often include at least limited facilities for legal research as well as links to law libraries. The sites listed here allow you to find law schools in which you might be interested.

American Bar Association–Approved Law Schools
http://www.abanet.org/legaled/approvedlawschools/approved.html
Includes 200 institutions that are searchable by state and via a clickable map.

Association of American Law Schools
http://www.aals.org
Provides links to 204 member schools and 28 nonmember schools.

Jurist (University of Pittsburgh School of Law)
http://jurist.law.pitt.edu/lawschools
Offers an alphabetical listing of U.S. law schools with links.

Rominger Legal Services Law School Directory
http://www.romingerlegal.com/lawschools.htm
Provides an alphabetical listing and a state-by-state directory of law schools.

Washburn University School of Law, Law School Directory
http://www.washlaw.edu/lawschools
Lists both American and foreign law schools, organized alphabetically.

SUGGESTED READINGS AND CLASSIC WORKS

Arrigo, Bruce A. *The Contours of Psychiatric Justice: A Postmodern Critique of Mental Illness, Criminal Insanity, and the Law.* Hamden, CT: Garland, 1996.

Bavidge, Michael. *Mad or Bad?* New York: St. Martin's Press, 1989.

Bazelon, D. *Questioning Authority: Justice and Criminal Law,* reprint ed. New York: New York University Press, 1990.

Dershowitz, Alan M. *The Abuse Excuse: And Other Cop-Outs, Sob Stories, and Evasions of Responsibility.* Boston: Little, Brown, 1994.

———. *Reasonable Doubts: The O. J. Simpson Case and the Criminal Justice System.* New York: Simon and Schuster, 1996.

Elliott, Carl. *The Rules of Insanity: Moral Responsibility and the Mentally Ill Offender.* Binghamton: State University of New York Press, 1996.

Finkel, Norman. *Insanity on Trial*. New York: Plenum, 1988.

Halleck, Seymour L. "The Assessment of Responsibility in Criminal Law and Psychiatric Practice." In *Law and Mental Health: International Perspectives*, edited by David N. Weisstub. New York: Pergamon, 1987.

Huckabee, Harlow M. *Lawyers, Psychiatrists and Criminal Law: Cooperation or Chaos?* Springfield, IL: Charles C. Thomas, 1980.

Moore, Michael. *Law and Psychiatry: Rethinking the Relationship*. New York: Cambridge University Press, 1985.

Moran, Richard, ed. *The Annals of the American Academy of Political and Social Science: The Insanity Defense*. London: Sage, 1985.

Morris, Norval. *Madness and the Criminal Law*. Chicago: University of Chicago Press, 1982.

Paull, Donald. *Fitness to Stand Trial*. Springfield, IL: Charles C. Thomas, 1993.

Pennock, J. Roland, and John Chapman. *Due Process*. New York: New York University Press, 1977.

Robinson, Daniel N. *Wild Beasts and Idle Humours: The Insanity Defense from Antiquity to the Present*. Cambridge, MA: Harvard University Press, 1996.

Rothwax, Harold J. *Guilty: The Collapse of Criminal Justice*. New York: Random House, 1996.

Simon, Rita, and David Aaronson. *The Insanity Defense: A Critical Assessment of Law and Policy in the Post-Hinckley Era*. New York: Praeger, 1988.

Steadman, Henry J., Margaret A. McGreevy, and Joseph P. Morrisey. *Before and after Hinckley: Evaluating Insanity Defense Reform*. New York: Guilford Press, 1993.

Szasz, Thomas. *Psychiatric Justice*. Syracuse, NY: Syracuse University Press, 1989.

NOTES

1. *Pope v. State*, 679 So. 2d 710 (1996).
2. Ibid.
3. Sanford H. Kadish and Stephen J. Schulhofer, *Criminal Law and Its Processes: Cases and Materials*, 6th ed. (New York: Little, Brown, 1995), 821.
4. Model Penal Code, Section 2.09.
5. George Gedda, "Cuba Hijacker Acquitted for Duress," Associated Press, July 26, 1997.
6. Some jurisdictions specify that the "other" must be an immediate family member.
7. *State v. Toscano*, 74 N.J. 421, 378 A.2d 755 (1977).
8. James F. Stephen, *A History of the Criminal Law of England*, Vol. II (London: MacMillan, 1883), p. 107.
9. *People v. Walker*, 18 Cal. Rptr. 2d 431 (1993).
10. California Penal Code, Section 22.
11. See *People v. Low*, 732 P.2d 622 (Colo. 1987).
12. *Davis v. State*, 265 Ind. 476, 355 N.E.2d 836 (1976).
13. *Gordon v. State*, 52 Ala. 308, 23 Am. Rep. 575 (1875).
14. Although one who purchases baking powder thinking it is heroin may suffer only from his own mistake, actual possession of a controlled substance is an element of most trafficking offenses.
15. *Gordon v. State*, 52 Ala. 308, 23 Am. Rep. 575 (1875).
16. *Ratzlaf v. United States*, 114 S. Ct. 655, 126 L. Ed. 2d 615 (1994).
17. *Ratzlaf et ux. v. United States*, 510 U.S. 135 (1993).
18. Ibid., syllabus.
19. *United States v. Squires*, 440 F.2d 859 (2d Cir. 1971).
20. *Long v. State*, 44 Del. 262, 65 A.2d 489 (1949).
21. *People v. Tolbert*, 56 Cal. Rptr. 2d 604 (1996).
22. "Girl Charged," Associated Press, February 28, 1994.
23. Ira Mickenberg, "A Pleasant Surprise: The Guilty but Mentally Ill Verdict Has Both Succeeded in Its Own Right and Successfully Preserved the Traditional Role of the Insanity Defense," *University of Cincinnati Law Review* 55 (1987): 943, 987–91.
24. "Ten-Year-Old Faces Murder Trial as Adult," *Fayetteville (N.C.) Observer-Times*, August 27, 1989.
25. *In re Ramon M.*, 22 Cal. 3d 419, 584 P.2d 524, 149 Cal. Rptr. 387 (1978).

26. Details for this story come from Ellen Wulfhorst, "U.S. Judge Blasts FBI Case against Albany Muslims," Reuters, August 24, 2004, http://www.ccmep.org/2004_articles/civil%20liberties/082404_us_judge.htm (accessed January 4, 2005).

27. "Indictment against Mosque Leaders Unsealed," Associated Press, August 5, 2004.

28. *United States* v. *Russell*, 411 U.S. 423 (1973).

29. Ibid.

30. *Cruz* v. *State*, 465 So. 2d 516, 518 (Fla. 1985).

31. Rollin M. Perkins and Ronald N. Boyce, *Criminal Law*, 3rd ed. (Mineola, NY: Foundation Press, 1982), 1167.

32. Ibid.

33. *Sorrells* v. *United States*, 287 U.S. 435 (1932).

34. *Sherman* v. *United States*, 356 U.S. 369 (1958).

35. *Jacobson* v. *United States*, 503 U.S. 540 (1992).

36. Ibid.

37. Stephen J. Morse, "The 'New Syndrome Excuse Syndrome,'" "*Criminal Justice Ethics* (winter/spring 1995): 7.

38. Ibid.

39. Ibid., 3.

40. *State* v. *Kelly*, 97 N.J. 178 (N.J. 1984).

41. *State* v. *Norman*, 324 N.C. 253, 378 S.E.2d 9 (1989).

42. Ibid.

43. California Evidence Code, Section 1107.

44. *State* v. *Hodges*, 716 P.2d 563, 567 (Kan. 1986), *supra*, 716 P.2d at p. 567, citing Lenore Walker, *The Battered Woman* (New York: Harper and Row, 1979), 19–31.

45. This list is drawn from Alan M. Dershowitz, *The Abuse Excuse: And Other Cop-Outs, Sob Stories, and Evasions of Responsibility* (Boston: Little, Brown, 1994), 321–41; Richard G. Singer and Martin R. Gardner, *Crimes and Punishment: Cases, Materials, and Readings in Criminal Law*, 2nd ed. (New York: Matthew Bender, 1996), 903–20; and Morse, "The 'New Syndrome Excuse Syndrome,'" 3.

46. *Werner* v. *State*, 711 S.W.2d 639 (Tex. Crim. App. 1986), in which the son of a Nazi concentration camp survivor claimed that Holocaust syndrome caused him to be overly assertive in confrontational situations. The court hearing the case disallowed the claim.

47. *State* v. *Marks*, 647 P.2d 1292 (Kan. Supreme Ct., 1982), in which expert testimony about rape trauma syndrome was allowed to counter a consent defense.

48. *State* v. *Kenneth J. Sharp, Jr.*, 418 So. 2d 1344 (La. Sup. Ct., 1982).

49. "Drunk Driving Charge Dismissed: PMS Cited," *Fayetteville* (N.C.) *Observer-Times*, June 7, 1991, 3A.

50. As reported in Arnold Binder, *Juvenile Delinquency: Historical, Cultural, Legal Perspectives* (New York: Macmillan, 1988), 494.

51. See, for example, Dershowitz, *The Abuse Excuse*, 30–31.

52. These numbers are not meant to be exact but are only exemplary.

53. Morse, "The 'New Syndrome Excuse Syndrome,'" 7.

54. Ibid., 9.

55. Dershowitz, *The Abuse Excuse*, 20–21.

56. *Time* (September 27, 1993): 32.

57. Dershowitz, *The Abuse Excuse*, 27.

58. Clarence Thomas, "Crime and Punishment: And Personal Responsibility," *National Times* (September 1994): 31.

59. Ibid.

60. Dershowitz, *The Abuse Excuse*, 41.

61. G. Williams, "The Theory of Excuses," *Criminal Law Review* 19 (1982): 732, 741–42.

62. *United States* v. *Taylor*, 437 F.2d 371 (4th Cir. 1971).

63. "Experts Testify du Pont 'Psychotic,'" Associated Press, September 22, 1996.

64. Aliah Wright, "Du Pont Incompetent," Associated Press, September 24, 1996.

65. *Pate* v. *Robinson*, 383 U.S. 375, 86 S. Ct. 836, 15 L. Ed. 2d 815 (1966).

66. Ibid.

67. *Dusky* v. *United States*, 362 U.S. 402, 80 S. Ct. 788, 789, 4 L. Ed. 2d 824, 825 (1960).

68. U.S. Code, Title 18, Section 4241, subsection C.

69. *Cooper* v. *Oklahoma*, 116 S. Ct. 1373, 134 L. Ed. 2d 498 (1996).

70. See U.S. Code, Title 18, Section 4241.

71. Arizona Penal Code, Sections 13-4501, 13-4503, 13-4507, and 13-4510.

72. Arizona Penal Code, Section 13-4022.

73. David Bazelon, *Questioning Authority: Justice and Criminal Law*, reprint ed. (New York: New York University Press, 1990).

74. Jerome Hall, *General Principles of Criminal Law*, 2nd ed. (Indianapolis: Bobbs-Merrill, 1960), 449.

75. Court TV website, CourtTV.com (accessed September 21, 1996).

76. Note that this is quite a different question than assuming that children under the age of seven cannot form the *mens rea* needed for criminal liability.

77. *United States v. Pohlot*, 827 F.2d 889 (3d Cir. 1987).

78. Ibid.

79. American Psychiatric Association, *Diagnostic and Statistical Manual of Mental Disorders*, 4th ed. (Washington, DC: American Psychiatric Association, 1994).

80. American Psychiatric Association website, http://www.psych.org/ (accessed September 20, 1996).

81. *People v. Schmidt*, 110 N.E. 945, 949 (N.Y. 1915).

82. *Ferrers' Case*, 19 How. St. Tr. 886 (1760).

83. *Hadfield's Case*, 27 How. St. Tr. 1282 (1800).

84. Much of the material in this section is taken from *United States v. Freeman*, 357 F.2d 606 (2d Cir. 1966), which provides an excellent summation of the M'*Naughten* case and of the development of the M'*Naughten* rule.

85. Phrenology is the study of the shape of the human skull in an attempt to assess personality characteristics. Monomania is a theory that holds that "a disorder affect[s] only one compartment of the mind without affecting the mind as a whole." See Perkins and Boyce, *Criminal Law*, 964, citing earlier sources.

86. Ibid.

87. 8 Eng. Rep. 718 (1843).

88. Perkins and Boyce, *Criminal Law*.

89. Ibid.

90. Texas Penal Code, Section 8.01.

91. "Yates Claimed She Killed Kids to Keep Them from Going to Hell," Court TV online, March 1, 2002, http://www.courttv.com/trials/yates/030102_pm.html (accessed November 2, 2004).

92. "Psychologist: Yates Was Insane," Court TV online, February 27, 2002, http://www.courttv.com/trials/yates/022702_ap.html (accessed November 2, 2004).

93. Perkins and Boyce, *Criminal Law*.

94. *Durham v. United States*, 94 U.S. App. D.C. 228, 214 F.2d 862, 874–75 (1954).

95. *United States v. Freeman*, 357 F.2d 606, 618–622 (2d Cir. 1966).

96. *United States v. Brawner*, 153 U.S. App. D.C. 1, 471 F.2d 969, 998–1002 (1972).

97. Ibid.

98. Model Penal Code, Commentary, Comment on Section 4.01 at 156–60 (Tentative Draft No. 4, 1955).

99. Model Penal Code, Section 4.01(1).

100. U.S. Code, Title 18, Section 17.

101. U.S. Code, Title 18, Sections 17 and 4242(b).

102. See, for example, *United States v. Pohlot*, 827 F.2d 889, 897 (3d Cir. 1987), cert. denied, 484 U.S. 1011, 108 S. Ct. 710, 98 L. Ed. 2d 660 (1988).

103. *United States v. Cameron*, 907 F.2d 1051, 1065 (11th Cir. 1990).

104. Mickenberg, "A Pleasant Surprise."

105. Ibid.

106. *State v. Porter*, 213 Mo. 43, 111 W.W. 529 (1908).

107. A. Levine, "Denying the Settled Insanity Defense: Another Necessary Step in Dealing with Drug and Alcohol Abuse," *Boston University Law Review* 76 (1998): 75–76.

108. L. Johnson, "Settled Insanity Is Not a Defense: Has the Colorado Supreme Court Gone Crazy? *Bieber v. People*," *Kansas Law Review* 43 (1994): 259–60.

109. Charlotte Carter-Yamauchi, *Drugs, Alcohol and the Insanity Defense: The Debate over "Settled Insanity"* (Honolulu: Legislative Reference Bureau, 1998): 22.

110. *United States v. Pohlot*, 827 F.2d 889 (3d Cir. 1987), cert. denied.

111. Peter Arenella, "The Diminished Capacity and Diminished Responsibility Defenses: Two Children of a Doomed Marriage," *Columbia Law Review* 77 (1977): 830.

112. *United States v. Brawner*, 471 F.2d 969 (1972).

113. Bryan A. Garner, ed., *Black's Law Dictionary*, 6th ed. (New York: Thompson West, 2004), p. 458.

114. Model Penal Code, Section 4.03.

115. Carol Pogash, "Myth of the 'Twinkie Defense': The Verdict in the Dan White Case Wasn't Based on His Ingestion of Junk Food," November 23, 2003, SF Gate of the San Francisco Chronicle, found at http://www.sfgate.com/cgi-bin/article.cgi?f=/c/a/2003/11/23/INGRE343501.DTL&ao=all.

116. California Penal Code, Section 25(a).

117. California Penal Code, Section 28(b).

118. California Penal Code, Section 25(c).

119. *Bulletin of the American Academy of Psychiatry and the Law* 19, no. 4 (1991).

120. American Bar Association Standing Committee on Association Standards for Criminal Justice, *Proposed Criminal Justice Mental Health Standards* (Chicago: American Bar Association, 1984).

121. American Psychiatric Association website, http://www.psych.org/ (accessed September 20, 1996), from which much of the material in this section is derived.

122. Ibid.

123. Ibid.

124. Carter-Yamauchi, *Drugs, Alcohol and the Insanity Defense*, 11, citing J. Kaplan, R. Weisberg, and G. Binder, *Criminal Law: Cases and Materials*, 3rd ed. (New York: Aspen, 1996), 745, and others.

125. Even those who have committed no crime can be confined under civil procedures if found dangerous to themselves or others. See, for example, *Kansas* v. *Hendricks*, 521 U.S. 346 (1997).

126. American Psychiatric Association website, http://www.psych.org/ (accessed September 20, 1996).

127. *Commonwealth* v. *Burgess*, 450 Mass. 366 (Mass. 2008).

128. *Foucha* v. *Louisiana*, 504 U.S. 71 (1992).

129. Ibid.

130. See, for example, *People* v. *Beck*, 96 C.D.O.S. 5794 (California's First Appellate District, 1996).

131. *Shannon* v. *United States*, 114 S. Ct. 2419, 129 L. Ed. 2d 459 (1994).

132. Idaho Code, Section 18-207(1).

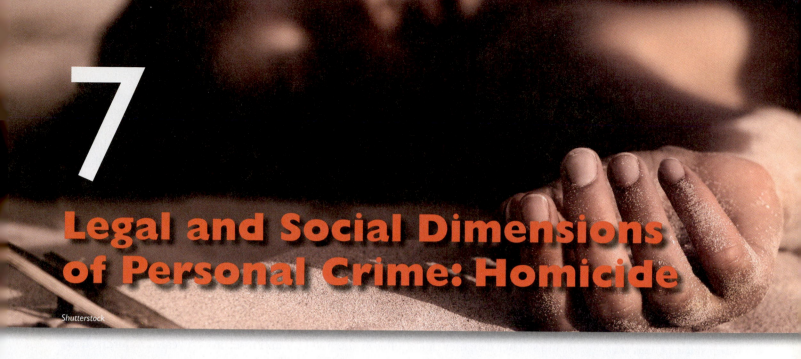

Shutterstock

7

Legal and Social Dimensions of Personal Crime: Homicide

CHAPTER OUTLINE

Introduction

Criminal Homicide

Murder

Manslaughter

Negligent Homicide

Suicide

OBJECTIVES

After reading this chapter, you should be able to

- Distinguish between criminal homicide and noncriminal homicide.
- Distinguish between first-degree murder and second-degree murder.
- Provide a legally acceptable definition of death.
- Identify causation problems that are characteristic of criminal homicide prosecutions.
- Explain the concept of *corpus delicti* as it relates to criminal homicide.
- Explain the concept of malice aforethought.
- Explain the felony murder rule.
- Summarize what is required to prove a charge of first-degree murder.
- Explain the concept of assisted suicide, and describe the nature of criminal liability as it attaches to assisted suicide.

"Murder" is never more than a shortening of life; if [a] defendant's culpable act has significantly decreased [the] span of human life, the law will not hear him say that [the] victim would thereafter have died in any event.

—*People v. Phillips, 64 Cal. 2d 574, 414 P.2d 353 (Cal. 1966)*

The typical murderer is a young man in his 20s who kills another man only slightly older.

—*Marvin Wolfgang[1]*

INTRODUCTION

Most homicide cases are heart-wrenching, but few are as difficult to come to terms with emotionally as that of 31-year-old Farinoosh "Roya" Dalili.[2] Officials claim that on March 3, 1997, Dalili jumped from the tenth floor of the Marriott Hotel in Torrence, California, holding her three-year-old daughter, Nagen, in her arms in a suicide attempt. Although badly injured, the mother survived. Her daughter did not. Prosecutors charged Dalili with first-degree murder in her daughter's death.

Dalili attended the three-week-long trial that ensued while lying prone in the courtroom in a hospital-style bed, with more than 200 pins holding her broken bones together. During testimony, she blamed the suicide attempt on depression brought on by spousal abuse. Her husband denied the allegation.

Describing the events that led up to the death of her daughter, Dalili said, "There was a rush and a voice that was telling me, 'Do it. Do it.' . . . I don't remember jumping." Dalili also testified that she recalled being alone on the window ledge just before jumping and could see her daughter in a stroller in the hotel room. Prosecutors revealed to jurors, however, that the woman told investigators she cradled her daughter in her arms as she jumped. "I know that now, that I took her with me," Dalili had said. Defense attorneys countered with claims that the child probably saw her mother jump and followed her out of the window.

Jurors refused to find Dalili guilty of first-degree murder, convicting her instead of involuntary manslaughter. Although prosecutor Alex Karkanen had sought a prison term, she was sentenced to a year of house arrest and five years of probation. "The victim is dead," Karkanen told reporters, "because of what the defendant did."

In February 2000, Dalili again tried to take her life by driving her car off Palos Verdes Drive East in San Pedro, California. She was apparently distraught over a pending civil suit filed by her ex-husband charging her with the wrongful death of the couple's daughter.[3] A guardrail foiled the attempt.

CRIMINAL HOMICIDE

Some deaths are accidental. Others are caused by human intent, recklessness, or negligence. An **accidental death**, or one that is caused by unexpected or unintended means, can be distinguished from an **accidental killing**, which is the result of a purposeful human act lawfully undertaken in the reasonable belief that no harm will result.

Homicide is the killing of one human being by another human being. (By definition, suicides are not included.) More precisely, homicide can be defined as "the killing of one human being by the act, procurement, or omission of another human being."[4] There are three basic types of homicide: justifiable, excusable, and criminal. **Justifiable homicides** are those that are permitted under law, as in the case of a state-ordered execution or a military killing of an enemy soldier in the line of duty. A death caused by the legitimate use of self-defense is sometimes classified as a justifiable homicide, although it may also be considered an excusable homicide.

Excusable homicides are those homicides that may involve some fault but not enough for the act to be considered criminal. A death caused by a vehicular accident in which the driver was not negligent, for example, would probably be excusable. The term **criminal homicide** refers only to those homicides to which criminal liability may attach. Generally speaking, any homicide that is not classified as justifiable or excusable may be considered criminal.

The early common law only recognized murder, and all murderers were punished with death. Over time the distinction between **murder** and **manslaughter**, and the latter's lesser

---

accidental death
A death that is caused by unexpected or unintended means.

accidental killing
A death that is the result of a purposeful human act lawfully undertaken in the reasonable belief that no harm would result.

homicide
The killing of a human being by the act, procurement, or omission of another human being.

justifiable homicide
(1) Homicide that is permitted under the law. (2) A killing justified for the good of society. (3) The killing of another in self-defense when danger of death or serious bodily harm exists. (4) The killing of a person according to one's duties or out of necessity but without blame.

[handwritten: common]

excusable homicide
A killing conducted in a manner that the criminal law does not prohibit. Also, a killing that may involve some fault but is not criminal homicide.

criminal homicide
The purposeful, knowing, reckless, or negligent killing of one human being by another. Also, a form of homicide for which criminal liability may be incurred. Criminal homicide may be classified as murder, manslaughter, or negligent homicide.

murder
The unlawful killing of a human being, carried out with malice or planned in advance. According to common law, the killing of one human being by another with malice aforethought.

[handwritten: both unlawful]

manslaughter
The unlawful killing of a human being without malice. Manslaughter differs from murder in that malice and premeditation are lacking.

punishment of life imprisonment, developed, as did the justifications and excuses defenses. Eventually both murder and manslaughter were subdivided into graded offenses. Some distinctions were made between voluntary and involuntary manslaughter and between first-degree and second-degree murder. Each of these grades will be discussed in greater detail later in this chapter. Most states today have followed the Model Penal Code and have passed laws recognizing three types of criminal homicide: (1) murder (of which there may be various degrees), (2) manslaughter (of which there may be various kinds), and (3) **negligent homicide** (which some consider to be a variety of involuntary manslaughter). This chapter is structured in terms of these three categories. In general, the circumstances surrounding the killing and the mental state of the actor at the time of the killing determine the type (or degree) of criminal homicide that can be charged. The terminology applied to different categories and subcategories of homicide, however, varies considerably between jurisdictions.

negligent homicide
The killing of a human being by criminal negligence or by the failure to exercise reasonable, prudent care. Also, a criminal offense committed by one whose negligence is the direct and proximate cause of another's death.

Corpus Delicti

The *corpus delicti* of a criminal homicide consists of two things: the death of a human being and the fact that the death was caused by the criminal act or agency of another person. (See Chapter 3 for a detailed discussion of the concept of *corpus delicti*.) Included within this definition is the requirement that the victim's death was the natural and probable consequence of another person's unlawful conduct.[5]

Under common law, an individual could not be convicted of any grade of criminal homicide unless the body of the deceased or at least portions of it were found and sufficiently identified to establish the fact of the victim's death. This requirement has since been modified in most states. Today, to conduct a successful prosecution on a charge of criminal homicide, the state must establish the *corpus delicti* of the crime of homicide, that is, the prosecution must establish the cause of death and show that death was caused by the criminal act of another.

> *Oh dear, I never realized what a terrible lot of explaining one has to do in a murder!*
>
> —Agatha Christie, Spider's Web (1956)

Although discovery of the body of the murder victim may not be necessary to prove criminal homicide in courts today, a conviction requires prosecutors to prove that the death in question was caused "by the act, agency, procurement, or omission of the accused."[6] In *Williams v. State*,[7] for example, the defendant was convicted after he confessed to shooting the victim at close range with a shotgun, although the victim's body was never recovered. In addition, several witnesses testified that the victim was dead and that they helped the defendant dispose of the body. A Texas appellate court, which upheld Williams's conviction, ruled that the state had successfully established that the victim was dead, even though no body had been found, and that the state had established that the victim's death was caused by the criminal act of the accused—thus meeting the requirements for proving criminal homicide under state law.

The Taking of a Life

During the final stage of labor, Californian Mary Chavez walked into her bathroom and sat on the toilet. Her baby dropped from her womb into the bowl and drowned. The baby never had a chance to cry, and evidence later showed that the umbilical cord had not been cut before its death. Evidence also indicated that the baby had breathed for a brief period of time after its head emerged but that it was probably dead before the birth process was completed. Chavez was convicted of murder but appealed, claiming that she had not killed a "human being," as her baby had not yet become a fully functioning independent entity at the time of its death. A California court of appeals, however, in upholding her murder conviction, ruled that "a viable child in the process of being born is a human being within the meaning of the homicide statutes whether or not the birth process has been fully completed."[8]

> *Murder is not the crime of criminals, but that of law-abiding citizens.*
>
> —Emmanuel Teney, professor of psychiatry, Wayne State University

Under common law, an essential element of homicide was the "killing of a human being." By definition, the victim must have been alive before the homicidal act occurred. Hence, under common law, the killing of an unborn child was not chargeable as homicide because the fetus was not considered "alive" in the sense of a "walking, breathing, human being." As one court noted: "Where the birth process has not begun, the courts are reluctant to consider the fetus a human being for homicide purposes."[9] If, however, a baby was born alive and then died as the result of an act committed against the mother before the birth (as, for example, where the mother was shot but gave birth after the shooting), then the baby's death could be considered criminal homicide. Many states still follow that common law rule. Texas, for example, requires that a person "cause the death of an individual" before the crime of murder can be said to have occurred.[10] Because causing the death of a living individual is a requirement for the act of murder, the act of decapitating a dead body is not considered homicide.[11]

The "alive" requirement has been modified in some states, where the killing of a fetus is now considered homicide. California's penal code, for example, defines murder as the "unlawful killing of a human being, or a fetus, with malice aforethought."[12] The change in the California law came after the case of *Keeler* v. *Superior Court*, in which a California court held that the killing of an unborn fetus is not murder, as "a killing cannot be a criminal homicide unless the victim is a living human being."[13] By 1996, following California's lead, 13 states had amended the wording of their homicide statutes to include a viable fetus under the notion of a living human being. For purposes of such statutes, the term *viable* is said to mean that if the fetus had been born prematurely at the time it was killed, it would have had at least a 75 percent chance of survival for at least a limited period of time outside the womb. Other states, such as California, Minnesota, Massachusetts, and South Carolina, have adopted even more stringent statutes, which say that, except for legal abortions, the killing of any developing fetus beyond a given age (usually six or seven weeks) constitutes homicide.

In 2004, the California Supreme Court ruled that the killing of a fetus constitutes second-degree murder, even when the killer had no idea that the expectant mother was pregnant. In the case of *People* v. *Taylor*,[14] Harold Taylor, a decorated Vietnam veteran, was convicted of the shooting death of his ex-girlfriend, Patty Fansler, in 1999. Neither Fansler, who weighed 200 pounds, nor Taylor were aware of the fact that Fansler was three months' pregnant at the time of her death. In their written opinion, the California justices reasoned that "[i]f the gunman simply walked down the hall of an apartment building and fired through the closed doors, he would be liable for the murder of all the victims struck by his bullets—including a fetus of one of his anonymous victims who happened to be pregnant."[15] Moreover, said the court, "[w]hen a defendant commits an act, the natural consequences of which are dangerous to human life, with a conscious disregard for life in general, he acts with implied malice towards those he ends up killing. . . . There is no requirement the defendant specifically know of the existence of each victim." The ruling effectively upheld Taylor's conviction and sentence of 65 years to life in prison.

At the federal level, the Unborn Victims of Violence Act[16]—better known as Laci and Conner's Law, after Laci Peterson and her unborn son (whom she had planned to name Conner)—was signed into law in 2004 by then-President George W. Bush. The law makes it a separate federal crime to "kill or attempt to kill" a fetus "at any stage of development" during an assault on a pregnant woman. The law also specifically prohibits the prosecution "of any person for conduct relating to an abortion for which the consent of the pregnant woman, or a person authorized by law to act on her behalf, has been obtained or for which such consent is implied by law."

In some states, illegal abortions may be chargeable as murder, and all jurisdictions have statutes prohibiting abortion except as permitted by therapeutic abortion laws. It is generally a felony to either solicit or to perform an illegal abortion. Section 274 of the California

Penal Code, for example, says that every person who provides, supplies, or administers to any woman; or procures any woman to take any medicine, drug, or substance; or uses or employs any instrument or other means, with intent to procure the miscarriage of the woman, except as provided for in the state's Therapeutic Abortion Act, is punishable by imprisonment in a state prison. In addition, Section 275 of California's code makes it a crime for a woman to solicit any person to perform an illegal abortion.

Defining Death

A central issue in criminal homicide cases is the definition of death, which is needed before criminal prosecution begins in order to establish that death has actually occurred. The Model Penal Code provides no definition of death. The code's *Commentary* cites two reasons for this failure: (1) Contemporary scientific understandings of death were not available when the code was first drafted, making death difficult to define at the time; and (2) the delicate contemporary interplay between criminal law and advances in medical science is still too nebulous to reduce to statutory formulation.[17]

The common law rule was that death, or "cessation of life," occurs when a person's heartbeat and respiration cease (Figure 7–1).[18] In 1968, a report defining the characteristics of a permanently nonfunctioning brain was published by a committee of the Harvard Medical School and became the basis for the concept of **brain death**.[19] Brain death is used today by some courts to establish the death of homicide victims. Under the standard of brain death, death is said to occur when a blood-flow test called a *cerebral angiogram*, or an electroencephalogram (EEG), produces no evidence of physiological or electrical brain activity for a given period of time (usually 12 hours). Brain death can occur even though the victim's heart continues to beat and respiration persists.[20]

Many jurisdictions have adopted the **Uniform Determination of Death Act (UDDA)**,[21] which provides that "[a]n individual who has sustained either: (1) irreversible cessation of circulatory and respiratory functions, or (2) irreversible cessation of all functions of the

brain death
Death determined by a "flat" reading on an electroencephalograph (EEG), usually after a 24-hour period, or by other medical criteria.

Uniform Determination of Death Act (UDDA)
A standard supported by the American Medical Association, the American Bar Association, and the National Conference of Commissioners on Uniform State Laws, which provides that "[a]n individual who has sustained either: (1) irreversible cessation of circulatory and respiratory functions, or (2) irreversible cessation of all functions of the entire brain, including the brain stem, is dead."[i] The UDDA provides a model for legislation and has been adopted in various forms by many states.

FIGURE 7–1

Determining Death.

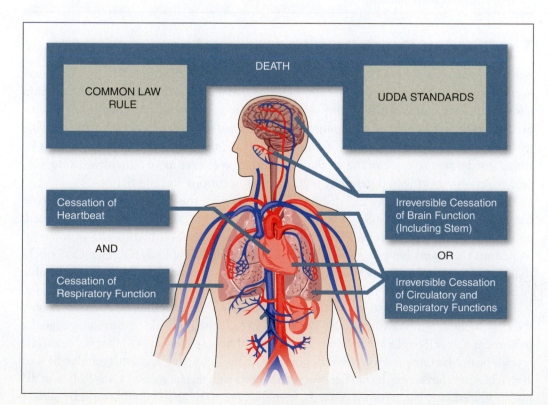

DEATH

COMMON LAW RULE

UDDA STANDARDS

Cessation of Heartbeat

AND

Cessation of Respiratory Function

Irreversible Cessation of Brain Function (Including Stem)

OR

Irreversible Cessation of Circulatory and Respiratory Functions

entire brain, including the brain stem, is dead."[22] The UDDA, an evolutionary formulation of the Uniform Brain Death Act originally proposed by the National Conference of Commissioners on Uniform State Laws, is supported by the American Medical Association, the American Bar Association, and the National Conference of Commissioners itself. [23]

Today, more than 30 states have adopted an approach using "cessation of brain function" in defining death—established through either statute or a state supreme court ruling. Even so, there is "deep disagreement" even among physicians as to "whether brain death is synonymous with death," as "[d]eath of the brain is not the same as death in a traditional sense."[24] EEG measurement of brain function, the primary criterion by which brain death is assessed today, is capable of recording only the brain's surface electrical activity and not other electrical activity, which may be occurring deeper in the brain.

Moreover, the UDDA accepts two separate, readily distinguishable clinical situations as death, both of which can be manifested successively in the same individual. Complicating matters still more from both legal and medical perspectives is the fact that a pregnant woman meeting the criteria for brain death can often be sustained on life-support systems until the fetus matures enough to be able to live outside the womb. Many states have defined brain death by statute. The applicable Texas statute, Section 671.001 of the Texas Health and Safety Code, is shown here.

TEXAS HEALTH AND SAFETY CODE

Section 671.001. Standard used in determining death.

(a) A person is dead when, according to ordinary standards of medical practice, there is irreversible cessation of the person's spontaneous respiratory and circulatory functions.

(b) If artificial means of support preclude a determination that a person's spontaneous respiratory and circulatory functions have ceased, the person is dead when, in the announced opinion of a physician, according to ordinary standards of medical practice, there is irreversible cessation of all spontaneous brain function. Death occurs when the relevant functions cease.

(c) Death must be pronounced before artificial means of supporting a person's respiratory and circulatory functions are terminated.

The Time of Death

Sometimes victims of homicidal acts suffer injuries but do not die immediately. Death may occur sometime after the fatal injury. In such cases, homicide prosecutions under common law required the death of the victim within a year and a day from the time that the ultimately fatal act took place. The requirement was termed the **year-and-a-day rule**. The rule was based on the belief that proof of causation (that is, the ability to show that actions by the accused were the cause of the victim's death) becomes ever more difficult with the passage of time—resulting in potentially unjustified prosecutions and convictions.[25]

Because the science of cause of death has improved since the rule's inception, its purpose has been obviated and the rule has been abolished in England, where it was first recognized, and in most U.S. jurisdictions. Some state legislatures have abolished it, and in some jurisdictions the courts have done away with it. For example, the U.S. Supreme Court held that the Tennessee Supreme Court could abolish the rule retroactively because a reasonable person should have known that the rule was so outdated as to no longer be in effect.[26]

Regardless, the rule persists in a minority of states. In 1991, for example, Guilford County (North Carolina) Superior Court Judge Peter M. McHugh cited the rule in dismissing a murder indictment against Terry Dale Robinson.[27] Evidence in the case plainly showed that Robinson had brutally beaten his estranged wife, Gina Robinson, with his hands, feet, and a shotgun that he used as a club. After the beating, he ran her over several times with an automobile. Gina Robinson did not die immediately but remained comatose from the time of the assault until her death—almost

year-and-a-day rule
A common law requirement that homicide prosecutions could not take place if the victim did not die within a year and a day from the time that the fatal act occurred.

three years later. After her death, prosecutors sought to indict her former husband on murder charges, but the defendant's lawyer moved to dismiss the indictment, citing the fact that the victim's death occurred more than a year and a day after the assault. Although the trial court agreed with the attorney, the state challenged the ruling. Upon appeal, the North Carolina Court of Appeals reinstated the indictment and ordered that Robinson be tried for murder. The appellate court said, "We hold, on the facts before us, that the relevant date of Mrs. Robinson's murder . . . is the date upon which she died."[28] California is another example. But in that state, the rule has been modified to three years and a day.[29]

> *Some people are alive simply because it is illegal to kill them.*
>
> —Anonymous

Proximate Cause and Homicide

Criminal homicide must be the result of an **affirmative act**, an omission to act, or criminal negligence. For criminal liability to accrue, the cause of death must not be so remote as to fail to constitute natural and probable consequences of the defendant's act. In other words, for charges of homicide to be brought successfully, a person's death must be the proximate result of a human act. Proximate cause is discussed in greater detail in Chapter 3. Suffice it to say here that, in homicide cases, a determination of proximate cause requires that death be a natural and probable consequence of the act in question. A test that is frequently used can be stated this way: If the original act had not occurred, would the victim have died? If, for example, a victim is shot by the accused, resulting in a nonfatal wound, but the victim later dies during an operation to remove the bullet, the shooting is considered to constitute the proximate cause of death.[30] Similarly, in *People* v. *Moan*,[31] a victim who was already very ill suffered an injury that accelerated his death. Nonetheless, the injury was considered the proximate cause of death. Hence an act that is determined to be the proximate cause of death need not be the only or sole cause of a person's death.[32]

affirmative act
Voluntary, conscious conduct. An affirmative act is not an omission or a failure to act.

Where concurring causes contribute to a victim's death, an accused may be held criminally liable by reason of conduct that directly contributes to the fatal result. In one case, for example, the removal of artificial life-support systems from a homicide victim after all electrical activity in the brain had ceased was not found to be an independent, intervening cause of death that would relieve the defendant of criminal responsibility.[33] Similarly, in an Illinois case, the defendant raped and severely beat an 85-year-old woman. Following the incident, the victim was moved to a nursing home, where she became depressed and refused to eat. Because of injuries sustained during the beating, the victim could not be fed through a nasal tube, and the woman consequently died of asphyxiation during an attempted feeding. The rapist was convicted of homicide, and an appellate court, upholding the conviction, stated that his criminal acts had set in motion a series of events that eventually caused the victim's death.[34]

Other courts have held that delays in medical treatment, whether avoidable or not, are not in fact intervening forces and cannot legally be considered superseding causes of death that would relieve murder defendants from criminal responsibility.[35] An accused cannot be found guilty of criminal homicide, however, when death is brought about by grossly erroneous medical or surgical treatment rather than by the wound inflicted by the accused. Finally, when the conduct of two or more people concurrently contributes to the death of a human being, the conduct of each person can be viewed as a proximate cause regardless of the extent to which each contributed to the death.[36]

MURDER

Murder is the first of the three types of criminal homicide. The elements of the crime of murder are

- An unlawful killing
- Of a human being
- With malice aforethought

FIGURE 7–2

Premeditation.

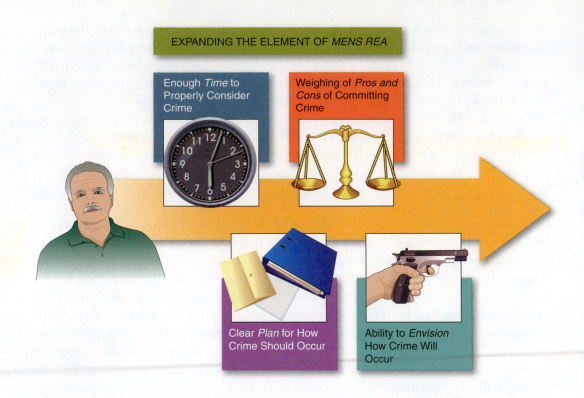

EXPANDING THE ELEMENT OF *MENS REA*

Enough *Time* to Properly Consider Crime

Weighing of *Pros and Cons* of Committing Crime

Clear *Plan* for How Crime Should Occur

Ability to *Envision* How Crime Will Occur

FIGURE 7–2

Premeditation.

first-degree murder
A willful, deliberate, and premeditated unlawful killing.

premeditation
The act of deliberating, meditating on, or planning a course of action, such as a crime.

second-degree murder
Depending on the jurisdiction, either (1) a murder committed during the perpetration or attempted perpetration of an enumerated felony, such as arson, rape, robbery, or burglary; or (2) any murder not classified by statute as first-degree murder.

malice
A legal term that refers to the intentional doing of a wrongful act without just cause or legal excuse. In cases of homicide, the term means "an intention to kill."

malice aforethought
An unjustifiable, inexcusable, and unmitigated person-endangering state of mind.[ii]

In most states, murder is divided into two categories: first degree and second degree. Generally speaking, **first-degree murder** includes any willful, deliberate, and premeditated unlawful killing. The term **premeditation** (which is discussed in greater detail later in this chapter) means the act of deliberating, meditating on, or planning a course of action, such as a crime. For purposes of the criminal law, premeditation requires the opportunity for *reflection* between the time the intent to act is formed and the act itself is committed (Figure 7–2). Hence, murder is clearly first degree when it is committed by poisoning or by lying in wait, or when it involves torture. First-degree murder is usually punishable by death or by life in prison.

In states in which only two degrees of murder are recognized, all murders other than first degree are said to constitute **second-degree murder**. Some states, such as Pennsylvania, recognize three or more degrees of murder. Where three degrees of murder are found, they are usually (1) murders that are committed willfully and deliberately and are premeditated; (2) murders committed during the perpetration or attempted perpetration of an enumerated felony, such as arson, rape, robbery, or burglary; and (3) all other types of murder.

Malice Aforethought

An essential element of the crime of murder is malice. Under common law, the "grand criterion" that "distinguished murder from other killing" was malice on the part of the killer, and this malice was not necessarily "malevolent to the deceased particularly" but "any evil design in general; the dictate of a wicked, depraved, and malignant heart."[37] As a contemporary legal term, **malice** refers to the intentional commission of a wrongful act without just cause or legal excuse. Malice encompasses both the intentional carrying out of a hurtful act without cause and the hostility of one individual toward another. In cases of homicide, the term means "an intention to kill."

First-degree murder is often described as requiring **malice aforethought**, a historical term that connotes a malicious design to kill or injure. In early English history, "aforethought" required that a person think about, envision, plan, or premeditate homicide before the time of the killing. Hence *malice aforethought* and *premeditation* were essentially equivalent terms.

Since then, however, the term *malice aforethought* has undergone considerable evolution, and today it includes several states of mind. It may, for example, encompass the causing of death during the commission of specified felonies, whether or not the offender premeditated the killing. As explained in the now-classic 1968 decision of *Green v. U.S.*, "malice aforethought is an unjustifiable, inexcusable, and unmitigated person-endangering state of mind."[38] In contemporary murder statutes, the term *malice aforethought* is generally understood to mean a killing while in possession of any one of the following five mental states: (1) an intent to kill, (2) an intent to inflict great bodily injury, (3) an intent to commit a felony (as in felony murder), (4) an intent to resist a lawful arrest, or (5) an awareness that one is engaged in conduct that carries with it a high risk of someone else's death. The fifth mental state, which describes unjustifiable conduct that is extremely reckless, is sometimes called **depraved heart murder** when it results in the death of a human being.[39]

Although, technically speaking, malice aforethought is planned malice, emphasis today is on the *malice* aspect of the term rather than on any kind of planning that includes the opportunity for reflection. Hence, in modern context, the term can be understood as "the intention to kill, actual or implied, under circumstances which do not constitute excuse or justification or mitigate the offense to manslaughter."[40] It is important to realize that neither malice nor malice aforethought requires an ill will or hatred of the victim.

Other distinctions can also be drawn. When an accused consciously desires to cause death, for example, the intent to kill is *actual* or *express*. It is *implied* when the defendant intends to cause great bodily harm or where the natural tendency of the defendant's behavior is to cause death or great bodily harm. California law, for example, says that "malice may be express or implied. It is expressed when there is manifested a deliberate intention unlawfully to take away the life of a fellow creature. It is implied, when no considerable provocation appears, or when the circumstances attending the killing show an abandoned and malignant heart."[41]

Malice may exist where the killing is unpremeditated, and malice may be inferred from surrounding circumstances. Pointing a firearm at an individual and firing it, for example, creates the presumption that the defendant actually intended to kill the victim. Malice may also be established by proving that the defendant intended to inflict serious bodily injury, even though he or she did not consciously desire the death of the victim.[42]

As mentioned earlier, under some circumstances a defendant may be guilty of murder if he or she acts in a manner that creates an unusually high risk of another's death and that does in fact result in death. Driving more than 100 miles per hour in a school zone while young children are present, for example, could establish malice in the form of a "depraved mind" or an "abandoned and malignant heart." A similar situation could exist when someone puts a healthy newborn baby in a trash bin and abandons it, or fires a weapon into a passing automobile. In *Commonwealth v. Malone*,[43] the accused was found guilty of murder when he killed the victim while playing a game of "Russian roulette." The game involved loading a pistol with one round and, after spinning the chamber, placing the gun to the victim's head and pulling the trigger. In holding the defendant criminally responsible, the court ruled that the defendant had acted with the awareness that his conduct created an extremely high risk of death to the victim. There is, however, disagreement as to whether a defendant must have been actually aware of the high risk involved or whether it is enough that his or her conduct created that risk. Most states require a subjective realization of the risk, on the theory that anything less is too removed from the notion of an "intent to kill" to justify a charge of murder.

depraved heart murder
(1) Unjustifiable conduct that is extremely negligent and results in the death of a human being, or (2) the killing of a human being with extreme atrocity.

Every unpunished murder takes away something from the security of every man's life.

—Daniel Webster,
American statesman and orator (1830)

Capital Murder

Thirty-three states and the federal government[44] presently authorize the death penalty for some types of murder. In some states, murders for which the death penalty is authorized

capital murder
Murder for which the death penalty is authorized by law.

are treated as a separate class of murder called **capital murder**. In Florida, Georgia, Idaho, Louisiana, Mississippi, Missouri, Nebraska, New Hampshire, New Mexico, North Carolina, Tennessee, and Wyoming, all murders in the first degree fall into the capital crimes category. The most common statutory requirement of first-degree murder is that the killing had to have been *premeditated* and *deliberate*.

The concepts of premeditation and deliberation are attempts to encapsulate the mental state of the offender at the time of the crime. The idea that only those who kill with clear intention, or who envision killing before the commission of their crimes, should be subject to capital punishment is well supported by decisions of the U.S. Supreme Court. In the case of *Edmund* v. *Florida* (1982),[45] for example, the Court held that the Eighth Amendment prohibition against cruel and unusual punishment prohibits the use of the death penalty on a defendant who does not him- or herself kill, attempt to kill, or intend that a killing take place or that lethal force be employed. In *Edmund*, the defendant waited in a getaway car while two accomplices went into a farmhouse and murdered an elderly couple who lived there. Because Edmund was guilty of murder only by a combination of the felony murder rule and rules on accomplice liability, the Court stated that it would be cruel and unusual punishment for him to be treated the same as if he had intentionally caused the harm.

The Court, however, did allow application of the death penalty in *Tison* v. *Arizona* (1987).[46] In *Tison*, the accomplice knew that the principal (his brother) might kill in furtherance of a joint plan designed to help their father escape from prison. The Court noted that the brothers possessed the mental state required for murder under Arizona law in that they exhibited an extreme indifference to the value of human life. Taken together, the *Edmund* and *Tison* cases demonstrate that an accomplice to murder can be given the death penalty if he or she had the requisite mental state for capital murder, but not if he or she was merely an accomplice with no desire that deadly force be used or that a killing take place. *Tison* and *Edmund*, along with another case, *Coker* v. *Georgia* (1977),[47] led to the conclusion that the U.S. Supreme Court will not allow imposition of the death penalty for crimes other than unlawful homicides committed with murderous intent. In *Coker*, for example, the Court held that the death penalty could not be imposed for the brutal rape of an adult woman. The Court, however, left open the question of whether someone who rapes a child can receive the death penalty. The Court answered this question in the 2008 case of *Kennedy v. Louisiana*[48] when it overturned Kennedy's sentence of death for the rape of his eight-year-old stepdaughter. The rape was so brutal that the victim's cervix was separated from her vagina, causing her rectum to protrude into her vagina, and the flesh of her body was torn from her vagina to her anus. Louisiana law permitted the imposition of death for the rape of minors but the Court found that death for child rape was contrary to contemporary notions of decency and hence disproportionate to the crime. *Kennedy* filled in the missing gap in this area of death penalty jurisprudence. Today, the death penalty may only be imposed for murder and crimes against the state, such as treason and espionage.

premeditated murder
Murder that was planned in advance (however briefly) and willfully carried out.

Premeditated murder is murder in which the intent to kill is formed pursuant to preexisting reflection rather than as the result of a sudden impulse or the heat of passion. The word *premeditated* means that the defendant must have considered the act before the killing. As noted in one court case, *premeditated* means "formed or determined upon as a result of careful thought and weighing of considerations for and against the proposed course of conduct." In that case, the court stated that the true test of premeditation was not the duration of time available for thought but the extent of reflection.[49]

aggravated murder
Murder plus one or more aggravating factors as specified by law. Aggravated murder is generally capital murder.

Following the lead of the Model Penal Code, some states have rejected premeditation and deliberation as the basis for identifying a murder as one that deserves the death penalty. Those states have legislatively defined capital murder as murder plus one or more specific aggravating factors, constituting what is sometimes called **aggravated murder**. The term *aggravated murder* is found in the statutes of some states (such as Utah, Washington, and

Ohio), although other states depict capital murder as "first-degree murder with aggravating factors" or with "special circumstances." Illinois law, for example, defines capital murder as first-degree murder with any one of 15 aggravating circumstances, whereas capital murder in Ohio consists of "aggravated murder with one of eight aggravating circumstances."[50]

Essentially, the concept of aggravated murder encompasses the notion that certain identifiable factors surrounding the circumstances of a particular murder may so enhance the culpability of the murderer that punishment of the first degree is warranted. Although the term *aggravated murder* is used to describe murders that are punishable by death in most jurisdictions, the term can also refer to murders punishable by life imprisonment in jurisdictions where the death penalty is lacking. (See Chapter 14 for more information on capital punishment.)

Felony Murder

In early summer of 1999, 45-year-old Miami taxi driver Webert St. Jean died of a heart attack while being robbed of $12. His alleged assailants, 22-year-old Alex Marrero and an unidentified second man, were apparently unarmed at the time but threatened to harm the cabbie if he resisted. St. Jean was forced from his cab and ran to a nearby home to call for help, but he collapsed and died before police arrived. St. Jean had taken medication to control high blood pressure. Following his death, police put out an arrest warrant for Marrero and his accomplice, charging them with first-degree murder. "They murdered him just as surely as if they stabbed him or shot him," said Miami police spokesperson Lieutenant Bill Schwartz. "If a criminal act places someone in such a stressful enough situation that their body can't handle it and as a result that person dies, the persons committing the crime are culpable."[51] Marrero surrendered to police shortly after the warrant was issued, but his accomplice remained at large.

Under common law, a defendant was guilty of murder if, while perpetrating a felony, or in the attempt to perpetrate a felony, another person died as a consequence of the crime or as a consequence of the attempt. Even if the other person's death was not intentional or foreseen, as in the case of a kidnapping victim who inadvertently suffocated or drowned, the offender could still be found guilty of murder and was often hanged. The **felony murder rule** was abolished by England in 1957, and it never existed in France or Germany.

Even though the felony murder rule has been widely criticized, it is still retained in various forms in most states today, where felony murder is often synonymous with first-degree murder (Figure 7–3). Defenders of the rule contend that it reaffirms the sanctity of human life. They say that the rule reflects society's judgment that the commission of a felony resulting in death is more serious and deserving of greater punishment than the commission of a felony that does not result in death. The felony murder rule is also intended to deter negligent and accidental killings during the commission of a felony. Critics of the rule complain that an unintended act cannot be effectively deterred, and they point out that deaths during the commission of felonies—the crimes "targeted" by felony murder laws—are quite rare.[52]

In most states, a death that results from the commission of an enumerated felony—that is, arson, rape, robbery, or burglary—constitutes first-degree murder. If the death results from the commission of a felony that is not listed or enumerated in the jurisdiction's felony murder statute, then the murder is either second-degree murder or manslaughter.

Because the felony murder rule applies whether the defendant kills the victim intentionally, recklessly, negligently, accidentally, or unforeseeably (rather than purposefully or intentionally), it creates a form of strict criminal liability for any death that results from the intentional commission of a felony. Courts have struggled with the felony murder rule

felony murder rule
A rule that establishes murder liability for a defendant if another person dies during the commission of certain felonies.

There are four kinds of homicide: felonious, excusable, justifiable, and praiseworthy, but it makes no great difference to the person slain whether he fell by one kind or another—the classification is for the advantage of the lawyers.

—Ambrose Bierce, The Devil's Dictionary (1911)

FIGURE 7–3

Felony Murder.

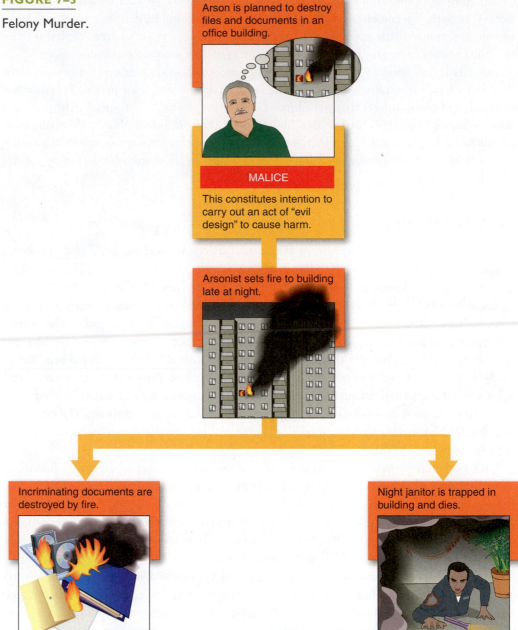

because a murder conviction under the rule does not require malice or intent. Generally speaking, courts have justified felony murder rules in two ways: (1) by holding that the rule dispenses with the requirement for malice, and (2) by holding that malice is implied from the intentional commission of a felony.

Under common law, all felonies were subject to the felony murder rule. Over the past 100 years or so, however, the felony murder rule has generally become more limited in scope in most jurisdictions (Table 7–1). Every state has numerous statutory felonies that were unknown at common law, and most pose virtually no unusual threat of death. Accordingly, the felony murder rule is today applied only to certain felonies. Generally, there are three schemes for identifying those felonies to which the rule applies, including those acts that (1) are inherently dangerous to life or health, (2) are held to be *malum in se*, and (3) were felonies under common law. *Malum in se* acts, for purposes of the felony murder rule, include "all felonies, all breaches of public order, injuries to person or property, outrages upon public

TABLE 7–1   The *Mens Rea* of Homicide at Common Law and under the Model Penal Code

Common Law *Mens Rea*	Crime	Model Penal Code *Mens Rea*
Malice aforethought	Murder	Purposeful, knowing, and reckless with extreme indifference to the value of life
All other unexcused homicides	Manslaughter	Reckless, except the extreme indifference standard for murder
Not recognized at common law	Negligent	Negligence

decency or good morals, and breaches of official duty, when done willfully or corruptly."[53] Most jurisdictions use an **inherently dangerous** test to decide when the felony murder rule applies. Felonies are inherently dangerous when, by their very nature or by the nature of their commission, they may result in death or serious bodily harm to a person. Also, the rules of proximate cause discussed earlier generally apply in felony murder situations, as the felony murder rule requires a causal relationship between the felony and the death. It is not sufficient that a death merely occurs at the same time as the felony. In some way, the felony must give rise to the killing.

inherently dangerous
A legal term used to describe an act or course of behavior (usually a felony) that, by its very nature, is likely to result in death or serious bodily harm to either the person involved in the behavior or to someone else.

MANSLAUGHTER

Manslaughter is the second of the three general types of criminal homicide discussed in this chapter. Manslaughter is the unlawful killing of a human being without malice. Manslaughter differs from murder in that malice and premeditation are lacking. Hence the elements of the crime of manslaughter are

- An unlawful killing
- Of a human being
- Without malice

Voluntary Manslaughter

Manslaughter occurs without deliberation, planning, or premeditation and may be voluntary or involuntary. "Voluntary manslaughter is the unlawful killing of a human being, without malice, which is done intentionally upon a sudden quarrel or in the heat of passion."[54] In other words, **voluntary manslaughter** is a homicide associated with a sudden fit of rage or passion. Such a killing, although intentional, is neither premeditated nor motivated by a basic evil intent (that is, malice). Voluntary manslaughter would otherwise be murder, except that it is committed in response to **adequate provocation**, as when a person finds his or her spouse in bed with another (Figure 7–4). Provocation is said to be "adequate" if it "would cause a reasonable person to lose self-control."[55] Adequate provocation is also termed *reasonable provocation*. Under common law, only a limited set of circumstances fell into the category of "reasonable provocation." Among them were mutual combat, serious assault or battery, an unlawful arrest, the commission of a crime against a close relative or family member, and the witnessing of one's spouse in an act of adultery. Generally, provocative words alone did not provide adequate provocation to reduce a willful killing to manslaughter. *Commonwealth* v. *Schnopps* (1981), presented in the Capstone Case feature, represents an exception to this rule.

Voluntary manslaughter can be more formally defined as a killing committed without lawful justification, in which the defendant acted under a sudden and intense passion resulting from serious provocation. Although the provocation may have been made by the person who was killed, voluntary manslaughter can also be charged when someone other than the

voluntary manslaughter
An unlawful killing of a human being, without malice, that is done intentionally during a sudden quarrel or in the heat of passion. Also, a killing committed without lawful justification, wherein the defendant acted under a sudden and intense passion resulting from adequate provocation.

adequate provocation
Provocation that "would cause a reasonable person to lose self-control." Also called *reasonable provocation*.

FIGURE 7–4

Murder and Voluntary Manslaughter Compared.

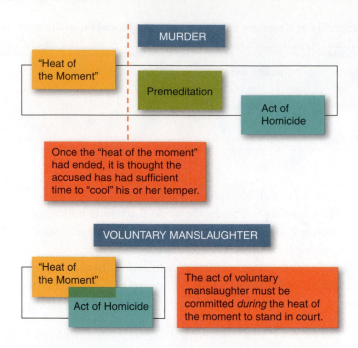

decedent incited the killer's passion. When a defendant, for example, endeavors to shoot an adulterous spouse caught in the act but instead kills a bystander who tries to prevent the shooting, he or she may still be charged with voluntary manslaughter.

Voluntary manslaughter is usually committed with one of the states of mind required for malice aforethought, but the presence of adequate provocation negates the state of mind—resulting in a lesser charge or a lowered sentence. The Texas law that defines murder, for example, reads: "At the punishment stage of a trial, the defendant may raise the issue as to whether he caused the death under the immediate influence of *sudden passion* arising from an *adequate cause*. If the defendant proves the issue in the affirmative by a preponderance of the evidence, the offense is a felony of the second degree [voluntary manslaughter]."[57] As used here, **adequate cause** means a cause that would commonly produce a degree of anger, rage, or terror in a person of ordinary temper, sufficient to render the mind of the defendant incapable of objective reflection. **Sudden passion** means passion directly caused by and rising out of provocation by the victim or of another acting with the victim. It includes the understanding that the passion arises at the time of the killing and is not solely the result of former provocation. In Texas, as in other jurisdictions that follow similar conventions, the burden is on the defendant to establish the existence of the necessary factors to reduce the crime from murder to voluntary manslaughter.

To reduce what would otherwise be murder to voluntary manslaughter in the state of Texas, four requirements must be met: (1) The defendant must have acted in response to a provocation that would be sufficient to cause a reasonable person to lose self-control, (2) the defendant must have acted in the "heat of passion," (3) any lapse of time between the provocation and the killing must not have been great enough that a reasonable person would have "cooled off" or regained control of him- or herself, and (4) the defendant must not, in fact, have "cooled off" by the time of the killing. As the last three requirements indicate, provocation must occur close in time to the killing for a lesser degree of murder to be charged. A murder that occurs six months after an incident of provocation, for example, would probably not be reduced to voluntary manslaughter in most jurisdictions.

The Model Penal Code approach to voluntary manslaughter is similar except for the lack of a "sudden passion" requirement. Section 210.3 (b) of the code says: "Criminal homicide constitutes manslaughter when . . . a homicide which would otherwise be murder

adequate cause
In cases of voluntary manslaughter, a cause that would commonly produce a degree of anger, rage, or terror in a person of ordinary temper, sufficient to render the mind of the defendant incapable of objective reflection.

sudden passion
In cases of voluntary manslaughter, passion directly caused by and rising out of provocation by the victim or of another acting with the victim. Sudden passion includes the understanding that the passion arises at the time of the killing and is not solely the result of former provocation.

APPLYING THE CONCEPT

CAPSTONE CASE

Is Learning about Marital Infidelity from One's Spouse in Heated, Hurtful Language as Provocative as Catching a Spouse Engaged in a Sex Act with a Lover?

Commonwealth v. Schnopps,
417 N.E. 2d 1213 (Mass. 1981)

THE CASE On October 13, 1979, Marilyn R. Schnopps was fatally shot by her estranged husband George A. Schnopps. A jury convicted Schnopps of murder in the first degree, and he was sentenced to the mandatory term of life imprisonment. Schnopps claims that the trial judge erred by refusing to instruct the jury on voluntary manslaughter. We agree. We reverse and order a new trial. . . .

We summarize those facts. Schnopps testified that his wife had left him three weeks prior to the slaying. He claims that he first became aware of the problems in his fourteen-year marriage at a point about six months before the slaying. According to the defendant, on that occasion he took his wife to a club to dance, and she spent the evening dancing with a coworker. On arriving home, the defendant and his wife argued over her conduct. She told him that she no longer loved him and that she wanted a divorce. Schnopps became very upset. He admitted that he took out his shotgun during the course of this argument, but he denied that he intended to use it.

During the next few months, Schnopps argued frequently with his wife. The defendant accused her of seeing another man, but she steadfastly denied the accusations. On more than one occasion Schnopps threatened his wife with physical harm. He testified he never intended to hurt his wife but only wanted to scare her so that she would end the relationship with her coworker.

One day in September, 1979, the defendant became aware that the suspected boyfriend used a "signal" in telephoning Schnopps' wife. Schnopps used the signal, and his wife answered the phone with "Hi, Lover." She hung up immediately when she recognized Schnopps' voice. That afternoon she did not return home. Later that evening, she informed Schnopps by telephone that she had moved to her mother's house and that she had the children with her. She told Schnopps she

would not return to their home. Thereafter she "froze [him] out," and would not talk to him. During this period, the defendant spoke with a lawyer about a divorce and was told that he had a good chance of getting custody of the children, due to his wife's "desertion and adultery."

On the day of the killing, Schnopps had asked his wife to come to their home and talk over their marital difficulties. Schnopps told his wife that he wanted his children at home and that he wanted the family to remain intact. Schnopps cried during the conversation and begged his wife to let the children live with him and to keep their family together. His wife replied, "No, I am going to court, you are going to give me all the furniture, you are going to have to get the Hell out of here, you won't have nothing." Then, pointing to her crotch, she said, "You will never touch this again, because I have got something bigger and better for it."

On hearing those words, Schnopps claims that his mind went blank, and that he went "berserk." He went to a cabinet and got out a pistol he had bought and loaded the day before, and he shot his wife and himself [killing her and injuring himself]. The issue raised by Schnopps' appeal is whether in these circumstances the judge was required to instruct the jury on voluntary manslaughter. Instructions on voluntary manslaughter must be given if there is evidence of provocation deemed adequate in law to cause the accused to lose his self-control in the heat of passion and if the killing followed the provocation before sufficient time had elapsed for the accused's temper to cool.

Schnopps argues that "[t]he existence of sufficient provocation is not foreclosed absolutely because a defendant learns of a fact from oral statements rather than from personal observation." Schnopps asserts that his wife's statements constituted a "peculiarly immediate and intense offense to a spouse's sensitivities." He concedes that the words at issue are indicative of past as well as present adultery. Schnopps claims, however, that his wife's admission of adultery was made for the first time on the day of the killing, and hence the evidence of provocation was sufficient to trigger jury consideration of voluntary manslaughter as a possible verdict.

The Commonwealth quarrels with the defendant's claim, asserting that the defendant knew of his wife's infidelity for some months, and hence the killing did not follow immediately upon the provocation. Therefore, the Commonwealth concludes, a manslaughter instruction would have been improper. . . .

THE FINDING Withdrawal of the issue of voluntary manslaughter in this case denied the jury the opportunity to pass on the defendant's credibility in the critical aspects of his testimony. The portion of Schnopps' testimony concerning provocation created a factual dispute between Schnopps and the Commonwealth. It was for the jury, not the judge, to resolve the factual issues raised by Schnopps' claim of provocation.

We do not question the propriety of the verdict returned by the jury. However, based on the defendant's testimony, voluntary manslaughter was a possible verdict. Therefore, it was error to withhold "from the consideration of the jury another verdict which, although they might not have reached it, was nevertheless open to them upon the evidence."

For the reasons stated, the judgment of the Superior Court is reversed, the verdict of murder in the first degree is set aside, and the case remanded for a new trial. [On retrial Schnopps was again found guilty of murder in the first degree. He appealed again and lost.[56]]

What Do *You* Think?

1. Were the wife's comments so shocking as to be tantamount to the defendant's actually catching her in an adulterous act with her lover?

2. What are the implications of extending the provocation doctrine in infidelity cases from actually witnessing a spouse committing adultery to learning about it verbally?

Additional Applications

Does the sight of an ex-girlfriend in bed with another man constitute adequate provocation?

People v. McCarthy, 547 N.E.2d 459 (Ill. 1989)

The Case: Defendant David McCarthy and Adrianne Neal began dating in 1974—while both were high school freshmen—and lived together (with one or two brief interruptions) from 1978 or 1979 until 1983. The couple also had two children

together, the first born in 1978 and the second in 1981. In April 1983, Adrianne and the children moved out of the apartment they had been sharing with McCarthy and, after a brief stay with Adrianne's mother, moved into an apartment of their own. Two months later, following a dispute over the children, McCarthy entered Adrianne's apartment late at night through a back door and, finding her lying in bed with another man she had recently begun dating, shot her five times at close range. Following a jury trial, McCarthy was convicted of murder and sentenced to 34 years in prison.

At trial, McCarthy requested a jury instruction on voluntary manslaughter in addition to murder. Admitting to the shooting, he testified that he had been deeply distraught over his breakup with Adrianne and had gone to the apartment that night only to talk to Adrianne and ask her to reconcile with him. He was carrying a gun, he added, only because he had intended to shoot himself if she refused to reconcile. Upon seeing his long-time girlfriend in bed with another man, however, he was "deeply hurt" and had been suddenly provoked to violence. Hearing this evidence, the trial judge nonetheless declined to instruct the jury on voluntary manslaughter. The absence of a marital relationship between the defendant and his victim, the court reasoned, precluded the use of such an instruction in the case.

The Finding: The Supreme Court of Illinois upheld the trial court's refusal of the requested instruction. State law, the court reasoned, has long recognized the availability of a voluntary manslaughter charge in instances involving adultery with the offender's spouse. Further, "[m]any of the same reasons that warrant recognition of adultery with a spouse as sufficient provocation" might "also be applicable" to other long-standing romantic relationships. Yet in this case, the court found, "we need not determine . . . whether the category of serious provocation . . . should be enlarged to include unmarried persons who share a marital-type relationship" because "the victim had broken off her relationship with the defendant some two months before the homicide occurred." Just as divorced persons may not claim the benefit of the voluntary manslaughter instruction, the Illinois court concluded, "we decline . . . to fashion a rule that would permit [its use] when the relationship in question has effectively ended."

Can "words alone" be adequate provocation in some circumstances?

Girouard v. State, 583 A.2d 718 (Md. App. 1991)

The Case: Steven and Joyce Girouard, both U.S. Army personnel, had been married for about two months when, on October 28, 1987, Steven killed Joyce by stabbing her

19 times with a long-handled kitchen knife. As found by the trial court, Steven attacked Joyce after an extended "verbal attack" of insults and taunts. As the appeals court described the couple's interactions right before Steven's knife attack:

> Joyce followed [Steven] into the bedroom, stepped up onto the bed and onto Steven's back, pulled his hair and said, "What are you going to do, hit me?" She continued to taunt him by saying, "I never did want to marry you and you are a lousy f**k and you remind me of my dad." The barrage of insults continued with her telling Steven that she wanted a divorce, that the marriage had been a mistake and that she had never wanted to marry him. She also told him she had seen his commanding officer and filed charges against him for abuse. She then asked Steven, "What are you going to do?" Receiving no response, she continued her verbal attack. She added that she had filed charges against him in the Judge Advocate General's Office (JAG) and that he would probably be court martialed.

At that point, Steven asked Joyce if she had "really done all those things," and she responded in the affirmative. He then left the bedroom and retrieved the kitchen knife, which he concealed with a pillow. Upon his returning to the bedroom, the court found, Joyce continued to taunt her husband. She reiterated that the marriage had been a mistake, that "she did not love him" and that the divorce "would be better for her." Asked again what he was going to do, Steven lunged at his wife and stabbed her 19 times. Immediately thereafter, Steven tried to slit his own wrists—but failing in this suicide attempt, he then called police and confessed to the dispatcher that he had just murdered his wife.

At trial, a psychologist testified for the defense that Steven had "basically reached the limit of his ability to swallow his anger. . . . What ensued was a very extreme explosion of rage that was intermingled with a great deal of panic." The trial court, however, found Steven guilty of second-degree murder and sentenced him to 22 years in prison. On appeal, Steven's counsel argued that the victim's verbal abuse of the defendant was sufficient to warrant a reduction of charges to voluntary manslaughter.

The Finding: The Court of Appeals unanimously affirmed Steven's conviction on second-degree-murder charges. Joyce's provocation of Steven in this case, the court reasoned, had been "needless," but the sole issue in the case was whether "the taunting words uttered by Joyce were enough to inflame the passion of a *reasonable* man so that that man would be sufficiently infuriated so as to strike out in hot-blooded passion to kill her." Mere words or gestures—"however offensive, insulting, or abusive they may be"—are not sufficient to meet this objective standard. The court added: "We cannot in good conscience countenance holding that a verbal domestic argument ending in the death of one spouse can result in a conviction of manslaughter. . . . [S]ocial necessity dictates our holding. Domestic arguments easily escalate into furious fights. We perceive no reason for a holding in favor of those who find the easiest way to end a domestic dispute is by killing the offending spouse." ■

---

is committed under the influence of extreme mental or emotional disturbance for which there is reasonable explanation or excuse. The reasonableness of such explanation or excuse shall be determined from the viewpoint of a person in the actor's situation under the circumstances as he believes them to be."

Involuntary Manslaughter

In December 1999, 45-year-old John Mickle was attacked and killed by two pit bull dogs as he walked through a Winnsboro, South Carolina, neighborhood at three o'clock in the morning.[58] Mickle was attacked about 200 yards from the dogs' home. Mickle was bitten more than 1,000 times, and his windpipe was also crushed. His body was discovered around sunrise by a patrolling sheriff's deputy. A few days later, the dog's owner, Frank Paul Speagle, 22, was charged with involuntary manslaughter. Authorities said he should have known that the animals were dangerous and should have kept them confined or leashed. A jury ultimately acquitted Speagle when witnesses to the attack could not be found.

Involuntary manslaughter is an unlawful homicide that is unintentionally caused and that either (1) is the result of an unlawful act other than a dangerous felony (or of a lawful

involuntary manslaughter
An unintentional killing for which criminal liability is imposed but that does not constitute murder. Also, the unintentional killing of a person during the commission of a lesser unlawful act, or the killing of someone during the commission of a lawful act, which nevertheless results in an unlawful death.

act done in an unlawful way) or (2) occurs as the result of criminal negligence or reckless-ness. The central distinguishing feature between voluntary and involuntary manslaughter is the absence in involuntary manslaughter of the intention to kill or to commit any un-lawful act that might reasonably produce death or great bodily harm. In other words, in cases of voluntary manslaughter, killing is intentional, whereas it is unintentional in instances of involuntary manslaughter. Pennsylvania law, for example, says: "A person is guilty of involuntary manslaughter when, as a direct result of the doing of an unlawful act in a reckless or grossly negligent manner, or the doing of a lawful act in a reckless or grossly negligent manner, he causes the death of another person."[59] An "unlawful act other than a dangerous felony" generally refers to a misdemeanor involving danger of injury.

Everybody is a potential murderer. I've never killed anyone, but I frequently get satisfaction reading the obituary notices.

—Clarence S. Darrow, American lawyer (1937)

Unlawful Act

An involuntary manslaughter conviction may be based on an acciden-tal death caused by the defendant during the commission of an unlawful act. The unlawful act may be any misdemeanor or felony that is not included under the felony murder rule. In some states, when death occurs as the result of an unlawful act that is a misdemeanor involving danger of injury, a charge of misdemeanor manslaughter may be brought under what is known as the *misdemeanor manslaughter rule*, which still operates in about a dozen states. Whether the unlawful act is a felony or a misdemeanor, there must be a causal re-lationship between the act and the death of the victim. In those situations in which the wrongful act is a serious felony, however, the requirement of proximate cause is generally suspended. The Model Penal Code does not define *manslaughter* in relationship to other unlawful behavior except to say generally that "[c]riminal homicide constitutes manslaugh-ter when . . . it is committed recklessly."[60] The Model Penal Code does recognize the fact that the act that causes death is unlawful and that this may have an evidentiary bearing on whether it is reckless.

Criminal Negligence

Unintentional killings may constitute involuntary man-slaughter when they result from criminal negligence—which in itself may be unlawful—or from gross negligence. Some state laws describe a special category of involuntary manslaugh-ter called **criminally negligent homicide**. Although the definition may sound a bit circular, criminally negligent homicide is usually defined as homicide resulting from criminal negli-gence. The Code of Alabama, for example, says: "A person commits the crime of criminally negligent homicide if he causes the death of another person by criminal negligence."[61]

Criminal negligence is negligence of such a nature and to such a degree that it is punish-able as a crime. Criminal negligence is defined by statute in most jurisdictions and consists of flagrant and reckless disregard of the safety of others or of willful indifference to the safety and welfare of others. Whether criminal negligence is present depends on all the circumstances surrounding an act or a failure to act. Criminal negligence is usually regarded as a form of **gross negligence**, which is a conscious disregard of one's duties, resulting in injury or damage to another. However, when the defendant uses an object or undertakes a course of action that is inherently dangerous, courts are generally more willing to find him or her criminally negligent, even though the negligence may not be gross. This is especially true in cases involving automo-biles and firearms. Gross negligence goes well beyond the purview of what is sometimes termed *ordinary negligence*. **Ordinary negligence** is said to be "the want of ordinary care," or negligence that could have been avoided if one had exercised ordinary, reasonable, or proper care. Ordi-nary negligence is not willful or purposeful but, rather, unthinking. It is based on the idea that the actor should have known the results or consequences of his or her actions, whereas gross negligence rests on the belief that the actor was in fact cognizant of the results of his or her acts.

For an unintentional killing to constitute involuntary manslaughter, gross negligence or criminal negligence is required. In addition, there is generally the requirement that a

criminally negligent homicide
Homicide that results from crimi-nal negligence.

gross negligence
The conscious disregard of one's duties, resulting in injury or dam-age to another.

ordinary negligence
The want of ordinary care, or negligence that could have been avoided if one had exercised ordi-nary, reasonable, or proper care.

CRIMINAL LAW IN THE NEWS

Abortion Doctors Charged with Murder in Maryland

Two abortion doctors have been charged with murder under a Maryland law that was previously only used when the fetus died in a pregnant woman who was stabbed or shot.

The physicians were allegedly part of a two-state scheme to evade New Jersey's ban on abortions after the first trimester. Under that scheme, women with late-term pregnancies were prepared for their abortions at clinics in New Jersey; then they drove to Maryland, which allows later-term abortions, and the procedures were completed there.

Maryland, however, is one of 38 states with a fetal homicide law, which allows murder charges for the killing of fetuses that could live outside the womb.

Steven C. Brigham, MD, who runs a chain of abortion clinics in several states, faces five counts of first-degree murder, five counts of second-degree murder, and one count of conspiracy to commit murder. Nicola I. Riley, MD, a Utah physician who began working for Dr. Brigham in 2010, faces one count each of first- and second-degree murder and conspiracy to commit murder.

The two-state scheme came to light in August 2010, when one of Dr. Brigham's New Jersey patients experienced a life-threatening emergency at one of his Maryland clinics. The patient was an 18-year-old New Jerseyan who was 21 weeks pregnant, surpassing that state's 14-week maximum for office-based procedures. She received preliminary injections at Dr. Brigham's Voorhees, New Jersey, clinic, to dilate her cervix and start the abortion. Then she drove 60 miles to Dr. Brigham's clinic in Elkton, Maryland, just across the state line, to complete the procedure there.

Because Dr. Brigham did not have a Maryland license to practice, Dr. Riley was at the Elkton clinic to finish the procedure. But the patient suffered a ruptured uterus and other internal injuries and had to be rushed to Union Hospital in Elkton and then flown to Johns Hopkins Hospital in Baltimore.

The Elkton incident came to the attention of New Jersey's physician disciplinary board, which charged that Dr. Brigham's two-state scheme violated the state's ban on late-term abortions.

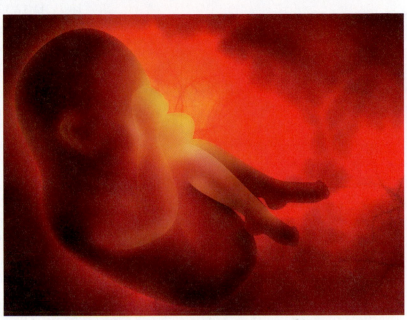

A fetus in the womb. How could abortion doctors be charged with a crime under fetal homicide laws, such as the one in New Jersey? *Fotolia LLC*

At an October 2011 hearing with the medical board, Dr. Brigham's attorney argued that the board had cleared him of similar charges in 1996 in a two-state scheme involving a New York clinic. At that time, the attorney said, the board defined an abortion as "the evacuation of the fetus and placenta from the uterus"; therefore, starting the procedure in New Jersey "does not constitute performing an abortion." But the 2011 board did not buy that argument and suspended Dr. Brigham's New Jersey license.

Meanwhile, Elkton police were also alarmed about the August incident and raided Dr. Brigham's clinic, finding 35 late-term aborted fetuses there. The fetuses reportedly ranged from 20 to as much as 35 weeks—very near a full-term pregnancy of 38 weeks.

Edward D.E. Rollins, a county state's attorney in Maryland, announced the murder indictments in late December 2011. He conceded that the state fetal homicide law would be entering "uncharted territory" because the statute had not been used against physicians before. In fact, the law specifically states that it is not intended to infringe on a woman's right to have an abortion. And rather than precisely define when a fetus is viable, the law says it is when "there is a reasonable likelihood" it could survive outside the womb.

In late January, Dr. Brigham's lawyers filed a motion to throw out the murder indictment, using his two-state scheme as one of his legal defenses. The motion contends that because abortion drugs were injected in New Jersey, the fetuses were already dead before they reached Maryland, and therefore Maryland could not have jurisdiction.

Resources

"N.J. Physician Disciplinary Board Suspends License of Controversial Abortion Doctor,
NJ.com, October 13 2010,
http://www.nj.com/news/index.ssf/2010/10/nj_asks_physician_disciplinary.html.

"Two Doctors Charged with Murder under Md. Fetal Homicide Law,"
Washington Post, December 30, 2011,
http://www.washingtonpost.com/local/two-doctors-charged-with-murder-under-md-fetal-homicide-law/2011/12/30/gIQAFkIURP_story.html.

"Lawyers in Abortion Murder Case Say Fetal Deaths Occurred in N.J.,"
Baltimore Sun, January 27, 2012,
http://articles.baltimoresun.com/2012-01-27/news/bs-md-abortion-doctor-motion-20120127_1_elkton-clinic-steven-c-brigham-fetal-deaths.

very substantial danger of serious bodily harm or death existed at the time of the offense. The Model Penal Code and a minority of jurisdictions require that the defendant has acted "recklessly," and the code defines *recklessly* as a "gross deviation from the standard of conduct that a law-abiding person would observe in the defendant's situation."[62]

The courts appear to be in disagreement as to whether a defendant is liable for manslaughter if he or she is unaware of the risk imposed by his or her conduct. In one case in Washington State, the defendant was found guilty of manslaughter for the death of her infant even though she did not realize that the infant's abscessed tooth had become gangrenous, which led to his death.[63] The Model Penal Code, in contrast, requires an actual knowledge by its definition of *recklessness*. Under the code, a person acts recklessly only when he or she "consciously disregards" a substantial and unjustified risk.[64]

There must, of course, be a causal link between the defendant's criminal negligence and the ensuing death. The defendant's conduct must not only be the cause in fact of the death but also the proximate cause of the death. For example, if the defendant is speeding through a residential area and hits a parked car, which secretly contains explosives, the defendant will not be liable for the death of an individual a block away who is killed by flying glass. In this situation, the fact that the car contained explosives was not reasonably foreseeable, nor was the fact that an individual a block away would be killed.

Unlike in civil law, the contributory negligence of the victim is not a defense to an involuntary manslaughter charge. It may, however, have a bearing on whether the defendant was grossly negligent or whether the defendant's conduct was the proximate cause of the death of the victim.

NEGLIGENT HOMICIDE

Negligent homicide is the third of the three general types of criminal homicide discussed in this chapter. Negligent homicide does not exist in the codes of all jurisdictions, but in many states, deaths resulting from degrees of negligence below that required for a charge of manslaughter may give rise to prosecutions for the crime of negligent homicide. Negligent homicide is quite separate from the crime of involuntary manslaughter (discussed previously), with which it is easily confused. The confusion stems from the fact that negligence may characterize both offenses. However, whereas involuntary manslaughter charges may be based on criminal negligence or gross negligence, the offense of negligent homicide, in contrast, allows for prosecution where the defendant's conduct was negligent but the degree of negligence involved did not amount to gross or criminal negligence or recklessness. Hence *negligent homicide* can be defined as the killing of a person without intent to kill, when the killing takes place while the offender is performing a negligent act or when the offender fails to exercise reasonable, prudent care.

The Model Penal Code provides that "[c]riminal homicide constitutes negligent homicide when it is committed negligently. In cases of negligent homicide, the failure of the defendant to perceive the risk involved is not a defense."[65] Under the Model Penal Code and the codes of a number of states, negligent homicide is a third-degree felony, and it is considered less serious than manslaughter.

Vehicular Homicide

Many unintentional deaths involve automobile accidents in which at least one surviving driver may have been to blame. Because of the difficulty of obtaining involuntary manslaughter convictions in such cases, some states have created the lesser offense of **vehicular homicide**, which, like negligent homicide, requires a substantially lower degree of negligence than involuntary manslaughter. As Florida law says, "Vehicular homicide is the killing of a human being by the operation of a motor vehicle by another in a reckless manner likely to cause the death of, or great bodily harm to, another."[66]

Additionally, many states have enacted statutes creating the crime of causing a death while driving intoxicated. Unlike vehicular homicide, which is generally a lesser included offense of involuntary manslaughter, causing a death by driving while intoxicated frequently results in the imposition of greater punishment than would an involuntary manslaughter conviction.

vehicular homicide
The killing of a human being as a result of another person's operation of a motor vehicle in a reckless manner likely to cause death or great bodily harm.

SUICIDE

Because suicide involves the intentional death of a human being and because it is sometimes brought about with the assistance of another person, it deserves special mention in this chapter. Under early common law, suicide was murder, and anyone who assisted another in committing suicide was a party to murder. Generally, the modern position is that suicide is not murder because of the requirement that a murder must be the killing of another individual. Thirty-five states, however, have created the statutory crime of aiding or assisting suicide. Section 401 of the California Penal Code, for example, provides that any person who deliberately aids, advises, or encourages another to commit suicide is guilty of a felony. Nine states criminalize assisted suicide through common law,[67] although successful prosecutions based on common law may be difficult to obtain. Three states have abolished common law crimes and do not have statutes criminalizing assisted suicide. Only two states, Oregon and Washington, permit physician-assisted suicide.

Most statutes regarding the crime of aiding suicide refer only to passive action. Anyone who takes active steps to end the life of another person is guilty of murder, even if the actions were taken at the request of the decedent. It has been difficult for the courts to determine when a defendant crosses the line between aiding suicide and committing murder. If, for example, a defendant buys potentially deadly drugs for someone else to take, such conduct is generally considered only to constitute aiding. If, however, the defendant actually gives the drugs to the other person, such an action is generally considered to be active conduct and, therefore, murder.

Suppose, for example, that a young couple makes a suicide pact. To accomplish the suicides, the defendant drives his automobile off a cliff, with his girlfriend in the front seat. The defendant survives, but his girlfriend dies. In such a case, the defendant would most likely be charged with murder. If, however, the girlfriend lives and the driver of the automobile dies, then she would probably be guilty only of aiding or encouraging the suicide because she was not actively involved in the attempt to commit it.

CRIMINAL LAW IN THE NEWS

Faith-Healing Parents Convicted in Son's Death

As members of a small Oregon sect, the Followers of Christ, Jeff and Marci Beagley ruled out traditional medical care in favor of faith healing. When their 16-year-old son Neil died in June 2008 without receiving medical attention, they were convicted of criminally negligent homicide and sent to prison.

The cause of Neil Beagley's death was kidney failure due to a congenital condition in his urinary tract, which could have been treated by inserting a catheter to remove a blockage, but he never saw a physician. When the teenager suddenly became very ill, at least 60 members of the faith gathered around him, anointed his body with oil, and used "laying on of hands" while praying for him. No one ever called for medical help.

Neil Beagley's death was the second case tried under a 1999 Oregon law specifically passed to stop an alarmingly high mortality rate due to untreated illnesses among children in the Followers of Christ. An Oregon medical examiner found that children in this 1,000-member sect had a death rate 26 times higher than children in the general population. The new law excludes faith healing as a defense in some manslaughter and criminal mistreatment cases.

The first case tried under the law involved the death of Neil Beagley's 15-month-old cousin just three months before the boy died. Ava Worthington, whose parents were also in the Followers of Christ, died from untreated pneumonia and a blood infection without medical care. The parents were charged with felony manslaughter but were acquitted. The only charge that stuck was a misdemeanor: a criminal mistreatment verdict against only the father. He was ordered to provide medical care for his other children and sentenced to 60 days in jail and five years of probation.

Prosecutors pushed for a much tougher sentence when the Beagley case came to trial.

Even though Neil Beagley had specified that he did not want medical attention, Horner argued that he was just mimicking his dad's views—Jeff Beagley said getting medical care showed a "lack of faith"—and that the parents could still have overruled their son. After more than three days of deliberation, the jury found the couple guilty of criminally negligent homicide.

The defense argued that judging from Neil Beagley's initial symptoms, he could have had a cold or the flu and there was no way to know he was dying. But the prosecution argued that—viewing what happened to Amy Worthington a few months before—the parents should have known that seemingly mild symptoms could mask a fatal disease.

Testifying for the defense, a biomedical ethics expert at Oregon State University called for probation along with education and counseling for the Beagleys. But the prosecutor

Jeff Beagley leaving the courthouse. What led to his conviction of criminally negligent homicide? *Newscom*

pushed for a stiff sentence to deter future deaths of children in the sect. "The court has the opportunity to deliver a clear message that this idea that one can let a child die while they're praying without medical attention is not supportable," said Greg Horner, the chief deputy district attorney.

The parents were sentenced to 16 months each in prison and their time was ultimately reduced by 98 days each for good behavior. When the Beagleys were released in March 2011, the Oregon legislature passed another law removing religious belief as an affirmative defense for homicide. In September 2011, another couple in the Followers of Christ was convicted of not providing medical care in the death of their child. Dale and Shannon Hickman were found guilty of second-degree manslaughter and each received six years in prison, the harshest sentence yet under the 1999 law.

Resources

"Faith-healing parents guilty in son's death,"
The Associated Press, February 2, 2010,
**http://www.msnbc.msn.com/id/35207710/ns/
us_news-crime_and_courts.**

"Jeffrey and Marci Beagley Sentenced to 16 Months of Prison for Their Son's Faith-Healing Death,"
Oregonian, March 8, 2010 (updated August 9, 2010),
**http://www.oregonlive.com/clackamascounty/index.
ssf/2010/03/jeffrey_and_marci_beagley_sent.html.**

"Faith healing couple to be released from prison,"
KATU, March 30, 2011,
**http://oregoncity.katu.com/news/news/
faith-healing-couple-be-released-prison/439481.**

On June 26, 1997, the U.S. Supreme Court upheld the constitutionality of two assisted-suicide laws. In *Vacco v. Quill*,[68] plaintiffs claimed that a New York law banning physician-assisted suicide violated the Fourteenth Amendment's equal protection clause. The claim rested on the observation that New York law allows people who wish to hasten their own deaths to do so by directing the removal of life-support systems, but it does not permit terminally ill people to self-administer prescribed lethal drugs to end their lives. The Court disagreed and upheld the New York ban.

The other 1997 case was that of *Washington v. Glucksberg*.[69] In *Glucksberg*, the Court upheld a Washington law that made "[p]romoting a suicide attempt" a felony and provided that "[a] person is guilty of [that crime] when he knowingly causes or aids another person to attempt suicide." Respondents in the case were four Washington physicians who occasionally treated terminally ill patients. In papers filed with the Court, the physicians declared that they would assist such patients in ending their lives were it not for the state's assisted-suicide ban. They, along with three gravely ill plaintiffs and a nonprofit organization that counsels people considering physician-assisted suicide, filed suit against the state, seeking a declaration that the Washington ban is unconstitutional. The basis of their action rested on the claim that the Fourteenth Amendment's due-process clause establishes a liberty interest that extends to a personal choice by a mentally competent, terminally ill adult to commit physician-assisted suicide. The Supreme Court disagreed, ruling that Washington's prohibition against causing or aiding a suicide does not violate the due-process clause. In the words of the Court: "An examination of our Nation's history, legal traditions, and practices demonstrates that Anglo-American common law has punished or otherwise disapproved of assisting suicide for over seven hundred years; that rendering such assistance is still a crime in almost every State; that such prohibitions have never contained exceptions for those who were near death; that the prohibitions have in recent years been reexamined and, for the most part, reaffirmed in a number of States; and that the President recently signed the Federal Assisted Suicide Funding Restriction Act of 1997, which prohibits the use of federal funds in support of physician-assisted suicide." The Court concluded: "In light of that history, this Court's decisions lead to the conclusion that respondents' asserted 'right' to assistance in committing suicide is not a fundamental liberty interest protected by the Due Process Clause." Subsequently, voters in Washington decriminalized assisted suicide by referendum.[70]

Mercy killings, in which a person actively seeks to end the life of someone who is suffering, are frequently prosecuted as homicides. In February 2000, for example, Kim Kevin Howell, 43, of Queen Creek, Arizona, was arrested and charged with murder after allegedly ending the life of his terminally ill friend, James Leon Scott.[71] The 43-year-old Scott lay dying of bladder cancer at a veterans' hospital in Loma Linda, California, when Howell allegedly pulled a ventilator tube from his neck. Howell told authorities that he had a long-standing pact with Scott in which both men agreed that if one friend ever lingered on life support, the other would pull the plug. Unbeknownst to Howell, however, his friend's family had already made the decision to stop the blood pressure medication that was keeping Scott alive and had given doctors a do-not-resuscitate order. The order would have allowed Scott's blood pressure to drop naturally until he died. "I knew about their agreement," said Scott's mother. "Everybody knew about their agreement. But it never entered my mind he would really do it."[72]

No discussion of assisted suicide would be complete without mention of Dr. Jack Kevorkian, the flamboyant Michigan physician who was sent to prison for second-degree murder in the 1998 poisoning death of Thomas Youk. Youk was suffering from Lou Gehrig's disease and had requested Kevorkian's assistance to end his life. His videotaped suicide was shown on national television.[73]

Kevorkian, whose case is discussed in the common law section of Chapter 1, has acknowledged assisting in 130 deaths since 1990.[74] In 2004, the U.S. Supreme Court rejected an appeal by Kevorkian without comment.[75] The appeal claimed that the physician had

APPLYING THE CONCEPT

CAPSTONE CASE

Does It Violate Equal Protection for a State to Permit Terminally Ill Persons to Terminate Life-Sustaining Treatments But to Criminalize Assisting Terminally Ill People Not on Life Support to Die?

Vacco v. Quill,
521 U.S. 793 (1997)

Chief Justice Rehnquist delivered the opinion of the Court.

In New York, as in most States, it is a crime to aid another to commit or attempt suicide, but patients may refuse even lifesaving medical treatment. The question presented by this case is whether New York's prohibition on assisting suicide therefore violates the Equal Protection Clause of the Fourteenth Amendment. We hold that it does not.

THE CASE   Respondents Timothy E. Quill, Samuel C. Klagsbrun, and Howard A. Grossman are physicians who practice in New York. . . . They urged that because New York permits a competent person to refuse life sustaining medical treatment, and because the refusal of such treatment is "essentially the same thing" as physician assisted suicide, New York's assisted suicide ban violates the Equal Protection Clause. The District Court disagreed. The Court of Appeals for the Second Circuit reversed. The court determined that, despite the assisted suicide ban's apparent general applicability, "New York law does not treat equally all competent persons who are in the final stages of fatal illness and wish to hasten their deaths," because "those in the final stages of terminal illness who are on life support systems are allowed to hasten their deaths by directing the removal of such systems; but those who are similarly situated, except for the previous attachment of life sustaining equipment, are not allowed to hasten death by self administering prescribed drugs." In the court's view, "[t]he ending of life by [the withdrawal of life support systems] is nothing more nor less than assisted suicide." . . . The Court of Appeals then examined whether this supposed unequal treatment was rationally related to any legitimate state interests and concluded that "to the extent that [New York's statutes]

prohibit a physician from prescribing medications to be self administered by a mentally competent, terminally ill person in the final stages of his terminal illness, they are not rationally related to any legitimate state interest." We granted *certiorari* . . . and now reverse.

THE FINDING   The Equal Protection Clause commands that no State shall "deny to any person within its jurisdiction the equal protection of the laws." This provision creates nonsubstantive rights. Instead, it embodies a general rule that States must treat like cases alike but may treat unlike cases accordingly. ("[T]he Constitution does not require things which are different in fact or opinion to be treated in law as though they were the same"). If a legislative classification or distinction "neither burdens a fundamental right nor targets a suspect class, we will uphold [it] so long as it bears a rational relation to some legitimate end." On their faces, neither New York's ban on assisting suicide nor its statutes permitting patients to refuse medical treatment treat anyone differently than anyone else or draw any distinctions between persons. Everyone, regardless of physical condition, is entitled, if competent, to refuse unwanted lifesaving medical treatment; no one is permitted to assist a suicide. Generally speaking, laws that apply evenhandedly to all "unquestionably comply" with the Equal Protection Clause. The Court of Appeals, however, concluded that some terminally ill people—those who are on life support systems—are treated differently than those who are not, in that the former may "hasten death" by ending treatment, but the latter may not "hasten death" through physician assisted suicide. This conclusion depends on the submission that ending or refusing lifesaving medical treatment "is nothing more nor less than assisted suicide." Unlike the Court of Appeals, we think the distinction between assisting suicide and withdrawing life sustaining treatment, a distinction widely recognized and endorsed in the medical profession and in our legal traditions, is both important and logical; it is certainly rational.

The distinction comports with fundamental legal principles of causation and intent. First, when a patient refuses life sustaining medical treatment, he dies from an underlying fatal disease or pathology; but if a patient ingests lethal medication prescribed by a physician, he is killed by that medication. Furthermore, a physician who withdraws, or honors a patient's refusal to begin, life sustaining medical treatment purposefully intends, or may so intend, only to respect his patient's wishes and "to cease doing useless and futile or degrading things to the patient when [the patient] no longer stands to benefit from them." The same is true when a doctor provides aggressive palliative care; in some cases, painkilling drugs may hasten a patient's death, but the physician's purpose and intent is, or may be, only to ease his patient's pain. A doctor who assists a suicide, however, "must, necessarily and indubitably, intend primarily that the patient be made dead. Similarly, a patient who commits suicide with a doctor's aid necessarily has the specific intent to end his or her own life, while a patient who refuses or discontinues treatment might not."

In a companion case, *Washington* v. *Glucksberg*, the Court similarly held that there is no due process liberty right to commit suicide or to assist another in suicide. This does not mean, however, that the states can't act to protect suicide and assisted suicide. Actually, it is not a protection; it is a decriminalization that occurs. The first state to protect physicians from prosecution for protecting suicide of terminally ill patients was Oregon in 1994. The United States challenged Oregon's Death with Dignity Act as violating the federal controlled substances act in federal court. The Act was upheld in *Gonzales* v. *Oregon*, 546 U.S. 243 (2005).

What Do *You* Think?

1. Why did the Court of Appeals for the Second Circuit hold that "New York law does not treat equally all competent persons who are in the final stages of fatal illness and wish to hasten their deaths"? On what basis did the U.S. Supreme Court disagree?

2. What important distinction did the U.S. Supreme Court draw between assisting suicide and withdrawing life-sustaining treatment? Do you agree that the distinction is valid? Why or why not?

Additional Applications

Are legal protections for assisted suicide emerging at the state level?

Baxter v. *Montana*, 224 P.3d 1211 (Mont. 2009)

The Case: Robert Baxter, a retired truck driver suffering from incurable lymphocytic leukemia, brought suit in Montana state court, challenging the constitutionality of the state's homicide statutes as applied to physicians who provide aid in dying to mentally competent, terminally ill patients. Joined in his suit by four physicians and Compassion & Choices (a nonprofit advocacy group), Baxter argued that, although federal constitutional law may not provide a right to assisted suicide, Article II of Montana's state constitution—which guarantees individual dignity and privacy—nonetheless grants terminally ill patients in that state a "right to die with dignity." In a landmark December 2008 ruling, a Montana trial court agreed: it held that the Montana Constitution's rights of individual privacy and human dignity, acting together, give a terminally ill patient a right to use the assistance of a physician to obtain a prescription for a lethal dose of medication. What's more, the patient's right to die with dignity was upheld to necessarily extend to protect the patient's physician from prosecution under the state's homicide laws. On appeal, the state challenged this trial court's interpretation of state constitutional law.

The Finding: In a highly anticipated ruling in December 2009, the Montana Supreme Court (which, under prevailing federalism principles, is the final judicial authority on the meaning of that state's constitution) opted to decide the case solely on statutory grounds, thereby sidestepping the broader question of whether the state's constitution protects a right to assisted suicide. The act of suicide, the court noted, is not actually a crime under Montana law. Consequently, "the only person who might conceivably be prosecuted for criminal behavior is the physician who prescribes a lethal dose of medication." Yet in that instance, the court reasoned, the laws of Montana already allow that physician to assert the defense of consent—because the state legislature has not plainly stated that assisting a suicide is "against public policy." Thus in effect, the court concluded, physicians in the state are already shielded from prosecution for helping to hasten the death of a consenting, terminally ill patient. ∎

received ineffective legal counsel. The Court rejected another Kevorkian claim in 2002 that his prosecution was unconstitutional. The doctor was paroled in 2006 at the age of 78.

The question of whether there is a constitutional right to have someone assist in suicide was the subject of *Vacco* v. *Quill* (1997), highlighted in the Capstone Case.

SUMMARY

- Homicide is the killing of a human being by another human being. Criminal homicides are those homicides for which criminal liability accrues. Generally, any homicide that is not excusable or justifiable is considered criminal homicide.

- This chapter describes three general categories of homicide: murder, manslaughter, and negligent homicide.

- An essential element of criminal homicide is the killing of a human being. Accordingly, the victim must have been alive before the homicidal act occurred. The "alive" requirement has been modified in some jurisdictions.

- A major problem in homicide cases is in defining death. The common law rule was that death occurs when a person's heartbeat and respiratory functions cease.

- Many jurisdictions have adopted the Uniform Determination of Death Act (UDDA) in defining death. The UDDA says that death occurs when an individual has sustained either (1) irreversible cessation of circulatory and respiratory functions or (2) irreversible cessation of all functions of the entire brain, including the brain stem.

- Criminal homicides must be the result of an affirmative act, an omission to act, or criminal negligence. The act causing the death need not be the only cause of death.

- Murder is the unlawful killing of another person with malice aforethought. The statutory elements of the crime of murder are (1) an unlawful killing (2) of a human being (3) with malice.

- Felony murders are deaths that result from the commission of a dangerous felony.

- Manslaughter is the unlawful killing of a human being without malice. The statutory elements of the crime of manslaughter are (1) an unlawful killing (2) of a human being (3) without malice. Manslaughter may be of two types: voluntary or involuntary.

- Voluntary manslaughter is the unlawful killing of a human being, without malice, which is done intentionally during a sudden quarrel or in the heat of passion. Voluntary manslaughter is homicide committed in response to adequate provocation.

- Provocation is said to be "adequate" if it would cause a reasonable person to lose self-control. Adequate provocation is also called *reasonable provocation*.

- Involuntary manslaughter is an unintended killing caused during the commission of an unlawful act not amounting to a dangerous felony or as the result of criminal negligence or recklessness.

- Criminal negligence, as it is defined by statute in most jurisdictions, consists of flagrant and reckless disregard of the safety of others or of willful indifference to the safety and welfare of others.

- In many states, deaths resulting from degrees of negligence below that required for a charge of manslaughter may give rise to prosecutions for the crime of negligent homicide.

- Vehicular homicide is the killing of a human being as the result of another person's operation of a motor vehicle in a reckless manner likely to cause death or great bodily harm.

- Many states have created the statutory crime of aiding suicide, although someone who actively ends the life of a suicidal individual may be guilty of murder.

KEY TERMS

accidental death, 210

accidental killing, 210

adequate cause, 222

adequate provocation, 221

affirmative act, 215

aggravated murder, 218

brain death, 213

capital murder, 218

criminal homicide, 210

criminally negligent homicide, 226

depraved heart murder, 217

excusable homicide, 210

felony murder rule, 219

first-degree murder, 216

gross negligence, 226

homicide, 210

inherently dangerous, 221

involuntary manslaughter, 225

justifiable homicide, 210

malice, 216

malice aforethought, 216

manslaughter, 210

murder, 210

negligent homicide, 211

ordinary negligence, 226

premeditated murder, 218

premeditation, 216

second-degree murder, 216

sudden passion, 222

Uniform Determination of Death Act (UDDA), 213

vehicular homicide, 229

voluntary manslaughter, 221

year-and-a-day rule, 214

QUESTIONS FOR DISCUSSION

1. What distinguishes noncriminal homicide from criminal homicide?

2. What are the three types of criminal homicide? Describe them.

3. Define *death* in legal terms.

4. What causation problems characterize criminal homicide prosecutions?

5. Explain the concept of *corpus delicti* as it relates to criminal homicide.

6. What is the difference between murder and voluntary manslaughter?

7. What is meant by *malice aforethought*?

8. What is the felony murder rule?

9. When a first-degree murder statute reads "willful, deliberate, and premeditated," does the statute require anything more than that the killing be intentional? Explain.

10. The defendant took a pistol with him on a visit to the hospital to see his terminally ill father. At his father's request, he killed him with a single shot to the head. What crime, if any, is the defendant guilty of? (See *State* v. *Forrest*, 362 S.E.2d 252 [N.C. 1987].)

CRITICAL THINKING AND APPLICATION PROBLEMS

Zack and Amber have been married for 15 years. They have one child, Angel, who is ten. The health of their relationship has been typical, marked by occasional disagreements about money and family issues, but nothing so serious as to threaten their marriage.

Zack, a local police officer, returned home from work early one day because he was feeling ill. When he entered the home he discovered his wife, a stay-home mother, in the kitchen with a man, Dallas, whom he recognized to be a police officer colleague. Amber was naked and Dallas was shirtless. After a moment of shock, Zack became enraged, pulled out his sidearm, and shot Amber. Dallas ran out the back door of the home. Zack gave chase but ended his pursuit in the backyard, returned to the home, called for an ambulance, and attempted to save Amber, who had a pulse. She died before the ambulance arrived.

Dallas ran to his car, which he had parked two blocks away in an attempt to keep his visit with Amber secret. He unlocked the car, started it, and quickly drove away. Distraught over what had just happened, he was not mindful of his speed nor was he watching the road. Three miles from where he started, he struck and killed nine-year-old Megan, who was crossing the street in a school zone. Dallas had been traveling at 50 miles per hour. The speed limit was 15 miles per hour in the school zone.

1. Applying the Model Penal Code or your state's laws, has Zack committed murder with the death of Amber? Manslaughter? Some other crime? Explain your answers fully.

2. Appling the Model Penal Code or your state's laws, has Dallas committed murder with the death of Megan? Manslaughter? Some other crime? Explain your answers fully.

LEGAL RESOURCES ON THE WEB

Some websites list law-related job opportunities. Although some jobs require a law degree, many employers are looking for candidates with undergraduate credentials to work in support roles.

Counsel.Net Legal Jobs
http://www.counsel.net/jobs
Contains a series of free job-posting boards for law firms and other businesses. An e-mail alert system, called JobAlert, notifies job hunters of legal jobs as they become available.

EmplawyerNet
http://www.emplawyernet.com
Offers free career planning and contains a database of more than 5,000 law-related job openings.

Federal Judiciary Employment Opportunities
http://www.uscourts.gov/employment/vacancies.html
Includes information on a wide variety of federal government jobs in law-related fields.

LawInfo Career Center
http://jobs.lawinfo.com
Allows attorneys and others involved with the law to post their résumés. Also lists job openings.

Lawyers Weekly Jobs
http://www.lawyersweeklyjobs.com
Includes job postings for attorneys, paralegals, legal secretaries, and other positions within the legal field.

SUGGESTED READINGS AND CLASSIC WORKS

Brennan, Susan L., and Richard Delgado. "Death: Multiple Definitions or a Single Standard?" *Southern California Law Review* 54 (1981): 1323.

Cole, Kevin. "Killings during Crime: Toward a Discriminating Theory of Strict Liability." *American Criminal Law Review* 28 (1990): 73.

Crump, David, and Susan Crump. "In Defense of the Felony Murder Doctrine." *Harvard Journal of Law and Public Policy* 8 (spring 1985): 359–398.

Hart, H. L. A. *The Concept of Law*. London: Oxford University Press, 1961.

Weinberg, JoAnna K. "Whose Right Is It Anyway? Individualism, Community, and the Right to Die: A Commentary on the New Jersey Experience." *Hastings Law Journal* 40 (November 1988): 119.

NOTES

1. Marvin Wolfgang, "A Sociological Approach to Criminal Homicide," *Federal Probation* 23 (March 1961): 48.

2. See "Jumper Avoids Prison in Daughter's Death," Associated Press, July 15, 1998; and "Woman Testifies from Bed She Doesn't Remember Suicide Leap," Associated Press, May 26, 1998.

3. "Woman's Second Suicide Attempt Foiled," Channel 2000, February 26, 2000, http://cbs2.com/news/stories/news-20000226–202413.html (accessed March 23, 2003).

4. *Black's Law Dictionary* (Abridged 5th ed. 1983), p. 375.

5. *Follis v. State*, 101 S.W.2d 242 (1947).

6. *Jones v. State*, 151 Tex. Crim. 114, 205 S.W.2d 603 (1947).

7. *Williams v. State*, 629 S.W.2d 791 (Tex. Ct. App. 5th Cir. 1981).

8. *People v. Chavez*, 176 P.2d 92 (Cal. App. 1947).

9. *Keeler v. Superior Court*, 470 P.2d 617 (Cal. 1970).

10. Texas Penal Code, Section 19.02.

11. *Lovelady v. State*, 14 Tex. App. 545 (Tex. Ct. Crim. App. 1883).

12. California Penal Code, Section 187.

13. *Keeler v. Superior Court*, 2 Cal. 3d 619, 87 Cal. Rptr. 481, 470 P.2d 617 (Cal. 1970).

14. *People v. Taylor*, 04 C.D.O.S. 2890.

15. Ibid.

16. Public Law 108-212.

17. Model Penal Code, Section 210.1, *Commentary*, 11.

18. *Thomas v. Anderson*, 215 P.2d 478, 96 Cal. App. 2d 371 (1950).

19. See Council on Ethical and Judicial Affairs, *Code of Medical Ethics: Current Opinions with Annotations* (Chicago: American Medical Association, 1995), and related publications.

20. *State v. Fierro*, 603 P.2d 74 (Ariz. 1979).

21. See National Conference of Commissioners on Uniform State Laws, *Uniform Determination of Death Act and Report* 12 Uniform Laws Annotated 320 (1990 Supp).

22. Ibid.

23. The National Conference of Commissioners on Uniform State Laws is a nonprofit association comprising state commissions on uniform laws from each state, the District of Columbia, the Commonwealth of Puerto Rico, and the U.S. Virgin Islands. The National Conference of Commissioners on Uniform State Laws has worked for the uniformity of state laws since 1892. The conference promotes the principle of uniformity by drafting and proposing specific statutes in areas of the law where uniformity between the states is desirable. No uniform law is effective until a state legislature adopts it.

24. P. A. Byrne, S. O'Reilly, and P. M. Quay, "Brain Death: An Opposing Viewpoint," *Journal of the American Medical Association* 242 (1979): 1985–90.

25. See the dissenting opinion in *Commonwealth v. Ladd*, 166 A.2d 501 (Pa. 1960).

26. *Rogers v. Tennessee*, 532 U.S. 451 (2001)

27. Guilford County (North Carolina), No. 91CRS20076, October 31, 1991.

28. North Carolina Court of Appeals, No. 9118SC1298, May 18, 1993.

29. California Penal Code, Section 194.

30. *People v. Freudenberg*, 121 Cal. App. 2d 564 (1953).

31. *People v. Moan*, 65 Cal. 532 (1884).

32. *People v. Fowler*, 178 Cal. 657 (1918); and *People v. Lewis*, 124 Cal. 551 (1899).

33. *People v. Saldana*, 47 Cal. App. 3d 954 (1975).

34. *People v. Brackett*, 510 N.E.2d 877 (Ill. 1987).

35. *People v. McGee*, 31 Cal. 2d 229, 187 P.2d 706 (1947).

36. *People v. Vernon*, 89 Cal. App. 3d 853 (1979).

37. *Commonwealth v. Malone*, 47 A.2d 445 (Pa. 1946).

38. *Green v. U.S.*, 132 U.S. App. D.C. 98, 405 F.2d 1368 (1968).

39. In some jurisdictions, the term *depraved heart murder* means the killing of a human being with extreme atrocity.

40. *People v. Morrin*, 187 N.W.2d 434 (Mich. 1971).

41. California Penal Code, Section 188.

42. *People v. Geiger*, 159 N.W.2d 383 (Mich. 1968).

43. *Commonwealth v. Malone*, 47 A.2d. 445 (Pa. 1946).

44. "Facts about the Death Penalty," Death Penalty Information Center, May 23, 2012, http://www.deathpenaltyinfo.org/documents/FactSheet.pdf.

45. *Edmund v. Florida*, 458 U.S. 782 (1982).

46. *Tison v. Arizona*, 107 S. Ct. 1676 (1987).

47. *Coker v. Georgia*, 433 U.S. 584 (1977).

48. *Kennedy v. Louisiana*, 554 U.S. 407 (2008).

49. *People* v. *Daniels*, 52 Cal. 3d 815 (1991).

50. Tracy L. Snell, "Capital Punishment, 1995," Bureau of Justice Statistics bulletin, December 1996.

51. Todd Venezia, "$12 Heist Nets Murder Charge," APB Online, May 5, 1999, http://www.apbonline.com/911/1999/05/07/taxi0507_01.html (accessed May 2, 2001).

52. Statistically speaking, only about 0.5 percent of all robberies involve homicide. Joshua Dressler, *Understanding Criminal Law*, 2nd ed. (Boston: Matthew Bender, 1995), 451.

53. Rollin M. Perkins and Ronald N. Boyce, *Criminal Law*, 3rd ed. (Mineola, NY: Foundation Press, 1982), 109.

54. Kansas Statutes Annotated, Section 21-3403.

55. John Kaplan and Robert Weisberg, *Criminal Law: Cases and Materials*, 2nd ed. (Boston: Little, Brown, 1991), 248.

56. *Commonwealth* v. *Schnopps*, 390 Mass. 722 (1984).

57. Texas Penal Code, Section 19.02. Emphasis added.

58. "Pit Bull Owner Charged in Mauling of Neighbor," Associated Press, December 10, 1999.

59. Crimes Code of Pennsylvania, Section 2504(a).

60. Model Penal Code, Section 210.3.

61. Alabama Code, 13A-6-4.

62. Model Penal Code, Section 210.3(1)(b).

63. *State* v. *Williams*, 484 P.2d 1167 (Wash. App. 1971).

64. Model Penal Code, Section 2.02(2)(c).

65. Model Penal Code, Section 2.02(d).

66. Florida Statutes Annotated, Section 782.071.

67. As reported by Euthanasia.com, http://www.euthanasia.com/bystate.html (accessed April 24, 2001).

68. *Vacco* v. *Quill*, 521 U.S. 793 (1997).

69. *Washington* v. *Glucksberg*, 521 U.S. 702 (1997).

70. Jacob Goldstein, "Washington Passes Initiative 1000, Legalizing Physician-Assisted Suicide," *Wall Street Journal*, November 5, 2008, http://blogs.wsj.com/health/2008/11/05/washington-passes-initiative-1000-legalizing-physician-assisted-suicide.

71. Todd Venezia, "Cops Say Mercy Killing Was Murder," APB News online, February 7, 2000, http://www.apbnews.com/newscenter/breakingnews (accessed May 2, 2001).

72. "Family Upset after Man Pulls Plug on Dying Friend," Associated Press, February 13, 2000.

73. "Supreme Court Turns Down Kevorkian," CNN.com Law Center, November 2, 2004, http://www.cnn.com/2004/LAW/11/01/scotus.rulings.ap (accessed February 10, 2005).

74. David Shepardson, "Kevorkian Loses Appeal in Top Court," *Detroit News*, November 2, 2004, http://www.detnews.com/2004/metro/0411/02/b01-322446.htm (accessed January 10, 2005).

75. *Kevorkian* v. *Warren*, 04-380. U.S. Supreme Court (2004).

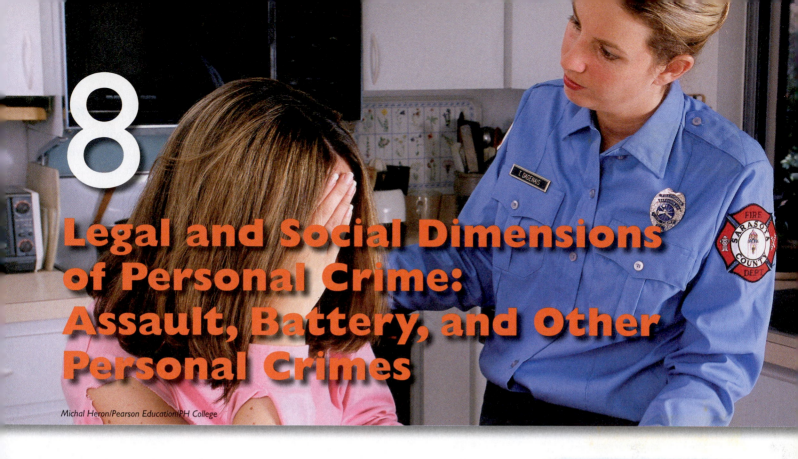

8

Legal and Social Dimensions of Personal Crime: Assault, Battery, and Other Personal Crimes

Michal Heron/Pearson Education/PH College

CHAPTER OUTLINE

Introduction

Assault, Battery, and Mayhem

Sex Offenses

Kidnapping and False Imprisonment

OBJECTIVES

After reading this chapter, you should be able to

- Describe the crime of assault.
- Describe the crime of battery.
- Identify the two types of common law assault, and list the elements of each.
- Explain the type or extent of injury to a victim required to prove the crime of battery.
- Describe the crime of mayhem.
- Explain the nature and elements of the crime of rape.
- Explain the difference between common law rape and modern statutes describing sexual assault.
- Describe the crime of false imprisonment.
- Describe the crime of kidnapping.

A battery committed by a person while in a state of voluntary intoxication is no less criminal by reason of his having been in such condition.

—Justice Traynor, in People v. Hood, 1 Cal. 3d 444 (1969)

Rape is nothing more or less than a conscious process of intimidation by which all men keep all women in a state of fear.

—Susan Brownmiller, Against Our Will (1975)

INTRODUCTION

In 1996, Georgia resident Miguel Ortiz was convicted of rape, aggravated **sodomy**, incest, and battery—crimes committed against his 15-year-old niece.[1] The victim lived with Ortiz, his wife, and their three children. Two of Ortiz's brothers and the victim's mother also lived in the household. One day, as the victim accompanied her uncle on some errands, Ortiz detoured, turned off on a rural road, and stopped his car. While on the isolated dirt road, Ortiz beat, raped, and sodomized his young niece. As they left the scene, Ortiz and the victim were involved in a single car accident in which their vehicle flipped over. The victim immediately ran from the car and sought assistance from the occupants of another vehicle, telling Trina Edwards and Ebony Reid that her uncle had just tried to rape her.

The victim's eye was swollen, she was not wearing any shoes, her clothing was unbuttoned, and she was crying and scared. She told Reid that her uncle had raped her, but then she claimed that he did not rape her. She changed her story one more time, saying he "kind of raped" her. The victim was driven to a nearby house, where medical and law enforcement personnel were summoned. She told Mattie Jo Duke, the responding emergency medical technician (EMT), that her uncle had raped her. The victim also told Investigator Lanny Dean that her uncle had raped her. At the hospital, medical personnel prepared a rape kit, and physical evidence gathered with the kit supported the victim's claim. Ortiz, a former offender, was sentenced to a lengthy prison term under Georgia's two-strikes law.

ASSAULT, BATTERY, AND MAYHEM

The emphasis in this chapter is on the legal and social dimensions of personal crimes, excluding homicide. As the chapter-opening story illustrates, there is often confusion—even in the victim's mind—about whether a crime should be reported and about the personal and social consequences of reporting the crime. Note also that there is considerable overlap between many of the crimes discussed in this chapter. A rape, for example, is also an aggravated form of a battery.

The crimes of assault and battery are a good starting point for the discussion of personal crimes. Although today the terms *assault* and *battery* are often used together or interchangeably, under common law they were different and distinct crimes. An **assault**, simply put, is an attempted or threatened battery. A **battery**, on the other hand, is a consummated

sodomy
Oral or anal copulation between people of the same or different gender or between a human being and an animal.

assault
Attempted or threatened battery. A willful attempt or willful threat to inflict injury on another person. Also, the act of intentionally frightening another person into fearing immediate bodily harm. One statutory definition of assault reads "an unlawful attempt, coupled with a present ability, to commit a violent injury on the person of another."[i]

battery
(1) Unlawful physical violence inflicted on another without his or her consent. (2) An intentional and offensive touching or wrongful physical contact with another, without consent, that results in some injury or offends or causes discomfort.

A beating taking place. What's the difference between assault and battery?

Paul Bradbury/AgeFotostock

assault. As one law text succinctly explains, "When we speak of an assault we usually have in mind a battery which was attempted or threatened. The attempt may have failed or it may have succeeded. If it failed, it constitutes an assault only. If it succeeded, it is an assault and battery."[2] Some state penal codes do not contain the word *assault*, replacing it with the term *attempted battery*.

Put more formally, an assault is a willful attempt or willful threat to inflict injury on another person. It may also include the act of intentionally frightening another person into fearing immediate bodily harm. Battery can be defined as unlawful physical violence inflicted on another without his or her consent or as an intentional and offensive touching or wrongful physical contact with another, without consent, that results in some injury or offense to that person. Battery requires actual unauthorized contact with the victim. Generally, an assault is included in any actual battery—hence the crime of "assault and battery."

From an analytical viewpoint, however, one major difference between criminal assault and battery is that assault is a specific-intent crime whereas battery is not. To commit an assault, a person must have intended to either commit a battery (attempted battery) or must have intentionally frightened the victim into fearing immediate bodily harm. Battery is a general-intent crime. It may be the natural consequence of the commission of some other offense, or it can result from gross negligence or recklessness. **Mayhem**, a third term of relevance here, is a battery that causes great bodily harm or disfigurement (Figure 8–1). Statutory extracts in this chapter include representative laws on assault, battery, and mayhem from California.

mayhem
The intentional infliction of injury on another that causes the removal of, seriously disfigures, or impairs the function of a member or organ of the body.

Assault

Under common law, two types of assault could be distinguished: an attempted battery and a threatened battery. In the first type of assault, the defendant *attempted* to commit a battery. The second type of assault, that of *threatened* battery, occurred when the defendant placed another in fear of imminent injury. The difference between the two is that the first was an actual attempt to commit a battery, whereas the second criminalized conduct that made another person fear an assault. A number of states today, including California, do not

FIGURE 8–1

Assault, Battery, and Mayhem.

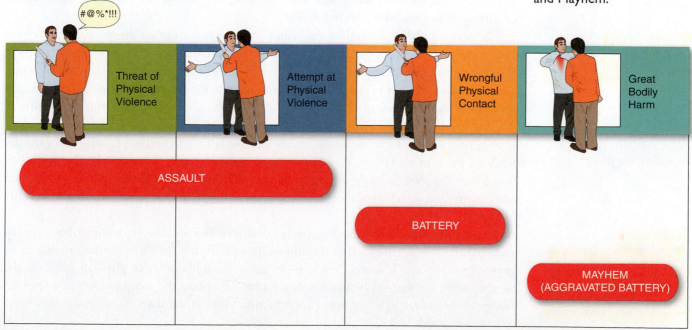

recognize the second type of assault. The common law elements of the attempted battery–type of assault are

- An unlawful attempt
- With present ability
- To commit a battery

The modern definition of assault is more sophisticated, as reflected in the Model Penal Code's assault provision. It provides that an assault occurs when a person:

> attempts to cause or purposely, knowingly or recklessly causes bodily injury to another; or negligently causes bodily injury to another with a deadly weapon; or attempts by physical menace to put another in fear of imminent serious bodily injury. [3]

Each of these elements is discussed in this section. It should be noted, however, that in an attempted battery–type assault, the victim need not be aware of the attempt. The victim, for example, may be unconscious at the time of the assault. To constitute assault, there must be an overt act from which the inference can be drawn that a violent injury was intended; mere words alone are insufficient. Be aware, however, that a defendant may be prosecuted for the related crime of threat or terroristic threat in some jurisdictions. The only act required under these laws is the act of delivering the threat. Accordingly, the defendant's words, along with the other elements of the crime (typically the threat must be of violence that was intended to, and in fact caused, a reasonable fear in the victim) are adequate for conviction.

Similarly, any attempt to commit an injury or an offensive touching must be unlawful. Accordingly, the attempt to inflict injury on a person in a valid self-defense situation is not an unlawful attempt. The use of force by law enforcement officers in effecting a valid arrest is also not unlawful, nor is the reasonable use of force in a boxing match or football game. If, however, the force used or attempted to be used is not authorized or is used in an unauthorized manner, it may be unlawful. Although fights and threatening gestures are a regular and expected part of professional boxing matches, for example, physical altercations are expected to remain within clearly specified bounds—and players who exceed those bounds may face criminal penalties or noncriminal sanctions. In a 1997 rematch for the World Boxing Association's heavyweight title, for example, Mike Tyson bit off part of defending champion Evander Holyfield's right ear. Following the match, the Nevada State Athletic Commission suspended Tyson indefinitely.

present ability
As used in assault statutes, a term meaning that the person attempting assault is physically capable of immediately carrying it out.

The **present ability** element of the crime of assault requires that the defendant be physically capable of carrying out the attempted act and that the method he or she intends or threatens to use will in fact inflict an injury or offensive touching if carried out. Simply put, present ability, as used in assault statutes, means that the offender is physically capable of immediate battery. Present ability relates solely to the ability of the person attempting or threatening the unlawful injury or offensive touching. It does not, in most jurisdictions, refer to the fact that for some reason or condition unknown to and not controlled by the defendant, the intended injury could not actually be inflicted. If, for example, the defendant fires a pistol at someone in an automobile, but, unknown to the defendant, the automobile was constructed with bulletproof glass and armor plating, the defendant would still be guilty of assault.

bodily injury
Physical harm to a human being. In cases of assault and battery, the term refers to the unlawful application of physical force on the person of the victim—even when no actual physical harm results.

The term **bodily injury**, which appears in many assault and battery statutes, has a special meaning. It does not mean that the injury attempted must be a severe one or must cause great physical pain. It merely refers to an unlawful application of physical force on the person of the victim. As one court noted, for assault crimes the terms *violence* and *force* are synonymous and include any application of force, even if it entails no pain or bodily harm or leaves no mark. [4]

Placing Another in Fear

The second type of assault under common law, the threatened battery–type, was the placing of another in fear of imminent injury. In some jurisdictions, the crime is described as *intentional-frightening assault*. As noted earlier, not all jurisdictions recognize this form of assault. The threatened battery–type assault requires that the defendant intend to create fear of imminent injury in the victim. As discussed previously, words alone do not suffice, and some overt act must occur before the crime can be said to have been committed. Telling a person, for example, "I'm going to kill you!" is not an assault unless accompanied by some overt act, such as pointing a gun at the person.

Conditional Assault

Either type of assault may be made conditional upon meeting the assailant's demands. For example, the bank robber's statement "One false move and I'll shoot!" is a conditional assault.

To constitute an assault, the condition must be one that the defendant is not entitled to place on the victim. For example, a property owner who assumes a threatening stance and tells a trespasser, "Leave my property or I'll throw you off!" does not commit an assault because property owners have a limited right to protect their property. If the condition is one that the defendant has no right to place on the victim, however, the action constitutes an assault. The statement "Hand me your money or I'll shoot," for example, qualifies as such a condition and may constitute an assault—especially when the person making it is armed or is thought to be armed.

Aggravated Assault

In most jurisdictions, a simple assault is one unaccompanied by aggravating circumstances. Simple assaults are classified as misdemeanors. All jurisdictions, however, have recognized various types of felonious assaults, which they call *aggravated assaults*. Aggravated assaults are generally assaults with intent to commit some other offense, such as rape or murder. As a result, aggravated assault is sometimes called *assault with intent*, and indictments for specific offenses, such as assault with intent to kill, are not unusual. Aggravated assault was not an offense under common law.

Special categories of assaults—such as assault with a dangerous weapon, assault on a peace officer, assault on a school official or teacher, assault on a prison guard or correctional worker, and so on—have also been classified in various jurisdictions as aggravated assault. Hence the term **aggravated assault** may mean (1) an assault that is committed with the intention of committing an additional crime or (2) an assault that involves special circumstances (Figure 8–2). To prove an aggravated assault, the prosecution must successfully show that an assault took place as part of another, more serious offense or that an assault occurred with an aggravating element specified by law. These ideas are embodied in the Model Penal Code's definition of aggravated assault. Aggravated assault is when a person:

> **aggravated assault**
> An assault that is committed with the intention of committing an additional crime, such as assault with intent to commit a felony; assault with intent to murder; assault with intent to commit rape, sodomy, mayhem, robbery, or grand larceny; and assault with intent to commit any other felony. Also, an assault that involves special circumstances specified by law.

(A) attempts to cause serious bodily injury to another, or causes such injury purposely, knowingly or recklessly under circumstances manifesting extreme indifference to the value of human life; or

(B) attempts to cause or purposely or knowingly causes bodily injury to another with a deadly weapon.[5]

Where assault is considered to be aggravated when committed with a dangerous weapon, the weapons are usually said to be of two types: (1) those that are inherently dangerous or

FIGURE 8–2

Aggravated Assault.

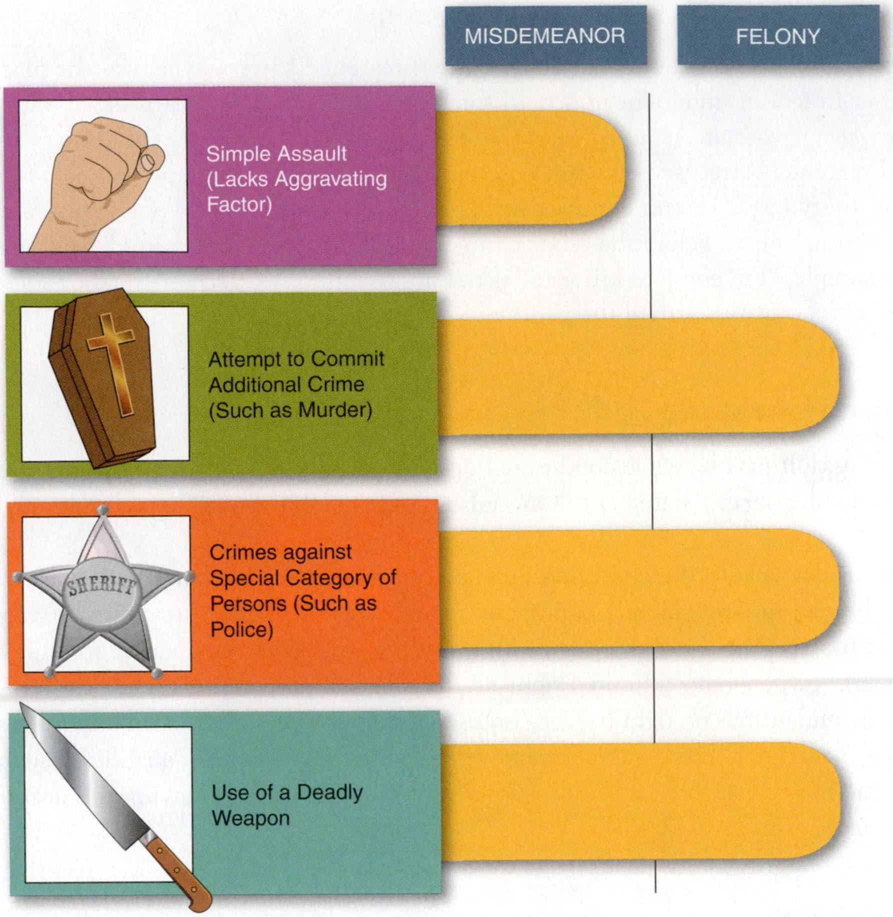

MISDEMEANOR	FELONY

Simple Assault (Lacks Aggravating Factor)

Attempt to Commit Additional Crime (Such as Murder)

Crimes against Special Category of Persons (Such as Police)

Use of a Deadly Weapon

deadly (as a loaded gun would be) and (2) those that are not dangerous per se but that can be used in a dangerous fashion (such as a rope used in a strangling). Some courts have held that a dog used in an attack is a dangerous weapon,[6] others have held that hands and fists can be deadly weapons even if the person has not had martial arts or combat training,[7] and still others have held that human teeth are *not* deadly weapons.[8]

Attempted Assault

Although a common law assault was in most cases an attempted battery, the law pertaining to criminal attempts generally does not apply to assaults.[9] This is partially the result of historical exigencies, under which the common law on assaults developed earlier and independently of the common law on criminal attempts. As a result, a major difference between attempts and assaults, which continues to be recognized today, is that for a criminal assault to occur, the defendant must be closer to completing the offense than is required for a criminal attempt. The concept of *proximity to completion* refers to criminal-attempt crimes in which the court looks at the nearness to completion of the intended crime in order to determine if a criminal attempt has taken place. More than a hundred years ago, the Ohio Supreme Court addressed the distinction this way: "An assault is an act done toward the commission of a battery; it must precede the battery, but it does so immediately. The next movement would, at least to all appearances, complete the battery. . . . [A]n act constituting an attempt to commit a felony may be more remote."[10] A few courts have attempted to reconcile the law of attempts with the law on assault, creating the logically improbable term *attempted assault*. In such cases, an attempt to assault means "an effort to accomplish a battery that had proceeded beyond the stage of preparation, but had not come close enough to completion to constitute an assault."

Another major difference between attempt and assault is that an accused may be convicted of a criminal attempt even if he or she could not carry out the primary offense. An attempted battery–type of assault requires an unlawful attempt with the present ability to commit the battery. Accordingly, a defendant could be convicted of an attempted murder without committing the crime of assault with the intent to commit murder if the defendant's conduct constitutes a substantial step toward completion of the murder but the defendant lacks present ability to commit the murder. Similarly, were he to make unwanted physical advances under certain circumstances, a man who is physically unable to complete the act of intercourse might still be conceptually guilty of an attempt to commit an assault with intent to rape. In one case, a man went to his car to retrieve a gun with which he intended to threaten his wife at her place of work. When he returned to the building, however, his wife had locked the doors and he could not enter. He was convicted of attempt to commit an assault with a dangerous weapon.[11]

Antistalking Statutes

In 1997, 41-year-old Cheryl Vivier donned a beard, glasses, and a baseball cap and posed as a fisherman.[12] With two handguns in her waistband, she entered the office of the Alligator Lakeside Inn in Saint Cloud, Florida. George Long, her 45-year-old ex-boyfriend and co-owner of the motel, was working behind the desk. A struggle ensued, and Long wrestled one of the guns away from Vivier before she pulled the other from her clothing and shot him four times in the chest. Long died at the scene, and Vivier shot herself soon afterward. The two had dated for several years before breaking up a few months earlier. After the breakup, Vivier had relentlessly pursued Long and had been arrested for trespassing and charged with aggravated stalking under Florida law.

The strict requirements needed to establish the crime of criminal assault have led many to believe that traditional criminal laws are not adequate to encompass the conduct of stalkers. Accordingly, many jurisdictions have extended the scope of their assault statutes to include intentional scaring or stalking. The first antistalking statute was enacted in California. California's statute reads as follows: "Any person who willfully, maliciously, and repeatedly follows or harasses another person, and who makes a credible threat with the intent to place that person in reasonable fear of death or great bodily injury is guilty of the crime of **stalking**."[13] The statute defines *harassment* as "a knowing and willful course of conduct directed toward a specific person which seriously harms, annoys, torments, or terrorizes that person, and which serves no legitimate purpose." *Credible threat* means a verbal or written threat implied by a pattern of conduct or a combination of verbal or written statements and conduct made with the intent and apparent ability to carry out the threat so as to cause the person who is the target of the threat to reasonably fear for his or her safety or for the safety of his or her immediate family.[14] Stalking is punishable in California by a fine of up to $1,000, imprisonment in a county jail for up to one year, or both.

Stalking activities now extend into cyberspace. Linda Fairstein, chief of the Sex Crimes Prosecution Unit of the Manhattan District Attorney's Office, recently noted, "Cyberspace has become a fertile field for illegal activity. By the use of new technology and equipment which cannot be policed by traditional methods, cyberstalking has replaced traditional methods of stalking and harassment." In addition, said Fairstein, "cyberstalking has led to offline incidents of violent crime." Police and prosecutors, she said, "need to be aware of the escalating numbers of these events and devise strategies to resolve these problems through the criminal justice system."[15]

stalking
The intentional frightening of another through following, harassing, annoying, tormenting, or terrorizing activities.

California has amended its stalking law to expressly include stalking via the Internet.[16] Under the modified California stalking law, a person commits stalking if he or she "willfully, maliciously, and repeatedly follows or harasses another person and . . . makes a credible threat with the intent to place that person in reasonable fear of his or her safety, or the safety of his or her immediate family." A "credible threat" includes one made through the use of an electronic communication device, a threat implied by a pattern of conduct, or a combination of verbal, written, or electronically communicated statements. Electronic communication devices include telephones, cellular phones, computers, video recorders, fax machines, and pagers. Recently, Florida has also added cyberactivity as a specific means by which the crime of stalking can be perpetrated.[17]

Many other state stalking statutes are broad enough to encompass stalking by e-mail or via electronic devices, including computers. Some statutes define prohibited conduct to include the communication of threats and harassment without specifying the means of delivery and therefore include electronically communicated threats and harassment by electronic devices.

A report by the U.S. attorney general's office says that "current trends and evidence suggest that cyberstalking is a serious problem that will grow in scope and complexity as more people take advantage of the Internet and other telecommunications technologies."[18] The report defines *cyberstalking* as "the use of the Internet, e-mail, or other electronic communications devices to stalk another person." It goes on to say that, although cyberstalking shares important characteristics with offline stalking, there are major differences:

- Offline stalking generally requires the perpetrator and the victim to be located in the same geographic area; cyberstalkers may be located across the street or across the country.
- Electronic communication technologies make it much easier for a cyberstalker to encourage third parties to harass or threaten a victim (for example, impersonating the victim and posting inflammatory messages to bulletin boards and in chat rooms, causing viewers of that message to send threatening messages back to the victim).
- Electronic communication technologies also lower the barriers to harassment and threats; a cyberstalker does not need to physically confront the victim.

In many cases, the cyberstalker and his or her victim(s) had prior relationships, and cyberstalking begins when the victim attempts to break off the relationship. However, there have also been many instances of cyberstalking by strangers. Given the enormous amount of personal information available through the Internet, a cyberstalker can easily locate private information about a potential victim with a few mouse clicks or keystrokes.[19] Learn more about how the law sees stalking in the following Capstone Case, *Clements* v. *State*.

Battery

As noted earlier, the crime of battery is either the causing of bodily injury or the offensive touching of the person of another. According to Florida law, for example, "The offense of battery occurs when a person: (1) actually and intentionally touches or strikes another person against the will of the other; or (2) intentionally causes bodily harm to another person." Battery has three elements:

- The willful and unlawful
- Use of force, violence, or offensive contact
- Against the person of another

Any unjustified offensive touching constitutes a battery. As one court noted: "No injury to the victim need occur; indeed the touching need not have left any mark at all upon the victim."[20] It is not necessary for the victim to actually fear physical harm as the result of

APPLYING THE CONCEPT

CAPSTONE CASE

Does Applying Stalking Laws between Spouses Unconstitutionally Interfere with the Marriage Relationship?

Clements v. State, 19 S.W. 3rd 442 (Texas App. 2000)

After a trial before the court, the trial judge sentenced appellant to 12 months [of] probation for stalking. Appellant [appeals on several grounds.] We affirm.

THE CASE Nathan and Jennifer Clements were married in September 1995, after a six-year courtship. Both were active members of the Christadelphian Church throughout their relationship. During the summer of 1996, Jennifer claims Nathan became possessive and controlling. Although he knew they frightened Jennifer, Nathan purchased guns and often left the guns on Jennifer's pillow. Nathan also scratched the name of one of Jennifer's male friends onto a bullet and told Jennifer that she could either give the bullet to her friend herself or Nathan would give it to him from the barrel of a gun. In November 1996, Nathan accused Jennifer of having affairs. Nathan stated that if he ever caught her with someone else, he would not hesitate to use one of his weapons.

In December 1996, Nathan told Jennifer she had 10 minutes to decide whether she would quit her job or be thrown out of their apartment. Jennifer then packed her things and left. Shortly after Jennifer left the apartment she began receiving phone calls from Nathan at her place of employment, Texas Instruments. From December 8, 1996, to January 1997, Jennifer received 26 phone messages from Nathan. Also during that time, Jennifer twice called Nathan to ask him to stop calling and harassing her. Jennifer testified that the telephone calls caused her to be in fear for her safety.

On December 18, 1996, Jennifer went to their apartment to retrieve her belongings. She hired a police officer to escort her because she was afraid for her safety. Although Nathan was not at the apartment, shortly after she left, Nathan left a message for Jennifer that he knew she brought a police officer with her to the apartment.

On December 19, 1996, Jennifer saw Nathan as she was leaving her new apartment. Nathan pulled next to her in his vehicle and began to honk his horn and yell at her. She drove to the Meadow Place police department because she was afraid Nathan would hurt her. At the police station, Nathan got out of his vehicle and began hitting Jennifer's window. Nathan could see Jennifer was in a hysterical state. Jennifer testified that she was afraid she would suffer bodily injury or death.

Because no one from the police station came out to offer assistance, Jennifer then drove to her place of employment because she knew there would be security personnel available. Nathan continued to follow Jennifer to Texas Instruments. Jennifer testified that Nathan was about an inch from her vehicle while she was driving and that he did not follow any traffic rules. Upon arriving at Texas Instruments, Nathan followed her around the parking lot at high rates of speed until Jennifer was able to contact a security officer.

Alice Wooten, a security officer at Texas Instruments, observed two vehicles traveling at high rates of speed in the Texas Instruments parking lot. When Wooten approached Jennifer, she noticed Jennifer was crying, shaking, and appeared terrified. Jennifer told Wooten that her husband was following her. Nathan left Texas Instruments before Wooten could speak with him.

In January 1997, Nathan filed an answer to Jennifer's original petition for divorce. In his original answer to Jennifer's original petition for divorce, Nathan acknowledged Jennifer was in fear. Nathan also stated only death or the return of Christ would end their marriage.

[The court detailed other interactions between the two that caused Jennifer to fear for her safety.]

Throughout this time period Jennifer was aware that according to his faith, Nathan believed he would not be permitted to remarry until Jennifer died, even after they legally divorced. As a result of Nathan's actions, Jennifer requested that her employer transfer her to another location. Nathan was convicted of stalking in March 1999.

(continued)

THE FINDING

The Stalking Statute: The current stalking statute, under which appellant was prosecuted, provides:

a. A person commits an offense if the person, on more than one occasion and pursuant to the same scheme or course of conduct that is directed specifically at another person, knowingly engages in conduct, including following the person, that:

    1. the actor knows or reasonably believes the other person will regard as threatening:

      (A) bodily injury or death for the other person;

      (B) bodily injury or death for a member of the other person's family or household;

      or

      (C) that an offense will be committed against the other person's property;

    2. causes the other person or member of the other person's family or household to be placed in fear of bodily injury or death or fear that an offense will be committed against the other person's property; and

    3. would cause a reasonable person to fear:

      (A) bodily injury or death for herself;

      (B) bodily injury or death for a member of the person's family or household; or

      (C) that an offense will be committed against the person's property.

Tex. Penal Code Ann. § 42.072 (Vernon Supp. 1999). This statute became effective on January 23, 1997.

LEGAL SUFFICIENCY

. . .

Appellant contends the evidence is legally insufficient for three reasons: . . . (2) the trial court erroneously admitted and considered incidents that occurred on dates other than April 4, 1997, the date alleged in the information, and (3) even considering the evidence in a light most favorable to the prosecution, no rational trier of fact could have found Nathan guilty. . . .

Dates Other Than April 4, 1997 Secondly, Nathan contends the trial court erred in admitting and considering incidents that occurred prior to the date alleged in the information, April 4, 1997. We disagree. The State was required to prove Jennifer was placed in fear of bodily injury or death at the time of Nathan's conduct. Tex. Penal Code Ann. § 42.072. Therefore, the incidents that occurred prior to January 23, 1997, the effective date of the stalking statute, and April 4, 1997, the date alleged in the information, establish Jennifer's state of mind at the time of the offense. These events did not, however, establish the elements of the stalking statute. Only the events that occurred after the effective date of the statute established the elements of the offense.

The Evidence Finally, Nathan argues that, even considering the evidence in a light favorable to the prosecution,

no rational trier of fact could have found appellant guilty where: (1) Jennifer said Nathan did not follow her, as alleged in the information, (2) there is no evidence Nathan ever threatened to injure or kill Jennifer, (3) there is no evidence Nathan ever harmed Jennifer, (4) there is no evidence Jennifer ever communicated to Nathan, or that Nathan should have known his actions were regarded by Jennifer as threatening . . . (6) there is no evidence that Nathan did anything to frighten Jennifer on April 4, 1997, and (7) there is no evidence Nathan's actions would cause a reasonable person to be placed in fear of injury or death.

Jennifer Said Nathan Did Not Follow Her, as Alleged in the Information The current stalking statute does not define the term "follow," so we apply the plain meaning of the term. We conclude that by repeatedly appearing at Jennifer's apartment when he did not reside there, and by causing himself to be where he knew Jennifer would be and engaging in conduct that he knew would cause Jennifer to be placed in fear, Nathan's conduct falls within the plain meaning of the term "follow."

There Is No Evidence Nathan Ever Harmed Jennifer The stalking statute does not require that Jennifer be harmed by Nathan.

There Is Legally Sufficient Evidence Jennifer Communicated to Nathan and That Nathan Knew His Actions Were Regarded by Jennifer as Threatening On more than one occasion, Jennifer asked Nathan to stop harassing her. Additionally, in his response to Jennifer's petition for divorce, filed January 9, 1997, Nathan acknowledged Jennifer was in fear. Moreover, Nathan saw that Jennifer was hysterical, crying, and shaking after he followed her to the police department and to Texas Instruments. Finally, Nathan was aware that Jennifer hired a police officer to accompany her to remove her things from their apartment. This shows not only that Nathan should have known Jennifer regarded his actions as threatening, but that she communicated to him the threatening nature of his actions. . . .

There Is Legally Sufficient Evidence Nathan Frightened Jennifer on April 4, 1997 Jennifer testified that she saw Nathan run across the parking lot toward the swimming pool area near her apartment on April 4, 1997, and that this caused her to be in fear of bodily injury or death. Jennifer called the police upon returning to her apartment.

Jennifer also testified that she had seen Nathan several other times at her apartment complex, and on at least one of those occasions he yelled at her. Jennifer testified that on those other occasions, Nathan saw her become hysterical and cry and shake. As such, there is legally sufficient evidence that Nathan frightened Jennifer on April 4, 1997.

There Is Legally Sufficient Evidence Nathan's Actions Would Cause a Reasonable Person to Be Placed in Fear of Injury or Death Considering the pattern of behavior Nathan exhibited, such as leaving numerous phone messages for Jennifer, appearing several times at her apartment and other places where he knew she would be, and engaging in conduct that he knew would frighten her, we find a reasonable person would also have been placed in fear of bodily injury or death.

We conclude a rational fact finder could have found all the essential elements of the crime of stalking beyond a reasonable doubt. As such, we find the evidence to be legally sufficient to support Nathan's conviction for stalking.

We overrule point of error one.

FACTUAL SUFFICIENCY

. . .

Having reviewed the entire record, we conclude Nathan's conviction for stalking is not contrary to the overwhelming weight of the evidence as to be clearly wrong and unjust. As such, we find the evidence to be factually sufficient to support Nathan's conviction.

We overrule point of error two.

CONSTITUTIONALITY OF STALKING STATUTE

In point of error three, Nathan contends the stalking statute is unconstitutional. Specifically, Nathan argues that the statute is unconstitutionally vague under the First Amendment and is overbroad and impinges upon protected speech and the marriage relationship. . . .

Vagueness All laws carry a presumption of validity. However, unless criminal laws are sufficiently clear, they are considered unconstitutionally vague. The party challenging a statute has the burden to establish its unconstitutionality.

To pass a vagueness challenge, a criminal statute must give a person of ordinary intelligence a reasonable opportunity to know what is prohibited. Further, the law must establish guidelines for law enforcement. Where First Amendment freedoms are implicated, the law must be sufficiently definite to avoid chilling protected expression. If an act implicates First Amendment guarantees, the doctrine of vagueness demands a greater degree of specificity than in other contexts. A criminal law may be held facially invalid even though it may not be unconstitutional as applied to a defendant's conduct.

The language of the 1997 statute is not unconstitutionally vague. We find this statute to thoroughly specify what conduct is prohibited and subject to prosecution. For example, one way in which a person can be convicted of stalking is by engaging in conduct he knows or reasonably believes will be regarded by the other person as threatening bodily injury or death. Tex. Penal Code Ann. §§ 42.072(a)(1)(A). It can also be an offense under the statute for a person to knowingly engage in conduct that would cause a reasonable person to fear bodily injury or death. Tex. Penal Code Ann. §§ 42.072(a)(3)(A). Therefore, the stalker is on notice of the prohibited conduct if he knows or believes the other person will regard that conduct as threatening bodily injury or death. As such, the previous vagueness problem no longer exists.

OVERBREADTH A statute, even if clear and precise, is overbroad if in its reach it prohibits constitutionally protected conduct. . . .

Nathan argues the current stalking statute prohibits his constitutionally protected conduct of attempting to "save" his marriage. We disagree. The current stalking statute specifically prohibits conduct, such as conduct that causes another person to be placed in fear of bodily injury or death. . . . Here, Nathan was not engaged in constitutionally protected conduct because his conduct placed Jennifer in fear of bodily injury or death. . . .

We hold the current stalking statute to be constitutional.

We overrule point of error three. . . . [Discussion on remaining points of error omitted.]

We affirm.

Michael H. Schneider, Chief Justice.

What Do You Think?

1. What are the elements of the crime of stalking under the statute discussed in this case?

2. Do you agree with the court of appeals that the statute is not unconstitutionally vague?

3. Is the evidence in this case sufficient to support a stalking conviction?

Additional Applications

May "tweeting" be prosecuted as stalking?

United States v. Cassidy, 814 F.Supp.2d 574 (D.Md. 2011)

The Case: On February 23, 2011, a federal grand jury indicted William Cassidy, a California resident, on one count of interstate stalking in violation of 18 U.S.C. Section 2261A(2)(A)—a 2006 law that makes it a crime to use "any interactive computer service . . . to engage in a course of conduct that causes [and is intended to cause] substantial emotional distress" to "a person in another State." According to the Federal Bureau of Investigation

(continued)

(FBI), Cassidy had "cyberstalked" Alyce Zeoli, a Buddhist religious leader, by sending out over 7,000 harassing tweets—including some with violent imagery of death—about Zeoli and her religious group. Because of these tweets, the complaint alleged, Zeoli had become fearful for her personal safety; indeed, other than for brief trips out to see her psychiatrist, Zeoli did not leave her Maryland home for roughly 18 months after Cassidy's tweeting had begun.

In a pretrial motion, Cassidy moved to quash the indictment, arguing (among other things) that applying the 2006 federal cyberstalking law to his online activity violated his First Amendment freedom of speech.

The Finding: In a controversial December 2011 ruling, U.S. District Judge Roger Titus dismissed the indictment against Cassidy on First Amendment grounds. Cassidy's tweets, Titus wrote, were clearly in "bad taste" and "inflicted substantial emotional distress." Yet the government failed to show that they were "true threats," which fall outside of the First Amendment; what's more, Titus noted, Zeoli is "not merely a private individual" but rather "an easily identifiable public figure that leads a religious sect"—and many of Cassidy's offending tweets "relate to [that sect's] beliefs and [her] qualifications as its leader." Consequently, the federal indictment here "sweeps into the type of expression that the Supreme Court has consistently tried to protect." Twitter and other online platforms for expression, Titus concluded, "are today's equivalent of a bulletin board that one is free to disregard." And like with any offensive bulletin board, a person distressed by graphic or disturbing messages conveyed via Twitter "ha[s] the ability to protect 'her own sensibilities by averting' her eyes."

Is it stalking to track a spouse with a GPS device?

Colorado v. Sullivan, 53 P.3d 1181 (Colo. App. 2002)

The Case: In the midst of contentious divorce proceedings, Robert Sullivan installed a global positioning system (GPS) device in his wife's car so that he could "maintai[n] a watch" over her and "gathe[r] information about her activities." The GPS device was not capable of providing information to Sullivan about his wife's whereabouts in real time; yet at least twice, Sullivan removed the device, downloaded its stored data, and then replaced it in his wife's car. Based on this GPS tracking, Sullivan was convicted at trial under a Colorado law that defines harassment by stalking as "repeatedly . . . plac[ing] under surveillance" another person "in a manner that would cause a reasonable person to suffer serious emotional distress" and "does cause that person . . . to suffer serious emotional distress." On appeal, Sullivan argued that the mere downloading of GPS information about his wife's previous movements—and thus only finding out about her activities after the fact—could not properly be understood as "repeated surveillance" under the state's antistalking law.

The Finding: A three-judge state appeals panel unanimously affirmed Sullivan's conviction for harassment by stalking. Unlike laws in other states, the court conceded, Colorado's antistalking statute itself is silent on the precise meaning of "repeated surveillance." Yet the common meaning of "surveillance," it held, is "to keep watch over someone or something," which GPS devices now allow even "without the necessity of [the defendant's] concurrent physical presence." Likewise, the word "repeatedly" is commonly understood to mean "more than one time"—which, in this case, fit the circumstances, as the GPS device "recorded the wife's movements on more than a single occasion" and Sullivan had downloaded information from the device at least twice. In enacting the law, the panel concluded, Colorado's state legislature clearly intended that "stalking behavior be stopped before it escalates into more serious conduct." In light of that legislative intent, "[w]e perceive no significant difference between [the defendant] physically following the wife and . . . using a device designed to achieve the same result." ∎

the touching or the injury. The unwelcomed touching of a woman's breast, for example, is a battery. To determine if the touching is offensive, the court considers whether a reasonable person would be offended by the touching. In essence, the law against battery demands respect for the integrity of one's personal space.

Although in most cases battery is an intentional crime, it may also be committed recklessly or with criminal negligence.[21] The Texas Penal Code, for example, makes it a crime to "intentionally, knowingly, or recklessly [cause] bodily injury to another."[22]

The doctrine of transferred intent applies to the crime of battery. Accordingly, if an assailant intends to injure one person and by mistake or accident injures another, he or she is guilty of battery. If, for example, a defendant intended to hit his girlfriend with a baseball bat but in swinging the bat accidentally hit her son instead, the defendant would be guilty of battery on the son (via transferred intent) and also guilty of assault (attempted battery) on his girlfriend.

In some cases, a **constructive touching** is considered sufficient to sustain a battery charge. In one case, for example, a defendant was convicted of battery when he hit a horse that the "victim" was riding. In another case, a defendant was convicted of battery when he got a young female child to touch his penis. Constructive touching is touching that is implied by law to replace the touching requirement (for example, where the defendant gets the young female to do the touching or where the defendant touches a hat that the victim is wearing). Additionally, the force necessary to produce the touching can be applied indirectly, as where the defendant sets in motion a force or scheme that results in unwanted touching.[23]

> **constructive touching**
> A touching that is inferred or implied from prevailing circumstances. Also, a touching for purposes of the law.

In most jurisdictions, the crime of battery is a misdemeanor unless there are special conditions associated with it that aggravate the crime. The most common special conditions include battery on a peace officer, battery with the intent to inflict death or serious bodily injury, battery that results in serious bodily injury, and sexual battery. *Serious bodily injury* includes loss of consciousness, concussion, bone fracture, protracted loss or impairment of any bodily member or organ, a wound that requires extensive suturing, and disfigurement. **Sexual battery** occurs when a person unlawfully touches an intimate part of another person's body against that person's will and for the purpose of sexual arousal, gratification, or abuse. Section 243.4(a) of the California Penal Code says, for example: "Any person who touches an intimate part of another person while that person is unlawfully restrained by the accused or an accomplice, and if the touching is against the will of the person touched and is for the purpose of sexual arousal, sexual gratification, or sexual abuse, is guilty of sexual battery." Other states, such as Indiana, don't require that an intimate area be touched, only that a touching has occurred with the intent of arousing or satisfying a sexual desire.[24] Sexual battery may also include cases of forced intimate touching in which the victim is institutionalized for medical treatment and is seriously disabled or medically incapacitated.

> **sexual battery**
> The unlawful touching of an intimate part of another person against that person's will and for the purpose of sexual arousal, gratification, or abuse.

The effective consent of the victim, also referred to as *legal consent*, or the defendant's reasonable belief that the victim legally consented to the conduct in question is a defense to the charge of battery if the conduct did not threaten to inflict or actually inflict serious bodily injury. **Effective consent** is consent that has been obtained in a legal manner. The person giving consent must be of legal age and mentally capable of giving consent. Effective consent cannot be obtained by fraud or by force, and it cannot be given by a person who does not have the capacity to consent (that is, to understandingly consent). No battery occurs, for example, when two people engage in friendly "horseplay," as both consent to physical interaction. A person cannot, however, effectively consent to the infliction of serious bodily injury. Hence the fact that a deathly ill "victim" begged another person to shoot him to put him out of his misery cannot be used as a defense if the other person obliges. Similarly, a child cannot effectively consent to sexual contact. Accordingly, sexual contact with a child is at least a battery (or a sexual battery, depending on the wording used by the jurisdiction in which the activity occurs). A workable defense to a charge of battery might also be offered where it can be shown that the victim knew the conduct was a risk of his or her occupation or the conduct was a recognized medical treatment or a scientific experiment conducted by recognized methods.

> **effective consent**
> Consent that has been obtained in a legal manner. Also called *legal consent*.

It is important to note that, in contrast to common law and to the laws of many jurisdictions, the Model Penal Code defines *assault* to include both assault and battery. The code says, "A person is guilty of assault if he: (a) attempts to cause or purposely, knowingly, or recklessly causes bodily injury to another."[25] States such as Texas that follow the Model Penal Code use similar wording in their statutes.

Aggravated Battery

aggravated battery
A battery that is committed with the use of a deadly weapon, that is committed with the intention of committing another crime, or that results in serious injury.

As is the case with the crime of assault, some jurisdictions have created the statutory crime of **aggravated battery**. Aggravated battery did not exist under common law. Like the crime of aggravated assault, aggravated battery may involve the use of a deadly weapon, may involve acts committed with the intention of committing another crime (that is, rape or murder), or may include cases of battery that result in serious injury. In cases of serious injury, the degree of harm inflicted on the victim determines whether a crime is chargeable as simple or aggravated battery. Kansas law, for example, provides that aggravated battery is "[i]ntentionally causing great bodily harm to another person or disfigurement of another person."[26] Florida law says that a person commits aggravated battery if he or she (1) intentionally or knowingly causes great bodily harm, permanent disability, or permanent disfigurement; or (2) uses a deadly weapon.[27] Although the definition of a deadly weapon may be open to dispute, some courts have held that hands can be deadly weapons,[28] as can a simple pair of pantyhose used in an attempt to strangle someone.

A few states define the crime of aggravated battery to include the battery of special categories of people, such as those who are pregnant or have a physical handicap or who are teachers or emergency personnel operating in a professional capacity. In some jurisdictions, battery is a misdemeanor, whereas aggravated battery is a felony.

Mayhem

In 1993, John Wayne Bobbitt returned home and allegedly sexually assaulted his wife, Lorena.[29] Later, while he was sleeping, she cut off his penis with a kitchen knife. Lorena Bobbitt, who admitted to severing her husband's organ and throwing it out of a car window as she drove off, was charged with maiming her husband. She soon became a media celebrity. She was acquitted of all criminal charges in 1994 after expert witnesses testified that she was psychologically unable to resist the impulse to attack her husband.

Common law did not recognize aggravated forms of assault and battery. The crime of mayhem developed as an alternative, and it was useful in punishing a perpetrator for a violent attack that did not end in death. To constitute mayhem, the injury suffered by the victim had to be serious and permanent. Under early common law, the injury had to be one that lessened the ability of the victim to defend him- or herself. Later, the types of injuries qualifying for prosecution under mayhem were broadened to include those that were disfiguring. In most jurisdictions today, mayhem requires an intent on the part of the defendant to cause injury to, or death of, the victim. There are three elements to the crime of mayhem:[30]

- An unlawful battery
- Involving maliciously inflicting or attempting to inflict violent injury
- With one or more disabling or disfiguring injuries resulting from the illegal action

California law says: "Every person who unlawfully and maliciously deprives a human being of a member of his body, or disables, disfigures, or renders it useless, or cuts or disables the tongue, or puts out an eye, or slits the nose, ear, or lip, is guilty of mayhem."[31] A more serious form of mayhem, that of aggravated mayhem, can be defined as "causing permanent disability or disfigurement of another human being, or depriving another human being of a limb, organ, or member of his or her body under circumstances manifesting extreme indifference to the physical or psychological well-being of that person."[32]

Whereas most jurisdictions have enacted the common law crime of mayhem in their criminal statutes, the Model Penal Code does not recognize mayhem as a separate offense. Under the code, it falls into the category of aggravated assault.[33] A few jurisdictions have enacted torture statutes, which may be closely related to mayhem laws. The California torture statute, for example, reads: "Every person who, with the intent to cause cruel or extreme pain and suffering for the purpose of revenge, extortion, persuasion, or for any sadistic purpose, inflicts great bodily injury . . . upon the person of another, is guilty of torture."[34] Mayhem, in California, is punishable by imprisonment in the state prison for a term of life, as you can see in the following excerpt of California law.

CALIFORNIA PENAL CODE

Section 203. Every person who unlawfully and maliciously deprives a human being of a member of his body, or disables, disfigures, or renders it useless, or cuts or disables the tongue, or puts out an eye, or slits the nose, ear, or lip, is guilty of mayhem.

Section 204. Mayhem is punishable by imprisonment in the state prison for two, four, or eight years.

Section 205. A person is guilty of aggravated mayhem when he or she unlawfully, under circumstances manifesting extreme indifference to the physical or psychological well-being of another person, intentionally causes permanent disability or disfigurement of another human being or deprives a human being of a limb, organ, or member of his or her body. For purposes of this section, it is not necessary to prove an intent to kill. Aggravated mayhem is a felony punishable by imprisonment in the state prison for life with the possibility of parole.

SEX OFFENSES

Few areas of criminal law have attracted as much attention and as much controversy in the past 25 years as the attempt to place legislative controls on sexual behavior. Efforts to estimate the extent of sexual crime in our society also stir controversy. One reason for the controversy is that in recent years attitudes about sexual relationships have been in a state of flux. People generally agree, however, that unwanted and nonconsensual sexual activity should be subject to criminal prosecution and that sex with children under the age of legal consent should be criminalized. Statistics show that nonconsensual sexual behavior is relatively common. In one study, for example, researchers found that 27 percent of college-age women had been victims of rape or attempted rape and that a number of the women had been victimized more than once.[35] **Criminal sexual conduct** is a gender-neutral term that is applied today to a wide variety of sex offenses, including rape, sodomy, criminal sexual conduct with children, and deviate sexual behavior.

criminal sexual conduct
A gender-neutral term applied today to a wide variety of sex offenses, including rape, sodomy, criminal sexual conduct with children, and deviate sexual behavior.

Rape

Although the penal codes of many states today recognize that both males and females can be sexually assaulted, common law defined the crime of **rape** as "the carnal knowledge of a woman forcibly and against her will."[36] The term *carnal knowledge* meant sexual intercourse. It has been replaced with the term *sexual intercourse* in many contemporary statutes. For centuries, courts required that a woman must "resist to the utmost of her ability" and that resistance must continue until the woman was physically overcome or until the offense was complete. No state adheres to the "utmost resistance" requirement today, although most continue to require some "reasonable resistance" on the part of a conscious victim, while recognizing that resistance can be overcome through threats.

Under common law, any sexual penetration of the female vagina by the male penis was sufficient to complete the crime of rape. It was not necessary that emission occur, or as one

rape
Under common law, unlawful sexual intercourse with a female without her consent. Today, rape statutes in a number of jurisdictions encompass unlawful sexual intercourse between members of the same gender.

English court put it, "the least penetration makes it rape . . . although there be no *emissio seminis*."[37] Common law convictions for the crime of rape required that the penetration be of the vagina; penetration of the anus or mouth was referred to as **deviate sexual intercourse**. In contrast, the modern tendency is to define *rape* as any nonconsensual sexually motivated penetration of any orifice of the victim's body.

In most jurisdictions today, the elements of the crime of rape are

1. Sexual intercourse with a person who is not the spouse of the perpetrator
2. Through force, through the threat of force, or by guile
3. And without the lawful consent of the victim

deviate sexual intercourse
Any contact between any part of the genitals of one person and the mouth or anus of another.

Under common law, a husband could not rape his wife because it was believed that when a woman married, she consented to sexual intercourse. This rule, called the *marital exemption*, held that "a wife is irrebuttably presumed to consent to sexual relations with her husband, even if forcible and without consent."[38] In contrast, today **spousal rape** is a crime in all 50 states.[39] However, partial spousal rape exceptions and other hurdles to proving spousal rape persist. For example, the Model Penal Code and some states recognize a partial spousal rape exception for spouses who are living together. The Model Penal Code applies the exception to any man and woman living together "as man and wife," even if not married. For the exception not to apply, a couple must be legally separated.[40]

Rape is the only crime in which the victim becomes the accused.

—Freda Adler, Sisters in Crime (1975)

spousal rape
The rape of one's spouse.

This doesn't mean that husbands couldn't be prosecuted for rape at the common law or under the Model Penal Code, even if the spouses are living together. A husband who assists another in raping his wife was at the common law guilty of the crime as an accomplice. He would also be guilty as an accomplice to rape under the laws of all states today.

In the past, many rape statutes emphasized the role of force in the crime of rape, giving rise to the term **forcible rape**. Forcible rape is nonconsensual sexual intercourse accomplished against a person's will by means of force, violence, duress, menace, or fear of immediate and unlawful bodily injury to the victim. Maryland law, for example, reads: "A person is guilty of rape in the second degree if the person engages in vaginal intercourse with another person (1) [b]y force or threat of force against the will and without the consent of the other person."[41] In most jurisdictions, the crime of rape requires that the unlawful intercourse must be committed by force, fraud, or forcible compulsion, except for those situations in which the victim is incapable of giving legal consent. Consent cannot be given by a victim who is a minor, who is mentally incompetent, or who is unconscious.

forcible rape
Rape that is accomplished against a person's will by means of force, violence, duress, menace, or fear of immediate and unlawful bodily injury to the victim.

Over time, recognition grew in Western legal circles that force could exist without violence and that a rape victim might be compelled to submit to an assailant even though no overt force was employed. As one Maryland court reasoned:

Certainly, then, a marriage license should not be viewed as a license for a husband to forcibly rape his wife with impunity. A married woman has the same right to control her own body as does an unmarried woman.

—Sol Wachtler, People v. Liberta, 64 N.Y.2d 152, 164, 474 N.E.2d 567, 485 N.Y.S.2d 207 (1984)

Force is an essential element of the crime and to justify a conviction, the evidence must warrant a conclusion either that the victim resisted and her resistance was overcome by force or that she was prevented from resisting by threats to her safety. But no particular amount of force, either actual or constructive, is required to constitute rape. Necessarily that fact must depend upon the prevailing circumstances. As in this case, force may exist without violence. If the acts and threats of the defendant were reasonably calculated to create in the mind of the victim—having regard to the circumstances in which she was placed—a real apprehension, due to fear, of imminent bodily harm, serious enough to impair or overcome her will to resist, then such acts and threats are the equivalent of force. . . . Since resistance is necessarily relative, the presence or absence of it must depend on the facts and circumstances in each case. . . . But the real test, which must be recognized in all cases, is whether the assault was committed without the consent and against the will of the prosecuting witness.[42]

This approach was adopted by the drafters of the Model Penal Code, as reflected in their statement in the *Commentaries*, "The central element in the definition of rape is the absence of the female's consent."[43] Even so, state laws vary considerably in their description of the crime of rape. Utah law, for example, says simply, "A person commits rape when the actor has sexual intercourse with another person without the victim's consent."[44] Some states define rape to include both force and absence of consent. Still others require only force or coercion and make little or no reference to consent. A few, like Utah, make no reference to force, requiring only a lack of consent.

Most jurisdictions also distinguish between various degrees of rape. First-degree, or aggravated, rape is often defined to include one or more of the following: (1) an armed offender, (2) serious bodily injury to the victim, (3) an additional felony where the rape occurs during the commission of some other crime, or (4) gang rape. The category of second-degree rape generally includes any other type of rape.

Lawful Consent

In individual cases the question of whether intercourse was consensual may be a difficult one to answer. If the victim is incapable of giving legally effective consent, then intercourse with the victim is rape even if he or she expressed words indicating consent. The fact that the victim consented to sexual foreplay does not mean that the victim consented to intercourse, nor does the fact that the victim had in the past consented to intercourse with the defendant constitute consent on the present occasion. A difficult question arises in situations in which the victim remains silent and offers no resistance to the act. Most jurisdictions require that the victim, if conscious and able to communicate, must in some manner manifest his or her objection to the act for it to constitute rape.

A lack of consent can be established by any acts of the victim that would lead a reasonable person to believe that he or she does not consent to the intercourse. In most jurisdictions, a reasonable mistake as to whether the victim consented is a defense to rape. In a case that made headlines during 1993, Joel Valdez, dubbed the "condom rapist," was found guilty of rape after a jury in Austin, Texas, rejected his claim that the act became consensual once he complied with his victim's request to use a condom. Valdez, who was drunk and armed with a knife at the time of the offense, claimed that his victim's request was a consent to sex. After that, he said, "we were making love."[45]

Evidence that the victim has a bad reputation for chastity is inadmissible because consent is not an issue in a case involving statutory rape.

—State v. DeLawder, 344 A.2d 212 (Md. Ct. Spec. App., 1975)

Statutory Rape

All jurisdictions have laws defining **statutory rape**. Under such laws, anyone who has intercourse with a child below a certain specified age is guilty of statutory rape, whether or not the child consented. Statutory rape, in most jurisdictions, is a strict liability crime. As mentioned earlier in this book, strict liability crimes can be committed when the offender engages in activity that is legally prohibited, even if the offender is unaware of breaking the law or did not intend to do so. Hence a man who has sexual intercourse with a consenting female under the age specified by statute can still be found guilty of statutory rape even though he thought she was older. Most jurisdictions hold that even a reasonable belief on the part of the defendant that the victim was over the age of consent at the time of the offense is no defense to a charge of statutory rape.[46] In some instances, men have been convicted of statutory rape even though they had been duped by a female below the age of consent into thinking that the girl was older. The Model Penal Code and a minority of jurisdictions, however, do allow the defense of reasonable mistake as to age.[47]

statutory rape
Sexual intercourse, whether consensual or not, with a person under the age of consent, as specified by statute.

Same-Sex Rape

The common law definition of *rape* required both (1) penetration and (2) an unwilling *female* victim. Accordingly, it was generally held that there was no crime of homosexual rape under common law. Today, however, a majority of jurisdictions have rape statutes that are gender neutral. In those jurisdictions, intercourse between people of the same gender may be rape if all of the other elements of the crime are present. A few states, such as New York, have gender-neutral rape laws by virtue of court ruling rather than statutory legislation.[48]

Similarly, a woman can be convicted of the rape of another woman when she forces a man to have nonconsensual sexual intercourse with the victim. In a 1971 California case, for example, a female defendant who forced her husband to have intercourse with a young girl at gunpoint was convicted of rape.[49]

Rape Shield Laws   In the not too distant past, it was common practice in American courts for defendants charged with the crime of rape to cross-examine victims about prior acts of "unchastity." Evidence of this sort was allowed because it was believed to have bearing on the issue of consent. As one California court put it in a 1970 instruction to a jury, "It may be inferred that a woman who has previously consented to sexual intercourse would be more likely to consent again. Such evidence may be considered by you only for such bearing as it may have on the question of whether or not she gave her consent to the alleged sexual act and in judging her credibility."[50]

During the past 20 or 30 years, many jurisdictions have passed **rape shield laws** intended to protect victims of rape. A typical rape shield provision requires that the relevance of any evidence regarding the past sexual conduct of a rape victim be demonstrated before it can be presented in court. Whether a rape victim was a virgin, sexually experienced, or even a prostitute before the alleged rape, for example, may be irrelevant. In some cases, however, such as when a defendant claims that the person charging him with rape is a prostitute and had actually consented to an act of prostitution, the victim's sexual history may be regarded as relevant.

Rape shield laws concern themselves more with appropriate courtroom procedure than they do with criminal behavior. In general, any evidence that has a tendency to prove or disprove the facts at issue is said to have **probative value**. Rape shield laws mandate that the probative value, or worth, of any particular information about a woman's sexual history be demonstrated before such evidence can be presented at trial.

Sexual Assault

A recent trend in the United States is to combine all nonconsensual sexual offenses into one crime called **sexual assault**, which in some jurisdictions may also be termed *criminal sexual conduct* or *sexual abuse*. Where such broad laws exist, sexual assault encompasses far more than the common law crime of rape. Sexual assault may include the common law crimes of rape, deviate sexual intercourse, unlawful sexual contact, **fellatio** (oral stimulation of the male penis), and statutory rape. For purposes of law, *deviate sexual intercourse*, as mentioned earlier in this chapter, means any contact between any part of the genitals of one person and the mouth or anus of another person or the penetration of the genitals or the anus of another person with an object. It can also include any form of sexual intercourse between a human being and an animal. **Sexual contact** means any touching of the anus, breast, or any part of the genitals of another person with intent to arouse or gratify the sexual desire of any person. Sexual contact generally means a touching short of intercourse.

The Model Penal Code and a few jurisdictions give a much more limited meaning to the term *sexual assault*. The Model Penal Code, for example, contains separate sections defining the crime of rape (Section 213.1), deviate sexual intercourse (Section 213.2), and statutory rape (Section 213.3), but also contains a section (213.4) defining sexual assault. Under the code, sexual assault, which is classified as a misdemeanor, occurs whenever a person has sexual contact with another person (not his or her spouse) while knowing that contact to be offensive to the other person. Sexual assault under the code also includes sexual contact that occurs when

rape shield law
A statute intended to protect victims of rape by limiting a defendant's in-court use of a victim's sexual history.

probative value
The worth of any evidence to prove or disprove the facts at issue.

sexual assault
A statutory crime that combines all sexual offenses into one offense (often with various degrees). It is broader than the common law crime of rape.

fellatio
Oral stimulation of the penis.

sexual contact
Any touching of the anus, breast, or any part of the genitals of another person with intent to arouse or gratify the sexual desire of any person.

the victim is (1) suffering from mental disease or defect that leaves him or her unable to consent; (2) unaware that a sexual act is being committed; (3) less than 10 years old; (4) substantially impaired through actions of the offender, such as the administering of drugs; or (5) less than 16 years old and the actor is at least four years older; and under a few other circumstances.

KIDNAPPING AND FALSE IMPRISONMENT

In early 1997, former New York City resident Joshua Torres, age 23, began serving a sentence of 58 years to life in prison for the 1995 kidnap-murder of 20-year-old Kimberly Antonakos. Torres had been convicted a month earlier of abducting Antonakos from in front of her home and attempting to extort ransom money from her father. During the kidnapping, Antonakos had been grabbed and thrown into the trunk of a car and then driven to an abandoned house in Queens, where she was held for three days in an unheated basement, all the while gagged and tied to a pole.[51] After the young woman's father failed to respond to a $75,000 ransom demand because his answering machine did not record the kidnapper's call, Torres doused Antonakos with gasoline and burned her to death. Sentencing judge Thomas Demakos, who admitted being moved to tears by testimony in the case, said that the crime cried out for the death penalty, which was not in effect in New York State when the murder took place. Torres was sentenced instead to 25 years to life for murder, another 25 years to life for kidnapping, and 8 to 25 years for arson—all to be served consecutively.

Kidnapping

Kidnapping and false imprisonment are crimes that intimately invade a person's privacy and take away his or her liberty—often in abrupt and forceful fashion. *Kidnapping* is generally defined as the unlawful removal of a person from the place where he or she is found, against that person's will, and through the use of force, fraud, threats, or some other form of intimidation.

Under early common law, kidnapping consisted of the forcible abduction or stealing away of a person from his own country and into another. Somewhat later the requirement was modified to require involuntary movement merely from one county to another. Today most jurisdictions hold that any unlawful movement of the victim that is "substantial" is sufficient to satisfy the movement (asportation) requirement inherent in the crime of kidnapping. Today the most common legal issue in kidnapping cases is whether a person is forcefully moved against his or her will and not the degree of movement or distance involved.[52] Regardless, the question of movement can be thorny, as you will read later in this chapter.

Generally speaking, the elements of kidnapping are

- An unlawful taking and carrying away, also known as asportation
- Of a human being
- By force, fraud, threats, or intimidation
- And against the person's will

In some jurisdictions, kidnapping may also be committed by the use of *deadly* force to confine the victim or by confining the victim for purposes of extortion, ransom, or sexual assault. Kidnapping for ransom (or *aggravated kidnapping*, as these crimes are sometimes called) is a more serious form of kidnapping and is usually punished more severely than the crime of simple kidnapping (Figure 8–3). The same may be true when state statutes specify that the release of a victim in a place that is not safe raises the degree of the crime committed.

The laws of some jurisdictions provide for more than one type of kidnapping. California law, for example, recognizes four different kidnapping offenses: (1) forcible kidnapping,

kidnapping
The unlawful removal of a person from the place where he or she is found, against that person's will, and through the use of force, fraud, threats, or some other form of intimidation. Also, an aggravated form of false imprisonment that is accompanied by either a moving or secreting of the victim.

FIGURE 8–3

Aggravated Kidnapping.

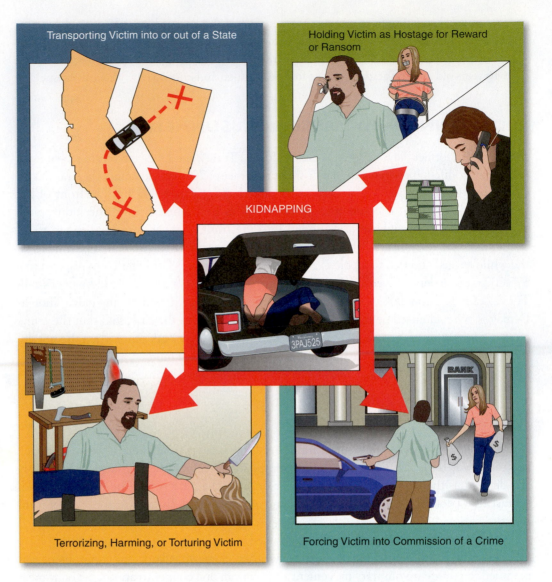

Transporting Victim into or out of a State

Holding Victim as Hostage for Reward or Ransom

KIDNAPPING

Terrorizing, Harming, or Torturing Victim

Forcing Victim into Commission of a Crime

(2) kidnapping with intent to commit certain specified felonies, (3) kidnapping with intent to take the victim out of state, and (4) bringing a kidnapped victim into the state. California law also specifies penalty enhancements for kidnappings that are committed for the purposes of committing a sexual offense, ransom, extortion, or robbery, and for kidnapping a child under the age of 14.

In an effort to combat the abduction of children, which is sometimes called *child stealing*, Florida law also provides that "[c]onfinement of a child under the age of thirteen is against his will within the meaning of this subsection if such confinement is without the consent of his parent or legal guardian."[53] The abduction of children might occur in instances of contested divorce or child-custody battles.

Just as the laws of different jurisdictions vary as to what constitutes kidnapping, they also vary on how the confinement must be accomplished for the law to apply. A few jurisdictions do not classify an unwilling movement of an individual accomplished through fraud as kidnapping, holding instead that force, intimidation, or threat must be used for the offense to qualify as kidnapping. Similarly, if all of the elements are present except a substantial movement of the victim, then the offense may be an attempted kidnapping. The general rule, however, is that movement or confinement accomplished by force or threat is sufficient to constitute the crime of kidnapping.[54] In some cases, the mere persuading of a minor or incompetent person to remain in one place or to move is sufficient to constitute kidnapping. If a victim at first willingly accompanies the offender, the crime of kidnapping still occurs if force or restraint is later used to move the victim farther.

Kidnapping occurs only if there has been asportation, or movement, of the victim. In those situations in which the movement of the victim is merely incidental to the commission of another crime, a few jurisdictions allow the prosecution of the defendant for both the intended crime and for kidnapping.[55] Some jurisdictions, though, hold that a kidnapping has not been committed unless the forced movement substantially increases the risk to the victim beyond the risk created by the other crime.[56] In one Michigan case, for example, the defendant walked into a store, pulled a gun, and compelled the victim to go into another room to open a safe. Although the defendant was clearly guilty of armed robbery, a court held that he had not committed kidnapping—not because of the short distance involved in the forced movement, but because movement of the victim was merely incidental to commission of the armed robbery. Had the defendant used the victim as a shield as he left the scene of the robbery, however, it is likely that he would also have been guilty of kidnapping.

A federal kidnapping law, sometimes called the Lindbergh Law,[57] was created in response to the kidnapping of the infant son of Charles A. Lindbergh, who was the first person to make a nonstop solo trans-Atlantic flight. The Lindbergh baby was taken from the family's New Jersey home in 1932 by Bruno Richard Hauptmann. The child was later found dead, and Hauptmann was convicted of the crime and executed in 1936. Other federal laws make it a crime to take a hostage[58] or to knowingly receive, possess, or dispose of any money or property that has been delivered as ransom on behalf of a victim of kidnapping.[59]

False Imprisonment

False imprisonment, which is basically the unlawful violation of the personal liberty of another, is similar to kidnapping except that it does not involve the "carrying away" of the victim. Not all states have false imprisonment statutes, and in those that do, it is usually classified as a misdemeanor. The elements of false imprisonment are

false imprisonment
The unlawful restraint of another person's liberty. Also, the unlawful detention of a person without his or her consent. Also called *false arrest.*

- An unlawful restraint by one person
- Of another person's freedom of movement
- Without the victim's consent or without legal justification

The defendant must have compelled the victim to remain against his or her will or to go where he or she did not want to go.[60] Although the confinement must be accomplished by actual physical restraint, the application of force is not essential. Confinement may be accomplished by threats or by some other action of the defendant that restrains the victim's freedom of movement. One court, for example, found a defendant guilty of false imprisonment for intentionally driving a car too fast for his passenger to leave.[61]

In cases in which the confinement is accomplished by threat, the victim must be aware of the threat. Similarly, it is not false imprisonment to prevent a person from going in one direction, as long as the person may go in a different direction and is aware of this opportunity. Also, confinement must be unlawful in that there must be no legal authority for the confinement. An arrest that is made without proper legal authority constitutes false arrest—a form of false imprisonment.

False imprisonment is a lesser included offense of the crime of kidnapping. Some authors note that kidnapping is also an aggravated form of false imprisonment—as this excerpt from Florida law reveals: "The term 'false imprisonment' means forcibly, by threat, or secretly confining, abducting, imprisoning, or restraining another person without lawful authority and against his will."[62] As with kidnapping, the statute also provides that "[c]onfinement of a child under the age of thirteen is against his will within the meaning of this section if such confinement is without the consent of his parent or legal guardian."[63] Federal law imposes a duty on states to enforce the child-custody determinations made by other states under the Parental Kidnapping Prevention Act.[64] Some jurisdictions, which define *false imprisonment* simply as "restraining another unlawfully so as to interfere substantially with his liberty," would consider false imprisonment achieved through the use of force or threats as "aggravated false imprisonment."

Under common law, both kidnapping and false imprisonment were misdemeanors. Today, however, kidnapping is generally regarded far more seriously, and false imprisonment remains a lesser crime (Figure 8–4). Florida law, for example, reads: "A person who kidnaps a person is guilty of a felony of the first degree, punishable by imprisonment for a term of years not exceeding life."[65]

The case of *Schweinle v. State* (1996) in the Capstone Case illustrates the relationship and differences between false imprisonment and kidnapping.

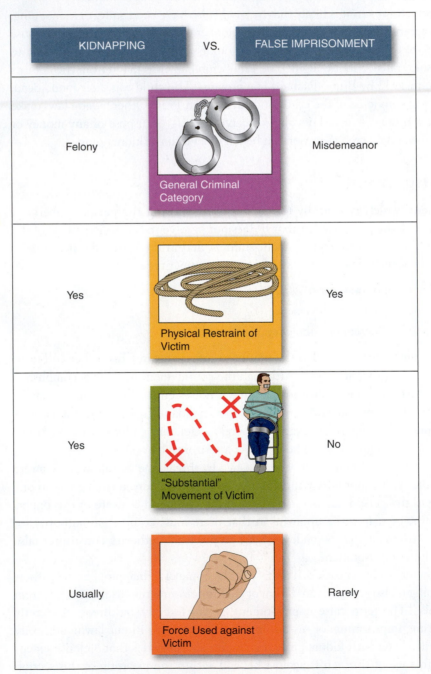

FIGURE 8–4

Kidnapping versus False Imprisonment.

APPLYING THE CONCEPT

CAPSTONE CASE

Is a Defendant Charged with Aggravated Kidnapping Entitled to Have the Jury Also Consider the Lesser Charge of False Imprisonment?

Schweinle v. State, 915 S.W.2d 17 (Texas Ct. App. 1996)

THE CASE   Defendant was convicted . . . of aggravated kidnapping, and he appealed. The Houston Court of Appeals, 893 S.W.2d 708, affirmed, and defendant petitioned for review. The Court of Criminal Appeals held that defendant was entitled to charge of false imprisonment as lesser included offense.

Reversed and remanded. . . .

A jury convicted appellant of aggravated kidnapping and assessed his punishment at confinement for fifteen years in the penitentiary. The conviction was affirmed. We granted discretionary review to determine whether evidence of extraneous offenses and expert testimony regarding "battered woman syndrome" was improperly admitted in the guilt-innocence phase, and whether a lesser included offense was raised by the evidence. . . .

Appellant and the complainant became engaged after a brief courtship, and the complainant, who had formerly lived with her parents, moved into appellant's house. However, the couple began arguing, and the complainant moved back to her parents' house, although she would occasionally spend the night with appellant. On October 23, 1991, they had planned that appellant would pick up some food for dinner, and the complainant would meet appellant at his father's liquor store, where appellant worked. The complainant was alone at her parents' house changing clothes when she heard a door slam. Appellant came into the bedroom, enraged because the complainant had not met him at the liquor store as planned. The complainant testified appellant told her she was coming with him, that he had some food in the car and she was going to eat every bite of it. He grabbed her by the arm, dragged her down the hall and slapped her. The complainant told appellant she did not want to go with him, but appellant insisted she was coming with him and walked her to the truck. As appellant was driving, he smeared a steak sandwich in the complainant's face and pointed a gun at her, telling her

he would shoot her if she tried to escape. Appellant drove the truck to a subdivision near his house in which roads had been built but no houses constructed. There, he threw another sandwich at her and hit her in the stomach with his fist. He then drove to his house, where he continued to beat her with a belt and a rolled-up newspaper covered with duct tape. The next morning appellant took the complainant to her parents' house.

THE FINDING   In ground four, appellant contends the Court of Appeals erred by holding that the lesser included offense of false imprisonment was not raised by the evidence. Whether a charge on a lesser included offense is required is determined by a two-pronged test. First, we must determine whether the offense constitutes a lesser included offense. Tex. Code Crim. Proc. Ann. art. 37.09 provides that an offense is a lesser included offense if, *inter alia:* "It is established by proof of the same or less than all the facts required to establish the commission of the offense charged." Second, the lesser included offense must be raised by the evidence at trial. In other words, there must be some evidence which would permit a rational jury to find that if guilty, the defendant is guilty only of the lesser offense. . . . Anything more than a scintilla of evidence from any source is sufficient to entitle a defendant to submission of the issue. . . .

Under V.T.C.A. Penal Code, Section 20.03, a person commits the offense of kidnapping if he intentionally or knowingly abducts another. "'Abduct' means to restrain a person with intent to prevent his liberation by: (A) secreting or holding him in a place where he is not likely to be found; or (B) using or threatening to use deadly force. . . . Restrain' means to restrict a person's movements without consent, so as to interfere substantially with his liberty, by moving him from one place to another or by confining him. Restraint is 'without consent' if it is accomplished by force, intimidation, or deception. . . ."

A person commits the offense of false imprisonment if he "intentionally or knowingly restrains another person."

(continued)

Kidnapping is accomplished by abduction, which includes restraint, but false imprisonment is committed by restraint only. Thus, false imprisonment is a lesser included offense of kidnapping and aggravated kidnapping.

The next step of the analysis is to determine whether there was evidence that if guilty, appellant was guilty only of restraining the complainant, without intending to prevent her liberation by either secreting or holding her in a place where she was not likely to be found or using or threatening to use deadly force. The Court of Appeals held appellant was required to rebut or negate both theories of abduction which could have occurred anytime during the ongoing offense. It noted that appellant argued he needed only to refute that he pointed the gun at the complainant in the truck and that he kept her at his house. It held that keeping the complainant isolated at the undeveloped subdivision constituted restraint in a place where she was not likely to be found. It determined that the only evidence which refuted this theory was appellant's testimony that the complainant freely chose to go with him and stayed in the truck of her own free will. However, it reasoned that because this evidence refuted both abduction and restraint, appellant failed to show if guilty, he was guilty of *only* the lesser included offense. . . .

The Court of Appeals' analysis is flawed in two respects. First, the Court of Appeals determined that the subdivision where appellant stopped his truck to throw more food on the complainant and beat her was a place where she was not likely to be found, without considering whether a rational jury could have reached the opposite conclusion under the evidence. In *Saunders v. State*, 840 S.W.2d 390 (Tex. Cr. App.1992), this Court held that a lesser included offense may be raised if evidence either affirmatively refutes or negates an element establishing the greater offense, or the evidence on the issue is subject to two different interpretations, and one of the interpretations negates or rebuts an element of the greater. In the instant case, the Court of Appeals did not refer to any facts in the record which demonstrated that the subdivision was or was not a place where the complainant was not likely to be found. . . .

Pictures of this area were admitted into evidence. From this evidence, a rational jury could have believed that the street where appellant stopped his truck was not a place where the complainant was not likely to be found.

Secondly, by holding that appellant did not raise the lesser included offense because his testimony refuted both the greater and lesser offenses, the Court of Appeals erred under *Bignall*. In that case, this Court held that the defendant was entitled to submission of the lesser included offense of theft based on defense testimony that no one had a gun, despite his evidence showing he was not guilty of any

offense. This Court held that a rational jury could have believed that part of the State's evidence that Bignall was involved in the theft, and that part of Bignall's evidence that no one had a gun, and concluded that appellant was guilty only of theft. We pointed out that the defendant's denial of committing any offense does not automatically foreclose submission of a lesser included offense. *Bignall*, 887 S.W.2d at 24.

Applying those principles to this case, a rational jury could have believed the complainant's testimony that she did not go freely with appellant. Appellant testified that he did not threaten to shoot the complainant, did not touch the gun during the drive from her parents' house to his, and did not point the gun at her at any time. He admitted that the gun was lying on the seat of his truck during the offense, but explained that he habitually carried the gun in his truck either on the seat next to him or on the floor next to the gearshift. He testified that when they reached his house, he retrieved the gun from the truck, took it inside as he always did, and placed it on his pinball machine where he often kept it. The complainant testified that she knew appellant kept a gun in his truck and that it was not unusual for it to be lying on the seat. From this evidence, a rational jury could have found that despite the presence of a gun on the seat, appellant did not use or threaten to use deadly force to prevent the complainant's liberation.

Similarly, the jury could have believed that appellant held the complainant in his house against her will but believed appellant's house was not a place where the complainant was not likely to be found. Evidence was presented that the complainant had a key to appellant's house, had formerly lived there, and had spent the night there the past three or four nights before the offense. In addition, the complainant's mother testified that when she came home on the night of the offense and found the house in disarray and her daughter missing, she became afraid for her daughter's safety and drove by appellant's house. From this evidence, a jury could have rationally concluded that the complainant was restrained at appellant's house, but his house was not a place where she was not likely to be found. In sum, the jury could have found that appellant had restrained but not abducted the complainant and thus was guilty only of false imprisonment. Therefore, the Court of Appeals erred by holding this lesser included offense was not raised by the evidence.

Accordingly, we reverse the judgment of the Court of Appeals and remand the case to that court to conduct a harm analysis pursuant to Tex. Code Crim. Proc. Ann. art. 36.19. Appellant's grounds for review one, two, and three are dismissed without prejudice.

What Do You Think?

1. What are the differences between false imprisonment and kidnapping?

2. Based on the facts contained in the court's opinion, did the accused commit any offense other than kidnapping and false imprisonment? If so, what?

Additional Applications

Can a parent be charged with false imprisonment of his own children?

State v. Teynor, 414 N.W.2d 76 (Wisc. App. 1983)

The Case: On July 23, 1985, Clarence Teynor went to his ex-wife's apartment in Holmen, Wisconsin, and, according to the ex-wife's testimony at trial, violently pushed her against a stove and demanded to "take his family home." Frightened and worried, she gathered the couple's three children—who were living with her in the apartment, under a temporary custody order—and rode with Teynor in his truck to the former family farm, located about 80 miles away. Once at the farmhouse, Teynor received a call that police would soon arrive; consequently, he drove the children out into the woods, where they remained until police arrived.

Teynor was arrested and charged with (among other things) the false imprisonment of the three children in violation of Section 940.30 of the Wisconsin statutes. On appeal, he argued that his status as the victims' parent shielded him from prosecution for the alleged crimes.

The Finding: The Court of Appeals of Wisconsin upheld Teynor's conviction. Under Wisconsin law, the court found, parents of a minor child do enjoy the general right "to direct the child's activities and where the child shall live." What's more, "parental status affords . . . a privilege which may be asserted as a defense to prosecution for any crime by a parent against his or her child if the conduct is reasonable discipline of the child." Nonetheless, the panel continued, the state legislature, when passing Wisconsin's false imprisonment statute, clearly did not intend to exempt parents from prosecution for "nonconsensual restraint or confinement of the child." Consequently, in that state, "a parent may commit the offense of false imprisonment against the parent's child." And in this particular case, the court added, Teynor could not have claimed a parental exemption in any event, for when his ex-wife was awarded temporary custody of their children, Teynor effectively lost any special authority that he previously had held over the victims in the case.

Can a nursing home administrator be charged with false imprisonment for refusing to discharge a resident without payment?

Massey v. Texas, 624 S.W.2d 576 (Tex. App. 1981)

The Case: On Friday, December 3, 1976, John Allen went to the Forest Manor Nursing Home in Dallas, Texas, and attempted to have his father discharged from the facility. According to testimony at trial, however, a facility administrator responded: "Yeah, you can take him out if you give me six hundred and seventy-five dollars. I know you can't raise that." The following Monday (December 6), Allen again tried to gain his father's release from the facility—this time being told by Forest Manor administrator Wanda Massey (on a recorded call): "Bring me his money to pay for him being here, and you can have him." Following this conversation, Dallas police were apparently called, and after a series of conversations involving Massey, Allen, the police, and an attorney at an elder rights organization, Massey agreed to release the father that day. Evidence at trial suggested that Allen's father—a partially paralyzed elderly man who struggled to communicate effectively with others—remained unaware of much of this dispute throughout the duration of the events.

Several months later, following extensive local newspaper coverage about poor conditions at Dallas-area nursing homes, the Dallas district attorney charged defendant Wanda Massey with false imprisonment of Allen's father during the three-day period of December 3–6, 1976. At trial, the jury found Massey guilty of "restraint by intimidation" and sentenced her to nine days in jail and a $685 fine. On appeal, Massey challenged the sufficiency of the evidence to sustain her false imprisonment conviction.

The Finding: On appeal, the Court of Criminal Appeals in Texas reversed Massey's conviction and ordered a judgment of acquittal. In its opinion, the appeals court left unchallenged the prosecutor's premise that a nursing home administrator could be held criminally liable for refusing to release a resident for failure to pay. Yet in this particular case, the court found, an insufficient factual record existed to support the jury's finding that Massey had "intentionally or knowingly" restrained Allen's father by intimidation. The jury, the court emphasized, had been confronted at trial with a significant number of factual disputes between the parties. Police records did not corroborate with precision the prosecution's presentation of the events of December 3–6. And most important, the appeals court suggested, Allen's father—who was the victim of the crime alleged in the case—was likely never fully aware of the specifics of the dispute surrounding him. Consequently, the panel concluded, he likely never felt "intimidated" by Massey into staying at the facility longer than he desired. ■

SUMMARY

- Although the terms *assault* and *battery* are often used together or interchangeably, they should be distinguished for purposes of the criminal law. An assault is an attempted or threatened battery. A battery is a consummated assault. Mayhem is a battery that causes great bodily harm.

- Under common law, two types of assault could be distinguished: an attempted battery and a threatened battery. In the first type of assault, a defendant attempted to commit a battery. The second type of assault, that of threatened battery, occurred when a defendant placed another in fear of imminent injury. The first was an actual attempt to commit a battery, whereas the latter criminalized conduct that made another person fear an assault.

- Some jurisdictions have combined assault and battery crimes into one offense called *assault*.

- The "present ability" element of the crime of assault requires that the person attempting assault is physically capable of immediately carrying it out.

- The term *aggravated assault* may mean (1) an assault that is committed with the intention of committing an additional crime or (2) an assault that involves special circumstances.

- Many jurisdictions have enacted antistalking statutes designed to prevent the intentional harassing, annoying, or threatening of another person.

- The crime of battery is an intentional crime, but it may be committed through reckless or criminally negligent conduct. To constitute battery, the offense need cause no injury, and the victim need not fear the force intended to be applied.

- Sexual battery occurs when a person unlawfully touches an intimate part of another person's body against that person's will and for the purpose of sexual arousal, gratification, or abuse.

- Traditionally, *rape* has been defined as unlawful sexual intercourse with a female without her effective consent. Under common law, a husband could not rape his wife because it was believed that when a woman married, she consented to sexual intercourse. The rape statutes of an increasing number of jurisdictions today, however, are not gender specific and also permit charges of spousal rape.

- Statutory rape is sexual intercourse, by an adult, with a child who has not yet reached the legal age of consent.

- Some jurisdictions have consolidated sexual offenses into one broad crime of sexual assault.

- Kidnapping is the unlawful removal of a person from the place where he or she is found, against that person's will, and through the use of force, fraud, threats, or some other form of intimidation.

- False imprisonment is the unlawful violation of the personal liberty of another. False arrest, or an arrest that is made without proper legal authority, is a form of false imprisonment.

KEY TERMS

aggravated assault, 243

aggravated battery, 252

assault, 240

battery, 240

bodily injury, 242

constructive touching, 251

criminal sexual conduct, 253

deviate sexual intercourse, 254

effective consent, 251

false imprisonment, 259

fellatio, 256

forcible rape, 254

kidnapping, 257

mayhem, 241

present ability, 242

probative value, 256

rape, 253

rape shield law, 256

sexual assault, 256

sexual battery, 251

sexual contact, 256

sodomy, 240

spousal rape, 254

stalking, 245

statutory rape, 255

QUESTIONS FOR DISCUSSION

1. What are the differences between the common law crimes of assault and battery?

2. What are the two types of common law assault, and what are the elements of each?

3. How does mayhem differ from other types of battery?

4. Explain the type or extent of injury to a victim required for the crime of battery.

5. Explain the difference between common law rape and modern statutes describing sexual assault. What does it mean to say that a rape statute is not "gender specific"?

6. Give an example of false imprisonment. How does false imprisonment differ from kidnapping? How does it differ from false arrest?

CRITICAL THINKING AND APPLICATION PROBLEMS

Use the following facts to respond to problems 1 and 2:

Rob Burr entered a bank, displayed a weapon, and ordered the teller, Marcia, to put all the money that she had in a bag that he handed to her. He then ordered her to take him to the bank's safe so that he could "get all the money in there." After she walked him to the safe, he ordered her inside with him. Once inside, he ordered her to put the money from the safe into another bag. She complied with all of his directives. On the way out of the bank he ordered Margaret, a 21-year-old teller, to accompany him. He drove her to a woods 15 miles from the bank, where he raped her and left her on the side of the road. She walked to a nearby home, where she contacted the police. The women identified Robb from a photo array, and he was arrested. He was subsequently charged with robbery, kidnapping both Marcia and Margaret, false imprisonment of both Marcia and Margaret, and the rape of Margaret.

1. Did Rob commit the crimes of kidnapping and false imprisonment of Marcia? Explain fully.

2. Did Rob commit the crimes of kidnapping and false imprisonment of Margaret? Explain fully.

3. You work for a state legislator as a policy adviser on law and judiciary issues. Your state's criminal code doesn't have a spousal rape exception. The legislator you work for has been lobbied by a family rights organization to introduce legislation that would create a spousal rape exception for spouses who live together, but not for spouses who are legally separated. Unfamiliar with the subject, she asks you to brief her on the subject by: (1) articulating the reasons a "partial spousal rape exception" should be enacted, and (2) the reasons it should not be. Prepare this document. Your discussion should include philosophical, moral, legal, and practical dimensions of the issue.

LEGAL RESOURCES ON THE WEB

A growing number of websites provide the opportunity to participate in law-related simulations. iCourthouse, for example, allows participants to serve on virtual juries. Cases are drawn from real life and permit virtual jury panel members to experience at least some of the ins and outs of jury service. iCourthouse and other similar services are listed here.

American Mock Trial Association (AMTA)
http://www.collegemocktrial.org
AMTA sponsors annual mock trial tournaments for undergraduates. The organization seeks to help students understand the work of a trial attorney.

iCourthouse
http://www.icourthouse.com
This site describes itself as "a greatly streamlined version of the court system in the real world. . . . The cases are real, the jurors are real, and the verdicts are real. . . . iCourthouse is always in session."

Mock Trial Online
http://www.abc.net.au/mocktrial
This Australian site conducts a full mock trial over the Internet. Mock Trial Online is a joint project involving the Law Society of New South Wales, ABC Online, and the British Council.

SUGGESTED READINGS AND CLASSIC WORKS

Alexander, Shana. *Anyone's Daughter.* New York: Viking Press, 1979.

Augustine, Rene L. "Marriage: The Safe Haven for Rapists." *Journal of Family Law* 29 (1991): 559.

Berger, Vivian. "A Not So Simple Rape." *Criminal Justice Ethics* 7 (1988): 69.

Diamond, John. "Kidnapping: A Modern Definition." *American Journal of Criminal Law* 13 (fall 1985): 1.

Estrich, Susan. *Real Rape.* Cambridge: Harvard University Press, 1987.

Harman, John D. "Consent, Harm, and Marital Rape." *Journal of Family Law* 22 (1983): 423.

Kadish, Sanford H., ed. *Encyclopedia of Crime and Justice* 3 (New York: Free Press, 1983).

Kirk, William, and Richard Hawkins. "The Meaning of Arrest for Wife Assaulters." *Criminology* 27 (February 1989): 163.

NOTES

1. Adapted from *Ortiz* v. *State,* 470 S.E. 2d 874, 876 (Ga. 1996).
2. Rollin M. Perkins and Ronald N. Boyce, *Criminal Law,* 3rd ed. (Mineola, NY: Foundation Press, 1982), 151, citing *State* v. *Jones,* 133 S.C. 167, 130 S.E. 747 (1925).
3. Model Penal Code Section 211.
4. *People* v. *James,* 9 Cal. App. 2d 162 (1935).
5. M.P.C. §211.
6. *State* v. *Bowers,* 239 Kan. 417, 721 P.2d 268 (1986).
7. *People* v. *Ross,* 831 P.2d 1310, 1314 (Colo. 1992).
8. *Commonwealth* v. *Davis,* 406 N.E.2d 417, 419 (Mass. App. Ct. 1980).
9. Joshua Dressler, *Understanding Criminal Law,* 2nd ed. (New York: Matthew Bender, 1995), 350.
10. *Fox* v. *State,* 34 Ohio St. 377, 380 (1878).
11. *State* v. *Wilson,* 218 Or. 575, 346 P.2d 115 (1959).
12. "Woman Kills Ex-Boyfriend, Self," Associated Press, January 22, 1997.
13. California Penal Code, Section 646.9.

14. Ibid.

15. *Cyberstalking: A New Challenge for Law Enforcement and Industry* (Washington, DC: U.S. Attorney General's Office, August 1999).

16. California Penal Code, Section 646.9.

17. Florida Statutes, Section 784.048 (2003).

18. *Cyberstalking.*

19. Ibid.

20. *State* v. *Bowers*, 239 Kan. 417, 721 P.2d 268 (1986).

21. *Fish* v. *Michigan*, 62 F.2d 659 (6th Cir. 1933).

22. Texas Penal Code, Section 22.01, subparagraphs (1) and (3).

23. *State* v. *Monroe*, 28 S.E. 547 (N.C. 1897).

24. IC 35-42-4-8.

25. Model Penal Code, Section 211.1.

26. Kansas Statutes Annotated, Section 21-3414(a) (1) (A).

27. Florida Statutes, Section 784.045.

28. *Dixon* v. *State*, 1992 Fla. App. LEXIS 2401; 17 Fla. L. W. D. 700 (1992). The original decision was rendered by a three-member panel of the appellate court. The full court later ruled that "bare hands . . . are not deadly weapons for purposes of alleging or proving the crime of aggravated battery."

29. In November 1993, a jury found Bobbitt not guilty of raping his wife.

30. Harvey Wallace and Cliff Roberson, *Principles of Criminal Law* (White Plains, NY: Longman, 1996), 164.

31. California Penal Code, Section 203.

32. California Penal Code, Section 205.

33. Model Penal Code, Section 211.1.

34. California Penal Code, Section 206.

35. Mary P. Koss, Christine A. Gidycz, and Nadine Wisniewski, "The Scope of Rape: Incidence and Prevalence of Sexual Aggression and Victimization in a National Sample of Higher Education Students," *Journal of Counseling and Clinical Psychology* 55 (1987): 162.

36. Joseph R. Nolan and Jacqueline M. Nolan-Haley, *Black's Law Dictionary: Definitions of the Terms and Phrases of American and English Jurisprudence, Ancient and Modern*, 6th ed. (St. Paul: West, 1990), 212.

37. East's Pleas of the Crown 436 (1803).

38. *State* v. *Bell*, 90 N.M. 134, 560 P.2d 925, 931 (1977).

39. "Spousal Rape Twenty Years Later," *The National Center for Victims of Crime*, Winter 1999/2000, http://www.ncvc.org/ncvc/main.aspx?dbName=DocumentViewer&DocumentID=32701.

40. Model Penal Code Section 213 generally; Section 213.6 for the legal separation provision.

41. Maryland Code, Article 27, Section 463(a)(1).

42. *State* v. *Rusk*, 424 A.2d 720 (Md. 1981), citing *Hazel* v. *State*, 221 Md. 464, 157 A.2d 922 (1960).

43. American Law Institute, *Model Penal Code and Commentaries* (1985).

44. Utah Code Annotated, Section 76-402.

45. "Jury Convicts Condom Rapist," *USA Today*, May 14, 1993.

46. *State* v. *Randolph*, 528 P.2d 1008 (Wash. 1974).

47. Model Penal Code, Section 213.6 (1).

48. *People* v. *Liberta*, 474 N.E.2d 567 (N.Y. 1984).

49. *People* v. *Hernandez*, 18 Cal. App. 3d 651, 96 Cal. Rptr. 71 (1971).

50. *People* v. *Rincon-Pineda*, 14 Cal. 3d at 951–952 (1970).

51. "Judge Gives Max in Burned Alive Case," United Press, December 10, 1996.

52. *State* v. *Padilla*, 474 P.2d 821 (Ariz. 1970).

53. Ibid.

54. Texas Penal Code, Section 20.01(1)(a).

55. *State* v. *Jacobs*, 380 P.2d 998 (Ariz. 1952).

56. *People* v. *Adams*, 192 N.W.2d 19 (Mich. 1971).

57. 18 U.S. Code Annotated, Section 1201(a).

58. 18 U.S. Code Annotated, Section 1203.

59. 18 U.S. Code Annotated, Section 1202.

60. *People* v. *Agnew*, 16 Cal. 2d 655 (1940).

61. *Dupler* v. *Seubert*, 69 Wis. 2d 373, 230 N.W.2d 626, 631 (1975).

62. Florida Penal Code, Section 787.02.

63. Ibid.

64. 28 U.S. Code Annotated, Section 1738A.

65. Florida Penal Code, Section 787.01(2).

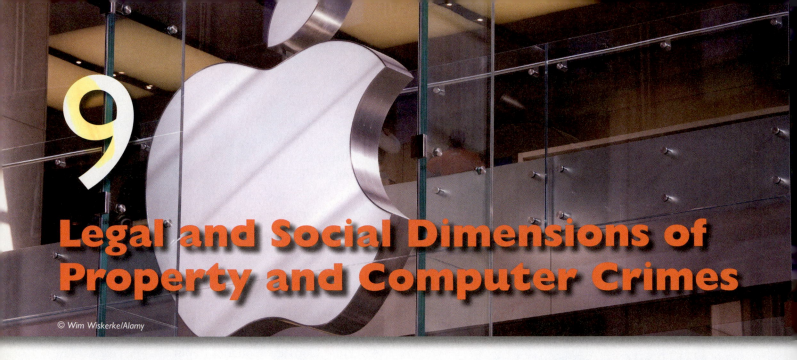
© Wim Wiskerke/Alamy

9

Legal and Social Dimensions of Property and Computer Crimes

CHAPTER OUTLINE

Introduction

Theft Crimes

Consolidation of Theft Crimes

Grading of Theft Crimes

Burglary

Arson

Computer and High-Technology Crimes

OBJECTIVES

After reading this chapter, you should be able to

- Describe the crime of embezzlement.
- Explain the differences between larceny and embezzlement, and tell why they are important.
- Describe the rules regarding the keeping of found property.
- Identify the types of property that were subject to the common law crime of larceny.
- Explain the difference between embezzlement and false pretenses.
- Expound upon the historical need that led to the formulation of the "breaking bulk" doctrine.
- Explain what it means to say that "only people you trust can embezzle from you."
- Summarize the advantages and disadvantages of consolidating the wrongful acquisition crimes into a single crime of theft.
- Identify the test used by courts in robbery cases to determine whether property was taken from the presence of the victim.
- Distinguish between robbery and extortion.
- Describe the crime of burglary and explain the concept of constructive entry as applied to burglary crimes.
- Identify the common elements of modern-day arson statutes and distinguish the modern definition from the common law definition.
- Describe computer and high-technology crimes and identify the five types of computer crime discussed in this chapter.

It is not a crime to make a fool of another by delivering fewer goods than ordered.
—Rex v. Wheatly, 97 E.R. 746 (1761)

More money has been stolen at the point of a fountain pen than at the point of a gun.
—Woody Guthrie

As surely as the future will bring new forms of technology, it will bring new forms of crime.
—Cynthia Manson and Charles Ardai[1]

INTRODUCTION

On July 29, 1999, Wisconsin resident Waverly C. Burns, 43, was sentenced to 21 months' imprisonment and three years of supervised release by U.S. District Court Judge Barbara B. Crabb. Burns had pleaded guilty to identity theft and was sentenced under the 1998 federal Identity Theft and Assumption Deterrence Act.[2] The law, which became effective on October 30, 1998, criminalizes the unauthorized use of another person's identification with the intent to commit a crime. Under the law, anyone who obtains money or property valued at $1,000 or more over a one-year period can be sentenced to up to 15 years in prison.

Burns had gained employment with Clean Power in Madison, Wisconsin, by using the identity of a man named James W. Clark. Through his job, Burns gained access to the Tenney Building, which houses the offices of the Wisconsin Supreme Court. On January 3, 1999, Burns entered the court's offices and took six computer monitors owned by the state of Wisconsin. His conviction resulted from an investigation conducted by the Social Security Administration's Office of Inspector General and the Wisconsin Capitol Police.

THEFT CRIMES

Theft crimes, along with drug crimes, are the most commonly occurring crime in the United States. In 2010 there were nearly 6.2 million larcenies (ordinary thefts) and over 700,000 motor vehicle thefts, as opposed to a little more than 1.2 million violent crimes (murder, rape, robbery, and aggravated assault). Consequently, law enforcement officers and courts devote considerable resources to theft crimes.[3]

The modern concept of identity theft is very new, and laws specifically targeting it are only a few years old. On the other hand, the law of **theft** has a long and colorful history. Crimes of theft are generally property crimes, and this chapter discusses a variety of property crimes, including larceny, burglary, criminal trespass, arson, computer crimes involving misappropriation, and, of course, identity theft.

As one author notes, "Theft is a general term embracing a wide variety of misconduct by which a person is improperly deprived of his property. The purpose of theft law is to promote security of property by threatening aggressors with punishment."[4] For purposes of this chapter, we will change this definition of theft slightly to read "a general term embracing a wide variety of misconduct by which a person is *unlawfully* deprived of his or her property."

Crimes of theft are sometimes called **acquisitive offenses**, *wrongful acquisition crimes*, or *crimes of misappropriation* because they involve the unlawful acquisition or appropriation of someone else's property. The *Commentaries* to the Model Penal Code (MPC) note that laws defining theft as a crime are the result of "a long history of expansion of the role of the criminal law in protecting property."[5] Although common law originally concerned itself only with crimes of violence, the law expanded, through application of the principle of trespass, "to cover all taking of another's property from his possession without his consent, even though no force was used."[6]

At first, only **larceny** was punished as a crime under common law. Larceny was defined as "the wrongful taking and carrying away by any person of the mere personal goods of another, from any place, with a felonious intent to convert them to his own use, and make them his own property, without the consent of the owner."[7] Larceny was a capital crime under common law.

Under early law, only personal belongings, such as tools, livestock, money, clothes, and household items, could be stolen. Real estate, in the sense of land and all that it naturally contained, was not thought subject to larceny, even though it could be temporarily "converted" for another's use. Squatters and those who trespassed on property that did not

theft
A general term embracing a wide variety of misconduct by which a person is unlawfully deprived of his or her property.

acquisitive offense
A crime that involves the unlawful acquiring or appropriation of someone else's property. Larceny, extortion, embezzlement, false pretenses, robbery, and the receiving of stolen property are all acquisitive offenses. Also called *wrongful acquisition crime* and *crime of misappropriation*.

larceny
The trespassory or wrongful taking and carrying away (asportation) of the personal property of another with intent to steal.

belong to them were dealt with under laws against poaching and laws against trespass, but they were not said to have "stolen" the land. Even someone who severed items (such as ore, trees, or crops) from the land of another and carried them away was not subject to prosecution for the crime of larceny. In contrast, once a crop had been harvested, or a tree cut down and made into lumber, then it was considered to be in the possession of its rightful owner, and any unlawful carrying away of the material constituted larceny.

Similarly, under common law, anyone who killed a wild animal on land belonging to another might be guilty of the crime of poaching but could not be convicted of larceny even if he carried the animal away—because the landowner did not have true possession of the animal before it was killed. The stealing of domestic animals, on the other hand, was larceny, as carrying them away removed them from the possession of their rightful owners. Early common law distinguished between the stealing of animals of a higher nature, such as cows, pigs, horses, and chickens (which was larceny), and the stealing of animals of a base nature, such as cats, dogs, and monkeys (which was not larceny). These distinctions were, of course, entirely artificial, but they served to limit the use of the death penalty to more serious cases of theft.

The early law of theft rarely extended beyond larceny. Outright cheating and the misappropriation of goods entrusted into the care of another were not regarded as crimes, although civil remedies existed under common law by which proper ownership of misappropriated goods might be restored. More than 200 years ago, for example, one English court held that "[i]t is not a crime to make a fool of another by delivering fewer goods than ordered,"[8] even if the buyer trusts the seller and only later finds out that he or she has been duped. The watchword of the day was *caveat emptor*, or "let the buyer beware," and one who shortchanged another was generally not criminally liable under early common law.

Judged by today's standards, common law might seem inadequate. It should be understood, however, that at the time "business transactions were relatively few and comparatively simple. Individuals had time to make their own investigations and they usually did so, and it was not considered sound business or good common sense to rely on the mere oral statement of another."[9] In other words, in earlier times the burden of ensuring accurate transactions lay upon the purchaser, not the seller, and it was assumed that buyers would carefully watch any measuring process involved in the transaction and that they would take the time to inspect the number and quality of goods they received before paying for them.

As commerce increased, criminal law expanded to punish new forms of theft. By then, however, the law regarding larceny had become so fixed that new crimes had to be invented to fill the gaps. Crimes like embezzlement, extortion, and obtaining property by false pretenses came to be recognized. A fundamental principle of common law crimes against property was that they concerned themselves with the wrongful acquisition of property, and the terms *wrongful acquisition crimes* and *acquisitive offenses* came into vogue.

Most acquisitive offenses, including larceny, embezzlement, false pretenses, robbery, and the receiving of stolen property, required such precise elements that early courts were slow to expand those crimes to cover novel and emerging situations. Even today, courts and legislatures have difficulty fitting certain offenses, such as computer and high-technology crimes, into the category of theft. The problem stems from the fact that it is sometimes difficult to demonstrate that something has been stolen when the "rightful" owner seems to still be in possession of it (as can happen with the theft of software). It is complicated by the fact that "in a commercial society no clear line can be drawn between greedy antisocial acquisitive behavior on the one hand, and on the other hand, aggressive selling, advertising, and other entrepreneurial activity that is highly regarded or at least commonly tolerated."[10]

The modern trend in some jurisdictions has been to consolidate all acquisitive crimes into the single crime of theft. In such jurisdictions, the consolidated crime of theft includes what had been the common law crimes of larceny, embezzlement, obtaining property by false pretenses, receiving stolen property, robbery, extortion (sometimes called *blackmail*),

TABLE 9–1 Comparison of Crimes Against Property

Crime	Mens Rea	Act
Larceny	Intent to deprive owner of property	Trespassory taking and carrying away of the property of another
Embezzlement	Intent to deprive owner of property	Conversion of lawfully entrusted property
Robbery	Intent to deprive owner of property	Taking property from another under threat of force or through intimidation
Forgery	Intent to create false document and to prejudice another's legal rights with document	The creation of a false document or material alteration of genuine document and use of document in way that prejudices another's rights
False Pretenses	To knowingly make false statement of material fact with intent to acquire title or possession of property that is known to belong to another with intent to defraud	Making the false material statement and obtaining title or possession of property known to belong to another
Receiving Stolen Property	Knowledge that the property is stolen and acquisition with intention of depriving owner of the property	To receive property that is known to be stolen
Extortion	Intent to deprive owner of property by making a threat of future harm	To acquire property belonging to another through threat
Identity Theft	Knowing use of identifying information of another with intent to assume his or her identity and intent to deprive another of property	To use identifying information of another, to assume identity, and to take property
Burglary	Intentional breaking and entering the property of another with intent to commit a crime inside	Breaking and entering the property of another and the commission or attempted commission of a crime

and burglary. Other jurisdictions treat each of these crimes separately. In this chapter, we discuss each, along with forgery and identity theft (Table 9–1).

Larceny

As discussed earlier, larceny was the first and most basic of the property crimes to develop under common law. Simply put, larceny is the wrongful taking of personal property from the possession of another. Under English common law, larceny initially consisted of the "unconsented to" taking of the property of another from that person's possession. As such, larceny was a crime against possession, not ownership, as the person from whom the item was stolen could still be said to have ownership, even if he or she was no longer in possession of the stolen property. A successful larceny resulted in *dispossessing* the rightful owner of something of value, but it did not terminate inherent rights of ownership—meaning that once stolen property had been recovered, it could lawfully be returned to its rightful owner.

I hate this "crime doesn't pay" stuff. Crime in the United States is perhaps one of the biggest businesses in the world today.

—Peter Kirk, University of California

Possession and Custody   Today, larceny is generally understood as the

- Trespassory (wrongful) taking
- And carrying away (asportation)
- Of the personal property of another
- With intent to steal

Taken together, these four elements constitute the modern crime of larceny.

Almost all jurisdictions have divided larceny into two categories: petit (or petty) and grand. Grand larceny usually consists of the stealing of property that has a market value in excess of a certain specified amount, or the theft of certain statutorily listed property, such as firearms and cattle. Sections 486–87 of the California Penal Code, for example, read:

> Theft is divided into two degrees, the first of which is termed grand theft; the second, petty theft. . . . Grand theft is theft committed in any of the following cases: (a) When the money, labor, or real or personal property taken is of a value exceeding four hundred dollars ($400). . . . (b) Notwithstanding subdivision (a), grand theft is committed in any of the following cases: (1) (A) When domestic fowls, avocados, olives, citrus or deciduous fruits, other fruits, vegetables, nuts, artichokes, or other farm crops are taken of a value exceeding one hundred dollars ($100). . . . (2) When fish, shellfish, mollusks, crustaceans, kelp, algae, or other aquacultural products are taken from a commercial or research operation which is producing that product, of a value exceeding one hundred dollars ($100). (3) Where the money, labor, or real or personal property is taken by a servant, agent, or employee from his or her principal or employer and aggregates four hundred dollars ($400) or more in any consecutive twelve-month period. (c) When the property is taken from the person of another. (d) When the property taken is an automobile, firearm, horse, mare, gelding, any bovine animal, any caprine animal, mule, jack, jenny, sheep, lamb, hog, sow, boar, gilt, barrow, or pig.

Some states are very specific in defining just what constitutes grand larceny. Section 487e of the California Penal Code, for example, reads: "Every person who feloniously steals, takes, or carries away a dog of another which is of a value exceeding four hundred dollars ($400) is guilty of grand theft."[11]

Subject Matter of Larceny

Under common law, only tangible personal property could be subject to the crime of larceny. **Tangible property** is property that has physical form and is capable of being touched. It is "movable" property in the sense that it can be taken and carried away. **Personal property** is anything of value that is subject to ownership and that is not land or **fixtures** (that is, items that are permanently affixed to the land).[12] As mentioned earlier, under common law, crops and minerals were not considered to be personal property until they were severed from the land, but domestic animals were considered to be tangible personal property and thus were subject to larceny.

Such thinking leads to another principle, which is that in order to constitute larceny, the thing stolen must have some value—however slight. This principle is generally recognized in societies around the globe. In some contemporary Islamic societies (such as Kuwait and Saudi Arabia), for example, it is not criminal to steal liquor, pigs, or pork, as such things are regarded as "unclean" under the Muslim Koran and are therefore without value.

Common law excluded **intangible property** from the realm of larceny. Intangible property is property that has no value in and of itself but that represents value. A deed to a piece of occupied land, for example, is a kind of intangible property. Although a deed might be taken and carried away without the owner's consent, the rightful owner would still retain both legal ownership and possession of the land itself—that is, the thing that had real value. The owner need merely to apply to the local courthouse for a new copy of the deed, and the person holding the stolen deed would find it to be of no value in trying to sell the land to someone else.

The distinction between tangible and intangible property was especially valid in early society, where populations were sparse and individuals and families were generally known to one another. In modern complex society, however, proof of ownership may be more difficult to establish. Hence, although most of today's larceny arrests are still made for the stealing of tangible property, larceny law has become much more complex. In many American jurisdictions today, goods and services, minerals, crops, fixtures, trees, utilities, software, intellectual

---

tangible property
Property that has physical form and can be touched, such as land, goods, jewelry, and furniture. Also, movable property that can be taken and carried away.

personal property
Anything of value that is subject to ownership and that is not land or fixture.

fixture
An item that is permanently affixed to the land.

intangible property
Property that has no intrinsic value but that represents something of value. Intangible personal property may include documents, deeds, records of ownership, promissory notes, stock certificates, computer software, and intellectual property.

and property rights, and other intangibles can all be stolen and are the subject of various laws designed to deter theft. Some jurisdictions have enacted larceny statutes designed to criminalize the misappropriation of property that, although it has value, cannot be touched. Texas law, for example, says quite succinctly: "'Property' means: (A) **real property**; (B) tangible or intangible personal property, including anything severed from land; or (C) a document, including money, that represents or embodies anything of value."[13] The Model Penal Code, although a bit more complex, defines *property* as follows: "'[P]roperty' means anything of value, including real estate, tangible and intangible personal property, contract rights choses-in-action [things to which an owner has a contractual or legal right] and other interests in or claims to wealth, admission or transportation tickets, captured or domestic animals, food and drink, electric and other power."[14] Whether intellectual property satisfies the property requirement for a theft statute was the issue in the U.S. Supreme Court case of *Dowling* v. *United States*, 473 U.S. 207 (1985), which is presented in a Capstone Case in this chapter.

Under the Model Penal Code and the laws of a number of states, the theft of electricity from the company that generates it constitutes larceny, as does the theft of computer software, processing time, or proprietary information. Other jurisdictions have created special laws criminalizing the theft of intellectual property and other intangibles. The misappropriation of the fruits of high technology are discussed later in this chapter.

Trespassory Taking

At common law, there could be no larceny unless there was a trespassory taking of property. *Taking* generally consists of a physical seizure by which one exercises dominion and control over the property in question.[15] To constitute larceny, however, the taking must also be trespassory. A **trespassory taking** is merely a taking without the consent of the victim. Consent induced by fraud may constitute trespassory taking. It is important to note that a trespassory taking, as the term is used in conjunction with larceny cases, has no relationship to the idea of trespass where real estate or land is concerned. Under common law, a trespassory taking was called *trespass de bonis asportatis* (trespass for goods carried away) to distinguish it from other forms of trespass.

As English society became more impersonal and more mercantile, the common law crime of larceny, based as it was on possession, became less adequate. Under early common law, if a defendant was already in possession of the property said to be stolen, he or she could not be found guilty of larceny because there would be no trespassory taking.[16] So, for example, a person entrusted with cargo could not be said to have taken it without the consent of the victim, even if he or she later diverted shipment of the cargo and sold it without delivering it to its planned destination. The need to stimulate commerce and to protect foreign merchants who might contract with carriers and haulers who, of necessity, were unknown to them mandated modifications in the understanding of larceny. New rules were needed, and they came in the area of bailments—an aspect of the law concerned with the relationship between an owner and one to whom the owner had entrusted his or her property for purposes such as sale, storage, transport, repair, processing, or investment. Because bailments involved contractual arrangements, disagreements between owners and bailees had previously been under the purview of civil law. Widespread economic changes, however, and the requirements they placed on the English judicial system soon brought bailments into the realm of criminal law.

The change came in an oft-cited 1473 case, commonly called the *Carrier's Case*.[17] In this case, an English court struggled with the question of a carrier who was given possession of a wagon of goods to deliver for the owner. The carrier "broke the bulk" of the goods, or separated and stole items from the wagon. To bring such activities within the purview of larceny, the court hearing the case held that, although the carrier had rightful possession of the packaged goods, "constructive possession" returned to the owner as soon as he broke

real property
Land and fixtures.

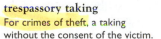

trespassory taking
For crimes of theft, a taking without the consent of the victim.

APPLYING THE CONCEPT

CAPSTONE CASE

Is It Theft to Sell Someone Else's Copyrighted Songs without Permission?

Dowling v. United States, 473 U.S. 207 (1985)
JUSTICE BLACKMUN delivered the opinion of the Court.

THE CASE   The National Stolen Property Act provides for the imposition of criminal penalties upon any person who "transports in interstate or foreign commerce any goods, wares, merchandise, securities or money, of the value of $5,000 or more, knowing the same to have been stolen, converted or taken by fraud." In this case, we must determine whether the statute reaches the interstate transportation of "bootleg" phonorecords, "stolen, converted or taken by fraud" only in the sense that they were manufactured and distributed without the consent of the copyright owners of the musical compositions performed on the records.

After a bench trial [the defendant was convicted of several copyright and theft offenses that] stemmed from an extensive bootleg record operation involving the manufacture and distribution by mail of recordings of vocal performances by Elvis Presley. The evidence demonstrated that sometime around 1976, Dowling, to that time an avid collector of Presley recordings, began in conjunction with codefendant William Samuel Theaker to manufacture phonorecords of unreleased Presley recordings. They used material from a variety of sources, including studio outtakes, acetates, soundtracks from Presley motion pictures, and tapes of Presley concerts and television appearances. Until early 1980, Dowling and Theaker had the records manufactured at a record-pressing company in Burbank, Cal. When that company later refused to take their orders, they sought out other record-pressing companies in Los Angeles and, through codefendant Richard Minor, in Miami, Fla. The bootleg entrepreneurs never obtained authorization from or paid royalties to the owners of the copyrights in the musical compositions.

In the beginning, Dowling, who resided near Baltimore, handled the "artistic" end of the operation, contributing his knowledge of the Presley subculture, seeking out and selecting the musical material, designing the covers and labels, and writing the liner notes, while Theaker, who lived in Los Angeles and had some familiarity with the music industry, took care of the business end, arranging for the record pressings, distributing catalogs, and filling orders. In early 1979, however, having come to suspect that the FBI was investigating the west coast operation, Theaker began making shipments by commercial trucking companies of large quantities of the albums to Dowling in Maryland.

Throughout 1979 and 1980, the venturers did their marketing through Send Service, a labeling and addressing entity, which distributed at least 50,000 copies of their catalog and advertising flyers to addresses on mailing lists provided by Theaker and Dowling. Theaker would collect customers' orders from post office boxes in Glendale, Cal., and mail them to Dowling in Maryland, who would fill the orders. The two did a substantial business: the stipulated testimony establishes that throughout this period Dowling mailed several hundred packages per week and regularly spent $1,000 per week in postage. The men also had occasion to make large shipments from Los Angeles to Minor in Miami, who purchased quantities of their albums for resale through his own channels. . . .

THE FINDING   Federal crimes, of course, "are solely creatures of statute." Accordingly, when assessing the reach of a federal criminal statute, we must pay close heed to language, legislative history, and purpose in order strictly to determine the scope of the conduct the enactment forbids. Due respect for the prerogatives of Congress in defining federal crimes prompts restraint in this area, where we typically find a "narrow interpretation" appropriate. See *Williams* v. *United States*, 458 U.S. 279, 290 (1982). Chief Justice Marshall early observed:

> The rule that penal laws are to be construed strictly, is perhaps not much less old than construction itself. It is founded on the tenderness of the law for the rights of individuals; and on the plain principle that the power of punishment is vested in the legislative, not in the judicial department. It is the legislature, not the Court, which is to define a crime, and ordain its punishment.

Thus, the Court has stressed repeatedly that when choice has to be made between two readings of what conduct Congress has made a crime, it is appropriate, before we choose the harsher alternative, to require that Congress should have spoken in language that is clear and definite.

Applying that prudent rule of construction here, we examine at the outset the statutory language. Section 2314 [one of the statutory provisions for which the defendant was convicted] requires, first, that the defendant have transported "goods, wares, [or] merchandise" in interstate or foreign commerce; second, that those goods have a value of "$5,000 or more"; and, third, that the defendant "[know] the same to have been stolen, converted or taken by fraud." Dowling does not contest that he caused the shipment of goods in interstate commerce or that the shipments had sufficient value to meet the monetary requirement. He argues, instead, that the goods shipped were not "stolen, converted or taken by fraud." In response, the Government does not suggest that Dowling wrongfully came by the phonorecords actually shipped or the physical materials from which they were made; nor does it contend that the objects that Dowling caused to be shipped, the bootleg phonorecords, were "the same" as the copyrights in the musical compositions that he infringed by unauthorized distribution of Presley performances of those compositions. The Government argues, however, that the shipments come within the reach of § 2314 because the phonorecords physically embodied performances of musical compositions that Dowling had no legal right to distribute. According to the Government, the unauthorized use of the musical compositions rendered the phonorecords "stolen, converted or taken by fraud" within the meaning of the statute.

We must determine, therefore, whether phonorecords that include the performance of copyrighted musical compositions for the use of which no authorization has been sought nor royalties paid are consequently "stolen, converted or taken by fraud" for purposes of § 2314. We conclude that they are not.

The courts interpreting § 2314 have never required, of course, that the items stolen and transported remain in entirely unaltered form. See, e.g., *United States* v. *Moore,* 571 F.2d 154, 158 (CA3) (counterfeit printed Ticketron tickets "the same" as stolen blanks from which they were printed). Nor does it matter that the item owes a major portion of its value to an intangible component. . . .

It follows that interference with copyright does not easily equate with theft, conversion, or fraud. The Copyright Act even employs a separate term of art to define one who misappropriates a copyright: Anyone who violates any of the exclusive rights of the copyright owner, that is, anyone who trespasses into his exclusive domain by using or authorizing the use of the copyrighted work in one of the five ways set forth in the statute, is an infringer of the copyright. 17 U. S. C. § 501(a). There is no dispute in this case that Dowling's unauthorized inclusion on his bootleg albums of performances of copyrighted compositions constituted infringement of those copyrights. It is less clear, however, that the taking that occurs when an infringer arrogates the use of another's protected work comfortably fits the terms associated with physical removal employed by § 2314. The infringer invades a statutorily defined province guaranteed to the copyright holder alone. But he does not assume physical control over the copyright; nor does he wholly deprive its owner of its use. While one may colloquially link infringement with some general notion of wrongful appropriation, infringement plainly implicates a more complex set of property interests than does run-of-the-mill theft, conversion, or fraud. As a result, it fits but awkwardly with the language Congress chose—"stolen, converted or taken by fraud"—to describe the sorts of goods whose interstate shipment § 2314 makes criminal. And, when interpreting a criminal statute that does not explicitly reach the conduct in question, we are reluctant to base an expansive reading on inferences drawn from subjective and variable understandings.

In light of the ill-fitting language, we turn to consider whether the history and purpose of § 2314 evince a plain congressional intention to reach interstate shipments of goods infringing copyrights. Our examination of the background of the provision makes more acute our reluctance to read § 2314 to encompass merchandise whose contraband character derives from copyright infringement.

Congress enacted § 2314 as an extension of the National Motor Vehicle Theft Act, ch. 89, 41 Stat. 324, currently codified at 18 U. S. C. § 2312. Passed in 1919, the earlier Act was an attempt to supplement the efforts of the States to combat automobile thefts. Particularly in areas close to state lines, state law enforcement authorities were seriously hampered by car thieves' ability to transport stolen vehicles beyond the jurisdiction in which the theft occurred. Legislating pursuant to its commerce power, Congress made unlawful the interstate transportation of stolen vehicles, thereby filling in the enforcement gap by "[striking] down State lines which serve as barriers to protect [these interstate criminals] from justice."

"By 1919, the law of most States against local theft had developed so as to include not only common-law larceny but embezzlement, false pretenses, larceny by trick,

(continued)

and other types of wrongful taking. The advent of the automobile, however, created a new problem with which the States found it difficult to deal. The automobile was uniquely suited to felonious taking whether by larceny, embezzlement or false pretenses. It was a valuable, salable article which itself supplied the means for speedy escape. 'The automobile [became] the perfect chattel for modern large-scale theft.' This challenge could be best met through use of the Federal Government's jurisdiction over interstate commerce. The need for federal action increased with the number, distribution and speed of the motor vehicles until, by 1919, it became a necessity. The result was the National Motor Vehicle Theft Act."

Congress acted to fill an identical enforcement gap when in 1934 it "[extended] the provisions of the National Motor Vehicle Theft Act to other stolen property" by means of the National Stolen Property Act (Act of May 22, 1934). Again, Congress acted under its commerce power to assist the States' efforts to foil the "roving criminal," whose movement across state lines stymied local law enforcement officials. As with its progenitor, Congress responded in the National Stolen Property Act to "the need for federal action" in an area that normally would have been left to state law.

No such need for supplemental federal action has ever existed, however, with respect to copyright infringement, for the obvious reason that Congress always has had the bestowed authority to legislate directly in this area. Article I, § 8, cl. 8, of the Constitution provides that Congress shall have the power:

> To promote the Progress of Science and useful Arts, by securing for limited Times to Authors and Inventors the exclusive Right to their respective Writings and Discoveries.

By virtue of the explicit constitutional grant, Congress has the unquestioned authority to penalize directly the distribution of goods that infringe copyright, whether or not those goods affect interstate commerce. Given that power, it is implausible to suppose that Congress intended to combat the problem of copyright infringement by the circuitous route hypothesized by the Government. Of course, the enactment of criminal penalties for copyright infringement would not prevent Congress from choosing as well to criminalize the interstate shipment of infringing goods. But in dealing with the distribution of such goods, Congress has never thought it necessary to distinguish between intrastate and interstate activity. Nor does any good reason to do so occur to us. In sum, the premise of § 2314—the need to fill with federal action an enforcement chasm created by limited state jurisdiction—simply does not apply to the conduct the Government seeks to reach here.

What Do *You* Think?

1. When you use the word *stolen*, what do you mean by it?
2. Do you agree with the Court's interpretation of the word? Why or why not?

Additional Applications

Are photocopies of documents containing trade secrets "goods" under the National Stolen Property Act?

United States v. *Bottone*, 365 F.2d 389 (2d Cir. 1966)

The Case: After a jury trial in New York federal district court, Caesar Bottone and two co-defendants were convicted of transporting stolen goods in violation of 18 U.S.C. Section 2314 (the National Stolen Property Act [NSPA]). The convictions stemmed from the defendants' roles in an elaborate scheme to steal proprietary materials—both biological specimens and company documents detailing secret production processes—from a New York–based manufacturer of antibiotics and steroids. On appeal, the defendants challenged the applicability of the NSPA specifically to their theft of company documents. Their basic argument: the documents that they had moved across state lines were not "goods" under the NSPA because those documents were merely photocopies of company materials that, after a temporary removal to one of the defendant's homes for copying, had been returned to their original locations. Because no tangible company property had actually been "stolen," they asserted, the NSPA had not actually been violated.

The Finding: A panel of the U.S. Court of Appeals for the Second Circuit unanimously upheld the convictions and rejected the defendants' reading of Section 2314. "To be sure," the panel wrote, "where no tangible objects were ever taken or transported, a court would be hard pressed to conclude that 'goods' had been stolen and transported within the meaning of [the NSPA]." Indeed, the court continued, the NSPA would presumably not extend to a case "where a carefully guarded secret formula was memorized, carried away in the recesses of a thievish mind and placed in writing only after a boundary has been crossed." Yet in this case, "tangible goods [were] stolen and transported and the only obstacle to condemnation is a clever intermediate . . . use of a photocopy machine." When, as here, "the physical form of the stolen goods is secondary in every respect to the matter recorded in them, the transformation of the information in the stolen papers into a tangible object never possessed by the original owner should be deemed immaterial."

To rule otherwise, the panel concluded, would simply "offend common sense."

Are computer source codes "goods" under the National Stolen Property Act?

United States v. *Aleynikov*, 2012 U.S. App. LEXIS 7439 (2nd Cir. 2012)

The Case: In December 2010, Sergey Aleynikov, a former computer programmer for Goldman Sachs, was convicted in a New York federal district court for transporting stolen property in interstate commerce under 18 U.S.C. Section 2314. Federal prosecutors had charged Aleynikov with violating the NSPA by stealing and transferring approximately 500,000 lines of proprietary computer source code from Goldman Sachs' high-frequency trading system shortly before leaving for a rival firm. On his last day at Goldman Sachs, Aleynikov allegedly encrypted the code and uploaded it to a server in Germany; later, he downloaded it to his home computer and, eventually, copied it to a personally owned flash drive that he took to Chicago (the headquarters of his new employer). On appeal, Aleynikov argued that computer source code copied from Goldman Sachs' systems did not constitute a "good" within the meaning of the NSPA.

The Finding: In a unanimous April 2012 ruling, a three-judge panel of the U.S. Court of Appeals for the Second Circuit reversed Aleynikov's NSPA conviction. Writing for the court, Chief Judge Dennis Jacobs reasoned that Aleynikov "stole purely intangible property embodied in a purely intangible format"—which, following the Supreme Court's *Dowling* decision as well as *Bottone* (described earlier), meant that his conduct fell outside the NSPA's criminal prohibition. Aleynikov's theft of computer code was analogous to the infringement of copyright discussed in *Dowling*, Jacobs wrote. Consequently, charges under the NSPA could be sustained only if Aleynikov was shown to have "physically seized anything tangible from Goldman, such as a compact disc or thumb drive containing source code." Here, prosecutors never alleged that Aleynikov had "'assume[d] physical control' over anything;" consequently, by definition, Aleynikov "did not violate the NSPA."

---

the bulk. The owner of the goods, said the court, had entrusted the carrier with bales, but not with the content of those bales. Accordingly, breaking bulk was a misappropriation and constituted a trespassory taking of possession. The carrier was found guilty of larceny.

The "breaking bulk" doctrine was later expanded to cover situations in which the carrier or other bailee, such as a warehouse person, is given a quantity of bulk goods and appropriates some but not all of them. Some American jurisdictions continue to follow this doctrine, although others have enacted the statutory offense of larceny by bailee.

A trespassory taking can also be understood as a taking of possession, even when the thief does not take physical possession of the stolen merchandise. If, for example, a person out playing tennis finds an unattended tennis racket and offers to sell it to a passerby, he is still guilty of larceny if the passerby consummates the transaction and walks off with the racket. In such a case, the unwary purchaser assumes that the person offering to sell the racket is the lawful owner, and the thief need never touch the racket in order for it to be stolen. If, on the other hand, the legitimate owner of the tennis racket returns before it can be carried off by the purchaser, the defendant may be guilty of receiving money under false pretenses, although he could not be found guilty of larceny.

Other issues arise when a person finds lost or mislaid property. If a person takes the property and intends to keep it at the time it is carried away, he or she has committed a trespassory taking and is thus guilty of larceny. In 1997, for example, a Brinks armored truck overturned on Interstate 95 in the desperately poor Overtown section of Miami, Florida. The truck, loaded with an estimated $3.7 million, split open, dropping an unknown amount of money onto the highway and spilling dollar bills, quarters, and fifty-pound bags of money onto a street below the overpass on which the accident happened. Money floated into trees, covered the highway, and showered down onto people, cars, and houses. Those on the scene said it seemed to be raining money. "People walking by, people driving by, anybody that was a witness got money," said Florida Highway Patrol spokesperson Lieutenant Ernesto Duarte.[18] "Things like this don't happen very often, and people are going to try to take advantage," said Duarte. "It's funny, but it's dangerous. People jumped out of cars and grabbed bags full of money. Residents all got money." Police estimated that about $550,000 disappeared before police arrived on the scene.

In the Miami incident, the rightful owner of the spilled cash was clearly known to the people who picked it up. Hence those who took the money and kept it committed larceny. Miami Police Lieutenant Bill Schwartz put it concisely when he said, "The money does not belong to them. It is theft, whether you picked up a quarter or $100,000. Collecting the quarters, nickels, and dimes will be hard," said Schwartz. "But the big bills, we'll be counting on people's consciences."[19] The detective also noted that previously poor people found suddenly "strutting the street with wads of cash" could be investigated.

On the other hand, if a finder of lost property does not know who the owner is and has no reason to believe that he or she can find the property's owner, then the finder may legally be considered the new owner of the property. If a person finds lost property, he or she may take possession of the lost item without incurring criminal liability if he or she intends to return it to the rightful owner. Hence a person who discovers a lost wallet may lawfully take the wallet home with him if he intends to call the local "lost and found" bureau (or other authority) and to return the wallet and all of its contents to its lawful owner.

Similar rules apply to one to whom property has been delivered by mistake; that is, a defendant who receives misdelivered property has a duty to return it and has no right to keep what was not intended for him. A person who receives misdelivered property is guilty of larceny if he or she realizes the mistake and intends to keep the property. Under the Model Penal Code, however, and the laws of some states, a defendant's intent at the time he or she receives the property is irrelevant, and the defendant becomes liable for theft if he or she, with the purpose of depriving the owner thereof, fails to take reasonable measures to restore the property to the person entitled to it.[20]

asportation
The trespassory taking and carrying away (as of personal property in the crime of larceny or of the victim in kidnapping).

Carrying Away In most jurisdictions, to constitute larceny, the property that is "taken" must be "carried away." The technical term for "carrying away" is **asportation**. Even the slightest movement of an object, if done in a "carrying-away" manner, is sufficient to constitute asportation.[21]

Objects may, however, be moved in a manner other than one consistent with a carrying away of those items. Jewelry on a jewelry counter, for example, might be picked up, turned over for examination, and even tried on without carrying-away movements. As soon as the object is concealed, however, as in the case of shoplifters who "palm" small items by hiding them in their closed hands, a carrying-away movement can be said to have occurred. Similarly, a fallen bicycle may be picked up off the ground, righted, and moved back into a bicycle stand by a good Samaritan. If the person mounts the bicycle and begins to ride off, however, a carrying-away movement occurs.

In many jurisdictions, the asportation requirement is viewed merely as a means of ensuring that the defendant had dominion and control over the property in question. If, for example, a thief puts his hand into the pocket of an intended victim and begins to lift the victim's wallet, asportation sufficient for prosecution has occurred even though the wallet is not completely removed from the victim's pocket.

Some jurisdictions have eliminated the requirement that an object be "carried away" for a charge of larceny to be brought. The unlawful taking of the property of another with intent to steal constitutes larceny in those jurisdictions. Carrying away may not occur, for example, in cases of misdelivery, as when furniture is delivered to the wrong address. In such a case, accepting delivery of misdelivered property may involve no physical movement of the property beyond the placement of the furniture by delivery people. In such cases, larceny could still be said to have occurred without the need for legal fictions in support of the carrying away requirement.

Property of Another   Larceny can only be committed against a person who has possession of the property in question. It is sometimes said that a person cannot be convicted of larceny if the property he or she carried away was his or her own. It is important, however, to draw distinctions between the concepts of (1) ownership, (2) possession, and (3) custody. Because the crime of larceny builds on possession rather than ownership, it is possible, in at least some jurisdictions, for the rightful owner of property to unlawfully steal his or her own property when it is in the temporary possession or custody of another. As one court put it: "The phrase 'of another' in the definition of larceny has reference to possession rather than to title or ownership. . . . Even the owner himself may commit larceny by stealing his own goods if they are in the possession of another and he takes them from the possessor wrongfully with intent to deprive him of a property interest therein."[22]

When a demand of return is made, of course, property must be returned to its rightful owner unless some other condition exists that would lawfully preclude such a return. Conditions barring return of property might include a lien on the property, a contract granting possession of the property to another person for a specified period of time, or the fact that the property has been pawned or that it has been repaired and an outstanding repair bill must still be paid. A person who owns a car may, for example, sign a rental contract whereby he agrees to temporarily relinquish possession of the vehicle. If the owner then secretly steals the vehicle back when the renter is asleep, he may be guilty of larceny.

Property that is free and clear of all attachments, however, may still be stolen by its rightful owner if it is in the possession of another. Imagine, for example, that the owner of some property—say, gold jewelry—entrusts it into the care of another for safekeeping. If the owner were then to enter the place where the jewelry was being stored and secretly remove it (in order, perhaps, to later file a fraudulent insurance claim), the owner would then be guilty of larceny because she had unlawfully taken the property from another's possession.

Custody over an item is not the same thing as ownership or possession. A person who owns something may legally possess it but may also relinquish custody of it temporarily. A woman who hands her purse to a man, asking him to hold it while she goes on a ride at an amusement park, for example, has relinquished custody of her purse but is still the owner and maintains possession from a legal point of view. If she asks the man to hold her purse for safekeeping while she vacations for a few weeks, the man may be said to have both custody of the purse and temporary possession of it. He is still not the purse's owner, however. Assuming that the man complies with the woman's wishes and returns the purse when asked, no legal issues arise. If, however, he sells the purse to another or gives it to his wife as a present, he has taken possession of it and has misappropriated it. Even so, he is still not the lawful owner of the purse, nor is his wife.

Under common law, a defendant who was a co-owner of the taken property could not be found guilty of larceny. A few jurisdictions, however, have changed this rule by statute.

Intent to Steal   Larceny is a crime that can only be committed intentionally. It cannot be committed negligently or recklessly. If, for example, a defendant picks up a notebook computer on an airport luggage return rack, thinking that it is hers, and walks off with it, she is not guilty of larceny. An unreasonable, but honest, belief in ownership or right to possession is sufficient to constitute a valid defense to larceny. Such a defense is called the **claim of right** and is recognized in most jurisdictions.

claim of right
A defense against a charge of larceny that consists of an honest belief in ownership or right to possession.

The "intent to steal" element of the crime of larceny is sometimes said to mean that the offender intends to permanently dispossess the rightful owner of the property in question. It would, however, be more accurate to say that the offender intends to wrongfully deprive one who lawfully has possession of an item (even though he or she may not be the owner) to the continued useful possession of that item. So, for example, a man could not be charged with larceny if he "borrows" a tie he finds on a restaurant coat stand upon learning that the restaurant has a dress code and then returns the tie when leaving the restaurant.[23] On the other hand, one who "borrows" a full can of paint and later returns it empty is guilty of larceny because he or she has deprived the legitimate owner of the value that had been inherent in the paint contained within the can.

The requirement of "intent to steal" of the crime of larceny often makes it difficult to obtain larceny convictions in joyriding situations because the "stolen" vehicle is only "borrowed" and may be returned even before the owner notices that it is missing. Accordingly, most jurisdictions have statutorily created the crime of joyriding, which involves the unauthorized use of a motor vehicle, even when no "intent to steal"—in the sense of permanently depriving the rightful owner of possession of the vehicle—can be demonstrated. The Model Penal Code, for example, provides that a person commits a misdemeanor if he or she operates another's automobile, airplane, motorcycle, or other motor-propelled vehicle without the consent of the owner.[24]

Embezzlement

embezzlement
The misappropriation of property already in the possession of the defendant. Also, the unlawful conversion of the personal property of another by a person to whom it has been entrusted by (or for) its rightful owner.

conversion
The unauthorized assumption of the right of ownership. Conversion is a central feature of the crime of embezzlement, as in the unlawful *conversion* of the personal property of another, by a person to whom it has been entrusted.

As mentioned earlier, larceny requires a trespassory *taking* of another's property. Under some circumstances, however, property may be misappropriated without the need for trespassory taking. **Embezzlement** is the unlawful conversion of the personal property of another by a person to whom it has been entrusted by, or for, its rightful owner. Embezzlement is fundamentally a violation of trust. Because an embezzler already has lawful possession of the property in question, embezzlement is not a crime against possession but one against ownership. The central feature of the crime of embezzlement is unlawful **conversion**. Although the original "taking" of possession occurs legally, embezzled property is converted to an unauthorized use. If, for example, a woman's employer gives her money to take to the bank for deposit into the company's account, but the employee takes the money and spends it instead, she is guilty of embezzlement. One can be guilty of embezzlement only if the embezzled property belongs to another, as transferring ownership of an item to one who already owns it is not a crime. In some jurisdictions, embezzlement is known as *fraudulent conversion* because it involves the misappropriation of property entrusted to one's care (Figure 9–1).

To be able to embezzle, an employee must occupy a position of financial trust and must be sufficiently familiar with company procedures to steal and to cover up his or her wrongdoings. As a consequence, most embezzlers appear to be law-abiding citizens until they are discovered. Embezzlers are sometimes called *white-collar criminals* because of the relatively prestigious positions they often occupy within the business world. Criminologists sometimes say that embezzlement is a crime that takes place where there is a meeting of desire and opportunity. Donald Cressy, for example, observed that most embezzlers are average middle-class employees, but that there are four events that may coalesce and lead them to steal from their employers and violate the financial trust placed in them:[25]

1. The embezzler-to-be is placed in a position of financial trust, and he or she accepts this position with no intention of using it to steal.

2. The embezzler-to-be develops a personal problem that he or she is too embarrassed to share with anyone and that appears to be solvable by obtaining extra money.

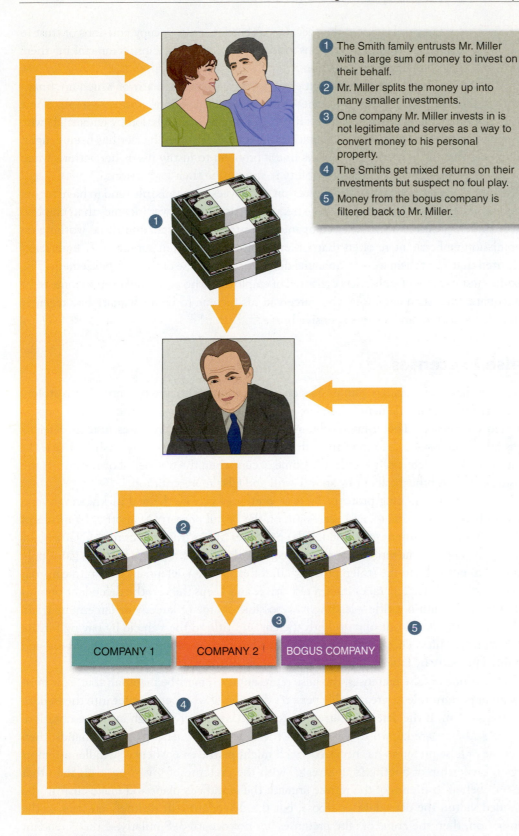

FIGURE 9–1

Embezzlement.

1. The Smith family entrusts Mr. Miller with a large sum of money to invest on their behalf.
2. Mr. Miller splits the money up into many smaller investments.
3. One company Mr. Miller invests in is not legitimate and serves as a way to convert money to his personal property.
4. The Smiths get mixed returns on their investments but suspect no foul play.
5. Money from the bogus company is filtered back to Mr. Miller.

COMPANY 1   COMPANY 2   BOGUS COMPANY

3. The embezzler-to-be develops technical skills relating to his or her position and in that learning process discovers the methods needed to secretly violate the trust placed in him or her.

4. The embezzler-to-be acquires the mind-set that justifies embezzlement. Embezzlers routinely rationalize their conduct in order to maintain their self-image of being a trusted person. The embezzler may, for example, consider the embezzlement a form of borrowing or a temporary taking of the money. Many embezzlers fully intend to return the money "someday."

The rise of computer crime and armed robbery has not eliminated the lure of caged cash.

—Technology writer James Chiles

Cressy also noted that because embezzlers must occupy positions of trust in order to steal, their positions insulate them from suspicion, often making them feel immune from detection.

Cressy's critics note that everyone has problems, many of which are financial, and that not everyone—even those in positions of trust—steals. Some critics note that the personal problems cited as leading to law violation by embezzlers who are apprehended may merely be explanations offered after the embezzler has been caught. Others say that an embezzler will always find a problem to justify his or her actions when caught because people have a natural ability to rationalize their bad actions.

Research on embezzlement cases shows that employees who embezzle tend to have higher levels of indebtedness, change jobs more frequently, and have lower incomes than employees in similar positions with other companies. Contract employees and those working on commission embezzle more often than other employees. A recent survey of 97 embezzlers indicated that 75 of them were in financial difficulty at the time of their embezzlement. The next highest number of embezzlers consisted of employees who perceived their income to be inadequate. One such employee who perceived his income to be inadequate had recently purchased a Lear jet and a very expensive home.[26]

False Pretenses

false pretenses
Knowingly and unlawfully obtaining title to, and possession of, the lawful property of another by means of deception and with intent to defraud. Also called *obtaining property by false pretenses.*

In cases of larceny, offenders gain possession of, but not title to, the property that is stolen. In the crime of embezzlement, offenders gain ownership of property they already possess through conversion. The crime of obtaining property by false pretenses, usually referred to as **false pretenses**, is a form of theft that also involves transfer of ownership or title. In contrast to embezzlement, however, the crime occurs when the transfer of ownership or the passing of title is brought about by an unlawful and false representation.

The crime of obtaining property by false pretenses can be defined as knowingly and unlawfully obtaining title to, and possession of, the lawful property of another by means of deception and with intent to defraud. False pretenses differs from the crime of "larceny by trick" (existent in some jurisdictions), in which the defendant, through trickery, gains only possession, not title, to the stolen property. If, for example, a defendant obtains a car from an automobile dealership, takes it for a test-drive, and keeps the car, the defendant obtains only possession and not title—leading to a possible charge of larceny or larceny by trick. If, however, the defendant obtains both the car and title to the vehicle by paying for the car with a worthless check, then the defendant has both committed a check offense and obtained property by false pretenses.

In the crime of false pretenses, the false representation must be material; that is, it must play an important role in a reasonable person's decision of whether to enter into the fraudulent transaction. If the defendant attempts to deceive another through misrepresentation, but the real facts are known to the other at the time that ownership changes hands, then no crime of false pretenses has occurred. Such might be the case where a swindler attempts to gain ownership of a retiree's "nest egg," with the pretense of investing it on the other person's behalf. If friends of the retiree unmask the swindler's plans and make clear to the intended victim the defendant's purpose, but the defendant still willingly engages in the transaction, then the crime of false pretenses has not occurred. Similarly, if the defendant attempts to swindle another but fails, then he or she might be guilty of an *attempt* to gain property by false pretenses but not of the crime itself.

Although misrepresentation is often made orally or in writing, it is also possible to misrepresent oneself and the facts surrounding a transaction merely by keeping quiet. Hence if an offender says something without intending to mislead another but is misunderstood, then he or she may be found guilty of false pretenses if the misunderstanding results in a transfer of ownership of something of value *and* the transfer was facilitated by the defendant's silence and failure to correct the misunderstanding. Finally, it is not an indictable offense for a person to use misrepresentation to obtain payments or property that is already due to him or her. So, for example, a person to whom a debt is owed may use deceit to obtain payment without violating any law.

As noted earlier, for the crime of false pretenses to be committed, title must also pass to the defendant. If sale of the property occurs, then title has passed. If the property is merely loaned or leased to the defendant, there has been no passing of title. An exception to this general rule exists where money is involved. When an individual loans money to another person because of false representation, it is generally not expected that the *same* money will be returned, and the crime of false pretenses may be charged.[27]

The three most common defenses to false pretenses are that (1) the victim was too gullible and should have been more wary, (2) the victim suffered no pecuniary (monetary) loss, and (3) there was no intent to defraud. In a few cases, the defendants argued that the representation, although false, was one that would not have deceived an ordinarily intelligent person. Most jurisdictions do not recognize such a defense, however, on the theory that one of the purposes of criminal law is to protect those who cannot protect themselves. Most jurisdictions also do not recognize the defense of no pecuniary loss.

If the defendant believes that his or her representation is true, he or she cannot be convicted of false pretenses even if the belief is unreasonable in the eyes of others. Accordingly, to constitute the crime of false pretenses there must an intentional deception. A false representation, however, may be made by a person who makes a statement alleging that a certain fact is true, when he or she does not know whether the statement is, in fact, true.

Forgery

The legal principles underlying the crime of false pretenses extend to many other illegal activities, including the writing of bad checks, credit card fraud, the unlawful altering of wills, counterfeiting, and any other crimes through which ownership of property is obtained by fraud. Some of these crimes, however, have been separately codified by legislative action and are worthy of separate mention.

One such offense is forgery. **Forgery** is the making of a false written instrument or the material alteration of an existing genuine written instrument. Forgery is complete when the perpetrator either makes or passes a false instrument with intent to defraud. The gist of the crime of forgery is the actual intent to defraud, and the act of defrauding is itself not required. The common law crime of forgery, however, included the act of "uttering" a forged document, and the crime was sometimes referred to as *forgery and uttering*. **Uttering** is the offering, passing, or attempted passing of a forged document with knowledge that the document is false and with intent to defraud. Today, most jurisdictions have established a separate statutory crime of uttering a forged document.[28]

> **forgery**
> The making of a false written instrument or the material alteration of an existing genuine written instrument.

> **uttering**
> The offering, passing, or attempted passing of a forged instrument with knowledge that the document is false and with intent to defraud.

The elements of forgery are

- A false signature or material alteration
- Signed or altered without authority
- Of a writing or other instrument that, if genuine, would have legal significance
- With intent to defraud

The elements of the crime of uttering, passing, publishing, or attempting to pass are

- Possession or creation of a forged document that, if genuine, would have legal significance
- Uttering, passing, publishing, or attempting to pass the forged document
- With intent to defraud

For an instrument to be subject to forgery, the instrument, were it to be genuine, must create some legal right or obligation with apparent legal significance. If the instrument has no legal significance, then it is not subject to forgery. Instruments said to have legal significance include checks, wills, college transcripts, college diplomas, insurance proof-of-loss forms, divorce decrees, badges, stamps, credit cards, credit card receipts, and trademarks.

A genuine document that has been materially altered is also considered to be a forged document. To constitute forgery, however, the alteration must be material and unauthorized. Changing the date on a check that has already been issued, for example, would not be a material alteration unless the change in date had some legal significance. To have legal significance, the alteration must result in some material change in the rights and obligations of the parties involved. If the document is only partially completed, for example, the completion of the document may be forgery if completed in an unauthorized manner. Filling the date in on a check that had been issued undated normally would not be forgery, nor would writing the correct amount on a signed but uncompleted charge card receipt left behind at the place of purchase. Modifying the amount for which a check has been written (for example, by adding extra zeros) or altering a charge card receipt before submitting it for payment (for example, adding a tip to a receipt that is untotaled) would be forgery if the action is secretly done and is unauthorized.

In cases involving forgery of a signature, the prosecution must establish that the defendant lacked the authority to sign the other person's name. Authority to sign may be implied from prior transactions. If, for example, one spouse regularly picks up the other spouse's paychecks, forges the spouse's name on the checks, and cashes them, authority to sign might be implied by past actions, and there would be no forgery. There are, however, situations in which people commit forgery even when they sign their own names to documents. If someone receives a check made out in his name but he knows that the check was intended for another person by the same name, he commits forgery when he signs his name to the check and cashes it (uttering).

criminal simulation
The making of a false document or object that does not have any apparent legal significance.

Many jurisdictions have enacted the statutory crime of **criminal simulation**.[29] Criminal simulation is different from forgery in that the item or document falsified need not have any apparent legal significance. Making a piece of furniture to pass off as an antique, for example, constitutes the crime of criminal simulation. Criminal simulation, like forgery, requires an intent to defraud or harm another. It is generally a misdemeanor.

Laws against forgery and against criminal simulation are now undergoing sweeping changes as jurisdictions modify existing laws to keep pace with the creation of valuable electronic documents. Such documents, which may never be printed on paper, provide for critically needed authentication and identification during financial and other transactions conducted via computer and over telephone and radio communications. Emerging laws of relevance to such activities are discussed later in this chapter.

Receiving Stolen Property

receiving stolen property
(1) Knowingly taking possession of or control over property that has been unlawfully stolen from another. (2) Accepting property that the receiver knew was stolen or that he or she should have known was stolen.

Receiving stolen property is another form of theft. **Receiving stolen property** can be defined as knowingly taking possession of, or control over, property that has been unlawfully stolen from another. *Receiving*, for purposes of the law, means taking possession of, acquiring control over, or taking title to any property.

Under early common law, receiving stolen property was not a crime. Later, English statutes provided for accomplice liability for the act of receiving stolen property. It wasn't until 1827, however, that an English statute was passed making the receiving of stolen property a separate offense. Today, all American jurisdictions have the statutory crime of receiving stolen property, although in some jurisdictions, it is combined under a general theft statute. There are four elements to the crime of receiving stolen property:[30]

- Receiving
- Stolen property
- Which the receiver knew was stolen
- Where the property was received with the intent to deprive the rightful owner of its possession

If the property in question has not been stolen, then the crime of receiving stolen property cannot take place. Property that has been stolen and recovered can no longer be considered stolen property. If law enforcement officers recover stolen property and then attempt to entrap a person into receiving stolen property by selling it or delivering it to him or her, the crime of receiving stolen property cannot be charged. This conclusion is based on the principle that once property has been recovered by lawful authorities, it is no longer stolen.

Similarly, in almost all jurisdictions, the crime of receiving stolen property requires that the defendant know that the property was stolen. Such knowledge may be established by circumstantial evidence, as when a defendant pays an unreasonably low price for the merchandise. In a few jurisdictions, it is sufficient to show that a defendant should have been aware that there was a likelihood that the property in question was stolen (perhaps because the price asked for the item was unreasonably low), and he or she made no efforts to verify ownership. Under such circumstances the person buying the item would not be merely an innocent purchaser in the eyes of the law.

The crime of receiving stolen property is different from the theft of the property itself, and a defendant who steals property cannot be convicted of receiving the same property; that is to say, a thief cannot receive stolen property from him- or herself.[31]

Robbery

The Federal Bureau of Investigation (FBI) classifies robbery as a violent personal crime. We classify it here as a property crime, rather than as a personal crime, because the *object* of robbery is the unlawful acquisition of property, even though the property may be forcefully taken from the personal possession of another. **Robbery** is the unlawful taking of property that is in the immediate possession of another by force or threat of force. Because an "unlawful taking" constitutes larceny, robbery can also be defined as a form of larceny, or as larceny from a person by violence, intimidation, or placing the person in fear. From another point of view, robbery is simply an aggravated form of larceny, and in addition to the elements necessary to constitute larceny, the crime of robbery requires two more features: (1) that the property be taken from a person or removed from the victim's presence and (2) that the taking occur through the use of force or by putting the victim in fear. As the last element indicates, actual force need not be used, and the threatened use of force suffices to constitute robbery. Hence the elements of the crime of robbery are

robbery
The unlawful taking of property that is in the immediate possession of another by force or by threat of force. Also, larceny from a person by violence or intimidation or by placing the person in fear.

- The felonious taking of personal property
- From the person or immediate presence of another
- Against the will of the victim
- And accomplished by means of force or by putting the victim in fear

Some crimes, such as pocket picking and purse snatching, also involve the unlawful taking of property from the immediate possession of another person. They are crimes of larceny, however, and not robbery, because the stolen property is taken before the victim is aware of what is happening. No violence or intimidation is used in committing such crimes. If a purse snatcher or pickpocket misses the target on the first "grab," however, and a struggle ensues before the purse or wallet is taken, then the offender is guilty of robbery.

In cases of robbery, it is generally easy to establish that property has been taken *from a person*—as happens in instances of armed robbery, where the robber demands a person's wallet or jewelry that he or she is wearing. Problems arise, however, when property is not taken from a person but is merely removed *from the presence of the victim*. The test to determine if the property is taken from the presence of the victim is whether the victim, at the time of the offense, was in a location where he or she could have prevented the taking had he or she not been intimidated or forcibly restrained from doing so.

When property is stolen from a person who is unconscious or dead, the crime is larceny rather than robbery because no force is used and the "victim" is not threatened. If, however, the person from whom valuables are stolen is unconscious, and if the cause of unconsciousness was some intentional action on the part of the thief, then most courts would hold that robbery has occurred. On the other hand, if the person is in a state of voluntarily self-induced unconsciousness (as might happen with one who drinks too much), then stealing property from his or her person would likely be larceny, not robbery. Courts have also held that one who kills another and then steals possessions from the deceased's body is guilty of robbery (as well as murder) if the passage of time between the killing and the robbery is not substantial. A murderer who returns to an undiscovered corpse a week after the killing, however, and steals items from the body of the victim would be committing larceny and not robbery.

It is important to note that robbery, in most jurisdictions, requires either using or threatening to use force *or* putting the victim in fear. One or the other will suffice. *Fear* means "intimidation." Some states use an objective standard to determine whether intimidation occurred; they ask whether the circumstances would have induced fear in the mind of a reasonable person. Other states use a subjective standard; they ask whether the person robbed actually experienced fear. Accordingly, in such jurisdictions, if the victim is unusually timid, robbery can occur even though the average person would not have felt apprehensive under similar circumstances.

Most jurisdictions recognize various degrees of robbery. First-degree robbery, for example, may be armed robbery—that is, robbery committed with the use of a dangerous or deadly weapon or robbery in which the victim is seriously injured. First-degree robbery is sometimes termed *aggravated robbery*. Second-degree robbery, sometimes called *strong-arm robbery*, may be robbery in which no weapon is used or where the victim is not seriously injured. Some states, like New York, make even finer distinctions and have three or more degrees of robbery defined by statute.

In deciding what degree of robbery a defendant can be charged with, it is important to know (1) what constitutes a deadly weapon and (2) what constitutes a serious injury. *Serious bodily injury* has often been interpreted to mean an injury that requires medical treatment. The definition of a *deadly weapon* has proved more complex. Some state statutes specify that armed robbery is any robbery committed with a firearm, making the definition of a deadly weapon relatively straightforward. Most statutes, however, avoid use of the term *firearm* and refer instead to *deadly weapon* or *dangerous weapon*. The dangerousness (or deadliness) of weapons has often been assessed on the basis of their construction and purpose, as well as the use to which they are put during the offense. Hence guns, knives, screwdrivers, hammers, axes, clubs, sticks, and even dogs and high-heeled shoes and boots have been found to be deadly weapons within the meaning of robbery statutes. Some courts have gone so far as to conclude that a deadly weapon is anything that appears to be such from the point of view of the victim, meaning that even toy guns (and, in at least one case, a hairbrush hidden in a robber's pocket and held to look like a gun) can meet the criteria for a deadly weapon. Finally, some courts have found that a robber in possession of a deadly weapon at the time of the robbery, such as a gun or a knife, has committed armed robbery even though the weapon remained concealed and was never brought to the attention of the victim.

Extortion

Some years ago, Vermont attorney John Harrington threatened to accuse Armand Morin of adultery unless Morin paid $175,000. At the time of the threat, Harrington represented Morin's wife in divorce proceedings. Upon learning from Mrs. Morin that Mr. Morin routinely engaged in sexual relations with women staying alone at the couple's motel, Harrington arranged for a woman named Mrs. Mazza to register at Morin's motel and approach him in a friendly manner. Mrs. Mazza was instructed by the attorney to be "receptive and available," but not aggressive, so as to avoid any claims of entrapment. Shortly after she registered, Mr. Morin went to Mrs. Mazza's motel room. An hour later, attorney Harrington and a private investigator burst into the room and photographed Mr. Morin and Mrs. Mazza together in bed naked. Conversation between the two had also been secretly recorded by Mrs. Mazza and was later turned over to the attorney.

Armed with photographs and the recorded conversation, Harrington sent a letter to Mr. Morin marked "personal and confidential," in which he proposed that his client would waive all alimony proceedings on receipt of $175,000. The letter also included a compromising photo showing Mr. Morin with Mrs. Mazza. Morin took the letter to the police, who then arrested the attorney and charged him with extortion. The relevant Vermont statute provided that a "person who maliciously threatens to accuse another of a crime or offense, or with an injury to his person or property, with intent to extort money or other pecuniary advantage, or with intent to compel the person so threatened to do an act against his will," is guilty of extortion. At trial, Harrington argued that he had been acting merely as an attorney, attempting to secure a divorce for his client "on the most favorable terms possible." Nonetheless, a jury found him guilty of extortion.

Harrington appealed, but the appellate court upheld his conviction, ruling that the attorney had threatened to accuse Morin of the *crime* of adultery—rather than attempting simply to negotiate a divorce settlement—thereby bringing his behavior under the purview of the state's extortion statute. In the words of the appellate court: "A demand for settlement of a civil action, accompanied by a malicious threat to expose the wrongdoer's criminal conduct, if made with intent to extort payment against his will, constitutes the crime alleged in the indictment."[32]

Under early common law, **extortion** was the corrupt collection of an unlawful fee by a public officer under color of office or the attempt to collect such a fee. It was then a misdemeanor. Today, almost all American jurisdictions have expanded the crime of extortion via statute to cover anyone who uses the threat of future actions to wrongfully obtain property, services, or the relinquishment of another's right to something. Hence the contemporary crime of extortion can be defined as the taking of personal property by a threat of future harm. Statutory extortion is a felony in most jurisdictions.

Extortion differs from the crime of robbery in that robbery occurs when property is taken by force or threat of immediate violence. In extortion, the defendant obtains property by threat of *future* violence. The threat of violence can be to cause physical harm to the victim or to others whom the victim values. Some jurisdictions allow the threatened harm to extend to various other forms of injury, as in Vermont, where the threatened accusation of a crime will suffice. **Blackmail** is a form of extortion in which a threat is made to disclose a crime or other social disgrace. Even a threat to cause economic injury or social embarrassment may be sufficient to constitute extortion in most jurisdictions. A threat to bring a lawsuit or to take other official action, unless the property is given or returned to the defendant, may also constitute extortion. It is a defense under such circumstances, however, if

extortion
The taking of personal property by threat of future harm.

blackmail
A form of extortion in which a threat is made to disclose a crime or other social disgrace.

the defendant honestly and lawfully claimed the property as restitution or indemnification for harm done, to which the lawsuit or other official action relates, or as compensation for property or other lawful services.[33]

Jurisdictions differ as to whether property must actually be received in order to complete the crime of extortion. In some states, such as Kentucky, the uttering or issuing of the threat itself completes the offense. In others, the crime is not considered complete until the offender receives the property—although he or she may be charged with attempted extortion or an attempt to extort.

It is worthwhile to note that extortion differs from the offense of **compounding a crime**, also known as *compounding a felony*, which "consists of the receipt of property or other valuable consideration in exchange for an agreement to conceal or not prosecute one who has committed a crime."[34] Compounding usually involves a mutual agreement between parties, whereas extortion is based on a qualified threat.

compounding a crime
The receipt of property or other valuable consideration in exchange for agreeing to conceal or not prosecute one who has committed a crime.[i] Also called *compounding a felony*.

Identity Theft: A Twenty-First-Century Version of Theft

In July 2000, California Attorney General Bill Lockyer announced the arrest of six individuals for an alleged Medi-Cal fraud ring that bilked the state out of more than $1.39 million. A criminal complaint filed in Los Angeles County Superior Court accused the defendants of illegally obtaining physicians' medical licenses and other personal identification from Los Angeles–area hospitals. The defendants were also accused of submitting fraudulent applications to the California Department of Health Services to request the Medi-Cal provider numbers needed to bill the state's Medi-Cal program. The defendants allegedly later obtained names and identifying information for several thousand hospital patients who were Medi-Cal beneficiaries without the knowledge or consent of the hospitals or the patients involved. According to Lockyer, the defendants then submitted fraudulent Medi-Cal claims representing that the victimized doctors had rendered services to these patients.

To mask their operations, the defendants allegedly established phony businesses and used mail drops to receive state checks (known in California as state "warrants"). Finally, using bogus identification, the defendants apparently opened bank accounts in the doctors' names and cashed the checks.[35]

identity theft
The unauthorized use of another individual's personal identity to fraudulently obtain money, goods, or services; to avoid the payment of debt; or to avoid criminal prosecution.

Identity theft is rapidly becoming the most important new theft crime of the twenty-first century. It can be defined as the unauthorized use of another individual's personal identity to fraudulently obtain money, goods, or services; to avoid the payment of debt; or to avoid criminal prosecution.

At the federal level, the Federal Trade Commission (FTC) runs a clearinghouse for complaints by victims of identity theft. Although the FTC does not have the authority to bring criminal cases, the commission provides victims of identity theft with information to help them resolve the financial and other problems that can result from such illegal activity. The FTC may also refer victim complaints to other appropriate government agencies and private organizations for action.

According to the FTC, many people have confronted, directly or through a third person, some form of identity theft.[36] Someone either has used their name to open up a credit card account or has used their identifying information—name, Social Security number, mother's maiden name, or other personal information—to commit fraud or to engage in other unlawful activities.

Other common forms of identity theft include taking over an existing credit card account and making unauthorized charges to it (typically, the identity thief forestalls discovery by the victim by contacting the credit card issuer and changing the billing address on the account), taking out loans in another person's name, writing fraudulent checks using another person's name or account number, and using personal information to access and transfer money out of another person's bank or brokerage account. In extreme cases, the identity thief may completely take over the victim's identity—opening a bank account, getting multiple credit cards, buying a car, getting a home mortgage, and even working under the victim's assumed name.

The FTC says that identity theft can be perpetrated based on simple low-tech practices, such as stealing someone's mail or "dumpster diving" through his or her trash to collect credit card offers or to obtain identifying information such as account numbers or Social Security numbers. Far more sophisticated practices are sometimes used, however. In a practice known as *skimming*, identity thieves use computers to read and store the information encoded on the magnetic strip of an ATM or credit card when that card is inserted through either a specialized card reader or a legitimate payment mechanism. Once stored, the information can be reencoded onto any other card with a magnetic strip, instantly transforming a blank card into a machine-readable ATM or credit card identical to that of the victim.[37]

The FTC also notes that the Internet has dramatically altered the potential impact of identity theft. Among other things, the Internet provides access to collections of identifying information gathered through both illicit and legal means. The global publication of identifying details, which were previously unavailable to most people, increases the potential misuse of that information. Similarly, the Internet expands exponentially the ability for a third party to disseminate the identifying information, making it available for others to exploit.[38]

In an effort to combat identity theft, the federal Identity Theft and Assumption Deterrence Act (also known as the *Identity Theft Act*)[39] was signed into law in 1998. The act, mentioned briefly at the start of this chapter, does not apply to thefts of less than $50,000. The act makes it a federal offense to knowingly transfer or use, without lawful authority, a means of identification of another person with the intent to commit, or to aid or abet, any unlawful activity that constitutes a violation of federal law or that constitutes a felony under any applicable state or local law.[40] The statute further defines *means of identification* to include "any name or number that may be used, alone or in conjunction with any other information, to identify a specific individual," including, among other things, name, address, Social Security number, driver's license number, biometric data, access devices (for example, credit cards), electronic identification number or routing code, and telecommunications identifying information. Under the law, a conviction for identity theft carries a maximum penalty of 15 years' imprisonment and a possible fine and forfeiture of any personal property used or intended to be used to commit the crime. The states also have statutes criminalizing identity theft. Following are three examples of identity theft statutes from Arizona, Connecticut, and New York. New York's statute is more detailed than the other two. Is there a practical or legal difference among them?

ARIZONA CRIMINAL CODE

Section 2708. Taking identity of another person; classification.

(a) A person commits taking the identity of another person if the person knowingly takes the name, birth date or Social Security number of another person, without the consent of that other person, with the intent to obtain or use the other person's identity for any unlawful purpose or to cause loss to a person.

(b) Taking the identity of another person is a class 5 felony.

CONNECTICUT PUBLIC ACT NO. 99-99

(a) A person is guilty of identity theft when such person intentionally obtains personal identifying information of another person without the authorization of such other person and uses that information for any unlawful purpose including, but not limited to, obtaining, or attempting to obtain, credit, goods, services or medical information in the name of such other person without the consent of such other person. As used in this section, "personal identifying information" means a motor vehicle operator's license number, Social Security number, employee identification number, mother's maiden name, demand deposit number, savings account number or credit card number.

(b) Identity theft is a class D felony.

NEW YORK PENAL LAW CHAPTER 619 (A.4939)

A person is guilty of identity theft in the third degree when he or she knowingly and with intent to defraud assumes the identity of another person by presenting himself or herself as that other person, or by acting as that other person or by using personal identifying information of that other person, and thereby:

In the third degree (Penal Law § 190.78)

1. Obtains goods, money, property or services or uses credit in the name of such other person or causes financial loss to such person or another person; or

2. Commits a Class A misdemeanor or higher level crime.

(Class A misdemeanor)

In the second degree (Penal Law § 190.79)

1. Obtains goods, money, property or services or uses credit in the name of such other person in an aggregate amount that exceeds five hundred dollars; or

2. Causes financial loss to such person or to another person or persons in an aggregate amount that exceeds five hundred dollars; or

3. Commits or attempts to commit a felony or acts as an accessory to the commission of a felony; or

4. Commits the crime of identity theft in the third degree as defined in section 190.78 of this article and has been previously convicted within the last five years of identity theft in the first, second or third degrees, unlawful possession of personal identification information in the first, second or third degrees, or grand larceny in the first, second, third or fourth degrees.

(Class E felony)

In the first degree (Penal Law § 190.80)

1. Obtains goods, money, property or services or uses credit in the name of such other person in an aggregate amount that exceeds two thousand dollars; or

2. Causes financial loss to such person or to another person or persons in an aggregate amount that exceeds two thousand dollars; or

3. Commits or attempts to commit a Class D felony or higher level crime or acts as an accessory in the commission of a class D or higher level felony; or

4. Commits the crime of identity theft in the second degree as defined in section 190.79 of this article and has been previously convicted within the last five years of identity theft in the first, second or third degrees or unlawful possession of personal identification information in the first, second or third degrees, or grand larceny in the first, second, or third degrees.

(Class D felony)

Schemes to commit identity theft may also run afoul of other federal statutes, including those relating to credit card fraud, computer fraud, mail fraud, wire fraud, financial institution fraud, or Social Security fraud. Each offense under these statutes is a federal felony and carries substantial penalties—in some cases as much as 30 years in prison, combined with possible fines and criminal forfeiture.

CONSOLIDATION OF THEFT CRIMES

Because of the complexities that can surround any given instance of theft, it has traditionally been difficult for prosecutors to know how to properly charge some defendants. The fine distinctions drawn by statutes, combined with the many statutory varieties of theft in some jurisdictions, have exacerbated the problem. As a result, suggestions arose by attorneys and legal scholars some years ago to consolidate the crimes of larceny, embezzlement, and false pretenses. The suggestions were based on the belief that the misappropriation of property by stealth, conversion, and deception represents different aspects of one general type of harm. The 1962 draft of the Model Penal Code (MPC) incorporated a consolidated theft provision (Section 223.1) that has since been adopted by many states. The MPC provision covers larceny, embezzlement, and false pretenses, as well as extortion, blackmail, and receiving stolen property. In effect, the MPC provision encompasses all nonviolent crimes involving the misappropriation of property, and places robbery (because it involves violence or the threat of violence) in a separate category.

Today, in recognition of the common principles underlying theft offenses, a fair number of jurisdictions, including New York, Texas, and California, have statutorily consolidated all or most common law theft crimes under one heading. As is the case with the Model Penal Code, such laws generally combine two or more of the crimes of larceny, embezzlement, extortion, receiving stolen property, and false pretenses into one crime called *theft* or, as in New York, *larceny*. The New York law, in contrast to the consolidated theft statutes of some other states, does not include the crime of receiving stolen property, although it does incorporate the offense of acquiring lost property.

GRADING OF THEFT CRIMES

As noted in an early chapter, some crimes (e.g., battery) may be punished differently depending on various factors. Sometimes these factors are written directly into the criminal code as variations in the name of the crime, the grade of the crime (e.g., felony, misdemeanor, infraction), and the punishment. For example, many states grade battery by the harm that is caused, by the status of the victim (e.g., a member of the public, a law enforcement officer), or another factor. Similarly, theft crimes are often graded by the value of the property that was stolen or embezzled. Theft statutes may also grade offenses by the nature of the property stolen.

The Model Penal Code, for example, incorporates both the value and the nature of the property into its grading scheme. It provides that theft of property valued at more than $500, or the theft of a firearm, car, airplane, motorcycle, or motorboat, is a felony of the third degree. Theft of property valued between $50 and $500 is a misdemeanor, and if less than $50, a petty misdemeanor. Although grading is common, the Model Penal Code's simplified grading scheme has not been widely adopted. State grading of theft crimes varies considerably. In addition to statutory grading, judges may consider the value of what is stolen, as well as other circumstances surrounding the crime, at sentencing. For example, if a state's theft laws grade thefts of property valued at $5,000 and greater as the highest form of theft with one to three years of possible imprisonment, a convictee who has stolen $5 million is far more likely to be sentenced at the high end of the range than an individual who is convicted of stealing $5,000, assuming all other factors are identical between the two convictees.

BURGLARY

Jerry Gonzales was dating Krissi Caldwell. Her parents did not approve, and he was not permitted in their home. The couple decided to kill her parents, and Caldwell let Gonzales into their home, where he shot both of her parents several times. The father survived, but the mother died. Gonzales was tried for the crime of murder committed in the course of committing a burglary. His attorney argued, in his defense, that the crime Gonzales committed was not burglary because the entry was made with Krissi Caldwell's consent.

Burglary is another wrongful acquisition crime directed against property. Burglary involves more than theft, however, and under common law it was considered to be a crime against habitation (or one's dwelling). Under common law, burglary consisted of the breaking and entering of the dwelling house of another at night with intent to commit a felony. In most jurisdictions today, however, the crime of **burglary** is statutorily defined as the

burglary
The breaking and entering of a building, locked automobile, boat, and so on, with the intent to commit a felony or theft. Also, the entering of a structure for the purposes of committing a felony or theft.

- Breaking
- And entering
- Of a building, locked automobile, boat, and so on
- With the intent to commit a felony or theft

Most jurisdictions divide the crime of burglary into burglary in the first and second degrees. Burglary in the first degree is burglary of an inhabited dwelling. All other burglaries are second-degree burglaries. Some jurisdictions maintain the nighttime distinction, classifying burglaries of inhabited dwellings that occur at night as more serious than other burglaries.

The "breaking" requirement does not necessitate any damage to the property burglarized, although it is usually interpreted as requiring the use of actual or constructive force to create an opening in the thing burglarized. The opening of any part of a structure with the slightest amount of force will suffice. Hence, whereas an entry through an already open door is not sufficient to meet the "breaking" requirement of burglary in most jurisdictions, the simple act of opening a closed door, even one that is unlocked, is sufficient. Many jurisdictions hold that the application of force to enlarge an already existing opening also satisfies the "breaking" requirement, whereas other jurisdictions hold that enlargement is not sufficient.[41] Some years ago, one court explained the amount of force necessary to constitute a breaking this way: "The gist of burglarious breaking is the application of force to remove some obstacle to entry, and the amount of force employed is not material. The exercise of the slightest force is sufficient. The breaking consists of the removal by the intruder, by the exercise of force, of an obstruction which, if left untouched, would prevent entrance. Hence, the application of force to push further open an already partly open door or window to enable a person to enter a room or building, is a breaking sufficient to constitute burglary if the other essential elements of the offense are present."[42] In other words, although a breaking needs only the tiniest physical force, the concept of breaking requires more than merely passing over or through an imaginary line or threshold separating one defined space from another (Figure 9–2).

Obtaining entry by fraud, by threatening to use force against another person, by entering through a chimney, and by having a co-conspirator open a door from within have all been held sufficient to constitute *constructive* breaking. Jurisdictions differ, however, on whether a defendant who has entered without a breaking—whether constructive or actual—commits the crime of burglary when he or she uses force to exit the structure—as when a person hides in a department store washroom before closing and breaks out of the store during the night with purloined merchandise. Most jurisdictions hold that the use of force merely to exit does not constitute burglary,[43] although a few follow an old common law rule that "breaking out of a building in making an exit is sufficient"[44] for the "breaking" requirement.

Generally speaking, breaking must be trespassory. Accordingly, a defendant who has permission to enter a structure cannot be found guilty of burglary in most jurisdictions.[45] Courts will examine any purported consent to determine whether the defendant in fact had permission to be on the premises at the time in question and to be in the particular part of the structure he or she entered. To constitute a defense, consent to enter must have been given by the owner of the structure entered or by a person legally authorized to act on

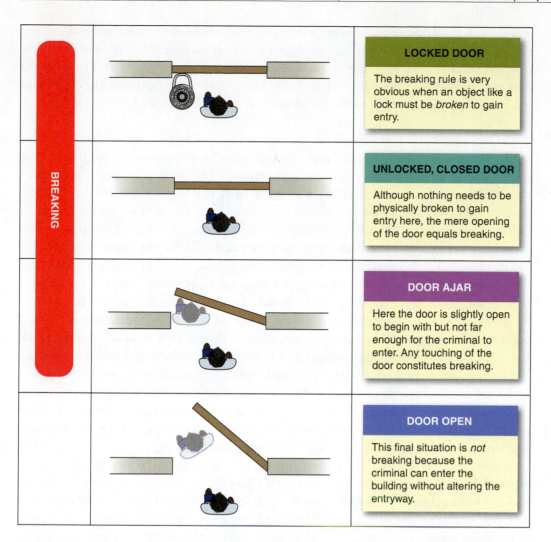

FIGURE 9–2

Defining "Breaking" in Terms of Burglary.

LOCKED DOOR

The breaking rule is very obvious when an object like a lock must be *broken* to gain entry.

UNLOCKED, CLOSED DOOR

Although nothing needs to be physically broken to gain entry here, the mere opening of the door equals breaking.

DOOR AJAR

Here the door is slightly open to begin with but not far enough for the criminal to enter. Any touching of the door constitutes breaking.

DOOR OPEN

This final situation is *not* breaking because the criminal can enter the building without altering the entryway.

behalf of the owner. Consent is not effective if given by a person the defendant knows is not legally authorized to provide it. In the *Gonzales* case, discussed earlier in this section, an appellate court held that Jerry Gonzales did not have effective consent to enter the Caldwell home and that a burglary charge (among other charges) was appropriate. The holding was based on the fact that Gonzales knew that Krissi Caldwell's parents did not want him in their home.[46]

In *Folsom* v. *State* (1995), which appears in a Capstone Case in this chapter, the question before the court was whether an estranged spouse's forcible entry into the marital home was trespassory.

In addition to breaking, an actual or constructive entry into the structure is required for a burglary to occur. The slightest intrusion by the burglar or by any part of the burglar's body into the burglarized structure is sufficient to satisfy the requirement of an actual entry. Entry can also be accomplished by the insertion of a tool or other instrument into the structure burglarized. Drilling a hole into the floor of a granary, for example, in order to steal the grain that runs through the hole would be considered an entry for purposes of the crime of burglary.[47] A **constructive entry** occurs when the defendant causes another person (or a robot) to enter the structure to commit the crime or to achieve the felonious purpose. Sending an innocent six-year-old child into a house, for example, to retrieve something for the burglar would be a constructive entry. In one early case, an individual was convicted of burglary when he sent his dog into a house to retrieve the desired object. All American jurisdictions recognize the concept of a constructive entry in burglary cases.

constructive entry
In the crime of burglary, an entry that occurs when the defendant causes another person to enter a structure to commit a crime or for a felonious purpose.

Courts have required that there be a causal relationship between the breaking and the entry. For example, in the case of *Regina* v. *Davis*, the defendant opened a window to crawl through. Before doing so, however, he noticed an open door and entered the structure through the door instead of the window. The court held that the defendant was not guilty of burglary because the breaking (raising the window) was not the means of entry.[48]

Under common law, the burglarized structure had to be an occupied dwelling. Currently, in most jurisdictions, the burglarized structure must be an occupied dwelling to constitute first-degree burglary. Courts have generally held that as long as the structure that is burglarized is used to sleep in on a regular basis, it is an occupied dwelling for purposes of the law,[49] and it does not matter if the building is also used for business or other functions. During the temporary absence of the residents, an occupied dwelling is still considered "occupied," but it ceases to be an occupied dwelling when the residents permanently move out.[50] All jurisdictions now recognize at least one form of burglary that does not require that the structure in question be a dwelling. Most still require, however, that it be a building, although the definition of a *building* may be liberally interpreted. In one case, for example, a car wash, which was completely open on both ends, was considered to be a building.[51] In many states, including California, even though an automobile is not a building in the everyday sense of the word, a locked vehicle is also subject to being "burglarized."

Common law required that the breaking and entry had to occur during hours of darkness. It did not matter if the dwelling was brightly illuminated with artificial light. No jurisdictions presently limit breaking-and-entering offenses to nighttime hours, although in many jurisdictions, burglary during the hours between sunset and sunrise is a higher degree of burglary than one committed under the same circumstances during daylight.

Under common law, dictates against burglary were intended to protect owners of property and those dwelling therein. The target of burglary under common law, therefore, always had to be the property of *another*. The rule still applies, and one cannot burglarize one's own house. Even where individuals share living space, it is generally recognized as legally impossible for one occupant to commit burglary against the others. A more complicated situation exists, however, where a property owner breaks into property rented to a tenant. In recognition of just such a possibility, the *Commentaries* to the Model Penal Code say that the essential elements of burglary are[52]

- An unprivileged entry
- Into a building or occupied structure
- With criminal purpose

The *Commentaries* thus eliminate the need for the property to be that of another and dispense with the need for a "breaking," as the term has been traditionally understood. The California burglary law reflects a similar contemporary understanding of the essence of the crime of burglary, and the Capstone Case of *Folsom* v. *State* elaborates on it.

Under common law, to constitute burglary the defendant must have intended to commit a felony, such as rape, murder, or a theft offense, at the time of the entry. Presently, most jurisdictions follow this requirement. The theft offense in many jurisdictions, however, may be a misdemeanor (for example, petty theft). In some jurisdictions, all that is necessary is that the defendant intended to commit any crime, and in a few, it is not necessary that the burglar intended to commit that crime in the burglarized structure. Entering a structure in order to be a lookout or to hide until another crime can be completed elsewhere, for example, may constitute burglary in some jurisdictions. Intent, however, does not require that an identifiable offense actually be committed. Hence, someone who breaks and enters someone else's house with murderous intent still commits burglary even if he or she is unable to find the intended victim.

APPLYING THE CONCEPT

CAPSTONE CASE

Can Someone Commit Burglary of His or Her Home?

Folsom v. State, 668 So. 2d 114 (Ala. Crim. App. 1995)

THE CASE   The appellant, Paul Folsom, was convicted of sexual abuse in the first degree and of burglary in the first degree . . . .

The appellant asserts that there was not sufficient evidence to convict him of burglary. He specifically contends that because his wife, from whom he was separated at the time of the offense, owned the house, and because he had lived there during the marriage, he could not lawfully be convicted of burglary.

The state's evidence tended to show that the appellant and Patricia Criddle were married in August 1992 and that the appellant then moved into Criddle's house. Shortly after the marriage, the appellant became abusive and Criddle asked him to leave. The appellant had stayed in the house for approximately 35 days. The appellant gave Criddle the house keys in September 1992, and Criddle filed for divorce in October 1992. Criddle testified that on several occasions the appellant came to her house and kicked the door open. On December 13, 1992, the appellant kicked the back door open and lunged at Criddle with a knife.

The issue whether a spouse can burglarize the residence of the other spouse was addressed in depth in this court's opinion in *White v. State*, 587 So. 2d 1218 (Ala. Cr. App. 1990). This court stated:

> In Alabama, burglary, like trespass, is an offense against the possession, and hence the test for the purpose of determining in whom the ownership of the premises should be laid in an indictment is not the title, but the occupancy or possession at the time the offense was committed. A person "enters or remains unlawfully" in or upon premises when he is not licensed, invited or privileged to do so. Under Alabama law, a person who is licensed or privileged to enter premises cannot commit criminal trespass or burglary.

At the time of the crime, the defendant and his wife were separated. Some authorities broadly state that a man cannot burglarize his wife's home, and it is considered that the burglary statute is not designed to protect against entries by persons occupying a marital or immediate familial relationship with the legal possessor of property. So, it is held that in the absence of a legal separation agreement, or restraining order, or court decree limiting or ending the consortium rights of the parties, each spouse has a legal right to be with the other spouse on premises possessed by either or both spouses so long as the marriage exists, and entry onto such premises by either spouse cannot be a burglary, although a court order will negate any rights to enter the premises.

While the offense [of burglary] is not committed by one who breaks and enters his own dwelling or other building, it has, however, also been held that the mere existence of the marriage relationship does not preclude the one spouse from committing burglary against the other spouse.

We agree with the holding of the Florida Supreme Court in *Cladd v. State*, 398 So. 2d 442, 443-44 (Fla. 1981):

> The sole issue presented for review is whether a husband, who is physically but not legally separated from his wife, can be guilty of burglary when he enters premises, possessed only by the wife and in which he has no ownership or possessory interest, without the wife's consent and with intent to commit an offense therein. . . . We hold that under the particular facts of this case, the defendant could be guilty of burglary of his estranged wife's apartment. . . .
>
> The factual situation is narrow. The defendant and his wife had been separated for approximately six months, although there was no formal separation agreement or restraining order. He had no ownership or possessory interest in his wife's apartment and had at no time lived there. One morning, he broke through the locked door of her apartment with a crowbar, struck her, and attempted to throw her over the second floor stair railing. . . .

We reject the defendant's contention that the marriage relationship and the right of consortium deriving therefrom preclude the State from ever establishing the nonconsensual entry requisite to the crime of burglary. . . . Since burglary is an invasion of the possessory property

(continued)

rights of another, where premises are in the sole possession of the wife, the husband can be guilty of burglary if he makes a nonconsensual entry into her premises with intent to commit an offense, the same as he can be guilty of larceny of his wife's separate property. In *State v. Herndon* discussing a wife's separate property rights, we held that a husband could be charged with the larceny of his wife's separate property, and we explained:

> In a society like ours, where the wife owns and holds property in her own right, where she can direct the use of her personal property as she pleases, where she can engage in business and pursue a career, it would be contrary to every principle of reason to hold that a husband could *ad lib* appropriate her property. If the common-law rule was of force, the husband could collect his wife's paycheck, he could direct its use, he could appropriate her separate property and direct the course of her career or business if she has one. We think it has not only been abrogated by law, it has been abrogated by custom, the very thing out of which the common law was derived.
>
> The defendant's consortium rights did not immunize him from burglary where he had no right to be on the premises possessed solely by his wife independent of an asserted right to consortium. . . .

The facts were sufficient to present the case to the jury on the issue whether the appellant was guilty of burglary.

The appellant further contends that there was not sufficient evidence to find him guilty of sexual abuse. Criddle testified that the appellant kicked open the door to her house, dragged her to the bedroom, forcibly placed an object in her vagina, and then had sexual intercourse with her. The victim's testimony alone was sufficient to present the case to the jury on the issue whether the appellant was guilty of sexual abuse. . . .

For the foregoing reasons, the judgment in this cause is due to be, and it is hereby, affirmed.

What Do *You* Think?

1. At what point does marriage give a spouse the right to enter the property of his or her marriage partner?

2. What test did the court apply in order to determine that the husband had no right to enter the home?

3. Are there other relationships that should also hold special legal status, as they establish privileges similar to those of legal spouses at issue in this case? What challenges are involved in enforcing such privileges?

Additional Applications

Does a state's civil anti-ousting statute preclude a charge of burglary for breaking into a spouse's home?

State v. Lilly, 717 N.E.2d 322 (Ohio 1999)

The Case: In the early morning hours of January 27, 1997, defendant Harold Lilly, Jr., drove to his estranged wife's apartment in West Carrollton, Ohio, and, entering through a door that he had intentionally left unlocked the day before, destroyed some of Mrs. Lilly's personal belongings and took her purse. A state court jury convicted Lilly of burglary and he was sentenced to five years' imprisonment. On appeal, Lilly challenged the burglary charge in light of an 1887 Ohio civil statute which provided that "[n]either husband nor wife . . . can be excluded from the other's dwelling, except upon a decree or order of injunction made by a court of competent jurisdiction." Lilly conceded that he did not live in his wife's apartment, and further, that his wife had not given him permission to enter on the night in question. Nonetheless, Lilly argued, he was not under any court order to stay away; consequently, under Ohio's civil anti-ousting law, he had a statutory right to enter his wife's residence at will. By extension, his entry did not constitute a criminal trespass (a statutory element of burglary) under Ohio's criminal law.

The Finding: On appeal, the Ohio Supreme Court rejected Lilly's argument and held that a spouse can indeed be prosecuted for burglary of the other spouse's residence despite the state's anti-ousting law. Writing for the majority, Justice Evelyn Lundberg Stratton found that the 1887 civil statute was likely passed for a specific purpose: to prevent one estranged spouse from ejecting the other from a marital home that the ejected spouse may have originally owned. Accordingly, Lundberg Stratton noted, the legislature placed the anti-ousting provision in the domestic relations chapter—not the criminal law chapters—of the Revised Code. Beyond that, she noted, the legislature has never signaled any intention to apply the state's civil marital property laws in criminal contexts. And at least seven other states have similar civil anti-ousting statutes on the books, and all of those jurisdictions likewise distinguish their criminal laws and thus allow burglary charges against a spouse. Based on this history and context, the Ohio court concluded, the state's anti-ousting statute was completely irrelevant in Lilly's criminal case. Consequently, his conviction for burglary was permitted to stand.

Is intent to violate a restraining order sufficient to meet the independent crime element of burglary?

People v. Rhorer, 967 P.2d 147 (Colo. 1998)

The Case: Colorado's burglary statute provides that a person commits second-degree burglary if he "knowingly breaks an entrance into, or enters, or remains unlawfully in a building or occupied structure with intent to commit therein a crime against a person or property." On September 7, 1992, defendant Rex Rhorer broke a bedroom window at the home of his ex-girlfriend, Debbie Martinez; at the time, Rhorer was prohibited from having contact with Martinez under a court-issued no-contact order. Following Rhorer's arrest, prosecutors charged him with second-degree burglary and menacing, but at trial, the jury returned a verdict of not guilty on the menacing charge. On the burglary charge, by contrast, Rhorer was found guilty, on the grounds that he had broken into Martinez's home with the intent to violate the restraining order (a third-degree misdemeanor). On appeal, Rhorer argued that a restraining-order violation was not a separate crime "against a person or property"; thus, he was not guilty of burglary as defined in Colorado law.

The Finding: The Supreme Court of Colorado upheld Rhorer's burglary conviction, finding that his restraining-order violation could indeed count as the independent crime required by the state's burglary statute. Restraining orders, the court noted, are issued pursuant to the state's Domestic Abuse Act, and the legislature provides criminal penalties for violations regardless of whether those violations occur in the context of a breaking and entering as well. Consequently, the court held, Rhorer's "intent to violate the no-contact order by breaking into Martinez's home constituted an 'intent to commit therein a crime against person or property'"; as such, it "was an appropriate predicate crime under the second degree burglary statute."

Violations of restraining orders as independent crimes: A different approach?

State v. Colvin, 645 N.W.2d 449 (Minn. 2002)

The Case: On February 25, 1999, Peter Colvin entered his ex-wife's home in Rochester, Minnesota, through an unlocked window and proceeded to "watc[h] television and drin[k] a beer." Colvin did not damage any property or resist leaving when asked to do so; his presence in his ex-wife's house, however, violated a temporary restraining order that had been issued against him four months before. Consequently, state prosecutors charged him with first-degree burglary; Minnesota law defined that crime as entering a dwelling without consent when "another person, not an accomplice, is present in it" and the defendant "intended to commit some independent crime other than trespass." The trial court found Colvin guilty of the charge; on appeal, Colvin argued that intent to violate a restraining order cannot satisfy the independent crime element of burglary under state law.

The Finding: On review, the Supreme Court of Minnesota reversed Colvin's conviction, holding that entry in violation of a restraining order, although satisfying the no-consent element of burglary, could *not* also satisfy the independent crime element as well. Established state case law, the court noted, already holds that entry into a home with the intent to trespass cannot serve as an independent crime for purposes of supporting a burglary charge. Nonviolent entry into a home in violation of a protection order—without more—is similarly linked to the nonconsent element of burglary; consequently, that act standing alone cannot serve as the independent crime necessary to justify a burglary charge under Minnesota law.

---

criminal trespass
The entering or remaining on the property or in the building of another when entry was forbidden. Also, failing to depart after receiving notice to do so.

criminal mischief
The intentional or knowing damage or destruction of the tangible property of another.

looting
Burglary committed within an affected geographic area during an officially declared state of emergency or during a local emergency resulting from an earthquake, fire, flood, riot, or other disaster.

The crime of burglary is completed when entry is made. A defendant who, for example, enters a building to steal something but, after entry, changes his or her mind is still guilty of burglary. Generally, the crime of burglary is a felony, although most jurisdictions also recognize the statutory crimes of criminal trespass and looting.

Criminal trespass is a lesser included offense of burglary. Criminal trespass is the entering or remaining on the property or in the building of another when entry is forbidden or failing to depart after receiving notice to do so.[53] A similar statutory crime against property is **criminal mischief**. Criminal mischief is the intentional or knowing damage or destruction of the tangible property of another. It is committed by those who deface or destroy property. In most jurisdictions, it is a misdemeanor. **Looting**, another crime against property, can be defined as burglary committed within an affected geographic area during an officially declared state of emergency or during a local emergency resulting from an earthquake, fire, flood, riot, or other disaster. Some jurisdictions also criminalize the possession of burglary tools—that is, the possession of tools that serve a special purpose in breaking and entering a secured structure. The possession of burglary tools is only a crime when it can be shown that the possessor had the intent to use those tools for the purpose of burglary.

Arson

arson
The knowing and malicious burning of the personal property of another or the burning of one's own property if the purpose is to collect insurance money.

Under common law, **arson** was the malicious burning of the dwelling of another. Hence the crime was committed against habitation, not against property. The common law punishment for those convicted of arson, at least for a time, was death by burning. The modern trend has been to expand the scope of arson crimes to include many items other than structures, effectively transforming the crime into one against property. In the Washington State statute, for example, arson includes the burning of hay, a bridge, a motor vehicle, and many other things. To constitute arson in the contemporary sense of the offense, there is no requirement that an entire structure be burned or even that a fire, in the normal sense of the word, ensue. Arson occurs with even the slightest malicious burning, although a discoloration or blackening by heat or smoke would not be regarded as sufficient to constitute a "burning."

In almost all modern jurisdictions, arson requires the knowing and malicious burning of the fixture or personal property of another, and it includes the burning of one's own property if the purpose is to collect insurance money. Arson cannot be committed by negligent or reckless conduct, and there is no felony arson rule, as there is in the case of felony murder. In determining the pecuniary loss in arson cases, courts generally consider the fair market value of the property at the time it was destroyed or, in the case of damaged property, the cost of restoring it. Most states, like Washington, have divided arson into first and second degrees, with first-degree arson being the more aggravated form of arson.

Most jurisdictions also have statutes to punish those who recklessly start a fire or who unlawfully cause a fire. Such offenses differ from arson in that they may not include the requirement of "knowing and malicious" for the crime of arson. Section 452 of the California Penal Code, for example, provides that a person is guilty of unlawfully causing a fire when he or she recklessly sets fire to, burns, or causes to be burned any structure, forest land, or other property. Accordingly, a person may be convicted of unlawfully causing a fire because of recklessness. Under California law, the crime is a misdemeanor.

Computer and High-Technology Crimes

intellectual property
A form of creative endeavor that can be protected through patent, copyright, trademark, or other legal means. Intellectual property includes proprietary knowledge, trade secrets, confidentiality agreements, know-how, ideas, inventions, creations, technologies, processes, works of art and literature, and scientific discoveries or improvements.

computer crime
A crime that employs computer technology as central to its commission and that could not take place without such technology. Also called *cybercrime*.

The nature of criminal activity sometimes changes faster than laws can keep up with it. The burgeoning growth of technology, and especially computer technology, has brought with it new types of property crimes. Many such crimes involve the theft of electronic forms of **intellectual property**, specifically, the proprietary information stored in computers and digital devices and on electromagnetic, optical, and other storage media. During the past 20 years, all of the states, the federal government, and the District of Columbia have enacted statutes for **computer crime** designed to facilitate the prosecution of high-technology and computer-related crimes.

Many traditional forms of crime, including fraud, drug dealing, theft, espionage, pornography, and extortion, can be committed using computers and the Internet. The fact that computers can be used to commit crimes, however, does not necessarily make those crimes computer crimes. Only crimes that could not be committed without computer technology may properly be termed *computer crimes*. Crimes that simply target computer machinery (such as the theft of computer equipment, and the arson of computer facilities) or that utilize computer facilities for the commission of more mundane crimes (such as theft, black-mail, and extortion) may be more appropriately prosecuted under other laws.

In the late 1990s FBI agents arrested 21-year-old Adam Quinn Pletcher and charged him with trying to extort $5.25 million from Microsoft founder and chairman Bill Gates.[54] Pletcher, a loner who spent hours in front of his computer, allegedly sent several letters to Gates demanding the money and threatening to kill him or his wife, Melinda, if he didn't respond via an online dating service called NetGirl. The service, run by America Online, was to serve as a secure medium for the exchange of messages between Gates and the extortionist. FBI agents nabbed Pletcher after he sent Gates a disk that held erased files still containing the names of Pletcher's parents. Some months earlier, Pletcher had made headlines in Chicago when he was accused of running scams on his Internet webpage, in-cluding (1) selling fake driver's licenses, (2) promising people that he could get them cars at bargain prices and then pocketing their money, (3) running an illegal raffle that solicited $10 chances to win an expensive automobile, and (4) offering "free" pagers that cost more than $50 in service charges. By all accounts, Pletcher was a hacker—a technologically so-phisticated loner.

Although the attempt to extort money from Gates was prosecuted under "traditional" law, not all crimes committed with the use of computers can be so handled. The rapid growth in the number of crimes that took advantage of developing computer technology in the 1960s and 1970s—before the enactment of computer crime statutes—often forced prosecutors to use traditional tools in their arsenal and to charge computer criminals with larceny and other property crimes, even though the types of crimes being committed did not fit well with traditional understandings of crimes against property. As a consequence, it was not unusual to hear defendants argue, when charged with the larceny of software or data, that nothing of substance had actually been "carried away" because the allegedly stolen information generally remained on the computers from which it was said to have been stolen. Defendants and their attorneys typically argued that no crime had actually been committed because "property," under many larceny statutes of the time, meant only "tangible property," and electronic impulses, including computer programs and data, could not constitute tangible property.

In one exemplary case from the early 1960s, Robert F. Hancock, an employee of Dallas-based Texas Instruments Automatic Computers, was arrested and charged with stealing computer programs.[55] Hancock's story was fairly straightforward. In September 1964, Hancock began sharing an apartment with a man named Smith. Hancock told Smith that his job was classified and said that he could not talk about it for security reasons. Nonetheless, Smith and Hancock frequently discussed computers, computer programming, and the impact of computerization on society. Eventually, Hancock told Smith that he was in possession of computer programs that would be of great value to Texaco, one of Texas Instruments' clients. Hancock asked Smith to go to Houston and approach executives at Texaco about buying the programs. He gave Smith a list of the programs that he had and also gave him one program on disk to verify the authenticity of those on the list. Smith made the trip and talked to two Texaco representatives, who told him that they could not enter into confidential negotiations.

A few days later, Hancock asked Smith to again contact Texaco executives, which he did. A man named Sims, who said he worked for Texaco, told Smith by telephone that his company was interested in the programs and asked Smith to bring them with him and be ready to discuss price. When he arrived in Houston, Smith was met at the airport by a man calling himself Don Sims, who said he worked with the computer department at Texaco. Sims looked at the index of programs presented by Smith, while Sims's companion examined the sample program. When Sims asked for a price, Smith offered the programs for $5 million. Sims then took all the materials from Smith and identified himself as an investigator, Dale Simpson. About the same time, a Texas Instruments security officer in Dallas was telling Hancock that he was being suspended for giving Smith the programs to sell.

Hancock was charged with felony theft under Texas law, tried, and convicted. He appealed his conviction, arguing, among other things, that computer programs are not corporeal property and are therefore not subject to theft. The appellate court, however, held that the Texas Penal Code defines *property*, as related to the crime of theft, to include "all writings of every description, provided such property possesses any ascertainable value." The court wrote: "It is evident that the computer programs as alleged and the evidence in support thereof show that such property is included and comes within the meaning of the statutes defining the offenses of theft."[56]

As this example shows, computer crimes were not going unpunished before the enactment of a virtual plethora of computer crime statutes in the 1970s and 1980s. Because computer crimes generally violate traditional laws as well as laws specifically designed to combat them, many prosecutors successfully prosecuted early computer crimes under embezzlement, larceny, and fraud statutes. Federal prosecutors also sometimes made use of existing wire-fraud and mail-fraud laws.

Early Computer Crime Cases

Not all computer crime prosecutions under existing laws were successful in the early days of high technology, as the 1977 Virginia case of *Lund* v. *Commonwealth* shows.[57] Charles Walter Lund, a graduate student in statistics at Virginia Technological University, improperly used the university's computer to work on his doctoral thesis, billing the costs back to various university departments. He was charged with grand larceny and larceny by false pretense for "stealing" computer time and computer services. Although convicted at trial, the Virginia Supreme Court reversed Lund's conviction, holding that computer time and services were not goods and chattels (personal property) within the meaning of the state's larceny statute. Because they could not be carried away, said the court, computer time and services were merely intangibles. In 1978, partially in reaction to the *Lund* case and others like it, the Virginia general assembly enacted penal code Section 18.2–98.1, which reads: "Computer time or services or data processing services or information or data stored in connection therewith is hereby defined to be property which may be the subject of larceny under Section 18.2–95 or 18.2–96, or embezzlement under Section 18.2–111, or false pretenses under Section 18.2–178 [of the state's penal code]."

In another 1972 case, *Ward* v. *Superior Court*,[58] a California computer company employee was charged with grand theft of a trade secret belonging to another computer company. The trade secret was a computer program, valued by its owner at $5,000, which made it possible to provide a remote plotting service, through a switching attachment, over telephone lines to customers who had a specially designed plotter and transceiver unit. Because the program eliminated the need for an expensive transmitting unit, it gave its owner a substantial competitive advantage. Ward accessed and printed out the program from a terminal in his own company, using a third company's site and billing numbers. He was charged under two sections of the California Penal Code, one of which made it an offense to steal, take, or carry away any article representing a trade secret and the other of which made it an offense to mail a copy of any article representing a trade secret. Although the trial court reasoned that an article must be tangible in order for it to be carried away and that electronic impulses transmitted over telephone lines are not tangible, it held that Ward had illegally copied an article that represented a trade secret.

Other courts were more reluctant to judicially create a new category of crime. In *People* v. *Weg*,[59] for example, the defendant—a computer programmer for the New York City Board of Education—allegedly stole data from the system he administered for his own commercial benefit. Although charged with theft of services under New York Penal Code Section 165.15(8), the court held that the Board of Education's computer was not "business" equipment. The court made clear that it felt that both the statutory context and the legislative history of the New York law clearly indicated that the legislature had meant to protect equipment in commercial use but that the Board of Education's computers did not come under such a definition. If the legislature wanted to make unauthorized use of computers a crime, said the court, it could do so, as some other states had already done.

Although some early defendants in the computer crime arena were able to avoid criminal liability by playing on the shortcomings of traditional statutes defining property crimes, most were not. As the Electronic Frontier Foundation, a San Francisco–based organization founded in 1990 and dedicated to protecting civil liberties on the World Wide Web, observes, "Without going into detailed discussion of [many] cases, we can make these general observations: (1) despite some ingenious defense arguments, most courts and prosecutors had little difficulty applying traditional concepts to computer offenses; (2) federal prosecutors frequently turned to wire fraud and mail fraud charges where state prosecutors would have charged fraud, larceny, or embezzlement; and (3) courts sometimes refused to apply traditional definitions to new offenses where there was no readily apparent loss by the victim."[60]

Computer Crime Laws

By 1990, all 50 states and the federal government had enacted computer crime statutes. The first state to pass a computer crime law was Florida, which passed one in 1978. The last state to enact a computer crime law was Massachusetts, which passed its statute in 1990.

Federal statutes of relevance to crimes committed with or against computer equipment and software include the following:

- Federal Wiretap Act of 1968[61]
- National Stolen Property Act[62]
- Computer Fraud and Abuse Act of 1984[63] and its amendments, especially Section 290001 of Title 29 of the Violent Crime Control and Law Enforcement Act of 1994[64] (the Computer Abuse Amendments Act of 1994)
- Electronic Communications Privacy Act of 1986[65]
- Communications Decency Act[66]
- No Electronic Theft Act of 1997[67]
- Digital Theft Deterrence and Copyright Damages Improvement Act of 1999[68]
- Cyber Security Enhancement Act of 2002[69]

For the most part, federal laws protect equipment owned by the federal government or a financial institution or computers that are accessed across state lines without prior authorization.[70] The Computer Fraud and Abuse Act defines as criminal the intentional unauthorized access to a computer used exclusively by the federal government or any other computer used by the government when such conduct affects the government's use. The same statute also defines as criminal the intentional and unauthorized access to two or more computers in different states involving conduct that alters or destroys information and causes loss to one or more parties in excess of $1,000.[71] Central to the law is a provision that makes it a federal crime to access, without authorization, any data-processing system if the data-processing system is involved in or used in relationship to interstate commerce. The act also makes it a crime to use a public telephone system to access, without authority, any data-processing system, and the act prohibits those who have the authority to access a data-processing system from using that authority in an unauthorized manner. Punishment specified under federal law is a maximum sentence of five years and a fine of up to $250,000 upon conviction. The Computer Abuse Amendments Act of 1994, however, adds the provision that "any person who suffers damage or loss by reason of a violation of [this] section . . . may maintain a civil action against the violator to obtain compensatory damages and injunctive relief or other equitable relief."[72]

The Cyber Security Enhancement Act (CSEA) of 2002, which is part of the Homeland Security Act of 2002, directed the U.S. Sentencing Commission to take several factors into account in creating new sentencing guidelines for computer criminals. The law told commission members to consider not only the financial loss caused by computer crime but also the level of planning involved in the offense, whether the crime was committed for commercial or private advantage, and whether malicious intent existed on the part of the perpetrator. Under the law, computer criminals can face up to life in prison if they put human lives in jeopardy. The law also makes it easier for police agencies to obtain investigative information from Internet service providers (ISPs) and shields from lawsuits ISPs that hand over user information to law enforcement officers without a warrant. The information in question, however, should be that which poses an immediate risk of injury or death.

The Digital Theft Deterrence and Copyright Damages Improvement Act of 1999 amended Section 504(c) of the Copyright Act and increased the amount of damages that could be awarded in cases of copyright infringement, a crime that is intimately associated with software piracy. Enacted in 1997, the No Electronic Theft Act (NETA or NETAct) criminalizes the willful infringement of copyrighted works, including by electronic means, even when the infringing party derives no direct financial benefit from the infringement (such as when pirated software is freely distributed online). The law was created in response to a 1994 case in which David LaMacchia, a Massachusetts Institute of Technology (MIT) student, distributed more than $1 million worth of copyrighted commercial software on an unauthorized MIT Internet bulletin board. LaMacchia could not be prosecuted under the federal Copyright Act because he did not profit from the distribution.[73] NETA makes it a federal crime to distribute or possess unauthorized electronic copies of copyrighted materials valued at more than $1,000. Possessing ten or more illegal documents worth more than $2,500 carries a three-year prison term and a $250,000 fine. In keeping with NETA requirements, the U.S. Sentencing Commission enacted amendments to its guidelines in 2000 to increase the penalties associated with electronic theft.

The 1996 Communications Decency Act (CDA) is Title 5 of the Telecommunications Act of 1996.[74] It sought to protect minors from harmful material on the Internet. A portion of the CDA criminalized the knowing transmission of obscene or indecent messages to any recipient under 18 years of age. Another section prohibited knowingly sending or displaying to a person under 18 any message "that, in context, depicts or describes, in terms patently offensive as measured by contemporary community standards, sexual or excretory activities or organs." The law provided acceptable defenses for those who took "good faith . . . effective . . . actions" to restrict access by minors to prohibited communications and to those who restricted such access by requiring certain designated forms of age proof, such as a verified credit card or an adult identification number.

Shortly after the law was passed, however, the American Civil Liberties Union (ACLU) and a number of other plaintiffs filed suit against the federal government, challenging the constitutionality of the law's two provisions relating to the transmission of obscene materials to minors. In 1996, a three-judge federal district court entered a preliminary injunction against enforcement of both challenged provisions, ruling that they contravened First Amendment guarantees of free speech. The government then appealed to the U.S. Supreme Court. The Court's 1997 decision, *Reno* v. *ACLU*,[75] upheld the lower court's ruling and found that the CDA's "indecent transmission" and "patently offensive display"

CRIMINAL LAW IN THE NEWS

Kim Dotcom of Megaupload Arrested for Online Piracy

At 6 foot, 6 inches and 322 pounds, Web entrepreneur Kim Dotcom has made a career of being larger than life, and his spectacular arrest on January 20, 2012, in his sprawling mansion in New Zealand lived up to that image.

New Zealand police cut through a series of locks to get to the 38-year-old native German, whose given name was Kim Schmitz. Though there were reports he had a shotgun handy, Dotcom surrendered peacefully.

Concurrent with the arrest, authorities in nine countries shut down worldwide operations of Megaupload, Dotcom's hugely popular file-sharing website. Executing 20 warrants, they seized hundreds of servers and closed 18 domain names.

U.S. prosecutors orchestrated the whole operation, executing an indictment against Dotcom and others at Megaupload for criminal copyright infringement. The company is accused of stealing $500 million worth of copyrighted material from music, film, and television rights holders over five years of operation.

The film and recording industries pushed to prosecute Megaupload, pointing to a disturbing erosion of their royalty income through unauthorized use on the Internet. The criminal investigation, begun in 2010, is based on a lawsuit filed by the Motion Picture Association of America against Megaupload.

The indictment points to a new, gloves-off stage in the battle against unauthorized use of copyrighted material on the Internet. A decade ago, when copyright holders sued the file-sharing service Napster and shut it down, no criminal charges were filed, no one was arrested, and no one went to prison.

In addition to criminal copyright violations, Dotcom and his associates are charged with money laundering and racketeering, which alone could bring 10 years in prison. Dotcom asserts Megaupload is no different than YouTube, which escaped infringement charges in 2010. But he started his career as a hacker and he has been convicted of insider trading and embezzlement.

Megaupload made its money by serving as a "digital locker" that stored users' files, which then could be accessed by anyone entering the site. At its peak, the site logged 50 million visits daily, making up 4% of all Internet traffic.

The company gave payments to site users whose content generated high traffic. Prosecutors allege this content was often pirated. For example, one copyright infringer allegedly uploaded nearly 17,000 videos to the site, which then gleaned 334 million views.

Kim Dotcom, the Web entrepreneur arrested in New Zealand in 2012 on charges of Internet piracy. What kinds of theft crimes does the Internet facilitate? How do they differ from more traditional forms of theft? *Source: Newscom*

Under the Digital Millennium Copyright Act, websites are protected from prosecution if they are unaware of pirated content and take down content when copyright holders inform them of violations. But prosecutors charge that Megaupload staff knew full well they were harboring pirated content and did not completely take down content when requested, leaving hundreds of copies still on the site, in some cases.

But some experts think prosecutors may be overreaching. Professor James Grimmelmann of New York Law School said he hopes Dotcom is found guilty, but added that many of the activities in the indictment appear to be legitimate business strategies for Internet sites, such as offering premium subscriptions, running ads, and rewarding active users.

Jennifer Granick, an attorney blogging for Stanford's Center for Internet and Society, said it's going to be hard to win infringement charges based on users' content, rather than content directly pirated by Megaupload. She added that some legal arguments in the case are based on civil copyright law, which is not applicable to criminal copyright law.

New Zealand authorities are squeamish about cooperating too closely with U.S. officials. Over U.S. objections, a New Zealand judge granted Dotcom bail, requiring that he remain in the area and not use the Internet. U.S. officials will argue for his extradition in a hearing scheduled for March 2013.

(continued)

Resources

"Megaupload File Sharing Site Shut Down for Piracy by Feds," *LA Times*, January 19, 2012, **http://latimesblogs.latimes.com/ entertainmentnewsbuzz/2012/01/file-sharing-megaupload-shut-down-for-piracy-by-feds.html.**

"Why the Feds Smashed Megaupload," Ars Technica, February 8, 2012,

http://arstechnica.com/tech-policy/news/2012/01/ why-the-feds-smashed-megaupload.ars.

"Kim Dotcom's Wild Ride Hits Digital Piracy Wall," Newsday, February 27, 2012, **http://www.newsday.com/business/technology/ kim-dotcom-s-wild-ride-hits-digital-piracy-wall-1.3560434.**

provisions abridge "the freedom of speech" protected by the First Amendment. Justice John Paul Stevens wrote for the majority: "It is true that we have repeatedly recognized the governmental interest in protecting children from harmful materials. But that interest does not justify an unnecessarily broad suppression of speech addressed to adults."

Most other federal legislation aimed at keeping online pornography away from the eyes of children has not fared any better when reviewed by the High Court. Enforcement of the 1998 Child Online Protection Act (COPA), for example, was partially barred by a 2004 U.S. Supreme Court ruling that held that measures in the law were too restrictive and jeopardized free speech interests.[76] Subsequent lower court litigation on different issues also found the statute unconstitutional. And although the Children's Internet Protection Act (CIPA) of 2000,[77] which requires public and school libraries receiving certain kinds of federal funding to install pornography filters on their Internet-linked computers, was approved, most observers acknowledge that the Court has placed the Internet in the same category as newspapers and other print media, where almost no regulation is permitted.

Most computer crime laws—whether federal or state—criminalize unauthorized access, although penalties for simple access (or access without harm) are usually not harsh.[78] Access was one of the legal issues raised by the defendant in *People* v. *Rice* (2008), which is highlighted in a Capstone Case in this chapter.

Most state computer crime laws are comprehensive statutes, often taking the form of an independent title in a state's criminal code called the Computer Crimes Act or the Computer Crime Prevention Act.[79] In contrast, some states have created a patchwork quilt of modifications to existing laws to cover a variety of crimes, such as computer trespass and theft with a computer. Ohio, for example, has inserted a series of computer crime definitions in its general theft statute; has added one section on denying access to a computer; and has placed computer systems, networks, and software used in committing any offense within its general definition of "contraband."[80] Many state computer crime statutes occupy a middle ground and can be found under other statutory categories, such as crimes against property, fraud, theft (as is the case in California), or business and commercial offenses. Arizona, for example, has placed its computer crime provisions under the section of its penal code entitled Organized Crime and Fraud, whereas North Dakota places such legislation under its Racketeer Influenced and Corrupt Organizations (RICO) statute.

Because legislatures often found themselves creating new laws to deal with emerging and rapid social and technological changes, computer crime laws frequently set forth a number of definitions unique to such legislation. Typically defined by such laws are terms like these: (1) *access*, (2) *computer*, (3) *computer network*, (4) *computer program*, (5) *computer software*, (6) *computer system*, and (7) *computer data*. A few states have attempted to define specific terminology such as (1) *computer control language* (Maryland), (2) *computer database* (Maryland), (3) *computer hacking* (South Carolina), (4) *system hacker* (Tennessee), (5) *computer supplies* (Wisconsin), (6) *database* (New Jersey and Pennsylvania), (7) *private personal data*

APPLYING THE CONCEPT

CAPSTONE CASE

Is It a Computer Crime for an Individual to Enter Untrue Answers into an Automated, Computerized Telephone System for the Purpose of Defrauding Another?

People v. *Rice*, Colo. App. 3rd, 2008.

THE CASE Defendant, Nina B. Rice, appeals from the judgment of conviction entered upon a jury verdict finding her guilty of computer crime. . . .

I. Background Evidence at trial established that, in 2003, defendant filed for unemployment compensation benefits with the Colorado Department of Labor and Employment. To do so, she utilized the Department's CUBLine, an interactive computer system with which unemployment claimants communicate over the telephone.

For over five months, defendant contacted the CUB-Line to make biweekly claims for unemployment benefits. Each time she contacted the CUBLine, the computer system asked defendant if she had worked during the week for which she claimed unemployment benefits. Each time, she pressed the number on her telephone corresponding to an answer of "no." In fact, she was employed at the time, and she concedes that she lied in her CUB-Line responses.

Defendant was charged by information with the crimes of theft and computer crime. The theft count alleged that defendant intended to permanently deprive the Department of money, and the computer crime count alleged that she accessed a computer for the purpose of obtaining money from the Department or committing theft. At trial, she testified that she believed the money she received from her unemployment claims belonged to her and had been withheld from her paychecks issued by her previous employer.

The jury was unable to reach a verdict on the theft count and found defendant guilty of computer crime. The jury also convicted defendant of false swearing, a lesser nonincluded offense submitted to the jury at defendant's request. Defendant was subsequently sentenced to five years' probation. This appeal followed.

II. Sufficiency of the Evidence Defendant contends the evidence was insufficient to support the jury's verdict of guilty on the computer crime count. Specifically, she contends the evidence was insufficient to establish that she "accessed" a computer or computer system within the meaning of the term "access" as used in section 18-5.5-102(1)(c)-(d), C.R.S. 2007. We disagree. . . .

The prosecution charged defendant with computer crime pursuant to subsections (c) and (d) of section 18-5.5-102(1). Under those subsections,

A person commits computer crime if the person knowingly:

. . .

(c) Accesses any computer, computer network, or computer system, or any part thereof to obtain, by means of false or fraudulent pretenses, representations, or promises, money; property; services; passwords or similar information through which a computer, computer network, or computer system or any part thereof may be accessed; or other thing of value; or

(b) Accesses any computer, computer network, or computer system, or any part thereof to commit theft. . . .

§ 18-5.5-102(1)(c)-(d).

Here, the prosecution presented evidence that defendant made biweekly unemployment benefits claims by calling an automated phone system, the CUBLine, maintained by the Department. An employee of the Department testified that the CUBLine is a "computerized system, which uses interactive voice response technology." She further testified that an unemployment benefits claimant identifies himself or herself by entering a Social Security number and a personal identification number using numbers on a telephone when prompted by the system. The system then asks the claimant a number of questions related to "weekly eligibility requirements, such as . . . did you work during the weeks you are claiming?" The claimant responds by pressing "1" for "yes"

(continued)

and "9" for "no." This procedure is described in a brochure that was admitted into evidence at trial and, according to the record, was given to defendant to review before she made her first biweekly claim. When the computer system determines a claimant is eligible for unemployment benefits, a computer prints a check that is automatically sent to the claimant. Typically, an eligible claimant completes a claim and receives a check without interacting with a person. . . .

Defendant contends that she did not "access" a computer within the meaning of section 18-5.5-102(1)(c)-(d) by making a phone call and pressing telephone buttons in response to the CUBLine questions. We disagree. . . .

THE FINDING   "Access" is not defined in the Colorado Criminal Code. However, it is a term of common usage, and persons of ordinary intelligence need not guess at its meaning. We, therefore, begin with the dictionary definition in determining the plain and ordinary meaning of "access." *Black's Law Dictionary* 14 (8th ed. 2004) defines the word "access" as "[a]n opportunity or ability to enter, approach, pass to and from, or communicate with."

Viewing the evidence in the light most favorable to the prosecution, we conclude defendant accessed, within the ordinary meaning of the term, a computer system, because she communicated with the CUBLine by inputting data in response to computer-generated questions. Also, the CUBLine was described in testimony at trial sufficient to support a finding that it was a "computer system" as that term is defined in section 18-5.5-101(6), C.R.S. 2007. . . .

In any event, we disagree with defendant's various arguments in support of a narrower definition of "access." . . .

Second, because we conclude the term "access," as used in section 18-5.5-102(1)(c)-(d), is not ambiguous, we reject defendant's contention that the rule of lenity requires us to adopt her interpretation.

Third, we reject defendant's contention that section 18-5.5-102(1)(c)-(d) would be rendered unconstitutionally vague if the term "access" were given its ordinary meaning. . . .

The ordinary meaning of "access" is not confusing or overly technical, and is readily understandable by an ordinary person of reasonable intelligence. . . .

[The court then reversed and remanded the case for other reasons.]

What Do You Think?

1. Would an ordinary person agree that making selections in a telephone system qualifies as accessing a computer system or network?

2. Excluding the crimes she was charged with, what other crime(s) did the defendant commit?

Additional Applications

Does the Computer Fraud and Abuse Act (CFAA) provide a vehicle for prosecuting "cyber-bullying"?

United States v. *Drew*, 259 F.R.D. (C.D.Cal. 2009)

The Case: In an elaborate act of online deception, defendant Lori Drew of O'Fallon, Missouri, and others set up a MySpace account under a fictitious identity (a supposed 16-year-old O'Fallon resident named "Josh Evans") and, using that online pseudonym, carried on a flirtatious online relationship with 13-year-old Megan Meier, a former classmate of Drew's daughter. After the online relationship between "Josh" and Megan had developed for some time, Drew and her co-conspirators had "Josh" tell Megan that he was moving away from O'Fallon. Several days later, "Josh" told Megan that he no longer liked her and that "the world would be a better place without her in it." Later that same day, Megan committed suicide.

Federal prosecutors charged Lori Drew with several violations of the Computer Fraud and Abuse Act (CFAA). At trial, the jury deadlocked on a felony conspiracy charge and acquitted Drew of accessing a computer to intentionally inflict emotional distress. The jury found Drew guilty, however, on one misdemeanor CFAA count of intentionally violating an Internet website's terms of service by deliberately creating a false profile and using it to communicate with another user. After the verdict, Drew moved for a directed judgment of acquittal on the grounds that an intentional violation of a site's terms of service alone does not violate 18 U.S.C. Section 1030(a)(2)(C)'s prohibition of "intentionally access[ing] a computer without authorization."

The Finding: The federal trial judge overturned the jury verdict and granted Drew's motion for acquittal. "[T]he owner of an Internet website," the judge found, clearly "has the right to establish the extent to (and the conditions under) which members of the public will be allowed access." Yet "[t]reating a violation of a website's terms of service, without more, to be sufficient to constitute 'intentionally access[ing] a computer without authorization . . . ' would result in transforming [the CFAA] into an overwhelmingly overbroad enactment that would convert a multitude of otherwise innocent Internet users into misdemeanant criminals." And in that situation, "there is absolutely no limitation or criteria as to which of the breaches should merit criminal prosecution." Federal prosecutors would then be "improperly free 'to pursue their personal predilections.'"

Is an employee's violation of corporate computer-use policies a crime under the CFAA?

United States v. *Nosal*, 676 F.3d 854 (9th Cir. 2012)

The Case: Shortly after leaving a job at Korn/Ferry, a leading executive search firm, to start a competing business, defendant David Nosal convinced some of his former colleagues to access Korn/Ferry's proprietary databases in order to download confidential source lists, names, and contacts and transfer that information to him. After discovering the scheme, federal prosecutors indicted Nosal on 20 criminal counts, including charges that Nosal had violated the CFAA by aiding and abetting others in exceeding their "authorized access" to company computers with intent to defraud. Nosal moved to dismiss the CFAA counts, arguing that the statute's prohibition on "exceed[ing] authorized access" applies only to "hackers," not those with authorized access who "misuse information they obtain by means of such access." The trial court ultimately agreed and dismissed the CFAA charges; on appeal, the government argued that the trial court had erred in failing to apply the CFAA to any knowing violations of corporate computer-use policies by authorized users.

The Finding: Sitting *en banc*, the U.S. Court of Appeals for the Ninth Circuit affirmed the trial court's dismissal of CFAA charges in an April 2012 ruling. Writing for the majority, Judge Alex Kozinski noted that the CFAA's prohibition on exceeding authorized access to computer databases "can be read [in] either of two ways." Yet the "more sensible" and "more plausible" reading, he concluded, is to limit the CFAA only to instances of unauthorized *access* to information rather than unauthorized *use*. Interpreting the statute otherwise, Kozinski argued, "would transform the CFAA from an anti-hacking statute into an expansive misappropriation statute," and if Congress "had meant to expand the scope of criminal liability to everyone who uses a computer in violation of computer use restrictions—which may well include everyone who uses a computer—we would expect it to use language better suited to that purpose." Kozinski added: "Minds have wandered since the beginning of time and the computer gives employees new ways to procrastinate, by chatting with friends, playing games, shopping or watching sports highlights. Such activities are routinely prohibited by many computer-use policies . . . . [n]evertheless, under the [government's proposed] interpretation of the CFAA, such minor dalliances would become federal crimes." ∎

(Connecticut and Delaware), and (8) *supporting documentation* (Wisconsin). Pennsylvania's computer crime law, which is fairly concise and similar in purpose to the computer crime laws of many other jurisdictions, is reproduced here. (Note the definition of the word *property* under the Pennsylvania law.)

TITLE 18, PENNSYLVANIA CONSOLIDATED STATUTES

Section 3933. Unlawful use of computer.

(a) Offense defined. A person commits an offense if he:

1. accesses, alters, damages, or destroys any computer, computer system, computer network, computer software, computer program or data base or any part thereof, with the intent to interrupt the normal functioning of an organization or to devise or execute any scheme or artifice to defraud or deceive or control property or services by means of false or fraudulent pretenses, representations, or promises;

2. intentionally and without authorization accesses, alters, interferes with the operation of, damages, or destroys any computer, computer system, computer network, computer software, computer program, or computer data base or any part thereof; or

3. intentionally or knowingly and without authorization gives or publishes a password, identifying code, personal identification number, or other confidential information about a computer, computer system, computer network, or data base.

(b) Grading. An offense under subsection (a)(1) is a felony of the third degree. An offense under subsection (a)(2) or (3) is a misdemeanor of the first degree.

(c) Definitions. As used in this section the following words and phrases shall have the meanings given to them in this subsection:

"Access." To intercept, instruct, communicate with, store data in, retrieve data from, or otherwise make use of any resources of a computer, computer system, computer network, or data base.

"Computer." An electronic, magnetic, optical, hydraulic, organic, or other high speed data processing device or system which performs logic, arithmetic, or memory functions and includes all input, output, processing, storage, software, or communication facilities which are connected or related to the device in a system or network.

"Computer network." The interconnection of two or more computers through the usage of satellite, microwave, line, or other communication medium.

"Computer program." An ordered set of instructions or statements and related data that, when automatically executed in actual or modified form in a computer system, causes it to perform specified functions.

"Computer software." A set of computer programs, procedures, and associated documentation concerned with the operation of a computer system.

"Computer system." A set of related, connected, or unconnected computer equipment, devices, and software.

"Data base." A representation of information, knowledge, facts, concepts, or instructions which are being prepared or processed or have been prepared or processed in a formalized manner and are intended for use in a computer, computer system, or computer network, including, but not limited to, computer printouts, magnetic storage media, punched cards, or data stored internally in the memory of the computer.

"Financial instrument." Includes, but is not limited to, any check, draft, warrant, money order, note, certificate of deposit, letter of credit, bill of exchange, credit or debit card, transaction authorization mechanism, marketable security, or any computer system representation thereof.

"Property." Includes, but is not limited to, financial instruments, computer software, and programs in either machine or human readable form, and anything of value, tangible or intangible.

"Services." Includes, but is not limited to, computer time, data processing, and storage functions.
(Dec. 2, 1983, P.L.248, No.67, eff. 60 days; Dec. 11, 1986, P.L.1517, No.164, eff. 60 days)

An example of a federal statute criminalizing computer crime follows.

TITLE 18 U.S. CODE

Section 1030. Fraud and related activity in connection with computers

(a) Whoever—

1. having knowingly accessed a computer without authorization or exceeding authorized access, and by means of such conduct having obtained information that has been determined by the United States Government pursuant to an Executive order or statute to require protection against unauthorized disclosure for reasons of national defense or foreign relations, or any restricted data, as defined in paragraph y of section 11 of the Atomic Energy Act of 1954, with reason to believe that such information so obtained could be used to the injury of the United States, or to the advantage of any foreign nation willfully communicates, delivers, transmits, or causes to be communicated, delivered, or transmitted, or attempts to communicate, deliver, transmit or cause to be communicated, delivered, or transmitted the same to any person not entitled to receive it, or willfully retains the same and fails to deliver it to the officer or employee of the United States entitled to receive it;

2. intentionally accesses a computer without authorization or exceeds authorized access, and thereby obtains—

    (a) information contained in a financial record of a financial institution, or of a card issuer as defined in section 1602(n) of title 15, or contained in a file of a consumer reporting agency on a consumer, as such terms are defined in the Fair Credit Reporting Act (15 U.S.C. 1681 et seq.);

    (b) information from any department or agency of the United States; or

    (c) information from any protected computer if the conduct involved an interstate or foreign communication;

3. intentionally, without authorization to access any nonpublic computer of a department or agency of the United States, accesses such a computer of that department or agency that is exclusively for the use of the Government of the United States or, in the case of a computer not exclusively for such use, is used by or for the Government of the United States and such conduct affects that use by or for the Government of the United States;

4. knowingly and with intent to defraud, accesses a protected computer without authorization, or exceeds authorized access, and by means of such conduct furthers the intended fraud and obtains anything of value, unless the object of the fraud and the thing obtained [consist] only of the use of the computer and the value of such use is not more than $5,000 in any 1-year period;

5. (a) knowingly causes the transmission of a program, information, code, or command, and as a result of such conduct, intentionally causes damage without authorization, to a protected computer;

    (b) intentionally accesses a protected computer without authorization, and as a result of such conduct, recklessly causes damage; or

    (c) intentionally accesses a protected computer without authorization, and as a result of such conduct, causes damage;

6. knowingly and with intent to defraud trafficks (as defined in section 1029) in any password or similar information through which a computer may be accessed without authorization, if—

    (a) such trafficking affects interstate or foreign commerce; or

    (b) such computer is used by or for the Government of the United States; or

7. with intent to extort from any person, firm, association, educational institution, financial institution, government entity, or other legal entity, any money or other thing of value, transmits in interstate or foreign commerce any communication containing any threat to cause damage to a protected computer; shall be punished as provided in subsection (c) of this section.

(b) Whoever attempts to commit an offense under subsection (a) of this section shall be punished as provided in subsection (c) of this section.

(c) The punishment for an offense under subsection (a) or (b) of this section is—

1. (a) a fine under this title or imprisonment for not more than ten years, or both, in the case of an offense under subsection (a)(1) of this section which does not occur after a conviction for another offense under this section, or an attempt to commit an offense punishable under this subparagraph; and (B) a fine under this title or imprisonment for not more than twenty years, or both, in the case of an offense under subsection (a)(1) of this section which occurs after a conviction for another offense under this section, or an attempt to commit an offense punishable under this subparagraph;

2. (a) a fine under this title or imprisonment for not more than one year, or both, in the case of an offense under subsection (a)(2), (a)(3), (a)(5)(C), or (a)(6) of this section which does not occur after a conviction for another offense under this section, or an attempt to commit an offense punishable under this subparagraph;

    (b) a fine under this title or imprisonment for not more than 5 years, or both, in the case of an offense under subsection (a)(2), if—

      i. the offense was committed for purposes of commercial advantage or private financial gain;

      ii. the offense was committed in furtherance of any criminal or tortious act in violation of the Constitution or laws of the United States or of any State; or

      iii. the value of the information obtained exceeds $5,000; and

(c) a fine under this title or imprisonment for not more than ten years, or both, in the case of an offense under subsection (a)(2), (a)(3), or (a)(6) of this section which occurs after a conviction for another offense under this section, or an attempt to commit an offense punishable under this subparagraph; and (3)(A) a fine under this title or imprisonment for not more than five years, or both, in the case of an offense under subsection (a)(4), (a)(5)(A), (a)(5)(B), or (a)(7) of this section which does not occur after a conviction for another offense under this section, or an attempt to commit an offense punishable under this subparagraph; and

(d) a fine under this title or imprisonment for not more than ten years, or both, in the case of an offense under subsection (a)(4), (a)(5)(A), (a)(5)(B), (a)(5)(C), or (a)(7) of this section which occurs after a conviction for another offense under this section, or an attempt to commit an offense punishable under this subparagraph.

(d) The United States Secret Service shall, in addition to any other agency having such authority, have the authority to investigate offenses under subsections (a)(2)(A), (a)(2)(B), (a)(3), (a)(4), (a)(5), and (a)(6) of this section. Such authority of the United States Secret Service shall be exercised in accordance with an agreement which shall be entered into by the Secretary of the Treasury and the Attorney General.

(e) As used in this section—

1. the term "computer" means an electronic, magnetic, optical, electrochemical, or other high speed data processing device performing logical, arithmetic, or storage functions, and includes any data storage facility or communications facility directly related to or operating in conjunction with such device, but such term does not include an automated typewriter or typesetter, a portable handheld calculator, or other similar device;

2. the term "protected computer" means a computer—

   (a) exclusively for the use of a financial institution or the United States Government, or, in the case of a computer not exclusively for such use, used by or for a financial institution or the United States Government and the conduct constituting the offense affects that use by or for the financial institution or the Government; or

   (b) which is used in interstate or foreign commerce or communication;

3. the term "State" includes the District of Columbia, the Commonwealth of Puerto Rico, and any other commonwealth, possession or territory of the United States;

4. the term "financial institution" means—

   (a) an institution, with deposits insured by the Federal Deposit Insurance Corporation;

   (b) the Federal Reserve or a member of the Federal Reserve including any Federal Reserve Bank;

   (c) a credit union with accounts insured by the National Credit Union Administration;

   (d) a member of the Federal home loan bank system and any home loan bank;

   (e) any institution of the Farm Credit System under the Farm Credit Act of 1971;

   (f) a broker-dealer registered with the Securities and Exchange Commission pursuant to section 15 of the Securities Exchange Act of 1934;

   (g) the Securities Investor Protection Corporation;

   (h) a branch or agency of a foreign bank (as such terms are defined in paragraphs (1) and (3) of section 1(b) of the International Banking Act of 1978); and

   (i) an organization operating under section 25 or section 25(a) of the Federal Reserve Act;

5. the term "financial record" means information derived from any record held by a financial institution pertaining to a customer's relationship with the financial institution;

6. the term "exceeds authorized access" means to access a computer with authorization and to use such access to obtain or alter information in the computer that the accesser is not entitled so to obtain or alter;

7. the term "department of the United States" means the legislative or judicial branch of the Government or one of the executive departments enumerated in section 101 of title 5;

8. the term "damage" means any impairment to the integrity or availability of data, a program, a system, or information, that—

    (a) causes loss aggregating at least $5,000 in value during any 1-year period to one or more individuals;

    (b) modifies or impairs, or potentially modifies or impairs, the medical examination, diagnosis, treatment, or care of one or more individuals;

    (c) causes physical injury to any person; or

    (d) threatens public health or safety; and

9. the term "government entity" includes the Government of the United States, any State or political subdivision of the United States, any foreign country, and any state, province, municipality, or other political subdivision of a foreign country. . . .

The Electronic Frontier Foundation (EFF) points out that "state statutes do not always give computer offenses specific names."[81] The EFF notes that such laws "use a variety of descriptions to state exactly what they are prohibiting." It found that the following descriptive titles are among the most commonly used: (1) access to defraud, (2) access to obtain money, (3) computer fraud, (4) offenses against computer users, (5) offenses against intellectual property, (6) offenses against computer equipment and supplies, (7) unauthorized access, and (8) unauthorized or unlawful computer use.

Generally speaking, computer crime laws attempt to apply the concept of common law trespass to computers. Hence computer crimes are usually defined as unauthorized entry onto someone else's property. Where no criminal intent beyond curiosity or mischief exists, the crime may be a minor offense, such as computer hacking. Where criminal intent exists, however, the laws of most jurisdictions allow prosecution for both the unauthorized access and some other crime, usually a fraud or theft or an attempt to commit a fraud or theft. Similarly, most computer crime laws contain provisions making it illegal to interfere with another person's legitimate access to computer services or to information stored in a computer. Most states, however, provide for an affirmative defense of authorization when a reasonable belief that access was authorized can be demonstrated.

Types of Computer Crimes

A contemporary term for computer crime is *cybercrime*. Simply put, cybercrime is crime committed with or through the use of computers. Generally speaking, there are five types of cybercrime found in today's law, although the names given each type vary considerably between jurisdictions. The five types are (1) computer fraud; (2) computer trespass; (3) theft of computer services; (4) personal trespass by computer; and (5) computer tampering, or the dissemination of computer viruses, worms, and Trojan horses (Figure 9–3).

Even though titles vary, each type of computer offense has distinguishable elements. Distilling the laws of a variety of jurisdictions, it can be said that the elements of **computer fraud** make it unlawful for any person to

- Use a computer or computer network
- Without authority
- And with the intent to (1) obtain property or services by false pretenses, (2) embezzle or commit larceny, or (3) convert the property of another

The elements of **computer trespass** criminalize the activities of any person who

- Uses a computer or computer network
- Without authority
- And with the intent to (1) remove computer data, computer programs, or computer software from a computer or computer network; (2) cause a computer to malfunction; (3) alter or erase any computer data, computer programs, or computer software; (4) effect the creation

computer fraud
A statutory provision, found in many states, that makes it unlawful for any person to use a computer or computer network without authority and with the intent to (1) obtain property or services by false pretenses, (2) embezzle or commit larceny, or (3) convert the property of another.

computer trespass
The offense of using a computer or computer network without authority and with the intent to (1) remove computer data, computer programs, or computer software from a computer or computer network; (2) cause a computer to malfunction; (3) alter or erase any computer data, computer programs, or computer software; (4) effect the creation or alteration of a financial instrument or of an electronic transfer of funds; (5) cause physical injury to the property of another; or (6) make or cause to be made an unauthorized copy of data stored on a computer or of computer programs or computer software.

FIGURE 9–3

Types of Computer Crime.

Image bottom right © 3355m/Fotolia

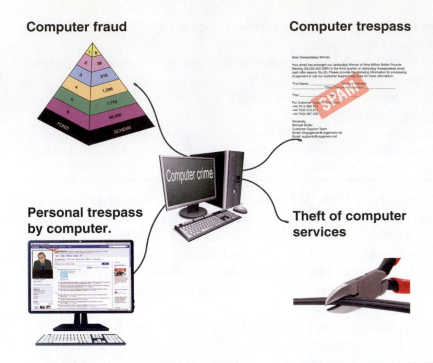

FIGURE 9–3

Types of Computer Crime.

Image bottom right © 3355m/Fotolia

or alteration of a financial instrument or of an electronic transfer of funds; (5) cause physical injury to the property of another; or (6) make or cause to be made an unauthorized copy of data stored on a computer or of computer programs or computer software.

theft of computer services
The willful use of a computer or computer network with the intent to obtain computer services without authority.

Laws against the **theft of computer services** make it unlawful for any person to

- Willfully use a computer or computer network
- With intent to obtain computer services
- Without authority

personal trespass by computer
The use of a computer or computer network without authority and with the intent to cause physical injury to an individual.

The elements of **personal trespass by computer** make it illegal for a person to

- Use a computer or computer network
- Without authority
- And with the intent to cause physical injury to an individual

Some states, depending on the seriousness of the behavior involved or the degree of harm that results, define greater and lesser degrees of each type of offense.

Although many states deal with computer viruses, worms, and Trojan horses (sometimes called *rogue programs*) under laws against computer trespass, some states have now enacted special legislation on **computer tampering** to deal with such threats. Many such special laws were passed after the arrest of Robert Morris, whose 1988 release of an Internet worm that spread to computers throughout the country (and the world) in a matter of hours, slowing them down and necessitating special administrative measures, became a watershed event in the history of computing. Morris's experiment in malicious programming cost thousands of hours of operator time to repair and an untold amount of monetary damage. Following Morris's arrest and prosecution, California modified its computer crime legislation to specifically refer to both worms and viruses, calling them "computer contaminants."[82] Maine and Texas both changed their laws to include computer viruses, and other states used terminology like *destructive computer programs* and *computer tampering* to describe the same phenomena.

computer tampering
Illegally inserting or attempting to insert a "program" into a computer, while knowing or believing that the "program" contains information or commands that will or may damage or destroy that computer (or its data), or any other computer (or its data) accessing or being accessed by that computer, *or* that will or may cause loss to the users of that computer or the users of a computer that accesses or that is accessed by such "program."[ii]

Computer tampering has four elements. Laws against computer tampering make it illegal for a person to

- Insert or attempt to insert a "program" into a computer
- While knowing or believing

- That the "program" contains information or commands
- That will or may damage or destroy that computer (or its data) or any other computer (or its data) accessing or being accessed by that computer, *or* that will or may cause loss to the users of that computer or the users of a computer that accesses or that is accessed by such "program"

Individual computer-tampering statutes may define the terms *program* and *loss* more precisely, although they do not do so in all cases.[83]

Federal Cybercrime Enforcement Agencies

Numerous federal agencies are involved in the battle against computer crime. Primary among them are the Computer Crime and Intellectual Property Section (CCIPS) of the U.S. Department of Justice and the FBI's Infrastructure Protection and Computer Intrusion Squad (IPCIS). CCIPS was founded in 1991 as the Computer Crime Unit but was elevated to "section" status within the Criminal Division of the U.S. Department of Justice in 1996.

The CCIPS staff consists of about two dozen lawyers who focus exclusively on the issues raised by computer and intellectual property crime. CCIPS staffers work closely on computer crime cases with assistant U.S. attorneys known as computer and telecommunications coordinators (CTCs) in U.S. attorney offices around the country.[84] CCIPS attorneys take a lead role in litigating some computer crime and intellectual property investigations and a coordinating role in some national investigations. Section attorneys advise federal prosecutors and law enforcement agents, comment on and propose legislation, coordinate international efforts to combat computer crime, litigate cases, and train federal law enforcement groups.

The FBI's IPCIS is responsible for investigating unauthorized intrusions into major computer networks belonging to telecommunications providers, private corporations, U.S. government agencies, and public and private educational facilities.[85] The squad also investigates the illegal interception of signals (especially cable and satellite signal theft) and the infringement of copyright laws related to software.

Internet-Based Crime

In February 2000, the President's Working Group on Unlawful Conduct on the Internet released a report entitled *The Electronic Frontier: The Challenge of Unlawful Conduct Involving the Use of the Internet*.[86] The group reported that "similar to the technologies that have preceded it, the Internet provides a new tool for wrongdoers to commit crimes, such as fraud, the sale or distribution of child pornography, the sale of guns or drugs or other regulated substances without regulatory protections, or the unlawful distribution of computer software or other creative material protected by intellectual property rights. In the most extreme circumstances, cyberstalking and other criminal conduct involving the Internet can lead to physical violence, abductions, and molestation."[87] Some criminal activities, the group observed, "employ both the product delivery and communications features of the Internet." Pedophiles, for example "may use the Internet's file transfer utilities to distribute and receive child pornography and use its communications features to make contact with children."

The group said that, "although the precise extent of unlawful conduct involving the use of computers is unclear, the rapid growth of the Internet and e-commerce has made such unlawful conduct a critical priority for legislators, policymakers, industry, and law enforcement agencies."[88] One reason is the Internet's potential to reach vast audiences easily, meaning that the potential scale of unlawful conduct is often much wider in cyberspace than the same conduct would be in the offline world.

The group attempted to assess the extent to which existing federal laws adequately address unlawful conduct involving the use of the Internet. It developed four general principles to guide its analysis (Figure 9–4). Those principles, which can also serve as guidelines for future legislation at both the state and federal level, are as follows:

- *Online–offline consistency.* Substantive regulation of unlawful conduct (for example, legislation providing for civil or criminal penalties for given conduct) should, as a rule, apply in the same way to conduct in the cyberworld as it does to conduct in the physical world. If an activity is prohibited in the physical world but not on the Internet, then the Internet becomes a safe haven for that unlawful activity. Similarly, conduct that is not prohibited in the physical world should not be subject to prohibition merely because it is carried out in cyberspace. Thus unlawful conduct involving the use of the Internet should not be treated as a special form of conduct outside the scope of existing laws. For example, fraud that is perpetrated through the use of the Internet should not be treated any differently, as a matter of substantive criminal law, from fraud that is perpetrated through the use of the telephone or the mail. To the extent that existing laws treat online and offline conduct inconsistently, they should be amended to remove inconsistencies.

- *Appropriate investigatory tools.* To effectively enforce substantive laws that apply to online conduct, law enforcement authorities need appropriate tools for detecting and investigating unlawful conduct involving the Internet. To the extent that existing investigative authority is tied to a particular technology, for example, it may need to be modified or clarified so that it also applies to the Internet. Moreover, the Internet, like other new technologies before it, may justify new forms of investigative authority. Before the invention of the telephone, for example, law enforcement agencies had no need for wiretaps, but once it was clear that

FIGURE 9–4

Deterring Computer Crime.

the telephone was being used to facilitate illegal activity, that new authority (circumscribed with protections for civil liberties and other societal interests) became necessary and appropriate. In like manner, features of the Internet that make it different from prior technologies may justify the need for changes in laws and procedures that govern the detection and investigation of computer crimes.

- *Technology neutrality.* To the extent that specific regulation of online activity may be necessary, any such regulation should be drafted in a technology-neutral way. Regulation tied to a particular technology may quickly become obsolete and require further amendment. In particular, laws written before the widespread use of the Internet may be based on assumptions regarding then-current technologies and thus may need to be clarified or updated to reflect new technological capabilities or realities. For example, regulation of "wire communications" may not account for the fact that communications may now occur through wireless means or by satellite. Technology-specific laws and regulations may also "lock in" a particular technology, hindering the development of superior technology.

- *Consideration of other social interests.* Any government regulation of conduct involving the use of the Internet requires a careful consideration of different social interests. In addition to society's strong interests in investigating and prosecuting unlawful conduct, society also has strong interests in promoting free speech, protecting children, protecting reasonable expectations of privacy, providing broad access to public information, and supporting legitimate commerce.

Of course, the Internet presents new issues relating to online expectations of privacy and confidentiality that may not have analogs in the offline world. Accordingly, concluded the working group, "rules and regulations designed to protect the safety and security of Internet users should be carefully tailored to accomplish their objectives without unintended consequences, such as stifling the growth of the Internet or chilling its use as a free and open communication medium."[89]

The group concluded that existing substantive federal laws appear to be generally adequate to protect Internet users from unlawful conduct. As noted earlier in this chapter, many such laws generally do not distinguish between unlawful conduct committed through the use of the Internet and the same conduct committed through the use of other, more traditional means of communication. For example, laws governing fraud, such as credit card fraud, identity theft, securities fraud, and unfair and deceptive trade acts or practices, apply with equal force to both online and offline conduct. Similarly, laws prohibiting the distribution and possession of child pornography and the luring of minors across state lines for unlawful sexual activity have been used with success to prosecute and convict those who use the Internet to distribute such material or to communicate with child victims in violation of statutory prohibitions. Laws in other areas, including the sale of firearms, the interstate transmission of gambling information, the sale of alcohol, securities fraud, and the theft of intellectual property, also generally apply to online as well as offline conduct.

One special problem associated with Internet activity that was noted by the working group involves questions about jurisdiction. Although crimes on the Internet may victimize local populations, the medium over which these crimes are committed permits a defendant to be located anywhere in the world. The group noted that "in the physical world, one cannot visit a place without some sense of its geographic location. Whether a particular street address or an area of the world, human travel is spatially based." By contrast, the group said, "because one can access a computer remotely without knowing where, in physical space, that computer is located, many people have come to think of the collection of worldwide computer linkages as 'cyberspace.'"

Significantly, cybercriminals are no longer hampered by the existence of national or international boundaries because information and property can be easily transmitted through communications and data networks. As a result, a criminal no longer needs to be at the actual scene of the crime (or anywhere nearby) to prey on his or her victims. A computer server running a webpage designed to defraud senior citizens, for example, might be located in Thailand, and victims of the scam could be scattered throughout numerous countries. A child pornographer might distribute photographs or videos via e-mail making its way through the communications networks of several countries before reaching the intended recipients. Likewise, evidence of a crime can be stored at a remote location, either for the purpose of concealing the crime from law enforcement and others or simply because of the design of the network. To clarify its point about jurisdictional issues, the working group gave this example: "A cyberstalker in Brooklyn, New York, may send a threatening e-mail to a person in Manhattan. If the stalker routes his communication through Argentina, France, and Norway before reaching his victim, the New York Police Department may have to get assistance from the Office of International Affairs at the Department of Justice in Washington, D.C., which, in turn, may have to get assistance from law enforcement in (say) Buenos Aires, Paris, and Oslo just to learn that the suspect is in New York." In this example, the working group points out, the perpetrator needs no passport and passes through no checkpoints as he commits his crime, whereas law enforcement agencies are burdened with cumbersome mechanisms for international cooperation—mechanisms that often derail or slow investigations.

The group adds that such jurisdictional issues do "not mean that traditional legal structures cannot be meaningfully applied to the Internet. Even though connections may be of short duration, computers are still physically located in particular places. The challenge to law enforcement is identifying that location and deciding which laws apply to what conduct." Some state computer crime statutes specifically provide that prosecution for computer crimes can take place in any jurisdiction where the computer used in the offense was located, in any area where an affected computer network functions, or in any jurisdiction "from which, to which, or through which any use of a computer or computer network was made, whether by wires, electromagnetic waves, microwaves, or any other means of communication."[90]

The report concludes by calling for increased interstate and federal–state cooperation. The fundamental question, says the group, is "how sovereign nations can meaningfully enforce national laws and procedures on a global Internet." Because the gathering of information in other jurisdictions and internationally will be crucial to investigating and prosecuting cybercrimes, the group concludes that "all levels of government will need to develop concrete and reliable mechanisms for cooperating with each other."

SUMMARY

- This chapter discusses property crimes, including larceny, burglary, criminal trespass, arson, and computer crimes involving misappropriation.

- Most property crimes are crimes of theft. They are sometimes called *acquisitive offenses*, *wrongful acquisition crimes*, or *crimes of misappropriation* because they involve the unlawful acquiring or appropriation of someone else's property.

- Larceny was the only form of theft originally punished under early common law. In early times, it was a capital offense.

- In most jurisdictions today, the statutory crime of larceny consists of the wrongful taking and carrying away (or *asportation*) of the personal property of another with the intent to permanently deprive the owner of possession of the property.

- Almost all jurisdictions have divided larceny into petit, or petty, larceny and grand larceny. Grand larceny (also known as *grand theft*) usually consists of the theft of property that has a market value of more than a certain amount or of the theft of certain property listed in the statute, such as firearms and cattle.

- Embezzlement is the unlawful conversion of the personal property of another by a person to whom it has been entrusted by (or for) its rightful owner. Embezzlement is fundamentally a violation of trust. Like larceny, one can be guilty of embezzlement only if the embezzled property belongs to another. Embezzlement is also known as *fraudulent conversion*.

- The crime of obtaining property by false pretenses, usually referred to simply as *false pretenses*, occurs when the taking of property with the passing of title is predicated on a false representation of a material fact. The crime occurs when a person uses false pretenses to obtain both possession of and title to the property in question.

- Forgery is the making of a false instrument or the material alteration of an existing genuine instrument. Forgery is complete when one either makes or passes a false instrument with the intent to defraud. The gist of the crime of forgery is the intent to defraud.

- Uttering is the offering, passing, or attempted passing of a forged document with the knowledge that the document is false and with the intent to defraud. Today, most jurisdictions have established the separate statutory crime of uttering a forged document.

- Receiving stolen property is another form of theft. Receiving stolen property can be defined as taking possession of, or control over, property that has been unlawfully stolen from another, knowing that it has been stolen.

- Robbery is an aggravated form of larceny. In addition to the elements necessary to constitute larceny, robbery involves two additional aspects: (1) The property must be taken from a person or removed from the presence of the victim, and (2) the taking must be by use of force or by putting the victim in fear.

- Under early common law, extortion was the corrupt collection of an unlawful fee by a public officer under color of office. It was a misdemeanor. Almost all American jurisdictions today have expanded the crime of extortion to cover anyone who uses a future threat to wrongfully obtain property. The contemporary crime of extortion can be defined as the taking of personal property by a threat of future harm. Statutory extortion is a felony in most jurisdictions.

- Blackmail is a form of extortion in which a threat is made to disclose a crime or other social disgrace. Even a threat to cause economic injury or social embarrassment may be sufficient to constitute blackmail in most jurisdictions.

- Identity theft, which is the unauthorized use of another individual's personal identity to fraudulently obtain money, goods, or services, is quickly becoming the most important new theft crime of the twenty-first century. Common forms of identity theft include taking over an existing credit card account and making unauthorized charges to it, taking out loans in another person's name, writing fraudulent checks using another person's name or account number, and using personal information to access and transfer money out of another person's bank or brokerage account.

- Under common law, burglary was the breaking and entering of the dwelling house of another in the nighttime with the intent to commit a felony. In most jurisdictions today, however, the crime of burglary is statutorily defined as the breaking and entering of a building, locked automobile, boat, and so on, with the intent to commit a felony or theft. Many jurisdictions divide burglary into burglary in the first or second degree. First-degree burglary is the burglary of an inhabited dwelling, and all other burglaries are second-degree burglaries.

- Looting, another crime against property, can be defined as burglary committed within an affected geographic area during an officially declared state of emergency or during a local emergency resulting from an earthquake, fire, flood, riot, or other disaster.

- Under common law, arson was the malicious burning of a structure of another. The modern trend is to increase the types of items that may be subject to arson. In almost all jurisdictions today, arson is defined in terms of knowingly and maliciously causing a fire. Arson cannot be committed by negligent or reckless conduct.

- Computer crime is a form of crime that could not be committed without computer technology. All 50 states and the federal government have enacted special laws, known as *computer crime statutes*, against cybercrime.

- Generally speaking, there are five types of cybercrime found in today's law: (1) computer fraud; (2) computer trespass; (3) theft of computer services; (4) personal trespass by computer; and (5) computer tampering, or the dissemination of computer viruses and worms.

KEY TERMS

acquisitive offense, 269

arson, 298

asportation, 278

blackmail, 287

burglary, 292

claim of right, 279

compounding a crime, 288

computer crime, 298

computer fraud, 311

computer tampering, 312

computer trespass, 311

constructive entry, 293

conversion, 280

criminal mischief, 297

criminal simulation, 284

criminal trespass, 297

embezzlement, 280

extortion, 287

false pretenses, 282

fixture, 272

forgery, 283

identity theft, 288

intangible property, 272

intellectual property, 298

larceny, 269

looting, 297

personal property, 272

personal trespass by computer, 312

real property, 273

receiving stolen property, 284

robbery, 285

tangible property, 272

theft, 269

theft of computer services, 312

trespassory taking, 273

uttering, 283

QUESTIONS FOR DISCUSSION

1. How do larceny and embezzlement differ, and why are these differences important?

2. What are the rules regarding the keeping of found property?

3. What types of property were subject to the common law crime of larceny?

4. What is the difference between embezzlement and false pretenses?

5. What was the nature of the historical need that led to the formulation of the "breaking bulk" doctrine?

6. It is often stated that "only people you trust can embezzle from you." Do you agree or disagree with this statement? Explain your answer.

7. What are the advantages to consolidating the wrongful acquisition crimes into a single crime of theft? What are the disadvantages?

8. What test do the courts use in robbery cases to determine whether property was taken from the presence of the victim?

9. How does extortion differ from robbery?

10. Explain the concept of constructive entry as applied to burglary crimes.

11. What are the five types of computer crime discussed in this chapter? What are the unique features of each?

CRITICAL THINKING AND APPLICATION PROBLEMS

Use the following facts to answer problems 1 and 2:

X. Torshun, a 21-year-old male and student at State University, used a screwdriver to break into a home owned by Claud I. Us, the city's mayor, and his wife, Messa Lina-Us. The couple was not home during the burglary. X took a laptop computer and $500 in cash from the home. The laptop and cash belonged to Messa. Against the advice of his wife, Claud reported the burglary to the police. In the days following the burglary, X searched the files on the computer for something of value. While searching the computer's files, he discovered video files of Messa having sex with three different men. Seizing the opportunity to make money, he contacted Messa by phone and threatened to release the photos and videos if she didn't pay him $25,000. Frightened that the release of the videos would end her marriage, destroy her husband's political career, and deeply embarrass her, she agreed to pay X. Unknown to Messa, the police had X under surveillance for the burglary, had a wiretap order for his phone, overheard the conversation, and arrested him immediately following Messa's payment to him.

1. What crime(s) has X committed? Explain fully how each element of the crime(s) you identify has been satisfied.

2. Change the facts so that a different property crime than you identified in your answer to problem 1 occurs. Explain how the elements of that crime are satisfied by your facts.

3. Assume that two thieves "steal" the same amount of money from their victims. Thief A takes $1,000 in cash from the purse of a victim when she isn't looking. Thief B is a financial adviser who has been given access to a victim's bank account for the purpose of investing the victim's money. Thief B withdraws the $1,000 from the victim's account and deposits it in Thief B's bank account with the intent to keep it. Assume that neither thief has a criminal record and that they are otherwise similar, for example, in age and financial condition. Should their punishments be identical? Explain your answer fully.

LEGAL RESOURCES ON THE WEB

Some websites contain a wealth of material describing high-technology crime and computer crime—as well as descriptions of statutes intended to curb such activity.

CERT Coordination Center
http://www.cert.org
CERT focuses on computer security concerns for Internet users.

Computer Crime and Intellectual Property Section (CCIPS), U.S. Department of Justice
http://www.cybercrime.gov
CCIPS is a central resource in the federal government's fight against cybercrime. A weekly e-mail newsletter is available through the site.

Computer Incident Advisory Capability (CIAC), U.S. Department of Energy
http://www.doecirc.energy.gov/ciac
The center provides solutions for U.S. government agencies that are facing security challenges in information technology.

Computer Security Division, National Institute of Standards and Technology (NIST)
http://csrc.nist.gov
The mission of NIST's Computer Security Division is to provide standards and technology to protect information systems against threats to the confidentiality of information, to protect the integrity of information and processes, and to safeguard the availability of

information and services in order to build trust and confidence in information technology (IT) systems.

Computer Security Laboratory, University of California, Davis
http://seclab.cs.ucdavis.edu

The laboratory's mission is to improve the current state of computer security through research and teaching.

National Infrastructure Protection Center (NIPC)
http://ecommerce.hostip.info/pages/770/National-Infrastructure-Protection-Center-NIPC.html

NIPC manages computer-intrusion investigations at the federal level.

SUGGESTED READINGS AND CLASSIC WORKS

American Law Institute. *Model Penal Code and Commentaries*, vol. 2. Philadelphia: American Law Institute, 1980.

Brickley, Kathleen F. "The Jurisprudence of Larceny: An Historical Inquiry and Interest Analysis." *Vanderbilt Law Review* 33 (1980): 1101.

Cressy, Donald. *Other People's Money*. Belmont, CA: Wadsworth, 1953.

Fletcher, George P. "The Metamorphosis of Larceny." *Harvard Law Review* 89 (1976): 469.

Gabor, Thomas, and Andre Normandeau. *Armed Robbery: Cops, Robbers, and Victims*. Springfield, IL: Charles C. Thomas, 1987.

Goldberger, Peter. "Forgery." In *Encyclopedia of Crime and Justice*, edited by Sanford Kadish. New York: Free Press, 1983.

Hall, Jerome. *Theft, Law, and Society*, 2nd ed. Indianapolis: Bobbs-Merrill, 1952.

Roberson, Cliff. *Preventing Employee Misconduct*. Lexington, MA: Lexington Books, 1986.

Schmalleger, Frank, and Michael Pittarno, eds.. *Crimes of the Internet*. Upper Saddle River, NJ: Pearson, 2009.

Weinreb, Lloyd L. "Manifest Criminality, Criminal Intent, and the Metamorphosis of Larceny." *Yale Law Journal* 90 (1980): 294.

NOTES

1. Cynthia Manson and Charles Ardai, *Future Crime: An Anthology of the Shape of Crime to Come* (New York: Donald I. Fine, 1992), ix.

2. U.S. Code, Title 18, Section 1028(a)(7).

3. Uniform Crime Reports, Federal Bureau of Investigation, U.S. Department of Justice, 2010.

4. Louis B. Schwartz, "Theft," in *The Encyclopedia of Crime and Justice*, edited by Sandord Kadish (New York: Macmillian Library Reference, 1983), 4: 1537–1551.

5. American Law Institute, *Model Penal Code and Commentaries*, comment to Section 223.1 at 127–32 (1980).

6. Ibid.

7. East's *Pleas of the Crown* 553 (1803).

8. *Rex v. Wheatly*, 97 E.R. 746 (1761).

9. Rollin M. Perkins and Ronald N. Boyce, *Criminal Law*, 3rd ed. (Mineola, NY: Foundation Press, 1982), 289.

10. Schwartz, "Theft," 1537.

11. The statute also effectively eliminates any common law vestiges of the classification of dogs as "base" animals.

12. *State v. Jackson*, 11 S.E.2d 149 (N.C. 1940).

13. Texas Penal Code, Section 28.01(3).

14. Model Penal Code, Section 223.0(6).

15. *Thompson v. State*, 10 So. 520 (Ala. 1891).

16. *Commonwealth v. Tluchak*, 70 A.2d. 657 (Pa. 1950).

17. *Carrier's Case*, Y.B. Rasch. 13 Edw. IV, f. 9, pl. 5 (Eng. 1473).

18. Frances Robles, "Truck Crash Turns I-95 into Road to Riches," *Miami Herald*, January 9, 1997.

19. Ibid.

20. Model Penal Code, Section 223.5.

21. *State v. Jones*, 65 N.C. 395 (1871).

22. Ibid., 297, 298.

23. Although not "larceny," other laws might criminalize such behavior.

24. Model Penal Code, Section 223.9.

25. Donald Cressy, *Other People's Money* (Belmont, CA: Wadsworth, 1953).

26. The material in this section was adapted from Cliff Roberson, *Preventing Employee Misconduct: A Self-Defense Manual for Business* (Lexington, MA: Lexington Books, 1986).

27. *United States v. Nelson*, 227 F.2d 72 (D.C. Cir. 1955).

28. See, for example, California Penal Code, Section 475.

29. See, for example, Texas Penal Code, Section 32.22.

30. *State v. George*, 173 S.W. 1077 (Mo. 1915).

31. *People v. Taylor*, 4 Cal. App. 2d 214 (1935).

32. *State v. Harrington*, 260 A.2d 692 (Vt. 1970).

33. Model Penal Code, Section 223.4.

34. Stephen A. Saltzburg and others, *Criminal Law: Cases and Materials* (Charlottesville, VA: Michie, 1994), 562.

35. California Attorney General's Office, press release, July 7, 2000.

36. Prepared Statement of the Federal Trade Commission on Identity Theft made before the Subcommittee on Technology, Terrorism, and Government Information of the Committee on the Judiciary of the United States Senate, Washington, DC, March 7, 2000, from which some of the wording in this section is taken.

37. Ibid.

38. Ibid.

39. U.S. Code, Title 18, Section 1028(a)(7).

40. Ibid.

41. *State v. Sorenson*, 138 N.W. 411 (Iowa 1912).

42. *State v. Hill*, 520 P.2d 946 (Wash. App. 1974), citing *State v. Rosencrans*, 167 P.2d 170, 172 (Wash. 1946).

43. *Rolland v. Commonwealth*, 82 Pa. 306 (1876).

44. John S. Baker, Jr., and others, *Hall's Criminal Law: Cases and Materials*, 5th ed. (Charlottesville, VA:

Michie, 1993), 496, citing *Lawson v. Commonwealth*, 169 S.W. 587 (Ky. 1914), and *People v. Toland*, 111 N.E. 760 (N.Y. 1916). See also *Rolland v. Commonwealth*, 82 Pa. 324 (1876).

45. *Smith v. State*, 362 P.2d 1071 (Alaska 1961).

46. *State v. Gonzales*, 905 S.W.2d 4 (Tex. App. Eastland 1995).

47. *Mattox v. State*, 101 N.E. 1009 (Ind. 1913).

48. *Regina v. Davis*, 6 Cox Crim. Cas. 369 (1854).

49. *State v. Hudson*, 430 P.2d 386 (N.M. 1967).

50. *Henderson v. State*, 86 So. 439 (Fla. 1920).

51. *People v. Blair*, 288 N.E.2d 443 (Ill. 1952).

52. American Law Institute, *Model Penal Code and Commentaries*, Part II, Section 221.1 (1980).

53. Texas Penal Code, Section 30.05.

54. Steve Miletich, *Seattle Post-Intelligencer*, via Simon and Schuster NewsLink online, May 21, 1997.

55. Some of the materials in this section are adapted from the Electronic Frontier Foundation website, http://www.eff.org.

56. *Hancock v. State*, 402 S.W.2d 906, 18 A.L.R. 3d 1113 (Tex. Crim. 1966).

57. *Lund v. Commonwealth*, 217 Va. 688, 232 S.E.2d 745 (1977).

58. *Ward v. Superior Court*, 3 Computer Law Serv. Rep. 206 (Cal. Super Ct. 1972).

59. *People v. Weg*, 113 Misc.2d 1017, 450 N.Y.S.2d 957 (N.Y. City Crim. Ct. 1982).

60. Electronic Frontier Foundation website, http://www .eff.org.

61. U.S. Code, Title 18, Section 2510.

62. And as amended by the National Information infrastructure Protection Act of 1996; Public Law 104-294.

63. U.S. Code, Title 18, Section 1030 (Public Law 98-473).

64. Public Law 103-322.

65. Public Law 99-508.

66. Title 5 of the Telecommunications Act of 1996, Public Law 104-104, 110 Stat. 56.

67. Public Law 105-147.

68. Public Law 106-160.

69. Section 225 of the Homeland Security Act, Public Law 107-296.

70. U.S. Code, Title 18, Section 1029.

71. As described in M. Gemiganni, "Viruses and Computer Law," *Communications of the ACM* 32 (June 1989): 669.

72. This section is taken in part from Frank Schmalleger, *Criminology Today: An Interactive Introduction*, 4th ed. (Upper Saddle River, NJ: Prentice Hall, 2006).

73. See "David LaMacchia Cleared; Case Raises Civil Liberties Issues," *The Tech* (MIT), February 7, 1995, http://tech.mit.edu/V115/N0/lamacchia.00n.html (accessed January 20, 2005).

74. Public Law 104-104, 110 Stat. 56.

75. *Reno* v. *ACLU*, 521 U.S. 844 (1997).

76. *Ashcroft* v. *ACLU*, 542 U.S. 656 (2004).

77. Public Law 106-554.

78. For a good discussion of the development of computer crime laws, see Richard C. Hollinger and Lonn LanzaKaduce, "The Process of Criminalization: The Case of Computer Crime Laws," *Criminology* 26 (1988): 101.

79. See, for example, the Alabama Computer Crime Act, Alabama Code, Sections 13-A-8-100 to 103; the Florida Computer Crimes Act, Florida Statutes, Sections 815.01 to 815.07; and the Illinois Computer Crime Prevention Law, Illinois Revised Statutes, Chapter 38, Section 5/16D-1 to 5/16D-7.

80. See Ohio Revised Code Annotated, Sections 2913.01, 2913.81, and Ohio Revised Code Annotated, Section 2901.01 (m)(10).

81. Visit the Electronic Frontier Foundation on the Web at http://www.eff.org.

82. California Penal Code, Section 502 (b)(10).

83. See, for example, Illinois Revised Statutes, Chapter 38, Section 5/16D-3 (a)(4), from which the elements used in our definition of *computer tampering* are derived.

84. Adapted from the Computer Crime and Intellectual Property Section of the Criminal Division of the U.S. Department of Justice home page, http://www.cybercrime.gov.

85. Adapted from the FBI's Washington Field Office Infrastructure Protection and Computer Intrusion Squad home page, http://www.fbi.gov/programs/ipcis/ipcis.htm.

86. The President's Working Group on Unlawful Conduct on the Internet, *The Electronic Frontier: The Challenge of Unlawful Conduct Involving the Use of the Internet* (Washington, DC: White House, 2000), http://www.usdoj.gov/criminal/cybercrime/unlawful.htm (accessed March 29, 2009).

87. Ibid.

88. Ibid.

89. Ibid.

90. Georgia Code, Section 16-9-94.

© David Grossman/Alamy

10

Offenses against Public Order and the Administration of Justice

OBJECTIVES

After reading this chapter, you should be able to

- Describe what constitutes breach of peace and disorderly conduct, including fighting and affray.
- Explain the concept of fighting words, and show how fighting words can be distinguished from protected forms of speech.
- Describe the crimes of riot and unlawful assembly.
- Describe what constitutes vagrancy and loitering.
- Summarize weapons-carrying violations.
- Describe what constitutes illegal entry into the United States.
- Distinguish among treason, sedition, and espionage.
- Summarize obstruction of justice and the crime of escape.
- Describe what constitutes perjury and contempt.
- Describe what constitutes misconduct in office.
- Summarize various environmental crimes.

> *One declares so many things to be a crime that it becomes impossible for men to live without breaking laws.*
>
> —Ayn Rand, Atlas Shrugged (1957)

> *The criminal law is society's most destructive and intrusive form of intervention.*
>
> —Law Reform Commission of Canada (1977)

> *Vulgar statements directed at police officers . . . [are] not sufficient to constitute disorderly conduct.*
>
> —People v. Stephen, 153 Misc. 2d 382, 581 N.Y.S.2d 981 (N.Y. Crim. Ct. 1992)

INTRODUCTION

On October 30, 1991, at about 4 o'clock in the morning, New York City Police Officer William McGill was on patrol at the corner of 150th Street and Broadway. While walking by a store that was still open, Officer McGill observed a young man whom he later learned was named Paul Stephen. Stephen was standing in the store, and as the officer walked by, Stephen clutched his genital area and yelled, "F—you! If you were in jail, I'd f—you! You'd be my bitch. . . ." Stephen followed the officer out into the street repeating the statements and yelling: "If you didn't have that gun and badge, I'd kick your ass, I'd kill you!" A crowd of 15 to 20 people joined the defendant, yelling, "Yeah, f—the police!"[1]

Officer McGill decided to arrest Stephen for disorderly conduct. While the officer was attempting to restrain Stephen, the defendant struggled violently, flailing his arms, twisting and turning his body, and butting the officer in the chest with his head. Stephen was jailed for a short while. When he appeared in court, his attorney argued that his conduct was protected under the U.S. Constitution's First Amendment guarantee of free speech and by Article I, Section 8, of the New York State Constitution. A portion of the trial court's opinion follows:[2]

> It has long been recognized that the guarantees of freedom of expression under the First and Fourteenth Amendments of the Federal Constitution are not absolute and do not prevent States from punishing certain "well-defined and narrowly limited classes of speech. . . ." Where words present a clear and present danger of inciting those listening to lawless action, they are not entitled to constitutional protections and may be punished. . . .
>
> In this case, there is no indication that either defendant or any member of the crowd was armed or preparing to lay hands upon the officer. Accordingly, defendant's statements are protected speech and do not fall within the incitement exception to the First Amendment. . . .
>
> The second class of unprotected speech relevant to this case is that category of speech constituting "fighting words," words "which by their very utterance inflict injury or tend to incite an immediate breach of the peace," or which are likely to provoke the average person to retaliation. (*Chaplinsky* v. *New Hampshire, supra*, 315 U.S. at 572, 62 S. Ct. at 769). The People contend that defendant's words to the officer fall squarely within this class of actionable conduct.
>
> While the original *Chaplinsky* formulation of "fighting words" may have given some impression of establishing a category of words which could be proscribed regardless of the context in which they were used, developing First Amendment doctrine in the half century since *Chaplinsky* was decided has continually resorted to analyzing provocative expression contextually. . . . Thus, whether particular speech constitutes "fighting words" cannot be determined outside of the context in which the speech occurs.
>
> In the context within which these words were uttered, defendant's remarks, even with the accompanying gestures, could not be said to have a direct tendency to provoke the police officer to retaliate with acts of violence or other breach of the peace. No reasonable person witnessing the situation would have thought it likely that the police officer would have been driven to attack defendant as a direct consequence of his comments.
>
> Moreover, the Supreme Court has held that the "fighting words" doctrine applies more narrowly to police officers, as police officers are trained and expected to exercise more restraint in response to provocation than do other citizens. (*City of Houston* v. *Hill*, 482 U.S. 451, 107 S. Ct. 2502, 96 L. Ed. 2d 398 [1987]). One of the reasons we expect the police to be less sensitive to provocation, according to the Supreme Court, is because: "[t]he freedom of individuals verbally to oppose or challenge police action without thereby risking arrest is one of the principal characteristics by which we distinguish a free nation from a police state. . . ." Thus, even if reasonable civilians might

have been provoked into retaliatory action by defendant's comments, one could expect that a trained police officer would remain calm (as he apparently did). Thus, defendant's remarks, while odious, do not come within the small class of "fighting words" for which the government may mete out punishment. . . .

As defendant's threatening comments and gestures did not present a clear and present danger of either of these types of immediate harm, and amounted to pure, protected speech, this prosecution infringes defendant's rights of free expression under the First and Fourteenth Amendments of the Federal Constitution. Accordingly, the motion to dismiss the charge of Penal Law Section 240.20(1) on Federal Constitutional grounds is granted.

Defendant next argues that because the officer lacked authority to arrest him for disorderly conduct, the resisting arrest charge must be dismissed as facially insufficient. . . . In this case, assuming the facts stated in the accusatory instrument to be true, the officer arrested the defendant for exercising his constitutional rights to express his views regarding members of the police department, albeit in an extremely derisive way. Because on these facts, no violation of disorderly conduct occurred, the officer was not authorized to arrest the defendant. . . . As the officer was not authorized to make an arrest at the time the defendant struggled with the officer, an essential element of resisting arrest is lacking. . . . Accordingly, the charge of resisting arrest is dismissed for facial insufficiency.

> *Although the preservation of liberty depends in part upon the maintenance of social order, the First Amendment requires that officers and municipalities respond with restraint in the face of verbal challenges to police action, since a certain amount of expressive disorder is inevitable in a society committed to individual freedom and must be protected if that freedom would survive.*
>
> —*Justice William J. Brennan, writing for the majority in City of Houston v. Hill, 482 U.S. 451 (1987)*

CRIMES AGAINST PUBLIC ORDER

This chapter and Chapter 12 discuss crimes against the social order. Between the two chapters, four categories of social-order crimes are discussed: (1) crimes against public order and safety, which include disorderly conduct, breach of peace, unlawful fighting, and so on; (2) crimes against justice and the administration of government, including treason and perjury; (3) crimes against the environment; and (4) crimes against public decency and morality, including obscenity, prostitution, sodomy, and other sex-related offenses. Our coverage of social-order offenses begins in this chapter with a discussion of crimes against the public order and safety and includes discussions of crimes against the administration of justice and crimes against the environment. The final category of social-order crimes, those committed against public morality, is discussed in Chapter 12.

Public-order offenses are those that disturb or invade society's peace and tranquility. Public-order offenses include the following: breach of peace (sometimes called *disturbing the peace*), disorderly conduct, fighting, affray (fighting in public), vagrancy, loitering, illegally carrying weapons, keeping a disorderly (or "bawdy") house, public intoxication (whether by alcohol or other controlled substances), disturbance of public assembly, inciting to riot, rioting, unlawful assembly, rout, and obstructing public passage. Laws criminalizing such activities rest on the assumption that public order is inherently valuable and should be maintained—and that disorder is not to be tolerated and should be reduced, when it occurs, through the application of the criminal law. This modern-day assumption derives from an early English common law principle that held that anyone intentionally violating the peace decreed by the king, and desired by him for all of his subjects throughout the realm, could be called to answer to the king's representatives.

Breach of Peace and Disorderly Conduct

As some authors point out, all crimes, when viewed from a philosophical perspective, are breaches of peace and disruptions of public order.[3] A murder, for example, not only victimizes the individual killed but also violates the orderliness of social interaction and lessens the overall integrity of the social order. Some crimes, however, do not just *theoretically* disturb public tranquility but are themselves *actual* disturbances of public tranquility or cause such disturbances—and these are the crimes that concern us here.

Under common law, **breach of peace** was the term used to describe any unlawful activity that unreasonably disturbed the peace and tranquility of the community. *Breach of peace*, as used today, is "a flexible term, occasionally defined by statute, for a violation of public order; [or] an act calculated to disturb the public peace."[4] Breach of peace can also be described as "a public offense done by violence, or one causing or likely to cause an immediate disturbance of public order."[5] The term itself "embraces a great variety of conduct destroying or menacing public order and tranquility. It includes not only violent acts, but acts and words likely to produce violence in others."[6]

All jurisdictions have statutes that prohibit conduct likely to cause breaches of the public peace. At common law, the main thrust of strictures against breach of peace was to discourage acts that were not otherwise deemed criminal but that tended to disturb the peace and tranquility of the community. As English jurist William Blackstone observed, "Peace is the very end and foundation of civil society."[7] Contemporary statutes, building on the common law emphasis on public tranquility, specifically prohibit disorderly conduct, unlawful fighting, challenging a person to fight, the use of "fighting words," and so on. Certain types of conduct may be considered a breach of peace in one jurisdiction but be called disorderly conduct in another. Accordingly, there is significant overlap between the two offenses, as will be obvious from our discussion in this section. The California breach-of-peace statute contains the phrase "offensive words," referring to the use of fighting words. **Fighting words**, as the story that opens this chapter points out, are utterances that are intended to provoke those at whom they are directed. Impugning another's parentage provides an oft-cited example of fighting words. Fighting words are not protected by the free speech clause of the First Amendment to the U.S. Constitution, a position made clear by the U.S. Supreme Court in the 1942 case of *Chaplinsky* v. *New Hampshire*.[8] In *Chaplinsky*, the Court ruled that "it is well understood that the right of free speech is not absolute at all times and under all circumstances. There are certain well-defined and narrowly limited classes of speech, the prevention and punishment of which have never been thought to raise any Constitutional problem. These include the lewd and obscene, the profane, the libelous, and the insulting or 'fighting' words—those that by their very utterance inflict injury or tend to incite an immediate breach of the peace." As the Court explained, "It has been well observed that such utterances are no essential part of any exposition of ideas, and are of such slight social value as a step to truth that any benefit that may be derived from them is clearly outweighed by the social interest in order and morality." In short, the Court was saying that the use of "epithets or personal abuse is not in any proper sense communication of information or opinion safeguarded by the Constitution" and may be punished as a criminal act.

Whereas breach of peace is a general term, **disorderly conduct** refers to specific, purposeful, and unlawful behavior that tends to cause public inconvenience, annoyance, or alarm. Because there was no disorderly conduct crime under common law, the modern-day crime of disorderly conduct has been created by statute. One of the constitutional problems associated with attempting to outlaw disorderly conduct, however, is accurately describing just what forms of behavior constitute the offense. At least one court has observed that disorderly conduct is "[a] term of loose and indefinite meaning (except as defined by statutes), but signifying generally any behavior that is contrary to law, and more particularly such as tends to disturb the peace or decorum, scandalize the community, or shock the public sense of morality."[9]

In October 2001, for example, not long after the September 11 terrorist attacks, William Harvey, 54, of Long Island City, New York, was arrested near the World Trade Center site and charged with disorderly conduct for staging a speech in which he heralded Osama bin

---

breach of peace
Any unlawful activity that unreasonably disturbs the peace and tranquility of the community. Also, "an act calculated to disturb the public peace."[i]

fighting words
Words that, by their very utterance, inflict injury or tend to incite an immediate breach of peace. Fighting words are not protected by the free speech clause of the First Amendment to the U.S. Constitution.

disorderly conduct
Specific, purposeful, and unlawful behavior that tends to cause public inconvenience, annoyance, or alarm.

APPLYING THE CONCEPT

CAPSTONE CASE

Are Words That Are So Insulting That They May Lead a Reasonable Person to Violence Protected Speech under the First Amendment?

Chaplinsky v. *New Hampshire*, 315 U.S. 568 (1942)
Mr. Justice Murphy delivered the opinion of the Court.

THE CASE   Appellant, a member of the sect known as Jehovah's Witnesses, was convicted in the municipal court of Rochester, New Hampshire, for violation of Chapter 378, Section 2, of the Public Laws of New Hampshire: "No person shall address any offensive, derisive or annoying word to any other person who is lawfully in any street or other public place, nor call him by any offensive or derisive name, nor make any noise or exclamation in his presence and hearing with intent to deride, offend or annoy him, or to prevent him from pursuing his lawful business or occupation."

The complaint charged that appellant, "with force and arms, in a certain public place in said city of Rochester, to-wit, on the public sidewalk on the easterly side of Wakefield Street, near unto the entrance of the City Hall, did unlawfully repeat the words following, addressed to the complainant, that is to say, "You are a God damned racketeer" and "a damned Fascist and the whole government of Rochester are Fascists or agents of Fascists," the same being offensive, derisive and annoying words and names. . . .

By motions and exceptions, appellant raised the questions that the statute was invalid under the Fourteenth Amendment of the Constitution of the United States in that it placed an unreasonable restraint on freedom of speech, freedom of the press, and freedom of worship, and because it was vague and indefinite. These contentions were overruled, and the case comes here on appeal.

There is no substantial dispute over the facts. Chaplinsky was distributing the literature of his sect on the streets of Rochester on a busy Saturday afternoon. Members of the local citizenry complained to the City Marshal, Bowering, that Chaplinsky was denouncing all religion as a "racket." Bowering told them that Chaplinsky was lawfully engaged, and then warned Chaplinsky that the crowd was getting restless. Some time later, a disturbance occurred and the traffic officer on duty at the busy intersection started with

Chaplinsky for the police station, but did not inform him that he was under arrest or that he was going to be arrested. On the way, they encountered Marshal Bowering, who had been advised that a riot was under way and was therefore hurrying to the scene. Bowering repeated his earlier warning to Chaplinsky, who then addressed to Bowering the words set forth in the complaint.

Chaplinsky's version of the affair was slightly different. He testified that when he met Bowering, he asked him to arrest the ones responsible for the disturbance. In reply, Bowering cursed him and told him to come along. Appellant admitted that he said the words charged in the complaint, with the exception of the name of the Deity.

Over appellant's objection, the trial court excluded, as immaterial, testimony relating to appellant's mission "to preach the true facts of the Bible," his treatment at the hands of the crowd, and the alleged neglect of duty on the part of the police. This action was approved by the court below, which held that neither provocation nor the truth of the utterance would constitute a defense to the charge.

THE FINDING   It is now clear that "Freedom of speech and freedom of the press, which are protected by the First Amendment from infringement by Congress, are among the fundamental personal rights and liberties which are protected by the Fourteenth Amendment from invasion by state action." *Lovell* v. *Griffin*, 303 U.S. 444, 450. Freedom of worship is similarly sheltered. *Cantwell* v. *Connecticut*, 310 U.S. 296, 303.

Appellant assails the statute as a violation of all three freedoms, speech, press and worship, but only an attack on the basis of free speech is warranted. The spoken, not the written, word is involved. And we cannot conceive that cursing a public officer is the exercise of religion in any sense of the term. . . . Allowing the broadest scope to the language and purpose of the Fourteenth Amendment, it is well understood that the right of free speech is not absolute at all times and under all circumstances. There are certain

(continued)

well-defined and narrowly limited classes of speech, the prevention and punishment of which have never been thought to raise any Constitutional problem. These include the lewd and obscene, the profane, the libelous, and the insulting or "fighting" words—those which, by their very utterance, inflict injury or tend to incite an immediate breach of the peace. It has been well observed that such utterances are no essential part of any exposition of ideas and are of such slight social value as a step to truth that any benefit that may be derived from them is clearly outweighed by the social interest in order and morality.

"Resort to epithets or personal abuse is not in any proper sense communication of information or opinion safeguarded by the Constitution, and its punishment as a criminal act would raise no question under that instrument." . . . We are unable to say that the limited scope of the statute as thus construed contravenes the Constitutional right of free expression. It is a statute narrowly drawn and limited to define and punish specific conduct lying within the domain of state power, the use in a public place of words likely to cause a breach of the peace. This conclusion necessarily disposes of appellant's contention that the statute is so vague and indefinite as to render a conviction thereunder a violation of due process. A statute punishing verbal acts, carefully drawn so as not unduly to impair liberty of expression, is not too vague for a criminal law. Nor can we say that the application of the statute to the facts disclosed by the record substantially or unreasonably impinges upon the privilege of free speech. Argument is unnecessary to demonstrate that the appellations "damned racketeer" and "damned Fascist" are epithets likely to provoke the average person to retaliation and thereby cause a breach of the peace. . . .

. . . Our function is fulfilled by a determination that the challenged statute, on its face and as applied, does not contravene the Fourteenth Amendment.

Affirmed.

What Do *You* Think?

1. Do you think that the language used by Chaplinsky should be subject to governmental regulation? Why or why not?

2. Do you believe that all manner of speech should be protected by the First Amendment? If not, what limits would you put on such protections?

3. What are "fighting words"? Why aren't they protected by the First Amendment? Do you think they should be? Explain.

Must police officers tolerate more verbal abuse than others?

Lewis v. New Orleans, 415 U.S. 130 (1974)

The Case: During a January 1970 traffic stop in New Orleans, Louisiana, defendant Lewis allegedly engaged in a profanity-laced verbal exchange with a city police officer. According to the officer's description—which was vigorously denied by the defendant at trial—Lewis "started yelling and screaming" and referred to him as "you god damn m f..police." Lewis was consequently convicted of violating a city ordinance that made it unlawful for any person "wantonly to curse or revile or . . . use obscene or opprobrious language toward or with reference to any member of the city police while in the actual performance of his duty." On appeal, the Supreme Court of Louisiana upheld Lewis's conviction, finding that the ordinance as written applied only to unprotected "fighting words." On review at the U.S. Supreme Court, however, Lewis argued that the ordinance violated the First Amendment by prohibiting some forms of constitutionally protected expression.

The Finding: In a 6–3 ruling, the U.S. Supreme Court reversed Lewis's conviction. Writing for five members of the Court, Justice William Brennan found that the ordinance "plainly has a broader sweep than the constitutional definition of 'fighting words' announced in *Chaplinsky v. New Hampshire*." The law's proscription on "opprobrious language," Brennan found, "embraces words that do not 'by their very utterance inflict injury or tend to incite an immediate breach of the peace.'" The category of "opprobrious language" could include words that merely "convey . . . disgrace," Brennan wrote; consequently, the ordinance "is susceptible of application to protected speech . . . and is facially invalid."

Concurring in the result, Justice Lewis Powell also suggested that under the *Chaplinsky* "fighting words" doctrine, language aimed specifically at police officers may be entitled to broader First Amendment protection. "Quite apart from the ambiguity inherent in the term 'opprobrious,'" Powell wrote, "words may or may not be 'fighting words' depending upon the circumstances of their utterance." He continued: "It is unlikely . . . that the words said to have been used here would have precipitated a physical confrontation between the middle-aged woman who spoke them and the police officer in whose presence they were uttered." What's more, "a properly trained officer may reasonably be expected to 'exercise a higher degree of restraint' than the average citizen, and thus be less likely to respond belligerently. . . ."

Must an officer actually respond with anger in order for the "fighting words" doctrine to apply?

Bousquet v. Arkansas, 548 S.W.2d 125 (1977)

The Case: Upset that an off-duty police officer (working as a security guard) was following her at a Little Rock, Arkansas, department store, defendant Mary Bousquet angrily confronted the officer, asking: "Are you going to follow me upstairs? . . . I'm talking to you mother f****** pig!" A short time later, she added: "Follow me outside you mother f***** and son-of-a- bitch." After aiming additional profanities at the officer—and ultimately grabbing him by the shirt and pushing him—Bousquet was arrested at the scene; she was later found guilty of violating the state's prohibition on "us[ing] abusive or obscene language, or mak[ing] an obscene gesture, in a manner likely to provoke a violent or disorderly response." On appeal, Bousquet argued that her verbal outbursts were not "fighting words," and thus should be considered as protected speech, because, in the specific circumstances of her arrest, the officer was not actually "aroused to immediate, violent anger" by her words.

The Finding: The Supreme Court of Arkansas rejected Bousquet's First Amendment argument and upheld her conviction for disorderly conduct. To apply the *Chaplinsky* fighting words doctrine, the court held, it was "not necessary that the person addressed must have reacted violently." What's more, trial courts need not make specific findings of fact that "under the circumstances existing, the words spoken by the accused were likely to incite violent retaliation from the person to whom the words were spoken." Instead, the state court held, officials need only show that the words in question "were likely to provoke an *average person* to retaliate and cause a breach of the peace" (emphasis added). Using that standard, Bousquet's language constituted "fighting words" that lie outside the First Amendment. ■

Laden and told onlookers that the attacks had been in retaliation for the U.S treatment of Islamic countries.

Although Harvey said that he was asserting his First Amendment rights to free speech, Judge Neil E. Ross of the Manhattan Criminal Court found that Harvey created a public disturbance. "It is the reaction which speech engenders, not the content of the speech, that is the heart of disorderly conduct," Ross said.[10] The judge concluded that it was reasonable to infer that Harvey was aware of the substantial risk of public alarm that his speech would engender and that he consciously chose to disregard that risk.

To lose First Amendment protection, speech must actually cause, or be likely to cause, a breach of peace. Speech that is offensive but doesn't amount to fighting words or that doesn't create a clear and present danger to people may not be censored or punished. Two Supreme Court decisions illustrate this point. In *Texas* v. *Johnson*[11] the Supreme Court upheld the right of Johnson to burn the flag of the United States as a form of political protest even though most people in the United States find this form of expression distasteful, if not disturbing. That Johnson was engaged in political speech, which benefits from the First Amendment's greatest protection, at the 1984 Republican National Convention, was important to the Court. In another example, the Court upheld the First Amendment rights of the members of the Westboro Baptist Church of Topeka, Kansas, to protest at the funerals of fallen U.S. soldiers. Believing that God hates the United States, they rejoiced in the deaths of members of the U.S. military. To make their point they picketed at the funerals of deceased members of the armed forces. Their signs read "Thank God for Dead Soldiers," "Fags Doom Nations," "You Are Going To Hell," and other generally offensive messages. The church group notified the police of their intention to picket, complied with the police's rules for staging the demonstration, and didn't interfere with the funeral or block any sidewalks or streets. Nonetheless, the father of a slain soldier whose funeral was picketed sued the picketers for intentional infliction of emotional distress and four other torts. Although hurtful and offensive, the Court said of the picketing:

> Westboro believes that America is morally flawed; many Americans might feel the same about Westboro. Westboro's funeral picketing is certainly hurtful and its contribution to public discourse may be negligible. But Westboro addressed matters of public import on public property, in a peaceful manner, in full compliance with the guidance of local officials. The speech was indeed planned to coincide with Matthew Snyder's funeral, but did not itself disrupt that funeral, and Westboro's choice to conduct its picketing at that time and place did not alter the nature of its speech.
>
> Speech is powerful. It can stir people to action, move them to tears of both joy and sorrow, and—as it did here—inflict great pain. On the facts before us, we cannot react to that pain by punishing the speaker. As a Nation we have chosen a different course— to protect even hurtful speech on public issues to ensure that we do not stifle public debate. That choice requires that we shield Westboro from tort liability for its picketing in this case.[12]

Fighting and Affray

One form of disorderly conduct that is often described by statute is unlawful public fighting. Although some fights may be officially sanctioned, as in the case of regulated sporting events, spontaneous and unregulated physical altercations that occur in a place open to public view constitute disorderly conduct. Many jurisdictions have statutes outlawing **affray**, which can be defined as "the fighting of persons in a public place to the terror of the people."[13] The term *affray* derives from the word *afraid* and means an altercation that tends to alarm the community.

Fighting is a mutual event and thus differs from assault. If one person attacks another, the attacker may be guilty of assault because the accosted person may be an innocent victim. But when two people willingly and publicly fight one another, both are guilty of the crime of affray. **Prize fighting**, which is unlawful public fighting undertaken for the purpose of winning an award or a prize, is specifically prohibited by statute in many jurisdictions. Participants in boxing matches that occur under public auspices, however, are exempted from prosecution—as long as they follow the rules of the game.

affray
A fight between two or more people in a public place to the terror of others.[ii]

prize fighting
Unlawful public fighting undertaken for the purpose of winning an award or a prize.

Alcohol and Drug Crimes

Alcohol abuse is commonplace in American society today. The problem, however, is not new to modern times. Records show that the early Puritans who came to this country in the 1600s, for example, stocked their ship, the *Arabella*, with 10,000 gallons of wine and 42 tons of beer but only 11 tons of water.[14]

Our contemporary view of drunkenness builds on earlier American conceptions and "translates the behavioral description of the habitual drunkard into . . . [that of] the alcoholic."[15] But the understanding we have of the drunkard is not the understanding of the seventeenth and eighteenth centuries. In that early view, the drunkard's sin was the love of "excess" drink to the point of drunkenness, and drunkenness was seen as the result of individual choice.

From a theoretical viewpoint, the modern understanding of problem drinking is framed in terms of the alcoholic, a person who cannot consistently choose whether to drink or not. The alcoholic is seen as essentially powerless, suffering from the disease of alcoholism. "The core of the disease concept [is] the idea that habitual drunkards are alcohol addicts, persons who have lost control over their drinking and who must abstain entirely from alcohol."[16] The idea that alcoholism is a disease was officially endorsed by the American Medical Association in 1956.

Statistically speaking, nearly 17.6 million adults in the United States are alcoholics or have alcohol problems,[17] and 500,000 of those are between the age of 9 and 12. Americans spend over $90 billion on alcohol each year, and the average adult American consumes more than 25 gallons of beer, 2 gallons of wine, and 1.5 gallons of distilled spirits every year.[18] In 2000, almost 7 million persons age 12 to 20 were binge drinkers, and one survey found that 25 million Americans surveyed reported driving under the influence of alcohol. Among young adults age 18 to 25 years, almost 23% drove under the influence of alcohol. The latest death statistics released by the National Highway Traffic Safety Administration (NHTSA) show that 17,488 people were killed in alcohol-related traffic accidents last year. Alcohol and alcohol-related problems cost the American economy at least $100 million in health-care costs and lost productivity every year. Finally, four out of every ten criminal offenders report alcohol as a factor in violence, and three out of four incidents of spousal violence are reported to involve alcohol use by the offender.

A few decades ago, the two most common crimes involving alcohol were public drunkenness and **driving while intoxicated (DWI)**. Although both crimes are still quite common, DWI ordinances have generally been expanded to encompass the operation of a motor vehicle while under the influence of drugs. **Driving under the influence (DUI)** is an offense that can be committed by a person under the influence of either alcohol or drugs (or both).

> **driving while intoxicated (DWI)**
> Unlawfully operating a motor vehicle while under the influence of alcohol.

In most jurisdictions, there are two separate crimes within the DUI category. The first type of DUI is the crime of driving while under the influence of alcohol or drugs. DUI occurs whenever a person operates a motor vehicle while under the influence; the person's blood alcohol level is immaterial as long as his or her ability to operate a motor vehicle is impaired. The second type of DUI is the crime of operating a motor vehicle with a blood alcohol level specified by statute to be at or above a certain level. The second form of statutory DUI does not require that the individual's driving skills be impaired but only that his or her blood alcohol level has reached a certain measurable level. In recognition of this distinction, some jurisdictions have modified their statutes to include the phrase *driving with an unlawful blood alcohol level* (DUBAL). The normal blood alcohol level for most DUBAL crimes is generally set by law as either 0.10% or 0.08% (alcohol content of blood by volume), with a lower level usually specified for operating an aircraft or boat.

> **driving under the influence (DUI)**
> Unlawfully operating a motor vehicle while under the influence of alcohol or drugs (or both).

A few jurisdictions use tests of blood alcohol level only to establish a presumption that a person has been operating a vehicle while under the influence of alcohol. In those jurisdictions, evidence may be admitted as to the effect that a certain level of blood alcohol is likely to have had on the defendant. Another variation, used in a few jurisdictions, considers blood alcohol levels below 0.06% to establish the presumption that a person was not under the influence of alcohol, levels of 0.07% to 0.1% to establish a presumption that the driver was under the influence, and levels of over 0.1% as irrefutable evidence that the person was under the influence of alcohol.

Some jurisdictions, such as California, have statutorily established a third type of DUI, which involves the operation of a motor vehicle by a person who is addicted to the use of any drug, unless the person is on an approved drug-maintenance program.[19] Most jurisdictions make it a crime for a juvenile to operate a motor vehicle, boat, or airplane with any trace of alcohol in his or her blood. Others use a level of 0.05% for juveniles. Generally, a person's first DUI conviction is counted as a misdemeanor, but subsequent offenses are felonies.

As with all statutes, some terminology is specific to DUI statutes. The term *under the influence* means, for example, that "alcohol or drugs or a combination thereof [has] so affected the nervous system, the brain, or muscles as to impair to an appreciable degree the ability of the person to operate a motor vehicle in an ordinary and cautious manner."[20] "Driving," for purposes of DUI statutes, generally requires some intentional movement of the driver's vehicle. The movement may be as simple as coasting down a hill or pedaling a moped.

A movement of a vehicle over a distance of a few feet has been held sufficient to constitute "driving." The definition of *motor vehicles* generally includes animal-drawn vehicles, go-carts, forklifts, snowmobiles, bulldozers, mopeds, and mobile cranes.[21] Almost all jurisdictions, however, also have statutes that prohibit operating an aircraft, boat, or locomotive while under the influence of alcohol or drugs. The operator or driver is usually defined as the person who "drives," or is in actual physical control of the vehicle (Figure 10–1).

Most jurisdictions provide for the administrative suspension of a DUI defendant's driver's license for refusal to take a test for the physical presence of alcohol. In California, for example, before asking a driver to submit to a chemical test, arresting officers must advise the person that refusal to submit to, or failure to complete, a chemical test for the presence of alcohol in the body will result in suspension or revocation of the person's driver's license and mandatory imprisonment upon conviction of DUI. Suspects are also advised that a refusal to take, or a failure to complete, such a test may be used in court as evidence that the driver was driving while under the influence. Defendants are similarly told that they have no right to consult with an attorney before taking the test or before making a choice of which test to take (Breathalyzer, blood analysis, or urinalysis).[22]

Public drunkenness is the second most common alcohol-related offense. To constitute the crime of public drunkenness, one must, while in a public place, be in a state of intoxication to such a degree that one is unable to care for oneself. It is not, however, a crime in most jurisdictions to be intoxicated in a private place, such as one's home. Some jurisdictions have established the statutory crime of being drunk and disorderly. As the name

public drunkenness
The offense of being in a state of intoxication in a place accessible to the public.

FIGURE 10–1

Driving Under the Influence.

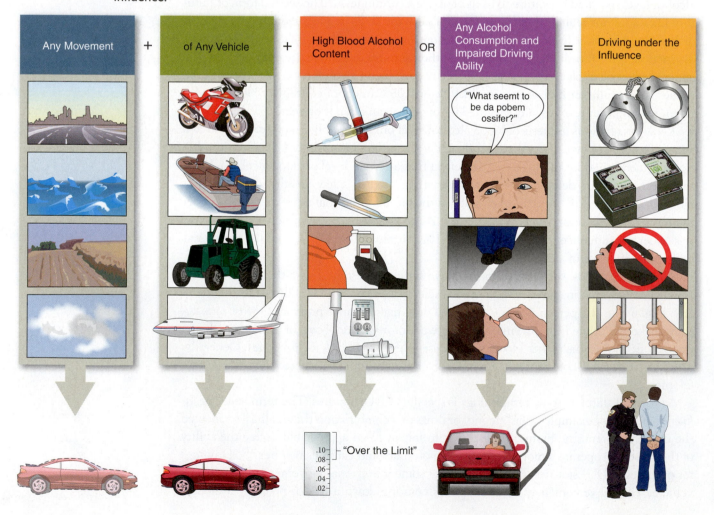

implies, this crime generally requires that the person be both drunk and disorderly for the offense to occur.

Riot and Unlawful Assembly

In most jurisdictions, an **unlawful assembly** is when three or more people assemble for the purpose of committing an unlawful act or of committing a lawful act in a violent, boisterous, or tumultuous manner. Unlawful assembly is a specific-intent crime and therefore requires that those who are assembled must intend to commit an unlawful act or a lawful act in a prohibited manner.

A **rout** can be described as the preparatory stage of a riot.[23] A rout occurs when an unlawful assembly makes an attempt to advance toward the commission of an act that would be a riot. The difference between an unlawful assembly and a rout is that a rout requires both an unlawful assembly and an overt act. A **riot** is the culmination of unlawful assembly and rout and can be defined as a tumultuous disturbance of the peace by three or more people assembled of their own authority (Figure 10–2).[24]

The federal Anti-Riot Act of 1968 provides the following definition:

> [T]he term "riot" means a public disturbance involving: (1) an act or acts of violence by one or more persons, part of an assemblage of three or more persons, which act or acts shall constitute a clear and present danger of, or shall result in, damage or injury to the property of any other person or to the person of any other individual or (2) a threat or threats of the commission of an act or acts of violence by one or more persons part of an assemblage of three or more persons having, individually or collectively, the ability of immediate execution of such threat or threats, where the performance of the threatened act or acts of violence would constitute a clear and present danger of, or would result in, damage or injury to the property of any other person or to the person of any other individual.[25]

The federal Anti-Riot Act makes it illegal for any person to travel between states or to enter the country or to use "any facility of interstate or foreign commerce" (such as the mail, telephones, radio, fax machines, the Internet, or television) to incite, organize, promote, encourage, participate in, or carry out a riot. As the wording of the act indicates, to constitute a riot, there must be at least *threats* to use force or violence, and the threats or use of force must actually disturb the peace. Public peace is considered

unlawful assembly
A gathering of three or more people for the purpose of doing an unlawful act or for the purpose of doing a lawful act in a violent, boisterous, or tumultuous manner.

rout
The preparatory stage of a riot.

riot
A tumultuous disturbance of the peace by three or more people assembled of their own authority.[iii]

FIGURE 10–2

Riot and Related Offenses.

INCITING A RIOT

Inciting is verbally provoking others to riot. The person at the podium is using intentionally inflammatory language to get a riot started.

ROUT

The rout is preparation for the riot itself. Here the potential rioters have armed themselves with dangerous objects.

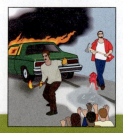

RIOT

A riot consists of an overt act committed by an assembly of people. Rioters here are destroying a car and opening a fire hydrant.

DISTURBANCE OF PUBLIC ASSEMBLY

This type of disturbance is caused to any place a group is lawfully assembling. These rioters are vandalizing a church and yelling obscenities at the group.

LYNCHING

When rioters take any person from the custody of the law, a lynching has occurred. This prisoner has been taken from a jail by the rioters.

"disturbed" when the actions of the group excite terror, alarm, and consternation in the neighborhood.[26]

As noted earlier, unlawful assembly, rout, and riot all require a common purpose by three or more people. The requirement of *three* or more people stems from common law, although some states have statutorily reduced the required number of participating individuals to two. In any case, a single individual acting alone cannot commit these offenses. However, a single individual acting alone can commit the crime of urging or **inciting a riot**. Inciting a riot is the use of words or other means to intentionally provoke a riot. To establish the crime of urging or inciting a riot, the prosecution must prove that the defendant's acts were done with the intent to cause a riot.

Although rarely seen today, the crime of **lynching** is defined as taking, by means of riot, a person from the lawful custody of a peace officer. Any participation in the lynching is sufficient to constitute the offense. The taking of the person from lawful custody is the gist of the crime of lynching. Although *lynching* is now synonymous with *hanging* in common parlance, the law does not require that the person taken be harmed or that harm be intended. Because lynching requires that the taking of the person be by means of a riot, lynching is not a crime that a single individual, acting alone, can commit. The crime of **rescuing a prisoner**, however, which has been codified in some jurisdictions, may be committed by a single individual acting alone. The crime is committed when one or more people rescue or attempt to rescue a person being held in lawful custody.

Another offense against the public order is **disturbance of public assembly**, sometimes termed *disturbing a public or religious meeting*. The crime occurs when one or more people purposely disturb a public gathering collected for a lawful purpose. Disturbing public assembly is a statutory crime in most jurisdictions and generally involves the *willful* disturbance of a public or religious meeting without legal authority. California's statute is like those in many other states. Compare it to the Model Penal Code, Section 250.1.

inciting a riot
The use of words or other means to intentionally provoke a riot.

lynching
The taking, by means of riot, of any person from the lawful custody of a peace officer.

rescuing a prisoner
A crime that is committed when one or more people rescue or attempt to rescue any person being held in lawful custody.

disturbance of public assembly
A crime that occurs when one or more people act unlawfully at a public gathering collected for a lawful purpose in such a way as to purposefully disturb the gathering.

CALIFORNIA PENAL CODE

Section 403. Every person who, without authority of law, willfully disturbs or breaks up any assembly or meeting that is not unlawful in its character, other than an assembly or meeting referred to in Section 302 of the Penal Code or Section 18340 of the Elections Code, is guilty of a misdemeanor.

Section 404. (a) Any use of force or violence, disturbing the public peace, or any threat to use force or violence, if accompanied by immediate power of execution, by two or more persons acting together, and without authority of law, is a riot.
(b) As used in this section, disturbing the public peace may occur in any place of confinement. Place of confinement means any state prison, county jail, industrial farm, or road camp, or any city jail, industrial farm, or road camp, or any juvenile hall, juvenile camp, juvenile ranch, or juvenile forestry camp.

Section 404.6. Every person who with the intent to cause a riot does an act or engages in conduct which urges a riot, or urges others to commit acts of force or violence, or the burning or destroying of property, and at a time and place and under circumstances which produce a clear and present and immediate danger of acts of force or violence or the burning or destroying of property, is guilty of a misdemeanor punishable by a fine not exceeding one thousand dollars ($1,000), or by imprisonment in a county jail not exceeding one year, or by both that fine and imprisonment.

Section 405. Every person who participates in any riot is punishable by a fine not exceeding one thousand dollars, or by imprisonment in a county jail not exceeding one year, or by both such fine and imprisonment.

Section 405a. The taking by means of a riot of any person from the lawful custody of any peace officer is a lynching.

Section 405b. Every person who participates in any lynching is punishable by imprisonment in the state prison for two, three, or four years.

Section 406. Whenever two or more persons, assembled and acting together, make any attempt or advance toward the commission of an act which would be a riot if actually committed, such assembly is a rout.

Section 407. Whenever two or more persons assemble together to do an unlawful act, or do a lawful act in a violent, boisterous, or tumultuous manner, such assembly is an unlawful assembly.

Section 408. Every person who participates in any rout or unlawful assembly is guilty of a misdemeanor.

Section 409. Every person remaining present at the place of any riot, rout, or unlawful assembly, after the same has been lawfully warned to disperse, except public officers and persons assisting them in attempting to disperse the same, is guilty of a misdemeanor.

Vagrancy and Loitering

Under common law, **vagrancy** was the act of going about from place to place by a person without visible means of support, who was idle, and who, although able to work for his or her maintenance, refused to do so and lived without labor or on the charity of others.[27] As such, the common law crime of vagrancy made it an offense simply to wander from place to place without any visible means of support. It focused on the idle and those avoiding work. Later English statutes required all able-bodied men to work. In 1937, one English court explained the history of vagrancy laws:

> The early Vagrancy Acts came into being under peculiar conditions utterly different to those of the present time. From the time of the Black Death in the middle of the 14th century till the middle of the 17th century, and indeed, although in diminishing degree, right down to the reform of the Poor Law in the first half of the nineteenth century, the roads of England were crowded with masterless men and their families, who had lost their former employment through a variety of causes, had no means of livelihood, and had taken to a vagrant life. The main causes were the gradual decay of the feudal system under which the labouring classes had been anchored to the soil, the economic slackening of the legal compulsion to work for fixed wages; the break up of the monasteries in the reign of Henry VIII, and the consequent disappearance of the religious orders which had previously administered a kind of "public assistance" in the form of lodging, food and alms; and, lastly, the economic changes brought about by the Enclosure Acts. Some of these people were honest labourers who had fallen upon evil days, others were the "wild rogues," so common in Elizabethan times and literature, who had been born to a life of idleness and had no intention of following any other. It was they and their confederates who formed themselves into the notorious "brotherhood of beggars," which flourished in the 16th and 17th centuries. They were a definite and serious menace to the community, and it was chiefly against them and their kind that the harsher provisions of the vagrancy laws of the period were directed.[28]

Seen in these terms, a **vagrant** (also called a *vagabond*) was "a wanderer; an idle person who, being able to maintain himself by lawful labor, either refuses to work or resorts to unlawful practices, e.g., begging, to gain a living."[29] The term *common vagrant* was often applied at common law to distinguish one whose condition or mode of life was that of a vagrant from one who might be temporarily vagrant.

vagrancy
Under common law, the act of going about from place to place by a person without visible means of support, who was idle, and who, though able to work for his or her maintenance, refused to do so and lived without labor or on the charity of others.[iv]

vagrant
A wanderer; an idle person who, being able to maintain him- or herself by lawful labor, either refuses to work or resorts to unlawful practices, such as begging, to gain a living.[v] Also called *vagabond*.

Early American laws against vagrancy were based on their English counterparts, as well as on strong cultural beliefs in the efficacy of a work ethic and fears that idleness would lead to crime. North Carolina law of four decades ago, for example, classified as vagrants:

> (1) Persons wandering or strolling about in idleness who are able to work and have no property to support them. (2) Persons leading an idle immoral or profligate life, who have no property to support them and who are able to work and do not work. (3) All persons able to work having no property to support them and who have not some visible and known means of a fair, honest, and reputable livelihood. (4) Persons having a fixed abode who have no visible property to support them and who live by stealing or by trading in, bartering for, or buying stolen property. (5) Professional gamblers living in idleness. (6) All able-bodied men having no visible means of support who shall live in idleness upon the wages or earnings of their mother, wife, or minor children, except of male children over eighteen years old. (7) Keepers and inmates of bawdy houses, assignation houses, lewd and disorderly houses, and other places where illegal sexual intercourse is habitually carried on: Provided, that nothing here is intended or shall be construed as abolishing the crime of keeping a bawdy house, or lessening the punishment by law for such crime.[30]

When common law vagrancy was enacted into law in the United States, vagrancy statutes were often successfully attacked as being vague and overbroad and as encouraging "arbitrary enforcement by failing to describe with sufficient particularity what a suspect must do in order to satisfy the statute."[31] Some authors have observed that "[s]tatutory language was intentionally rather vague, presumably to allow police broad discretion to arrest persons they deemed undesirable to the community."[32] Although vagrancy had often been described in early vagrancy statutes as being "an act," the truth of the matter was that such statutes criminalized the **status** of vagrant. As we have observed earlier in this text, generally speaking, to be something is not a crime, although to do something may be. Hence to be a vagrant cannot be criminal, although the less one does, the more vagrant one may appear to be.

As a result of such flaws, most vagrancy statutes were eventually invalidated by state courts—and by the U.S. Supreme Court, which in the 1972 case of *Papachristou* v. *City of Jacksonville*[33] held that many traditionally worded vagrancy statutes were void for vagueness because they failed "to give a person of ordinary intelligence fair notice that his contemplated conduct is forbidden by the statute and because [they] encourage arbitrary and erratic arrests and convictions." The Jacksonville city ordinance voided by the Supreme Court in 1972 read as follows: "Rogues and vagabonds, or dissolute persons who go about begging; common gamblers, persons who use juggling or unlawful games or plays, common drunkards, common night walkers, thieves, pilferers or pickpockets, traders in stolen property, lewd, wanton and lascivious persons, keepers of gambling places, common railers and brawlers, persons wandering or strolling around from place to place without any lawful purpose or object, habitual loafers, disorderly persons, persons neglecting all lawful business and habitually spending their time by frequenting houses of ill fame, gaming houses, or places where alcoholic beverages are sold or served, persons able to work but habitually living upon the earnings of their wives or minor children shall be deemed vagrants and, upon conviction in the Municipal Court, shall be punished as provided for class D offenses."[34] A little more than a decade later, in *Kolender* v. *Lawson*,[35] the U.S. Supreme Court found a California statute, which prohibited loitering or wandering about without apparent reason or business and refusing to identify oneself when asked to do so by police, unconstitutional because it vested too much discretionary power in the hands of the police.

States that today retain vagrancy statutes have typically rephrased their description of the crime to require some specific form of behavior. The California vagrancy statute, for example, which is reprinted here, couches vagrancy in terms of **loitering**, which it says "means to delay, to linger, or to idle about a school or public place without lawful business for being

---

status
A person's state of being.

loitering
The act of delaying, lingering, or idling about without a lawful reason for being present.

present." By specifying the circumstances under which loitering could occur, legislatures have sought to de-emphasize a person's status as a determinant of criminality.

CALIFORNIA PENAL CODE

Section 653g. Every person who loiters about any school or public place at or near which children attend or normally congregate and who remains at any school or public place at or near which children attend or normally congregate, or who reenters or comes upon a school or place within seventy-two hours, after being asked to leave by the chief administrative official of that school or, in the absence of the chief administrative official, the person acting as the chief administrative official, or by a member of the security patrol of the school district who has been given authorization, in writing, by the chief administrative official of that school to act as his or her agent in performing this duty, or a city police officer, or sheriff or deputy sheriff, or Department of the California Highway Patrol peace officer is a vagrant, and is punishable by a fine of not exceeding one thousand dollars ($1,000) or by imprisonment in the county jail for not exceeding six months, or by both the fine and the imprisonment.

As used in this section, "loiter" means to delay, to linger, or to idle about a school or public place without lawful business for being present.

Teenage Curfew

In 2000, 15-year-old Colin Hodgkins had a late dinner at the Steak 'n Shake in Marion County, Indiana, where he and some friends had stopped after attending a school soccer game. As Colin was leaving the restaurant, he was arrested for violating the state's curfew law.[36] He was taken by the police to the local high school, where he was questioned and required to undergo drug tests before being released to his mother. At the time, Indiana law prohibited minors from being out in public after 11:00 p.m. without parental accompaniment.

Hodgkins's mother filed suit against the state, arguing that the Indiana statute violated her son's First Amendment rights by preventing him and other teenagers from attending midnight mass or a late political rally. When the district court agreed with her, the state amended the statute to make such late-night activities exceptions to the curfew.[37] Colin then challenged the amended statute, and the U.S. Court of Appeals for the Seventh Circuit agreed that the statute dissuaded minors from engaging in protected activities because they risked arrest, detention, and drug tests if they did so.[38] In the words of the court, "[W]e hold that the curfew law, even with the new affirmative defenses for First Amendment activity, is not narrowly tailored to serve a significant governmental interest and fails to allow for ample alternative channels for expression. The statute restricts a minor's access to any public forum during curfew hours, and the affirmative defense for participating in First Amendment activities does not significantly reduce the chance that a minor might be arrested for exercising First Amendment rights."[39]

In 2003 the U.S. Court of Appeals for the Second Circuit overruled a similar city ordinance that had been enacted by the city of Vernon, Connecticut.[40] Nonetheless, at last count about 500 cities in the United States had curfew regulations in effect,[41] and courts are split on the constitutionality of such statutes.[42]

In 2000, a Texas court upheld a curfew ordinance that was enacted by the city of San Antonio.[43] The San Antonio Youth Curfew ordinance prohibits youths under the age of 17 from being in public places within the city between the hours of 10:30 p.m. and 6:00 a.m. on Sunday through Thursday and between the hours of 12:00 midnight and 6:00 a.m. on Friday or Saturday. In the 2000 case, a teenager had been stopped by the police for violating the city's curfew law. He was subsequently searched, and the police found marijuana on his person.

About the same time, a curfew law passed by the District of Columbia was found unconstitutional because it was not narrowly tailored to serve the District's compelling interest in addressing the problems of crime and victimization by and against minors in the least intrusive manner.[44]

As these cases show, the constitutionality of curfew statutes is unclear. The laws that have been overturned were generally seen as being too vague and as restricting the First Amendment rights of the teenagers involved. Many officials believe, however, that such laws are needed to combat criminal activity by juveniles.[45]

Weapons Possession

All 50 states, the federal government, and many local governments have laws regulating gun possession, ownership, use, sale, transportation, and manufacture. Some of the laws are regulatory, whereas others fall into the criminal code.

Second Amendment

The right to bear arms is derived from the English common law, where it stood as a protection against the English monarch. The Framers of the U.S. Constitution embodied the right in the Second Amendment:

> A well regulated militia, being necessary to the security of a free state, the right of the people to keep and bear arms, shall not be infringed.

The Amendment refers to both a militia and a right to bear arms. Legal and linguistic scholars have studied and debated the relationship between the two rights for over 200 years. One interpretation of the Second Amendment is that the right to bear arms is conjoined with the right to a militia. That is, the militia has a right to possess arms. In this interpretation individuals do not possess a right to bear arms. An opposing interpretation is that the two clauses are independent from one another, establishing the right of the individual to bear arms.

Another question about the Second Amendment is whether it is a fundamental right that is "incorporated." If fundamental and incorporated, it acts to limit the authority of states to regulate gun possession and ownership in the same way it limits the federal government's authority.

These questions, although controversial and the subject of intense litigation over the years, were left unanswered by the Supreme Court until 2008 and 2010. In 2008 the Supreme Court answered the individual right question in the case of *District of Columbia* v. *Heller*.[46] Heller, a special police officer who carried a gun on the job, applied for a permit to possess a handgun at home. Washington, D.C., had banned handguns at the time, with limited exceptions; and although it permitted the possession of legally purchased and registered rifles, they were required to be unloaded and to have trigger locks. Heller's application for a permit was denied. Consequently, he filed suit seeking an injunction against the law, but lost at the trial level and won a reversal at the appellate level. The city appealed the decision and the Supreme Court, in a 5–4 decision, held that the right to bear arms is an individually held right, that it is independent of membership in a militia, and that the reference to a "free state" in the Amendment wasn't a reference to the United States or the individual states, but a reference to a free people. Although threats to freedom come from both invaders and tyrants, the Court reasoned that neighbors and strangers can also be a threat. Hence, the Court found self-defense to have been another reason the Framers included the Second Amendment in the Constitution. Accordingly, the Court concluded that individual people have the right to possess arms. Further, the Court struck down the requirement that guns in the home must be disassembled and trigger locked as an excessive infringement upon a homeowner's ability to self-defend.

The Court was clear, however, in finding that the right to bear arms, as is true of all rights, is limited. Forbidding ownership and possession by felons and the mentally ill, carrying weapons in and around schools and government buildings, regulating the manufacture and sale of all firearms, forbidding extreme weapons (grenade launchers, machine guns, etc.), and other laws that have existed for hundreds of years are reasonable restrictions of the right. Although this decision went far in defining the law of the area, there remains a murky area. To what extent may possession be regulated outside the home? How extensive may background checks and requirements for gun ownership be? How may governments regulate the transportation of weapons that may otherwise be possessed in the home? What about regulating ammunition? Given these unanswered questions, it is possible for a government to construct a web of restrictions that make it practically impossible to possess a gun in the home without actually regulating home possession or ownership.

Heller arose in a federal district. Thus, the Court didn't have to address the question of whether the right to bear arms is fundamental and applies to limit the states. But only two years later the Court answered the question in *McDonald* v. *Chicago*,[47] another 5–4 decision, which is presented as a Capstone Case in this chapter.

State Laws   Although *Heller* and *McDonald* make it clear that a person has a right to possess a handgun in the home, the Court also recognized the authority of governments to create reasonable restrictions on the right to bear arms. Indeed, federal, state, and local governments have enacted a variety of laws regulating guns beyond possession in the home, such as public possession laws. In many states, individuals may carry concealed weapons.

A **concealed weapon** is one that is carried on or near one's person and is not discernible by ordinary observation. In recent years, however, and in response to growing crime rates and citizens' fears of victimization, numerous states have enacted laws permitting the carrying of concealed weapons by citizens who meet certain licensing requirements. Such requirements typically include handgun training and background checks or a demonstrated need to carry a weapon for protection.

> **concealed weapon**
> A weapon that is carried on or near one's person and is not discernible by ordinary observation.

Moreover, many municipalities have enacted local ordinances even more restrictive than the laws of the states in which they are located. Most state gun control statutes (1) outlaw concealed weapons; (2) limit access to, or ownership of, handguns; (3) severely restrict ownership of modified shotguns and rifles, such as those that have been "sawed off"; and (4) criminalize possession of high explosives and weapons of mass destruction. Most states also have laws controlling the possession of guns by underage youths and laws that make it a crime to carry guns on school property or to discharge a firearm under specified circumstances. Many state codes go to considerable lengths in describing those to whom handgun and weapons laws do not apply, such as law enforcement officers, correctional personnel, and military personnel.

Federal Laws   The so-called Brady Law may be the most significant federal gun control legislation passed to date. The Brady Law—formally called the Brady Handgun Violence Prevention Act[48]—is named after former President Ronald Reagan's White House press secretary James Brady, who was shot in the head during John Hinckley's attempted assassination of Reagan in 1981. The Brady Law, signed by President Bill Clinton in 1994, provided for a five-day waiting period before the purchase of a handgun[49] and for the establishment of a national instant criminal background-checking system to be used by firearms dealers before the transfer of any handgun. An original provision of the law required that,

APPLYING THE CONCEPT

CAPSTONE CASE

Is the Right to Bear Arms as Found in *District of Columbia* v. *Heller* a Fundamental Right That Applies to the States?

McDonald v. *Chicago*, 561 U.S. 3025 (2010)

THE CASE Otis McDonald, Adam Orlov, Colleen Lawson, and David Lawson (Chicago petitioners) are Chicago residents who would like to keep handguns in their homes for self-defense but are prohibited from doing so by Chicago's firearms laws. . . . .

Chicago enacted its handgun ban to protect its residents "from the loss of property and injury or death from firearms." The Chicago petitioners and their *amici*, however, argue that the handgun ban has left them vulnerable to criminals. Chicago Police Department statistics, we are told, reveal that the City's handgun murder rate has actually increased since the ban was enacted and that Chicago residents now face one of the highest murder rates in the country and rates of other violent crimes that exceed the average in comparable cities.

Several of the Chicago petitioners have been the targets of threats and violence. For instance, Otis McDonald, who is in his late seventies, lives in a high-crime neighborhood. He is a community activist involved with alternative policing strategies, and his efforts to improve his neighborhood have subjected him to violent threats from drug dealers. Colleen Lawson is a Chicago resident whose home has been targeted by burglars. "In Mrs. Lawson's judgment, possessing a handgun in Chicago would decrease her chances of suffering serious injury or death should she ever be threatened again in her home." McDonald, Lawson, and the other Chicago petitioners own handguns that they store outside of the city limits, but they would like to keep their handguns in their homes for protection. . . .

THE FINDING . . . [W]e now turn directly to the question whether the Second Amendment right to keep and bear arms is incorporated in the concept of due process. In answering that question, as just explained, we must decide whether the right to keep and bear arms is fundamental to *our* scheme of ordered liberty . . . .

Our decision in *Heller* points unmistakably to the answer. Self-defense is a basic right, recognized by many legal systems from ancient times to the present day, and in *Heller*, we held that individual self-defense is "the *central component*" of the Second Amendment right. Explaining that "the need for defense of self, family, and property is most acute" in the home, we found that this right applies to handguns because they are "the most preferred firearm in the nation to 'keep' and use for protection of one's home and family . . . .

Heller makes it clear that this right is "deeply rooted in this Nation's history and tradition." *Heller* explored the right's origins, noting that the 1689 English Bill of Rights explicitly protected a right to keep arms for self-defense, 554 U. S. 570 (2008) (slip op., at 19–20), and that by 1765, Blackstone was able to assert that the right to keep and bear arms was "one of the fundamental rights of Englishmen . . . ."

The right to keep and bear arms was considered no less fundamental by those who drafted and ratified the Bill of Rights. "During the 1788 ratification debates, the fear that the federal government would disarm the people in order to impose rule through a standing army or select militia was pervasive in Antifederalist rhetoric. . . ."

By the 1850's, the perceived threat that had prompted the inclusion of the Second Amendment in the Bill of Rights—the fear that the National Government would disarm the universal militia—had largely faded as a popular concern, but the right to keep and bear arms was highly valued for purposes of self-defense. . . .

After the Civil War, many of the over 180,000 African Americans who served in the Union Army returned to the States of the old Confederacy, where systematic efforts were made to disarm them and other blacks. . . .

Union Army commanders took steps to secure the right of all citizens to keep and bear arms, but the 39th Congress concluded that legislative action was necessary. Its efforts to safeguard the right to keep and bear arms demonstrate that the right was still recognized to be fundamental. . . .

[The court continued by discussing the many times Congress and the states recognized, through legislation and state constitutional provisions, the right to bear arms as evidence of its fundamental importance.]

We therefore hold that the Due Process Clause of the Fourteenth Amendment incorporates the Second Amendment right recognized in *Heller*. The judgment of the Court of Appeals is reversed, and the case is remanded for further proceedings.

What Do *You* Think?

1. Large cities have serious problems with gangs and violent crimes. Guns are often used in violent crimes and are an important feature of gang life. Should these concerns outweigh the right to possess a weapon for self-defense?

2. Many developed industrialized nations don't permit gun ownership or possession. Most of these nations have lower rates of violent crime than the United States. Is this evidence of the need to regulate weapons possession in the United States?

3. The right to possess a handgun in the home, ready for use, is clearly established. What limits, if any, would you recognize in regard to the types of weapons a person may possess, the requirements for obtaining a gun (registration, waiting period, criminal history, etc.), how a gun may be transported (must it be in the trunk of a car, trigger locked, etc.?), and restrictions for possession in public places (concealed, unloaded, etc.)?

Additional Applications

Does the Second Amendment protect a right to practice shooting at a firing range?

Ezell v. *City of Chicago*, 651 F.3d 684 (7th Cir. 2011)

The Case: Just four days after the U.S. Supreme Court's *McDonald* decision, the city council in Chicago repealed the city's ban on handgun possession and adopted in its place a comprehensive Responsible Gun Owners Ordinance that, among other things, banned all gun firing ranges within city limits. Several plaintiffs (including three Chicago residents, a firing range designer, and two gun-rights groups) sought a preliminary injunction against enforcement of the ordinance, arguing that the Second Amendment protects the right to maintain proficiency in firearms use—including the right to practice marksmanship at a firing range—and thus the

city's total ban on firing ranges is unconstitutional. The federal district court denied the motion for an injunction; the plaintiffs then appealed to the U.S. Court of Appeals for the Seventh Circuit.

The Finding: In July 2011, a three-judge appellate panel reversed the district court and ordered that the injunction be issued. The Second Amendment right to possess firearms announced in *Heller* and *McDonald*, the appellate panel held, "implies a corresponding right to acquire and maintain proficiency in their use," as "the core right wouldn't mean much without the training and practice that make it effective." And by choosing to ban all gun ranges, rather than opting to craft more narrowly tailored restrictions, the city imposed a "severe burden" on "core Second Amendment right[s]" without demonstrating a corresponding "extremely strong public-interest justification" in doing so. Indeed, the court concluded, the city "rested its entire defense of the range ban on speculation about accidents and theft"; consequently, the court noted, its regulation is "wholly out of proportion to the public interests the City claims it serves."

Does the Second Amendment right to bear arms apply only to "citizens"?

Fletcher v. *Haas*, 2012 U.S. Dist. LEXIS 44623 (D.C.Mass. 2012)

The Case: Chapter 140 of the Massachusetts General Laws requires a state-issued permit before a resident can own or purchase a firearm, yet the state denies permits to all resident aliens (legal and illegal alike). Christopher Fletcher and Eoin Pryal—lawful permanent residents who emigrated to the United States from the United Kingdom—both applied for, and were denied, licenses to possess firearms at home for self-defense purposes. Following the Supreme Court's decisions in *Heller* and *McDonald*, they filed suit in federal district court, seeking to enjoin enforcement on Second Amendment grounds of the state's ban on gun possession by permanent resident aliens. Massachusetts officials defended their policy on the grounds that the Second Amendment applies only to U.S. citizens.

The Finding: In a March 2012 order, U.S. District Judge Douglas Woodlock ruled in favor of Fletcher and Pryal, holding that Second Amendment protections extend to permanent resident aliens. It is true, Woodlock observed, that the Supreme Court in *Heller* "described the right protected by the Second Amendment as belonging variously to 'citizens,'

(continued)

'Americans,' 'all members of the political community' and 'law abiding citizens.'" Yet as the *McDonald* Court made clear, such terms were "used rhetorically, rather than categorically" in *Heller*; what's more, the Second Amendment was "incorporated" against the states in *McDonald* by virtue of the Fourteenth Amendment's due process clause, which speaks explicitly in terms of the rights of "persons." As permanent resident aliens, Judge Woodlock found, both Fletcher and Pryal were "firmly on the path to full citizenship" and had "developed sufficient connection with this country to be considered part of [the] community." Consequently, Massachusetts could not deny them gun permits on the basis of their citizenship status.

Does the Second Amendment grant individuals a right to carry concealed weapons?

United States v. *Hart*, 726 F. Supp. 2d 56 (D. Mass. 2010)

The Case: On July 9, 2009, defendant Michael Hart was initially stopped by Massachusetts state troopers on suspicion of carrying a concealed weapon; after a sustained interaction, Hart was then arrested and charged with felony possession of a firearm and ammunition. At trial in federal court, Hart sought to suppress the gun and ammunition; among other things, Hart argued that the Second Amendment as interpreted in *Heller* and *McDonald* prohibits police officers from conducting a stop on the sole basis of a reasonable suspicion that the suspect is carrying a concealed weapon.

The Finding: In a July 2010 ruling, U.S. District Judge D. J. Young denied Hart's motion to suppress. The U.S. Supreme Court's recent rulings, Young held, "d[o] not hold, nor even suggest, that concealed weapons laws are unconstitutional." Indeed, *Heller* "notes that 'the majority of the 19th-century courts [that] consider[ed] the question held that prohibitions on carrying concealed weapons were lawful under the Second Amendment or state analogues.'" What's more, *McDonald* stressed that "the Second Amendment protects the right to possess a handgun in the home for the purpose of self-defense." Therefore, Young concluded, "it was not a violation of Hart's Second Amendment rights to stop him on the basis of the suspicion of a concealed weapon."

Can courts consider gun ownership in deciding to order pretrial detention for criminal defendants on dangerousness grounds?

United States v. *Meeks*, 2011 U.S. Dist. LEXIS 108020 (E.D.Mich. 2011)

The Case: Following extensive judicial proceedings, the U.S. Court of Appeals for the Sixth Circuit ruled in June 2010 that the U.S. government could hold nine defendants—all members of an antigovernment extremist organization—for an indefinite period pending their trial on charges of conspiring to use weapons of mass destruction to attack government officials. In ruling for the denial of bond, the Sixth Circuit cited the defendants' ongoing dangerousness; among other factors supporting that finding, the court pointed to defendant Meeks's possession of 1,000 tracer rounds of ammunition and a "substantial arsenal of weapons," including five semi-automatic weapons and 16 long guns. In seeking a new bond hearing, the defendants argued, among other things, that the Sixth Circuit's reliance on the guns and ammunition found in Meeks's home to establish dangerousness placed an "undue burden" on their Second Amendment rights as announced in *Heller* and *McDonald*.

The Finding: In a September 2011 ruling, U.S. District Judge Victoria Roberts rejected the defendants' Second Amendment arguments. *Heller* and *McDonald*, Judge Roberts wrote, address only the constitutionality of statutes that regulate gun ownership and possession; they do *not* change settled law regarding whether courts can consider gun ownership in determining whether a particular criminal defendant is too dangerous to release before trial. And on this point, she noted, the law is clear: several federal circuit courts of appeals have upheld findings of dangerousness based in part upon weapons found in defendants' homes. In this case, Judge Roberts continued, the Sixth Circuit clearly considered a broad range of additional factors beyond the defendants' gun possession when making its determination on dangerousness. Adding the fact of weapons possession to the overall mix does not violate the Second Amendment. As Roberts concluded: "[C]ourts can consider all facts potentially relevant to dangerousness, including otherwise lawful and constitutionally protected behavior, when making pretrial detention determinations." ∎

until the instant background-checking system could be established, licensed gun dealers were to notify the chief law enforcement officer in their area of all applications to purchase a handgun. In 1997, however, in the combined cases of *Printz* v. *United States*[50] and *Mack* v. *United States*,[51] the U.S. Supreme Court held that to impose such a requirement on local law enforcement officers was unconstitutional. Under the constitutional principle of dual sovereignty, said the Court, the "Framers of the Constitution rejected the concept of a central government that would act upon and through the States, and instead designed a system in which the State and Federal Governments would exercise concurrent authority over the people." Under the dual sovereignty principle, the justices held, the federal government is prohibited from exercising direct control over state officers. Were it to be able to do so, said the Court, "the Federal Government's power would be augmented immeasurably and impermissibly." Writing for the majority, Justice Scalia noted that "the Court's jurisprudence makes clear that the Federal Government may not compel the States to enact or administer a federal regulatory program."

Although the cooperation of local law enforcement officers in conducting background checks can no longer be required, the general thrust of the Brady Law remains in effect. A federal National Instant Criminal Background Check System (Instacheck, or NICS) has since become operational and is used by gun dealers throughout the country. The system, run by the Federal Bureau of Investigation's Criminal Justice Information Services (CJIS) Division, performs fast computerized criminal background checks and effectively zeros out the waiting period required for purchases. It has made gun sales cash-and-carry transactions in areas where they are not further restricted by state or local law.[52] Under Instacheck, a licensed importer, licensed manufacturer, or licensed dealer can verify the identity of an applicant using a valid photo ID (such as a driver's license) and can contact the system to receive a unique identification number authorizing the purchase before transfer of the handgun is made. Three years after the Brady Law went into effect, the Justice Department noted that the law had blocked gun sales to 186,000 criminals and others not allowed to buy firearms under its provisions.[53]

The Violent Crime Control and Law Enforcement Act of 1994 further regulated the sale of weapons within the United States, banning the manufacture of 19 military-style assault weapons, including those with specific combat features, such as high-capacity ammunition clips that are capable of holding more than ten rounds. The act also specifically prohibited the sale or transfer of a gun to a juvenile, as well as the possession of a gun by a juvenile, and it prohibited gun sales to, and possession by, people who are subject to family violence restraining orders. Congress did not renew the assault weapons ban, however, and it expired in September 2004.

In the Gun-Free School Zones Act of 1990,[54] Congress made it a federal offense "for any individual knowingly to possess a firearm at a place that the individual knows, or has reasonable cause to believe, is a school zone."[55] The law was passed to assuage parents' concerns that their children might be in mortal danger due to the presence of guns in the hands of school-age children and interlopers on school property.

In 1995, however, in a blow to federal efforts at gun control, the U.S. Supreme Court agreed with a lower court ruling that dismissed charges against a 12th-grade student who had carried a concealed .38-caliber handgun and five bullets into the Edison High School in San Antonio, Texas. The student had been charged with violating the federal Gun-Free School Zones Act. Arguing that the federal government has the power to control commerce between the states (based on Article I, Section 8, Clause 3, of the U.S. Constitution, which delegates to Congress the power "[t]o regulate Commerce with foreign Nations, and among the several States, and with the Indian Tribes"), government lawyers told the Court that it was necessary for the federal government to take steps intended to control violence in schools because "the occurrence of violent crime in school zones" has brought about a "decline in the quality of education" that "has an adverse impact on interstate commerce and the foreign commerce of the United States."

Although the Court agreed that this was a rational conclusion, it ruled that education, in the context of the law, was a local and not a national concern. Hence, said the justices, "To uphold the Government's contentions here, we would have to pile inference upon inference in a manner that would bid fair to convert congressional authority under the Commerce Clause to a general police power of the sort retained by the States."[56]

Immigration Crimes

Immigration and customs laws exist in both regulatory and criminal form. It is unlawful to bring some drugs, plants, animals, and other substances into the United States. The immigration and travel of people in and out of the United States is also regulated.

One consequence of the terrorist attacks of September 11, 2001, has been a closer examination of official policies restricting entry into the United States by foreign nationals. People living in this country illegally have also become subject to increased scrutiny. Myrna and Brady Dick, for example, had moved into a new home in the suburbs of Kansas City, Missouri, in 2004 when immigration officials informed Myrna that they intended to deport her to her native Mexico.[57] The Dicks were expecting their first child, and neither had had any previous record of law violation. According to Myrna's attorney, government officials accused her of claiming false citizenship in 1998 while returning to the United States after a short visit to her parents' home in Mexico. At the time, she was a resident alien but had apparently completed a reentry form by indicating that she was an American citizen. Immigration officials refused to comment specifically about her case but agreed that many people are now being investigated who would have been ignored in years past.

One of the complexities of entry law today is that there are effectively three classes of aliens who are physically present in the United States: (1) those who are here legally, (2) those who are here illegally, and (3) those who are technically regarded as not here at all. The seeming contradiction of having someone here physically but legally "knocking at the gates" is a result of a long and convoluted interplay of laws, treaties, and policies that have turned the simple word *entry* into a term of art. Determining whether an alien has "entered" or "departed" the United States can have a profound effect on his or her fate. It can affect whether the alien is deportable or excludable, has a right to a bond hearing and release from custody, or is able to apply for other immigration benefits.[58]

Until 1875, there were no entry requirements for aliens coming to the United States. At that time, the entry of an alien or noncitizen was not an issue because there were no grounds for exclusion. In 1875 and again in subsequent years, Congress chose to exclude various classes of aliens and passed laws relating to their deportation. However, grounds for deportation and exclusion did not always overlap. Throughout the history of entry law, some aliens could be excludable but not deportable. Until the early part of the twentieth century, this conflict between grounds for exclusion and grounds for deportation was not clearly evident because exclusion grounds applied only to the initial entry of an alien as an immigrant and not to subsequent "reentries."

Before 1875, the only requirement to be a legal resident of the United States was physical presence. In effect, if you could get off the boat or walk across the border, you were a permanent resident.[59] In 1907, Congress made most grounds of excludability applicable to "aliens" as opposed to "alien immigrants." This change required the courts to determine which entry counted for purposes of the alien's qualifications to be in the United States: the first entry as an immigrant or a subsequent entry. Analyzing congressional intent, the courts eventually took the latter view. This meant that, although unforeseeable at the time, an alien's brief trip outside the United States, whether for pleasure or for business, might later trigger severe consequences.

The harsh consequences of applying exclusion grounds to any entry of an alien were not lost on the courts. They began stretching exceptions contained in the law and thus created new interpretations. The most important concept was that of departure. Courts quickly realized that if they could find that an alien had not "departed" the United States, no new entry need be found, and grounds for exclusion could be avoided. Although never statutorily defined, the concept of departure plays an important role in the law of entry today.

Along with the concept of entry came the concept of parole. Unlike its criminal law cousin, an alien requesting parole wishes to be let in (to the United States), not let out (of jail). A parole allows an alien to remain in the United States, usually for a temporary period of time, but without most rights granted under the immigration laws. Although an alien who has been granted parole status is physically here, the alien is legally considered to be outside the country.

In 1963, the U.S. Supreme Court created an exception to entry law for legal residents of the United States. Where a legal resident makes a trip that is "innocent, casual, and brief," and not foreseeable as meaningfully interruptive of his or her residency, no entry is made.[60] Similar concepts have been adopted for various immigration programs.

In the United States recently, there has been a large and growing class of alien defendants who have been sentenced for violations of Section 1326 of Title 8 of the U.S. Code. That statute holds that a previously deported alien who reenters the country without obtaining the prior consent of the attorney general to reapply for admission shall be imprisoned for up to two years, fined, or both.

The crime of illegally reentering the United States after having been deported under the Immigration and Nationality Act[61] has five elements, which create the offense of illegally reentering the United States after having been deported (Figure 10–3). The first element deals with the status of the person. A violation of the law occurs when the person reentering is an alien. In *United States* v. *Meza-Soria*, the Ninth Circuit held that the government must prove alienage beyond a reasonable doubt and that the defendant is entitled to hold the government to its burden of proof on the issue of alienage.[62]

The second element of the offense provides that an alien is "not subject to prosecution[63] for illegal reentry into the United States unless he was actually 'arrested' at some previous time."[64]

The third element requires that there be a "prior deportation" of the alien from the country. In *United States* v. *Ventura-Candelario*, the U.S. District Court for the Southern District of New York held that the defendant was "removed" within the meaning of the statute, allowing enhanced punishment for illegal reentry because the term *removal* encompassed the term *deportation*.[65]

The fourth element requires that the alien must be "found, entering or attempting to enter" into the United States. The Eighth Circuit held in *United States* v. *Diaz-Diaz* that there is an illegal reentry in violation of the statute even if the charge is based on defendant's "being found" in the United States rather than actual reentry.[66]

The fifth and final element of the offense is satisfied if the alien reenters the United States without the consent of the attorney general.[67]

A contested contemporary question is how much authority states have over immigration. The federal government has long held that immigration is an exclusive federal power. Indeed, Article I appears to grant the authority to the federal government. Article I, Section 8, delegates the authority to make naturalization rules, to regulate commerce with foreign nations, and to establish import and excise taxes. Of course, treaties and other international matters are delegated to the president and Congress as a shared power, to the exclusion of the states. But the most compelling language is found in Article I, Section 9,

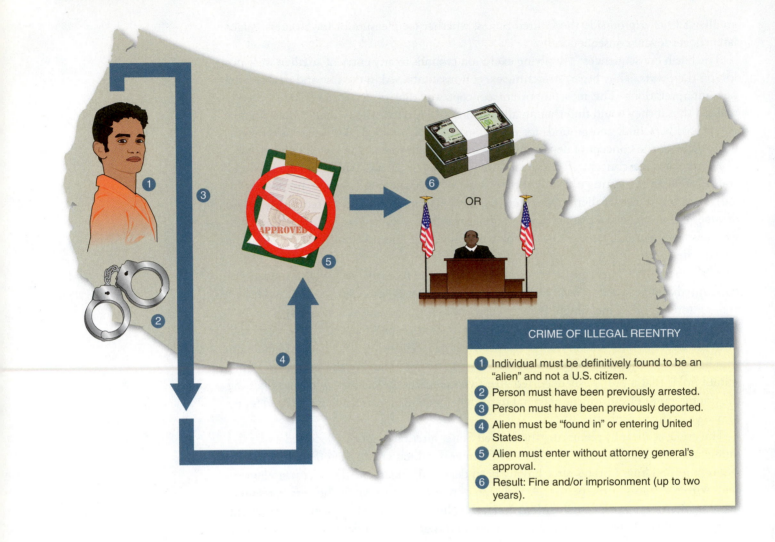

CRIME OF ILLEGAL REENTRY

1 Individual must be definitively found to be an "alien" and not a U.S. citizen.
2 Person must have been previously arrested.
3 Person must have been previously deported.
4 Alien must be "found in" or entering United States.
5 Alien must enter without attorney general's approval.
6 Result: Fine and/or imprisonment (up to two years).

FIGURE 10–3

Illegal Reentry.

which provides that "The Migration and Importation of such Persons as any of the State now existing shall think proper to admit, shall not be prohibited by the Congress prior to the Year one thousand eight hundred and eight, but a Tax or duty may be imposed on such importation, not exceeding ten dollars for each Person."

Although it is clear that the federal government has the authority to decide who may be admitted, it is unclear whether the states share authority with the federal government to enforce immigration laws when they are impacted by immigration. Unhappy with the efforts of the federal government to enforce its own laws, some states and localities have become aggressive in this area under the theory that authority over immigration is cooperatively shared. Arizona is such a state. In 2010 Arizona enacted the Support our Law Enforcement and Safe Neighborhoods Act. The law expanded the authority of state and local law enforcement officers over immigration. It included, among other things, a requirement that police officers who have made otherwise lawful stops or arrests must conduct an investigation of the detainee's immigration status if probable cause exists to believe the detainee is not in the United States lawfully. The law also made it a misdemeanor under Arizona law for a person to fail to comply with federal alien registration law and for illegal aliens to seek or obtain employment. Local law enforcement officers were authorized under the law to make warrantless arrests of individuals who committed crimes and were deportable under federal law. The law specifically excludes the use of race or ethnicity in the probable-cause determination. The United States filed suit against the state of Arizona seeking an injunction against the enforcement of the law, claiming that it encroaches on federal jurisdiction. The United States won in the lower courts, Arizona appealed, and the Supreme Court granted *certiorari*. The Supreme Court issued its decision in *Arizona* v. *United States*, in 2012, upholding the detention provision but invalidating the warrantless arrest and misdemeanor provisions, holding that these provisions were preempted by federal law.

Although such federalism conflicts are most common in the states that border Mexico, there are examples further north as well. For example, one sheriff in Ohio sent the United States a bill for the expenses associated with housing illegal aliens in his county's jail, sought to empower his deputies with the authority to enforce immigration laws, regularly sought out and detailed undocumented aliens, and had stickers placed on department vehicles asking citizens to call the department to report illegal aliens.[68]

CRIMES AGAINST THE ADMINISTRATION OF GOVERNMENT

A second class of social-order offense consists of crimes against the administration of government. Offenses in this category include treason, misprision of treason, rebellion, espionage, sedition, perjury, subornation of perjury, criminal contempt, obstruction of justice, resisting arrest, escape, misconduct in office, and bribery. We discuss each of these offenses in the pages that follow.

Treason

Treason can be defined as the attempt to overthrow the government of the society of which one is a member. Under early common law, it was considered high treason to kill the king or to promote a revolt in the kingdom. Treason under common law was neither a felony nor a misdemeanor but thought to be in a class by itself. Much the same is true today, and treason is the only crime specifically mentioned in the U.S. Constitution, which says, "Treason against the United States, shall consist only in levying War against them, or in adhering to their Enemies, giving them Aid and Comfort."[69] Federal statutes use wording similar to that of the Constitution: "Whoever, owing allegiance to the United States, levies war against them or adheres to their enemies, giving them aid and comfort within the United States or elsewhere, is guilty of treason and shall suffer death, or shall be imprisoned not less than five years and fined under this title but not less than ten thousand dollars ($10,000); and shall be incapable of holding any office under the United States."[70] Because treason is a breach of allegiance, a person who has lost or renounced his or her American citizenship cannot commit treason against the United States.[71]

The crime of treason requires some overt act, such as affirmative encouragement of the enemy. Disloyal thoughts alone are not sufficient to constitute treason. In addition, treason is a specific-intent offense, and conviction for treason requires that the defendant must have intended to betray the government. If the defendant acts with knowledge that his or her conduct will benefit the enemy, specific intent can be demonstrated. The U.S. Constitution stipulates: "No Person shall be convicted of Treason unless on the Testimony of two Witnesses to the same overt Act, or on Confession in open Court."[72]

Treason is also a crime under the laws of most states. Some states, such as California, have legislatively created the crime of treason, whereas in others the crime is constitutionally defined. Florida's constitution, for example, which mirrors wording in the U.S. Constitution, says: "Treason against the state shall consist only in levying war against it, adhering to its enemies, or giving them aid and comfort, and no person shall be convicted of treason except on the testimony of two witnesses to the same overt act or on confession in open court."[73]

Misprision of treason is the concealment or nondisclosure of the known treason of another. It is punishable under federal law and under the laws of most states. **Rebellion** consists of "deliberate, organized resistance, by force and arms, to the laws or operations of the government, committed by a subject."[74] Under federal law, rebellion is committed when a person incites or engages in any rebellion against the United States.[75] A related crime is that of advocating the overthrow of government. Federal law prohibits knowingly or willfully advocating the overthrow or destruction of the government of the United States or of any state.[76]

Related to treason is the crime of **espionage**, or spying for a foreign government. Espionage is defined under the federal Espionage Act[77] as "gathering, transmitting or losing" information or secrets related to the national defense with the intent or the reasonable belief that such information will be used against the United States.

Espionage against the United States did not end with the cold war. In 1994, for example, agent Aldrich Hazen Ames of the Central Intelligence Agency (CIA) and his wife, Rosario, were arrested and charged with conspiracy to commit espionage in a plot to sell U.S. government secrets to the Russian KGB. The Ames couple apparently told their Russian handlers of CIA operatives within the former Soviet Union and revealed the extent of American knowledge of KGB plans. Their activities had gone undetected for nearly a decade. Following arrest, the couple pleaded guilty to charges of espionage and tax fraud. Aldrich Ames was sentenced to life in prison; his wife received a five-year term. Two years later, in 1996, CIA station chief Harold Nicholson was arrested as he was preparing to leave Washington's Dulles Airport, allegedly on his way to meet his Russian handlers. Nicholson is the highest-ranking CIA employee ever to be charged with espionage. Also in 1996, 43-year-old Earl Edwin Pitts, a 13-year FBI veteran, was taken into custody at the FBI academy in Quantico, Virginia, and arraigned on charges of attempted espionage and conspiracy.[78] Pitts was charged with spying for the Russians and is said to have turned over lists of Russian agents within the United States who had been compromised. Nicholson and Pitts pleaded guilty to espionage charges in early 1997.[79] Both were sentenced to lengthy prison terms.

Finally, the crime of **sedition** consists of a communication or agreement intended to defame the government or to incite treason. Under federal law, the crime of seditious conspiracy is described as follows: "If two or more persons in any State or Territory, or in any place subject to the jurisdiction of the United States, conspire to overthrow, put down, or to destroy by force the Government of the United States, or to levy war against them, or to oppose by force the authority thereof, or by force to prevent, hinder, or delay the execution of any law of the United States, or by force to seize, take, or possess any property of the United States contrary to the authority thereof, they shall each be fined under this title or imprisoned not more than twenty years, or both."[80]

Perjury and Contempt

Under common law, **perjury** was the willful giving of false testimony under oath in a judicial proceeding. Most jurisdictions have enlarged the conduct prohibited under the crime of perjury to include any false testimony given under any lawfully administered oath. Accordingly, perjury may be committed if false testimony or a false statement is made under oath before any body that has lawful authority to administer an oath to witnesses who appear before it. Pennsylvania law, for example, says: "A person is guilty of perjury, a felony of the third degree, if in any official proceeding he makes a false statement under oath or equivalent affirmation, or swears or affirms the truth of a statement previously made, when the statement is material and he does not believe it to be true."[81] Jurisdictions that have broadened the law of perjury sometimes call the offense *false swearing*.

---

rebellion
Deliberate, organized resistance, by force and arms, to the laws or operations of the government, committed by a subject of that government.[vi]

espionage
The unlawful act of spying for a foreign government.

sedition
A crime that consists of a communication or agreement intended to defame the government or to incite treason.

perjury
The willful giving of false testimony under oath in a judicial proceeding. Also, false testimony given under any lawfully administered oath.

To constitute perjury or false swearing, however, the false statement, as noted by the Pennsylvania law just cited, must be material; that is, a false statement made under oath that concerns a matter that has no bearing on the proceedings at hand is not perjury. Pennsylvania law, for example, says: "Falsification is material, regardless of the admissibility of the statement under rules of evidence, if it could have affected the course or outcome of the proceeding. It is no defense that the declarant mistakenly believed the falsification to be immaterial. Whether a falsification is material in a given factual situation is a question of law."[82]

Common law required that perjury be proved by the testimony of at least two witnesses. Most jurisdictions have relaxed this rule and allow a perjury conviction to be obtained by the testimony of a single witness if supplemented by other indirect evidence. Jurisdictions are divided, however, as to whether retraction of perjured testimony is a defense. Many hold that it is a defense if the witness retracts his or her statement in the same proceedings and before the falsity has been discovered. In other jurisdictions, retraction is relevant only in mitigation.

Subornation of perjury occurs when one person procures another to commit perjury. Federal law, for example, reads: "Whoever procures another to commit any perjury is guilty of subornation of perjury, and shall be fined under this title or imprisoned not more than five years, or both."[83] To commit this crime, the defendant must have known that the testimony to be given by a witness would be false, and the defendant must have caused the witness to actually give the false testimony.[84] An attorney, for example, who calls a witness whom the attorney knows will commit perjury is guilty of subornation of perjury in some jurisdictions. In other jurisdictions, he or she would be considered to be a principal under the law of principals and thus guilty of perjury.

> **subornation of perjury**
> The unlawful procuring of another person to commit perjury.

Criminal contempt consists of deliberate conduct calculated to obstruct or embarrass a court of law or conduct intended to degrade the role of a judicial officer in administering justice. Criminal contempt harms the judicial process itself. It differs from civil contempt in that criminal contempt is a violation of criminal law[85] (that is, a violation of common law and of the statutory criminal law of most jurisdictions), whereas civil contempt is a sanction available to a court that can be imposed on a person who is recalcitrant to meet the court's lawful demands made on behalf of another party. Violating a court order to pay alimony, for example, may lead to a civil contempt charge, whereas being verbally abusive within the courtroom might constitute criminal contempt. In addition, two types of criminal contempt can be distinguished: (1) direct contempt, which consists of acts committed in the presence of the court; and (2) indirect contempt, which consists of acts committed outside the court's presence. Direct contempt might consist, for example, of a physical assault on a judge while a hearing or trial is in progress. Indirect contempt might involve actions by a juror outside the courtroom that are contrary to the court's instructions, such as discussing the case with family or friends when ordered not to do so.

> **criminal contempt**
> Deliberate conduct calculated to obstruct or embarrass a court of law. Also, conduct intended to degrade the role of a judicial officer in administering justice.

Although it is generally recognized that both forms of contempt are crimes, instances of direct contempt are usually dealt with summarily; that is, the judge in whose court the contempt occurs informs the "contemnor" of the contempt accusation and asks him or her why he or she should not be found guilty of contempt. Lacking a satisfactory answer, the court will enter a judgment against the offender and will impose punishment. Individuals charged with indirect contempt must be afforded an opportunity to prepare a defense and may be represented by counsel.

Obstruction of Justice

Obstruction of justice, or the attempt to interfere with the administration of public justice, was a misdemeanor under common law. Today, obstruction of justice is statutorily defined

> **obstruction of justice**
> An unlawful attempt to interfere with the administration of the courts, the judicial system, or law enforcement officers or with the activities of those who seek justice in a court or whose duties involve the administration of justice.

by both the states and the federal government and may be either a felony or a misdemeanor, depending on the seriousness of the offense. As with common law, the statutory crime of obstruction of justice might involve jury tampering; interfering with the activities of an officer of the law or of the court; tampering with or suppressing evidence; threatening witnesses; or bribing judges, jurors, or witnesses. Additionally, some states have made it a crime to refuse to render aid to law enforcement personnel in the official performance of their duties or to give false or misleading evidence to investigators. Many states have also created the crimes of endeavoring to obstruct justice and conspiring to obstruct justice.

Obstruction of justice may involve activities such as picketing or parading or using sound amplifiers with intent to disrupt or influence judges, jurors, or witnesses. Section 1507 of the federal criminal code says, for example: "Whoever, with the intent of interfering with, obstructing, or impeding the administration of justice, or with the intent of influencing any judge, juror, witness, or court officer, in the discharge of his duty, pickets or parades in or near a building housing a court of the United States, or in or near a building or residence occupied or used by such judge, juror, witness, or court officer, or with such intent uses any sound-truck or similar device or resorts to any other demonstration in or near any such building or residence, shall be fined under this title or imprisoned not more than one year, or both."[86]

The most common form of obstruction of justice is **resisting arrest**. All states make it a crime to resist a lawful arrest. Some even require that a person submit to arrest by a police officer who is carrying out his or her duties, even though the arrest may be unlawful (the defense of resisting unlawful arrest is discussed in Chapter 5). Oregon law, for example, says: "A person commits the crime of resisting arrest if the person intentionally resists a person known by the person to be a peace officer in making an arrest."[87] Some states employ more generic statutes that take the focus off arrest and place it on resisting any public officer in the performance of his or her duties. North Carolina law, for example, says: "If any person shall willfully and unlawfully resist, delay or obstruct a public officer in discharging or attempting to discharge a duty of his office, he shall be guilty of a Class 2 misdemeanor."[88]

resisting arrest
The crime of obstructing or opposing a peace officer who is making an arrest.

Escape

Under common law, prisoners who left lawful custody without permission committed the crime of **escape**. If force was used in the escape, the offense was termed *prison break* or *breach of prison*. Although all jurisdictions have enacted statutes criminalizing escape, some state statutes apply only to those who leave correctional custody without permission, whereas others apply as well to those who leave the custody of law enforcement personnel. Generally, escape laws require intent on the part of the escapee, but even where they don't, the courts have typically held that intent is a necessary element of the crime of escape. Otherwise it would be possible to imagine, for example, the arrest and conviction of a sleeping work crew prisoner whom authorities inadvertently left behind when they returned to prison.

Some jurisdictions make it lawful for prisoners to escape if they are under extreme duress or facing threats. Hence a prisoner who believes he is about to be murdered or raped by other inmates might lawfully escape in order to avoid being attacked. If such were to happen, however, the law would likely require that he turn himself in to authorities as soon as possible.

All jurisdictions make it illegal for anyone to help with an escape. Visitors to penal institutions, for example, may be guilty of the crime of aiding escape if they smuggle items into the facility that might be used in an escape attempt. Inmates who provide other prisoners with the tools or other means needed for an escape may also be charged with aiding or facilitating escape, as may correctional personnel who help inmates escape.

escape
The unlawful leaving of official custody or confinement without permission. Also, the failure to return to custody or confinement following an official temporary leave.

Misconduct in Office and Bribery

A public official who, under color of law or in his or her official capacity, acts in such a way as to exceed the bounds of the office may be guilty of **misconduct in office**. The term *misconduct in office* includes acts "which the office holder had no right to perform, acts performed improperly, and failure to act in the face of an affirmative duty to act."[89] Doing that which the officeholder has no right to do is called *malfeasance*. *Misfeasance* refers to official acts performed improperly, and *nonfeasance* describes failing to do that which should be done.

Misconduct can sometimes be the result of bribery. **Bribery** consists of "the offense of giving or receiving a gift or reward intended to influence a person in the exercise of a judicial or public duty."[90] As the definition notes, both the act of giving and the act of taking can constitute bribery—and a person who offers a bribe is just as guilty of the crime of bribery as the one who accepts it. The crime of bribery concerns only *official* acts, and no crime occurs when merely personal actions outside the official sphere are influenced by a bribe. Hence, under the laws of most jurisdictions, only public officeholders, state officials, or state employees acting in some official capacity can be found guilty of accepting bribes. Bribes may be offered, for example, to a jailer in an attempt to win the release of a prisoner, to a judge or juror to ensure the acquittal of a defendant in a criminal trial or a favorable verdict in a civil hearing or civil trial, to an elections official to win or influence an election, to a government decision maker to win a government contract, or to a legislator to gain passage of a favored bill.

misconduct in office
Acts that a public officeholder (1) has no right to perform, (2) performs improperly, or (3) fails to perform in the face of an affirmative duty to act.

bribery
The offense of giving or receiving a gift or reward intended to influence a person in the exercise of a judicial or public duty.[vii]

ENVIRONMENTAL CRIMES

Modernization, urbanization, industrialization, and population increases have proven very destructive to the world's natural environment. In response, nations around the world have enacted environmental laws, both civil and criminal. Today, the federal government of the United States and state and local governments have a plethora of environmental laws (Figure 10–4). Generally, environmental laws are intended (1) to protect and preserve the natural environment, for example, animals, flora, fauna, and water; (2) to protect the health of people; and (3) to protect, preserve, and enrich the value of the nation's natural resources. Because there is no individual victim, environmental crimes are generally considered crimes against the public.

Advancements in technology have improved the human condition in many ways. However, such advances have also created new, large risks. The *Deepwater Horizon* oil spill of 2010, the largest ocean oil spill in history, is an example. The spill, which followed an explosion of British Petroleum's *Deepwater Horizon* oil platform in the Gulf of Mexico, killed 11 people and resulted in millions of gallons of crude oil rushing into the ocean. Marine and other wildlife were killed, tourism was significantly injured, and significant resources were spent to contain and clean up the disaster. The federal government began an extensive investigation of the disaster and the response to it. At year-end 2011 three British Petroleum employees had been charged with crimes ranging from manslaughter to concealing information from Congress. Each pled not guilty, and they are awaiting trial. Additionally, the Obama administration put a temporary freeze on new government contracts with BP.[91]

One long-running example of a civil case involving huge environmental damages stems from the grounding of the tanker *Exxon Valdez*, which hit a reef in Prince William Sound, Alaska, in 1989 and spilled nearly 11 million gallons of oil, fouling beaches and killing fish and other wildlife. In 1994, an Anchorage jury awarded fishermen, seafood companies, and

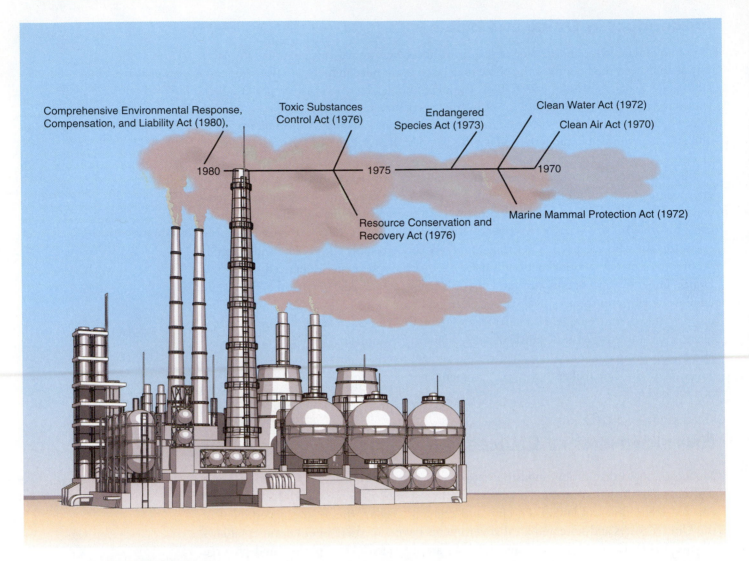

FIGURE 10-4

Federal Environmental Laws.

other plaintiffs $2.5 billion in punitive damages, but Exxon disputed the award, arguing that it had already paid billions to clean up the spill and compensate fishermen and others.

In 2008, the U.S. Supreme Court held Exxon liable for the much smaller amount of $507.5 million in punitive damages.[92] Writing for the Court, Justice David Souter issued an order vacating the $2.5 billion award and remanding the case back to a lower court. The Court found that the original damage award was excessive with respect to maritime common law.

The captain of the *Valdez*, Joseph Hazelwood, was charged with several felonies and misdemeanors. He was acquitted of all charges except misdemeanor negligent discharge of oil. He was fined $50,000 and sentenced to community service. The conviction was subsequently overturned by the Court of Appeals of Alaska and then reinstated by the Supreme Court of Alaska.[93]

Although most environmental violations are handled as administrative and civil cases, the number of criminal cases is increasing. At the federal level, the Department of Justice has a division that is responsible for prosecuting environmental crimes. Other agencies, such as the Environmental Protection Agency (EPA), play a role in the enforcement of the nation's environmental laws. Defendants charged with environmental crimes or violations of the U.S. Federal Criminal Code sometimes flee the court's jurisdiction rather than face prosecution or serve a sentence. When defendants become fugitives from justice, they are sought by the EPA's Criminal Investigation Division, which posts wanted posters on its environmental crimes website. Each poster provides a brief case summary and instructions on how to report information related to the fugitive's identity or current location.

There are many federal environmental statutes. The most significant include the Clean Water Act; the Clean Air Act; the Comprehensive Environmental Response, Compensation, and Liability Act; the Toxic Substances Control Act; the Resource Conservation and Recovery Act; and the Marine Mammal Protection Act.

The Clean Water Act

The Clean Water Act (CWA),[94] enacted in 1972 and subsequently amended on several occasions, is intended to protect the nation's navigable waterways. With few exceptions, the CWA does not explicitly apply to other surface waters.

The statute and its implementing regulations place limits on the pollutants that may be discharged into the water and establish a permitting system. The CWA provides for both civil and criminal remedies for both negligent and knowing violations, with the latter being punished more severely. Criminal remedies include fines and imprisonment. If an offender knows that his or her actions in violation of the CWA threaten any individual with death or serious injury, then the punishment is enhanced to a possible 15 years in prison. The CWA is a long and complex act. Adding to its complexity is a host of administrative regulations that different federal agencies have enacted to implement the act.

A controversial dimension of the CWA has been the interpretation of the term *navigable waterways* by the federal agencies responsible for enforcing the act. Over time, agencies, through their rule-making powers, have increased the reach of the CWA significantly by defining *navigable waterways* very broadly.

The Clean Air Act

Complementing the CWA is the Clean Air Act (CAA).[95] The objective of the CAA, enacted in 1970 with several subsequent amendments, is to reduce and control air pollution. The CAA's reach includes emissions by automobiles, industry, and aircraft. It also has provisions intended to control acid rain and to address ozone depletion. The statute also requires control of noise pollution caused by federal activities. The CAA expanded upon federal legislation dating back to the Air Quality Act of 1955.

The Comprehensive Environmental Response, Compensation, and Liability Act

Another significant federal environmental law is the Comprehensive Environmental Response, Compensation, and Liability Act (CERCLA),[96] popularly known as Superfund. Through CERCLA, enacted in 1980 with subsequent amendment, hazardous waste sites are identified, studied, and abated. CERCLA also taxes certain industries, such as the petroleum industry, to generate revenue to pay for cleanups. Both civil and criminal remedies exist for unlawful toxic waste disposal and for falsifying reports or otherwise violating CERCLA.

The Toxic Substances Control Act

Although many federal laws address toxins, the Toxic Substances Control Act (TSCA), enacted in 1976, is the most comprehensive piece of legislation on the subject. The sale, manufacture, development, and distribution of toxins are all subject to the reach of the TSCA. Through the act, the Environmental Protection Agency has the authority to screen all chemicals imported to the United States, and the manufacture of new chemicals that could pose a threat to human health or to the environment must be reported.

Knowing and willful violations of the TSCA, false reporting under the act, failing to maintain records as required by the act, and failing to submit reports required by the act are all subject to either civil, administrative, or criminal remedies.

The Endangered Species Act

Through the Endangered Species Act (ESA) of 1973,[97] the federal government provides for the conservation of ecosystems and any species that live in them that are endangered or threatened with extinction. The act specifically prohibits the importation, exportation, possession, sale, destruction, injury, and transport of endangered fish and wildlife. The statute has both civil and criminal enforcement provisions.

The Resource Conservation and Recovery Act

The Resource Conservation and Recovery Act (RCRA),[98] an amendment to the federal Solid Waste Disposal Act, was enacted in 1976 to address a problem of enormous magnitude: the huge volumes of municipal and industrial solid and hazardous waste generated nationwide.[99]

A national survey conducted by the EPA in 1996 estimated that 279 million metric tons of hazardous waste were generated nationwide in 1995, more than a 500-fold increase over the preceding 50 years. Unfortunately, this phenomenal growth in waste production was not mirrored by advancements in the field of waste management. Much of the waste produced entered the environment, where it posed a serious threat to ecological systems and public health.

In the mid-1970s, the U.S. Congress took action to ensure that industrial wastes were managed properly. This realization began the process that resulted in the passage of the Resource Conservation and Recovery Act. The RCRA was enacted as an amendment to the already existing Solid Waste Disposal Act of 1965, which did not effectively address the management of wastes. The new law placed controls on the generation, transportation, treatment, storage, and disposal of hazardous wastes, and it established a framework for the management of nonhazardous waste.

The RCRA has been further amended to reflect the nation's changing needs. Some of the more important amendments are the Hazardous and Solid Waste Amendments (HSWA) of 1984, which expanded the scope and requirements of the RCRA. The amendments were enacted largely in response to concerns that existing methods of hazardous waste disposal, particularly land disposal, were not safe. The amendments also required the EPA to develop a comprehensive program for regulating underground tanks and underground tank systems as needed to protect human health and the environment. They addressed the problem of leaking underground storage tanks by requiring tank notification, tank standards, reporting and record-keeping requirements for existing tanks, corrective action when necessary, and the development of compliance and enforcement programs. Other important amendments to the RCRA were the Federal Facilities Compliance Act of 1992, which was passed to strengthen the authority to enforce the RCRA at federally owned facilities, and the Land Disposal Flexibility Act of 1996, which amended the RCRA to provide regulatory flexibility for the land disposal of certain wastes.

The four goals of the RCRA are to

- Protect human health and the environment from the hazards posed by waste disposal
- Conserve energy and natural resources through waste recycling and recovery
- Reduce or eliminate, as expeditiously as possible, the amount of waste generated, including hazardous waste
- Ensure that wastes are managed in a manner that protects human health and the environment

The Marine Mammal Protection Act

The Marine Mammal Protection Act (MMPA) is the ESA's close cousin. It was enacted in 1972, with subsequent amendments, and, as the name indicates, it is intended to protect marine mammals from extinction. In its investigation of marine mammals, Congress found the following to be true:

1. [C]ertain species and population stocks of marine mammals are, or may be, in danger of extinction or depletion as a result of man's activities;

2. [S]uch species and population stocks should not be permitted to diminish beyond the point at which they cease to be a significant functioning element in the ecosystem of which they are a part, and, consistent with this major objective, they should not be permitted to diminish below their optimum sustainable population. Further measures should be immediately taken to replenish any species or population stock which has already diminished below that population. In particular, efforts should be made to protect essential habitats, including the rookeries, mating grounds, and areas of similar significance for each species of marine mammal from the adverse effect of man's actions;

3. [T]here is inadequate knowledge of the ecology and population dynamics of such marine mammals and of the factors which bear upon their ability to reproduce themselves successfully;

4. [N]egotiations should be undertaken immediately to encourage the development of international arrangements for research on, and conservation of, all marine mammals;

5. [M]arine mammals and marine mammal products either—
   A. move in interstate commerce, or
   B. affect the balance of marine ecosystems in a manner which is important to other animals and animal products which move in interstate commerce, and that the protection and conservation of marine mammals and their habitats [are] therefore necessary to insure the continuing availability of those products which move in interstate commerce . . .

6. [M]arine mammals have proven themselves to be resources of great international significance, esthetic and recreational as well as economic, and it is the sense of the Congress that they should be protected and encouraged to develop to the greatest extent feasible commensurate with sound policies of resource management and that the primary objective of their management should be to maintain the health and stability of the marine ecosystem. Whenever consistent with this primary objective, it should be the goal to obtain an optimum sustainable population keeping in mind the carrying capacity of the habitat.[100]

The goal of the statute is to ensure that the minimum sustainable population of each species is maintained. The statute prohibits the hunt, capture, harassment, and killing of threatened mammals in U.S. waters and by U.S. citizens on the high seas. It is enforceable through both civil and criminal actions.

Other Environmental Laws

These are just a few of the many federal environmental laws. Many others exist at the federal, state, and local levels of government. In addition to statutory law, much environmental law can be found in the regulations of administrative agencies. At the federal level, the Environmental Protection Agency has been delegated the authority to issue regulations and to enforce federal environmental law, but it is only one of many federal agencies that possess such authority. Similarly, many state and local agencies have enforcement authority and have been delegated rule-making authority.

SUMMARY

- This chapter discusses crimes against public order and crimes against the administration of government. Both types of offenses can be generally classified as social-order crimes. A third category of social-order crimes, offenses against public morality, is discussed in Chapter 12.

- Public-order offenses are those that disturb or invade society's peace and tranquility. They include breach of peace, disorderly conduct, fighting, affray, vagrancy, loitering, illegally carrying weapons, keeping a disorderly house, public intoxication, disturbance of public assembly, inciting to riot, rioting, unlawful assembly, rout, and obstructing public passage.

- Laws criminalizing public-order offenses rest on the assumption that public order is inherently valuable and should be maintained—and that disorder is not to be tolerated and should be reduced, when it occurs, through the application of the criminal law.

- Some court decisions have focused specifically on fighting words, or those utterances that are an affront to the public peace and that are intended to provoke those at whom they are directed. According to the U.S. Supreme Court, fighting words are not protected under free speech constitutional guarantees.

- Public intoxication is a common offense, and many people are arrested annually for driving while intoxicated (DWI) or driving under the influence (DUI).

- Vagrancy, a crime under common law, has been largely recast today in terms of loitering. Traditional vagrancy laws often ran afoul of the constitutional prohibition against vagueness because they criminalized a person's status rather than his or her conduct.

- A special category of public-order offense is that of illegally carrying weapons. Considerable debate exists within the United States today over the issue of gun control, with persuasive arguments being advanced on both sides of the controversy.

- Another class of social-order offense discussed in this chapter is that of crimes against the administration of government. Offenses in this category include treason, misprision of treason, rebellion, espionage, sedition, perjury, subornation of perjury, criminal contempt, obstruction of justice, resisting arrest, escape, misconduct in office, and bribery.

- Environmental laws are intended (1) to protect and preserve the natural environment; (2) to protect the health of people; and (3) to protect, preserve, and enrich the value of the nation's natural resources. There are many federal environmental statutes. The most significant include the Clean Water Act; the Clean Air Act; the Comprehensive Environmental Response, Compensation, and Liability Act; the Toxic Substances Control Act; the Resource Conservation and Recovery Act; and the Marine Mammal Protection Act. Because there is no individual victim, environmental crimes are generally considered crimes against the public.

KEY TERMS

affray, 330

breach of peace, 326

bribery, 351

concealed weapon, 339

criminal contempt, 349

disorderly conduct, 326

disturbance of public assembly, 334

driving under the influence (DUI), 331

driving while intoxicated (DWI), 331

escape, 350

espionage, 348

fighting words, 326

inciting a riot, 334

loitering, 336

lynching, 334

misconduct in office, 351

obstruction of justice, 349

perjury, 348

prize fighting, 330

public drunkenness, 332

QUESTIONS FOR DISCUSSION

1. What are the three categories of social-order crimes? How do they differ? With which two categories is this chapter most concerned?

2. What are fighting words? How can they be distinguished from protected forms of speech?

3. Explain the differences among rout, riot, and unlawful assembly.

4. What is vagrancy? Why have traditional laws against vagrancy been held to be unconstitutional?

5. Should the possession of handguns be regulated? Summarize the arguments on both sides of the issue.

6. What is the difference between treason and espionage?

7. Explain the differences among perjury, bribery, and contempt. How does criminal contempt differ from civil contempt?

8. What federal statutes are intended to protect the environment?

CRITICAL THINKING AND APPLICATION PROBLEMS

Consider a state law that reads as follows:

Breach of Peace—Incitement

a. Any person who utters a statement in the presence of another person that a reasonable person would find offensive is guilty of breach of peace, a class B misdemeanor.

b. Any person who utters a statement to another person that would be found to be threatening to life or limb by a reasonable person and that would likely provoke a reasonable person to respond with violence is guilty of breach of peace, a Class A misdemeanor.

1. Does section (a) violate the First Amendment's Free Speech Clause? Explain your answer.

2. Does section (b) violate the First Amendment's Free Speech Clause? Explain your answer.

LEGAL RESOURCES ON THE WEB

Many courts now offer websites containing information on court structure, administrative procedures, and coming changes in court procedure. A few of those sites are listed here.

California Courts
http://www.courts.ca.gov/
Website of the California judicial branch.

Conference of State Court Administrators (COSCA)
http://cosca.ncsc.dni.us
COSCA was organized in 1953 and is dedicated to the improvement of state court systems. Its membership consists of the state court administrator in each state, the District of Columbia, Puerto Rico, American Samoa, and the U.S. Virgin Islands.

Federal Judiciary
http://www.uscourts.gov

Website of the Administrative Office of the U.S. Courts.

Florida State Courts
http://www.flcourts.org
A statewide information system serving Florida's judiciary.

National Center for State Courts
http://www.ncsc.org/
The National Center for State Courts is an independent nonprofit organization dedicated to the improvement of justice.

U.S. Court of Appeals for the First Circuit
http://www.ca1.uscourts.gov

U.S. Court of Appeals for the Second Circuit
http://www.ca2.uscourts.gov

U.S. Court of Appeals for the Third Circuit
http://www.ca3.uscourts.gov

U.S. Court of Appeals for the Fourth Circuit
http://www.ca4.uscourts.gov

U.S. Court of Appeals for the Fifth Circuit
http://www.ca5.uscourts.gov

U.S. Court of Appeals for the Sixth Circuit
http://www.ca6.uscourts.gov

U.S. Court of Appeals for the Seventh Circuit
http://www.ca7.uscourts.gov

U.S. Court of Appeals for the Eighth Circuit
http://www.ca8.uscourts.gov

U.S. Court of Appeals for the Ninth Circuit
http://www.ca9.uscourts.gov

U.S. Court of Appeals for the Tenth Circuit
http://www.ca10.uscourts.gov

U.S. Court of Appeals for the Eleventh Circuit
http://www.ca11.uscourts.gov

U.S. Court of Appeals for the Armed Forces
http://www.armfor.uscourts.gov
This appellate court is empowered to review court-martial cases.

U.S. Court of Appeals for the District of Columbia Circuit
http://www.cadc.uscourts.gov

U.S. Court of Appeals for the Federal Circuit
http://www.cafc.uscourts.gov

U.S. Supreme Court
http://www.supremecourtus.gov
Provides public access to the Court's decisions, argument calendar, schedules, rules, visitors' guides, building photos, and bar admission forms. Although dockets have in the past been available by phone, this is the first venture onto the Internet for the nation's highest court. Decision texts are available online by noon on the day they are announced.

SUGGESTED READINGS AND CLASSIC WORKS

Adler, Jeffery S. "A Historical Analysis of the Law of Vagrancy." *Criminology* 27 (May 1989): 209.

Chambliss, William J. *Crime and the Legal Process*. New York: McGraw-Hill, 1969.

Feinberg, Joel. *The Moral Limits of the Criminal Law*. New York: Oxford University Press, 1986.

Lapierre, Wayne R. *Guns, Crime, and Freedom*. Washington, DC: Regnery, 1994.

Nisbet, Lee, ed. *The Gun Control Debate: You Decide*. Amherst, NY: Prometheus, 1991.

Vago, Steven. *Law and Society*, 4th ed. Upper Saddle River, NJ: Prentice Hall, 1994.

NOTES

1. *People v. Stephen*, 153 Misc. 2d 382, 581 N.Y.S.2d 981 (1992).

2. Ibid.

3. Rollins M. Perkins and Ronald N. Boyce, *Criminal Law*, 3rd ed. (Mineola, NY: Foundation Press, 1982), 477.

4. Ibid.

5. Ibid.

6. *Cantwell v. Connecticut*, 310 U.S. 296, 308, 60 S. Ct. 900 (1940).

7. Sir William Blackstone, *Commentaries on the Laws of England* (Oxford: Clarendon Press, 1765), 1:349.

8. *Chaplinsky v. New Hampshire*, 315 U.S. 568 (1942).

9. *State v. Cherry*, 173 N.W.2d 887, 888 (Neb. 1970).

10. *People v. Harvey*, 2001 NY078439.

11. *Texas v. Johnson*, 491 U.S. 397 (1989)

12. *Snyder v. Phelps*, 562 U.S. ____ (2011).

13. Wesley Gilmer, *The Law Dictionary*, 6th ed. (Cincinnati: Anderson, 1986), 54.

14. H. Lee, *How Dry Were We: Prohibition Revisited* (Upper Saddle River, NJ: Prentice Hall, 1963).

15. Ibid.

16. Stanton Peele, "The Cultural Context of Psychological Approaches to Alcoholism: Can We Control the Effects of Alcohol?" *American Psychologist* 39 (1984): 1137–1151.

17. Medline Plus, "Alcoholism," http://www.nlm.nih.gov/medlineplus/alcoholism.html (accessed April 4, 2009).

18. The details in this paragraph come from Drug Rehabs.org, http://www.drug-rehabs.org/alcohol-statistics.php (accessed April 3, 2009); and "Alcohol Statistics," http://www.alcohol-information. com/Alcohol_Statistics.html (accessed April 3, 2009).

19. California Penal Code, Section 23152(c).

20. *People v. Byrd*, 125 Ca. 3d 1054 (1985).

21. *People v. Jordan*, 75 Ca. 3d Supp. 1 (1979).

22. California Penal Code, Section 23157.

23. Derald D. Hunt, *California Criminal Law Manual*, 8th ed. (Edina, MN: Burgess, 1996).

24. Ibid.

25. U.S. Code Annotated, Title 18, Section 210(a)(1).

26. California Penal Code, Sections 404 and 406.

27. Ibid.

28. *Ledwith v. Roberts*, 1 K.B. 232, 271 (1937).

29. Gilmer, *The Law Dictionary*, 334.

30. North Carolina General Statutes, Article 43, Section 14-336 (1969).

31. *Papachristou v. City of Jacksonville*, 405 U.S. 156 (1972).

32. John M. Scheb and John M. Scheb II, *American Criminal Law* (St. Paul: West, 1996), 284.

33. *Papachristou v. City of Jacksonville*, 405 U.S. 156 (1972).

34. City of Jacksonville (Florida) Ordinance Code, Section 257 (rescinded).

35. *Kolender v. Lawson*, 461 U.S. 353 (1983).

36. Indiana Code, Sections 31-37-3-2 and 31-37-3-3.5.

37. See *Hodgkins v. Goldsmith*, No. IP99-1528-C-T/G, 2000 WL 892964, at 8-7 (S.D.Ind. July 3, 2000).

38. *Hodgkins v. Peterson*, 355 F.3d 1048 (7th Cir. 2004).

39. Ibid., at 73.

40. *Ramos v. Town of Vernon*, 331 F.3d 315 (2d Cir. 2003).

41. As reported in *Legal Affairs* (May/June 2004), 12.

42. Examples of cases in which curfews were upheld include *Schliefer* v. *Charlottesville*, 159 F.3d 843 (4th Cir. 1988), cert. den. 119 S. Ct. 1252 (1999), and *Hutchins* v. *District of Columbia*, 188 F.3d 531 (D.C. Cir. 1999).

43. In *re P.*, 2000 Tex. App. Lexis 2199.

44. *Hutchins* v. *District of Columbia*, 942 F. Supp. 665, 1996 U.S. Dist. LEXIS 16467.

45. For a discussion of the constitutionality of curfews as applied to the U.S. territory American Samoa, see Daniel E. Hall, "Curfews, Culture, and Custom in American Samoa: An Analytical Map for Applying the Constitution to U.S. Territories," *Asian-Pacific Law and Policy Journal* 2 (winter 2001): 69–107.

46. *District of Columbia* v. *Heller*, 554 U.S. 570 (2008).

47. *McDonald* v. *Chicago*, 561 U.S. 3025 (2010).

48. U.S. Code, Title 18, Section 922.

49. Ibid.

50. *Printz* v. *United States*, 521 U.S. 98 (1997).

51. *Mack* v. *United States*, 521 U.S. 98 (1997). Combined with *Printz* v. *United States*, 521 U.S. 98 (1997).

52. To learn more about the system, see Michael F. Cahn, James M. Tien, and David M. Einstein, *Assessment and Resolution of Replicated Firearm Eligibility Checks* (Washington, DC: Structured Decisions Corporation, 2004).

53. "Brady Bill Backers Hail 3rd Anniversary Friday," Reuters, February 28, 1997.

54. U.S. Code, Title 18, Section 922.

55. U.S. Code, Title 18, Section 922(q)(1)(A) (1988 ed., Supp. V).

56. *United States* v. *Lopez*, 514 U.S. 549 (1995).

57. Details for this story come from Donald Bradley, "Deportation Turns Couple's Dream into Nightmare," *Kansas City Star*, April 30, 2004, http://www .thestate.com/mld/thestate/news/nation/8559396. htm (accessed February 3, 2005).

58. *San Diego Law Review* 31 (1994): 911.

59. Joyce C. Vialet, Congressional Research Service, *CRS Report for Congress: A Brief History of U.S. Immigration Policy* (no. 91-141 EPW, Supp. 1991), reprinted in *House Committee on the Judiciary*, 102nd Congress, 2nd Session, Immigration and Nationality Act 548, 550–553.

60. *Rosenberg* v. *Fleuti*, 374 U.S. 449 (1963).

61. U.S. Code, Title 8, Section 1326.

62. *United States* v. *Meza-Soria*, 935 F.2d 166, 169 (9th Cir. 1991).

63. Under U.S. Code, Title 8, Section 1326(a).

64. See *United States* v. *Smith*, 36 F.3d 128 (5th Cir. 1994).

65. *United States* v. *Ventura-Candelario*, 981 F. Supp. 868, 869 (S.D.N.Y. 1997).

66. *United States* v. *Diaz-Diaz*, 135 F.3d 572, 575–576 (8th Cir. 1998).

67. See *United States* v. *Scantleberry-Frank*, 158 F.3d 612 (1st Cir. 1998).

68. See Daniel E. Hall and John Feldmeier, *Constitutional Law: Governmental Powers and Individual Freedoms*, 2nd ed. (Upper Saddle River, NJ: Pearson/Prentice Hall Publishing, 2012), chap. 2 for more about this topic.

69. U.S. Constitution, Article III, Section 3, Clause 1.

70. U.S. Code, Title 18, Section 2381.

71. *Kawakita* v. *United States*, 343 U.S. 717 (1952).

72. U.S. Constitution, Article III, Section 3.

73. Florida Constitution, Section 20.

74. Ibid.

75. U.S. Code, Title 18, Section 2383-84.

76. U.S. Code, Title 18, Section 2385.

77. U.S. Code, Title 18, Section 793.

78. Steven Komarow, "FBI Agent Is Accused of Spying for Russians," *USA Today*, December 19, 1996.

79. "Ex-CIA Officer Pleads Guilty to Spying," Reuters, March 4, 1997.

80. U.S. Code, Title 18, Section 2384.

81. Pennsylvania Code, Title 18, Section 4902(a).

82. Pennsylvania Code, Title 18, Section 4902(b).

83. U.S. Code, Title 18, Section 1622.

84. *Niehoff* v. *Sahagin*, 103 A.2d 211 (Me. 1954).

85. See *Bloom* v. *Illinois*, 391 U.S. 194, 88 S. Ct. 1477 (1968).

86. U.S. Code, Title 18, Section 1507.

87. Oregon Revised Statutes, Section 162.315(1).

88. North Carolina General Statutes, Chapter 14, Section 223.

89. Joseph R. Nolan and Jacqueline M. Nolan-Haley, *Black's Law Dictionary: Definitions of the Terms and Phrases of American and English Jurisprudence, Ancient and Modern*, 6th ed. (St. Paul: West, 1990), 999.

90. Ibid.

91. "3 BP Employees Plead Not Guilty on Gulf Oil Spill Charges," *CBS News*, November 28, 2012, http://www.cbsnews.com/8301-201_162-57556049/3-bp-employees-plead-not-guilty-on-gulf-oil-spill-charges/ (accessed December 5, 2012).

92. *Exxon Shipping Co.* v. *Baker*, 554 U.S. 471 (2008).

93. See Timothy Egan, "Court Overturns Conviction of *Exxon Valdez*'s Captain," *New York Times*, July 11, 1992, http://www.nytimes.com/1992/07/11/us/court-overturns-conviction-of-exxon-valdez-s-captain.html; *Alaska v. Hazelwood*, 866 P.2d 827 (Ala. 1993); and *Hazelwood v. Alaska*, Ala. Ct. App. A-3452 (July 2, 1998).

94. U.S. Code, Title 33, Section 1319(a).

95. U.S. Code, Title 42, Section 85 et seq.

96. U.S. Code, Title 42, Section 9601 et seq.

97. U.S. Code, Title 16, Section 1531 et seq.

98. The Resource Conservation and Recovery Act (RCRA) of 1976; U.S. Code, Title 42, Section 321 et seq. (P.L. 94-580).

99. Much of the information and some of the wording in this section come from the Environmental Protection Agency, "RCRA Statute, Regulations and Enforcement," http://epa.gov/compliance/civil/rcra/rcraenfstatreq.html (accessed January 7, 2009).

100. U.S. Code, Title 16, Section 1361 et seq.

© Photofusion Picture Library/Alamy

11

Offenses against Public Morality

OBJECTIVES

After reading this chapter, you should be able to

- Explain the concept of victimless crime.
- Describe prostitution and its legal status across the United States.
- Describe the nation's drug problem, antidrug legislation, and various methods for combatting the drug problem.
- Explain what constitutes pornography, obscenity, and lewdness.

> *Whatever differences of opinion may exist as to the extent and boundaries of the police power . . . there seems to be no doubt that it does extend to . . . the preservation of good order and the public morals.*
>
> —Boston Beer Co. *v.* Massachusetts, 97 U.S. 25, 33, 24 L. Ed. 989 (1878)

> *We do not allow a leper to live in our midst of his own volition, and the unfortunate woman, living in a respectable neighborhood and plying her terrible trade, is a leprous sore on the community which will fester until it leavens others with its dreadful poison.*
>
> —Mrs. C. M. Weymann, secretary of the Women's Legislative Council, describing Sacramento, California, prostitutes, 1913[1]

INTRODUCTION

About ten years ago, the city of Erie, Pennsylvania, enacted an ordinance making it an offense to knowingly or intentionally appear in public in a "state of nudity." At the time, a company known as Pap's A.M. operated an Erie nightclub called Kandyland, which featured totally nude erotic dancing by women. To comply with the new ordinance, Kandyland dancers were forced to change their dance routines by wearing "pasties" and "G-strings." Pap's, seeking to overturn the ordinance, filed suit against Erie and city officials. Initially, a Pennsylvania court struck down the city ordinance as unconstitutional, but a state appellate court reversed the decision. The Pennsylvania Supreme Court, in turn, reversed the decision of the appellate court, finding that the ordinance's public nudity sections violated the dancers' First Amendment right to freedom of expression. The Pennsylvania Supreme Court held that nude dancing is a form of expressive conduct entitled to protection under the First Amendment and reasoned that the Erie ordinance impacted "negatively on the erotic message of the dance."[2]

The city appealed to the U.S. Supreme Court, which overturned the decision by Pennsylvania's high court in March 2000.[3] The Court allowed that "nude dancing . . . is expressive conduct that falls within the outer ambit of the First Amendment's protection." However, the justices said, the purpose the city had in mind when enacting the ordinance was unrelated to the suppression of expressive conduct but was aimed instead at the "negative secondary effects" of such dancing. Negative secondary effects include crime, lowered property values, the potential for substance abuse in the vicinity of the bar, and other undesirable consequences "caused by the presence of adult entertainment establishments like Kandyland." Moreover, said the Court, the ordinance "does not target nudity that contains an erotic message; rather, it bans all public nudity, regardless of whether that nudity is accompanied by expressive activity." The Court concluded by saying that "even if Erie's public nudity ban has some minimal effect on the erotic message by muting that portion of the expression that occurs when the last stitch is dropped, the dancers at Kandyland and other such establishments are free to perform wearing pasties and G-strings. Any effect on the overall expression is therefore [minimal]." The Court's decision is summarized in a Capstone Case later in this chapter.

CRIMES AGAINST PUBLIC DECENCY AND MORALITY

Although most crimes have specific and identifiable *individual* victims, some crimes do not. Such offenses fall into a category of social-order offenses called *crimes against public decency and morality*.

Legal strictures against behavior that negatively affects public decency and morality originated in medieval days, when secular rulers and church leaders became concerned with institutionalizing accepted notions of good and evil—and especially with controlling human sexual behavior to have it conform to existing notions of propriety. At that time, authorities were mostly concerned with crimes of adultery and prostitution. Morals offenses, as in the example that opened this chapter, are often identified by municipal codes, although many have also been codified in state statutes.

Crimes against public decency and morality are sometimes termed **victimless crimes** by virtue of the fact that they generally involve willing participants. The key to understanding the meaning of the term *victimless crimes* is to recognize that, although the behavior of those involved in such crimes may violate the criminal law, it is, in almost all cases, consensual behavior that is freely engaged in by all of the parties involved. Persons committing the act of prostitution, for example, are often willing—even eager—participants in the crime. The same is

victimless crime
An offense committed against the social values and interests represented in and protected by the criminal law *and* in which parties to the offense willingly participate.

true for those participating in drug sales, drug purchases, drug use, gambling, and so on. Hence we can define a *victimless crime* as an offense committed against the social values and interests represented in and protected by the criminal law *and* in which parties to the offense willingly participate. In short, victimless crimes are those with willing participants (Figure 11–1).

Crimes against public decency and morality typically include not only prostitution, drug use, and gambling, but also pornography, obscenity, and various other consensual sex offenses, such as bestiality, deviate sexual relations, lewdness, indecency, seduction, fornication, adultery, and bigamy. Although they do not have readily identifiable *complaining* victims, it is important to recognize that those who are not directly involved in such

FIGURE 11–1

Crimes with a Victim versus Victimless Crime.

offenses may still see themselves as victimized by the activity. The spouses of men who visit prostitutes, for example, are victims of prostitution in the sense that they may be exposed to sexually transmitted diseases, the marriage bond may be weakened by the husband's criminal activity, and the affected families may have fewer financial resources as a result of the man's expenditures for illicit sexual services. Moreover, because prostitution (and other such crimes) lowers the moral quality of life for everyone even tangentially related to the parties involved in the crime, and because it demeans the status of women in society and may endanger underage children, the offense is arguably not without victims.

PROSTITUTION

In July 1995, English movie star Hugh Grant was arrested in Hollywood, California, for felonious fellatious activity with prostitute Divine Brown.[4] While some of Grant's fans asked, "Why would he do such a thing?" others asked, "Why not?" Three weeks later, when Grant made an appearance on NBC's *Tonight Show*, female fans lined the streets with signs reading, "We forgive you, Hugh!"[5]

Prostitution is sometimes said to be the world's "oldest profession." In early England, it was an ecclesiastical crime (that is, one coming under church jurisdiction rather than the jurisdiction of lay courts), and not a common law offense. In the American colonies, the Protestant ethic greatly influenced criminal law as it developed and quickly led to a definition of prostitution as a criminal offense. At the federal level, the Mann Act,[6] also known as the White Slave Traffic Act, was passed in 1910 and prohibited the interstate transportation of "any woman or girl" for "an immoral purpose." The "moral purity movement" of the early twentieth century, whose members were influential in seeing the Mann Act passed into law, led to the enactment of a series of so-called Red Light Abatement Acts in many western states between 1914 and 1920. Today, prostitution is a crime in all states except Nevada, where counties with a population less than 400,000 are empowered to license houses of prostitution. Several counties have elected to license brothels. Where allowed, Nevada has a comprehensive regulatory scheme that includes zoning and licensing houses of prostitution, monthly testing of prostitutes for HIV and other sexually transmitted diseases, mandatory condom use, and prostitution house owner liability for the transmission of diseases by prostitutes known to have tested positive.[7] Unlicensed prostitution is a misdemeanor in Nevada.

North Carolina law defines **prostitution** as "the offering or receiving of the body for sexual intercourse for hire [as well as] the offering or receiving of the body for indiscriminate sexual intercourse without hire."[8] Georgia law, on the other hand, limits the crime of prostitution to sexual intercourse for hire. Georgia law reads, "A person commits the offense of prostitution when he performs or offers or consents to perform an act of sexual intercourse for money."[9] Many states substitute the term *sexual act* or *sexual conduct* for *sexual intercourse* or interpret the term *sexual intercourse* to mean any overt sexual activity. As both the North Carolina and Georgia definitions indicate, however, a conviction for prostitution does not require that the sexual act in question actually take place. An offer to perform the act, or consent to do so, is sufficient to constitute prostitution. **Soliciting prostitution** is the act of asking, enticing, or requesting another to commit the crime of prostitution. In most situations, of course, voluntary sexual intercourse between consenting adults is not a crime. It is primarily the acts of solicitation of and payment for sexual services that violate the criminal law.[10]

Generally speaking, the elements of the crime of prostitution are

- Engaging in or offering to perform
- A sexual act
- For hire

prostitution
"The offering or receiving of the body for sexual intercourse for hire." Also, "the offering or receiving of the body for indiscriminate sexual intercourse without hire."[i] Some states limit the crime of prostitution to sexual intercourse for hire.

soliciting prostitution
The act of asking, enticing, or requesting another to commit the crime of prostitution.

Prostitutes can be of either gender, and in most states both the prostitute and his or her customer can be found guilty of prostitution.

The crime of **promoting prostitution** is a statutory offense in almost all jurisdictions. It is intended to punish those who profit or attempt to profit by using others to engage in prostitution. Generally, the following acts constitute the crime of promoting prostitution: (1) owning, controlling, managing, supervising, or otherwise keeping a house of prostitution; (2) procuring a person for a house of prostitution; (3) encouraging, inducing, or otherwise purposely causing another to become or remain a prostitute; (4) soliciting a person to patronize a prostitute; (5) procuring a prostitute for another; or (6) transporting a person with the purpose of promoting that person's involvement in prostitution.[11]

Other offenses are associated with the crime of prostitution. A person who has or exercises control over the use of any place or conveyance that offers seclusion or shelter for the practice of prostitution commits the offense of **keeping a place of prostitution** when he or she knowingly grants or permits the use of such place for the purpose of prostitution.[12]

Under common law, a place of prostitution was known as a *bawdy house*, and the term is still used in some states today. Both the owner and the keeper of a bawdy house were guilty of a misdemeanor under the common law.

According to contemporary Georgia law, "A person commits the offense of **pimping** when he performs any of the following acts: (1) offers or agrees to procure a prostitute for another; (2) offers or agrees to arrange a meeting of persons for the purpose of prostitution; (3) directs another to a place knowing such direction is for the purpose of prostitution; (4) receives money or other thing of value from a prostitute, without lawful consideration, knowing it was earned in whole or in part from prostitution; or (5) aids or abets, counsels, or commands another in the commission of prostitution or aids or assists in prostitution where the proceeds or profits derived therefrom are to be divided on a pro rata basis."[13] Similarly, "a person commits the offense of **pandering** when he or she solicits a person to perform an act of prostitution or when he or she knowingly assembles persons at a fixed place for the purpose of being solicited by others to perform an act of prostitution."[14]

Some jurisdictions have also enacted special laws criminalizing "massage parlor" activities akin to prostitution. Georgia law, for example, says: "(a) A person, including a masseur or masseuse, commits the offense of masturbation for hire when he erotically stimulates the genital organs of another, whether resulting in orgasm or not, by manual or other bodily contact exclusive of sexual intercourse or by instrumental manipulation for money or the substantial equivalent thereof. (b) A person committing the offense of masturbation for hire shall be guilty of a misdemeanor."[15]

PORNOGRAPHY, OBSCENITY, AND LEWDNESS

The word *obscenity* comes from the Latin word *caenum* ("filth"), and the word *pornography* is taken from the Greek word *porne* ("prostitute"). All jurisdictions have laws that punish the sale, possession, and distribution of obscene material, and most have statutes defining lewdness or public indecency.

Pornography can be defined as "the depiction of sexual behavior in such a way as to excite the viewer sexually."[16] Obscenity is a bit more difficult to define. A simple definition of **obscenity** is that it is extreme pornography. But the distinction between protected speech and obscenity can be confounding. As Supreme Court Justice Potter Stewart famously quipped in the 1964 decision *Jacobellis* v. *Ohio*[17] "I shall not today attempt further to define the kinds of material I understand to be embraced within that shorthand description . . . and perhaps I could never succeed in intelligibly doing so. But I know it when I see it, and the motion picture involved in this case is not that."

---

promoting prostitution
The statutory offense of (1) owning, controlling, managing, supervising, or otherwise keeping a house of prostitution; (2) procuring a person for a house of prostitution; (3) encouraging, inducing, or otherwise purposely causing another to become or remain a prostitute; (4) soliciting a person to patronize a prostitute; (5) procuring a prostitute for another; or (6) transporting a person with the purpose of promoting that person's involvement in prostitution.

I was naughty. I wasn't bad. Bad is hurting people, doing evil. Naughty is not hurting anyone. Naughty is being amusing.

—Biddle Barrows, the "Mayflower Madam" (1986)

---

keeping a place of prostitution
Knowingly granting or permitting the use of a place for the purpose of prostitution.

pimping
Aiding, abetting, counseling, or commanding another in the commission of prostitution. Also, the act of procuring a prostitute for another.

pandering
Soliciting a person to perform an act of prostitution.

pornography
The "depiction of sexual behavior in such a way as to excite the viewer sexually."[iii]

obscenity
That which appeals to the prurient interest and lacks serious literary, artistic, political, or scientific value.[iii]

The Supreme Court resolved some of the ambiguity in the 1973 case of *Miller v. California*.[18] The *Miller* definition of obscenity, which continues in use today, is:

1. The average person, applying contemporary community standards, would find that the work, taken as a whole, appeals to the **prurient interest**.

2. The work depicts or describes, in a patently offensive way, sexual conduct specifically defined by the applicable statute.

3. The work, taken as a whole, lacks serious literary, artistic, political, or scientific value.

> **prurient interest**
> A morbid interest in sex; an "[o]bsession with lascivious and immoral matters."[iv]

The *Miller* test requires the application of community standards, thereby opening the door to differing definitions of obscenity in the United States. This element of the test has been challenged by the Internet, which is not only the largest provider of pornography but is inherently global. Courts continue to wrestle with the question of whether Internet content should be evaluated by the standards of every community where the material is viewed or only by the standards of the home jurisdiction of the source.

> *Sex and obscenity are not synonymous. Obscene material is material which deals with sex in a manner appealing to prurient interest; i.e., material having a tendency to excite lustful thoughts.*
>
> *—Justice William J. Brennan, writing for the majority in Roth v. United States, 354 U.S. 476 (1957)*

The *Miller* test doesn't draw a bright line between what is obscene and what is not. Indeed, the community standard provision makes it impossible to give definite examples of obscenity. No doubt the standard is shifting, in part because technology has created a landscape where pornography is ubiquitous. Prosecutors no longer have the time to prosecute dirty pictures when there are so many cases of genuine child pornography and extreme sexual violence to pursue. Consequently, the types of material that would likely be found obscene today are depictions of bestiality and rape. But exceptions to these examples can be easily imagined. For example, photographs or reenactments of rape in a documentary about the Rape of Nanking, a historical event in 1937 where Japanese military personnel raped tens of thousands of Chinese women during the Second Sino-Japanese War, could be protected because of its educational value.

The Model Penal Code (MPC) incorporates the obscenity definition from *Miller* in Section 251.4:

1. Obscene Defined. Material is obscene if, considered as a whole, its predominant appeal is to prurient interest, that is, a shameful or morbid interest in nudity, sex or excretion, and if in addition it goes substantially beyond customary limits of candor in describing or representing such matters. Predominant appeal shall be judged with reference to ordinary adults unless it appears from the character of the material or the circumstances of its dissemination to be designed for children or other specially susceptible audience. Undeveloped photographs, molds, printing plates, and the like, shall be deemed obscene notwithstanding that processing or other acts may be required to make the obscenity patent or to disseminate it.

2. Offenses. Subject to the affirmative defenses provided in Subsection (3), a person commits a misdemeanor if he knowingly or recklessly:

   a. sells, delivers or provides, or offers or agrees to sell, deliver or provide, any obscene writing, picture, records or other representation or embodiment of the obscene; or

   b. presents or directs an obscene play, dance or performance, or participates in that portion thereof which makes its obscene; or

   c. publishes, exhibits or otherwise makes available any obscene material; or

   d. possesses any obscene material for purposes of sale or other commercial dissemination; or

   e. sells, advertises or otherwise commercially disseminates material, whether or not obscene, by representing or suggesting that it is obscene.

   A person who disseminates or possesses obscene material in the course of his business is presumed to do so knowingly or recklessly.

3. Justifiable and Non-Commercial Private Dissemination. It is an affirmative defense to prosecution under this Section that dissemination was restricted to:
   a. institutions or persons having scientific, educational, governmental or other similar justification for possessing obscene material; or
   b. non-commercial dissemination to personal associates of the actor.
4. Evidence; Adjudication of Obscenity. In any prosecution under this Section evidence shall be admissible to show:
   a. the character of the audience for which the material was designed or to which it was directed;
   b. what the predominant appeal of the material would be for ordinary adults or any special audience to which it was directed, and what effect, if any, it would probably have on conduct of such people;
   c. artistic, literary, scientific, educational or other merits of the material;
   d. the degree of public acceptance of the material in the United States;
   e. appeal to the prurient interest, or absence thereof, in advertising or other promotion of the material; and
   f. the good repute of the author, creator, publisher or other person from whom the material originated.

   Expert testimony and testimony of the author, creator, publisher or other person from whom the material originated, relating to factors entering into the determination of the issue of obscenity, shall be admissible. The Court shall dismiss a prosecution for obscenity if it is satisfied that the material is not obscene.

Note the language in the MPC that requires a trial judge to dismiss a case where the court is not satisfied that the material is obscene. This is an additional safeguard intended to protect free speech.

Although the production, mailing, and sale of obscene material may be subject to criminal sanctions, the U.S. Supreme Court has made it clear that overarching issues of privacy protect a person's right to read or view such materials within the confines of his or her own home. In the 1969 case of *Stanley v. Georgia*,[19] for example, the Court stated: "Whatever may be the justification for other statutes regulating obscenity, we do not think they reach into the privacy of one's own home. If the First Amendment means anything, it means a State has no business telling a man, sitting alone in his own home, what books he may read or what films he may watch." The "right of privacy," however, does not protect the public exhibition of obscene matter or the involvement of minors.[20]

One special area of recent concern in pornography legislation is the sexual exploitation of children, or **child pornography**. In 1982, in the case of *New York v. Ferber*,[21] the U.S. Supreme Court held that a New York law against the distribution of child pornography was valid even though the material in question didn't appeal to the prurient interest of the average person and was not displayed in what could be regarded as a patently offensive manner. Stated another way, child pornography may be regulated even if it doesn't rise to the level of obscenity. This is an exception to the First Amendment's protection of pornography.

In addition to the individual states, the United States has enacted several statutes aimed at regulating child pornography. Title XVI ("Child Pornography") of the federal Violent Crime Control and Law Enforcement Act of 1994, for example, sets penalties for international trafficking in child pornography. The law reads: "A person who, outside the United States, employs, uses, persuades, induces, entices, or coerces any minor to engage in, or who has a minor assist any other person to engage in, or who transports any minor with the intent that the minor engage in any sexually explicit conduct for the purpose of producing any visual depiction of such conduct, intending that the visual depiction will be imported into the United States or into waters within twelve miles of the coast of the United States, shall be . . . fined under this title, imprisoned not more than ten years, or both."[22] A second conviction is

---

Pornography is the undiluted essence of anti-female propaganda.

—Susan Brownmiller, Against Our Will (1975)

If the First Amendment means anything it means that a state has no business telling a man, sitting alone in his own house, what books he may read or what films he may watch.

—Justice Thurgood Marshall, Stanley v. Georgia, 394 U.S. 557 (1969)

---

child pornography
The depiction of sexual behavior involving children.

punishable by up to 20 years in prison. Pornography involving children is also prohibited by the Child Protection Act of 1984, which makes it a crime to knowingly receive through the mail a "visual depiction [involving] a minor engaging in sexually explicit conduct."

An emerging area of concern is the availability of pornography via the Internet. In 1997, the U.S. Supreme Court found key provisions of the Communications Decency Act of 1996 (CDA)[23] unconstitutional because they unduly prohibited free speech. The law, Title V of the Telecommunications Act of 1996,[24] criminalized the activities of anyone making indecent or patently offensive words or pictures accessible by children online. In striking down key provisions of the CDA, the Court, in the case of *Reno v. ACLU*,[25] found it impossible to broadly curtail the access of minors to indecent material on the Internet without unduly limiting free speech guarantees. Justice John Paul Stevens, speaking for the majority, wrote: "It is true that we have repeatedly recognized the governmental interest in protecting children from harmful materials. But that interest does not justify an unnecessarily broad suppression of speech addressed to adults." The Court also noted the availability of parental control software, which has proliferated throughout the technological marketplace and lessened the pressure for government action to regulate the availability of material on the Internet.

A new twist was presented to the Supreme Court in the 2002 case *Ashcroft v. Free Speech Coalition*.[26] In that case, the Court invalidated the Child Pornography Prevention Act's prohibition of pornographic *virtual* images of children and of pornography employing youthful-looking actors who were of legal age. The Court's rationale was that actual children were not involved in the production of this material.

Subsequently, in 2008, the Supreme Court reviewed the Prosecutorial Remedies and Other Tools to End the Exploitation of Children Today Act of 2003 (PROTECT Act), which prohibited the pandering of child pornography. The law was upheld, as you will see in *United States v. Williams* (2008), featured in the Capstone Case.

Similar to laws against pornography and obscenity are strictures against **lewdness**. Whereas pornography refers to some *thing* that is obscene, lewdness refers to *behavior* that is obscene. Lewd behavior consists of intimate activity by a single individual where such activity is intended to be sexually arousing. A lewd act might be captured on videotape, causing the tape to be classified as pornography. New Jersey law defines *lewd acts* to "include the exposing of the genitals for the purpose of arousing or gratifying the sexual desire of the actor or of any other person."[27] Under common law, it was a misdemeanor for persons to intentionally expose their private parts in a public place. Most of today's laws follow in this tradition.

Lewd behavior is sometimes also termed *lasciviousness*. **Lascivious** refers to something that is obscene or lewd or tends to cause lust. Lewd and lascivious conduct is sometimes also termed *public indecency* or **indecent exposure**. Georgia law, for example, states: "A person commits the offense of public indecency when he or she performs any of the following acts in a public place: (1) An act of sexual intercourse; (2) A lewd exposure of the sexual organs; (3) A lewd appearance in a state of partial or complete nudity; or (4) A lewd caress or indecent fondling of the body of another person."[28] The New Jersey statute on lewdness, which takes a somewhat different approach, follows. Compare it with Model Penal Code, Section 251.1.

> The Internet threatens to give every child a free pass into the equivalent of every adult bookstore and every adult video store in the country.
>
> —U.S. Justice Department attorney Seth P. Waxman, arguing before the U.S. Supreme Court in Reno v. ACLU, 521 U.S. 844 (1997)

lewdness
Obscene behavior.

lascivious
That which is obscene or lewd or tends to cause lust.

indecent exposure
The willful exposure of the private parts of one person to the sight of another person in a public place with the intent to arouse or gratify sexual desires. Also, the commission, in a place accessible to the public, of (1) an act of sexual intercourse; (2) a lewd exposure of the sexual organs; (3) a lewd appearance in a state of partial or complete nudity; or (4) a lewd caress or indecent fondling of the body of another person.[v] Also called *public indecency*.

NEW JERSEY CODE, SECTION 14-4

(a) A person commits a disorderly person's offense if he does any flagrantly lewd and offensive act which he knows or reasonably expects is likely to be observed by other non-consenting persons who would be affronted or alarmed.

(b) A person commits a crime of the fourth degree if:

    (1) He exposes his intimate parts for the purpose of arousing or gratifying the sexual desire of the actor or of any other person under circumstances where the actor knows or reasonably expects

APPLYING THE CONCEPT

CAPSTONE CASE

Is the Act of Offering to Sell or Give Child Pornography Protected Speech under the First Amendment?

United States v. Williams, 553 U.S. (2008)

Justice Scalia delivered the opinion of the Court.

THE CASE Section 2252A(a)(3)(B) of Title 18, United States Code, criminalizes, in certain specified circumstances, the pandering or solicitation of child pornography. This case presents the question whether that statute is overbroad under the First Amendment or impermissibly vague under the Due Process Clause of the Fifth Amendment. . . .

THE FINDING We have long held that obscene speech—sexually explicit material that violates fundamental notions of decency—is not protected by the First Amendment. But to protect explicit material that has social value, we have limited the scope of the obscenity exception and have overturned convictions for the distribution of sexually graphic but nonobscene material. Over the last 25 years, we have confronted a related and overlapping category of proscribable speech: child pornography. This consists of sexually explicit visual portrayals that feature children. We have held that a statute which proscribes the distribution of all child pornography, even material that does not qualify as obscenity, does not on its face violate the First Amendment. Moreover, we have held that the government may criminalize the possession of child pornography, even though it may not criminalize the mere possession of obscene material involving adults.

The broad authority to proscribe child pornography is not, however, unlimited. Four Terms ago, we held facially overbroad two provisions of the federal Child Pornography Protection Act of 1996 (CPPA). *Free Speech Coalition*, 535 U. S., at 258. The first of these banned the possession and distribution of "any visual depiction" that "is, or appears to be, of a minor engaging in sexually explicit conduct," even if it contained only youthful-looking adult actors or virtual images of children generated by a computer. This was invalid, we explained, because the child-protection rationale for speech restriction does not apply to materials produced without children. . . .

After our decision in *Free Speech Coalition*, Congress went back to the drawing board and produced [the statute being reviewed today,] . . . relevant portions of which now read as follows:

> "(a) Any person who—
> "(3) knowingly—
>
> . . . . .
>
> "(B) advertises, promotes, presents, distributes, or solicits through the mails, or in interstate or foreign commerce by any means, including by computer, any material or purported material in a manner that reflects the belief, or that is intended to cause another to believe, that the material or purported material is, or contains—
>
> "(i) an obscene visual depiction of a minor engaging in sexually explicit conduct; or
>
> "(ii) a visual depiction of an actual minor engaging in sexually explicit conduct,
>
> . . . . .
>
> "shall be punished as provided in subsection (b)."

§2252A(a)(3)(B) (2000 ed., Supp. V). . . .

Section 2256(2)(A) defines "sexually explicit conduct" as

> "actual or simulated—
>
> "(i) sexual intercourse, including genital-genital, oral-genital, anal-genital, or oral-anal, whether between persons of the same or opposite sex;
>
> "(ii) bestiality;
>
> "(iii) masturbation;
>
> "(iv) sadistic or masochistic abuse;
>
> "(v) lascivious exhibition of the genitals or pubic area of any person."

Violation of §2252A(a)(3)(B) incurs a minimum sentence of 5 years imprisonment and a maximum of 20 years. 18 U. S. C. §2252A(b)(1).

The Act's express findings indicate that Congress was concerned that limiting the child-pornography prohibition to material that could be *proved* to feature actual children, as our decision in *Free Speech Coalition* required, would enable many child pornographers to evade conviction. The emergence of new technology and the repeated retransmission of picture files over the Internet could make it nearly impossible to prove that a particular image was produced using real children. . . .

The following facts appear in the opinion of the Eleventh Circuit. . . . On April 26, 2004, respondent Michael Williams, using a sexually explicit screen name, signed in to a public Internet chat room. A Secret Service agent had also signed in to the chat room under the moniker "Lisa n Miami." The agent noticed that Williams had posted a message that read: "Dad of toddler has 'good' pics of her an [sic] me for swap of your toddler pics, or live cam." The agent struck up a conversation with Williams, leading to an electronic exchange of nonpornographic pictures of children. (The agent's picture was in fact a doctored photograph of an adult.) Soon thereafter, Williams messaged that he had photographs of men molesting his 4-year-old daughter. Suspicious that "Lisa n Miami" was a law-enforcement agent, before proceeding further Williams demanded that the agent produce additional pictures. When he did not, Williams posted the following public message in the chat room: "HERE ROOM; I CAN PUT UPLINK CUZ IM FOR REAL—SHE CANT." Appended to this declaration was a hyperlink that, when clicked, led to seven pictures of actual children, aged approximately 5 to 15, engaging in sexually explicit conduct and displaying their genitals. The Secret Service then obtained a search warrant for Williams's home, where agents seized two hard drives containing at least 22 images of real children engaged in sexually explicit conduct, some of it sadomasochistic.

Williams was charged with one count of pandering child pornography under §2252A(a)(3)(B) and one count of possessing child pornography under §2252A(a)(5)(B). He pleaded guilty to both counts but reserved the right to challenge the constitutionality of the pandering conviction. The District Court rejected his challenge and sentenced him to concurrent 60-month sentences on the two counts. The United States Court of Appeals for the Eleventh Circuit reversed the pandering conviction, holding that the statute was both overbroad and impermissibly vague. . . .

According to our First Amendment overbreadth doctrine, a statute is facially invalid if it prohibits a substantial amount of protected speech. The doctrine seeks to strike a balance between competing social costs. On the one hand, the threat of enforcement of an overbroad law deters people from engaging in constitutionally protected speech, inhibiting the free exchange of ideas. On the other hand, invalidating a law that in some of its applications is perfectly constitutional—particularly a law directed at conduct so antisocial that it has been made criminal—has obvious harmful effects. In order to maintain an appropriate balance, we have vigorously enforced the requirement that a statute's overbreadth be *substantial*, not only in an absolute sense, but also relative to the statute's plainly legitimate sweep. . . .

The first step in overbreadth analysis is to construe the challenged statute; it is impossible to determine whether a statute reaches too far without first knowing what the statute covers. Generally speaking, §2252A(a)(3)(B) prohibits offers to provide and requests to obtain child pornography. The statute does not require the actual existence of child pornography. In this respect, it differs from the statutes in *Ferber*, *Osborne*, and *Free Speech Coalition*, which prohibited the possession or distribution of child pornography. Rather than targeting the underlying material, this statute bans the collateral speech that introduces such material into the child-pornography distribution network. Thus, an Internet user who solicits child pornography from an undercover agent violates the statute, even if the officer possesses no child pornography. Likewise, a person who advertises virtual child pornography as depicting actual children also falls within the reach of the statute. . . .

A number of features of the statute are important to our analysis:

First, the statute includes a scienter requirement. The first word of §2252A(a)(3)—"knowingly"—[applies to the provisions under which Williams was prosecuted]. . . .

Second, the statute's string of operative verbs— "advertises, promotes, presents, distributes, or solicits"—is reasonably read to have a transactional connotation. That is to say, the statute penalizes speech that accompanies or seeks to induce a transfer of child pornography—via reproduction or physical delivery—from one person to another. . . .

To be clear, our conclusion that all the words in this list relate to transactions is not to say that they relate to *commercial* transactions. One could certainly "distribute" child pornography without expecting payment in return. Indeed, in much Internet file sharing of child pornography each participant makes his files available for free to other participants—as Williams did in this case. . . . To run afoul of the statute, the speech need only accompany or seek to induce the transfer of child pornography from one person to another.

Third, the phrase "in a manner that reflects the belief" includes both subjective and objective components. "[A] manner that reflects the belief" is quite different from "a manner that would give one cause to believe." The first formulation suggests that the defendant must actually have

(continued)

held the subjective "belief" that the material or purported material was child pornography. Thus, a misdescription that leads the listener to believe the defendant is offering child pornography, when the defendant in fact does not believe the material is child pornography, does not violate this prong of the statute. (It may, however, violate the "manner . . . that is intended to cause another to believe" prong if the misdescription is intentional.) There is also an objective component to the phrase "manner that reflects the belief." The statement or action must objectively manifest a belief that the material is child pornography; a mere belief, without an accompanying statement or action that would lead a reasonable person to understand that the defendant holds that belief, is insufficient.

Fourth, the other key phrase, "in a manner . . . that is intended to cause another to believe," contains only a subjective element: The defendant must "intend" that the listener believe the material to be child pornography and must select a manner of "advertising, promoting, presenting, distributing, or soliciting" the material that *he* thinks will engender that belief—whether or not a reasonable person would think the same. . . .

Fifth, the definition of "sexually explicit conduct" (the visual depiction of which, engaged in by an actual minor, is covered by the Act's pandering and soliciting prohibition even when it is not obscene) is very similar to the definition of "sexual conduct" in the New York statute we upheld against an overbreadth challenge in *Ferber*. . . .

We now turn to whether the statute, as we have construed it, criminalizes a substantial amount of protected expressive activity. . . .

Offers to engage in illegal transactions are categorically excluded from First Amendment protection. . . .

To be sure, there remains an important distinction between a proposal to engage in illegal activity and the abstract advocacy of illegality. The Act before us does not prohibit advocacy of child pornography but only offers to provide or requests to obtain it. There is no doubt that this prohibition falls well within constitutional bounds. The constitutional defect we found in the pandering provision at issue in *Free Speech Coalition* was that it went *beyond* pandering to prohibit possession of material that could not otherwise be proscribed. . . .

In sum, we hold that offers to provide or requests to obtain child pornography are categorically excluded from the First Amendment. . . .

It was also suggested at oral argument that the statute might cover documentary footage of atrocities being committed in foreign countries, such as soldiers raping young children. Perhaps so, if the material rises to the high level

of explicitness that we have held is required. That sort of documentary footage could of course be the subject of an as-applied challenge. The courts presumably would weigh the educational interest in the dissemination of information about the atrocities against the government's interest in preventing the distribution of materials that constitute "a permanent record" of the children's degradation whose dissemination increases "the harm to the child." Assuming that the constitutional balance would have to be struck in favor of the documentary, the existence of that exception would not establish that the statute is *substantially* overbroad. The "mere fact that one can conceive of some impermissible applications of a statute is not sufficient to render it susceptible to an overbreadth challenge." . . . In the vast majority of its applications, this statute raises no constitutional problems whatever.

[The Court continued, also finding that the statute was not overly vague.]

What Do *You* Think?

1. Should speech in the form of an offer to engage in a criminal act be sufficient to establish criminal liability?

2. Does your answer to question 1 change if there is no apparent ability to commit the act?

3. Should there be a hard-line rule that applies to all crimes, or should the First Amendment be interpreted flexibly, allowing legislatures to distinguish among crimes, depending on perceived risks and harm?

Additional Applications

Can the federal government ban sexually explicit cartoons depicting minors?

United States v. *Whorley*, 550 F.3d 326 (4th Cir. 2008)

The Case: On March 30, 2004, Dwight Whorley—already on probation for a previous federal conviction on child pornography charges—used computers in a Virginia state employment office to print out sexually explicit Japanese-style anime cartoons from his personal Yahoo e-mail account. Twenty of the cartoons depicted prepubescent children engaging in graphic sexual acts—including intercourse, masturbation, and oral sex—with adults. After state employees alerted police, Whorley was charged with, among other things, 20 counts of knowingly receiving obscene materials in interstate commerce in violation of 18 U.S. Code Sec. 1462. Whorley was also charged with 20 counts of "knowingly receiving ... obscene visual depictions of minors engaging in sexually explicit conduct" in violation of 18 U.S. Code Sec. 1466A(a)(1). Whorley was convicted by a jury on all 40 counts (along with 34 other counts as well) and sentenced to 20 years' imprisonment. On appeal, Whorley challenged his convictions under 18 U.S. Code Sections 1462 and 1466 on First Amendment grounds.

The Finding: A three-judge panel of the U.S. Court of Appeals for the Fourth Circuit upheld the challenged convictions. Writing for the appeals court, Judge Paul Niemeyer rejected Whorley's contention that the First Amendment allows prosecution only for receipt of visual depictions of *actual* children. "[T]here is, of course, no suggestion," Niemeyer wrote, "that the cartoons in this case depict actual children; they were cartoons." What's more, the U.S. Supreme Court in *New York* v. *Ferber* (1982) and *Ashcroft* v. *Free Speech Coalition* (2002) focused specifically on depictions of "real children" when explaining that child pornography lies outside the protection of the First Amendment. Still, Niemeyer reasoned, other precedents including *Miller* v. *California* (1973) hold that the government may ban *obscene* materials—including those lacking visual depictions of actual persons—without running afoul of the free speech clause. The cartoons at issue here, Niemeyer concluded, met the *Miller* definition of obscenity. Thus, Whorley's convictions were permitted to stand.

What is the relevant "community standard" for obscenity distributed on the Internet?

United States v. *Kilbride*, 534 F.3d 1240 (9th Cir. 2009)

The Case: Operators of a bulk e-mail advertising business since 2003, defendants Jeffrey Kilbride and James Schaffer were found guilty by an Arizona federal district court of violating federal anti-obscenity laws by distributing two sexually explicit images in e-mail solicitations for subscription-based adult websites. At trial, the federal district judge instructed the jury to apply the "contemporary community standards" test for obscenity formulated in *Miller* v. *California* (1973), explaining that the "community" in question "is not defined by a precise geographic area" and instead reflects the views of "society at large, or people in general." On appeal, Kilbride and Schaffer argued that the trial judge's instructions about the relevant "community" impermissibly invited jurors to speculate about "some broad global standard" when defining the legal protections for sexually explicit e-mails. Jurors, they argued, should have been instructed to apply a national community standard in the case.

The Finding: In a 2009 ruling, the U.S. Court of Appeals for the Ninth Circuit agreed that the trial court had erred in its application of *Miller*. In obscenity prosecutions involving nonelectronic materials, the appeals court explained, federal district judges have considerable flexibility in crafting instructions for jurors about the relevant community to be considered under *Miller*. Cases involving sexually explicit e-mails, by contrast, call for more precise trial court guidance because Internet communications may be distributed far beyond their originating location, often without the knowledge or consent of the original sender. U.S. Supreme Court precedent, the panel noted, currently provides "no explicit holding" as to the "appropriate geographic definition of contemporary community standards" in Internet obscenity cases. Still, the Ninth Circuit concluded, a close parsing of various justices' opinions in recent First Amendment cases "persuades us . . . that a national community standard must be applied in regulating obscene speech on the Internet, including obscenity disseminated via email." ∎

---

he is likely to be observed by a child who is less than thirteen years of age where the actor is at least four years older than the child.

(2) He exposes his intimate parts for the purpose of arousing or gratifying the sexual desire of the actor or of any other person under circumstances where the actor knows or reasonably expects he is likely to be observed by a person who because of mental disease or defect is unable to understand the sexual nature of the actor's conduct.

(c) As used in this section: "lewd acts" shall include the exposing of the genitals for the purpose of arousing or gratifying the sexual desire of the actor or of any other person.

Nude dancing has been the subject of considerable litigation because it presents a conflict between the police power of the states and local governments and an individual's First Amendment free speech rights. As you learned at the beginning of the chapter, the

APPLYING THE CONCEPT

CAPSTONE CASE

Is Fully Nude Dancing in a Strip Club Protected Speech under the First Amendment?

City of Erie v. Pap's A.M., 529 U.S. 277 (2000)

Justice O'Connor announced the judgment of the Court. . . .

THE CASE On September 28, 1994, the city council for the city of Erie, Pennsylvania, enacted Ordinance 75-1994, a public indecency ordinance that makes it a summary offense to knowingly or intentionally appear in public in a "state of nudity." Respondent Pap's, a Pennsylvania corporation, operated an establishment in Erie known as "Kandyland" that featured totally nude erotic dancing performed by women. To comply with the ordinance, these dancers must wear, at a minimum, "pasties" and a "G-string." On October 14, 1994, two days after the ordinance went into effect, Pap's filed a complaint against the city of Erie, the mayor of the city, and members of the city council, seeking declaratory relief and a permanent injunction against the enforcement of the ordinance. . . .

Being "in a state of nudity" is not an inherently expressive condition. As we explained in *Barnes*, however, nude dancing of the type at issue here is expressive conduct, although we think that it falls only within the outer ambit of the First Amendment's protection. . . .

To determine what level of scrutiny applies to the ordinance at issue here, we must decide "whether the State's regulation is related to the suppression of expression." If the governmental purpose in enacting the regulation is unrelated to the suppression of expression, then the regulation need only satisfy the "less stringent" standard from *O'Brien* for evaluating restrictions on symbolic speech. If the government interest is related to the content of the expression, however, then the regulation falls outside the scope of the *O'Brien* test and must be justified under a more demanding standard. In *Barnes*, we analyzed an almost identical statute, holding that Indiana's public nudity ban did not violate the First Amendment, although no five Members of the Court agreed on a single rationale for that conclusion. We now clarify that government restrictions on public nudity such as the ordinance at issue here should be evaluated under the framework set forth in *O'Brien* for content-neutral restrictions on symbolic speech.

The city of Erie argues that the ordinance is a content-neutral restriction that is reviewable under *O'Brien* because the ordinance bans conduct, not speech; specifically, public nudity. Respondent counters that the ordinance targets nude dancing and, as such, is aimed specifically at suppressing expression, making the ordinance a content-based restriction that must be subjected to strict scrutiny. . . .

THE FINDING The ordinance here, like the statute in *Barnes*, is on its face a general prohibition on public nudity. By its terms, the ordinance regulates conduct alone. It does not target nudity that contains an erotic message; rather, it bans all public nudity, regardless of whether that nudity is accompanied by expressive activity. . . .

The State's interest in preventing harmful secondary effects is not related to the suppression of expression. In trying to control the secondary effects of nude dancing, the ordinance seeks to deter crime and the other deleterious effects caused by the presence of such an establishment in the neighborhood. . . .

Similarly, even if Erie's public nudity ban has some minimal effect on the erotic message by muting that portion of the expression that occurs when the last stitch is dropped, the dancers at Kandyland and other such establishments are free to perform wearing pasties and G-strings. Any effect on the overall expression is *de minimis*. And as *Justice Stevens* eloquently stated for the plurality in *Young* v. *American Mini Theatres, Inc.*, 427 U. S. 50, 70 (1976), "even though we recognize that the First Amendment will not tolerate the total suppression of erotic materials that have some arguably artistic value, it is manifest that society's interest in protecting this type of expression is of a wholly different, and lesser, magnitude than the interest in untrammeled political debate," and "few of us would march our sons or daughters off to war to preserve the citizen's right to see" specified anatomical areas exhibited at establishments like Kandyland. If States are to be able to regulate secondary effects, then *de minimis* intrusions on expression such as those at issue here cannot be sufficient to render the ordinance content based.

We conclude that Erie's asserted interest in combating the negative secondary effects associated with adult entertainment establishments like Kandyland is unrelated to the suppression of the erotic message conveyed by nude dancing. The ordinance prohibiting public nudity is therefore valid if it satisfies the four-factor test from *O'Brien* for evaluating restrictions on symbolic speech. . . .

Applying that standard here, we conclude that Erie's ordinance is justified under *O'Brien*. The first factor of the *O'Brien* test is whether the government regulation is within the constitutional power of the government to enact. Here, Erie's efforts to protect public health and safety are clearly within the city's police powers. The second factor is whether the regulation furthers an important or substantial government interest. The asserted interests of regulating conduct through a public nudity ban and of combating the harmful secondary effects associated with nude dancing are undeniably important. . . .

The ordinance also satisfies *O'Brien*'s third factor, that the government interest is unrelated to the suppression of free expression, as discussed *supra*, at 7–15. The fourth and final *O'Brien* factor—that the restriction is no greater than is essential to the furtherance of the government interest—is satisfied as well. The ordinance regulates conduct, and any incidental impact on the expressive element of nude dancing is *de minimis*. The requirement that dancers wear pasties and G-strings is a minimal restriction in furtherance of the asserted government interests, and the restriction leaves ample capacity to convey the dancer's erotic message. . . .

What Do *You* Think?

1. Although the complete logic of the Pennsylvania Supreme Court is not provided in this summary opinion, why do you think that court found nude dancing to be a protected form of expression? On what basis might such an argument be made?

2. Did the U.S. Supreme Court contradict the Pennsylvania Supreme Court's finding relative to the nature of nude dancing as expressive conduct? If not, then how did the U.S. Supreme Court reach a conclusion that was different from that of Pennsylvania's high court?

Additional Applications

Is nude sunbathing protected "speech"?

Minnesota v. Turner, 382 N.W.2d 252 (Minn. App. 1986)

The Case: On September 8, 1993, Lee Ann Turner was arrested for sunbathing topless at a Minneapolis city park; her actions violated a local ordinance that prohibited exposure in a public park of the "female breast below the top of the areola" by anyone over the age of 10. Challenging her arrest, Turner argued that her decision to "go topless" was an expression of "political beliefs" protected by the First Amendment. She also challenged the ordinance's ban on First Amendment overbreadth grounds.

The Finding: A unanimous three-judge Minnesota appeals panel rejected Turner's First Amendment claims in a 1986 ruling. Noting that the ordinance in question explicitly exempted "theatrical, musical, or other artistic performances" from its coverage, the state appeals panel found that Minneapolis' "important or substantial" interests in "controlling public nudity and protect[ing] societal norms" justified its incidental restriction on symbolic political expression. Although Turner's available *means* of expression were thus limited, the court concluded, she nonetheless remained free to "write or speak out for change" and "communicate with Congress, the state legislature, or the Minneapolis Park Board [to] advocate [for] repeal or modification of any law or ordinance." The First Amendment does not limit government regulation of nudity "in contexts other than artistic expression" only to incidents of lewdness or indecency. And to date, no controlling court precedent has ever announced "a constitutional right to sunbathe nude."

Can a city restrict the specific *content* of nude dancing?

Schultz v. City of Cumberland, 228 F.3d 831 (7th Cir. 2000)

The Case: After struggling unsuccessfully for years to force the closure of the "Island Bar"—the only strip club in Cumberland, Wisconsin—Cumberland's city council in January 1998 enacted Ordinance 12.15, which established a comprehensive licensing and registration system for sexually oriented businesses. Section VIII(A) of the ordinance made it illegal to, among other things, "knowingly and intentionally, in a sexually oriented business, appea[r] in a state of nudity or depic[t] specified sexual activities," including sex acts both "normal or perverted" and "the fondling or other erotic touching of human genitals, pubic region, buttocks, anus or female breasts."

(continued)

In February 1998, Joseph Schultz—the owner of the Island Bar—and Tonya Norwood, an Island Bar exotic dancer, filed suit in federal district court seeking a permanent injunction against enforcement of Section VIII(A). In November 1998, a federal district court issued such an injunction; the U.S. Court of Appeals for the Seventh Circuit then took the case on appeal.

The Finding: Writing for a three-judge panel, Judge Michael Kanne affirmed the lower court's blocking of Section VIII(A)'s restrictions on depictions of "specified sexual activities." In "patent contrast to the regulations [at issue] in *Barnes* [v. *Glen Theatre*] and [*City of*] *Erie* [v. *Pap's A.M.*]," Kanne wrote, the Cumberland regulation "is not a content-neutral prohibition on . . . nudity" but rather a regulation that "by its plain terms specifically targets erotic expression." The First Amendment, he explained, provides city governments with considerable latitude to regulate a general category of conduct—such as public nudity—in a content-neutral manner. What's more, cities may place reasonable time, place, and manner restrictions on expressive conduct when doing so is justified by a need to meet important governmental objectives. Nonetheless, Section VIII(A) "goes several steps further," he noted, by "outlaw[ing] the performance of a strikingly wide array of sexually explicit dance movements" and thereby "depriv[ing] the performer of a repertoire of expressive elements with which to craft an erotic, sensual performance." Analyzed under the traditional "strict scrutiny test," the panel concluded, Section VIII(A)'s ban on specified movements in nude dancing violates the First Amendment. ∎

city of Erie, Pennsylvania, enacted an ordinance that was eventually reviewed by the U.S. Supreme Court in the case of *City of Erie* v. *Pap's A.M* (see the accompanying Capstone Case).

OTHER CONSENSUAL SEX OFFENSES

Although they may strike anyone with modern sensibilities as strange or outdated, laws against **fornication** and **adultery** continue to exist in some states. Holdovers from an earlier age, many such laws were passed in the late nineteenth or early twentieth centuries, when a strong family and sexual chastity were highly valued. As a result, many consensual sex offenses are still termed *offenses against the family*.

Contemporary Georgia law, for example, says: "An unmarried person commits the offense of fornication when he voluntarily has sexual intercourse with another person and, upon conviction thereof, shall be punished as for a misdemeanor."[29] As the law indicates, fornication can only be committed by an unmarried person. Sexual intercourse that occurs between a male and a female, at least one of whom is married to someone else, is adultery. In the words of the Official Code of Georgia: "A married person commits the offense of adultery when he voluntarily has sexual intercourse with a person other than his spouse and, upon conviction thereof, shall be punished as for a misdemeanor."[30]

In many jurisdictions, consensual sex offenses also included the crimes of homosexuality, bestiality, sodomy, and buggery. Homosexual behavior may be as old as humankind. Although legal today, the practice of homosexuality was against the law in this country in most places for many years.

Homosexuality has been traditionally viewed as unnatural sexual behavior and was frequently termed a **crime against nature**. *Crime against nature*, however, is also a general term that can include homosexual or heterosexual acts of anal intercourse, oral intercourse, and **bestiality** (sexual relations with animals). It may even apply to heterosexual intercourse in positions other than the conventional "missionary" position.

Concerning bestiality, Georgia law says: "A person commits the offense of bestiality when he performs or submits to any sexual act with an animal involving the sex

fornication
Voluntary sexual intercourse between two people, one of whom is unmarried.

adultery
Sexual intercourse between a male and a female, at least one of whom is married to someone else.

crime against nature
A general term that can include homosexual or heterosexual acts of anal intercourse, oral intercourse, and bestiality and that may even apply to heterosexual intercourse in positions other than the conventional "missionary" position.

bestiality
Sexual relations with animals.

organs of the one and the mouth, anus, penis, or vagina of the other."[31] Bestiality under Georgia law is punishable "by imprisonment for not less than one nor more than five years."[32]

Because crime against nature was long considered an unspeakable crime, statutes rarely provided precise definitions of the activities they outlawed. The Rhode Island law titled "Abominable and detestable crime against nature," for example, reads: "Every person who shall be convicted of the abominable and detestable crime against nature, either with mankind or with any beast, shall be imprisoned not exceeding twenty (20) years nor less than seven (7) years."[33] Idaho law is similar. It says: "Every person who is guilty of the infamous crime against nature, committed with mankind or with any animal, is punishable by imprisonment in the state prison not less than five (5) years."[34] The Idaho Penal Code goes on to say: "Any sexual penetration, however slight, is sufficient to complete the crime against nature."[35] The lack of precise statutory definition of crimes against nature has strong historical precedent. Blackstone's *Commentaries on the Laws of England*, for example, said that "the very mention of [such offense] is a disgrace to human nature" and referred to crime against nature as "a crime not fit to be named."[36]

Where statutory interpretations are lacking, courts have generally offered their own definitions of *crime against nature*. One North Carolina court, for example, held, "The crime against nature is sexual intercourse contrary to the order of nature. It includes acts with animals and acts between humans per anum and per os."[37] Another ruled that "[c]rime against nature embraces sodomy, buggery, and bestiality, as those offenses were known and defined at common law."[38] Some definitions have been less specific. In 1965, one Southern court ruled: "Conduct declared criminal by this section [crime against nature] is sexual intercourse contrary to the order of nature."[39] In prosecutions brought under crime-against-nature statutes, courts have often held that "[i]n charging the offense of crime against nature, because of its vile and degrading nature, there has been some laxity of the strict rules of pleading. It has never been the usual practice to describe the particular manner or the details of the commission of the act."[40]

States used a variety of terms in describing homosexual behavior or "deviate" sexual intercourse. South Carolina, for example, criminalized the "abominable crime of **buggery**." Although South Carolina provided no further statutory definition of the offense, buggery was generally understood to mean anal intercourse. Some states, such as Minnesota, had laws against sodomy. Minnesota's antisodomy law read: "'Sodomy' means carnally knowing any person by the anus or by or with the mouth. . . . Whoever . . . voluntarily engages in or submits to an act of sodomy with another may be sentenced to imprisonment for not more than one year or to payment of a fine of not more than three thousand dollars ($3,000), or both."[41]

buggery
Anal intercourse.

In *Bowers* v. *Hardwick*,[42] a 1986 case involving homosexual behavior, the U.S. Supreme Court upheld Georgia's law against sodomy, even though the act occurred in the privacy of an individual's home. The case was often cited as supporting legislation that prohibited "deviate" heterosexual and/or homosexual conduct in private between consenting adults. Twelve years after *Bowers*, however, the Georgia Supreme Court, in the case of *Powell* v. *State*,[43] invalidated Georgia's statutory sodomy prohibition, holding that it violated rights to privacy guaranteed under the state's constitution.

In 2003, in a potentially far-reaching decision in *Lawrence* v. *Texas*,[44] the U.S. Supreme Court struck down a Texas same-sex sodomy law on due-process grounds and swept aside its earlier ruling in *Bowers*. Because the Texas law banned homosexual sodomy, but not sodomy between heterosexuals, many felt that the Court would invalidate the Texas law on the basis of constitutional guarantees of equality. Instead, the Court took a much broader approach, saying that the issue under consideration "involves the liberty of the person both in its spatial and more transcendent dimensions." Writing for the majority, Justice Anthony Kennedy noted that, in *Bowers*, the Court had failed "to appreciate the extent of the liberty

CRIMINAL LAW IN THE NEWS

Federal Appeals Court Overturns California's Ban on Same-Sex Marriages

Proposition 8, a ban on same-sex marriages that California voters approved in 2008, was ruled unconstitutional by a federal appeals court in February 2012. But the court held off on allowing marriages of gay and lesbian couples to go forward, citing the possibility of more legal challenges.

Proponents of the ban said they would request a rehearing of the appeals case and, if that failed, ask the U.S. Supreme Court to take the case. Some legal analysts, however, said the appeals decision did not have the markings of a Supreme Court case because it was crafted along narrow legal lines that reflected unique events within the state.

For eight years, California has been immersed in a back-and-forth struggle over same-sex marriages that involved the courts, the legislature, and voting booths. It started in 2004, when San Francisco began issuing marriage licenses to same-sex couples. Almost 4,000 licenses were issued before the state supreme court stopped the action and voided the marriages.

In the next three years, the legislature passed two bills authorizing same-sex marriage, only to be vetoed by Governor Arnold Schwarzenegger. But in March 2008, the California Supreme Court ruled 4–3 that same-sex marriages could not be denied under the California Constitution, and about 18,000 gay and lesbian couples took marriage vows in the next eight months.

Then came Proposition 8, rewriting the California Constitution to remove same-sex couples from the legal definition of marriage. The measure went on the November 2008 ballot, and the ensuing campaign became the most expensive on any social issue ever. The measure was approved by 52% of voters.

Following their loss at the ballot box, same-sex marriage proponents filed a lawsuit in federal court to overturn the measure. This led to a trial, presided over by Judge R. Vaughn Walker, examining the nature of sexual orientation and the origin of marriage. Walker's decision struck down Proposition 8, asserting that preventing gay couples from marrying violated the equal protection and due-process clauses of the U.S. Constitution.

After issuing his decision and retiring from the bench, Walker publicly revealed for the first time that he was gay. He said he had been in a relationship for ten years

A gay couple at their commitment ceremony. What is the legal status of same-sex marriages in the United States? *Fotolia LLC*

but did not indicate he wanted to marry. Opponents filed a motion to vacate his decision due to bias. But a federal judge denied the motion, arguing that the presumption that a gay judge couldn't rule on same-sex marriage was like saying a female judge could not rule on cases involving women.

A two-member majority of the federal appeals panel affirmed Walker's decision but took a narrower view. Although it also cited the equal protection clause of the U.S. Constitution, it focused on California's situation leading up to Proposition 8.

In the opinion, Judge Stephen Reinhardt declared that the majority of voters had trampled over the basic, inalienable rights of a minority. They noted that California gay couples previously had a constitutional right to marry, accorded by the California Supreme Court eight months earlier—and then, for no legitimate reason, Proposition 8 had taken that right away. The court found no evidence that banning same-sex marriage would promote children's welfare or make parents more responsible, as the sponsors of Proposition 8 had claimed.

One of the Supreme Court rulings the appeals majority cited to make its point was a 1996 case, *Romer v. Evans*. In that case, the High Court struck down an amendment to the Colorado Constitution making it illegal for authorities to prohibit discrimination against gays. The High Court stated it was "not in our Constitutional tradition" to enact laws that single out "a certain class of citizens for disfavored legal status."

However, the dissenting judge on the appeals panel said his colleagues were overreaching. The courts should defer to the voice of the people and recognize that

Proposition 8 advanced "legitimate state interests," wrote Judge N. Randy Smith.

Resources

"California Proposition 8 Same-Sex-Marriage Ban Ruled Unconstitutional," *Washington Post*, February 7, 2012, http://www.washingtonpost.com/politics/calif-same-sex-marriage-ban-ruled-unconstitutional/2012/02/07/gIQAMNwkwQ_story.html.

"Appeals Court Rules California's Same-Sex Marriage Ban Unconstitutional," Fox News, February 7, 2012, http://www.foxnews.com/politics/2012/02/07/appeals-court-rules-californias-same-sex-marriage-ban-unconstitutional/.

"U.S. Appeals Court Rules Prop. 8 Unconstitutional," *San Francisco Chronicle*, February 8, 2012, http://www.sfgate.com/cgi-bin/article.cgi?f=/c/a/2012/02/08/MN1H1N3T1H.DTL.

at stake." At the heart of liberty, said the *Lawrence* Court, "is the right to define one's own concept of existence, of meaning, of the universe, and of the mystery of human life." In effect, the Court concluded that private sexual acts between consenting adults are a part of the personal liberties protected by the due-process clause of the Constitution. Such liberties include personal decisions about marriage, procreation, family relationships, and education.[45] The *Lawrence* decision effectively struck down all antisodomy laws, except those involving force or victimized individuals who, by reason of age or impairment, are not able to give effective legal consent.

In dissenting, Justice Antonin Scalia wrote that the Court's decision in *Lawrence* "effectively decrees the end of all morals legislation." Scalia went on to say that the decision opened the door to legalizing gay marriage because "preserving the traditional institution of marriage is just a kinder way of describing the State's moral disapproval of same-sex couples." See the Capstone Case of *Lawrence* v. *Texas* for a more thorough understanding of why the Supreme Court took the unusual action of directly reversing, as opposed to distinguishing from, its prior decision.

The Court's ruling in *Lawrence* also brought into question the American military's ban on sodomy. In 2004, in the case of *United States* v. *Marcum*, the nation's highest military court found in favor of the military's antisodomy policies. *Marcum*, however, involved a claim of coercion by a subordinate and was not a true test of the military's policies in light of *Lawrence*.

Another public morality crime is **bigamy**—the crime of marrying one person while still legally married to another person. Bigamy is categorized as a crime against the family. Although not a crime under early common law, bigamy was an ecclesiastical offense (that is, a crime against the church). In 1603, the British Parliament declared bigamy a capital offense. Today, under the Model Penal Code and the laws of many states, it is a misdemeanor.

bigamy
The crime of marrying one person while still legally married to another person.

Generally, the crime of bigamy is not committed if a person marries without divorcing from a prior spouse if the defendant's wife or husband has been absent for an extended period (generally about seven years) and the defendant honestly believes that the husband or wife is dead—or if there was a judgment of divorce or dissolution that was later declared void. Bigamy does not necessarily fall into the category of victimless crimes because the second spouse of one who is already legally married may be unaware of the previous marriage. Even so, as one court recently held: "At common law and under this section bigamy is an offense against society rather than against the lawful spouse of the offender."[46]

Some jurisdictions have also created the companion crime of marrying the spouse of another. As the name implies, this offense occurs when a person knowingly and willfully marries the husband or wife of another. A similar offense, **polygamy**, is the marrying of, or

polygamy
The state of having more than one wife or husband at the same time.

APPLYING THE CONCEPT

CAPSTONE CASE

May a State Make Private, Consensual Sex between Adults of the Same Sex a Crime?

Lawrence v. Texas, 539 U.S. 558 (2003)

Justice Kennedy delivered the opinion of the Court.

THE CASE   Liberty protects the person from unwarranted government intrusions into a dwelling or other private places. In our tradition the State is not omnipresent in the home. And there are other spheres of our lives and existence, outside the home, where the State should not be a dominant presence. Freedom extends beyond spatial bounds. Liberty presumes an autonomy of self that includes freedom of thought, belief, expression, and certain intimate conduct. The instant case involves liberty of the person both in its spatial and more transcendent dimensions. . . .

The question before the Court is the validity of a Texas statute making it a crime for two persons of the same sex to engage in certain intimate sexual conduct.

In Houston, Texas, officers of the Harris County Police Department were dispatched to a private residence in response to a reported weapons disturbance. They entered an apartment where one of the petitioners, John Geddes Lawrence, resided. The right of the police to enter does not seem to have been questioned. The officers observed Lawrence and another man, Tyron Garner, engaging in a sexual act. The two petitioners were arrested, held in custody over night, and charged and convicted before a Justice of the Peace.

The complaints described their crime as "deviate sexual intercourse, namely anal sex, with a member of the same sex (man)." The applicable state law is Tex. Penal Code Ann. § 21.06(a) (2003). It provides: "A person commits an offense if he engages in deviate sexual intercourse with another individual of the same sex." The statute defines "deviate sexual intercourse" as follows:

a.   any contact between any part of the genitals of one person and the mouth or anus of another person; or

b.   the penetration of the genitals or the anus of another person with an object." § 21.01(1).

* * *

We granted certiorari to consider three questions:

1.   "Whether Petitioners' criminal convictions under the Texas 'Homosexual Conduct' law—which criminalizes sexual intimacy by same-sex couples, but not identical behavior by different-sex couples—violate the Fourteenth Amendment guarantee of equal protection of laws?

2.   "Whether Petitioners' criminal convictions for adult consensual sexual intimacy in the home violate their vital interests in liberty and privacy protected by the Due Process Clause of the Fourteenth Amendment?

3.   "Whether *Bowers v. Hardwick*, 478 U.S. 186 (1986), should be overruled?"

THE FINDING   The petitioners were adults at the time of the alleged offense. Their conduct was in private and consensual.

We conclude the case should be resolved by determining whether the petitioners were free as adults to engage in the private conduct in the exercise of their liberty under the Due Process Clause of the Fourteenth Amendment to the Constitution. For this inquiry we deem it necessary to reconsider the Court's holding in *Bowers*.

In *Griswold* the Court invalidated a state law prohibiting the use of drugs or devices of contraception and counseling or aiding and abetting the use of contraceptives. The Court described the protected interest as a right to privacy and placed emphasis on the marriage relation and the protected space of the marital bedroom.

After *Griswold* it was established that the right to make certain decisions regarding sexual conduct extends beyond the marital relationship. In *Eisenstadt v. Baird*, 405 U.S. 438, (1972), the Court invalidated a law prohibiting the distribution of contraceptives to unmarried persons. The case was decided under the Equal Protection Clause; but with respect to unmarried persons, the Court went on to state the fundamental proposition that the law impaired the exercise of their personal rights. It quoted from the statement of the Court of Appeals finding the law to be in conflict with fundamental human rights, and it followed with this statement of its own:

"It is true that in *Griswold* the right of privacy in question inhered in the marital relationship. . . . If the right of privacy means anything, it is the right of the individual, married or single, to be free from unwarranted governmental intrusion into matters so fundamentally affecting a person as the decision whether to bear or beget a child."

The opinions in *Griswold* and *Eisenstadt* were part of the background for the decision in *Roe v. Wade*, 410 U.S. 113, (1973). As is well known, the case involved a challenge to the Texas law prohibiting abortions, but the laws of other States were affected as well. Although the Court held the woman's rights were not absolute, her right to elect an abortion did have real and substantial protection as an exercise of her liberty under the Due Process Clause. . . .

In *Carey v. Population Services Int'l*, 431 U.S. 678, (1977), the Court confronted a New York law forbidding sale or distribution of contraceptive devices to persons under 16 years of age. Although there was no single opinion for the Court, the law was invalidated. . . .

The facts in *Bowers* had some similarities to the instant case. A police officer, whose right to enter seems not to have been in question, observed Hardwick, in his own bedroom, engaging in intimate sexual conduct with another adult male. The conduct was in violation of a Georgia statute making it a criminal offense to engage in sodomy. One difference between the two cases is that the Georgia statute prohibited the conduct whether or not the participants were of the same sex, while the Texas statute, as we have seen, applies only to participants of the same sex. . . . The Court began its substantive discussion in *Bowers* as follows: "The issue presented is whether the Federal Constitution confers a fundamental right upon homosexuals to engage in sodomy and hence invalidates the laws of the many States that still make such conduct illegal and have done so for a very long time." That statement, we now conclude, discloses the Court's own failure to appreciate the extent of the liberty at stake. To say that the issue in *Bowers* was simply the right to engage in certain sexual conduct demeans the claim the individual put forward, just as it would demean a married couple were it to be said marriage is simply about the right to have sexual intercourse. The laws involved in *Bowers* and here are, to be sure, statutes that purport to do no more than prohibit a particular sexual act. Their penalties and purposes, though, have more far-reaching consequences, touching upon the most private human conduct, sexual behavior, and in the most private of places, the home. The statutes do seek to control a personal relationship that, whether or not entitled to formal recognition in the law, is within the liberty of persons to choose without being punished as criminals.

This, as a general rule, should counsel against attempts by the State, or a court, to define the meaning of the relationship or to set its boundaries absent injury to a person or abuse of an institution the law protects. It suffices for us to acknowledge that adults may choose to enter upon this relationship in the confines of their homes and their own private lives and still retain their dignity as free persons. When sexuality finds overt expression in intimate conduct with another person, the conduct can be but one element in a personal bond that is more enduring. The liberty protected by the Constitution allows homosexual persons the right to make this choice. . . .

At the outset it should be noted that there is no long-standing history in this country of laws directed at homosexual conduct as a distinct matter. Beginning in colonial times there were prohibitions of sodomy derived from the English criminal laws passed in the first instance by the Reformation Parliament of 1533. The English prohibition was understood to include relations between men and women as well as relations between men and men. . . . The absence of legal prohibitions focusing on homosexual conduct may be explained in part by noting that according to some scholars the concept of the homosexual as a distinct category of person did not emerge until the late 19th century. Thus early American sodomy laws were not directed at homosexuals as such but instead sought to prohibit nonprocreative sexual activity more generally. This does not suggest approval of homosexual conduct. It does tend to show that this particular form of conduct was not thought of as a separate category from like conduct between heterosexual persons.

Laws prohibiting sodomy do not seem to have been enforced against consenting adults acting in private. A substantial number of sodomy prosecutions and convictions for which there are surviving records were for predatory acts against those who could not or did not consent, as in the case of a minor or the victim of an assault. . . .

To the extent that there were any prosecutions for the acts in question, 19th-century evidence rules imposed a burden that would make a conviction more difficult to obtain even taking into account the problems always inherent in prosecuting consensual acts committed in private. . . . The policy of punishing consenting adults for private acts was not much discussed in the early legal literature. We can infer that one reason for this was the very private nature of the conduct. Despite the absence of prosecutions, there may have been periods in which there was public criticism of homosexuals as such and an insistence that the criminal laws be enforced to discourage their practices. But far from possessing "ancient roots," American laws

(continued)

targeting same-sex couples did not develop until the last third of the 20th century. The reported decisions concerning the prosecution of consensual, homosexual sodomy between adults for the years 1880–1995 are not always clear in the details, but a significant number involved conduct in a public place.

It was not until the 1970's that any State singled out same-sex relations for criminal prosecution, and only nine States have done so. Post-*Bowers* even some of these States did not adhere to the policy of suppressing homosexual conduct. Over the course of the last decades, States with same-sex prohibitions have moved toward abolishing them.

In summary, the historical grounds relied upon in *Bowers* are more complex than the majority opinion and the concurring opinion by Chief Justice Burger indicate. Their historical premises are not without doubt and, at the very least, are overstated.

It must be acknowledged, of course, that the Court in *Bowers* was making the broader point that for centuries there have been powerful voices to condemn homosexual conduct as immoral. The condemnation has been shaped by religious beliefs, conceptions of right and acceptable behavior, and respect for the traditional family. For many persons these are not trivial concerns but profound and deep convictions accepted as ethical and moral principles to which they aspire and which thus determine the course of their lives. These considerations do not answer the question before us, however. The issue is whether the majority may use the power of the State to enforce these views on the whole society through operation of the criminal law. "Our obligation is to define the liberty of all, not to mandate our own moral code." . . .

In our own constitutional system the deficiencies in *Bowers* became even more apparent in the years following its announcement. The 25 States with laws prohibiting the relevant conduct referenced in the *Bowers* decision are reduced now to 13, of which 4 enforce their laws only against homosexual conduct. In those States where sodomy is still proscribed, whether for same-sex or heterosexual conduct, there is a pattern of nonenforcement with respect to consenting adults acting in private. The State of Texas admitted in 1994 that as of that date it had not prosecuted anyone under those circumstances. . . .

Equality of treatment and the due process right to demand respect for conduct protected by the substantive guarantee of liberty are linked in important respects, and a decision on the latter point advances both interests. If protected conduct is made criminal and the law which does so remains unexamined for its substantive validity,

its stigma might remain even if it were not enforceable as drawn for equal protection reasons. When homosexual conduct is made criminal by the law of the State, that declaration in and of itself is an invitation to subject homosexual persons to discrimination both in the public and in the private spheres. The central holding of *Bowers* has been brought in question by this case, and it should be addressed. Its continuance as precedent demeans the lives of homosexual persons.

The stigma this criminal statute imposes, moreover, is not trivial. The offense, to be sure, is but a class C misdemeanor, a minor offense in the Texas legal system. Still, it remains a criminal offense with all that imports for the dignity of the persons charged. The petitioners will bear on their record the history of their criminal convictions. Just this Term we rejected various challenges to state laws requiring the registration of sex offenders. We are advised that if Texas convicted an adult for private, consensual homosexual conduct under the statute here in question, the convicted person would come within the registration laws of at least four States were he or she to be subject to their jurisdiction. This underscores the consequential nature of the punishment and the state-sponsored condemnation attendant to the criminal prohibition. Furthermore, the Texas criminal conviction carries with it the other collateral consequences always following a conviction, such as notations on job application forms, to mention but one example.

The present case does not involve minors. It does not involve persons who might be injured or coerced or who are situated in relationships where consent might not easily be refused. It does not involve public conduct or prostitution. It does not involve whether the government must give formal recognition to any relationship that homosexual persons seek to enter. The case does involve two adults who, with full and mutual consent from each other, engaged in sexual practices common to a homosexual lifestyle. The petitioners are entitled to respect for their private lives. . . .

The judgment of the Court of Appeals for the Texas Fourteenth District is reversed, and the case is remanded for further proceedings not inconsistent with this opinion.

It is so ordered.

What Do *You* Think?

1. The Court overruled *Bowers* v. *Hardwick* for several reasons, including these: (a) The historical premises relied upon in *Bowers* were not without doubt and, at the very least, were overstated; (b) an emerging recognition that liberty gave substantial protection to

(continued)

adult persons in deciding how to conduct their private lives in matters pertaining to sex ought to have been apparent when *Bowers* was decided; (c) the foundations of *Bowers* had subsequently sustained serious erosion from more recent Supreme Court decisions, and criticism of *Bowers* by some scholars and state courts had been substantial and continuing; (d) to the extent that *Bowers* had relied on values shared with a wider civilization, the reasoning and holding in *Bowers* had been rejected by various courts outside the United States; and (e) there had been no individual or societal reliance on *Bowers* of the sort that could have counseled against overturning *Bowers'* holding once there were compelling reasons to do so. Do you agree with the foregoing rationale provided by the Court for overruling *Bowers* v. *Hardwick*?

2. Was this a case where the U.S. Supreme Court changed its ruling based on public and international criticism? Why or why not?

Additional Applications

Did *Lawrence* effectively invalidate all applications of state antisodomy statutes?

In re *R.L.C.*, 643 S.E.2d 920 (N.C. 2007)

The Case: In the spring and summer of 2003, defendant R.L.C., a 14-year-old male, was dating O.P.M., a 12-year-old female. In the course of their relationship, the two juveniles had sexual intercourse and also engaged in oral sex on two occasions in the back seat of O.P.M.'s parents' sport utility vehicle. Under North Carolina law, their engagement in sexual intercourse was legal; their oral sex acts, however, were defined in the state's general crimes-against-nature statute as Class I felonies. Following an investigation by Alamance County sheriff's deputies, R.L.C. was charged in November 2004 with violating the antisodomy statute. After a juvenile court trial, R.L.C. was found to be criminally delinquent and sentenced to six months of unsupervised probation. R.L.C. appealed, arguing (among other things) that the Supreme Court's *Lawrence* ruling prohibited his prosecution under the statute.

The Finding: Applying a rational basis test, the Supreme Court of North Carolina distinguished *Lawrence* in upholding application of the state's antisodomy statute, at least in regard to minors. The *Lawrence* decision, the state court emphasized, held that application of a Texas antisodomy statute to "two adult men engaged in private,

consensual homosexual conduct" furthers "no legitimate state interest which can justify . . . intrusion into the personal and private life of the individual." By contrast, Justice Edward Thomas Brady wrote, applying North Carolina's anti-sodomy statute to juveniles promotes both the maintenance of "proper notions of morality among our State's youth" and "the government's desire for a healthy young citizenry." Many minors, Justice Brady noted, "are unable to make reasoned decisions based upon their limited life experience and education whether to engage in these sexual activities." Consequently, the state's ban on sodomy, at least as applied to juveniles, passes constitutional muster even after *Lawrence* as a reasonable means of promoting the state's legitimate interests.

Can states still punish fornication between consenting adults in light of *Lawrence*?

Martin v. *Ziherl*, 607 S.E.2d 367 (Va. 2005)

The Case: In a civil tort action filed in Virginia state court, Mugent Martin sought compensatory and punitive damages from her ex-boyfriend, Kristopher Ziherl, for knowingly infecting her with herpes during their two-year-long consensual sexual relationship. Martin asserted claims of negligence, intentional battery, and intentional infliction of emotional distress; under Virginia case law, however, injured parties cannot be awarded tort damages for injuries suffered while engaging in illegal activities—and Virginia Code Section 18.2-344 defined sexual intercourse between two unmarried adults as a criminal act. Consequently, her appeal to the Supreme Court of Virginia ultimately turned on a question of post-*Lawrence* constitutional law: specifically, was Virginia's criminal fornication statute still valid in light of the U.S. Supreme Court's *Lawrence* ruling?

The Finding: Extending *Lawrence*, the Supreme Court of Virginia effectively struck down the state's criminal fornication statute. After *Lawrence*, Judge Elizabeth Lacy wrote, there is "no principled way to conclude . . . that the Virginia statute criminalizing intercourse between unmarried persons does not improperly abridge a personal relationship that is within the liberty interest of persons to choose." Unmarried adults, the court reasoned, now have a Fourteenth Amendment right under *Lawrence* to "make the choice to engage in . . . intimate sexual conduct"; consequently, the sexual activity between Martin and Ziherl at issue in this case was not illegal under Virginia law and Martin's tort claim was not precluded under prevailing case law.

cohabiting with, more than one spouse at a time in the purported exercise of the right of plural marriage. In most jurisdictions, polygamy is a felony.

incest
Unlawful sexual intercourse with a relative through blood or marriage.

Incest, another sexually defined offense, consists of unlawful sexual intercourse with a relative through blood or marriage, such as one's brother, sister, mother, or father. One court defined incest as "sexual intercourse within or outside the bonds of marriage between persons related within certain prohibited degrees."[47] Although strong religious and social taboos have traditionally existed against incestuous behavior, a number of movies have tended to popularize, and even glamorize, acts of consensual incest.[48] Kathryn Harrison's memoir for Random House, *The Kiss*, also reveals details of an incestuous but consensual affair between daughter (over age 20) and father. In contrast, David Beatty, former executive director of the National Victims Center, sees the use of incest as entertainment as troublesome, particularly when it is presented as morally neutral. "In most cases when you're talking about incest, there is nothing romantic about it," says Beatty. "What you're talking about is two victims. If we start accepting incest as a literary motif, we lose public outrage, and when we lose that, we start to condone it. I find it very troubling."[49]

Incest is sometimes termed *prohibited sexual contact*. Although many cases of incest are consensual, others are not and can involve child sexual abuse or other serious crimes. Georgia's incest law reads: "A person commits the offense of incest when he engages in sexual intercourse with a person to whom he knows he is related either by blood or by marriage as follows: (1) Father and daughter or stepdaughter; (2) Mother and son or stepson; (3) Brother and sister of the whole blood or of the half blood; (4) Grandparent and grandchild; (5) Aunt and nephew; or (6) Uncle and niece."[50] The law also stipulates that "[a] person convicted of the offense of incest shall be punished by imprisonment for not less than one nor more than 20 years."

Until courts and legislatures began to strike them down in the 1970s and 1980s,[51] *seduction* statutes in some jurisdictions made it a crime for a man to seduce a "virtuous and innocent young woman, upon promise of marriage."[52] Marriage between the parties was generally a bar to prosecution. Although growing gender equality has largely eliminated criminal sanctions associated with such activity, some states still permit claims for civil damages when seduction occurs. Georgia law, for example, says: "The seduction of a daughter, unmarried and living with her parent, whether followed by pregnancy or not, shall give a right of action to the father or to the mother if the father is dead, or absent permanently, or refuses to bring an action. No loss of services need be alleged or proved. The seduction is the gist of the action, and in well-defined cases exemplary damages shall be granted."[53] Under Georgia law, civil compensation may be available in seduction cases even when no promise of marriage was made.

GAMBLING AND GAMING

Gambling is sometimes categorized under the heading "organized crime and vice offenses." We treat it here as an offense against morality because it has all of the characteristics of such an offense—although it may also frequently be associated with organized criminal activity. **Gambling** can be defined as the wagering of money, or of some other thing of value, on the outcome or occurrence of an event. It is illegal where made so by law. Gambling is sometimes called *gaming* in recognition of the fact that it may involve games of chance—that is, contests or events whose outcomes are determined at least in part by luck or chance.

gambling
The wagering of money, or of some other thing of value, on the outcome or occurrence of an event. Also called *gaming*.

Gambling was not a crime under common law unless conducted in such a manner that it constituted a public nuisance. Today, games of chance, including those based on lotteries as well as those making use of slot machines, are regulated in all jurisdictions, and violations of those regulations constitute the statutory crime of gambling. The laws of U.S. jurisdictions vary considerably, however, as to what constitutes illegal gambling. North Carolina law, for example, says: "any person or organization that operates any game of chance or any person who plays at or bets on any game of chance at which any money, property or other thing of value is bet, whether the same be in stake or not, shall be guilty of a Class 2 misdemeanor. This section shall not apply to a person who plays at or bets on any lottery game being lawfully conducted in any state."[54]

States that have stringent antigaming laws generally also have statutes making it illegal to keep or own slot machines (unless disabled), "punchboards," gaming tables, and other gambling accouterments.

In the state of Nevada, on the other hand, many games of chance—such as blackjack, poker, and "shooting dice"—are authorized but strictly regulated and closely controlled. In a number of other jurisdictions, only state-run lotteries are permitted. Some states allow on-track participants to bet on dog and horse races, whereas in other states no gambling or lottery of any type is allowed (although exceptions are frequently made for church raffles, bingo games, and fundraisers sponsored by nonprofit organizations). Under federal law, Native Americans are allowed to conduct games of chance on Indian reservations that are recognized by the U.S. government as independent jurisdictions. As a general rule, however, it is fair to conclude that in most jurisdictions any form of gambling not specifically authorized by statute is considered illegal, although state laws regulating gambling vary considerably.

Several federal statutes also restrict gambling, including these: (1) U.S. Code, Title 18, Section 1955, which prohibits on federally controlled property illegal gambling that is in violation of the local or state law; (2) Title 18, Section 1084, which prohibits the interstate transmission by wire communications of wagering information by persons engaged in illegal betting; (3) Title 18, Section 1952, which prohibits similar activities using the U.S. Postal Service; and (4) Title 18, Section 1953, which regulates the interstate transportation of gambling devices. A federal study of gambling, conducted some years ago, came to the conclusion that (1) illegal gambling is a growing industry in the United States, (2) the legalization of commercial gambling has not reduced illegal gambling, and (3) social gambling has generally been decriminalized by society.[55]

CONTROLLED SUBSTANCES

The word **drug** is a generic term applicable to a wide variety of substances that have any physical or psychotropic effect on the human body. Over the years, drugs have been defined by social convention. Whereas today, for example, most everyone would agree that heroin and cocaine are drugs, they were not always seen as such. Similarly, although alcohol, nicotine, and even caffeine probably fall into the "drug" category in the minds of most people today, their categorization as drugs is relatively recent, having occurred during the past two or three decades.[56] Both the law and social convention make strong distinctions between drugs that are socially acceptable and those that are not (Table 11–1).

Another important distinction can be made between two major classes of drugs: (1) those that are biologically active and (2) those that are psychologically active. Psychotropic substances, or drugs that affect the mind, are said to have psychoactive properties. Bioactive substances, on the other hand, are drugs that affect the body. Although bioactive drugs are subject to considerable regulation and control, most drug laws concern themselves with the manufacture, sale, and possession of psychoactive substances. The term **controlled substance** refers to specifically defined bioactive or psychoactive chemical substances that come under the purview of the criminal law. It is interesting to recognize that all of today's controlled substance laws are the result of legislative action. Common law had nothing to say about drugs other than alcohol.

drug
Any of a wide variety of substances having a physical or psychotropic effect on the human body.

controlled substance
A specifically defined bioactive or psychoactive chemical substance that comes under the purview of the criminal law.

TABLE 11–1   Drug Terminology

Drug: Any chemical substance defined by social convention as bioactive or psychoactive. Not all drugs are socially recognized as such, although those that are may not be well understood. Among recognized drugs, some are legal and readily available, whereas others are closely controlled.

Controlled substance: A specifically defined bioactive or psychoactive chemical substance that is proscribed by law.

Drug abuse: The frequent, overindulgent, or long-term use of a controlled substance in a way that creates problems in the user's life or in the lives of those with whom the user associates.

Psychological addiction: A craving for a specific drug that results from long-term substance abuse. People who are psychologically addicted use the drug in question as a "crutch" to deal with the events in their lives. Also called *psychological dependence.*

Physical addiction: A biologically based craving for a specific drug that results from frequent use of the substance. Also called *physical dependence.*

Addict: Generally, someone who abuses drugs and is psychologically dependent, physically dependent, or both.

Soft drugs: Psychoactive drugs with relatively mild effects whose potential for abuse and addiction is substantially less than that for hard drugs. By social convention, soft drugs include marijuana, hashish, and some tranquilizers and mood elevators.

Hard drugs: Psychoactive substances with serious potential for abuse and addiction. By social convention, hard drugs include heroin, methaqualone (Quaaludes), sopors, LSD, mescaline, peyote, psilocybin, and MDA. Cocaine and its derivative, crack, and methamphetamine (speed) are often placed in the hard-drug category.

Recreational drug user: A person who uses drugs relatively infrequently and whose use occurs primarily among friends and in social contexts that define drug use as pleasurable. Most addicts began as recreational users.

Source: Frank Schmalleger, *Criminal Justice Today: An Introductory Text for the Twenty-first Century,* 8th ed. © 2005. Reprinted and electronically reproduced by permission of Pearson Education, Inc., Upper Saddle River, NJ.

Anti–Drug Abuse Legislation

Anti–drug abuse legislation in the United States dates back to around 1875, when the city of San Francisco enacted a statute prohibiting the smoking of opium.[57] A number of western states were quick to follow the city's lead. The San Francisco law and many laws that came after it, however, clearly targeted Chinese immigrants and were rarely applied to other ethnic groups that may have been involved in the practice.

The first major piece of federal antidrug legislation came in 1914 with enactment of the Harrison Act. The Harrison Act required those dealing in opium, morphine, heroin, cocaine, and specified derivatives of those drugs to register with the federal government and to pay a tax of $1 per year. The only people permitted to register, however, were physicians, pharmacists, and members of the medical profession. Nonregistered drug traffickers faced a maximum fine of $2,000 and up to five years in prison.

Because the Harrison Act allowed physicians to prescribe controlled substances for the purpose of medical treatment, heroin addicts and other drug users could still legally purchase the drugs they needed. By 1920, however, court rulings had established that drug "maintenance" only prolonged addiction and did not qualify as "treatment."[58] The era of legally available heroin had ended.

By the 1930s, government attention came to be riveted on marijuana. In 1937, at the urging of the Federal Bureau of Narcotics, Congress passed the Marijuana Tax Act. As the title of the law indicates, the Marijuana Tax Act placed a levy on cannabis—at the rate of $100 per ounce. Individuals who didn't pay the tax were subject to prosecution. With passage of the Boggs Act in 1951, however, marijuana, along with a number of other drugs, entered the class of federally prohibited controlled substances. The Boggs Act also removed heroin from the list of medically useful substances and required the removal, within 120 days after the act's passage, of any medicines containing heroin from pharmacies across the country.[59]

The Controlled Substances Act of 1970

The Narcotic Control Act of 1956 increased penalties for drug trafficking and possession and made the sale of heroin to anyone under age 18 a capital offense. By 1970, America's drug problem was clear to almost everyone, and legislators assumed a highly punitive approach to controlling drug abuse. Under President Richard Nixon, legislation designed to encompass all aspects of drug abuse and to permit federal intervention at all levels of use was enacted. Termed the Comprehensive Drug Abuse Prevention and Control Act of 1970,[60] the bill still forms the basis of federal enforcement efforts today. Title II of the legislation is the Controlled Substances Act (CSA). The CSA sets up five schedules that classify psychoactive drugs according to their degree of psychoactivity and abuse potential (Figure 11–2):[61]

- *Schedule I controlled substances* have no established medical usage, cannot be used safely, and have great potential for abuse. Federal law requires that any research employing Schedule I substances be fully documented and that the substances themselves be stored in secure vaults. Included in this category are heroin, LSD, mescaline, peyote, methaqualone (Quaaludes), psilocybin, marijuana, and hashish, as well as other powerful drugs. Penalties for a first-offense possession and sale of Schedule I controlled substances under the federal Narcotic Penalties and Enforcement Act of 1986 range up to life imprisonment and a $10 million fine. Penalties increase for subsequent offenses.

- *Schedule II controlled substances* are defined as drugs with high abuse potential for which there is a currently accepted pharmacological or medical use. Most Schedule II substances are also considered to be addictive. Drugs that fall into this category include opium, morphine, codeine, cocaine, phencyclidine (PCP), and their derivatives. Certain other stimulants, such as methylphenidate (Ritalin) and phenmetrazine (Preludin), and a few barbiturates with high abuse potential also come under Schedule II. Legal access to Schedule II substances requires written nonrefillable prescriptions, vault storage, and thorough record keeping by vendors. Penalties for first-offense possession and sale of Schedule II controlled substances range up to 20 years' imprisonment and a $5 million fine under the federal Narcotic Penalties and Enforcement Act. Penalties increase for subsequent offenses.

- *Schedule III controlled substances* involve lower abuse potential than do those in previous schedules. They are drugs with an accepted medical use but whose use may lead to a high level of psychological dependence or to moderate or low physical dependence. Schedule III substances include many of the drugs found in Schedule II, but in derivative or diluted form. Common low-dosage antidiarrheals, such as opium-containing paregoric, and cold medicines or pain relievers with low concentrations of codeine fall into this category. Anabolic steroids, whose abuse by professional athletes has come under increased scrutiny, were added to the list of Schedule III controlled substances by congressional action in 1991. Legitimate access to Schedule III drugs is through a doctor's prescription (written or oral), with refills authorized in the same manner. Maximum penalties associated with first-offense possession and sale of Schedule III controlled substances under federal law include five years' imprisonment and fines of up to $1 million.

- *Schedule IV controlled substances* have a relatively low potential for abuse (when compared to higher schedules), are useful in established medical treatments, and involve only a limited risk of psychological or physical dependency. Depressants and mild tranquilizers, such as Valium, Librium, and Equanil, fall into this category, as do some stimulants. Schedule IV substances are medically available in the same fashion as Schedule III drugs. Maximum penalties associated with first-offense possession and sale of Schedule IV substances under federal law include three years in prison and fines of up to $1 million.

- *Schedule V controlled substances* are prescription drugs with a low potential for abuse and with only a very limited possibility of psychological or physical dependence. Cough medicines (antitussives) and antidiarrheals containing small amounts of opium, morphine, or codeine are found in Schedule V. A number of Schedule V medicines may be purchased through

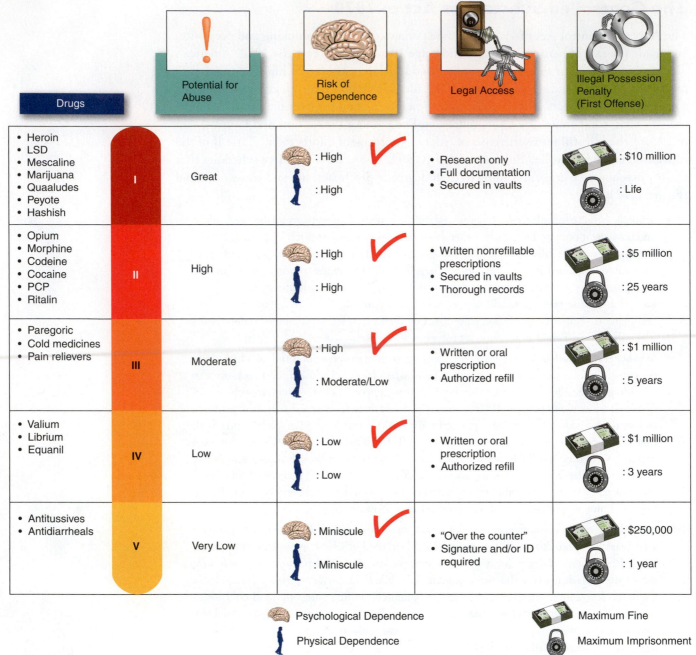

Drugs	Potential for Abuse	Risk of Dependence	Legal Access	Illegal Possession Penalty (First Offense)
• Heroin • LSD • Mescaline • Marijuana • Quaaludes • Peyote • Hashish **I**	Great	: High ✓ : High	• Research only • Full documentation • Secured in vaults	: $10 million : Life
• Opium • Morphine • Codeine • Cocaine • PCP • Ritalin **II**	High	: High ✓ : High	• Written nonrefillable prescriptions • Secured in vaults • Thorough records	: $5 million : 25 years
• Paregoric • Cold medicines • Pain relievers **III**	Moderate	: High ✓ : Moderate/Low	• Written or oral prescription • Authorized refill	: $1 million : 5 years
• Valium • Librium • Equanil **IV**	Low	: Low ✓ : Low	• Written or oral prescription • Authorized refill	: $1 million : 3 years
• Antitussives • Antidiarrheals **V**	Very Low	: Miniscule ✓ : Miniscule	• "Over the counter" • Signature and/or ID required	: $250,000 : 1 year

Psychological Dependence   Maximum Fine

Physical Dependence   Maximum Imprisonment

FIGURE 11–2

Schedules of the Federal Controlled Substances Act.

retail vendors with only minimal controls or on the signature of the buyer (with some form of identification required). Maximum federal penalties for first-offense possession and sale of Schedule V substances include one year in prison and a $250,000 fine.

Because each of the federal schedules depends primarily on a drug's abuse potential, it is important to understand this concept. One state law says that *potential for abuse* "means that a substance has properties of a central nervous system stimulant or depressant or an hallucinogen that creates a substantial likelihood of its being: (a) Used in amounts that create a hazard to the user's health or the safety of the community; (b) Diverted from legal channels and distributed through illegal channels; or (c) Taken on the user's own initiative rather than on the basis of professional medical advice."[62] The law goes on to say that "[p]roof of potential for abuse can be based upon a showing that these activities are already taking place, or upon a showing that the nature and properties of the substance make it reasonable to assume that there is a substantial likelihood that such activities will take place, in other than isolated or occasional instances."[63]

Pharmacologists, chemists, and botanists are constantly discovering and creating new drugs. Likewise, street-corner "chemists" in clandestine laboratories churn out inexpensive **designer drugs**—psychoactive substances with widely varying effects and abuse potential. Hence the Controlled Substances Act also includes provisions for determining what newly developed drugs should be controlled and into which schedule they should be placed. Under the CSA, criteria for assigning a new drug to one of the existing schedules include (1) the drug's actual or relative potential for abuse; (2) scientific evidence of the drug's pharmacological effects; (3) the state of current scientific knowledge regarding the substance; (4) its history and current pattern of abuse; (5) the scope, duration, and significance of abuse; (6) what, if any, risk there is to the public health; (7) the drug's psychic or physiological dependence liability; and (8) whether the substance is an immediate precursor of a substance already controlled.

In recent years, numerous federal and state laws (see Figure 11–3) have been enacted to combat the growing popularity of so-called date-rape drugs such as Rohypnol and GHB (gamma hydroxybutyric acid). GHB is popularly known as *Liquid X*, *Georgia Home Boy*, *Grievous Bodily Harm*, and *Scoop*.

Rohypnol (whose generic name is flunitrazepam) is a powerful sedative manufactured by Hoffmann-La Roche Inc. A member of the benzodiazepine family of depressants, it is legally prescribed in 64 countries for insomnia and as a preoperative anesthetic. Seven to ten times more powerful than Valium and virtually tasteless, Rohypnol has become popular with some college students and with "young men [who] put doses of Rohypnol in women's drinks without their consent in order to lower their inhibitions."[64] As one woman who was sexually attacked while under the drug's influence said, "You know something is going on, but you can't do anything about it."[65] Available on the black market, Rohypnol dissolves easily in drinks and can leave anyone who consumes it either severely disoriented or unconscious for hours. The drug is variously known as *roples*, *roche*, *ruffles*, *roofies*, and *rophies* on the street.

Penalties for trafficking in flunitrazepam were increased under the Drug-Induced Rape Prevention and Punishment Act of 1996.[66] In January 2000, the federal Date Rape Prevention Drug Act was signed into law.[67] The law amended the Controlled Substances Act by adding GHB to Schedule I and ketamine to Schedule III. Ketamine is another abused general anesthetic often used as a party drug. It is sometimes called *Special K*.

designer drug
A chemical substance that (1) has a potential for abuse similar to or greater than that of controlled substances, (2) is designed to produce a desired pharmacological effect, and (3) is produced to evade the controlling statutory provisions.

The Anti–Drug Abuse Act of 1988

In 1988, the federal Anti–Drug Abuse Act was passed into law. Under the law, penalties for "recreational" drug users were substantially increased,[68] and it became more difficult for suspected drug dealers to purchase weapons. The law also denied federal benefits to convicted drug offenders, ranging from loans (including student loans) to contracts and licenses.[69] Earned benefits such as Social Security, retirement, and health and disability benefits were not affected by the legislation, nor were welfare payments or existing public housing arrangements. (However, separate legislation does provide for termination of public housing tenancy for drug offenses.) Under the law, civil penalties of up to $10,000 may be assessed against convicted "recreational" users for possession of even small amounts of drugs.

The 1988 legislation also included the possibility of capital punishment for drug-related murders. The killing of a police officer by offenders seeking to avoid apprehension or prosecution is specifically cited in the law as carrying a possible sentence of death, although other murders by major drug dealers also fall under the capital punishment provision.[70] On May 14, 1991, David Chandler, a 37-year-old Alabama marijuana kingpin, became the

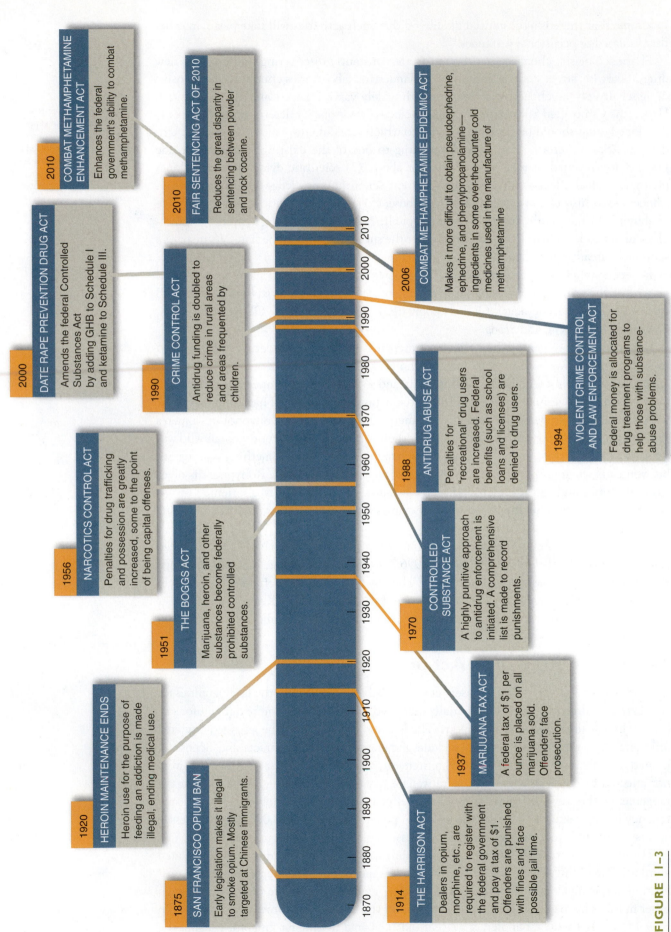

2010 COMBAT METHAMPHETAMINE ENHANCEMENT ACT
Enhances the federal government's ability to combat methamphetamine.

2010 FAIR SENTENCING ACT OF 2010
Reduces the great disparity in sentencing between powder and rock cocaine.

2000 DATE RAPE PREVENTION DRUG ACT
Amends the federal Controlled Substances Act by adding GHB to Schedule I and ketamine to Schedule III.

2006 COMBAT METHAMPHETAMINE EPIDEMIC ACT
Makes it more difficult to obtain pseudoephedrine, ephedrine, and phenylpropanolamine—ingredients in some over-the-counter cold medicines used in the manufacture of methamphetamine

1990 CRIME CONTROL ACT
Antidrug funding is doubled to reduce crime in rural areas and areas frequented by children.

1956 NARCOTICS CONTROL ACT
Penalties for drug trafficking and possession are greatly increased, some to the point of being capital offenses.

1988 ANTIDRUG ABUSE ACT
Penalties for "recreational" drug users are increased. Federal benefits (such as school loans and licenses) are denied to drug users.

1994 VIOLENT CRIME CONTROL AND LAW ENFORCEMENT ACT
Federal money is allocated for drug treatment programs to help those with substance-abuse problems.

1951 THE BOGGS ACT
Marijuana, heroin, and other substances become federally prohibited controlled substances.

1970 CONTROLLED SUBSTANCE ACT
A highly punitive approach to antidrug enforcement is initiated. A comprehensive list is made to record punishments.

1920 HEROIN MAINTENANCE ENDS
Heroin use for the purpose of feeding an addiction is made illegal, ending medical use.

1937 MARIJUANA TAX ACT
A federal tax of $1 per ounce is placed on all marijuana sold. Offenders face prosecution.

1875 SAN FRANCISCO OPIUM BAN
Early legislation makes it illegal to smoke opium. Mostly targeted at Chinese immigrants.

1914 THE HARRISON ACT
Dealers in opium, morphine, etc., are required to register with the federal government and pay a tax of $1. Offenders are punished with fines and face possible jail time.

1870 1880 1890 1900 1910 1920 1930 1940 1950 1960 1970 1980 1990 2000 2010

FIGURE 11–3

Federal Drug Legislation Timeline.

first person sentenced to die under the law.[71] Chandler had been convicted of ordering the murder of a police informant in 1990.

Other Federal Antidrug Legislation

Other significant federal antidrug legislation exists in the form of the Crime Control Act of 1990 and the Violent Crime Control and Law Enforcement Act of 1994. The 1990 law targeted drug crime through a number of initiatives. Specifically, it (1) doubled the appropriations authorized for drug law enforcement grants to states and local communities; (2) enhanced drug control and education programs aimed at the nation's schools; (3) expanded specific drug enforcement assistance to rural states; (4) expanded regulation of precursor chemicals used in the manufacture of illegal drugs; (5) sanctioned anabolic steroids under the Controlled Substances Act; (6) included provisions to enhance control over international money laundering; (7) created "drug-free school zones" by enhancing penalties for drug offenses occurring in close proximity to schools; and (8) enhanced the ability of federal agents to seize property used in drug transactions or purchased with drug proceeds.

The Violent Crime Control and Law Enforcement Act of 1994 provided $245 million for rural anticrime and antidrug efforts; set aside $1.6 billion for direct funding to localities around the country for anticrime efforts, including drug treatment programs; budgeted $383 million for drug treatment programs for state and federal prisoners; created a treatment schedule for all drug-addicted federal prisoners; required postconviction drug testing of all federal prisoners on release; allocated $1 billion for drug court programs for nonviolent offenders with substance-abuse problems; and mandated new stiff penalties for drug crimes committed by gangs. The act also tripled penalties for using children to deal drugs near schools and playgrounds and enhanced penalties for drug dealing in designated "drug-free zones" near playgrounds, schoolyards, video arcades, and youth centers. Finally, the law also expanded the federal death penalty to include offenders involved in large-scale drug trafficking, and it mandated life imprisonment for criminals convicted of three violent felonies or drug offenses.

State-Level Antidrug Laws

Antidrug laws at the state level show a surprising degree of uniformity. Such uniformity is due to the fact that almost all states have adopted some version of the Uniform Controlled Substances Act, which was proposed in 1972 by the National Conference of Commissioners on Uniform State Laws. The Uniform Controlled Substances Act is similar to the federal Drug Abuse and Prevention Control Act in that it also groups controlled substances into five schedules. The schedules are quite similar to those under federal law.

Most jurisdictions have also categorized controlled substances into penalty groups, with penalties ranging from first-degree felonies to misdemeanors. The possession of drugs or substances listed in Schedules I and II are generally felonies, and the possession of drugs or substances listed in Schedules III to V may be either felonies or misdemeanors. Under the laws of most jurisdictions, the crime of possessing a controlled substance involves a person's possession or right to exercise control over a controlled substance, his or her knowledge of the presence of the controlled substance and of its nature as a controlled substance, and possession of a usable quantity of the controlled substance. Generally speaking, the elements of the offense of unlawful possession of a controlled substance are as follows:

- Possession (except as otherwise provided by law)
- Of any controlled substance (as classified by law)
- Unless upon the written prescription of a physician, dentist, podiatrist, or veterinarian licensed to prescribe such a drug

Other than possession, jurisdictions generally criminalize the manufacture, sale, and purchase of a controlled substance. Florida law, for example, says that "it is unlawful for any person to sell, manufacture, or deliver, or possess with intent to sell, manufacture, or deliver, a controlled substance."[72] Similar to the laws of other states, Florida law also criminalizes the sale, manufacture, and possession with intent to sell or deliver a controlled substance "within one thousand feet of the real property comprising a public or private elementary, middle, or secondary school between the hours of 6 a.m. and 12 a.m." It also says that "it is unlawful for any person to sell, manufacture, or deliver, or possess with intent to sell, manufacture, or deliver, a controlled substance in, on, or within two hundred feet of the real property comprising a public housing facility, within two hundred feet of the real property comprising a public or private college, university, or other postsecondary educational institution, or within two hundred feet of any public park." As in other states, Florida law also makes it "unlawful for any person to purchase, or possess with intent to sell, a controlled substance," except as allowed by law (that is, with a license, through prescription, and so on). Finally, Florida law states: "It is unlawful for any person to be in actual or constructive possession of a controlled substance unless such controlled substance was lawfully obtained from a practitioner or pursuant to a valid prescription or order of a practitioner while acting in the course of his professional practice or to be in actual or constructive possession of a controlled substance except as otherwise authorized by this chapter."

Most jurisdictions have also created special penalties for adults who sell drugs to juveniles and for adults who employ juveniles in the illegal drug trade. Florida law, for example, says: "Except as authorized by this chapter, it is unlawful for any person eighteen years of age or older to deliver any controlled substance to a person under the age of eighteen years, or to use or hire a person under the age of eighteen years as an agent or employee in the sale or delivery of such a substance, or to use such person to assist in avoiding detection or apprehension for a violation of this chapter."

As in the case of federal law, most states have created special procedures for quickly adding individual designer drugs to controlled substance categories. Florida law, for example, describes designer drugs as "chemical substances which have a potential for abuse similar to or greater than that for substances controlled but which are designed to produce a desired pharmacological effect and to evade the controlling statutory provisions." Generally, such new substances are officially untested, and it cannot be immediately determined whether they have useful medical or chemical purposes. Because designer drugs can be created more rapidly than they can be identified and controlled by legislative action, many states, like Florida, authorize their attorney general to identify and classify any new substances that have a potential for abuse and to add such substances to existing schedules.[73]

Generally speaking, most states, like the federal government, also control the sale and possession of **precursor chemicals**, or those chemicals that may be used in the manufacture of a controlled substance. Similarly, most states have enacted antiparaphernalia laws similar to the Model Drug Paraphernalia Act, which prohibits possession, manufacture, delivery, or advertising of drug paraphernalia. Drug paraphernalia may include "bongs," hypodermic needles, "roach clips," crack pipes, and other specially described items normally used in the distribution and consumption of controlled substances.

Asset Forfeiture

Forfeiture is an enforcement strategy that federal statutes and some state laws support—and one that bears special mention. Antidrug forfeiture statutes at both the state and federal level provide a special category of forfeiture laws. Such statutes authorize judges to seize "all monies, negotiable instruments, securities, or other things of value furnished or intended to be furnished by any person in exchange for a controlled substance . . . [and] all proceeds

---

precursor chemical
A chemical that may be used in the manufacture of a controlled substance.

forfeiture
An enforcement strategy supported by federal statutes and some state laws that authorizes judges to seize "all monies, negotiable instruments, securities, or other things of value furnished or intended to be furnished by any person in exchange for a controlled substance . . . [and] all proceeds traceable to such an exchange."[vi]

traceable to such an exchange."[74] Forfeiture statutes find a legal basis in the relation-back doctrine. The relation-back doctrine assumes that because the government's right to illicit proceeds relates back to the time they are generated, anything acquired through the expenditure of those proceeds also belongs to the government.[75]

The first federal laws to authorize forfeiture as a criminal sanction were both passed in 1970. They are the Continuing Criminal Enterprise (CCE) statute and the Organized Crime Control Act. A section of the Organized Crime Control Act, known as the **RICO statute** (for Racketeer Influenced and Corrupt Organizations), was designed to prevent criminal infiltration of legitimate businesses and has since been extensively applied in federal drug-smuggling cases. In 1978, Congress authorized *civil forfeiture* of any assets acquired through narcotics trafficking in violation of federal law. Many states modeled their own legislation after federal law and now have similar statutes (Figure 11–4).

Forfeiture statutes have provided considerable grist for the judicial mill. In 1993, in the case of *United States* v. *92 Buena Vista Ave.*,[76] for example, the U.S. Supreme Court established an "innocent owner defense" in forfeiture cases, whereby federal authorities were forbidden from seizing drug transaction assets that were later acquired by a new and innocent owner. In the same year, in the case of *Austin* v. *United States*,[77] the Court placed limits on the government's authority to use forfeiture laws against drug criminals, finding that seizures of property must not be excessive when compared to the seriousness of the offense charged. Otherwise, the justices wrote, the Eighth Amendment's ban on excessive fines could be contravened. The justices, however, refused to establish a rule by which excessive fines could be judged, saying that "[t]he Court declines to establish a test for determining whether a forfeiture is constitutionally 'excessive,' since prudence dictates that the lower courts be

RICO statute

A section of the federal Organized Crime Control Act known as the Racketeer Influenced and Corrupt Organizations provision. Some states have passed their own RICO-like statutes.

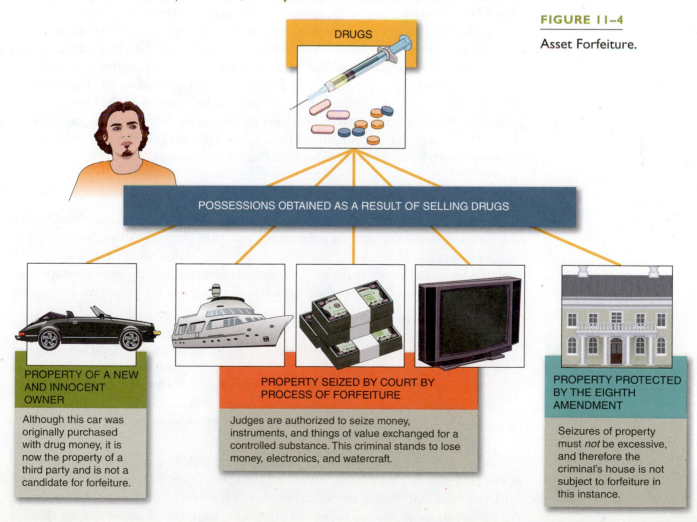

FIGURE 11–4

Asset Forfeiture.

DRUGS

POSSESSIONS OBTAINED AS A RESULT OF SELLING DRUGS

PROPERTY OF A NEW AND INNOCENT OWNER

Although this car was originally purchased with drug money, it is now the property of a third party and is not a candidate for forfeiture.

PROPERTY SEIZED BY COURT BY PROCESS OF FORFEITURE

Judges are authorized to seize money, instruments, and things of value exchanged for a controlled substance. This criminal stands to lose money, electronics, and watercraft.

PROPERTY PROTECTED BY THE EIGHTH AMENDMENT

Seizures of property must *not* be excessive, and therefore the criminal's house is not subject to forfeiture in this instance.

allowed to consider that question." The *Austin* ruling was supported by two other 1993 cases, *Alexander* v. *United States*[78] and *United States* v. *James Daniel Good Real Property*.[79] In *Alexander*, the Court found that forfeitures under the RICO statute must be limited according to the rules established in *Austin*, and in the second case, the Court held that "[a]bsent exigent circumstances, the Due Process Clause requires the Government to afford notice and a meaningful opportunity to be heard before seizing real property subject to civil forfeiture."

In 1996, however, in a case that may have relevance for drug law enforcement, the U.S. Supreme Court upheld the seizure of private property used in the commission of a crime, even though the property belonged to an innocent owner not involved in the crime. The case, *Bennis* v. *Michigan*,[80] involved the government's seizure of a car that had been used by the owner's husband in procuring the services of a prostitute. In effect, the justices ruled, an innocent owner is not protected from criminal conviction–related property forfeiture.

Also in 1996, in the case of *United States* v. *Ursery*,[81] the Supreme Court rejected claims that civil forfeiture laws constitute a form of double jeopardy. In *Ursery*, the defendant's house had been seized by federal officials who claimed that it had been used to facilitate drug transactions. The government later seized other personal items owned by Ursery, saying that they had been purchased with the proceeds of drug sales and that Ursery had engaged in money-laundering activities to hide the source of his illegal income. The court of appeals reversed Ursery's drug conviction and the forfeiture judgment, holding that the double jeopardy clause of the U.S. Constitution prohibits the government from both punishing a defendant for a criminal offense and forfeiting his property for that same offense in a separate civil proceeding. In reaffirming Ursery's conviction, however, the U.S. Supreme Court ruled that "a forfeiture [is] not barred by a prior criminal proceeding after applying a two-part test asking, first, whether Congress intended the particular forfeiture to be a remedial civil sanction or a criminal penalty, and second, whether the forfeiture proceedings are so punitive in fact as to establish that they may not legitimately be viewed as civil in nature, despite any congressional intent to establish a civil remedial mechanism." The Court concluded that "civil forfeitures are neither 'punishment' nor criminal for purposes of the Double Jeopardy clause." In distinguishing civil forfeitures and criminal punishments, the majority opinion held that "Congress has long authorized the Government to bring parallel criminal actions and . . . civil forfeiture proceedings based upon the same underlying events . . . , and this Court consistently has concluded that the Double Jeopardy Clause does not apply to such forfeitures because they do not impose punishment."

Medical Marijuana

In 1996, voters in California passed Proposition 215, known as the Compassionate Use Act, which allowed doctors to prescribe marijuana for medicinal purposes. About the same time, a similar measure passed in Arizona, and in November 1999, Maine voters passed a referendum permitting some sick people to use small amounts of marijuana. The thrust of voter-approved California Proposition 215 is contained in the following language taken from the proposition:

A. To ensure that seriously ill Californians have the right to obtain and use marijuana for medical purposes where that medical use is deemed appropriate and has been recommended by a physician who has determined that the person's health would benefit from the use of marijuana in the treatment of cancer, anorexia, AIDS, chronic pain, spasticity, glaucoma, arthritis, migraine, or any other illness for which marijuana provides relief.

B. To ensure that patients and their primary caregivers who obtain and use marijuana for medical purposes upon the recommendation of a physician are not subject to criminal prosecution or sanction.

The medical marijuana initiative was essentially derailed by the U.S. Supreme Court in the 2001 case of *United States* v. *Oakland Cannabis Buyers' Cooperative*.[82] In that case, the Court held that there is no medical necessity exception to the Controlled Substances Act's prohibitions on manufacturing and distributing marijuana. Because that act classifies marijuana as a Schedule I controlled substance, the Court said, it provides only one express exception to the prohibitions on manufacturing and distributing the drug: government-approved research projects. The Court also rejected the cooperative's arguments that a common law medical necessity defense should permit use of the drug by desperately ill patients. Subsequently, in 2005, the Supreme Court held that the United States may criminalize the use of marijuana for medical purposes, even when expressly allowed by state law.[83]

In spite of the supremacy of federal law, three states--Colorado, Massachusetts, and Washington--joined California and several other states in the decriminalization of marijuana, in different forms, through popular referenda in 2012. Regardless of state law, the federal government possesses the authority to punish individuals who possess or sell marijuana, potentially rendering state noncriminalization efforts moot. Whether Congress will react to the growing trend to decriminalize marijuana in the states by decriminalizing it under federal law remains to be seen.

A CRITIQUE OF LAWS REGULATING PUBLIC MORALITY

Numerous legal scholars have criticized the notion of crimes against public decency and morality—calling them "legal moralism"—and saying that they represent little more than attempts "to achieve conformity with private moral standards through use of the criminal law."[84] The well-known legal theorist Sanford H. Kadish, for example, wrote in 1967 of "the crisis of overcriminalization," in which attempts to legislate what should be issues of private morality have "been attended by grave consequences." Because crimes against public decency are consensual, says Kadish, the police, to obtain evidence, are obliged to resort to behavior that tends to degrade and demean both themselves personally and law enforcement as an institution.[85] "Because local officials may use moral crusades as a means of deflecting criticism of their own inept administrations," says Kadish, "these laws invite discriminatory enforcement against persons selected for prosecution on grounds unrelated to the evil against which these laws are purportedly addressed." Shutting down massage parlors or bath houses, for example, may merely serve as a diversionary strategy in the political arena, while diverting enforcement resources from more critical areas. A "war on drugs" can be seen in the same light. "Our indiscriminate policy of using the criminal law against selling what people insist on buying has spawned large-scale, organized systems, often of national scope, comprising an integration of the stages of production and distribution of the illicit product on a continuous and thoroughly businesslike basis," says Kadish. "Not only are these organizations especially difficult for law enforcement to deal with; they have the unpleasant quality of producing other crimes as well." Kadish adds: "There is, finally, a cost of inestimable importance, one which tends to be a product of virtually all the misuses of the criminal law. . . . That is the substantial diversion of police, prosecutorial, and judicial time, personnel, and resources. At a time when the volume of crime is steadily increasing, the burden on law enforcement agencies is becoming more and more onerous."[86]

Although the issues Kadish identifies are significant ones, American legislative history shows that lawmaking bodies across the country have generally assumed the authority to criminalize any conduct that they thought might be damaging to the health, safety, and morality of the community—sometimes even when such legislative restrictions were obviously in violation of constitutional protections. When a moral perspective becomes widely persuasive, even closely held constitutional principles may be modified. Our nation's experience with constitutional prohibitions on the manufacture, transportation, and sale of alcoholic beverages shows, for example, that legislative restrictions on morality are essentially arbitrary and may not always be workable. Although one could argue that all laws—even those condemning murder, rape, and other violent crimes—are based on socially shared conceptualizations of morality, the real question that needs to be answered is this: How far into the private lives of citizens may government-sanctioned views of morality properly intrude?

SUMMARY

- Crimes against public decency and morality constitute a third type of social-order offense. The first two types, crimes against public order and crimes against the administration of government, were discussed in Chapter 10.

- Crimes against public decency and morality typically include not only prostitution, gambling, and drug use, but also pornography, obscenity, and various other consensual sex offenses—such as bestiality, deviate sexual relations, lewdness, indecency, seduction, fornication, adultery, and bigamy.

- Crimes against public decency and morality are sometimes termed *victimless crimes* by virtue of the fact that they generally involve willing participants.

- Pornography is the depiction of sexual behavior in such a way as to excite the viewer sexually. *Obscenity*, a related crime, can be defined as that which appeals to the prurient interest (a morbid interest in sex) and lacks serious literary, artistic, political, or scientific value. Sex and obscenity are not synonymous, and obscenity is not constitutionally protected under First Amendment free speech guarantees.

- *Obscene matter* means material, taken as a whole, that to the average person, applying contemporary community standards, appeals to the prurient interest; depicts or describes sexual conduct in a patently offensive way; and lacks serious literary, artistic, political, or scientific value.

- An emerging concern in the area of crimes against public decency and morality is the availability of pornography via the Internet. Lawmakers (especially at the federal level) have attempted to restrict access to pornographic materials.

- *Crime against nature* refers to "intercourse contrary to the order of nature." It can include homosexuality, bestiality, and even heterosexual intercourse in positions other than the conventional "missionary" position.

- Drug use and abuse and lawfully controlled substances represent an area of special interest to many Americans today. Controlled substances are specifically defined as bioactive or psychoactive chemical substances that come under the purview of the criminal law.

- Under federal law and the laws of many states, controlled substances are classified according to five schedules. Schedules are an attempt to categorize controlled substances according to their abuse potential.

- Laws regulating public morality have sometimes been criticized as contributing to a "crisis of overcriminalization." *Overcriminalization* refers to the idea that laws regulating public morality may result in a substantial diversion of police, prosecutorial, and judicial time, personnel, and resources.

KEY TERMS

adultery, 376
bestiality, 376
bigamy, 379
buggery, 377
child pornography, 368
controlled substance, 385
crime against nature, 376
designer drug, 389
drug, 385
forfeiture, 392
fornication, 376
gambling, 384
incest, 384
indecent exposure, 369
keeping a place of prostitution, 366
lascivious, 369
lewdness, 369
obscenity, 366
pandering, 366
pimping, 366
polygamy, 379
pornography, 366
precursor chemical, 392
promoting prostitution, 366
prostitution, 365
prurient interest, 367
RICO statute, 393
soliciting prostitution, 365
victimless crime, 363

QUESTIONS FOR DISCUSSION

1. What are victimless crimes? Do you agree that some crimes are truly victimless? Why or why not?

2. Should prostitution remain illegal in most jurisdictions? Explain.

3. Should marijuana use be legalized under certain conditions? If so, what conditions?

4. What is meant by the "crisis of overcriminalization"? Do you agree that such a crisis exists relative to the crimes discussed in this chapter? Why or why not?

CRITICAL THINKING AND APPLICATION PROBLEMS

Consider the following scenario:

Rita Zenlo is a 34-year-old woman who is undergoing emotional counseling for sexual abuse she suffered as a child. Her counselor advised her to keep a personal journal, and to write about her memories and feelings. Rita found the exercise to be cathartic and wrote hundreds of pages describing in graphic detail the abuse she experienced at the hands of male relatives in the ninth, tenth, and eleventh years of her life. Believing that her writings may be helpful to others who have been raped and sexually molested, Rita created a website where she posted her writings. She named the website "A Victim's Reflection." A local police officer discovered the URL for Rita's website on a computer that had been seized during the search of the home of a man suspected of possessing child pornography. When the police checked the browsing history of the suspect, it was discovered that he had visited Rita's site 88 times. The police reviewed her site and discovered that it contained graphic accounts of rape and sexual assault of Rita when she was a child. The police contacted Rita and demanded that she remove the material describing her rape and molestation. She refused and has been charged with violating the state's obscenity law, which is identical to the Model Penal Code obscenity provision. Rita's defense is that her postings are protected speech under the First Amendment.

1. Assignment: Discuss Rita's defense in detail. Are her postings protected speech? Explain your answer. Include a discussion of applicable Supreme Court case(s) in your answer.

LEGAL RESOURCES ON THE WEB

Increasing numbers of law journals and abstracting services are now available on the Web or via e-mail subscription. Following are a sampling of such publications. You can perform a full-text search of law journals and of law journal abstracts on the Internet via the University Law Review Project at http://www.lawreview.org.

Alabama Law Review
http://www.law.ua.edu/lawreview
Published by the University of Alabama School of Law. Full-text reproductions of articles are available.

American University International Law Review
http://www.wcl.american.edu/journal/ilr
An international law journal produced by law students at American University. The *Review* publishes articles, critical essays, comments, and case notes on a wide variety of international law topics.

American University Law Review
http://www.wcl.american.edu/journal/lawrev

The oldest and the largest journal at American University's Washington College of Law. The articles published in the *Law Review* are not limited to one particular area of law. Some full-text articles are available online.

Florida State University Law Review
http://www.law.fsu.edu/journals/lawreview

Published by the Florida State University College of Law. Adobe PDF versions of articles are available online.

Mercer Law Review
http://www.law.mercer.edu/academics/lawreview

Published by students at the Walter F. George School of Law of Mercer University, Georgia. Full-text articles from recent issues are available online.

Murdoch University Electronic Journal of Law
http://www.murdoch.edu.au/elaw

Published by Murdoch University in Perth, Australia. This law journal is available entirely online.

New England Law Review
http://www.nesl.edu/lawrev

Published on the Web by the New England School of Law.

Ohio State Journal of Criminal Law
http://moritzlaw.osu.edu/osjcl/issues.php

A peer-evaluated, faculty–student cooperative journal published by the Michael E. Moritz College of Law at Ohio State University.

Stanford Law and Policy Review
http://www.stanford.edu/group/SLPR

Published twice a year by the law students of Stanford Law School. This academic journal concentrates on issues of law and public policy.

Washington and Lee Law Review
http://law.wlu.edu/lawreview

Published quarterly by students of the Washington and Lee University School of Law. Full-text articles are available online.

Web Journal of Current Legal Issues
http://webjcli.ncl.ac.uk

The *Web Journal of Current Legal Issues* is published bimonthly on the Web by the University of Newscastle, Tyne, United Kingdom, in association with Blackstone Press, Ltd. The journal focuses on current legal issues in judicial decisions, law reform, legislation, legal research, policy-related sociolegal research, legal information, information technology, and the practice of law.

SUGGESTED READINGS AND CLASSIC WORKS

Adler, Freda. *Sisters in Crime: The Rise of the New Female Criminal.* New York: McGraw-Hill, 1975.

Attorney General's Commission on Pornography. *Final Report.* Washington, DC: U.S. Government Printing Office, 1986.

Bazelon, David L. "The Morality of the Criminal Law." *Southern California Law Review* 49 (1976): 385.

Donnerstein, Edward. "Pornography and Violence against Women." *Annals of the New York Academy of Sciences* 347 (1980): 277.

Geis, Gilbert. *Not the Law's Business: An Examination of Homosexuality, Abortion, Prostitution, Narcotics, and Gambling in the United States*. New York: Schocken, 1979.

Kutchinksy, Berl. "The Effects of Easy Availability of Pornography on the Incidence of Sex Crimes." *Journal of Social Issues* 29 (1973): 95.

Myers, Laura. "Incest: No One Wants to Know." *Student Lawyer* (November 1980): 30.

Office of National Drug Control Policy. *The National Drug Control Strategy: 1997*. Washington, DC: U.S. Government Printing Office, 1997.

Schur, Edwin M., and Hugo Adam Bedau. *Victimless Crimes: Two Sides of a Controversy*. Upper Saddle River, NJ: Prentice Hall, 1974.

Shulgin, Alexander T. *Controlled Substances: A Chemical and Legal Guide to the Federal Drugs Laws*, 2nd ed. Berkeley, CA: Ronin, 1992.

NOTES

1. "Club Women Urge Segregation: See No Other Sane Recourse," *Sacramento Bee*, January 15, 1913.
2. *Pap's v. Erie*, 553 Pa. 348, 719 A.2d 273 (1998).
3. *City of Erie v. Pap's A M.*, 529 U.S. 277 (2000).
4. Fellatio may be felonious even when consensual.
5. *Time* (July 24, 1995): 58.
6. U.S. Code Annotated, Title 18, Section 2421.
7. N.R.S. 201 et seq.
8. General Statutes of North Carolina, Section 14-203.
9. Official Code of Georgia Annotated, Section 16-6-9.
10. Note, however, that North Carolina law (and the law of some other states) makes "indiscriminate sexual intercourse" a crime—even when no money changes hands.
11. Model Penal Code, Section 251.2(2).
12. Official Code of Georgia Annotated, Section 16-6-10.
13. Ibid., Section 16-6-11.
14. Ibid., Section 16-6-12.
15. Ibid., Section 16-6-16.
16. William Kornblum and Joseph Julian, *Social Problems*, 8th ed. (Upper Saddle River, NJ: Prentice Hall, 1995), 115.
17. *Jacobellis v. Ohio*, 378 U.S. 184.
18. *Miller v. California*, 413 U.S. 15 (1973).
19. *Stanley v. Georgia*, 394 U.S. 557 (1969).
20. *Paris Adult Theatre v. Slaton*, 413 U.S. 49 (1973).
21. *New York v. Ferber*, 458 U.S. 747 (1982).
22. Violent Crime Control and Law Enforcement Act of 1994, Title XVI, Section 160001, Subsection 2258.
23. U.S. Code Annotated, Title 47, Section 223(a)(1) (B)(ii) (Supp. 1997).
24. Public Law 104-104, 110 Statute 56.
25. *Reno v. ACLU*, 521 U.S. 844 (1997).
26. *Ashcroft v. Free Speech Coalition*, 535 U.S. 234 (2002).
27. New Jersey Code of Criminal Justice, Section 14-4.
28. Official Code of Georgia Annotated, Section 16-6-8.
29. Ibid., Section 16-6-18.
30. Ibid., Section 16-6-19.
31. Ibid., Section 16-6-6.
32. Ibid.
33. Rhode Island General Laws, Section 11-10-1.
34. Idaho Penal Code, Section 18-6605.
35. Ibid., Section 18-6606.
36. William Blackstone, *Commentaries on the Laws of England*, Vol. 4 (Oxford: Clarendon Press, 1769), p. 215.
37. *State v. Chance*, 3 N.C. App. 459, 165 S.E.2d 31 (1969).
38. *State v. Stokes*, 1 N.C. App. 245, 161 S.E.2d 53 (1968).
39. *State v. Whittemore*, 255 N.C. 583, 122 S.E.2d 396 (1961).
40. *State v. Stokes*, 1 N.C. App. 245, 161 S.E.2d 53 (1968).

41. Minnesota Statutes, Section 609.293 (Sodomy).

42. *Bowers* v. *Hardwick*, 478 U.S. 186 (1986).

43. *Powell* v. *State*, 270 Ga. 327, 510 S.E.2d 18 (1998).

44. *Lawrence* v. *Texas*, 539 U.S. 558 (2003).

45. Tony Mauro, "U.S. Supreme Court Strikes Down Law Banning Gay Sex," *Legal Times*, June 27, 2003.

46. *State* v. *Williams*, 220 N.C. 445, 17 S.E.2d 769 (1941).

47. *Haller* v. *State*, 232 S.W.2d 829 (Ark. 1950).

48. See, for example, *Lone Star* (1996), *The House of Yes* (1997), *This World* (1997), *Then the Fireworks* (1997), and *The Locusts* (1997).

49. Karen De Witt, "Incest as a Selling Point," *New York Times* News Service, March 30, 1997.

50. Official Code of Georgia Annotated, Section 16-6-22.

51. Most seduction statutes were rescinded or invalidated by court decree during the 1970s or 1980s.

52. General Statutes of North Carolina, Section 14-180.

53. Official Code of Georgia Annotated, Section 51-1-16.

54. North Carolina General Statutes, Section 14-292.

55. G. R. Blakey and H. A. Kurland, "Development of Federal Law on Gambling," *Cornell Law Review* 63 (1978): 923.

56. Some of the material in this section has been adapted from Frank Schmalleger, *Criminal Justice Today: An Introductory Text for the Twenty-first Century*, 10th ed. (Upper Saddle River, NJ: Prentice Hall, 2008).

57. The President's Commission on Organized Crime, *Organized Crime Today* (Washington, DC: U.S. Government Printing Office, 1986).

58. *Webb* v. *United States*, 249 U.S. 96, 63 L. Ed. 497, 39 S. Ct. 217 (1919).

59. Drug Enforcement Administration, *Drug Enforcement: The Early Years* (Washington, DC: DEA, December 1980), 41.

60. U.S. Code, Title 21, Section 801 et seq.

61. For a good summary of the law, see Drug Enforcement Administration, "Drugs of Abuse," http:// usdoj.gov/dea/concern/abuse/contents.htm (accessed April 5, 2009).

62. Florida Statutes, Section 893.02.

63. Ibid.

64. "'Rophies' Reported Spreading Quickly throughout the South," *Drug Enforcement Report* (June 23, 1995): 1–5.

65. Jodi S. Cohen, "Drug May Be Used in Sexual Assaults," *USA Today*, June 20, 1996.

66. Public Law 104-3305.

67. Public Law 106-172.

68. This provision became effective on September 1, 1989.

69. "Congress Gives Final OK to Major Antidrug Bill," *Criminal Justice Newsletter* 19, no. 21 (November 1, 1988): 1–4.

70. Ibid., 2.

71. "Drug Lord Sentenced to Death," *USA Today*, May 15, 1991.

72. Florida Statutes, Section 893.13.

73. Most states also permit the attorney general to remove a substance previously added to a schedule if he or she finds that the substance does not meet the requirements for inclusion in that schedule.

74. U.S. Code, Title 21, Section 881(a)(6).

75. Michael Goldsmith, *Civil Forfeiture: Tracing the Proceeds of Narcotics Trafficking* (Washington, DC: Police Executive Research Forum, 1988), 3.

76. *United States* v. *92 Buena Vista Ave.*, 113 S. Ct. 1126, 122 L. Ed. 2d 469 (1993).

77. *Austin* v. *United States*, 113 S. Ct. 2801, 15 L. Ed. 2d 448 (1993).

78. *Alexander* v. *United States*, 113 S. Ct. 2766, 125 L. Ed. 2d 441 (1993).

79. *United States* v. *James Daniel Good Real Property*, 114 S. Ct. 492, 126 L. Ed. 2d 490 (1993).

80. *Bennis* v. *Michigan*, 116 S. Ct. 1560, 134 L. Ed. 2d 661 (1996).

81. *United States* v. *Ursery*, 116 S. Ct. 2135, 135 L. Ed. 2d 549 (1996).

82. *United States* v. *Oakland Cannabis Buyers' Cooperative*, 532 U.S. 483, 121 S. Ct. 1711, 149 L. Ed. 2d 722 (2001).

83. *Gonzales* v. *Raich*, 545 U.S. 1 (2005).

84. Sanford H. Kadish, "The Crisis of Overcriminalization," *Annals of the American Academy of Political and Social Science* 374 (1967): 157.

85. Ibid.

86. Ibid.

© Mark McEvoy/Alamy

12

Terrorism and Human Trafficking

> [T]he constitutional Bill of Rights [is not] a suicide pact.
>
> —*Justice Robert Jackson, dissenting in* Terminiello v. City of Chicago, *337 U.S. 1 (1949)*

OBJECTIVES

After reading this chapter, you should be able to

- Define *terrorism*.
- Explain how the same act may be both a traditional crime and terrorism.
- Summarize terrorism laws and the constitutional issues raised by the war on terrorism.
- Identify several ways that recent acts of terrorism in the United States have led to changes in the laws of surveillance, detection, and detention, and describe the constitutional issues raised by these changes.
- Describe the crime of human trafficking.

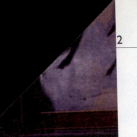

The commission of a traditional crime, such as murder, with the intention of coercing a population or influencing a government through fear or intimidation.

INTRODUCTION

Of all crimes, terrorism has received the greatest attention in the past decade. Historically, **terrorism** has been a greater threat to the people of other nations than to the inhabitants of the United States (Figure 12–1). But this is changing. Beginning with the bombing of the U.S. embassy in Beirut, Lebanon, in April 1983, acts of violence against U.S. targets have brought terrorism to the center of the American psyche (Table 12–1). Indeed, recent acts of terrorism, particularly the September 11, 2001, attacks on the World Trade Center and the Pentagon, have led to the creation of new terrorism laws; a plethora of new security practices at airports, power plants, water treatment facilities, and other public locations; an increase in private security; and increased cooperation and information sharing between federal and state law enforcement and security agencies. The changes have not only been extensive, but they've been expensive, too. It is estimated that the financial costs of 9/11 have exceeded a trillion dollars.[1] It is easy to imagine, for example, that the expense of hunting and executing Osama bin Laden ran into the hundreds of millions of dollars.

In the first portion of this chapter, terrorism and related crimes will be defined, major terrorism laws will be discussed, and the most significant constitutional issues that have surfaced in the war against terrorism will be examined. The second half of this chapter examines the very serious crimes of human smuggling and trafficking.

TERRORISM, TREASON, AND SEDITION

Terrorism has become the systematic weapon of a war that knows no borders or seldom has a face.

—*Jacques Chirac, former president of France*

Terrorism is a crime against the public, just like the crimes discussed in Chapter 10. Because of its significance, it is being treated separately in this book. As is true of other crimes against the public, the government may be the target, but individuals are harmed or murdered and property is destroyed.

FIGURE 12–1

Number of Terrorist Attacks, Top 15 Countries, in 2011.

National Counterterrorism Center, *Report on Terrorism, 2011.*

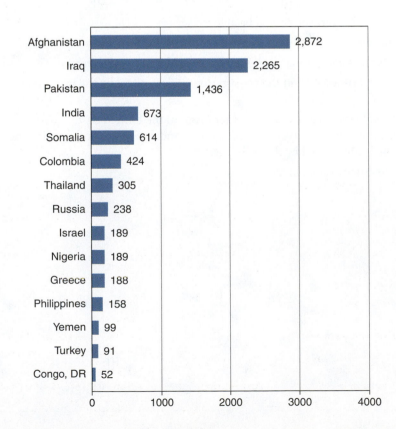

Regardless of the personal and property dimensions of the crime, which are separate chargeable offenses, the crime of terrorism is defined by its public nature. Terrorists intend to harm or disrupt government. They usually have political, ideological, or religious intentions; are zealots; and often have no regard for life or property. Some terrorists act on behalf of their governments; others act on their own. Terrorism is not new. Terror has been used to influence governments and their citizens for ages. It often transcends national boundaries. For this reason, terrorism is the subject of a considerable number of international as well as domestic laws.

A related crime is **treason**, the only crime mentioned in the Constitution of the United States. Article III, Section 3 provides that treason against the United States "shall consist only in levying War against them, or in adhering to their Enemies, giving them Aid and Comfort. No person shall be convicted of Treason unless on the Testimony of two Witnesses to the same overt Act, or on Confession in open Court." Article III doesn't declare treason to be a crime; it simply defines what acts may be declared treasonous by legislation, and it requires two witnesses or a confession to prove it. As discussed in Chapter 10, it is a federal statute that declares treason to be a crime: "Whoever, owing allegiance to the United States, levies war against them or adheres to their enemies, giving them aid and comfort within the United States or elsewhere, is guilty of treason and shall suffer death, or shall be imprisoned not less than five years and fined under this title but not less than ten

treason
The crime of levying war against, or supporting the enemy of, one's nation. It is the only crime specifically mentioned in the U.S. Constitution.

TABLE 12–1 Recent Acts of Terrorism against the United States

Incident	Date	Impact
Countless attacks on U.S. personnel in Iraq and Afghanistan during the two recent wars	Continuing	Thousands murdered, millions of dollars in property damage
Attack on U.S. embassy in Libya Attacks on World Trade Center and Pentagon	September 11, 2012 September 11, 2001	American ambassador and three others killed Nearly 5,000 dead, World Trade Center destroyed, Pentagon damaged, U.S. psyche changed
Attack on USS *Cole* in Yemen	October 12, 2000	17 murdered, many injured, ship damaged
Attacks on U.S. embassies in Kenya and Tanzania	August 7, 1998	291 murdered (12 U.S. citizens), 5,000 injured, embassies damaged
Bombing at Olympics in Georgia, USA	July 27, 1996	One murdered, many injured, property damaged
Attack on U.S. military base in Saudi Arabia	June 25, 1996	19 murdered, over 500 injured, and property damaged
Car bombing in Saudi Arabia	November 13, 1995	Seven murdered, including five U.S. personnel
Destruction of Murrah Federal Building in Oklahoma City	April 19, 1995	168 murdered, over 600 injured, building destroyed
Bombing of World Trade Center in New York	February 26, 1993	Six murdered, over 1,000 injured
Bombing of Pan Am flight 103	December 21, 1988	All passengers murdered, including 189 Americans, 11 on the ground also murdered
Bombing of marine barracks in Beirut, Lebanon	October 23, 1983	241 U.S. service personnel and 58 foreign service personnel murdered, property damage
Bombing of U.S. embassy in Beirut, Lebanon	April 18, 1983	17 Americans and 46 others murdered, property damage

thousand dollars ($10,000); and shall be incapable of holding any office under the United States."[2]

Although treason has been a crime since the early days of the nation, few have been convicted of the offense. This is in part due to the requirement that there be two witnesses to the same overt act—a significant hurdle to prosecutors.

Sedition, also defined in Chapter 10, is the act of inciting violence or insurrection against a government. Sedition has been a crime in the United States since the Alien and Sedition Acts of the late 1700s. The four laws that made up the Alien and Sedition Acts were enacted by a Federalist-controlled Congress and signed into law by President John Adams during a war with France. They prohibited the publication of false, scandalous, and malicious stories about the government and were used to silence members of the increasingly popular Republican Party, which opposed the anti-French positions of the Federalists. Many opposed the Alien and Sedition Acts as violative of the First Amendment and as infringing on the Tenth Amendment authority of the states to regulate such conduct. Both Thomas Jefferson and James Madison opposed the laws. Eventually, the laws expired and were not reauthorized in their original form. Those who were convicted and fined under them had their monies returned,[3] and when he took office, President Thomas Jefferson pardoned everyone who was convicted under the laws.

Several sedition laws exist today. These include the general prohibition of seditious conspiracies[4] and the Logan Act, which prohibits individuals from engaging in diplomacy with foreign governments. Other related crimes, such as espionage and subversive conduct, can also be found in the U.S. Code.[5]

Terrorism Laws

The federal government and the governments of all the states have terrorism laws. As mentioned, acts of terrorism usually involve crimes against people and crimes against property. But terrorism is more than an attack on an individual or an individual's property. It is an attack on a government, using people or property as tools.

Federal terrorism laws distinguish international from other forms of terrorism. The primary terrorism statute, 18 U.S.C. § 2331, that defines and distinguishes international and domestic terrorism is as follows:

(1) [T]he term "international terrorism" means activities that—

(A) involve violent acts or acts dangerous to human life that are a violation of the criminal laws of the United States or of any State, or that would be a criminal violation if committed within the jurisdiction of the United States or of any State;

(B) appear to be intended—

　(i) to intimidate or coerce a civilian population;

　(ii) to influence the policy of a government by intimidation or coercion; or

　(iii) to affect the conduct of a government by mass destruction, assassination, or kidnapping; and

(C) occur primarily outside the territorial jurisdiction of the United States, or transcend national boundaries in terms of the means by which they are accomplished, the persons they appear intended to intimidate or coerce, or the locale in which their perpetrators operate or seek asylum;

(2) [T]he term "national of the United States" has the meaning given such term in section 101(a)(22) of the Immigration and Nationality Act;

(3) [T]he term "person" means any individual or entity capable of holding a legal or beneficial interest in property;

CRIMINAL LAW IN THE NEWS

American Woman Embraces Islam on the Internet, Becomes "Jihad Jane"

Colleen LaRose is not like most Americans who join extreme Muslim causes. She has no Muslim background and apparently had no interest in it until she went on the Internet and took the cyber-personality of "Jihad Jane." When her real identity was exposed, she was arrested and later admitted to conspiring to murder a Swedish cartoonist who had satirized the prophet Mohammad.

LaRose grew up in Texas. Divorced twice at a young age, she was moving from city to city when, at age 41, she became romantically involved with Kurt Gorman, a businessman visiting from Pennsylvania. In 2004, he took her back to his hometown outside Philadelphia, where she helped take care of his elderly father.

While Gorman went to work each day, LaRose began her obsession with the Internet and developed a secret affinity for Muslim causes. Neither the townsfolk nor Gorman himself knew anything about it. "From what I can tell, she didn't seem to have much of a tie to Islam other than what she learned over the Internet," said U.S. Representative Charles Dent (R-Pa.), a neighbor of hers. Jihad Jane, saying she was a recent convert to Islam, posted online pictures of herself covered in a long black burka, with just her blue eyes peeking out.

According to federal prosecutors, LaRose "worked obsessively on her computer to communicate with, recruit and incite other jihadists." In June 2008, she posted a video on YouTube saying she was "desperate to do something somehow to help" suffering Muslims. Jihadists from Europe responded that she should join them and help kill Swedish cartoonist Lars Vilks, who had depicted Muhammad's face on the body of a dog.

In August 2009, LaRose abruptly left her Pennsylvania home and, according to prosecutors, traveled to somewhere in Europe, where she planned to marry an alleged co-conspirator. She wrote online that it would be "an honor & great pleasure to die or kill for" her intended spouse, the indictment said. LaRose joined an online community hosted by Vilks, but apparently she never went to Sweden, and after two months took a plane back to the United States.

LaRose was arrested in October 2009 at Philadelphia International Airport and put in prison, but authorities kept her arrest secret for five months. Her indictment,

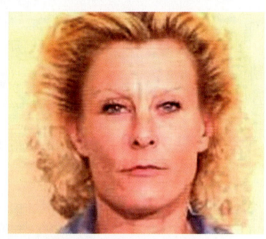

"Jihad Jane." What is the legal definition of terrorism?
AFP/Getty Images/Newscom

unsealed in March 2010, charged her with conspiracy to provide material support to terrorists, conspiracy to kill a person in a foreign country, making false statements to the Federal Bureau of Investigation (FBI), and attempted identity theft.

On the same day that Rose's arrest was announced, five of her alleged co-conspirators were arrested in Ireland. One of them was Jamie Paulin-Ramirez, a Coloradan who was a lot like LaRose. Known on the Internet as "Jihad Jamie," she went to Ireland and married an Algerian man she had never met before, apparently as a cover for the alleged plot. Paulin-Ramirez was later charged as a co-defendant with LaRose.

LaRose pleaded guilty to all the charges against her in February 2011. Her sentencing has not yet taken place, but she faces a possible life term in prison.

Assistant U.S. Attorney General David Kris said LaRose's alleged co-conspirators saw her American looks and U.S. citizenship as a way to go unnoticed. "Today's guilty plea, by a woman from suburban America who plotted with others to commit murder overseas and to provide material support to terrorists, underscores the evolving nature of the threat we face," he said in an announcement.

Resources

"Jihad Jane, Colleen LaRose, Recruited Terrorists and Plotted Murder, Prosecutors Say,"
Huffington Post, May 9, 2010,
http://www.huffingtonpost.com/2010/03/09/jihad-jane-colleen-larose_n_492586.html.

(continued)

"'Jihad Jane' Pleads Guilty to Murder Attempt on Swedish Cartoonist,"
The Guardian, February 1, 2011,
http://www.guardian.co.uk/world/2011/feb/02/jihad-jane-pleads-guilty-cartoonist-murder.

"'Jihad Jane' Admits to Conspiracy to Support Terrorists, Murder,"
Christian Science Monitor, February 1, 2011,
http://www.csmonitor.com/USA/Latest-News-Wires/2011/0201/Jihad-Jane-admits-to-conspiracy-to-support-terrorists-murder.

(4) [T]he term "act of war" means any act occurring in the course of—

(A) declared war;

(B) armed conflict, whether or not war has been declared, between two or more nations; or

(C) armed conflict between military forces of any origin; and

(5) [T]he term "domestic terrorism" means activities that—

(A) involve acts dangerous to human life that are a violation of the criminal laws of the United States or of any State;

(B) appear to be intended—

(i) to intimidate or coerce a civilian population;

(ii) to influence the policy of a government by intimidation or coercion; or

(iii) to affect the conduct of a government by mass destruction, assassination, or kidnapping; and

(C) occur primarily within the territorial jurisdiction of the United States.

HOMELAND SECURITY ACT, U.S. CODE

Title 6, Section 101(15). The term "terrorism" means any activity that—

(a) involves an act that—

(i) is dangerous to human life or potentially destructive of critical infrastructure or key resources; and

(ii) is a violation of the criminal laws of the United States or of any State or other subdivision of the United States; and

(b) appears to be intended—

(i) to intimidate or coerce a civilian population;

(ii) to influence the policy of a government by intimidation or coercion; or

(iii) to affect the conduct of a government by mass destruction, assassination, or kidnapping.

OHIO REVISED CODE

Title 29, Section 2909.21

(a) "Act of terrorism" means an act that is committed within or outside the territorial jurisdiction of this state or the United States, that constitutes a specified offense if committed in this state or constitutes an offense in any jurisdiction within or outside the territorial jurisdiction of the United States containing all of the essential elements of a specified offense, and that is intended to do one or more of the following:

(1) Intimidate or coerce a civilian population;

(2) Influence the policy of any government by intimidation or coercion;

(3) Affect the conduct of any government by the act that constitutes the offense.

From these and other laws, the following common elements of the crime of terrorism can be extracted:

- The commission of an already established crime
- Intended to coerce a population or influence a government
- Through intimidation or fear

Note that several other terrorism-related crimes exist; their definitions and penalties can be found in the applicable subject-specific statutes. For example, bioterrorism, aiding terrorists, financing terrorists, and using weapons of mass destruction in terrorism are separate federal crimes.

In addition to defining the crime of terrorism, there are many statutes defining the authority and responsibilities of law enforcement officers and agencies that investigate, prevent, and prosecute acts of terrorism. In some cases, terrorism law is embedded in a statute that addresses a different subject. One of the most significant federal laws is the **Foreign Intelligence Surveillance Act of 1978 (FISA)**.[6] FISA stands apart from other federal criminal laws because it recognizes the special nature of foreign intelligence work. Under FISA, secret court orders authorizing foreign surveillance by officers of the United States are permitted, even though such orders would not be permitted in standard criminal cases within the United States. The rationale for the distinction is that such orders are not intended to further a prosecution but to advance the gathering of foreign intelligence needed to protect the nation. FISA, which has been amended in recent years, is discussed in more detail later in this chapter.

Another important law is the Antiterrorism and Effective Death Penalty Act of 1996 (AEDPA). This statute was enacted in response to the bombing of the Alfred P. Murrah Federal Building in Oklahoma City in 1995. AEDPA amended existing laws to limit federal *habeas corpus* relief in two ways. First, it limited the time for filing to one year. Second, it limited the total number of petitions that may be filed in a single case. It also mandated closed-circuit television access for victims in cases in which the trial venue is changed.

Other significant federal laws addressing terrorism and sedition include the Immigration and Naturalization Act,[7] the Seditious Conspiracy (to overthrow the U.S. government) Act,[8] a statute prohibiting members of the U.S. armed forces from acting against the United States,[9] the federal treason statute,[10] and the Homeland Security Act.[11] Many other statutes are aimed at other subjects but have terrorism provisions.

In response to the attacks on the United States on September 11, 2001, Congress enacted the Uniting and Strengthening America by Providing Appropriate Tools Required to Intercept and Obstruct Terrorism Act of 2001, popularly known as the **USA PATRIOT Act**. The act, which was reauthorized in 2006, amended many existing laws, including FISA and the Electronic Communications Privacy Act of 1986. The changes included the following:

- The attorney general was given greater authority to deport suspected alien terrorists.
- Federal law enforcement officials were given expanded authority to secure data about individuals held by third parties, including physicians, Internet providers, and libraries, based only on an assertion that the data will further an ongoing terrorism investigation. Previously, the government had to prove that the individual was an agent of a foreign power.
- The authority of federal law enforcement officials to monitor e-mail, voicemail, and other forms of communication was increased.
- The authority of federal courts to issue pen register and trap orders (which determine the origin of electronic communications) was expanded from regional to national.
- The authority of law enforcement officers to obtain Internet histories of suspected terrorists without probable cause (requiring only relevance to ongoing investigations) was established.

Foreign Intelligence Surveillance Act of 1978 (FISA)
The Foreign Intelligence Surveillance Act of 1978 is the primary federal statute governing the collection of foreign intelligence by federal law enforcement agencies. Significant amendments to FISA were passed in 2001 through the USA PATRIOT Act and again in 2008.

habeas corpus
Literally, "you have the body"; a writ challenging the legality of incarceration, or a writ ordering a prisoner to be brought before a court to determine the legality of the prisoner's detention.

USA PATRIOT Act
A federal statute enacted immediately following, and in response to, the terrorist attacks on the United States on September 11, 2001. The statute increased federal law enforcement authority to prevent, detect, and prosecute terrorists.

FIGURE 12–2

Reducing the Scope and Capability of Terrorist Organizations.

National Strategy for Combating Terrorism (Washington, DC: White House, 2003), p. 13.

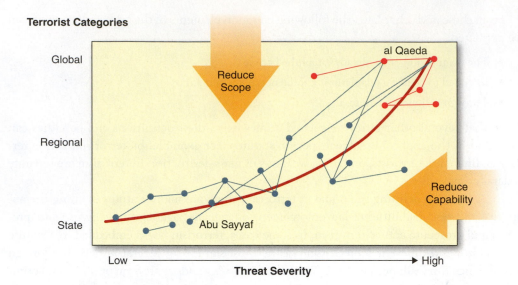

- Authority was given to the courts to issue wiretaps that law enforcement officers may move from one communication source to another (roving wiretaps) without securing new authorization.

- Several new terrorism crimes were created, including foreign use of fraudulent credit cards, harboring terrorists, terrorism-related money laundering, and terrorism against mass transit.

- Law enforcement agencies were granted the authority to share with intelligence agencies previously secret foreign intelligence obtained by grand juries.

- Civil claims against the United States were permitted for some breaches of privacy.

- The authority of law enforcement officers to forfeit and confiscate property used in terrorism was increased.

In 2006, the federal government published its *National Strategy for Combating Terrorism*, which targeted terrorist organizations through efforts to reduce their capabilities while simultaneously reducing their scope of influence (Figure 12–2).

CONSTITUTIONAL ISSUES

Terrorism doesn't just blow up buildings; it blasts every other issue off the political map. The spectre of terrorism, real and exaggerated, has become a shield of impunity, protecting governments around the world from scrutiny for their human rights abuses.

—Naomi Klein, Canadian writer

Although this is a text on criminal law, not criminal procedure, several important constitutional criminal procedure issues resulting from the "war on terror" should be mentioned. In response to the attacks of September 11, 2001, the USA PATRIOT Act was enacted, the Department of Homeland Defense was established, and President George W. Bush took immediate military action. The latter included issuing Military Order 1, which authorized the secretary of defense to detain members of al Qaeda who were suspected of planning or participating in terrorism against the United States. President Bush also provided for the establishment of military tribunals to try suspected terrorists. Consequently, the secretary of defense issued Military Commission Order 1, which elaborated on the president's order. This order set out the procedures to be used by military tribunals, provided for forfeiture of property by convicted terrorists, and established death as one possible punishment for convicted terrorists.

Within a short time, many suspected terrorists were arrested and detained, most of them overseas. Many were held at Guantanamo Bay, Cuba, which had, according to a study conducted by the Brookings Institution, approximately 250 detainees in 2008.[12] Eventually, the military tribunals began conducting hearings. Both of these actions raised constitutional issues so serious that the U.S. Supreme Court granted *certiorari* in several cases. The current

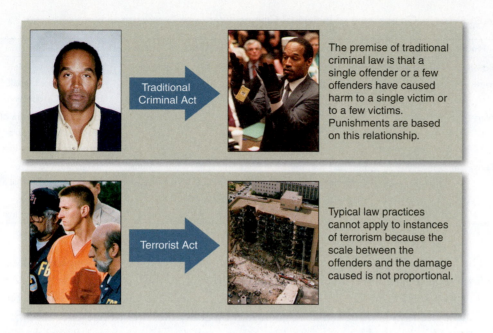

The premise of traditional criminal law is that a single offender or a few offenders have caused harm to a single victim or to a few victims. Punishments are based on this relationship.

Traditional Criminal Act

Terrorist Act

Typical law practices cannot apply to instances of terrorism because the scale between the offenders and the damage caused is not proportional.

FIGURE 12–3

Traditional Forms of Crime versus Terrorism.

(top left) Los Angeles Police Department/ AP Wide World Photos; *(top right)* AP Photo/Vince Bucci, Pool; *(bottom left)* Bob E. Daemmrich/Corbis; *(bottom right)* AP Wide World Photos.

"war on terror" is unique because it has given rise to legal issues that do not fall squarely into traditional criminal procedure, nor do they appear to be fully answered by the laws of war. One scholar explained the problem as follows:

> Like all wars, the global war on terror proclaimed by the Bush administration—or better, the U.S.-led worldwide war against Islamic extremists whose weapon of choice is terror—has put strain on the rule of law. This is in part because of the ways in which American constitutional law is entangled with the modern laws of war and their long-standing assumption that the principal actors are states. The modern laws of war are a part of the law of nations that emerged in the writings of seventeenth—and eighteenth—century jurists.[13]

As you can see, the nonstate character of terrorism confounds the application to terrorism of the laws of war. The traditional criminal justice model doesn't easily apply either (Figure 12–3). The criminal justice model is premised on the notion of a single actor or a few actors who harm or steal from a single victim or a few victims. In this context, the U.S. criminal justice system's due-process model (its constitutional, adversarial, accusatorial, legal-guilt nature) is intended to protect individual liberties, sometimes at the expense of failing to punish wrongdoers. There is an inherent cost-benefit assumption underlying the traditional criminal justice system. The prices to be paid under the due-process model of the traditional system are essentially a difficult investigatory and crime-prevention process and the rare release of a guilty defendant for legal reasons (for example, when evidence needed for conviction is suppressed for Fourth Amendment reasons). In some cases, the guilty person may pose a threat to others, but even that is rare.

Terrorism is different. In combating terrorism, the government's focus is as much on prevention as it is on prosecution and punishment. This is because the social costs of not detecting and preventing terrorism are more akin to the damages inflicted by war than the costs associated with traditional crimes; that is, hundreds, if not thousands, can lose their lives in a single terrorist incident, property damage can be extraordinary, and the potential for lasting damage is significant. Because courts are less knowledgeable and experienced in national security matters, and to maintain the separation of powers, courts normally extend great deference to the judgments of the executive branch in matters of national security, foreign affairs, and war. Indeed, the Supreme Court has said that deference to the executive in terrorism cases may be justified.[14] See Table 12–2 for a summary of the differences among individual crimes, war, and terrorism.

TABLE 12–2 Comparison of Individual Crimes, War, and Terrorism

Model	Actors	Motive of Actors	Target of Action	Support	Harm
Individual crime	Individual or small group	Personal: money, anger, vengeance, etc.	Individuals or property	Individual actors	One or a few people killed or injured, small amounts of property loss
War	State	Political	State	State	States, large numbers of people killed or injured, significant property loss
Terrorism	Individual or small group	Personal but often furthering a state's or religion's objectives	State indirectly through people and property	Individual, group, state	States, small to large numbers of people killed or injured, small to moderate property loss

The Supreme Court's decisions in recent years have begun to give contour to this largely undeveloped area of law (Table 12–3). The first decision of the Court addressed the detention of suspected terrorists. In *Hamdi* v. *Rumsfeld*,[15] a U.S. citizen (who also held Saudi Arabian citizenship) was seized in Afghanistan by U.S. allies and turned over to U.S. authorities, who detained him in several locations, including Guantanamo Bay and a naval jail in Virginia. The United States claimed that he was an unlawful combatant, as defined by law, who was waging war on the United States and that, accordingly, he could be detained without hearing or trial. Hamdi's father filed a *habeas corpus* petition on his son's behalf, and the case made its way to the Supreme Court.

The Court held that the Fourteenth Amendment's due-process protections applied to citizen detainees and that Hamdi was entitled to a hearing to determine if cause existed to support the finding that he was an unlawful combatant. Although the Court held that Hamdi had a right to counsel, it also held that access to judicial review is not required by the due-process clause. Rather, access to an impartial fact finder, even if military, is adequate. The United States responded by creating the Combatant Status Review Tribunals, which are similar in makeup to tribunals created under the auspices of the Geneva Conventions.

TABLE 12–3 Summary of U.S. Supreme Court Detainee Cases

Case	Holding	Consequence	Date
Boumediene v. *Bush*	The MCA's suspension of the writ of *habeas corpus* for noncitizen detainees violates the Constitution. Note: The Supreme Court chose not to hear petitions from several detainees in 2012.	Over 200 *habeas* petitions filed. Boumediene himself was ordered released in 2009 after more than seven years of detention.[17]	2008
Hamdan v. *Rumsfeld*	The use of executive-created military commissions to try suspected terrorists is not authorized by Congress and is therefore invalid.	Congress and president enacted Military Commissions Act (MCA) authorizing such bodies.	2006
Hamdi v. *Rumsfeld*	Citizen detainees are entitled to review of detention. Judicial review is not required. Assistance of counsel at review is required.	President established Combatant Status Review Tribunal.	2004
Rasul v. *Bush*	Noncitizen detainees enjoy right of *habeas corpus* review of detention if United States has authority over venue of detention. This applies to Guantanamo Bay, Cuba.	President established Combatant Status Review Tribunal.	2004

The Court issued *Rasul* v. *Bush*[16] on the same day as *Hamdi*. In this case, the Court held that noncitizen detainees enjoy the right of *habeas corpus* review if the United States has jurisdiction over the venue of their detention. Because the United States has a treaty with Cuba providing for U.S. control over the base, the Court found that noncitizen detainees at Guantanamo Bay have a right to have their detention reviewed.

In response to public concerns about the treatment of the detainees at Guantanamo Bay and Congress's and the president's concerns about unwarranted judicial intervention into the matter, two pieces of legislation were enacted. The Detainee Treatment Act prohibits cruel, inhumane, and degrading treatment of prisoners in the custody of the United States.[18] It also established procedures that are to be followed in detainee cases and stripped federal courts of the jurisdiction to hear appeals from detainees. In the 2006 case *Hamdan* v. *Rumsfeld*,[19] Hamdan, who had served as Osama bin Laden's personal driver, had appeared before the Combatant Status Review Tribunal, had been found to be an enemy combatant, and was scheduled to be tried before a military commission established under the authority of President Bush's military order. Hamdan challenged his trial by military commission, alleging that it violated both international law (the Geneva Conventions) and domestic law (the Uniform Code of Military Justice). The United States asserted that Congress's general authorization to go to war included the authority to establish the military commissions. The Court disagreed. It found that the congressional authorization to use force didn't include the authority to establish the commissions and that, therefore, the commissions stood in violation of both international and domestic law.

Congress and President Bush reacted quickly to the *Hamdan* decision in the form of the Military Commissions Act (MCA) of 2006,[20] which authorized the use of military commissions to try noncitizen detainees who had been determined to be enemy combatants by the Combatant Status Review process. The MCA also limited *habeas corpus* relief of the detainees who had been found to be enemy combatants and who were not located geographically in the United States. The provision suspending *habeas corpus* for the detainees was addressed by the Supreme Court in the case of *Boumediene* v. *Bush* (2008),[21] where it held the MCA's limitation of the right to *habeas corpus* to be unconstitutional because the U.S. Constitution applied to Guantanamo Bay, Cuba. Subsequently, hearings were held and several detainees, including Boumediene, were ordered to be released by courts. The MCA was amended in 2009 to provide for greater hearing rights for the detainees.

Besides the detainee issues, other constitutional issues are beginning to surface in the "war on terror." In particular, the expanded surveillance and investigative authorities of law enforcement, both at home and abroad, raise privacy concerns. An example of this can be found in the 2008 case of *Doe* v. *Mukasey*.[22] This case involved a provision of the USA PATRIOT Act that forbids electronic service providers (telephone companies and Internet service providers) from disclosing to their customers (and others) that the government has demanded to see their files. Under the USA PATRIOT Act, federal law enforcement agencies (the Federal Bureau of Investigation in this case) possess the authority to issue an administrative subpoena (known as a *national security letter*) to service providers demanding to see individual files. Probable cause is not required, as long as the data are relevant to a national security investigation.

In a complex decision, the U.S. Court of Appeals for the Second Circuit found that the nondisclosure requirement violated, in part, the First Amendment's free speech clause and devised a plan of review that requires the government to demonstrate that harm may occur as a result of disclosure in addition to relevance to a national security investigation. Because the USA PATRIOT Act and other antiterrorism laws challenge historical notions of civil rights in the United States, a considerable amount of litigation can be expected in the future. The 2010 Supreme Court decision in *Holder* v. *Humanitarian Law Project*, shown as a Capstone Case in this chapter, addresses the question of providing nonviolent support for organizations labeled as terrorist by the United States.

APPLYING THE CONCEPT

CAPSTONE CASE

Does It Violate the First Amendment's Free Speech Clause to Make It a Crime to Provide Support in Humanitarian, Nonviolent Activities to a Terrorist Organization?

Holder v. Humanitarian Law Project,
561 U.S. ___ (2010)

Chief Justice Roberts delivered the opinion of the Court.

* * *

THE CASE This litigation concerns 18 U.S.C. §2339B, which makes it a federal crime to "knowingly provid[e] material support or resources to a foreign terrorist organization." Congress has amended the definition of "material support or resources" periodically, but at present it is defined as follows:

> "[T]he term 'material support or resources' means any property, tangible or intangible, or service, including currency or monetary instruments or financial securities, financial services, lodging, training, expert advice or assistance, safehouses, false documentation or identification, communications equipment, facilities, weapons, lethal substances, explosives, personnel (1 or more individuals who may be or include oneself), and transportation, except medicine or religious materials."

The authority to designate an entity a "foreign terrorist organization" rests with the Secretary of State. . . .

In 1997, the Secretary of State designated 30 groups as foreign terrorist organizations. Two of those groups are the Kurdistan Workers' Party (also known as the Partiya Karkeran Kurdistan, or PKK) and the Liberation Tigers of Tamil Eelam (LTTE). . . .

Plaintiffs in this litigation are two U.S. citizens and six domestic organizations . . . . Plaintiffs claimed that they wished to provide support for the humanitarian and political activities of the PKK and the LTTE in the form of monetary contributions, other tangible aid, legal training, and political advocacy, but that they could not do so for fear of prosecution under §2339B. . . .

As relevant here, plaintiffs claimed that the material-support statute was unconstitutional on two grounds: First,

it violated their freedom of speech and freedom of association under the First Amendment, because it criminalized their provision of material support to the PKK and the LTTE, without requiring the Government to prove that plaintiffs had a specific intent to further the unlawful ends of those organizations. Second, plaintiffs argued that the statute was unconstitutionally vague. . . .

THE FINDING The First Amendment issue before us is more refined than either plaintiffs or the Government would have it. It is not whether the Government may prohibit pure political speech, or may prohibit material support in the form of conduct. It is instead whether the Government may prohibit what plaintiffs want to do—provide material support to the PKK and LTTE in the form of speech.

Everyone agrees that the Government's interest in combating terrorism is an urgent objective of the highest order. Plaintiffs' complaint is that the ban on material support, applied to what they wish to do, is not "necessary to further that interest." The objective of combating terrorism does not justify prohibiting their speech, plaintiffs argue, because their support will advance only the legitimate activities of the designated terrorist organizations, not their terrorism. . . .

The PKK and the LTTE are deadly groups. "The PKK's insurgency has claimed more than 22,000 lives." . . .

Money is fungible, and "[w]hen foreign terrorist organizations that have a dual structure raise funds, they highlight the civilian and humanitarian ends to which such moneys could be put." But "there is reason to believe that foreign terrorist organizations do not maintain legitimate *financial* firewalls between those funds raised for civil, nonviolent activities, and those ultimately used to support violent, terrorist operations." . . .

Providing foreign terrorist groups with material support in any form also furthers terrorism by straining the United

States' relationships with its allies and undermining cooperative efforts between nations to prevent terrorist attacks. . . .

In analyzing whether it is possible in practice to distinguish material support for a foreign terrorist group's violent activities and its nonviolent activities, we do not rely exclusively on our own inferences drawn from the record evidence. We have before us an affidavit stating the Executive Branch's conclusion on that question. The State Department informs us that "[t]he experience and analysis of the U.S. government agencies charged with combating terrorism strongly suppor[t]" Congress's finding that all contributions to foreign terrorist organizations further their terrorism. . . .

That evaluation of the facts by the Executive, like Congress's assessment, is entitled to deference. This litigation implicates sensitive and weighty interests of national security and foreign affairs. The PKK and the LTTE have committed terrorist acts against American citizens abroad, and the material-support statute addresses acute foreign policy concerns involving relationships with our Nation's allies. . . .

We turn to the particular speech plaintiffs propose to undertake. First, plaintiffs propose to "train members of [the] PKK on how to use humanitarian and international law to peacefully resolve disputes." Congress can, consistent with the First Amendment, prohibit this direct training. It is wholly foreseeable that the PKK could use the "specific skill[s]" that plaintiffs propose to impart, §2339A(b)(2), as part of a broader strategy to promote terrorism. . . .

Second, plaintiffs propose to "teach PKK members how to petition various representative bodies such as the United Nations for relief." . . .

The Government acts within First Amendment strictures in banning this proposed speech because it teaches the organization how to acquire "relief," which plaintiffs never define with any specificity, and which could readily include monetary aid. . . .

All this is not to say that any future applications of the material-support statute to speech or advocacy will survive First Amendment scrutiny. It is also not to say that any other statute relating to speech and terrorism would satisfy the First Amendment. In particular, we in no way suggest that a regulation of independent speech would pass constitutional muster, even if the Government were to show that such speech benefits foreign terrorist organizations. We also do not suggest that Congress could extend the same prohibition on material support at issue here to domestic organizations. We simply hold that, in prohibiting the particular forms of support that plaintiffs seek to provide to foreign terrorist groups, §2339B does not violate the freedom of speech.

[The Court also concluded that the right to association is not violated by the statute and that the statute is not impermissibly vague.]

What Do You Think?

1. Should U.S. law distinguish between the legitimate and terrorist activities of organizations for purposes of determining whether a person may provide support?

2. Where is the limit? What if the secretary of state were to declare thousands of foreign organizations to be terrorist in nature, including those that advocate violence but have not committed any violence?

Additional Applications

Is a doctor's pledge to provide medical services to al Qaeda "material support" under Section 2339B?

United States v. Farhane and Sabir, 634 F.3d 127 (2nd Cir. 2011)

The Case: Rafiq Sabir, a U.S. citizen and U.S.-trained emergency room doctor, swore an oath of allegiance to al Qaeda in May 2005 and promised to be on call to treat wounded members of that organization while in Saudi Arabia. Shortly after pledging to provide this support—but before traveling to the Middle East—Sabir was arrested and charged under the material support provisions of Section 2339B. After a four-week jury trial, a federal district court in 2007 found Sabir guilty of conspiracy and criminal attempt and sentenced him to 300 months' incarceration. On appeal, Sabir argued, among other things, that the statutory definition of "material support or resources" in Section 2339 is unconstitutionally vague because it explicitly exempts the supplying of "medicine" from its coverage. What's more, Sabir claimed that the statute is overbroad in limiting his substantive due-process and First Amendment rights as a doctor to practice medicine.

The Finding: A panel of the U.S. Court of Appeals for the Second Circuit rejected Sabir's arguments and upheld the trial court's verdicts. Regarding vagueness, the appeals panel concluded that the "medicine exception" in the material support statute clearly applied only to "medical supplies" rather than the practice of medicine in general. Indeed, the panel found, Sabir's offer to serve as an on-call physician for al Qaeda fell clearly within the statutory prohibition on the supplying of "personnel" to a

(*continued*)

terrorist group; thus, Sabir was sufficiently on notice that his activities violated the law. As for Sabir's overbreadth claim, the panel held that any rights possessed by doctors to practice medicine—even if rooted in the First and Fourteenth Amendments—nonetheless must yield to Congress's power in Article I of the Constitution to make laws "necessary and proper" for the nation's defense. Notably, the panel emphasized, Sabir had not been prosecuted for "performing routine duties as a hospital emergency room physician, treating admitted persons who coincidentally happened to be al Qaeda members." To the contrary, Sabir had pledged to "obey al Qaeda's leaders, including Osama bin Laden, and . . . protect his fellow 'brothers on the path of jihad' and 'on the path of al Qaeda.'"

Does a foreign organization have a due-process right to challenge its "terrorist" designation in court?

32 County Sovereignty Committee v. Department of State, 292 F.3d 797 (D.C. Cir. 2002)

The Case: In 2002, the U.S. Secretary of State designated the "Real IRA," a militant group seeking an end to British rule in Northern Ireland, as a foreign terrorist organization under the Antiterrorism and Effective Death Penalty Act of 1996. The secretary's publication of the designation in the *Federal Register* also listed three other Irish political organizations—the 32 County Sovereignty Committee, the 32 County Sovereignty Movement, and the Irish Republican Prisoners Welfare Association—as "aliases" of the Real IRA. In this action, the designated alias organizations challenged their designation and requested judicial review of the secretary's actions.

The Finding: A panel of the U.S. Court of Appeals for the District of Columbia Circuit rejected the foreign organizations' legal claims. In substance, the panel held, the organizations were asserting a Fifth Amendment due-process challenge to administrative rule making by the secretary of state, yet foreign organizations have "no constitutional rights, under the due process clause or otherwise," unless they have "come within the United States and developed substantial connections with this country." Although some American members of these organizations "personally rented post office boxes and utilized a bank account to transmit funds and information," the organizations themselves nonetheless did not "posses[s] any controlling interest in property located within the United States, nor do they demonstrate any other form of presence here." The secretary of state, therefore, "did not have to provide [the organizations] with any particular process before designating them as foreign terrorist organizations." ∎

HUMAN SMUGGLING AND TRAFFICKING IN PERSONS

In February 2007, 34-year-old Juan Balderas-Orosco pleaded guilty in federal court in Austin, Texas, to smuggling women into the United States to work as prostitutes.[23] According to court documents, Balderas-Orosco and 11 associates illegally brought hundreds of women into the United States from Latin American countries and forced each of them to have sex with as many as 40 men a day. The women were moved among more than a dozen brothels in Texas and Oklahoma to keep them disoriented and to prevent them from making friends in the community who might help them.

According to the United Nations (UN),[24] human smuggling and trafficking in persons are two of the fastest-growing areas of international criminal activity today. There are important distinctions that must be made between these two forms of crime. Following federal law, the U.S. State Department defines **human smuggling** as "the facilitation, transportation, attempted transportation or illegal entry of a person(s) across an international border, in violation of one or more country's laws, either clandestinely or through deception, such as the use of fraudulent documents." In other words, *human smuggling* refers to illegal immigration in which an agent is paid to help a person cross a border clandestinely.[25] Human smuggling may be conducted to obtain financial or other benefits for the smuggler, although sometimes people engage in smuggling for other motives, such as to reunite their families.[26] Human smuggling generally occurs with the consent of those being smuggled, and they often pay a smuggler for his or her services. Once they've entered the country, they usually

human smuggling
Illegal immigration in which an agent is paid to help a person cross a national border clandestinely.

have no further contact with the smuggler. The State Department notes that the vast majority of people who are assisted in illegally entering the United States are smuggled rather than trafficked.

Although smuggling might not involve active coercion, it can be deadly. In January 2007, for example, truck driver Tyrone Williams, 36, a Jamaican citizen living in Schenectady, New York, was sentenced to life in prison for causing the deaths of 19 illegal immigrants in the nation's deadliest known human-smuggling attempt.[27] Williams locked more than 70 immigrants in a container truck during a 2003 trip from South Texas to Houston but abandoned the truck about 100 miles from its destination. The victims died from dehydration, overheating, and suffocation in the Texas heat before the truck was discovered and its doors opened.

In contrast to smuggling, **trafficking in persons (TIP)** can be compared to a modern-day form of slavery, prompting former Secretary of State Condoleezza Rice to say that "defeating human trafficking is a great moral calling of our day."[28] Trafficking involves the exploitation of unwilling or unwitting people through force, coercion, threat, or deception; it includes human rights abuses such as debt bondage, deprivation of liberty, or lack of control over freedom and labor. Trafficking is often undertaken for purposes of sexual or labor exploitation.

U.S. government officials estimate that 800,000 to 900,000 victims are trafficked globally each year and that 17,500 to 18,500 are trafficked into the United States.[29] Women and children comprise the largest group of victims, and they are often physically and emotionally abused. Although TIP is often an international crime that involves the crossing of borders, it is important to note that TIP victims can be trafficked within their own countries and communities. Traffickers can move victims between locations within the same country and often sell them to other trafficking organizations.

The International Labor Organization (ILO), the UN agency charged with addressing labor standards, employment, and social protection issues, estimates that there are 12.3 million people in forced labor, bonded labor, forced child labor, and sexual servitude throughout the world today.[30] Other estimates range as high as 27 million.[31] The status of legislation criminalizing trafficking in persons in various countries can be seen in Figure 12–4.

trafficking in persons (TIP)
The exploitation of unwilling or unwitting people through force, coercion, threat, or deception.

FIGURE 12–4

Criminalization of Trafficking in Persons— Status of National Legislation.

United National Office on Drugs and Crime, Global Report on Trafficking in Persons (UNODC, 2009), p. 9.

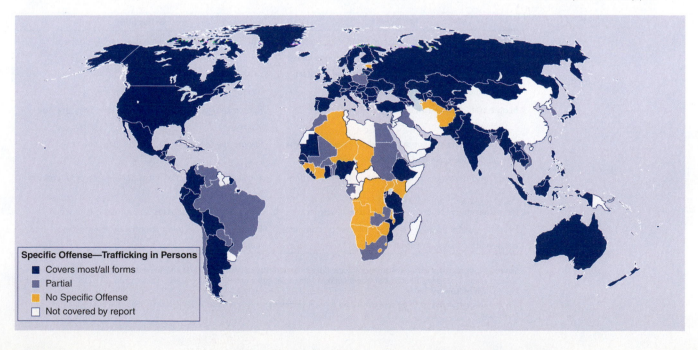

Specific Offense—Trafficking in Persons
- Covers most/all forms
- Partial
- No Specific Offense
- Not covered by report

Defeating human trafficking is a great moral calling and we will never subjugate it to the narrow demands of the day.

—Condoleezza Rice, former secretary of state

It is sometimes difficult to distinguish between a smuggling and a trafficking case because trafficking often includes an element of smuggling (that is, the illegal crossing of a national border). Moreover, some trafficking victims may believe they are being smuggled when they are really being trafficked but are unaware of their eventual fate. This happens, for example, when women trafficked for sexual exploitation believe they are agreeing to work in legitimate industries for decent wages—part of which they may agree to pay to the trafficker who smuggles them. They don't know that, upon arrival, the traffickers will keep them in bondage, subject them to physical force or sexual violence, force them to work in the sex trade, and take most or all of their earnings. UN literature notes that Chinese syndicates are notorious for continuing to control the lives of migrants at their destination, disciplining them by force, and extracting heavy payment for smuggling services—holding "their clients as virtual hostages until the fees have been paid."[32]

The U.S. Department of State's 2012 *Trafficking in Persons Report* says that "[t]he challenge facing all who work to end modern slavery is not just that of punishing traffickers and protecting those who are victimized by this crime, but of putting safeguards in place to ensure the freedom of future generations."[33] At the individual level, the report notes that human trafficking "is not abstract; it is about people. Every single occurrence of modern slavery is happening to a person—someone's sister, mother, brother, father, daughter, or son."[34]

The distinctions between smuggling and trafficking are sometimes very subtle, but key components that generally distinguish trafficking from smuggling are the elements of fraud, force, or coercion. However, under U.S. law, if the person is under 18 and induced to perform a commercial sex act, then it is considered trafficking, regardless of whether fraud, force, or coercion was involved. Table 12–4 provides a guide that distinguishes human trafficking from smuggling.

According to the UN, human smuggling and trafficking have become a worldwide industry that "employs" millions of people and leads to the annual turnover of billions of

TABLE 12–4 Distinguishing between Human Trafficking and Smuggling

Trafficking	Smuggling
Must contain an element of force, fraud, or coercion (actual, perceived, or implied), unless person is under 18 years of age and involved in commercial sex acts.	The person being smuggled is generally cooperating.
Forced labor and/or exploitation.	No forced labor or other exploitation.
People trafficked are victims.	People smuggled are violating the law. They are not victims.
People are enslaved, are subjected to limited movement or isolation, or have had documents confiscated.	People are free to leave, change jobs, etc.
Need not involve the actual movement of the victims.	Facilitates the illegal entry of people from one country into another.
No requirement to cross an international border.	Smuggling always crosses an international border.
Person must be involved in labor/services or commercial sex acts (that is, must be "working").	Person must only be in country or attempting to enter illegally.

Source: Adapted from U.S. Department of State, Bureau for International Narcotics and Law Enforcement Affairs, Human Smuggling and Trafficking Center. *Distinctions between Human Smuggling and Human Trafficking* (Washington, DC: U.S. Government Printing Office, January 2005).

Note: This chart is meant to be conceptual and is not intended to provide precise legal distinctions between smuggling and trafficking.

dollars.[35] The UN also notes that many of the routes used by smugglers have become well established and are widely known. For example, routes from Mexico and Central America to the United States, from West Asia through Greece and Turkey to Western Europe, and within East and Southeast Asia are regularly traveled. More often than not, the UN says, the ongoing existence of flourishing smuggling routes is facilitated by weak legislation, lax border controls, corrupt officials, and the power and influence of organized crime.

Although there are significant differences between TIP and human smuggling, the underlying conditions that give rise to both of these illegal activities are often similar. Extreme poverty, lack of economic opportunity, civil unrest, and political uncertainty are all factors that contribute to social environments in which TIP and human smuggling occur.

> *[F]or those of us who are in [a] position to do something to combat human slavery, however small our contribution, neutrality is a sin.*
>
> —Joseph E. Schmitz, former inspector general of the Department of Defense

FEDERAL IMMIGRATION AND TRAFFICKING LEGISLATION

The United States had what were essentially open national borders until the 1880s, when limited federal controls on immigration began. One of the nation's first immigration laws was the Chinese Exclusion Act, which became law in 1882 and was enforced for ten years. The law was enacted in response to the large numbers of mostly male Chinese laborers who had immigrated to the western United States in the mid-1800s looking for work and who often took jobs on the railroads and in the mining industry.

One of the first comprehensive pieces of federal immigration legislation was the 1924 Immigration Act. It limited the number of immigrants who could be admitted from any one country to 2% of the number of people from that country who were already living in the United States. Quotas were calculated using the Census of 1890. The law also barred immigration from specific parts of the Asia-Pacific Triangle, which included Japan, China, the Philippines, Laos, Thailand, Cambodia, and Korea.

The Immigration and Nationality Act (INA) of 1952 established the Immigration and Naturalization Service (INS) and continued numerical quotas.[36] The INA provided criminal penalties for anyone bringing or attempting to bring unauthorized aliens into the United States. Thirteen years later, the Immigration and Nationality Act amendments of 1965 abolished national-origin quotas.[37]

Recognizing human smuggling and TIP as serious social issues, Congress passed the Trafficking Victims Protection Act (TVPA) on October 28, 2000.[38] The TVPA is a comprehensive statute that addresses the significant problem of trafficking of persons for the purpose of subjecting them to commercial sex acts or forced labor. The legislation also increases the protections afforded to victims of trafficking.

The TVPA defines *severe forms of trafficking* as: "a.) **sex trafficking** in which a commercial sex act is induced by force, fraud, or coercion, or in which the person induced to perform such an act has not attained 18 years of age; or b.) the recruitment, harboring, transportation, provision, or obtaining of a person for labor or services, through the use of force, fraud, or coercion for the purpose of subjection to involuntary servitude, peonage, debt bondage, or slavery."[39]

sex trafficking
The recruitment, harboring, transportation, provision, or obtaining of a person for the purpose of a commercial sex act.

Under the TVPA, human trafficking does not require the crossing of an international border, nor does it even require the transportation of victims from one locale to another. That's because victims of severe forms of trafficking are not always illegal aliens; they may be U.S. citizens, legal residents, or visitors. Victims do not have to be women or children; they may also be adult males.

The Homeland Security Act (HSA) of 2002 dissolved the INS and transferred most of its functions to the Department of Homeland Security (DHS). Three DHS branches exist today in place of the INS: (1) Citizenship and Immigration Services (CIS), (2) Customs and Border Protection (CBP), and (3) Immigration and Customs Enforcement (ICE).

The Trafficking Victims Protection Reauthorization Act (TVPRA) of 2003 added a new initiative to the original law to collect foreign data on trafficking investigations, prosecutions, convictions, and sentences. The most recent data show that in 2006, reporting jurisdictions prosecuted 5,808 persons for trafficking-related offenses and secured 3,160 convictions.[40] The number of reported foreign prosecutions is the lowest since reporting began in 2003.

Finally, Section 7202 of the Intelligence Reform and Terrorism Prevention Act of 2004 established the Human Smuggling and Trafficking Center within the U.S. State Department. The secretary of state, the secretary of homeland security, the attorney general, and members of the national intelligence community oversee the center. The center was created to achieve greater integration and overall effectiveness in the U.S. government's enforcement of issues related to human smuggling, trafficking in persons, and criminal support of clandestine terrorist travel.

SUMMARY

- The crime of terrorism is defined in various ways, but the core elements are the commission of a traditional crime with the intent to coerce a population or influence a government through fear or intimidation.

- The related crime of sedition involves the act of planning or attempting to cause insurrection against a government. America's early sedition laws would not survive First Amendment review today because they focused on speech rather than conduct.

- The crime of treason is levying war against, or providing support for the enemies of, one's own nation. Treason is the only crime mentioned in the U.S. Constitution, which requires two witnesses to the same act to prove the crime.

- The USA PATRIOT Act and other post–September 11 antiterrorism laws are posing new constitutional questions that are not easily answered. These laws do not fit easily into the criminal justice model or the war laws model. Instead, a hybrid model is beginning to emerge.

- Recent court cases have established the right of suspected terrorist detainees to have their detentions reviewed. Traditional combatants of war possess no such right. However, the detainees possess few of the constitutional rights of traditional criminal defendants.

- Federal law defines human smuggling as "the facilitation, transportation, attempted transportation or illegal entry of a person(s) across an international border, in violation of one or more country's laws, either clandestinely or through deception, such as the use of fraudulent documents." Human smuggling generally occurs with the consent of those being smuggled.

- In contrast to smuggling, trafficking in persons involves the exploitation of unwilling or unwitting people through force, coercion, threat, or deception and includes human rights abuses, such as debt bondage, deprivation of liberty, or lack of control over freedom and labor.

KEY TERMS

foreign intelligence
surveillance act
of 1978 (FISA), 407

habeas corpus, 407

human smuggling, 414

sex trafficking, 417

terrorism, 402

trafficking in persons
(TIP), 415

treason, 403

USA PATRIOT Act, 407

QUESTIONS FOR DISCUSSION

1. What are the elements of the crimes of terrorism, sedition, and treason?

2. What does the U.S. Constitution require in treason cases?

3. Should suspected terrorists be treated as combatants in a war, as traditional criminal defendants, or otherwise?

4. Why does terrorism confound the existing constitutional models?

5. Do citizen detainees of the United States in the current "war on terror" have a right to have their detentions reviewed? If so, by whom? Do noncitizen detainees possess the same rights?

6. Explain the difference between human smuggling and trafficking in persons. Which one is more likely to involve threat or coercion?

CRITICAL THINKING AND APPLICATION PROBLEMS

1. Modern terrorism confounds the historic legal distinction between crimes and war. Do you believe the current war on terrorism should be governed by the rules of criminal law or by the rules of war? Explain your answer.

2. Roxy Consuelo persuaded a group of young Filipino women to move to Oceanella, a small island nation in the South Pacific Ocean. Charismatic and well spoken, Roxy promised the women well paying jobs, homes, and the prospect of continuing their education. She told them the only obstacle to their success in Oceanella was immigration law, which didn't permit them to move to Oceanella. But she told them it was easy, safe, and common for immigrants to enter Oceanella illegally, to live good lives, and to eventually qualify for legal status. Kim Kalaw, nineteen years old, was one of the women convinced to move. After difficult travel, Kim and fourteen other women arrived at Oceanella early in the morning by boat. The fifteen girls were rushed, under cover of darkness, to a factory where a business partner of Roxy had agreed to receive the women. However, the factory was boarded-up and the partner was not to be found. Roxy called the partner and learned that his factory had been closed by the police the day before and that the partner was a fugitive from justice. He suggested that Roxy contact "Rusty," whose business was only a block away. He said that, even though Roxy didn't know him, she "could trust Rusty." Roxy called him, negotiated a price of $5,000 U.S. per woman, delivered the women into Rusty's care, and returned to Asia. Rusty told the women that they were not allowed to leave his compound, lest they would be arrested by Oceanella police and jailed for violating immigration law. He told them that they were expected to work to pay for their room and board. Over a period of two weeks he visited each woman at night, coercing each, under threat of turning them into the police or onto the streets, into having sex with him. Over months he coerced each girl into prostitution, serving as many as twenty men per day. One year after their arrival Kim escaped the compound, found a police officer, and reported what had happened. The police arrested Roxy and Rusty

and the High Prosecutor of Oceanella has charged both with trafficking in persons and human smuggling. Using the basic elements of those crimes you learned in this chapter, discuss whether the two defendants are each guilty of neither, one, or both of the charged offenses. Explain your answers.

LEGAL RESOURCES ON THE WEB

Many antiterrorism websites are accessible through the Internet. The following are among the best:

Antiterrorism.org
http://www.antiterrorism.org/main.html
Part of the International Association of Counterterrorism and Security Professionals security websites group, this website includes the association's bookstore and company resources.

Belfer Center for Science and International Affairs (BCSIA)
http://belfercenter.ksg.harvard.edu/
BCSIA offers research, education, and training related to international security affairs, environmental and resource issues, and science and technology policy. Recognizing that science and technology are the driving forces behind threats and opportunities in international affairs, BCSIA integrates insights from social and natural scientists, technologists, and practitioners with experience in government, diplomacy, the military, and business to address critical issues.

International Relations and Security Network
http://www.isn.ethz.ch/isn
The International Relations and Security Network (ISN) is one of the world's leading open-access information services for international relations (IR) and security professionals.

Center for Defense Information (CDI)
http://www.cdi.org/program/index.cfm?programid=39
CDI's Terrorism Program examines "all aspects of fighting terrorism, from near-term issues of response and defense to long-term questions about how the United States should shape its future international security strategy." Research topics include conventional arms, defense and foreign policy, international peacekeeping, military forces and strategy, and nuclear issues.

CIA and the War on Terrorism
https://www.cia.gov/news-information/cia-the-war-on-terrorism/index.html
This website offers historical reports and analysis of the fight against terrorism and the Central Intelligence Agency's role in that effort.

Institute for the Study of Violent Groups (ISVG)
http://www.isvg.org/
The ISVG is a federally funded terrorism research center. It performs open-source collection, exploitation, and analysis on terrorist, extremist, and transnational criminal threats.

James Martin Center for Nonproliferation Studies (CNS)
http://cns.miis.edu/pubs/terror.htm
CNS combats the spread of weapons of mass destruction through research activities and information dissemination. CNS materials on terrorism include historical backgrounds and chronologies, legislation and testimony, and relevant publications.

Ready.gov
http://www.ready.gov/
One of the primary mandates of the U.S. Department of Homeland Security is to educate the public about how to be prepared in case of a national emergency—including a possible

terrorist attack. This accessible website offers checklists, plans, brochures, and videos on emergency readiness for families and businesses.

Terrorism Research Center

http://www.terrorism.com

The Terrorism Research Center offers many online resources dealing with terrorism, terrorist organizations, and antiterrorism efforts.

U.S. Department of State: Travel Warnings and Consular Information

http://travel.state.gov/travel/cis_pa_tw/cis_pa_tw_1168.html

Available at this site are updated advisories for those considering foreign travel.

U.S. Government Counterterrorism Publications

http://www.counterterrorismtraining.gov/pubs/index.html

Offered here are publications designed "to help law enforcement decision makers and other first responders develop agency policies, programs, and trainings. Organized by topic, these publications come from government, nonprofit, and private sources and address emerging counter-terrorism issues, research findings and statistics, policy and program development, and technical assistance and skill-building."

SUGGESTED READINGS AND CLASSIC WORKS

Advisory Panel to Assess Domestic Response Capabilities for Terrorism Involving Weapons of Mass Destruction. *First Annual Report to the President and Congress*. Santa Monica, CA: RAND, 1999, http://www.rand.org/organization/nsrd/terrpanel.

———. *Second Annual Report to the President and Congress*. Santa Monica, CA: RAND, 2000, http://www.rand.org/organization/nsrd/terrpanel.

———. *Third Annual Report to the President and Congress*. Santa Monica, CA: RAND, 2001, http://www.rand.org/organization/nsrd/terrpanel.

Brian Michael Jenkins, *New Challenges to U.S. Counterterrorism Efforts: An Assessment of the Current Terrorist Threat–Testimony Presented before the Senate Homeland Security and Governmental Affairs Committee on July 11, 2012* (Santa Monica, CA: RAND, July 2012), http://www.rand.org/pubs/testimonies/CT377.html.

National Commission on Terrorism. *Countering the Changing Threat of International Terrorism*. Washington, DC: National Commission on Terrorism, 1999.

National Commission on Terrorist Attacks upon the United States (9/11 Commission). *Final Report*. Washington, DC: 9/11 Commission, 2004, http://media.pearsoncmg.com/ph/chet/chet_criminal_justice_1/assets/schmalleger/911_Report.pdf.

National Strategy for Combating Terrorism. Washington, DC: White House, 2006.

U.S. Commission on National Security in the Twenty-first Century. *The Phase I Report: New World Coming—American Security in the Twenty-first Century*. Washington, DC: U.S. Commission on National Security in the Twenty-first Century, 1999.

———. *The Phase II Report: Seeking a National Strategy—A Concert for Preserving Security and Promoting Freedom*. Washington, DC: U.S. Commission on National Security in the Twenty-first Century, 2000.

———. *The Phase III Report: Roadmap for National Security*. Washington, DC: U.S. Commission on National Security in the Twenty-first Century, 2001.

U.S. Department of State. *Trafficking in Persons Report, 2012*. Washington, DC: U.S. Department of State, 2012, http://www.state.gov/g/tip/rls/tiprpt/2012.

NOTES

1. Belasco, A., "The Cost of Iraq, Afghanistan, and Other Global War on Terror Operations since 9/11." Congressional Research Service, March 29, 2011, http://www.fas.org/sgp/crs/natsec/RL33110.pdf.

2. U.S. Code, Title 18, Section 2381.

3. 70 Am. Jur. 2d 70.

4. U.S. Code, Title 18, Section 2384.

5. U.S. Code, Title 18, Section 792 et seq.; and U.S. Code, Title 50, Section 783.

6. U.S. Code, Title 50, Section 36.

7. U.S. Code, Title 8, Section 101 et seq.

8. U.S. Code, Title 18, Section 2384.

9. U.S. Code, Title 18, Section 2389.

10. U.S. Code, Title 18, Section 2381.

11. U.S. Code, Title 6, Section 101.

12. *The Current Detainee Population at Guantanamo: An Empirical Study* (Washington, DC: Brookings Institution, 2008), http://www.brookings.edu/reports/2008/1216_detainees_wittes.aspx (accessed March 2009).

13. Peter Berkowitz, ed., *Terrorism, the Laws of War, and the Constitution* (Stanford, CA: Hoover Institution Press, 2005), ix, x.

14. *Zadvydas v. Davis*, 533 U.S. 678, 696 (2001).

15. *Hamdi v. Rumsfeld*, 542 U.S. 507 (2004).

16. *Rasul v. Bush*, 542 U.S. 466 (2004).

17. The New York Times, Times Topics, Lakhdar Boumediene, May 25, 2012. http://topics.nytimes.com/top/reference/timestopics/people/b/lakhdar_boumediene/index.html.

18. U.S. Code, Title 42, Section 21D.

19. *Hamdan v. Rumsfeld*, 548 U.S. 557 (2006).

20. U.S. Code, Title 10, Section 948.

21. *Boumediene v. Bush*, 553 U.S. 723 (2008)

22. *Doe v. Mukasey*, 549 F.3d 861 (2d Cir. 2008).

23. Details for this story come from "Man Pleads Guilty to Smuggling Women for Prostitution in Brothel Ring," Associated Press, February 10, 2007, http://www.usatoday.com/news/nation/2007-02-10-immigrant-brothel_x.htm (accessed May 20, 2009).

24. Bureau for International Narcotics and Law Enforcement Affairs, Human Smuggling and Trafficking Center, *Distinctions between Human Smuggling and Human Trafficking* (Washington, DC: Human Smuggling and Trafficking Center, January 1, 2005).

25. Raimo Väyrynen, "Illegal Immigration, Human Trafficking, and Organized Crime," United Nations University/World Institute for Development Economics Research, discussion paper no. 2003/72 (October 2003), 16.

26. Much of the material in this section is adapted from Frank Schmalleger, *Criminology Today: An Integrative Introduction* (Upper Saddle River, NJ: Prentice Hall, 2009), 620–623.

27. Details for this story come from "Immigrant Smuggler Faulted in 19 Deaths Sentenced to Life in Prison," Associated Press, January 18, 2007, http://www.usatoday.com/news/nation/2007-01-18-smuggler_x.htm (accessed May 20, 2009).

28. Office of the Under Secretary for Democracy and Global Affairs, *Trafficking in Persons Report* (Washington, DC: U.S. Department of State, June 2007).

29. Ibid., 8.

30. Ibid.

31. Ibid.

32. Bureau for International Narcotics and Law Enforcement Affairs, *Distinctions between Human Smuggling and Human Trafficking*, 16.

33. Office of the Under Secretary for Democracy and Global Affairs, *Trafficking in Persons Report, 2012* (Washington, DC: U.S. Department of State, 2012), 7.

34. Ibid., p. 10.

35. United Nations Office on Drugs and Crime, *Global Report on Trafficking in Persons* (New York: UNODC:, 2009), 5.

36. U.S. Code, Title 8, Section 1324.

37. Public Law 89-236.

38. Trafficking Victims Protection Act of 2000, Div. A of Public Law 106-386, Section 108, as amended.

39. Office of the Under Secretary for Democracy and Global Affairs, *Trafficking in Persons Report*, 7.

40. Ibid., 36.

© Paul Doyle/Alamy

13

Victims and the Law

CHAPTER OUTLINE

Introduction

Who Is a Victim?

A Short History of the Victim

Victims' Rights Legislation

The Growth of Victims' Rights

Victim Statistics

Restitution

OBJECTIVES

After reading this chapter, you should be able to

- Define *victim*.
- Explain how the status of victims has changed over time.
- Summarize victims' rights and services.
- Summarize the impact that a victims' rights amendment to the U.S. Constitution might have on the American justice system.
- Describe how victim impact statements are used.

Justice, though due to the accused, is due to the accuser also.

—Justice Benjamin Cardozo, Snyder v. Massachusetts, 291 U.S. 97, 122 (1934)

Let victim rights ring across America.

—National Organization for Victim Assistance[1]

No more essential duty of government exists than the protection of the lives of its people. Fail in this, and we fail in everything.

—Harper's magazine (July 1984)

INTRODUCTION

Around 9:45 a.m. on August 24, 2000, an intruder broke into the Merced, California, home of John and Stephanie Carpenter.[2] At home were the couple's five children: Anna, 13; Vanessa, 11; Jessica Lynne, 14; Ashley, 9; and John William, 8. The parents were out of the house—the father at work; the mother running errands.

The intruder, 27-year-old Jonathon David Bruce, was a stranger to the family but had a hatred of children. Bruce picked up a short-handled spading fork from the family garden, entered the house naked, and surprised the children, attacking them as they slept or watched television. Before the attack ended, John William and Ashley were dead. More than 100 stab wounds covered Ashley's body, while John William died from more than 40 wounds. The older children managed to flee, running to a neighbor's house to call 911. "Somebody's in my house that I don't know; they're stabbing my brother and sister with a pitchfork," 14-year-old Jessica Lynne Carpenter cried to an emergency dispatcher moments after escaping the attack with her two sisters. "I don't know who it is. I just woke up and he was in the house."[3] When police arrived, Bruce was sprayed with mace but still charged at officers with the spading fork. He was shot 13 times and died at the scene.

The attack on the Carpenter children, a senseless tragedy, serves as a reminder that no one is safe from crime. Nonetheless, John William and Ashley Carpenter were unusual victims of violent crimes. They were children from a middle-class family who died at the hands of a stranger. Surveys of crime victims, such as the **National Crime Victimization Survey (NCVS)**, which will be discussed later in this chapter, show that males, the poor, members of racial minorities, and young adults are more likely to be victimized than are others.

Before we can meaningfully discuss victims' issues or crime statistics, it is necessary to clarify the term *victim*.

national crime victimization survey (NCVS)
A survey, conducted annually by the Bureau of Justice Statistics, that provides data on households that report having been affected by crime.

WHO IS A VICTIM?

The concept of a victim is foreign to civil law, which speaks instead in terms of people who have been injured or wronged. The word *victim* denotes someone who has been harmed through the kind of activity proscribed by the criminal law.[4]

Although everyone has an intuitive appreciation of what it means to be a victim, the term *crime victim* can be more formally defined. The Violent Crime Control and Law Enforcement Act of 1994, for example, says that the word **victim** means "any individual against whom an offense has been committed."[5] For certain purposes, however, federal law expands the term to include "a parent or legal guardian if the victim is below the age of eighteen years or incompetent" and "one or more family members or relatives designated by the court if the victim is deceased or incapacitated."

A federal Bureau of Prisons (BOP) policy directive defines the term *victim* as "someone who suffers direct or threatened physical, emotional, or financial harm as the result of the commission of a crime." According to the BOP, "the term 'victim' also includes the immediate family of a minor or homicide victim."[6] An even more elaborate definition of the term *victim* is found in Alaskan law.

victim
"[A]ny individual against whom an offense has been committed," or for certain procedural purposes, "a parent or legal guardian if the victim is below the age of eighteen years or incompetent" or "one or more family members or relatives designated by the court if the victim is deceased or incapacitated."[i]

ALASKA STATUTES

Section 12.55.185. In this chapter, unless the context requires otherwise, "victim" means:

(a) a person against whom an offense has been perpetrated;

(b) one of the following, not the perpetrator, if the person specified in (A) of this paragraph is a minor, incompetent, or incapacitated:

(i) An individual living in a spousal relationship with the person specified in (A) of this paragraph; or

(ii) A parent, adult child, guardian, or custodian of the person;

(c) one of the following, not the perpetrator, if the person specified in (A) of this paragraph is dead:

(i) A person living in a spousal relationship with the deceased before the deceased died;

(ii) An adult child, parent, brother, sister, grandparent, or grandchild of the deceased; or

(iii) Any other interested person, as may be designated by a person having authority in law to do so.

A SHORT HISTORY OF THE VICTIM

Throughout much of early human history, victims had few, if any, "official" support mechanisms. Nonetheless, early social norms generally supported the actions of victims who, before the emergence of organized law enforcement and formal judicial systems, were able to exact revenge on those who had victimized them. Such early victims typically sought the support of friends and family members in hunting down and punishing the perpetrator. Moreover, early tribal codes generally required victims' families to care for the needs of victims or their survivors. This early period in history, during which victims took an active role in determining the fate of offenders and during which the care of victims was socially mandated, has been termed the **Golden Age of the Victim**. The Golden Age lent a sense of closure to the victimization experience and had the effect of making victims feel "whole again" (Figure 13–1).

golden age of the victim
A historical epoch during which victims had well-recognized rights, including a personal say in imposing punishments on apprehended offenders.

Eventually, however, crimes came to be seen as offenses against society, and the needs of the victim were largely forgotten. By the late Middle Ages in England, the concept of the king's peace had emerged, under which all offenses were seen as violations of laws decreed by the monarch. Under the king's peace, it became the duty of local officials, including sheriffs and constables, to apprehend offenders and to arrange for their trial and punishment. As a consequence, victims were effectively removed from any direct involvement in deciding the

FIGURE 13–1

Eras of Victims' Rights.

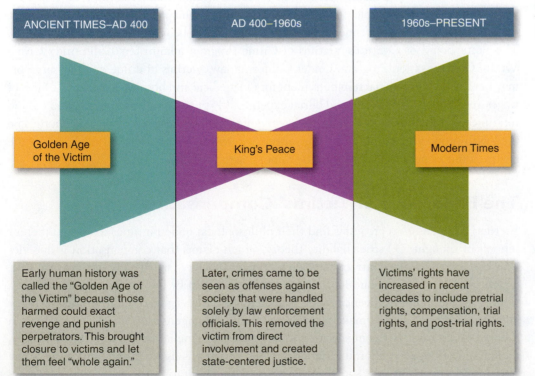

ANCIENT TIMES–AD 400	AD 400–1960s	1960s–PRESENT
Golden Age of the Victim	King's Peace	Modern Times
Early human history was called the "Golden Age of the Victim" because those harmed could exact revenge and punish perpetrators. This brought closure to victims and let them feel "whole again."	Later, crimes came to be seen as offenses against society that were handled solely by law enforcement officials. This removed the victim from direct involvement and created state-centered justice.	Victims' rights have increased in recent decades to include pretrial rights, compensation, trial rights, and post-trial rights.

The mugger who is arrested is back on the street before the police officer; but the person mugged may not be back on the street for a long time, if ever.

—*Mario Cuomo (April 1985)*

offender's fate. From that point onward in the Western legal tradition, victims were expected only to provide evidence of a crime and to testify against those who had offended them. Society's moral responsibility toward making victims "whole again" was largely forgotten, and victims as a class were moved to the periphery of the justice process. Victim-centered justice had been transformed into state-centered justice, under which the victim played a mere token role as the personal target of criminal activity.

The situation remained relatively unchanged until the 1960s, when a renewed interest in victims led to a resurgence of efforts meant to assist them. Popular sentiments were soon translated into a flurry of laws designed to provide compensation to victims of violent crimes. The first modern victims' compensation statute was adopted by New Zealand in 1963. Known as the Criminal Injuries Compensation Act, it provided a mechanism for claims to be filed by victims of certain specified violent crimes. Under the law, a three-member government board was created with the authority to make awards to victims. A year later, partially in response to a movement led by victims' rights advocate Margaret Fry, Great Britain passed a similar law. In 1965, California passed the first American legislation intended to assist victims of crime. About the same time, the New York city council passed a "good Samaritan" statute designed to pay up to $4,000 to anyone suffering physical injury while going to the aid of a crime victim. Many states then joined the victims' compensation bandwagon, and today all 50 states and the District of Columbia have passed legislation providing for monetary payments to crime victims—although legislatures have rarely funded programs at levels that would pay all requests.

Modern state victims' compensation programs require applicants to meet certain eligibility requirements, and most set award maximums. A number of states set minimum loss limits (similar to an insurance policy's deductible) and have established a "needs test" whereby only financially needy crime victims are eligible for compensation. Likewise, some states deny awards to family members of the offender, as in the case in which a son assaults a father. All states provide for the possibility of payment for medical assistance, lost wages, and living expenses. However, victims who are responsible in some significant way for their own victimization are generally not eligible for reimbursement under existing laws.

In California, for example, qualifying victims of crime may receive financial assistance for losses resulting from a crime when those losses cannot be reimbursed by other sources. The State Board of Control's Victims of Crime Program administers California's Crime Victim Compensation Program. Under California law, victims of crime or their survivors may be eligible for financial reimbursement for (1) medical and hospital expenses, (2) loss of wages and support, (3) funeral and burial expenses, (4) professional counseling, and (5) job retraining or rehabilitation. California law requires that applications from adult victims be filed within one year of the date of the crime, whereas applications resulting from a crime against a minor must be filed before the minor's 19th birthday.

The Philosophy of Victims' Compensation

Victims' compensation programs find their philosophical underpinnings in seven different schools of thought: (1) strict liability theory, which claims that compensation is due victims because the social contract between victim and society (specifically, the government, which has a duty to safeguard its citizens) has been broken by the experience of victimization; (2) government negligence theory, which holds that the government was negligent for allowing harm and should make appropriate forms of compensation; (3) equal protection theory, which says that compensation should serve to ameliorate imbalances in society, including the huge variation in crime risk faced by citizens living in different parts of the nation and under different social conditions; (4) humanitarian theory, which advocates compensation because of the suffering victims undergo; (5) social welfare theory, which says that victims should be compensated if they are in need; (6) crime-prevention theory, which holds that compensation programs encourage more citizens to report crime, thereby resulting in more effective law enforcement programs; and (7) political motives theory, which says that victims' compensation is in vogue with the voting public and that any politician who seeks public office must inevitably support the concept.[7]

Victims' Assistance Programs Today

Victims experience many hardships extending beyond their original victimization, including the trauma of testifying, uncertainty about their role in the justice process, lost time at work, trial delays, fear of retaliation by the defendant, and a general lack of knowledge about what is expected of them as the wheels of justice grind forward (Figure 13–2). Problems that follow from initial victimization are referred to as **postcrime victimization**, or *secondary victimization*. The insensitivity of police, employers, and family members can exacerbate the difficulties crime victims face. Even hospitals that charge high fees for medical records and social service agencies that swamp applicants in a plethora of forms can contribute to the victim's sense of continuing victimization.

In recent years, numerous victims' assistance programs, designed to provide comfort and help to victims of crime, have developed across the nation. The earliest of these programs began as grassroots movements designed to counsel victims of rape. In 1975, a national survey identified only 23 victims' assistance programs in the United States.[8] By 1986, the number had grown to more than 600, and estimates today place the number of such programs at more than 1,000. Some authors have drawn a distinction between victim-service programs, which emphasize therapeutic counseling, and **victim-assistance programs**, which provide a wide array of services.

Most victim-/witness-assistance programs are small and are staffed by local volunteers. They typically counsel victims and witnesses, orient them to the justice process, and provide a variety of other services, such as transportation to court, child care during court appearances, and referrals to social service agencies when additional assistance is needed. A survey found that most such organizations explain the court process to victims (71.2% of all organizations surveyed), make referrals to other agencies (68.4%), provide court escorts (65.2%), help victims complete victims' compensation forms (64.1%), attempt to educate

postcrime victimization
Problems for the victim that follow from an initial victimization, such as loss of employment, inability to pay medical bills, and insensitivity of family members. Also called *secondary victimization*.

victim-assistance program
A service organization that works to provide comfort and assistance to victims of crime and to witnesses.

FIGURE 13–2

The Aftermath of a Criminal Offense for the Victim.

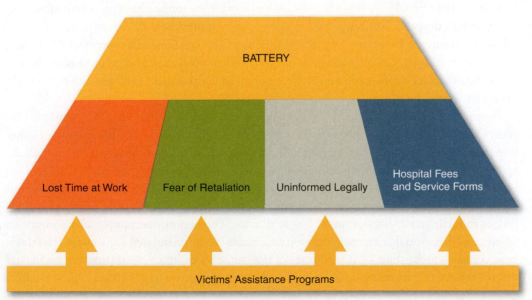

BATTERY

Lost Time at Work | Fear of Retaliation | Uninformed Legally | Hospital Fees and Service Forms

Victims' Assistance Programs

the public about the needs of victims (60.9%), advocate with employers on behalf of victims (60.3%), and provide transportation to court (59.2%).[9]

Victims' assistance programs in California are eligible to receive funding through the Office of Criminal Justice Planning from the state's Victim-Witness Assistance Fund if they provide *all* of the following services: (1) crisis intervention; (2) emergency assistance (that is, directly or indirectly providing food, housing, clothing, and, when necessary, cash); (3) resource and referral counseling to agencies within the community that are appropriate to meet the victim's needs; (4) direct counseling of the victim on problems resulting from the crime; (5) assistance in the processing, filing, and verifying of claims filed by victims; (6) assistance in obtaining the return of a victim's property held as evidence by law enforcement agencies; (7) orientation to the criminal justice system; (8) court escort; (9) presentations to and training of criminal justice system agencies; (10) public presentations and publicity; (11) the monitoring of appropriate court cases to keep victims and witnesses apprised of the progress and outcome of their case; (12) notification to friends, relatives, and employers of the occurrence of the crime and the victim's condition, upon request of the victim; (13) notification to the employer of the victim or witness, if requested by the victim or witness, informing the employer that the employee was a victim of, or witness to, a crime and asking the employer to minimize any loss of pay or other benefits that may result because of the crime or the employee's participation in the criminal justice system; and (14) upon request of the victim, assisting in obtaining restitution for the victim, in ascertaining the victim's economic loss, and in providing the probation department, district attorney, and court with information relevant to his or her losses prior to the imposition of sentence.[10]

To meet California's nondiscrimination guidelines, victims' assistance programs that receive state funding must also provide (1) translation services for non-English-speaking or hearing-impaired victims and witnesses; (2) follow-up contact to determine whether clients received the necessary assistance; (3) field visits to a client's home, place of business, or other location, whenever necessary to provide services; (4) service to victims and witnesses of all types of crime; (5) volunteer participation to encourage community involvement; and (6) services for elderly victims of crime, appropriate to their special needs.

Two large nonprofit public groups that serve the needs of victims on a national scale are the National Organization for Victim Assistance (NOVA) and the National Center for Victims of Crime (NCVC). Both are located in the Washington, D.C., area and provide leadership in victim education, lobby Congress, and hold conferences and workshops designed to assist local victim-/witness-assistance programs.

Founded in 1975, NOVA is a private umbrella organization working on behalf of victims of crime and disaster. NOVA is guided by four official purposes: (1) to serve as a national advocate in support of victims' rights and services, (2) to provide direct services to victims, (3) to be an educational resource providing support to victim-assistance professionals, and (4) to be of service to its members. NOVA's avowed central focus is to educate policymakers about victims' rights.[11]

Begun in December 1985, the NCVC has as its mission (1) to serve as a national resource center for victims and their advocates; (2) to establish training programs and other self-help opportunities to help victims and their advocates deal effectively with the judicial system, understand victims' rights, seek reparation, and cope with grief; and (3) to encourage and promote research concerning victims of violent crime through the establishment of a national databank and resource library.[12] The NCVC is a nonprofit organization with offices in Arlington, Virginia, and New York City. The center maintains a comprehensive library and a national computer database collection of victim-related legislation. The database contains more than 27,000 statutes of relevance to violence, victimization, and other victim-related criminal justice issues in all 50 states and at the federal level.

VICTIMS' RIGHTS LEGISLATION

Legislative milestones in the American movement for **victims' rights** include the federal Victim and Witness Protection Act of 1982, which was enacted "to enhance and protect the necessary role of crime victims and witnesses in the criminal justice process." Other federal legislation of importance to victims includes the Victims of Crime Act of 1984, the Violence against Women Act of 1994 (part of the Violent Crime Control and Law Enforcement Act of 1994), the Victims' Rights and Restitution Act, the Child Victims' Bill of Rights of 1990, and the Crime Victims' Rights Act of 2004.

The 1984 Victims of Crime Act (VOCA) resulted from recommendations made in 1982 by the President's Task Force on Victims of Crime. VOCA established a federal crime victims' compensation fund, which provides payments for medical expenses attributable to a physical injury, loss of wages, and funeral expenses resulting from "a compensable crime." The fund is administered through the federal Office for Victims of Crime (OVC)—another VOCA product—which began operations in 1985. Since its beginnings, OVC has served as the federal government's focal point for all issues affecting crime victims across the nation. Today, OVC is one of five agencies within the U.S. Department of Justice's Office of Justice Programs. OVC offers a broad range of programs and activities designed to help crime victims cope with the personal and financial problems that result from victimization.

OVC also plays a pivotal leadership role in the victims' movement. The office supplements, reinforces, and encourages the expansion of state compensation and assistance programs throughout the country. OVC administers VOCA funding to all populations affected by victimization, including underserved populations, such as sexually exploited children and victims residing on remote Indian reservations. The office also awards grants to sponsor training and technical assistance on cutting-edge substantive issues of interest to victims' advocates as well as to criminal justice system personnel who regularly interact with victims. OVC's leadership role at the federal level encompasses activities designed to draw public attention to the needs of crime victims and to promote victims' rights through legislation and public policy.

OVC operates the Office for Victims of Crime Resource Center, a component of the National Criminal Justice Reference Service (NCJRS). The OVC Resource Center provides victim-related information on such issues as domestic violence, child abuse, elderly victims, bias-related violence, victims' rights, and victims' compensation to practitioners, policymakers, researchers, crime victims, and other interested parties. The resource center collects, maintains, and disseminates information about national, state, and local victim-related organizations and about state programs that receive funds authorized by VOCA.

The Violent Crime Control and Law Enforcement Act of 1994 contained significant victims' rights legislation. The act, which was the culmination of six years of bipartisan work in the U.S. Congress, was the largest crime bill in the nation's history. It provided funding for 100,000 new police officers, $9.7 billion in funding for prisons, and $6.1 billion in funding for prevention programs. The 1994 crime bill also provided $2.6 billion in additional funding for the Federal Bureau of Investigation (FBI), Drug Enforcement Administration, Immigration and Naturalization Service, U.S. attorneys, Treasury Department, and other Justice Department components, as well as the federal courts.

Some of the most significant victims' rights provisions of the Violent Crime Control and Law Enforcement Act of 1994 include the following: (1) the Violence against Women Act, which provides financial support for police, prosecutors, and victims' services in cases

victims' rights
The fundamental right of victims to be equitably represented throughout the criminal justice process.

right of allocution
A statutory provision permitting crime victims to speak at the sentencing of convicted offenders. A federal right of allocution was established for victims of federal violent and sex crimes under the Violent Crime Control and Law Enforcement Act of 1994.

involving sexual violence or domestic abuse; (2) a **right of allocution** provision, permitting victims of federal violent and sex crimes to speak at the sentencing of their assailants; (3) a requirement that federal sex offenders and child molesters pay restitution to their victims; (4) increased penalties for frauds perpetrated against older victims; and (5) additional money for the federal Crime Victims' Fund (established under the Victims of Crime Act of 1984) and the victim-support programs it funds.

The federal Crime Victims' Rights Act,[13] part of the Justice for All Act of 2004, has been described as "the most far-reaching victims' rights bill ever considered by the U.S. Congress."[14] It was signed into law by President George W. Bush on October 30, 2004. Relevant portions of the legislation follow.

CRIME VICTIMS' RIGHTS ACT

Section 3771. Crime victims' rights

(a) RIGHTS OF CRIME VICTIMS.—A crime victim has the following rights:

1. The right to be reasonably protected from the accused.
2. The right to reasonable, accurate, and timely notice of any public court proceeding, or any parole proceeding, involving the crime or of any release or escape of the accused.
3. The right not to be excluded from any such public court proceeding, unless the court, after receiving clear and convincing evidence, determines that testimony by the victim would be materially altered if the victim heard other testimony at that proceeding.
4. The right to be reasonably heard at any public proceeding in the district court involving release, plea, sentencing, or any parole proceeding.
5. The reasonable right to confer with the attorney for the Government in the case.
6. The right to full and timely restitution as provided in law.
7. The right to proceedings free from unreasonable delay.
8. The right to be treated with fairness and with respect for the victim's dignity and privacy.

(b) RIGHTS AFFORDED.—In any court proceeding involving an offense against a crime victim, the court shall ensure that the crime victim is afforded the rights described in subsection (a). Before making a determination described in subsection (a)(3), the court shall make every effort to permit the fullest attendance possible by the victim and shall consider reasonable alternatives to the exclusion of the victim from the criminal proceeding. The reasons for any decision denying relief under this chapter shall be clearly stated on the record.

(c) BEST EFFORTS TO ACCORD RIGHTS.

1. GOVERNMENT.—Officers and employees of the Department of Justice and other departments and agencies of the United States engaged in the detection, investigation, or prosecution of crime shall make their best efforts to see that crime victims are notified of, and accorded, the rights described in subsection (a).
2. ADVICE OF ATTORNEY.—The prosecutor shall advise the crime victim that the crime victim can seek the advice of an attorney with respect to the rights described in subsection (a).
3. NOTICE.—Notice of release otherwise required pursuant to this chapter shall not be given if such notice may endanger the safety of any person. . . .
4. LIMITATION ON RELIEF.—In no case shall a failure to afford a right under this chapter provide grounds for a new trial. . . .

DEFINITIONS.—For the purposes of this chapter, the term 'crime victim' means a person directly and proximately harmed as a result of the commission of a Federal offense or an offense in the District of Columbia. In the case of a crime victim who is under 18 years of age, incompetent, incapacitated, or deceased, the legal guardians of the crime victim or the representatives of the crime victim's estate, family members, or any other persons appointed as suitable by the court may assume the crime victim's rights under this chapter, but in no event shall the defendant be named as such guardian or representative.

THE GROWTH OF VICTIMS' RIGHTS

When the victims' movement began, the idea of legal rights for victims of crime was novel. At the time, victims' advocates built a platform of victims' rights on six principles:

- Victims and witnesses have a right to protection from intimidation and harm.
- Victims and witnesses have a right to be informed concerning the criminal justice process.
- Victims and witnesses have a right to reparations.
- Victims and witnesses have a right to preservation of property and employment.
- Victims and witnesses have a right to due process in criminal court proceedings.
- Victims and witnesses have a right to be treated with dignity and compassion.

The rights of victims have advanced considerably since the 1970s, and more than 30 states and the federal government have enacted legislation or have modified their constitutions in recognition of victims' rights. Some states have done both.

A key focus of victims' rights advocates today is the passage of a federal constitutional amendment.[15] One organization that is central to the push for such an amendment is the National Victims' Constitutional Amendment Passage (or NVCAP). NVCAP is supported in its efforts by 48 state attorneys general, the International Association of Chiefs of Police, the Fraternal Order of Police, the National Criminal Justice Association, the American Correctional Association, the American Probation and Parole Association, and other criminal justice–related organizations.[16]

Not everyone thinks a victims' rights amendment to the Constitution is a good idea. Elisabeth Semel, a San Diego attorney and a member of the National Association of Criminal Defense Lawyers, said of an earlier version of the resolution: "We have a constitutional system that is intended to be out of balance—that's what the presumption of innocence is all about. The proposed amendment would have an impact at a stage when someone merely is accused of a crime, not convicted of one."[17]

Son of Sam Laws

Notoriety-for-profit statutes, also called **Son of Sam laws**, provide additional support for the rights of victims. Notoriety-for-profit laws are intended to deny convicted offenders the opportunity to further capitalize on their crimes. The laws work by setting the stage for civil action against infamous offenders who might otherwise profit from the sale of their "story." A few state laws also target the sale of memorabilia associated with crimes. Most such laws hold potential profits in an escrow account, allowing victims or their survivors the time necessary to file suit (Figure 13–3).

In 1977, New York became the first state to enact a Son of Sam law.[18] The original New York statute was developed in response to efforts by convicted serial killer David Berkowitz to profit from the sale of his life's story. (Berkowitz took the name "Son of Sam" because of the way in which he "heard" instructions in his head telling him whom to kill.) The New York law required that publishers turn over proceeds of a convict's book to an escrow account for the benefits of any victim. The law defined *person convicted of a crime* to include "any person who has voluntarily and intelligently admitted the commission of a crime for which such person is not prosecuted."

Notoriety-for-profit laws exist today in 43 states and at the federal level. Generally, such statutes apply to any convicted felon and provide that when an offender enters into a contract to receive profits from the recounting of the crime—as in a book, movie, television show, or other depiction of the crime—all profits, which would otherwise be paid to the offender, must instead be held for the benefit of the offender's victims. In some cases, media

Son of Sam law
A statute that provides support for the rights of victims by denying convicted offenders the opportunity to further capitalize on their crimes. Son of Sam laws set the stage for civil action against infamous offenders who might otherwise profit from the sale of their story. Also called *notoriety-for-profit law.*

FIGURE 13–3
Son of Sam Laws.

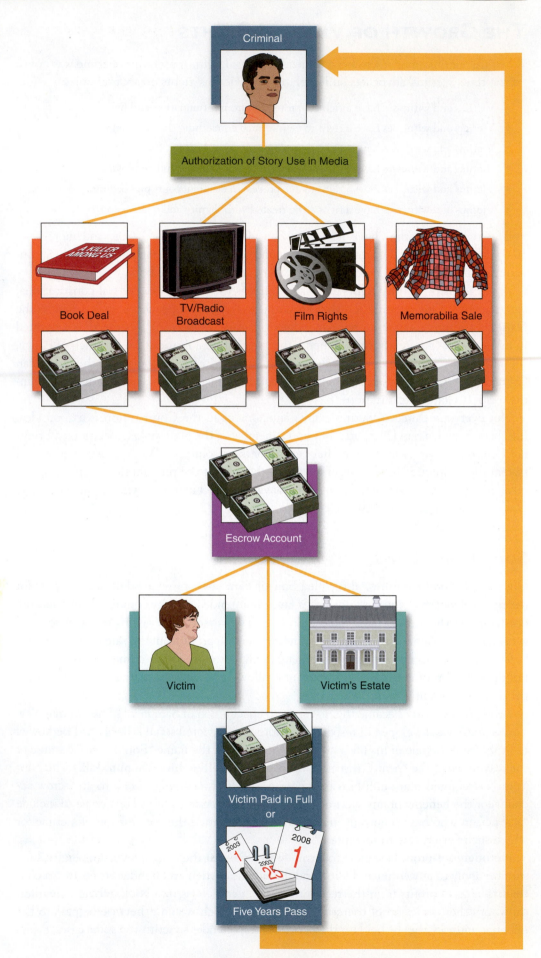

proceeds that would otherwise be payable to the offender must be contributed to the state's victims' compensation fund.

Son of Sam laws are predicated on the belief that permitting violent criminals to profit from a retelling of their crimes in the mass media is fundamentally offensive to society's sense of propriety.[19] Profiteering is made especially repugnant by the fact that victims often continue to suffer financially and are sometimes forced to endure added emotional pain from publicity following their victimization.

The need for notoriety-for-profit laws was explained succinctly by California Senator Charles Calderon, chairman of the state's Senate Judiciary Committee. "There used to be a saying: 'If you do the crime, you do the time,'" said Calderon. "Now it's 'If you do the crime, you do prime time.'"[20]

Son of Sam laws, although widespread, have been challenged under the First Amendment's guarantee of the right to freedom of expression. In 1991, the U.S. Supreme Court, in the case of *Simon & Schuster, Inc. v. New York State Crime Victims Board*,[21] found New York's original notoriety-for-profit law to be unconstitutional. The Court held that the New York law was overly broad and could have been applied to a wide array of authors—including many whom the law obviously did not intend to target. Attorneys for Simon and Schuster pointed out that historical figures as diverse as Saint Augustine, Malcolm X, and Henry David Thoreau could have had profits from their writings escrowed in the state of New York because of misdeeds they admitted committing.

Following that 1991 case, New York and several other states enacted new legislation intended to overcome the Court's objections. Key provisions of the revised New York law specify that (1) sanctions apply to any economic benefit an offender may derive from crime, not just to proceeds from the sale of an offender's story; (2) once notified of pending financial payments to an offender, victims have three years in which to obtain a civil judgment for damages; and (3) the state's Crime Victim Compensation Board can freeze and seize all profits before victims have the opportunity to sue. Other states have amended their notoriety-for-profit laws by including provisions designating all profits derived from the offender's criminal activities as subject to attachment or by making their laws applicable only to literary or media works depicting the violent crimes of which the offender was convicted.

In 2004, citing the *Simon & Schuster* case, the California Supreme Court overturned important portions of that state's Son of Sam law.[22] The California case,[23] which involved the 1963 kidnapping of Frank Sinatra, Jr., entered the court system in 1998 when Sinatra brought suit against Columbia Pictures to prevent the company from paying $1.5 million for the rights to a film about the four-day kidnapping, which occurred when he was 19 years old. Sinatra's attorneys argued that California law required convicted kidnapper Barry Keenan to forgo any profits from the crime and said that the money should instead go to a state trust set up to compensate crime victims. In finding that the California Son of Sam statute was similar to New York's flawed law, the California justices wrote that the state's law was overinclusive and unfairly "reaches beyond a criminal's profits from the crime or its exploitation to reach all income from the criminal's speech or expression on any theme or subject, if the story of the crime is included." The decision let stand, however, that portion of California law that prohibits felons from profiting from the selling of memorabilia, property, and rights that were enhanced by criminal notoriety.[24]

Procedures required for compensation under Son of Sam laws vary from state to state. In most states, the victim must sue the offender in civil court and obtain a judgment for damages before being eligible to file a claim against the offender's potential profits. In other states, claims may be made through the state's victims' compensation program. Some states require that the offender be convicted before his or her profits can be frozen, while other states provide for the attachment of profits upon indictment or at some other preliminary

APPLYING THE CONCEPT

CAPSTONE CASE

May a State Redirect the Profits from a Criminal's Commercial Writings to the Victims of the Criminal?

Simon & Schuster, Inc. v. *New York State Crime Victims Board,* 502 U.S.105 (1991)

New York's Son of Sam law requires that an accused or convicted criminal's income from works describing his crime be deposited in an escrow account. These funds are then made available to the victims of the crime and the criminal's other creditors. We consider whether this statute is consistent with the First Amendment.

THE CASE   In the summer of 1977, New York was terrorized by a serial killer popularly known as the Son of Sam. The hunt for the Son of Sam received considerable publicity, and by the time David Berkowitz was identified as the killer and apprehended, the rights to his story were worth a substantial amount. Berkowitz's chance to profit from his notoriety while his victims and their families remained uncompensated did not escape the notice of New York's Legislature. The State quickly enacted the statute at issue.

The statute was intended to "ensure that monies received by the criminal under such circumstances shall first be made available to recompense the victims of that crime for their loss and suffering." As the author of the statute explained, "It is abhorrent to one's sense of justice and decency that an individual . . . can expect to receive large sums of money for his story once he is captured—while five people are dead, [and] other people were injured as a result of his conduct."

This case began in 1986, when the Board first became aware of the contract between petitioner Simon & Schuster and admitted organized crime figure Henry Hill.

Looking back from the safety of the Federal Witness Protection Program, Henry Hill recalled: "At the age of twelve my ambition was to be a gangster. To be a wiseguy. To me, being a wiseguy was better than being president of the United States." N. Pileggi, *Wiseguy: Life in a Mafia Family* 19 (1985) (hereinafter *Wiseguy*). Whatever one might think of Hill, at the very least it can be said that he realized his dreams. After a career spanning twenty-five years, Hill admitted engineering some of the most daring crimes of his day, including the 1978–1979 Boston College basketball point-shaving scandal and the theft of $6 million from Lufthansa Airlines in 1978, the largest successful cash robbery in American history. *Wiseguy* 9. Most of Hill's crimes were more banausic: He committed extortion, he imported and distributed narcotics, and he organized numerous robberies.

Hill was arrested in 1980. In exchange for immunity from prosecution, he testified against many of his former colleagues. Since his arrest, he has lived under an assumed name in an unknown part of the country.

In August 1981, Hill entered into a contract with author Nicholas Pileggi for the production of a book about Hill's life. The following month, Hill and Pileggi signed a publishing agreement with Simon and Schuster. Under the agreement, Simon and Schuster agreed to make payments to both Hill and Pileggi. Over the next few years, according to Pileggi, he and Hill "talked at length virtually every single day, with not more than an occasional Sunday or holiday skipped. We spent more than three hundred hours together; my notes of conversations with Henry occupy more than six linear file feet." Because producing the book required such a substantial investment of time and effort, Hill sought compensation.

The result of Hill and Pileggi's collaboration was *Wiseguy,* which was published in January 1986. The book depicts, in colorful detail, the day-to-day existence of organized crime, primarily in Hill's first-person narrative. Throughout *Wiseguy,* Hill frankly admits to having participated in an astonishing variety of crimes. He discusses, among other things, his conviction for extortion and the prison sentence he served. In one portion of the book, Hill recounts how members of the Mafia received preferential treatment in prison:

> The dorm was a separate three-story building outside the wall, which looked more like a Holiday Inn than a prison. There were four guys to a room, and we had comfortable beds and private baths. There were

two dozen rooms on each floor, and each of them had mob guys living in them. It was like a wiseguy convention—the whole Gotti crew, Jimmy Doyle and his guys, Ernie Boy Abbamonte and Joe Crow Delvecchio, Vinnie Aloi, Frank Cotroni.

It was wild. There was wine and booze, and it was kept in bath-oil or after-shave jars. The hacks in the honor dorm were almost all on the take, and even though it was against the rules, we used to cook in our rooms. Looking back, I don't think Paulie went to the general mess five times in the two and a half years he was there. We had a stove and pots and pans and silverware stacked in the bathroom. We had glasses and an ice-water cooler where we kept the fresh meats and cheeses. When there was an inspection, we stored the stuff in the false ceiling, and once in a while, if it was confiscated, we'd just go to the kitchen and get new stuff.

We had the best food smuggled into our dorm from the kitchen. Steaks, veal cutlets, shrimp, red snapper. Whatever the hacks could buy, we ate. It cost me two, three hundred a week. Guys like Paulie spent five hundred to a thousand bucks a week. Scotch cost thirty dollars a pint. The hacks used to bring it inside the walls in their lunch pails. We never ran out of booze, because we had six hacks bringing it in six days a week. Depending on what you wanted and how much you were willing to spend, life could be almost bearable. *Wiseguy* 150–151.

Wiseguy was reviewed favorably: *The Washington Post* called it an "amply detailed and entirely fascinating book that amounts to a piece of revisionist history," while *New York Daily News* columnist Jimmy Breslin named it "the best book on crime in America ever written." The book was also a commercial success: Within nineteen months of its publication, more than a million copies were in print. A few years later, the book was converted into a film called *Goodfellas,* which won a host of awards as the best film of 1990.

From Henry Hill's perspective, however, the publicity generated by the book's success proved less desirable. The Crime Victims Board learned of *Wiseguy* in January 1986, soon after it was published.

On January 31, the Board notified Simon and Schuster: "It has come to our attention that you may have contracted with a person accused or convicted of a crime for the payment of monies to such person." The Board ordered Simon and Schuster to furnish copies of any contracts it had entered into with Hill, to provide the dollar amounts and dates of all payments it had made to Hill, and to suspend all payments to Hill in the future. Simon and Schuster complied with this order. By that time, Simon and

Schuster had paid Hill's literary agent $96,250 in advances and royalties on Hill's behalf and was holding $27,958 for eventual payment to Hill.

The Board reviewed the book and the contract and on May 21, 1987, issued a Proposed Determination and Order. The Board determined that *Wiseguy* was covered by § 632-a of the Executive Law, that Simon and Schuster had violated the law by failing to turn over its contract with Hill to the Board and by making payments to Hill, and that all money owed to Hill under the contract had to be turned over to the Board to be held in escrow for the victims of Hill's crimes. The Board ordered Hill to turn over the payments he had already received and ordered Simon and Schuster to turn over all money payable to Hill at the time or in the future. . . .

Because the Federal Government and most of the States have enacted statutes with similar objectives, the issue is significant and likely to recur. We accordingly granted *certiorari,* 498 U.S. (1991), and we now reverse.

THE FINDING   A statute is presumptively inconsistent with the First Amendment if it imposes a financial burden on speakers because of the content of their speech. As we emphasized in invalidating a content-based magazine tax, "official scrutiny of the content of publications as the basis for imposing a tax is entirely incompatible with the First Amendment's guarantee of freedom of the press."

This is a notion so engrained in our First Amendment jurisprudence that last Term we found it so "obvious" as to not require explanation. It is but one manifestation of a far broader principle: "Regulations which permit the Government to discriminate on the basis of the content of the message cannot be tolerated under the First Amendment." In the context of financial regulation, it bears repeating, as we did in *Leathers* [a precedential case], that the Government's ability to impose content-based burdens on speech raises the specter that the Government may effectively drive certain ideas or viewpoints from the marketplace. The First Amendment presumptively places this sort of discrimination beyond the power of the Government. As we reiterated in *Leathers,* "The constitutional right of free expression is . . . intended to remove governmental restraints from the arena of public discussion, putting the decision as to what views shall be voiced largely into the hands of each of us . . . in the belief that no other approach would comport with the premise of individual dignity and choice upon which our political system rests."

The Son of Sam law is such a content-based statute. It singles out income derived from expressive activity for a burden the State places on no other income, and it is directed only at works with a specified content. Whether

(continued)

the First Amendment "speaker" is considered to be Henry Hill, whose income the statute places in escrow because of the story he has told, or Simon and Schuster, which can publish books about crime with the assistance of only those criminals willing to forgo remuneration for at least five years, the statute plainly imposes a financial disincentive only on speech of a particular content. . . .

The Board next argues that discriminatory financial treatment is suspect under the First Amendment only when the legislature intends to suppress certain ideas. This assertion is incorrect; our cases have consistently held that "illicit legislative intent is not the *sine qua non* of a violation of the First Amendment." Simon and Schuster need adduce "no evidence of an improper censorial motive." As we concluded in *Minneapolis Star*, "we have long recognized that even regulations aimed at proper governmental concerns can restrict unduly the exercise of rights protected by the First Amendment."

Finally, the Board claims that even if the First Amendment prohibits content-based financial regulation specifically of the media, the Son of Sam law is different, because it imposes a general burden on any "entity" contracting with a convicted person to transmit that person's speech.

This argument falters on both semantic and constitutional grounds. Any "entity" that enters into such a contract becomes by definition a medium of communication, if it wasn't one already. In any event, the characterization of an entity as a member of the "media" is irrelevant for these purposes. The Government's power to impose content-based financial disincentives on speech surely does not vary with the identity of the speaker.

The Son of Sam law establishes a financial disincentive to create or publish works with a particular content. In order to justify such differential treatment, "the State must show that its regulation is necessary to serve a compelling state interest and is narrowly drawn to achieve that end."

The Board disclaims, as it must, any state interest in suppressing descriptions of crime out of solicitude for the sensibilities of readers. As we have often had occasion to repeat, "The fact that society may find speech offensive is not a sufficient reason for suppressing it. Indeed, if it is the speaker's opinion that gives offense, that consequence is a reason for according it constitutional protection. . . . If there is a bedrock principle underlying the First Amendment, it is that the Government may not prohibit the expression of an idea simply because society finds the idea itself offensive or disagreeable." The Board thus does not assert any interest in limiting whatever anguish Henry Hill's victims may suffer from reliving their victimization.

There can be little doubt, on the other hand, that the State has a compelling interest in ensuring that victims of

crime are compensated by those who harm them. Every State has a body of tort law serving exactly this interest. The State's interest in preventing wrongdoers from dissipating their assets before victims can recover explains the existence of the State's statutory provisions for prejudgment remedies and orders of restitution. We have recognized the importance of this interest before. . . . The State likewise has an undisputed compelling interest in ensuring that criminals do not profit from their crimes. . . . The parties debate whether book royalties can properly be termed the profits of crime, but that is a question we need not address here. For the purposes of this case, we can assume without deciding that the income escrowed by the Son of Sam law represents the fruits of crime. We need only conclude that the State has a compelling interest in depriving criminals of the profits of their crimes, and in using these funds to compensate victims.

The Board attempts to define the State's interest more narrowly, as "ensuring that criminals do not profit from storytelling about their crimes before their victims have a meaningful opportunity to be compensated for their injuries." Here the Board is on far shakier ground. The Board cannot explain why the State should have any greater interest in compensating victims from the proceeds of such "storytelling" than from any of the criminal's other assets. Nor can the Board offer any justification for a distinction between this expressive activity and any other activity in connection with its interest in transferring the fruits of crime from criminals to their victims. Thus even if the State can be said to have an interest in classifying a criminal's assets in this manner, that interest is hardly compelling.

We have rejected similar assertions of a compelling interest in the past. In *Arkansas Writers' Project* and *Minneapolis Star*, we observed that while the State certainly has an important interest in raising revenue through taxation, that interest hardly justified selective taxation of the press, as it was completely unrelated to a press/non-press distinction. [W]e recognized the State's interest in preserving privacy by prohibiting residential picketing, but refused to permit the State to ban only nonlabor picketing. This was because "nothing in the content-based labor-nonlabor distinction has any bearing whatsoever on privacy." Much the same is true here. The distinction drawn by the Son of Sam law has nothing to do with the State's interest in transferring the proceeds of crime from criminals to their victims.

Like the government entities in the above cases, the Board has taken the effect of the statute and posited that effect as the State's interest. If accepted, this sort of circular defense can sidestep judicial review of almost any statute, because it makes all statutes look narrowly tailored. As Judge Newman pointed out in his dissent from the opinion of the Court of Appeals, such an argument "eliminates the entire inquiry concerning the validity of content-based discriminations. Every content-based discrimination could be upheld by simply observing that the state is anxious to regulate the designated category of speech."

In short, the State has a compelling interest in compensating victims from the fruits of the crime, but little if any interest in limiting such compensation to the proceeds of the wrongdoer's speech about the crime. We must therefore determine whether the Son of Sam law is narrowly tailored to advance the former, not the latter, objective.

As a means of ensuring that victims are compensated from the proceeds of crime, the Son of Sam law is significantly overinclusive. As counsel for the Board conceded at oral argument, the statute applies to works on any subject, provided that they express the author's thoughts or recollections about his crime, however tangentially or incidentally. In addition, the statute's broad definition of "person convicted of a crime" enables the Board to escrow the income of any author who admits in his work to having committed a crime, whether or not the author was ever actually accused or convicted.

These two provisions combine to encompass a potentially very large number of works. Had the Son of Sam law been in effect at the time and place of publication, it would have escrowed payment for such works as *The Autobiography of Malcolm X*, which describes crimes committed by the civil rights leader before he became a public figure; *Civil Disobedience*, in which Thoreau acknowledges his refusal to pay taxes and recalls his experience in jail; and even the *Confessions of Saint Augustine*, in which the author laments "my past foulness and the carnal corruptions of my soul," one instance of which involved the theft of pears from a neighboring vineyard. See A. Haley & Malcolm X, *The Autobiography of Malcolm X* 108–125 (1964); H. Thoreau, *Civil Disobedience* 18–22 (1849, reprinted 1969); *The Confessions of Saint Augustine* 31, 36–37 (Franklin Library ed. 1980). Amicus Association of American Publishers, Inc., has submitted a sobering bibliography listing hundreds of works by American prisoners and ex-prisoners, many of which contain descriptions of the crimes for which the authors were incarcerated, including works by such authors as Emma Goldman and Martin Luther King, Jr. A list of prominent figures whose autobiographies would be subject to the statute if written is not difficult to construct: The list could include Sir Walter Raleigh, who was convicted of treason after a dubiously conducted 1603 trial; Jesse Jackson, who was arrested in 1963 for trespass and resisting arrest after attempting to be served at a lunch counter

in North Carolina; and Bertrand Russell, who was jailed for seven days at the age of 89 for participating in a sit-down protest against nuclear weapons. The argument that a statute like the Son of Sam law would prevent publication of all of these works is hyperbole—some would have been written without compensation—but the Son of Sam law clearly reaches a wide range of literature that does not enable a criminal to profit from his crime while a victim remains uncompensated.

Should a prominent figure write his autobiography at the end of his career, and include in an early chapter a brief recollection of having stolen (in New York) a nearly worthless item as a youthful prank, the Board would control his entire income from the book for five years and would make that income available to all of the author's creditors, despite the fact that the statute of limitations for this minor incident had long since run. That the Son of Sam law can produce such an outcome indicates that the statute is, to say the least, not narrowly tailored to achieve the State's objective of compensating crime victims from the profits of crime.

The Federal Government and many of the States have enacted statutes designed to serve purposes similar to that served by the Son of Sam law. Some of these statutes may be quite different from New York's, and we have no occasion to determine the constitutionality of these other laws. We conclude simply that in the Son of Sam law, New York has singled out speech on a particular subject for a financial burden that it places on no other speech and no other income. The State's interest in compensating victims from the fruits of crime is a compelling one, but the Son of Sam law is not narrowly tailored to advance that objective. As a result, the statute is inconsistent with the First Amendment.

The judgment of the Court of Appeals is accordingly Reversed.

What Do *You* Think?

1. Henry Hill's financial relationship with Simon and Schuster was the subject of the case described in this section. From what crimes did Hill intend to profit? How did he intend to profit?

2. What was the significance of this case for notoriety-for-profit laws? On what basis did the Court find the New York law unconstitutional?

3. Do you agree with the Court's conclusion that "[h]ad the Son of Sam law been in effect at the time and place of publication, it would have escrowed payment for such works as *The Autobiography of Malcolm X*, . . .

(continued)

Civil Disobedience, . . . and even the *Confessions of Saint Augustine*"?

4. How might new notoriety-for-profit laws be written (or existing ones revised) to make them acceptable under U.S. Supreme Court scrutiny?

Additional Applications

After *Simon & Schuster*, may states apply civil forfeiture statutes to seize royalties from a criminal's tell-all book?

Arizona v. Gravano, 60 P.3d 246 (Ariz.App. 2002)

The Case: Sammy "The Bull" Gravano, already notorious for his earlier involvement in organized crime activities in New York, was arrested in February 2000 in Maricopa County, Arizona, for distributing MDMA (commonly called "Ecstasy") in violation of state law. Subsequent to this arrest, Arizona officials filed a civil complaint against Gravano under the state's Racketeering and Forfeiture Reform Acts, seeking control over a variety of Gravano's assets—including money paid to him in connection with the 1997 publication of the Harper-Collins best seller *Underboss: Sammy the Bull Gravano's Story of Life in the Mafia.* Arizona's civil forfeiture laws authorized state seizure of any "monies, negotiable instruments, securities and other property" traceable to criminal racketeering activity, including crimes previously committed in other states. Challenging the state's action, however, Gravano argued that any money derived from *Underboss* was protected against seizure by the First Amendment as interpreted in *Simon & Schuster*.

The Finding: Distinguishing the Supreme Court's *Simon & Schuster* ruling explicitly, a three-judge Arizona appeals court panel in 2002 upheld the state's seizure of Gravano's book royalties. Writing for the appeals panel, Judge Lawrence Winthrop argued that unlike Son of Sam laws found in many states (including Arizona, as a footnote pointed out), Arizona's civil forfeiture statutes were not aimed specifically at the proceeds of expressive activity but rather at *any* tangible property gained through racketeering. Consequently, Winthrop explained, "whether proceeds of an expressive work are forfeitable under the statutory scheme does not depend upon the content of the work" as in *Simon & Schuster* but rather upon the demonstration of a "causal connection between racketeering and the proceeds" in question. In Gravano's case, Winthrop noted, such a causal connection existed

because "the storyteller's notoriety from racketeering is what ma[de] the story [in *Underboss*] so marketable." The state's civil forfeiture laws were "content-neutral" toward expression; thus, state officials faced no First Amendment obstacle to proceeding.

Under the Victim and Witness Protection Act (VWPA), 18 U.S.C., Sec. 3663, may a court specifically order the payment of restitution to victims from future book or movie proceeds?

United States v. Jackson, 978 F.2d 903 (5th Cir. 1992)

The Case: In a highly publicized case, defendants Juan Jackson and Genaro Ruiz Camacho were convicted in federal district court in 1991 on interstate kidnapping charges in connection with the abduction and brutal murders of a Pleasant Grove, Texas, woman and her three-year-old child. (In a parallel proceeding, Camacho was also tried and convicted in Texas state court for capital murder.) Applying federal statutory guidelines, the trial judge sentenced both defendants to life in prison. Beyond that, the judge—citing the Victim and Witness Protection Act (VWPA) and reasoning that the defendants might someday receive income from a book or movie based on their high-profile crimes—ordered that Jackson and Camacho pay a combined $1,250,000 in restitution to the victims' families. On appeal, Jackson and Camacho argued, among other things, that the trial judge's restitution order—issued in apparent anticipation of future book or movie royalties—violated the First Amendment as interpreted in *Simon & Schuster*.

The Finding: In a 1992 ruling, a panel of the U.S. Court of Appeals for the Fifth Circuit reversed the district court's restitution order and remanded the case for additional findings of fact. Noting that the VWPA grants a trial court wide discretion in determining specific restitution amounts, the appeals panel nonetheless expressed concern that the trial judge here had considered the defendants' possible future royalties rather than just the victim's "lost income and . . . funeral expenses" as required under the VWPA. On remand, the appeals panel held, the trial court should make specific findings of fact to support the amount of restitution that the defendants must pay. What's more, the appeals panel warned: "Under the Supreme Court's holding in *Simon & Schuster*, the district court cannot limit a restitution order solely to the income the defendants earn on speech associated with their criminal activities." ∎

stage in the criminal justice process. If found not guilty, however, all funds are usually returned to the person acquitted.

Victim-Impact Statements

Another result of the victims' rights movement has been an ongoing call for the use of **victim impact statements** before the sentencing of convicted offenders. Victim impact statements generally take the form of written documents that describe the losses, suffering, and trauma experienced by crime victims or by surviving family members. Jurisdictions that have laws supporting the use of victim impact statements expect judges to consider them in arriving at an appropriate sanction for the offender.

The drive to include victim impact statements in sentencing decisions, already mandated in federal courts by the 1982 Victim and Witness Protection Act, was substantially enhanced by the "right of allocution" provision of the Violent Crime Control and Law Enforcement Act of 1994. That law requires that "if sentence is to be imposed for a crime of violence or sexual abuse" in a federal court, the court must "address the victim personally if the victim is present at the sentencing hearing and determine if the victim wishes to make a statement or present any information in relation to the sentence."[25]

Additional wording in the 1994 law made clear that "[i]t is the sense of the Senate that (1) the law of a State should provide for a victim's right of allocution at a sentencing hearing and at any parole hearing if the offender has been convicted of a crime of violence or sexual abuse; [and] (2) such a victim should have an opportunity equivalent to the opportunity accorded to the offender to address the sentencing court or parole board and to present information in relation to the sentence imposed or to the early release of the offender."[26]

Approximately 20 states now have laws that permit direct victim involvement at the sentencing phase of criminal trials, and all 50 states and the District of Columbia "allow for some form of submission of a victim impact statement either at the time of sentencing or to be contained in the presentence investigation reports" made by court officers.[27] Where written victim impact statements are not available, courts may invite the victim to testify directly before sentencing.

Hearing from victims, however, does not guarantee that a sentencing court will sympathize with them. A study of victim impact statements found, for example, that sentencing decisions were rarely influenced by them: "These statements did not produce sentencing decisions that reflected more clearly the effects of crime on victims. Nor did we find much evidence that—with or without impact statements—sentencing decisions were influenced by our measures of the effects of crime on victims, once the charge and the defendant's prior record were taken into account."[28] The authors concluded that victim impact statements have little effect on courts because judges and other "officials have established ways of making decisions which do not call for explicit information about the impact of crime on victims."

The Constitutionality of Victim Impact Statements

Victim impact statements met a significant constitutional challenge in 1987 in the case of *Booth v. Maryland*.[29] The case involved Irvin Bronstein, 78, and his wife Rose, 75, who were robbed and brutally murdered in their home in Baltimore, Maryland, in 1983. Arrested were John Booth and Willie Reid, acquaintances of the Bronsteins, who were caught stealing to support heroin habits. Booth and Reid were both convicted of murdering the Bronsteins. Booth, however, decided to allow the jury (rather than the judge) to set his sentence. As required by state law, the jury considered a victim impact statement that was part of a presentence report prepared by probation officers. The victim impact statement used in the case was a powerful one, describing the wholesome personal qualities of the Bronsteins and the emotional suffering their children had experienced as a result of the murders.

victim impact statement The in-court use of victim- or survivor-supplied information by sentencing authorities who want to make an informed sentencing decision. Also, a written document that describes the losses, suffering, and trauma experienced by the crime victim or by the victim's survivors. In jurisdictions in which victim impact statements are used, judges are expected to consider them in arriving at an appropriate sentence for the offender.

Booth received a death sentence but appealed, and his case eventually reached the U.S. Supreme Court. The Court overturned his sentence, reasoning that victim impact statements, at least in capital cases, violate the Eighth Amendment's ban on cruel and unusual punishments. In a close (5–4) decision, the majority held that information in victim impact statements leads to the risk that the death penalty might be imposed in an arbitrary and capricious manner.

In 1991, however, in what was to be a complete about-face, the U.S. Supreme Court recanted the *Booth* ruling, explaining that it had been based on "a misreading of precedent."[30] Like *Booth*, *Payne* v. *Tennessee*[31] began with a double murder. In this case, a 28-year-old mother and her two-year-old daughter were stabbed to death in Millington, Tennessee.[32] A second child, three-year-old Nicholas Christopher, himself severely wounded in the incident, witnessed the deaths of his mother and young sister. In a trial following the killings, the prosecution established that Pervis Tyrone Payne, a 20-year-old retarded man, had killed the mother and child after the woman resisted his sexual advances. Payne was convicted of both murders. At the sentencing phase of the trial, Mary Zvolanek, Nicholas's grandmother, testified that the boy continued to cry out daily for his dead sister. Payne received two death sentences.

Interestingly, by this time *Booth* had already been decided and might have been used by a Tennessee appellate court to overturn Payne's conviction or to send his case back to a lower court for resentencing. Nonetheless, Payne's conviction was upheld by the Tennessee Supreme Court in an opinion that then-Justice Thurgood Marshall said did little to disguise the Tennessee court's contempt for the High Court's majority opinion in *Booth*.

This time, however, due largely to an increasingly conservative majority, the U.S. Supreme Court agreed with the Tennessee justices, holding that "[v]ictim impact evidence is simply another form or method of informing the sentencing authority about the specific harm caused by the crime in question, evidence of a general type long considered by sentencing authorities." Chief Justice William Rehnquist wrote for the majority: "Courts have always taken into consideration the harm done by the defendant in imposing sentence." In a concurring opinion, Justice Antonin Scalia rejected the earlier ruling in *Booth*, saying that it "significantly harms our criminal justice system." *Booth*, said Scalia, had been decided with "plainly inadequate rational support." Although generally acceptable, there are due-process limits to the admission of victim impact evidence. Victim evidence that is unnecessarily duplicative or prejudicial may be excluded by trial courts. As to the number of victims that may testify, there is no precise formula. If there are few victims, all may testify. But in trials with hundreds or thousands of victims, it is impossible and likely unfair to the defendant for all to testify. Trial judges must make these decisions after considering the relative value-added status of the victims. The final number allowed to testify has been large in some cases, however. For example, in the sentencing hearing of Timothy McVeigh, the Oklahoma City bombing terrorist convicted of killing 168 people, including a day care full of children, and injuring more than 400 other people, over three dozen victims testified.[33] McVeigh was sentenced to death and executed in 2001.

VICTIM STATISTICS

It is difficult to know precisely how much crime is committed yearly in the United States. On the one hand, many crimes go unreported. On the other, victims may describe their victimization experiences in terms that do not readily fit statistical categories used for determining "official" counts of crime. In addition, numerous false reports are filed, and "real" victims sometimes hesitate to report their victimization.

Two major surveys provide annual crime statistics for the United States in an effort to measure the extent of criminal victimization throughout the nation. The first survey is conducted by the Federal Bureau of Investigation's **Uniform Crime Reporting (UCR) Program**, which now incorporates the National Incident-Based Reporting System (NIBRS). The UCR/NIBRS surveys collect data from police departments across the country about the number of crimes reported or known to the police. The second survey, conducted by the Bureau of Justice Statistics, is the National Crime Victimization Survey (NCVS). The NCVS is based on victim self-reports that are made to survey interviewers. It obtains information about crimes that are not always known to the police. Hence the NCVS typically uncovers more criminal activity than the UCR/NIBRS. Even so, the NCVS still probably underestimates the total number of crimes occurring in the country, especially those regarding gunshot and knife assaults, domestic violence, and rape. Undercounting may be due to fear of reprisal, the reluctance of victims to speak to "officials," and the general unavailability of many victims.

Comparisons between UCR/NIBRS and NCVS data can be difficult. For one thing, the NCVS excludes many crimes that the UCR/NIBRS counts. Not measured by the NCVS, for example, are murder (as murder victims cannot self-report), arson, drunk driving, child abuse and neglect, and crimes against children under age 12. Also, the NCVS samples U.S. households and largely omits the homeless and others who are not attached to traditional households.

Uniform Crime Reporting (UCR) Program
A data-collection program run by the Federal Bureau of Investigation that tallies crime statistics annually. Reports under the program consist primarily of data on crimes reported to the police and of arrests.

The National Crime Victimization Survey

For all of its shortcomings, the NCVS is the government's primary source of information about criminal victimization. Twice each year, data are obtained from a nationally representative sample (roughly 50,000 households, comprising about 100,000 people) on the frequency, characteristics, and consequences of criminal victimization throughout the United States. To collect NCVS information, the Bureau of Justice Statistics annually polls people over age 12 about rape, robbery, assault, larceny, burglary, and motor vehicle theft. Partly because of the difficulty in obtaining certain kinds of information through a survey, the NCVS does not collect data on certain crime categories (such as child abuse and drug abuse) and inevitably undercounts others (such as rape and domestic violence). Nonetheless, NCVS data consistently show that about 63% of all crimes are never brought to the attention of the police.

NCVS findings report the likelihood of victimization by rape, sexual assault, robbery, assault, theft, household burglary, and motor vehicle theft for the population as a whole, as well as for special segments of the population, such as women, the elderly, members of various racial groups, and city dwellers. As such, the NCVS provides the largest national forum for victims to describe the impact of crime and the social and physical characteristics of violent offenders.[34]

NCVS Findings   The 2010 data indicate the lowest level of victimization since 1973—the first year the data were collected. Although the rate of reported victimization had been declining for years, at about 4% per year, the decline between 2009 and 2010 was 13%. The sharp decline is somewhat puzzling, particularly given the nation's challenging economic condition.

As was true in the past, the data also paint a vivid picture of crime in America and show that males, blacks, Hispanics, the young, the poor, and inner-city dwellers are the most vulnerable to crimes of violence.[35] In 2010, U.S. residents age 12 or older experienced an estimated 18.7 million violent and property crime victimizations, according to the NCVS. These criminal victimizations included an estimated 14.8 million property crimes,

3.8 million violent crimes, and 138,000 personal thefts. In that year, the rate of violent crime was 14.9 victimizations per 1,000 individuals age 12 or older across the nation, and the property crime rate was 120 per 1,000 households.

According to NCVS data, males experienced higher rates of victimizations than females. In 2010, males experienced 15.7 violent victimizations per 1,000 males age 12 or older. The rate of violent victimizations for females was 14.2 per 1,000 females age 12 or older. Although different, the rate of victimization between males and females is the closest it has been since the data has been collected by the NCVS.

People in the older age groups generally experience lower rates of violent victimization than those in younger age groups. In 2010, households that were headed by a person age 65 or older experienced lower rates of property victimization than households headed by a younger person.

There is a strong correlation between income and crime. As income declines, the rate of burglary and theft in the household increased. Households at the lowest income levels, less than $7,500, experienced the highest rate of property crimes, 169 per 100,000, compared to 119 per 100,000 in households with a total income of $75,000 or more.

Black victims experienced higher rates of violence than whites or people of other races. The rate of violent victimization for blacks was 20.8, 13.6 for white, 15.6 for Hispanic, 42.2 for Native American or Alaskan, 6.3 for Asian, and 52.6 for people of two or more races per 1,000 people age 12 or older.

Of offenders who victimized males in 2010, 5% were described as intimates and 47% as strangers. In contrast, of offenders who victimized females, 21% were described as intimates and 29% as strangers. Males and females were equally likely to be victimized by an offender they previously knew.

In 2010, 22% of all violent victimizations, 61% of all serious violent victimizations, 12% of rapes and sexual assaults, and 20% of all assaults involved a weapon, with firearms being the most commonly used weapon. During 2010, 51% of all violent victimizations and 39% of all property crimes were reported to the police. Rape or sexual assault was less likely to be reported to the police (50%) than robbery (58%) and aggravated assault (60%). Motor vehicle theft was the property crime most likely to be reported to the police; about 83% of these victimizations were reported.

Violence against Women

Violence against women first came to be viewed as a serious social problem in the early 1970s, in part because of the reemergence of the women's movement. In unprecedented numbers, scholars trained in such diverse disciplines as philosophy, literature, law, and sociology began to examine violence against women in the context of a feminist ideology.[36] One result of this heightened interest in women's victimization was the creation of the federal Violence against Women Office; another was initiation of a National Violence against Women (NVAW) Survey.

The NVAW Survey also gathers information on men's victimization. Using a definition of rape that includes forced vaginal, oral, and anal sex, the survey found that nearly one in six U.S. women has experienced an attempted or completed rape at some point in her life. The survey also found that 0.3% of surveyed women said they experienced a completed or attempted rape in the previous 12 months. These estimates equate to approximately 302,100 women who are forcibly raped each year in the United States.

Because some rape victims experienced more than one rape in the 12 months preceding the survey, the incidence of rape (number of separate victimizations) exceeded the prevalence of rape (number of rape victims). Specifically, women who were raped in the previous 12 months averaged 2.9 rapes. According to survey estimates, approximately 876,100 rapes were perpetrated against women in the United States during the 12 months preceding the survey.

The annual rape victimization estimates generated by the NVAW Survey are higher than comparable victimization estimates generated by the National Crime Victimization Survey. However, direct comparisons between the NVAW Survey and the NCVS are difficult to make because the two surveys differ substantially with respect to methodological issues.

The NVAW Survey also found that women experience significantly more partner violence than men do: 25% of surveyed women, compared with 8% of surveyed men, said they were raped and/or physically assaulted by a current or former spouse, cohabiting partner, or date in their lifetime; 1.5% of surveyed women and 0.9% of surveyed men said they were raped and/or physically assaulted by such a perpetrator in the previous 12 months. Women were also found to be much more likely to have been injured by intimate partners.

Generally speaking, the NVAW Survey shows that violence against women is primarily partner violence. Seventy-six percent of the women who were raped and/or physically assaulted since age 18 were assaulted by a current or former husband, cohabiting partner, or date, compared with 18% of surveyed men.

Using a definition of stalking that requires the victim to feel a high level of fear, the survey found that stalking is more prevalent than previously thought: 8% of surveyed women and 2% of surveyed men said they were stalked at some time in their lives. One percent of surveyed women and 0.4% of surveyed men said they were stalked in the previous 12 months.

Young Black Male Victims

According to data from both the UCR/NIBRS and the NCVS, black males ages 12 to 24 experience violent crime at a rate significantly higher than the rates for other population groups. According to the NCVS, black males ages 16 to 19 are particularly at risk and have violent victimization rates double that of white males and three times that of white females in the same age range.[37] Although black males between the ages of 16 and 24 comprise only about 1% of the population age 12 and over, they suffer 5% of all NCVS-reported violent victimizations. Moreover, whereas the rate of violent victimizations experienced by young white males has remained relatively constant during the past decade, it has increased substantially among young black males. Generally speaking, black males age 16 to 19 sustain one violent crime for every two or three people annually.

> *Black males age twelve to twenty-four [are] almost fourteen times as likely to be homicide victims as [are] members of the general population.*
>
> —Bureau of Justice Statistics

Handgun violence is especially prevalent in the violent victimization of young black males. NCVS data show that for victimizations involving a weapon, among male victims ages 16 to 19, 50% of black victims and 22% of white victims face a handgun. The average rate of handgun victimizations per 1,000 black males ages 16 to 19 is 39.7—or four times the rate for white males.

NCVS data do not include information on homicide, as victim self-reports are impossible in homicide cases. The FBI's Uniform Crime Reporting Program, however, shows that, although black males ages 12 to 24 comprise 1.3% of the population, they suffer 17.2% of all single-victim homicides. This translates into a homicide rate of 114.9 per 100,000 black males in the 12–24 age range—a rate almost 14 times higher than that of the general population.

Elderly Victims

Adults age 65 or older have the lowest victimization rates for all types of crime.[38] Although those age 65 or older comprise about 14% of all people interviewed in the NCVS, they

An elderly crime victim. Why are the elderly particularly susceptible to crimes motivated by economic gain?

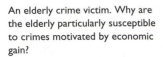

© Bubbles Photolibrary/Alamy

report less than 2% of all victimizations. In a given year, according to NCVS data, adults 65 or older living in the United States experience about 1.5 million criminal victimizations.[39]

Not only are victimization rates low among the elderly, but they are declining. The 2010 violent victimization rate of the elderly was 2.4 per 1,000.[40]

The violent crime rate is nearly 18 times higher for people under age 25 than for people over 65. For example, the rate for robbery is nearly six times higher for those under age 25 than for those age 65 or older.

As for personal crime victimizations, adults over 65 are significantly less likely to become victims of all forms of household crime than individuals in younger age groups. Personal larceny with contact (purse snatching and pocket picking) is an exception. Those who are 65 or older are about as likely as those under age 65 to be victims of personal larceny with contact.

The elderly, however, appear to be particularly susceptible to crimes motivated by economic gain. Such crimes include robbery and personal theft, as well as the household crimes of larceny, burglary, and motor vehicle theft. Like the general population, the elderly are most susceptible to household crimes and least susceptible to violent crimes. Unlike younger victims of violence, however, elderly victims of violence are about as likely to be robbed as assaulted. Robberies comprise 38% of the violent crimes committed against the elderly but account for only 20% of the violence experienced by people younger than age 65.

Violent offenders injure about a third of all victims, and elderly victims of violent crime are more likely than younger victims to suffer a serious injury. Among violent crime victims age 65 or older, 9% suffer serious injuries such as broken bones and loss of consciousness. By comparison, 5% of younger victims suffer similar injuries. In addition, when injured, almost half of all older victims (but only a fourth of younger ones) receive medical care in a hospital.

Most victims of violent crime are attacked by a stranger rather than by a relative or someone whom the victim knows. However, elderly violent crime victims are more likely than younger victims to face assailants who are strangers. Robbery victims age 65 or older are especially more likely than younger victims to be vulnerable to offenders whom they do not know.

Similarly, elderly victims of violent crime are almost twice as likely as younger victims to be raped, robbed, or assaulted at or near their home. Half of the elderly victims of violence and a quarter of those under age 65 are victimized at or near their home. The vulnerability of the elderly to violent crime at or near the home may reflect the lifestyle of the elderly, who may live alone and tend to spend more time at home.

About 38% of elderly victims of violent crime (compared to 35% of younger victims) report facing an armed offender. When facing an armed offender, older victims are somewhat more likely to face an offender with a gun (41% versus 36%). Most victims of violent crime, regardless of age, face lone assailants, but about half the robbery victims age 65 or older are accosted by multiple robbers (a substantially greater figure than for those under 65). In cases of aggravated assault, the reverse is true (younger victims of aggravated assault are more likely than older victims to face multiple offenders).

Elderly victims are less likely than younger victims to act to protect themselves during a violent crime. Victims age 65 or older take self-protective measures during 58% of victimizations, compared with 73% of younger victims who take such action. Moreover, older victims are less likely to use physical force against offenders (such as attacking or chasing an offender or offering physical resistance). Those elderly people who do protect themselves typically use nonviolent means, including arguing or reasoning with the offender, screaming, or running away.

Elderly victims of robbery and personal theft are more likely than younger victims to report victimization to the police. Seven out of ten elderly victims (versus five out of ten victims under age 65) report a robbery or attempted robbery to the police. No measurable difference, however, distinguishes older from younger victims in reporting aggravated assault or household crimes to the police.

Among the elderly, NCVS data show that certain groups are generally more likely to be victimized than others. Elderly men generally have higher victimization rates than elderly women. Elderly women, however, have higher rates of personal larceny with contact, such as purse snatching. Adults ages 65 to 74 have higher rates of victimization than those age 75 or older. Elderly blacks are more likely than elderly whites to be crime victims. However, rates of personal larceny that do not involve contact between the victim and the offender are higher for whites.

The elderly with the lowest incomes experience higher rates of violence than do others. Elderly people with the highest family incomes experience the highest rates of personal theft or household crime. Similarly, elderly people who are either separated or divorced have the highest rates of victimization for all types of crime, and elderly city dwellers have higher rates of victimization for all types of crime than do others in the same age group. Elderly renters are more likely than homeowners to experience both violence and personal theft. However, elderly homeowners are more likely than renters to be victims of household crime.

The Uniform Crime Reporting Program

The FBI's Uniform Crime Reporting Program collects data about offenses known to law enforcement in two major categories: violent crime and property crime. It also collects information regarding clearances of these offenses (i.e., crimes that have been solved). Expanded offense data, which include detailed information about victims, offenders, circumstances, and trends in crime volume and crime rate per 100,000 inhabitants, are collected under the program's National Incident-Based Reporting System.

Under the UCR Program, violent crime comprises four offenses: murder and nonnegligent manslaughter, forcible rape, robbery, and aggravated assault. *Violent crimes* are defined by the UCR Program as those offenses that involve force or the threat of force.

The UCR Program uses a hierarchy rule that requires that only the most serious offense in a multiple-offense criminal incident be counted. In descending order of severity, the violent crimes are murder and nonnegligent manslaughter, forcible rape, robbery, and aggravated assault, followed by the property crimes of burglary, larceny-theft, and motor vehicle theft.

So, for example, if a criminal incident occurs in which a man is murdered, his girlfriend is raped, and the couple's car is stolen, only the murder will be recorded in the program's official data (although the perpetrator can be charged by prosecutors with all of the various offenses that he committed). The hierarchy rule does not apply to the offense of arson.

According to UCR statistics, an estimated 1,246,248 violent crimes occurred throughout the nation in 2010 (Figure 13–4), or 403 violent crimes per 100,000 inhabitants, a 6% decrease from the year before and 13% below 2001.[41] Aggravated assaults accounted for 62.5% of violent crimes and constituted the single largest category of violent crime reported to law enforcement agencies. Robbery comprised 29.5% of the violent crime total, and

FIGURE 13–4

Violent Crimes Known to
the Police, 2003–2010.

Federal Bureau of Investigation,
Crime in the United States, 2010
(Washington, DC: Federal Bureau of
Investigation, 2011).

Estimated Number of Offenses

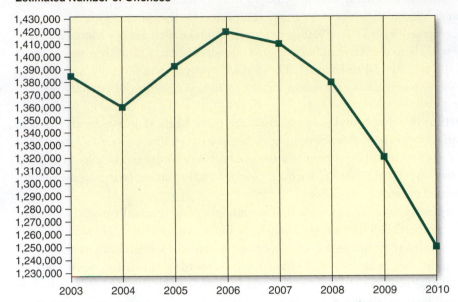

forcible rape accounted for 6.8%. Murder accounted for 1.2% of all estimated violent crimes in 2010. It should also be mentioned that in 2010, offenders used firearms in 67.5% of the nation's murders, 41.4% of reported robberies, and 20.6% of aggravated assaults.

The UCR Program defines *murder and nonnegligent manslaughter* as the willful (nonnegligent) killing of one human being by another. For data-reporting purposes, the classification of this offense is based solely on police investigation as opposed to the determination of a court, medical examiner, coroner, jury, or other judicial body. The UCR Program does not include the following possible situations when reporting murder and nonnegligent manslaughter: deaths caused by negligence, suicide, or accident; justifiable homicides; and attempts to murder or assaults to murder (which are scored as aggravated assaults).

In 2010, an estimated 14,748 people were murdered throughout the United States, meaning that there were an estimated 4.8 murders per 100,000 inhabitants. Almost 90% of the murders that occurred in the United States in 2010 were within or adjacent to urban or metropolitan areas.

Forcible rape, as defined by the UCR Program, is the carnal knowledge of a female forcibly and against her will. Although state laws might include same-sex sexual assaults in their rape and sexual assault statutory provisions, the FBI data definition counts only rapes of females by males.[42] The UCR data category also includes assaults and attempts to commit rape by force or threat of force, but statutory rape (without force) and other sex offenses are excluded. The UCR data-collection program counts one offense for each female victim of a forcible rape, attempted forcible rape, or assault with intent to rape, regardless of the victim's age. A rape by force involving a female victim and a familial offender is counted as a forcible rape, and not as an act of incest. In 2010, the estimated number of forcible rapes totaled 84,767, and the rate of forcible rapes was estimated at 54.2 offenses per 100,000 female inhabitants. Rapes committed through the use of force or the threat of force comprised 93% of reported rape offenses, and rape attempts accounted for 7% of reported rapes.

The UCR Program defines *robbery* as the taking or attempting to take of anything of value from the care, custody, or control of a person by force or threat of force or violence and/or by putting the victim in fear. In 2010, the estimated number of robberies reported by the FBI totaled 367,832, or 119 per 100,000 inhabitants (Figure 13–5), and the average dollar loss per robbery offense was $1,239. The highest average dollar loss was for banks, which lost $4,410 per offense.

The UCR Program defines *aggravated assault* as an unlawful attack by one person upon another for the purpose of inflicting severe or aggravated bodily injury. The program further specifies that this type of assault is usually accompanied by the use of a weapon or by other means likely to produce death or great bodily harm. Attempted aggravated assault that involves the display of—or threat to use—a gun, knife, or other weapon is included in this crime category because serious personal injury would likely result if the assault were completed. When aggravated assault and larceny-theft occur together, the offense falls under the category of robbery.

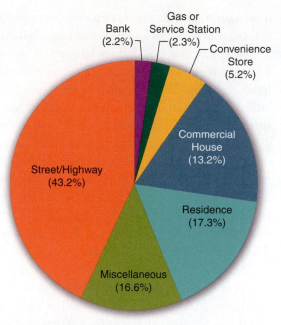

FIGURE 13–5

Robbery Locations, 2010.

Note: Because of rounding, the percentages may not add up to 100.

Federal Bureau of Investigation, *Crime in the United States, 2010* (Washington, DC: Federal Bureau of Investigation, 2011).

During 2010, there were an estimated 778,901 aggravated assaults throughout the nation. The rate of aggravated assaults was 252.3 offenses per 100,000 inhabitants in 2010, and 20.6% of the aggravated assaults for which law enforcement agencies provided expanded data involved a firearm; 27.4% were committed with hands, fists, or feet; 19% with knives and other cutting instruments; and the remainder with other weapons.

Under the UCR Program, the property crime category includes the offenses of burglary, larceny-theft, motor vehicle theft, and arson (Figure 13–6). The object of theft-type offenses is the taking of money or property, but no force or threat of force is used against victims. The property crime category includes arson because that offense involves the destruction of property. If, however, people are killed in arson crimes, the offenses would be counted as homicides under the program.

Throughout the nation in 2010, there were an estimated 9,082,887 property crime offenses, and the rate of property crimes was estimated at 2,941.9 offenses per 100,000

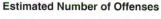

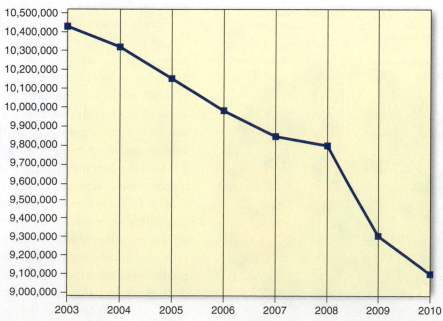

FIGURE 13–6

Property Crimes, 2003–2010.

Federal Bureau of Investigation, *Crime in the United States, 2010* (Washington, DC: Federal Bureau of Investigation, 2011).

inhabitants. Larceny-theft offenses accounted for two-thirds (68.1%) of all property crimes, and those crimes cost an estimated $15.7 billion in total losses.

The UCR Program defines *burglary* as the unlawful entry of a structure to commit a felony or theft. To classify an offense as a burglary, the use of force to gain entry need not have occurred. The program has three subclassifications for burglary: forcible entry, unlawful entry where no force is used, and attempted forcible entry. The UCR definition of *structure* includes, for example, apartment, barn, house trailer or houseboat when used as a permanent dwelling, office, railroad car (but not automobile), stable, and vessel (ship).

In 2010, there were an estimated 2,159,878 burglaries, and burglary accounted for 23.8% of the estimated number of property crimes committed that year. Of all burglaries, 60.5% involved forcible entry, 33.2% were unlawful entries (without force), and the remainder (6.3%) were forcible entry attempts. In 2010, burglary offenses cost victims an estimated $4.6 billion in lost property; overall, the average dollar loss per burglary offense was $2,119. The burglary of residential properties accounted for 73.9% of all burglary offenses.

The UCR Program defines *larceny-theft* as the unlawful taking, carrying, leading, or riding away of property from the possession or constructive possession of another. Examples are thefts of bicycles and motor vehicle parts and accessories, shoplifting, pocket picking, and the stealing of any property or article that is not taken by force and violence or by fraud (Figure 13–7). Attempted larcenies are included. Embezzlement, confidence games, forgery, check fraud, and similar crimes are excluded.

During 2010, there were an estimated 6,185,867 million larceny-thefts nationwide, and larceny-thefts accounted for an estimated 68.1% of all property crimes in that year. The rate of larceny-thefts was 2,003.5 per 100,000 U.S. inhabitants in 2010, and the crime of larceny-theft cost victims an estimated $6.1 billion in lost property. The average value of property taken during larceny-thefts was $988 per offense.

The UCR Program defines *motor vehicle theft* as the theft or attempted theft of a motor vehicle. Under the program, a motor vehicle is a self-propelled vehicle that runs on land surfaces and not on rails. Examples of motor vehicles include sport-utility vehicles, automobiles, trucks, buses, motorcycles, motor scooters, all-terrain vehicles, and snowmobiles. Motor vehicle theft does not include farm equipment, bulldozers, airplanes, construction equipment, or watercraft such as motorboats, sailboats, houseboats, or jet skis. The taking of a motor vehicle for temporary use by someone with lawful access is excluded from this definition.

There were an estimated 737,142 million thefts of motor vehicles nationwide in 2010, and the national rate for motor vehicle thefts was 238.8 per 100,000 residents. The estimated total value of motor vehicles stolen in 2010 was $4.5 billion, averaging $6,152 per vehicle stolen. Among vehicle types, automobiles accounted for 73% of the motor vehicles reported stolen in 2010.

The UCR Program defines *arson* as any willful or malicious burning or attempting to burn, with or without intent to defraud, of a dwelling house, a public building, a motor vehicle or aircraft, the personal property of another, and so on. Only fires that investigation

FIGURE 13–7

Larceny-Theft Offense Distribution, 2010.

Due to rounding, the percentages may not add up to 100.

Federal Bureau of Investigation, *Crime in the United States, 2010* (Washington, DC: Federal Bureau of Investigation, 2011).

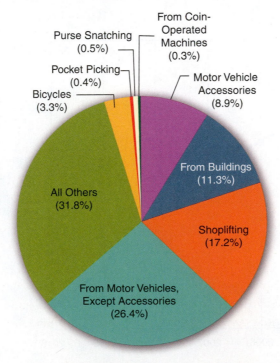

Purse Snatching (0.5%)
From Coin-Operated Machines (0.3%)
Pocket Picking (0.4%)
Bicycles (3.3%)
Motor Vehicle Accessories (8.9%)
From Buildings (11.3%)
All Others (31.8%)
Shoplifting (17.2%)
From Motor Vehicles, Except Accessories (26.4%)

determines to have been willfully set—not fires labeled as suspicious or of unknown origin—are included in arson data collection.

In 2010, 14,197 law enforcement agencies provided at least partial arson data. They reported 48,619 arsons. Arsons involving structures (residential, storage, public, and so on) accounted for 45.5% of the total number of arson offenses. Mobile property was involved in 26% of arsons, and other types of property (such as crops, timber, and fences) accounted for 28.5% of reported arsons. The average dollar loss due to arsons was $17,612, and arsons of industrial/manufacturing structures resulted in the highest average dollar losses (an average of $133,717 per arson). Nationwide, the rate of arson was 19.67 offenses for every 100,000 inhabitants.

RESTITUTION

The 1982 President's Task Force on Victims of Crime recognized the inequitable financial consequences that often follow criminal victimization with these words: "It is simply unfair that victims should have to liquidate their assets, mortgage their homes, or sacrifice their health or education or that of their children while the offender escapes responsibility for the financial hardship he has imposed. It is unjust that a victim should have to sell his car to pay bills while the offender drives to his probation appointments. The victim may be placed in a financial crisis that will last a lifetime. If one of the two must go into debt, the offender should do so."[43] The report recommended that legislation be passed requiring **restitution** in all criminal cases. The report also suggested that mandates be established requiring judges to order that convicted offenders be required to pay restitution in cases in which victims have suffered financially, unless compelling reasons to the contrary can be demonstrated.

restitution
A court requirement that a convicted offender pay money or provide services to the victim of the crime or provide services to the community.

A year later, the American Bar Association (ABA), in its *Guidelines for Fair Treatment of Crime Victims and Witnesses*, recommended that "victims of a crime involving economic loss, loss of earnings, or [loss of] earning capacity should be able to expect the sentencing body to give priority consideration to restitution as a condition of probation."[44]

The President's Task Force and the ABA were both recognizing growing sentiment, brought about throughout the nation by the burgeoning victims' rights movement of the 1970s, in support of offender restitution. Although offenders in times past were often required to make restitution payments to their victims, the development of the concept of the king's peace (discussed earlier) and the associated vision of crime as an offense against society (rather than as primarily a violation of the individual) led to the abandonment of mandated offender restitution and its replacement with fines paid to government authorities.

One of the original proponents of restitution as a sentencing philosophy was criminologist Stephen Schafer. Schafer, who wrote the book *The Victim and His Criminal* in 1968, discussed three types of restitution: (1) compensatory fines, which can be imposed in addition to other court-ordered punishments and compensate the victim for the actual amount of loss; (2) double or treble damages, in which offenders are required, as punishment, to pay the victim back more than the amount of the original injury; and (3) restitution in lieu of other punishment, where the offender discharges any criminal responsibility by compensating the victim. The latter form of restitution imposes no other criminal penalties if the offender meets his or her restitution obligations.[45]

Restitution differs considerably in nature from government-sponsored victims' assistance. Although both may result in financial payments to victims, court-ordered offender restitution is a sentencing option that forces the offender to assume at least some financial responsibility for the crime committed. Restitution advocates argue that criminal offenders should be required to shoulder a substantial portion of the financial burden required to make victims "whole again." Requiring offenders to make restitution payments, they say, helps restore victims to their previous condition of "wholeness" and also places at least partial responsibility for the process back on offenders who caused the loss of "wholeness" to begin with. Advocates of court-ordered restitution, which works through fines and garnishments, claim that, as a sentence, restitution benefits everyone because it lessens society's share of the financial costs of assisting victims and because it enhances the sense of social and individual responsibility that convicted offenders are made to experience.

The Restoration Movement

The change in perspective that the American system of justice underwent in the 1970s and 1980s meant that restitution was no longer seen "solely as a punitive or rehabilitative measure" but came to be understood "as a matter of justice to crime victims."[46] A maturing of the victims' movement led to the development of the concept of restoration, which was built on a restorative justice model.[47] Restorative justice (defined and discussed more fully in Chapter 14) builds on restitution and other sentencing strategies to benefit all parties affected by the criminal event—that is, the victim, society, and the offender.

A report by the U.S. Department of Justice explains restoration this way: "Crime was once defined as a 'violation of the State.' This remains the case today, but we now recognize that crime is far more. It is—among other things—a violation of one person by another. While retributive justice may address the first type of violation adequately, restorative justice is required to effectively address the later. . . . Thus (through restorative justice) we seek to attain a balance between the legitimate needs of the community, the . . . offender, and the victim."[48]

Vermont began a Sentencing Options Program in 1995 built around the concept of reparative probation. The Vermont program provides an example of how the restorative justice model can be put into practice. According to state officials, the Vermont reparative options program, which "requires the offender to make reparations to the victim and to the community, marks the first time in the United States that the restorative justice model has been embraced by a state department of corrections and implemented on a statewide scale."[49] Vermont's reparative program builds on "community reparative boards," consisting of five or six citizens from the community where the crime was committed, and requires face-to-face public meetings between the offender and board representatives. Keeping in mind the program's avowed goals of "making the victim(s) whole again" and having the offender "make amends to the community," board members determine the specifics of the offender's sentence. Options include restitution, community service, victim–offender mediation, victim empathy programs, driver improvement courses, and similar programs. Some advocates of the restoration philosophy of sentencing point out that restitution payments and work programs that benefit the victim may also have the added benefit of rehabilitating the offender. The hope is that such sentences can teach offenders personal responsibility through structured financial obligations, job requirements, regularly scheduled payments, and the like.

One proponent of the restorative justice model points out that a central question that still needs to be answered is, Who or what is restored? According to restoration advocate John V. Wilmerding, "[w]hile various groups embracing different perspectives may say that using the term restorative justice implies that victims, communities, offenders, or even the entire 'trinity' of these benefit from 'restoration,' in fact none of these interpretations suffices completely, for each is vulnerable to criticisms from those with differing opinions or felt philosophical loyalties." A better answer to the question, says Wilmerding, is "equity." He writes: "Heralded in antiquity, crystallized in the major religious philosophies, and brought to bear upon practical social theory during the American Revolution was the premise that a cardinal component of justice is equity, and that some kinds of processes are uniquely suited to restoring equity. And while some of these justice processes might also be said to foster the conservation and even the creation of equity, it may be posited that the restoration of equity is indeed the most important central calling within the modern compensatory trend popularly known as restorative justice."[50] As a consequence of such thinking, Wilmerding suggests use of the term *equity restorative justice* in place of *restorative justice*.

SUMMARY

- A victim is any person against whom an offense has been committed. For certain procedural purposes, a parent or legal guardian is considered to be the victim if the actual victim is below the age of 18 years or is incompetent. A victim may also be one or more family members or relatives designated by the court if the actual victim is deceased or incapacitated.

- During the Golden Age of the Victim, which blossomed a few hundred years ago in England, victims had well-recognized rights, including a personal say in imposing punishments on apprehended offenders.

- A rebirth of the Golden Age began during the 1960s, when a renewed interest in victims worldwide led to a resurgence of efforts intended to assist them.

- Victims' compensation programs are part of the new Golden Age. They exist in many states to help pay the medical and other costs associated with the victimization experience.

- During the past two decades, a flurry of victims' rights legislation has been passed by state governments and by the federal government. The most significant victims' legislation to date has been the 1984 federal Victims of Crime Act (VOCA), which established a federal crime victims' compensation fund as well as the federal Office for Victims of Crime (OVC).

- A key focus of victims' rights advocates today is the passage of a federal constitutional amendment, which proponents claim would give victims and offenders equal standing in criminal proceedings.

- Son of Sam laws, also known as *notoriety-for-profit laws*, provide additional support for the rights of victims by denying convicted offenders the opportunity to further capitalize on their crimes. Such laws set the stage for civil action against infamous offenders who might otherwise profit from the sale of their "story" to media representatives or from the sale of crime memorabilia.

- Victim impact statements, which are supported by laws in many states and (for certain crimes) under federal jurisdiction, provide for the in-court use of victim- or survivor-supplied information by sentencing authorities who want to make an informed sentencing decision. A federal right of allocution permits victims to make in-court statements during the sentencing of offenders who have committed violent or sex crimes.

- Statistics describing the extent of crime in the United States are available from two major sources: the Bureau of Justice Statistics, which publishes the annual National Crime Victimization Survey (NCVS), and the FBI's Uniform Crime Reporting (UCR) Program.

- The NCVS depends primarily on victim self-reports made to surveyors, whereas the UCR Program gathers data on reported crimes and on arrests from police departments nationwide.

- Crime surveys show that, whereas the incidence of crime rose after the 1960s, crime rates declined in most categories during the late 1990s and early 2000s.

- Court-ordered restitution is one method by which victims can recoup some of the costs of their victimization. Restitution supports the restorative justice model, which holds that it is necessary to attain a balance among the legitimate needs of the community, the offender, and the victim.

KEY TERMS

golden age of the
victim, 425

national crime victimization
survey (NCVS), 424

postcrime victimization, 427

restitution, 449

right of allocution, 430

Son of Sam law, 431

Uniform Crime Reporting
(UCR) Program, 441

victim, 424

victim impact statement, 439

victims' rights, 429

victim-/witness-assistance
program, 427

QUESTIONS FOR DISCUSSION

1. Do you believe that the definition of the term *victim* offered by this chapter is adequate? Why or why not?

2. How did the status of crime victims during the historical Golden Age of the Victim differ from the status of victims today? Discuss how a changed view of the nature of crime has affected the status of victims.

3. What is meant by victims' rights? Should today's crime victims have more rights? Explain.

4. Do you believe that a victims' rights amendment to the U.S. Constitution is needed to balance the rights of crime victims with those of suspects? Why or why not?

5. If you were a sentencing judge, what kinds of information would you like a victim impact statement to contain?

CRITICAL THINKING AND APPLICATION PROBLEMS

You work for a state legislator, Amy Vicrites. I. M. Swindler was convicted of defrauding thousands of people of hundreds of millions of dollars in retirement funds. He was convicted, sentenced to 40 years in prison, and fined $500,000, and is currently serving his prison sentence in one of your state's prisons. As a consequence of the fine, successful lawsuits by the victims, and legal fees, Swindler is now broke. Indeed, over $200 million in losses to the victims have been lost. Swindler is charismatic and his case was a cause célèbre. As a result, he is still popular. To make money he posted the following items for sale on eBay:

A. *Worked Rich, Retired Broke*. He wrote a book detailing his crimes, the investigation of his crimes, his trial, and his incarceration. Price: $75.

B. Book with Autograph: A copy of *Worked Rich, Retired Broke* with his autograph. Price: $125.

Your state has a victims' rights statute. The State Victim Support Agency sued Swindler under the law, seeking all of the revenues from his sales, which are estimated to be about $200,000. Swindler defended against the lawsuit by alleging that the law violated his First Amendment free speech rights by targeting his writings. The trial court, appellate court, and state supreme court all found for Swindler, dismissing the suit. Your boss, Vicrites, is furious, as are many people in the state. She has asked you to review the law and to revise the language to bring it into conformity with the First Amendment. She wants to retain the authority to prevent criminals from making money on their crimes in the future. She accepts that nothing can be done with Swindler.

Your Assignment: Revise the following statute in a way that retains the authority of the state to take the revenues earned from crimes by the perpetrators of crimes, to be distributed to the victims of the crimes or to the state if the victims have been fully compensated.

Criminal Anti-Profit and Revenue Redistribution Law

Any person, organization, or entity that earns a profit from the writing, publishing, creating, distributing, or posting of a book, video, or other media about a crime for which there has been a conviction in a court of the state shall withhold 100% of the royalties and other revenues due to the person convicted of the crime(s) that is the subject of the writing, if any. The monies withheld under this provision shall be sent to the State Victim Support Agency and it shall distribute those funds to the victims of the crime or deposit them into the state's victim support fund, as provided for elsewhere in these laws.

LEGAL RESOURCES ON THE WEB

Many victims' organizations have created websites. Some of the better-known sites are listed here.

National Center for Victims of Crime
http://www.ncvc.org

An extensive online resource for victim information and advocacy. Contains many links and much information about the organization's advocacy efforts.

National Crime Victims Research and Treatment Center
http://www.musc.edu/cvc

A website that works to increase understanding of the impact of criminal victimization on adults, children, and their families. Contains information about the center and its work as well as links to related sites.

National Organization for Victim Assistance (NOVA)
http://www.try-nova.org

NOVA is a private nonprofit organization of victim-/witness-assistance programs and practitioners, criminal justice agencies and professionals, mental health professionals, researchers, former victims and survivors, and others who are committed to the recognition and implementation of victims' rights and services. You can set up a free NovaOne online account that allows you to register for NOVA conferences and events, become a NOVA member, renew membership, and access member-only content.

Office for Victims of Crime (OVC)
http://www.ovc.gov

A U.S. Department of Justice site with information about crime victims and resources for crime victims. Contains an extensive collection of links to relevant information.

Victim-Assistance Online
http://www.vaonline.org

Victim-Assistance Online is a nonprofit information, research, and networking resource for victim-assistance specialists, professionals in related disciplines, and all interested in the field of victimology. The Victim-Assistance Online website offers research, reviews, and link directories to more than 40 victim assistance–related topics, including more than 3,000 links to organizations, agencies, and services around the world. The site also includes a virtual library, offering an index of online articles, documents, handbooks, and guides.

Victim Offender Mediation Association (VOMA)
http://www.igc.org/voma

The VOMA website offers information about the field of victim–offender mediation and reconciliation programs.

SUGGESTED READINGS AND CLASSIC WORKS

Coates, Robert B., Boris Kalanj, and Mark S. Umbreit. *Victim Meets Offender: The Impact of Restorative Justice and Mediation.* Monsey, NY: Willow Tree Press, 1994.

Davis, Gwynn. *Making Amends: Mediation and Reparation in Criminal Justice.* New York: Routledge, 1992.

Davis, Robert C., Arthur J. Lurigio, and Wesley Skogan, eds. *Victims of Crime,* 2nd ed. Newbury Park, CA: Sage, 1996.

Fattah, Ezzat A., ed. *From Crime Policy to Victim Policy: Reorienting the Justice System.* New York: St. Martin's Press, 1986.

————.*The Plight of Crime Victims in Modern Society.* New York: St. Martin's Press, 1989.

Fletcher, George P. *With Justice for Some.* Reading, MA: Addison-Wesley, 1995.

Hagan, John. *Victims before the Law: The Organizational Domination of Criminal Law.* Toronto: Butterworth, 1983.

McShane, Marilyn D., and Frank P. Williams III, eds. *Victims of Crime and the Victimization Process,* reprint ed. New York: Garland, 1997.

Neiderbach, Shelley. *Invisible Wounds: Crime Victims Speak.* Binghamton, NY: Haworth Press, 1986.

Poliny, Valiant. *A Public Policy Analysis of the Emerging Victims' Rights Movement.* San Francisco: Austin and Winfield, 1995.

Roberts, Albert R. *Helping Crime Victims: Research, Policy, and Practice.* Newbury Park, CA: Sage, 1990.

Schafer, Stephen. *Compensation and Restitution to Victims of Crime,* 2nd ed. Montclair, NJ: Patterson Smith, 1970.

Viano, Emilio C., ed. *Critical Issues in Victimology: International Perspectives.* New York: Springer, 1992.

Weed, Frank J. *Certainty of Justice: Reform in the Crime Victim Movement.* Hawthorne, NY: Aldine De Gruyter, 1995.

Young, Marlene A. *Victim Assistance: Frontiers and Fundamentals.* Dubuque, IA: Kendall Hunt, 1993.

Young, Marlene A., and John H. Stein, eds. *2001: The Next Generation in Victim Assistance.* Dubuque, IA: Kendall Hunt, 1994.

NOTES

1. Slogan for Victim Rights Week, 1997. See NOVA's website, http://www.access.digex.net/-nova.
2. Kimi Yoshino, "Children's Wounds Detailed," *Fresno Bee,* August 20, 2000, http://www.fresnobee.com/localnews/story/0,1724,190173,00.html (accessed June 3, 2003).
3. "Pitchfork Attacker Kills Kid," *Fresno Bee,* August 24, 2000.
4. As found in Stephen A. Saltzburg and others, *Criminal Law: Cases and Materials* (Charlottesville, VA: Michie, 1994), 38.
5. Violent Crime Control and Law Enforcement Act of 1994, Title XXIII, Section 230101.
6. Federal Bureau of Prisons, Directive 1490.03.
7. Robert Elias, *Victims of the System: Crime Victims and Compensation in American Politics and Criminal Justice* (New Brunswick, NJ: Transaction, 1983), 24–26.
8. Albert R. Roberts, *Helping Crime Victims* (Newbury Park, CA: Sage, 1990).
9. Ibid., 31.
10. California Penal Code, Section 13835.4.

11. National Organization for Victim Assistance website, http://www.trynova.org/about/mission/ (accessed April 1, 2009).

12. National Center for Victims of Crime website, http://www.ncvc.org.

13. H.R. 5107.

14. "Crime Victim Advocates Applaud Enactment of 'Ground-Breaking' Federal Victim Rights Law," NVCAP/MADD press release, November 1, 2004.

15. It takes a two-thirds vote by each chamber of Congress to send a proposed amendment to the states, where ratification by 38 legislatures is required.

16. See National Victims' Constitutional Amendment Passage, "Criminal Justice Professionals Continue to Support the Crime Victims' Rights Amendment, http://www.nvcap.org (accessed February 1, 2009).

17. Richard Carelli, "Victims' Rights," Associated Press online, northern edition, October 18, 1996.

18. Some of the material in this section is adapted from Infolink, National Center for Victims of Crime online, http://www.ncvc.org (accessed June 10, 2009).

19. See James Stark and Howard W. Goldstein, *The Rights of Crime Victims* (New York: Bantam Books, 1985).

20. "Trial and Error: Ten Things the O. J. Simpson Case Has Taught Us—for Better or Worse—about the Criminal Justice System," January 18, 1997, KQED at http://www.kqed.org (accessed October 4, 2002).

21. *Simon & Schuster, Inc. v. New York State Crime Victims Board*, 112 S. Ct. 501 (1992).

22. California Civil Code, Section 2225(b) (1).

23. *Keenan v. Superior Court*, 72 Cal. App. 4th 681 (1999).

24. Mike McKee, "California Justices Junk 'Son of Sam' Restrictions," *Recorder*, February 22, 2002, Law.com (accessed January 22, 2004).

25. Violent Crime Control and Law Enforcement Act of 1994, Title XXIII, Subtitle A, Section 230101.

26. Ibid., Section 230102.

27. National Center for Victims of Crime/Mothers against Drunk Driving/American Prosecutors Research Institute, *Impact Statements: A Victim's Right to Speak: A Nation's Responsibility to Listen* (Washington, DC: National Center for Victims of Crime, July 1994).

28. Robert C. Davis and Barbara E. Smith, "The Effects of Victim Impact Statements on Sentencing Decisions:

A Test in an Urban Setting," *Justice Quarterly* 11, no. 3 (September 1994): 453–69.

29. *Booth v. Maryland*, 107 S. Ct. 2529 (1987).

30. "Supreme Court Closes Term with Major Criminal Justice Rulings," *Criminal Justice Newsletter* 22, no. 13 (July 1, 1991): 2.

31. *Payne v. Tennessee*, 501 U.S. 808 (1991).

32. See "What Say Should Victims Have?" *Time* (May 27, 1991): 61.

33. Susan Bandes, *Victims, "Closure," and the Sociology of Emotion*, Public Law and Legal Theory Working Paper No. 208, University of Chicago Law School, 2008. Available at http://www.law.uchicago.edu/files/files/pl208.pdf.

34. Michael Rand and Shannan Catalano, *Criminal Victimization, 2006* (Washington, DC: Bureau of Justice Statistics, 2007).

35. The information in this section, and some of the wording, is taken from Jennifer L. Truman, *Criminal Victimization, 2010* (Washington, DC: Bureau of Justice Statistics, 20011).

36. Much of the information in this section, and some of the wording, is taken from Patricia Tjaden and Nancy Thoennes, *Prevalence, Incidence, and Consequences of Violence against Women: Findings from the National Violence against Women Survey* (Washington, DC: Bureau of Justice Statistics, 1998).

37. Lisa D. Bastian and Bruce M. Taylor, "Young Black Male Victims: National Crime Victimization Survey," a BJS Crime Data Brief (Washington, DC: Bureau of Justice Statistics, 1994).

38. Data in this section come from *Elderly Crime Victims: National Crime Victimization Survey* (Washington, DC: Bureau of Justice Statistics, March 1994); and Patsy A. Klaus, *Crimes against Persons Age 65 or Older* (Washington, DC: Bureau of Justice Statistics, revised January 2000).

39. Jennifer L. Truman, *Criminal Victimization, 2010* (Washington, DC: Bureau of Justice Statistics, 2011).

40. Ibid.

41. Much of the information in this section, and some of the wording, is taken from Federal Bureau of Investigation, *Crime in the United States, 2010* (Washington, DC: Federal Bureau of Investigation, 20011).

42. Of course, the reporting rule does not preclude the bringing of rape or sexual assault charges against anyone perpetrating same-sex assaults or against women who rape men.

43. President's Task Force on Victims of Crime, *Final Report* (Washington, DC: U.S. Government Printing Office, 1982).

44. *Guidelines for Fair Treatment of Crime Victims and Witnesses* (Chicago: American Bar Association, 1983), 22.

45. Stephen Schafer, *The Victim and His Criminal: A Study in Functional Responsibility* (New York: Random House, 1968).

46. Susan Hillenbrand, "Restitution and Victim Rights in the 1980s," in *Victims of Crime: Problems, Policies and Programs*, edited by Arthur J. Lurigio, Wesley G. Skogan, and Robert C. Davis (Newbury Park, CA: Sage, 1990), 192.

47. Restorative justice is sometimes also termed *community justice* or *relational justice*.

48. Gordon Bazemore and Mark S. Umbreit, *Balanced and Restorative Justice: Program Summary* (Washington, DC: Office of Juvenile Justice and Delinquency Prevention, October 1994), foreword.

49. E-mail communications with the Office of Reparative Programs, Department of Corrections, State of Vermont, July 3, 1995.

50. John Wilmerding, "Toward a Campaign for Equity-Restorative Justice," e-mail communication, January 3, 1997.

© Corbis Premium RF/Alamy

14

Punishment and Sentencing

CHAPTER OUTLINE

OBJECTIVES

After reading this chapter, you should be able to

- Explain the different sentencing rationales.
- Summarize the constitutional issues involved in sentencing.
- Summarize the advantages and disadvantages of plea bargaining.
- Summarize the features of three-strikes laws, and expound on their relative effectiveness.
- Explain restorative justice, and describe how it differs from retribution as a purpose of criminal punishment.
- Explain the issues associated with the death penalty and the arguments for and against it.
- Explain how *habeas corpus* appeals are limited in capital cases, and provide the rationale underlying such limitations.
- Summarize the Eighth Amendment's three clauses and give examples of recent Supreme Court decisions concerning the application of the Eighth Amendment to capital punishment and other specific forms of punishment.
- Describe alternative sentencing options.

We will not punish a man because he hath offended, but that he may offend no more; nor does punishment ever look to the past, but to the future; for it is not the result of passion, but that the same thing be guarded against in time to come.

—Seneca (3 BC–AD 65)

Punishment, that is justice for the unjust.

—Saint Augustine (AD 345–430)

457

INTRODUCTION

sentencing
The process through which a sentencing authority imposes a lawful punishment or other sanction on a person convicted of violating the criminal law.

This chapter describes the purposes of criminal punishment and the sentencing of offenders. **Sentencing** is the last stage of a criminal trial. It can be defined as the process through which a sentencing authority imposes a lawful punishment or other sanction on a person convicted of violating the criminal law. The great Christian author C. S. Lewis, writing about the justice system, once penned these words: "It is only as deserved or undeserved that a sentence can be just or unjust." As you read through the following chapter-opening story, which is taken directly from the opinion of the Utah Supreme Court in the case of *State v. Wood* (1993),[1] ask yourself just what kind of punishment, if any, might be "deserved" in this case.

On October 25, 1988, Lance Conway Wood, newly released from the Utah State Prison, moved into the Cedar City (Utah) two-bedroom apartment of his girlfriend, Brenda Stapely, and her roommate, Paula Jones. Soon after, Michael Archuleta, also just released from prison, moved into the same apartment to be with his girlfriend, Paula Jones. Wood and Archuleta had known each other in prison.

On November 21, 1988, Wood and Archuleta purchased soft drinks at a local convenience store. After adding whiskey to their drinks, the two men engaged in a conversation with Gordon Church, who was seated in his car in a nearby parking lot. Church drove Wood and Archuleta up and down Main Street and then up Cedar Canyon. After returning to Cedar City, Church left Wood and Archuleta at their apartment complex.

Wood and Archuleta walked to the apartment of Anthony Sich, who lived above the apartment rented to Stapely and Jones. Wood told Sich that he was going into the mountains and asked if he could borrow a pair of gloves. Sich sent Wood to retrieve the gloves from his car, and while Wood was outside, Church returned and invited him and Archuleta to go for another drive.

Church drove Wood and Archuleta back to Cedar Canyon and pulled off the road. Wood and Archuleta exited the car first and began to walk down a path. Archuleta told Wood that he wanted to rob Church, and Wood acquiesced. Church overtook the two men, and the three continued walking up the trail. As the men started back down the trail toward the car, Archuleta grabbed Church and put a knife to his neck. Although Wood attempted to stop Archuleta by grabbing his arm, Archuleta made a surface cut on Church's neck. Church broke free and ran, but Archuleta chased after and tackled him, again putting the knife to his neck and threatening to kill him. Archuleta cut Church's throat again so that the two cuts formed an "X" on the front of Church's neck.

Archuleta bent Church forward over the hood of the car and, with the knife still at Church's throat, had anal intercourse with him. At Church's request, Archuleta used a condom. Archuleta then turned to Wood, who was standing by the trunk of the car, and asked if he "wanted any." Wood declined. Archuleta went to the trunk of the car and opened it. He told Wood that he was looking for something with which he could bind Church. Wood removed a spare tire and a fan from the trunk, while Archuleta retrieved tire chains and battery cables. Wood remained at the rear of the car, while Archuleta returned to the front, where he wrapped the tire chains around Church. Archuleta also fastened the battery cable clamps to Church's genitals. Wood maintained before and at trial that he removed the clamps from Church as soon as he realized what Archuleta had done.

Archuleta led Church to the rear of the car and forced him into the trunk. Wood and Archuleta replaced the spare tire and fan and drove to a truck stop near Cedar City where they purchased gas. They continued north on Interstate 15 until they reached the Dog Valley exit. They parked along a deserted dirt road where Archuleta told Wood, "You know we have to kill him."

Archuleta removed Church from the trunk and attempted to kill him by breaking his neck. When that failed, Church suffered several blows to the head with a tire iron and a jack. The tire iron was then shoved and kicked so far into Church's rectum that it pierced his liver. A state medical examiner testified that the cause of death was injuries to the head and skull due to a blunt force and the internal injuries caused by the tire iron inserted into Church's rectum.

Wood told police that he waited inside the car while Archuleta killed Church. Evidence adduced at trial, however, showed that Wood's pants and jacket were splattered with blood in a cast-off pattern indicating that Wood was within two or three feet of Church, who was on the ground during the beating, and that Wood was facing Church when the blows were struck. A blood spot appeared on the back of Archuleta's jacket, and Wood's shoes bore a transfer or contact blood stain caused by contact with a bloody object. Investigators found strands of human hair consistent with Church's hair wrapped around Wood's shoelaces. The injuries to Church's lower jaw were consistent with being kicked by someone wearing Wood's shoes. Three paired lesions on Church's back were caused by a dull-tipped instrument, such as the red-handled side cutters found in the pocket of Wood's jeans.

After Church died, Wood and Archuleta dragged his body to some nearby trees, where they covered it with branches. They swept their path with branches on the way back to the car to conceal any footprints. With Wood at the wheel, the pair again drove north on I-15 and abandoned Church's car in Salt Lake City.

Wood called his friend Christy Worsfold and asked if he and Archuleta could come to her apartment for a few minutes. When the men arrived at the apartment, Worsfold immediately noticed that Archuleta's pants were caked with blood. Wood explained that they had been rabbit hunting the night before, their car had broken down, and they had hitchhiked to Salt Lake. The two men then went to a thrift store, where Archuleta bought some clean pants, and Archuleta repeated the rabbit hunting story to the store clerk.

Archuleta discarded his bloody jeans in a drainage ditch near the 45th South on-ramp to I-15 in Salt Lake County. He and Wood then went into a nearby Denny's restaurant, where Wood left the gloves he had borrowed from Sich. After eating, the two hitchhiked as far as the Draper exit, where Archuleta pulled out Church's wallet, scattered its contents, and handed the wallet to Wood. They next hitchhiked to Salem, where they visited Archuleta's father. From there, they hitchhiked to Cedar City, arriving at about 11:30 p.m.

Wood immediately went upstairs to Sich's apartment and told him about the murder. When Sich advised him to contact the police, Wood responded, "[M]aybe I could get some kind of federal protection." Sich and Wood walked to a local convenience store, where Wood called Brenda Stapely, who was in Phoenix, and told her that Archuleta had killed someone. Stapely contacted John Graff, Wood's parole officer, and told him to call Wood at the store. Graff called Wood and arranged to meet him at the convenience store. Just before Graff's arrival with the police, Wood discarded Church's wallet.

Wood and Sich accompanied Graff and a police officer to the corrections department office, where Wood recounted the events of the previous night. The police arrested Archuleta for the murder and, after several interviews with Wood, also charged Wood with murder in the first degree, aggravated sexual assault, object rape, forcible sexual abuse, aggravated kidnapping, aggravated assault, and possession of a stolen vehicle. . . . Wood was tried by a jury for first-degree murder, aggravated sexual assault, and aggravated kidnapping. The jury found him guilty on all three counts. Because the jury could not reach a unanimous verdict as to the death penalty, the court imposed a life sentence for first-degree murder and two consecutive mandatory minimum sentences of ten years to life for aggravated sexual assault and aggravated kidnapping.[2]

> *The purpose of the law in punishing people is to prevent others from committing a like crime or crimes. Its prime purpose is to deter people from committing offences.*
>
> —*The King v. Porter, 55 Commw. L.R. 182, 186–188 (1933)*

As we asked at the start of this chapter: Would you say that the punishment imposed on Wood was appropriate? Might some other punishment have been "deserved"? You may be interested to know that, in this case, the Utah Supreme Court upheld Wood's conviction and sentence.

SENTENCING RATIONALES

One fundamental way of distinguishing crimes from violations of the civil law, or torts, is to recognize that crimes are subject to punishment. As one legal scholar says, "The best candidate for a conceptual proposition about the criminal law is that the infliction of 'punishment' is sufficient to render a legal process criminal in nature."[3] Noted legal scholar and professor at Columbia University School of Law George P. Fletcher notes, "As a test for when processes are criminal, the Supreme Court unhesitatingly invokes the concept of 'punishment' as the relevant criterion."[4] Hence, regardless of the classification given to a statute by a legislature ("criminal," "civil," or "administrative"), if punishment is associated with violation of the law, the U.S. Supreme Court has ruled that constitutional guarantees of due process must apply.

The need to assign blame and the need to punish wrongdoers may be fundamental human qualities. Criminal law itself may be rooted in deep moral and psychological principles basic to the human way of life. Within this context, it is important to realize that punishment, as a mechanism of the criminal law, can be distinguished from other attempts to discourage undesirable conduct, such as taxes, licensing requirements, civil liability, and administrative regulations. Well-known legal philosopher H. L. A. Hart identifies five distinguishing features of criminal punishment that set it apart from other sanctions:[5]

1. It must involve pain or other consequences normally considered unpleasant.
2. It must be for an offense against legal rules.
3. It must be imposed against an actual or supposed offender for his offense.
4. It must be intentionally administered by human beings other than the offender.
5. It must be imposed and administered by an authority constituted by a legal system against which the offense is committed.

More important, perhaps, than any definition of *punishment* is the purpose of punishment under criminal law. Lewis's notion of punishment "as deserved," alluded to at the start of this chapter, underlies the purpose of most criminal punishments and supports what is today called the just deserts philosophy. **Just deserts** is a popular model of criminal sentencing that holds that criminal offenders deserve the punishment they receive at the hands of the state and that suggests that punishments should be appropriate to the type and severity of crime committed. Although at first glance the just deserts philosophy may appeal to common sense, it is important to realize that punishment is not the only goal of sentencing. There are five primary sentencing rationales that operate in American criminal justice today (Figure 14–1):

1. Retribution
2. Deterrence
3. Rehabilitation
4. Restoration
5. Incapacitation

Each is discussed in the following pages.

Retribution

One goal of criminal sentencing is retribution. **Retribution** is the most punishment-oriented of all sentencing goals and underlies the just deserts philosophy. As one writer observes, "The distinctive aspect of retributivism is that the moral desert of an offender is a *sufficient* reason to punish him or her. . . . Retributivism is a very straightforward theory of

just deserts
A model of criminal sentencing that holds that criminal offenders deserve the punishment they receive at the hands of the state and that suggests that punishments should be appropriate to the type and severity of crime committed.

retribution
The act of taking revenge on a criminal perpetrator. The most punishment-oriented of all sentencing goals, retribution claims that we are justified in punishing offenders because they deserve it.

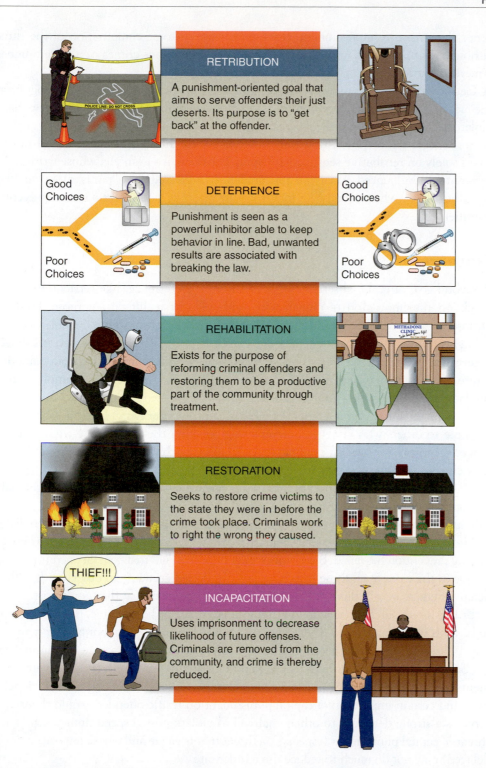

FIGURE 14–1

The Five Purposes of Sentencing.

RETRIBUTION

A punishment-oriented goal that aims to serve offenders their just deserts. Its purpose is to "get back" at the offender.

DETERRENCE

Good Choices

Poor Choices

Punishment is seen as a powerful inhibitor able to keep behavior in line. Bad, unwanted results are associated with breaking the law.

Good Choices

Poor Choices

REHABILITATION

Exists for the purpose of reforming criminal offenders and restoring them to be a productive part of the community through treatment.

METHADONE CLINIC

RESTORATION

Seeks to restore crime victims to the state they were in before the crime took place. Criminals work to right the wrong they caused.

INCAPACITATION

THIEF!!!

Uses imprisonment to decrease likelihood of future offenses. Criminals are removed from the community, and crime is thereby reduced.

punishment: We are justified in punishing because and only because offenders deserve it."[6] Still, retribution may call for even harsher punishments than those that are merely "deserved." The purpose of retribution is to "get back" at the offender by meting out a punishment that is in some primal way satisfying to the social group and to the victim or his or her survivors.

In older times, even minor offenses could be severely punished. The punishment for simple theft, for example, could be death—a sanction often imposed on the spot, before a pursuing mob, once the offender had been caught. The Old Testament dictum of "an eye for an eye, a tooth for a tooth" may have been intended to reduce the severity of punishment, bringing it in line with what was deserved. Punishments imposed by today's criminal law

Although the Law of God may ordain that some men must die; the law of man is always insufficient to determine who those might be.

—Charles Black

generally consist of imprisonment, fines, probation, or some combination of the three—although death remains an option for some especially serious crimes in a large number of American jurisdictions.

Central to an understanding of retribution as a sentencing philosophy is recognition of the fact that it holds offenders responsible for their behavior and supports the view that law violators freely choose their illegal courses of action.

Some legal philosophers, however, have suggested that punishment should never be based solely on retributive sentiments. Jeremy Bentham, for example, whose writings have substantially influenced American jurisprudence, suggested that "punishment ought not be inflicted . . . where it must be inefficacious: where it cannot act so as to prevent the mischief."[7]

Deterrence

deterrence
A goal of criminal sentencing that seeks to prevent others from committing crimes similar to the one for which an offender is being sentenced.

specific deterrence
A goal of criminal sentencing that seeks to prevent a particular offender from engaging in repeat criminality.

general deterrence
A goal of criminal sentencing that seeks to prevent others from committing crimes similar to the one for which a particular offender is being sentenced by making an example of the person sentenced.

A second goal of criminal sentencing is deterrence. Deterrence, like retribution, also depends on the imposition of punishment—although for a different purpose. Under the philosophy of deterrence, punishment is seen as a powerful inhibitor, capable of keeping behavior in line. Two types of **deterrence** can be identified: specific and general. **Specific deterrence** is intended to deter the individual sentenced to punishment from committing future offenses. A burglar sentenced to a number of years in prison, for example, may find the lack of freedom such a painful experience that he or she refrains from committing any new crimes once released. **General deterrence**, on the other hand, uses punishment as an example to others who may be contemplating breaking the law. Hence the burglar sentenced to prison stands as an example to associates that they, too, may face a similar fate if they choose the same course of action.

Critics of deterrence say that there is little evidence that punishment deters criminal behavior. In fact, say critics, many criminals seem to commit one offense after another, a fact that calls into question the efficacy of deterrence as a sentencing philosophy. Other writers disagree: "If I interview a thousand prisoners, I collect information about a thousand men in whose cases general prevention has failed. But I cannot infer from this data that general prevention is ineffective in the cases of all those who have not committed crimes."[8] In other words, although deterrent effects may be difficult to measure, that doesn't mean that they don't exist.

Still other researchers have found that for deterrence to be effective, punishment needs to be both swift and certain.[9] Delayed punishment or punishments that may or may not be imposed seem to lessen the deterrent effects of any efforts intended to reduce criminal activity. Severity of punishment may also be important as a deterrent effect, but severe punishments may be more significant deterrents of minor offenses than of major ones. Hence the swift and certain imposition of capital punishment on traffic offenders would theoretically serve as a strong deterrent to others inclined to violate posted speed limits, although the threat of capital punishment (especially a threat that is vague and whose imposition is often delayed) may not do much to reduce the murder rate.

Rehabilitation

rehabilitation
The attempt to reform a criminal offender. Also, the state in which a reformed offender is said to be.

Rehabilitation, also a goal of criminal sentencing, is quite different in its purpose than retribution or deterrence. The purpose of rehabilitation is to reform criminal offenders, restoring them to productive lives within the community. Rehabilitation programs, which may also include a punishment component (as punishment *can* result in behavioral change), often involve job or skills training, educational coursework leading to high school completion, counseling, and psychological treatment. From the point of view of rehabilitation, the nature of the criminal offense is of less significance than the supposed likelihood of reforming the offender—except insofar as the offense committed provides a clue to the need for specific rehabilitative strategies.

The term *rehabilitation*, although widely used, may be something of a misnomer, as it literally means to return a person (or thing) to a former state. A criminal offender's "former state" may, of course, not have been a desirable one from the point of view of those stressing rehabilitation. Many offenders grew up in crime-prone areas and may have been inculcated early in life with values that easily led to law-violating behavior. Perhaps a more appropriate term for what advocates of rehabilitation have in mind is *resocialization*, a word sometimes associated with the process of rehabilitation.

Although hopes for the successful rehabilitation of offenders ran high for two or three decades after World War II, studies of recidivism rates among released prisoners dispelled the notion that rehabilitation could be easily achieved. *Recidivism* refers to the rate at which formerly adjudicated offenders return to crime. It is more formally expressed as the rate at which released prisoners are reconvicted of new offenses during a specified period of time following release—often five years. One of the best-known studies of recidivism rates was conducted by Robert Martinson in the early 1970s. Martinson surveyed 231 studies evaluating correctional treatment programs between the years 1945 and 1967, and his report, published in 1974,[10] proclaimed the failure of rehabilitative efforts. Martinson's findings, which showed recidivism rates of between 70 and 90%, led to development of the "nothing works" doctrine, a perspective on criminal sentencing that held that efforts at rehabilitation were doomed to failure.

Restoration

Restoration, the fourth goal of criminal sentencing, emphasizes the emotional and financial cost of crime to its victims and seeks to restore crime victims to a state akin to that which they were in before victimization. **Restoration** is a sentencing goal that seeks to make victims and the community "whole again." It frequently builds on the use of fines, restitution, and community service—forms of punishment that may be imposed on offenders by a sentencing judge. Court-ordered restitution requires convicted offenders to repay their victims through an agency of the court, such as the clerk of courts office. Restitution payments, like fines, may be collected on an installment basis, as arranged by the court. Court-ordered restitution became an option under federal law with passage of the 1982 Victim and Witness Protection Act, which permits federal courts to impose restitution as part of a sentence.

restoration
A sentencing goal that seeks to make victims and the community "whole again."

Although restoration has been a goal of sentencing for many years, emphasis today is on the notion of **restorative justice**, a concept that identifies a triad of needs: (1) the need to compensate victims, (2) the need to place appropriate responsibility on the criminal offender, and (3) the need to attempt reintegration of the offender with the community. A report on restorative justice by the U.S. Department of Justice explains the term this way: "Crime was once defined as a 'violation of the state.' This remains the case today, but we now recognize that crime is far more. It is—among other things—a violation of one person by another. While retributive justice may address the first type of violation adequately, restorative justice is required to effectively address the latter. . . . Thus, [through restorative justice] we seek to attain a balance between the legitimate needs of the community, the . . . offender, and the victim."[11] Some of the most significant differences between retributive and restorative justice are listed in Table 14–1.

restorative justice
A sentencing model that builds on restitution and community participation in an attempt to make the victim "whole again."

Incapacitation

A final sentencing philosophy can be found in incapacitation. **Incapacitation** is a strategy that makes use of imprisonment or some other sentencing option to reduce the likelihood that an offender will be capable of committing future offenses. As one writer says, "[I]ncapacitation

incapacitation
The use of imprisonment or other means to reduce the likelihood that an offender will be capable of committing future offenses.

TABLE 14–1 Differences between Retributive and Restorative Justice

Retributive Justice	Restorative Justice
Crime is an act against the state, a violation of a law, an abstract idea.	Crime is an act against another person or the community.
The criminal justice system controls crime.	Crime control lies primarily in the community.
Offender accountability is defined as taking punishment.	Offender accountability is defined as assuming responsibility and taking action to repair harm.
Crime is an individual act with individual responsibility.	Crime has both individual and social dimensions of responsibility.
Victims are peripheral to the process of resolving a crime.	Victims are central to the process of resolving a crime.
The offender is defined by deficits.	The offender is defined by the capacity to make reparation.
The emphasis is on an adversarial relationship.	The emphasis is on dialogue and negotiation.
Pain is imposed to punish and deter.	Restitution is a means of restoring both parties; the goal is reconciliation and restoration.
The community is on the sidelines, represented abstractly by the state.	The community is a facilitator in the restorative process.
The response to crime is focused on the offender's past behavior.	The response is focused on the harmful consequences of the offender's behavior; the emphasis is on the future and on reparation.
The process depends on proxy professionals.	Both the offender and the victim are directly involved.

Source: Adapted from Gordon Bazemore and Mark S. Umbreit, *Balanced and Restorative Justice: Program Summary* (Washington, DC: Office of Juvenile Justice and Delinquency Prevention, October 1994), 7.

---

habitual offender
A person sentenced under the provisions of a statute declaring that those who are convicted of a given offense and are shown to have previously been convicted of another specified offense(s) shall receive a more severe penalty than that for the current offense alone.

career offender
Under federal sentencing guidelines, a person who (1) is at least 18 years old at the time of the most recent offense, (2) is convicted of a felony that is either a crime of violence or a controlled substance offense, and (3) has at least two prior felony convictions of either a crime of violence or a controlled substance offense.

three-strikes legislation
Statutory provisions that mandate lengthy prison terms for criminal offenders convicted of a third violent crime or felony.

is founded on the basic premise that those who are removed from a community, particularly through incarceration, cannot victimize society during a time of physical separation."[12]

In modern guise, incapacitation was embodied in **habitual offender** statutes that were passed in many states during the 1940s and 1950s and were recommended in the 1973 report of the National Advisory Commission on Criminal Justice Standards and Goals. The commission advised that "[s]tate penal code revisions should contain separate provisions for sentencing offenders when, in the interest of public protection, it is considered necessary to incapacitate them for substantial periods of time." The report went on to define a dangerous offender as "a person over twenty-one years of age whose criminal conduct is found by the court to be characterized by: (a) a pattern of repetitive behavior which poses a serious threat to the safety of others, (b) a pattern of persistent aggressive behavior with heedless indifference to the consequences, or (c) a particularly heinous offense involving the threat or infliction of serious bodily harm."

In a similar vein, federal sentencing guidelines say that defendants can be counted as **career offenders** if "(1) the defendant was at least eighteen years old at the time of the . . . offense, (2) the . . . offense is a crime of violence or trafficking in a controlled substance, and (3) the defendant has at least two prior felony convictions of either a crime of violence or a controlled substance offense."[13] In 1990, the category of armed career criminal was added to federal sentencing guidelines, subjecting those who fall into that category to some of the most severe sanctions available under federal law.

As a consequence of efforts at incapacitation, prisons throughout the United States were used during the 1980s as warehouses for huge numbers of prisoners that judges and paroling authorities were reluctant to release onto the nation's streets. The trend toward warehousing, which continues today, can be seen in **three-strikes legislation**, which mandates long prison sentences for offenders who are convicted of a third felony offense.

California has one of the nation's toughest three-strikes laws, requiring life sentences for "three-time losers." Shortly after passage, however, California's three-strikes law was called into question by a California Supreme Court ruling,[14] which held that judges could disregard prior convictions at sentencing when they believed that a mandatory life prison sentence would be unwarranted. In 1997, however, the California Supreme Court ruled that a three-strikes defendant could be punished under the law for past juvenile convictions for violent felonies.[15] Specifically, the court held that prior adjudication of a delinquent offender 16 years of age or older, for an offense that would count as a strike if it were the result of an adult conviction, could count as a strike once that person attained adult status under state law (that is, age 18).

In further refinements to the applicability of the state's three-strikes law, the California Supreme Court ruled in 1998 that a single criminal act involving multiple charges could count as more than one felony offense for purposes of the law.[16] Also in 1998, the state's supreme court put limits on judges' discretion in exempting repeat offenders from receiving lengthy sentences under the three-strikes law. The court ruled that a defendant whose past and present conduct showed him or her to be within "the spirit of the three-strikes law" must be given the full sentence required by the statute.[17] That year, in further support of California's law, the U.S. Supreme Court upheld a provision of the statute that doubles prison sentences for a second strike, saying that the sentencing requirement does not violate double jeopardy provisions of the U.S. Constitution.[18]

A year later, the U.S. Supreme Court refused to hear the case of Michael Wayne Riggs, who was caught stealing vitamin pills from a California supermarket and was sentenced to 25 years in prison based on a record of drug crimes, robbery, and other felonies. Many saw the Court's refusal to hear the case as an endorsement of California's three-strikes sentencing scheme.[19]

On March 7, 2000, California voters passed Proposition 21, which broadened legal categories for determining what felonies can count under that state's three-strikes law. As a result of the change, violent and serious felonies now officially include gang-related felonies and conspiracies under California law.

Supporters of three-strikes laws argue that they lower crime rates by ensuring that those convicted under them are denied the opportunity to continue their criminal careers. In 2003, in two separate cases,[20] the U.S. Supreme Court lent considerable support to California's three-strikes sentencing scheme when it upheld the three-strikes convictions of Gary Ewing and Leandro Andrade. Ewing, sentenced to 25 years to life in prison following conviction for felony grand theft of three golf clubs, had four prior felony convictions at the time he was convicted. Andrade, who had a long prison record, was sentenced to 50 years in prison (two 25-year terms to be served consecutively) for two petty-theft convictions. Under California law, a person who commits petty theft can be charged with a felony if he or she has prior felony convictions. The charge is known as "petty theft with prior convictions." Justice Sandra Day O'Connor, writing for the Court, noted that states should be able to decide when repeat offenders "must be isolated from society . . . to protect the public safety," even when nonserious crimes trigger the lengthy sentence. The Court also found that it is not cruel and unusual punishment to impose a possible life term for a nonviolent felony when a defendant has a history of serious or violent convictions.

As a sentencing strategy, incapacitation works best when it incapacitates those who are most likely to commit repeat offenses. Hence three-strikes and other similar "get-tough-on-crime" policies represent a philosophy of **selective incapacitation** under which only the most dangerous offenders are separated from society for long periods of time.

Incapacitation that makes use of imprisonment can be very costly. Proponents of California's three-strikes legislation, however, argue that increased prison costs are a small price to pay for substantial reductions in crime rates. Reduced crime rates, they say, will quickly translate into substantial savings in the social costs associated with crime. In 1996, for example, California's then-Governor Pete Wilson said that the state's three-strikes law

selective incapacitation
A sentencing strategy that imprisons or otherwise removes from society a select group of offenders, especially those considered to be most dangerous.

had reduced crime, had kept potential repeat offenders out of the state, and had saved millions of dollars in costs associated with crime.[21] The governor cited a report released by the California Department of Corrections, which concluded that, over the first two years of the program's existence, three-strikes sentences had resulted in the incarceration of 1,342 additional offenders and had increased the cost to taxpayers for new prison beds by $41 million. In contrast, said Wilson, social costs associated with new crimes had been reduced by $150 million during the same time period. Imprisonment of another 14,497 offenders on second-strike convictions, the governor added, prevented them from committing more than $1.7 billion in crime each year.[22] Even so, in 2012 California voters approved Proposition 36, which revised the state's three-strikes law to impose life sentences only when the third or last felony conviction is for a serious or violent crime. Exceptions include third strikes involving nonviolent sex or drug offenses, or those that involve a firearm.

Although lengthy prison terms may sound retributive, it is important to remember that a sentencing philosophy of incapacitation requires only restraint and not punishment. Hence sentencing options that make use of home confinement, the electronic monitoring of offenders at home and at work, and other methods of restricting an offender's movements could all come under the rubric of incapacitation. Realistically, however, retributive influences are being increasingly brought to bear on incarcerated populations. Some states, for example, have limited prisoner access to weightlifting equipment, curtailed furlough programs, and reduced opportunities for prison-based entertainment, including restrictions on the availability of television sets and limitations on programming. Hence a mix of efforts directed at both incapacitation and retribution—with a built-in smattering of hopes for both deterrent and rehabilitative effects—tends to characterize American sentencing philosophy today.

CONSTITUTIONAL LIMITATIONS

Several constitutional provisions come into play during sentencing and punishment. For example, you will soon learn that the Sixth Amendment's right to a jury trial has significantly affected sentencing procedure in recent years. Of course, due process is omnipresent, providing a safety net of fairness. But the most significant provisions in the Constitution in regard to sentencing and punishment are found in the Eighth Amendment, which reads:

> Excessive bail shall not be required, nor excessive fines imposed, nor cruel and unusual punishments inflicted.

There are three clauses in the Eighth Amendment. The prohibition of cruel and unusual punishments, the prohibition of excessive fines, and the prohibition of excessive bail. The first two have been incorporated and therefore apply to the states. The excessive bail clause has not been incorporated. Most scholars believe, however, that it will be incorporated in the near future, and today all of the states provide for bail with common exceptions, such as when a detainee poses a threat to others, is likely to obstruct justice, or is a flight risk. Courts have universally recognized these exceptions.

In regard to cruel and unusual punishments, the Supreme Court has held that the concept of cruelty is changing, reflecting contemporary standards of decency. So what was acceptable in 1791, when the Eighth Amendment became effective, may not be acceptable today. Indeed there has been an explosion in Eighth Amendment jurisprudence in recent decades. Today, inmates enjoy protections never imagined by the Framers, including the right to medical care, a minimum amount of space, exercise/physical acitivity, a healthy diet, and access to legal materials, among other rights. The Eighth Amendment also distinguishes between pretrial detainees, who have greater rights, and convicted prisoners, and many forms of punishment that were once common are considered cruel today. Several limitations created by the Eighth Amendment will be mentioned in this chapter.

IMPOSING CRIMINAL SANCTIONS

At the beginning of this chapter, we said that sentencing is the process through which a sentencing authority imposes a lawful punishment or other sanction on a person convicted of violating the criminal law. In almost all cases, the sentencing authority is a judge, although in some jurisdictions and for certain types of crimes, juries may be called on to recommend an appropriate sentence.

Until recently, judges in most U.S. jurisdictions had considerably more leeway in sentencing decisions than they do today. As little as 30 years ago, most jurisdictions in the United States followed the practice of indeterminate sentencing. An **indeterminate sentence** is "a type of sentence to imprisonment in which the commitment, instead of being for a specified single time quantity, such as three years, is for a range of time, such as two to five years, or five years maximum and zero minimum."[23] Like other sentences, indeterminate sentences for multiple offenses could be imposed either concurrently or consecutively. A **consecutive sentence** is "one of two or more sentences imposed at the same time, after conviction for more than one offense, and which is served in sequence with the other sentences,"[24] that is, consecutive sentences are served one after the other. Conversely, a **concurrent sentence** is one that is served at the same time another sentence is being served (Figure 14–2).

Indeterminate sentences were the rule throughout most of the United States for well over a hundred years. They were imposed in the belief that an offender facing a flexible sentence would be motivated to *earn* an early release from confinement through good behavior. Under the indeterminate model, the inmate's behavior while incarcerated is the primary determinant of the amount of time served. Hence inherent in indeterminate sentencing strategies is the hope of rehabilitation through self-motivation.

As disappointment with the rehabilitative ideal grew, however, many states and the federal government increasingly switched to determinate sentencing approaches. In 1978, California, a bellwether state, joined the determinate sentencing bandwagon with passage of the California Determinate Sentencing Act. A **determinate sentence** sets a single standard "time quantity"[25] of imprisonment. In determinate sentencing jurisdictions, judges have little leeway in imposing sentences, and criminal law violators are sentenced to predetermined punishments generally set by law. The California law, for example, allows judges to impose a short, average-length, or long sentence for each offense of which a defendant is convicted. Judges must, however, impose the average-length sentence unless extenuating circumstances indicate that either the shorter or longer sentence is more appropriate. Any deviation from the standard sentence requires judges to explain in writing, and for the record, why that deviation was made. Imposition of a long sentence requires judges in California to hold a formal fact-finding hearing before sentence is passed.

Another reason for the growth of determinate sentencing schemes, which are also variously termed *fixed*, *mandatory*, and *structured sentencing*, was a perceived need to ensure three fundamental sentencing principles: proportionality, equity, and social debt. **Proportionality** refers to the belief that the severity of sanctions should bear a direct relationship to the seriousness of the crime committed. Under the principle of proportionality, offenders committing similar crimes should receive similar sentences. Under indeterminate sentencing practices, however, two offenders who commit virtually the same offense but come before different judges may receive very different sentences, resulting in sentencing disparities and perceived inequities. Hence the notoriety of "hanging judges," who imposed strict punishments on convicted offenders, is often contrasted with the leniency of "soft judges," who could be depended on to "go easy" on those who stood before them. **Equity,** a related concept, is based on a concern with social equality and means that similar crimes should be punished with the same degree of severity, regardless of the social or personal characteristics of offenders. According to the equity principle, extralegal factors (such as gender, race, financial status, age, physical appearance, and education) should not

indeterminate sentence
A relatively unspecific term of incarceration stated as a minimum and maximum time to be served (such as a term of imprisonment of "from one to ten years").[i]

consecutive sentence
One of two or more sentences imposed at the same time, after conviction for more than one offense, and served in sequence with the other sentences.

concurrent sentence
One of two or more sentences imposed at the same time, after conviction for more than one offense, and to be served simultaneously.[ii]

determinate sentence
A fixed term of incarceration specified by law. Also called *presumptive* or *fixed sentence*.

proportionality
A sentencing principle that holds that the severity of sanctions should bear a direct relationship to the seriousness of the crime committed.

equity
A sentencing principle, based on concerns with social equality, that holds that similar crimes should be punished with the same degree of severity, regardless of the social or personal characteristics of the offenders.

FIGURE 14–2

Types of Sentences.

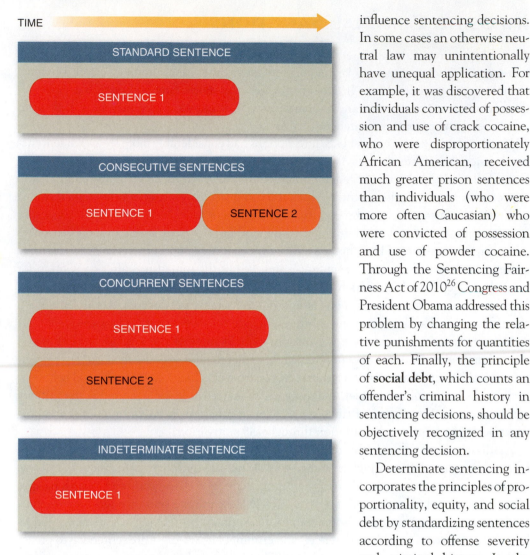

influence sentencing decisions. In some cases an otherwise neutral law may unintentionally have unequal application. For example, it was discovered that individuals convicted of possession and use of crack cocaine, who were disproportionately African American, received much greater prison sentences than individuals (who were more often Caucasian) who were convicted of possession and use of powder cocaine. Through the Sentencing Fairness Act of 2010[26] Congress and President Obama addressed this problem by changing the relative punishments for quantities of each. Finally, the principle of **social debt**, which counts an offender's criminal history in sentencing decisions, should be objectively recognized in any sentencing decision.

Determinate sentencing incorporates the principles of proportionality, equity, and social debt by standardizing sentences according to offense severity and criminal history. In determinate sentencing jurisdictions, judicial deviation from determinate sentencing standards, although possible, typically must be predicated on a finding by the judge of specific aggravating or mitigating factors enumerated by sentencing laws. **Aggravating factors** are "circumstances relating to the commission of a crime which cause its gravity to be greater than that of the average instance of the given type of offense."[27] Conversely, **mitigating factors** are "circumstances surrounding the commission of a crime which do not in law justify or excuse the act, but which in fairness may be considered as reducing the blameworthiness of the defendant."[28] Some typical aggravating and mitigating factors that judges may take into consideration in arriving at sentencing decisions in determinate sentencing jurisdictions are listed in Table 14–2.

social debt
A sentencing principle that objectively counts an offender's criminal history in sentencing decisions.

aggravating factor
A circumstance relating to the commission of a crime that causes its gravity to be greater than that of the average instance of the given type of offense.[iii] Also, an element of an offense or of an offender's background that could result in a harsher sentence under the determinate sentencing model than would otherwise be called for by sentencing guidelines.

mitigating factor
A circumstance surrounding the commission of a crime that does not in law justify or excuse the act but that in fairness may be considered as reducing the blameworthiness of the offender.[iv] Also, an element of an offense or of an offender's background that could result in a lesser sentence under the determinate sentencing model than would otherwise be called for by sentencing guidelines.

Federal Sentencing Practices

The movement toward determinate sentencing was led by the federal government, which in 1984 passed the Sentencing Reform Act.[29] The act established the U.S. Sentencing Commission under the leadership of Judge William W. Wilkins, Jr., and mandated the development of determinate sentencing guidelines. Guidelines developed by the commission took effect on November 1, 1987, and combined the seriousness of an offense with an offender's past criminal record in computing the length of prison time to which a federal court should sentence a convicted offender.

TABLE 14–2 Aggravating and Mitigating Factors

AGGRAVATING FACTORS
- The defendant induced others to participate in the commission of the offense.
- The offense was especially heinous, atrocious, or cruel.
- The defendant was armed with or used a deadly weapon at the time of the crime.
- The offense was committed for the purpose of avoiding or preventing a lawful arrest or effecting an escape from custody.
- The offense was committed for hire.
- The offense was committed against a present or former law enforcement officer or correctional officer while engaged in the performance of official duties or because of the past exercise of official duties.
- The defendant took advantage of a position of trust or confidence to commit the offense.

MITIGATING FACTORS
- The defendant has no record of criminal convictions punishable by more than 60 days of imprisonment.
- The defendant has made substantial or full restitution.
- The defendant has been a person of good character or has had a good reputation in the community.
- The defendant aided in the apprehension of another felon or testified truthfully on behalf of the prosecution.
- The defendant acted under strong provocation, or the victim was a voluntary participant in the criminal activity or otherwise consented to it.
- The offense was committed under duress, coercion, threat, or compulsion, which was insufficient to constitute a defense but significantly reduced the defendant's culpability.
- The defendant was suffering from a mental or physical condition that was insufficient to constitute a defense but significantly reduced culpability for the offense.

Federal sentencing guidelines are built around a table containing 43 rows, each corresponding to one offense level. The penalties associated with each level overlap those of levels above and below in order to discourage unnecessary litigation. A person charged with a crime involving $11,000, for example, on conviction is unlikely to receive a penalty substantially greater than if the amount involved had been somewhat less than $10,000—a sharp contrast to the old system. A change of six levels roughly doubles the sentence imposed under the guidelines, regardless of the level at which one starts.

The federal sentencing table, which is reproduced in Table 14–3, contains six columns corresponding to the criminal history category into which an offender falls. Criminal history categories are determined on the basis of points earned by offenders through previous convictions. Each prior sentence of imprisonment for more than one year and one month counts as three points. Two points are assigned for each prior prison sentence over six months or if the defendant committed the offense while on probation, parole, or work release. The system also assigns points for other types of previous convictions and for offenses committed less than two years after release from imprisonment. Points are added to determine the criminal history category into which an offender falls. Thirteen points or more are required for the highest category. At each offense level, sentences in the highest criminal history category are generally two to three times as severe as for the lowest category. Defendants may also move into the highest criminal history category (number VI) by being designated career offenders.

Although based on determinate principles, current federal sentencing practices continue to reflect the traditional goals of sentencing. Federal law, for example, specifies that "[t]he court, in determining the particular sentence to be imposed, shall consider . . . the need for the sentence imposed: (A) to reflect the seriousness of the offense, to promote respect for the law, and to provide just punishment for the offense; (B) to afford adequate deterrence to criminal conduct; (C) to protect the public from further crimes of the defendant; and (D) to provide the defendant with needed educational or vocational training, medical care, or other correctional treatment in the most effective manner."[30]

TABLE 14–3 The Federal Sentencing Table

Months of Imprisonment

Criminal History Category (Criminal History Points)

OFFENSE LEVEL	I (0 or 1)	II (2 or 3)	III (4, 5, 6)	IV (7, 8, 9)	V (10, 11, 12)	VI (13 or higher)
1	0–6	0–6	0–6	0–6	0–6	0–6
2	0–6	0–6	0–6	0–6	0–6	1–7
3	0–6	0–6	0–6	0–6	2–8	3–9
4	0–6	0–6	0–6	2–8	4–10	6–12
5	0–6	0–6	1–7	4–10	6–12	9–15
6	0–6	1–7	2–8	6–12	9–15	12–18
7	0–6	2–8	4–10	8–14	12–18	15–21
8	0–6	4–10	6–12	10–16	15–21	18–24
9	4–10	6–12	8–14	12–18	18–24	21–27
10	6–12	8–14	10–16	15–21	21–27	24–30
11	8–14	10–16	12–18	18–24	24–30	27–33
12	10–16	12–18	15–21	21–27	27–33	30–37
13	12–18	15–21	18–24	24–30	30–37	33–41
14	15–21	18–24	21–27	27–33	33–41	37–46
15	18–24	21–27	24–30	30–37	37–46	41–51
16	21–27	24–30	27–33	33–41	41–51	46–57
17	24–30	27–33	30–37	37–46	46–57	51–63
18	27–33	30–37	33–41	41–51	51–63	57–71
19	30–37	33–41	37–46	46–57	57–71	63–78
20	33–41	37–46	41–51	51–63	63–78	70–87
21	37–46	41–51	46–57	57–71	70–87	77–96
22	41–51	46–57	51–63	63–78	77–96	84–105
23	46–57	51–63	57–71	70–87	84–105	92–115
24	51–63	57–71	63–78	77–96	92–115	100–125
25	57–71	63–78	70–87	84–105	100–125	110–137
26	63–78	70–87	78–97	92–115	110–137	120–150
27	70–87	78–97	87–108	100–125	120–150	130–162
28	78–97	87–108	97–121	110–137	130–162	140–175
29	87–108	97–121	108–135	121–151	140–175	151–188
30	97–121	108–135	121–151	135–168	151–188	168–210
31	108–135	121–151	135–168	151–188	168–210	188–235
32	121–151	135–168	151–188	168–210	188–235	210–262
33	135–168	151–188	168–210	188–235	210–262	235–293
34	151–188	168–210	188–235	210–262	235–293	262–327
35	168–210	188–235	210–262	235–293	262–327	292–365
36	188–235	210–262	235–293	262–327	292–365	324–405
37	210–262	235–293	262–327	292–365	324–405	360–life
38	235–293	262–327	292–365	324–405	360–life	360–life
39	262–327	292–365	324–405	360–life	360–life	360–life
40	292–365	324–405	360–life	360–life	360–life	360–life
41	324–405	360–life	360–life	360–life	360–life	360–life
42	360–life	360–life	360–life	360–life	360–life	360–life
43	Life	Life	Life	Life	Life	Life

Source: U.S. Sentencing Commission.

In 1989, in the case of *Mistretta* v. *United States*,[31] the constitutionality of federal sentencing guidelines was tested. Mistretta, a federal prisoner, argued that Congress had overstepped its bounds in creating the U.S. Sentencing Commission and assigning to the commission the power to determine federal sentencing practices. Mistretta's claim was built on the doctrine of nondelegation, which holds that a clause in the U.S. Constitution mandates that no branch of government can engage in the excessive assignment of its discretionary powers to another agency. The Court, however, rejected Mistretta's argument, saying that, in a complex society, "Congress cannot do its job absent an ability to delegate power under broad general directives." Congress, concluded the Court, is not excessive in its delegation of authority if it is sufficiently precise in its assignment of responsibilities to external agencies. The Federal Sentencing Guidelines survived many constitutional attacks, such as the claim that they violate Article III by divesting judges of inherent sentencing discretion. Then, in 2005, the Supreme Court found the mandatory nature of the guidelines to be unconstitutional. This will be discussed in more detail later in this chapter.

The Role of the Jury in Sentencing

In 2000, in the U.S. Supreme Court case of *Apprendi* v. *New Jersey*,[32] the Court questioned the fact-finding authority of judges in making sentencing decisions, ruling that other than the fact of a prior conviction, any fact that increases the penalty for a crime beyond the prescribed statutory maximum is, in effect, an element of the crime that must be submitted to a jury and proved beyond a reasonable doubt. The justices wrote that "under the Due Process Clause of the Fifth Amendment and the notice and jury trial guarantees of the Sixth Amendment, any fact (other than prior conviction) that increases the maximum penalty for a crime must be charged in an indictment, submitted to a jury, and proven beyond a reasonable doubt." The *Apprendi* case raised the question of whether judges can legitimately deviate from established sentencing guidelines or apply sentence enhancements based on judicial determinations of aggravating factors that deviate from those guidelines—especially when such deviations are based on findings of fact that might otherwise be made by a jury.

In the 2002 case of *Harris* v. *United States*,[33] however, the Court found that the brandishing and discharging of a weapon under federal law are sentencing factors to be found by a judge, not elements of an offense to be found by a jury. The sentence imposed in *Harris* did not extend beyond the statutory maximum for the crime of which the defendant was convicted, and the Court reasoned that incremental changes in the minimum penalty that are specified in the law "are precisely what one would expect to see in provisions meant to identify matters for the sentencing judge's consideration."

Similarly, in the 2002 case of *United States* v. *Cotton*,[34] the Court found that sentences imposed by a federal judge were not improper, even though the judge based those sentences on a drug quantity not alleged in the original indictment brought against the defendants. The *Cotton* defendants had been charged with conspiracy to distribute and to possess with intent to distribute a "detectable amount" of cocaine and cocaine base in the city of Baltimore. Under federal law, the penalty for such offenses is "not more than 20 years." After the jury returned a finding of guilt, the judge made an independent determination of drug quantity (more than 500 grams of cocaine base) and then imposed enhanced penalties (up to life) as allowed under federal law. The judge's finding was based on "overwhelming and uncontroverted evidence" that the defendants "were involved in a vast drug conspiracy."

Also in 2002, the Supreme Court issued its decision in *Ring* v. *Arizona*,[35] holding that Arizona's capital sentencing scheme was incompatible with the Sixth Amendment right to a trial by jury. The *Ring* decision effectively overturned death-penalty sentencing practices in as many as nine states. *Ring* established that juries, not judges, must decide the facts that lead to a death sentence. In the 2004 case of *Schriro* v. *Summerlin*,[36] however, the Court found that the *Ring* ruling did not apply retroactively to hundreds of death sentences that were already final when *Ring* was decided.

Also in 2004, in the case of *Blakely* v. *Washington*,[37] the U.S. Supreme Court extended *Apprendi* and *Ring* by effectively invalidating sentencing schemes that allow judges rather than juries to determine any factor that increases a criminal sentence, except for prior convictions. The Court found that because the facts supporting Blakely's increased sentence (a determination that he had acted with deliberate cruelty in kidnapping his estranged wife) were neither admitted by Blakely nor found by a jury, the sentence violated Blakely's Sixth Amendment right to trial by jury. The *Blakely* decision required that the sentencing laws of at least eight states and the federal government be rewritten—a process that began soon after the decision was rendered.

Finally, in two related cases in 2005, the U.S. Supreme Court greatly expanded judicial discretion at the federal level when it declared federal sentencing guidelines advisory rather than mandatory. The Court found that federal sentencing guidelines unconstitutionally forced judges to increase sentences based on their own factual findings rather than on those of a jury.

In one of the two cases, *United States* v. *Booker*,[38] a Wisconsin federal jury convicted Freddie J. Booker of possessing and distributing crack cocaine and also determined that Booker had 92.5 grams of crack in his possession. Under federal sentencing guidelines, that amount of the drug would have limited Booker's maximum prison sentence to 21 years and 10 months. During sentencing, however, the trial judge determined that Booker had distributed an additional 566 grams of crack cocaine, had perjured himself at trial, and had 23 prior convictions. Consequently, the judge sentenced Booker to 30 years behind bars. Interestingly, even though the judge-ordered sentencing enhancement exceeded what the federal guidelines would have called for based on the facts found by the jury alone, federal law allows for such a sentence based only on what the jury found in the case.

In *Booker* and its sister case, *United States* v. *Fanfan*,[39] the majority held that the federal sentencing guidelines must become "effectively advisory." The Court's opinions allow judges to consider guideline ranges for sentencing but permit them to tailor the sentence in light of other statutory concerns as well. According to Indiana University School of Law sentencing expert professor Frank Bowman III, the Court's decisions restore virtually unlimited discretion to federal judges in imposing sentences. "After today," said Bowman, "judges have the greatest sentencing power they've ever had in the history of the republic."[40]

Truth in Sentencing

The 1984 Federal Comprehensive Crime Control Act, which adopted determinate sentencing for nearly all federal offenders, also addressed the issue of honesty in sentencing. Under the old federal system, a sentence of ten years in prison might actually have meant only a few years spent behind bars before the offender was released. On average, good-time credits and parole reduced time served to about one-third of actual sentences (Figure 14–3).[41] Sentencing practices in most states reflected the federal model. Although sentence reductions may have benefited offenders, they often outraged victims, who felt betrayed by the sentencing process and viewed it as misleading at best and dishonest at worst.

The federal emphasis on honesty in sentencing was emulated by many states, creating a sentencing environment of "what you get is what you serve." The idea that sentences that are imposed should closely match the time inmates actually serve is called **truth in sentencing**. Truth in sentencing, described more formally as "a close correspondence between the sentence imposed upon those sent to prison and the time actually served prior to prison release,"[42] has become an important policy focus of many state legislatures and

truth in sentencing
"A close correspondence between the sentence imposed upon those sent to prison and the time actually served prior to prison release."[v]

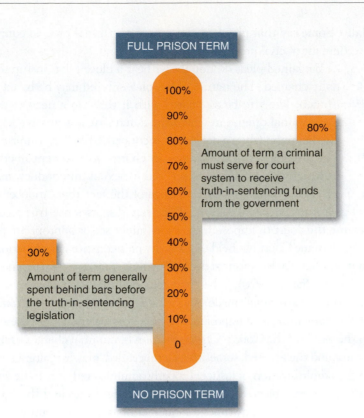

FIGURE 14-3

The Impact of Truth-in-Sentencing Laws.

FULL PRISON TERM

100%
90%
80%
70%
60%
50%
40%
30%
20%
10%
0

80%

Amount of term a criminal must serve for court system to receive truth-in-sentencing funds from the government

30%

Amount of term generally spent behind bars before the truth-in-sentencing legislation

NO PRISON TERM

the federal Congress. The Violent Crime Control and Law Enforcement Act of 1994, for example, set aside $4 billion in federal prison construction funds, called "Truth in Sentencing Incentive Funds," for states that adopt truth-in-sentencing laws guaranteeing that certain violent offenders will serve at least 85% of their sentences. A study found that, given the current situation in most states, meeting federal truth-in-sentencing requirements would increase the time actually spent in prison for the average prison-bound offender by almost 50%.[43]

Some states have chosen to approach truth in sentencing in another way. In 1994, for example, the New Jersey Supreme Court imposed a truth-in-sentencing rule on New Jersey judges that, although it doesn't require lengthened sentences, mandates that judges publicly disclose how much time a convicted defendant is likely to spend behind bars. Judges must also state when a defendant could get out of prison on good behavior.[44]

PLEA BARGAINING

Many sentences are imposed as a result of bargained pleas, that is, as the result of agreements among the prosecutor, defense attorney, and court as to what an appropriate sentence might be for an offender who pleads guilty. Fully 80 to 90% of sentences in some jurisdictions result from **plea bargaining**.[45] In a study of 37 big-city prosecutors,[46] the Bureau of Justice Statistics found that for every 100 adults arrested on a felony charge, half were eventually convicted of either a felony or a misdemeanor. Of all convictions, 94% were the result of a plea. Only 6% of convictions were the product of a criminal trial.

Plea bargaining circumvents the trial process and dramatically reduces the time required for the resolution of a criminal case. As such, it greatly increases the number of criminal cases that can be processed by a court. Without plea bargaining, most criminal courts would become mired in the legal formalities required by trials, and case backlogs would increase

plea bargaining
The process of negotiating an agreement among the defendant, the prosecutor, and the court as to what an appropriate plea and associated sentence should be in a given case.

substantially. Some say that plea bargaining is the criminal process equivalent to the out-of-court settlement of civil process.

If criminals wanted to grind justice to a halt, they could do it by banding together and all pleading not guilty.

—Dorothy Wright Wilson, former dean, University of Southern California Law Center

Bargained pleas do not always bear a close relationship to the crimes originally charged. The nature of the plea entered may be based more on the punishment likely to be associated with it than on a need to accurately describe the criminal offense in which the defendant was involved.[47] Plea bargains are also common when a defendant is concerned with minimizing the socially stigmatizing impact of the offense. A charge of "indecent liberties," for example, in which the defendant is accused of sexual misconduct, may be pleaded out as assault. Such a plea, which takes advantage of the fact that "indecent liberties" can be thought of as a form of sexual assault, effectively disguises the true nature of the offense while allowing the court to impose what many might see as appropriate punishment.

The U.S. Supreme Court has held that a guilty plea constitutes conviction.[48] The Court has also given its consent to the informal decision-making processes of bargained pleas. In the case of *Brady* v. *United States* (1970),[49] the court reasoned that such pleas were acceptable if they were voluntarily and knowingly made. A year later, in *Santobello* v. *New York*,[50] the High Court ruled that plea bargaining is an important and necessary component of the American system of justice. In the words of the Court: "The disposition of criminal charges by agreement between the prosecutor and the accused, sometimes loosely called 'plea bargaining,' is an essential component of the administration of justice. Properly administered, it is to be encouraged. If every criminal charge were subjected to a full-scale trial, the States and the Federal Government would need to multiply by many times the number of judges and court facilities."[51]

To validate a negotiated plea, judicial consent is required. Judges are often likely to accept pleas that are the result of a bargaining process because such pleas reduce the workload of the court. Although few judges are willing to guarantee a sentence before a plea is entered, most prosecutors and criminal trial lawyers know what sentences to expect from typical pleas.

After a guilty plea has been entered, it may be withdrawn with the consent of the court. In the case of *Henderson* v. *Morgan* (1976),[52] for example, the U.S. Supreme Court permitted a defendant to withdraw a plea of guilty nine years after it had been given. In *Henderson*, the defendant had originally entered a plea of guilty to second-degree murder but attempted to withdraw it before sentencing. The defendant's reasons for wanting to withdraw the plea included his belief that he had not been completely advised as to the nature of the charge or the sentence he might receive as a result of the plea.

Some Supreme Court decisions, however, have enhanced the prosecutor's authority in the bargaining process by declaring that negotiated pleas cannot be capriciously withdrawn by defendants.[53] Other rulings have supported discretionary actions by prosecutors, in which sentencing recommendations were retracted even after bargains had been struck.[54] Some lower court cases have upheld the government's authority to withdraw from a negotiated plea when the defendant fails to live up to certain conditions.[55] These conditions may include requiring the defendant to provide information on other criminal involvement, criminal cartels, the activities of smugglers, and so on.

Because they circumvent the trial process, plea bargains could be abused by prosecutors, defense attorneys, and judges who are more interested in a speedy resolution of cases than they are in seeing justice done. Carried to the extreme, plea bargaining may result in defendants being convicted of crimes they did not commit. Although it probably happens only rarely, it is conceivable that innocent defendants (especially those with prior criminal records) who—for whatever reason—think a jury will convict them may plead guilty to lessened charges to avoid a trial. In an effort to protect defendants against hastily arranged pleas, the Federal Rules of Criminal Procedure require judges to (1) inform the defendant of the various rights he or she is surrendering by pleading guilty, (2) determine that the plea is voluntary, (3) require disclosure of any plea agreements, and (4) make sufficient inquiry to ensure there is a factual basis for the plea.[56]

TRADITIONAL SENTENCING OPTIONS

Sentencing is fundamentally a risk-management strategy designed to protect the public while serving the ends of rehabilitation, deterrence, retribution, and restoration. Because the goals of sentencing are difficult to agree on, so too are sanctions. Lengthy prison terms do little for rehabilitation, and community-release programs can hardly protect the innocent from offenders bent on continuing criminality. Assorted sentencing philosophies continue to permeate state-level judicial systems. Each state has its own sentencing laws, and frequent revisions of those statutes are not uncommon. Because of huge variations from one state to another in the laws and procedures that control the imposition of criminal sanctions, sentencing has been called "the most diversified part of the Nation's criminal justice process."[57] There is at least one common ground, however: the four traditional sanctions that continue to dominate the thinking of most legislators and judges when dealing with the criminal law. The four traditional sanctions are

- Imprisonment
- Probation
- Fines
- Death

Imprisonment, probation, and fines are sanctions that are generally available to judges in most indeterminate sentencing jurisdictions. The option selected typically depends on the severity of the offense and the judge's best guess as to the likelihood of future criminal involvement on the part of the defendant. Sometimes two or more options are combined, as when an offender might be fined and also sentenced to prison or placed on probation and also fined in suppvort of restitution payments. **Probation** is actually a sentence of imprisonment that is deferred. It is granted through a judgment suspending the prison sentence imposed on a convicted offender, and the offender's continued freedom is conditioned on his or her meeting certain behavioral requirements, such as avoiding future law violations. Probationers might be closely monitored or not. Often the conditions of probation are used to restore the offender to the community and to accomplish other rehabilitative purposes. For example, alcohol and drug offenders may be required to enroll in substance-abuse counseling and to report for periodic substance-abuse testing.

Jurisdictions that operate under determinate sentencing guidelines generally limit a judge's choice to only one sentencing option and often specify the extent to which that option can be applied. Dollar amounts of fines, for example, are rigidly set, and prison terms are specified for each type of offense. The death penalty remains an option in a fair number of jurisdictions—both determinate and indeterminate—but only for a highly select group of offenders.

The Bureau of Justice Statistics recently reported on the sentencing practices of state felony courts.[58] Highlights of the study show that state courts annually convict about 1.1 million people of felonies. The study also found that

- For every 100 persons arrested for a violent felony, 31 were convicted.
- Forty percent of convicted felons were sentenced to a period of confinement in state prison.
- Thirty percent were sent to local jails.
- An estimated 28% of convicted felons were sentenced to probation with no jail or prison time.

probation
A sentence of imprisonment that is suspended. Also, the conditional freedom granted by a judicial officer to an adjudicated or adjudged adult or juvenile offender, as long as the person meets certain conditions of behavior.

In addition, the study found the following:

- About a third of convicted felons were drug offenders, and about one in five was a violent offender.
- Ninety-four percent of felony convictions occurred in state courts, the remaining 6% in federal courts.
- Ninety-five percent of convicted felons pleaded guilty; the remaining 5% were found guilty by a jury or judge.
- The average sentence length for convicted felons to state prison was almost five years.
- Females accounted for a quarter of felony property offenders.

The same survey revealed that the average age of persons convicted of a felony in state courts was 32 years. People in their 20s accounted for 40% of convicted felons, which was more than double their percentage in the adult population (18%). Persons under the age of 30 accounted for 48% of felony convictions for property offenses but 61% of felony weapon convictions. Men accounted for a larger percentage of persons convicted of a felony (82%), compared to their percentage in the adult population (49%). Whites represented 82% of the adult population in the United States, compared to 59% of persons convicted of a felony. Blacks were 12% of the adult population but 38% of convicted felons.

Although the number of active sentences handed out to felons may seem low to some, the number of criminal defendants receiving active prison time has increased dramatically over time. When viewed historically, statistics reveal that court-ordered prison commitments have increased nearly eightfold in the past 30 years.

The Eighth Amendment draws the outer limits of traditional sentencing. For example, the excessive fines clause was used to invalidate a forfeiture of more than $357,000 because the defendant failed to report taking more than $10,000 in cash out of the United States. The Court found the forfeiture to be grossly disproportionate.[59] The precise relationship between the amount of a fine and the gravity of the crime is unknown. This is true of imprisonment as well; only grossly disproportionate prison sentences violate the Eighth Amendment. Accordingly, legislatures and sentencing judges possess wide latitude when crafting punishments. For example, life imprisonment without the possibility of parole for possession of 672 grams of cocaine was upheld by the Supreme Court.[60]

The question whether a juvenile could be sentenced to life imprisonment without the possibility of parole was decided by the Supreme Court in the 2012 case *Miller v. Alabama*.

LESS TRADITIONAL SENTENCING OPTIONS

Disheartened by the prison system and other traditional sentencing options, judges and prison wardens occasionally turn to less traditional forms of punishment. For example, individuals who have harmed others while driving drunk have been required to speak to others convicted of driving while intoxicated. Inmates, particularly in local jails, are often required to perform service to the community.

Some officials require prison and jail inmates to provide hard labor while shackled in so-called chain gangs. Some jail inmates are required to sleep in tents.[61] Others are served food with poor taste that satisfies basic nutritional requirements.[62] The list of less traditional sentencing options is nearly unlimited. However, the Eighth Amendment's cruel and unusual punishments clause, as well as statutory and administrative law, limits the punishments that may be imposed. For example, imposing hard and painful labor with shackling was found to be cruel.[63]

APPLYING THE CONCEPT

CAPSTONE CASE

Is It Cruel and Unusual Punishment under the Eighth Amendment to Incarcerate a Juvenile Murderer for Life with No Possibility of Parole?

Miller v. Alabama, 567 U.S. __ (2012)
Justice KAGAN delivered the opinion of the Court.

THE CASE   The two 14-year-old offenders in this case were convicted of murder and sentenced to life imprisonment without the possibility of parole. In neither case did the sentencing authority have any discretion to impose a different punishment. State law mandated that each juvenile die in prison even if a judge or jury would have thought that his youth and its attendant characteristics, along with the nature of his crime, made a lesser sentence (for example, life *with* the possibility of parole) more appropriate. Such a scheme prevents those meting out punishment from considering a juvenile's "lessened culpability" and greater "capacity for change," *Graham v. Florida*, 560 U. S. ___ (2010), and runs afoul of our cases' requirement of individualized sentencing for defendants facing the most serious penalties. We therefore hold that mandatory life without parole for those under the age of 18 at the time of their crimes violates the Eighth Amendment's prohibition on "cruel and unusual punishments." . . .

In November 1999, petitioner Kuntrell Jackson, then 14 years old, and two other boys decided to rob a video store. En route to the store, Jackson learned that one of the boys, Derrick Shields, was carrying a sawed-off shotgun in his coat sleeve. Jackson decided to stay outside when the two other boys entered the store. Inside, Shields pointed the gun at the store clerk, Laurie Troup, and demanded that she "give up the money." Troup refused. A few moments later, Jackson went into the store to find Shields continuing to demand money. At trial, the parties disputed whether Jackson warned Troup that "[w]e ain't playin'," or instead told his friends, "I thought you all was playin.'" When Troup threatened to call the police, Shields shot and killed her. The three boys fled empty-handed.

Arkansas law gives prosecutors discretion to charge 14-year-olds as adults when they are alleged to have committed certain serious offenses. The prosecutor here exercised that authority by charging Jackson with capital felony murder and aggravated robbery. . . .

One night in 2003, Miller was at home with a friend, Colby Smith, when a neighbor, Cole Cannon, came to make a drug deal with Miller's mother. The two boys followed Cannon back to his trailer, where all three smoked marijuana and played drinking games. When Cannon passed out, Miller stole his wallet, splitting about $300 with Smith. Miller then tried to put the wallet back in Cannon's pocket, but Cannon awoke and grabbed Miller by the throat. Smith hit Cannon with a nearby baseball bat, and once released, Miller grabbed the bat and repeatedly struck Cannon with it. Miller placed a sheet over Cannon's head, told him "'I am God, I've come to take your life,'" and delivered one more blow. The boys then retreated to Miller's trailer, but soon decided to return to Cannon's to cover up evidence of their crime. Once there, they lit two fires. Cannon eventually died from his injuries and smoke inhalation. . . .

THE FINDING   The Eighth Amendment's prohibition of cruel and unusual punishment "guarantees individuals the right not to be subjected to excessive sanctions." That right, we have explained, "flows from the basic 'precept of justice that punishment for crime should be graduated and proportioned'" to both the offender and the offense. . . .

The cases before us implicate two strands of precedent reflecting our concern with proportionate punishment. The first has adopted categorical bans on sentencing practices based on mismatches between the culpability of a class of offenders and the severity of a penalty. So, for example, we have held that imposing the death penalty for nonhomicide crimes against individuals, or imposing it on mentally retarded defendants, violates the Eighth Amendment. See *Kennedy v. Louisiana*, 554 U. S. 407 (2008); *Atkins v. Virginia*, 536 U. S. 304 (2002). Several of the cases in this group have specially focused on juvenile offenders, because of their lesser culpability. Thus, *Roper* held that the Eighth Amendment bars capital punishment

(continued)

for children, and *Graham* concluded that the Amendment also prohibits a sentence of life without the possibility of parole for a child who committed a nonhomicide offense. *Graham* further likened life without parole for juveniles to the death penalty itself, thereby evoking a second line of our precedents. In those cases, we have prohibited mandatory imposition of capital punishment, requiring that sentencing authorities consider the characteristics of a defendant and the details of his offense before sentencing him to death. Here, the confluence of these two lines of precedent leads to the conclusion that mandatory life-without-parole sentences for juveniles violate the Eighth Amendment.

To start with the first set of cases: *Roper* and *Graham* establish that children are constitutionally different from adults for purposes of sentencing. Because juveniles have diminished culpability and greater prospects for reform, we explained, "they are less deserving of the most severe punishments." Those cases relied on three significant gaps between juveniles and adults. First, children have a "lack of maturity and an underdeveloped sense of responsibility," leading to recklessness, impulsivity, and heedless risk-taking. Second, children "are more vulnerable . . . to negative influences and outside pressures," including from their family and peers; they have limited "contro[l] over their own environment" and lack the ability to extricate themselves from horrific, crime-producing settings. And third, a child's character is not as "well formed" as an adult's; his traits are "less fixed" and his actions less likely to be "evidence of irretrievabl[e] deprav[ity]." . . .

Our decisions rested not only on common sense—on what "any parent knows"—but on science and social science as well. In *Roper*, we cited studies showing that "'[o]nly a relatively small proportion of adolescents" who engage in illegal activity "develop entrenched patterns of problem behavior." And in *Graham*, we noted that "developments in psychology and brain science continue to show fundamental differences between juvenile and adult minds"—for example, in "parts of the brain involved in behavior control." We reasoned that those findings—of transient rashness, proclivity for risk, and inability to assess consequences—both lessened a child's "moral culpability" and enhanced the prospect that, as the years go by and neurological development occurs, his "deficiencies will be reformed."

Roper and *Graham* emphasized that the distinctive attributes of youth diminish the penological justifications for imposing the harshest sentences on juvenile offenders, even when they commit terrible crimes. Because "[t]he heart of the retribution rationale" relates to an offender's blameworthiness, "the case for retribution is not as strong with a minor as with an adult." Nor can deterrence do the work in this context, because "the same characteristics that render juveniles less culpable than adults"—their immaturity, recklessness, and impetuosity—make them less likely to consider potential punishment. Similarly, incapacitation could not support the life-without-parole sentence in *Graham*: Deciding that a "juvenile offender forever will be a danger to society" would require "mak[ing] a judgment that [he] is incorrigible"—but "incorrigibility is inconsistent with youth." And for the same reason, rehabilitation could not justify that sentence. Life without parole "forswears altogether the rehabilitative ideal." It reflects "an irrevocable judgment about [an offender's] value and place in society," at odds with a child's capacity for change. . . .

But the mandatory penalty schemes at issue here prevent the sentencer from taking account of these central considerations. By removing youth from the balance—by subjecting a juvenile to the same life-without-parole sentence applicable to an adult—these laws prohibit a sentencing authority from assessing whether the law's harshest term of imprisonment proportionately punishes a juvenile offender. That contravenes *Graham*'s (and also *Roper*'s) foundational principle: that imposition of a State's most severe penalties on juvenile offenders cannot proceed as though they were not children.

And *Graham* makes plain these mandatory schemes' defects in another way: by likening life-without-parole sentences imposed on juveniles to the death penalty itself. Life-without-parole terms, the Court wrote, "share some characteristics with death sentences that are shared by no other sentences." Imprisoning an offender until he dies alters the remainder of his life "by a forfeiture that is irrevocable." And this lengthiest possible incarceration is an "especially harsh punishment for a juvenile," because he will almost inevitably serve "more years and a greater percentage of his life in prison than an adult offender." . . .

Of special pertinence here, we insisted in these rulings that a sentencer have the ability to consider the "mitigating qualities of youth." . . .

We therefore hold that the Eighth Amendment forbids a sentencing scheme that mandates life in prison without possibility of parole for juvenile offenders. . . .

What Do You Think?

1. Do you believe the Court's determinations about the immaturity and the possibility of change of juvenile offenders are correct?

2. The Court didn't foreclose the possibility of life imprisonment for juveniles, only life imprisonment without the possibility of parole. What factors do you think the Court expects future parole decision makers to take into consideration?

Additional Applications

Does the Eighth Amendment now prohibit *all* life-without-parole sentences for juvenile offenders?

State v. *Long*, 2012 Ohio 3052 (Ohio App. 2012)

The Case: Following a jury trial in Hamilton County, Ohio, 17-year-old Eric Long was convicted in 2011 of committing two aggravated murders; consequently, the state trial judge sentenced Long to two terms of life imprisonment without the possibility of parole. On appeal, Long argued (among other things) that his life-without-parole sentences violated the Eighth Amendment's prohibition on cruel and unusual punishment in light of *Miller v. Alabama*.

The Finding: In one of the first published lower court interpretations of *Miller*, an Ohio appeals court in July 2012 unanimously upheld the trial court's life-without-parole sentences. Writing for the state appeals panel, Hamilton County Court of Appeals Judge Lee Hildebrandt noted the recent *Miller* holding that "a mandatory life-without-parole sentence for juvenile offenders violates the Eighth Amendment." Yet Long's life-without-parole sentences in this case, Hildebrandt wrote, "unlike that in *Miller*, w[ere] not mandated by operation of law." Rather, Ohio state law gave the trial court here "discretion to impose either life without parole eligibility or a lesser sentence of life with parole eligibility"—and as *Miller* requires, the trial court here considered "Long's youth and its attendant characteristics, along with the nature of his crime" before opting in favor of the maximum sentences. Consequently, Judge Hildebrandt concluded, Long's sentence "did not run afoul of the Eighth Amendment's proscriptions affecting juvenile offenders."

After *Miller*, may courts sentence juveniles to consecutive fixed prison terms that together exceed an offender's life expectancy?

Bunch v. *Smith*, 2012 U.S. App. LEXIS 13756 (6th Cir. 2012)

The Case: After finding 16-year-old Chaz Bunch guilty on multiple charges of aggravated robbery, kidnapping, rape, and firearms violations, an Ohio state court sentenced Bunch to consecutive fixed prison terms that together totaled 89 years of incarceration. Explaining the lengthy aggregate sentence, the trial court told Bunch: "I just have to make sure that you don't get out of the penitentiary. I've got to do everything I can to keep you there, because it would be a mistake to have you back in society."

On appeal, Bunch argued that the trial judge had violated the Eighth Amendment's prohibition on cruel and unusual punishment by sentencing him to "the functional equivalent of life without parole." After exhausting his state appeals, Bunch filed a petition in federal court, seeking federal *habeas* relief on Eighth Amendment grounds.

The Finding: In a July 2012 decision, a panel of the U.S. Court of Appeals for the Sixth Circuit rejected Bunch's request for federal *habeas* relief. On *habeas* review, the appeal panel noted, Bunch had to show that the trial court's decision violated "clearly established Federal law"—but no authoritative court ruling has yet established that "consecutive, fixed-term sentences for juveniles who commit multiple non-homicide offenses are unconstitutional when they amount to the practical equivalent of life without parole." The Supreme Court's 2010 ruling in *Graham v. Florida*, the panel reasoned, was "not clearly applicable," because *Graham* involved only an imposition of a life-without-parole sentence for a single nonhomicide offense. What's more, the panel noted, "the Supreme Court's recent decision in *Miller v. Alabama* . . . does not warrant a different result" because *Miller* "extended the reasoning in *Graham* to mandatory sentences of life without parole for juveniles convicted of homicide offenses" but "did not address juvenile offenders, like Bunch, who received consecutive, fixed-term sentences for committing multiple non-homicide offenses." Thus, "even if we assume that *Miller* also applies to Bunch's case on collateral review, Bunch is still not entitled to *habeas* relief." ∎

Most less traditional punishments involve a physical component, perhaps pain or discomfort. A punishment does not violate the Eighth Amendment because the offender experiences pain. It is the infliction of unnecessary and wanton pain that is forbidden. A punishment is unconstitutional when it inflicts more pain than is necessary to achieve a legitimate penological purpose, including rehabilitation, incapacitation, or retribution. Hard labor, for example, is not *per se* cruel.[64] Solitary confinement is lawful, and whipping, which is no longer employed, has been held both constitutional[65] and unconstitutional when applied by prison guards to inmates.[66]

It is possible for a punishment to not be painful but still violate the Eighth Amendment because it encroaches excessively on an offender's fundamental physical rights. For example, the mandatory chemical castration of male sex offenders and the sterilization of women convicted of child neglect would likely violate the Eighth Amendment, although the Supreme Court has not addressed these specific issues.

SENTENCE ENHANCEMENTS

Many states and the federal government have statutes that enhance or increase a sentence beyond the sentencing range found in the specific statute under which an offender is convicted. As mentioned earlier, some laws require increased sentences for habitual offenders. Typically, a sentence is enhanced if the offender has been convicted of two or more prior felonies in a given time, for example, ten years. These laws are known by many names, including habitual offender and three strikes. In some instances the enhancement is life imprisonment. Generally, these laws have been held by the courts to be consonant with the Eighth Amendment even when they impose life imprisonment for lesser felonies because the offenders have been convicted of multiple offenses. For example, life imprisonment with the possibility of parole for stealing items valued at $150 when it was the offender's third conviction was upheld.[67]

hate crime
A criminal offense in which the defendant's conduct was motivated by hatred, bias, or prejudice, based on the actual or perceived race, color, religion, national origin, ethnicity, gender, or sexual orientation of another individual or group of individuals. Also called *bias crime.*

In addition to habitual offender laws, it is also common for sentences of **hate-crime** convictions to be enhanced. Hate crimes are criminal offenses in which the defendant's conduct was motivated by hatred, bias, or prejudice, based on the actual or perceived race, color, religion, national origin, ethnicity, gender, or sexual orientation of another individual or group of individuals.[68] A more extensive definition can be found in the California Penal Code, which defines a *hate crime* as "any act of intimidation, harassment, physical force, or the threat of physical force directed against any person, or family, or their property or advocate, motivated either in whole or in part by the hostility to the real or perceived ethnic background, national origin, religious belief, gender, age, disability, or sexual orientation, with the intention of causing fear and intimidation."[69] Hate crimes are not separate offenses, however, and many types of felonies can be prosecuted as hate crimes.

Hate-crime laws, which have developed during the past decade or two, simply enhance or increase the penalties associated with serious offenses that fall into the hate-crimes category. At the federal level, the Hate Crimes Sentencing Enhancement Act of 1994[70] is typical of such legislation. The act provides for enhanced sentences when a federal offense is determined to be a hate crime.

The federal Hate Crime Statistics Act, signed into law by then-President George W. Bush in April 1990, mandates an annual statistical tally of hate crimes throughout the country. Data collection under the law began in January 1991. Yearly statistics show approximately 6,600 reported instances of hate crimes, including about a dozen murders. Most hate crimes (approximately 47%) appear to be motivated by racial bias, and religious hatred (20%) and sexual orientation–related crimes (19%) account for most of the remainder.[71] Many hate crimes that are reported fall into the category of intimidation, although vandalism, simple assault, and aggravated assault also account for a fair number of hate-crime offenses. Notable in recent years has been a spate of church burnings throughout the South where congregations have been predominantly African American. A few robberies and rapes are also classified under the hate-crime umbrella in any given year. Hate crimes are sometimes also called *bias crimes.* One form of bias crime that bears special mention is homophobic homicide, which is the murder of homosexuals by those opposed to their lifestyles.

Some hate crimes are committed by organized hate groups. According to the Intelligence Project of the Southern Poverty Law Center, 926 organized hate groups operated in the United States in 2008.[72] Included among them were the Ku Klux Klan, neo-Nazi groups, and racist skinhead organizations. A number of other so-called patriot organizations, many with separatist leanings based on race or ethnicity, also existed throughout the country.

Some hate-crime laws have not passed constitutional muster, often because they have run afoul of First Amendment concerns over free speech. In 1992, for example, in the case of *R.A.V. v. City of St. Paul*,[73] the U.S. Supreme Court invalidated a St. Paul, Minnesota, city ordinance designed to prevent the bias-motivated display of symbols or objects, such as Nazi swastikas or burning crosses. Also in 1992, in the case of *Forsyth County, Ga. v. Nationalist Movement*,[74] the Court held that a county requirement regulating parades was unconstitutional because it also regulated freedom of speech—in this case a plan by an affiliate of the Ku Klux Klan to parade in opposition to a Martin Luther King, Jr., birthday celebration.

In 2003, however, in a case that provided an interesting contrast to *R.A.V.*, the Court held that states may make it a crime to burn a cross with intent to intimidate, as long as the relevant law clearly places the burden on prosecutors of proving that the cross burning was intended as a threat and not as a form of symbolic expression. The case was *Virginia v. Black*.[75]

Some writers have noted that statutes intended to control hate crimes may contravene constitutional guarantees if they (1) are too vague, (2) criminalize thought more than action, (3) attempt to control what would otherwise be free speech, and (4) deny equal protection of the laws to those who wish to express their personal biases.[76]

Examples of effective hate-crime legislation can be found in a Wisconsin law that increases penalties for most crimes when the offender "[i]ntentionally selects the person against whom the crime . . . is committed or selects the property that is damaged or otherwise affected by the crime . . . in whole or in part because of the actor's belief or perception regarding the race, religion, color, disability, sexual orientation, national origin or ancestry of that person or the owner or occupant of that property, whether or not the actor's belief or perception was correct."[77] Wisconsin's penalty-enhancement statute was upheld in the 1993 case of *Wisconsin v. Mitchell*.[78] In that case, the U.S. Supreme Court held that Mitchell, a black man whose severe beating of a white boy was racially motivated, could be punished with additional severity as permitted by Wisconsin law because he acted out of "race hatred." The Court called the assault "conduct unprotected by the First Amendment" and upheld the Wisconsin statute, saying that because "the statute has no 'chilling effect' on free speech, it is not unconstitutionally overbroad."

Other examples of sentence enhancements exist. For example, the federal sentencing guidelines recommend an increase of sentence for terrorism crimes.[79]

CAPITAL PUNISHMENT

The last of the four traditional sanctions—although by far the least commonly used—is **capital punishment**, or a sentence of death. A death sentence is, of course, the most extreme sentencing option available in the United States today. In 1995, the state of New York reinstated the death penalty after a 30-year hiatus, and today 38 states and the federal government make capital punishment an option when serious crimes are committed (Figure 14–4). Approximately 3,800 death-row inmates are housed in the nation's prisons, and around 100 executions are carried out yearly. The number of annual executions has been steadily rising as changes in the law and recent Supreme Court decisions have facilitated an increasing rate of legal death.

capital punishment
The imposition of a sentence of death.

FIGURE 14–4

States with Capital Punishment and Alternative Methods of Execution.

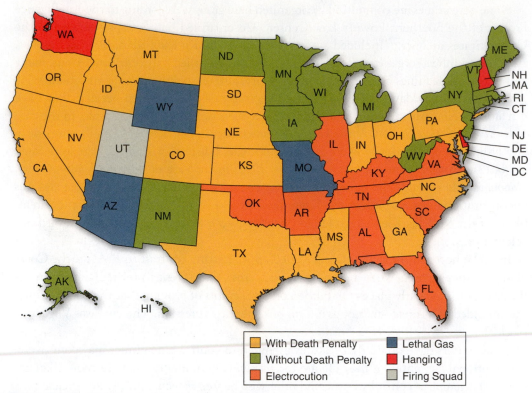

Note 1: The New York Court of Appeals has held that a portion of New York's death penalty sentencing statute (CPL 400.27) was unconstitutional (*People v. Taylor*, 9 N.Y.3d 129 (2007)). As a result, no defendants can be sentenced to death until the legislature corrects errors in the statute.
Note 2: All states in which capital punishment is a sentencing option use lethal injection as the primary method of execution. Alternative choices available to the condemned are indicated on the map.
Note 3: Oklahoma is the only state in which two alternatives to lethal injection are offered to condemned inmates. Lethal injection, electrocution, or firing squad are all choices in that state.

Death is not only an unusually severe punishment, unusual in its pain, in its finality, and in its enormity, but it serves no penal purpose more effectively than a less severe punishment.

—Justice William J. Brennan, dissenting in Gregg v. Georgia, 428 U.S. 153 (1976)

Capital punishment, as a sentencing possibility, was absent from federal law for a number of years before its reestablishment under the 1988 Anti–Drug Abuse Act, which included the possibility of capital punishment for drug-related murders. The 1994 Federal Violent Crime Control and Law Enforcement Act dramatically raised the number of crimes punishable by death under federal jurisdiction to around 60 distinct offenses. Candidates for death under the 1994 act are those who commit first-degree murder, espionage, kidnapping in which death results, murder of a foreign official, bank robbery in which death results, hostage taking resulting in death, murder for hire, genocide, carjacking that leads to death, "civil rights murders," the murder of federal law enforcement officials, foreign murder of U.S. nationals, sexual abuse resulting in death, sexual exploitation of children resulting in death, the murder of state or local officials (including state and local law enforcement officers and state correctional officers), murder by an escaped prisoner, the murder of federal witnesses or of court officers or jurors, and shipboard violence or violence at international airports resulting in death. A subsection of the 1994 Federal Violent Crime Control and Law Enforcement Act,[80] entitled the Drive-By Shooting Prevention Act of 1994, specifies that "[a] person who, in furtherance or to escape detection of a major drug offense and with the intent to intimidate, harass, injure, or maim, fires a weapon into a group of two or more persons and who, in the course of such conduct, kills any person shall, if the killing . . . is a first-degree murder . . . , be punished by death or imprisonment for any term of years or for life, fined under this title, or both." Similarly, the Violent Crime Control Act also states that "[a] person who, while confined in a Federal correctional institution under a sentence for a term of life imprisonment, commits the murder of another shall be punished by death or by life imprisonment."

Capital punishment can be analyzed from three quite different points of view: (1) a legal perspective, which includes constitutional issues; (2) a philosophical, moral, and ethical perspective; and (3) empirical analysis of data on deterrence, public opinion, and so on.

Although our emphasis in this textbook here is on the criminal law, philosophical considerations of the morality of capital punishment and empirical studies of death-penalty efficacy are important issues in their own right. In 2000, for example, Governor George Ryan of Illinois suspended executions in his state and called for an examination of the fairness of capital punishment after discovering that more death-row inmates had been found innocent and released than had been executed since Illinois returned to the use of capital punishment in 1977. In fact, 130 people in 26 states have been released from U.S. death rows since 1972 after proof of their innocence was substantiated,[81] and an analysis of every capital conviction and appeal over a 22-year period published in 2000 by Columbia Law School Professor James Liebman found an extremely high rate of prejudicial error in the American capital punishment system.[82] Liebman found serious reversible errors in nearly seven out of every ten capital cases.

New forensic technologies, such as DNA testing, now make it possible to almost conclusively demonstrate innocence in many cases. In 2004, in recognition of the power that DNA testing holds to exonerate the innocent, President Bush signed the Innocence Protection Act[83] into law. The legislation was included in a larger bill called the Justice for All Act of 2004.[84] The Innocence Protection Act provides federal funds to eliminate the backlog of unanalyzed DNA samples in the nation's crime laboratories[85] and sets aside money to improve the capacity of federal, state, and local crime laboratories to conduct DNA analyses.[86] The act also ensures access to postconviction DNA testing for those serving time in prison or on death row and sets forth conditions under which a federal prisoner asserting innocence may obtain postconviction DNA testing of specific evidence. A new trial or resentencing is required under the legislation "if the DNA test results, when considered with all other evidence in the case (regardless of whether such evidence was introduced at trial), establish by compelling evidence that a new trial would result in an acquittal."[87] Similarly, the legislation requires the preservation of biological evidence by federal law enforcement agencies for any defendant under a sentence of imprisonment or death.

The Eighth Amendment and Capital Punishment

Among death-penalty cases decided by the U.S. Supreme Court, one of the earliest was *Wilkerson v. Utah* (1878),[88] which questioned shooting as a method of execution and raised Eighth Amendment claims that firing squads constituted a form of cruel and unusual punishment. The Court disagreed, however, contrasting the relatively civilized nature of firing squads with the many forms of torture often associated with capital punishment around the time the Bill of Rights was written. Similarly, electrocution found acceptance as a permissible form of execution in *In re Kemmler* (1890).[89] In *Kemmler*, the Court defined cruel and unusual methods of execution as follows: "Punishments are cruel when they involve torture or a lingering death; but the punishment of death is not cruel, within the meaning of that word as used in the Constitution. It implies there is something inhuman and barbarous, something more than the mere extinguishing of life."[90] Almost 60 years later, the Court ruled that a second attempt at the electrocution of a convicted person, when the first did not work, did not violate the Eighth Amendment.[91] The Court reasoned that the initial failure was the consequence of accident or unforeseen circumstances and not the result of an effort on the part of executioners to be intentionally cruel.

CRIMINAL LAW IN THE NEWS

DNA Testing Topples Old Convictions, Raising New Concerns

Former inmate Henry James Jr. owes his newfound freedom to a scientist pottering in a Louisiana crime lab. The man came across missing evidence from James's 1981 case, in which he was convicted of sexually assaulting a neighbor at knifepoint.

When the sample was tested for DNA, it conclusively proved James was not the assailant and he was exonerated in October 2011. James said that walking out of Louisiana's notorious Angola Prison after 30 years "was a feeling of a miracle."

Since the late 1980s, when DNA testing was

A symbolic representation of human DNA. Is DNA evidence foolproof? SOURCE: Fotolia LLC

first used to double-check convictions, it has exonerated almost 300 convicted inmates. But these stunning upsets raise yet more questions. Did prosecutors conceal evidence to push through a conviction? Should exonerated inmates be compensated? And should every request for DNA testing be granted?

Michael Morton, who was convicted 25 years ago for the murder of his wife in Dallas, spent years futilely asking for evidence to test. When DNA tests were finally made, they absolved him and implicated a man living nearby.

Morton, who was released in October 2011, alleged that Ken Anderson, the prosecutor in the 1986 case, concealed evidence that confirmed his innocence. Anderson denied the charge, but in February 2012, Texas Supreme Court Chief Justice Wallace Jefferson granted Morton's request to open a court of inquiry to investigate the matter. "Revenge is a natural instinct, but it's not what I'm asking for here," Morton said. "It's just accountability."

Often, suing the prosecutors is the only way to get any compensation in these cases. In Kentucky, an exonerated inmate sued local authorities and won settlements totaling $4.6 million in 2000. The Supreme Court, however,

put this approach into question in March 2011, when it struck down a huge award for John Thompson, a former death-row inmate exonerated for armed robbery and murder.

Prosecutors admitted that a blood test showing Thompson's innocence had been withheld from his lawyers. He sued the New Orleans District Attorney's office for misconduct and got $14 million. But in a 5–4 ruling, the Supreme Court overturned the award, ruling that the district attorney's office was not liable because there was no pattern of "deliberate indifference."

States like Texas now require payments to exonerated inmates, based on years of incarceration. Originally, Texas ruled out inmates who had pleaded guilty, but because many exonerated inmates had been forced into confessions, that provision was removed. In 2007, the state doubled compensations to $50,000 per year of imprisonment.

Texas has also limited prosecutors' ability to oppose postconviction DNA testing, but the new law still meets with some resistance. In October 2011, Anthony Melendez, who had been convicted for the 1982 slayings of three teenagers, asked District Attorney Abel Reyna for

DNA samples. But Reyna told the Waco *Tribune Herald* that, generally, he doesn't support DNA testing, because it might overrule what a jury has already decided.

There is no doubt that DNA testing has profoundly changed the way criminal evidence is processed. The tests are sometimes all that is needed to breathe new life into long-forgotten cases, even in cases of multiple convictions with samples for just some of the crimes.

Thomas Haynesworth was convicted of five different rapes in Virginia in 1984. A sample for one of the cases was tested in 2009 and showed he was innocent. It identified the real perpetrator, a known serial rapist, who was then linked to the other cases that lacked DNA evidence. With the help of other evidence, Haynesworth was exonerated for all the rapes in March 2011, after 27 years behind bars.

Resources

"Cleared of Murder, Morton Seeks Accountability," *Texas Tribune*, December 19, 2011, http://www.texastribune.org/texas-dept-criminal-justice/michael-morton/morton-officially-cleared-murder/.

"Supreme Court Rules against Exonerated Death Row Inmate Who Sued Prosecutors," *Washington Post*, March 29, 2011, http://www.washingtonpost.com/politics/supreme-court-rules-against-exonerated-death-row-inmate-who-sued-prosecutors/2011/03/29/AF8tZPwB_story.html.

"Exonerated after 30 Years, Henry James Jr. Says He Never Lost Hope," *Times-Picayune*, October 21, 2011, http://www.nola.com/crime/index.ssf/2011/10/exonerated_after_30_years_henr.html.

In 1971, in the case of *McGautha* v. *California*,[92] the Court rejected a defendant's claim that the due-process clause of the Constitution prohibited "committing to the untrammeled discretion of the jury the power to pronounce life or death in capital cases." In effect, in *McGautha*, the Court upheld the power of juries to make decisions regarding life and death.

However, only one year later, in the landmark case of *Furman* v. *Georgia*,[93] the Court ruled that "evolving standards of decency"[94] necessitated a reconsideration of Eighth Amendment guarantees. In a 5–4 ruling, with no majority opinion,[95] the *Furman* decision invalidated Georgia's death-penalty statute on the basis that it allowed a jury *unguided* discretion in the imposition of a capital sentence. The majority of justices concluded that the Georgia statute, which permitted a jury to simultaneously decide issues of guilt or innocence while it weighed sentencing options, permitted an arbitrary and capricious application of the death penalty. The *Furman* case had the effect of striking down every death-penalty statute then in existence, although it did little to provide clear guidance to states interested in reestablishing the practice of capital punishment.

Following *Furman*, states that reenacted death-penalty laws did so in one of two ways: They either imposed mandatory death sentences for certain types of crimes or created a two-step procedure whereby the determination of guilt was separated from the penalty phase of a criminal trial. In 1976, in the case of *Woodson* v. *North Carolina*,[96] a law requiring the death penalty for specific crimes was overturned. In *Woodson*, the Court held that "the fundamental respect for humanity underlying the Eighth Amendment . . . requires consideration of the character and record of the individual offender and the circumstances of the particular offense."

Also in 1976, however, in the case of *Gregg* v. *Georgia*, the Court approved Georgia's newly developed two-step trial procedure.[97] In that case, the Court upheld the two-stage procedural requirements as necessary for ensuring the separation of the highly personal information needed in sentencing decisions from the kinds of information reasonably permissible in jury trials where issues of guilt or innocence alone are being decided. As a consequence of *Gregg*, death-penalty trials in most jurisdictions today involve two stages. In the first stage, guilt or innocence is decided. If the defendant is convicted of a crime for

> *We are concerned here only with the imposition of capital punishment for the crime of murder, and when a life has been taken deliberately by the offender, we cannot say that the punishment is invariably disproportionate to the crime. It is an extreme sanction suitable to the most extreme of crimes.*
>
> —Justice Potter Stewart, Gregg v. Georgia, 428 U.S. 153 (1976)

which execution is possible, a second ("penalty") phase ensues. The penalty phase generally permits the introduction of new evidence that may have been irrelevant to the question of guilt but that may be relevant to punishment, such as drug use or childhood abuse. Although in most death penalty jurisdictions juries determine the punishment, the trial judge sets the sentence in the second phase of capital murder trials in Arizona, Idaho, Montana, and Nebraska. Four states—Alabama, Delaware, Florida, and Indiana—allow juries only to recommend a sentence to the judge.

Decisions following *Gregg* set limits on the use of death as a penalty for all but the most severe crimes. In the case of *Coker* v. *Georgia* (1977),[98] for example, the Court struck down a state law imposing the death penalty for the rape of an adult woman, concluding that capital punishment under such circumstances would be "grossly disproportionate" to the crime committed. Somewhat later, in *Edmund* v. *Florida* (1982),[99] the Court overturned the death sentence of an individual convicted of felony murder, ruling that the Constitution forbids executing a defendant "who does not himself kill, attempt to kill, or intend that a killing take place or that lethal force be employed." In *Edmund*, the defendant was a getaway-car driver whose accomplices committed murder while he waited in the vehicle. In 1987, in *Tison* v. *Arizona*,[100] a divided Court held that felony murder rules might lead to death sentences when defendants "could have foreseen that lethal force might be used" in a crime, even though they were not the ones to employ it. In the Capstone Case of *Kennedy* v. *Louisiana* (2008), the Supreme Court answered the long-awaited question of whether child rapists could be punished with death.

In two 1990 rulings, *Blystone* v. *Pennsylvania*[101] and *Boyde* v. *California*,[102] the Court upheld state statutes that had been interpreted to require death penalties where juries find a lack of mitigating factors to offset aggravating circumstances. Similarly, in the 1990 case of R. Gene Simmons, an Arkansas mass murderer convicted of killing 16 relatives during a 1987 shooting rampage, the Court granted inmates under sentence of death the right to waive appeals. Before the *Simmons* case, any interested party could file a brief on behalf of condemned persons—with or without their consent.[103]

Although capital punishment is not unconstitutional, long delays associated with its imposition may be. In 1998, the U.S. Supreme Court refused to hear a case in which an execution had been delayed for 23 years. Justice Stephen Breyer observed that "twenty-three years under sentence of death is unusual—whether one takes as a measuring rod current practice or the practice in this country and in England at the time our Constitution was written."[104] Breyer noted that his concern arose from the fact that the defendant "has experienced that delay because of the State's own faulty procedures and not because of frivolous appeals on his own part."

The U.S. Supreme Court has held that certain personal characteristics of the perpetrator, such as mental disability and age, can be a bar to execution. In 2001, for example, in the case of *Penry* v. *Johnson*,[105] the U.S. Supreme Court found that a Texas state trial court had failed to allow a jury to properly consider a murder defendant's low IQ and childhood abuse as mitigating factors when it found that his crime warranted the death penalty. Shortly after the Court's decision, Texas Governor Rick Perry vetoed legislation that would have banned the execution of mentally retarded death-row inmates throughout the state.[106]

Limits on Death-Row Appeals

habeas corpus
Literally, "you have the body." A writ challenging the legality of incarceration, or a writ ordering a prisoner to be brought before a court to determine the legality of the prisoner's detention.

The federal Constitution allows people who are in custody to challenge the legality of their confinement by seeking a writ of **habeas corpus**. *Habeas corpus* is a Latin term that literally means "you have the body," and a writ of *habeas corpus* is an order requiring a prisoner to be brought before a court for the purpose of determining the legality of the prisoner's detention. Also known as the *Great Writ*, *habeas corpus* has been interpreted to mean that

APPLYING THE CONCEPT

CAPSTONE CASE

Is It Cruel under the Eighth Amendment to Execute Convicted Child Rapists?

Kennedy v. *Louisiana*, 554 U.S. (2008)
Justice Kennedy delivered the opinion of the Court.

THE CASE The National Government and, beyond it, the separate States are bound by the proscriptive mandates of the Eighth Amendment to the Constitution of the United States, and all persons within those respective jurisdictions may invoke its protection. Patrick Kennedy, the petitioner here, seeks to set aside his death sentence under the Eighth Amendment. He was charged by the respondent, the State of Louisiana, with the aggravated rape of his then-8-year-old stepdaughter. After a jury trial petitioner was convicted and sentenced to death under a state statute authorizing capital punishment for the rape of a child under 12 years of age. This case presents the question whether the Constitution bars respondent from imposing the death penalty for the rape of a child where the crime did not result, and was not intended to result, in death of the victim. We hold the Eighth Amendment prohibits the death penalty for this offense. The Louisiana statute is unconstitutional.

Petitioner's crime was one that cannot be recounted in these pages in a way sufficient to capture in full the hurt and horror inflicted on his victim or to convey the revulsion society, and the jury that represents it, sought to express by sentencing petitioner to death. At 9:18 a.m. on March 2, 1998, petitioner called 911 to report that his stepdaughter, referred to here as L. H., had been raped. He told the 911 operator that L. H. had been in the garage while he readied his son for school. Upon hearing loud screaming, petitioner said, he ran outside and found L. H. in the side yard. Two neighborhood boys, petitioner told the operator, had dragged L. H. from the garage to the yard, pushed her down, and raped her. Petitioner claimed he saw one of the boys riding away on a blue 10-speed bicycle.

When police arrived at petitioner's home between 9:20 and 9:30 a.m., they found L. H. on her bed, wearing a T-shirt and wrapped in a bloody blanket. She was bleeding profusely from the vaginal area. Petitioner told police he had carried her from the yard to the bathtub and then to the bed. Consistent with this explanation, police found a thin line of blood drops in the garage on the way to the house and then up the stairs. Once in the bedroom, petitioner had used a basin of water and a cloth to wipe blood from the victim. This later prevented medical personnel from collecting a reliable DNA sample.

L. H. was transported to the Children's Hospital. An expert in pediatric forensic medicine testified that L. H.'s injuries were the most severe he had seen from a sexual assault in his four years of practice. A laceration to the left wall of the vagina had separated her cervix from the back of her vagina, causing her rectum to protrude into the vaginal structure. Her entire perineum was torn from the posterior fourchette to the anus. The injuries required emergency surgery. . . .

THE FINDING Evolving standards of decency must embrace and express respect for the dignity of the person, and the punishment of criminals must conform to that rule. See *Trop, supra,* at 100 (plurality opinion). As we shall discuss, punishment is justified under one or more of three principal rationales: rehabilitation, deterrence, and retribution. It is the last of these, retribution, that most often can contradict the law's own ends. This is of particular concern when the Court interprets the meaning of the Eighth Amendment in capital cases. When the law punishes by death, it risks its own sudden descent into brutality, transgressing the constitutional commitment to decency and restraint.

For these reasons we have explained that capital punishment must "be limited to those offenders who commit 'a narrow category of the most serious crimes' and whose extreme culpability makes them 'the most deserving of execution.'" Though the death penalty is not invariably unconstitutional, see *Gregg* v. *Georgia,* 428 U.S. 153 (1976), the Court insists upon confining the instances in which the punishment can be imposed.

Applying this principle, we held in *Roper* and *Atkins* that the execution of juveniles and mentally retarded persons

(continued)

are punishments violative of the Eighth Amendment because the offender had a diminished personal responsibility for the crime. The Court further has held that the death penalty can be disproportionate to the crime itself where the crime did not result, or was not intended to result, in death of the victim. In *Coker*, for instance, the Court held it would be unconstitutional to execute an offender who had raped an adult woman. See also *Eberheart, supra* (holding unconstitutional in light of *Coker* a sentence of death for the kidnapping and rape of an adult woman). And in *Enmund* v. *Florida*, 458 U.S. 782 (1982), the Court overturned the capital sentence of a defendant who aided and abetted a robbery during which a murder was committed but did not himself kill, attempt to kill, or intend that a killing would take place. On the other hand, in *Tison* v. *Arizona*, the Court allowed the defendants' death sentences to stand where they did not themselves kill the victims but their involvement in the events leading up to the murders was active, recklessly indifferent, and substantial.

In these cases the Court has been guided by "objective indicia of society's standards, as expressed in legislative enactments and state practice with respect to executions." *Roper*, 543 U.S., at 563; see also *Coker, supra*, at 593–597 (plurality opinion) (finding that both legislatures and juries had firmly rejected the penalty of death for the rape of an adult woman); *Enmund, supra*, at 788 (looking to "historical development of the punishment at issue, legislative judgments, international opinion, and the sentencing decisions juries have made"). The inquiry does not end there, however. Consensus is not dispositive. Whether the death penalty is disproportionate to the crime committed depends as well upon the standards elaborated by controlling precedents and by the Court's own understanding and interpretation of the Eighth Amendment's text, history, meaning, and purpose.

Based both on consensus and [on] our own independent judgment, our holding is that a death sentence for one who raped but did not kill a child, and who did not intend to assist another in killing the child, is unconstitutional under the Eighth and Fourteenth Amendments. . . .

[The Court then examined the legislative and sentencing trends for child rapists and concluded that the evidence points in the direction of U.S. society not favoring capital punishment for child rapists.]

As we have said in other Eighth Amendment cases, objective evidence of contemporary values as it relates to punishment for child rape is entitled to great weight, but it does not end our inquiry. "[T]he Constitution contemplates that in the end our own judgment will be brought to bear on the question of the acceptability of the death penalty under the Eighth Amendment." We turn, then, to the resolution of the question before us, which is informed by our precedents and our own understanding of the Constitution and the rights it secures. . . .

It must be acknowledged that there are moral grounds to question a rule barring capital punishment for a crime against an individual that did not result in death. These facts illustrate the point. Here the victim's fright, the sense of betrayal, and the nature of her injuries caused more prolonged physical and mental suffering than, say, a sudden killing by an unseen assassin. The attack was not just on her but on her childhood. For this reason, we should be most reluctant to rely upon the language of the plurality in *Coker*, which posited that, for the victim of rape, "life may not be nearly so happy as it was" but it is not beyond repair. 433 U.S., at 598. Rape has a permanent psychological, emotional, and sometimes physical impact on the child. See C. Bagley & K. King, *Child Sexual Abuse: The Search for Healing* 2–24, 111–112 (1990); Finkelhor & Browne, "Assessing the Long-Term Impact of Child Sexual Abuse: A Review and Conceptualization" in *Handbook on Sexual Abuse of Children* 55–60 (L. Walker ed. 1988). We cannot dismiss the years of long anguish that must be endured by the victim of child rape.

It does not follow, though, that capital punishment is a proportionate penalty for the crime. The constitutional prohibition against excessive or cruel and unusual punishments mandates that the State's power to punish "be exercised within the limits of civilized standards." Evolving standards of decency that mark the progress of a maturing society counsel us to be most hesitant before interpreting the Eighth Amendment to allow the extension of the death penalty, a hesitation that has special force where no life was taken in the commission of the crime. It is an established principle that decency, in its essence, presumes respect for the individual and thus moderation or restraint in the application of capital punishment.

To date the Court has sought to define and implement this principle, for the most part, in cases involving capital murder. One approach has been to insist upon general rules that ensure consistency in determining who receives a death sentence. See *California* v. *Brown*, 479 U.S. 538, 541 (1987) ("[D]eath penalty statutes [must] be structured so as to prevent the penalty from being administered in an arbitrary and unpredictable fashion"). At the same time the Court has insisted, to ensure restraint and moderation in use of capital punishment, on judging the "character and record of the individual offender and the circumstances of the particular offense as a constitutionally indispensable part of the process of inflicting the penalty of death." . . .

Our concern here is limited to crimes against individual persons. We do not address, for example, crimes defining and punishing treason, espionage, terrorism, and drug kingpin activity, which are offenses against the State. As it relates to crimes against individuals, though, the death penalty should not be expanded to instances where the victim's life was not taken. We said in *Coker* of adult rape:

> We do not discount the seriousness of rape as a crime. It is highly reprehensible, both in a moral sense and in its almost total contempt for the personal integrity and autonomy of the female victim. . . . Short of homicide, it is the 'ultimate violation of self.' . . . [But] [t]he murderer kills; the rapist, if no more than that, does not. . . . We have the abiding conviction that the death penalty, which 'is unique in its severity and irrevocability,' is an excessive penalty for the rapist who, as such, does not take human life.

The same distinction between homicide and other serious violent offenses against the individual informed the Court's analysis in *Enmund*, where the Court held that the death penalty for the crime of vicarious felony murder is disproportionate to the offense. The Court repeated there the fundamental, moral distinction between a "murderer" and a "robber," noting that while "robbery is a serious crime deserving serious punishment," it is not like death in its "severity and irrevocability."

Consistent with evolving standards of decency and the teachings of our precedents we conclude that, in determining whether the death penalty is excessive, there is a distinction between intentional first-degree murder on the one hand and nonhomicide crimes against individual persons, even including child rape, on the other. The latter crimes may be devastating in their harm, as here, but "in terms of moral depravity and of the injury to the person and to the public," *Coker*, they cannot be compared to murder in their "severity and irrevocability."

In addition, by in effect making the punishment for child rape and murder equivalent, a State that punishes child rape by death may remove a strong incentive for the rapist not to kill the victim. Assuming the offender behaves in a rational way, as one must to justify the penalty on grounds of deterrence, the penalty in some respects gives less protection, not more, to the victim, who is often the sole witness to the crime. It might be argued that, even if the death penalty results in a marginal increase in the incentive to kill, this is counterbalanced by a marginally increased deterrent to commit the crime at all. Whatever balance the legislature strikes, however, uncertainty on the point makes the argument for the penalty less compelling than for homicide crimes.

Each of these propositions, standing alone, might not establish the unconstitutionality of the death penalty for the crime of child rape. Taken in sum, however, they demonstrate the serious negative consequences of making child rape a capital offense. These considerations lead us to conclude, in our independent judgment, that the death penalty is not a proportional punishment for the rape of a child.

What Do *You* Think?

1. Do you agree with the Court that, in terms of crimes against individuals, only the taking of a life is serious enough to impose death on the perpetrator?

2. The Court looks to "objective evidence" as guidance. Do you see flaws in this reasoning? Don't legislators make decisions that do not necessarily reflect the values of their constituents?

3. Can you speculate as to why so few states have lacked statutes imposing death on child rapists?

Additional Applications

Does *Kennedy* apply to the military?

United States v. *Toussant*, 2008 CCA LEXIS 564 (U.S. Army Crim. App. 2008)

The Case: In February 2008, military prosecutors filed charges against U.S. Army Master Sergeant Robert Toussant for repeatedly raping a female under the age of 16—an offense punishable by death under Article 120 of the Uniform Code of Military Justice (UCMJ). Challenging the charges on interlocutory appeal, Sgt. Toussant argued that the Supreme Court's recent ruling in *Kennedy* v. *Louisiana* prohibited death as an authorized punishment for rape of a child under the UCMJ. Consequently, Toussant argued, court-martial proceedings against him on those charges could not proceed.

The Finding: In a December 2008 decision, the U.S. Army Court of Criminal Appeals rejected Toussant's interpretation of *Kennedy* and held that his court-martial on child rape charges could proceed. The U.S. Supreme Court, the military court found, had clarified after its initial *Kennedy* ruling that that decision "was limited to the civilian context." What's more, the Army panel found, the Supreme Court has "recognized the long standing existence of the death penalty for rape in the military" in finding that it "need not decide whether certain considerations might justify differences in the application of the Cruel and Unusual Punishments Clause to military cases." Absent a clear mandate from the Supreme Court to apply *Kennedy* in military contexts, the military appeals panel concluded, capital charges for child rape could still be brought by military prosecutors against Toussant. ∎

death-row prisoners and other state inmates whose convictions have been upheld by state appellate courts can petition federal court in order to argue that their rights were violated at trial.

In a move to reduce delays in the carrying out of death sentences, the U.S. Supreme Court, in the case of *McCleskey* v. *Zandt* (1991),[107] limited the number of appeals a condemned person may bring to the courts. Saying that repeated filings for the sole purpose of delay promotes "disrespect for the finality of convictions" and "disparages the entire criminal justice system," the Court established a two-pronged criterion for future appeals. According to *McCleskey*, in any petition beyond the first, filed with a federal court, capital defendants must demonstrate (1) good cause why the claim now being made was not included in the first filing and (2) how the absence of that claim may have harmed the petitioner's ability to mount an effective defense (Figure 14–5). Two months later, the Court reinforced *McCleskey* when it ruled, in *Coleman* v. *Thompson*,[108] that state prisoners could not cite "procedural default," such as a defense attorney's failure to meet a state's filing deadline for appeals, as the basis for an appeal to federal court.

FIGURE 14–5

Limits on Death-Row Appeals.

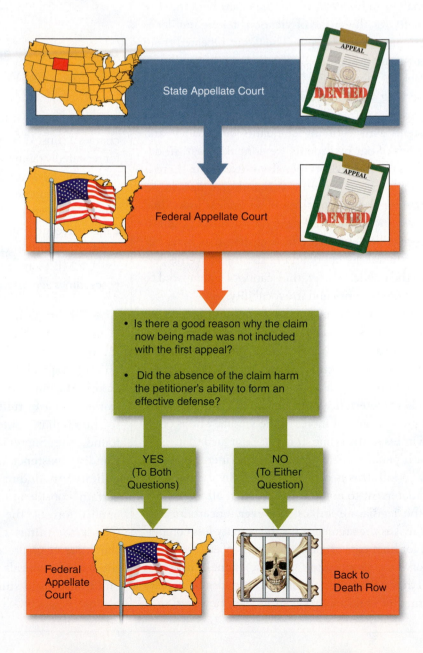

In 1995, in the case of *Schlup* v. *Delo*,[109] the Court continued to define standards for continued appeals from death-row inmates under federal jurisdiction, ruling that before appeals based on claims of new evidence can be heard, "a petitioner must show that, in light of the new evidence, it is more likely than not that no reasonable juror would have found him guilty beyond a reasonable doubt."[110] A "reasonable juror" was defined as one who "would consider fairly all of the evidence presented and would conscientiously obey the trial court's instructions requiring proof beyond a reasonable doubt."

In 1996, a unanimous Supreme Court upheld a provision of the Antiterrorism and Effective Death Penalty Act of 1996 that sharply restricts appeals by death-row prisoners and other convicts. Provisions of the antiterrorism legislation deny a second federal *habeas* appeal for most death-row inmates who claim violations of their constitutional rights. The law, however, does allow prisoners to petition the Supreme Court directly during their first round of appeals but requires that additional appeals be approved by a three-judge U.S. appeals court panel before they can make their case to a trial court. Specifically, Title I of the Antiterrorism and Effective Death Penalty Act of 1996 requires dismissal of a claim presented in a state prisoner's second or successive federal *habeas* application if that claim was also presented in a prior application; compels dismissal of a claim that was not presented in a prior federal application unless certain conditions apply; and creates a gatekeeping mechanism whereby the prospective applicant files in the court of appeals a motion for leave to file a second or successive *habeas* application in the district court, and a three-judge panel determines whether the application makes a *prima facie* showing that it satisfies the requirements of the law. Under the law, the panel's decisions cannot be appealed to the Supreme Court.

The 1996 case *Felker* v. *Turpin*[111] involved Ellis Wayne Felker, 47, a Georgia inmate who had been scheduled to die for the 1981 rape and murder of a 19-year-old college student. Felker challenged the new law, claiming that it unconstitutionally restricted the jurisdiction of the U.S. Supreme Court and improperly suspended his ability to file *habeas corpus* applications with the Court. The Court ruled, however, that the law does not improperly limit its ability to consider successive appeals by inmates challenging their convictions or sentences. "We hold that the act does not preclude this court from entertaining an application for *habeas corpus* relief, although it does affect the standards governing the granting of such relief," Chief Justice William Rehnquist wrote in the opinion issued by the Court. Justice Rehnquist went on to describe the new restrictions as part of a recent trend independently initiated by the Court and aimed at preventing abuses. "The added restrictions that the act places on second *habeas* petitions are well within the compass of this evolutionary process and we hold that they do not amount to a 'suspension' of the writ," Rehnquist said.

In most instances, failure to comply with application deadlines for appeals or petitions for *habeas corpus* relief are fatal. However, the extreme facts of the Capstone Case *Maples v. Thomas* led to a different result.

Death as Cruel and Unusual

Although the majority of justices on the U.S. Supreme Court in recent years have seemed largely convinced of the constitutionality of a sentence of death, a few have viewed capital punishment as a barbarous punishment that has no place in civilized society. In 1994, for example, Justice Harry A. Blackmun spoke out against capital punishment in a Texas case.[112] In a dissenting opinion, Blackmun wrote: "From this day forward, I no longer shall tinker with the machinery of death. . . . Rather than continue to coddle the Court's delusion that the desired level of fairness has been achieved . . . I feel morally and intellectually obligated simply to concede that the death penalty experiment has failed. . . . The basic

In order for a punishment to constitute cruel or unusual punishment, it must involve torture or a lingering death, or the infliction of unnecessary and wanton pain.

—*Supreme Court of Florida, Jones v. Butterworth, 714 So. 2d 404 (1998)*

APPLYING THE CONCEPT

CAPSTONE CASE

Is a Capital Convictee Responsible for His Attorney's Failure to File His Appeal?

Maples v. Thomas, 565 U.S. ___ (2012)
Justice Ginsburg delivered the opinion of the Court.

THE CASE Cory R. Maples is an Alabama capital prisoner sentenced to death in 1997 for the murder of two individuals. At trial, he was represented by two appointed lawyers, minimally paid and with scant experience in capital cases. Maples sought postconviction relief in state court, alleging ineffective assistance of counsel and several other trial infirmities. His petition, filed in August 2001, was written by two New York attorneys serving pro bono, both associated with the same New York–based large law firm. An Alabama attorney, designated as local counsel, moved the admission of the out-of-state counsel pro hac vice. As understood by New York counsel, local counsel would facilitate their appearance, but would undertake no substantive involvement in the case.

In the summer of 2002, while Maples' postconviction petition remained pending in the Alabama trial court, his New York attorneys left the law firm; their new employment disabled them from continuing to represent Maples. They did not inform Maples of their departure and consequent inability to serve as his counsel. Nor did they seek the Alabama trial court's leave to withdraw. Neither they nor anyone else moved for the substitution of counsel able to handle Maples' case.

In May 2003, the Alabama trial court denied Maples' petition. Notices of the court's order were posted to the New York attorneys at the address of the law firm with which they had been associated. Those postings were returned, unopened, to the trial court clerk, who attempted no further mailing. With no attorney of record in fact acting on Maples' behalf, the time to appeal ran out.

Thereafter, Maples petitioned for a writ of habeas corpus in federal court. The District Court and, in turn, the Eleventh Circuit, rejected his petition, pointing to the procedural default in state court, i.e., Maples' failure timely to appeal the Alabama trial court's order denying him postconviction relief. Maples, it is uncontested, was blameless for the default.

THE FINDING The sole question this Court has taken up for review is whether, on the extraordinary facts of Maples' case, there is "cause" to excuse the default. . . .

Alabama sets low eligibility requirements for lawyers appointed to represent indigent capital defendants at trial. Appointed counsel need only be a member of the Alabama bar and have "five years' prior experience in the active practice of criminal law." Nor does the State provide, or require appointed counsel to gain, any capital-case-specific professional education or training.

Appointed counsel in death penalty cases are also undercompensated. . . .

Nearly alone among the States, Alabama does not guarantee representation to indigent capital defendants in postconviction proceedings. The State has elected, instead, "to rely on the efforts of typically well-funded [out-of-state] volunteers. . . .

As a rule, a state prisoner's habeas claims may not be entertained by a federal court "when (1) 'a state court [has] declined to address [those] claims because the prisoner had failed to meet a state procedural requirement,' and (2) 'the state judgment rests on independent and adequate state procedural grounds.' . . .

We confine our consideration to the question whether Maples has shown cause to excuse the missed notice of appeal deadline.

Cause for a procedural default exists where "something external to the petitioner, something that cannot fairly be attributed to him[,] . . . 'impeded [his] efforts to comply with the State's procedural rule.'" Negligence on the part of a prisoner's postconviction attorney does not qualify as "cause." That is so, we reasoned in Coleman, because the attorney is the prisoner's agent, and under "well-settled principles of agency law," the principal bears the risk of negligent conduct on the part of his agent. . . .

A markedly different situation is presented, however, when an attorney abandons his client without notice, and thereby occasions the default. Having severed the principal-agent relationship, an attorney no longer acts, or fails to act, as the client's representative. . . .

We agree that, under agency principles, a client cannot be charged with the acts or omissions of an attorney who has abandoned him. Nor can a client be faulted for failing to act on his own behalf when he lacks reason to believe his attorneys of record, in fact, are not representing him. We therefore inquire whether Maples has shown that his attorneys of record abandoned him, thereby supplying the "extraordinary circumstances beyond his control," necessary to lift the state procedural bar to his federal petition. . . .

. . . [T]he record admits of only one reading: At no time before the missed deadline was [Maples' attorney] serving as Maples' agent "in any meaningful sense of that word." The case was remanded to the trial court with an order to determine if his attorneys' failure caused his prejudice, part of the legal test that is applied in such cases.]

What Do *You* Think?

1. Should any criminal defendant be responsible for the mistakes of defense counsel under agency theory?

2. Do you believe the outcome would have been different if the state would have proved that Maples knew his attorneys were not actively pursuing his appeal?

Additional Applications

What constitutes "abandonment" by counsel after *Maples*?

Moormann v. Schriro, 672 F.3d 644 (9th Cir. 2012)

The Case: Robert Moormann, sentenced to death in 1985 for the murder of his adoptive mother in Arizona, was scheduled for execution by state officials on February 29, 2012. Two days before the scheduled execution, with all state appeals and regular federal *habeas* claims now exhausted, Moormann filed with the U.S. Court of Appeals for the Ninth Circuit for an emergency stay and permission to file a new petition for *habeas* relief in light of *Maples*. Moormann's primary argument (now raised by new counsel) was that the *Maples* decision—announced just weeks earlier—established for the first time that "abandonment" by counsel justified additional federal court review. And in Moormann's earlier state postconviction proceedings, his new counsel argued, defense lawyers had "failed so utterly to raise a colorable claim [of mitigating evidence] that either one or both of them effectively had 'abandoned'" their client within the meaning of the Supreme Court's new *habeas* rule.

The Finding: In an expedited February 28, 2012, ruling, a three-judge Ninth Circuit panel denied Moormann's request for a stay and subsequent federal review under *Maples*. Emphasizing the "very high" procedural barriers that exist to last-minute *habeas* relief generally, Judge Mary Schroeder wrote that Moormann had ultimately failed to make the necessary *prima facie* showing that his postconviction counsel had abandoned him within the meaning of *Maples*. As Judge Schroeder saw it, the specific allegations raised here by Moormann's "current and diligent" counsel—that earlier lawyers had failed to carry out even a minimal investigation into whether Moormann had suffered from a "difficult childhood, mental disabilities, and a possibly incestuous relationship with the victim"—had indeed raised questions about whether "serious negligence" by counsel had occurred. Still, Schroeder continued, *Maples* established only an exception from general procedural default rules for instances in which lawyers "ceased acting . . . as attorneys" so that "in reality, [the client] ha[s] been reduced to *pro se* status." In this case, the court found, Moormann had "always [been] represented by active counsel" throughout his postconviction appeals; thus, Schroeder concluded, no valid *Maples* claim had been presented.

Does a significant state-created delay in notifying a prisoner of court action justify an exception to habeas petition deadlines?

Earl v. Fabian, 556 F.3d 717 (8th Cir. 2009)

The Case: Christopher Earl, convicted in Minnesota state court in 2004 on ten counts of aiding and abetting first-degree murder, was sentenced to three consecutive life terms without the possibility of parole. For security reasons, Minnesota corrections officials then transferred Earl to an undisclosed correctional facility in Florida, where his counsel was unable to contact him directly throughout postconviction proceedings. (State officials refused to inform Earl's public defender of where he could be reached; consequently, counsel had to rely on the state Department of Corrections' assurance that it would forward all written correspondence to Earl in a timely manner.)

In January 2007, Earl filed a petition for a writ of *habeas corpus* with the federal district court, asserting that prosecutors had improperly used a videotaped confession against him at trial. Earl's *habeas* petition was denied because it was 35 days late under the applicable one-year filing deadline—yet on appeal, Earl argued that Minnesota officials had effectively caused the delay by failing at least twice to deliver key correspondence from his counsel as promised. (One letter from Earl's counsel—informing Earl that

(continued)

the state supreme court had affirmed his convictions—was allegedly delayed for seven months. Another letter—informing Earl that rehearing had been denied—allegedly failed to reach Earl for a year.)

The Finding: A three-judge panel of the U.S Court of Appeals for the Eighth Circuit vacated the district court's dismissal of Earl's *habeas* petition and remanded the case for additional fact-finding. "[T]here has been no suggestion," the appeals panel noted, that Minnesota officials had "intentionally restricted [Earl's] access to the courts." Nonetheless, "an inmate has a liberty interes[t] protected by the due process clause in uncensored communication"—and state officials, "[h]aving rendered Earl incommunicado . . . assumed the responsibility to transmit information about his case and counsel's correspondence to him in a timely fashion." Thus on remand, the Eighth Circuit panel concluded, the trial court must "make findings on what mechanism the state of Minnesota relied on to send notice to Earl, what actually happened to delay notice, and when Earl actually received notice that his judgment had become final." The "ultimate issue" on appeals, the panel emphasized, is "whether the state created an impediment that prevented Earl from filing his *habeas* petition." ∎

question—does the system accurately and consistently determine which defendants 'deserve' to die?—cannot be answered in the affirmative." In response to Blackmun's objections, Justice Antonin Scalia said that Blackmun missed the mark because his "explanation often refers to 'intellectual, moral, and personal' perceptions, but never to the text and tradition of the Constitution. It is the latter rather than the former," wrote Scalia, "that ought to control." Mention of capital crimes in the Fifth Amendment[113] is sufficient evidence, argued Scalia, that the Constitution permits imposition of the penalty of death under appropriate circumstances.

More open to debate is the constitutionality of *methods* for the imposition of capital punishment. In a 1993 hearing, *Poyner* v. *Murray*,[114] the U.S. Supreme Court hinted at the possibility of reopening questions first raised in *Kemmler*. The case challenged Virginia's use of the electric chair as a form of cruel and unusual punishment. Syvasky Lafayette Poyner, who originally brought the case before the Court, lost his bid for a stay of execution and was electrocuted in March 1993. Nonetheless, in *Poyner*, Justices David Souter, Harry Blackmun, and John Paul Stevens wrote: "The Court has not spoken squarely on the underlying issue since *In re Kemmler* . . . and the holding of that case does not constitute a dispositive response to litigation of the issue in light of modern knowledge about the method of execution in question."

In a more recent ruling, members of the Court questioned the constitutionality of hanging, suggesting that it may be a form of cruel and unusual punishment. In that case, *Campbell* v. *Wood* (1994), the defendant, Charles Campbell, raped a woman, got out of prison, and then found the woman and murdered her. His request for a stay of execution was denied because Washington State law offered Campbell a choice among various methods of execution, and therefore an alternative to hanging. Similarly, in 1996, the Court upheld California's death penalty statute, which provides for lethal injection as the primary method of capital punishment in that state.[115] The constitutionality of the statute had been challenged by two death-row inmates who claimed that a provision in the law that permitted condemned prisoners the choice of lethal gas in lieu of injection brought the statute within the realm of allowing cruel and unusual punishments.

Questions about the constitutionality of electrocution as a means of execution arose in 1997, when flames shot from the head and the leather mask covering the face of Pedro Medina during his Florida execution. Similarly, in 1999, blood poured from behind the mask covering Allen Lee "Tiny" Davis's face as he was put to death in Florida's electric chair. State officials claimed that the 344-pound Davis had suffered a nosebleed brought on by hypertension and the blood-thinning medication that he had been taking. In 2001, the Georgia Supreme Court declared electrocution to be unconstitutional, ending its use in that state.[116] The Georgia court cited testimony from lower court records showing that electrocution may not result in a quick death or in immediate cessation of consciousness.

Today, lethal injection is the primary method of executing offenders in the United States. Lethal injection is a process whereby the condemned offender is given multiple drugs, at least one intended to anaesthetize the individual and the others intended to induce respiratory and heart failure. Although intended to be more humane that former methods, lethal injection is imperfect. In some cases, veins are difficult to find, extending the time to execution. Injections into muscles, rather than veins, can also be a problem. One study found that some offenders slowly suffocate, experiencing significant pain, while they are unable to communicate. These problems led the creator of the lethal injection to question whether it's time to change the procedure.[117] In spite of the problems that have occurred in some instances, the Supreme Court found lethal injection, as administered at the time, to be consonant with the Eighth Amendment in *Baze* v. *Rees* (2008).[118]

INTERMEDIATE SANCTIONS

Although traditional sentencing options have included imprisonment, fines, probation, and—for murder and treason—death, significant numbers of innovative sentencing options, also called **intermediate sanctions** or *alternative sanctions*, have become available to judges in many jurisdictions during the past few decades. Intermediate sanctions—which may be imposed in lieu of other, more traditional sanctions—include the use of split sentencing, shock probation and shock parole, shock incarceration, mixed sentencing, community service, intensive supervision, and home confinement.

A **split sentence** requires a convicted offender to serve a brief period of confinement in a local, state, or federal correctional facility, followed by a term of court-ordered probation. "Ninety days in jail, to be followed by a probationary term of two years," might be a typical split sentence. Split sentences are frequently imposed on youthful offenders who commit minor crimes in hopes that the threat of further sanctions might deter them from additional law violation.

Shock probation is much like split sentencing in that the offender serves a relatively short period of time in correctional custody and is then released by court order. An important difference is that under shock probation programs, an offender must *apply* for release after entering confinement and can never be sure whether his or her request will be granted. If it is, release may come as something of a shock to an offender who might otherwise be anticipating a relatively long prison term. *Shock parole* is similar in purpose and design to shock probation. The main difference is that release decisions made under shock probation programs are made by a judge, whereas release decisions under shock parole programs are made by a paroling authority, such as a state parole board.

Shock incarceration, another form of alternative sanction, makes use of "boot camp" correctional programs that are intended to impress on youthful offenders the realities of prison life. Shock incarceration programs are modeled after military basic training and typically employ "drill sergeant"–type instructors selected for their ability to control and harass their charges. Such programs are highly regimented and make use of strict discipline, rigorous physical training, and hard labor in an effort to convince young offenders of the need to avoid future violations of the criminal law. Although shock incarceration programs are generally of short duration (often only weeks or months), program "failures" may be moved into the general prison population and be ordered to serve longer terms of confinement.

Although most states allow judges to place offenders into shock incarceration settings, some jurisdictions delegate that authority to corrections officials. Two states, Louisiana and Texas, authorize judges and corrections personnel joint authority in the decision-making

intermediate sanctions
The use of split sentencing, shock probation and parole, home confinement, shock incarceration, and community service in lieu of other, more traditional sanctions, such as imprisonment and fines. Intermediate sanctions are becoming increasingly popular as prisons become more crowded. Also called *alternative sanctions*.

split sentence
A sentence explicitly requiring the convicted person to serve a period of confinement in a local, state, or federal facility, followed by a period of probation.

shock probation
The practice of sentencing offenders to prison, allowing them to apply for probationary release, and granting release in surprise fashion. Offenders who receive shock probation may not be aware that they will be released on probation and may expect to spend a much longer time behind bars.

shock incarceration
A sentencing option that makes use of "boot camp"–type prisons in order to impress on convicted offenders the realities of prison life.

process.[119] Some states, such as Massachusetts, have begun to accept classes of female inmates into boot camp settings. The Massachusetts program, which first accepted women in 1993, requires inmates to spend nearly four months in the program.

A comprehensive 1995 study of boot camp prisons examined shock incarceration programs in eight states: Florida, Georgia, Illinois, Louisiana, New York, Oklahoma, South Carolina, and Texas.[120] The study found that boot camp programs are especially popular because "they are . . . perceived as being tough on crime" and "have been enthusiastically embraced as a viable correctional option." The report concluded, however, that "the impact of boot camp programs on offender recidivism is at best negligible."

mixed sentence
A sentence that requires a convicted offender to serve weekends (or other specified periods of time) in a confinement facility (usually a jail), while undergoing probation supervision in the community.

A **mixed sentence**, another alternative sentencing option, requires offenders to perform some type of community service along with brief periods of time in confinement—often served on weekends. The community service component of mixed sentencing may require offenders to spend a specified number of hours per week working in government offices, cleaning public parks, washing police cars, or renovating state or county buildings. Offenders with special skills, such as nurses, physicians, or accountants, may be ordered to serve the community in a capacity in keeping with their abilities. Mixed sentencing is typically employed only with minor offenders, and there is considerable disagreement among justice professionals as to whether such punishment reduces recidivism, provides an effective deterrent, or rehabilitates offenders. Sometimes probationers are ordered to perform community service without having to serve time behind bars. **Community service** is a sentencing alternative that requires an offender to spend at least part of his or her time working for a public agency.

community service
A sentencing alternative that requires offenders to spend at least part of their time working for a community agency.

intensive supervision
A form of probation supervision involving frequent face-to-face contacts between the probationary client and probation officers.

Intensive supervision, also called *intensive probation supervision (IPS)*, is an alternative form of sentencing that imposes especially strict requirements on offenders sentenced to probation. Such requirements may include a mandatory curfew, required employment, routine and unannounced alcohol and drug testing, community service requirements, and frequent face-to-face meetings with probation officers. Some intensive probation supervision programs also include "prison awareness visits" during which individuals assigned to the program must tour correctional facilities in order to witness firsthand the unsavory conditions of confinement in a penal institution.

home confinement
A form of punishment in which individuals are confined to their homes and may be monitored electronically to be sure they do not leave during the hours of confinement. Absence from the home during working hours is often permitted. Also called *house arrest*.

Home confinement, the last alternative sanction we will discuss, has grown substantially in popularity in recent years. Home confinement, also called *house arrest*, requires that offenders be confined in their homes and sometimes makes use of electronic monitoring to ensure that they do not leave during the hours of confinement. Home confinement programs generally permit those so sentenced to travel to and from work, medical appointments, or treatment programs. Participants sometimes wear ankle or arm bracelets that send out a signal, which can be monitored from equipment installed in their residences for that purpose. Some electronic monitoring devices are attached to an offender's telephone and require the confined individual to insert a device into a "reader" connected to the phone or to make some other predefined response to telephone calls intended to determine the offender's location.

House arrest can be an effective response to the rising cost of imprisonment. Estimates show that whereas imprisonment may cost taxpayers as much as $50,000 per year per offender, traditional home confinement programs cost only $1,500 to $7,000 per offender per year, depending on the jurisdiction and the type of supervision employed. Electronic monitoring increases the cost of home confinement by about $1,000.[121] Advocates of house arrest argue that it is also socially cost-effective[122] because it provides no opportunity for the kinds of negative socialization that occur in prison.

Intermediate sanctions are generally available to relatively unthreatening, nonviolent, and first-time offenders. In 1994, California legislators reaffirmed their commitment to intermediate sanctions with passage of the Community-Based Punishment Act. The act, passed alongside the state's punitive three-strikes legislation, has as its goal the release of nonviolent offenders—a group that continues to comprise a majority of the California prison population.

SUMMARY

- This chapter describes criminal sentencing and punishment. Sentencing is the process through which a sentencing authority imposes a lawful punishment or other sanction on a person convicted of violating the criminal law.

- One fundamental way of distinguishing crimes from violations of the civil law, or torts, is to recognize that crimes are subject to punishment. When criminal punishment is associated with violation of the law, the U.S. Supreme Court has ruled that constitutional guarantees of due process must apply.

- A perceived need for retribution, as a goal of criminal sentencing, may be fundamental to the human condition. In its present guise, retribution is found in the just deserts philosophy, which holds that criminal offenders deserve the punishment they receive at the hands of the state and suggests that punishment should be appropriate to the type and severity of the crime committed.

- Other goals of criminal sentencing include deterrence, rehabilitation, restoration, and incapacitation.

- Three-strikes laws and habitual offender statutes, which are built on a policy of selective incapacitation, reflect a growing society-wide emphasis on both retribution and deterrence.

- Restoration, a sentencing goal that seeks to make victims and the community "whole again," frequently builds on the practice of restitution and embodies many of the principles of restorative justice.

- Two major approaches to sentencing are found in the indeterminate and determinate models. An indeterminate sentence is a type of sentence to imprisonment in which the commitment, instead of being for a specified single time quantity, such as three years, is for a range of time, such as two to five years or five years maximum and zero minimum. A determinate sentence sets a single standard time quantity of imprisonment.

- Determinate sentencing schemes typically take into consideration both aggravating and mitigating factors in reaching sentencing decisions. Aggravating factors are circumstances relating to the commission of a crime that cause its gravity to be greater than that of the average instance of the given type of offense. Conversely, mitigating factors are circumstances surrounding the commission of a crime that do not in law justify or excuse the act but which in fairness may be considered as reducing the blameworthiness of the defendant.

- A recent movement toward truth in sentencing at both the state and federal levels has tended to ensure that the time inmates actually serve in prison closely matches the sentences that were imposed.

- Traditional sentencing options have generally included imprisonment, probation, fines, and death. Studies show that 44% of sentenced felons receive active prison terms.

- Hate-crime laws, which have developed during the past 20 years, increase the penalties associated with bias crimes.

- The U.S. Supreme Court has created an environment in which capital punishment remains a viable sentencing option for especially heinous crimes in which mitigating factors are lacking. Death sentences today are usually imposed via a two-step process, which first determines a defendant's guilt and later decides the sentence.

- *Habeas corpus* appeals are used by death-row prisoners and other state inmates whose convictions have been upheld by state appellate courts to petition federal courts in order to argue that their rights were violated at trial. Recent initiatives in both federal law and U.S. Supreme Court precedents, however, have had the effect of limiting *habeas* opportunities.

KEY TERMS

aggravating factor, 468

capital punishment, 481

career offender, 464

community service, 496

concurrent sentence, 467

consecutive sentence, 467

determinate sentence, 467

deterrence, 462

equity, 467

general deterrence, 462

habeas corpus, 486

habitual offender, 464

hate crime, 480

home confinement, 496

incapacitation, 463

indeterminate sentence, 467

intensive supervision, 496

intermediate sanctions, 495

just deserts, 460

mitigating factor, 468

mixed sentence, 496

plea bargaining, 473

probation, 475

proportionality, 467

rehabilitation, 462

restoration, 463

restorative justice, 463

retribution, 460

selective incapacitation, 465

sentencing, 458

shock incarceration, 495

shock probation, 495

social debt, 468

specific deterrence, 462

split sentence, 495

three-strikes legislation, 464

truth in sentencing, 472

QUESTIONS FOR DISCUSSION

1. What are the purposes of criminal sentencing? What sentencing strategies are most closely associated with each sentencing purpose?

2. How is each purpose of criminal sentencing served by indeterminate sentencing? By determinate sentencing? Which sentencing model (determinate or indeterminate) is more appropriate today? Why?

3. Do you believe that three-strikes laws can be an effective deterrent to crime? Are three-strikes laws economically efficient? Explain your answers.

4. What is restorative justice, and how does it build on restitution? How does it differ from retribution as a purpose of criminal punishment?

5. Do you believe that capital punishment should continue to remain a viable sentencing option for especially heinous crimes? Why or why not?

6. How are *habeas corpus* appeals limited in capital cases? Explain the underlying rationale.

CRITICAL THINKING AND APPLICATION PROBLEMS

B. A. Dapple was charged and tried with two crimes arising out of the same set of facts, distribution of a controlled substance and possession of an unregistered firearm. He was also charged with being a habitual offender. The jury returned a verdict of guilty on the distribution charge and not guilty on the firearms charge. The judge conducted a sentencing hearing at which she concluded that Dapple used the firearm while distributing the drugs. She increased his sentence as a result, sentencing him at the higher end of the scale for distribution, nine years. The statute provides for five to ten years for distribution of a controlled substance. She then ordered the jury to hear evidence that Dabble is a habitual offender. In her state, three felony convictions in a ten-year period make an offender "habitual." The jury heard the evidence of Dabble's two prior convictions, one for aggravated battery and the other for rape, and found Dabble to be a habitual offender. State law required the imposition of death for habitual offenders when one or more of the convictions was of a violent crime. Accordingly, the state judge sentenced Dabble to death on the habitual offender charge.

1. Assignment: Discuss all Sixth Amendment and Eighth Amendment issues you find, citing applicable cases.

LEGAL RESOURCES ON THE WEB

Many Internet sites provide information about criminal sentencing and capital punishment. Some of the more comprehensive sites are listed here.

ACLU Death Penalty Page
http://www.aclu.org/DeathPenalty/DeathPenaltyMain.cfm

The ACLU's Death Penalty Page offers comprehensive resources on activism against the death penalty in the United States. It includes a link to the ACLU's death-penalty briefing paper and the *ACLU Abolitionist*.

Cornell University Law School Death Penalty Project
http://www.lawschool.cornell.edu/research/death-penalty-project/index.cfm

The project, which began in 1997, encompasses several elements, including a capital punishment clinic, a commitment to provide continuing education programs for capital defense attorneys, and the collection and study of data in this field. The site provides links to death-penalty cases, publications, and other resources.

Death Penalty Information Center (DPIC)
http://www.deathpenaltyinfo.org

This site contains a wealth of information on the death penalty, including current law, statistics, and historical information.

Derechos Human Rights: Death Penalty Information
http://www.derechos.org/dp

This site lists all the countries that currently retain the death penalty.

Sentencing Project
http://www.sentencingproject.org

The Sentencing Project is an independent source of criminal justice policy analysis, data, and program information for the public and policymakers. Its website provides resources relevant to sentencing policy, imprisonment, felony disenfranchisement, drug policy, and women in the justice system.

U.S. Sentencing Commission
http://www.ussc.gov

The U.S. Sentencing Commission's guidelines provide federal judges with clear direction for the sentencing of defendants in their courts. The commission's website provides information about meetings, public hearings, and sentencing policy deliberations.

SUGGESTED READINGS AND CLASSIC WORKS

de Graaff, Peter. "The Poverty of Punishment," *Current Issues in Criminal Justice* 5, no. 1 (July 1993): 13–28.

Gorecki, Jan. *Capital Punishment: Criminal Law and Social Evolution.* New York: Columbia University Press, 1983.

Gorr, Michael J., and Sterling Harwood, eds. *Controversies in Criminal Law: Philosophical Essays on Responsibility and Procedure.* Boulder, CO: Westview Press, 1992.

Husak, Douglas N. *Philosophy of Criminal Law.* Totowa, NJ: Rowman and Littlefield, 1987.

Kadish, Sanford H. *Blame and Punishment: Essays in the Criminal Law.* New York: Macmillan, 1987.

Shavell, Steven. *Criminal Law and Optimal Use of Nonmonetary Sanctions as a Deterrent.* Cambridge, MA: Harvard Law School, 1985.

Zimring, Franklin E., and Gordon Hawkins. *Capital Punishment and the American Agenda.* New York: Cambridge University Press, 1989.

NOTES

1. *State v. Wood*, 868 P.2d 70 (Utah 1993).
2. Ibid.
3. George P. Fletcher, *Rethinking Criminal Law* (Boston: Little, Brown, 1978), 408.
4. Ibid., p. 408.
5. H. L. A. Hart, *Punishment and Responsibility* (New York: Oxford University Press, 1968).
6. Michael S. Moore, "The Moral Worth of Retribution," in *Responsibility, Character and Emotions: New Essays in Moral Psychology*, F. Schoeman, ed. (Cambridge: Cambridge University Press, 1987).
7. Jeremy Bentham, *An Introduction to the Principles of Morals and Legislation* (1789; repr., Oxford: Clarendon Press, 1996).
8. J. Andenaes, "The General Preventive Effects of Punishment," *University of Pennsylvania Law Review* 114 (1966): 955–57.
9. See, for example, Franklin Zimring and Gordon Hawkins, *Deterrence: The Legal Threat in Crime Control* (Chicago: University of Chicago Press, 1973).
10. Robert Martinson, "What Works: Questions and Answers about Prison Reform," *Public Interest*, no. 35 (1974): 22–54.
11. Gordon Bazemore and Mark S. Umbreit, *Balanced and Restorative Justice: Program Summary* (Washington, DC: Office of Juvenile Justice and Delinquency Prevention, October 1994), foreword.
12. John S. Baker, Jr., and others, *Hall's Criminal Law: Cases and Materials*, 5th ed. (Charlottesville, VA: Michie, 1993), 842.
13. U.S. Sentencing Commission, *Federal Sentencing Guidelines Manual* (Washington, DC: U.S. Government Printing Office, 1987), 207.
14. *People v. Superior Court of San Diego (Romero)*, 13 Cal. 4th 497 (1996).
15. *People v. Davis*, 15 Cal. 4th 1096, 1103 (1997). See also *People v. Garcia*, 21 Cal. 4th 1 (1999).
16. *People v. Benson*, 18 Cal. 4th 24 (1998).
17. *People v. Williams*, 17 Cal. 4th 148 (1998).
18. *Monge v. California*, 118 S. Ct. 2246 (1998).
19. *Riggs v. California*, 119 S. Ct. 890 (1999), *cert. denied*.
20. *Ewing v. California*, 123 S. Ct. 1179, 155 L. Ed. 2d 108 (2003); and *Lockyer v. Andrade*, 123 S. Ct. 1166, 155 L. Ed. 2d 144 (2003).
21. "Wilson Praises '3 Strikes' Law," United Press online, March 6, 1996.
22. For a detailed survey of the impact of three-strikes legislation on the California justice system, see Board of Corrections, *"Three Strikes, You're Out": Impact on California's Criminal Justice System and Options for Ongoing Monitoring* (Sacramento: Board of Corrections, September 1996).
23. Bureau of Justice Statistics, *Dictionary of Criminal Justice Data Terminology*, 2nd ed. (Washington, DC: U.S. Department of Justice, 1981), 107.
24. Ibid., 46.
25. Ibid., 107.
26. Public Law 110-220 (2010).
27. Ibid., 15.

28. Ibid., 16.

29. Public Law 98-473 (1984).

30. U.S. Code, Title 18, Section 3553.

31. *Mistretta v. United States*, 488 U.S. 361, 371 (1989).

32. *Apprendi v. New Jersey*, 530 U.S. 466 (2000).

33. *Harris v. United States*, 122 S. Ct. 2406, 153 L. Ed. 2d 524 (2002).

34. *United States v. Cotton*, 535 U.S. 625 (2002).

35. *Ring v. Arizona*, 536 U.S. 584 (2002).

36. *Schriro v. Summerlin*, 542 U.S. 348 (2004).

37. *Blakely v. Washington*, 542 U.S. 296 (2004).

38. *United States v. Booker*, 543 U.S. 220 (2005).

39. *United States v. Fanfan*, 543 U.S. 220 (2005).

40. Tony Mauro, "Supreme Court: Sentencing Guidelines Advisory, Not Mandatory," Law.com, January 1, 2005 (accessed July 4, 2010).

41. U.S. Sentencing Commission, *Federal Sentencing Guidelines Manual*, 2.

42. Lawrence A. Greenfeld, "Prison Sentences and Time Served for Violence," Bureau of Justice Statistics, *Selected Findings*, no. 4 (April 1995).

43. Ibid.

44. Thomas Martello, "Truth in Sentencing," Associated Press, northern edition, April 26, 1994.

45. Barbara Boland and Ronald Sones, *Prosecution of Felony Arrests, 1981* (Washington, DC: Bureau of Justice Statistics, 1986). See also U.S. Department of Justice, Bureau of Justice Statistics, *The Prosecution of Felony Arrests* (Washington, DC: U.S. Government Printing Office, 1983).

46. Barbara Boland and others, *The Prosecution of Felony Arrests, 1982* (Washington, DC: U.S. Government Printing Office, May 1988).

47. For a now-classic discussion of such considerations, see David Sudnow, "Normal Crimes: Sociological Features of the Penal Code in a Public Defender Office," *Social Problems* 12 (1965): 255.

48. *Kercheval v. United States*, 274 U.S. 220, 223, 47 S. Ct. 582, 583 (1927); *Boykin v. Alabama*, 395 U.S. 238 (1969); and *Dickerson v. New Banner Institute, Inc.*, 460 U.S. 103 (1983).

49. *Brady v. United States*, 397 U.S. 742 (1970).

50. *Santobello v. New York*, 404 U.S. 257 (1971).

51. Ibid.

52. *Henderson v. Morgan*, 426 U.S. 637 (1976).

53. *Santobello v. New York*, 404 U.S. 257 (1971).

54. *Mabry v. Johnson*, 467 U.S. 504 (1984).

55. *United States v. Baldacchino*, 762 F.2d 170 (1st Cir. 1985); *United States v. Reardon*, 787 F.2d 512 (10th Cir. 1986); and *United States v. Donahey*, 529 F.2d 831 (11th Cir. 1976).

56. *Federal Rules of Criminal Procedure*, no. 11.

57. *Report to the Nation on Crime and Justice*, 2nd ed. (Washington, DC: U.S. Department of Justice, 1988), 90.

58. Matthew R. Durose and Patrick A. Langan, *Felony Sentences in State Courts, 2004* (Washington, DC: Bureau of Justice Statistics, July 2007).

59. *United States v. Bajakajian*, 524 U.S. 321 (1998).

60. *Harmelin v. Michigan*, 501 U.S. 957 (1991)

61. There are many instances of housing inmates in tents. See, for example, "Arizona Criminals Find Jail Too In-Tents," CNN.com, July 27, 1999 (accessed July 28, 2000), featuring Maricopa County, Arizona's well-known tent city run by Sheriff Joe Arpaio.

62. Thomas Gnau, "Sheriff Jones Is Larger Than Life—and Loving It," *Journal News* (Hamilton, OH), November 5, 2006.

63. *Weems v. United States*, 217 U.S. 349 (1910)

64. *Pervear v. Commonwealth*, 72 U.S. (5 Wall) 475 (1867); and *Kehrli v. Sprinkle*, 524 F.2d 328 (10th Cir. 1975).

65. *Delaware v. Cannon*, 55 Del. 587, 190 A.2d 574 (1963).

66. *Jackson v. Bishop*, 404 F.2d 571 (8th Cir. 1968). For more on corporal punishment, see Daniel E. Hall, "When Caning Meets the Eighth Amendment: Whipping Offenders in the United States," *Widener Journal of Public Law* 4 (1994): 403.

67. *Lockyer v. Andrade*, 538 U.S. 63 (2003)

68. H.R. 4797, 102d Cong., 2d Sess. (1992).

69. California Penal Code, Section 13519.6.

70. Violent Crime Control and Law Enforcement Act of 1994, Section 280003.

71. Federal Bureau of Investigation, *Uniform Crime Reports, 2010* (Washington, DC: FBI, 2011).

72. David Holthouse, "The Year in Hate," *The Intelligence Report* (Montgomery, AL: Southern Poverty Law Center, 2009). Available at http://www.splcenter.org/intel/intelreport/article.jsp?aid=1027 (accessed July 9, 2010).

73. *R.A.V. v. City of St. Paul, Minn.*, 112 S. Ct. 2538 (1992).

74. *Forsyth County, Ga. v. Nationalist Movement*, 112 S. Ct. 2395 (1992).

75. *Virginia v. Black*, 538 U.S. 343 (2003).

76. John Kleinig, "Penalty Enhancements for Hate Crimes," *Criminal Justice Ethics* (summer/fall 1992): 3–6.

77. Wisconsin Statutes, Chapter 939, Section 645(1)(b).

78. *Wisconsin v. Mitchell*, 508 U.S. 47 (1993).

79. See *United States Sentencing Guidelines Manual*, Section 3A1.4.

80. Violent Crime Control and Law Enforcement Act of 1994, Section 60008.

81. Death Penalty Information Center, "Innocence and the Death Penalty." Available at http://www.deathpenaltyinfo.org/innocence-and-death-penalty (accessed July 9, 2010).

82. James S. Liebman, Jeffrey Fagan, and Valerie West, "A Broken System: Error Rates in Capital Cases, 1973–1995," *Texas Law Review* (October 2000), i, 4–5.

83. Title IV of the Justice for All Act of 2004.

84. H.R. 5107.

85. At the time the legislation was enacted, Congress estimated that 300,000 rape kits remained unanalyzed in police department evidence lockers across the country.

86. The act also provides funding for the DNA Sexual Assault Justice Act (Title III of the Justice for All Act of 2004) and the Rape Kits and DNA Evidence Backlog Elimination Act of 2000 (U.S. Code, Title 42, Section 14135)—authorizing more than $500 million for programs to improve the capacity of crime labs to conduct DNA analysis, reduce non-DNA backlogs, train evidence examiners, support sexual assault forensic examiner programs, and promote the use of DNA to identify missing persons.

87. Section 3600(g)(2).

88. *Wilkerson v. Utah*, 99 U.S. 130 (1878).

89. *In re Kemmler*, 136 U.S. 436 (1890).

90. Ibid., 447.

91. *Louisiana ex rel. Francis v. Resweber*, 329 U.S. 459 (1947).

92. *McGautha v. California*, 402 U.S. 183 (1971).

93. *Furman v. Georgia*, 408 U.S. 238 (1972).

94. A position first ascribed in *Trop v. Dulles*, 356 U.S. 86 (1958).

95. Each justice filed a separate opinion.

96. *Woodson v. North Carolina*, 428 U.S. 280 (1976).

97. *Gregg v. Georgia*, 428 U.S. 153 (1976).

98. *Coker v. Georgia*, 433 U.S. 584 (1977).

99. *Edmund v. Florida*, 458 U.S. 782 (1982).

100. *Tison v. Arizona*, 481 U.S. 137 (1987).

101. *Blystone v. Pennsylvania*, 494 U.S. 299 (1990).

102. *Boyde v. California*, 494 U.S. 370 (1990).

103. *Whitmore ex rel. Simmons v. Arkansas*, 495 U.S. 149 (1990).

104. *Elledge v. Florida*, 525 U.S. 944 (1998).

105. *Penry v. Johnson*, 532 U.S. 782 (2001).

106. Mike de Brauw, "Texas Has a New 'Governor Death': Perry Opposes Legislation to Reform the Death Penalty," *New Abolitionist* (July 2001).

107. *McCleskey v. Zandt*, 499 U.S. 467, 493–494 (1991).

108. *Coleman v. Thompson*, 501 U.S. 722, 729 (1991).

109. *Schlup v. Delo*, 513 U.S. 298 (1995).

110. Some Supreme Court watchers have concluded that *Schlup* v. *Delo* constitutes a relaxation of previous doctrine, under which the Court required prisoners to show "clear and convincing evidence" of why their cases should be heard.

111. *Felker v. Turpin, Warden*, 519 U.S. 589 (1996).

112. Quotations in this paragraph are taken from opinions in the U.S. Supreme Court case of *Callins v. Collins*, 510 U.S. 1141 (1994), in which *certiorari* was denied.

113. The Fifth Amendment says that no person "shall be deprived of life . . . without due process of law."

114. *Poyner v. Murray*, 508 U.S. 931 (1993), *cert. denied.*

115. *Director Gomez et al. v. Fierro and Ruiz*, 519 U.S. 918 (1996).

116. See *Dawson v. State*, S01A1041 (2001); and *Moore v. State*, S01A1210 (2001).

117. Elizabeth Cohen, "Lethal Injection Creator: Maybe It's Time to Change the Formula," CNN Health, May 7, 2007, http://articles.cnn.com/2007-05-07/health/lethal.injection_1_sodium-thiopental-lethal-injection-lethal-three-drug-cocktail?_s=PM:HEALTH (accessed July 15, 2012).

118. *Baze v. Rees*, 553 U.S. 35 (2008).

119. *Multisite Evaluation of Shock Incarceration* (Washington, DC: National Institute of Justice, 1995).

120. Ibid.

121. Joan Petersilia, "House Arrest," *Crime File Study Guide* (Washington, DC: National Institute of Justice, 1988).

122. *BI Home Escort: Electronic Monitoring System*, advertising brochure, BI Incorporated, Boulder, CO (no date).

Appendix A

HOW TO BRIEF A CASE

Throughout this textbook, the authors cite a number of important cases. The full-text court opinions for many of these cases can be found online at the website that supports this book. Your instructor may ask that you prepare a brief of some of these cases or that you brief other cases that may be assigned.

Generally speaking, two types of briefs are used in the legal profession. The first is extensive and summarizes cases, statutes, regulations, and related legal materials that are pertinent to a legal issue that is under consideration. It is usually offered to a judge or to the court in support of the position of the submitting party.

A second type of brief—the kind with which we are concerned here—is simply a concise summary of the relevant facts of a single case. A brief of this sort is prepared in order to analyze a case and to present needed information in an abbreviated format that is convenient for use in class or as part of legal research. To prepare a brief for use in class, you need to read the court's written opinion and take notes on the case, being careful to arrange them in a specific format. A case brief, which may be only one or two pages in length, generally includes seven parts: (1) the case citation, (2) a short statement of the facts of the case, (3) a brief procedural history of the case, (4) a summation of the issue or issues involved, (5) the court's decision, (6) an overview of the rationale provided by the court for its decision, and (7) notes to yourself about the case. Each of these parts is briefly discussed here.

Case Citation

The citation includes the name of the case (usually found italicized or underlined at the top of the page in a case reporter or in large boldfaced type at the beginning of an opinion published online), conventional information needed to find the case through legal research, a reference to the court that issued the opinion, and the date the case was decided. A typical citation might look like this:

State v. *Smith,* 58 So. 2d 853 (Ala. Crim. App. 1997)

In this instance, 58 refers to the volume number of the reporter in which the case has been published, and *So. 2d* is the name of the reporter—in this case, the second series of the *Southern Reporter.* The number 853 refers to the page number in the reporter where the decision begins, *Ala. Crim. App.* references the court issuing the decision (in this case, the Alabama Court of Criminal Appeals), and 1997 is the year in which the case was decided. Often court names are not given, as one familiar with legal citation can deduce the court from the name of the reporter. In that case, a citation may look like this:

People v. *Versaggi,* 83 N.Y.2d 123 (1994)

Practiced legal researchers will probably understand that N.Y. in this citation refers to the New York Court of Appeals. Anyone who is not sure can check the reporter referenced by the citation, in which the court's entire name is given.

The citation format used in this book follows the convention of italicizing the names of the plaintiff (in these examples, the state or the "People") and the defendant. Note that the *v.*, which appears between the names of the parties (and stands for *versus*) is not italicized. Other formats may differ. To learn more about legal citations, you might want to consult a printed guide, such as *A Uniform System of Citation,*[1] known in the legal profession as the *Bluebook.*[2] The *Bluebook* is the result of the collaborative efforts of the Columbia Law Review Association, the Harvard Law Review Association, the University of Pennsylvania Law Review, and the Yale Law Review. As an alternative, you might also survey the appropriate format for legal citations through an online service, such as Boston College's Law Library (http://www.bc.edu/schools/law/library).

Relational electronic databases now under development will soon allow rapid online retrieval of case opinions by employing technologically advanced computerized search capabilities. Newly emerging citation styles, needed to take full advantage of the capabilities of such electronic case databases, have begun to augment the standard citation format.

In recognition of such changes, the 2012 edition of the *Bluebook* addresses citability of opinions found on the Internet. It suggests, "The citation should consist of all the elements required for the basic document type (e.g., case, constitution, statute, regulation), followed by the appropriate signal, and as complete an ID or address for the online electronic source as is available."[3] An example might be:

LLR No. 9405161.PA, P10 [http://www.versuslaw.com]

In this example, from the Versus Law website, *LLR* refers to Lawyer's Legal Research, an electronic citation format created by the Versus Law staff. The number after the *LLR* designator refers to a specific case (in this instance, a 1994 Pennsylvania Supreme Court case, *Commonwealth* v. *Berkowitz*), and the letters after the period reference the jurisdiction (Pennsylvania). *P10* identifies the tenth paragraph in the case, and the URL for Versus Law is provided in brackets.

On August 6, 1996, in an effort to further standardize case citations, the ABA's House of Delegates passed a motion to recommend a universal citation system to the courts. The resolution recommends that courts adopt a universal citation system using sequential decision numbers for each year and internal paragraph numbers within the decision. The numbers should be assigned by the court and included in the decision at the time it is made publicly available by the court. The standard form of citation, shown for a decision in a federal court of appeals, would be as follows:

> *Smith* v. *Jones*, 1996 5Cir 15, ¶ 18, 22 F.3d 955

In this example, *1996* is the year of the decision; *5Cir* refers to the U.S. Court of Appeals for the Fifth Circuit; *15* indicates that this citation is to the 15th decision released by the court in the year; *18* is the paragraph number where the material referred to is located; and the remainder is the parallel citation to the volume and page in the printed case report, where the decision may also be found.

Facts

The facts of a case, for purposes of a legal brief, refer to only those facts that are *essential* to the court's decision. Facts should be presented in the form of a story and should relate what happened that led to the defendant's arrest. For example:

> The defendant, Robert Versaggi, who worked for Eastman Kodak Corporation as a computer technician at the time of his arrest, was charged with two counts of computer tampering in the second degree (under New York Penal Law § 156.20). Authorities alleged that Versaggi intentionally altered two computer programs designed to provide uninterrupted telephone service to the offices of Eastman Kodak Corporation. It was also alleged that, as a result of Versaggi's actions, approximately 2,560 of the lines at the Kodak Park Complex were shut down and use of another 1,920 lines was impaired

> for approximately an hour and a half on October 10, 1986, before company employees were able to restore service. As a result, a substantial number of the employees working at that large industrial complex, with the potential for dangerous chemical spills and accidents, were unable to receive calls, to call outside the complex, or to call 911 or similar emergency services. On November 19, 1986, a second interruption occurred. Essentially all service at Kodak's State Street office was shut down for four minutes before the computer reactivated itself. As a result, all outside telephone calls, from the company's customers and offices worldwide, were disconnected. Evidence against Versaggi consisted of telephone company and computer records showing that he accessed Kodak computers from his home computer at the time of both incidents and had instructed them to shut down.

History

The legal history of a case describes what occurred before the case reached its current level. Legal history should consist of a rendering of who was arrested, what he or she was charged with, and the findings of trial and appellate courts. In the case just cited, for example, the words of the New York Court of Appeals provide a concise legal history:

> Charged with two counts of computer tampering, [the defendant was found guilty by] Rochester City Court…of two counts of computer tampering in the second degree. [The court determined] that [the defendant] intentionally altered two computer programs designed to provide uninterrupted telephone service to the offices of the Eastman Kodak Corporation. The County Court affirmed.

Issue

The question before the court, or the legal issue that the court is being asked to resolve, should be plainly stated. It will always be a question about the law, the application of a specific law, or a general legal principle. Sometimes there is more than one issue. Even so, the issue can often be stated in one or two sentences, although occasionally a statement of the issue or issues requires more detail. Keep in mind that questions have been concisely stated if they can be answered with a "yes" or a "no." Frequently, the court states the issue itself in language like this: "The issue before the court is whether…," and such a statement can be incorporated directly into the brief. Continuing with the case of *People* v. *Versaggi*, for example, we might state the issue as follows:

Does merely entering commands without changing any programs or computer code constitute tampering or altering within the meaning of the statute? The defendant argued that he could not be guilty under New York law of tampering with a computer program because he did not alter or change any programs. He claimed that he merely entered commands, which allowed the disconnect instructions of each program to function. Hence, the issue for the court became deciding whether the defendant's conduct was encompassed within the language of the tampering statute.

One trick you can use to easily spot issues is to look for the word *whether*. The issue usually follows.

Decision (or Finding)

What did the court rule? How did it answer the question before it? You should remember that the decision of the court can always be stated in "yes" or "no" fashion and that an appellate court may affirm or reverse the decision of a lower court. Appellate courts may also send a case back to a lower court for review or retrial. In the case we have been using as an example, the decision might be stated as follows:

> Yes. The appellate court affirmed the judgment of the lower court and upheld the defendant's conviction.

Rationale

In their written opinions, courts explain the reasons they had for reaching their decision. It may be that the court applied or interpreted a particular statute, that it analyzed previous cases and decided the present one within the context of such historical decisions, or that the court chose to create a new precedent based on the majority's sense of justice and fairness. Summaries of such rationales, especially as they are stated in the written opinion of the court, should be contained in your brief. Hence an analysis of this case might conclude:

> The court reasoned that, although the word *alter*, as contained within the New York computer-tampering statute, means "to change or modify," the legislature had "attached expansive language to the verb,"

stating that the crime consisted of altering a computer program "in any manner." The term *computer program* was not defined by the statute, but the court reasoned that a computer program consists of "an ordered set of instructions" given to a computer telling it how to function. Hence, according to the court's interpretation, the defendant modified the computer's programming by sending it instructions via his modem and thereby violated the computer-tampering statute.

Your Notes

For purposes of further study, you should take notes for your own use. You might want to outline what you think about the case. Do you agree or disagree with the conclusion reached by the court? Why? Could the court have used a different rationale in reaching its decision? If so, what? Perhaps you will want to note dissenting or concurring opinions. Finally, you might want to note what lessons you learned from a review of the case.

> In 1986, the New York state legislature modified the state penal code to include five new crimes: unauthorized use of a computer (Penal Law § 156.05); computer trespass (Penal Law § 156.10); computer tampering (Penal Law §§ 156.20 and 156.25); unlawful duplication of computer-related material (Penal Law § 156.30); and criminal possession of computer-related material (Penal Law § 156.35). Versaggi could not logically be indicted for the crimes of unauthorized use of a computer because he had lawful access to the computer whose services he disrupted. Moreover, he had not duplicated any computer-related materials, nor had he in his possession any computer-related materials that he had not been authorized to possess. Hence he was charged with the crime of "computer trespass."

NOTES

1. *A Uniform System of Citation*, 17th ed. (Cambridge, MA: Harvard Law Review Association, 2001).
2. *Bluebook* format requires that the *v.* between parties be italicized.
3. *A Uniform System of Citation*, Section 2-110(2).

Appendix B

MODEL PENAL CODE EXCERPTS

SOURCE: Copyright 1985 by *The American Law Institute*; The Model Penal Code was adopted at the 1962 annual meeting of the American Law Institute. Reprinted with permission. All rights reserved.

Part I: General Provisions

Section 1.04.   Classes of Crimes; Violations.

(1) An offense defined by this Code or by any other statute of this State, for which a sentence of [death or of] imprisonment is authorized, constitutes a crime. Crimes are classified as felonies, misdemeanors or petty misdemeanors.

(2) A crime is a felony if it is so designated in this Code or if persons convicted thereof may be sentenced [to death or] to imprisonment for a term that, apart from an extended term, is in excess of one year.

(3) A crime is a misdemeanor if it is so designated in this Code or in a statute other than this Code enacted subsequent thereto.

(4) A crime is a petty misdemeanor if it is so designated in this Code or in a statute other than this Code enacted subsequent thereto or if it is defined by a statute other than this Code that now provides that persons convicted thereof may be sentenced to imprisonment for a term of which the maximum is less than one year. . . .

(5) [omitted]

Section 1.05.   All Offenses Defined by Statute; Application of General Provisions of the Code.

(1) No conduct constitutes an offense unless it is a crime or violation under this Code or another statute of this State.

(2) The provisions of Part I of the Code are applicable to offenses defined by other statutes, unless the Code otherwise provides.

(3) This Section does not affect the power of a court to punish for contempt or to employ any sanction authorized by law for the enforcement of an order or a civil judgment or decree.

[Sections 1.06 through 1.11 omitted]

Section 1.12.   Proof beyond a Reasonable Doubt; Affirmative Defenses; Burden of Proving Fact When Not an Element of an Offense; Presumptions.

(1) No person may be convicted of an offense unless each element of such offense is proved beyond a reasonable doubt. In the absence of such proof, the innocence of the defendant is assumed.

(2) Subsection (1) of this Section does not:
   (a) require the disproof of an affirmative defense unless and until there is evidence supporting such defense; or
   (b) apply to any defense that the Code or another statute plainly requires the defendant to prove by a preponderance of evidence.

(3) A ground of defense is affirmative, within the meaning of Subsection (2)(a) of this Section, when:
   (a) it arises under a section of the Code that so provides; or
   (b) it relates to an offense defined by a statute other than the Code and such statute so provides; or
   (c) it involves a matter of excuse or justification peculiarly within the knowledge of the defendant on which he can fairly be required to adduce supporting evidence.

(4) [omitted]

Article 2. General Principles of Liability

Section 2.01.   Requirement of Voluntary Act; Omission as Basis of Liability; Possession as an Act.

(1) A person is not guilty of an offense unless his liability is based on conduct that includes a voluntary act or the omission to perform an act of which he is physically capable.

(2) The following are not voluntary acts within the meaning of this Section;
   (a) a reflex or convulsion;
   (b) a bodily movement during unconsciousness or sleep;
   (c) conduct during hypnosis or resulting from hypnotic suggestion;
   (d) a bodily movement that otherwise is not a product of the effort or determination of the actor, either conscious or habitual.

(3) Liability for the commission of an offense may not be based on an omission unaccompanied by action unless:

    (a) the omission is expressly made sufficient by the law defining the offense; or

    (b) a duty to perform the omitted act is otherwise imposed by law.

(4) Possession is an act, within the meaning of this Section, if the possessor knowingly procured or received the thing possessed or was aware of his control thereof for a sufficient period to have been able to terminate his possession.

Section 2.02. General Requirements of Culpability.

(1) *Minimum Requirements of Culpability*. Except as provided in Section 2.05, a person is not guilty of an offense unless he acted purposely, knowingly, recklessly or negligently, as the law may require, with respect to each material element of the offense.

(2) *Kinds of Culpability Defined*.

    (a) *Purposely*. A person acts purposely with respect to a material element of an offense when:

        i. the element involves the nature of his conduct or a result thereof, it is his conscious object to engage in conduct of that nature or to cause such a result; and

        ii. the element involves the attendant circumstances, he is aware of the existence of such circumstances or he believes or hopes that they exist.

    (b) *Knowingly*. A person acts knowingly with respect to a material element of an offense when:

        i. the element involves the nature of his conduct or the attendant circumstances, he is aware that his conduct is of that nature or that such circumstances exist; and

        ii. the element involves a result of his conduct, he is aware that it is practically certain that his conduct will cause such a result.

    (c) *Recklessly*. A person acts recklessly with respect to a material element of an offense when he consciously disregards a substantial and unjustifiable risk that the material element exists or will result from his conduct. The risk must be of such a nature and degree that, considering the nature and purpose of the actor's conduct and the circumstances known to him, its disregard involves a gross deviation from the standard of conduct that a law-abiding person would observe in the actor's situation.

    (d) *Negligently*. A person acts negligently with respect to a material element of an offense when he should be aware of a substantial and unjustifiable risk that the material element exists or will result from his conduct. The risk must be of such a nature and degree that the actor's failure to perceive it, considering the nature and purpose of his conduct and the circumstances known to him, involves a gross deviation from the standard of care that a reasonable person would observe in the actor's situation.

(3) *Culpability Required Unless Otherwise Provided*. When the culpability sufficient to establish a material element of an offense is not prescribed by law, such element is established if a person acts purposely, knowingly or recklessly with respect thereto.

(4) *Prescribed Culpability Requirement Applies to All Material Elements*. When the law defining an offense prescribes the kind of culpability that is sufficient for the commission of an offense, without distinguishing among the material elements thereof, such provision shall apply to all the material elements of the offense, unless a contrary purpose plainly appears.

(5) [omitted]

(6) [omitted]

(7) *Requirement of Knowledge Satisfied by Knowledge of High Probability*. When knowledge of the existence of a particular fact is an element of an offense, such knowledge is established if a person is aware of a high probability of its existence, unless he actually believes that it does not exist.

(8) *Requirement of Willfulness Satisfied by Acting Knowingly*. A requirement that an offense be committed willfully is satisfied if a person acts knowingly with respect to the material elements of the offense, unless a purpose to impose further requirements appears.

(9) *Culpability as to Illegality of Conduct*. Neither knowledge nor recklessness or negligence as to whether conduct constitutes an offense or as to the existence, meaning or application of the law determining the elements of an offense is an element of such offense, unless the definition of the offense or the Code so provides.

(10) *Culpability as Determinant of Grade of Offense*. When the grade or degree of an offense depends on whether the offense is committed purposely, knowingly, recklessly or negligently, its grade or degree shall be the lowest for which the determinative kind of culpability is established with respect to any material element of the offense.

Section 2.03. Causal Relationship between Conduct and Result; Divergence between Result Designed or

Contemplated and Actual Result or between Probable and Actual Result.

(1) Conduct is the cause of a result when:

    (a) it is an antecedent but for which the result in question would not have occurred; and

    (b) the relationship between the conduct and result satisfies any additional causal requirements imposed by the Code or by the law defining the offense.

(2) When purposely or knowingly causing a particular result is an element of an offense, the element is not established if the actual result is not within the purpose or the contemplation of the actor unless:

    (a) the actual result differs from that designed or contemplated, as the case may be, only in the respect that a different person or different property is injured or affected or that the injury or harm designed or contemplated would have been more serious or more extensive than that caused; or

    (b) the actual result involves the same kind of injury or harm as that designed or contemplated and is not too remote or accidental in its occurrence to have a [just] bearing on the actor's liability or on the gravity of his offense.

(3) When recklessly or negligently causing a particular result is an element of an offense, the element is not established if the actual result is not within the risk of which the actor is aware or, in the case of negligence, of which he should be aware unless:

    (a) the actual result differs from the probable result only in the respect that a different person or different property is injured or affected or that the probable injury or harm would have been more serious or more extensive than that caused; or

    (b) the actual result involves the same kind of injury or harm as the probable result and is not too remote or accidental in its occurrence to have a [just] bearing on the actor's liability or on the gravity of his offense.

(4) When causing a particular result is a material element of an offense for which absolute liability is imposed by law, the element is not established unless the actual result is a probable consequence of the actor's conduct.

Section 2.04. Ignorance or Mistake.

(1) Ignorance or mistake as to a matter of fact or law is a defense if:

    (a) the ignorance or mistake negatives the purpose, knowledge, belief, recklessness or negligence required to establish a material element of the offense; or

    (b) the law provides that the state of mind established by such ignorance or mistake constitutes a defense.

(2) Although ignorance or mistake would otherwise afford a defense to the offense charged, the defense is not available if the defendant would be guilty of another offense had the situation been as he supposed. In such case, however, the ignorance or mistake of the defendant shall reduce the grade and degree of the offense of which he may be convicted to those of the offense of which he would be guilty had the situation been as he supposed.

(3) A belief that conduct does not legally constitute an offense is a defense to a prosecution for that offense based upon such conduct when:

    (a) the statute or other enactment defining the offense is not known to the actor and has not been published or otherwise reasonably made available prior to the conduct alleged; or

    (b) he acts in reasonable reliance upon an official statement of the law, afterward determined to be invalid or erroneous, contained in (i) a statute or other enactment; (ii) a judicial decision, opinion or judgment; (iii) an administrative order or grant of permission; or (iv) an official interpretation of the public officer or body charged by law with responsibility for the interpretation, administration or enforcement of the law defining the offense.

(4) The defendant must prove a defense arising under Subsection (3) of this Section by a preponderance of evidence.

Section 2.05. [omitted]

Section 2.06. Liability for Conduct of Another; Complicity.

(1) A person is guilty of an offense if it is committed by his own conduct or by the conduct of another person for which he is legally accountable, or both.

(2) A person is legally accountable for the conduct of another person when:

    (a) acting with the kind of culpability that is sufficient for the commission of the offense, he causes an innocent or irresponsible person to engage in such conduct; or

    (b) he is made accountable for the conduct of such other person by the Code or by the law defining the offense; or

(c) he is an accomplice of such other person in the commission of the offense.

(3) A person is an accomplice of another person in the commission of an offense if:
   (a) with the purpose of promoting or facilitating the commission of the offense, he
      i. solicits such other person to commit it, or
      ii. aids or agrees or attempts to aid such other person in planning or committing it, or
      iii. having a legal duty to prevent the commission of the offense, fails to make proper effort so to do; or
   (b) his conduct is expressly declared by law to establish his complicity.

(4) When causing a particular result is an element of an offense, an accomplice in the conduct causing such result is an accomplice in the commission of that offense if he acts with the kind of culpability, if any, with respect to that result that is sufficient for the commission of the offense.

(5) A person who is legally incapable of committing a particular offense himself may be guilty thereof if it is committed by the conduct of another person for which he is legally accountable, unless such liability is inconsistent with the purpose of the provision establishing his incapacity.

(6) Unless otherwise provided by the Code or by the law defining the offense, a person is not an accomplice in an offense committed by another person if:
   (a) he is a victim of that offense; or
   (b) the offense is so defined that his conduct is inevitably incident to its commission; or
   (c) he terminates his complicity prior to the commission of the offense and
      i. wholly deprives it of effectiveness in the commission of the offense; or
      ii. gives timely warning to the law enforcement authorities or otherwise makes proper effort to prevent the commission of the offense.

(7) An accomplice may be convicted on proof of the commission of the offense and of his complicity therein, though the person claimed to have committed the offense has not been prosecuted or convicted or has been convicted of a different offense or degree of offense or has an immunity to prosecution or conviction or has been convicted.

Section 2.07.   Liability of Corporations, Unincorporated Associations and Persons Acting, or under a Duty to Act, in Their Behalf.

(1) A corporation may be convicted of the commission of an offense if:
   (a) the offense is a violation or the offense is defined by a statute other than the Code in which a legislative purpose to impose liability on corporations plainly appears and the conduct is performed by an agent of the corporation acting in behalf of the corporation within the scope of his office or employment, except that if the law defining the offense designates the agents for whose conduct the corporation is accountable or the circumstances under which it is accountable, such provisions shall apply; or
   (b) the offense consists of an omission to discharge a specific duty of affirmative performance imposed on corporations by law; or
   (c) the commission of the offense was authorized, requested, commanded, performed or recklessly tolerated by the board of directors or by a high managerial agent acting in behalf of the corporation within the scope of his office or employment.

(2) When absolute liability is imposed for the commission of an offense, a legislative purpose to impose liability on a corporation shall be assumed, unless the contrary plainly appears.

(3) [omitted]

Section 2.08.   Intoxication.

(1) Except as provided in Subsection (4) of this Section, intoxication of the actor is not a defense unless it negatives an element of the offense.

(2) When recklessness establishes an element of the offense, if the actor, due to self-induced intoxication, is unaware of a risk of which he would have been aware had he been sober, such unawareness is immaterial.

(3) Intoxication does not, in itself, constitute mental disease within the meaning of Section 4.01.

(4) Intoxication that (a) is not self-induced or (b) is pathological is an affirmative defense if by reason of such intoxication the actor at the time of his conduct lacks substantial capacity either to appreciate its criminality [wrongfulness] or to conform his conduct to the requirements of law.

Section 2.09.   Duress.

(1) It is an affirmative defense that the actor engaged in the conduct charged to constitute an offense because he was coerced to do so by the use of, or a threat to use, unlawful force against his person or the person

of another, that a person of reasonable firmness in his situation would have been unable to resist.

(2) The defense provided by this Section is unavailable if the actor recklessly placed himself in a situation in which it was probable that he would be subjected to duress. The defense is also unavailable if he was negligent in placing himself in such a situation, whenever negligence suffices to establish culpability for the offense charged.

(3) It is not a defense that a woman acted on the command of her husband, unless she acted under such coercion as would establish a defense under this Section. [The presumption that a woman acting in the presence of her husband is coerced is abolished.]

(4) When the conduct of the actor would otherwise be justifiable under Section 3.02, this Section does not preclude such defense.

Section 2.10. Military Orders.

It is an affirmative defense that the actor, in engaging in the conduct charged to constitute an offense, does no more than execute an order of his superior in the armed services that he does not know to be unlawful.

Section 2.11. Consent.

(1) *In General.* The consent of the victim to conduct charged to constitute an offense or to the result thereof is a defense if such consent negatives an element of the offense or precludes the infliction of the harm or evil sought to be prevented by the law defining the offense.

(2) *Consent to Bodily Injury.* When conduct is charged to constitute an offense because it causes or threatens bodily injury, consent to such conduct or to the infliction of such injury is a defense if:
    (a) the bodily injury consented to or threatened by the conduct consented to is not serious; or
    (b) the conduct and the injury are reasonably foreseeable hazards of joint participation in a lawful athletic contest or competitive sport or other concerted activity not forbidden by law; or
    (c) the consent establishes a justification for the conduct under Article 3 of the Code.

(3) *Ineffective Consent.* Unless otherwise provided by the Code or by the law defining the offense, assent does not constitute consent if:

    (a) it is given by a person who is legally incompetent to authorize the conduct charged to constitute the offense; or

    (b) it is given by a person who by reason of youth, mental disease or defect or intoxication is manifestly unable or known by the actor to be unable to make a reasonable judgment as to the nature or harmfulness of the conduct charged to constitute the offense; or
    (c) it is given by a person whose improvident consent is sought to be prevented by the law defining the offense; or
    (d) it is induced by force, duress or deception of a kind sought to be prevented by the law defining the offense.

Section 2.12. De Minimis Infractions.

The Court shall dismiss a prosecution if, having regard to the nature of the conduct charged to constitute an offense and the nature of the attendant circumstances, it finds that the defendant's conduct:

(1) was within a customary license or tolerance, neither expressly negatived by the person whose interest was infringed nor inconsistent with the purpose of the law defining the offense; or

(2) did not actually cause or threaten the harm or evil sought to be prevented by the law defining the offense or did so only to an extent too trivial to warrant the condemnation of conviction; or

(3) presents such other extenuations that it cannot reasonably be regarded as envisaged by the legislature in forbidding the offense.

The Court shall not dismiss a prosecution under Subsection (3) of this Section without filing a written statement of its reasons.

Section 2.13. Entrapment.

(1) A public law enforcement official or a person acting in cooperation with such an official perpetrates an entrapment if for the purpose of obtaining evidence of the commission of an offense, he induces or encourages another person to engage in conduct constituting such offense by either:
    (a) making knowingly false representations designed to induce the belief that such conduct is not prohibited; or
    (b) employing methods of persuasion or inducement that create a substantial risk that such an offense will be committed by persons other than those who are ready to commit it.

(2) Except as provided in Subsection (3) of this Section, a person prosecuted for an offense shall be acquitted

if he proves by a preponderance of evidence that his conduct occurred in response to an entrapment. The issue of entrapment shall be tried by the Court in the absence of the jury.

(3) The defense afforded by this Section is unavailable when causing or threatening bodily injury is an element of the offense charged and the prosecution is based on conduct causing or threatening such injury to a person other than the person perpetrating the entrapment.

Article 3. General Principles of Justification

Section 3.01. Justification an Affirmative Defense; Civil Remedies Unaffected.

(1) In any prosecution based on conduct that is justifiable under this Article, justification is an affirmative defense.

(2) The fact that conduct is justifiable under this Article does not abolish or impair any remedy for such conduct that is available in any civil action.

Section 3.02. Justification Generally: Choice of Evils.

(1) Conduct that the actor believes to be necessary to avoid a harm or evil to himself or to another is justifiable, provided that:
  (a) the harm or evil sought to be avoided by such conduct is greater than that sought to be prevented by the law defining the offense charged; and
  (b) neither the Code nor other law defining the offense provides exceptions or defenses dealing with the specific situation involved; and
  (c) a legislative purpose to exclude the justification claimed does not otherwise plainly appear.

(2) When the actor was reckless or negligent in bringing about the situation requiring a choice of harms or evils or in appraising the necessity for his conduct, the justification afforded by this Section is unavailable in a prosecution for any offense for which recklessness or negligence, as the case may be, suffices to establish culpability.

Section 3.03. Execution of Public Duty.

(1) Except as provided in Subsection (2) of this Section, conduct is justifiable when it is required or authorized by:
  (a) the law defining the duties or functions of a public officer or the assistance to be rendered to such officer in the performance of his duties; or

  (b) the law governing the execution of legal process; or
  (c) the judgment or order of a competent court or tribunal; or
  (d) the law governing the armed services or the lawful conduct of war; or
  (e) any other provision of law imposing a public duty.

(2) The other sections of this Article apply to:
  (a) the use of force upon or toward the person of another for any of the purposes dealt with in such sections; and
  (b) the use of deadly force for any purpose, unless the use of such force is otherwise expressly authorized by law or occurs in the lawful conduct of war.

(3) The justification afforded by Subsection (1) of this Section applies:

  (a) when the actor believes his conduct to be required or authorized by the judgment or direction of a competent court or tribunal or in the lawful execution of legal process, notwithstanding lack of jurisdiction of the court or defect in the legal process; and
  (b) when the actor believes his conduct to be required or authorized to assist a public officer in the performance of his duties, notwithstanding that the officer exceeded his legal authority.

Section 3.04. Use of Force in Self-Protection.

(1) *Use of Force Justifiable for Protection of the Person.* Subject to the provisions of this Section and of Section 3.09, the use of force upon or toward another person is justifiable when the actor believes that such force is immediately necessary for the purpose of protecting himself against the use of unlawful force by such other person on the present occasion.

(2) *Limitations on Justifying Necessity for Use of Force.*
  (a) The use of force is not justifiable under this Section:
    i. to resist an arrest that the actor knows is being made by a peace officer, although the arrest is unlawful; or
    ii. to resist force used by the occupier or possessor of property or by another person on his behalf, where the actor knows that the person using the force is doing so under a claim of right to protect the property, except that this limitation shall not apply if:
      A. the actor is a public officer acting in the performance of his duties or a person

lawfully assisting him therein or a person making or assisting in a lawful arrest; or

   B. the actor has been unlawfully dispossessed of the property and is making a re-entry or recaption justified by Section 3.06; or

   C. the actor believes that such force is necessary to protect himself against death or serious bodily injury.

(b) The use of deadly force is not justifiable under this Section unless the actor believes that such force is necessary to protect himself against death, serious bodily injury, kidnapping or sexual intercourse compelled by force or threat; nor is it justifiable if:

   i. the actor, with the purpose of causing death or serious bodily injury, provoked the use of force against himself in the same encounter; or

   ii. the actor knows that he can avoid the necessity of using such force with complete safety by retreating or by surrendering possession of a thing to a person asserting a claim of right thereto or by complying with a demand that he abstain from any action that he has no duty to take, except that:

     A. the actor is not obliged to retreat from his dwelling or place of work, unless he was the initial aggressor or is assailed in his place of work by another person whose place of work the actor knows it to be; and

     B. a public officer justified in using force in the performance of his duties or a person justified in using force in his assistance or a person justified in using force in making an arrest or preventing an escape is not obliged to desist from efforts to perform such duty, effect such arrest or prevent such escape because of resistance or threatened resistance by or on behalf of the person against whom such action is directed.

(c) Except as required by paragraphs (a) and (b) of this Subsection, a person employing protective force may estimate the necessity thereof under the circumstances as he believes them to be when the force is used, without retreating, surrendering possession, doing any other act that he has no legal duty to do or abstaining from any lawful action.

(3) *Use of Confinement as Protective Force.* The justification afforded by this Section extends to the use of confinement as protective force only if the actor takes all reasonable measures to terminate the confinement as

soon as he knows that he safely can, unless the person confined has been arrested on a charge of crime.

Section 3.05.   Use of Force for the Protection of Other Persons.

(1) Subject to the provisions of this Section and of Section 3.09, the use of force upon or toward the person of another is justifiable to protect a third person when:

   (a) the actor would be justified under Section 3.04 in using such force to protect himself against the injury he believes to be threatened to the person whom he seeks to protect; and

   (b) under the circumstances as the actor believes them to be, the person whom he seeks to protect would be justified in using such protective force; and

   (c) the actor believes that his intervention is necessary for the protection of such other person.

(2) [omitted]

Section 3.06.   Use of Force for Protection of Property.

(1) *Use of Force Justifiable for Protection of Property.* Subject to the provisions of this Section and of Section 3.09, the use of force upon or toward the person of another is justifiable when the actor believes that such force is immediately necessary:

   (a) to prevent or terminate an unlawful entry or other trespass upon land or a trespass against or the unlawful carrying away of tangible, movable property, provided that such land or movable property is, or is believed by the actor to be, in his possession or in the possession of another person for whose protection he acts; or

   (b) to effect an entry or re-entry upon land or to retake tangible movable property, provided that the actor believes that he or the person by whose authority he acts or a person from whom he or such other person derives title was unlawfully dispossessed of such land or movable property and is entitled to possession, and provided, further, that:

     i. the force is used immediately or on fresh pursuit after such dispossession; or

     ii. the actor believes that the person against whom he uses force has no claim of right to the possession of the property and, in the case of land, the circumstances, as the actor believes them to be, are of such urgency that it would be an exceptional hardship to postpone the entry or re-entry until a court order is obtained.

(2) [omitted]

(3) *Limitations on Justifiable Use of Force.*
   (a) *Request to Desist.* The use of force is justifiable under this Section only if the actor first requests the person against whom such force is used to desist from his interference with the property, unless the actor believes that:
      i.   such request would be useless; or
      ii. it would be dangerous to himself or another person to make the request; or
      iii. substantial harm will be done to the physical condition of the property that is sought to be protected before the request can effectively be made.
   (b) *Exclusion of Trespasser.* The use of force to prevent or terminate a trespass is not justifiable under this Section if the actor knows that the exclusion of the trespasser will expose him to substantial danger of serious bodily injury.
   (c) *Resistance of Lawful Re-entry or Recaption.* The use of force to prevent an entry or re-entry upon land or the recaption of movable property is not justifiable under this Section, although the actor believes that such re-entry or recaption is unlawful, if:
      i.   the re-entry or recaption is made by or on behalf of a person who was actually dispossessed of the property; and
      ii. it is otherwise justifiable under Subsection (1)(b) of this Section.
   (d) *Use of Deadly Force.* The use of deadly force is not justifiable under this Section unless the actor believes that:
      i.   the person against whom the force is used is attempting to dispossess him of his dwelling otherwise than under a claim of right to its possession; or
      ii. the person against whom the force is used is attempting to commit or consummate arson, burglary, robbery or other felonious theft or property destruction and either:
         A. has employed or threatened deadly force against or in the presence of the actor; or
         B. the use of force other than deadly force to prevent the commission or the consummation of the crime would expose the actor or another in his presence to substantial danger of serious bodily injury.

(4) [omitted]

(5) *Use of Device to Protect Property.* The justification afforded by this Section extends to the use of a device for the purpose of protecting property only if:
   (a) the device is not designed to cause or known to create a substantial risk of causing death or serious bodily injury; and
   (b) the use of the particular device to protect the property from entry or trespass is reasonable under the circumstances, as the actor believes them to be; and
   (c) the device is one customarily used for such a purpose or reasonable care is taken to make known to probable intruders the fact that it is used.

(6) *Use of Force to Pass Wrongful Obstructor.* The use of force to pass a person whom the actor believes to be purposely or knowingly and unjustifiably obstructing the actor from going to a place to which he may lawfully go is justifiable, provided that:
   (a) the actor believes that the person against whom he uses force has no claim of right to obstruct the actor; and
   (b) the actor is not being obstructed from entry or movement on land that he knows to be in the possession or custody of the person obstructing him, or in the possession or custody of another person by whose authority the obstructor acts, unless the circumstances, as the actor believes them to be, are of such urgency that it would not be reasonable to postpone the entry or movement on such land until a court order is obtained; and
   (c) the force used is not greater than would be justifiable if the person obstructing the actor were using force against him to prevent his passage.

Section 3.07.   Use of Force in Law Enforcement.

(1) *Use of Force Justifiable to Effect an Arrest.* Subject to the provisions of this Section and of Section 3.09, the use of force upon or toward the person of another is justifiable when the actor is making or assisting in making an arrest and the actor believes that such force is immediately necessary to effect a lawful arrest.

(2) *Limitations on the Use of Force.*
   (a) The use of force is not justifiable under this Section unless:
      i.   the actor makes known the purpose of the arrest or believes that it is otherwise known by or cannot reasonably be made known to the person to be arrested; and
      ii. when the arrest is made under a warrant, the warrant is valid or believed by the actor to be valid.

(b) The use of deadly force is not justifiable under this Section unless:

  i. the arrest is for a felony; and

  ii. the person effecting the arrest is authorized to act as a peace officer or is assisting a person whom he believes to be authorized to act as a peace officer; and

  iii. the actor believes that the force employed creates no substantial risk of injury to innocent persons; and

  iv. the actor believes that:

    A. the crime for which the arrest is made involved conduct including the use or threatened use of deadly force; or

    B. there is a substantial risk that the person to be arrested will cause death or serious bodily injury if his apprehension is delayed.

(3) *Use of Force to Prevent Escape from Custody.* . . .

(4) *Use of Force by Private Person Assisting an Unlawful Arrest.* . . .

(5) *Use of Force to Prevent Suicide or the Commission of a Crime.* . . .

Section 3.08. Use of Force by Persons with Special Responsibility for Care, Discipline or Safety of Others. . . .

Section 3.09. Mistake of Law as to Unlawfulness of Force or Legality of Arrest; Reckless or Negligent Use of Otherwise Justifiable Force; Reckless or Negligent Injury or Risk of Injury to Innocent Persons.

(1) The justification afforded by Sections 3.04 to 3.07, inclusive, is unavailable when:

  (a) the actor's belief in the unlawfulness of the force or conduct against which he employs protective force or his belief in the lawfulness of an arrest that he endeavors to effect by force is erroneous; and

  (b) his error is due to ignorance or mistake as to the provisions of the Code, any other provision of the criminal law or the law governing the legality of an arrest or search.

(2) When the actor believes that the use of force upon or toward the person of another is necessary for any of the purposes for which such belief would establish a justification under Sections 3.03 to 3.08 but the actor is reckless or negligent in having such belief or in acquiring or failing to acquire any knowledge or belief that is material to the justifiability of his use of force, the justification afforded by those Sections is unavailable in a prosecution for an offense for which recklessness or negligence, as the case may be, suffices to establish culpability.

(3) When the actor is justified under Sections 3.03 to 3.08 in using force upon or toward the person of another but he recklessly or negligently injures or creates a risk of injury to innocent persons, the justification afforded by those Sections is unavailable in a prosecution for such recklessness or negligence towards innocent persons.

Article 4. Responsibility

Section 4.01. Mental Disease or Defect Excluding Responsibility.

(1) A person is not responsible for criminal conduct if at the time of such conduct as a result of mental disease or defect he lacks substantial capacity either to appreciate the criminality [wrongfulness] of his conduct or to conform his conduct to the requirements of law.

(2) As used in this Article, the terms "mental disease" or "defect" do not include an abnormality manifested only by repeated criminal or otherwise antisocial conduct.

Section 4.02. Evidence of Mental Disease or Defect Admissible When Relevant to Element of the Offense; Mental Disease or Defect Impairing Capacity as Ground for Mitigation of Punishment in Capital Cases.

(1) Evidence that the defendant suffered from a mental disease or defect is admissible whenever it is relevant to prove that the defendant did or did not have a state of mind that is an element of the offense.

(2) Whenever the jury or the Court is authorized to determine or to recommend whether or not the defendant shall be sentenced to death or imprisonment upon conviction, evidence that the capacity of the defendant to appreciate the criminality [wrongfulness] of his conduct or to conform his conduct to the requirements of law was impaired as a result of mental disease or defect is admissible in favor of sentence of imprisonment.

Section 4.03. Mental Disease or Defect Excluding Responsibility Is Affirmative Defense; Requirement of Notice; Form of Verdict and Judgment When Finding of Irresponsibility Is Made.

(1) Mental disease or defect excluding responsibility is an affirmative defense.

(2) Evidence of mental disease or defect excluding responsibility is not admissible unless the defendant, at the time of entering his plea of not guilty or within ten days thereafter or at such later time as the Court may for good cause permit, files a written notice of his purpose to rely on such defense.

(3) When the defendant is acquitted on the ground of mental disease or defect excluding responsibility, the verdict and the judgment shall so state.

Section 4.04.   Mental Disease or Defect Excluding Fitness to Proceed.

No person who as a result of mental disease or defect lacks capacity to understand the proceedings against him or to assist in his own defense shall be tried, convicted or sentenced for the commission of an offense so long as such incapacity endures.

Article 5. Inchoate Crimes

Section 5.01.   Criminal Attempt.

(1) *Definition of Attempt.* A person is guilty of an attempt to commit a crime if, acting with the kind of culpability otherwise required for commission of the crime, he:

(a) purposely engages in conduct that would constitute the crime if the attendant circumstances were as he believes them to be; or

(b) when causing a particular result is an element of the crime, does or omits to do anything with the purpose of causing or with the belief that it will cause such result without further conduct on his part; or

(c) purposely does or omits to do anything that, under the circumstances as he believes them to be, is an act or omission constituting a substantial step in a course of conduct planned to culminate in his commission of the crime.

(2) *Conduct Which May Be Held Substantial Step under Subsection (1)(c).* Conduct shall not be held to constitute a substantial step under Subsection (1)(c) of this Section unless it is strongly corroborative of the actor's criminal purpose. Without negativing the sufficiency of other conduct, the following, if strongly corroborative of the actor's criminal purpose, shall not be held insufficient as a matter of law:

(a) lying in wait, searching for or following the contemplated victim of the crime;

(b) enticing or seeking to entice the contemplated victim of the crime to go to the place contemplated for its commission;

(c) reconnoitering the place contemplated for the commission of the crime;

(d) unlawful entry of a structure, vehicle or enclosure in which it is contemplated that the crime will be committed;

(e) possession of materials to be employed in the commission of the crime, that are specially designed for such unlawful use or that can serve no lawful purpose of the actor under the circumstances;

(f) possession, collection or fabrication of materials to be employed in the commission of the crime, at or near the place contemplated for its commission, if such possession, collection or fabrication serves no lawful purpose of the actor under the circumstances;

(g) soliciting an innocent agent to engage in conduct constituting an element of the crime.

(3) *Renunciation of Criminal Purpose.* When the actor's conduct would otherwise constitute an attempt under Subsection (1)(b) or (1)(c) of this Section, it is an affirmative defense that he abandoned his effort to commit the crime or otherwise prevented its commission, under circumstances manifesting a complete and voluntary renunciation of his criminal purpose. The establishment of such defense does not, however, affect the liability of an accomplice who did not join in such abandonment or prevention.

Within the meaning of this Article, renunciation of criminal purpose is not voluntary if it is motivated, in whole or in part, by circumstances, not present or apparent at the inception of the actor's course of conduct, that increase the probability of detection or apprehension or that make more difficult the accomplishment of the criminal purpose. Renunciation is not complete if it is motivated by a decision to postpone the criminal conduct until a more advantageous time or to transfer the criminal effort to another but similar objective or victim.

Section 5.02.   Criminal Solicitation.

(1) *Definition of Solicitation.* A person is guilty of solicitation to commit a crime if with the purpose of promoting or facilitating its commission he commands, encourages or requests another person to engage in specific conduct that would constitute such crime or an attempt to commit such crime or would establish his complicity in its commission or attempted commission.

(2) *Uncommunicated Solicitation.* It is immaterial under Subsection (1) of this Section that the actor fails to communicate with the person he solicits to commit a

crime if his conduct was designed to effect such communication.

(3) *Renunciation of Criminal Purpose.* It is an affirmative defense that the actor, after soliciting another person to commit a crime, persuaded him not to do so or otherwise prevented the commission of the crime, under circumstances manifesting a complete and voluntary renunciation of his criminal purpose.

Section 5.03.   Criminal Conspiracy.

(1) *Definition of Conspiracy.* A person is guilty of conspiracy with another person or persons to commit a crime if with the purpose of promoting or facilitating its commission he:
  (a) agrees with such other person or persons that they or one or more of them will engage in conduct that constitutes such crime or an attempt or solicitation to commit such crime; or
  (b) agrees to aid such other person or persons in the planning or commission of such crime or of an attempt or solicitation to commit such crime.

(2) *Scope of Conspiratorial Relationship.* If a person guilty of conspiracy, as defined by Subsection (1) of this Section, knows that a person with whom he conspires to commit a crime has conspired with another person or persons to commit the same crime, he is guilty of conspiring with such other person or persons, whether or not he knows their identity, to commit such crime.

(3) *Conspiracy with Multiple Criminal Objectives.* If a person conspires to commit a number of crimes, he is guilty of only one conspiracy so long as such multiple crimes are the object of the same agreement or continuous conspiratorial relationship.

(4) *Joinder and Venue in Conspiracy Prosecutions.*
  (a) Subject to the provisions of paragraph (b) of this Subsection, two or more persons charged with criminal conspiracy may be prosecuted jointly if:
    i. they are charged with conspiring with one another; or
    ii. the conspiracies alleged, whether they have the same or different parties, are so related that they constitute different aspects of a scheme of organized criminal conduct. . . .

(5) *Overt Act.* No person may be convicted of conspiracy to commit a crime, other than a felony of the first or second degree, unless an overt act in pursuance of such conspiracy is alleged and proved to have been done by him or by a person with whom he conspired.

(6) *Renunciation of Criminal Purpose.* It is an affirmative defense that the actor, after conspiring to commit a crime, thwarted the success of the conspiracy, under circumstances manifesting a complete and voluntary renunciation of his criminal purpose.

(7) *Duration of Conspiracy.* For purposes of Section 1.06(4):
  (a) conspiracy is a continuing course of conduct that terminates when the crime or crimes that are its object are committed or the agreement that they be committed is abandoned by the defendant and by those with whom he conspired; and
  (b) such abandonment is presumed if neither the defendant nor anyone with whom he conspired does any overt act in pursuance of the conspiracy during the applicable period of limitation; and
  (c) if an individual abandons the agreement, the conspiracy is terminated as to him only if and when he advises those with whom he conspired of his abandonment or he informs the law enforcement authorities of the existence of the conspiracy and of his participation therein.

Section 5.05.   Grading of Criminal Attempt, Solicitation and Conspiracy; Mitigation in Cases of Lesser Danger; Multiple Convictions Barred. . . .

Article 6. Authorized Disposition of Offenders

Section 6.01.   Degrees of Felonies.

(1) Felonies defined by this Code are classified, for the purpose of sentence, into three degrees, as follows:
  (a) felonies of the first degree;
  (b) felonies of the second degree;
  (c) felonies of the third degree.
  A felony is of the first or second degree when it is so designated by the Code. A crime declared to be a felony, without specification of degree, is of the third degree.

(2) Notwithstanding any other provision of law, a felony defined by any statute of this State other than this Code shall constitute, for the purpose of sentence, a felony of the third degree.

Section 6.04.   Penalties against Corporations and Unincorporated Associations; Forfeiture of Corporate Charter or Revocation of Certificate Authorizing Foreign Corporation to Do Business in the State.

(1) The Court may suspend the sentence of a corporation or an unincorporated association that has been convicted of an offense or may sentence it to pay a fine authorized by Section 6.03.

(2) (a) The [prosecuting attorney] is authorized to institute civil proceedings in the appropriate court of general jurisdiction to forfeit the charter of a corporation organized under the laws of this State or to revoke the certificate authorizing a foreign corporation to conduct business in this State. The Court may order the charter forfeited or the certificate revoked upon finding

  i.   that the board of directors or a high managerial agent acting in behalf of the corporation has, in conducting the corporation's affairs, purposely engaged in a persistent course of criminal conduct and

  ii. that for the prevention of future criminal conduct of the same character, the public interest requires the charter of the corporation to be forfeited and the corporation to be dissolved or the certificate to be revoked.

(b) When a corporation is convicted of a crime or a high managerial agent of a corporation, as defined in Section 2.07, is convicted of a crime committed in the conduct of the affairs of the corporation, the Court, in sentencing the corporation or the agent, may direct the [prosecuting attorney] to institute proceedings authorized by paragraph (a) of this Subsection.

Part II: Definition of Specific Crimes

OFFENSES INVOLVING DANGER TO THE PERSON

Article 210. Criminal Homicide

Section 210.0.   Definitions.

In Articles 210–213, unless a different meaning plainly is required:

(1) "human being" means a person who has been born and is alive;

(2) "bodily injury" means physical pain, illness or any impairment of physical condition;

(3) "serious bodily injury" means bodily injury which creates a substantial risk of death or which causes serious, permanent disfigurement, or protracted loss or impairment of the function of any bodily member or organ;

(4) "deadly weapon" means any firearm or other weapon, device, instrument, material or substance, whether animate or inanimate, which in the manner it is used or is intended to be used is known to be capable of producing death or serious bodily injury.

Section 210.1.   Criminal Homicide.

(1) A person is guilty of criminal homicide if he purposely, knowingly, recklessly or negligently causes the death of another human being.

(2) Criminal homicide is murder, manslaughter or negligent homicide.

Section 210.2.   Murder.

(1) Except as provided in Section 210.3(1)(b), criminal homicide constitutes murder when:

  (a) it is committed purposely or knowingly; or

  (b) it is committed recklessly under circumstances manifesting extreme indifference to the value of human life. Such recklessness and indifference are presumed if the actor is engaged or is an accomplice in the commission of, or an attempt to commit, or flight after committing or attempting to commit robbery, rape or deviate sexual intercourse by force or threat of force, arson, burglary, kidnapping or felonious escape.

(2) Murder is a felony of the first degree [but a person convicted of murder may be sentenced to death, as provided in Section 210.6].

Section 210.3.   Manslaughter.

(1) Criminal homicide constitutes manslaughter when:

  (a) it is committed recklessly; or

  (b) a homicide which would otherwise be murder is committed under the influence of extreme mental or emotional disturbance for which there is reasonable explanation or excuse. The reasonableness of such explanation or excuse shall be determined from the viewpoint of a person in the actor's situation under the circumstances as he believes them to be.

(2) Manslaughter is a felony of the second degree.

Section 210.4.   Negligent Homicide.

(1) Criminal homicide constitutes negligent homicide when it is committed negligently.

(2) Negligent homicide is a felony of the third degree.

Section 210.5.   Causing or Aiding Suicide.

(1) *Causing Suicide as Criminal Homicide.* A person may be convicted of criminal homicide for causing another to commit suicide only if he purposely causes such suicide by force, duress or deception.

(2) *Aiding or Soliciting Suicide as an Independent Offense.* A person who purposely aids or solicits another to commit suicide is guilty of a felony of the second degree if his conduct causes such suicide or an attempted suicide, and otherwise of a misdemeanor.

Section 210.6.   Sentence of Death for Murder; Further Proceedings to Determine Sentence.

(1) *Death Sentence Excluded.* When a defendant is found guilty of murder, the Court shall impose sentence for a felony of the first degree if it is satisfied that:

(a) none of the aggravating circumstances enumerated in Subsection (3) of this Section was established by the evidence at the trial or will be established if further proceedings are initiated under Subsection (2) of this Section; or

(b) substantial mitigating circumstances, established by the evidence at the trial, call for leniency; or

(c) the defendant, with the consent of the prosecuting attorney and the approval of the Court, pleaded guilty to murder as a felony of the first degree; or

(d) the defendant was under 18 years of age at the time of the commission of the crime; or

(e) the defendant's physical or mental condition calls for leniency; or

(f) although the evidence suffices to sustain the verdict, it does not foreclose all doubt respecting the defendant's guilt.

(2) *Determination by Court or by Court and Jury.* . . .

Article 212. Kidnapping and Related Offenses; Coercion

Section 212.0.   Definitions.
In this Article, the definitions given in Section 210.0 apply unless a different meaning plainly is required.

Section 212.1.   Kidnapping.
A person is guilty of kidnapping if he unlawfully removes another from his place of residence or business, or a substantial distance from the vicinity where he is found, or if he unlawfully confines another for a substantial period in a place of isolation, with any of the following purposes:

(a) to hold for ransom or reward, or as a shield or hostage; or

(b) to facilitate commission of any felony or flight thereafter; or

(c) to inflict bodily injury on or to terrorize the victim or another; or

(d) to interfere with the performance of any governmental or political function.

Kidnapping is a felony of the first degree unless the actor voluntarily releases the victim alive and in a safe place prior to trial, in which case it is a felony of the second degree. A removal or confinement is unlawful within the meaning of this Section if it is accomplished by force, threat or deception, or, in the case of a person who is under the age of 14 or incompetent, if it is accomplished without the consent of a parent, guardian or other person responsible for general supervision of his welfare.

Section 212.2.   Felonious Restraint.
A person commits a felony of the third degree if he knowingly:

(a) restrains another unlawfully in circumstances exposing him to risk of serious bodily injury; or

(b) holds another in a condition of involuntary servitude.

Section 212.3.   False Imprisonment.
A person commits a misdemeanor if he knowingly restrains another unlawfully so as to interfere substantially with his liberty.

Section 212.4.   [omitted]

Section 212.5.   Criminal Coercion.

(1) *Offense Defined.* A person is guilty of criminal coercion if, with purpose unlawfully to restrict another's freedom of action to his detriment, he threatens to:

(a) commit any criminal offense; or

(b) accuse anyone of a criminal offense; or

(c) expose any secret tending to subject any person to hatred, contempt or ridicule, or to impair his credit or business repute; or

(d) take or withhold action as an official, or cause an official to take or withhold action.

It is an affirmative defense to prosecution based on paragraphs (b), (c) or (d) that the actor believed the accusation or secret to be true or the proposed official action justified and that his purpose was limited to compelling the other to behave in a way reasonably related to the circumstances which were the subject of the accusation, exposure or proposed official action, as by desisting from further misbehavior, making good a wrong done, refraining from taking any action or responsibility for which the actor believes the other disqualified.

(2) *Grading.* Criminal coercion is a misdemeanor unless the threat is to commit a felony or the actor's purpose is felonious, in which cases the offense is a felony of the third degree.

Article 213. Sexual Offenses

Section 213.0.   Definitions.

In this Article, unless a different meaning plainly is required:

(1) the definitions given in Section 210.0 apply;

(2) "Sexual intercourse" includes intercourse per os or per anum, with some penetration however slight; emission is not required;

(3) "deviate sexual intercourse" means sexual intercourse per os or per anum between human beings who are not husband and wife, and any form of sexual intercourse with an animal.

Section 213.1.   Rape and Related Offenses.

(1) *Rape.* A male who has sexual intercourse with a female not his wife is guilty of rape if:
   (a) he compels her to submit by force or by threat of imminent death, serious bodily injury, extreme pain or kidnapping, to be inflicted on anyone; or
   (b) he has substantially impaired her power to appraise or control her conduct by administering or employing without her knowledge drugs, intoxicants or other means for the purpose of preventing resistance; or
   (c) the female is unconscious; or
   (d) the female is less than 10 years old.
      Rape is a felony of the second degree unless (i) in the course thereof the actor inflicts serious bodily injury upon anyone, or (ii) the victim was not a voluntary social companion of the actor upon the occasion of the crime and had not previously permitted him sexual liberties, in which cases the offense is a felony of the first degree.

(2) *Gross Sexual Imposition.* A male who has sexual intercourse with a female not his wife commits a felony of the third degree if:
   (a) he compels her to submit by any threat that would prevent resistance by a woman of ordinary resolution; or
   (b) he knows that she suffers from a mental disease or defect which renders her incapable of appraising the nature of her conduct; or

   (c) he knows that she is unaware that a sexual act is being committed upon her or that she submits because she mistakenly supposes that he is her husband.

Section 213.2.   Deviate Sexual Intercourse by Force or Imposition.

(1) *By Force or Its Equivalent.* A person who engages in deviate sexual intercourse with another person, or who causes another to engage in deviate sexual intercourse, commits a felony of the second degree if:
   (a) he compels the other person to participate by force or by threat of imminent death, serious bodily injury, extreme pain or kidnapping, to be inflicted on anyone; or
   (b) he has substantially impaired the other person's power to appraise or control his conduct, by administering or employing without the knowledge of the other person drugs, intoxicants or other means for the purpose of preventing resistance; or
   (c) the other person is unconscious; or
   (d) the other person is less than 10 years old.

(2) *By Other Imposition.* A person who engages in deviate sexual intercourse with another person, or who causes another to engage in deviate sexual intercourse, commits a felony of the third degree if:
   (a) he compels the other person to participate by any threat that would prevent resistance by a person of ordinary resolution; or
   (b) he knows that the other person suffers from a mental disease or defect which renders him incapable of appraising the nature of his conduct; or
   (c) he knows that the other person submits because he is unaware that a sexual act is being committed upon him.

Section 213.3.   Corruption of Minors and Seduction.

(1) *Offense Defined.* A male who has sexual intercourse with a female not his wife, or any person who engages in deviate sexual intercourse or causes another to engage in deviate sexual intercourse, is guilty of an offense if:
   (a) the other person is less than [16] years old and the actor is at least [four] years older than the other person; or
   (b) the other person is less than 21 years old and the actor is his guardian or otherwise responsible for general supervision of his welfare; or
   (c) the other person is in custody of law or detained in a hospital or other institution and the actor has supervisory or disciplinary authority over him; or

(d) the other person is a female who is induced to participate by a promise of marriage which the actor does not mean to perform.

(2) *Grading.* An offense under paragraph (a) of Subsection (1) is a felony of the third degree. Otherwise an offense under this section is a misdemeanor.

Section 213.4.   Sexual Assault.

A person who has sexual contact with another not his spouse, or causes such other to have sexual conduct with him, is guilty of sexual assault, a misdemeanor, if:

(1) he knows that the contact is offensive to the other person; or

(2) he knows that the other person suffers from a mental disease or defect which renders him or her incapable of appraising the nature of his or her conduct; or

(3) he knows that the other person is unaware that a sexual act is being committed; or

(4) the other person is less than 10 years old; or

(5) he has substantially impaired the other person's power to appraise or control his or her conduct, by administering or employing without the other's knowledge drugs, intoxicants or other means for the purpose of preventing resistance; or

(6) the other person is less than [16] years old and the actor is at least [four] years older than the other person; or

(7) the other person is less than 21 years old and the actor is his guardian or otherwise responsible for general supervision of his welfare; or

(8) the other person is in custody of law or detained in a hospital or other institution and the actor has supervisory or disciplinary authority over him.

Sexual contact is any touching of the sexual or other intimate parts of the person for the purpose of arousing or gratifying sexual desire.

Section 213.5.   Indecent Exposure.

A person commits a misdemeanor if, for the purpose of arousing or gratifying sexual desire of himself or of any person other than his spouse, he exposes his genitals under circumstances in which he knows his conduct is likely to cause affront or alarm.

Section 213.6.   Provisions Generally Applicable to Article 213.

(1) *Mistake as to Age.* Whenever in this Article the criminality of conduct depends on a child's being below the age of 10, it is no defense that the actor did not know the child's age, or reasonably believed the child to be older than 10. When criminality depends on the child's being below a critical age other than 10, it is a defense for the actor to prove by a preponderance of the evidence that he reasonably believed the child to be above the critical age.

(2) *Spouse Relationships.* Whenever in this Article the definition of an offense excludes conduct with a spouse, the exclusion shall be deemed to extend to persons living as man and wife, regardless of the legal status of their relationship. The exclusion shall be inoperative as respects spouses living apart under a decree of judicial separation. Where the definition of an offense excludes conduct with a spouse or conduct by a woman, this shall not preclude conviction of a spouse or woman as accomplice in a sexual act which he or she causes another person, not within the exclusion, to perform.

(3) *Sexually Promiscuous Complainants.* It is a defense to prosecution under Section 213.3 and paragraphs (6), (7) and (8) of Section 213.4 for the actor to prove by a preponderance of the evidence that the alleged victim had, prior to the time of the offense charged, engaged promiscuously in sexual relations with others.

(4) *Prompt Complaint.* No prosecution may be instituted or maintained under this Article unless the alleged offense was brought to the notice of public authority within [3] months of its occurrence or, where the alleged victim was less than [16] years old or otherwise incompetent to make complaint, within [3] months after a parent, guardian or other competent person specially interested in the victim learns of the offense.

(5) *Testimony of Complainants.* No person shall be convicted of any felony under this Article upon the uncorroborated testimony of the alleged victim. Corroboration may be circumstantial. In any prosecution before a jury for an offense under this Article, the jury shall be instructed to evaluate the testimony of a victim or complaining witness with special care in view of the emotional involvement of the witness and the difficulty of determining the truth with respect to alleged sexual activities carried out in private.

OFFENSES AGAINST PROPERTY

Article 220. Arson, Criminal Mischief, and Other Property Destruction

Section 220.1.   Arson and Related Offenses.

(1) *Arson.* A person is guilty of arson, a felony of the second degree, if he starts a fire or causes an explosion with the purpose of:

   (a) destroying a building or occupied structure of another; or

   (b) destroying or damaging any property, whether his own or another's, to collect insurance for such loss. It shall be an affirmative defense to prosecution under this paragraph that the actor's conduct did not recklessly endanger any building or occupied structure of another or place any other person in danger of death or bodily injury.

(2) *Reckless Burning or Exploding.* A person commits a felony of the third degree if he purposely starts a fire or causes an explosion, whether on his own property or another's, and thereby recklessly:

   (a) places another person in danger of death or bodily injury; or

   (b) places a building or occupied structure of another in danger of damage or destruction.

(3) *Failure to Control or Report Dangerous Fire. . . .*

(4) *Definitions.* "Occupied structure" means any structure, vehicle or place adapted for overnight accommodation of persons, or for carrying on business therein, whether or not a person is actually present. Property is that of another, for the purposes of this section, if anyone other than the actor has a possessory or proprietary interest therein. If a building or structure is divided into separately occupied units, any unit not occupied by the actor is an occupied structure of another.

Section 220.2. [omitted]
Section 220.3. Criminal Mischief.

(1) *Offense Defined.* A person is guilty of criminal mischief if he:

   (a) damages tangible property of another purposely, recklessly, or by negligence in the employment of fire, explosives, or other dangerous means listed in Section 220.2(1); or

   (b) purposely or recklessly tampers with tangible property of another so as to endanger person or property; or

   (c) purposely or recklessly causes another to suffer pecuniary loss by deception or threat.

(2) *Grading.* Criminal mischief is a felony of the third degree if the actor purposely causes pecuniary loss in excess of $5,000, or a substantial interruption or impairment of public communication, transportation, supply of water, gas or power, or other public service. It is a misdemeanor if the actor purposely causes pecuniary loss in excess of $100, or a petty misdemeanor if he purposely or recklessly causes pecuniary loss in excess of $25. Otherwise criminal mischief is a violation.

Article 221. Burglary and Other Criminal Intrusion

Section 221.0. Definitions.

In this Article, unless a different meaning plainly is required:

(1) "occupied structure" means any structure, vehicle or place adapted for overnight accommodation of persons, or for carrying on business therein, whether or not a person is actually present.

(2) "night" means the period between thirty minutes past sunset and thirty minutes before sunrise.

Section 221.1. Burglary.

(1) *Burglary Defined.* A person is guilty of burglary if he enters a building or occupied structure, or separately secured or occupied portion thereof, with purpose to commit a crime therein, unless the premises are at the time open to the public or the actor is licensed or privileged to enter. It is an affirmative defense to prosecution for burglary that the building or structure was abandoned.

(2) *Grading.* Burglary is a felony of the second degree if it is perpetrated in the dwelling of another at night, or if, in the course of committing the offense, the actor:

   (a) purposely, knowingly or recklessly inflicts or attempts to inflict bodily injury on anyone; or

   (b) is armed with explosives or a deadly weapon.

Otherwise, burglary is a felony of the third degree. An act shall be deemed "in the course of committing" an offense if it occurs in an attempt to commit the offense or in flight after the attempt or commission.

(3) *Multiple Convictions.* A person may not be convicted both for burglary and for the offense which it was his purpose to commit after the burglarious entry or for an attempt to commit that offense, unless the additional offense constitutes a felony of the first or second degree.

Section 221.2. Criminal Trespass.

(1) *Buildings and Occupied Structures.* A person commits an offense if, knowing that he is not licensed or privileged to do so, he enters or surreptitiously remains in any building or occupied structure, or separately secured or occupied portion thereof. An offense under

this Subsection is a misdemeanor if it is committed in a dwelling at night. Otherwise it is a petty misdemeanor.

(2) *Defiant Trespasser.* A person commits an offense if, knowing that he is not licensed or privileged to do so, he enters or remains in any place as to which notice against trespass is given by:

(a) actual communication to the actor; or

(b) posting in a manner prescribed by law or reasonably likely to come to the attention of intruders; or

(c) fencing or other enclosure manifestly designed to exclude intruders.

An offense under this Subsection constitutes a petty misdemeanor if the offender defies an order to leave personally communicated to him by the owner of the premises or other authorized person. Otherwise it is a violation.

(3) *Defenses.* It is an affirmative defense to prosecution under this Section that:

(a) a building or occupied structure involved in an offense under Subsection (1) was abandoned; or

(b) the premises were at the time open to members of the public and the actor complied with all lawful conditions imposed on access to or remaining in the premises; or

(c) the actor reasonably believed that the owner of the premises, or other person empowered to license access thereto, would have licensed him to enter or remain.

Article 222. Robbery

Section 222.1. Robbery.

(1) *Robbery Defined.* A person is guilty of robbery if, in the course of committing a theft, he:

(a) inflicts serious bodily injury upon another; or

(b) threatens another with or purposely puts him in fear of immediate serious bodily injury; or

(c) commits or threatens immediately to commit any felony of the first or second degree.

An act shall be deemed "in the course of committing a theft" if it occurs in an attempt to commit theft or in flight after the attempt or commission.

(2) *Grading.* Robbery is a felony of the second degree, except that it is a felony of the first degree if in the course of committing the theft the actor attempts to kill anyone, or purposely inflicts or attempts to inflict serious bodily injury.

Article 223. Theft and Related Offenses

Section 223.0. Definitions.

In this Article, unless a different meaning plainly is required:

(1) "deprive" means: (a) to withhold property of another permanently or for so extended a period as to appropriate a major portion of its economic value, or with intent to restore only upon payment of reward or other compensation; or (b) to dispose of the property so as to make it unlikely that the owner will recover it.

(2) "financial institution" means a bank, insurance company, credit union, building and loan association, investment trust or other organization held out to the public as a place of deposit of funds or medium of savings or collective investment.

(3) "government" means the United States, any State, county, municipality, or other political unit, or any department, agency or subdivision of any of the foregoing, or any corporation or other association carrying out the functions of government.

(4) "movable property" means property the location of which can be changed, including things growing on, affixed to, or found in land, and documents, although the rights represented thereby have no physical location; "immovable property" is all other property.

(5) "obtain" means: (a) in relation to property, to bring about a transfer or purported transfer of a legal interest in the property, whether to the obtainer or another; or (b) in relation to labor or service, to secure performance thereof.

(6) "property" means anything of value, including real estate, tangible and intangible personal property, contract rights, choses-in-action and other interests in or claims to wealth, admission or transportation tickets, captured or domestic animals, food and drink, electric or other power.

(7) "property of another" includes property in which any person other than the actor has an interest which the actor is not privileged to infringe, regardless of the fact that the actor also has an interest in the property and regardless of the fact that the other person might be precluded from civil recovery because the property was used in an unlawful transaction or was subject to forfeiture as contraband. Property in possession of the actor shall not be deemed property of another who has only a security interest therein, even if legal title is in the creditor pursuant to a conditional sales contract or other security agreement.

Section 223.1. Consolidation of Theft Offenses; Grading; Provisions Applicable to Theft Generally.

(1) *Consolidation of Theft Offenses.* Conduct denominated theft in this Article constitutes a single offense. An accusation of theft may be supported by evidence that it was committed in any manner that would be theft under this Article, notwithstanding the specification of a different manner in the indictment or information, subject only to the power of the Court to ensure fair trial by granting a continuance or other appropriate relief where the conduct of the defense would be prejudiced by lack of fair notice or by surprise.

(2) *Grading of Theft Offenses.*

   (a) Theft constitutes a felony of the third degree if the amount involved exceeds $500, or if the property stolen is a firearm, automobile, airplane, motorcycle, motorboat, or other motor-propelled vehicle, or in the case of theft by receiving stolen property, if the receiver is in the business of buying or selling stolen property.

   (b) Theft not within the preceding paragraph constitutes a misdemeanor, except that if the property was not taken from the person or by threat, or in breach of a fiduciary obligation, and the actor proves by a preponderance of the evidence that the amount involved was less than $50, the offense constitutes a petty misdemeanor.

   (c) The amount involved in a theft shall be deemed to be the highest value, by any reasonable standard, of the property or services which the actor stole or attempted to steal. Amounts involved in thefts committed pursuant to one scheme or course of conduct, whether from the same person or several persons, may be aggregated in determining the grade of the offense.

(3) *Claim of Right.* It is an affirmative defense to prosecution for theft that the actor:

   (a) was unaware that the property or service was that of another; or

   (b) acted under an honest claim of right to the property or service involved or that he had a right to acquire or dispose of it as he did; or

   (c) took property exposed for sale, intending to purchase and pay for it promptly, or reasonably believing that the owner, if present, would have consented.

(4) *Theft from Spouse.* It is no defense that theft was from the actor's spouse, except that misappropriation of household and personal effects, or other property normally accessible to both.

Section 223.2. [omitted]

Section 223.3. Theft by Deception.

A person is guilty of theft if he purposely obtains property of another by deception. A person deceives if he purposely:

(1) creates or reinforces a false impression, including false impressions as to law, value, intention or other state of mind; but deception as to a person's intention to perform a promise shall not be inferred from the fact alone that he did not subsequently perform the promise; or

(2) prevents another from acquiring information which would affect his judgment of a transaction; or

(3) fails to correct a false impression which the deceiver previously created or reinforced, or which the deceiver knows to be influencing another to whom he stands in a fiduciary or confidential relationship; or

(4) fails to disclose a known lien, adverse claim or other legal impediment to the enjoyment of property which he transfers or encumbers in consideration for the property obtained, whether such impediment is or is not valid, or is or is not a matter of official record.

The term "deceive" does not, however, include falsity as to matters having no pecuniary significance, or puffing by statements unlikely to deceive ordinary persons in the group addressed.

Section 223.4. Theft by Extortion.

A person is guilty of theft if he purposely obtains property of another by threatening to:

(1) inflict bodily injury on anyone or commit any other criminal offense; or

(2) accuse anyone of a criminal offense; or

(3) expose any secret tending to subject any person to hatred, contempt or ridicule, or to impair his credit or business repute; or

(4) take or withhold action as an official, or cause an official to take or withhold action; or

(5) bring about or continue a strike, boycott or other collective unofficial action, if the property is not demanded or received for the benefit of the group in whose interest the actor purports to act; or

(6) testify or provide information or withhold testimony or information with respect to another's legal claim or defense; or

(7) inflict any other harm which would not benefit the actor.

It is an affirmative defense to prosecution based on paragraphs (2), (3) or (4) that the property obtained by threat of accusation, exposure, lawsuit or other invocation of official action was honestly claimed as restitution or indemnification for harm done in the circumstances to which such accusation, exposure, lawsuit or other official action relates, or as compensation for property or lawful services.

Section 223.5. Theft of Property Lost, Mislaid, or Delivered by Mistake.

A person who comes into control of property of another that he knows to have been lost, mislaid, or delivered under a mistake as to the nature or amount of the property or the identity of the recipient is guilty of theft if, with purpose to deprive the owner thereof, he fails to take reasonable measures to restore the property to a person entitled to have it.

Section 223.6. Receiving Stolen Property.

(1) *Receiving.* A person is guilty of theft if he purposely receives, retains, or disposes of movable property of another knowing that it has been stolen, or believing that it has probably been stolen, unless the property is received, retained, or disposed with purpose to restore it to the owner. "Receiving" means acquiring possession, control or title, or lending on the security of the property.

(2) *Presumption of Knowledge.* The requisite knowledge or belief is presumed in the case of a dealer who:

  (a) is found in possession or control of property stolen from two or more persons on separate occasions; or

  (b) has received stolen property in another transaction within the year preceding the transaction charged; or

  (c) being a dealer in property of the sort received, acquires it for a consideration which he knows is far below its reasonable value.

    "Dealer" means a person in the business of buying or selling goods including a pawnbroker.

Section 223.7. [omitted]

Section 223.8. Theft by Failure to Make Required Disposition of Funds Received.

A person who purposely obtains property upon agreement, or subject to a known legal obligation, to make specified payment or other disposition, whether from such property or its proceeds or from his own property to be reserved in equivalent amount, is guilty of theft if he deals with the property obtained as his own and fails to make the required payment or disposition. The foregoing applies notwithstanding that it may be impossible to identify particular property as belonging to the victim at the time of the actor's failure to make the required payment

or disposition. An officer or employee of the government or of a financial institution is presumed: (i) to know any legal obligation relevant to his criminal liability under this Section, and (ii) to have dealt with the property as his own if he fails to pay or account upon lawful demand, or if an audit reveals a shortage or falsification of accounts.

Section 223.9. Unauthorized Use of Automobiles and Other Vehicles.

A person commits a misdemeanor if he operates another's automobile, airplane, motorcycle, motorboat, or other motor-propelled vehicle without consent of the owner. It is an affirmative defense to prosecution under this Section that the actor reasonably believed that the owner would have consented to the operation had he known of it.

Article 224. Forgery and Fraudulent Practices

Section 224.0. Definitions.

In this Article, the definitions given in Section 223.0 apply unless a different meaning plainly is required.

Section 224.1. Forgery.

(1) *Definition.* A person is guilty of forgery if, with purpose to defraud or injure anyone, or with knowledge that he is facilitating a fraud or injury to be perpetrated by anyone, the actor:

  (a) alters any writing of another without his authority; or

  (b) makes, completes, executes, authenticates, issues or transfers any writing so that it purports to be the act of another who did not authorize that act, or to have been executed at a time or place or in a numbered sequence other than was in fact the case, or to be a copy of an original when no such original existed; or

  (c) utters any writing which he knows to be forged in a manner specified in paragraphs (a) or (b).

"Writing" includes printing or any other method of recording information, money, coins, tokens, stamps, seals, credit cards, badges, trademarks, and other symbols of value, right, privilege, or identification.

(2) *Grading.* Forgery is a felony of the second degree if the writing is or purports to be part of an issue of money, securities, postage or revenue stamps, or other instruments issued by the government, or part of an issue of stock, bonds or other instruments representing interests in or claims against any property or enterprise. Forgery is a felony of the third degree if the writing is or purports to be a will, deed, contract, release,

commercial instrument, or other document evidencing, creating, transferring, altering, terminating, or otherwise affecting legal relations. Otherwise forgery is a misdemeanor.

[Section 224.2 through Section 224.13 omitted]

Section 224.14.   Securing Execution of Documents by Deception.

A person commits a misdemeanor if by deception he causes another to execute any instrument affecting, purporting to affect, or likely to affect the pecuniary interest of any person.

OFFENSES AGAINST THE FAMILY

Article 230. Offenses against the Family

Section 230.1.   Bigamy and Polygamy.

(1) *Bigamy.* A married person is guilty of bigamy, a misdemeanor, if he contracts or purports to contract another marriage, unless at the time of the subsequent marriage:
  (a) the actor believes that the prior spouse is dead; or
  (b) the actor and the prior spouse have been living apart for five consecutive years throughout which the prior spouse was not known by the actor to be alive; or
  (c) a Court has entered a judgment purporting to terminate or annul any prior disqualifying marriage, and the actor does not know that judgment to be invalid; or
  (d) the actor reasonably believes that he is legally eligible to remarry.

(2) *Polygamy.* A person is guilty of polygamy, a felony of the third degree, if he marries or cohabits with more than one spouse at a time in purported exercise of the right of plural marriage. The offense is a continuing one until all cohabitation and claim of marriage with more than one spouse terminates. This section does not apply to parties to a polygamous marriage, lawful in the country of which they are residents or nationals, while they are in transit through or temporarily visiting this State.

(3) *Other Party to Bigamous or Polygamous Marriage.* A person is guilty of bigamy or polygamy, as the case may be, if he contracts or purports to contract marriage with another knowing that the other is thereby committing bigamy or polygamy.

Section 230.2.   Incest.

A person is guilty of incest, a felony of the third degree, if he knowingly marries or cohabits or has sexual intercourse with an ancestor or descendant, a brother or sister of the whole or half blood [or an uncle, aunt, nephew or niece of the whole blood]. "Cohabit" means to live together under the representation or appearance of being married. The relationships referred to herein include blood relationships without regard to legitimacy, and relationship of parent and child by adoption.

Section 230.3.   Abortion.

(1) *Unjustified Abortion.* A person who purposely and unjustifiably terminates the pregnancy of another otherwise than by a live birth commits a felony of the third degree or, where the pregnancy has continued beyond the twenty-sixth week, a felony of the second degree.

(2) *Justifiable Abortion.* A licensed physician is justified in terminating a pregnancy if he believes there is substantial risk that continuance of the pregnancy would gravely impair the physical or mental health of the mother or that the child would be born with grave physical or mental defect, or that the pregnancy resulted from rape, incest, or other felonious intercourse. All illicit intercourse with a girl below the age of 16 shall be deemed felonious for purposes of this subsection. Justifiable abortions shall be performed only in a licensed hospital except in case of emergency when hospital facilities are unavailable. [Additional exceptions from the requirement of hospitalization may be incorporated here to take account of situations in sparsely settled areas where hospitals are not generally accessible.]

(3) [omitted]

(4) *Self-Abortion.* A woman whose pregnancy has continued beyond the twenty-sixth week commits a felony of the third degree if she purposely terminates her own pregnancy otherwise than by a live birth, or if she uses instruments, drugs or violence upon herself for that purpose. Except as justified under Subsection (2), a person who induces or knowingly aids a woman to use instruments, drugs or violence upon herself for the purpose of terminating her pregnancy otherwise than by a live birth commits a felony of the third degree whether or not the pregnancy has continued beyond the twenty-sixth week.

(5) [omitted]

(6) [omitted]

(7) *Section Inapplicable to Prevention of Pregnancy.* Nothing in this Section shall be deemed applicable to the prescription, administration or distribution of drugs or other substances for avoiding pregnancy, whether by

preventing implantation of a fertilized ovum or by any other method that operates before, at or immediately after fertilization.

Section 230.4. Endangering Welfare of Children.

A parent, guardian, or other person supervising the welfare of a child under 18 commits a misdemeanor if he knowingly endangers the child's welfare by violating a duty of care, protection or support.

Section 230.5. Persistent Nonsupport.

A person commits a misdemeanor if he persistently fails to provide support which he can provide and which he knows he is legally obliged to provide to a spouse, child or other dependent.

OFFENSES AGAINST PUBLIC ADMINISTRATION

Article 240. Bribery and Corrupt Influence (omitted)

Article 241. Perjury and Other Falsification in Official Matters

Section 241.0. Definitions.

In this Article, unless a different meaning plainly is required:

(1) the definitions given in Section 240.0 apply; and

(2) "statement" means any representation, but includes a representation of opinion, belief or other state of mind only if the representation clearly relates to state of mind apart from or in addition to any facts which are the subject of the representation.

Section 241.1. Perjury.

(1) *Offense Defined.* A person is guilty of perjury, a felony of the third degree, if in any official proceeding he makes a false statement under oath or equivalent affirmation, or swears or affirms the truth of a statement previously made, when the statement is material and he does not believe it to be true.

(2) *Materiality.* Falsification is material, regardless of the admissibility of the statement under rules of evidence, if it could have affected the course or outcome of the proceeding. It is no defense that the declarant mistakenly believed the falsification to be immaterial. Whether a falsification is material in a given factual situation is a question of law.

(3) *Irregularities No Defense.* It is not a defense to prosecution under this Section that the oath or affirmation was administered or taken in an irregular

manner or that the declarant was not competent to make the statement. A document purporting to be made upon oath or affirmation at any time when the actor presents it as being so verified shall be deemed to have been duly sworn or affirmed.

(4) *Retraction.* No person shall be guilty of an offense under this Section if he retracted the falsification in the course of the proceeding in which it was made before it became manifest that the falsification was or would be exposed and before the falsification substantially affected the proceeding.

(5) *Inconsistent Statements.* Where the defendant made inconsistent statements under oath or equivalent affirmation, both having been made within the period of the statute of limitations, the prosecution may proceed by setting forth the inconsistent statements in a single count alleging in the alternative that one or the other was false and not believed by the defendant. In such case it shall not be necessary for the prosecution to prove which statement was false but only that one or the other was false and not believed by the defendant to be true.

(6) *Corroboration.* No person shall be convicted of an offense under this Section where proof of falsity rests solely upon contradiction by testimony of a single person other than the defendant.

Section 241.2. False Swearing.

(1) *False Swearing in Official Matters.* A person who makes a false statement under oath or equivalent affirmation, or swears or affirms the truth of such a statement previously made, when he does not believe the statement to be true, is guilty of a misdemeanor if:

  (a) the falsification occurs in an official proceeding; or

  (b) the falsification is intended to mislead a public servant in performing his official function.

(2) *Other False Swearing.* A person who makes a false statement under oath or equivalent affirmation, or swears or affirms the truth of such a statement previously made, when he does not believe the statement to be true, is guilty of a petty misdemeanor, if the statement is one which is required by law to be sworn or affirmed before a notary or other person authorized to administer oaths.

[Sections 241.3 through 241.8 omitted]

Section 241.9. Impersonating a Public Servant.

A person commits a misdemeanor if he falsely pretends to hold a position in the public service with purpose to induce another to submit to such pretended official authority or otherwise to act in reliance upon that pretense to his prejudice.

Article 242. Obstructing Governmental Operations; Escapes

Section 242.0.   Definitions.
In this Article, unless another meaning plainly is required, the definitions given in Section 240.0 apply.

Section 242.1.   Obstructing Administration of Law or Other Governmental Function.
A person commits a misdemeanor if he purposely obstructs, impairs or perverts the administration of law or other governmental function by force, violence, physical interference or obstacle, breach of official duty, or any other unlawful act, except that this Section does not apply to flight by a person charged with crime, refusal to submit to arrest, failure to perform a legal duty other than an official duty, or any other means of avoiding compliance with law without affirmative interference with governmental functions.

Section 242.2.   Resisting Arrest or Other Law Enforcement.
A person commits a misdemeanor if, for the purpose of preventing a public servant from effecting a lawful arrest or discharging any other duty, the person creates a substantial risk of bodily injury to the public servant or anyone else, or employs means justifying or requiring substantial force to overcome the resistance.

Section 242.3.   Hindering Apprehension or Prosecution.
A person commits an offense if, with purpose to hinder the apprehension, prosecution, conviction or punishment of another for crime, he:

(1) harbors or conceals the other; or

(2) provides or aids in providing a weapon, transportation, disguise or other means of avoiding apprehension or effecting escape; or

(3) conceals or destroys evidence of the crime, or tampers with a witness, informant, document or other source of information, regardless of its admissibility in evidence; or

(4) warns the other of impending discovery or apprehension, except that this paragraph does not apply to a warning given in connection with an effort to bring another into compliance with law; or

(5) volunteers false information to a law enforcement officer.

The offense is a felony of the third degree if the conduct which the actor knows has been charged or is liable to be charged against the person aided would constitute a felony of the first or second degree. Otherwise it is a misdemeanor.

[Sections 222.4 through 242.5 omitted]

Section 242.6.   Escape.

(1) *Escape.* A person commits an offense if he unlawfully removes himself from official detention or fails to return to official detention following temporary leave granted for a specific purpose or limited period. "Official detention" means arrest, detention in any facility for custody of persons under charge or conviction of crime or alleged or found to be delinquent, detention for extradition or deportation, or any other detention for law enforcement purposes; but "official detention" does not include supervision of probation or parole, or constraint incidental to release on bail.

(2) *Permitting or Facilitating Escape.* A public servant concerned in detention commits an offense if he knowingly or recklessly permits an escape. Any person who knowingly causes or facilitates an escape commits an offense.

(3) [omitted]

(4) *Grading of Offenses.* An offense under this Section is a felony of the third degree where:

(a) the actor was under arrest for or detained on a charge of felony or following conviction of crime; or

(b) the actor employs force, threat, deadly weapon or other dangerous instrumentality to effect the escape; or

(c) a public servant concerned in detention of persons convicted of crime purposely facilitates or permits an escape from a detention facility.

Otherwise an offense under this Section is a misdemeanor.

Section 242.7.   Implements for Escape; Other Contraband.

(1) *Escape Implements.* A person commits a misdemeanor if he unlawfully introduces within a detention facility, or unlawfully provides an inmate with, any weapon, tool or other thing which may be useful for escape. An inmate commits a misdemeanor if he unlawfully procures, makes, or otherwise provides himself with, or has in his possession, any such implement of escape. "Unlawfully" means surreptitiously or contrary to law, regulation or order of the detaining authority.

(2) *Other Contraband.* A person commits a petty misdemeanor if he provides an inmate with anything which the actor knows it is unlawful for the inmate to possess.

OFFENSES AGAINST PUBLIC ORDER AND DECENCY

Article 250. Riot, Disorderly Conduct, and Related Offenses

Section 250.1.   Riot; Failure to Disperse.

(1) *Riot.* A person is guilty of riot, a felony of the third degree, if he participates with [two] or more others in a course of disorderly conduct:

   (a) with purpose to commit or facilitate the commission of a felony or misdemeanor;

   (b) with purpose to prevent or coerce official action; or

   (c) when the actor or any other participant to the knowledge of the actor uses or plans to use a firearm or other deadly weapon.

(2) *Failure of Disorderly Persons to Disperse upon Official Order.* Where [three] or more persons are participating in a course of disorderly conduct likely to cause substantial harm or serious inconvenience, annoyance or alarm, a peace officer or other public servant engaged in executing or enforcing the law may order the participants and others in the immediate vicinity to disperse. A person who refuses or knowingly fails to obey such an order commits a misdemeanor.

Section 250.2.   Disorderly Conduct.

(1) *Offense Defined.* A person is guilty of disorderly conduct if, with purpose to cause public inconvenience, annoyance or alarm, or recklessly creating a risk thereof, he:

   (a) engages in fighting or threatening, or in violent or tumultuous behavior; or

   (b) makes unreasonable noise or offensively coarse utterance, gesture or display, or addresses abusive language to any person present; or

   (c) creates a hazardous or physically offensive condition by any act which serves no legitimate purpose of the actor.

"Public" means affecting or likely to affect persons in a place to which the public or a substantial group has access; among the places included are highways, transport facilities, schools, prisons, apartment houses, places of business or amusement, or any neighborhood.

(2) *Grading.* An offense under this section is a petty misdemeanor if the actor's purpose is to cause substantial harm or serious inconvenience, or if he persists in disorderly conduct after reasonable warning or request to desist. Otherwise disorderly conduct is a violation.

Section 250.3.   False Public Alarms.

A person is guilty of a misdemeanor if he initiates or circulates a report or warning of an impending bombing or other crime or catastrophe, knowing that the report or warning is false or baseless and that it is likely to cause evacuation of a building, place of assembly, or facility of public transport, or to cause public inconvenience or alarm.

Section 250.4.   Harassment.

A person commits a petty misdemeanor if, with purpose to harass another, he:

(1) makes a telephone call without purpose of legitimate communication; or

(2) insults, taunts or challenges another in a manner likely to provoke violent or disorderly response; or

(3) makes repeated communications anonymously or at extremely inconvenient hours, or in offensively coarse language; or

(4) subjects another to an offensive touching; or

(5) engages in any other course of alarming conduct serving no legitimate purpose of the actor.

Section 250.5.   Public Drunkenness; Drug Incapacitation.

A person is guilty of an offense if he appears in any public place manifestly under the influence of alcohol, narcotics or other drug, not therapeutically administered, to the degree that he may endanger himself or other persons or property, or annoy persons in his vicinity. An offense under this Section constitutes a petty misdemeanor if the actor has been convicted hereunder twice before within a period of one year. Otherwise the offense constitutes a violation.

Section 250.6.   Loitering or Prowling.

A person commits a violation if he loiters or prowls in a place, at a time, or in a manner not usual for law-abiding individuals under circumstances that warrant alarm for the safety of persons or property in the vicinity. Among the circumstances which may be considered in determining whether such alarm is warranted is the fact that the actor takes flight upon appearance of a peace officer, refuses to identify himself, or manifestly endeavors to conceal himself or any object. Unless flight by the actor or other circumstance makes it impracticable, a peace officer shall prior to any arrest for an offense under this section afford the actor an opportunity to dispel any alarm which would otherwise be warranted, by requesting him to identify himself and explain his presence and conduct. No person shall be convicted of an offense under this Section if the peace officer did not comply with the preceding sentence, or if it appears at trial that the explanation given by the actor was true and, if believed by the peace officer at the time, would have dispelled the alarm.

[Sections 250.7 and 250.8 omitted]

Section 250.9. Desecration of Venerated Objects.

A person commits a misdemeanor if he purposely desecrates any public monument or structure, or place of worship or burial, or if he purposely desecrates the national flag or any other object of veneration by the public or a substantial segment thereof in any public place. "Desecrate" means defacing, damaging, polluting or otherwise physically mistreating in a way that the actor knows will outrage the sensibilities of persons likely to observe or discover his action.

Section 250.10. Abuse of Corpse.

Except as authorized by law, a person who treats a corpse in a way that he knows would outrage ordinary family sensibilities commits a misdemeanor.

Section 250.11. Cruelty to Animals.

A person commits a misdemeanor if he purposely or recklessly:

(1) subjects any animal to cruel mistreatment; or

(2) subjects any animal in his custody to cruel neglect; or

(3) kills or injures any animal belonging to another without legal privilege or consent of the owner.

Subsections (1) and (2) shall not be deemed applicable to accepted veterinary practices and activities carried on for scientific research.

Section 250.12. Violation of Privacy.

(1) *Unlawful Eavesdropping or Surveillance.* A person commits a misdemeanor if, except as authorized by law, he:

(a) trespasses on property with purpose to subject anyone to eavesdropping or other surveillance in a private place; or

(b) installs in any private place, without the consent of the person or persons entitled to privacy there, any device for observing, photographing, recording, amplifying or broadcasting sounds or events in such place, or uses any such unauthorized installation; or

(c) installs or uses outside a private place any device for hearing, recording, amplifying or broadcasting sounds originating in such place which would not ordinarily be audible or comprehensible outside, without the consent of the person or persons entitled to privacy there.

"Private place" means a place where one may reasonably expect to be safe from casual or hostile intrusion or surveillance, but does not include a place to which the public or a substantial group thereof has access.

(2) *Other Breach of Privacy of Messages.* A person commits a misdemeanor if, except as authorized by law, he:

(a) intercepts without the consent of the sender or receiver a message by telephone, telegraph, letter or other means of communicating privately; but this paragraph does not extend to (i) overhearing of messages through a regularly installed instrument on a telephone party line or on an extension, or (ii) interception by the telephone company or subscriber incident to enforcement of regulations limiting use of the facilities or incident to other normal operation and use; or

(b) divulges without the consent of the sender or receiver the existence or contents of any such message if the actor knows that the message was illegally intercepted, or if he learned of the message in the course of employment with an agency engaged in transmitting it.

Article 251. Public Indecency

Section 251.1. Open Lewdness.

A person commits a petty misdemeanor if he does any lewd act which he knows is likely to be observed by others who would be affronted or alarmed.

Section 251.2. Prostitution and Related Offenses.

(1) *Prostitution.* A person is guilty of prostitution, a petty misdemeanor, if he or she:

(a) is an inmate of a house of prostitution or otherwise engages in sexual activity as a business; or

(b) loiters in or within view of any public place for the purpose of being hired to engage in sexual activity.

"Sexual activity" includes homosexual and other deviate sexual relations. A "house of prostitution" is any place where prostitution or promotion of prostitution is regularly carried on by one person under the control, management or supervision of another. An "inmate" is a person who engages in prostitution in or through the agency of a house of prostitution. "Public place" means any place to which the public or any substantial group thereof has access.

(2) *Promoting Prostitution.* A person who knowingly promotes prostitution of another commits a misdemeanor or felony as provided in Subsection (3). The following acts shall, without limitation of the foregoing, constitute promoting prostitution:

   (a) owning, controlling, managing, supervising or otherwise keeping, alone or in association with others, a house of prostitution or a prostitution business; or

   (b) procuring an inmate for a house of prostitution or a place in a house of prostitution for one who would be an inmate; or

   (c) encouraging, inducing, or otherwise purposely causing another to become or remain a prostitute; or

   (d) soliciting a person to patronize a prostitute; or

   (e) procuring a prostitute for a patron; or

   (f) transporting a person into or within this state with purpose to promote that person's engaging in prostitution, or procuring or paying for transportation with that purpose; or

   (g) leasing or otherwise permitting a place controlled by the actor, alone or in association with others, to be regularly used for prostitution or the promotion of prostitution, or failure to make reasonable effort to abate such use by ejecting the tenant, notifying law enforcement authorities, or other legally available means; or

   (h) soliciting, receiving, or agreeing to receive any benefit for doing or agreeing to do anything forbidden by this Subsection.

(3) [omitted]

(4) *Presumption from Living Off Prostitutes.* A person, other than the prostitute or the prostitute's minor child or other legal dependent incapable of self-support, who is supported in whole or substantial part by the proceeds of prostitution is presumed to be knowingly promoting prostitution in violation of Subsection (2).

(5) *Patronizing Prostitutes.* A person commits a violation if he hires a prostitute to engage in sexual activity with him, or if he enters or remains in a house of prostitution for the purpose of engaging in sexual activity.

Section 251.3. Loitering to Solicit Deviate Sexual Relations.

A person is guilty of a petty misdemeanor if he loiters in or near any public place for the purpose of soliciting or being solicited to engage in deviate sexual relations.

Section 251.4. Obscenity.

(1) *Obscene Defined.* Material is obscene if, considered as a whole, its predominant appeal is to prurient interest, that is, a shameful or morbid interest, in nudity, sex or excretion, and if in addition it goes substantially beyond customary limits of candor in describing or representing such matters. Predominant appeal shall be judged with reference to ordinary adults unless it appears from the character of the material or the circumstances of its dissemination to be designed for children or other specially susceptible audience. Undeveloped photographs, molds, printing plates, and the like, shall be deemed obscene notwithstanding that processing or other acts may be required to make the obscenity patent or to disseminate it.

(2) *Offenses.* Subject to the affirmative defense provided in Subsection (3), a person commits a misdemeanor if he knowingly or recklessly:

   (a) sells, delivers or provides, or offers or agrees to sell, deliver or provide, any obscene writing, picture, record or other representation or embodiment of the obscene; or

   (b) presents or directs an obscene play, dance or performance, or participates in that portion thereof which makes it obscene; or

   (c) publishes, exhibits or otherwise makes available any obscene material; or

   (d) possesses any obscene material for purposes of sale or other commercial dissemination; or

   (e) sells, advertises or otherwise commercially disseminates material, whether or not obscene, by representing or suggesting that it is obscene.

   A person who disseminates or possesses obscene material in the course of his business is presumed to do so knowingly or recklessly.

(3) *Justifiable and Non-commercial Private Dissemination.* It is an affirmative defense to prosecution under this Section that dissemination was restricted to:

   (a) institutions or persons having scientific, educational, governmental or other similar justification for possessing obscene material; or

   (b) non-commercial dissemination to personal associates of the actor.

(4) *Evidence; Adjudication of Obscenity.* In any prosecution under this Section evidence shall be admissible to show:

   (a) the character of the audience for which the material was designed or to which it was directed;

(b) what the predominant appeal of the material would be for ordinary adults or any special audience to which it was directed, and what effect, if any, it would probably have on conduct of such people;

(c) artistic, literary, scientific, educational or other merits of the material;

(d) the degree of public acceptance of the material in the United States;

(e) appeal to prurient interest, or absence thereof, in advertising or other promotion of the material; and

(f) the good repute of the author, creator, publisher or other person from whom the material originated.

Expert testimony and testimony of the author, creator, publisher or other person from whom the material originated, relating to factors entering into the determination of the issue of obscenity, shall be admissible. The Court shall dismiss a prosecution for obscenity if it is satisfied that the material is not obscene.

Glossary

abandonment The voluntary and complete abandonment of the intent and purpose to commit a criminal offense. Abandonment is a defense to a charge of attempted criminal activity. Also called *renunciation*.

abused child[1] A child who has been physically, emotionally, or sexually abused. Most states also consider a child who is forced into delinquent activity by a parent or guardian to be abused.

accessory One who knowingly gives assistance to a person who has committed a felony for the purpose of helping that individual avoid apprehension or detection. An accessory is liable for separate, lesser offenses following a crime.

accessory after the fact A person who did not participate in a crime but who furnished postcrime assistance to keep the offender from being detected or from being arrested.

accessory before the fact A person who aids and abets in preparation for crime commission, but who was not present at the crime scene.

accidental death A death that is caused by unexpected or unintended means.

accidental killing A death that is the result of a purposeful human act lawfully undertaken in the reasonable belief that no harm would result.

accomplice A person who, with intent to promote or facilitate the commission of a crime, gives assistance or encouragement to the principal. An accomplice is liable as a principal before and during a crime.

accomplice liability The degree of criminal blameworthiness of one who aids, abets, encourages, or assists another person in the commission of a crime.

acquisitive offense A crime that involves the unlawful acquiring or appropriation of someone else's property. Larceny, extortion, embezzlement, false pretenses, robbery, and the receiving of stolen property are all acquisitive offenses. Also called *wrongful acquisition crime* and *crime of misappropriation*.

actual possession Possession in which one has direct physical control over the object or objects in question.

actus reus An act in violation of the law; a guilty act.

adequate cause In cases of voluntary manslaughter, a cause that would commonly produce a degree of anger, rage, or terror in a person of ordinary temper, sufficient to render the mind of the defendant incapable of objective reflection.

adequate provocation Provocation that "would cause a reasonable person to lose self-control." Also called *reasonable provocation*.

adjudicatory hearing The fact-finding process wherein the juvenile court determines whether there is sufficient evidence to sustain the allegations in a petition.

ADMAX An acronym for administrative maximum. This term is used by the federal government to denote ultra-high-security prisons.

administration of justice The performance of any of the following activities: detection, apprehension, detention, pretrial release, post-trial release, prosecution, adjudication, correctional supervision, or rehabilitation of accused persons or criminal offenders.[2]

adultery Sexual intercourse between a male and a female, at least one of whom is married to someone else.

adversarial system The court system that pits the prosecution against the defense in the belief that truth can best be realized through effective debate over the merits of the opposing sides.

affirmative act Voluntary, conscious conduct. An affirmative act is not an omission or a failure to act.

affirmative defense An answer to a criminal charge in which a defendant takes the offensive and responds to the allegations with his or her own assertions based on legal principles. Affirmative defenses must be raised and supported by the defendant independently of any claims made by the prosecutor. Affirmative defenses include justifications and excuses.

affray A fight between two or more people in a public place to the terror of others.[3]

aggravated assault An assault that is committed with the intention of committing an additional crime, such as assault with intent to commit a felony; assault with intent to murder; assault with intent to commit rape, sodomy, mayhem, robbery, or grand larceny; and assault with intent to commit any other felony. Also, an assault that involves special circumstances specified by law.

aggravated battery A battery that is committed with the use of a deadly weapon, that is committed with the intention of committing another crime, or that results in serious injury.

---

[1] All boldfaced terms are explained whenever possible using definitions provided by the Bureau of Justice Statistics under a mandate of the Justice System Improvement Act of 1979. That mandate found its most complete expression in the *Dictionary of Criminal Justice Data Terminology* (Washington, DC: Bureau of Justice Statistics, 1982), the second edition of which provides the wording for many definitions in this text.

[2] Adapted from U.S. Code, Title 28, Section 20.3 (2[d]). Title 28 of the U.S. Code defines the term *administration of criminal justice*.

[3] Wesley Gilmer, *The Law Dictionary*, 6th ed. (Cincinnati: Anderson, 1986), 19.

aggravated murder Murder plus one or more aggravating factors as specified by law. Aggravated murder is generally capital murder.

aggravating factor A circumstance relating to the commission of a crime that causes its gravity to be greater than that of the average instance of the given type of offense.[4] Also, an element of an offense or of an offender's background that could result in a harsher sentence under the determinate sentencing model than would otherwise be called for by sentencing guidelines.

aggravating circumstances Circumstances relating to the commission of a crime that make it more grave than the average instance of that crime.

alibi A statement or contention by an individual charged with a crime that he or she was so distant when the crime was committed, or so engaged in other provable activities, that his or her participation in the commission of that crime was impossible.

alter ego rule A rule of law that, in some jurisdictions, holds that a person can only defend a third party under circumstances and only to the degree that the third party could act on his or her own behalf.

alternative sentencing The use of court-ordered community service, home detention, day reporting, drug treatment, psychological counseling, victim–offender programming, or intensive supervision in lieu of other, more traditional sanctions, such as imprisonment and fines.

anticipatory warrant A search warrant issued on the basis of probable cause to believe that evidence of a crime, although not currently at the place described, will likely be there when the warrant is executed.

apparent danger A form of imminent danger that is said to exist when the conduct or activity of an attacker makes the threat of danger obvious.

appeal The request that a court with appellate jurisdiction review the judgment, decision, or order of a lower court and set it aside (reverse it) or modify it.

appellate jurisdiction The lawful authority of a court to review a decision made by a lower court.

arraignment Strictly, the hearing before a court having jurisdiction in a criminal case in which the identity of the defendant is established, the defendant is informed of the charge and of his or her rights, and the defendant is required to enter a plea. Also, in some usages, any appearance in criminal court before trial.

arrest The act of taking an adult or juvenile into physical custody by authority of law for the purpose of charging the person with a criminal offense, a delinquent act, or a status offense, terminating with the recording of a specific offense. Technically, an arrest occurs whenever a law enforcement officer curtails a person's freedom to leave.

arson The knowing and malicious burning of the personal property of another or the burning of one's own property if the purpose is to collect insurance money.

asportation The trespassory taking and carrying away (as of personal property in the crime of larceny or of the victim in kidnapping).

assault Attempted or threatened battery. A willful attempt or willful threat to inflict injury on another person. Also, the act of intentionally frightening another person into fearing immediate bodily harm. One statutory definition of assault reads "an unlawful attempt, coupled with a present ability, to commit a violent injury on the person of another."[5]

attendant circumstances The facts surrounding an event.

bail The money or property pledged to the court or actually deposited with the court to effect the release of a person from legal custody.

bail bond A document guaranteeing the appearance of a defendant in court as required and recording the pledge of money or property to be paid to the court if he or she does not appear. The bail bond is signed by the person to be released and by anyone else acting in his or her behalf.

bailiff The court officer whose duties are to keep order in the courtroom, to secure witnesses, and to maintain physical custody of the jury.

balancing test A principle, developed by the courts and applied to the corrections arena by *Pell* v. *Procunier* (1974), that attempts to weigh the rights of an individual, as guaranteed by the Constitution, against the authority of any state to make laws or to otherwise restrict a person's freedom in order to protect the state's interests and its citizens.

battered woman's syndrome (BWS) A condition characterized by a history of repetitive spousal abuse and "learned helplessness" (the subjective inability to leave an abusive situation). Also, "a series of common characteristics that appear in women who are abused physically and psychologically over an extended period of time by the dominant male figure in their lives; a pattern of psychological symptoms that develop after somebody has lived in a battering relationship; or a pattern of responses and perceptions presumed to be characteristic of women who have been subjected to continuous physical abuse by their mate[s]."[6] Also called *battered person's syndrome*.

---

[4] Bureau of Justice Statistics, *Dictionary of Criminal Justice Data Terminology,* 2nd ed. (Washington, DC: U.S. Department of Justice, 1981), 46.

[5] California Penal Code, Section 240.

[6] *People* v. *Romero*, 8 Cal. 4th 728, 735 (1994); and *People* v. *Dillard*, 96 C.D.O.S. 3869 (1996).

battery (1) Unlawful physical violence inflicted on another without his or her consent. (2) An intentional and offensive touching or wrongful physical contact with another, without consent, that results in some injury or offends or causes discomfort.

bestiality Sexual relations with animals.

bigamy The crime of marrying one person while still legally married to another person.

bill of attainder A legislative pronouncement that an individual is guilty of a crime. Bills of attainder are prohibited to the federal and state governments by the U.S. Constitution.

Bill of Rights The first ten amendments to the U.S. Constitution, which were made part of the Constitution in 1791.

biological weapon A biological agent used to threaten human life (for example, anthrax, smallpox, or any infectious disease).[7]

Bivens action A civil suit, based on the case of *Bivens* v. *Six Unknown Federal Agents*, brought against federal government officials for denying the constitutional rights of others.

blackmail A form of extortion in which a threat is made to disclose a crime or other social disgrace.

blended sentence A juvenile court disposition that imposes both a juvenile sanction and an adult criminal sentence on an adjudicated delinquent. The adult sentence is suspended on the condition that the juvenile offender successfully completes the term of the juvenile disposition and refrains from committing any new offense.[8]

bodily injury Physical harm to a human being. In cases of assault and battery, the term refers to the unlawful application of physical force on the person of the victim—even when no actual physical harm results.

brain death Death determined by a "flat" reading on an electroencephalograph (EEG), usually after a 24-hour period, or by other medical criteria

breach of peace Any unlawful activity that unreasonably disturbs the peace and tranquility of the community. Also, "an act calculated to disturb the public peace."[9]

bribery The offense of giving or receiving a gift or reward intended to influence a person in the exercise of a judicial or public duty.[10]

buggery Anal intercourse.

burden of proof The mandate, operative in American criminal courts, that an accused person is presumed innocent until proven guilty and that the prosecution must prove the defendant's guilt beyond a reasonable doubt.

Bureau of Justice Statistics (BJS) A U.S. Department of Justice agency responsible for the collection of criminal justice data, including the annual National Crime Victimization Survey.

burglary The breaking and entering of a building, locked automobile, boat, and so on, with the intent to commit a felony or theft. Also, the entering of a structure for the purposes of committing a felony or theft.

"but for" rule A method for determining causality that holds that "without this, that would not be," or "*but for* the conduct of the accused, the harm in question would not have occurred."

canon of construction A rule that guides courts in interpreting constitutions, statutes, and other law.

capital murder Murder for which the death penalty is authorized by law.

capital offense A criminal offense punishable by death.

capital punishment The imposition of a sentence of death.

career offender Under federal sentencing guidelines, a person who (1) is at least 18 years old at the time of the most recent offense, (2) is convicted of a felony that is either a crime of violence or a controlled substance offense, and (3) has at least two prior felony convictions of either a crime of violence or a controlled substance offense.

case law The body of previous decisions, or precedents, that has accumulated over time and to which attorneys refer when arguing cases and that judges use in deciding the merits of new cases.

caseload The number of probation or parole clients assigned to one probation or parole officer for supervision.

castle exception An exception to the retreat rule that recognizes a person's fundamental right to be in his or her home and also recognizes the home as a final and inviolable place of retreat. Under the castle exception to the retreat rule, it is not necessary to retreat from one's home in the face of an immediate threat, even where retreat is possible, before resorting to deadly force in protection of the home.

causation in fact An actual link between an actor's conduct and a result.

chain of command The unbroken line of authority that extends through all levels of an organization, from the highest to the lowest.

change of venue The movement of a trial or lawsuit from one jurisdiction to another or from one location to another

---

[7] Technical Working Group on Crime Scene Investigation, *Crime Scene Investigation: A Guide for Law Enforcement* (Washington, DC: National Institute of Justice, 2000), p. 12.

[8] Howard N. Snyder and Melissa Sickmund, *Juvenile Offenders and Victims: 2006 National Report* (Washington, DC: Office of Juvenile Justice and Delinquency Prevention, 2006).

[9] Gilmer, *The Law Dictionary*, 54.

[10] Ibid.

within the same jurisdiction. A change of venue may be made in a criminal case to ensure that the defendant receives a fair trial.

child pornography The depiction of sexual behavior involving children.

circumstantial evidence The evidence that requires interpretation or that requires a judge or jury to reach a conclusion based on what the evidence indicates. From the close proximity of the defendant to a smoking gun, for example, the jury might conclude that he or she pulled the trigger.

civil death The legal status of prisoners in some jurisdictions who are denied the opportunity to vote, hold public office, marry, or enter into contracts by virtue of their status as incarcerated felons. While civil death is primarily of historical interest, some jurisdictions still limit the contractual opportunities available to inmates.

civil justice The civil law, the law of civil procedure, and the array of procedures and activities having to do with private rights and remedies sought by civil action. Civil justice cannot be separated from social justice because the justice enacted in our nation's civil courts reflects basic American understandings of right and wrong.

civil law The form of the law that governs relationships between parties.

civil liability The potential responsibility for payment of damages or other court-ordered enforcement as a result of a ruling in a lawsuit. Civil liability is not the same as criminal liability, which means "open to punishment for a crime."[11]

claim of right A defense against a charge of larceny that consists of an honest belief in ownership or right to possession.

classification system A system used by prison administrators to assign inmates to custody levels based on offense history, assessed dangerousness, perceived risk of escape, and other factors.

clear and convincing evidence The level of factual proof used in civil cases involving issues of personal liberty. The standard requires greater certainty than "more probable than not" but is not as demanding as "no reasonable doubt."

clearance rate A traditional measure of investigative effectiveness that compares the number of crimes reported or discovered to the number of crimes solved through arrest or other means (such as the death of the suspect).

closing argument An oral summation of a case presented to a judge, or to a judge and jury, by the prosecution or by the defense in a criminal trial.

co-conspirator hearsay rule This rule is an exception to the general rule that hearsay, or statements made out of court by a person who is not in court to testify, is inadmissible. In conspiracy trials, statements made by conspirators out of court and who are not available to testify are admissible.

common law Law originating from use and custom rather than from written statutes. The term refers to nonstatutory customs, traditions, and precedents that help guide judicial decision making.

community corrections The use of a variety of officially ordered program-based sanctions that permit convicted offenders to remain in the community under conditional supervision as an alternative to an active prison sentence.

community court A low-level court that focuses on quality-of-life crimes that erode a neighborhood's morale, that emphasizes problem solving rather than punishment, and that builds on restorative principles such as community service and restitution.

community policing "A philosophy that promotes organizational strategies, which support the systematic use of partnerships and problem-solving techniques, to proactively address the immediate conditions that give rise to public safety issues such as crime, social disorder, and fear of crime."[12]

community service A sentencing alternative that requires offenders to spend at least part of their time working for a community agency.

compelling interest A legal concept that provides a basis for suspicionless searches when public safety is at issue. In two cases, the U.S. Supreme Court held that public safety may sometimes provide a sufficiently compelling interest to justify limiting an individual's right to privacy.

competent to stand trial A finding by a court that the defendant has sufficient present ability to consult with his lawyer with a reasonable degree of rational understanding and that the defendant has a rational as well as factual understanding of the proceeding against him or her.

complicity Involvement in crime either as a principal or as an accomplice. The term also refers to the activities of conspirators and may therefore be taken to mean conduct that is intended to encourage or aid another person to commit a crime, to escape, or to avoid prosecution.

compounding a crime The receipt of property or other valuable consideration in exchange for agreeing to conceal or not prosecute one who has committed a crime.[13] Also called *compounding a felony.*

---

[11] Adapted from Gerald Hill and Kathleen Hill, *The Real Life Dictionary of the Law,* http://www.law.com (accessed June 11, 2008).

[12] Office of Community Oriented Policing Services, *Community Policing Defined* (Washington, DC: U.S. Department of Justice, 2009), p. 3.

[13] Stephen A. Saltzburg and others, *Criminal Law: Cases and Materials* (Charlottesville, VA: Michie, 1994), 562.

CompStat A crime-analysis and police-management process built on crime mapping that was developed by the New York City Police Department in the mid-1990s.

computer crime A crime that employs computer technology as central to its commission and that could not take place without such technology. Also called *cybercrime*.

computer fraud A statutory provision, found in many states, that makes it unlawful for any person to use a computer or computer network without authority and with the intent to (1) obtain property or services by false pretenses, (2) embezzle or commit larceny, or (3) convert the property of another.

computer tampering Illegally inserting or attempting to insert a "program" into a computer, while knowing or believing that the "program" contains information or commands that will or may damage or destroy that computer (or its data), or any other computer (or its data) accessing or being accessed by that computer, *or* that will or may cause loss to the users of that computer or the users of a computer that accesses or that is accessed by such "program."[14]

computer trespass The offense of using a computer or computer network without authority and with the intent to (1) remove computer data, computer programs, or computer software from a computer or computer network; (2) cause a computer to malfunction; (3) alter or erase any computer data, computer programs, or computer software; (4) effect the creation or alteration of a financial instrument or of an electronic transfer of funds; (5) cause physical injury to the property of another; or (6) make or cause to be made an unauthorized copy of data stored on a computer or of computer programs or computer software.

computer virus A computer program designed to secretly invade systems and either modify the way in which they operate or alter the information they store. Viruses are destructive software programs that may effectively vandalize computers of all types and sizes.

concealed weapon A weapon that is carried on or near one's person and is not discernible by ordinary observation.

concurrence The simultaneous coexistence of (1) an act in violation of the law and (2) a culpable mental state.

concurrent sentence One of two or more sentences imposed at the same time, after conviction for more than one offense, and to be served simultaneously.[15]

conditional release The release of an inmate from prison to community supervision with a set of conditions for remaining on parole. If a condition is violated, the individual can be returned to prison or face another sanction in the community.[16]

conditions of parole (probation) The general and special limits imposed on an offender who is released on parole (or probation). General conditions tend to be fixed by state statute, whereas special conditions are mandated by the sentencing authority (court or board) and take into consideration the background of the offender and the circumstances of the offense.

conduct In the criminal law, behavior and its accompanying mental state.

conflict model A criminal justice perspective that assumes that the system's components function primarily to serve their own interests. According to this theoretical framework, justice is more a product of conflicts among agencies within the system than it is the result of cooperation among component agencies.

consecutive sentence One of two or more sentences imposed at the same time, after conviction for more than one offense, and served in sequence with the other sentences.

consensus model A criminal justice perspective that assumes that the system's components work together harmoniously to achieve the social product we call *justice*.

consent A justification, offered as a defense to a criminal charge, claiming that the person suffering an injury either agreed to sustain the injury or accepted the possibility of injury before the activity was undertaken.

constructive entry In the crime of burglary, an entry that occurs when the defendant causes another person to enter a structure to commit a crime or for a felonious purpose.

constructive possession The ability to exercise control over property or objects, even though they are not in one's physical custody.

constructive touching A touching that is inferred or implied from prevailing circumstances. Also, a touching for purposes of the law.

controlled substance A specifically defined bioactive or psychoactive chemical substance that comes under the purview of the criminal law.

conversion The unauthorized assumption of the right of ownership. Conversion is a central feature of the crime of embezzlement, as in the unlawful *conversion* of the personal property of another, by a person to whom it has been entrusted.

corporate crime A violation of a criminal statute by a corporate entity or by its executives, employees, or agents acting on behalf of and for the benefit of the corporation, partnership, or other form of business entity.[17]

[14] Illinois Revised Statutes, Chapter 38, Section 5/16D-3 (a)(4).

[15] Bureau of Justice Statistics, *Dictionary of Criminal Justice Data Terminology*, 46.

[16] Jeremy Travis and Sarah Lawrence, *Beyond the Prison Gates: The State of Parole in America* (Washington, DC: Urban Institute Press, 2002), p. 3.

[17] Michael L. Benson, Francis T. Cullen, and William J. Maakestad, *Local Prosecutors and Corporate Crime* (Washington, DC: National Institute of Justice, 1992), 1.

corpus delicti The facts that show that a crime has occurred. Literally, "the body of the crime."

corpus delicti rule (1) The body or essence of a criminal offense that proves that the alleged crime has been committed, but not who committed the crime. (2) In practice, a principle of law that says that an out-of-court confession, unsupported by other facts, is insufficient to support a criminal conviction.

court of last resort The court authorized by law to hear the final appeal on a matter.

courtroom work group The professional courtroom actors, including judges, prosecuting attorneys, defense attorneys, public defenders, and others who earn a living serving the court.

crime Any act or omission in violation of penal law, committed without defense or justification, and made punishable by the state in a judicial proceeding.

crime against nature A general term that can include homosexual or heterosexual acts of anal intercourse, oral intercourse, and bestiality and that may even apply to heterosexual intercourse in positions other than the conventional "missionary" position.

crime-control model A criminal justice perspective that emphasizes the efficient arrest and conviction of criminal offenders.

Crime Index A now-defunct but once-inclusive measure of the UCR Program's violent and property crime categories, or what are called *Part I offenses*. The Crime Index, long featured in the FBI's publication *Crime in the United States*, was discontinued in 2004. The index had been intended as a tool for geographic (state-to-state) and historical (year-to-year) comparisons via the use of crime rates (the number of crimes per unit of population). However, criticism that the index was misleading arose after researchers found that the largest of the index's crime categories, larceny-theft, carried undue weight and led to an underappreciation of changes in the rates of more violent and serious crimes.

crime prevention The anticipation, recognition, and appraisal of a crime risk and the initiation of action to eliminate or reduce it.

crime typology A classification of crimes along a particular dimension, such as legal category, offender motivation, victim behavior, or characteristics of individual offenders.

criminal conspiracy An agreement between two or more people to commit or to effect the commission of an unlawful act or to use unlawful means to accomplish an act that is not unlawful.

criminal contempt Deliberate conduct calculated to obstruct or embarrass a court of law. Also, conduct intended to degrade the role of a judicial officer in administering justice.

criminal homicide The purposeful, knowing, reckless, or negligent killing of one human being by another. Also, a form of homicide for which criminal liability may be incurred. Criminal homicide may be classified as murder, manslaughter, or negligent homicide.

criminal intelligence The information compiled, analyzed, and/or disseminated in an effort to anticipate, prevent, or monitor criminal activity.[18]

criminal justice In the strictest sense, the criminal (penal) law, the law of criminal procedure, and the array of procedures and activities having to do with the enforcement of this body of law. Criminal justice cannot be separated from social justice because the justice enacted in our nation's criminal courts reflects basic American understandings of right and wrong.

criminal justice system The aggregate of all operating and administrative or technical support agencies that perform criminal justice functions. The basic divisions of the operational aspects of criminal justice are law enforcement, courts, and corrections.

criminal law The body of rules and regulations that defines and specifies punishments for offenses of a public nature or for wrongs committed against the state or society. Also called *penal law*.

criminal liability The degree of blameworthiness assigned to a defendant by a criminal court and the concomitant extent to which the defendant is subject to penalties prescribed by the criminal law.

criminal mischief The intentional or knowing damage or destruction of the tangible property of another.

criminal negligence (1) Behavior in which a person fails to reasonably perceive substantial and unjustifiable risks of dangerous consequences. (2) Negligence of such a nature and to such a degree that it is punishable as a crime. (3) Flagrant and reckless disregard for the safety of others, or willful indifference to the safety and welfare of others.

criminal sexual conduct A gender-neutral term applied today to a wide variety of sex offenses, including rape, sodomy, criminal sexual conduct with children, and deviate sexual behavior.

criminal simulation The making of a false document or object that does not have any apparent legal significance.

criminal solicitation The encouraging, requesting, or commanding of another person to commit a crime.

criminal trespass The entering or remaining on the property or in the building of another when entry was forbidden. Also, failing to depart after receiving notice to do so.

criminalize To make criminal; to declare an act or omission to be criminal or in violation of a law making it so.

---

[18] Office of Justice Programs, *The National Criminal Intelligence Sharing Plan* (Washington, DC: U.S. Department of Justice, 2005), 27.

criminally negligent homicide Homicide that results from criminal negligence.

criminology The scientific study of the causes and prevention of crime and the rehabilitation and punishment of offenders.

culpable ignorance The failure to exercise ordinary care to acquire knowledge of the law or of facts that may result in criminal liability.

cybercrime See *computer crime*.

cyberstalking The use of the Internet, e-mail, and other electronic communication technologies to stalk another person.[19]

cyberterrorism A form of terrorism that makes use of high technology, especially computers and the Internet, in the planning and carrying out of terrorist attacks.

damages (actual) A financial award in a civil suit intended to compensate for injuries to person or property.

danger law A law intended to prevent the pretrial release of criminal defendants judged to represent a danger to others in the community.

dangerous proximity test A test for assessing attempts, under which a person is guilty of an attempt when his or her conduct comes dangerously close to success.

dark figure of crime Crime that is not reported to the police and that remains unknown to officials.

date rape The unlawful forced sexual intercourse with a female against her will that occurs within the context of a dating relationship. Date rape, or acquaintance rape, is a subcategory of rape that is of special concern today.

deadly force A force likely to cause death or great bodily harm.

deadly weapon doctrine A rule that empowers a jury to infer a defendant's specific intent to take the life of the victim when the defendant used an item in such a manner that it is known to be capable of causing death or serious bodily injury.

defense Evidence and arguments offered by a defendant and his or her attorney(s) to show why that person should not be held liable for a criminal charge.

defense counsel A licensed trial lawyer hired or appointed to conduct the legal defense of a person accused of a crime and to represent him or her before a court of law.

degree The level of seriousness of an offense.

delayed-notification search See *"sneak and peek" search*.

deliberate indifference A wanton disregard by corrections personnel for the well-being of inmates. Deliberate indifference requires both actual knowledge that a harm is occurring and disregard of the risk of harm that is occurring. A prison official may be held liable under the Eighth Amendment for acting with deliberate indifference to inmate health or safety only if he or she knows that inmates face a substantial risk of serious harm and disregards that risk by failing to take reasonable measures to abate it.

delinquency In the broadest usage, juvenile actions or conduct in violation of criminal law, juvenile status offenses, and other juvenile misbehavior.

delinquent child A child who has engaged in activity that would be considered a crime if the child were an adult. The term *delinquent* is used to avoid the stigma associated with the term *criminal*.

dependent child A child who has no parents or whose parents are not available or are unable to care for him or her.

depraved heart murder (1) Unjustifiable conduct that is extremely negligent and results in the death of a human being, or (2) the killing of a human being with extreme atrocity.

design capacity The number of inmates a prison was intended to hold when it was built or modified.

designer drug A chemical substance that (1) has a potential for abuse similar to or greater than that of controlled substances, (2) is designed to produce a desired pharmacological effect, and (3) is produced to evade the controlling statutory provisions.

determinate sentence A fixed term of incarceration specified by law. Also called *presumptive* or *fixed sentence*.

deterrence A goal of criminal sentencing that seeks to prevent others from committing crimes similar to the one for which an offender is being sentenced.

deviate sexual intercourse Any contact between any part of the genitals of one person and the mouth or anus of another.

digital criminal forensics The lawful seizure, acquisition, analysis, reporting, and safeguarding of data from digital devices that may contain information of evidentiary value to the trier of fact in criminal events.[20]

diminished capacity A defense based on claims of a mental condition that may be insufficient to exonerate a defendant of guilt but that may be relevant to specific mental elements of certain crimes or degrees of crime. Also called *diminished responsibility*.

directed patrol A police-management strategy designed to increase the productivity of patrol officers through the scientific analysis and evaluation of patrol techniques.

[19] Violence against Women Office, *Stalking and Domestic Violence: Report to Congress* (Washington, DC: U.S. Department of Justice, 2001), 5.

[20] Adapted from Larry R. Leibrock, "Overview and Impact on 21st Century Legal Practice: Digital Forensics and Electronic Discovery," no date, http://www.courtroom21.net/FDIC.pps (accessed July 5, 2008).

direct evidence The evidence that, if believed, directly proves a fact. Eyewitness testimony and videotaped documentation account for the majority of all direct evidence heard in the criminal courtroom.

direct-supervision jail A temporary confinement facility that eliminates many of the traditional barriers between inmates and corrections staff. Physical barriers in direct-supervision jails are far less common than in traditional jails, allowing staff members the opportunity for greater interaction with, and control over, residents.

discretionary release The release of an inmate from prison to supervision that is decided by a parole board or other authority.

disorderly conduct Specific, purposeful, and unlawful behavior that tends to cause public inconvenience, annoyance, or alarm.

dispositional hearing The final stage in the processing of adjudicated juveniles in which a decision is made on the form of treatment or penalty that should be imposed on the child.

dispute-resolution center An informal hearing place designed to mediate interpersonal disputes without resorting to the more formal arrangements of a criminal trial court.

distinguish To argue or to find that a rule established by an earlier appellate court decision does not apply to a case currently under consideration even though an apparent similarity exists between the cases.

disturbance of public assembly A crime that occurs when one or more people act unlawfully at a public gathering collected for a lawful purpose in such a way as to purposefully disturb the gathering.

diversion The official suspension of criminal or juvenile proceedings against an alleged offender at any point after a recorded justice system intake, but before the entering of a judgment, and referral of that person to a treatment or care program administered by a nonjustice or private agency. Also, a release without referral.

domestic terrorism The unlawful use of force or violence by a group or an individual who is based and operates entirely within the United States and its territories without foreign direction and whose acts are directed at elements of the U.S. government or population.[21]

double jeopardy A second prosecution or a second punishment for the same offense. Double jeopardy is prohibited by the Fifth Amendment to the U.S. Constitution.

driving while intoxicated (DWI) Unlawfully operating a motor vehicle while under the influence of alcohol.

driving under the influence (DUI) Unlawfully operating a motor vehicle while under the influence of alcohol or drugs (or both).

drug Any of a wide variety of substances having a physical or psychotropic effect on the human body.

DSM-IV The fourth edition of the *Diagnostic and Statistical Manual of Mental Disorders*, published by the American Psychiatric Association.[22] The DSM-IV lists 12 major categories of mental disorders.

due process of law The procedures that effectively guarantee individual rights in the face of criminal prosecution; the due course of legal proceedings according to the rules and forms that have been established for the protection of private rights; formal adherence to fundamental rules for fair and orderly legal proceedings. Due process of law is a constitutional guarantee.

due process model A criminal justice perspective that emphasizes individual rights at all stages of justice system processing.

duress A condition under which one is forced to act against one's will. Also called *compulsion*.

Durham rule A rule for determining insanity that holds that an accused is not criminally responsible if his or her unlawful act was the product of mental disease or mental defect. Also called *product rule*.

effective consent Consent that has been obtained in a legal manner. Also called *legal consent*.

Electronic Communications Privacy Act (ECPA) A law passed by Congress in 1986 establishing the due process requirements that law enforcement officers must meet in order to legally intercept wire communications.

electronic evidence Information and data of investigative value that are stored in or transmitted by an electronic device.[23]

elements (of a crime) (1) The basic components of crime. (2) In a specific crime, the essential features of that crime, as specified by law or statute.

embezzlement The misappropriation of property already in the possession of the defendant. Also, the unlawful conversion of the personal property of another by a person to whom it has been entrusted by (or for) its rightful owner.

emergency search A search conducted by the police without a warrant, which is justified on the basis of some immediate and overriding need, such as public safety, the likely

---

[21] Federal Bureau of Investigation, *FBI Policy and Guidelines: Counterterrorism*, http://www.fbi.gov/contact/fo/jackson/cntrterr.htm (accessed August 26, 2002).

[22] American Psychiatric Association, *Diagnostic and Statistical Manual of Mental Disorders*, 4th ed. (Washington, DC: American Psychiatric Association, 1994).

[23] Adapted from Technical Working Group for Electronic Crime Scene Investigation, *Electronic Crime Scene Investigation: A Guide for First Responders* (Washington, DC: National Institute of Justice, 2001), p. 2.

escape of a dangerous suspect, or the removal or destruction of evidence.

entrapment An improper or illegal inducement to crime by agents of law enforcement. Also, a defense that may be raised when such inducements occur.

equity A sentencing principle, based on concerns with social equality, that holds that similar crimes should be punished with the same degree of severity, regardless of the social or personal characteristics of the offenders.

escape The unlawful leaving of official custody or confinement without permission. Also, the failure to return to custody or confinement following an official temporary leave.

espionage The unlawful act of spying for a foreign government.

evidence Anything useful to a judge or jury in deciding the facts of a case. Evidence may take the form of witness testimony, written documents, videotapes, magnetic media, photographs, physical objects, and so on.

evidence-based policing (EBP) The use of the best available research on the outcomes of police work to implement guidelines and evaluate agencies, units, and officers.[24]

evidence-based practice Crime-fighting strategies that have been scientifically tested and are based on social science research.

ex post facto Formulated, enacted, or operating retrospectively. Literally, "after the fact." As prohibited by the Constitution, no punitive law may be applied to acts committed before the law was enacted and effective.

excessive force The application of an amount or frequency of force greater than that required to compel compliance from a willing or unwilling subject.[25]

excusable homicide A killing conducted in a manner that the criminal law does not prohibit. Also, a killing that may involve some fault but is not criminal homicide.

exclusionary rule The understanding, based on U.S. Supreme Court precedent, that incriminating information must be seized according to constitutional specifications of due process or it will not be allowed as evidence in a criminal trial.

exculpatory evidence Any information having a tendency to clear a person of guilt or blame.

execution-of-public-duty defense A defense to a criminal charge, such as assault, that is often codified and that precludes the possibility of police officers and other public employees from being prosecuted when lawfully exercising their authority.

excuse A type of legal defense in which the defendant claims that some personal condition or circumstance at the time of the act was such that he or she should not be held accountable under the criminal law.

expert witness A person who has special knowledge and skills recognized by the court as relevant to the determination of guilt or innocence. Unlike lay witnesses, expert witnesses may express opinions or draw conclusions in their testimony.

express consent A verbally expressed willingness to engage in a specified activity.

extortion The taking of personal property by threat of future harm.

false imprisonment The unlawful restraint of another person's liberty. Also, the unlawful detention of a person without his or her consent. Also called *false arrest*.

false pretenses Knowingly and unlawfully obtaining title to, and possession of, the lawful property of another by means of deception and with intent to defraud. Also called *obtaining property by false pretenses*.

federal court system The three-tiered structure of federal courts, comprising U.S. district courts, U.S. courts of appeals, and the U.S. Supreme Court.

fellatio Oral stimulation of the penis.

felony A serious crime, generally one punishable by death or by incarceration in a state or federal prison facility as opposed to a jail.

felony murder rule A rule that establishes murder liability for a defendant if another person dies during the commission of certain felonies.

fighting words Words that, by their very utterance, inflict injury or tend to incite an immediate breach of peace. Fighting words are not protected by the free speech clause of the First Amendment to the U.S. Constitution.

first appearance An appearance before a magistrate during which the legality of the defendant's arrest is initially assessed and the defendant is informed of the charges on which he or she is being held. At this stage in the criminal justice process, bail may be set or pretrial release arranged. Also called *initial appearance*.

first-degree murder A willful, deliberate, and premeditated unlawful killing.

fixture An item that is permanently affixed to the land.

fleeing felon rule A now-defunct law enforcement practice that permitted officers to shoot a suspected felon who attempted to flee from a lawful arrest.

---

[24] Lawrence W. Sherman, *Evidence-Based Policing* (Washington, DC: Police Foundation, 1998), 3.

[25] International Association of Chiefs of Police, *Police Use of Force in America, 2001* (Alexandria, VA: IACP, 2001), 1.

fleeting-targets exception An exception to the exclusionary rule that permits law enforcement officers to search a motor vehicle based on probable cause but without a warrant. The fleeting-targets exception is predicated on the fact that vehicles can quickly leave the jurisdiction of a law enforcement agency.

forcible rape Rape that is accomplished against a person's will by means of force, violence, duress, menace, or fear of immediate and unlawful bodily injury to the victim.

Foreign Intelligence Surveillance Act of 1978 (FISA) The Foreign Intelligence Surveillance Act of 1978 is the primary federal statute governing the collection of foreign intelligence by federal law enforcement agencies. Significant amendments to FISA were passed in 2001 through the USA PATRIOT Act and again in 2008.

forgery The making of a false written instrument or the material alteration of an existing genuine written instrument.

forfeiture An enforcement strategy supported by federal statutes and some state laws that authorizes judges to seize "all monies, negotiable instruments, securities, or other things of value furnished or intended to be furnished by any person in exchange for a controlled substance . . . [and] all proceeds traceable to such an exchange."[26]

fornication Voluntary sexual intercourse between two people, one of whom is unmarried.

fruit of the poisonous tree doctrine A legal principle that excludes from introduction at trial any evidence later developed as a result of an illegal search or seizure.

fusion center A multiagency law enforcement facility designed to enhance cooperative efforts through a coordinated process for collecting, sharing, and analyzing information in order to develop actionable intelligence.

gain time The amount of time deducted from time to be served in prison on a given sentence as a consequence of participation in special projects or programs.

gambling The wagering of money, or of some other thing of value, on the outcome or occurrence of an event. Also called *gaming*.

general deterrence A goal of criminal sentencing that seeks to prevent others from committing crimes similar to the one for which a particular offender is being sentenced by making an example of the person sentenced.

general intent The form of intent that can be assumed from the defendant's behavior. General intent refers to an actor's physical conduct.

good-faith exception An exception to the exclusionary rule. Law enforcement officers who conduct a search or who seize evidence on the basis of good faith (that is, when they believe they are operating according to the dictates of the law) and who later discover that a mistake was made (perhaps in the format of the application for a search warrant) may still use the seized evidence in court.

good time The amount of time deducted from time to be served in prison on a given sentence as a consequence of good behavior.

grand jury A group of jurors who have been selected according to law and have been sworn to hear the evidence and to determine whether there is sufficient evidence to bring the accused person to trial, to investigate criminal activity generally, or to investigate the conduct of a public agency or official.

grievance procedure A formalized arrangement, usually involving a neutral hearing board, whereby institutionalized individuals have the opportunity to register complaints about the conditions of their confinement.

gross negligence The conscious disregard of one's duties, resulting in injury or damage to another.

guilty but mentally ill (GBMI) A verdict, equivalent to a finding of guilty, that establishes that "the defendant, although mentally ill, was sufficiently in possession of his faculties to be morally blameworthy for his acts."[27]

habeas corpus Literally, "you have the body"; a writ challenging the legality of incarceration, or a writ ordering a prisoner to be brought before a court to determine the legality of the prisoner's detention.

habitual offender A person sentenced under the provisions of a statute declaring that those who are convicted of a given offense and are shown to have previously been convicted of another specified offense(s) shall receive a more severe penalty than that for the current offense alone.

hands-off doctrine A policy of nonintervention with regard to prison management that U.S. courts tended to follow until the late 1960s. For 30 years, the doctrine languished as judicial intervention in prison administration dramatically increased, although there is now evidence that a new hands-off era is beginning.

harm Loss, disadvantage, injury, or anything so regarded by the person affected, including loss, disadvantage, or injury to any other person in whose welfare he or she is interested. Also called *resulting harm*.

hate crime A criminal offense in which the defendant's conduct was motivated by hatred, bias, or prejudice, based on

[26] U.S. Code, Title 21, Section 881(a)(6).

[27] Ira Mickenberg, "A Pleasant Surprise: The Guilty but Mentally Ill Verdict Has Both Succeeded in Its Own Right and Successfully Preserved the Traditional Role of the Insanity Defense," *University of Cincinnati Law Review* 55 (1987): 943, 987–991.

the actual or perceived race, color, religion, national origin, ethnicity, gender, or sexual orientation of another individual or group of individuals. Also called *bias crime*.

hearsay Something that is not based on the personal knowledge of a witness. Witnesses who testify about something they have heard, for example, are offering hearsay by repeating information about a matter of which they have no direct knowledge.

hearsay rule The long-standing precedent that hearsay cannot be used in American courtrooms. Rather than accepting testimony based on hearsay, the court will ask that the person who was the original source of the hearsay information be brought in to be questioned and cross-examined. Exceptions to the hearsay rule may occur when the person with direct knowledge is dead or is otherwise unable to testify.

home confinement A form of punishment in which individuals are confined to their homes and may be monitored electronically to be sure they do not leave during the hours of confinement. Absence from the home during working hours is often permitted. Also called *house arrest*.

homicide The killing of a human being by the act, procurement, or omission of another human being.

***Hudud* crime** A serious violation of Islamic law that is regarded as an offense against God.

human smuggling Illegal immigration in which an agent is paid to help a person cross a national border clandestinely.

identity theft The unauthorized use of another individual's personal identity to fraudulently obtain money, goods, or services; to avoid the payment of debt; or to avoid criminal prosecution.

ignorance of fact Lack of knowledge of some fact relating to the situation at hand.

ignorance of the law A lack of knowledge of the law or of the existence of a law relevant to the situation at hand.

illegally seized evidence Any evidence seized without regard to the principles of due process as described by the Bill of Rights. Most illegally seized evidence is the result of police searches conducted without a proper warrant or of improperly conducted interrogations.

impossibility A defense to a charge of attempted criminal activity that claims the defendant could not have factually or legally committed the envisioned offense even if he or she had been able to carry through the attempt to do so. It is, for example, factually impossible to kill someone who is already dead.

incapacitation The use of imprisonment or other means to reduce the likelihood that an offender will be capable of committing future offenses.

incest Unlawful sexual intercourse with a relative through blood or marriage.

inchoate crime An unfinished crime that generally leads to another crime. Also, a crime that consists of actions that are steps toward another offense. Also called *anticipatory offense*.

inciting a riot The use of words or other means to intentionally provoke a riot.

incompetent to stand trial A finding by a court that—as a result of a mental illness, defect, or disability—a defendant is unable to understand the nature and object of the proceeding against him or her or is unable to assist in the preparation of his or her own defense.

indecent exposure The willful exposure of the private parts of one person to the sight of another person in a public place with the intent to arouse or gratify sexual desires. Also, the commission, in a place accessible to the public, of (1) an act of sexual intercourse; (2) a lewd exposure of the sexual organs; (3) a lewd appearance in a state of partial or complete nudity; or (4) a lewd caress or indecent fondling of the body of another person.[28] Also called *public indecency*.

indeterminate sentence A relatively unspecific term of incarceration stated as a minimum and maximum time to be served (such as a term of imprisonment of "from one to ten years").[29]

indictment A formal written accusation submitted to the court by a grand jury alleging that a specified person has committed a specified offense, usually a felony.

individual rights The rights guaranteed to all members of American society by the U.S. Constitution (especially those rights found in the first ten amendments to the Constitution, known as the *Bill of Rights*). These rights are particularly important to criminal defendants facing formal processing by the criminal justice system.

individual-rights advocate One who seeks to protect personal freedoms within the process of criminal justice.

infancy defense A defense that claims that certain individuals should not be held criminally responsible for their activities by virtue of their youth. Also called *immaturity defense*.

inference A conclusion drawn from other facts. Juries often infer intent from a defendant's behavior.

information A formal written accusation submitted to a court by a prosecutor alleging that a specified person has committed a specified offense.

---

[28] Official Code of Georgia Annotated, Section 16-6-8.

[29] Bureau of Justice Statistics, *Dictionary of Criminal Justice Data Terminology*, 46.

infraction A violation of a state statute or local ordinance punishable by a fine or other penalty, but not by incarceration. Also called *summary offense*.

inherent coercion The tactics used by police interviewers that fall short of physical abuse but that nonetheless pressure suspects to divulge information.

inherently dangerous A legal term used to describe an act or course of behavior (usually a felony) that, by its very nature, is likely to result in death or serious bodily harm to either the person involved in the behavior or to someone else.

initial appearance See *first appearance*.

insanity An affirmative defense to a criminal charge; a social and legal term (rather than a medical one) that refers to "a condition which renders the affected person unfit to enjoy liberty of action because of the unreliability of his behavior with concomitant danger to himself and others."[30] Also, a finding by a court of law.

insanity defense A legal defense based on claims of mental illness or mental incapacity.

Insanity Defense Reform Act (IDRA) A part of the 1984 Crime Control and Prevention Act that mandated a comprehensive overhaul of the insanity defense as it operated in the federal courts. The IDRA made insanity an affirmative defense to be proved by the defendant by clear and convincing evidence and created a special verdict of not guilty by reason of insanity.

intake The first step in decision making regarding a juvenile whose behavior or alleged behavior is in violation of the law or could otherwise cause a juvenile court to assume jurisdiction.

intangible property Property that has no intrinsic value but that represents something of value. Intangible personal property may include documents, deeds, records of ownership, promissory notes, stock certificates, computer software, and intellectual property.

intellectual property A form of creative endeavor that can be protected through patent, copyright, trademark, or other legal means. Intellectual property includes proprietary knowledge, trade secrets, confidentiality agreements, know-how, ideas, inventions, creations, technologies, processes, works of art and literature, and scientific discoveries or improvements.

intelligence-led policing (ILP) The collection and analysis of information to produce an intelligence end product designed to inform police decision making at both the tactical and strategic levels.[31]

intensive probation supervision (IPS) A form of probation supervision involving frequent face-to-face contact between the probationer and the probation officer.

intensive supervision A form of probation supervision involving frequent face-to-face contacts between the probationary client and probation officers.

intermediate sanctions The use of split sentencing, shock probation or parole, shock incarceration, mixed sentencing, community service, intensive probation supervision, or home confinement in lieu of other, more traditional sanctions, such as imprisonment and fines. Also called *alternative sanctions*

internal affairs The branch of a police organization tasked with investigating charges of wrongdoing involving members of the department.

International Justice and Public Safety Information Sharing Network (NLETS) An important law enforcement information-sharing resource.

international terrorism The unlawful use of force or violence by a group or an individual who has some connection to a foreign power or whose activities transcend national boundaries against people or property in order to intimidate or coerce a government, the civilian population, or any segment thereof in furtherance of political or social objectives.[32]

interrogation The information-gathering activity of police officers that involves the direct questioning of suspects.

involuntary intoxication Intoxication that is not willful.

involuntary manslaughter An unintentional killing for which criminal liability is imposed but that does not constitute murder. Also, the unintentional killing of a person during the commission of a lesser unlawful act, or the killing of someone during the commission of a lawful act, which nevertheless results in an unlawful death.

irresistible impulse test A test for insanity that evaluates defense claims that at the time the crime was committed, a mental disease or disorder prevented the defendant from controlling his or her behavior in keeping with the requirements of the law.

Islamic law A system of laws, operative in some Arab countries, based on the Muslim religion and especially the holy book of Islam, the Koran.

jail A confinement facility administered by an agency of local government, typically a law enforcement agency, intended

---

[30] Joseph R. Nolan and Jacqueline M. Nolan-Haley, *Black's Law Dictionary: Definitions of the Terms and Phrases of American and English Jurisprudence, Ancient and Modern*, 6th ed. (St. Paul: West, 1990).

[31] Angus Smith, ed., *Intelligence-Led Policing* (Richmond, VA: International Association of Law Enforcement Intelligence Analysts, 1997), 1.
[32] Ibid.

for adults but sometimes also containing juveniles. Jails hold people who are being detained pending adjudication or who were committed after adjudication, usually those sentenced to a year or less.

judge An elected or appointed public official who presides over a court of law and who is authorized to hear and sometimes to decide cases and to conduct trials.

judicial review The authority of a court to review the actions of the executive and legislative branches and to declare as void those not consonant with the Constitution.

jurisdiction (1) The geographic district or subject matter over which the authority of a government body, especially a court, extends. (2) The authority of a court to hear and decide an action or lawsuit.

jurisprudence The philosophy of law. Also, the science and study of the law.

juror A member of a trial or grand jury who has been selected for jury duty and is required to serve as an arbiter of the facts in a court of law. Jurors are expected to render verdicts of "guilty" or "not guilty" as to the charges brought against the accused, although they may sometimes fail to do so (as in the case of a hung jury).

jury instructions Directions given by a judge to a jury concerning the law of the case.

jury selection The process whereby, according to law and precedent, members of a particular trial jury are chosen.

just deserts A model of criminal sentencing that holds that criminal offenders deserve the punishment they receive at the hands of the state and that suggests that punishments should be appropriate to the type and severity of crime committed.

justice The principle of fairness; the ideal of moral equity.

justice model A contemporary model of imprisonment based on the principle of just deserts.

justifiable homicide (1) Homicide that is permitted under the law. (2) A killing justified for the good of society. (3) The killing of another in self-defense when danger of death or serious bodily harm exists. (4) The killing of a person according to one's duties or out of necessity but without blame.

justification A type of legal defense in which the defendant admits to committing the act in question but claims it was necessary in order to avoid some greater evil.

juvenile A youth at or below the upper age of juvenile court jurisdiction in a particular state.

juvenile court Any court that has jurisdiction over matters involving juveniles.

juvenile disposition The decision of a juvenile court that concludes a dispositional hearing. The adjudicated juvenile might be committed to a juvenile correctional facility; be placed in a juvenile residence, shelter, or care or treatment program; be required to meet certain standards of conduct; or be released.

juvenile justice system The government agencies that function to investigate, supervise, adjudicate, care for, or confine youthful offenders and other children subject to the jurisdiction of the juvenile court.

juvenile offender A child who violates the criminal law or who commits a status offense. Also, a person subject to juvenile court proceedings because a statutorily defined event caused by the person was alleged to have occurred while the person was below the statutorily specified age limit of original jurisdiction of a juvenile court.

juvenile petition A document filed in juvenile court alleging that a juvenile is a delinquent, a status offender, or a dependent and asking that the court assume jurisdiction over the juvenile or that an alleged delinquent be transferred to a criminal court for prosecution as an adult.

Kansas City experiment The first large-scale scientific study of law enforcement practices. Sponsored by the Police Foundation, it focused on the practice of preventive patrol.

keeping a place of prostitution Knowingly granting or permitting the use of a place for the purpose of prostitution.

kidnapping The unlawful removal of a person from the place where he or she is found, against that person's will, and through the use of force, fraud, threats, or some other form of intimidation. Also, an aggravated form of false imprisonment that is accompanied by either a moving or secreting of the victim.

Knapp Commission A committee that investigated police corruption in New York City in the early 1970s.

knowing behavior Action undertaken with awareness.

knowing possession Possession with awareness of what one possesses.

landmark case A precedent-setting court decision that produces substantial changes both in the understanding of the requirements of due process and in the practical day-to-day operations of the justice system.

larceny The trespassory or wrongful taking and carrying away (asportation) of the personal property of another with intent to steal.

larceny-theft (UCR/NIBRS) The unlawful taking or attempted taking, carrying, leading, or riding away of property, from the possession or constructive possession of another. Motor vehicles are excluded. Larceny is the most common of the eight major offenses, although probably only a small percentage of all larcenies is actually reported to the police because of the small dollar amounts involved.

lascivious That which is obscene or lewd or tends to cause lust.

last-act test In the crime of attempt, a test that asks whether the accused had taken the last step or act toward commission of the offense, had performed all that he or she intended and was able to do in an attempt to commit the crime, but for some reason did not complete the crime.

latent evidence Evidence of relevance to a criminal investigation that is not readily seen by the unaided eye.

law "That which is laid down, ordained, or established . . . a body of rules of action or conduct prescribed by controlling authority, and having binding *legal* force."[33]

Law Enforcement Assistance Administration (LEAA) A now-defunct federal agency established under Title I of the Omnibus Crime Control and Safe Streets Act of 1968 to funnel federal funding to state and local law enforcement agencies.

lay witness An eyewitness, character witness, or other person called on to testify who is not considered an expert. Lay witnesses must testify to facts only and may not draw conclusions or express opinions.

legal cause A legally recognizable cause; the type of cause that is required to be demonstrated in court in order to hold an individual criminally liable for causing harm.

legalistic style A style of policing marked by a strict concern with enforcing the precise letter of the law. Legalistic departments may take a hands-off approach to disruptive or problematic behavior that does not violate the criminal law.

legislative history The record of debates, committee reports and meetings, legislators' statements, and other evidence of what the legislature intended when it enacted a particular statute.

less-lethal weapon A weapon that is designed to disable, capture, or immobilize—but not kill—a suspect. Occasional deaths do result from the use of such weapons, however.

lewdness Obscene behavior.

line operations In police organizations, the field activities or supervisory activities directly related to day-to-day police work.

loitering The act of delaying, lingering, or idling about without a lawful reason for being present.

looting Burglary committed within an affected geographic area during an officially declared state of emergency or during a local emergency resulting from an earthquake, fire, flood, riot, or other disaster.

lynching The taking, by means of riot, of any person from the lawful custody of a peace officer.

mala in se Acts that are regarded, by tradition and convention, as wrong in themselves.

mala prohibita Acts that are considered "wrongs" only because there is a law against them.

malice A legal term that refers to the intentional doing of a wrongful act without just cause or legal excuse. In cases of homicide, the term means "an intention to kill."

malice aforethought An unjustifiable, inexcusable, and unmitigated person-endangering state of mind.[34]

malware Malicious computer programs such as viruses, worms, and Trojan horses.

mandatory release The release of an inmate from prison that is determined by statute or sentencing guidelines and is not decided by a parole board or other authority.[35]

mandatory sentencing A structured sentencing scheme that allows no leeway in the nature of the sentence imposed. Under mandatory sentencing, clearly enumerated punishments are mandated for specific offenses or for habitual offenders convicted of a series of crimes.

manslaughter The unlawful killing of a human being without malice. Manslaughter differs from murder in that malice and premeditation are lacking.

mayhem The intentional infliction of injury on another that causes the removal of, seriously disfigures, or impairs the function of a member or organ of the body.

mens rea The specific mental state of the defendant at the time of the crime; a guilty mind.

mere possession Possession in which one may or may not be aware of what he or she possesses.

mere preparation An act or omission that may be part of a series of acts or omissions constituting a course of conduct planned to culminate in the commission of a crime but that fails to meet the requirements for a substantial step. Also, preparatory actions or steps taken toward the completion of a crime that are remote from the actual commission of the crime.

***Miranda* triggers** The dual principles of custody and interrogation, both of which are necessary before an advisement of rights is required.

***Miranda* warnings** The advisement of rights due criminal suspects by the police before questioning begins. *Miranda* warnings were first set forth by the U.S. Supreme Court in the 1966 case of *Miranda v. Arizona*.

misconduct in office Acts that a public officeholder (1) has no right to perform, (2) performs improperly, or (3) fails to perform in the face of an affirmative duty to act.

[33] Nolan and Nolan-Haley, *Black's Law Dictionary*, 1026. Italics added.

[34] Rollin M. Perkins and Ronald N. Boyce, *Criminal Law*, 3rd ed. (Mineola, NY: Foundation Press, 1982), 75.

[35] Travis and Lawrence, *Beyond the Prison Gates*, 3.

misdemeanor A minor crime; an offense punishable by incarceration, usually in a local confinement facility, for a period of which the upper limit is prescribed by statute in a given jurisdiction, typically one year or less.

misprision of felony The failure to report a known crime; the concealment of a crime.

mistake of fact Misinterpretation, misunderstanding, or forgetfulness of a fact relating to the situation at hand; belief in the existence of a thing or condition that does not exist.

mistake of law A misunderstanding or misinterpretation of the law relevant to the situation at hand.

mitigating circumstances Circumstances relating to the commission of a crime that may be considered to reduce the blameworthiness of the offender.

mitigating factor A circumstance surrounding the commission of a crime that does not in law justify or excuse the act but that in fairness may be considered as reducing the blameworthiness of the offender.[36] Also, an element of an offense or of an offender's background that could result in a lesser sentence under the determinate sentencing model than would otherwise be called for by sentencing guidelines.

mixed sentence A sentence that requires a convicted offender to serve weekends (or other specified periods of time) in a confinement facility (usually a jail), while undergoing probation supervision in the community.

M'Naghten rule A rule for determining insanity that asks whether the defendant knew what he or she was doing or whether the defendant knew that what he or she was doing was wrong.

model penal code (MPC) A model code of criminal laws intended to standardize general provisions of criminal liability, sentencing, defenses, and the definitions of specific crimes between and among the states. The Model Penal Code was developed by the American Law Institute.

morals Ethical principles, or principles meant to guide human conduct and behavior; principles or standards of right and wrong.

morals offense An offense that was originally defined to protect the family and related social institutions. Included in this category are crimes such as lewdness, indecency, sodomy, and other sex-related offenses, including seduction, fornication, adultery, bigamy, pornography, obscenity, cohabitation, and prostitution.

mores Unwritten, but generally known, rules that govern serious violations of the social code.

motive A person's reason for committing a crime.

motor vehicle theft (UCR/NIBRS) The theft or attempted theft of a motor vehicle. *Motor vehicle* is defined as a self-propelled road vehicle that runs on land surface and not on rails. The stealing of trains, planes, boats, construction equipment, and most farm machinery is classified as larceny under the UCR/NIBRS Program, not as motor vehicle theft.

multiculturalism The existence within one society of diverse groups that maintain unique cultural identities while frequently accepting and participating in the larger society's legal and political systems.[37] Multiculturalism is often used in conjunction with the term *diversity* to identify many distinctions of social significance.

murder The unlawful killing of a human being, carried out with malice or planned in advance. According to common law, the killing of one human being by another with malice aforethought.

national crime victimization survey (NCVS) A survey, conducted annually by the Bureau of Justice Statistics, that provides data on households that report having been affected by crime.

National Incident-Based Reporting System (NIBRS) An incident-based reporting system that collects detailed data on every single crime occurrence. NIBRS data are replacing the kinds of summary data that have traditionally been provided by the FBI's Uniform Crime Reporting Program.

natural law The rules of conduct inherent in human nature and in the natural order, which are thought to be knowable through intuition, inspiration, and the exercise of reason without the need to refer to man-made laws.

necessity A defense to a criminal charge that claims that it was necessary to commit some unlawful act in order to prevent or avoid a greater harm.

neglected child A child who is not receiving the proper level of physical or psychological care from his or her parents or guardians or who has been placed for adoption in violation of the law.

negligent homicide The killing of a human being by criminal negligence or by the failure to exercise reasonable, prudent care. Also, a criminal offense committed by one whose negligence is the direct and proximate cause of another's death.

1983 lawsuit A civil suit brought under Title 42, Section 1983, of the U.S. Code against anyone who denies others their constitutional right to life, liberty, or property without due process of law.

nolo contendere A plea of "no contest." A no-contest plea is used when the defendant does not wish to contest conviction.

---

[36] Bureau of Justice Statistics, *Dictionary of Criminal Justice Data Terminology*, 46.

[37] Adapted from Robert M. Shusta et al., *Multicultural Law Enforcement*, 2nd ed. (Upper Saddle River, NJ: Prentice Hall, 2002), 443.

Because the plea does not admit guilt, however, it cannot provide the basis for later civil suits that might follow a criminal conviction.

norms Unwritten rules that underlie and are inherent in the fabric of society.

not guilty by reason of insanity (NGRI) The plea of a defendant, or the verdict of a jury or judge in a criminal proceeding, that the defendant is not guilty of the offense charged because at the time the crime was committed, the defendant did not have the mental capacity to be held criminally responsible for his or her actions.

obscenity That which appeals to the prurient interest and lacks serious literary, artistic, political, or scientific value.[38]

obstruction of justice An unlawful attempt to interfere with the administration of the courts, the judicial system, or law enforcement officers or with the activities of those who seek justice in a court or whose duties involve the administration of justice.

offense A violation of the criminal law. Also, in some jurisdictions, a minor crime, such as jaywalking, that is sometimes described as *ticketable*.

omission to act An intentional or unintentional failure to act, which may impose criminal liability if a duty to act under the circumstances is specified by law.

opening statement The initial statement of the prosecution or the defense, made in a court of law to a judge, or to a judge and jury, describing the facts that he or she intends to present during trial to prove the case.

operational capacity The number of inmates a prison can effectively accommodate based on management considerations.

ordinary negligence The want of ordinary care, or negligence that could have been avoided if one had exercised ordinary, reasonable, or proper care.

organized crime The unlawful activities of the members of a highly organized, disciplined association engaged in supplying illegal goods or services, including gambling, prostitution, loan-sharking, narcotics, and labor racketeering, and in other unlawful activities.[39]

original jurisdiction The lawful authority of a court to hear or to act on a case from its beginning and to pass judgment on the law and the facts. The authority may be over a specific geographic area or over particular types of cases.

outrageous government conduct A kind of entrapment defense based on an objective criterion involving "the belief that the methods employed on behalf of the Government to bring about conviction cannot be countenanced."[40]

pandering Soliciting a person to perform an act of prostitution.

parens patriae A common law principle that allows the state to assume a parental role and to take custody of a child when he or she becomes delinquent, is abandoned, or is in need of care that the natural parents are unable or unwilling to provide.

parole The status of a convicted offender who has been conditionally released from prison by a paroling authority before the expiration of his or her sentence and placed under the supervision of a parole agency, and is required to observe the conditions of parole.

parole board A state paroling authority. Most states have parole boards that decide when an incarcerated offender is ready for conditional release. Some boards also function as revocation hearing panels.

parole (probation) violation An act or a failure to act by a parolee (or probationer) that does not conform to the conditions of his or her parole (or probation).

parole revocation The administrative action of a paroling authority removing a person from parole status in response to a violation of lawfully required conditions of parole, including the prohibition against committing a new offense, and usually resulting in a return to prison.

Part I offenses A UCR/NIBRS offense group used to report murder, rape, robbery, aggravated assault, burglary, larceny-theft, motor vehicle theft, and arson, as defined under the FBI's UCR/NIBRS Program.

Part II offenses A UCR/NIBRS offense group used to report arrests for less serious offenses. Agencies are limited to reporting only arrest information for Part II offenses, with the exception of simple assault.

parties to crime All those who take part in the commission of a crime, including those who aid and abet and are therefore criminally liable for the offense.

Peace Officer Standards and Training (POST) program The official program of a state or legislative jurisdiction that sets standards for the training of law enforcement officers. All states set such standards, although not all use the term *POST*.

penal code The written, organized, and compiled form of the criminal laws of a jurisdiction.

penal law See *criminal law*.

---

[38] David R. Simon, *The American Standard Law Dictionary*, 1995, via Cybernation online, http://www.e-legal.com (accessed July 4, 2009).

[39] The Organized Crime Control Act of 1970.

[40] Rollin M. Perkins and Ronald N. Boyce, *Criminal Law*, 3rd ed. (Mineola, NY: Foundation Press, 1982), 1167.

peremptory challenge The right to challenge a potential juror without disclosing the reason for the challenge. Prosecutors and defense attorneys routinely use peremptory challenges to eliminate from juries individuals who, although they express no obvious bias, are thought to be capable of swaying the jury in an undesirable direction.

perfect self-defense A claim of self-defense that meets all of the generally accepted legal conditions for such a claim to be valid. Where deadly force is used, perfect self-defense requires that in light of the circumstances, the defendant reasonably believed it to be necessary to kill the decedent to avert imminent death or great bodily harm and that the defendant was neither the initial aggressor nor responsible for provoking the fatal confrontation.

perjury The willful giving of false testimony under oath in a judicial proceeding. Also, false testimony given under any lawfully administered oath.

personal crime A crime committed against a person, including (according to the FBI's UCR Program) murder, rape, aggravated assault, and robbery. Also called *violent crime.*

personal property Anything of value that is subject to ownership and that is not land or fixture.

personal trespass by computer The use of a computer or computer network without authority and with the intent to cause physical injury to an individual.

petty crime See *quality-of-life offense.*

physical proximity test A test traditionally used under common law to determine whether a person was guilty of attempted criminal activity. The physical proximity test requires that the accused has it within his or her power to complete the crime almost immediately.

pimping Aiding, abetting, counseling, or commanding another in the commission of prostitution. Also, the act of procuring a prostitute for another.

Pinkerton's Rule A doctrine holding that all conspirators are liable for the acts of co-conspirators that are taken in furtherance of the conspiracy.

plain view A legal term describing the ready visibility of objects that might be seized as evidence during a search by police in the absence of a search warrant specifying the seizure of those objects. To lawfully seize evidence in plain view, officers must have a legal right to be in the viewing area and must have cause to believe that the evidence is somehow associated with criminal activity.

plea In criminal proceedings, the defendant's formal answer in court to the charge contained in a complaint, information, or indictment that he or she is guilty of the offense charged, is not guilty of the offense charged, or does not contest the charge.

plea bargaining The process of negotiating an agreement among the defendant, the prosecutor, and the court as to what an appropriate plea and associated sentence should be in a given case.

plurality requirement The logical and legal requirement that a conspiracy must involve two or more parties.

police-community relations (PCR) An area of police activity that recognizes the need for the community and the police to work together effectively and is based on the notion that the police derive their legitimacy from the community they serve. Many police agencies began to explore PCR in the 1960s and 1970s.

police corruption The abuse of police authority for personal or organizational gain.[41]

police discretion The opportunity of law enforcement officers to exercise choice in their daily activities.

police ethics The special responsibility to adhere to moral duty and obligation that is inherent in police work.

police management The administrative activities of controlling, directing, and coordinating police personnel, resources, and activities in the service of crime prevention, the apprehension of criminals, the recovery of stolen property, and the performance of a variety of regulatory and helping services.

police power The authority of a state to enact and enforce a criminal statute.[42]

police professionalism The increasing formalization of police work and the accompanying rise in public acceptance of the police.

police subculture A particular set of values, beliefs, and acceptable forms of behavior characteristic of American police with which the police profession strives to imbue new recruits. Socialization into the police subculture commences with recruit training and continues thereafter.

police use of force The use of physical restraint by a police officer when dealing with a member of the public.[43]

police working personality All aspects of the traditional values and patterns of behavior evidenced by police officers who have been effectively socialized into the police subculture. Characteristics of the police personality often extend to the personal lives of law enforcement personnel.

polygamy The state of having more than one wife or husband at the same time.

---

[41] Carl B. Klockars et al., *The Measurement of Police Integrity,* National Institute of Justice Research in Brief (Washington, DC: NIJ, 2000), 1.

[42] *Jacobson v. Massachusetts,* 197 U.S. 11 (1905).

[43] National Institute of Justice, *Use of Force by Police: Overview of National and Local Data* (Washington, DC: NIJ, 1999).

pornography The "depiction of sexual behavior in such a way as to excite the viewer sexually."[44]

postcrime victimization Problems for the victim that follow from an initial victimization, such as loss of employment, inability to pay medical bills, and insensitivity of family members. Also called *secondary victimization*.

positive law Law that is legitimately created and enforced by governments.

precedent A legal principle that ensures that previous judicial decisions are authoritatively considered and incorporated into future cases.

precursor chemical A chemical that may be used in the manufacture of a controlled substance.

preliminary hearing A proceeding before a judicial officer in which three matters must be decided: (1) whether a crime was committed, (2) whether the crime occurred within the territorial jurisdiction of the court, and (3) whether there are reasonable grounds to believe that the defendant committed the crime.

premeditated murder Murder that was planned in advance (however briefly) and willfully carried out.

premeditation The act of deliberating, meditating on, or planning a course of action, such as a crime.

preponderance of the evidence A standard for determining legal liability, which requires a probability of just over 50 percent that the defendant did what is claimed.

present ability As used in assault statutes, a term meaning that the person attempting assault is physically capable of immediately carrying it out.

presentence investigation (PSI) The examination of a convicted offender's background prior to sentencing. Presentence examinations are generally conducted by probation or parole officers and are submitted to sentencing authorities.

presumptive sentencing A model of criminal punishment that meets the following conditions: (1) The appropriate sentence for an offender convicted of a specific charge is presumed to fall within a range of sentences authorized by sentencing guidelines that are adopted by a legislatively created sentencing body, usually a sentencing commission; (2) sentencing judges are expected to sentence within the range or to provide written justification for failing to do so; and (3) there is a mechanism for review, usually appellate, of any departure from the guidelines.

pretrial release The release of an accused person from custody, for all or part of the time before or during prosecution, upon his or her promise to appear in court when required.

principal in the first degree A person whose acts directly resulted in the criminal misconduct in question.

principal in the second degree A person who was present at the crime scene and who aided, abetted, counseled, or encouraged the principal.

principle of legality An axiom that holds that behavior cannot be criminal if no law exists that defines it as such. Today, the principle of legality is commonly analyzed as a due-process principle.

prison A state or federal confinement facility that has custodial authority over adults sentenced to confinement.

prison argot The slang that is characteristic of prison subculture and prison life.

prison capacity The size of the correctional population an institution can effectively hold.[45] There are three types of prison capacity: rated, operational, and design.

prisoner reentry The managed return to the community of individuals released from prison. Also called *reentry*.

prisonization The process whereby newly institutionalized offenders come to accept prison lifestyles and criminal values. Although many inmates begin their prison experience with only a few values that support criminal behavior, the socialization experience they undergo while incarcerated leads to a much wider acceptance of such values.

prison subculture The values and behavioral patterns characteristic of prison inmates. Prison subculture has been found to be surprisingly consistent across the country.

private prison A correctional institution operated by a private firm on behalf of a local or state government.

private protective services The independent or proprietary commercial organizations that provide protective services to employers on a contractual basis.

privatization The movement toward the wider use of private prisons.

prize fighting Unlawful public fighting undertaken for the purpose of winning an award or a prize.

probable cause A set of facts and circumstances that would induce a reasonably intelligent and prudent person to believe that a particular other person has committed a specific crime. Also, reasonable grounds to make or believe an accusation. Probable cause refers to the necessary level of belief that would allow for police seizures (arrests) of individuals and full searches of dwellings, vehicles, and possessions.

probation A sentence of imprisonment that is suspended. Also, the conditional freedom granted by a judicial officer to

---

[44] William Kornblum and Joseph Julian, *Social Problems*, 8th ed. (Upper Saddle River, NJ: Prentice Hall, 1995), 115.

[45] Paige M. Harrison and Allen J. Beck, *Prisoners in 2005* (Washington, DC: Bureau of Justice Statistics, 2006), 7.

an adjudicated or adjudged adult or juvenile offender, as long as the person meets certain conditions of behavior.

probation revocation A court order taking away a convicted offender's probationary status and usually withdrawing the conditional freedom associated with that status in response to a violation of the conditions of probation.

probative value The worth of any evidence to prove or disprove the facts at issue.

problem police officer A law enforcement officer who exhibits problem behavior, as indicated by high rates of citizen complaints and use-of-force incidents and by other evidence.[46]

problem-solving policing A type of policing that assumes that many crimes are caused by existing social conditions within the community and that crimes can be controlled by uncovering and effectively addressing underlying social problems. Problem-solving policing makes use of community resources, such as counseling centers, welfare programs, and job-training facilities. It also attempts to involve citizens in crime prevention through education, negotiation, and conflict management.

procedural defense A defense that claims that the defendant was in some significant way discriminated against in the justice process or that some important aspect of official procedure was not properly followed in the investigation or prosecution of the crime charged.

procedural law The part of the law that specifies the methods to be used in enforcing substantive law.

promoting prostitution The statutory offense of (1) owning, controlling, managing, supervising, or otherwise keeping a house of prostitution; (2) procuring a person for a house of prostitution; (3) encouraging, inducing, or otherwise purposely causing another to become or remain a prostitute; (4) soliciting a person to patronize a prostitute; (5) procuring a prostitute for another; or (6) transporting a person with the purpose of promoting that person's involvement in prostitution.

property bond The setting of bail in the form of land, houses, stocks, or other tangible property. In the event that the defendant absconds before trial, the bond becomes the property of the court.

property crime A crime committed against property, including (according to the FBI's UCR Program) burglary, larceny, motor vehicle theft, and arson.

proportionality A sentencing principle that holds that the severity of sanctions should bear a direct relationship to the seriousness of the crime committed.

prosecutor An attorney whose official duty is to conduct criminal proceedings on behalf of the state or the people against those accused of having committed criminal offenses.

prosecutorial discretion The decision-making power of prosecutors, based on the wide range of choices available to them, in the handling of criminal defendants, the scheduling of cases for trial, the acceptance of negotiated pleas, and so on. The most important form of prosecutorial discretion lies in the power to charge, or not to charge, a person with an offense.

prostitution "The offering or receiving of the body for sexual intercourse for hire." Also, "the offering or receiving of the body for indiscriminate sexual intercourse without hire."[47] Some states limit the crime of prostitution to sexual intercourse for hire.

proximate cause The primary or moving cause that plays a substantial part in bringing about injury or damage. It may be a first cause that sets in motion a string of events whose ultimate outcome is reasonably foreseeable.

prurient interest A morbid interest in sex; an "[o]bsession with lascivious and immoral matters."[48]

psycholegal error The mistaken belief that if we identify a cause for conduct, including mental or physical disorders, then the conduct is necessarily excused.[49]

psychological manipulation The manipulative actions by police interviewers, designed to pressure suspects to divulge information, that are based on subtle forms of intimidation and control.

public defender An attorney employed by a government agency or subagency, or by a private organization under contract to a government body, for the purpose of providing defense services to indigents, or an attorney who has volunteered such service.

public drunkenness The offense of being in a state of intoxication in a place accessible to the public.

public-order advocate One who believes that under certain circumstances involving a criminal threat to public safety, the interests of society should take precedence over individual rights.

public-order offense An act that is willfully committed and that disturbs public peace or tranquility. Included are offenses such as fighting, breach of peace, disorderly conduct, vagrancy, loitering, unlawful assembly, public intoxication, obstructing public passage, and (illegally) carrying weapons.

---

[46] Samuel Walker, Geoffrey P. Albert, and Dennis J. Kenney, *Responding to the Problem Police Officer: A National Study of Early Warning Systems* (Washington, DC: National Institute of Justice, 2000).

[47] General Statutes of North Carolina, Section 14-203.

[48] California Penal Code, Section 311(a).

[49] Stephen J. Morse, "The 'New Syndrome Excuse Syndrome,'" *Criminal Justice Ethics* (winter/spring 1995): 7.

punitive damages A financial award in a civil suit that is intended to punish the defendant and/or to deter similar future misconduct. Punitive damages are monies beyond the actual damages suffered by the plaintiff.

quality-of-life offense A minor violation of the law (sometimes called a *petty crime*) that demoralizes community residents and businesspeople. Quality-of-life offenses involve acts that create physical disorder (for example, excessive noise and vandalism) or that reflect social decay (for example, panhandling and prostitution).

racial profiling "Any police-initiated action that relies on the race, ethnicity, or national origin rather than [1] the behavior of an individual, or [2] on information that leads the police to a particular individual who has been identified as being, or having been, engaged in criminal activity."[50]

rape Under common law, unlawful sexual intercourse with a female without her consent. Today, rape statutes in a number of jurisdictions encompass unlawful sexual intercourse between members of the same gender.

rape shield law A statute intended to protect victims of rape by limiting a defendant's in-court use of a victim's sexual history.

rated capacity The number of inmates a prison can handle according to the judgment of experts.

real evidence Evidence that consists of physical material or traces of physical activity.

reasonable doubt In legal proceedings, an actual and substantial doubt arising from the evidence, from the facts or circumstances shown by the evidence, or from the lack of evidence.[51] Also, that state of the case, which after the entire comparison and consideration of all the evidence, leaves the minds of the jurors in such a condition that they cannot say they feel an abiding conviction of the truth of the charge.[52]

real property Land and fixtures.

reasonable doubt standard The standard of proof necessary for conviction in criminal trials.

reasonable force A degree of force that is appropriate in a given situation and is not excessive; the minimum degree of force necessary to protect oneself, one's property, a third party, or the property of another in the face of a substantial threat.

reasonable person A person who acts with common sense and who has the mental capacity of an average, normal, sensible human being. The reasonable person criterion requires that the assumptions and ideas on which a defendant acted must have been reasonable in that the circumstances as they appeared to the defendant would have created the same beliefs in the mind of an ordinary person.

reasonable suspicion The level of suspicion that would justify an officer in making further inquiry or in conducting further investigation. Reasonable suspicion may permit stopping a person for questioning or for a simple pat-down search. Also, a belief, based on a consideration of the facts at hand and on reasonable inferences drawn from those facts, that would induce an ordinarily prudent and cautious person under the same circumstances to conclude that criminal activity is taking place or that criminal activity has recently occurred. Reasonable suspicion is a *general* and reasonable belief that a crime is in progress or has occurred, whereas probable cause is a reasonable belief that a *particular* person has committed a *specific* crime.

rebellion Deliberate, organized resistance, by force and arms, to the laws or operations of the government, committed by a subject of that government.[53]

recidivism The repetition of criminal behavior. In statistical practice, a recidivism rate may be any of a number of possible counts or instances of arrest, conviction, correctional commitment, or correctional status change related to repetitions of these events within a given period of time.

receiving stolen property (1) Knowingly taking possession of or control over property that has been unlawfully stolen from another. (2) Accepting property that the receiver knew was stolen or that he or she should have known was stolen.

reckless behavior An activity that increases the risk of harm.

reentry See *prisoner reentry*.

regional jail A jail that is built and run using the combined resources of a variety of local jurisdictions.

[14] rehabilitation The attempt to reform a criminal offender. Also, the state in which a reformed offender is said to be.

release on recognizance (ROR) The pretrial release of a criminal defendant on his or her written promise to appear in court as required. No cash or property bond is required.

remote location monitoring A supervision strategy that uses electronic technology to track offenders who are sentenced to house arrest or those who have been ordered to limit their movements while completing a sentence involving probation or parole.

---

[50] Deborah Ramirez, Jack McDevitt, and Amy Farrell, *A Resource Guide on Racial Profiling Data Collection Systems: Promising Practices and Lessons Learned* (Washington, DC: U.S. Department of Justice, 2000), 3.

[51] *Victor v. Nebraska*, 114 S. Ct. 1239, 127 L. Ed. 2d 583 (1994).

[52] State of California, Jury Instructions.

[53] Gilmer, *The Law Dictionary*, 334.

rescuing a prisoner A crime that is committed when one or more people rescue or attempt to rescue any person being held in lawful custody.

resisting arrest The crime of obstructing or opposing a peace officer who is making an arrest.

restitution A court requirement that an alleged or convicted offender pay money or provide services to the victim of the crime or provide services to the community.

restoration A sentencing goal that seeks to make victims and the community "whole again."

restorative justice A sentencing model that builds on restitution and community participation in an attempt to make the victim "whole again."

retreat rule A rule in many jurisdictions that requires that a person being attacked retreat in order to avoid the necessity of using force against the attacker if retreat can be accomplished with "complete safety."

retribution The act of taking revenge on a criminal perpetrator. The most punishment-oriented of all sentencing goals, retribution claims that we are justified in punishing offenders because they deserve it.

revocation hearing A hearing held before a legally constituted hearing body (such as a parole board) to determine whether a parolee or probationer has violated the conditions and requirements of his or her parole or probation.

right of allocution A statutory provision permitting crime victims to speak at the sentencing of convicted offenders. A federal right of allocution was established for victims of federal violent and sex crimes under the Violent Crime Control and Law Enforcement Act of 1994.

riot A tumultuous disturbance of the peace by three or more people assembled of their own authority.[54]

robbery The unlawful taking of property that is in the immediate possession of another by force or by threat of force. Also, larceny from a person by violence or intimidation or by placing the person in fear.

rout The preparatory stage of a riot.

rule of law the maxim that an orderly society must be governed by established principles and known codes that are applied uniformly and fairly to all of its members. Also called *supremacy of law*.

rules of evidence The court rules that govern the admissibility of evidence at criminal hearings and trials.

scienter Knowledge; guilty knowledge.

scientific jury selection The use of correlational techniques from the social sciences to gauge the likelihood that potential jurors will vote for conviction or for acquittal.

scientific police management The application of social sciences techniques to the study of police administration for the purpose of increasing effectiveness, reducing the frequency of citizen complaints, and enhancing the efficient use of available resources.

search incident to an arrest A warrantless search of an arrested individual conducted to ensure the safety of the arresting officer. Because individuals placed under arrest may be in possession of weapons, courts have recognized the need for arresting officers to protect themselves by conducting an immediate search of arrestees without obtaining a warrant.

second-degree murder Depending on the jurisdiction, either (1) a murder committed during the perpetration or attempted perpetration of an enumerated felony, such as arson, rape, robbery, or burglary; or (2) any murder not classified by statute as first-degree murder.

security threat group (STG) An inmate group, gang, or organization whose members act together to pose a threat to the safety of corrections staff or the public, who prey on other inmates, or who threaten the secure and orderly operation of a correctional institution.

sedition A crime that consists of a communication or agreement intended to defame the government or to incite treason.

selective incapacitation A sentencing strategy that imprisons or otherwise removes from society a select group of offenders, especially those considered to be most dangerous.

selective incorporation (aka incorporation) A constitutional doctrine that holds that rights found in the Bill of Rights, which were originally intended to only restrict the federal government, apply to the states through the Fourteenth Amendment's due-process clause. Only rights found by the Supreme Court to be fundamental and necessary to an ordered liberty are incorporated.

self-defense A defense to a criminal charge that is based on the recognition that a person has an inherent right to self-protection and that to reasonably defend oneself from unlawful attack is a natural response to threatening situations.

sentencing The process through which a sentencing authority imposes a lawful punishment or other sanction on a person convicted of violating the criminal law.

sequestered jury A jury that is isolated from the public during the course of a trial and throughout the deliberation process.

service style A style of policing marked by a concern with helping rather than strict enforcement. Service-oriented police agencies are more likely to refer citizens to community

---
[54] Ibid., 293.

resources, such as drug-treatment programs, than are other types of agencies.

sex trafficking The recruitment, harboring, transportation, provision, or obtaining of a person for the purpose of a commercial sex act.

sexual assault A statutory crime that combines all sexual offenses into one offense (often with various degrees). It is broader than the common law crime of rape.

sexual battery The unlawful touching of an intimate part of another person against that person's will and for the purpose of sexual arousal, gratification, or abuse.

sexual contact Any touching of the anus, breast, or any part of the genitals of another person with intent to arouse or gratify the sexual desire of any person.

sheriff The elected chief officer of a county law enforcement agency. The sheriff is usually responsible for law enforcement in unincorporated areas and for the operation of the county jail.

shock incarceration A sentencing option that makes use of "boot camp"–type prisons in order to impress on convicted offenders the realities of prison life.

shock probation The practice of sentencing offenders to prison, allowing them to apply for probationary release, and granting release in surprise fashion. Offenders who receive shock probation may not be aware that they will be released on probation and may expect to spend a much longer time behind bars.

"sneak and peek" search A search that occurs in the suspect's absence and without his or her prior knowledge. Also known as a *delayed-notification search.*

social control The use of sanctions and rewards within a group to influence and shape the behavior of individual members of that group. Social control is a primary concern of social groups and communities, and it is their interest in the exercise of social control that leads to the creation of both criminal and civil statutes.

social debt A sentencing principle that objectively counts an offender's criminal history in sentencing decisions.

social justice An ideal that embraces all aspects of civilized life and that is linked to fundamental notions of fairness and to cultural beliefs about right and wrong.

sodomy Oral or anal copulation between people of the same or different gender or between a human being and an animal.

soliciting prostitution The act of asking, enticing, or requesting another to commit the crime of prostitution.

Son of Sam law A statute that provides support for the rights of victims by denying convicted offenders the opportunity to further capitalize on their crimes. "Son of Sam" laws set the stage for civil action against infamous offenders who might otherwise profit from the sale of their story. Also called *notoriety-for-profit law.*

spam Unsolicited commercial bulk e-mail whose primary purpose is the advertisement or promotion of a commercial product or service.

span of control The number of police personnel or the number of units supervised by a particular officer.

specific deterrence A goal of criminal sentencing that seeks to prevent a particular offender from engaging in repeat criminality.

specific intent A thoughtful, conscious intention to perform a specific act in order to achieve a particular result.

Speedy Trial Act A 1974 federal law requiring that proceedings against a defendant in a criminal case begin within a specified period of time, such as 70 working days after indictment. Some states also have speedy trial requirements.

split sentence A sentence explicitly requiring the convicted person to serve a period of confinement in a local, state, or federal facility, followed by a period of probation.

spousal rape The rape of one's spouse.

staff operations In police organizations, activities (such as administration and training) that provide support for line operations.

stalking The intentional frightening of another through following, harassing, annoying, tormenting, or terrorizing activities.

stand your ground A statute that permits the use of deadly force to repel life- or limb-threatening force in public spaces with no duty to retreat.

stare decisis The legal principle that requires that courts be bound by their own earlier decisions and by those of higher courts having jurisdiction over them regarding subsequent cases on similar issues of law and fact. The term literally means "standing by decided matters."

state court administrator A coordinator who assists with case-flow management, operating funds budgeting, and court docket administration.

state court system A state judicial structure. Most states generally have at least three court levels: trial courts, appellate courts, and a state supreme court.

status A person's state of being.

status offender A child who commits an act that is contrary to the law by virtue of the offender's status as a child. Purchasing cigarettes, buying alcohol, and being truant are examples of such behavior.

status offense An act or conduct that is declared by statute to be an offense, but only when committed by or engaged in by a juvenile, and that can be adjudicated only by a juvenile court.

statutory law Law in the form of statutes or formal written codes made by a legislature or governing body with the power to make law.

statutory rape Sexual intercourse, whether consensual or not, with a person under the age of consent, as specified by statute.

strategic policing A type of policing that retains the traditional police goal of professional crime fighting but enlarges the enforcement target to include nontraditional kinds of criminals, such as serial offenders, gangs and criminal associations, drug-distribution networks, and sophisticated white-collar and computer criminals. Strategic policing generally makes use of innovative enforcement techniques, including intelligence operations, undercover stings, electronic surveillance, and sophisticated forensic methods.

strict liability A thoughtful, conscious intention to perform a specific act in order to achieve a particular result.

strict liability crime A violation of law for which one may incur criminal liability without fault or intention. Strict liability offenses do not require mens rea.

structured sentencing A model of criminal punishment that includes determinate and commission-created presumptive sentencing schemes, as well as voluntary/advisory sentencing guidelines.

subornation of perjury The unlawful procuring of another person to commit perjury.

subpoena A written order issued by a judicial officer or grand jury requiring an individual to appear in court and to give testimony or to bring material to be used as evidence. Some subpoenas mandate that books, papers, and other items be surrendered to the court.

substantial capacity test A test developed by the American Law Institute and embodied in the Model Penal Code that holds that "a person is not responsible for criminal conduct if at the time of such conduct as a result of mental disease or defect he lacks substantial capacity either to appreciate the criminality [wrongfulness] of his conduct or to conform his conduct to the requirements of the law."[55]

substantial step (1) Significant activity undertaken in furtherance of some goal. (2) An act or omission that is a significant part of a series of acts or omissions, constituting a course of conduct planned to culminate in the commission of a crime. (3) An important or essential step toward the commission of a crime that is considered sufficient to constitute the crime of criminal attempt. A substantial step is conduct that is strongly corroborative of the actor's criminal purpose. According to one court, a substantial step is "behavior of such a nature that a reasonable observer, viewing it in context, could conclude beyond a reasonable doubt that it was undertaken in accordance with a design to violate the statute."[56]

substantive criminal law The part of the law that defines crimes and specifies punishments.

sudden passion In cases of voluntary manslaughter, passion directly caused by and rising out of provocation by the victim or of another acting with the victim. Sudden passion includes the understanding that the passion arises at the time of the killing and is not solely the result of former provocation.

suspicionless search A search conducted by law enforcement personnel without a warrant and without suspicion. Suspicionless searches are permissible only if based on an overriding concern for public safety.

syndrome A complex of signs and symptoms presenting a clinical picture of a disease or disorder.[57]

syndrome-based defense A defense predicated on, or substantially enhanced by, the acceptability of syndrome-related claims.

tangible property Property that has physical form and can be touched, such as land, goods, jewelry, and furniture. Also, movable property that can be taken and carried away.

***Tazir* crime** A minor violation of Islamic law that is regarded as an offense against society, not God.

team policing The reorganization of conventional patrol strategies into "an integrated and versatile police team assigned to a fixed district."[58]

teen court An alternative approach to juvenile justice in which alleged offenders are judged and/or sentenced by a jury of their peers.

terrorism The commission of a traditional crime, such as murder, with the intention of coercing a population or influencing a government through fear or intimidation.

testimony The oral evidence offered by a sworn witness on the witness stand during a criminal trial.

theft A general term embracing a wide variety of misconduct by which a person is unlawfully deprived of his or her property.

---

[55] Model Penal Code, Section 4.01(1).

[56] *United States v. Buffington*, 815 F.2d 1292, 1302 (9th Cir.1987) (quoting *United States v. Mandujano*, 499 F.2d 370, 376 [5th Cir.1974], cert. denied, 419 U.S. 1114, 95 S.Ct. 792, 42 L.Ed.2d 812 [1975]).

[57] C F. Chapman, *Barron's Medical Dictionary for the Nonprofessional* (New York: Barron's Educational Series, 1984).

[58] Sam S. Souryal, *Police Administration and Management* (St. Paul, MN: West, 1977), 261.

theft of computer services The willful use of a computer or computer network with the intent to obtain computer services without authority.

three-strikes legislation Statutory provisions that mandate lengthy prison terms for criminal offenders convicted of a third violent crime or felony.

tort A private or civil wrong or injury; "the unlawful violation of a private legal right other than a mere breach of contract, express or implied."[59]

tortfeasor An individual, business, or other legally recognized entity that commits a tort.

total institution An enclosed facility separated from society both socially and physically, where the inhabitants share all aspects of their daily lives.

trafficking in persons (TIP) The exploitation of unwilling or unwitting people through force, coercion, threat, or deception.

transferred intent A legal construction by which an unintended act that results from intentional action undertaken in the commission of a crime may also be illegal.

transnational organized crime Unlawful activity undertaken and supported by organized criminal groups operating across national boundaries.

treason The crime of levying war against, or supporting the enemy of, one's nation. It is the only crime specifically mentioned in the U.S. Constitution.

trespassory taking For crimes of theft, a taking without the consent of the victim.

trial In criminal proceedings, the examination in court of the issues of fact and relevant law in a case for the purpose of convicting or acquitting the defendant.

trial *de novo* Literally, "new trial." The term is applied to cases that are retried on appeal, as opposed to those that are simply reviewed on the record.

truth in sentencing "A close correspondence between the sentence imposed upon those sent to prison and the time actually served prior to prison release."[60]

undisciplined child A child who is beyond parental control, as evidenced by his or her refusal to obey legitimate authorities, such as school officials and teachers.

Uniform Crime Reporting (UCR) Program A data-collection program run by the Federal Bureau of Investigation that tallies crime statistics annually. Reports under the program consist primarily of data on crimes reported to the police and of arrests.

Uniform Determination of Death Act (UDDA) A standard supported by the American Medical Association, the American Bar Association, and the National Conference of Commissioners on Uniform State Laws, which provides that "[a]n individual who has sustained either: (1) irreversible cessation of circulatory and respiratory functions, or (2) irreversible cessation of all functions of the entire brain, including the brain stem, is dead."[61] The UDDA provides a model for legislation and has been adopted in various forms by many states.

unlawful assembly A gathering of three or more people for the purpose of doing an unlawful act or for the purpose of doing a lawful act in a violent, boisterous, or tumultuous manner.

USA PATRIOT Act A federal statute enacted immediately following, and in response to, the terrorist attacks on the United States on September 11, 2001. The statute increased federal law enforcement authority to prevent, detect, and prosecute terrorists.

uttering The offering, passing, or attempted passing of a forged instrument with knowledge that the document is false and with intent to defraud.

vagrancy Under common law, the act of going about from place to place by a person without visible means of support, who was idle, and who, though able to work for his or her maintenance, refused to do so and lived without labor or on the charity of others.[62]

vagrant A wanderer; an idle person who, being able to maintain him- or herself by lawful labor, either refuses to work or resorts to unlawful practices, such as begging, to gain a living.[63] Also called *vagabond*.

vehicular homicide The killing of a human being as a result of another person's operation of a motor vehicle in a reckless manner likely to cause death or great bodily harm.

verdict The decision of the jury in a jury trial or of a judicial officer in a nonjury trial.

vicarious liability The criminal liability of one party for the criminal acts of another party.

victim "[A]ny individual against whom an offense has been committed," or for certain procedural purposes, "a parent or legal guardian if the victim is below the age of eighteen years or incompetent" or "one or more family members or relatives designated by the court if the victim is deceased or incapacitated."[64]

---

[59] General Statutes of Georgia, 51-1-1.

[60] Lawrence A. Greenfeld, "Prison Sentences and Time Served for Violence," Bureau of Justice Statistics, *Selected Findings*, no. 4 (April 1995).

[61] Uniform Determination of Death Act, Uniform Law Ann., Chapter 12 (1981 Supp.), 187.

[62] Adapted from Nolan and Nolan-Haley, *Black's Law Dictionary*, 1549.

[63] Gilmer, *The Law Dictionary*, 334.

[64] Violent Crime Control and Law Enforcement Act of 1994, Title XXIII, Section 230101.

victim-assistance program A service organization that works to provide comfort and assistance to victims of crime and to witnesses.

victim impact statement The in-court use of victim- or survivor-supplied information by sentencing authorities who want to make an informed sentencing decision. Also, a written document that describes the losses, suffering, and trauma experienced by the crime victim or by the victim's survivors. In jurisdictions in which victim impact statements are used, judges are expected to consider them in arriving at an appropriate sentence for the offender.

victimless crime An offense committed against the social values and interests represented in and protected by the criminal law *and* in which parties to the offense willingly participate.

victims' rights The fundamental right of victims to be equitably represented throughout the criminal justice process.

violent crime A UCR/NIBRS summary offense category that includes murder, rape, robbery, and aggravated assault.

void-for-vagueness principle A constitutional principle that refers to a statute defining a crime that is so unclear that a reasonable person of at least average intelligence could not determine what the law purports to command or prohibit.

voluntary/advisory sentencing guidelines Recommended sentencing policies that are not required by law.

voluntary intoxication Willful intoxication; intoxication that is the result of personal choice. Voluntary intoxication includes the voluntary ingestion, injection, or taking by any other means of any intoxicating liquor, drug, or other substance.

voluntary manslaughter An unlawful killing of a human being, without malice, that is done intentionally during a sudden quarrel or in the heat of passion. Also, a killing committed without lawful justification, wherein the defendant acted under a sudden and intense passion resulting from adequate provocation.

warrant In criminal proceedings, a writ issued by a judicial officer directing a law enforcement officer to perform a specified act and affording the officer protection from damages if he or she performs it.

watchman style A style of policing marked by a concern for order maintenance. Watchman policing is characteristic of lower-class communities where informal police intervention in the lives of residents is employed in the service of keeping the peace.

Wharton's rule A rule applicable to conspiracy cases holding that an agreement by two persons to commit a particular crime cannot be prosecuted as a conspiracy when the crime is of such a nature as to necessarily require the participation of two persons.

white-collar crime Violation of the criminal law committed by a person of respectability and high social status in the course of his or her occupation. Also, a nonviolent crime for financial gain utilizing deception and committed by anyone who has special technical or professional knowledge of business or government, irrespective of the person's occupation.

writ of *certiorari* A writ issued from an appellate court for the purpose of obtaining from a lower court the record of its proceedings in a particular case. In some states, this writ is the mechanism for discretionary review. A request for review is made by petitioning for a writ of *certiorari*, and the granting of review is indicated by the issuance of the writ.

writ of *habeas corpus* A writ that directs the person detaining a prisoner to bring him or her before a judicial officer to determine the lawfulness of the imprisonment.

year-and-a-day rule A common law requirement that homicide prosecutions could not take place if the victim did not die within a year and a day from the time that the fatal act occurred.

Table of Cases

Subject Index